NISSAN MAXIMA
1985-92 REPAIR MANUAL

CHILTON'S

Covers all U.S. and Canadian models of
Nissan Maxima

by Richard T. Smith

CHILTON Automotive Books

PUBLISHED BY **HAYNES NORTH AMERICA**, Inc.

AUTOMOTIVE
PARTS &
ACCESSORIES
ASSOCIATION MEMBER

Manufactured in USA
© 1992 Haynes North America, Inc.
ISBN 0-8019-8261-8
Library of Congress Catalog Card No. 91-058874
5678901234 9876543210

Haynes Publishing Group
Sparkford Nr Yeovil
Somerset BA22 7JJ England

Haynes North America, Inc
861 Lawrence Drive
Newbury Park
California 91320 USA

ABCDE
FGHIJ
K

12G1

Contents

Contents

SAFETY NOTICE

Proper service and repair procedures are vital to the safe, reliable operation of all motor vehicles, as well as the personal safety of those performing repairs. This manual outlines procedures for servicing and repairing vehicles using safe, effective methods. The procedures contain many NOTES, CAUTIONS and WARNINGS which should be followed, along with standard procedures to eliminate the possibility of personal injury or improper service which could damage the vehicle or compromise its safety.

It is important to note that repair procedures and techniques, tools and parts for servicing motor vehicles, as well as the skill and experience of the individual performing the work vary widely. It is not possible to anticipate all of the conceivable ways or conditions under which vehicles may be serviced, or to provide cautions as to all possible hazards that may result. Standard and accepted safety precautions and equipment should be used when handling toxic or flammable fluids, and safety goggles or other protection should be used during cutting, grinding, chiseling, prying, or any other process that can cause material removal or projectiles.

Some procedures require the use of tools specially designed for a specific purpose. Before substituting another tool or procedure, you must be completely satisfied that neither your personal safety, nor the performance of the vehicle will be endangered.

Although information in this manual is based on industry sources and is complete as possible at the time of publication, the possibility exists that some car manufacturers made later changes which could not be included here. While striving for total accuracy, the authors or publishers cannot assume responsibility for any errors, changes or omissions that may occur in the compilation of this data.

PART NUMBERS

Part numbers listed in this reference are not recommendations by Haynes North America, Inc. for any product brand name. They are references that can be used with interchange manuals and aftermarket supplier catalogs to locate each brand supplier's discrete part number.

SPECIAL TOOLS

Special tools are recommended by the vehicle manufacturer to perform their specific job. Use has been kept to a minimum, but where absolutely necessary, they are referred to in the text by the part number of the tool manufacturer. These tools can be purchased, under the appropriate part number, from your local dealer or regional distributor, or an equivalent tool can be purchased locally from a tool supplier or parts outlet. Before substituting any tool for the one recommended, read the SAFETY NOTICE at the top of this page.

ACKNOWLEDGMENTS

The publisher expresses appreciation to Nissan Motor Corp., USA, Carson, CA, for their generous assistance.

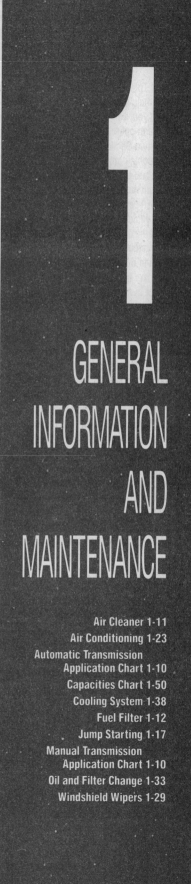

1

GENERAL INFORMATION AND MAINTENANCE

HOW TO USE THIS BOOK

Chilton's Total Car Care for Nissan Maxima is intended to help you learn more about the inner workings of your vehicle and save you money on its upkeep and operation.

The first two Sections will be the most used, since they contain maintenance and tune-up information and procedures. Studies have shown that a properly tuned and maintained vehicle can get at least 10 percent better gas mileage than an out-of-tune vehicle. The other Sections deal with the more complex systems of your vehicle. Operating systems from engine through brakes are covered in detail.

A secondary purpose of this book is a reference for owners who want to understand their vehicle and/or their mechanics better. In this case, no tools at all are required.

Before removing any bolts, read through the entire procedure. This will give you the overall view of what tools and supplies will be required. There is nothing more frustrating than having to walk to the bus stop on Monday morning because you were short 1 bolt on Sunday afternoon. So read ahead and plan ahead. Each operation should be approached logically and all procedures thoroughly understood before attempting any work.

All Sections contain adjustments, maintenance, removal and installation procedures, and repair or overhaul procedures. When repair is not considered practical, we tell you how to remove the part and then how to install the new or rebuilt replacement. In this way, you at least save the labor costs. Backyard repair of such components as the alternator is just not practical.

Two basic mechanic's rules should be mentioned here. One, whenever the left side of the vehicle or engine is referred to, it is meant to specify the driver's side of the vehicle. Conversely, the right side of the vehicle means the passenger's side. Secondly, most screws and bolt are removed by turning

counterclockwise and tightened by turning clockwise.

Safety is always the most important rule. Constantly be aware of the dangers involved in working on an automobile and take the proper precautions. (See the section in this Section Servicing Your Vehicle Safely and the SAFETY NOTICE on the acknowledgement page.)

Pay attention to the instructions provided. There are 3 common mistakes in mechanical work:

1. Incorrect order of assembly, disassembly or adjustment. When taking something apart or putting it together, doing things in the wrong order usually just costs you extra time; however, it CAN break something. Read the entire procedure before beginning disassembly. Do everything in the order in which the instructions say you should do it, even if you can't immediately see a reason for it. When you're taking apart something that is very intricate (for example, a carburetor), you might want to draw a picture of how it looks when assembled at one point in order to make sure you get everything back in its proper position. (We will supply exploded views whenever possible). When making adjustments, especially tune-up adjustments, do them in order; often, one adjustment affects another, and you cannot expect even satisfactory results unless each adjustment is made only when it cannot be changed by any order.

2. Overtorquing (or undertorquing). While it is more common for over-torquing to cause damage, undertorquing can cause a fastener to vibrate loose causing serious damage. Especially when dealing with aluminum parts, pay attention to torque specifications and utilize a torque wrench in assembly. If a torque figure is not available, remember that if you are using the right tool to do the job, you will probably not have to strain yourself to get a fastener tight enough. The pitch of most threads is so slight that the tension you put on the wrench will be multiplied many, many times in actual force on

what you are tightening. A good example of how critical torque is can be seen in the case of spark plug installation, especially where you are putting the plug into an aluminum cylinder head. Too little torque can fail to crush the gasket, causing leakage of combustion gases and consequent overheating of the plug and engine parts. Too much torque can damage the threads or distort the plug which changes the spark gap.

There are many commercial products available for ensuring that fasteners won't come loose, even if they are not torqued just right (a very common brand is Loctite®). If you're worried about getting something together tight enough to hold, but loose enough to avoid mechanical damage during assembly, one of these products might offer substantial insurance. Read the label on the package and make sure the products is compatible with the materials, fluids, etc. involved before choosing one.

3. Crossthreading. This occurs when a part such as a bolt is screwed into a nut or casting at the wrong angle and forced. Cross threading is more likely to occur if access is difficult. It helps to clean and lubricate fasteners and to start threading with the part to be installed going straight in. Then, start the bolt, spark plug, etc. with your fingers. If you encounter resistance, unscrew the part and start over again at a different angle until it can be inserted and turned several turns without much effort. Keep in mind that many parts, especially spark plugs, used tapered threads so gentle turning will automatically bring the part you're treading to the proper angle if you don't force it or resist a change in angle. Don't put a wrench on the part until its's been turned a couple of turns by hand. If you suddenly encounter resistance, and the part has not seated fully, don't force it. Pull it back out and make sure it's clean and threading properly.

Always take your time and be patient; once you have some experience, working on your vehicle will become an enjoyable hobby.

TOOLS AND EQUIPMENT

▶ SEE FIGS. 1 AND 2

The service procedures in this book presuppose a familiarity with hand tools and their proper use. However, it is possible that you may have a limited amount of experience with the sort of equipment needed to work on an automobile.

This section is designed to help you assemble a basic set of tools that will handle most of the jobs you may undertake.

In addition to the normal assortment of screwdrivers and pliers, automotive service work requires an investment in wrenches,

sockets and the handles needed to drive them, plus various measuring tools such as torque wrenches and feeler gauges.

You will find that virtually every nut and bolt on your vehicle is metric. Therefore, despite a few close size similarities, standard inch-size tools

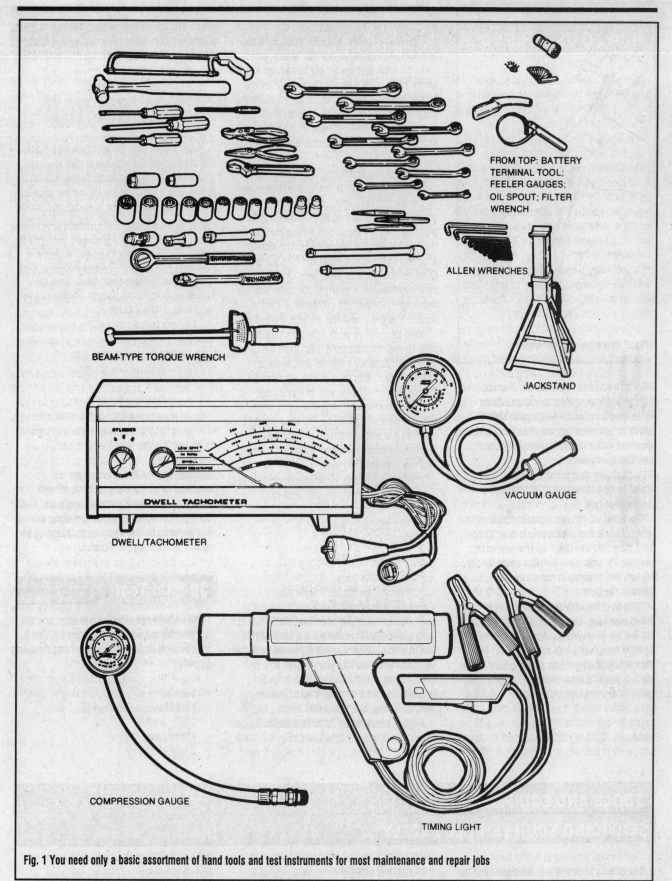

FROM TOP: BATTERY TERMINAL TOOL; FEELER GAUGES; OIL SPOUT; FILTER WRENCH

ALLEN WRENCHES

BEAM-TYPE TORQUE WRENCH

JACKSTAND

CYLINDER

LOW RPM IN RPM

DWELL
POINT RESISTANCE

DWELL TACHOMETER

DWELL/TACHOMETER

VACUUM GAUGE

COMPRESSION GAUGE

TIMING LIGHT

Fig. 1 You need only a basic assortment of hand tools and test instruments for most maintenance and repair jobs

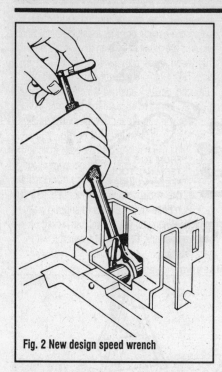

Fig. 2 New design speed wrench

will not fit and must not be used. You will need a set of metric wrenches as your most basic tool kit, ranging from about 6–22mm in size. High quality forged wrenches are available in 3 styles: open end, box end and combination open/box end. The combination tools are generally the most desirable as a starter set; the wrenches shown in the accompanying illustration are of the combination type.

The other set of tools inevitably required is a ratchet handle and socket set. This set should have the same size range as your wrench set. The ratchet, extensions and flex drives for the sockets are available in many sizes; it is advisable to choose a 3/8 in. drive set initially. One break in the inch/metric sizing war is that metric sized sockets sold in the U.S. have inch-sized drive (1/4 in., 3/8 in., 1/2 in. and etc.). Thus, if you already have an inch-sized socket set, you need only buy new metric sockets in the sizes needed. Sockets are available in 6- and 12-point versions; 6-point types are stronger and are a good choice for a first set. The choice of a drive handle for the sockets should be made with some care. If this is your first set, take the plunge and invest in a flex-head ratchet; it will get into

many places otherwise accessible only through a long chain of universal joints, extensions and adapters. An alternative is a flex handle, which lacks the ratcheting feature but has a head which pivots 180°; such a tool is shown below the ratchet handle in the illustration. In addition to the range of sockets mentioned, a rubber lined spark plug socket should be purchased. The correct size for the plugs in your vehicle's engine is 13/16 in.

The most important thing to consider when purchasing hand tools is quality. Don't be misled by the low cost of bargain tools. Forged wrenches, tempered screwdriver blades and fine tooth ratchets are much better investments than their less expensive counterparts. The skinned knuckles and frustration inflicted by poor quality tools make any job an unhappy chore. Another consideration is that quality tools come with an unbeatable replacement guarantee; if the tool breaks, you get a new one, no questions asked.

Most jobs can be accomplished using the tools on the accompanying lists. There will be an occasional need for a special tool, such as snaping pliers; that need will be mentioned in the text. It would not be wise to buy a large assortment of tools on the premise that someday they will be needed. Instead, the tools should be acquired 1 at a time, each for a specific job, both to avoid unnecessary expense and to be certain that you have the right tool.

The tools needed for basic maintenance jobs, in addition to the wrenches and sockets mentioned, include:

1. Jackstands, for support.
2. Oil filter wrench.
3. Oil filter spout or funnel.
4. Grease gun.
5. Battery post and clamp cleaner.
6. Container for draining oil.
7. Many rags for the inevitable spills.

In addition to these items there are several others which are not absolutely necessary but handy to have around. These include a transmission funnel and filler tube, a drop (trouble) light on a long cord, an adjustable (crescent) wrench and slip joint pliers.

A more advanced list of tools, suitable for tune-up work, can be drawn up easily. While the tools are slightly more sophisticated, they need

not be outrageously expensive. The key to these purchases is to make them with an eye towards adaptability and wide range. A basic list of tune-up tools could include:

1. Tachometer/dwell meter.
2. Spark plug gauge and gapping tool.
3. Feeler gauges for valve adjustment.
4. Timing light.

You will need both the wire type (spark plugs) and the flat type (valves) feeler gauges. The choice of a timing light should be made carefully. A light which works on the DC current supplied by the vehicle battery is the best choice; it should have a xenon tube for brightness. The light should have an inductive pickup which clamps around the No. 1 spark plug cable (the timing light illustrated has one of these pickups).

In addition to these basic tools, there are several other tools and gauges which you may find useful. These include:

1. A compression gauge. The screw-in type is slower to use but eliminates the possibility of faulty reading due to escaping pressure.
2. A manifold vacuum gauge.
3. A test light.
4. A combination volt/ohmmeter.
5. An induction meter, used to determine whether or not there is current flowing in a wire, an extremely helpful tool for electrical troubleshooting.

Finally, you will find a torque wrench necessary for all but the most basic of work. The beam type models are perfectly adequate. The click type (breakaway) torque wrenches are more accurate but are much more expensive and must be periodically recalibrated.

Special Tools

Special tools are available from:
    Kent-Moore Corporation
    29784 Little Mack
    Roseville, Michigan 48066

In Canada:
    Kent-Moore of Canada, Ltd.,
    2395 Cawthra
    Mississauga, Ontario
    Canada L5A 3P2

SERVICING YOUR VEHICLE SAFELY

It is virtually impossible to anticipate all of the hazards involved with automotive maintenance and service, but care and common sense will prevent most accidents.

The rules of safety for mechanics range from don't smoke around gasoline, to use the proper tool for the job. The trick to avoiding injuries is to develop safe work habits and take every

possible precaution. Always think through what you do before doing it!

Dos

▶ SEE FIG. 3

• Do keep a fire extinguisher and first aid kit within easy reach.

• Do wear safety glasses or goggles when cutting, drilling, grinding or prying, even if you have 20/20 vision. If you wear glasses for the sake of vision, they should be made of hardened glass that can serve also as safety glasses or wear safety goggles over your regular glasses.

• Do shield your eyes whenever you work around the battery. Batteries contain sulphuric acid. In case of contact with the eyes or skin, flush the area with water or a mixture of water and baking soda and get medical attention immediately.

• Do use safety stands for any under vehicle service. Jacks are for raising vehicles; safety stands are for making sure the vehicle stays raised until you want it to come down. Whenever the vehicle is raised, block the wheels remaining on the ground and set the parking brake.

• Do use a hydraulic floor jack of at least 1$\frac{1}{2}$ ton capacity when working on your Nissan. That little jack supplied with the vehicle is only designed for changing tires out on the rod.

• Do use adequate ventilation when working with any chemicals or hazardous materials. Like carbon monoxide, the asbestos dust resulting from brake lining wear can be poisonous in sufficient quantities.

• Do disconnect the negative battery cable when working on the electrical system. The secondary ignition system can contain up to 40,000 volts.

• Do follow manufacturer's directions whenever working with potentially hazardous materials. Both brake fluid and antifreeze are poisonous if taken internally.

• Do properly maintain your tools. Loose hammerheads, mushroomed punches and chisels, frayed or poorly grounded electrical cords, excessively worn screwdrivers, spread wrenches (open end), cracked sockets, slipping ratchets or faulty droplight sockets can cause accidents.

• Do use the proper size and type of tool for the job being done.

• Do when possible, pull on a wrench handle rather than push on it, and adjust your stance to prevent a fall.

• Do be sure adjustable wrenches are tightly closed on the nut or bolt and pulled so the face is on the side of the fixed jaw.

• Do select a wrench or socket that fits the nut or bolt. The wrench or socket should sit straight, not cocked.

• Do strike squarely with a hammer. Avoid glancing blows.

• Do set the parking brake and block the drive wheels if the work requires the engine running.

Don'ts

▶ SEE FIG. 4

• Don't run an engine in a garage or anywhere else without proper ventilation—EVER! Carbon monoxide is poisonous. It takes a long time to leave the human body and you can build up a deadly supply of it in your system by simply breathing in a little every day. You may not realize you are slowly poisoning yourself. Always use power vents, windows, fans or open the garage doors.

• Don't work around moving parts while wearing a necktie or other loose clothing. Short sleeves are much safer than long, loose sleeves. Hard-toed shoes with neoprene soles protect your toes and give a better grip on slippery surfaces. Jewelry such as watches, fancy belt buckles, beads or body adornment of any kind is not safe working around a vehicle. Long hair should be hidden under a hat or cap.

• Don't use pockets for tool boxes. A fall or bump can drive a screwdriver deep into your body. Even a wiping cloth hanging from the back pocket can wrap around a spinning shaft or fan.

• Don't use cinder blocks to support a vehicle! When you get the vehicle jacked up (with a hydraulic floor jack), support it with jackstands.

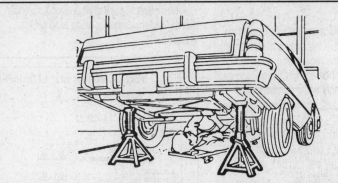

Fig. 3 Always support the vehicle securely with jackstands; don't use cinder blocks, tire-changing jacks or the like

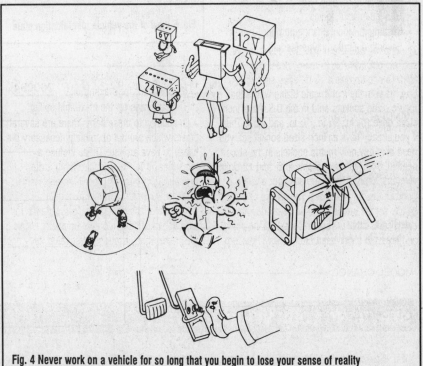

Fig. 4 Never work on a vehicle for so long that you begin to lose your sense of reality

• Don't smoke when working around gasoline, cleaning solvent or other flammable material.

• Don't smoke when working around the battery. When the battery is being charged, it gives off explosive hydrogen gas.

• Don't use gasoline to wash your hands. There are excellent soaps available. Gasoline may contain lead, and lead can enter the body through a cut, accumulating in the body until you are very ill. Gasoline also removes all the natural oils from the skin so bone dry hands will suck up oil and grease.

• Don't service the air conditioning system unless you are equipped with the necessary tools and training. The refrigerant, R–12, is compressed and in liquid form, and when released into the air will instantly freeze any surface it contacts, including your eyes. Although the refrigerant is normally non-toxic, R–12 becomes a deadly poisonous gas (phosgene) in the presence of an open flame. One good whiff of the vapors from burning refrigerant can be fatal.

SERIAL NUMBER IDENTIFICATION

Vehicle

♦ SEE FIGS. 5–7

The vehicle identification plate is located on the cowl at the rear of the engine compartment. The plate contains the model type, engine capacity, maximum horsepower, wheelbase and the engine and chassis serial numbers.

The vehicle or chassis serial number is broken down as shown in the illustration and described below. The vehicle identification number is also reproduced on a plate on the upper left surface of the instrument panel and can be seen from the outside through the windshield.

The V.I.N. is broken down as follows:

• First 3 digits/letters: Manufacturer
• Fourth letter: Engine type
• Fifth letter: Vehicle line
• Sixth digit: Model change number (0–9)
• Seventh digit: Body type (sedan)

• Eighth letter: Restraint system—S means standard; P means automatic.
• Ninth digit: Check digit 0–9 or X to verify that the serial number is being read off the vehicle itself

• Tenth letter: Model year in a letter code
• Eleventh letter: Manufacturing plant code
• Last 6 digits: Vehicle serial (chassis) number

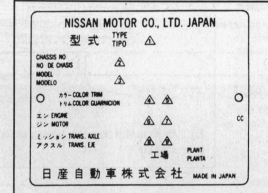

1. Type
2. Vehicle identification number (chassis number)
3. Model
4. Body color code
5. Trim color code
6. Engine model
7. Engine displacement
8. Transaxle model
9. Axle model

Fig. 5 View of the vehicle identification plate

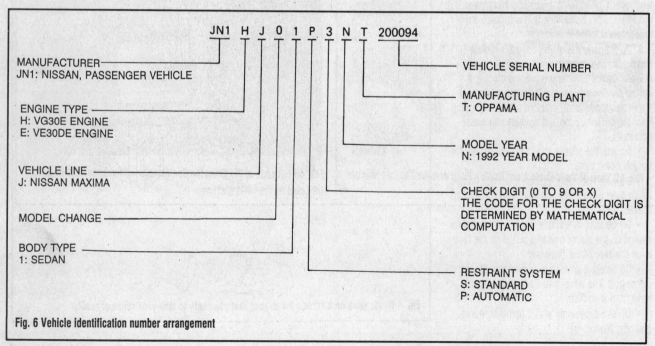

Fig. 6 Vehicle identification number arrangement

FIG. 6A View of the vehicle identification number plate

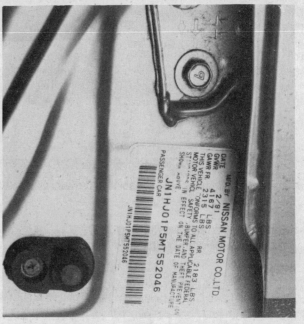

FIG. 6B View of the FMVSS certification label located on the bottom of the driver's door pillar

FIG. 6C View of the Vehicle Identification Plate and the Chassis Number

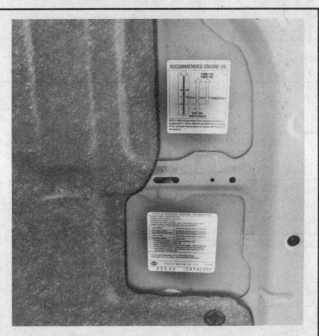

FIG. 6D Location of the Emission Control Information Label and Engine Oil Label on the 1991 Maxima

FIG. 6E Location of the Air Conditioning Label on the 1991 Maxima

Engine

♦ SEE FIGS. 8 AND 9

The engine serial number can be found on the driver's side edge of the right rear cylinder bank, looking from the driver's seat.

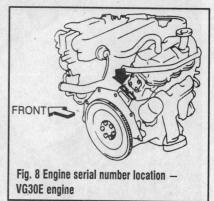

Fig. 8 Engine serial number location — VG30E engine

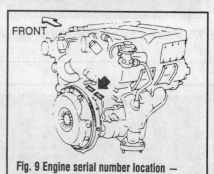

Fig. 9 Engine serial number location — VE30DE engine

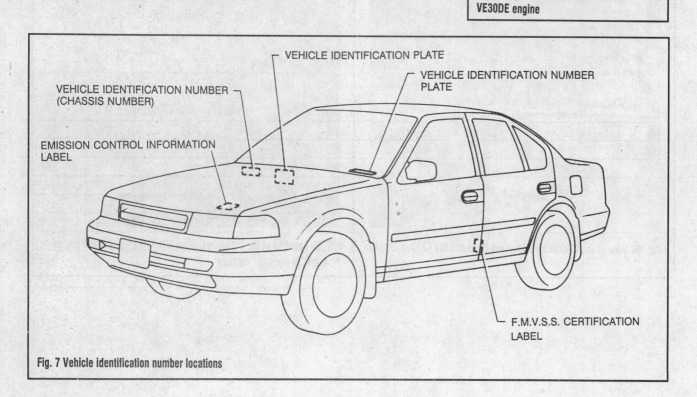

VEHICLE IDENTIFICATION PLATE

VEHICLE IDENTIFICATION NUMBER PLATE

VEHICLE IDENTIFICATION NUMBER (CHASSIS NUMBER)

EMISSION CONTROL INFORMATION LABEL

F.M.V.S.S. CERTIFICATION LABEL

Fig. 7 Vehicle identification number locations

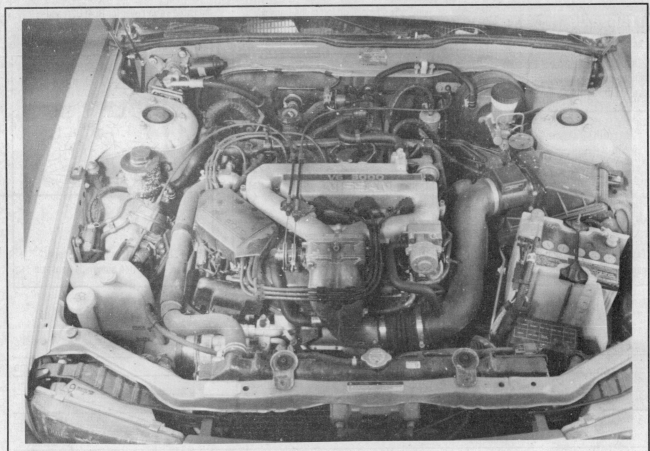

FIG. 8A View of the engine compartment with the various components on the 1991 VG30E engine

ENGINE IDENTIFICATION CHART

Year	Model	Engine Displacement Liter (cc)	Engine Series (ID/VIN)	Fuel System	No. of Cylinders	Engine Type
1985	Maxima	3.0 (2960)	VG30E	EFI	V6	SOHC
1986	Maxima	3.0 (2960)	VG30E	EFI	V6	SOHC
1987	Maxima	3.0 (2960)	VG30E	EFI	V6	SOHC
1988	Maxima	3.0 (2960)	VG30E	EFI	V6	SOHC
1989	Maxima	3.0 (2960)	VG30E	EFI	V6	SOHC
1990	Maxima	3.0 (2960)	VG30E	EFI	V6	SOHC
1991	Maxima	3.0 (2960)	VG30E	EFI	V6	SOHC
1992	Maxima	3.0 (2960)	VG30E	EFI	V6	SOHC
	Maxima	3.0 (2960)	VE30DE	EFI	V6	DOHC

EFI—Electronic Fuel Injection
SOHC—Single Overhead Cam
DOHC—Dual Overhead Cam

Transaxle

♦ SEE FIGS. 10–12

On the manual transaxle the serial number is stamped on the front upper face of the transaxle case. On the automatic transaxle the serial number is stamped on top of the transaxle housing for RE4FO4V model or on top of the transaxle valve cover for RL4FO2A and RE4FO2A models.

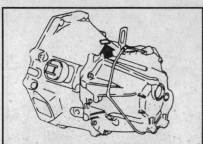

Fig. 10 Location of the transaxle serial number — manual transaxle

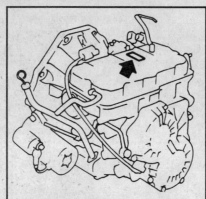

Fig. 11 Location of the transaxle serial number — RE4FO2A automatic transaxle

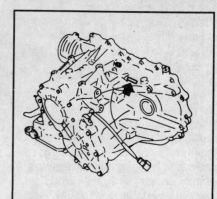

Fig. 12 Location of the transaxle serial number — RE4FO4A automatic transaxle

TRANSAXLE IDENTIFICATION CHART

Year	Model	Transaxle Identification	Transaxle Type
1985	Maxima	RS5F50A	Manual
	Maxima	RL4F02A	Automatic
1986	Maxima	RS5F50A	Manual
	Maxima	RL4F02A	Automatic
1987	Maxima	RS5F50A	Manual
	Maxima	RL4F02A	Automatic
1988	Maxima	RS5F50A	Manual
	Maxima	RL4F02A	Automatic
1989	Maxima	RS5F50A	Manual
	Maxima	RE4F02A	Automatic
1990	Maxima	RS5F50A	Manual
	Maxima	RE4F02A	Automatic
1991	Maxima	RS5F50A	Manual
	Maxima	RE4F02A	Automatic
1992	Maxima	RS5F50V	Manual
	Maxima	RE4F02A ①	Automatic
	Maxima	RE4F04V ②	Automatic

① Used with VG30E engine
② Used with VE30DE engine

ROUTINE MAINTENANCE

Routine maintenance is the self-explanatory term used to describe the sort of periodic work necessary to keep a vehicle in safe and reliable working order. A regular program aimed at monitoring essential systems ensure that the vehicle's components are functioning correctly (and will continue to do so until the next inspection, one hopes), and can prevent small problems from developing into major headaches. Routine maintenance also pays off big dividends in keeping major repair costs at a minimum, extending the life of the vehicle, and enhancing resale value, should you ever desire to part with your Nissan.

A very definite maintenance schedule is provided by Nissan, and must be followed, not only to keep the new vehicle warranty in effect, but also to keep the vehicle working properly. The Maintenance Intervals chart in this Section outlines the routine maintenance which must be performed according to intervals based on either accumulated mileage or time. Your vehicle also came with a maintenance schedule provided by Nissan. Adherence to these schedules will result in a longer life for your vehicle, and will, over the long run, save you money and time.

The checks and adjustments in the following sections generally require only a few minutes of attention every few weeks. The services to be performed can be easily accomplished in a morning. The most important part of any maintenance program is regularity. The few minutes or occasional morning spent on these seemingly trivial tasks will forestall or eliminate major problems later.

An air cleaner is used to keep airborne dirt and dust out of the air flowing through the engine. Proper maintenance is vital, as a clogged element will undesirably enrichen the fuel mixture, restrict air flow and power, and allow excessive contamination of the oil with abrasives.

The vehicles are equipped with a disposable,

Fig. 14 View of the air filter used on the 1989–92 Maxima

paper cartridge air cleaner element. The filter should be checked at every tune-up or sooner if the vehicle is operated in a dusty area. Loose dust can sometimes be removed by striking the filter against a hard surface several times or by blowing through it with compressed air. The filter should be replaced every 30,000 miles.

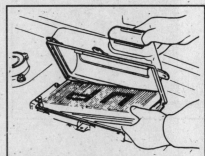

Fig. 15 When installing the air filter, make sure the work UP is facing upward

Air Cleaner

⬧ SEE FIGS. 13–15

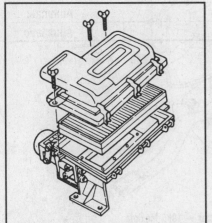

Fig. 13 View of the air filter used on 1985–88 Maxima

FIG. 14A Removing the air cleaner housing clips

FIG. 14B Removing the air cleaner from the housing

REMOVAL & INSTALLATION

1. Unscrew the wing nut(s), if equipped.
2. Lift off the housing cover and remove the filter element.
3. Before installing the original or the replacement filter, wipe out the inside of the housing with a clean rag or paper towel.
4. Install the paper air cleaner filter, seat the top cover on the bottom housing and tighten the wing nut(s), if equipped.

➡ **Make sure the word UP is facing up when you install the filter element.**

Fuel Filter

◆ SEE FIGS. 16–22

The fuel filter is a disposable plastic unit. It's located in the engine compartment, next to the power brake booster. The filter should be replaced at least every 30,000 miles. A dirty filter will starve the engine and cause poor running.

REMOVAL & INSTALLATION

1. On the 1985 Maxima, remove the rear seat.
2. Start the engine.
3. On the 1985 Maxima, disconnect the fuel pump electrical connector, located on the left side of the vehicle. On the 1986–92 models, remove the fuel pump fuse from the fuse block.

➡ **If using the CONSULT diagnostic tester on the 1992 VE30DE engine, place it in the WORK SUPPORT mode and depress the START button, with the engine idling, to release the fuel pressure.**

4. After the engine stalls, try to restart the engine; if the engine will not start, the fuel pressure has been released.

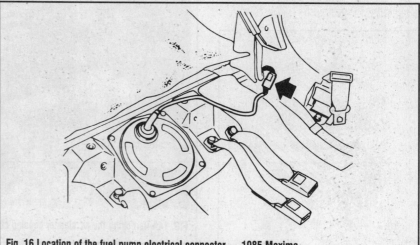

Fig. 16 Location of the fuel pump electrical connector — 1985 Maxima

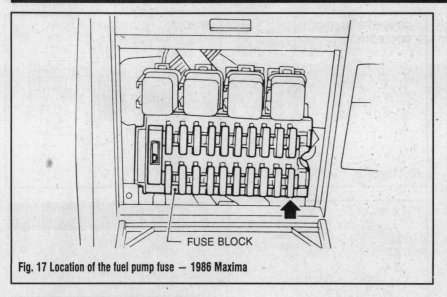

Fig. 17 Location of the fuel pump fuse — 1986 Maxima

FUSE BLOCK

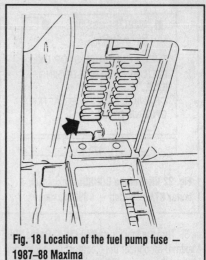

Fig. 18 Location of the fuel pump fuse — 1987–88 Maxima

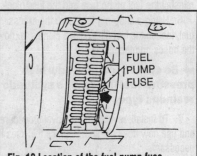

FUEL PUMP FUSE

Fig. 19 Location of the fuel pump fuse — 1989–91 Maxima

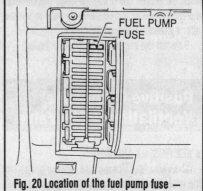

FUEL PUMP FUSE

Fig. 20 Location of the fuel pump fuse — 1992 Maxima

FIG. 21A Removing the fuel filter from the retainer located on the cowl

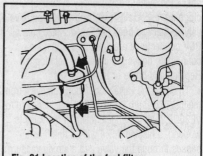

Fig. 21 Location of the fuel filter

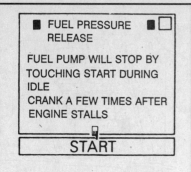

■ FUEL PRESSURE RELEASE ■ □

FUEL PUMP WILL STOP BY TOUCHING START DURING IDLE
CRANK A FEW TIMES AFTER ENGINE STALLS

START

Fig. 22 View of the CONSULT diagnostic tester START button — 1992 Maxima

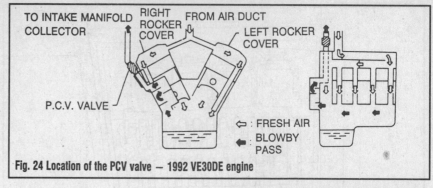

Fig. 24 Location of the PCV valve — 1992 VE30DE engine

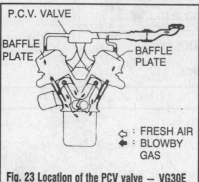

Fig. 23 Location of the PCV valve — VG30E engine

5. Turn the ignition switch **OFF**. On the 1985 Maxima, reconnect the electrical connector and replace the rear seat. On the 1986–92 Maximas, reinstall the fuel pump fuse into the fuse block.

6. Using a shop rag to absorb the excess fuel, loosen the fuel filter's hose clamps, remove the hoses and the filter.

➡ **Be sure to install a new high pressure fuel filter, not a synthetic resinous type.**

7. To install, reverse the removal procedures and use new hose clamps. Replace fuel lines if necessary.

8. On some 1989–91 vehicles the "Check Engine Light" will stay ON after installation is completed. The memory code in the control unit must be erased. To erase the code disconnect the battery cable for 10 seconds then reconnect after installation of fuel filter.

9. Start the engine and check for leaks.

Positive Crankcase Ventilation (PCV) Valve

▶ SEE FIGS. 23 AND 24

The valve feeds crankcase blowby gases into the intake manifold to be burned with the normal air/fuel mixture. The PCV valve has no strict interval for maintenance. However, it is wise to check the system occasionally in case of clogging, especially if you know that you have a vehicle that has been neglected. Make sure all PCV connections are tight. Check that the connecting hoses are clear and not clogged. Replace any brittle or broken hoses.

To check the valve's operation, remove it from the intake plenum for VG30E or cylinder head for VE30DE, with the engine idling. If the valve is working, a hissing noise will be heard as air passes through the valve and a strong vacuum will be felt when you place a finger over the valve opening.

REMOVAL & INSTALLATION

1. Squeeze the hose clamp with pliers and remove the hose.

2. If the valve has screw threads, use a wrench, to unscrew it and remove the valve.

3. Disconnect the ventilation hoses and flush with solvent.

4. Install the new PCV valve and replace the hoses and clamp.

Evaporative Canister

SERVICING

▶ SEE FIGS. 25 AND 26

Normally, the evaporation canister is maintenance free. Every 30,000 miles, check the fuel and vapor lines for proper connections and correct routing as well as condition. Replace damaged or deteriorated parts as necessary.

Battery

GENERAL MAINTENANCE

Loose, dirty or corroded battery terminals are a major cause of "no-start." Every 3 months or so, remove the battery terminals and clean them, giving them a light coating of petroleum jelly when finished. This will help retard corrosion.

Check the battery cables for signs of wear or chafing and replace any cable or terminal that looks marginal. Battery terminals can be easily cleaned and inexpensive terminal cleaning tools are an excellent investment that will pay for themselves many times over. They can usually be purchased from any well equipped auto store or parts department. Side terminal batteries require a different tool to clean the threads in the battery case. The accumulated white powder and corrosion can be cleaned from the top of the battery with an old tooth brush and a solution of baking soda and water.

Unless you have a maintenance-free battery, check the electrolyte level and check the specific gravity of each cell. Be sure the vent holes in each cell cap are not blocked by grease or dirt. The vent holes allow hydrogen gas, formed by the chemical reaction in the battery, to escape safely.

FLUID LEVEL

Check the battery electrolyte level at least once a month, more often in hot weather or during periods of extended operation. The level can be checked through the case of a translucent polypropylene battery; the cell caps must be removed on other models

If the battery level is low, add distilled water to the bottom of the split ring of each cell, then operate vehicle for about 1 hour and test the specific gravity.

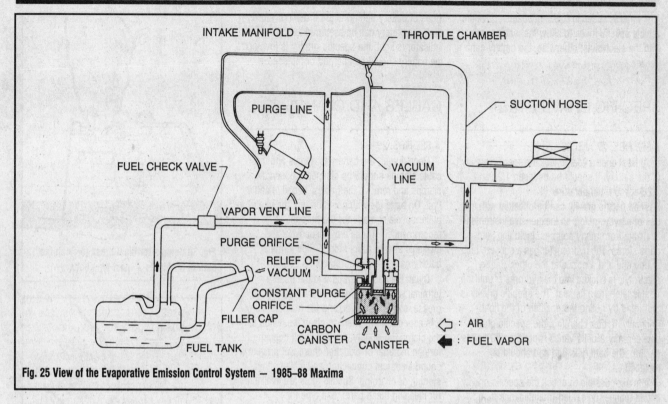

Fig. 25 View of the Evaporative Emission Control System — 1985–88 Maxima

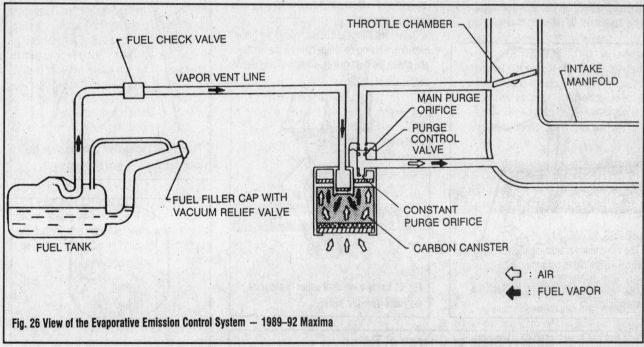

Fig. 26 View of the Evaporative Emission Control System — 1989–92 Maxima

If water is added in freezing weather, drive the vehicle several miles to allow the water to mix with the electrolyte; otherwise, the battery can freeze.

SPECIFIC GRAVITY TEST

♦ SEE FIGS. 27 AND 28

At least once a year, check the specific gravity of the battery. It should be between 1.20 and 1.26 at room temperature.

The specific gravity can be checked with the use of a hydrometer; an inexpensive instrument available from many sources, including auto parts stores. The hydrometer has a squeeze bulb at one end and a nozzle at the other. Battery electrolyte is sucked into the hydrometer until the float is lifted from its seat. The specific gravity is then read by noting the position of the float. Generally, if after charging, the specific gravity between any 2 cells varies more than 50 points (0.050), the battery is bad and should be replaced.

It is not possible to check the specific gravity in this manner on sealed (maintenance free) batteries. Instead, the indicator built into the top of the case must be relied on to display any signs of battery deterioration. If the indicator is dark, the battery can be assumed to be OK. If the indicator is light, the specific gravity is low, and the battery should be charged or replaced.

CABLES AND CLAMPS

♦ SEE FIGS. 29–32

Once a year, the battery terminals and the cable clamps should be cleaned. Loosen the clamps and remove the cables, negative cable first. On batteries with posts on top, the use of a puller specially made for the purpose is recommended. These are inexpensive and available at auto parts stores. Side terminal battery cables are secured with a bolt.

Clean the cable clamps and the battery terminal with a wire brush, until all corrosion, grease, etc., is removed and the metal is shiny. It is especially important to clean the inside of the clamp thoroughly, since a small deposit of foreign material or oxidation there will prevent a sound electrical connection and inhibit either starting or charging. Special tools are available for cleaning these parts, one type for conventional batteries and another type for side terminal batteries.

Before installing the cables, loosen the battery hold-down clamp or strap, remove the battery and check the battery tray. Clear it of any debris,

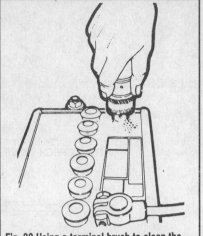
Fig. 30 Using a terminal brush to clean the battery terminals — post type battery

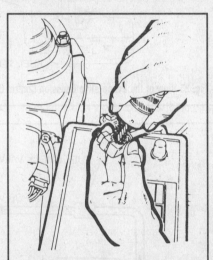
Fig. 31 Using a terminal brush to clean the cable terminals — post type battery

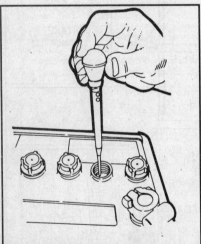
Fig. 27 Using an hydrometer to check the specific gravity

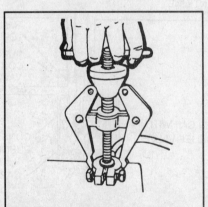
Fig. 29 Using a terminal puller to separate the cable from the battery

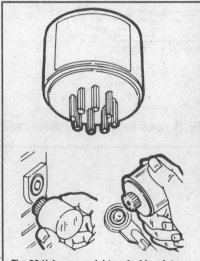
Fig. 32 Using a special terminal brush to clean the battery and cable terminals — side mount type battery

Battery State of Charge at Room Temperature

Specific Gravity Reading	Charged Condition
1.260–1.280	Fully Charged
1.230–1.250	¾ Charged
1.200–1.220	½ Charged
1.170–1.190	¼ Charged
1.140–1.160	Almost no Charge
1.110–1.130	No Charge

Fig. 28 Battery state of charge at room temperature

JUMP STARTING A DEAD BATTERY

The chemical reaction in a battery produces explosive hydrogen gas. This is the safe way to jump start a dead battery, reducing the chances of an accidental spark that could cause an explosion.

Jump Starting Precautions

1. Be sure both batteries are of the same voltage.
2. Be sure both batteries are of the same polarity (have the same grounded terminal).
3. Be sure the vehicles are not touching.
4. Be sure the vent cap holes are not obstructed.
5. Do not smoke or allow sparks around the battery.
6. In cold weather, check for frozen electrolyte in the battery. Do not jump start a frozen battery.
7. Do not allow electrolyte on your skin or clothing.
8. Be sure the electrolyte is not frozen.

CAUTION: Make certin that the ignition key, in the vehicle with the dead battery, is in the OFF position. Connecting cables to vehicles with on-board computers will result in computer destruction if the key is not in the OFF position.

Jump Starting Procedure

1. Determine voltages of the two batteries; they must be the same.
2. Bring the starting vehicle close (they must not touch) so that the batteries can be reached easily.
3. Turn off all accessories and both engines. Put both vehicles in Neutral or Park and set the handbrake.
4. Cover the cell caps with a rag—do not cover terminals.
5. If the terminals on the run-down battery are heavily corroded, clean them.
6. Identify the positive and negative posts on both batteries and connect the cables in the order shown.
7. Start the engine of the starting vehicle and run it at fast idle. Try to start the car with the dead battery. Crank it for no more than 10 seconds at a time and let it cool for 20 seconds in between tries.
8. If it doesn't start in 3 tries, there is something else wrong.
9. Disconnect the cables in the reverse order.
10. Replace the cell covers and dispose of the rags.

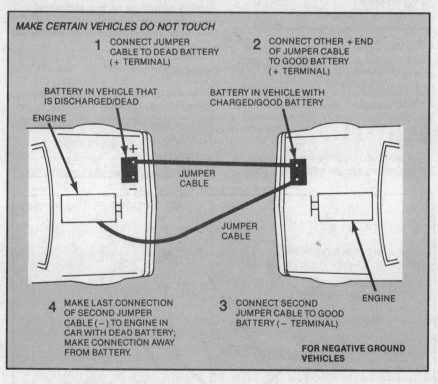

Side terminal batteries occasionally pose a problem when connecting jumper cables. There frequently isn't enough room to clamp the cables without touching sheet metal. Side terminal adaptors are available to alleviate this problem and should be removed after use

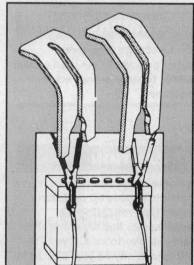

and check it for soundness. Rust should be wire brushed away, and the metal given a coat of anti-rust paint. Install the battery and tighten the hold-down clamp or strap securely but be careful not to overtighten, which will crack the battery case.

After the clamps and terminals are clean, reinstall the cables, negative cable last. Do not hammer on the clamps to install. Tighten the clamps securely but do not distort them. Give the clamps and terminals a thin external coat of petroleum jelly after installation, to retard corrosion.

Check the cables when the terminals are cleaned. If the cable insulation is cracked or broken, or if the ends are frayed, the cable should be replaced with a new cable of the same length and gauge.

CHARGING

1. Place the battery in a well ventilated area and remove the cell caps.
2. Make sure the fluid level is up to the split rings.
3. Connect a battery charger to the battery; red clamp on (+) positive and the black clamp on (–) negative or ground.
4. If using an adjustable charger, position the charge rate on 12V medium and charge until the specific is up to normal. Under no conditions should the battery be charged more than 6–8 hours; normal charging time is 4 hours, depending upon the charged state of the battery.

✱✱ WARNING

Too fast a charge rate, for an extended period of time, can cause the plates to sulfate and require replacement.

✱✱ CAUTION

Keep flame or sparks away from the battery; it gives off explosive hydrogen gas, rendering it a potential bomb. Battery electrolyte contains sulphuric acid. If you should splash any on your skin or in your eyes, flush the affected area with plenty of clear water. If it lands in your eyes, get medical help immediately.

REPLACEMENT

When necessary to replace the battery, select one with an amperage rating equal to or greater than the original. Deterioration, embrittlement and just plain aging of the battery cables, starter motor and associated wires makes the battery's job harder in successive years. The slow increase in electrical resistance over time makes it prudent to install a new battery with a greater capacity than the old.

Belts

INSPECTION

Check the belts driving the fan, air pump, air conditioning compressor and the alternator for cracks, fraying, wear and tension every 30,000 mile; replace as necessary.

ADJUSTING

▶ SEE FIGS. 33–35

Belt deflection at the midpoint of the longest span between pulleys should not be more than 1/2 in. (13mm) with 22 lbs. (10kg) of pressure applied to the belt.

1985–88

The power steering pump and air compressor belt tensions are adjusted with the idler pulley.

ALTERNATOR

1. Disconnect the negative battery cable.
2. Loosen the alternator's pivot bolt.
3. Loosen the alternator's mounting bolt.
4. Using a wooden lever, pry the alternator toward or away from the engine until the proper tension is achieved.
5. Tighten the alternator's pivot bolt locknut.
6. Tighten the alternator's mounting bolt.
7. Reconnect the negative battery cable.

EXCEPT ALTERNATOR

1. Disconnect the negative battery cable.
2. At the top of the slotted bracket holding the idler pulley, there is a bolt which is used to either raise or lower the pulley. To free the bolt for adjustment, it is necessary to loosen the locknut in the face of the idler pulley.
3. Loosen the idler pulley's mounting bolt.
4. Turn the adjusting bolt to adjust the belt tension.
5. After adjusting the belt tension, tighten the the idler pulley's mounting bolt.
6. Reconnect the negative battery cable.

✱✱ WARNING

An overly tight belt will wear out the pulley bearings on the assorted components.

1989–92

The belt tensions are adjusted using an adjustment bolt. The power steering pump and air compressor belt tensions are adjusted with the idler pulley.

ALTERNATOR

1. Disconnect the negative battery cable.

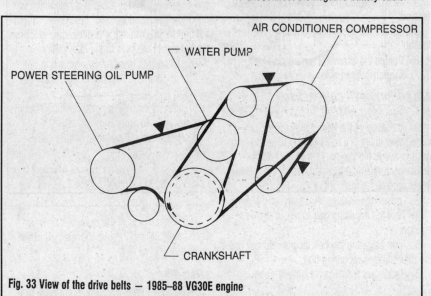

Fig. 33 View of the drive belts — 1985–88 VG30E engine

POWER STEERING OIL PUMP
WATER PUMP
AIR CONDITIONER COMPRESSOR
CRANKSHAFT

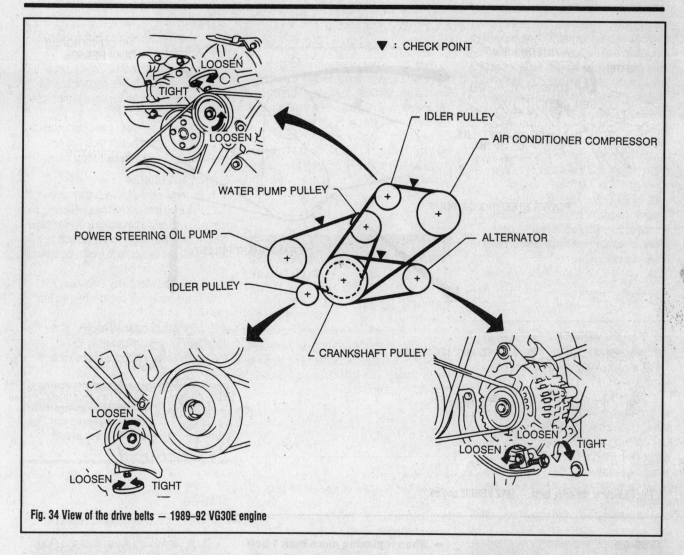

▼ : CHECK POINT

IDLER PULLEY

AIR CONDITIONER COMPRESSOR

WATER PUMP PULLEY

POWER STEERING OIL PUMP

ALTERNATOR

IDLER PULLEY

CRANKSHAFT PULLEY

LOOSEN

TIGHT

LOOSEN

LOOSEN

TIGHT

LOOSEN

LOOSEN

TIGHT

Fig. 34 View of the drive belts — 1989–92 VG30E engine

2. Loosen the alternator's adjusting bolt locknut.

3. Loosen the alternator's mounting bolt.

4. Turn the adjusting bolt to adjust the belt tension.

5. Tighten the alternator's adjusting bolt locknut.

6. Tighten the alternator's mounting bolt.

7. Reconnect the negative battery cable.

AIR CONDITIONER COMPRESSOR

1. Disconnect the negative battery cable.

2. At the top of the idler pulley for the air conditioner, there is a bolt which is used to either raise or lower the pulley. To free the bolt for adjustment, it is necessary to loosen the locknut in the face of the idler pulley.

3. Loosen the idler pulley's mounting bolt.

4. Turn the adjusting bolt to adjust the belt tension.

5. After adjusting the belt tension, tighten the the idler pulley's mounting bolt.

6. Reconnect the negative battery cable.

POWER STEERING PUMP

1. Disconnect the negative battery cable.

2. At the bottom of the idler pulley for the power steering pump, there is a bolt which is used to either raise or lower the pulley. To free the bolt for adjustment, it is necessary to loosen the locknut in the face of the idler pulley.

3. Loosen the idler pulley's mounting bolt.

4. Turn the adjusting bolt to adjust the belt tension.

5. After adjusting the belt tension, tighten the the idler pulley's mounting bolt.

6. Reconnect the negative battery cable.

REMOVAL & INSTALLATION

The replacement of the inner belt on multi-belted engines may require the removal of the outer belts.

1985–88

To replace a drive belt loosen the pivot and

mounting bolts of the component which the belt is driving, then, using a wooden lever or equivalent, pry the component inward to relieve the tension on the drive belt, always be careful where you locate the prybar not to damage the component. Slip the belt off the component pulley, match the new belt with the old belt for length and width, these measurements must be the same or problems will occur when adjust the new belt. After a new belt is installed correctly, adjust the tension.

➡ **When replacing more than 1 belt it is a good idea, to make note or mark what belt goes around what pulley. This will make installation fast and easy.**

On air conditioning compressor and power steering pump belt replacements, loosen the lock bolt for the adjusting bolt on idler pulley or power steering pump, then loosen the adjusting bolt. Pry pulley or pump inward to relieve the tension on the drive belt, always be careful where you locate the prybar not to damage the component or pulley.

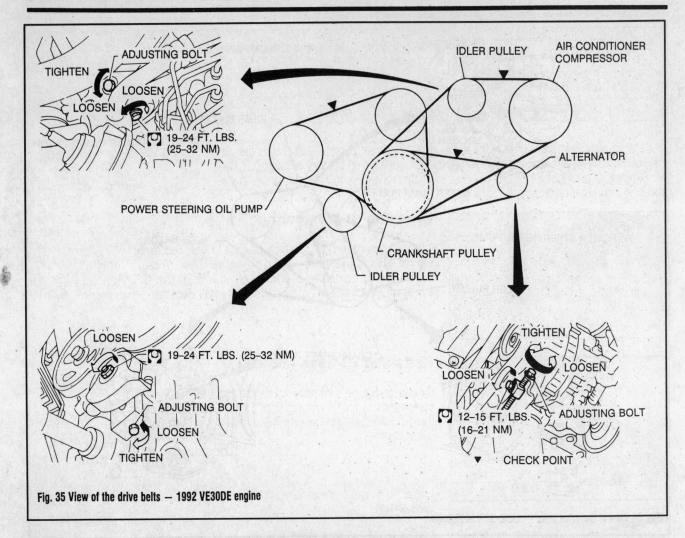

Fig. 35 View of the drive belts — 1992 VE30DE engine

1989–92

To replace a drive belt loosen the adjusting and mounting bolts of the component which the belt is driving, move the component inward to relieve the tension on the drive belt.

Slip the belt off the component pulley, match the new belt with the old belt for length and width, these measurements must be the same or problems will occur when adjust the new belt. After a new belt is installed correctly, adjust the tension.

➡ **When replacing more than 1 belt it is a good idea, to make note or mark what belt goes around what pulley; this will make installation fast and easy.**

On air conditioning compressor and power steering pump belt replacements, loosen the lock bolt for the adjusting bolt on idler pulley or power steering pump, then loosen the adjusting bolt.

HOW TO SPOT WORN V-BELTS

V–Belts are vital to efficient engine operation—they drive the fan, water pump and other accessories. They require little maintenance (occasional tightening) but they will not last forever. Slipping or failure of the V–belt will lead to overheating. If your V–belt looks like any of these, it should be replaced.

Cracking or Weathering

This belt has deep cracks, which cause it to flex. Too much flexing leads to heat build—up and premature failure. These cracks can be caused by using the belt on a pulley that is too small. Notched belts are available for small diameter pulleys.

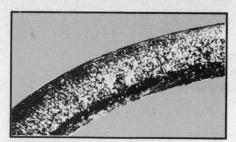

Softening (Grease and Oil)

Oil and grease on a belt can cause the belt's rubber compounds to soften and separate from the reinforcing cords that hold the belt together. The belt will first slip, then finally fail altogether.

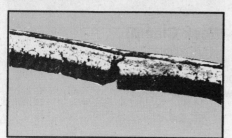

Glazing

Glazing is caused by a belt that is slipping. A slipping belt can cause a run-down battery, erratic power steering, overheating or poor accessory performance. The more the belt slips, the more glazing will be built up on the surface of the belt. The more the belt is glazed, the more it will slip. If the glazing is light, tighten the belt.

Worn Cover

The cover of this belt is worn off and is peeling away. The reinforcing cords will begin to wear and the belt will shortly break. When the belt cover wears in spots or has a rough jagged appearance, check the pulley grooves for roughness.

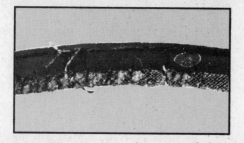

Separation

This belt is on the verge of breaking and leaving you stranded. The layers of the belt are separating and the reinforcing cords are exposed. It's just a matter of time before it breaks completely.

HOW TO SPOT BAD HOSES

Both the upper and lower radiator hoses are called upon to perform difficult jobs in an inhospitable environment. They are subject to nearly 18 psi at under hood temperatures often over 280°F, and must circulate nearly 7500 gallons of coolant an hour—3 good reasons to have good hoses.

Swollen Hose

A good test for any hose is to feel it for soft or spongy spots. Frequently these will appear as swollen areas of the hose. The most likely cause is oil soaking. This hose could burst at any time, when hot or under pressure.

Cracked Hose

Cracked hoses can usually be seen but feel the hoses to be sure they have not hardened; a prime cause of cracking. This hose has cracked down to the reinforcing cords and could split at any of the cracks.

Frayed Hose End (Due to Weak Clamp)

Weakened clamps frequently are the cause of hose and cooling system failure. The connection between the pipe and hose has deteriorated enough to allow coolant to escape when the engine is hot.

Debris In Cooling System

Debris, rust and scale in the cooling system can cause the inside of a hose to weaken. This can usually be felt on the outside of the hose as soft or thinner areas.

Hoses

The upper and lower radiator hoses and all heater hoses should be checked for deterioration, leaks and loose hose clamps every 15,000 miles.

REMOVAL & INSTALLATION

❄ CAUTION

When draining the coolant, keep in mind that cats and dogs are attracted by the ethylene glycol antifreeze, and are quite likely to drink any that is left in an uncovered container or in puddles on the ground. This will prove fatal in sufficient quantity. Always drain the coolant into a sealable container. Coolant should be reused unless it is contaminated or several years old.

1. After engine is cold, remove the radiator cap and drain the radiator into a clean pan if you are going to reuse the old coolant.

2. Remove the hose clamps and remove the hose by either cutting it off or twisting it to break its seal on the radiator and engine coolant inlets.

3. When installing the new hose, do not overtighten the hose clamps or you might cut the hose or destroy the neck of the radiator.

4. Refill the radiator with coolant, run the engine with the radiator cap on and then recheck the coolant level after the engine has reached operating temperature which is about 5 minutes.

➡ **It always is good idea, to replace hose clamps when replacing radiator hoses.**

Air Conditioning System

❄ CAUTION

The air conditioning system contains refrigerant under high pressure. Severe personal injury may result from improper service procedures. Wear safety goggles when servicing the refrigeration system.

SAFETY WARNINGS

Because of the importance of the necessary safety precautions that must be exercised when working with air conditioning systems and R–12 refrigerant, a recap of the safety precautions are outlined.

1. Avoid contact with a charged refrigeration system, even when working on another part of the air conditioning system or vehicle. If a heavy tool comes into contact with a section of copper tubing or a heat exchanger, it can easily cause the relatively soft material to rupture.

2. When it is necessary to apply force to a fitting which contains refrigerant, as when checking that all system couplings are securely tightened, use a wrench on both parts of the fitting involved, if possible. This will avoid putting torque on refrigerant tubing; it is advisable, when possible, to use tube or line wrenches when tightening these flare nut fittings.

3. Do not attempt to discharge the system by merely loosening a fitting or removing the service valve caps and cracking the valves. Precise control is possible only when using the service gauges. Place a rag under the open end of the center charging hose while discharging the system to catch any drops of liquid that might escape. Wear protective gloves when connecting or disconnecting service gauge hoses.

4. Discharge the system only in a well ventilated area, as high concentrations of the gas can exclude oxygen and act as an anesthetic. When leak testing or soldering, this is particularly important, as toxic gas is formed when R–12 contacts any flame.

5. Never start a system without first verifying that both service valves are backseated, if equipped, and that all fittings are throughout the system are snugly connected.

6. Avoid applying heat to any refrigerant line or storage vessel. Charging may be aided by using water heated to less than 125°F (51°C) to warm the refrigerant container. Never allow a refrigerant storage container to sit out in the sun or near any other source of heat, such as a radiator.

7. Always wear goggles when working on a system to protect the eyes. If refrigerant contacts the eye, it is advisable in all cases to see a physician as soon as possible.

8. Frostbite from liquid refrigerant should be treated by first gradually warming the area with cool water and then gently applying petroleum jelly. A physician should be consulted.

9. Always keep refrigerant can fittings capped when not in use. Avoid sudden shock to the can which might occur from dropping it or from banging a heavy tool against it. Never carry a can in the passenger compartment of a vehicle.

10. Always completely discharge the system before painting the vehicle, if the paint is to be baked on or before welding anywhere near the refrigerant lines.

SYSTEM INSPECTION

The most important aspect of air conditioning service is the maintenance of pure and adequate charge of refrigerant in the system. A refrigeration system cannot function properly in a significant percentage of the charge is lost. Leaks are common because the severe vibration encountered in an automobile can easily cause a sufficient cracking or loosening of the air conditioning fittings. As a result, the extreme operating pressures of the system force refrigerant out.

The problem can be understood by considering what happens to the system as is operated with continuous leak. Because the expansion valve regulates the flow of refrigerant to the evaporator, the level of refrigerant is fairly constant. The receiver/drier stores any excess of refrigerant and so a loss will first appear as a reduction in the level of liquid. As this level nears the bottom of the vessel, some refrigerant vapor bubbles will begin to appear in the stream of liquid supplied to the expansion valve. This vapor decreases the capacity of the expansion valve very little as the valve opens to compensate for its presence. As the quantity of liquid in the condenser decreases, the operating pressure will drop there and throughout the high side of the system. As the R–12 continues to be expelled, the pressure available to force the liquid through the expansion valve will continue to decrease, and, eventually, the valve's orifice will prove to be too much of a restriction for adequate flow even with the needle fully withdrawn.

At this point, low side pressure will start to drop, and severe reduction in cooling capacity, marked by freeze-up of the evaporator coil, will result. Eventually, the operating pressure of the evaporator will be lower than the pressure of the atmosphere surrounding it, and air will be drawn into the system wherever there are leaks in the low side.

Because all atmospheric air contains at least some moisture, water will enter the system and mix with the R–12 and the oil. Trace amounts of moisture will cause sludging of the oil, and corrosion of the system. Saturation and clogging of the filter/drier, and freezing of the expansion valve orifice will eventually result. As air fills the system to a greater and greater extent, it will interfere more and more with the normal flows of refrigerant and heat.

A list of general precautions that should be observed while doing this follows:

1. Keep all tools as clean and dry as possible.

2. Thoroughly purge the service gauges and hoses of air and moisture before connecting them to the system; keep them capped when not in use.

3. Thoroughly clean any refrigerant fitting before disconnecting it, in order to minimize the entrance of dirt into the system.

4. Plan any operation that requires opening the system beforehand in order to minimize the length of time it will be exposed to open air. Cap or seal the open ends to minimize the entrance of foreign material.

5. When adding oil, pour it through an extremely clean and dry tube or funnel. Keep the oil capped whenever possible. Do not use oil that has not been kept tightly sealed.

6. Use only refrigerant 12. Purchase refrigerant intended for use in only automobile air conditioning system. Avoid the use of refrigerant 12 that may be packaged for another use such as cleaning or powering a horn, as it is impure.

7. Completely evacuate any system that has been opened to replace a component, other than when isolating the compressor or that has leaked sufficiently to draw in moisture and air. This requires evacuating air and moisture with a good vacuum pump for at least 1 hour.

➡ **If a system has been open for a considerable length of time it may be advisable to evacuate the system for up to 12 hours (overnight).**

8. Use a wrench on both halves of a fitting that is to be disconnected, so as to avoid placing torque on any of the refrigerant lines.

Antifreeze

In order to prevent heater core freeze-up during air conditioner operation, it is necessary to maintain permanent type antifreeze protection of 15°F (–9°C) or lower. A reading of –15°F (–26°C) is ideal since this protection also supplies sufficient corrosion inhibitors for the protection of the engine cooling system.

❄ WARNING

Do not use antifreeze longer than specified by the manufacturer.

Radiator Cap

For efficient operation of an air conditioned

cooling system, the radiator cap should have a holding pressure which meets manufacturer's specifications. A cap which fails to hold these pressures should be replaced.

Condenser

Any obstruction of or damage to the condenser configuration will restrict the air flow which is essential to its efficient operation. It is therefore, a good rule to keep this unit clean an in proper physical shape.

➡ **Bug screens are regarded as obstructions.**

Condensation Drain Tube

This single drain expels the condensation, which accumulates on the bottom of the evaporator housing, into the engine compartment.

If this tube is obstructed, the air conditioning performance can be restricted and condensation buildup can spill over onto the vehicle's floor.

REFRIGERANT LEVEL CHECKS

❄ CAUTION

The compressed refrigerant used in the air conditioning system expands into the atmosphere at a temperature of –2°F (–19°C) or lower. This will freeze any surface, including your eyes, that it contacts. In addition, the refrigerant decomposes into a poisonous gas in the presence of a flame. Do not open or disconnect any part of the air conditioning system.

Sight Glass Check

▶ SEE FIG. 36

You can safely make a few simple checks to determine if your air conditioning system needs service. The tests work best if the temperature is warm (about 70°F).

➡ **If your vehicle is equipped with an aftermarket air conditioner, the following system check may not apply. You should contact the manufacturer of the unit for instructions on systems checks.**

1. Place the automatic transmission in **P** or the manual transaxle in neutral. Set the parking brake.

2. Run the engine at a fast idle (about 1500 rpm) either with the help of a friend or by temporarily readjusting the idle speed screw.

3. Set the controls for maximum cold with the blower on High.

4. Locate the sight glass in one of the system lines. Usually it is on the left alongside the top of the radiator.

5. If you see bubbles, the system must be recharged. Very likely there is a leak at some point. If it is determined that the system has a leak, it should be corrected as soon as possible. Leaks may allow moisture to enter and cause a very expensive rust problem.

6. If there are no bubbles, there is either no refrigerant at all or the system is fully charged. Feel the 2 hoses going to the belt-driven

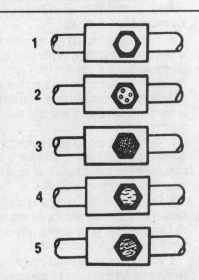

1. Clear sight glass—system correctly charged or overcharged
2. Occasional bubbles—refrigerant charge slightly low
3. Oil streaks on sight glass—total lack of refrigerant
4. Heavy stream of bubbles—series shortage of refrigerant
5. Dark or clouded sight glass—contaminant present

Fig. 36 Inspection of the refrigerant using the sight glass

compressor. If they are both at the same temperature, the system is empty and must be recharged.

7. If one hose (high-pressure) is warm and the other (low-pressure) is cold, the system may be all right. However, you are probably making these tests because you think there is something wrong, so proceed to the next step.

8. Have an assistant in the vehicle, turn the fan control ON and OFF to operate the compressor clutch. Watch the sight glass.

9. If bubbles appear when the clutch is disengaged and disappear when it is engaged, the system is properly charged.

10. If the refrigerant takes more than 45 seconds to bubble when the clutch is disengaged, the system is overcharged. This usually causes poor cooling at low speeds.

➡ **Run the air conditioner for a few minutes, every 2 weeks or so, during the cold months. This avoids the possibility of the compressor seals drying out from lack of lubrication.**

GAUGE SETS

Most of the service work performed in air conditioning requires the use of a set of 2 gauges, one for the high (head) pressure side of the system and the other for the low (suction) side.

The low side gauge records both pressure and vacuum. Vacuum readings are calibrated from 0–30 in. Hg and the pressure graduations read from 0 to no less than 60 psi.

The high side gauge measures pressure from 0 to at last 600 psi.

Both gauges are threaded into a manifold that contains 2 hand shut-off valves. Proper manipulation of these valves and the use of the attached test hoses allow the user to perform the following services:

1. Test high and low side pressures.
2. Remove air, moisture and contaminated refrigerant.
3. Purge the system (of refrigerant).
4. Charge the system (with refrigerant).

The manifold valves are designed so they have no direct effect on gauge readings, but serve only to provide for, or cut off, flow of refrigerant through the manifold. During all testing and hook-up operations, the valves are kept in a close position to avoid disturbing the refrigeration system. The valves are opened only to purge the system or refrigerant or to charge it.

DISCHARGING THE SYSTEM

➡ SEE FIGS. 37 AND 38

➡ **R–12 refrigerant is a chlorofluorocarbon which, when released into the atmosphere, can contribute to the depletion of the ozone layer in the upper atmosphere. Ozone filters out harmful radiation from the sun. If possible, an approved R–12 Recovery/Recycling machine that meets SAE standards should be**

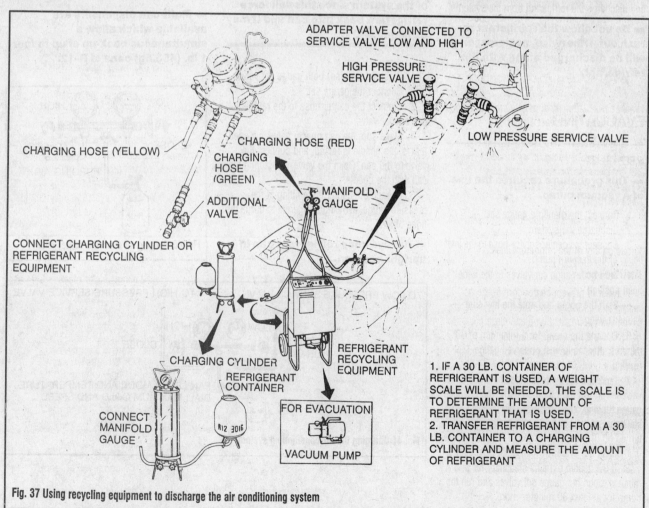

ADAPTER VALVE CONNECTED TO SERVICE VALVE LOW AND HIGH

HIGH PRESSURE SERVICE VALVE

LOW PRESSURE SERVICE VALVE

CHARGING HOSE (YELLOW)

CHARGING HOSE (RED)

CHARGING HOSE (GREEN)

ADDITIONAL VALVE

MANIFOLD GAUGE

CONNECT CHARGING CYLINDER OR REFRIGERANT RECYCLING EQUIPMENT

CHARGING CYLINDER

REFRIGERANT CONTAINER

REFRIGERANT RECYCLING EQUIPMENT

CONNECT MANIFOLD GAUGE

R12 3016

FOR EVACUATION

VACUUM PUMP

1. IF A 30 LB. CONTAINER OF REFRIGERANT IS USED, A WEIGHT SCALE WILL BE NEEDED. THE SCALE IS TO DETERMINE THE AMOUNT OF REFRIGERANT THAT IS USED.
2. TRANSFER REFRIGERANT FROM A 30 LB. CONTAINER TO A CHARGING CYLINDER AND MEASURE THE AMOUNT OF REFRIGERANT

Fig. 37 Using recycling equipment to discharge the air conditioning system

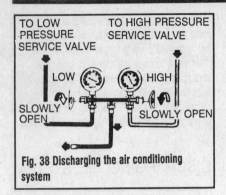

Fig. 38 Discharging the air conditioning system

employed when discharging the system. Follow the operating instructions provided with approved equipment exactly to properly discharge the system.

1. Close the high and low pressure valves of the manifold gauge fully.

2. Connect the 2 charging hoses of the manifold gauge to their respective service valves.

3. Slowly open both manifold gauge valves and discharge the refrigerant from the system.

➡ **Do not allow the refrigerant to rush out. Otherwise, compressor oil will be discharged along with the refrigerant.**

EVACUATING

♦ SEE FIG. 39

➡ **This procedure requires the use of a vacuum pump.**

1. Connect the manifold gauge set.

2. Discharge the system.

3. Connect the center service hose to the inlet fitting of the vacuum pump.

4. Turn both gauge set valves to the wide open position.

5. Start the pump and note the low side gauge reading.

6. Operate the pump for a minimum of 30 minutes after the lowest observed gauge reading.

7. Leak test the system. Close both gauge set valves. Turn off the pump and note the low side gauge reading. The needle should remain stationary at the point at which the pump was turned off. If the needle drops to 0 rapidly, there is a leak in the system which must be repaired.

8. If the needle remains stationary for 3–5 minutes, open the gauge set valves and run the pump for at least 30 minutes more.

9. Close both gauge set valves, stop the pump and disconnect the gauge set. The system is now ready for charging.

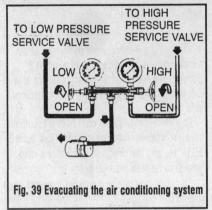

Fig. 39 Evacuating the air conditioning system

CHARGING

♦ SEE FIGS. 40–42

❄ CAUTION

Never charge refrigerant through high-pressure side (discharge side) of the system since this will force refrigerant back into can and it may exploded.

1. Close (clockwise) both gauge set valves.

2. Connect the gauge set.

3. Connect the center hose to the refrigerant can opener valve.

4. Make sure the can opener valve is closed, that is, the needle is raised, and connect the valve to the can. Open the valve, puncturing the can with the needle.

5. Loosen the center hose fitting at the pressure gauge, allowing refrigerant to purge the hose of air.

➡ **Always keep refrigerant can in upright position.**

6. Open the low side gauge set valve and the can valve.

7. Start the engine and turn the air conditioner to the maximum cooling mode. The compressor will operate and pull refrigerant gas into the system.

➡ **To help speed the process, the can may be placed, upright, in a pan of warm water, not exceeding 104°F (40°C).**

8. If more than 1 can of refrigerant is needed, close the can valve and gauge set low side valve when the can is empty and connect a new can to the opener. Repeat the charging process until the sight glass indicates a full charge.

9. When the charging process has been completed, close the gauge set valve and can valve. Run the system for at least 5 minutes to allow it to normalize.

10. Loosen both service hoses at the gauges to allow any refrigerant to escape. Remove the gauge set and install the dust caps on the service valves.

➡ **Multi-can dispensers are available which allow a simultaneous hook-up of up to four 1 lb. (453.6g) cans of R–12.**

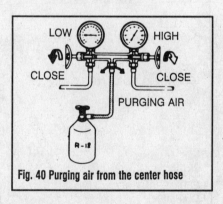

Fig. 40 Purging air from the center hose

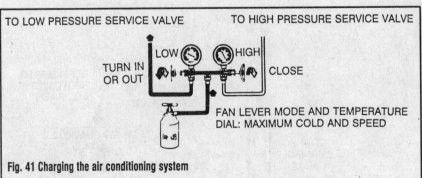

Fig. 41 Charging the air conditioning system

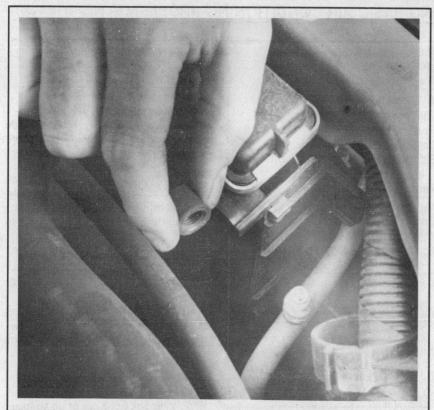

FIG. 41A Location of the air conditioner's low-pressure (suction) service valve

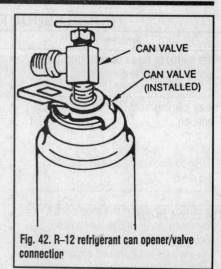

CAN VALVE

CAN VALVE (INSTALLED)

Fig. 42. R–12 refrigerant can opener/valve connection

✳✳ CAUTION

Never exceed the recommended maximum charge for the system.

Refrigerant Capacity
- 1985-88: 2.0–2.4 lbs. (0.9–1.09kg)
- 1989-90: 2.0–2.2 lbs. (0.9–0.99kg)
- 1991-92: 1.87–2.09 lbs. (0.85–0.95kg)

LEAK TESTING

Some leak tests can be performed with a soapy water solution. There must be at least a 1/2 lb. (0.23kg) charge in the system for a leak to be detected. The most extensive leak tests are performed with either a Halide flame type leak tester or the more preferable electronic leak tester.

In either case, the equipment is expensive and the use of a Halide detector can be extremely hazardous!

When using either method of leak detection, follow the manufacturer's instructions as the design and function of the detection may vary significantly.

FIG. 41B Location of the air conditioner's high-pressure (discharge) service valve

TROUBLESHOOTING BASIC AIR CONDITIONING PROBLEMS

Problem	Cause	Solution
There's little or no air coming from the vents (and you're sure it's on)	• The A/C fuse is blown • Broken or loose wires or connections • The on/off switch is defective.	• Check and/or replace • Check and/or repair connections • Replace switch
The air coming from the vents is not cool enough	• Windows and air vent wings open • The compressor belt is slipping • Heater is on • Condenser is clogged with debris • Refrigerant has escaped through a leak in the system • Receiver/drier is plugged	• Close windows and vent wings • Tighten or replace compressor belt • Shut heater off • Clean the condenser • Check system • Service system
The air has an odor	• Vacuum system is disrupted • Odor producing substances on the evaporator case • Condensation has collected in the bottom of the evaporator housing	• Have the system checked/repaired • Clean the evaporator case • Clean the evaporator housing drains
System is noisy or vibrating	• Compressor belt or mountings loose • Air in the system	• Tighten or replace belt; tighten mounting bolts • Have the system serviced

Sight glass condition
  Constant bubbles, foam or oil streaks
  Clean sight glass, but no cold air
  Clear sight glass, but air is cold
  Clouded with milky fluid
	
	• Undercharged system
	
	• No refrigerant at all
	• System is OK
	• Receiver drier is leaking dessicant
		
		• Charge the system
		
		• Check and charge the system
		
		• Have system checked

Large difference in temperature of lines	• System undercharged	• Charge and leak test the system
Compressor noise	• Broken valves • Overcharged • Incorrect oil level • Piston slap • Broken rings • Drive belt pulley bolts are loose	• Replace the valve plate • Discharge, evacuate and install the correct charge • Isolate the compressor and check the oil level. Correct as necessary. • Replace the compressor • Replace the compressor • Tighten with the correct torque specification
Excessive vibration	• Incorrect belt tension • Clutch loose • Overcharged • Pulley is misaligned	• Adjust the belt tension • Tighten the clutch • Discharge, evacuate and install the correct charge • Align the pulley
Condensation dripping in the passenger compartment	• Drain hose plugged or improperly positioned • Insulation removed or improperly installed	• Clean the drain hose and check for proper installation • Replace the insulation on the expansion valve and hoses
Frozen evaporator coil	• Faulty thermostat • Thermostat capillary tube improperly installed • Thermostat not adjusted properly	• Replace the thermostat • Install the capillary tube correctly • Adjust the thermostat
Low side low—high side low	• System refrigerant is low • Expansion valve is restricted	• Evacuate, leak test and charge the system • Replace the expansion valve

TROUBLESHOOTING BASIC AIR CONDITIONING PROBLEMS

Problem	Cause	Solution
Low side high—high side low	• Internal leak in the compressor—worn	• Remove the compressor cylinder head and inspect the compressor. Replace the valve plate assembly if necessary. If the compressor pistons, rings or cylinders are excessively worn or scored replace the compressor
	• Cylinder head gasket is leaking	• Install a replacement cylinder head gasket
	• Expansion valve is defective	• Replace the expansion valve
	• Drive belt slipping	• Adjust the belt tension
Low side high—high side high	• Condenser fins obstructed	• Clean the consenser fins
	• Air in the system	• Evacuate, leak test and charge the system
	• Expansion valve is defective	• Replace the expansion valve
	• Loose or worn fan belts	• Adjust or replace the belts as necessary
Low side low—high side high	• Expansion valve is defective	• Replace the expansion valve
	• Restriction in the refrigerant hose	• Check the hose for kinks—replace if necessary
	• Restriction in the receiver/drier	• Replace the receiver/drier
	• Restriction in the condenser	• Replace the condenser
Low side and high side normal (inadequate cooling)	• Air in the system	• Evacuate, leak test and charge the system
	• Moisture in the system	• Evacuate, leak test and charge the system

Windshield Wipers

♦ SEE FIG. 43

For maximum effectiveness and longest element life, the windshield and wiper blades should be kept clean. Dirt, tree sap, road tar and so on will cause streaking, smearing and blade deterioration if left on the glass. It is advisable to wash the windshield carefully with a commercial glass cleaner at least once a month. Wipe off the rubber blades with the wet rag afterwards. Do not attempt to move the wipers back and forth by hand; damage to the motor and drive mechanism will result.

If the blades are found to be cracked, broken or torn, they should be replaced immediately. Replacement intervals will vary with usage, although ozone deterioration usually limits blade life to about 1 year. If the wiper pattern is smeared or streaked, or if the blade chatters across the glass, the blades should be replaced. It is easiest and most sensible to replace them in pairs.

There are basically 3 types of wiper blade refills, which differ in their method of replacement. One type has 2 release buttons, approximately ⅓ of the way up from the ends of the blade frame. Pushing the buttons down releases a lock and allows the rubber blade to be

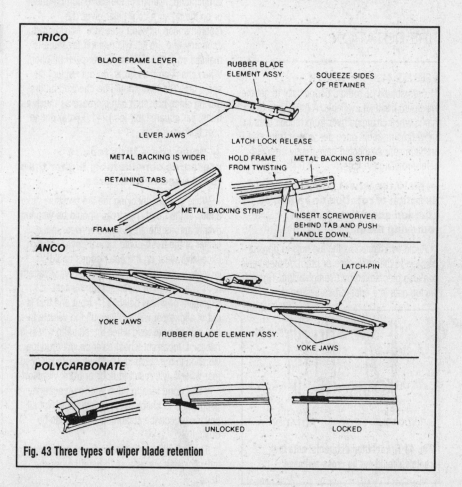

Fig. 43 Three types of wiper blade retention

removed from the frame. The new blade slides back into the frame and locks in place.

The second type of refill has 2 metal tabs which are unlocked by squeezing them together. The rubber blade can then be withdrawn from the frame jaws. A new 1 is installed by inserting it into the front frame jaws and sliding it rearward to engage the remaining frame jaws. There are usually 4 jaws. Be certain when installing that the refill is engaged in all of them. At the end of its travel, the tabs will lock into place on the front jaws of the wiper blade frame.

The third type is a refill made from polycarbonate. The refill has a simple locking device at one end which flexes downward out of the groove into which the jaws of the holder fit, allowing easy release. By sliding the new refill through all the jaws and pushing through the slight resistance when it reaches the end of its travel, the refill will lock into position.

Regardless of the type of refill used, make sure all of the frame jaws are engaged as the refill is pushed into place and locked. The metal blade holder and frame will scratch the glass if allowed to touch it.

Tire and Wheels

TIRE ROTATION

▶ SEE FIG. 44

Tires should be rotated periodically to get the maximum tread lift available. A good time to do this is when changing over from regular tires to snow tires or about once per year. If front end problems are suspected have them corrected before rotating the tires.

➡ **Mark the wheel position or direction of rotation on radial, or studded snow tires before removing them.**

Avoid overtightening the lug nuts to prevent damage to the brake disc or drum. Alloy wheels can also be cracked by overtightening. Tighten the lug nuts in a criss-cross sequence.

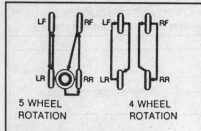

Fig. 44 Tire rotation diagrams; note that radials should not be cross-switched

TIRE DESIGN

▶ SEE FIG. 45

All 4 tires should be of the same construction type. Radial, bias or bias-belted tires should not be mixed. The wheels must be the correct width for the tire. Tire dealers have charts of tire and rim compatibility. A mismatch can cause sloppy handling and rapid tire wear. The tread width should match the rim width (inside bead to inside bead) within an inch. For radial tires, the rim width should be 80 percent or less of the tire (not tread) width. The height (mounted diameter) of the new tires can greatly change speedometer accuracy, engine speed at a given road speed, fuel mileage, acceleration, and ground clearance. Tire manufacturers furnish full measurement specifications.

TIRE INFLATION

▶ SEE FIGS. 46–48

The tires should be checked frequently for proper air pressure. Make sure the tires are cool, as you will get a false reading when the tires are heated because air pressure increases with temperature. A chart in the glove compartment or on the driver's door pillar gives the recommended inflation pressure. Maximum fuel economy and tire life will result if pressure is maintained at the highest figure given on chart. When checking pressures, do not neglect the spare tire. The tires should be checked before driving since pressure can increase as much as 6 lbs. per square inch (psi) (41.37kpa) due to heat buildup.

➡ **Some spare tires require pressures considerably higher than those used in other tires.**

While you are checking the tire pressure, take a look at the tread. The tread should be wearing evenly across the tire. Excessive wear in the center of the tread could indicate over-inflation. Excessive wear on the outer edges could indicate under inflation. An irregular wear pattern is usually a sign of incorrect front wheel alignment or wheel balance. A front end that is out of alignment will usually pull the vehicle to one side of a flat road when the steering wheel is released. Incorrect wheel balance will produce vibration in the steering wheel, while unbalanced rear wheels will result in floor or trunk vibration.

It is a good idea to have your own accurate gauge, and to check pressures weekly. Not all gauges on service station air pumps can be trusted.

Tires should be replaced when a tread wear indicator appears as a solid band across the tread.

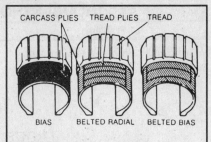

Fig. 45 Types of tire construction

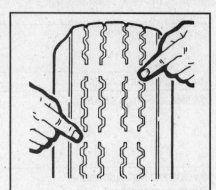

Fig. 46 Tread wear indicators sill appear when the tire is worn out

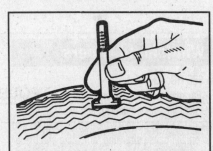

Fig. 47 Tread depth can be checked with an inexpensive gauge

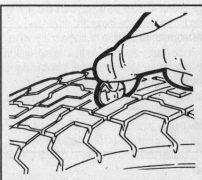

Fig. 48 A penny works as well as anything for checking tire tread depth; when you can see the top of Lincoln's head, it's time for a new tire

CARE OF SPECIAL WHEELS

Aluminum wheels should be cleaned and waxed regularly. Do not use abrasive cleaners, as they could damage the protective coating. Inspect wheel rims regularly for dents or corrosion, which may cause loss of pressure, damage the tire bead, or sudden wheel failure.

TROUBLESHOOTING BASIC WHEEL PROBLEMS

Problem	Cause	Solution
The car's front end vibrates at high speed	• The wheel are out of balance • Wheels are out of alignment	• Have wheel balanced • Have wheel alignment checked/adjusted
Car pulls to either side	• Wheels are out of alignment • Unequal tire pressure • Different size tires or wheels	• Have wheel alignment checked/adjusted • Check/adjust tire pressure • Change tires or wheels to same size
The car's wheel(s) wobbles	• Loose wheel lug nuts • Wheels out of balance • Damaged wheel • Wheels are out of alignment • Worn or damaged ball joint • Excessive play in the steering linkage (usually due to worn parts) • Defective shock absorber	• Tighten wheel lug nuts • Have tires balanced • Raise car and spin the wheel. If the wheel is bent, it should be replaced • Have wheel alignment checked/adjusted • Check ball joints • Check steering linkage • Check shock absorbers
Tires wear unevenly or prematurely	• Incorrect wheel size • Wheels are out of balance • Wheels are out of alignment	• Check if wheel and tire size are compatible • Have wheels balanced • Have wheel alignment checked/adjusted

TROUBLESHOOTING BASIC TIRE PROBLEMS

Problem	Cause	Solution
The car's front end vibrates at high speeds and the steering wheel shakes	• Wheel out of balance • Front end needs aligning	• Have wheels balanced • Have front end alignment checked
The car pulls to one side while cruising	• Unequal tire pressure (car will usually pull to the low side) • Mismatched tires • Front end needs aligning	• Check/adjust tire pressure • Be sure tires are of the same type and size • Have front end alignment checked
Abnormal, excessive or uneven tire wear See "How to Read Tire Wear"	• Infrequent tire rotation • Improper tire pressure • Sudden stops/starts or high speed on curves	• Rotate tires more frequently to equalize wear • Check/adjust pressure • Correct driving habits
Tire squeals	• Improper tire pressure • Front end needs aligning	• Check/adjust tire pressure • Have front end alignment checked

TIRE SIZE COMPARISON CHART

"Letter" sizes			Inch Sizes	Metric-inch Sizes		
"60 Series"	"70 Series"	"78 Series"	1965–77	"60 Series"	"70 Series"	"80 Series"
			5.50-12, 5.60-12	165/60-12	165/70-12	155-12
		Y78-12	6.00-12			
		W78-13	5.20-13	165/60-13	145/70-13	135-13
		Y78-13	5.60-13	175/60-13	155/70-13	145-13
			6.15-13	185/60-13	165/70-13	155-13, P155/80-13
A60-13	A70-13	A78-13	6.40-13	195/60-13	175/70-13	165-13
B60-13	B70-13	B78-13	6.70-13	205/60-13	185/70-13	175-13
			6.90-13			
C60-13	C70-13	C78013	7.00-13	215/60-13	195/70-13	185-13
D60-13	D70-13	D78-13	7.25-13			
E60-13	E70-13	E78-13	7.75-13			195-13
			5.20-14	165/60-14	145/70-14	135-14
			5.60-14	175/60-14	155/70-14	145-14
			5.90-14			
A60-14	A70-14	A78-14	6.15-14	185/60-14	165/70-14	155-14
	B70-14	B78-14	6.45-14	195/60-14	175/70-14	165-14
	C70-14	C78-14	6.95-14	205/60-14	185/70-14	175-14
D60-14	D70-14	D78-14				
E60-14	E70-14	E78-14	7.35-14	215/60-14	195/70-14	185-14
F60-14	F70-14	F78-14, F83-14	7.75-14	225/60-14	200/70-14	195-14
G60-14	G70-14	G77-14, G78-14	8.25-14	235/60-14	205/70-14	205-14
H60-14	H70-14	H78-14	8.55-14	245/60-14	215/70-14	215-14
J60-14	J70-14	J78-14	8.85-14	255/60-14	225/70-14	225-14
L60-14	L70-14		9.15-14	265/60-14	235/70-14	
	A70-15	A78-15	5.60-15	185/60-15	175/70-15	155-15
B60-15	B70-15	B78-15	6.35-15	195/60-15	175/70-15	165-15
C60-15	C70-15	C78-15	6.85-15	205/60-15	185/80-15	175-15
	D70-15	D78-15				
E60-15	E70-15	E78-15	7.35-15	215/60-15	195/70-15	185-15
F60-15	F70-15	F78-15	7.75-15	225/60-15	205/70-15	195-15
G60-15	G70-15	G78-15	8.15-15/8.25-15	235/60-15	215/70-15	205-15
H60-15	H70-15	H78-15	8.45-15/8.55-15	245/60-15	225/70-15	215-15
J60-15	J70-15	J78-15	8.85-15/8.90-15	255/60-15	235/70-15	225-15
	K70-15		9.00-15	265/60-15	245/70-15	230-15
L60-15	L70-15	L78-15, L84-15	9.15-15			235-15
	M70-15	M78-15				255-15
		N78-15				

NOTE: Every size tire is not listed and many size comparisons are approximate, based on load ratings. Wider tires than those supplied new with the vehicle, should always be checked for clearance.

FLUIDS AND LUBRICANTS

Fuel and Engine Oil Recommendations

OIL

◆ SEE FIGS. 49 AND 50

The SAE (Society of Automotive Engineers) grade number indicates the viscosity of the engine oil and thus its ability to lubricate at a given temperature. The lower the SAE grade number, the lighter the oil. The lower the viscosity, and the easier it is to crank the engine in cold weather.

Oil viscosities should be chosen from those oils recommended for the lowest anticipated temperatures during the oil change interval.

Multi-viscosity oils (10W-30, 20W-50, etc.) offer the important advantage of being adaptable to temperature extremes. They allow easy starting at low temperatures, yet they give good protection at high speeds and engine temperatures. This is a decided advantage in changeable climates or in long distance touring.

Choose the viscosity range carefully, based upon the lowest expected temperature for the time of year. If the lowest expected temperature is 0°F (–18°C), you should use 10W-30. If it is 50°F (10°C), as in spring and fall, you can use 20W-40 and 20W-50 for their extra guarantee of sufficient viscosity at high temperatures.

The API (American Petroleum Institute) designation indicates the classification of engine oil used under certain given operating conditions. Only oils designated for use Service SE should be used. Oils of the SE type perform a variety of functions inside the engine in addition to the basic function as a lubricant. Through a balanced system of metallic detergents and polymeric dispersants, the oil prevents the formation of high and low temperature deposits and also keeps sludge and particles of dirt in suspension. Acids, particularly sulfuric acid, as well as other by-products of combustion, are neutralized. Both the SAE grade number and the API designation can be found on top of the oil can.

➡ **The API has come out with a new designation of motor oil, SG. Oils designated for use Service SG are equally acceptable in your Nissan.**

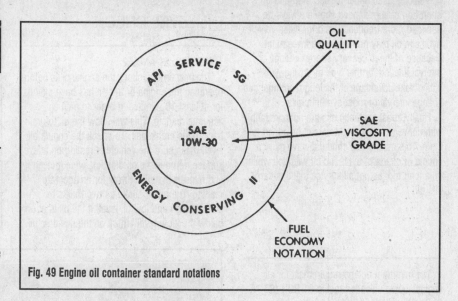

Fig. 49 Engine oil container standard notations

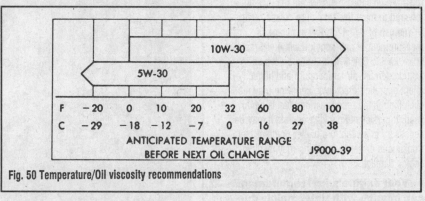

Fig. 50 Temperature/Oil viscosity recommendations

Non-detergent or straight mineral oils should not be used in your vehicle.

SYNTHETIC OIL

There are excellent synthetic and fuel efficient oils available that, under the right circumstances, can help provide better fuel mileage and better engine protection. However, these advantages come at a price, which can be 3–4 times the price per quart of conventional motor oils.

Before pouring any synthetic oils into your vehicle's engine, you should consider the condition of the engine and the type of driving you do. Also, check the vehicle's warranty conditions regarding the use of synthetics.

Generally, it is best to avoid the use of synthetic oil in both brand new and older, high mileage engines. New engines require a proper break-in, and the synthetics are so slippery that they can prevent this. Most manufacturers recommend that you wait at least 5000 miles before switching to a synthetic oil. Conversely, older engines are looser and tend to use more oil. Synthetics will slip past worn parts more readily than regular oil, and will be used up faster. If your vehicle already leaks and/or uses oil (due to worn parts and bad seals or gaskets), it will leak and use more with a slippery synthetic oil inside.

Consider your type of driving. If most of your accumulated mileage is on the highway at higher, steadier speeds, a synthetic oil will reduce friction and probably help deliver better fuel mileage. Under such ideal highway conditions, the oil change interval can be extended, as long as the oil filter will operate effectively for the extended life of the oil. If the filter can't do its job for this extended period, dirt and sludge will build up in your engine's crankcase, sump, oil pump and lines, no matter what type of oil is used. If using synthetic oil in this manner, you should continue to change the oil filter at the recommended intervals.

Vehicles used under harder, stop-and-go, short hop circumstances should always be serviced more frequently, and for these vehicles synthetic oil may not be a wise investment. Because of the necessary shorter change interval needed for this type of driving, you cannot take advantage of the long recommended change interval of most synthetic oils.

Finally, most synthetic oils are not compatible with conventional oils and cannot be added to them. This means you should always carry a couple of quarts of synthetic oil with you while on a long trip, as not all service stations carry this oil.

FUEL

The minimum octane requirement for all engines using unleaded fuel is 91 RON (87 CLC). All unleaded fuels sold in the U.S. are required to meet this minimum octane rating.

The use of a fuel too low in octane (a measurement of anti-knock quality) will result in spark knock. Since many factors such as altitude, terrain, air temperature and humidity affect operating efficiency, knocking may result even though the recommended fuel is being used. If persistent knocking occurs, it may be necessary to switch to a higher grade of fuel. Continuous or heavy knocking may result in engine damage.

➡ **Your engine's fuel requirement can change with time, mainly due to carbon buildup, which will in turn increase the temperatures in the combustion chamber and change the compression ratio. If your engine pings, knocks or runs on, switch to a higher grade of fuel. Sometimes just changing brands will cure the problem. If it becomes necessary to retard the timing from specifications, don't change it more than about 2°. Retarded timing will reduce power output and fuel mileage, in addition to increasing the engine temperature.**

Engine

OIL LEVEL CHECK

◆ SEE FIGS. 51 AND 52

The best time to check the engine oil is before operating the engine or after it has been sitting for at least 10 minutes in order to gain an accurate reading. This will allow the oil to drain back in the crankcase. To check the engine oil level, make sure the vehicle is resting on a level surface, remove the oil dipstick, wipe it clean and reinsert the stick firmly for an accurate reading. The oil dipstick has two marks to indicate high and low oil level. If the oil is at or below the "low level" mark on the dipstick, oil

should be added as necessary. The oil level should be maintained in the safety margin, neither going above the "high level" mark or below the "low level" mark.

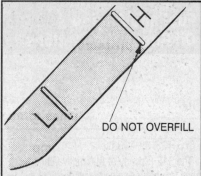

Fig. 51 Checking the engine oil level — VG30E engine

FIG. 51A View of the engine's oil dipstick in the dipstick tube

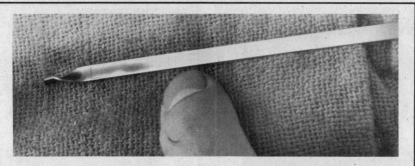

FIG. 51B View of the engine's dipstick indicating the proper fluid level on the VG30E engine

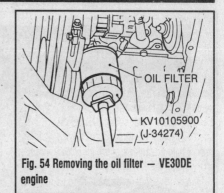

Fig. 54 Removing the oil filter — VE30DE engine

REFILL OIL TO "H" LEVEL. DO NOT OVERFILL

Fig. 52 Checking the engine oil level — VE30DE engine

OIL AND FILTER CHANGE

◆ SEE FIGS. 53–57

The Nissan factory maintenance intervals (every 7500 miles or 6 months) specify changing the oil filter at every second oil change after the initial service. We recommend replacing the oil filter with every oil change. For the small price of an oil filter, it's cheap insurance to replace the filter at every oil change. One of the larger filter manufacturers points out in its advertisements that not changing the filter leaves 1 quart (0.9L) of dirty oil in the engine. This claim is true and should be kept in mind when changing your oil.

➡ **When installing a new filter, use Nissan part No. 15208–60U00 or equivalent, for the VE30DE engine or Nissan PREMIUM or equivalent, for VG30E engine.**

1. Run the engine until it reaches normal operating temperature.
2. Raise and safely support the vehicle and support it on safety stands if necessary to gain access to the filter.
3. Slide a drain pan of at least 6 quarts (6L) capacity under the oil pan.

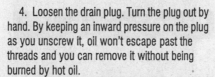

✳✳ CAUTION

The EPA warns that prolonged contact with used engine oil may cause a number of skin disorders, including cancer! You should make every effort to minimize your exposure to used engine oil. Protective gloves should be worn when changing the oil. Wash your hands and any other exposed skin areas as soon as possible after exposure to used engine oil. Soap and water, or waterless hand cleaner should be used.

4. Loosen the drain plug. Turn the plug out by hand. By keeping an inward pressure on the plug as you unscrew it, oil won't escape past the threads and you can remove it without being burned by hot oil.
5. Allow the oil to drain completely and then install the drain plug. Don't overtighten the plug or you'll be buying a new pan or a trick replacement plug for damaged threads.
6. Using an oil filter wrench, remove the oil filter. Keep in mind that it's holding about 1 quart (0.9L) of dirty, hot oil.
7. Empty the old filter into the drain pan and dispose of the filter and old oil.

OIL FILTER WRENCH

Fig. 53 Removing the oil filter — VG30E engine

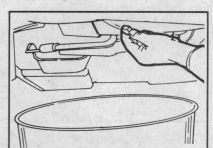

Fig. 55 By keeping an inward pressure on the drain plug, as you unscrew it, oil won't escape past the threads

Fig. 56 Coat the new oil filter gasket with clean oil

Fig. 57 Add oil through the capped opening in the rocker arm cover

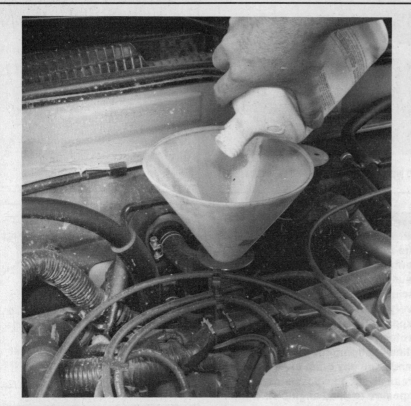

FIG. 56A Adding oil to the engine on the VG30E engine

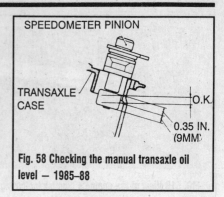

Fig. 58 Checking the manual transaxle oil level — 1985–88

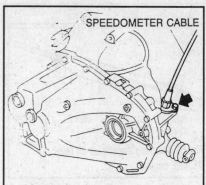

Fig. 59 Remove the speedometer cable to check the manual transaxle oil — 1985–88

➡ **One ecologically desirable solution to the used oil disposal problem is to find a cooperative gas station owner who will allow you to dump your used oil into his tank or take the oil to a reclamation center (often at garages and gas stations.**

8. Using a clean rag, wipe off the filter adapter on the engine block. Be sure the rag doesn't leave any lint which could clog an oil passage.

9. Coat the rubber gasket on the filter with fresh oil. Spin it onto the engine **by hand**; when the gasket touches the adapter surface give it another 1/2–3/4 turn. No more or you'll squash the gasket and it will leak.

10. Refill the engine with the correct amount of fresh oil.

11. Crank the engine over several times and then start it. If the oil pressure indicator light doesn't go out or the pressure gauge shows zero, shut the engine down and find out what's wrong.

12. If the oil pressure is OK and there are no leaks, shut the engine OFF and lower the vehicle.

Manual Transaxle

FLUID RECOMMENDATION

For manual transaxles be sure to use fluid with an API GL–4 rating.

LEVEL CHECK

1985–88

◆ SEE FIGS. 58 AND 59

Inspect the manual transaxle oil level at 12 months or 15,000 miles, at this point you should also correct the level. To check the oil level in the manual transaxle you have to remove speedometer cable at the clutch housing and look in the transaxle case to determine if fluid is needed. Refer below to the picture of the speedometer pinion for the correct level.

1989–92

◆ SEE FIG. 61

You should inspect the manual transaxle gear oil at 12 months or 15,000 miles, at this point you should correct the level or replace the oil as necessary. The lubricant level should be even with the bottom of the filler hole. Hold in on the filler plug when unscrewing it. When you are sure all of the threads of the plug are free of the transaxle case, move the plug away from the case slightly. If lubricant begins to flow out of the transaxle, then you know it is full. If not, add the correct gear oil as necessary

DRAIN AND REFILL

➡ **It is recommended that the manual transaxle fluid be changed every 30,000 miles if the vehicle is used in severe service. You may also want to change it if you have bought your vehicle used or if it has been driven in water deep enough to reach the transaxle case.**

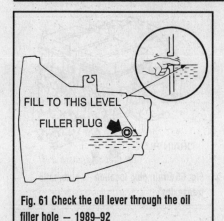

Fig. 61 Check the oil lever through the oil filler hole — 1989–92

1985–88

◆ SEE FIG. 60

1. Run the engine until it reaches normal operating temperature then turn key to the **OFF** position.

2. Raise and safely support the vehicle.

3. Remove speedometer cable at the clutch housing.

4. The drain plug is located on the bottom of the transaxle case. Place a pan under the drain plug and remove it.

❄❄ CAUTION

The oil will be HOT. Push up against the threads as you unscrew the plug to prevent leakage.

5. Allow the oil to drain completely. Clean off the plug and replace it; do not overtighten the plug.

6. Fill the transaxle with gear oil through the filler plug hole. Use API service GL–4 gear oil of the proper viscosity. This oil usually comes in a squeeze bottle with a long nozzle. If yours isn't, use a plastic squeeze bottle (the type used in the kitchen). Refer to the "Capacities" chart for the amount of oil needed.

7. The oil level should come up to the correct level.

8. Replace the speedometer cable at the clutch housing. Lower the vehicle, dispose of the old oil in the same manner as old engine oil.

9. Test drive the vehicle, stop and check for leaks.

1989–92

◆ SEE FIG. 62

1. Run the engine until it reaches normal operating temperature then turn key to the **OFF** position.

2. Raise and safely support the vehicle.

3. Remove the filler plug from the left side of the transaxle to provide a vent.

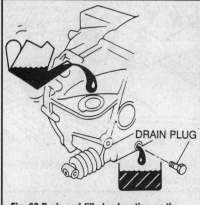

Fig. 60 Drain and fill plug location on the manual transaxle — 1985–88

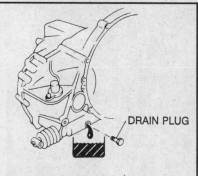

Fig. 62 Drain plug location on the manual transaxle — 1989–92

4. The drain plug is located on the bottom of the transaxle case. Place a pan under the drain plug and remove it.

❄❄ CAUTION

The oil will be HOT. Push up against the threads as you unscrew the plug to prevent leakage.

5. Allow the oil to drain completely. Clean off the plug and replace it; do not overtighten the plug.

6. Fill the transaxle with gear oil through the filler plug hole. Use API service GL–4 gear oil of the proper viscosity. This oil usually comes in a squeeze bottle with a long nozzle. If yours isn't, use a plastic squeeze bottle (the type used in the kitchen). Refer to the "Capacities" chart for the amount of oil needed.

7. The oil level should come up to the edge of the filler hole. You can stick your finger in to verify this. Watch out for sharp threads.

8. Replace the filler plug. Lower the vehicle, dispose of the old oil in the same manner as old engine oil.

9. Test drive the vehicle, stop and check for leaks.

Automatic Transaxle

FLUID RECOMMENDATIONS

All automatic transaxle, use Dexron® II ATF (automatic transaxle fluid)

LEVEL CHECK

◆ SEE FIGS. 63 AND 64

The fluid level in the automatic transaxle should be checked every 12 months or 15,000 miles, whichever comes first. The transaxle has a dipstick for fluid level checks.

1. Drive the vehicle until it is at normal operating temperature. The level should not be checked immediately after the vehicle has been driven for a long time at high speed or in city traffic in hot weather. In those cases, the transaxle should be given a 1/2 hour to cool down.

2. Stop the vehicle, apply the parking brake, then shift slowly through all gear positions, ending in **P**. Let the engine idle for about 5 minutes with the transaxle in **P**. The vehicle should be on a level surface.

3. With the engine still running, remove the dipstick, wipe it clean, then reinsert it, pushing it fully home.

4. Pull the dipstick again and, holding it horizontally, read the fluid level.

5. Cautiously feel the end of the dipstick to determine the temperature. Note that on Nissans there is a scale on each side, HOT on one, COLD on the other. If the fluid level is not in the correct area, more will have to be added.

6. Fluid is added through the dipstick tube. You will probably need the aid of a spout or a long necked funnel. Be sure whatever you pour through is perfectly clean and dry. Use an automatic transaxle fluid marked Dexron® II. Add fluid slowly, and in small amounts, checking the level frequently between additions. Do not overfill, which will cause foaming, fluid loss, slippage or possible transaxle damage. It takes only 1 pint (473mL) to raise the level from **L** to **H** when the transaxle is hot.

DRAIN AND REFILL

◆ SEE FIG. 65

➡ **It is recommended that the automatic transaxle fluid be changed every 30,000 miles if the vehicle is used in severe service.**

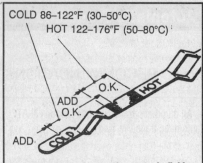

Fig. 63 Check the automatic transaxle fluid level

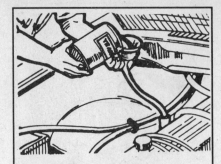

Fig. 64 Adding oil through the dipstick tube — automatic transaxle

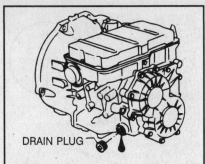

Fig. 65 Drain plug location — automatic transaxles

FIG. 63A View of the automatic transaxle's dipstick in the fluid charging tube

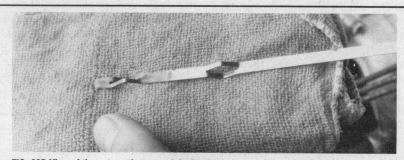

FIG. 63B View of the automatic transaxle's dipstick indicating the proper fluid level

You may also want to change it if you have bought your vehicle used or if it has been driven in water deep enough to reach the transaxle case.

1. Drive the vehicle enough to warm the transaxle fluid.
2. Raise and safely support the vehicle.
3. Place a drain pan under the transaxle.
4. Remove the drain plug located on the side of the transaxle case and allow the fluid to drain.
5. After draining, replace the drain plug and refill with new fluid.
6. Start the engine and correct the fluid level, as necessary.
7. Lower the vehicle and test drive.

Cooling System

FLUID RECOMMENDATION

▶ SEE FIGS. 66 AND 67

The cooling fluid or antifreeze, should be changed every 30,000 miles or 24 months. When replacing the fluid, use a mixture of 50 percent water and 50 percent ethylene glycol antifreeze.

Check the freezing protection rating at least once a year, preferably just before the winter sets in. This can be done with an antifreeze tester (most service stations will have one on hand and will probably check it for you, if not, they are available at an auto parts store). Maintain a protection rating of at least –20°F (–29°C) to prevent engine damage as a result of freezing and to assure the proper engine operating temperature.

It is also a good idea to have the the cooling system check for leaks, A pressure test gauge is available to perform such a task. Checking and repairing a coolant leak in the early stages while save time and money.

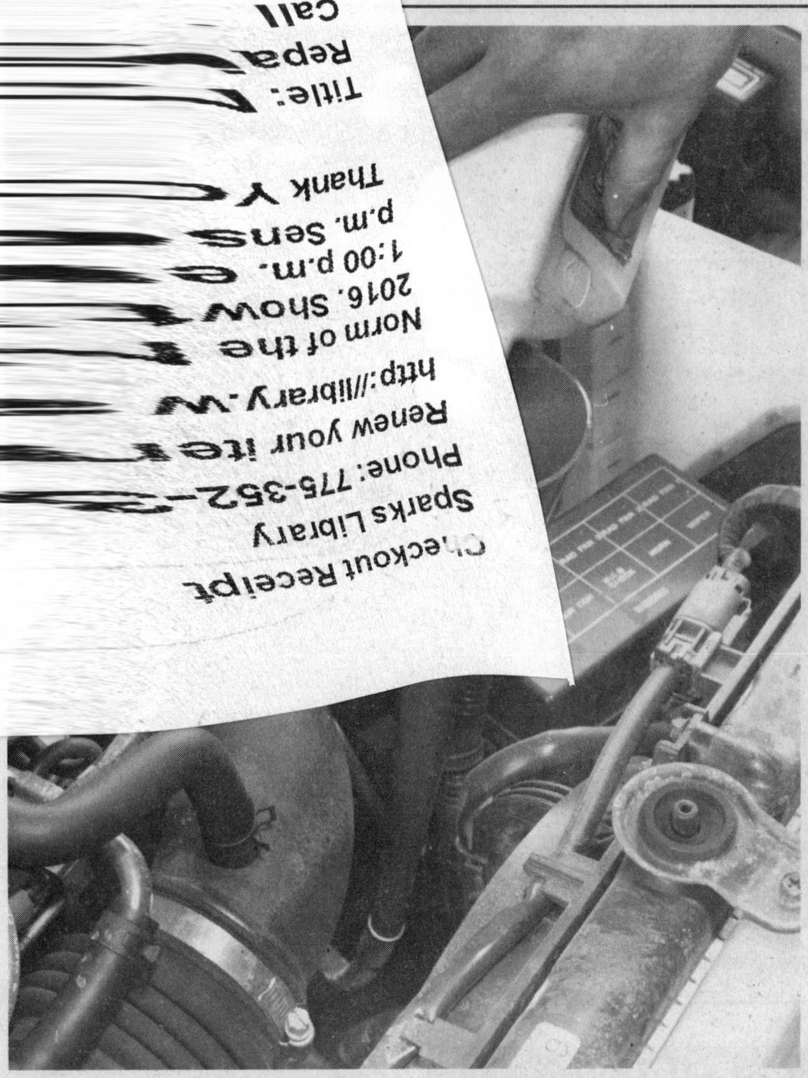

FIG. 63C Adding automatic transmission fluid to the automatic transaxle via charging pipe

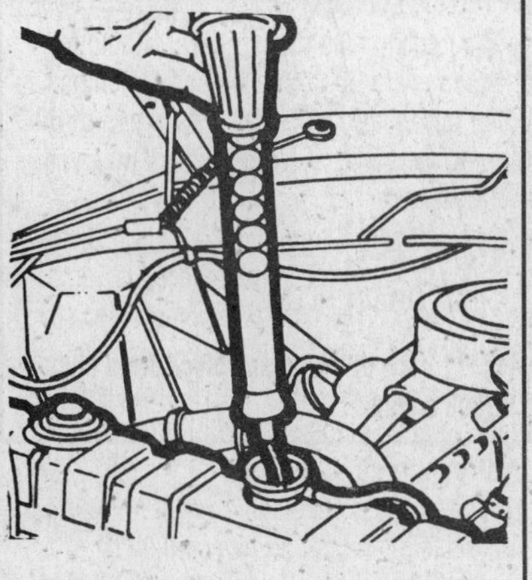

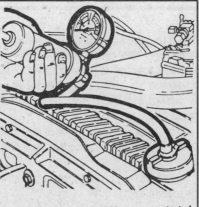

Fig. 66 Coolant protection can be checked with a simple float type tester

Fig. 67 The system should be pressure tested at least once a year

LEVEL CHECK

♦ SEE FIGS. 68 AND 69

Check the coolant level every 3000 miles or once a month. In hot weather operation, it may be a good idea to check the level once a week. Check for loose connections and signs of deterioration of the coolant hoses. Maintain the coolant level 3/4–1 1/4 in. (19–38mm) below the level of the filler neck when the engine is cold. If the engine is equipped with a coolant recovery bottle check the coolant level in the bottle when the engine is cold, the level should be up to the MAX mark. If the bottle is empty, check the level in the radiator and refill as necessary, then fill the bottle up to the MAX level.

❋❋ CAUTION

Never remove the radiator cap when the vehicle is hot or overheated. Wait until it has cooled. Place a thick cloth over the radiator cap to shield yourself from the heat and turn the radiator cap, slightly, until the sound of escaping pressure can be heard. Do not turn any more; allow the pressure to release gradually. When no more pressure can be heard escaping, remove the cap with the heavy cloth, cautiously.

➡ **Never add cold water to an overheated engine while the engine is not running.**

After filling the radiator, run the engine until it reaches normal operating temperature, to make sure the thermostat has opened and all the air is bled from the system.

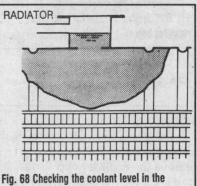

Fig. 68 Checking the coolant level in the radiator

FIG. 68A View of the cooling system overflow tank showing maximum system level

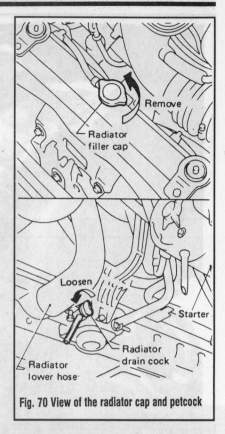

Fig. 70 View of the radiator cap and petcock

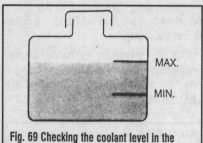

Fig. 69 Checking the coolant level in the recovery bottle

DRAIN AND REFILL

♦ SEE FIGS. 70–75

To drain the cooling system, allow the engine to cool down **before attempting to remove the radiator cap.** Then turn the cap until it hisses. Wait until all pressure is off the cap before removing it completely.

✳ CAUTION

To avoid burns and scalding, always handle a warm radiator cap with a heavy rag.

1. If equipped with a manual air conditioning, set the heater TEMP control lever to the fully HOT position. If equipped with automatic air conditioning turn ignition switch **ON** and set temperature at MAXIMUM. Then turn the ignition switch **OFF**.

2. With the radiator cap removed, drain the radiator by loosening the petcock at the bottom of the radiator.

3. Remove the drain plugs from both sides of the engine block.

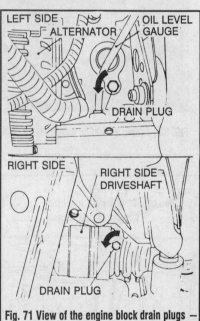

Fig. 71 View of the engine block drain plugs — VG30E engine

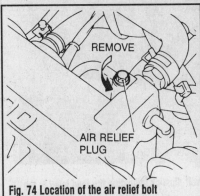

Fig. 73 Location of the air relief bolt location — 1985–88

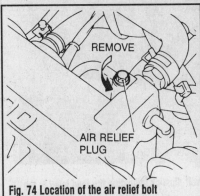

REMOVE

AIR RELIEF PLUG

Fig. 74 Location of the air relief bolt location — 1989–92 VG30E engine

AIR RELIEF PLUG

Fig. 75 Location of the air relief bolt location — 1992 VE30DE engine

> **CAUTION**
> When draining the coolant, keep in mind that cats and dogs are attracted by the ethylene glycol antifreeze, and are quite likely to drink any that is left in an uncovered container or in puddles on the ground. This will prove fatal in sufficient quantity. Always drain the coolant into a sealable container. Coolant should be reused unless it is contaminated or several years old.

4. Close the petcock. Be careful not to damage the petcock when closing.

5. Install the drain plugs to both sides of the engine block.

➡ **Slowly pour coolant through coolant filler neck to release air in the system with the air relief bolt or plug loosen.**

6. Refill the system with a 50/50 mix of ethylene glycol antifreeze; fill the system to 3/4–1 1/4 in. 19–38mm) from the bottom of the filler neck. Reinstall the radiator cap.

➡ **If equipped with a fluid reservoir tank, fill the reservoir tank up to the MAX level.**

7. Operate the engine at 2000 rpm for a few minutes and check the system for signs of leaks and for the correct level.

FLUSHING AND CLEANING THE SYSTEM

To flush the system you must first, drain the cooling system but do not close the petcock valve on the bottom of the radiator. You can

Brake and Clutch Master Cylinder

FLUID RECOMMENDATION

When adding or changing the fluid in the systems, use a quality brake fluid of the DOT 3 specifications.

➡ **Never reuse old brake fluid.**

LEVEL CHECK

◆ SEE FIGS. 76 AND 77

The brake and clutch master cylinders are

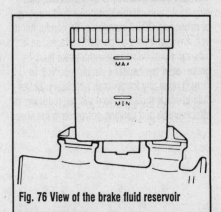

MAX

MIN

Fig. 76 View of the brake fluid reservoir

FIG. 76A View of the brake system's master cylinder reservoir showing the fluid level

Power Steering System

FLUID RECOMMENDATION

When adding or changing the power steering fluid, use Dexron® II ATF (Automatic Transmission Fluid).

LEVEL CHECK

▶ SEE FIG. 78

The power steering hydraulic fluid level is checked with a dipstick inserted into the pump reservoir cap. The level can be checked with the fluid either warm or cold. The vehicle should be parked on a level surface. Check the fluid level every 12 months or 15,000 miles, whichever comes first.

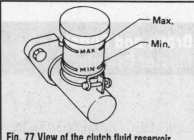

Fig. 77 View of the clutch fluid reservoir

located under the hood, in the left rear section of the engine compartment. They are made of translucent plastic so the levels may be checked without removing the tops. The fluid level in both reservoirs should be checked at least every 15,000 miles. The fluid level should be maintained at the upper most mark on the side of the reservoir. Any sudden decrease in the level indicates a possible leak in the system and should be checked out immediately.

When making additions of brake fluid, use only fresh, uncontaminated brake fluid meeting or exceeding DOT 3 standards. Be careful not to spill any brake fluid on painted surfaces, as it eats the paint. Do not allow the brake fluid container or the master cylinder reservoir to remain open any longer than necessary. Brake fluid absorbs moisture from the air, reducing its effectiveness and causing corrosion in the lines.

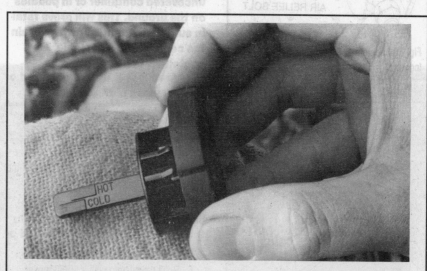

FIG. 78B View of the power steering pump's reservoir dipstick indicating the fluid level in the HOT or COLD condition

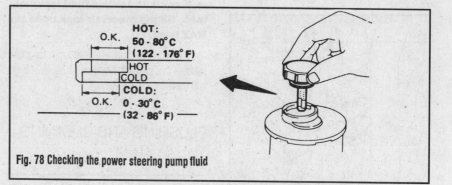

Fig. 78 Checking the power steering pump fluid

multipurpose grease every 7500 miles.

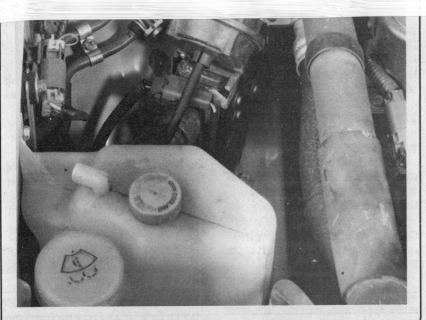

FIG. 78A Location of the power steering pump's reservoir and dipstick

TRAILER TOWING

General Recommendations

Your vehicle was primarily designed to carry passengers and cargo. It is important to remember that towing a trailer will place additional loads on your vehicle's engine, drive train, steering, braking and other systems. However, if you find it necessary to tow a trailer, using the proper equipment is a must.

Local laws may require specific equipment such as trailer brakes or fender mounted mirrors. Check your local laws.

➡ **A trailering brochure with information on trailer towing, special equipment required and optional equipment available can be obtained from your Nissan dealer**

Trailer Weight

Never allow the total trailer load to exceed 1000 lbs. (454kg) The total trailer load equals trailer weight plus its cargo weight.

Hitch Weight

Figure the hitch weight to select a proper hitch. Hitch weight is usually 9–11 percent of the trailer gross weight and should be measured with the trailer loaded. Hitches fall into 3 types: those that mount on the frame and rear bumper or the bolt-on or weld-on distribution type used for larger trailers. Axle mounted or clamp-on bumper hitches should never be used.

Check the gross weight rating of your trailer. Tongue weight is usually figured as 10 percent of gross trailer weight. Therefore, a trailer with a maximum gross weight of 1000 lbs. (454kg) will have a maximum tongue weight of 100 lbs. (45.4kg) Class I trailers fall into this category.

When you've determined the hitch that you'll need, follow the manufacturer's installation instructions, exactly, especially when it comes to fastener torques. The hitch will subjected to a lot of stress and good hitches come with hardened bolts. Never substitute an inferior bolt for a hardened bolt.

Cooling

ENGINE

One of the most common, if not THE most common, problems associated with trailer towing is engine overheating.

If you have a standard cooling system, without an expansion tank, you'll definitely need to get an aftermarket expansion tank kit, preferably one with at least a 2 quart (2L) capacity. These kits are easily installed on the radiator's overflow hose, and come with a pressure cap designed for expansion tanks.

Another helpful accessory is a Flex Fan. These fan are large diameter units are designed to provide more airflow at low speeds, with blades that have deeply cupped surfaces. The blades then flex or flatten out, at high speed, when less cooling air is needed. These fans are far lighter in weight than stock fans, requiring less horsepower to drive them. Also, they are far quieter than stock fans.

If you do decide to replace your stock fan with a flex fan, note that if your vehicle has a fan clutch, a spacer between the flex fan and water pump hub will be needed.

Aftermarket engine oil coolers are helpful for prolonging engine oil life and reducing overall engine temperatures. Both of these factors increase engine life.

While not absolutely necessary in towing Class I and some Class II trailers, they are recommended for heavier Class II and all Class III towing.

Engine oil cooler systems consist of an adapter, screwed on in place of the oil filter, a remote filter mounting and a multi-tube, finned heat exchanger, which is mounted in front of the radiator or air conditioning condenser.

TRANSAXLE

An automatic transaxle is usually recommended for trailer towing. Modern automatics have proven reliable and, of course, easy to operate, in trailer towing.

The increased load of a trailer, however, causes an increase in the temperature of the automatic transaxke fluid. Heat is the worst enemy of an automatic transaxle. As the temperature of the fluid increases, the life of the fluid decreases.

It is essential, therefore, that you install an automatic transaxle cooler.

The cooler, which consists of a multi-tube, finned heat exchanger, is usually installed in front of the radiator or air conditioning compressor and hooked inline with the transaxle cooler tank inlet line. Follow the cooler manufacturer's installation instructions.

Select a cooler of at least adequate capacity, based upon the combined gross weights of the vehicle and trailer.

Cooler manufacturers recommend that you use an aftermarket cooler in addition to, and not instead of, the present cooling tank in your radiator. If you do want to use it in place of the radiator cooling tank, get a cooler at least 2 sizes larger than normally necessary.

➡ **A transaxle cooler can, sometimes, cause slow or harsh shifting in the transmission during cold weather, until the fluid has a chance to come up to normal operating temperature. Some coolers can be purchased with or retrofitted with a temperature bypass valve which will allow fluid flow through the cooler only when the fluid has reached operating temperature or above.**

Handling A Trailer

Towing a trailer with ease and safety requires a certain amount of experience. It's a good idea to learn the feel of a trailer by practicing turning, stopping and backing in an open area such as an empty parking lot.

TOWING

Fig. 79 Towing hook location — front wheel drive vehicles

JACKING

♦ SEE FIG. 80

Never use the tire changing jack (the little jack supplied with the vehicle) for anything other than changing a flat out on the road. These jacks are simply not safe enough for any type of vehicle service except tire changing!

The service operations in this book often require that one end or the other, or both, of the vehicle be raised and safely supported. For this reason a hydraulic floor jack of at least $1\frac{1}{2}$ ton capacity is as necessary as a spark plug socket to you, the do-it-yourself owner/mechanic. The cost of these jacks (invest in a good quality unit) is actually quite reasonable considering how they pay for themselves again and again over the years.

Along with a hydraulic floor jack should be at least two sturdy jackstands. These are a necessity if you intend to work underneath the vehicle. Never work under the vehicle when it is only supported by a jack!

Drive-on ramps are an alternative method of raising the front end of the vehicle. They are commercially available or can be fabricated from heavy lumber or steel. Be sure to always block the wheels when using ramps.

❊❊ CAUTION

NEVER use concrete cinder blocks to support the vehicle. They are likely to break if the load is not evenly distributed. They should never be trusted when you are under the vehicle!

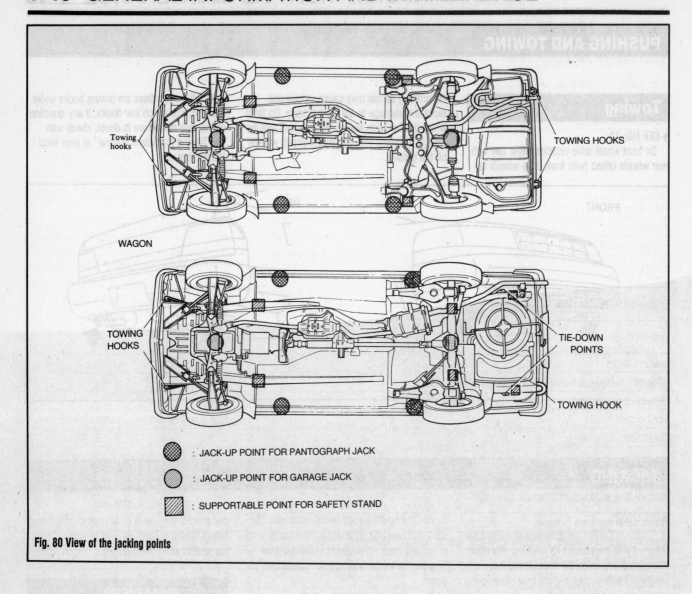

Fig. 80 View of the jacking points

1985–89 MAINTENANCE INTERVALS CHART—NORMAL SERVICE

MAINTENANCE OPERATION		7.5	15	30	45	60
Periodic maintenance should be performed	Miles × 1,000	7.5	15	30	45	60
at number of miles, kilometers or months,	(Kilometers × 1,000)	(12)	(24)	(48)	(72)	(96)
whichever comes first.	Months	6	12	24	36	48
Drive belts				I*		I*
Air cleaner filter			Replace every 30,000 miles (48,000 km).			
Vapor lines				I*		I*
Fuel lines (hoses, piping, connections, etc.)				I*		I*
Fuel filter			See NOTE (1)*.			
Engine coolant				R		R
Engine oil		R	Then replace every 7,500 miles (12,000 km) or 6 months.			
Engine oil filter (Use PREMIUM type.)		R	Then replace every second oil change.			
Spark plugs			Replace every 30,000 miles (48,000 km).			
Ignition wires			Inspect every 2 years*.			
Idle rpm			I*	I*	I*	I*
Exhaust gas sensor				I		I
Timing belt			Replace every 60,000 miles (96,000 km)			
Brake lines & hoses		I	I	I	I	
Brake pads & discs			Inspect every 15,000 miles (24,000 km).			
Manual and automatic transaxle gear oil			Inspect every 15,000 miles (24,000 km).			
Power steering lines & hoses			I	I	I	I
Steering gear & linkage, axle & suspension parts & front drive shaft boots			I	I	I	I
Locks, hinges & hood latch			L	L	L	L
Exhaust system			I	I	I	I
Seat belts, buckles, retractors, anchors & adjuster			I	I	I	I

NOTE: (1) If vehicle is operated under extremely adverse weather conditions or in areas where ambient temperatures are either extremely low or extremely high, the filters might become clogged. In such an event, replace them immediately.

(2) Maintenance items and intervals with "*" are recommended by NISSAN for reliable vehicle operation. The owner need not perform such maintenance in order to maintain the emission warranty or manufacturer recall liability. Other maintenance items and intervals are required.

Abbreviations: R = Replace
I = Inspect. Correct or replace if necessary.
L = Lubricate

1985–89 MAINTENANCE INTERVALS CHART—SEVERE SERVICE

Severe driving conditions

A — Repeated short distance driving
B — Extensive idling
C — Driving in dusty conditions
D — Driving in extremely low or high ambient temperatures
E — Towing a trailer
F — Driving in areas using road salt or other corrosive materials
G — Driving on rough and/or muddy roads

Driving condition	Maintenance item	Maintenance operation	Maintenance interval
. . C	Air cleaner filter	R	More frequently
A B C . E . . .	Engine oil & oil filter	R	Every 3,000 miles (5,000 km) or 3 months
A . C . E F G .	Brake pads & discs	I	Every 7,500 miles (12,000 km)
. . . . E . G .	Manual and automatic transaxle gear oil	R	Every 30,000 miles (48,000 km) or 24 months
. . . . . . G .	Steering gear & linkage, and axle & suspension parts	I	Every 7,500 miles (12,000 km) or 6 months
. . . D . F G .	Front drive shaft boots	I	Every 7,500 miles (12,000 km) or 6 months
. . C D . F G .	Steering linkage ball joints & front suspension ball joints	I	Every 7,500 miles (12,000 km) or 6 months
. . . . . F . .	Locks, hinges & hood latch	L	Every 7,500 miles (12,000 km) or 6 months
A . . . E F G .	Exhaust system	I	Every 7,500 miles (12,000 km) or 6 months

Maintenance operations: I = Inspect. Correct or replace if necessary   R = Replace   L = Lubricate

1990–92 MAINTENANCE INTERVALS CHART — SEVERE SERVICE

Abbreviations: R = Replace   I = Inspect. Correct or replace if necessary.   [ ]: At the mileage intervals only

MAINTENANCE OPERATION		MAINTENANCE INTERVAL															
Perform at number of miles,	Miles × 1,000	3.75	7.5	11.25	15	18.75	22.5	26.25	30	33.75	37.5	41.25	45	48.75	52.5	56.25	60
kilometers or months,	(km × 1,000)	(6)	(12)	(18)	(24)	(30)	(36)	(42)	(48)	(54)	(60)	(66)	(72)	(78)	(84)	(90)	(96)
whichever comes first.	Months	3	6	9	12	15	18	21	24	27	30	33	36	39	42	45	48
Drive belts	See NOTE (1)																I*
Air cleaner filter	See NOTE (2)								[R]								[R]
Vapor lines									I*								I*
Fuel lines									I*								I*
Fuel filter	See NOTE (3)*																
Engine coolant	See NOTE (4)																R*
Engine oil		R	R	R	R	R	R	R	R	R	R	R	R	R	R	R	R
Engine oil filter	See NOTE (5)	R	R	R	R	R	R	R	R	R	R	R	R	R	R	R	R
Spark plugs VE30DE engine (Use PLATINUM-TIPPED type)																	[R]
VE30E engine									[R]								[R]
Timing belt (VG30E engine only)																	[R]
Brake lines & cables					I				I				I				I
Brake pads, discs, drums & linings			I		I		I		I		I		I		I		I
Manual & automatic transaxle oil	See NOTE (6)				I				I				I				I
Steering gear & linkage, axle & suspension parts			I		I		I		I		I		I		I		I
Steering linkage ball joints & front suspension ball joints			I		I		I		I		I		I		I		
Exhaust system			I		I		I		I		I		I				I
Drive shaft boots			I		I		I		I		I		I		I		I
Air bag system	See NOTE (7)																

NOTE:
(1) After 60,000 miles (96,000 km) or 48 months, inspect every 15,000 miles (24,000 km) or 12 months.
(2) If operating mainly in dusty conditions, more frequent maintenance may be required.
(3) If vehicle is operated under extremely adverse weather conditions or in areas where ambient temperatures are either extremely low or extremely high, the filters might become clogged. In such an event, replace them immediately.
(4) After 60,000 miles (96,000 km) or 48 months, replace every 30,000 miles (48,000 km) or 24 months.
(5) Use Part No. 15208-60U00 or equivalent on VE30DE engine, and Nissan PREMIUM type or equivalent on VG30E engine.
(6) If towing a trailer, using a camper or a car-top carrier, or driving on rough or muddy roads, change (not just inspect) oil at every 30,000 miles (48,000 km) or 24 months.
(7) Inspect the air bag system 10 years after the date of manufacture as noted on the F.M.V.S.S. certification label.
(8) Maintenance items and intervals with "*" are recommended by NISSAN for reliable vehicle operation. The owner need not perform such maintenance in order to maintain the emission warranty or manufacturer recall liability. Other maintenance items and intervals are required.

1990–92 MAINTENANCE INTERVALS CHART — NORMAL SERVICE

Abbreviations: R = Replace   I = Inspect. Correct or replace if necessary.   **[ ]: At the mileage intervals only**

MAINTENANCE OPERATION					MAINTENANCE INTERVAL					
Perform at number of miles,	Miles × 1,000	7.5	15	22.5	30	37.5	45	52.5	60
kilometers or months,	(km × 1,000)	(12)	(24)	(36)	(48)	(60)	(72)	(84)	(96)
whichever comes first.	Months	6	12	18	24	30	36	42	48
Drive belts	See NOTE (1)								I*
Air cleaner filter					[R]				[R]
Vapor lines					I*				I*
Fuel lines					I*				I*
Fuel filter	See NOTE (2)*								
Engine coolant	See NOTE (3)								R*
Engine oil		R	R	R	R	R	R	R	R
Engine oil filter	See NOTE (4)	R			R		R		R
Spark plugs VE30DE engine (Use PLATINUM-TIPPED type)									[R]
VE30E engine					[R]				[R]
Timing belt (VG30E engine only)									[R]
Brake lines & cables				I		I		I	I
Brake pads, discs, drums & linings				I		I		I	I
Manual & automatic transaxle oil				I		I		I	I
Steering gear & linkage, axle & suspension parts									I
Exhaust system				I		I		I	I
Drive shaft boots			I			I		I	I
Air bag system	See NOTE (5)								

NOTE: (1) After 60,000 miles (96,000 km) or 48 months, inspect every 15,000 miles (24,000 km) or 12 months.
(2) If vehicle is operated under extremely adverse weather conditions or in areas where ambient temperatures are either extremely low or extremely high, the filters might become clogged. In such an event, replace them immediately.
(3) Afer 60,000 miles (96,000 km) or 48 months, replace every 30,000 miles (48,000 km) or 24 months.
(4) Use Part No. 15208-60U00 or equivalent on VE30DE engine, and Nissan PREMIUM type or equivalent on VG30E engine.
(5) Inspect the air bag system 10 years after the date of manufacture as noted on the F.M.V.S.S. certification label.
(6) Maintenance items and intervals with "*" are recommended by NISSAN for reliable vehicle operation. The owner need not perform such maintenance in order to maintain the emission warranty or manufacturer recall liability. Other maintenance items and intervals are required.

CAPACITIES

Year	Model	Engine ID/VIN	Engine Displacement liter (cc)	Engine Crankcase with Filter	Transmission (pts.)			Transfer case (pts.)	Drive Axle		Fuel Tank (gal.)	Cooling System (qts.)
					4-Spd	5-Spd	Auto.		Front (pts.)	Rear (pts.)		
1985	Maxima	VG30E	3.0 (2960)	4.5	NA	10	14.75	NA	NA	NA	15.87	9.75
1986	Maxima	VG30E	3.0 (2960)	4.5	NA	10	14.75	NA	NA	NA	15.87	9.75
1987	Maxima	VG30E	3.0 (2960)	4.5	NA	10	14.75	NA	NA	NA	17.12	9.75
1988	Maxima	VG30E	3.0 (2960)	4.5	NA	10	14.75	NA	NA	NA	17.12	9.75
1989	Maxima	VG30E	3.0 (2960)	4.5	NA	10	15.50	NA	NA	NA	18.50	8.75
1990	Maxima	VG30E	3.0 (2960)	4.5	NA	10	15.50	NA	NA	NA	18.50	8.75
1991	Maxima	VG30E	3.0 (2960)	4.12	NA	10	15.75	NA	NA	NA	18.50	8.75
1992	Maxima	VG30E	3.0 (2960)	4.12	NA	10	15.75	NA	NA	NA	18.50	8.75
	Maxima	VE30DE	3.0 (2960)	4	NA	10	20.00	NA	NA	NA	18.50	11.25

NA—Not available

2

ENGINE PERFORMANCE AND TUNE-UP

ENGINE TUNE-UP SPECIFICATIONS

Year	Engine ID/VIN	Engine Displacement liter (cc)	Spark Plugs Gap (in.)	Ignition Timing (deg.)		Fuel Pump (psi)	Idle Speed (rpm)		Valve Clearance	
				MT	AT		MT	AT	In.	Ex.
1985	VG30E	3.0 (2960)	0.039–0.043	20	20①	37⑤	700	700①②	0	0
1986	VG30E	3.0 (2960)	0.039–0.043	20	20①	37⑤	700②	700①②	0	0
1987	VG30E	3.0 (2960)	0.039–0.043	20	20①	37⑤	750③	700①②	0	0
1988	VG30E	3.0 (2960)	0.039–0.043	15	20①	37⑤	750③	700①②	0	0
1989	VG30E	3.0 (2960)	0.039–0.043	15	15④	36⑥	750	750④	0	0
1990	VG30E	3.0 (2960)	0.039–0.043	15	15④	36⑥	750	750④	0	0
1991	VG30E	3.0 (2960)	0.039–0.043	15	15④	36⑥	750	750④	0	0
1992	VG30E	3.0 (2960)	0.039–0.043	NA	15④	36⑥	NA	750④	0	0
	VE30DE	3.0 (2960)	0.039–0.043	15	15④	36⑥	750	750④	0	0

NOTE: The lowest cylinder pressure should be within 75% of the highest cylinder pressure reading. For example, if the highest cylinder is 134 psi, the lowest should be 101. Engine should be at normal operating temperature with throttle valve in the wide open position.
The underhood specifications sticker often reflects tune-up specification changes in production. Sticker figures must be used if they disagree with those in this chart.
NA—Not available

① Place transaxle in Drive
② 650 rpm at high altitude
③ 700 rpm at high altitude
④ Place transaxle in Neutral
⑤ The fuel pump pressure will normally drop as the engine vacuum increases.
⑥ 43 psi when the fuel pressure regulator valve vacuum hose is disconnected

TUNE-UP PROCEDURES

In order to extract the full measure of performance and economy from your engine it is essential that it is properly tuned at regular intervals. A regular tune-up will keep your engine running smoothly and will prevent the annoying breakdowns and poor performance often associated with an unmaintained engine.

The spark plugs should be replaced every 30,000 miles (48,000 km) or 24 months for VG30E engine or 60,000 miles (96,000 km) or 48 months for VE30DE engine.

This interval should be halved if the vehicle is operated under severe conditions such as prolonged idling, start-and-stop driving, or if starting or running problems are noticed. It is assumed that the routine maintenance described in Section 1 has been kept up, as this will have a decided effect on the results of a tune-up. All of the applicable steps of a tune-up should be followed in order, as the result is a cumulative one.

If the specifications on the underhood tune-up sticker in the engine compartment disagree with the Tune-Up Specifications chart in this Section, the figures on the sticker must be used. The sticker often reflects changes made during the production run.

Spark Plugs

◆ SEE FIGS. 1 AND 2

A typical spark plug consists of a metal shell surrounding a ceramic insulator. A metal electrode extends downward through the center of the insulator and protrudes a small distance. Located at the end of the plug and attached to the side of the outer metal shell is the side electrode. This side electrode bends in a 90 degrees so its tip is even with, parallel to, the tip of the center electrode. This distance between the 2 electrodes is called spark plug gap. The spark plug in no way produces a spark but merely provides a gap across which the current can arc. The coil produces approximately 50,000 volts which travels to the distributor where it is distributed through the spark plug wires to the plugs. The current passes along the center electrode and jumps the gap to the side electrode and, in so doing, ignites the air/fuel mixture in the combustion chamber. All plugs used, have a resistor built into the center electrode to reduce interference to any nearby radio and television receivers. The resistor also cuts down on erosion of plug electrodes caused by excessively long sparking. Resistor spark plug wiring is original equipment on all Maxima's.

Spark plug life and efficiency depend upon the condition of the engine and the temperatures to which the plug is exposed. Combustion chamber temperatures are affected by many factors such as compression ratio of the engine, fuel/air mixtures, exhaust emission equipment and the type of driving you do. Spark plugs are designed and classified by number according to the heat range at which they will operate most efficiently. The amount of heat that the plug absorbs is determined by the length of the lower insulator. The longer the insulator (it extends farther into the engine), the hotter the plug will operate. A plug that has a short path for heat transfer and remains too cool will quickly accumulate deposits of oil and carbon since it is not hot enough to burn them off. This leads to plug fouling and consequently to misfiring. A plug that has a long path for heat transfer will have no deposits but due to the excessive heat, the electrodes will burn away quickly and, in some instances, pre-ignition may result.

Preignition takes place when plug tips get so hot that they glow sufficiently to ignite the fuel/air mixture before the spark does. This early ignition will usually cause a pinging during low speeds and heavy loads. In sever cases, the heat may become enough to start the fuel/air mixture burning throughout the combustion chamber rather than just to the front of the plug as in

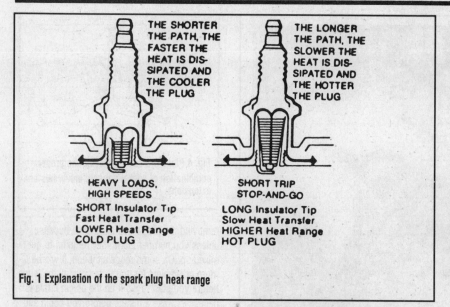

Fig. 1 Explanation of the spark plug heat range

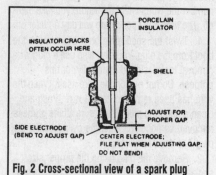

Fig. 2 Cross-sectional view of a spark plug

normal operation. At this time, the piston is rising in the cylinder making its compression stroke. The burning mass is compressed and an explosion results producing tremendous pressure. Something has to give, and it does. Pistons are often damaged. Obviously, this detonation (explosion) is a destructive condition that can be avoided by installing a spark plug designed and specified for your particular engine.

A set of spark plugs usually requires replacement after 30,000 miles (48,000 km) or 24 months for VG30E engine or 60,000 miles (96,000 km) or 48 months for VE30DE engine, depending on the type of driving. The electrode on a new spark plug has a sharp edge but, with use, this edge becomes rounded by erosion causing the plug gap to increase. In normal operation, plug gap increases about 0.001 in. in every 1000–2000 miles (1600–3200 km). As the gap increases, the plug's voltage requirement also increases. It requires a greater voltage to jump the wider gap and about 2–3 times as much voltage to fire a plug at high speeds and acceleration than at idle.

The higher voltage produced by the ignition coil is one of the primary reasons for the prolonged replacement interval for spark plugs. A consistently hotter spark prevents the fouling of plugs for much longer than could normally be expected. This spark is also able to jump across a larger gap more efficiently than a spark from a conventional system.

Worn plugs become obvious during acceleration. Voltage requirement is greatest during acceleration and a plug with an enlarged gap may require more voltage than the coil is able to produce. As a result, the engine misses and sputters until acceleration is reduced. Reducing acceleration reduces the plug's voltage requirement and the engine runs smoother. Slow, city driving is hard on plugs. The long periods of idle experienced in traffic creates an overly rich gas mixture. The engine isn't running fast enough to completely burn the gas and, consequently, the plugs are fouled with gas deposits and engine idle becomes rough. In many cases, driving under right conditions can effectively clean these fouled plugs.

➡ **There are several reasons why a spark plug will foul and you can usually learn which is at fault by just looking at the plug. A few of the most common reasons for plug fouling, and a description of the fouled plug's appearance.**

Accelerate your vehicle to the speed where the engine begins to miss and then slow down to the point where the engine smooths out. Run at this speed for a few minutes and then accelerate again to the point of engine miss. With each repetition this engine miss should occur at increasingly higher speeds and then disappear altogether. Do not attempt to shortcut this procedure by hard acceleration. This approach will compound problems by fusing deposits into a hard permanent glaze. Dirty, fouled plugs may be cleaned by sandblasting. Many shops have a spark plug sandblaster. After sandblasting, the electrode should be filed to a sharp, square shape and then gapped to specifications. Gapping a plug too close will produce rough idle while gapping it too wide will increase its voltage requirement and cause missing at high speeds and during acceleration.

The type of driving you do may require a change in spark plug heat range. If the majority of your driving is done in the city and rarely at high speeds, plug fouling may necessitate changing to a plug with a heat range number one lower than that specified by the vehicle manufacturer. For example, a 1985 VG30E engine requires a BCPR6ES–11 plug. Frequent city driving may foul these plugs making engine operation rough. A BCPR5ES–11 is the next hottest plug and its insulator is longer than the BCPR6ES–11 so it can absorb and retain more heat than the shorter BCPR6ES–11. This hotter BCPR5ES–11 burns off deposits even at low city speeds but would be too hot for prolonged turnpike driving. Using this plug at high speeds would create dangerous pre-ignition. On the other hand, if the aforementioned engine were used almost exclusively for long distance high speed driving, the specified BCPR6ES–11 might be too hot resulting in rapid electrode wear and dangerous pre-ignition. In this case, it might be wise to change to a colder BCPR7ES–11. If the vehicle is used for abnormal driving (as in the examples above) or the engine has been modified for higher performance. Then a change to a plug of a different heat range may be necessary. For a modified vehicle it is always wise to go to a colder plug as a protection against pre-ignition. It will require more frequent plug cleaning, but destructive detonation during acceleration will be avoided.

REMOVAL

◆ SEE FIGS. 3, 3A, 3B AND 4

When you're removing spark plugs, you should work on one at a time. Don't start by

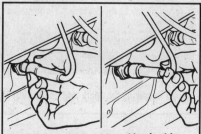

Fig. 3 Twist and pull on the rubber boot to remove the spark plug wires; never pull on the wire itself

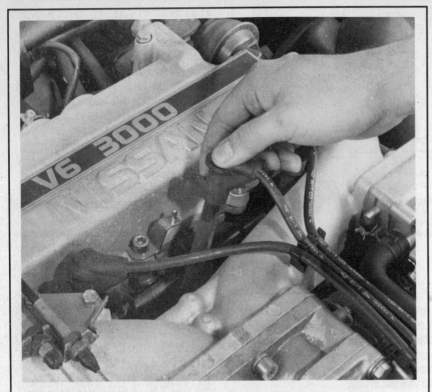

FIG. 3A Removing the spark plug wire from the spark plug on the 1991 VG30E engine

FIG. 3B Removing the spark plug on the 1991 VG30E engine

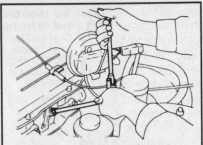

Fig. 4 Plugs are removed using the proper combination of socket wrench, universals and extensions

removing the plug wires all at once because unless you number them, they're going to get mixed up. On some models though, it will be more convenient for you to remove all the wires before you start to work on the plugs. If this is necessary, take a minute before you begin and number the wires with tape before you take them off. The time you spend here will pay off later on.

1. Twist the spark plug boot and remove the boot from the plug. You may also use a plug wire removal tool designed especially for this purpose. Do not pull on the wire itself. When the wire has been removed, take a wire brush and clean around the plug. Make sure all the grime is removed so none will enter the cylinder after the plug has been removed.

2. Remove the plug using the proper size socket, extensions and universals as necessary. The cylinder head is aluminum, which is easily stripped. Remove plugs ONLY when the engine is cold.

3. If removing the plug is difficult, drip some penetrating oil on the plug threads, allow it to work, then remove the plug. Also, be sure the socket is straight on the plug, especially on those hard to reach plugs.

INSPECTION

◆ SEE FIGS. 5–7

Check the plugs for deposits and wear. If they are not going to be replaced, clean the plugs thoroughly. Remember that any kind of deposit will decrease the efficiency of the plug. Plugs can be cleaned on a spark plug cleaning machine, which can sometimes be found in service stations or you can do an acceptable job of cleaning with a stiff brush.

➡ **Do not use a wire brush on platinum plugs used on the VE30DE engine.**

If the plugs are cleaned, the electrodes must be filed flat. Use an ignition points file, not an emery board or the like, which will leave deposits. The electrodes must be filed perfectly flat with sharp edges. Rounded edges reduce the spark plug voltage by as much as 50 percent.

Check the spark plug gap before installation. The ground electrode (the L-shaped one connected to the body of the plug) must be parallel to the center electrode and the specified size wire gauge (see Tune-Up Specifications) should pass through the gap with a slight drag. Always check the gap on new plugs, too. They are not always set correctly at the factory. Wire gapping tools usually have a bending tool attached. Use that to adjust the side electrode until the proper distance is obtained. Absolutely never bend the center electrode. Also, be careful not to bend the side electrode too far or too often. It may weaken and break off within the engine, requiring removal of the cylinder head to retrieve it.

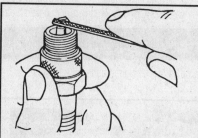

Fig. 5 Plugs that are in good condition can be filed and reused

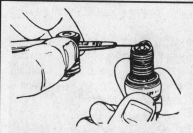

Fig. 6 Always use a wire gauge to check the electrode gap

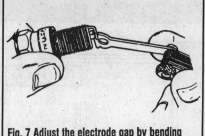

Fig. 7 Adjust the electrode gap by bending the side electrode

INSTALLATION

1. Lubricate the threads of the spark plugs with drop of oil. Install the plugs and tighten them hand tight. Take care not to crossthread them.

2. Tighten the spark plugs with the socket. Do not apply the same amount of force you would use for a bolt; just snug them in. If a torque wrench is available, tighten to 14–22 ft. lbs.

3. Install the wires on their respective plugs. Make sure the wires are firmly connected. You will be able to feel them click into place.

Spark Plug Wires

REPLACING AND TESTING

▶ SEE FIG. 8

Every 15,000 miles (24,000 km), inspect the spark plug wires for burns, cuts or breaks in the insulation. Check the boots and the nipples on the distributor cap. Replace any damaged wiring.

Every 2 years for 1985–88 VG30E engines or 3 years for 1989–92 VG30E engines, the resistance of the wires should be checked with an ohmmeter. Wires with excessive resistance will cause misfiring and may make the engine

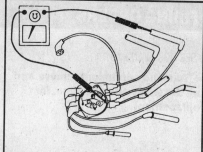

Fig. 8 Using an ohmmeter to check the resistance of the spark plugs wires — 30,000 ohms is the absolute limit of acceptability

difficult to start in damp weather. Generally, the useful life of the cables is 45,000–60,000 miles (72,000–96,000 km).

To check resistance, remove the distributor cap, leaving the wires in place. Connect one lead of an ohmmeter to an electrode within the cap. Connect the other lead to the corresponding spark plug terminal (remove it from the spark plug for this test). Replace any wire which shows a resistance over 30,000Ω. Resistance should not be over 25,000Ω, and 30,000Ω must be considered the outer limit of acceptability.

It should be remembered that resistance is also a function of length; the longer the wire, the greater the resistance. Thus, if the wires on your vehicle are longer than the factory originals, resistance will be higher, quite possibly outside the limits.

When installing new wires, replace them one at a time to avoid mixups. Start by replacing the longest one first. Install the boot firmly over the spark plug. Route the wire over the same path as the original. Insert the nipple firmly onto the tower on the distributor cap, then install the cap cover and latches to secure the wires.

FIRING ORDERS

♦ SEE FIGS. 9 AND 10

➡ **To avoid confusion, remove and tag the wires one at a time, for replacement.**

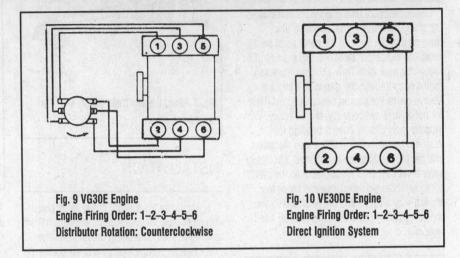

Fig. 9 VG30E Engine
Engine Firing Order: 1–2–3–4–5–6
Distributor Rotation: Counterclockwise

Fig. 10 VE30DE Engine
Engine Firing Order: 1–2–3–4–5–6
Direct Ignition System

ELECTRONIC IGNITION

Description and Operation

VG30E Engine

♦ SEE FIGS. 11, 11A, 11B AND 12

On the VG30E engine, a crank angle sensor mounted in the distributor is the basic component of the entire Electronic Concentrated Control System (ECCS). There are no adjustments necessary.

The crank angle sensor is equipped with a light emitting photo diode which monitors the

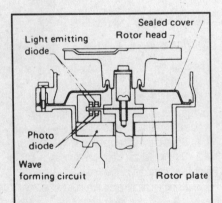

Fig. 11 Cross-sectional view of the distributor equipped with a crank angle sensor — VG30E engine

FIG. 11A View of the ignition coil on the 1991 VG30E engine

FIG. 11B View of the distributor on the 1991 VG30E engine

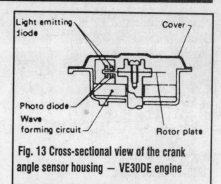

Fig. 13 Cross-sectional view of the crank angle sensor housing — VE30DE engine

of the left camshaft. It is the basic component of the entire Electronic Concentrated Control System (ECCS). There are no adjustments necessary.

The crank angle sensor is equipped with a light emitting photo diode which monitors the engine rotation. The light impulses, created by the rotation of the sensor's rotor plate, are converted into electrical square wave impulses and sent to the Electronic Control Unit (ECU).

The ECU monitors the engines functions through sensors, determines the engine's needs and sends cylinder firing impulses to the Power Transistor, which amplifies the impulses from the ECU.

The Power Transistor sends the amplified impulses to the correct ignition coil's primary circuit; thereby, turning the ignition coil ON and OFF.

The ON and OFF operation of the each ignition coil's primary circuit produces high voltage in it's secondary circuit. The secondary high voltage is sent directly to the spark plug.

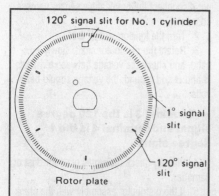

Fig. 12 View and description the of the crank angle sensor rotor plate–VG30E and VE30DE engines

engine rotation. The light impulses, created by the rotation of the sensor's rotor plate, are converted into electrical square wave impulses and sent to the Electronic Control Unit (ECU).

The ECU monitors the engines functions through sensors, determines the engine's needs and sends cylinder firing impulses to the Power Transistor, which amplifies the impulses from the ECU.

The Power Transistor sends the amplified impulses to the ignition coil's primary circuit, turning the ignition coil ON and OFF.

The ON and OFF operation of the ignition coil's primary circuit produces high voltage in it's secondary circuit. The secondary high voltage is sent to the distributor where it is distributed to the designated spark plug at the proper time.

VE30DE Engine

♦ SEE FIG. 13

On the VE30DE engine, a crank angle sensor is mounted in a housing and attached to the rear

Diagnosis and Testing

VG30E Engine

IGNITION COIL

1985–88

♦ SEE FIG. 15

On the 1985–88 vehicle, the ignition coil/power transistor assembly is located, in the engine compartment, on the front right fender.

1. Disconnect the negative battery cable.
2. Disconnect the electrical harness connector from the ignition coil.
3. Using an ohmmeter, adjust it to the low range.
4. Attach the probes to terminals **1** and **2**; there should be resistance of approximately

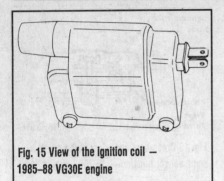

Fig. 15 View of the ignition coil — 1985–88 VG30E engine

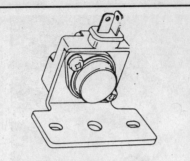

Fig. 14 View of the power transistor — 1985–88 VG30E engine

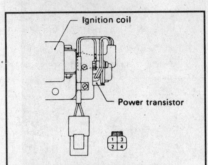

Fig. 18 Testing of the ignition coil/power transistor assembly — 1985–88 VG30E engine

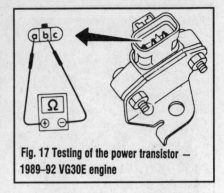

Fig. 17 Testing of the power transistor — 1989–92 VG30E engine

0.8Ω. If the test does not meet 0.8Ω, replace the ignition coil.

5. Connect the electrical harness connector to the ignition coil.

6. Connect the negative battery cable.

1989–92
♦ SEE FIG. 16

On the 1989–92 vehicle, the ignition coil is located on the front of the engine, in front of the distributor.

1. Disconnect the negative battery cable.

2. Disconnect the electrical harness connector from the ignition coil.

3. Using an ohmmeter, adjust it to the low range.

4. Attach the probes to terminals **1** and **2**; there should be resistance of approximately 1.0Ω. If the test does not meet 1.0Ω, replace the ignition coil.

5. Connect the electrical harness connector to the ignition coil.

6. Connect the negative battery cable.

POWER TRANSISTOR

1985–88
♦ SEE FIGS. 14 AND 18

On the 1985–88 vehicle, the power transistor is located, in the engine compartment, on the front right fender.

1. Disconnect the negative battery cable.

2. Disconnect the ignition coil/power transistor assembly electrical harness connector.

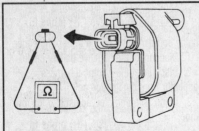

Fig. 16 Testing of the ignition coil — 1989–92 VG30E engine

3. Using an ohmmeter, adjust the setting to the low range, approximately 1.0Ω.

4. To test the ignition coil/power transistor assembly, perform the following procedures:

a. Place the positive (+) probe on terminal **2** and the negative (–) probe on terminal **3**; there should be continuity.

b. Place the positive (+) probe on terminal **2** and the negative (–) probe on terminal **4**; there should be continuity.

c. Place the positive (+) probe on terminal **3** and the negative (–) probe on terminal **4**; there should be continuity.

5. If the ignition coil/power transistor assembly does not perform according to the test, replace power transistor.

6. Reconnect the electrical harness connector.

7. Connect the negative battery cable.

1989–92
♦ SEE FIG. 17

On the 1989–92 vehicle, the power transistor is located on the front of the engine, in front of the distributor.

1. Disconnect the negative battery cable.

2. Disconnect the electrical harness connector from the power transistor.

3. Using an ohmmeter, adjust the setting to the low range, approximately 1.0Ω.

4. To test the power transistor, perform the following procedures:

a. Place the positive (+) probe on terminal **a** and the negative (–) probe on terminal **b**; there should be continuity.

b. Place the positive (+) probe on terminal **a** and the negative (–) probe on terminal **c**; there should be continuity.

c. Place the negative (–) probe on terminal **a** and the positive (+) probe on terminal **b**; there should not be continuity.

d. Place the negative (–) probe on terminal **a** and the positive (+) probe on terminal **c**; there should not be continuity.

5. If the power transistor does not perform according to the test, replace it.

6. Reconnect the electrical harness connector to the power transistor.

7. Connect the negative battery cable.

DISTRIBUTOR

1985–88
♦ SEE FIG. 22

1. Remove the distributor from the engine; do not disconnect the crank angle sensor harness connector.

2. Turn the ignition switch **ON**.

3. Rotate the distributor shaft, slowly by hand, and check the voltage between terminals **b** and **d** and ground; the voltage should be 0–5 volts.

➡ **Terminal 3 is the 120 degree signal and terminal 4 is the 1 degree signal.**

4. Visually check the signal plate for dust or damage.

5. If the distributor assembly with the crank angle sensor does not agree with the tests, replace the distributor with the crank angle sensor.

1989–92
♦ SEE FIG. 23

1. Remove the distributor from the engine; do not disconnect the crank angle sensor harness connector.

2. Turn the ignition switch **ON**.

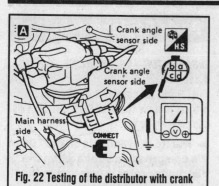

Fig. 22 Testing of the distributor with crank angle sensor — 1985–88 VG30E engine

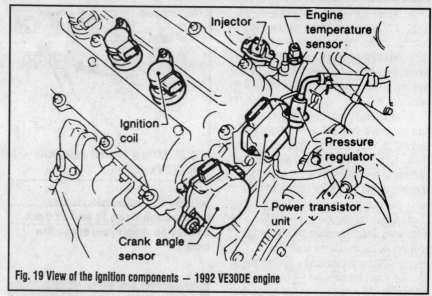

Fig. 19 View of the ignition components — 1992 VE30DE engine

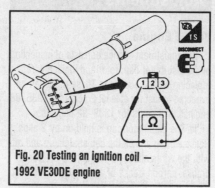

Fig. 20 Testing an ignition coil — 1992 VE30DE engine

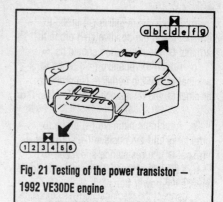

Fig. 21 Testing of the power transistor — 1992 VE30DE engine

Fig. 23 Testing of the distributor with crank angle sensor — 1989–92 VG30E engine

3. Rotate the distributor shaft, slowly by hand, and check the voltage between terminals **3** and **4** and ground; the voltage should be 0–5 volts.

➡ **Terminal 3 is the 120 degree signal and terminal 4 is the 1 degree signal.**

4. Visually check the signal plate for dust or damage.

5. If the distributor assembly with the crank angle sensor does not agree with the tests, replace the distributor with the crank angle sensor.

VE30DE Engine
▶ SEE FIG. 19

IGNITION COIL
▶ SEE FIG. 20

The VE30DE engine is equipped multiple ignition coils, each are attached directly to the spark plugs.

1. Disconnect the negative battery cable.

2. Disconnect the electrical connector(s) from the ignition coil(s).

3. Disconnect the ignition coil(s) from the spark plug(s).

4. Using an ohmmeter, adjust it to the low range. Attach the probes to the terminal **1** and terminal **2**, then measure the resistance; the resistance should be approximately 0.8Ω.

5. If the resistance is not approximately 0.8Ω, replace the ignition coil(s).

6. Connect the ignition coil(s) to the spark plug(s).

7. Connect the electrical connector(s) to the ignition coil(s).

8. Connect the negative battery cable.

POWER TRANSISTOR
▶ SEE FIG. 21

The power transistor is attached to the rear of the left cylinder head.

1. Disconnect the negative battery cable.

2. Disconnect the electrical harness connector(s) from the power transistor.

➡ **If necessary, remove the power transistor from the engine.**

3. Using an ohmmeter, adjust it to the low range and perform the following procedures:

a. Attach the positive (+) probe to terminal **d** and with the negative (–) probe, touch terminals **a, b, c, e, f** and **g**; the resistance of each terminal should not be 0 or ∞.

b. Attach the negative (–) probe to terminal **d** and with the positive (+) probe, touch terminals **a, b, c, e, f** and **g**; the resistance of each terminal should not be 0 or ∞.

c. Attach the positive (+) probe to terminal **d** and with the negative (–) probe, touch terminals **1, 2, 3, 4, 5** and **6**; the resistance of each terminal should not be 0 or ∞.

d. Attach the negative (–) probe to terminal **d** and with the positive (+) probe, touch terminals **1, 2, 3, 4, 5** and **6**; the resistance of each terminal should ∞.

e. Attach the positive (+) probe to terminal **a** and the negative (–) probe to terminal **1**; the resistance should not be 0 or ∞.

f. Attach the negative (–) probe to terminal **a** and the positive (+) probe to terminal **1**; the resistance should be ∞.

g. Attach the positive (+) probe to terminal **b** and the negative (–) probe to terminal **2**; the resistance should not be 0 or ∞.

h. Attach the negative (–) probe to terminal **b** and the positive (+) probe to terminal **2**; the resistance should be ∞.

i. Attach the positive (+) probe to terminal **c** and the negative (–) probe to terminal **3**; the resistance should not be 0 or ∞.

j. Attach the negative (–) probe to terminal **c** and the positive (+) probe to terminal **3**; the resistance should be ∞.

k. Attach the positive (+) probe to terminal **e** and the negative (–) probe to terminal **4**; the resistance should not be 0 or ∞.

l. Attach the negative (–) probe to terminal **e** and the positive (+) probe to terminal **4**; the resistance should be ∞.

m. Attach the positive (+) probe to terminal **f** and the negative (–) probe to terminal **5**; the resistance should not be 0 or ∞.

n. Attach the negative (–) probe to terminal **f** and the positive (+) probe to terminal **5**; the resistance should be ∞.

o. Attach the positive (+) probe to terminal **g** and the negative (–) probe to terminal **6**; the resistance should not be 0 or ∞.

p. Attach the negative (–) probe to terminal **g** and the positive (+) probe to terminal **6**; the resistance should be ∞.

4. If the any of the test results do not agree, replace the power transistor.

➡ **If the power transistor was removed from the engine, install it.**

5. Connect the electrical harness connectors to the power transistor.
6. Connect the negative battery cable.

CRANK ANGLE SENSOR

1992
◗ SEE FIG. 24

1. Remove the crank angle sensor from the engine; do not disconnect the crank angle sensor harness connector.
2. Disconnect the electrical harness connector from the power transistor.
3. Turn the ignition switch **ON**.
4. Rotate the crank angle sensor shaft, slowly by hand, and check the voltage between terminals **a** and **b** and ground; the voltage should be 0–5 volts.

➡ **Terminal "a" is the 120 degree signal and terminal "b" is the 1 degree signal.**

5. Visually check the signal plate for dust or damage.
6. If the crank angle sensor does not agree with the tests, replace the crank angle sensor.

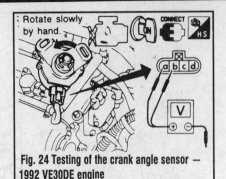

Fig. 24 Testing of the crank angle sensor — 1992 VE30DE engine

➡ **After the inspection tests, malfunction Code 11 and/or Code 21 may be displayed; erase the codes.**

Adjustments

VG30E Engine

The adjustment service consists of inspection of the distributor cap, rotor and ignition wires, replacing when necessary. These parts can be expected to last for at least 2 years for 1985–88 engines or 3 years for 1989–92 engines.

1. The distributor cap is held on by 2 clips. Release them and lift the cap straight up and off, with the wires attached. Inspect the cap for cracks, carbon tracks or a worn center contact. Replace it, if necessary, transferring the wires one at a time from the old cap to the new.
2. Pull the ignition rotor straight up to remove. Replace it if its contacts are worn, burned or pitted. Do not file the contacts. To replace, press it firmly onto the shaft. It only goes on one way, so be sure it is fully seated.
3. Make sure the crank angle sensor rotor plate is clean and no dirt is within the housing.
4. Inspect the wires for cracks or brittleness. Replace them one at a time to prevent cross wiring, carefully pressing the replacement wires into place. The cores of electronic wires are more susceptible to breakage than those of standard wires, so treat them gently.

VE30DE Engine

The adjustment service consists of inspection of the crank angle sensor housing, wiring and wiring connectors.

Make sure the crank angle sensor rotor plate is clean and no dirt is within the housing.

Parts Replacement

DISTRIBUTOR — VG30E ENGINE
◗ SEE FIGS. 25 AND 26

1. Rotate the crankshaft until the No. 1 cylinder is at the Top Dead Center (TDC) of it's compression stroke.

➡ **The No. 1 cylinder is on the TDC of it's compression stroke when the distributor rotor is pointing to the No. 1 spark plug wire on the distributor cap and the punched mark on the crankshaft sprocket is aligned with mark on the oil pump housing.**

2. Disconnect the negative battery cable.
3. Using chalk, mark the distributor rotor's position on the distributor housing. Also, make mark the distributor housing-to-engine position.
4. Remove the distributor cap.
5. Disconnect the crank angle sensor electrical connector.
6. Remove the hold-down bolt and remove the distributor housing.

To install:

7. Align the punched mark on the distributor shaft with the protruding mark on the distributor housing.
8. Install the distributor and align the mark on the distributor housing with the alignment mark on the engine. Align the rotor with the mark on the distributor housing.

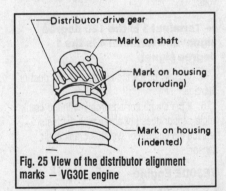

Fig. 25 View of the distributor alignment marks — VG30E engine

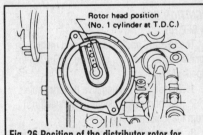

Fig. 26 Position of the distributor rotor for No. 1 cylinder at TDC of it's compression stroke — VG30E engine

9. Tighten the distributor hold-down bolt to 3.6–4.3 ft. lbs. (5–6 Nm) for 1985–88 or 10–12 ft. lbs. (14–17 Nm) for 1989–92.

10. Install the distributor cap and connect the electrical harness connector.

11. Connect the negative battery cable.

12. Start the engine and check the engine operation.

CRANK ANGLE SENSOR VE30DE ENGINE

♦ SEE FIGS. 27, 27A, 27B, 27C AND 28

1. Disconnect the negative battery cable.

2. Rotate the crankshaft until the No. 1 cylinder is at the Top Dead Center (TDC) of it's compression stroke. If necessary, remove the No. 1 spark plug, rotate the crankshaft until compression pressure is emitted from the No. 1 cylinder and it is on the TDC of it's compression stroke.

➡ **The No. 1 cylinder may be on the TDC of it's compression stroke when the mark on the crankshaft pulley is aligned with the pointer; if not rotate the crankshaft 360 degrees and realign the crankshaft pulley mark with the pointer.**

3. Using chalk, mark the crank angle sensor housing's position on the engine.

4. Disconnect the crank angle sensor electrical connector.

5. Remove the hold-down bolt and remove the crank angle sensor housing.

To install:

6. Align the crank angle sensor shaft with the camshaft on the cylinder head.

7. Install the crank angle senor housing and align the mark on the housing with the alignment mark on the engine.

8. Tighten the housing hold-down bolt to 9–12 ft. lbs. (13–16 Nm).

9. Connect the electrical harness connector.

10. Connect the negative battery cable.

11. Start the engine and check the engine operation.

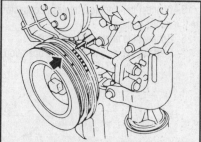

Fig. 27 Aligning the crankshaft pulley with the timing marker with the No. 1 cylinder on TDC of it's compression stroke — VE30DE engine

FIG. 27A Removing the distributor rotor from the distributor shaft on the 1991 VG30E engine

FIG. 27B Removing the sealed cover from the distributor on the 1991 VG30E engine

FIG. 27C View of the distributor's crank angle sensor assembly on the 1991 VG30E engine

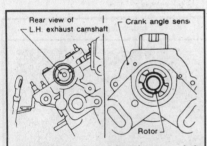

Fig. 28 Aligning the crank angle sensor shaft with the left exhaust camshaft when the No. 1 cylinder is on TDC of it's compression stroke — VE30DE engine

IGNITION COIL

VG30E Engine

1. Disconnect the negative battery cable.
2. Disconnect the electrical harness connector from the ignition coil.
3. Disconnect the ignition coil wire from the ignition coil.
4. Remove the ignition coil bolts and the coil.

➡ **On the 1985–88 vehicles, the power transistor must be removed with ignition coil.**

To install:
5. Install the ignition coil and tighten the bolts.
6. Connect the ignition coil wire to the ignition coil.

7. Connect the electrical harness connector to the ignition coil.
8. Connect the negative battery cable.
9. Start the engine and check the operation.

VE30DE Engine

1. Disconnect the negative battery cable.
2. Disconnect the electrical harness connector(s) from the ignition coil(s).
3. Disconnect the ignition coil(s) from the spark plug(s).

To install:
4. Connect the ignition coil(s) to the spark plug(s).
5. Connect the electrical harness connector(s) to the ignition coil(s).
6. Connect the negative battery cable.
7. Start the engine and check the operation.

POWER TRANSISTOR

VG30E Engine

1. Disconnect the negative battery cable.
2. Disconnect the electrical harness connectors from the power transistor.
3. Remove the power transistor bolts and the transistor.

➡ **On the 1985–88 vehicles, the ignition coil must be removed with power transistor.**

To install:
4. Install the power transistor and tighten the bolts.
5. Connect the electrical harness connectors to the power transistor.
6. Connect the negative battery cable.
7. Start the engine and check the operation.

VE30DE Engine

1. Disconnect the negative battery cable.
2. Disconnect the electrical harness connectors from the power transistor.
3. Remove the power transistor-to-engine bolts and the transistor.

To install:
4. Install the power transistor and tighten the bolts to 2.7–3.7 ft. lbs. (3.7–5.0 Nm).
5. Connect the electrical harness connectors to the power transistor.
6. Connect the negative battery cable.
7. Start the engine and check the operation.

IGNITION TIMING

Preliminary Procedures

1. Make sure the following items are in good order:
   a. Battery
   b. Ignition system
   c. Engine oil and coolant levels
   d. Fuses
   e. Electronic Control Unit harness connector
   f. Vacuum hoses
   g. Air intake system
   h. Fuel pressure
   i. Engine compression
   j. EGR control valve operation
   k. Throttle valve

2. If equipped with air conditioning, turn the air conditioning control **OFF**.

3. If equipped with an automatic transaxle, place the shift control in **N**.

4. If measuring the CO percentage, position the probe more than 15.7 in. (40 cm) into the tail pipe.

5. Turn **OFF** the headlights, the heater blower motor and the rear defogger.

6. Position the front wheels in the straight-ahead position.

7. Perform the checks after the radiator fan has stopped.

8. Apply the parking brakes and block the wheels.

Inspection and Adjustment

VG30E Engine

1985–88

▶ SEE FIG. 33

1. Start the engine and allow it to reach normal operating temperatures, until water temperature indicator points to the middle of the gauge.

2. Raise the hood and run the engine at about 2000 rpm for about 2 minutes, under no-load.

3. Perform the ECU self diagnosis check; if diagnostic problems exist, repair or replace the defective component.

4. Disconnect the idle-up solenoid harness connector; the idle-up solenoid is located on the front right side of the engine.

5. If the engine runs smoothly, race it 2–3 times under no-load and run it for about 1 min. at idle speed.

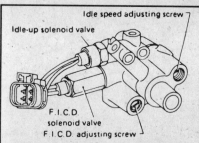

Fig. 33 View of the idle-up solenoid and harness connector — 1985–88 VG30E engines

6. Using a timing light, connect it to the engine according to the manufacturer's instructions.

7. If the timing is not at specifications, loosen the distributor hold-down bolt, turn the distributor until the timing marks align and tighten the hold-down bolt.

8. If the timing cannot be adjusted correctly, perform the idle speed adjustment and readjust the timing.

1989–92

▶ SEE FIGS. 29, 29A, AND 29B

1. Start the engine and allow it to reach

normal operating temperatures, until water temperature indicator points to the middle of the gauge.

2. Raise the hood and run the engine at about 2000 rpm for about 2 minutes, under no-load.

3. Perform the ECU self diagnosis check; if diagnostic problems exist, repair or replace the defective component.

4. If the engine runs smoothly, race it 2–3 times under no-load and run it for about 1 min. at idle speed.

5. Using a timing light, connect it to the engine according to the manufacturer's instructions.

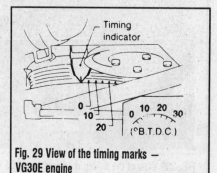

Fig. 29 View of the timing marks — VG30E engine

FIG. 29A Removing the plug to expose the crankshaft bolt on the 1991 VG30E engine

FIG. 29B View of the timing marks on the 1991 VG30E engine

Fig. 30 If using the CONSULT diagnostic tester, selecting the AAC VALVE ADJ in WORK SUPPORT mode — VE30DE engine

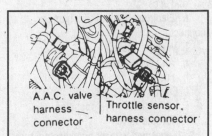

Fig. 31 Disconnecting the throttle sensor harness connector and the AAC valve harness connector

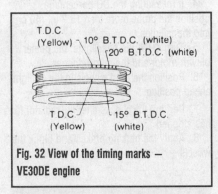

Fig. 32 View of the timing marks — VE30DE engine

6. If the timing is not at specifications, loosen the distributor hold-down bolt, turn the distributor until the timing marks align and tighten the hold-down bolt.

7. If the timing cannot be adjusted correctly, perform the idle speed adjustment and readjust the timing.

VE30DE Engine

◆ SEE FIGS. 30–32

1. Start the engine and allow it to reach normal operating temperatures, until water temperature indicator points to the middle of the gauge. Ensure that the engine speed stays below 1000 rpm.

2. Raise the hood and run the engine at about 2000 rpm for about 2 minutes, under no-load.

3. Perform the ECU self diagnosis check, in Mode II; if diagnostic problems exist, repair or replace the defective component.

4. Run the engine at 2000 rpm for about 2 minutes under no-load. Race the engine 2–3 times under no-load and run it for about 1 min. at idle speed.

5. If using the CONSULT diagnostic tester, perform the following procedures:

   a. Turn the engine **OFF** and disconnect the throttle sensor harness connector.

   b. Start the engine.

   c. Select the **AAC VALVE ADJ** in **WORK SUPPORT** mode.

   d. Touch the **START** button.

6. If not using the CONSULT diagnostic tester, perform the following procedures:

   a. Turn the engine **OFF** and disconnect the throttle sensor harness connector and the Auxiliary Air Control (AAC) valve harness connector.

   b. Start the engine.

7. Race the engine 2–3 times (2000–3000 rpm) under no-load and run it for about 1 min. at idle speed.

8. Using a timing light, connect it to the engine according to the manufacturer's instructions.

9. If the timing is not at specifications, loosen the crank angle sensor hold-down bolt, turn the crank angle sensor until the timing marks align and tighten the hold-down bolt.

10. If the timing cannot be adjusted correctly, perform the idle speed adjustment and readjust the timing.

VALVE LASH

These engines use hydraulic valve adjusters which cannot be adjusted in any way. If the engine exhibits valve noise, this indicates either excessive wear of valve train parts or clogged hydraulic tensioners, due to inadequate engine maintenance. You may also wish to check the torque of rocker shaft retaining bolts. See Section 3.

IDLE SPEED AND MIXTURE ADJUSTMENTS

Descriptions, adjustments and overhaul procedures for fuel systems can be found in Section 5.

Electronic Fuel Injection (EFI)

These vehicles use a rather complex electronic fuel injection system which is controlled by a series of temperature, altitude (for California) and air flow sensors which feed information into a Electronic Control Unit (ECU). The control unit then relays an electronic signal to the fuel injector nozzle at each cylinder, which allows a predetermined amount of fuel into the combustion chamber. To adjust the mixture controls on these units requires a CO meter and several special Nissan tools. Therefore, we will confine ourselves to idle speed adjustment.

IDLE SPEED ADJUSTMENT

VG30E Engine

1985–88
♦ SEE FIGS. 34 AND 35
1. Turn **OFF** the: headlights, heater blower, air conditioning and rear window defogger. If the vehicle has power steering, make sure the wheel is in the straight-ahead position. The ignition timing must be correct to get an effective idle speed adjustment. Adjust the timing if you do not know it to be correct. Connect a tachometer (a special adapter harness may be needed) according to the instrument manufacturer's directions.
2. Start engine and warm it, until water temperature indicator points to the middle of the gauge.
3. Run engine at about 2000 rpm for about 2 minutes under no load.

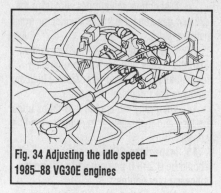

Fig. 34 Adjusting the idle speed — 1985–88 VG30E engines

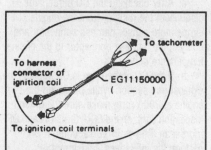

Fig. 35 Special tool adapter harness for tachometer installation — 1985–88 VG30E engines

4. Disconnect idle up solenoid harness connector and then race engine 2–3 times under no load, then run engine at idle speed.
5. Apply the parking brake securely and then place the automatic transaxle in **D** or the manual transaxle in neutral. Adjust the idle speed to the figure shown in the Tune-Up Specifications Chart by turning the idle-up solenoid's speed adjusting screw.
6. Stop engine and connect idle-up solenoid harness connector.
7. Run the engine at approximately 2000 rpm for about 2 minutes under no-load.
8. While operating the engine at 2000 rpm, make sure the green inspection light, on the ECU, turns ON and OFF more than 5 times in 10 seconds.

➡ If the ECU does not turn ON and OFF more than 5 times in 10 seconds, set the ECU diagnostic mode selector to Mode II, determine the problem(s), correct the problem(s) and readjust the idle speed.

9. Remove road test for proper operation.

1989–92
♦ SEE FIGS. 36–38
1. Before adjusting the idle speed, visually check the following items first: air cleaner for being clogged, hoses and ducts for leaks, EGR valve for proper operation, all electrical connectors, gaskets and idle switch.
2. Start the engine and warm it to operating temperature, until water temperature indicator points to the middle of the gauge.
3. Then race the engine to 2000–3000 rpm a few times under no-load and then allow it to return to the idle speed.
4. Connect a tachometer according to the instrument manufacturer's directions.
5. Check the idle speed in the neutral position for manual transaxle or **N** for an automatic transaxle.
6. If the idle speed has to be adjusted you must close the Auxiliary Air Control (AAC) valve by turning the diagnostic mode selector on the ECU fully clockwise.
7. Adjust the idle speed by turning the idle speed adjusting screw with transaxle in the Neutral position.
8. Operate the Auxiliary Air Control (AAC) valve by turning the diagnostic mode selector on the ECU fully counterclockwise and recheck the idle speed.
9. Run the engine at approximately 2000 rpm for about 2 minutes under no-load.
10. While operating the engine at 2000 rpm, make sure the green inspection light, on the ECU, turns ON and OFF more than 5 times in 10 seconds. Perform the following procedures:
   a. Then race the engine to 2–3 times under no-load and then allow it to return to the idle speed.

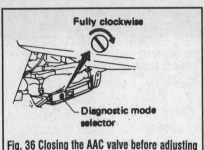

Fig. 36 Closing the AAC valve before adjusting the idle speed — 1989–92 VG30E engines

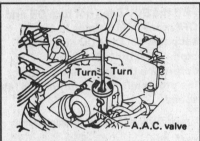

Fig. 37 Adjusting the idle speed — 1989–92 VG30E engines

Fig. 38 Opening the AAC valve after idle speed adjustment — 1989–92 VG30E engines

b. Set the ECU diagnostic mode selector to Mode II.

c. If the inspection (red and green) lights turn ON and OFF, simultaneously, more than 5 times, at 2000 rpm under no-load in 10 seconds, the vehicle is operating correctly.

d. If the inspection (red and green) lights do not turn ON and OFF, simultaneously, more than 5 times, at 2000 rpm under no-load in 10 seconds, proceed to Step 17.

11. If the ECU does not turn ON and OFF more than 5 times in 10 seconds, check the exhaust gas sensor harness by performing the following procedures:

a. Turn the ignition switch **OFF** and disconnect the negative battery cable.

b. Disconnect the ECU SMJ harness connector from the ECU.

c. Disconnect the exhaust gas sensor harness connector. Using a jumper wire, connect the main harness side terminal for the exhaust gas sensor to a ground.

d. Using an ohmmeter, check for continuity between terminal No. 29 of the ECU SMJ harness connector and ground. If continuity does not exist, readjust the idle speed. If continuity exists, proceed to Step 12.

12. Connect the SMJ harness connector to the ECU and perform the following procedures:

a. Disconnect the engine temperature sensor harness connector.

b. Using 2500Ω resistor, connect it between the terminals of the engine temperature sensor harness connector.

c. Disconnect the jumper wire from the exhaust gas sensor harness connector (main harness side).

13. Connect the negative battery cable. Start the engine and warm it to operating temperature, until water temperature indicator points to the middle of the gauge.

14. Then race the engine 2–3 times under no-load and then allow it to return to the idle speed.

15. Inspect the CO percentage; at idle it should be 0.2–8.0 percent and perform the following procedures:

a. After checking the CO percentage, disconnect the resistor from the engine temperature sensor harness connector and connect the harness connector to the engine temperature sensor.

b. If the CO percentage is OK, replace the exhaust gas sensor. While operating the engine at 2000 rpm, make sure the green inspection light, on the ECU, turns ON and OFF more than 5 times in 10 seconds. If OK, perform the idle speed adjustment.

c. If, while operating the engine at 2000 rpm, the green inspection light, on the ECU, does not turn ON and OFF more than 5 times in 10 seconds, go to Step 17.

16. If the CO percentage is not OK, connect the exhaust gas sensor harness connector to the exhaust gas sensor.

17. If problems continue to exist, check and/or correct the problems with the following:

a. Fuel pressure regulator

b. Air flow meter and it's circuit

c. Fuel injector(s) and circuit

d. Engine temperature sensor and circuit

18. If OK, perform the idle speed adjustment.

19. Road test the vehicle.

VE30DE Engine

♦ SEE FIGS. 39 AND 40

1. Make sure the following items are in good order:

a. Battery

b. Ignition system

c. Engine oil and coolant levels

d. Fuses

e. Electronic Control Unit harness connector

f. Vacuum hoses

g. Air intake system

h. Fuel pressure

i. Engine compression

j. EGR control valve operation

k. Throttle valve

2. If equipped with air conditioning, turn the air conditioning control **OFF**.

3. If equipped with an automatic transaxle, place the shift control in **N**.

4. If measuring the CO percentage, position the probe more than 15.7 in. (40cm) into the tail pipe.

5. Turn **OFF** the headlights, the heater blower motor and the rear defogger.

6. Position the front wheels in the straight-ahead position.

7. Perform the checks after the radiator fan has stopped.

8. Apply the parking brakes and block the wheels.

9. Start the engine and allow it to reach normal operating temperatures, until water temperature indicator points to the middle of the gauge. Ensure that the engine speed stays below 1000 rpm.

10. Raise the hood and run the engine at about 2000 rpm for about 2 minutes, under no-load.

11. Perform the ECU self diagnosis check, in Mode II; if diagnostic problems exist, repair or replace the defective component.

12. Run the engine at 2000 rpm for about 2 minutes under no-load. Race the engine 2–3 times under no-load and run it for about 1 min. at idle speed.

13. If using the CONSULT diagnostic tester, perform the following procedures:

a. Turn the engine **OFF** and disconnect the throttle sensor harness connector.

b. Start the engine.

c. Select the **AAC VALVE ADJ** in **WORK SUPPORT** mode.

d. Touch the **START** button.

14. If not using the CONSULT diagnostic tester, perform the following procedures:

a. Turn the engine **OFF** and disconnect the throttle sensor harness connector and the Auxiliary Air Control (AAC) valve harness connector.

b. Start the engine.

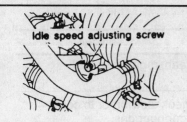

Fig. 39 Adjusting the idle speed adjusting screw — VE30DE engine

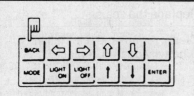

Fig. 40 View of the CONSULT diagnostic tester control board — VE30DE engine

15. Race the engine 2–3 times (2000–3000 rpm) under no-load and run it for about 1 min. at idle speed.

16. Using a timing light, connect it to the engine according to the manufacturer's instructions.

17. If the timing is not at specifications, loosen the crank angle sensor hold-down bolt, turn the crank angle sensor until the timing marks align and tighten the hold-down bolt.

18. If using the CONSULT diagnostic tester, read idle speed in the **AAC VALVE ADJ** in **WORK SUPPORT** mode, by touching the **START** button.

19. If not using the CONSULT diagnostic tester and idle speed is not correct, race the engine 2–3 times (at 2000–3000 rpm) under no-load and run it at idle. To correct the idle speed, adjust the idle speed adjusting screw.

20. If using the CONSULT diagnostic tester and the idle speed is correct, perform the following procedures:

  a. Touch **BACK**.

  b. Turn the ignition switch **OFF** and connect the throttle sensor harness connector.

21. If not using the CONSULT diagnostic tester and the idle speed is correct, perform the following procedures:

  a. Turn the ignition switch **OFF**.

  b. Connect the throttle sensor harness connector and the AAC valve harness connector.

22. Start the engine and race it 2–3 times (at 2000–3000 rpm) under no-load and run it at idle speed.

23. If using the CONSULT diagnostic tester, read the idle speed in the **DATA MONITOR** mode and the idle speed is correct, proceed to Step 25.

24. If not using the CONSULT diagnostic tester and the idle speed is not correct, perform the following procedures:

  a. Check and/or replace the AAC valve.

  b. Check and/or replace the AAC valve harness.

  c. Check the ECU function by substituting it with one that is good.

25. If using the CONSULT diagnostic tester, perform the following procedures:

  a. See **M/R F/C MNT** in the **DATA MONITOR** mode.

  b. Operate the engine at 2000 rpm for 2 minutes under no-load.

  c. With the engine running at 2000 rpm under no-load and the operating temperatures normal, check that the monitor fluctuates between **LEAN** and **RICH** more than 5 times in 10 seconds; if not, proceed to Step 27.

26. If not using the CONSULT diagnostic tester, perform the following procedures:

  a. Set the ECU in the self-diagnostic Mode II.

  b. Operate the engine at 2000 rpm for 2 minutes under no-load.

  c. With the engine running at 2000 rpm under no-load and the operating temperatures normal, check that the red light on the ECU or the check engine light on the instrument panel turns ON and OFF more than 5 times in 10 seconds; if not, proceed to Step 27.

27. If problems still exist, check, repair and/or replace the following item(s) and perform the idle speed adjustment:

  a. Exhaust gas sensor harness.

  b. ECU SMJ harness connector.

  c. Exhaust gas sensor.

  d. Fuel pressure regulator.

  e. Air flow meter and circuit.

  f. Fuel injectors and circuits.

  g. Engine temperature sensor and circuit.

  h. Electronic Control Unit (ECU).

TORQUE SPECIFICATIONS

Component	English	Metric
Crank angle sensor hold-down bolt		
VE30DE engine	9–12 ft. lbs.	13–16 Nm
Distributor hold-down bolt		
VG30E engine		
1985–88	3.6–4.3 ft. lbs.	5–6 Nm
1989–92	10–12 ft. lbs.	14–17 Nm
Power transistor-to-engine bolts		
VE30DE engine	2.7–3.7 ft. lbs.	3.7–5.0 Nm
Spark plug		
VG30E engine	14 ft. lbs.	22 Nm
VE30DE engine	14 ft. lbs.	22 Nm

Diagnosis of Spark Plugs

Problem	Possible Cause	Correction
Brown to grayish-tan deposits and slight electrode wear.	• Normal wear.	• Clean, regap, reinstall.
Dry, fluffy black carbon deposits.	• Poor ignition output.	• Check distributor to coil connections.
Wet, oily deposits with very little electrode wear.	• "Break-in" of new or recently overhauled engine. • Excessive valve stem guide clearances. • Worn intake valve seals.	• Degrease, clean and reinstall the plugs. • Refer to Section 3. • Replace the seals.
Red, brown, yellow and white colored coatings on the insulator. Engine misses intermittently under severe operating conditions.	• By-products of combustion.	• Clean, regap, and reinstall. If heavily coated, replace.
Colored coatings heavily deposited on the portion of the plug projecting into the chamber and on the side facing the intake valve.	• Leaking seals if condition is found in only one or two cylinders.	• Check the seals. Replace if necessary. Clean, regap, and reinstall the plugs.
Shiny yellow glaze coating on the insulator.	• Melted by-products of combustion.	• Avoid sudden acceleration with wide-open throttle after long periods of low speed driving. Replace the plugs.
Burned or blistered insulator tips and badly eroded electrodes.	• Overheating.	• Check the cooling system. • Check for sticking heat riser valves. Refer to Section 1. • Lean air-fuel mixture. • Check the heat range of the plugs. May be too hot. • Check ignition timing. May be over-advanced. • Check the torque value of the plugs to ensure good plug-engine seat contact.
Broken or cracked insulator tips.	• Heat shock from sudden rise in tip temperature under severe operating conditions. Improper gapping of plugs.	• Replace the plugs. Gap correctly.

3

ENGINE AND ENGINE OVERHAUL

ENGINE ELECTRICAL

Ignition Coil

TESTING

VG30E Engine

1985–88

♦ SEE FIG. 2

On the 1985–88 vehicle, the ignition coil/power transistor assembly is located, in the engine compartment, on the front right fender.

1. Disconnect the negative battery cable.
2. Disconnect the electrical harness connector from the ignition coil.
3. Using an ohmmeter, adjust it to the low range.
4. Attach the probes to terminals **1** and **2**; there should be resistance of approximately 0.8 ohm. If the test does not meet 0.8 ohm, replace the ignition coil.
5. Connect the electrical harness connector to the ignition coil.
6. Connect the negative battery cable.

1989–92

♦ SEE FIG. 3

On the 1989–92 vehicle, the ignition coil is located on the front of the engine, in front of the distributor.

1. Disconnect the negative battery cable.
2. Disconnect the electrical harness connector from the ignition coil.
3. Using an ohmmeter, adjust it to the low range.
4. Attach the probes to terminals **1** and **2**; there should be resistance of approximately 1.0 ohm. If the test does not meet 1.0 ohm, replace the ignition coil.
5. Connect the electrical harness connector to the ignition coil.
6. Connect the negative battery cable.

VE30DE Engine

♦ SEE FIGS. 6 AND 7

The VE30DE engine is equipped multiple ignition coils, each are attached directly to the spark plugs.

1. Disconnect the negative battery cable.
2. Disconnect the electrical connector(s) from the ignition coil(s).
3. Disconnect the ignition coil(s) from the spark plug(s).
4. Using an ohmmeter, adjust it to the low

range. Attach the probes to the terminal **1** and terminal **2**, then measure the resistance; the resistance should be approximately 0.8 ohm.

5. If the resistance is not approximately 0.8 ohm, replace the ignition coil(s).
6. Connect the ignition coil(s) to the spark plug(s).
7. Connect the electrical connector(s) to the ignition coil(s).
8. Connect the negative battery cable.

REMOVAL & INSTALLATION

VG30E Engine

1. Disconnect the negative battery cable.
2. Disconnect the electrical harness connector from the ignition coil.
3. Disconnect the ignition coil wire from the ignition coil.
4. Remove the ignition coil bolts and the coil.

➡ **On the 1985–88 vehicles, the power transistor must be removed with ignition coil.**

To install:
5. Install the ignition coil and tighten the bolts.
6. Connect the ignition coil wire to the ignition coil.

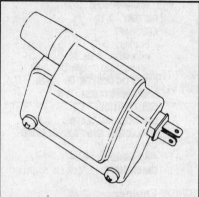

FIG. 2 View of the ignition coil — 1985–88 VG30E engine

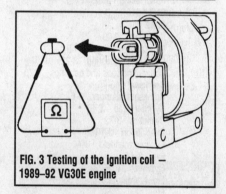

FIG. 3 Testing of the ignition coil — 1989–92 VG30E engine

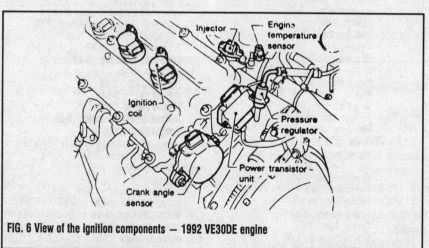

FIG. 6 View of the ignition components — 1992 VE30DE engine

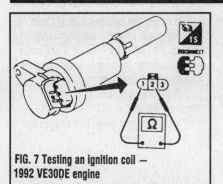

**FIG. 7 Testing an ignition coil —
1992 VE30DE engine**

7. Connect the electrical harness connector to the ignition coil.

8. Connect the negative battery cable.

9. Start the engine and check the operation.

VE30DE Engine

1. Disconnect the negative battery cable.

2. Disconnect the electrical harness connector(s) from the ignition coil(s).

3. Disconnect the ignition coil(s) from the spark plug(s).

To install:

4. Connect the ignition coil(s) to the spark plug(s).

5. Connect the electrical harness connector(s) to the ignition coil(s).

6. Connect the negative battery cable.

7. Start the engine and check the operation.

Power Transistor

TESTING

VG30E Engine

1985–88

♦ SEE FIGS. 1 AND 5

On the 1985–88 vehicle, the power transistor is located, in the engine compartment, on the front right fender.

1. Disconnect the negative battery cable.

2. Disconnect the ignition coil/power transistor assembly electrical harness connector.

3. Using an ohmmeter, adjust the setting to the low range, approximately 1.0 ohms.

4. To test the ignition coil/power transistor assembly, perform the following procedures:

   a. Place the positive (+) probe on terminal **2** and the negative (–) probe on terminal **3**; there should be continuity.

   b. Place the positive (+) probe on terminal **2** and the negative (–) probe on terminal **4**; there should be continuity.

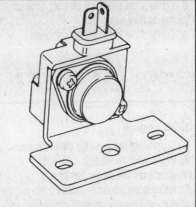

**FIG. 1 View of the power transistor —
1985–88 VG30E engine**

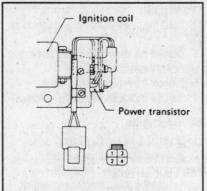

FIG. 5 Testing of the ignition coil/power transistor assembly — 1985–88 VG30E engine

   c. Place the positive (+) probe on terminal **3** and the negative (–) probe on terminal **4**; there should be continuity.

5. If the ignition coil/power transistor assembly does not perform according to the test, replace power transistor.

6. Reconnect the electrical harness connector.

7. Connect the negative battery cable.

1989–92

♦ SEE FIG. 4

On the 1989–92 vehicle, the power transistor is located on the front of the engine, in front of the distributor.

1. Disconnect the negative battery cable.

2. Disconnect the electrical harness connector from the power transistor.

3. Using an ohmmeter, adjust the setting to the low range, approximately 1.0 ohms.

4. To test the power transistor, perform the following procedures:

   a. Place the positive (+) probe on terminal **a** and the negative (–) probe on terminal **b**; there should be continuity.

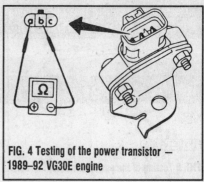

**FIG. 4 Testing of the power transistor —
1989–92 VG30E engine**

   b. Place the positive (+) probe on terminal **a** and the negative (–) probe on terminal **c**; there should be continuity.

   c. Place the negative (–) probe on terminal **a** and the positive (+) probe on terminal **b**; there should not be continuity.

   d. Place the negative (–) probe on terminal **a** and the positive (+) probe on terminal **c**; there should not be continuity.

5. If the power transistor does not perform according to the test, replace it.

6. Reconnect the electrical harness connector to the power transistor.

7. Connect the negative battery cable.

VE30DE Engine

♦ SEE FIG. 8

The power transistor is attached to the rear of the left cylinder head.

1. Disconnect the negative battery cable.

2. Disconnect the electrical harness connector(s) from the power transistor.

➡ **If necessary, remove the power transistor from the engine.**

3. Using an ohmmeter, adjust it to the low range and perform the following procedures:

   a. Attach the positive (+) probe to terminal **d** and with the negative (–) probe, touch terminals **a**, **b**, **c**, **e**, **f** and **g**; the resistance of each terminal should not be 0 or ∞.

   b. Attach the negative (–) probe to terminal **d** and with the positive (+) probe, touch terminals **a**, **b**, **c**, **e**, **f** and **g**; the resistance of each terminal should not be 0 or ∞.

   c. Attach the positive (+) probe to terminal **d** and with the negative (–) probe, touch terminals **1**, **2**, **3**, **4**, **5** and **6**; the resistance of each terminal should not be 0 or ∞.

   d. Attach the negative (–) probe to terminal **d** and with the positive (+) probe, touch terminals **1**, **2**, **3**, **4**, **5** and **6**; the resistance of each terminal should ∞.

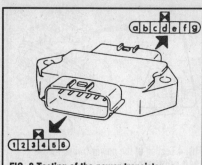

FIG. 8 Testing of the power transistor — 1992 VE30DE engine

e. Attach the positive (+) probe to terminal **a** and the negative (–) probe to terminal **1**; the resistance should not be 0 or ∞.

f. Attach the negative (–) probe to terminal **a** and the positive (+) probe to terminal **1**; the resistance should be ∞.

g. Attach the positive (+) probe to terminal **b** and the negative (–) probe to terminal **2**; the resistance should not be 0 or ∞.

h. Attach the negative (–) probe to terminal **b** and the positive (+) probe to terminal **2**; the resistance should be ∞.

i. Attach the positive (+) probe to terminal **c** and the negative (–) probe to terminal **3**; the resistance should not be 0 or ∞.

j. Attach the negative (–) probe to terminal **c** and the positive (+) probe to terminal **3**; the resistance should be ∞.

k. Attach the positive (+) probe to terminal **e** and the negative (–) probe to terminal **4**; the resistance should not be 0 or ∞.

l. Attach the negative (–) probe to terminal **e** and the positive (+) probe to terminal **4**; the resistance should be ∞.

m. Attach the positive (+) probe to terminal **f** and the negative (–) probe to terminal **5**; the resistance should not be 0 or ∞.

n. Attach the negative (–) probe to terminal **f** and the positive (+) probe to terminal **5**; the resistance should be ∞.

o. Attach the positive (+) probe to terminal **g** and the negative (–) probe to terminal **6**; the resistance should not be 0 or ∞.

p. Attach the negative (–) probe to terminal **g** and the positive (+) probe to terminal **6**; the resistance should be ∞.

4. If the any of the test results do not agree, replace the power transistor.

➡ **If the power transistor was removed from the engine, install it.**

5. Connect the electrical harness connectors to the power transistor.

6. Connect the negative battery cable.

REMOVAL & INSTALLATION

VG30E Engine

1. Disconnect the negative battery cable.

2. Disconnect the electrical harness connectors from the power transistor.

3. Remove the power transistor bolts and the transistor.

➡ **On the 1985–88 vehicles, the ignition coil must be removed with power transistor.**

To install:

4. Install the power transistor and tighten the bolts.

5. Connect the electrical harness connectors to the power transistor.

6. Connect the negative battery cable.

7. Start the engine and check the operation.

VE30DE Engine

1. Disconnect the negative battery cable.

2. Disconnect the electrical harness connectors from the power transistor.

3. Remove the power transistor-to-engine bolts and the transistor.

To install:

4. Install the power transistor and tighten the bolts to 2.7–3.7 ft. lbs. (3.7–5.0 Nm).

5. Connect the electrical harness connectors to the power transistor.

6. Connect the negative battery cable.

7. Start the engine and check the operation.

Distributor

A distributor equipped with a crank angle sensor is installed on the VG30E engine.

REMOVAL

1. Rotate the crankshaft until the No. 1 cylinder is at the Top Dead Center (TDC) of it's compression stroke.

➡ **The No. 1 cylinder is on the TDC of it's compression stroke when the distributor rotor is pointing to the No. 1 spark plug wire on the distributor cap and the punched mark on the crankshaft sprocket is aligned with mark on the oil pump housing.**

2. Disconnect the negative battery cable.

3. Using chalk, mark the distributor rotor's position on the distributor housing. Also, make mark the distributor housing-to-engine position.

4. Remove the distributor cap.

5. Disconnect the crank angle sensor electrical connector.

6. Remove the hold-down bolt and remove the distributor housing.

INSTALLATION

Engine Not Disturbed

◆ SEE FIGS. 9 AND 10

1. Align the punched mark on the distributor shaft with the protruding mark on the distributor housing.

2. Install the distributor and align the mark on the distributor housing with the alignment mark on the engine. Align the rotor with the mark on the distributor housing.

3. Tighten the distributor hold-down bolt to 3.6–4.3 ft. lbs. (5–6 Nm) for 1985–88 or 10–12 ft. lbs. (14–17 Nm) for 1989–92.

4. Install the distributor cap and connect the electrical harness connector.

5. Connect the negative battery cable.

6. Start the engine and check the engine operation.

Engine Disturbed

1. It is necessary to place the No. 1 cylinder in the firing position to correctly install the distributor. To locate this position, the ignition timing marks on the crankshaft front pulley are used.

2. Remove the No. 1 cylinder spark plug. Turn the crankshaft until the piston in the No. 1 cylinder is moving up on the compression stroke. This can be determined by placing your thumb over the spark plug hole and feeling the air being forced out of the cylinder. Stop turning the crankshaft when the timing marks that are used to time the engine are aligned.

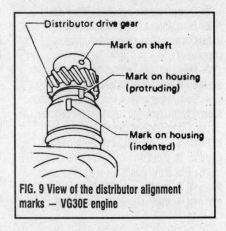

FIG. 9 View of the distributor alignment marks — VG30E engine

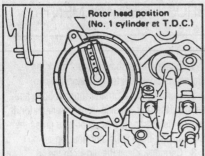

FIG. 10 Position of the distributor rotor for No. 1 cylinder at TDC of it's compression stroke — VG30E engine

3. Oil the distributor housing lightly where the distributor bears on the cylinder block.

4. Align the punched mark on the distributor shaft with the protruding mark on the distributor housing.

5. Install the distributor and align the mark on the distributor housing with the alignment mark on the engine. Align the rotor with the mark on the distributor housing.

6. Tighten the distributor hold-down bolt to 3.6–4.3 ft. lbs. (5–6 Nm) for 1985–88 or 10–12 ft. lbs. (14–17 Nm) for 1989–92.

7. Install the distributor cap and connect the electrical harness connector.

8. Connect the negative battery cable.

9. Start the engine and check the engine operation.

Crank Angle Sensor

A crank angle sensor is used on the VE30DE engine instead of a distributor.

1. Disconnect the negative battery cable.

2. Rotate the crankshaft until the No. 1 cylinder is at the Top Dead Center (TDC) of it's compression stroke. If necessary, remove the No. 1 spark plug, rotate the crankshaft until compression pressure is emitted from the No. 1 cylinder and it is on the TDC of it's compression stroke.

➡ **The No. 1 cylinder may be on the TDC of it's compression stroke when the mark on the crankshaft pulley is aligned with the pointer; if not rotate the crankshaft 360° and realign the crankshaft pulley mark with the pointer.**

3. Using chalk, mark the crank angle sensor housing's position on the engine.

4. Disconnect the crank angle sensor electrical connector.

5. Remove the hold-down bolt and remove the crank angle sensor housing.

INSTALLATION

Engine Not Disturbed

▶ SEE FIGS. 11 AND 12

1. Align the crank angle sensor shaft with the camshaft on the cylinder head.

2. Install the crank angle senor housing and align the mark on the housing with the alignment mark on the engine.

3. Tighten the housing hold-down bolt to 9–12 ft. lbs. (13–16 Nm).

4. Connect the electrical harness connector.

5. Connect the negative battery cable.

6. Start the engine and check the engine operation.

Engine Disturbed

1. It is necessary to place the No. 1 cylinder in the firing position to correctly install the distributor. To locate this position, the ignition timing marks on the crankshaft front pulley are used.

2. Remove the No. 1 cylinder spark plug. Turn the crankshaft until the piston in the No. 1 cylinder is moving up on the compression stroke. This can be determined by placing your thumb over the spark plug hole and feeling the air being forced out of the cylinder. Stop turning the crankshaft when the timing marks that are used to time the engine are aligned.

3. Oil the distributor housing lightly where the distributor bears on the cylinder block.

4. Align the crank angle sensor shaft with the camshaft on the cylinder head.

5. Install the crank angle senor housing and align the mark on the housing with the alignment mark on the engine.

6. Tighten the housing hold-down bolt to 9–12 ft. lbs. (13–16 Nm).

7. Connect the electrical harness connector.

8. Connect the negative battery cable.

9. Start the engine and check the engine operation.

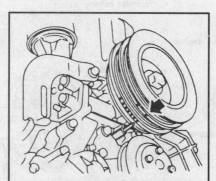

FIG. 11 Aligning the crankshaft pulley with the timing marker with the No. 1 cylinder on TDC of it's compression stroke — VE30DE engine

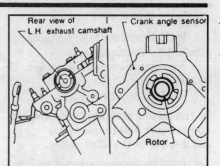

FIG. 12 Aligning the crank angle sensor shaft with the left exhaust camshaft when the No. 1 cylinder is on TDC of it's compression stroke — VE30DE engine

Alternator

ALTERNATOR PRECAUTIONS

To prevent damage to the alternator and regulator, the following precautionary measures must be taken when working with the electrical system.

1. Never reverse battery connections.

2. Booster batteries for starting must be connected properly. Make sure the positive cable of the booster battery is connected to the positive terminal of the battery that is getting the boost. This applies to both negative and ground cables.

3. Disconnect the battery cables before using a fast charger; the charger has a tendency to force current through the diodes in the opposite direction for which they are designed. This burns out the diodes.

4. Never use a fast charger as a booster for starting the vehicle.

5. Do not ground the alternator output terminal.

6. Do not operate the alternator on an open circuit with the field energized.

7. Do not attempt to polarize an alternator.

REMOVAL & INSTALLATION

1985–88

1. Disconnect the negative battery terminal.

2. Disconnect the lead wires and connector from the alternator.

3. Loosen the drive belt adjusting bolt and remove the belt.

4. Unscrew the alternator attaching bolts and remove the alternator from the vehicle.

To install:

5. Mount the alternator to the engine and partially tighten the attaching bolts.

6. Reconnect the lead wires and connector to the alternator.

7. Install the alternator drive belt.

➡ **The power steering pump and air compressor belt tensions are adjusted with the idler pulley.**

8. Adjust the alternator belt by performing the following procedures:

a. Using a wooden lever, pry the alternator toward or away from the engine until the proper tension is achieved.

b. Tighten the alternator's pivot bolt locknut.

c. Tighten the alternator's mounting bolt to 12–15 ft. lbs. (16–21 Nm).

➡ **The alternator belt tension is quite critical. A belt that is too tight may cause alternator bearing failure; one that is too loose will cause a gradual battery discharge.**

9. Connnect the battery cable. Start the engine and check for proper operation.

1989–92

1. Disconnect the negative battery terminal.
2. Disconnect the lead wires and connector from the alternator.

3. Loosen the drive belt adjusting bolt locknut and remove the belt.

4. Unscrew the alternator attaching bolts and remove the alternator from the vehicle.

To install:

5. Mount the alternator to the engine and partially tighten the attaching bolts.

6. Reconnect the lead wires and connector to the alternator.

7. Install the alternator drive belt.

➡ **The belt tensions are adjusted using an adjustment bolt.**

8. Adjust the alternator belt by performing the following procedures:

a. Turn the adjusting bolt to adjust the belt tension.

b. Tighten the alternator's adjusting bolt locknut to 12–15 ft. lbs. (16–21 Nm).

c. Tighten the alternator's mounting bolt to 16–22 ft. lbs. (22–29 Nm).

➡ **The alternator belt tension is quite critical. A belt that is too tight may cause alternator bearing failure; one that is too loose will cause a gradual battery discharge.**

9. Connnect the battery cable. Start the engine and check for proper operation.

BRUSH REPLACEMENT

◆ SEE FIGS. 13-22

1. Using a scratch awl, matchmark the alternator end-shells to the stator housing.

2. Remove the alternator through bolts and separate the rear housing from the alternator; it may be necessary to use prypars to press the rear housing from the stator housing.

3. Carefully, clean the dirt from the components; compressed air may be very helpful for cleaning.

4. Inspect the brushes for wear and the brush holder for smoothness of brush movement; replace the brushes if the length is less than 0.276 in. (7.0mm) for VG30E engine or 0.236 in. (6.0mm) for VE30DE engine. Check the brush lead wire(s) for wear; replace the brushes, if the wires are worn.

5. Using spring gauge, inspect the brush spring tension; the spring tension must be 3.88–9.17 oz. (1.079–2.550 N) for VG30E engine or 3.60–12.34 oz. (1.000–3.432 N) for VE30DE engine.

6. To install new brushes, perform the following procedures:

a. Using a soldering iron, separate the brush lead wire from the brush holder.

b. Insert the new brush lead wire through the hole in the brush holder.

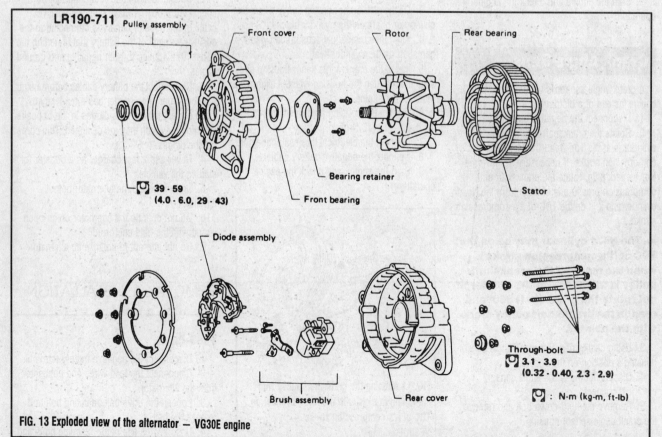

FIG. 13 Exploded view of the alternator — VG30E engine

c. Position the brush so it extends 0.413–0.453 in. (10.5–11.5mm) from the brush holder.

d. Wrap the brush lead wire 1½ times around the terminal groove and solder the wire.

➡ **When soldering, be careful not to allow the solder to adhere to the insulating tube, for it will weaken the tube and cause it to break.**

7. For the alternator used on the VG30E engine, perform the following procedures:

a. Using a small wire at the rear cover, push the brushes into the brush holder and insert the wire through the rear cover and secure the brushes in position.

b. Install the rear cover to the stator housing, align the matchmarks and install the through bolts.

c. Tighten the through bolts and remove the wire securing the brushes.

8. For the alternator used on the VE30DE engine, perform the following procedures:

a. Fit the brushes into the brush older, depress them and install the assembly onto the rotor shaft; be careful not to scratch the sliprings.

b. Install the through bolts and tighten.

FIG. 13A View of the alternator and engine mount location on the 1991 VG30E engine

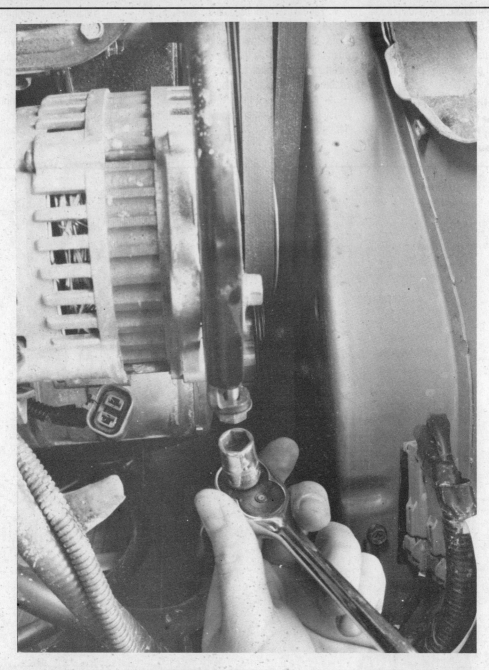

FIG. 13B Removing the alternator on the 1991 VG30E engine

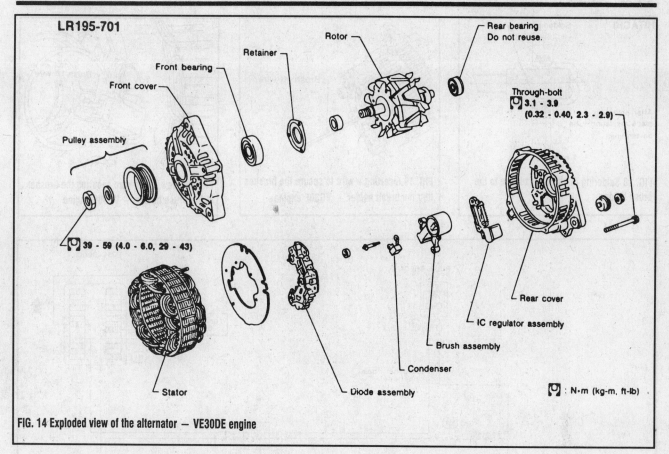

LR195-701

Front cover

Front bearing

Retainer

Rotor

Rear bearing
Do not reuse.

Pulley assembly

Through-bolt
⊡ 3.1 - 3.9
(0.32 - 0.40, 2.3 - 2.9)

⊡ 39 - 59 (4.0 - 6.0, 29 - 43)

Rear cover

IC regulator assembly

Brush assembly

Condenser

Stator

Diode assembly

⊡ : N·m (kg-m, ft-lb)

FIG. 14 Exploded view of the alternator — VE30DE engine

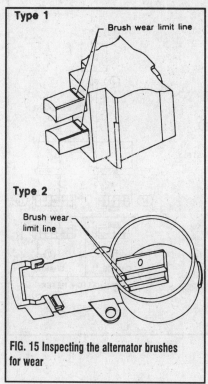

Type 1

Brush wear limit line

Type 2

Brush wear
limit line

FIG. 15 Inspecting the alternator brushes
for wear

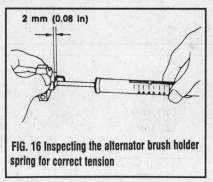

2 mm (0.08 in)

FIG. 16 Inspecting the alternator brush holder
spring for correct tension

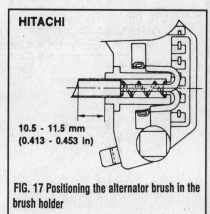

HITACHI

10.5 - 11.5 mm
(0.413 - 0.453 in)

FIG. 17 Positioning the alternator brush in the
brush holder

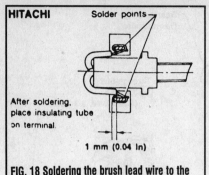
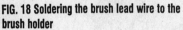

HITACHI

Solder points

After soldering, place insulating tube on terminal.

1 mm (0.04 In)

FIG. 18 Soldering the brush lead wire to the brush holder

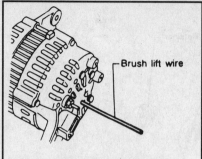

Brush lift wire

FIG. 19 Inserting a wire to secure the brushes into the brush holder — VG30E engine

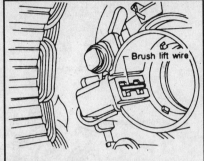

Brush lift wire

FIG. 20 View of the wire securing the brushes in the brush holder — VG30E engine

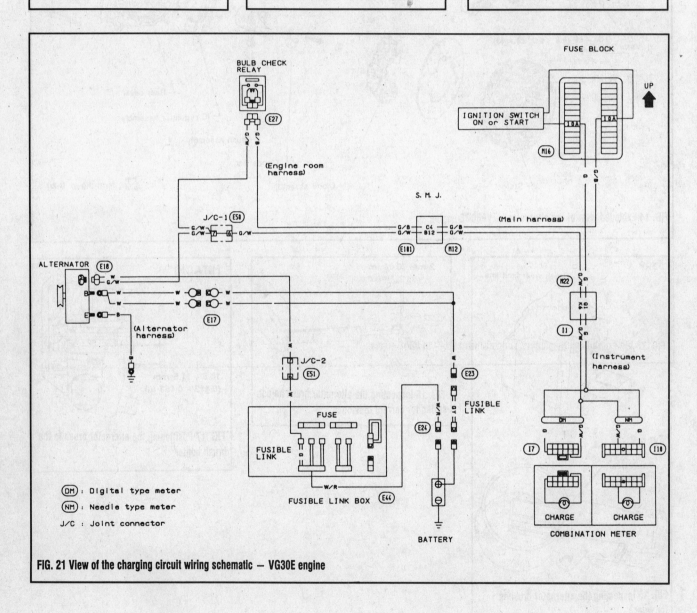

FIG. 21 View of the charging circuit wiring schematic — VG30E engine

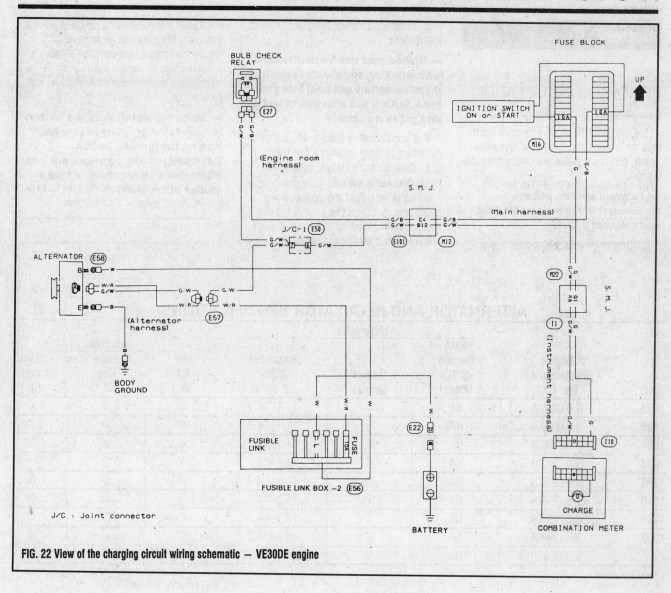

FIG. 22 View of the charging circuit wiring schematic — VE30DE engine

Battery

REMOVAL & INSTALLATION

1. Disconnect the negative (ground) cable from the terminal, and then the positive cable. Special pullers are available to remove the cable clamps.

➡ **To avoid sparks, always disconnect the ground cable first, and connect it last.**

2. Remove the battery hold-down clamp.

3. Remove the battery, being careful not to spill the acid.

➡ **Spilled acid can be neutralized with a baking soda/water solution. If you somehow get acid into your eyes, flush it out with lots of water and get to a doctor.**

4. Clean the battery posts thoroughly before reinstalling or when installing a new battery.
5. Clean the cable clamps, using a wire brush, both inside and out.
6. Install the battery and the hold-down clamp or strap. Connect the positive and then the negative cable. Do not hammer them in place. The terminals should be coated lightly (externally) with non-metallic grease to prevent corrosion. There are also felt washers impregnated with an anti-corrosion substance which are slipped over the battery posts before installing the cables; these are available in auto parts stores.

➡ **Make absolutely sure the battery is connected properly before you turn on the ignition switch. Reversed polarity can burn out your alternator and regulator within a matter of seconds.**

ALTERNATOR AND REGULATOR SPECIFICATIONS

| Year | Engine Displacement liter (cc) | Alternator | | | Regulator | | |
		Field Current @ 12v (amps)	Output (amps)	Regulated Volts @ 75°F	Air Gap (in.)	Point Gap (in.)	Back Gap (in.)
1985	3.0 (2960)	NA	③	14.1–14.7	②	②	②
1986	3.0 (2960)	NA	③	14.1–14.7	②	②	②
1987	3.0 (2960)	NA	③	14.1–14.7	②	②	②
1988	3.0 (2960)	NA	③	14.1–14.7	②	②	②
1989	3.0 (2960)	NA	④	14.1–14.7	②	②	②
1990	3.0 (2960)	NA	④	14.1–14.7	②	②	②
1991	3.0 (2960)	NA	④	14.1–14.7	②	②	②
1992	3.0 (2960)	NA	④	14.1–14.7	②	②	②
	3.0 (2960) ①	NA	⑤	14.1–14.7	②	②	②

NA—Not available
① VE30DE engine
② Integrated circuit regulator assembly
③ 22 amp at 1300 rpm
   65 amp at 2500 rpm
   87 amp at 5000 rpm
④ 23 amp at 1300 rpm
   63 amp at 2500 rpm
   84 amp at 5000 rpm
⑤ 34 amp at 1300 rpm
   80 amp at 2500 rpm
   91 amp at 5000 rpm

Starter

♦ SEE FIGS. 23 AND 24

The gear reduction starter has a set of ratio reduction gears; the brushes on the gear reduction starter are located on a plate behind the starter drive housing. The extra gears make the starter pinion gear turn at about 1/2 the speed of the starter, giving the starter twice the turning power of a conventional starter.

REMOVAL & INSTALLATION

1. Disconnect the negative battery cable from the battery.
2. On the VE30DE engine, remove the air duct.
3. Disconnect the starter wiring at the starter, taking note of the positions for correct installation.
4. On the VE30DE engine, remove the connector brackets.
5. Remove the starter-to-engine bolts and remove the starter from the vehicle.

To install:
6. Install the starter to the engine.

7. Tighten the attaching bolts. Be careful not overtorque the mounting bolts as this will crack the nose of the starter case.
8. Install the starter wiring in the correct location.
9. On the VE30DE engine, install the air duct and the connector brackets.
10. Connect the negative battery cable.
11. Start the engine a few times to make sure of proper operation.

SOLENOID REPLACEMENT

➡ **The starter solenoid is also know as the magnetic switch assembly.**

S114-461A

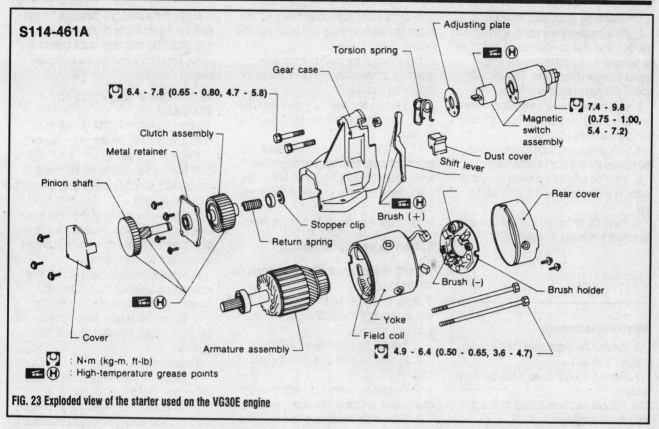

FIG. 23 Exploded view of the starter used on the VG30E engine

S114-756

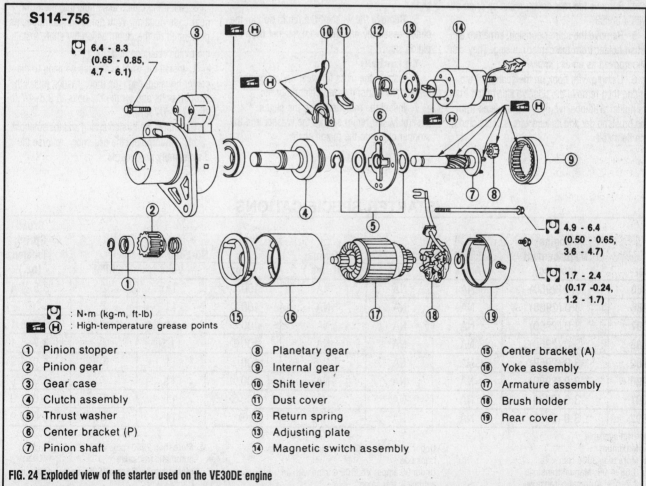

① Pinion stopper
② Pinion gear
③ Gear case
④ Clutch assembly
⑤ Thrust washer
⑥ Center bracket (P)
⑦ Pinion shaft

⑧ Planetary gear
⑨ Internal gear
⑩ Shift lever
⑪ Dust cover
⑫ Return spring
⑬ Adjusting plate
⑭ Magnetic switch assembly

⑮ Center bracket (A)
⑯ Yoke assembly
⑰ Armature assembly
⑱ Brush holder
⑲ Rear cover

FIG. 24 Exploded view of the starter used on the VE30DE engine

1. Remove the starter from the engine.

2. Place the starter in a vise or equivalent, to hold the starter in place while you are working on the solenoid; do not tighten the vise to tight around the case of the starter. The case will crack if you tighten the vise to much.

3. Loosen the solenoid's **M** (motor) terminal locknut and separate the motor wire connector from the solenoid's terminal.

4. Remove the solenoid-to-starter screws and remove the solenoid from the starter.

5. Install the solenoid and torque the solenoid-to-starter screws to 4.7–5.8 ft. lbs. (6.4–7.8 Nm).

6. Install the **M** (motor) wire and locknut to the bottom terminal of the starter.

OVERHAUL

Brush Replacement

1. Remove the starter, then the solenoid or magnetic switch.

2. Remove the dust cover, E-ring and thrust washers.

3. Remove the starter through-bolts and brush holder setscrews.

4. Remove the rear cover; it can be pried off with a prybar.

5. Remove the starter housing, armature and brush holder from the center housing. They can be removed as an assembly.

6. Using a wire hook on the spring, lift the spring then remove the positive side brush from its holder. The positive brush is insulated from the brush holder and its lead wire is connected to the field coil.

7. Using a wire hook on the spring, lift the spring and remove the negative brush from the holder.

8. Replace all the brushes in the starter assembly; a solder iron may be necessary to replace the brushes.

9. Insert the new brushes in the brush holder.

10. Install the brush holder into the center housing.

11. Install the brush holder setscrews, rear cover and starter through bolts; torque the through bolts to 3.6–4.7 ft. lbs. (4.9–6.4 Nm).

12. Install the thrust washers, E-ring and dust cover.

13. Install the solenoid or magnetic switch.

Starter Drive Replacement

EXCEPT VE30DE ENGINE WITH AUTOMATIC TRANSAXLE

Starter model S114–756 is used on all engines, except the VE30DE engine with an automatic transaxle.

1. Remove the starter from the engine.

2. Remove the front cover from the gear case.

3. Remove the pinion metal retainer-to-gear case screws and the retainer/clutch assembly.

4. Remove the stopper clip from the pinion shaft.

5. Remove the washer, the return spring, the clutch assembly and the metal retainer from the pinion shaft.

To install:

6. Inspect the parts for wear and/or damage; replace the parts, if worn, chipped or etc.

7. Install the metal retainer, the clutch assembly, the return spring, the washer and the stopper clip onto the pinion shaft.

8. Install the pinion assembly into the gear case and tighten the metal retainer screws.

9. Install the front cover to the gear case.

10. Install the starter into the engine and check it's operation.

VE30DE ENGINE WITH AUTOMATIC TRANSAXLE

Starter model S114–461A is used on the VE30DE engine with an automatic transaxle.

1. Remove the starter.

2. Remove the solenoid and the torsion spring. Matchmark the frontgear case housing to the center housing.

3. Remove the center housing-to-front gear case housing bolts, then separate the front gear case housing from the center housing. Do not disassemble the entire starter.

4. Remove the pinion gear-to-clutch shaft assembly retaining ring and pull the clutch assembly from the front gear case housing.

5. Remove the pinion spacer, the pinion gear and thrust washer from the front gear case housing.

To install:

6. Inspect the parts for wear and/or damage; replace the parts, if worn, chipped or etc.

7. Install the thrust washer, the pinion gear and the spacer into the front gear case housing.

8. Slide the clutch assembly into the front gear case housing. With the pinion components positioned on the clutch assembly shaft, install the pinion retaining ring.

9. Install the front gear case housing to the center housing, align the matchmarks, install the through bolts and torque the bolts to 3.6–4.7 ft. lbs. (4.9–6.4 Nm).

10. Install the torsion spring and the solenoid.

11. To complete the assembly, reverse the disassembly procedures.

STARTER SPECIFICATIONS

Year	Engine Displacement liter (cc)	Lock Test Amps	Lock Test Volts	Torque (ft. lbs.)	No-Load Test Amps	No-Load Test Volts	No-Load Test RPM	Brush Spring Tension (oz.)
1985	3.0 (2960)	NA	NA	NA	100 ①	11	②	3.5–4.4
1986	3.0 (2960)	NA	NA	NA	100 ①	11	②	③
1987	3.0 (2960)	NA	NA	NA	100 ①	11	②	3.7–5.1
1988	3.0 (2960)	NA	NA	NA	100 ①	11.5	②	3.7–5.1
1989	3.0 (2960)	NA	NA	NA	100 ①	11	②	4.0–4.9
1990	3.0 (2960)	NA	NA	NA	100 ①	11	②	4.0–4.9
1991	3.0 (2960)	NA	NA	NA	100 ①	11	②	4.0–4.9
1992	3.0 (2960)	NA	NA	NA	④	11	⑤	4.0–4.9

NA—Not available
① Maximum
② More than 3000 rpm
③ 3.68–4.96: Manual transaxle
   3.7–5.1: Automatic transaxle
④ Under 100 amps: VG30E engine or a manual transaxle
   Under 90 amps: VE30DE engine with an automatic transaxle
⑤ More than 2950 rpm: VE30DE engine with an automatic transaxle
   More than 3000 rpm: VG30E engine or manual transaxle

Sending Units and Sensors

♦ SEE FIGS. 25–29

REMOVAL & INSTALLATION

Fuel Temperature Sensor

The fuel temperature sensor, used on 1985–88 VG30E engine, is a part of the fuel pressure regulator and senses the fuel temperature. When the fuel temperature is higher than the specified level, the ECU enriches the fuel/air mixture. Never remove the fuel temperature sensor from the fuel pressure regulator; always replace it as an assembly.

Water Temperature Switch No. 1

The water temperature switch No. 1, used on

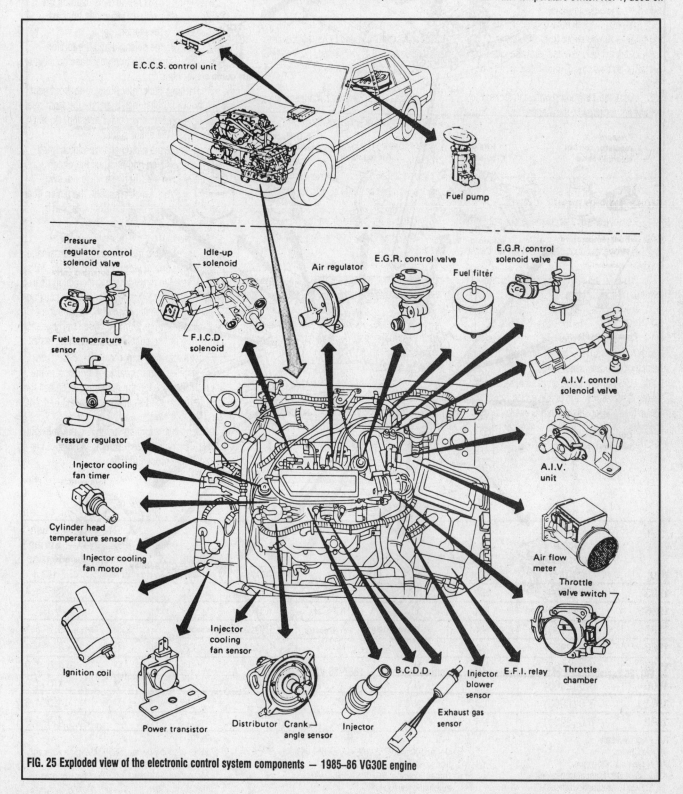

FIG. 25 Exploded view of the electronic control system components — 1985–86 VG30E engine

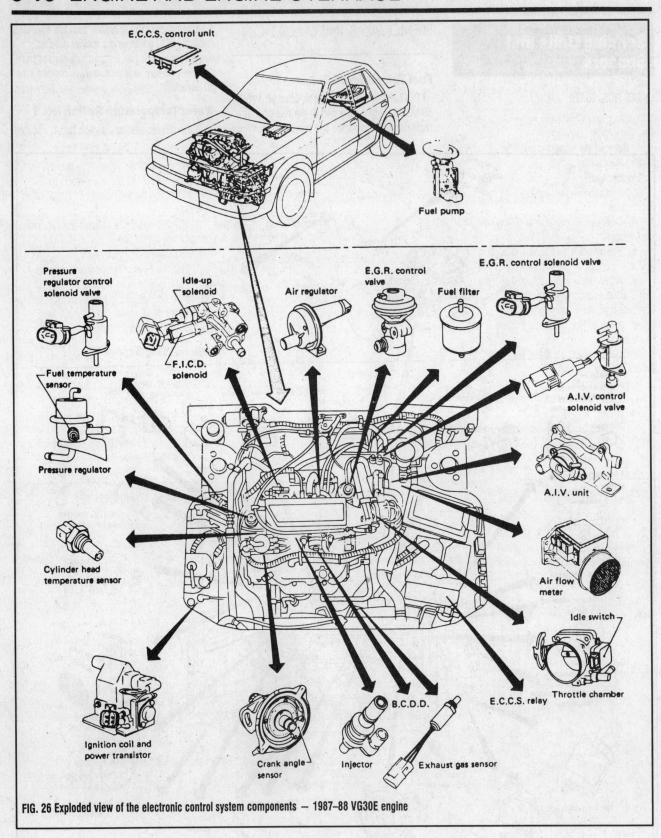

FIG. 26 Exploded view of the electronic control system components — 1987–88 VG30E engine

the 1985–88 vehicles, is located at the lower left corner of the radiator and controls the operation of the No. 1 cooling fan, which is located on the left side of the cooling fan assembly.

1. Disconnect the negative battery cable.
2. Drain the cooling system.
3. Disconnect the water temperature switch No. 1 electrical connector.
4. Remove the water temperature switch No. 1 from the radiator.

To Install:

5. To test the switch, perform the following procedures:

   a. Connect an ohmmeter to the electrical connectors.

   b. Position the switch in a beaker of water.

   c. When the water is heated to 194°F (90°C), the switch will turn **ON** causing the ohmmeter to show continuity.

   d. If the switch does not test correctly, replace it.

6. Coat the switch threads with sealant and install into the radiator.
7. Fill the cooling system.
8. Connect the electrical connector to the water temperature switch No. 1.
9. Connect the negative battery cable.

Water Temperature Switch No. 2

The water temperature switch No. 2, used on the 1985–88 vehicles, is located at the upper right corner of the radiator and controls the operation of the No. 2 cooling fan, which is located on the right side of the cooling fan assembly.

1. Disconnect the negative battery cable.
2. Drain the cooling system to a level below the water temperature switch No. 2.
3. Disconnect the water temperature switch No. 2 electrical connector.
4. Remove the water temperature switch No. 2 from the radiator.

To install:

5. To test the switch, perform the following procedures:

   a. Connect an ohmmeter to the electrical connectors.

   b. Position the switch in a beaker of water.

   c. When the water is heated to 212°F (100°C), the switch will turn **ON** causing the ohmmeter to show continuity.

   d. If the switch does not test correctly, replace it.

6. Coat the switch threads with sealant and install into the radiator.
7. Fill the cooling system.

8. Connect the electrical connector to the water temperature switch No. 2.
9. Connect the negative battery cable.

Cylinder Head Temperature Sensor

The cylinder head temperature sensor is built into the front of the cylinder head; it monitors changes in the cylinder head temperature and transmits a signal to the ECU.

1. Disconnect the negative battery cable.
2. Disconnect the electrical harness connector from the cylinder head temperature sensor.
3. Remove the cylinder head temperature sensor from the engine.

To Install:

4. Install the cylinder head temperature sensor and torque to 9–12 ft. lbs. (12–16 Nm).
5. Install the electrical harness connector to the cylinder head temperature sensor and connect the negative battery cable.

Exhaust Gas Sensor

The exhaust gas sensor is built into the exhaust manifold to monitor the amount of oxygen in the exhaust gas.

1. If the engine has been operated, wait until the exhaust manifold has cooled.
2. Disconnect the electrical connector from the exhaust gas sensor.

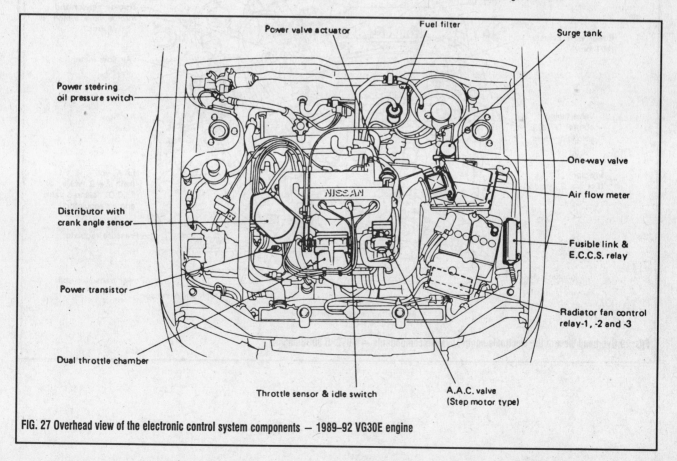

FIG. 27 Overhead view of the electronic control system components — 1989–92 VG30E engine

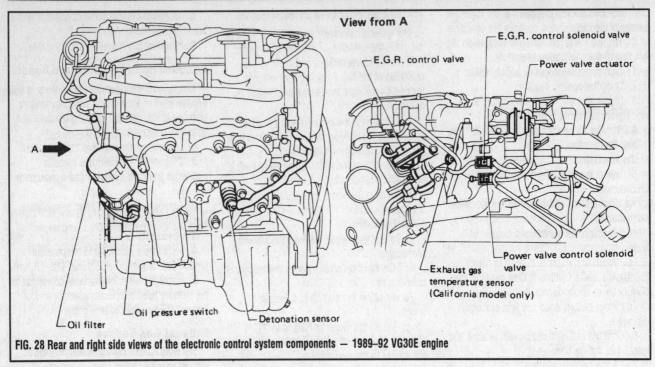

FIG. 28 Rear and right side views of the electronic control system components — 1989–92 VG30E engine

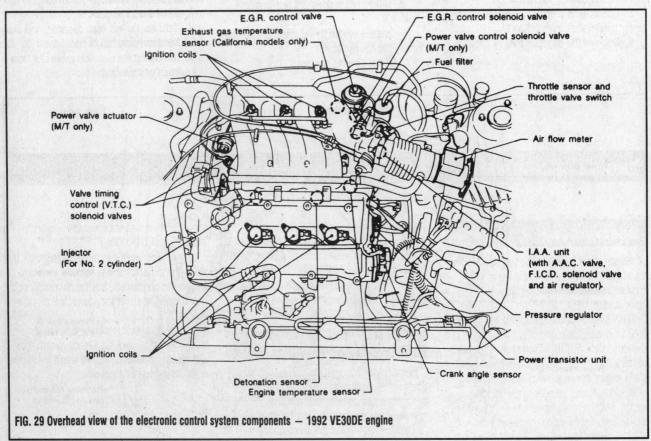

FIG. 29 Overhead view of the electronic control system components — 1992 VE30DE engine

3. Remove the exhaust gas sensor from the exhaust manifold.

4. To install, reverse the removal procedures, coat the threads with a non-seizing compound and torque the exhaust gas sensor to 30–37 ft. lbs. (40–50 Nm).

Throttle Valve (Idle) Switch

♦ SEE FIG. 30

The throttle valve (idle) switch is attached to the throttle chamber and actuates in response to the accelerator pedal movement. The switch has an idle contact and a full throttle contact. The idle contact is used for engine control; it closes when the throttle valve is positioned at idle and opens when it is at any other position.

1. Disconnect the negative battery cable.

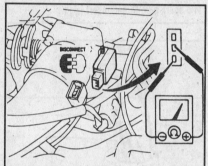

FIG. 30 Using a voltmeter to set the throttle valve (idle) switch

2. Disconnect the electrical connector from the throttle valve (idle) switch.

3. Remove the throttle valve (idle) switch-to-throttle chamber screws and the switch.

To install:

4. Install the throttle valve (idle) switch loosely to the throttle chamber.

5. Connect the negative battery cable and turn **ON** the ignition switch.

6. Using an voltmeter, check and/or adjust the switch to the following conditions:

a. With the throttle fully closed, the voltage should be 9–10 volts.

b. With the throttle open, the voltage should be 0 volts.

7. When the voltage conditions are met, tighten the throttle valve (idle) switch screws.

8. Connect the electrical connector to the throttle valve (idle) switch.

Air Flow Meter

The air flow meter is mounted in the air intake system at the rear of the engine. It measures the mass flow rate of intake air by monitoring the cooling rate of air passing over a heated wire within the meter.

1. Disconnect the negative battery cable.

2. Remove the air intake duct from the air flow meter.

3. Disconnect the electrical connector from the air flow meter.

4. Remove the air flow meter bolts and the air flow meter.

To install:

5. Install the air flow meter and tighten the bolts.

6. Connect the electrical connector to the air flow meter.

7. Install the air duct to the air flow meter.

8. Connect the negative battery cable.

Oil Pressure Switch

The oil pressure switch is at the right rear of the engine, next the to oil filter.

➡ **If the engine is hot, allow it to cool before performing this procedure.**

1. Disconnect the negative battery cable.

2. Raise and safely support the vehicle.

3. Disconnect the electrical connector from the oil pressure switch.

4. Remove the oil pressure switch from the engine.

To install:

5. Using proper sealant, lubricate the oil pressure switch threads.

6. Install the oil pressure switch and torque it to 9–12 ft. lbs. (13–17 Nm).

7. Connect the electrical connector to the oil pressure switch.

8. Connect the negative battery cable.

ENGINE MECHANICAL

Description

Nissan offers 2 engines to power it's Maxima: the standard VG30E engine and the newly engineered VE30DE engine which was introduced in 1992.

The VG30E engine consists of a belt driven, 3.0L V6 engine, equipped with a Single Overhead Cam (SOHC) which operates 2 valves per cylinder. Other features are hydraulic valve lifters, a cast iron block with aluminum heads.

In 1992, Nissan introduced the VE30DE engine which is more powerful than the VG30E engine and offers a much quicker response. The VE30DE engine is similar to the VG30E engine, except it is equipped with a Dual Overhead Cams (DOHC) 24 valve design which boosts the power output. The 4 valves per cylinder and dual overhead cams concept, combined with the advanced technology of variable induction and variable valve timing, assure you of responsive power for driving around town or passing on the highway. Advances in the variable induction system have produced maximum power and optimized fuel efficiency at all engine speeds.

Engine Overhaul Tips

Most engine overhaul procedures are fairly standard. In addition to specific parts replacement procedures and complete specifications for your individual engine, this Section also is a guide to accepted rebuilding procedures. Examples of standard rebuilding practice are shown and should be used along with specific details concerning your particular engine.

Competent and accurate machine shop services will ensure maximum performance, reliability and engine life.

In most instances it is more profitable for the do-it-yourself mechanic to remove, clean and inspect the component, buy the necessary parts and deliver these to a shop for actual machine work.

On the other hand, much of the rebuilding work (crankshaft, block, bearings, piston rods and other components) is well within the scope of the do-it-yourself mechanic.

TOOLS

The tools required for an engine overhaul or parts replacement will depend on the depth of your involvement. With a few exceptions, they will be the tools found in a mechanic's tool kit (see Section 1). More in-depth work will require any or all of the following:

- a dial indicator (reading in thousandths) mounted on a universal base
- micrometers and telescope gauges
- jaw and screw-type pullers
- scraper
- valve spring compressor
- ring groove cleaner
- piston ring expander and compressor
- ridge reamer
- cylinder hone or glaze breaker
- Plastigage®
- engine stand

The use of most of these tools is illustrated in this Section. Many can be rented for a one-time use from a local parts jobber or tool supply house specializing in automotive work.

Occasionally, the use of special tools is called for. See the information on Special Tools and Safety Notice in the front of this book before substituting another tool.

INSPECTION TECHNIQUES

Procedures and specifications are given in this Section for inspecting, cleaning and assessing the wear limits of most major components. Other procedures such as Magnaflux® and Zyglo® can be used to locate material flaws and stress cracks. Magnaflux® is a magnetic process applicable only to ferrous materials. The Zyglo® process coats the material with a fluorescent dye penetrant and can be used on any material. Check for suspected surface cracks can be more readily made using spot check dye. The dye is sprayed onto the suspected area, wiped off and the area sprayed with a developer. Cracks will show up brightly.

OVERHAUL TIPS

Aluminum has become extremely popular for use in engines, due to its low weight. Observe the following precautions when handling aluminum parts:

- Never hot tank aluminum parts (the caustic hot tank solution will eat the aluminum.
- Remove all aluminum parts (identification tag, etc.) from engine parts prior to the tanking.
- Always coat threads lightly with engine oil or anti-seize compounds before installation, to prevent seizure.
- Never overtorque bolts or spark plugs especially in aluminum threads.

Stripped threads in any component can be repaired using any of several commercial repair kits (Heli-Coil®, Microdot®, Keenserts®, etc.).

When assembling the engine, any parts that will be frictional contact must be prelubed to provide lubrication at initial start-up. Any product specifically formulated for this purpose can be used but engine oil is not recommended as a prelube.

When semi-permanent (locked, but removable) installation of bolts or nuts is desired, threads should be cleaned and coated with Loctite® or other similar, commercial non-hardening sealant.

REPAIRING DAMAGED THREADS

♦ SEE FIGS. 31-35

Several methods of repairing damaged threads are available. Heli-Coil® (shown here), Keenserts® and Microdot® are among the most widely used. All involve basically the same principle — drilling out stripped threads, tapping the hole and installing a prewound insert — making welding, plugging and oversize fasteners unnecessary.

Two types of thread repair inserts are usually supplied: a standard type for most Inch Coarse, Inch Fine, Metric Course and Metric Fine thread sizes and a spark lug type to fit most spark plug port sizes. Consult the individual manufacturer's catalog to determine exact applications. Typical thread repair kits will contain a selection of prewound threaded inserts, a tap (corresponding to the outside diameter threads of the insert) and an installation tool. Spark plug inserts usually differ because they require a tap equipped with pilot threads and a combined reamer/tap section. Most manufacturers also supply blister-packed thread repair inserts separately in addition to a master kit containing a variety of taps and inserts plus installation tools.

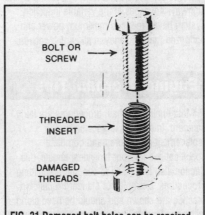

FIG. 31 Damaged bolt holes can be repaired with thread repair inserts

Before effecting a repair to a threaded hole, remove any snapped, broken or damaged bolts or studs. Penetrating oil can be used to free frozen threads. The offending item can be removed with locking pliers or with a screw or stud extractor. After the hole is clear, the thread can be repaired, as shown in the series of accompanying illustrations.

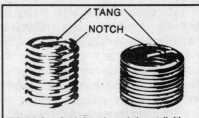

FIG. 32 Standard thread repair insert (left) and spark plug thread insert (right)

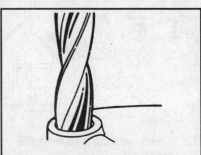

FIG. 33 Drill out the damaged threads with specified drill. Drill completely through the hole or to the bottom of a blind hole

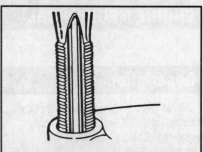

FIG. 34 With the tap supplied, tap the hole to receive the thread insert. Keep the tap well oiled and back it out frequently to avoid clogging the threads

Standard Torque Specifications and Fastener Markings

In the absence of specific torques, the following chart can be used as a guide to the maximum safe torque of a particular size/grade of fastener.

- There is no torque difference for fine or coarse threads.
- Torque values are based on clean, dry threads. Reduce the value by 10% if threads are oiled prior to assembly.
- The torque required for aluminum components or fasteners is considerably less.

U.S. Bolts

SAE Grade Number	1 or 2			5			6 or 7		
Number of lines always 2 less than the grade number.									
Bolt Size (inches)—(Thread)	**Maximum Torque**			**Maximum Torque**			**Maximum Torque**		
	Ft./Lbs.	Kgm	Nm	Ft./Lbs.	Kgm	Nm	Ft./Lbs.	Kgm	Nm
¼ — 20	5	0.7	6.8	8	1.1	10.8	10	1.4	13.5
— 28	6	0.8	8.1	10	1.4	13.6			
⁵⁄₁₆ — 18	11	1.5	14.9	17	2.3	23.0	19	2.6	25.8
— 24	13	1.8	17.6	19	2.6	25.7			
⅜ — 16	18	2.5	24.4	31	4.3	42.0	34	4.7	46.0
— 24	20	2.75	27.1	35	4.8	47.5			
⁷⁄₁₆ — 14	28	3.8	37.0	49	6.8	66.4	55	7.6	74.5
— 20	30	4.2	40.7	55	7.6	74.5			
½ — 13	39	5.4	52.8	75	10.4	101.7	85	11.75	115.2
— 20	41	5.7	55.6	85	11.7	115.2			
⁹⁄₁₆ — 12	51	7.0	69.2	110	15.2	149.1	120	16.6	162.7
— 18	55	7.6	74.5	120	16.6	162.7			
⅝ — 11	83	11.5	112.5	150	20.7	203.3	167	23.0	226.5
— 18	95	13.1	128.8	170	23.5	230.5			
¾ — 10	105	14.5	142.3	270	37.3	366.0	280	38.7	379.6
— 16	115	15.9	155.9	295	40.8	400.0			
⅞ — 9	160	22.1	216.9	395	54.6	535.5	440	60.9	596.5
— 14	175	24.2	237.2	435	60.1	589.7			
1 — 8	236	32.5	318.6	590	81.6	799.9	660	91.3	894.8
— 14	250	34.6	338.9	660	91.3	849.8			

Metric Bolts

Relative Strength Marking	4.6, 4.8			8.8		
Bolt Markings						
Bolt Size Thread Size x Pitch (mm)	**Maximum Torque**			**Maximum Torque**		
	Ft./Lbs.	Kgm	Nm	Ft./Lbs.	Kgm	Nm
6 x 1.0	2–3	.2–.4	3–4	3–6	.4–.8	5–8
8 x 1.25	6–8	.8–1	8–12	9–14	1.2–1.9	13–19
10 x 1.25	12–17	1.5–2.3	16–23	20–29	2.7–4.0	27–39
12 x 1.25	21–32	2.9–4.4	29–43	35–53	4.8–7.3	47–72
14 x 1.5	35–52	4.8–7.1	48–70	57–85	7.8–11.7	77–110
16 x 1.5	51–77	7.0–10.6	67–100	90–120	12.4–16.5	130–160
18 x 1.5	74–110	10.2–15.1	100–150	130–170	17.9–23.4	180–230
20 x 1.5	110–140	15.1–19.3	150–190	190–240	26.2–46.9	160–320
22 x 1.5	150–190	22.0–26.2	200–260	250–320	34.5–44.1	340–430
24 x 1.5	190–240	26.2–46.9	260–320	310–410	42.7–56.5	420–550

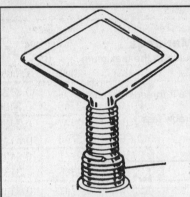

FIG. 35 Screw the threaded insert onto the installation tool until the tang engages the slot. Screw the insert into the tapped hole until it is ¼–½ turn below the top surface. After installation break off the tang with a hammer and punch

Checking Engine Compression

◆ SEE FIG. 36

A noticeable lack of engine power, excessive oil consumption and/or poor fuel mileage measured over an extended period are all indicators of internal engine war. Worn piston rings, scored or worn cylinder bores, blown head gaskets, sticking or burnt valves and worn valve seats are all possible culprits here. A check of each cylinder's compression will help you locate the problems.

As mentioned in the Tools and Equipment section of Section 1, a screw-in type

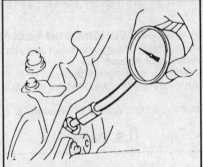

FIG. 36 The screw-in type compression gauge is more accurate

compression gauge is more accurate than the type you simply hold against the spark plug hole, although it takes slightly longer to use. It's worth it to obtain a more accurate reading. Follow the procedures below.

1. Warm the engine to normal operating temperatures.
2. Remove all the spark plugs.
3. Disconnect the high tension lead from the ignition coil or the distributor harness connection if equipped.
4. If equipped, disconnect all injector connections.
5. Screw the compression gauge into the No. 1 spark plug hole until the fitting is snug.

➡ **Be careful not to crossthread the plug hole. On aluminum cylinder heads use extra care, as the threads in these heads are easily ruined.**

6. Ask an assistant to depress the accelerator pedal fully. Then, while you read the

compression gauge, ask the assistant to crank the engine until at least 4 compression strokes occur, using the ignition switch.

7. Read the compression gauge at the end of each series of cranks and record the highest of these readings. Repeat this procedure for each of the engine's cylinders. Compare the highest reading of each cylinder to the compression pressure specification in the Tune-Up Specifications chart in Section 2.

A cylinder's compression pressure is usually acceptable if it is not less than 80 percent of maximum. The difference between any 2 cylinders should be no more than 12–14 lbs.

8. If a cylinder is unusually low, pour a tablespoon of clean engine oil into the cylinder through the spark plug hole and repeat the compression test. If the compression rises after adding the oil, it appears that the cylinder's piston rings or bore are damaged or worn. If the pressure remains low, the valves may not be seating properly (a valve job is needed) or the head gasket may be blown near that cylinder. If compression in any 2 adjacent cylinders is low, and if the addition of oil doesn't help the compression, there is leakage past the head gasket. Oil and coolant water in the combustion chamber can result from this problem. There may be evidence of water droplets on the engine dipstick when a head gasket has blown.

➡ **Maximum cylinder compression should be 173 psi at 300 rpm. or minimum cylinder compression is 128 psi at 300 rpm. When analyzing compression test results, look for uniformity among cylinders, rather than specific pressures.**

GENERAL ENGINE SPECIFICATIONS

Year	Engine ID/VIN	Engine Displacement liter (cc)	Fuel System Type	Net Horsepower @ rpm	Net Torque @ rpm (ft. lbs.)	Bore × Stroke (in.)	Compression Ratio	Oil Pressure @ rpm
1985	VG30E	3.0 (2960)	EFI	152 @ 5200	167 @ 3600	3.43 × 3.27	9.0:1	57 @ 4000
1986	VG30E	3.0 (2960)	EFI	152 @ 5200	167 @ 3600	3.43 × 3.27	9.0:1	57 @ 4000
1987	VG30E	3.0 (2960)	EFI	160 @ 5200	174 @ 4000	3.43 × 3.27	9.0:1	43 @ 2000
1988	VG30E	3.0 (2960)	EFI	160 @ 5200	168 @ 3600	3.43 × 3.27	9.0:1	59 @ 3200
1989	VG30E	3.0 (2960)	EFI	160 @ 5200	182 @ 2800	3.43 × 3.27	9.0:1	59 @ 3200
1990	VG30E	3.0 (2960)	EFI	160 @ 5200	182 @ 2800	3.43 × 3.27	9.0:1	59 @ 3200
1991	VG30E	3.0 (2960)	EFI	160 @ 5200	182 @ 2800	3.43 × 3.27	9.0:1	59 @ 3200
1992	VG30E	3.0 (2960)	EFI	160 @ 5200	182 @ 2800	3.43 × 3.27	9.0:1	59 @ 3200
	VE30DE	3.0 (2960)	EFI	190 @ 5600	190 @ 4000	3.43 × 3.27	10.0:1	67 @ 3000

NOTE: Horsepower and torque are SAE net figures. They are measured at the rear of the transmission with all accessories installed and operating. Since the figures vary when a given engine is installed in different models, some are representative rather than exact.
EFI—Electronic Fuel Injection

VALVE SPECIFICATIONS

Year	Engine ID/VIN	Engine Displacement liter (cc)	Seat Angle (deg.)	Face Angle (deg.)	Spring Test Pressure (lbs. @ in.)	Spring Installed Height (in.)	Stem-to-Guide Clearance (in.)		Stem Diameter (in.)	
							Intake	Exhaust	Intake	Exhaust
1985	VG30E	3.0 (2960)	45	45.5	①	NA	0.0008–0.0021	0.0016–0.0029	0.2742–0.2748	0.3128–0.3134
1986	VG30E	3.0 (2960)	45	45.5	①	NA	0.0008–0.0021	0.0016–0.0029	0.2742–0.2748	0.3136–0.3138
1987	VG30E	3.0 (2960)	45	45.5	①	NA	0.0008–0.0021	0.0016–0.0029	0.2742–0.2748	0.3136–0.3138
1988	VG30E	3.0 (2960)	45	45.5	①	NA	0.0008–0.0021	0.0016–0.0029	0.2742–0.2748	0.3136–0.3138
1989	VG30E	3.0 (2960)	45	45.5	①	NA	0.0008–0.0021	0.0016–0.0029	0.2742–0.2748	0.3136–0.3138
1990	VG30E	3.0 (2960)	45	45.5	①	NA	0.0008–0.0021	0.0016–0.0029	0.2742–0.2748	0.3136–0.3138
1991	VG30E	3.0 (2960)	45	45.5	①	NA	0.0008–0.0021	0.0016–0.0029	0.2742–0.2748	0.3136–0.3138
1992	VG30E	3.0 (2960)	45	45.5	①	NA	0.0008–0.0021	0.0016–0.0029	0.2742–0.2748	0.3136–0.3138
	VE30DE	3.0 (2960)	45	45.5	②	NA	0.0008–0.0017	0.0016–0.0025	0.2352–0.2354	0.2344–0.2346

NA—Not available
① Outer: 117.7 lbs. @ 1.181 in.
  Inner: 57.3 lbs. @ 0.984 in.
② 120.4 lbs. @ 1.059 in.

CAMSHAFT SPECIFICATIONS

All measurements given in inches.

Year	Engine ID/VIN	Engine Displacement liter (cc)	Journal Diameter 1	2	3	4	5	Elevation In.	Ex.	Bearing Clearance	Camshaft End Play
1985	VG30E	3.0 (2960)	1.8472–①1.8480	1.8472–①1.8480	1.8472–①1.8480	—	—	1.5566–1.5640	1.5566–1.5640	0.0059②	0.0012–0.0024
1986	VG30E	3.0 (2960)	1.8472–①1.8480	1.8472–①1.8480	1.8472–①1.8480	—	—	1.5566–1.5640	1.5566–1.5640	0.0059②	0.0012–0.0024
1987	VG30E	3.0 (2960)	1.8472–①1.8480	1.8472–①1.8480	1.8472–①1.8480	—	—	1.5566–1.5640	1.5566–1.5640	0.0059②	0.0012–0.0024
1988	VG30E	3.0 (2960)	1.8472–①1.8480	1.8472–①1.8480	1.8472–①1.8480	—	—	1.5566–1.5640	1.5566–1.5640	0.0059②	0.0012–0.0024
1989	VG30E	3.0 (2960)	1.8472–①1.8480	1.8472–①1.8480	1.8472–①1.8480	—	—	1.5566–1.5640	1.5566–1.5640	0.0059②	0.0012–0.0024
1990	VG30E	3.0 (2960)	1.8472–①1.8480	1.8472–①1.8480	1.8472–①1.8480	—	—	1.5566–1.5640	1.5566–1.5640	0.0059②	0.0012–0.0024
1991	VG30E	3.0 (2960)	1.8472–①1.8480	1.8472–①1.8480	1.8472–①1.8480	—	—	1.5566–1.5640	1.5566–1.5640	0.0059②	0.0012–0.0024
1992	VG30E	3.0 (2960)	1.8472–①1.8480	1.8472–①1.8480	1.8472–①1.8480	—	—	1.5566–1.5640	1.5566–1.5640	0.0059②	0.0012–0.0024
	VE30DE	3.0 (2960)	1.0211–1.0218	1.0211–1.0218	1.0211–1.0218	1.0211–1.0218	1.0211–1.0218	1.4834–1.4909	1.4834–1.4909	0.0059②	0.0028–0.0058

① Middle three journals: 1.8472–1.8480 in.
  Rear (last) journal: 1.6701–1.6709 in.
  Left camshaft, front journal: 1.8866–1.8874 in.
② Limit

CRANKSHAFT AND CONNECTING ROD SPECIFICATIONS

All measurements are given in inches.

| Year | Engine ID/VIN | Engine Displacement liter (cc) | Crankshaft | | | | Connecting Rod | | |
			Main Brg. Journal Dia.	Main Brg. Oil Clearance	Shaft End-play	Thrust on No.	Journal Diameter	Oil Clearance	Side Clearance
1985	VG30E	3.0 (2960)	①	0.0011–0.0022	0.0020–0.0067	4	1.9670–1.9675	0.0004–0.0020	0.0079–0.0138
1986	VG30E	3.0 (2960)	①	0.0011–0.0022	0.0020–0.0067	4	1.9670–1.9675	0.0004–0.0020	0.0079–0.0138
1987	VG30E	3.0 (2960)	①	0.0011–0.0022	0.0020–0.0067	4	1.9670–1.9675	0.0006–0.0021	0.0079–0.0138
1988	VG30E	3.0 (2960)	①	0.0011–0.0022	0.0020–0.0067	4	1.9670–1.9675	0.0006–0.0021	0.0079–0.0138
1989	VG30E	3.0 (2960)	①	0.0011–0.0022	0.0020–0.0067	4	1.9670–1.9675	0.0006–0.0021	0.0079–0.0138
1990	VG30E	3.0 (2960)	①	0.0011–0.0022	0.0020–0.0067	4	1.9670–1.9675	0.0006–0.0021	0.0079–0.0138
1991	VG30E	3.0 (2960)	①	0.0011–0.0022	0.0020–0.0067	4	1.9670–1.9675	0.0006–0.0021	0.0079–0.0138
1992	VG30E	3.0 (2960)	①	0.0011–0.0022	0.0020–0.0067	4	1.9667–1.9675	0.0006–0.0021	0.0079–0.0138
	VE30DE	3.0 (2960)	①	0.0011–0.0022	0.0020–0.0067	4	②	0.0011–0.0019	0.0079–0.0138

① Grade No. 0: 2.4790–2.4793 in.
　Grade No. 1: 2.4787–2.4790 in.
　Grade No. 2: 2.4784–2.4787 in.
② Grade No. 0: 1.9672–1.9675 in.
　Grade No. 1: 1.9670–1.9672 in.
　Grade No. 2: 1.9667–1.9670 in.

PISTON AND RING SPECIFICATIONS

All measurements are given in inches.

| Year | Engine ID/VIN | Engine Displacement liter (cc) | Piston Clearance | Ring Gap | | | Ring Side Clearance | | |
				Top Compression	Bottom Compression	Oil Control	Top Compression	Bottom Compression	Oil Control
1985	VG30E	3.0 (2960)	0.0010–0.0018	0.008–0.017	0.007–0.017	0.008–0.030	0.0016–0.0029	0.0012–0.0025	0.0006–0.0075
1986	VG30E	3.0 (2960)	0.0010–0.0018	0.008–0.017	0.007–0.017	0.008–0.030	0.0016–0.0029	0.0012–0.0025	0.0006–0.0075
1987	VG30E	3.0 (2960)	0.0010–0.0018	0.008–0.017	0.007–0.017	0.008–0.030	0.0016–0.0029	0.0012–0.0025	0.0006–0.0075
1988	VG30E	3.0 (2960)	0.0010–0.0018	0.008–0.017	0.007–0.017	0.008–0.030	0.0016–0.0029	0.0012–0.0025	0.0006–0.0075
1989	VG30E	3.0 (2960)	0.0006–0.0014	0.008–0.017	0.007–0.017	0.008–0.030	0.0016–0.0029	0.0012–0.0025	0.0006–0.0075
1990	VG30E	3.0 (2960)	0.0006–0.0014	0.008–0.017	0.007–0.017	0.008–0.030	0.0016–0.0029	0.0012–0.0025	0.0006–0.0075
1991	VG30E	3.0 (2960)	0.0006–0.0014	0.008–0.017	0.007–0.017	0.008–0.030	0.0016–0.0029	0.0012–0.0025	0.0006–0.0075
1992	VG30E	3.0 (2960)	0.0006–0.0014	0.008–0.017	0.007–0.017	0.008–0.030	0.0016–0.0029	0.0012–0.0025	0.0006–0.0075
	VE30DE	3.0 (2960)	0.0006–0.0014	0.008–0.015	0.019–0.027	0.008–0.027	0.0016–0.0031	0.0012–0.0025	NA

NA—Not available

TORQUE SPECIFICATIONS

All readings in ft. lbs.

Year	Engine ID/VIN	Engine Displacement liter (cc)	Cylinder Head Bolts	Main Bearing Bolts	Rod Bearing Bolts	Crankshaft Damper Bolts	Flywheel Bolts	Manifold Intake	Manifold Exhaust	Spark Plugs	Lug Nut
1985	VG30E	3.0 (2960)	③	⑤	33–40	90–98	72–80	12–14	13–16	14–22	58–72
1986	VG30E	3.0 (2960)	③	⑤	33–40	90–98	72–80	12–14	13–16	14–22	58–72
1987	VG30E	3.0 (2960)	③	⑤	33–40	90–98	72–80	12–14	13–16	14–22	72–87
1988	VG30E	3.0 (2960)	③	⑤	⑥	90–98	72–80	12–14	13–16	14–22	72–87
1989	VG30E	3.0 (2960)	③	⑤	⑥	90–98	61–69	①	13–16	14–22	72–87
1990	VG30E	3.0 (2960)	③	⑤	⑥	90–98	61–69	①	13–16	14–22	72–87
1991	VG30E	3.0 (2960)	③	⑤	⑥	90–98	61–69	①	13–16	14–22	72–87
1992	VG30E	3.0 (2960)	③	⑤	⑥	90–98	61–69	①	13–16	14–22	72–87
	VE30DE	3.0 (2960)	④	⑤	⑦	123–130	61–69	②	⑧	14–22	72–87

① 1st: 2.2–3.6 ft. lbs. (3–5 Nm)
  2nd: 12–14 ft. lbs. (16–20 Nm)
  3rd: 17–20 ft. lbs. (24–27 Nm)
② Nuts: 17–20 ft. lbs. (24–27 Nm)
  Bolts: 12–14 ft. lbs. (16–20 Nm)
③ 1st: 22 ft. lbs. (29 Nm)
  2nd: 43 ft. lobs. (59 Nm)
  3rd: Loosen all bolts
  4th: 22 ft. lbs. (29 Nm)
  5th: 40–47 ft. lbs. (54–64 Nm)
④ 1st: Apply liquid gasket sealant to cylinder block
  2nd: 29 ft. lbs. (39 Nm)
  3rd: Bolt A—90 ft. lbs. (123 Nm)
     Bolt B—90 ft. lbs. (123 Nm)

  4th: Loosen all bolts
  5th: 25–33 ft. lbs. (34–44 Nm)
  6th: Bolt A—90 ft. lbs. (123 Nm)
     Bolt B—90 ft. lbs. (123 Nm)
  7th: Install cylinder head outside bolts
⑤ Tighten in 2–3 steps
  67–74 ft. lbs. (90–100 Nm)
⑥ 1st: 10–12 ft. lbs. (14–16 Nm)
  2nd: 28–33 ft. lbs. (38–44 Nm)
⑦ 1st: 10–12 ft. lbs. (14–16 Nm)
  2nd: 43–48 ft. lbs. (59–65 Nm)
⑧ 1st: 13–16 ft. lbs. (18–22 Nm)
  2nd: 17–20 ft. lbs. (24–27 Nm)

Engine

REMOVAL & INSTALLATION

It is recommended the engine and transaxle be removed as a single unit. If need be, the units may be separated after removal.

VG30E Engine

▶ SEE FIGS. 37-40

1. Matchmark the hood hinge relationship and remove the hood.
2. Release the fuel system pressure. Disconnect the negative battery cable and raise and safely support the vehicle.
3. Drain the coolant from the cylinder block and the radiator. Drain the crankcase and the automatic transaxle, if equipped.
4. Remove the air cleaner, the air intake tube, the air flow meter and disconnect the throttle linkage.
5. Disconnect and/or remove the following:
• Drive belts
• Ignition wire from the ignition coil/power transistor to the distributor
• Ignition coil ground wire and the engine ground cable

• Electrical connector from the distributor
• Engine electrical harness connectors
• Fuel and fuel return hoses
• Upper and lower radiator hoses
• Heater inlet and outlet hoses
• Engine vacuum hoses
• Carbon canister hoses
• Any interfering engine accessory: power steering pump, air conditioning compressor and alternator

6. Remove the carbon canister.
7. Remove the auxiliary fan, washer tank and radiator (with the fan assembly).
8. If equipped with a manual transaxle, remove the clutch release cylinder from the clutch housing.
9. On the 1989–92 models, remove the buffer rods without altering the length of the rods. Disconnect the speedometer cable.
10. Remove the spring pins from the transaxle gear selector rods.
11. Install engine slingers to the block and connect a suitable lifting device to the slingers. Do not tension the lifting device at this point.
12. Disconnect the exhaust pipe at both the manifold connections and the clamp holding the exhaust pipe to the engine.
13. If equipped with a manual transaxle, drain the transaxle gear oil.

14. Disconnect the right and left side halfshafts from their side flanges and remove the bolt holding the radius link support.
15. Lower the shifter and selector rods and remove the bolts from the motor mount brackets. Remove the nuts holding the front and rear motor mounts to the frame.
16. Lower the engine/transaxle assembly down and onto an engine stand.
To install:
17. Raise the engine/transaxle assembly in to the vehicle. When raising the engine onto the mounts, make sure to keep is a level as possible.
18. Check the clearance between the frame and clutch housing and make sure the engine mount bolts are seated in the groove of the mounting bracket.
19. After installing the motor mounts on the 1989–92 models, adjust and install the buffer rods; the front should be 3.50–5.58 in. (89–91mm) and the rear should be 3.90–3.98 in (99–101mm).
20. Raise the shifter and selector rods to their normal operating positions.
21. Connect the halfshafts.
22. Connect the exhaust pipe to the manifold connection and the clamp holding the exhaust pipe to the engine.
23. Disconnect the lifting device and remove the engine slingers.

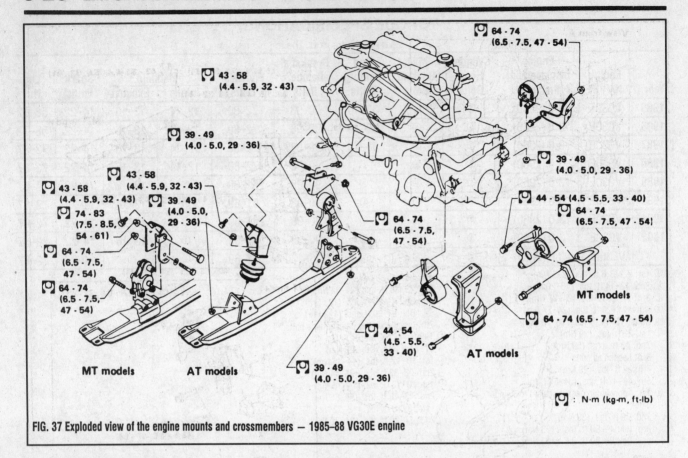

FIG. 37 Exploded view of the engine mounts and crossmembers — 1985–88 VG30E engine

24. Insert the spring pins into the transaxle gear selector rods.

25. Connect the speedometer cable.

26. If equipped with a manual transaxle, mount the clutch cylinder onto the clutch housing.

27. Install the auxiliary fan, washer tank, grille and radiator (with the fan assembly).

28. Install the carbon canister.

29. Install and/or connect all hoses, belts, electrical harness connectors and components that were necessary to be removed.

30. Connect the throttle cable, then install the air cleaner, the air flow meter and air intake duct.

31. Fill the transaxle, the engine and the cooling system to the proper levels.

32. Install the hood and connect the negative battery cable.

33. Make all the necessary engine adjustments. Charge the air conditioning system, if discharged. Road test the vehicle for proper operation.

VE30DE Engine

♦ SEE FIGS. 41 AND 42

1. Matchmark the hood hinge relationship and remove the hood.

2. Release the fuel system pressure. Disconnect the negative battery cable and raise and safely support the vehicle.

3. Drain the coolant from the cylinder block and the radiator. Drain the crankcase and the automatic transaxle, if equipped.

4. Remove the air cleaner, the air intake tube, the air flow meter and disconnect the throttle linkage.

5. Disconnect and/or remove the following:
- Drive belts
- Engine ground cable
- Electrical connector from the crank angle sensor
- Engine electrical harness connectors
- Fuel and fuel return hoses
- Upper and lower radiator hoses
- Heater inlet and outlet hoses
- Engine vacuum hoses
- Carbon canister hoses
- Any interfering engine accessory: power steering pump, air conditioning compressor and alternator

6. Remove the carbon canister.

7. Remove the auxiliary fan, washer tank and radiator (with the fan assembly).

8. If equipped with a manual transaxle, remove the clutch release cylinder from the clutch housing.

9. Disconnect the speedometer cable.

10. Remove the spring pins from the transaxle gear selector rods.

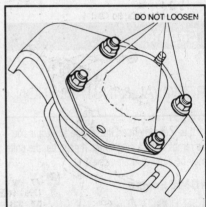

FIG. 38 Do not loosen the front engine mounting insulation cover securing bolts — 1985–88 VG30E engine

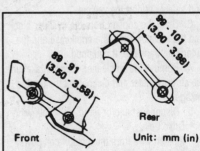

FIG. 40 Adjust the buffer rods when installing the engine — 1989–92 VG30E engine

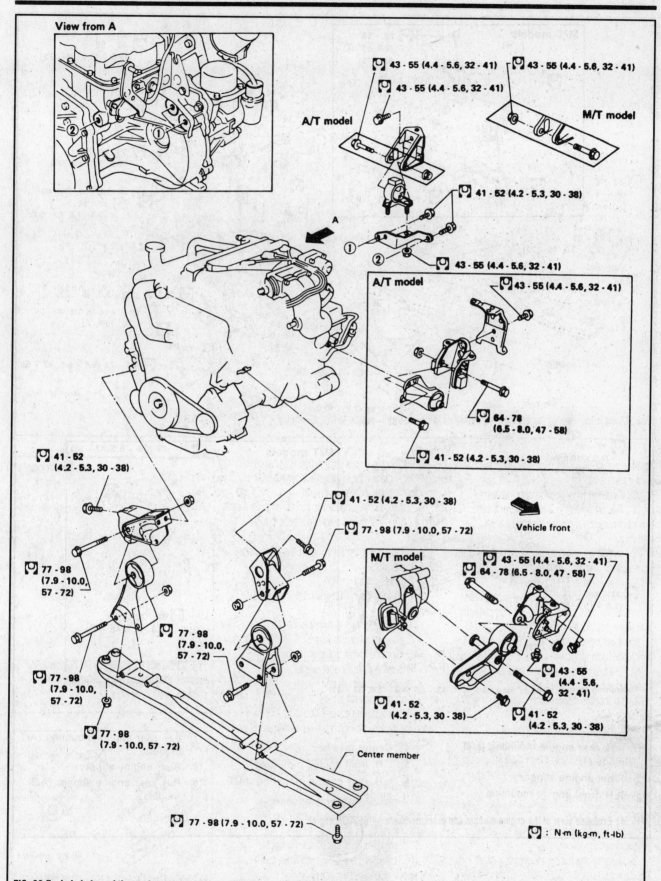

FIG. 39 Exploded view of the engine mounts and crossmembers — 1985–88 VG30E engine

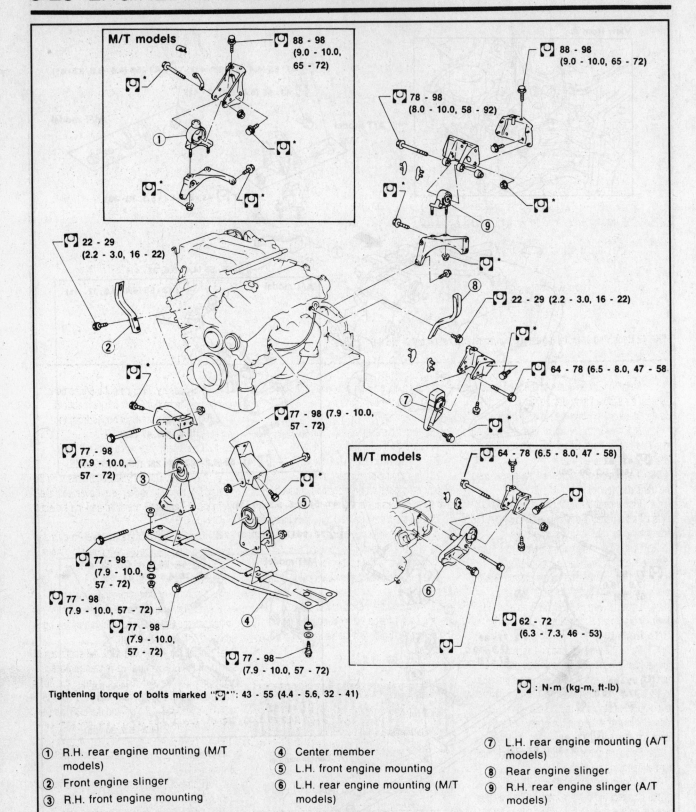

Tightening torque of bolts marked "⬚*": 43 - 55 (4.4 - 5.6, 32 - 41)

⬚ : N·m (kg-m, ft-lb)

① R.H. rear engine mounting (M/T models)
② Front engine slinger
③ R.H. front engine mounting

④ Center member
⑤ L.H. front engine mounting
⑥ L.H. rear engine mounting (M/T models)

⑦ L.H. rear engine mounting (A/T models)
⑧ Rear engine slinger
⑨ R.H. rear engine slinger (A/T models)

FIG. 41 Exploded view of the engine mounts and crossmembers — VE30DE engine

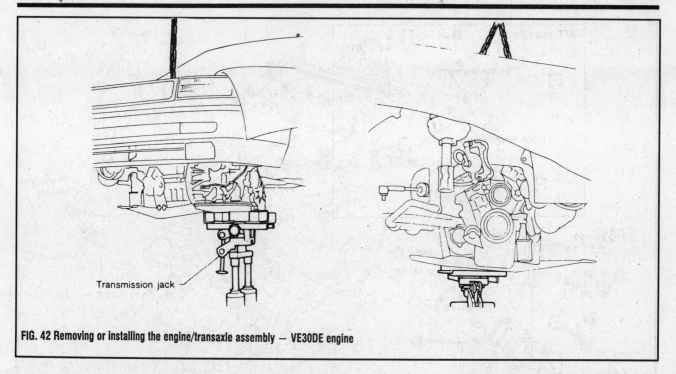

FIG. 42 Removing or installing the engine/transaxle assembly — VE30DE engine

11. Install engine slingers to the block and connect a suitable lifting device to the slingers. Do not tension the lifting device at this point.

12. Disconnect the exhaust pipe at both the manifold connections and the clamp holding the exhaust pipe to the engine.

13. If equipped with a manual transaxle, drain the transaxle gear oil.

14. Disconnect the right and left side halfshafts from their side flanges and remove the bolt holding the radius link support.

15. Lower the shifter and selector rods and remove the bolts from the motor mount brackets. Remove the nuts holding the front and rear motor mounts to the frame.

16. Lower the engine/transaxle assembly down and onto an engine stand.

To install:

17. Raise the engine/transaxle assembly in to the vehicle. When raising the engine onto the mounts, make sure to keep is a level as possible.

18. Check the clearance between the frame and clutch housing and make sure the engine mount bolts are seated in the groove of the mounting bracket.

19. Raise the shifter and selector rods to their normal operating positions.

20. Connect the halfshafts.

21. Connect the exhaust pipe to the manifold connection and the clamp holding the exhaust pipe to the engine.

22. Disconnect the lifting device and remove the engine slingers.

23. Insert the spring pins into the transaxle gear selector rods.

24. Connect the speedometer cable.

25. If equipped with a manual transaxle, mount the clutch cylinder onto the clutch housing.

26. Install the auxiliary fan, washer tank, grille and radiator (with the fan assembly).

27. Install the carbon canister.

28. Install and/or connect all hoses, belts, electrical harness connectors and components that were necessary to be removed.

29. Connect the throttle cable, then install the air cleaner, the air flow meter and air intake duct.

30. Fill the transaxle, the engine and the cooling system to the proper levels.

31. Install the hood and connect the negative battery cable.

32. Make all the necessary engine adjustments. Charge the air conditioning system, if discharged. Road test the vehicle for proper operation.

Rocker Arm (Valve) Cover

REMOVAL & INSTALLATION

VG30E Engine

1985–88

◆ SEE FIGS. 49 AND 50

1. Disconnect the negative battery cable.

2. If necessary, disconnect the electrical connectors from the upper intake manifold.

3. Remove the breather hoses from the rocker arm covers.

4. If the spark plug wires are in the way, disconnect them and move them aside.

5. If the EGR control valve interferes with the removal of the right rocker arm cover, remove it from the upper intake manifold and the exhaust manifold.

6. Remove the rocker arm cover-to-cylinder head bolts and the rocker arm cover(s); then, discard the gasket(s).

To install:

7. Clean the gasket mounting surfaces.

8. Install new rocker arm cover gasket(s). Install the rocker arm cover and torque the bolts to 0.7–2.2 ft. lbs. (1–3 Nm).

9. Install the spark plug wire, if disconnected.

10. If the EGR control valve was removed, use a new gasket and install it. Torque the EGR control valve-to-upper intake manifold bolts to 13–17 ft. lbs. (18–23 Nm) and the EGR tube-to-exhaust manifold nut to 25–33 ft. lbs. (34–44 Nm).

11. Install the breather hoses to the rocker arm covers.

12. Connect the electrical connectors to the upper intake manifold.

13. Connect the negative battery cable.

14. Start the engine and check for oil leaks.

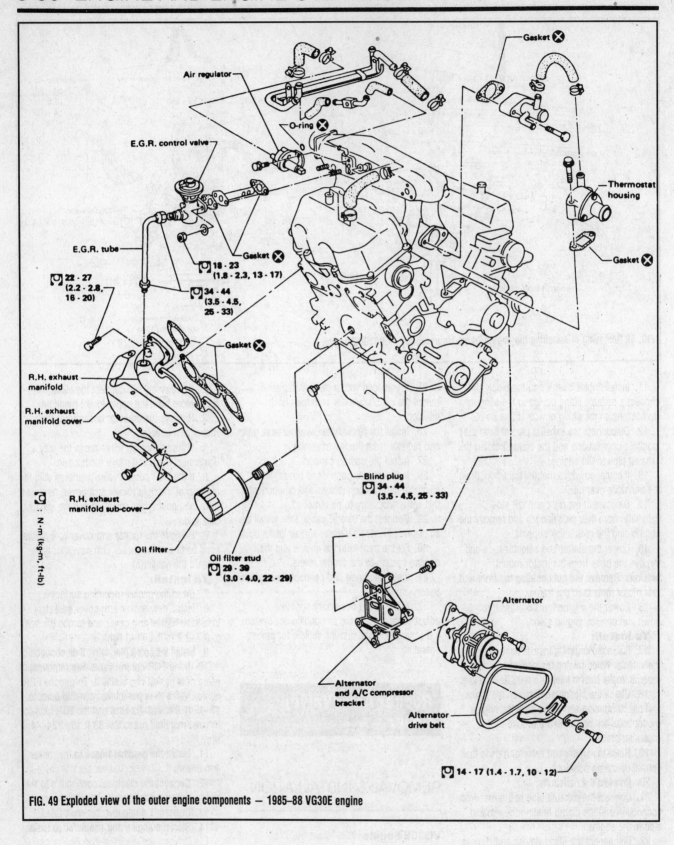

FIG. 49 Exploded view of the outer engine components — 1985–88 VG30E engine

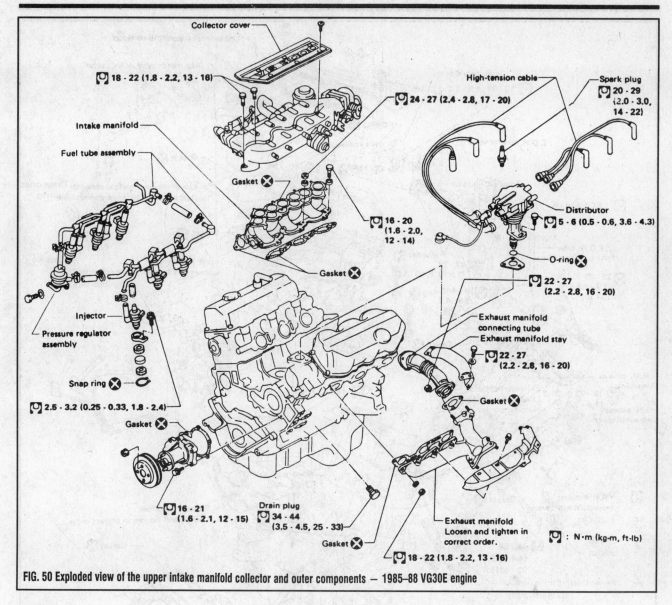

FIG. 50 Exploded view of the upper intake manifold collector and outer components — 1985–88 VG30E engine

1989–92

Right Side

▶ SEE FIGS. 51 AND 52

1. Disconnect the negative battery cable.

2. Remove the breather hose from the rocker arm cover.

3. If the spark plug wires are in the way, disconnect them and move them aside.

4. Remove the rocker arm cover-to-cylinder head bolt and the rocker arm cover; then, discard the gasket(s).

To install:

5. Clean the gasket mounting surfaces.

6. Install a new rocker arm cover gasket. Install the rocker arm cover and torque the bolts to 0.7–2.2 ft. lbs. (1–3 Nm).

7. Install the spark plug wire, if disconnected.

8. Install the breather hose to the rocker arm cover.

9. Connect the negative battery cable.

10. Start the engine and check for oil leaks.

Left Side

1. Disconnect the negative battery cable.

2. Disconnect the air intake duct from the dual duct housing.

3. Disconnect the electrical connectors from the throttle body, the step motor AAC valve and the exhaust gas temperature sensor.

4. Disconnect and label the hoses from the rocker arm cover, the throttle body, the step motor AAC valve, the EGR control valve and the air cut valve.

5. If the spark plug wires are in the way, disconnect them and move them aside. Disconnect the accelerator cable from the throttle body.

6. Remove the upper intake manifold collector-to-intake manifold bolts, in sequence, and lift the assembly from the intake manifold. Discard the gasket.

7. Remove the rocker arm cover-to-cylinder head bolts and the rocker arm cover; then, discard the gasket.

To install:

8. Clean the gasket mounting surfaces.

9. Install a new rocker arm cover gasket. Install the rocker arm cover and torque the bolts to 0.7–2.2 ft. lbs. (1–3 Nm).

10. Use a new gasket and install the upper intake manifold collector-to-intake manifold; torque the bolts, in sequence, to 5.1–5.8 ft. lbs. (7–8 Nm).

11. Connect the spark plug wire, if disconnected. Connect the accelerator cable to the throttle body.

12. Connect the hoses to the rocker arm cover, the throttle body, the step motor AAC valve, the EGR control valve and the air cut valve.

13. Connect the electrical connectors to the throttle body, the step motor AAC valve and the exhaust gas temperature sensor.

14. Connect the negative battery cable.

15. Start the engine and check for oil leaks.

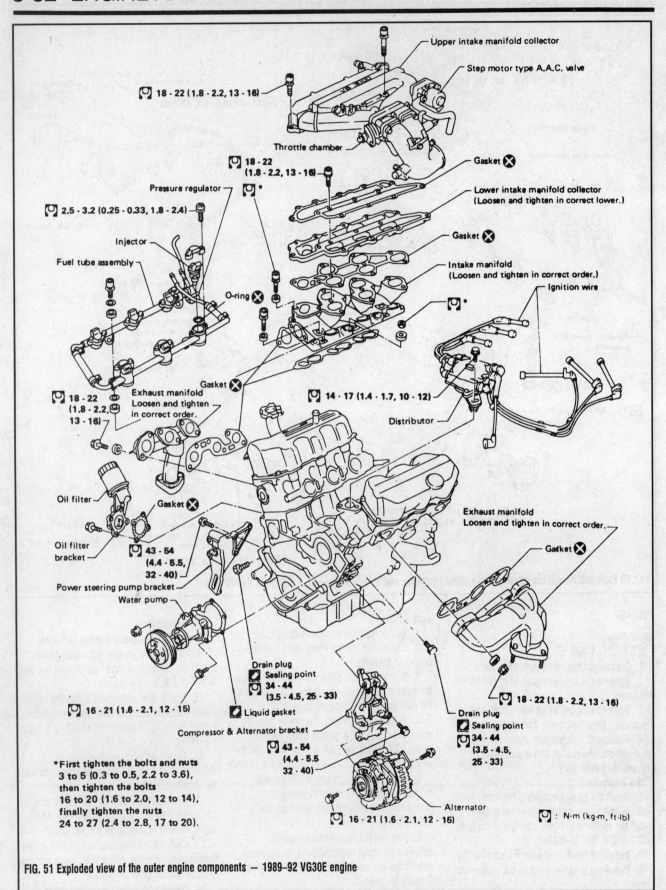

FIG. 51 Exploded view of the outer engine components — 1989–92 VG30E engine

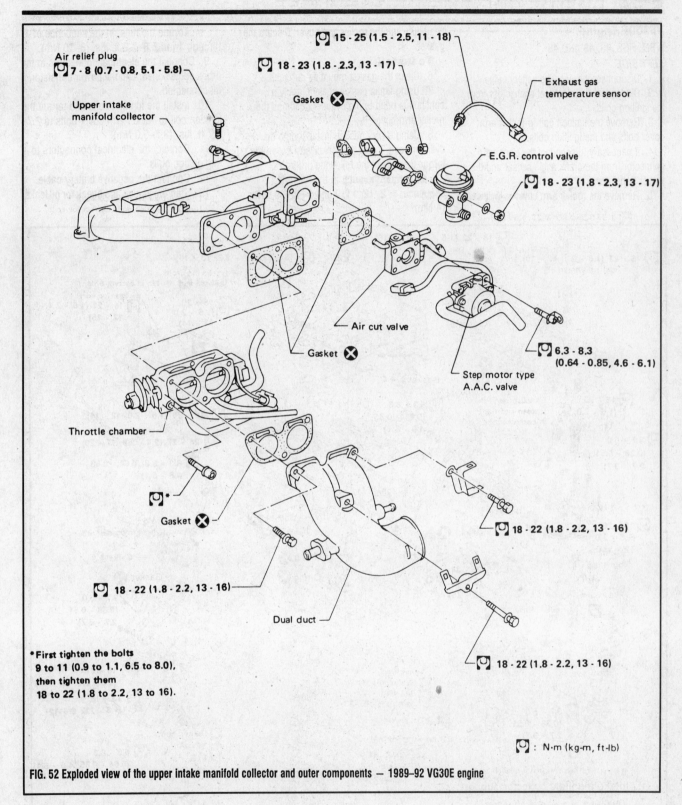

Air relief plug
7 - 8 (0.7 - 0.8, 5.1 - 5.8)

Upper intake
manifold collector

15 - 25 (1.5 - 2.5, 11 - 18)

18 - 23 (1.8 - 2.3, 13 - 17)

Gasket ⊗

Exhaust gas
temperature sensor

E.G.R. control valve

18 - 23 (1.8 - 2.3, 13 - 17)

Air cut valve

Gasket ⊗

6.3 - 8.3
(0.64 - 0.85, 4.6 - 6.1)

Step motor type
A.A.C. valve

Throttle chamber

*

Gasket ⊗

18 - 22 (1.8 - 2.2, 13 - 16)

18 - 22 (1.8 - 2.2, 13 - 16)

Dual duct

18 - 22 (1.8 - 2.2, 13 - 16)

*First tighten the bolts
9 to 11 (0.9 to 1.1, 6.5 to 8.0),
then tighten them
18 to 22 (1.8 to 2.2, 13 to 16).

: N·m (kg-m, ft-lb)

FIG. 52 Exploded view of the upper intake manifold collector and outer components — 1989–92 VG30E engine

VE30DE Engine

♦ SEE FIGS. 43, 46 AND 48

LEFT SIDE

1. Disconnect the negative battery cable.
2. Disconnect the electrical connectors from the ignition coils.
3. Remove the ignition coil-to-rocker arm cover bolts and the ignition coils.
4. If necessary, disconnect the electrical connector from the crank angle sensor and the power transistor.
5. Remove the rocker arm cover-to-cylinder head nuts and the rocker arm cover. Discard the gasket.

To install:

6. Clean the gasket mounting surfaces.
7. Using liquid gasket sealant, apply a continuous bead to the cylinder head and the rocker arm cover.
8. Using a new gasket, install it onto the cylinder head. Install the rocker arm cover and torque the nuts in the following order:

a. Torque the nuts, in the following sequence: 1, 2, 12, 11, 9 and 14 to 2.9 ft. lbs. (4 Nm).

b. Torque the nuts, in the sequence of 1 through 14 to 5.8–7.2 ft. lbs. (8–10 Nm).

9. Connect the electrical connectors to the crank angle sensor and the power transistor, if disconnected.
10. Install the ignition coils and torque the ignition coil-to-rocker arm cover bolts to 2.7–3.7 ft. lbs. (3.7–5.0 Nm).
11. Connect the electrical connectors to the ignition coils.
12. Connect the negative battery cable.
13. Start the engine and check for oil leaks.

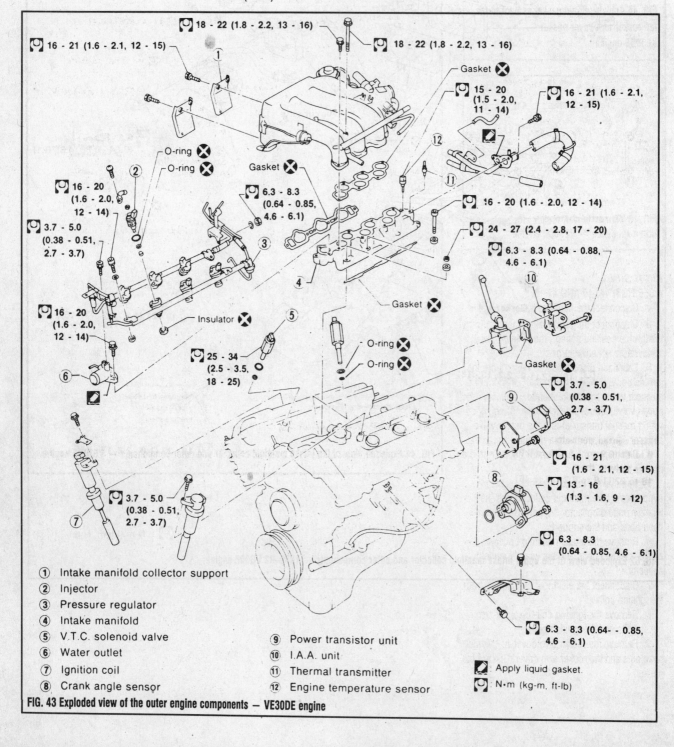

1. Intake manifold collector support
2. Injector
3. Pressure regulator
4. Intake manifold
5. V.T.C. solenoid valve
6. Water outlet
7. Ignition coil
8. Crank angle sensor
9. Power transistor unit
10. I.A.A. unit
11. Thermal transmitter
12. Engine temperature sensor

FIG. 43 Exploded view of the outer engine components — VE30DE engine

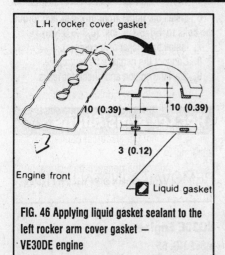

FIG. 46 Applying liquid gasket sealant to the left rocker arm cover gasket — VE30DE engine

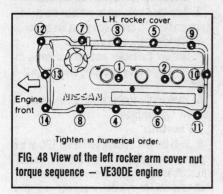

FIG. 48 View of the left rocker arm cover nut torque sequence — VE30DE engine

RIGHT SIDE

♦ SEE FIGS. 44, 45 AND 47

1. Disconnect the negative battery cable.

2. Disconnect the electrical connectors from the throttle position sensor, the exhaust gas temperature sensor and/or etc.

3. Label and disconnect the hoses from the throttle body, the EGR valve, the EGR control solenoid valve, the intake manifold collector, the power valve control solenoid valve (if equipped with a manual transaxle) and the power valve actuator (if equipped with a manual transaxle).

4. Disconnect the accelerator cable from the throttle body.

5. Remove the intake manifold collector support-to-intake manifold collector and the intake manifold collector support-to-cylinder head bolts and the supports.

6. Remove the intake manifold collector-to-intake manifold bolts and the intake manifold collector.

7. Disconnect the electrical connectors from the ignition coils.

8. Remove the ignition coil-to-rocker arm cover bolts and the ignition coils.

9. Remove the rocker arm cover-to-cylinder head nuts and the rocker arm cover. Discard the gasket.

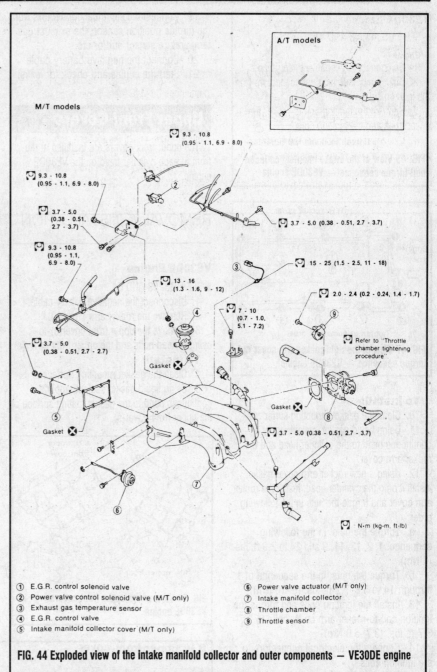

① E.G.R. control solenoid valve
② Power valve control solenoid valve (M/T only)
③ Exhaust gas temperature sensor
④ E.G.R. control valve
⑤ Intake manifold collector cover (M/T only)
⑥ Power valve actuator (M/T only)
⑦ Intake manifold collector
⑧ Throttle chamber
⑨ Throttle sensor

FIG. 44 Exploded view of the intake manifold collector and outer components — VE30DE engine

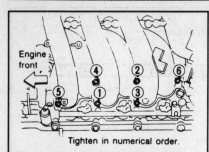

FIG. 45 View of the intake manifold collector bolt torque sequence — VE30DE engine

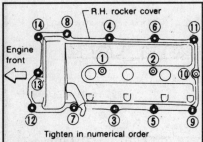

FIG. 47 View of the right rocker arm cover nut torque sequence — VE30DE engine

To Install:

10. Clean the gasket mounting surfaces.

11. Using liquid gasket sealant, apply a continuous bead to the cylinder head and the rocker arm cover.

12. Using a new rocker arm cover gasket, install it onto the cylinder head. Install the rocker arm cover and torque the nuts in the following order:

a. Torque the nuts, in the following sequence: 1, 2, 12, 11, 9 and 14 to 2.9 ft. lbs. (4 Nm).

b. Torque the nuts, in the sequence of 1 through 14 to 5.8–7.2 ft. lbs. (8–10 Nm).

13. Install the ignition coils and torque the ignition coil-to-rocker arm cover bolts to 2.7–3.7 ft. lbs. (3.7–5.0 Nm).

14. Connect the electrical connectors to the ignition coils.

15. Using a new gasket, install the intake manifold collector and torque the intake manifold collector-to-intake manifold bolts, in sequence, to 13–16 ft. lbs. (18–22 Nm).

16. Install the intake manifold collector support and torque the bolts to 12–15 ft. lbs. (16–21 Nm).

17. Connect the accelerator cable to the throttle body.

18. Connect the hoses to the throttle body, the EGR valve, the EGR control solenoid valve, the intake manifold collector, the power valve control solenoid valve (if equipped with a manual transaxle) and the power valve actuator (if equipped with a manual transaxle).

19. Connect the electrical connectors from the throttle position sensor, the exhaust gas temperature sensor and/or etc.

20. Connect the negative battery cable.

21. Start the engine and check for leaks.

Upper Front Covers

The upper front covers are installed at the front of each cylinder head on the VE30DE engine.

REMOVAL & INSTALLATION

VE30DE Engine

▶ SEE FIGS. 53 AND 54

1. Disconnect the negative battery cable.

2. Remove the rocker arm cover(s).

3. Remove the upper front cover(s)-to-cylinder head bolts and the upper front cover(s).

To install:

4. Clean the gasket mounting surfaces.

5. Using liquid gasket sealant, apply a continuous bead to the gasket mating surface of the upper front cover(s).

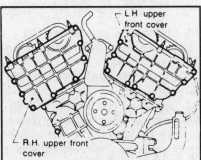

FIG. 54 View of the upper front covers — VE30DE engine

6. Install the upper front cover(s) and torque the bolts to 4.6–6.1 ft. lbs. (6.3–8.3 Nm).

7. Install the rocker arm cover(s).

8. Connect the negative battery cable.

9. Start the engine and check for leaks.

Rocker Arms/Shafts

REMOVAL & INSTALLATION

VG30E Engine

▶ SEE FIG. 55

1. Disconnect the negative battery cable.

2. Turn the crankshaft to position the No. 1 piston on the TDC of it's compression stroke.

3. Remove the rocker arm cover.

4. Remove the rocker arm/shaft assembly-to-cylinder head bolts by loosening the bolts in 2–3 steps.

5. Remove the rocker arm/shaft assembly from the cylinder head.

To install:

6. With the No. 1 piston set on the TDC of it's compression stroke, install the left side rocker arm/shaft assembly and torque the rocker arm/shaft assembly-to-cylinder head bolts, in 2–3 steps, to 13–16 ft. lbs. (18–22 Nm).

➡ **The left side of the engine incorporates cylinders No. 2, 4 and 6.**

7. Rotate the crankshaft 360° and position the No. 4 piston on the TDC of it's compression stroke. Install the right side rocker arm/shaft assembly and torque the rocker arm/shaft assembly-to-cylinder head bolts, in 2–3 steps, to 13–16 ft. lbs. (18–22 Nm).

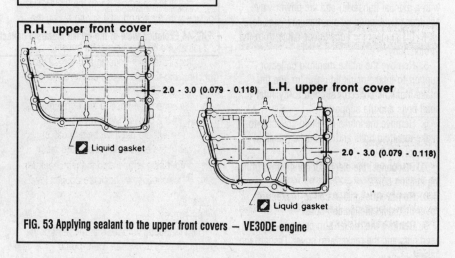

FIG. 53 Applying sealant to the upper front covers — VE30DE engine

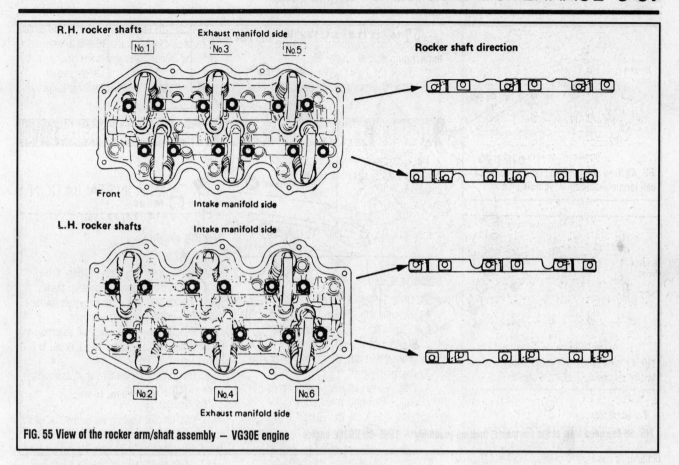

R.H. rocker shafts

Exhaust manifold side

No.1   No.3   No.5

Rocker shaft direction

Front

Intake manifold side

L.H. rocker shafts

Intake manifold side

No.2   No.4   No.6

Exhaust manifold side

FIG. 55 View of the rocker arm/shaft assembly — VG30E engine

➡ **The right side of the engine incorporates cylinders No. 1, 3 and 5.**

8. Install the rocker arm cover.

9. Connect the negative battery cable. Start the engine and check the engine operation.

VE30DE Engine

The VE30DE engine is equipped with floating rocker arms which can only be removed when the camshaft(s) are removed.

Thermostat

REMOVAL & INSTALLATION

VG30E Engine

➡ **It may be necessary to remove radiator shroud, coolant fan assembly and water suction pipe retaining bolts to gain access to the thermostat housing.**

1985–88

◆ SEE FIG. 56

The thermostat is located at the front of the engine, directly above the water pump.

1. Disconnect the negative battery cable.

2. Drain the cooling system to a level below the thermostat housing.

3. Disconnect the hose from the front of the thermostat housing.

4. Remove the 3 bolts from the front of the thermostat housing. Separate the front housing from the thermostat housing. Remove the gasket and the thermostat from the thermostat housing.

To install:

5. Clean the gasket mounting surfaces.

6. Install the thermostat into the thermostat housing with the thermostat spring facing the engine. Using a new gasket, coat with sealant and install it onto the thermostat housing.

7. Install the front housing and torque the front housing-to-thermostat housing bolts to 12–15 ft. lbs. (16–21 Nm).

8. Reconnect the hose to the front housing.

9. Refill the cooling system.

10. Connect the negative battery cable.

11. Start the engine and allow it to reach normal operating temperatures; then check for leaks. After cooling, recheck the coolant level.

1989–92

◆ SEE FIG. 57

The thermostat is located at the front of the engine, directly above the water pump.

1. Disconnect the negative battery cable.

2. Drain the cooling system to a level below the thermostat housing.

3. Disconnect the water hose from the water outlet housing.

4. Remove the water outlet housing-to-thermostat housing bolts. Separate the water outlet housing from the thermostat housing. Remove the thermostat from the thermostat housing.

To install:

5. Clean the gasket mounting surfaces.

6. Using liquid sealant, apply a bead to the water outlet housing.

7. Install the thermostat into the thermostat housing with the thermostat spring facing the hose and the thermostat pintle in the upward direction.

8. Install the water outlet housing and torque the water outlet housing-to-thermostat housing bolts to 12–15 ft. lbs. (16–21 Nm).

9. Reconnect the hose to the front housing.

10. Refill the cooling system.

11. Connect the negative battery cable.

12. Start the engine and allow it to reach normal operating temperatures; then check for leaks. After cooling, recheck the coolant level.

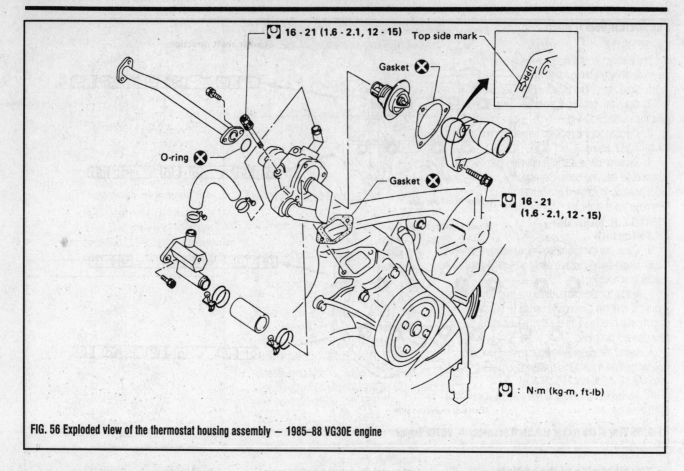

FIG. 56 Exploded view of the thermostat housing assembly — 1985–88 VG30E engine

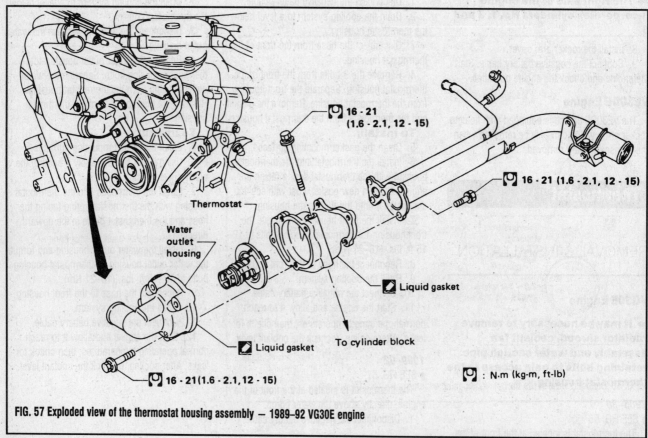

FIG. 57 Exploded view of the thermostat housing assembly — 1989–92 VG30E engine

VE30E Engine

♦ SEE FIG. 58

The thermostat is located at the rear of the engine, directly above the transaxle.

1. Disconnect the negative battery cable.
2. Drain the cooling system to a level below the thermostat housing.
3. Disconnect the radiator hose from the water inlet housing.
4. Remove the water inlet housing-to-thermostat housing bolts. Separate the water inlet housing from the thermostat housing. Remove the thermostat from the thermostat housing.

To install:

5. Clean the gasket mounting surfaces.
6. Using liquid sealant, apply a bead to the water inlet housing.
7. Install the thermostat into the thermostat housing with the thermostat spring facing the thermostat housing and the thermostat pintle in the upward direction.
8. Install the water inlet housing and torque the water inlet housing-to-thermostat housing bolts to 12–15 ft. lbs. (16–21 Nm).
9. Reconnect the radiator hose to the water inlet housing.
10. Refill the cooling system.
11. Connect the negative battery cable.
12. Start the engine and allow it to reach normal operating temperatures; then check for leaks. After cooling, recheck the coolant level.

Intake Manifold

REMOVAL & INSTALLATION

VG30E engine

1985–88

♦ SEE FIGS. 59–62

1. Release the fuel pressure and disconnect the battery cables.
2. Drain cooling system to a level below the intake manifold.
3. Disconnect the electrical connectors from the upper intake manifold.
4. Remove the breather hoses from the rocker arm covers.
5. If the spark plug wires are in the way, disconnect them and move them aside.
6. Remove the EGR control valve from the upper intake manifold and the exhaust manifold.
7. Remove the collector cover-to-upper intake manifold bolts and remove the cover.
8. Remove upper intake manifold-to-intake manifold bolts, in sequence, and remove the upper intake manifold from the engine.
9. If the fuel injector assembly is in the way, perform the following procedures:
   a. Disconnect the electrical connectors from the fuel injectors.

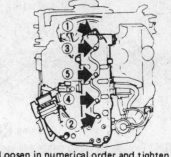

Loosen in numerical order and tighten in reverse order of removal.

FIG. 59 Loosening the upper intake manifold-to-intake manifold bolts, in sequence — 1985–88 VG30E engine

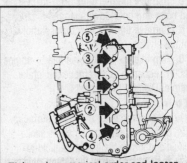

Tighten in numerical order and loosen in reverse order of removal.

FIG. 60 Torquing the upper intake manifold-to-intake manifold bolts, in sequence, in 2–3 steps — 1985–88 VG30E engine

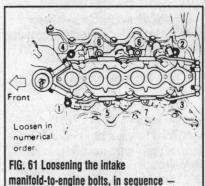

Front

Loosen in numerical order.

FIG. 61 Loosening the intake manifold-to-engine bolts, in sequence — 1985–88 VG30E engine

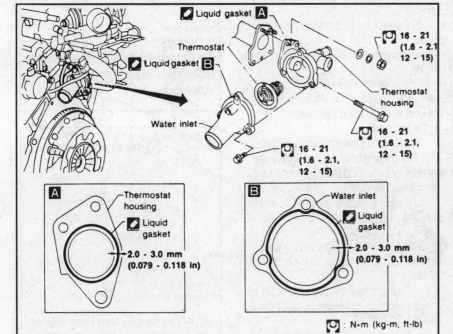

Liquid gasket A

Thermostat

Liquid gasket B

Water inlet

Thermostat housing

16 - 21
(1.6 - 2.1
12 - 15)

16 - 21
(1.6 - 2.1,
12 - 15)

16 - 21
(1.6 - 2.1,
12 - 15)

A

Thermostat housing

Liquid gasket

2.0 - 3.0 mm
(0.079 - 0.118 In)

B

Water inlet

Liquid gasket

2.0 - 3.0 mm
(0.079 - 0.118 In)

: N•m (kg-m, ft-lb)

FIG. 58 Exploded view of the thermostat housing assembly — VE30DE engine

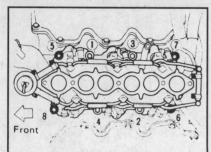

FIG. 62 Torquing the intake manifold-to-engine bolts, in sequence, in 2–3 steps — 1985–88 VG30E engine

b. Disconnect the fuel injector assembly from the fuel lines.

c. Remove the fuel injector(s)-to-cylinder head bolts and hold-down clamps.

d. Remove the fuel injector assembly from the engine.

10. Remove the intake manifold-to-engine bolts, in sequence, and remove the intake manifold. Discard the gaskets.

To install:

11. Clean the gasket mounting surfaces.

12. Using new gaskets, install the intake manifold and torque the intake manifold-to-engine, in sequence, using 2–3 steps, nuts to 17–20 ft. lbs. (24–27 Nm) or nuts to bolts to 12–14 ft. lbs. (16–20 Nm).

13. If the fuel injector assembly was removed, install it by perform the following procedures:

a. Install the fuel injector assembly to the engine.

b. Install the fuel injector(s)-to-cylinder head bolts and hold-down clamps; torque the hold-down bolts to 1.8–2.4 ft. lbs. (2.5–3.2 Nm).

c. Connect the fuel injector assembly to the fuel lines.

d. Connect the electrical connectors to the fuel injectors.

14. Install the upper intake manifold and torque the upper intake manifold-to-intake manifold bolts, in sequence, to 13–16 ft. lbs. (18–22 Nm).

15. Install the collector cover to the upper intake manifold.

16. Install the spark plug wire, if disconnected.

17. If the EGR control valve was removed, use a new gasket and install it. Torque the EGR control valve-to-upper intake manifold bolts to 13–17 ft. lbs. (18–23 Nm) and the EGR tube-to-exhaust manifold nut to 25–33 ft. lbs. (34–44 Nm).

18. Install the breather hoses to the rocker arm covers.

19. Connect the electrical connectors to the upper intake manifold.

20. Refill the cooling system. Connect the negative battery cable.

21. Start the engine and check for oil leaks.

1989–92

◆ SEE FIGS. 63-68

1. Disconnect the negative battery cable and relieve the fuel pressure.

2. Disconnect the air intake duct from the dual duct housing.

3. Disconnect the electrical connectors from the throttle body, the step motor AAC valve and the exhaust gas temperature sensor.

4. Disconnect and label the hoses from the rocker arm cover, the throttle body, the step motor AAC valve, the EGR control valve and the air cut valve.

5. If the spark plug wires are in the way, disconnect them and move them aside. Disconnect the accelerator cable from the throttle body.

6. Remove the upper intake manifold collector-to-intake manifold bolts, in sequence, and lift the assembly from the intake manifold. Discard the gasket.

7. Remove the lower intake manifold collector-to-intake manifold bolts, in sequence, and lift the assembly from the intake manifold. Discard the gasket.

8. If the fuel injector assembly is in the way, perform the following procedures:

a. Disconnect the electrical connectors from the fuel injectors.

b. Disconnect the fuel injector assembly from the fuel lines.

c. Remove the fuel rail-to-cylinder head bolts.

d. Remove the fuel rail assembly from the engine.

9. Remove the intake manifold-to-engine bolts, in sequence, lift the intake manifold from the engine and discard the gasket.

To install:

10. Clean the gasket mounting surfaces.

1. Use a new gasket and install the intake manifold by performing the following procedures:

a. Torque the intake manifold-to-engine nuts/bolts, in sequence, to 2.2–3.6 ft. lbs. (3–5 Nm).

b. Retorque the intake manifold-to-engine nuts/bolts, in sequence, to 12–14 ft. lbs. (16–20 Nm).

c. Finally, torque the intake manifold-to-engine nuts/bolts, in sequence, to 17–20 ft. lbs. (24–27 Nm).

12. If the fuel injector assembly was removed, perform the following procedures:

a. Install the fuel rail assembly to the engine.

b. Install the fuel rail-to-cylinder head bolts and torque the bolts to 1.8–2.4 ft. lbs. (2.5–3.2 Nm).

c. Connect the fuel injector assembly to the fuel lines.

d. Connect the electrical connectors to the fuel injectors.

13. Use a new gasket and install the lower intake manifold collector; torque the lower intake manifold collector-to-intake manifold bolts, in 2–3 steps, in sequence, to 13–16 ft. lbs. (18–22 Nm).

14. Use a new gasket and install the upper intake manifold collector-to-intake manifold; torque the bolts to 5.1–5.8 ft. lbs. (7–8 Nm).

15. Connect the spark plug wire, if disconnected. Connect the accelerator cable to the throttle body.

16. Connect the hoses to the rocker arm cover, the throttle body, the step motor AAC valve, the EGR control valve and the air cut valve.

17. Connect the electrical connectors to the throttle body, the step motor AAC valve and the exhaust gas temperature sensor.

18. Connect the negative battery cable.

19. Start the engine and check for oil leaks.

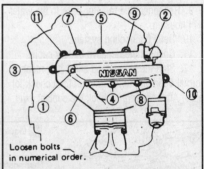

FIG. 63 Loosening the upper intake manifold collector bolts, in sequence — 1989–92 VG30E engine

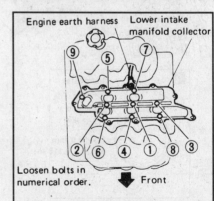

FIG. 64 Loosening the lower intake manifold collector bolts, in sequence — 1989–92 VG30E engine

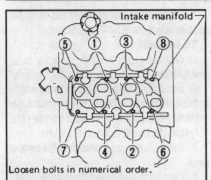

FIG. 65 Loosening the intake manifold-to-engine bolts, in sequence, in 2–3 steps — 1989–92 VG30E engine

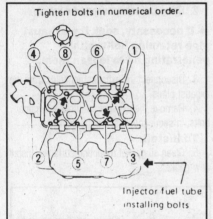

FIG. 66 Torquing the intake manifold-to-engine bolts, in sequence, in 2–3 steps — 1989–92 VG30E engine

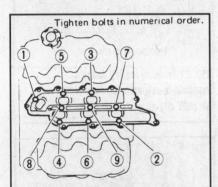

FIG. 67 Torquing the lower intake manifold collector-to-intake manifold bolts, in sequence, in 2–3 steps — 1989–92 VG30E engine

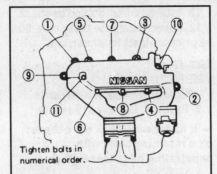

FIG. 68 Torquing the upper intake manifold collector-to-intake manifold bolts, in sequence, in 2–3 steps — 1989–92 VG30E engine

VE30DE Engine

◆ SEE FIG. 69

1. Disconnect the negative battery cable.

2. Disconnect the electrical connectors from the throttle position sensor, the exhaust gas temperature sensor and/or etc.

3. Label and disconnect the hoses from the throttle body, the EGR valve, the EGR control solenoid valve, the intake manifold collector, the power valve control solenoid valve (if equipped with a manual transaxle) and the power valve actuator (if equipped with a manual transaxle).

4. Disconnect the accelerator cable from the throttle body.

5. Remove the intake manifold collector support-to-intake manifold collector and the intake manifold collector support-to-cylinder head bolts and the supports.

6. Remove the intake manifold collector-to-intake manifold bolts and the intake manifold collector.

7. If necessary, disconnect the electrical connectors from the ignition coils.

8. If necessary, disconnect the electrical connector from the crank angle sensor and the power transistor.

9. If the fuel injector assembly is in the way, perform the following procedures:

   a. Disconnect the electrical connectors from the fuel injectors.

   b. Disconnect the fuel injector assembly from the fuel lines.

   c. Remove the fuel rail-to-cylinder head bolts.

   d. Remove the fuel rail assembly from the engine.

10. Remove the intake manifold-to-engine bolts, in sequence, by reversing the torquing sequence. Lift the intake manifold from the engine and discard the gasket.

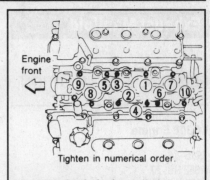

FIG. 69 Torquing the intake manifold-to-engine bolts, in sequence, in 2–3 steps — VE30DE engine

To install:

11. Clean the gasket mounting surfaces.

12. Install the intake manifold and torque the intake manifold-to-engine, in sequence, bolts to 12–14 ft. lbs. (16–20 Nm) and the nuts to 17–20 ft. lbs. (24–27 Nm).

13. If the fuel injector assembly was removed, perform the following procedures:

   a. Install the fuel rail assembly to the engine.

   b. Install the fuel rail-to-cylinder head bolts and torque the bolts to 12–14 ft. lbs. (16–20 Nm).

   c. Connect the fuel injector assembly to the fuel lines.

   d. Connect the electrical connectors to the fuel injectors.

14. Connect the electrical connectors to the ignition coils, if disconnected.

15. Using a new gasket, install the intake manifold collector and torque the intake manifold collector-to-intake manifold bolts, in sequence, to 13–16 ft. lbs. (18–22 Nm).

16. Install the intake manifold collector support and torque the bolts to 12–15 ft. lbs. (16–21 Nm).

17. Connect the accelerator cable to the throttle body.

18. Connect the hoses to the throttle body, the EGR valve, the EGR control solenoid valve, the intake manifold collector, the power valve control solenoid valve (if equipped with a manual transaxle) and the power valve actuator (if equipped with a manual transaxle).

19. If disconnected, connect the electrical connectors to the crank angle sensor and the power transistor.

20. If disconnected, connect the electrical connectors to the ignition coils.

21. Connect the electrical connectors from the throttle position sensor, the exhaust gas temperature sensor and/or etc.

22. Connect the negative battery cable.

23. Start the engine and check for leaks.

Exhaust Manifold

REMOVAL & INSTALLATION

VG30E Engine

1985–88

▶ SEE FIG. 70

1. Disconnect the negative battery cable.
2. Raise and safely support the vehicle.
3. Disconnect the exhaust manifolds from the exhaust pipe.
4. Remove the exhaust manifold sub-cover and manifold cover. Remove the EGR tube from the right exhaust manifold. Remove the exhaust manifold stay.
5. Disconnect the left exhaust manifold at the exhaust manifold crossover tube by removing retaining nuts and disconnect the right exhaust manifold from the connecting pipe.

➡ **Soak the exhaust pipe retaining bolts with penetrating oil, if necessary, to loosen them.**

6. Remove bolts for each manifold in sequence.

To install:

7. Clean all gasket mounting surfaces. Install new gaskets.
8. Install the exhaust manifolds to the engine and torque the exhaust manifold-to-engine bolts, alternately in 2 stages, in the exact reverse order of removal to 13–16 ft. lbs. (16–22 Nm).
9. Using new gaskets, connect the exhaust manifold connecting pipe to the exhaust manifolds and torque the nuts/bolts to 16–20 ft. lbs. (22–27 Nm).
10. Install the exhaust manifold stay and torque the bolts to 16–20 ft. lbs. (22–27 Nm). Torque the EGR tube nut-to-right exhaust manifold to 25–33 ft. lbs. (34–44 Nm).

11. Install the exhaust manifold covers.
12. Connect the negative battery cable. Start the engine and check for exhaust leaks.

1989–92

▶ SEE FIG. 71

1. Disconnect the negative battery cable.
2. Raise and safely support the vehicle.

➡ **If necessary, soak the exhaust pipe retaining bolts with penetrating oil to loosen them.**

3. Disconnect the exhaust manifolds from the exhaust pipes.

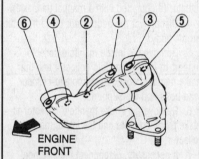

R.H. SIDE EXHAUST MANIFOLD

L.H. SIDE EXHAUST MANIFOLD

FIG. 71 Loosening the exhaust manifolds-to-engine bolts, in sequence — 1989–92 VG30E engine

4. Remove both exhaust manifolds-to-engine bolts, in sequence. Discard the gaskets.

To install:

5. Clean all gasket mounting surfaces. Install new gaskets.
6. Install the exhaust manifolds to the engine and torque the exhaust manifold-to-engine bolts, alternately in 2 stages, in the exact reverse order of removal to 13–16 ft. lbs. (16–22 Nm).
7. Install the exhaust manifolds to the exhaust pipes.
8. Connect the negative battery cable. Start the engine and check for exhaust leaks.

VE30DE Engine

▶ SEE FIGS. 72 AND 73

1. Disconnect the negative battery cable.
2. Raise and safely support the vehicle.

➡ **If necessary, soak the exhaust pipe retaining bolts with penetrating oil to loosen them.**

3. Disconnect the exhaust manifolds from the exhaust pipes.
4. Remove the exhaust manifold-to-engine bolts, in sequence. Discard the gaskets.

To install:

5. Clean all gasket mounting surfaces. Install new gaskets.

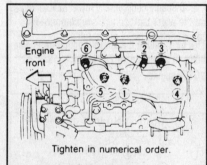

Tighten in numerical order.

FIG. 72 Torquing the left exhaust manifold-to-engine bolts, in sequence — VE30DE engine

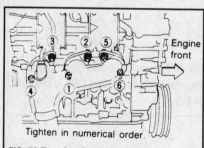

Tighten in numerical order.

FIG. 73 Torquing the right exhaust manifold-to-engine bolts, in sequence — VE30DE engine

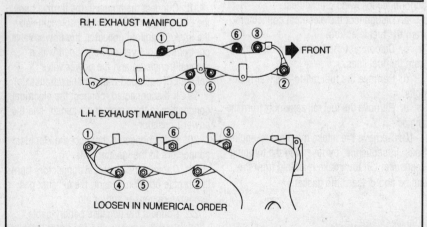

R.H. EXHAUST MANIFOLD

L.H. EXHAUST MANIFOLD

LOOSEN IN NUMERICAL ORDER

FIG. 70 Loosening the exhaust manifolds-to-engine bolts, in sequence — 1985–88 VG30E engine

6. Install the exhaust manifold to the engine and perform the following procedure:

a. Torque the exhaust manifold-to-engine bolts, in sequence, to 13–16 ft. lbs. (16–22 Nm).

b. Torque the exhaust manifold-to-engine bolts, in sequence, to 17–20 ft. lbs. (24–27 Nm).

7. Install the exhaust manifolds to the exhaust pipes.

8. Connect the negative battery cable. Start the engine and check for exhaust leaks.

Radiator

REMOVAL & INSTALLATION

VG30E Engine

1985–89

◆ SEE FIG. 74

1. Disconnect the negative battery cable.

2. Remove the front bumper. Remove the cap and drain the radiator via the drain plug in the bottom tank.

3. Disconnect upper and lower radiator hoses and the water temperature switch connectors at top and bottom tanks of the radiator.

4. Remove the fan/shroud assembly from the radiator.

➡ **To remove the electrical cooling fan unplug the fans electrical connections and remove the fan/ shroud as an assembly. If equipped with an automatic transaxle disconnect and plug the transaxle cooling lines at the radiator.**

5. Remove the 2 bolts that mount the top of the radiator via grommets and the 2 at the bottom which fasten the radiator to the mounts. Remove the radiator.

To install:

6. Position the fan/shroud assembly in the vehicle before installing the radiator.

7. Install the radiator in the vehicle and torque the mounting bolts evenly to 2.2–2.9 ft. lbs. (3–4 Nm).

8. Connect the upper and lower radiator hoses and the water temperature switch connectors at the top and bottom tanks of the radiator.

9. If equipped with an automatic transaxle, connect the oil cooler lines to the radiator. Check and/or refill the transaxle.

10. Refill the cooling system with 50/50 antifreeze/water mix and bleed the system.

11. Install the front bumper. Run engine and check the cooling system for leaks.

1989–92

◆ SEE FIG. 75

1. Disconnect the negative battery cable.

2. Remove the cap and drain the radiator via the drain plug in the bottom tank.

3. Disconnect upper and lower radiator hoses.

4. Disconnect the fan electrical connectors. Remove the fan/shroud assembly from the radiator.

5. If equipped with an automatic transaxle disconnect and plug the transaxle cooling lines at the radiator.

6. Disconnect the overflow hose from the radiator.

7. Remove the radiator from the vehicle.

To install:

8. Install the radiator into the vehicle.

9. Position the fan/shroud assembly in the vehicle and connect it to the radiator.

10. Connect the upper and lower radiator hoses.

11. If equipped with an automatic transaxle, connect the oil cooler lines to the radiator. Check and/or refill the transaxle.

12. Refill the cooling system with 50/50 antifreeze/water mix and bleed the system.

13. Run engine and check the cooling system for leaks.

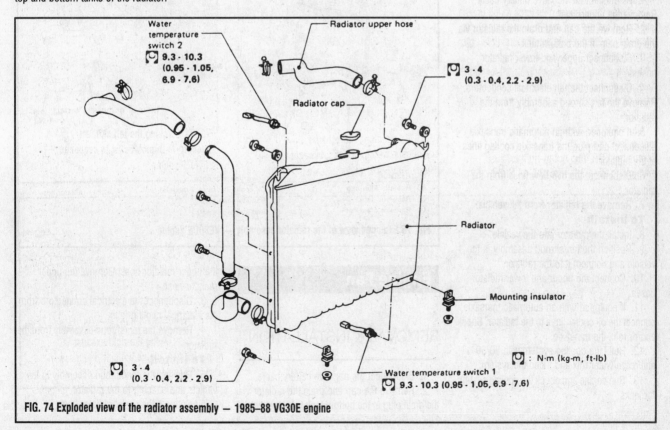

FIG. 74 Exploded view of the radiator assembly — 1985–88 VG30E engine

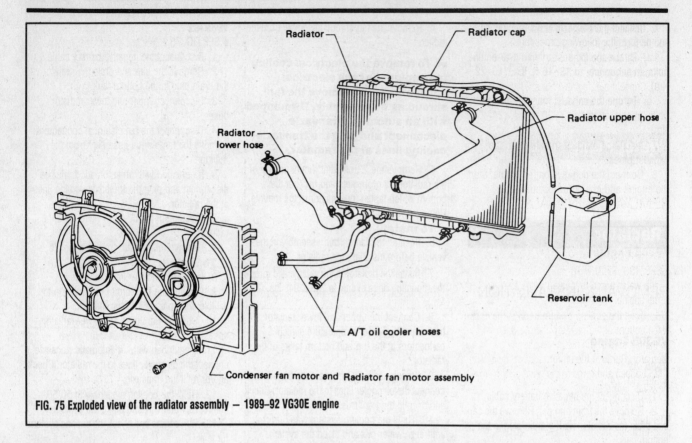

FIG. 75 Exploded view of the radiator assembly — 1989–92 VG30E engine

VE30DE Engine

♦ SEE FIG. 76

1. Disconnect the negative battery cable. Remove the undercover

2. Remove the cap and drain the radiator via the drain plug in the bottom tank.

3. Disconnect upper and lower radiator hoses.

4. Disconnect the fan electrical connectors. Remove the fan/shroud assembly from the radiator.

5. If equipped with an automatic transaxle disconnect and plug the transaxle cooling lines at the radiator.

6. Disconnect the overflow hose from the radiator.

7. Remove the radiator from the vehicle.

To install:

8. Install the radiator into the vehicle.

9. Position the fan/shroud assembly in the vehicle and connect it to the radiator.

10. Connect the upper and lower radiator hoses.

11. If equipped with an automatic transaxle, connect the oil cooler lines to the radiator. Check and/or refill the transaxle.

12. Refill the cooling system with 50/50 antifreeze/water mix and bleed the system.

13. Run engine and check the cooling system for leaks.

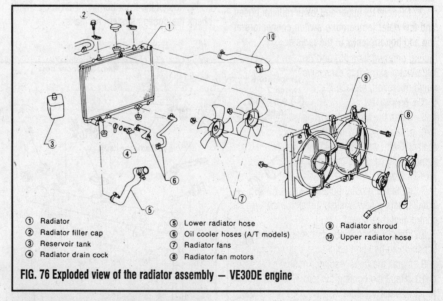

① Radiator
② Radiator filler cap
③ Reservoir tank
④ Radiator drain cock
⑤ Lower radiator hose
⑥ Oil cooler hoses (A/T models)
⑦ Radiator fans
⑧ Radiator fan motors
⑨ Radiator shroud
⑩ Upper radiator hose

FIG. 76 Exploded view of the radiator assembly — VE30DE engine

Engine Fan

REMOVAL & INSTALLATION

1. Disconnect the negative battery cable.

2. Remove the cap and drain the radiator via the drain plug in the bottom tank to a level below the upper radiator hose. Remove the upper radiator hose.

3. Disconnect the electrical connectors from the electrical cooling fans.

4. Remove the fan/shroud assembly from the radiator.

To install:

5. Position the fan/shroud assembly in the vehicle and attach it to the radiator.

6. Connect the upper radiator hose.

7. Connect the electrical connectors to the electrical cooling fans.

8. Refill the cooling system with 50/50 antifreeze/water mix and bleed the system.

9. Connect the negative battery cable. Run engine and check the cooling system for leaks.

Water Pump

REMOVAL & INSTALLATION

VG30E Engine

♦ SEE FIGS. 77 AND 78

The water pump is located in the front center of the engine.

1. Drain the cooling system through the cock at the bottom of the radiator and the drain plug, on the left side of the block, behind the alternator. Remove the upper radiator hose.

2. Loosen and remove the drive belt(s) from the water pump pulley.

3. To make the operation easier, remove the timing belt cover. If necessary, remove the thermostat housing and gasket for access.

➡ **Be careful to keep coolant off the timing belt.**

4. Remove the water pump-to-engine bolts (noting different lengths) and remove the pump. If the water pump has excessive end play or rough operation, replace it.

To Install:

5. Clean the gasket mounting surfaces.

6. Use a new gasket and coat the gasket with sealant. Reinstall the pump and torque the water pump-to-engine bolts evenly to 12–15 ft. lbs. (16–21 Nm).

7. If the thermostat housing was removed, install it with a new gasket. Install the cruise control unit if removed.

8. Install the tensioner, tensioner bracket, air conditioning belt and adjust the belt correctly.

9. Install the upper radiator hose.

10. Refill the cooling system. Connect the negative battery cable.

11. Start the engine, run to normal operating temperature and check for the correct coolant level and for leaks.

VE30DE Engine

♦ SEE FIGS. 79–81

The water pump is located in the front center of the engine.

1. Disconnect the negative battery cable.

2. Drain the cooling system to a level below the water pump.

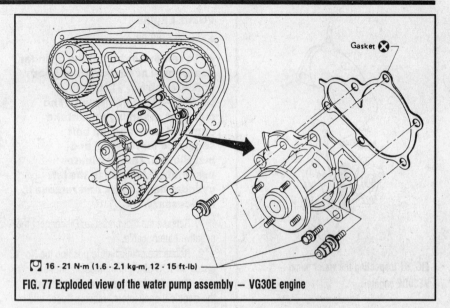

16 - 21 N·m (1.6 - 2.1 kg-m, 12 - 15 ft-lb)

FIG. 77 Exploded view of the water pump assembly — VG30E engine

FIG. 78 Checking the water pump for excessive end play and rough operation — VG30E engine

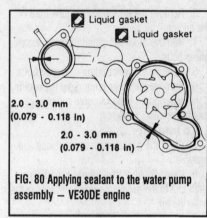

2.0 - 3.0 mm (0.079 - 0.118 in)

2.0 - 3.0 mm (0.079 - 0.118 in)

FIG. 80 Applying sealant to the water pump assembly — VE30DE engine

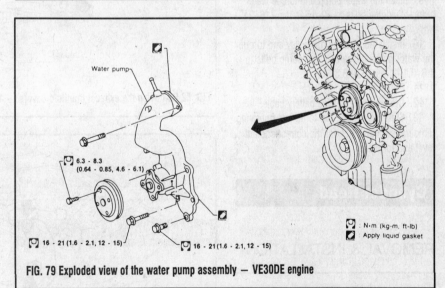

Water pump

6.3 - 8.3 (0.64 - 0.85, 4.6 - 6.1)

16 - 21 (1.6 - 2.1, 12 - 15)

16 - 21 (1.6 - 2.1, 12 - 15)

N·m (kg-m, ft-lb) Apply liquid gasket

FIG. 79 Exploded view of the water pump assembly — VE30DE engine

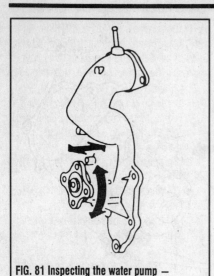

FIG. 81 Inspecting the water pump — VE30DE engine

3. Remove the drive belts from the front of the engine.

4. Remove the water pump pulley-to-water pump bolts.

5. Remove the water pump-to-engine bolts.

6. Remove the water pump from the engine. If the water pump has excessive end play or rough operation, replace it.

To install:

7. Clean the gasket mounting surfaces and grooves.

8. Using liquid sealant, apply a continuous bead of it to the gasket mounting surfaces of the water pump.

9. Install the water pump and torque water pump-to-engine bolts to 12–15 ft. lbs. (16–21 Nm).

10. Install the water pump pulley and torque the water pump pulley-to-water pump bolts to 4.6–6.1 ft. lbs. (6.3–8.3 Nm).

11. Refill the cooling system.

12. Connect the negative battery cable.

13. Start the engine, run to normal operating temperature and check for the correct coolant level and for leaks.

Cylinder Head

REMOVAL & INSTALLATION

➡ **To prevent distortion or warping of the cylinder head, allow the engine to cool completely before removing the head bolts.**

VG30E Engine

◆ SEE FIGS. 82-89

➡ **To remove or install the cylinder head, you'll need a cylinder head bolt wrench No. ST10120000 (J24239–01) or equivalent. The collector assembly and intake manifold have special bolt sequence for removal and installation. The distributor assembly is located in the left cylinder head, mark and remove it, if necessary.**

1. Release the fuel pressure. Disconnect the negative battery cable.

2. Rotate the crankshaft to position the No. 1 piston on TDC of it's compression stroke.

3. Drain the cooling system. Disconnect all the electrical connectors, vacuum hoses and water hoses connected to the intake manifold collector.

➡ **An engine block drain plug is located directly behind the alternator. On the 1989–92 engines, an extra drain plug is located on the right side, directly behind the right halfshaft.**

4. Remove the timing belt. Refer to the Timing Belt, Removal and Installation procedures.

➡ **Do not rotate either the crankshaft or camshaft from this point onward or the valves could be bent by hitting the pistons.**

5. Remove the intake manifold collector cover, for 1985–88, and the intake manifold collector. Refer to the section Intake Manifold Removal and Installation for correct bolt removal sequence.

6. Remove the intake manifold and fuel rail assembly.

7. Remove the exhaust manifold collector bracket. Remove the exhaust manifold covers. Disconnect the exhaust manifold when it connects to the exhaust connecting tube.

8. Remove the camshaft pulleys and the rear timing cover securing bolts.

9. Loosen the cylinder head bolts bolts, in sequence, using 2–3 steps.

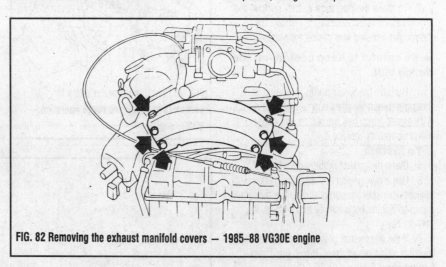

FIG. 82 Removing the exhaust manifold covers — 1985–88 VG30E engine

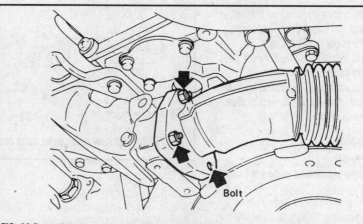

Bolt

FIG. 83 Removing the exhaust manifold connecting tube — 1985–88 VG30E engine

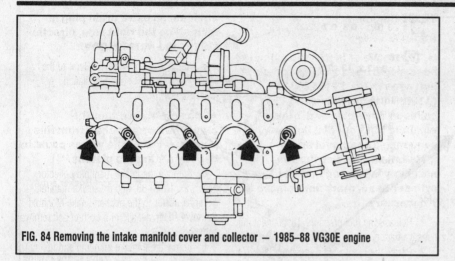

FIG. 84 Removing the intake manifold cover and collector — 1985–88 VG30E engine

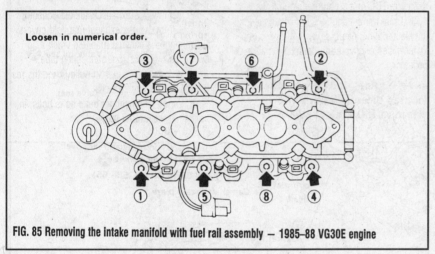

Loosen in numerical order.

FIG. 85 Removing the intake manifold with fuel rail assembly — 1985–88 VG30E engine

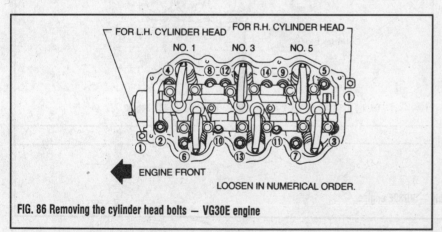

FOR L.H. CYLINDER HEAD — FOR R.H. CYLINDER HEAD

NO. 1   NO. 3   NO. 5

ENGINE FRONT

LOOSEN IN NUMERICAL ORDER.

FIG. 86 Removing the cylinder head bolts — VG30E engine

10. Remove the cylinder head with the exhaust manifold attached. If you need to remove the exhaust manifold, refer to the procedure in this section.

12. Check the positions of the timing marks and camshaft sprockets to make sure they have not shifted.

To install:

13. Clean the gasket mounting surfaces. Inspect the cylinder head(s) for warpage, wear, cracks and/or damage.

14. Make the following checks by performing the following procedures:

a. If the engine was disturbed, rotate the crankshaft to position the No. 1 piston on the TDC of it's compression stroke.

b. Align the mark on the crankshaft sprocket with the mark on the oil pump body.

c. Make sure the knock pin on the camshaft is set at the top.

15. Using a new gasket, install the cylinder head. Apply clean engine oil to the threads and seats of the bolts and install the bolts with washers in the correct position. Note that bolts 4, 5, 12, and 13 are 5.00 in. (127mm) long. The other bolts are 4.17 in. (106mm) long.

6. Torque the bolts according to the pattern for the cylinder head on each side in the following stages:

a. Torque all bolts, in order, to 22 ft. lbs. (29 Nm).

b. Torque all bolts, in order, to 43 ft. lbs. (59 Nm).

c. Loosen all bolts completely.

d. Torque all bolts, in order, to 22 ft. lbs. (29 Nm).

e. Torque all bolts, in order, to 40–47 ft. lbs. (54–64 Nm). If you have a special wrench available that torques bolts to a certain angle, torque them 60–65° tighter rather than going to 40–47 ft. lbs.

17. Install the rear timing cover bolts. Install the camshaft pulleys and torque the camshaft pulley-to-camshaft bolts to 58–65 ft. lbs. (78–88 Nm). Make sure the pulley marked R3 goes on the right and that marked L3 goes on the left.

18. Align the timing marks, if necessary, and then install the timing belt and adjust the belt tension.

19. Install the front upper and lower belt covers.

20. Make sure the rocker arm cover bolts, trays and washers are free of oil. Then, install the rocker arm covers.

21. For the 1985–88 engines, install the intake manifold and fuel tube. Torque nuts as follows:

a. Torque in numbered order to 26–43 inch lbs.

b. Torque in numbered order to 17–20 ft. lbs.

22. For the 1985–88 engines, torque the bolts on the intake manifold as follows:

a. Torque in numbered order to 26–43 inch lbs.

b. Torque in numbered order to 12–14 ft. lbs.

23. For the 1989–92 engines, torque the intake manifold-to-engine bolts as follows:

a. Torque, in sequence, to 2.2–3.6 ft. lbs. (3–5 Nm).

b. Torque, in sequence, to 12–14 ft. lbs. (16–20 Nm).

c. Torque, in sequence, to 17–20 ft. lbs. (24–27 Nm).

24. Install the exhaust manifold, if removed from the cylinder head.

25. Connect the exhaust manifold to the exhaust pipe connection. Install the exhaust collector bracket.

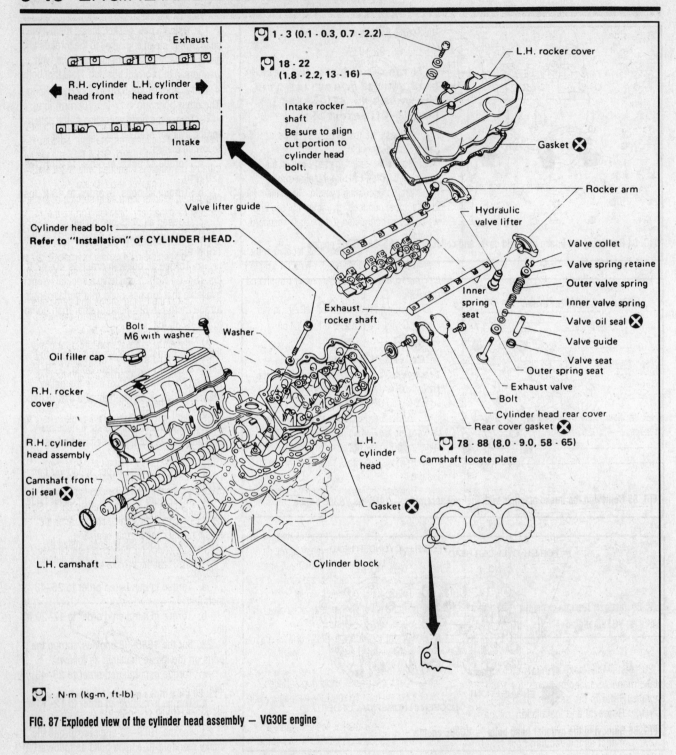

Exhaust

R.H. cylinder head front ← → L.H. cylinder head front

Intake

1 - 3 (0.1 - 0.3, 0.7 - 2.2)

18 - 22 (1.8 - 2.2, 13 - 16)

Intake rocker shaft
Be sure to align cut portion to cylinder head bolt.

L.H. rocker cover

Gasket

Rocker arm

Valve lifter guide

Hydraulic valve lifter

Cylinder head bolt
Refer to "Installation" of CYLINDER HEAD.

Valve collet

Valve spring retaine

Outer valve spring

Inner valve spring

Valve oil seal

Valve guide

Valve seat

Exhaust rocker shaft

Inner spring seat

Outer spring seat

Exhaust valve

Bolt

Bolt M6 with washer

Washer

Cylinder head rear cover

Rear cover gasket

Oil filler cap

78 - 88 (8.0 - 9.0, 58 - 65)

R.H. rocker cover

Camshaft locate plate

R.H. cylinder head assembly

L.H. cylinder head

Camshaft front oil seal

Gasket

L.H. camshaft

Cylinder block

: N·m (kg-m, ft-lb)

FIG. 87 Exploded view of the cylinder head assembly — VG30E engine

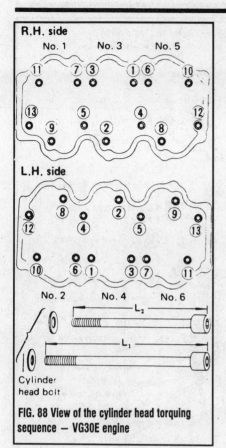

FIG. 88 View of the cylinder head torquing sequence — VG30E engine

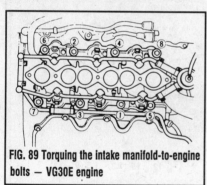

FIG. 89 Torquing the intake manifold-to-engine bolts — VG30E engine

26. Install the intake manifold collector and intake manifold collector cover, for 1985–88 engines. Refer to the section for Intake Manifold Removal and Installation for the correct torque pattern.

27. Connect all the vacuum hoses and water hoses to the intake collector.

28. Refill the cooling system. Connect the negative battery cable. Start the engine check the engine timing. After the engine reaches the normal operating temperature check for the correct coolant level.

29. Road test the vehicle for proper operation.

VE30DE Engine

♦ SEE FIGS. 90-103

➡ **To remove or install the cylinder head, you'll need a cylinder head bolt wrench No. ST10120000 (J24239–01) or equivalent.**

1. Release the fuel pressure. Disconnect the negative battery cable.

2. Rotate the crankshaft to position the No. 1 piston on TDC of it's compression stroke.

3. Drain the cooling system. Disconnect all the electrical connectors, vacuum hoses and water hoses connected to the intake manifold collector.

4. The crank angle sensor is located in the rear of the left cylinder head, mark it's position, disconnect the electrical connector from it and remove it.

5. Remove the timing chain. Refer to the Timing Chain, Removal and Installation procedures.

➡ **Do not rotate either the crankshaft or camshaft from this point onward or the valves could be bent by hitting the pistons.**

6. Remove the intake manifold collector. Refer to the section Intake Manifold Removal and Installation for correct bolt removal sequence.

7. Remove the intake manifold and fuel rail assembly.

8. Remove the exhaust manifold(s)-to-cylinder head(s) bolts and the exhaust manifolds.

9. Remove the camshaft sprockets-to-camshafts bolts and the camshaft sprockets.

10. Remove the exhaust camshafts, the camshaft brackets and the rocker arms.

11. Remove the outside cylinder head bolts.

12. Loosen the cylinder head-to-engine bolts, in sequence, using 2–3 steps.

13. Lift the cylinder head(s) from the engine and discard the gasket(s).

To Install:

14. Clean the gasket mounting surfaces. Inspect the cylinder head(s) for warpage, wear, cracks and/or damage.

15. Using liquid gasket sealant, apply a continuous bead to the mating surface of the cylinder block.

16. Install the cylinder head(s) and torque the head bolts by performing the following procedures:

  a. Torque all bolts, in sequence, to 29 ft. lbs. (39 Nm).

  b. Torque all bolts, in sequence, to 90 ft. lbs. (123 Nm).

  c. Loosen all bolts.

  d. Torque all bolts, in sequence, to 25–33 ft. lbs. (34–44 Nm).

  e. Torque all bolts, in sequence, to 87–94 ft. lbs. (188–127 Nm).

17. Install the outside cylinder head-to-engine bolts.

18. Install the exhaust camshafts, camshaft brackets and rocker arms; the right exhaust camshaft is identified with **96E RE** and the left exhaust camshaft is identified with **96E LE**.

19. Using a gasket sealant, apply a continuous bead to the mating surface of the left exhaust camshaft end bracket. Torque the exhaust camshaft bracket-to-cylinder head bolts to 6.7–8.7 ft. lbs. (9.0–11.0 Nm).

20. Position the right exhaust camshaft key at about 10 o'clock position and the left camshaft key at about 12 o'clock position.

21. Install the timing chains and sprockets; torque the timing chain sprocket-to-camshaft bolts to 80–87 ft. lbs. (108–118 Nm).

22. Install the exhaust manifold(s) and the exhaust manifold(s)-to-cylinder head(s) bolts.

23. Install the intake manifold and fuel rail assembly.

24. Install the intake manifold collector.

25. Align and install the crank angle sensor to the rear of the left cylinder head, connect the electrical connector to it.

26. Connect all the electrical connectors, vacuum hoses and water hoses to the intake manifold collector. Refill the cooling system.

27. Connect the negative battery cable. Start the engine check the engine timing. After the engine reaches the normal operating temperature check for the correct coolant level.

28. Road test the vehicle for proper operation.

FIG. 90 View of the cylinder head bolt wrench No. ST10120000 (J24239–01)

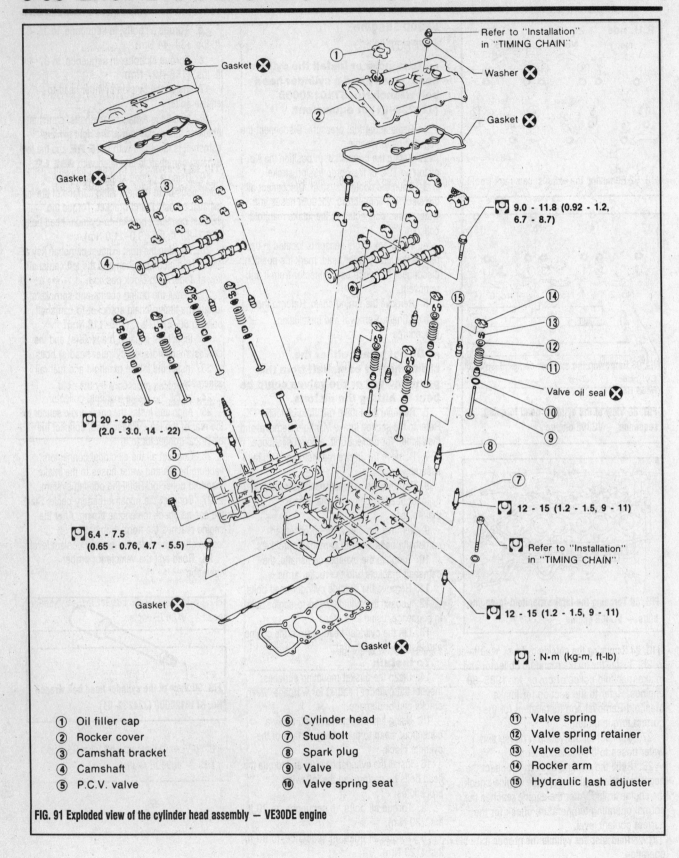

Refer to "Installation" in "TIMING CHAIN"

Washer ⊗

Gasket ⊗

Gasket ⊗

Gasket ⊗

9.0 - 11.8 (0.92 - 1.2, 6.7 - 8.7)

Valve oil seal ⊗

20 - 29 (2.0 - 3.0, 14 - 22)

12 - 15 (1.2 - 1.5, 9 - 11)

6.4 - 7.5 (0.65 - 0.76, 4.7 - 5.5)

Refer to "Installation" in "TIMING CHAIN".

12 - 15 (1.2 - 1.5, 9 - 11)

Gasket ⊗

Gasket ⊗

: N·m (kg-m, ft-lb)

① Oil filler cap
② Rocker cover
③ Camshaft bracket
④ Camshaft
⑤ P.C.V. valve

⑥ Cylinder head
⑦ Stud bolt
⑧ Spark plug
⑨ Valve
⑩ Valve spring seat

⑪ Valve spring
⑫ Valve spring retainer
⑬ Valve collet
⑭ Rocker arm
⑮ Hydraulic lash adjuster

FIG. 91 Exploded view of the cylinder head assembly — VE30DE engine

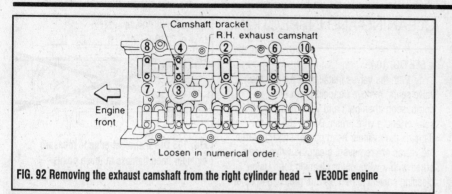

FIG. 92 Removing the exhaust camshaft from the right cylinder head — VE30DE engine

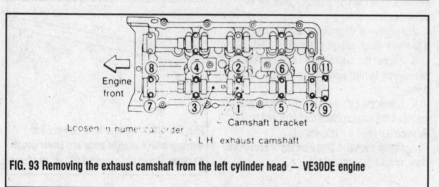

FIG. 93 Removing the exhaust camshaft from the left cylinder head — VE30DE engine

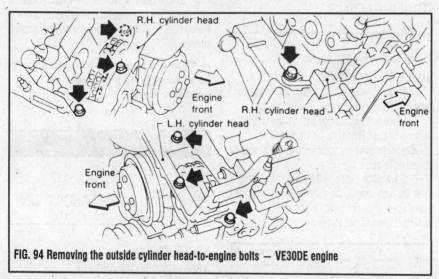

FIG. 94 Removing the outside cylinder head-to-engine bolts — VE30DE engine

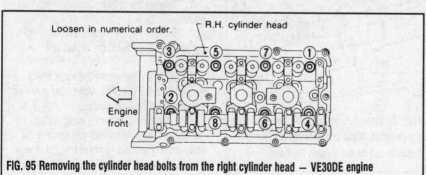

FIG. 95 Removing the cylinder head bolts from the right cylinder head — VE30DE engine

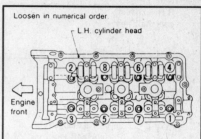

FIG. 96 Removing the cylinder head bolts from the left cylinder head — VE30DE engine

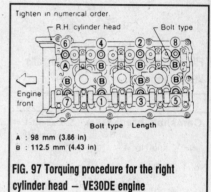

A : 98 mm (3.86 in)
B : 112.5 mm (4.43 in)

FIG. 97 Torquing procedure for the right cylinder head — VE30DE engine

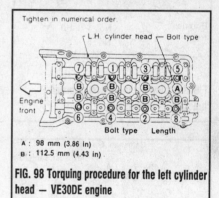

A : 98 mm (3.86 in)
B : 112.5 mm (4.43 in)

FIG. 98 Torquing procedure for the left cylinder head — VE30DE engine

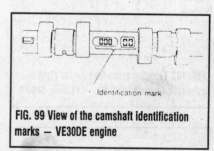

FIG. 99 View of the camshaft identification marks — VE30DE engine

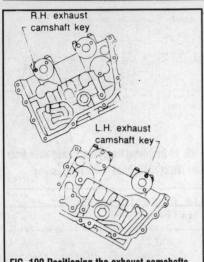

FIG. 100 Positioning the exhaust camshafts — VE30DE engine

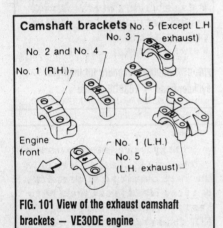

FIG. 101 View of the exhaust camshaft brackets — VE30DE engine

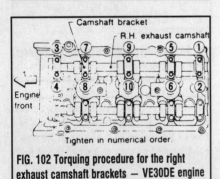

FIG. 102 Torquing procedure for the right exhaust camshaft brackets — VE30DE engine

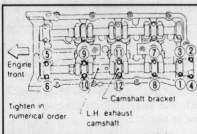

FIG. 103 Torquing procedure for the left exhaust camshaft brackets — VE30DE engine

CLEANING AND INSPECTION

♦ SEE FIG. 104

1. With the valves installed to protect the valve seats, remove deposits from the combustion chambers and valve heads with a scraper and a wire brush. Be careful not to damage the cylinder head gasket surface. After the valves are removed, clean the valve guide bores with a valve guide cleaning tool. Using cleaning solvent to remove dirt, grease and other deposits, clean all bolt holes; be sure the oil passages are clean.

2. Remove all deposits from the valves with a fine wire brush or buffing wheel.

3. Inspect the cylinder head for cracks or excessively burned areas in the exhaust outlet ports.

4. Check the cylinder head for cracks and inspect the gasket surface for burrs and nicks. Replace the head if it is cracked.

5. Check the valve seat inserts for excessive wear, cracks or looseness.

RESURFACING

Cylinder Head Flatness

♦ SEE FIGS. 105 AND 106

When a cylinder head is removed, check the flatness of the cylinder head gasket surface.

1. Place a straight-edge across the gasket surface of the cylinder head. Using feeler gauges, determine the clearance at the center of the straight-edge.

2. If warpage exceeds 0.004 in. (0.10mm) over the total length, the cylinder head must be resurfaced. Cylinder head height after resurfacing must not exceed specifications.

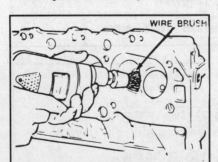

FIG. 104 Clean the combustion chambers with a wire brush. Make sure you remove the deposits and do not scratch the head

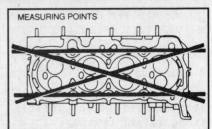

FIG. 105 Use a straight-edge to measure cylinder head flatness at these points

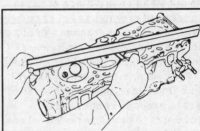

FIG. 106 Check cylinder head flatness and warpage with a straight-edge and feeler gauge. Warpage should not exceed 0.004 in. (0.10mm)

3. If necessary to refinish the cylinder head gasket surface, do not plane or grind off more than 0.008 in. (0.20mm) from the original gasket surface.

➡ Cylinder head resurfacing should be done only by a competent machine shop.

Valves

REMOVAL & INSTALLATION

VG30E Engine

♦ SEE FIGS. 107, 108 AND 110

1. Remove the cylinder head(s) from the engine.

2. Remove the rocker arm assembly-to-cylinder head bolts and the rocker arm assembly.

3. Using a wire, secure the valve lifters so they will not fall out of the valve lifter guide and remove the valve lifter guide.

4. Using the valve spring compressor, compress the valve springs and remove the valve (collet) keepers; a small magnet is very helpful for removing the keepers and spring seats.

➡ Valve spring compressors are available at most auto parts and auto tool shops.

5. Remove the valve spring compressor, the valve spring retainer, the outer spring, the inner spring and the spring seat.

6. Slide the valve out from the other side of the cylinder head.

➡ **Since it is very important that each valve and its spring, retainer, spring seat and keepers is reassembled in its original location, you must keep these parts in order. The best way to do this is to cut 12 holes in a piece of heavy cardboard or wood. Label each hole with the cylinder number and either IN or EX, corresponding to the location of each valve in the head. As you remove each valve, insert it into the holder, and assemble the seats, springs, keepers and retainers to the stem on the labeled side of the holder. This way each valve and its attending parts are kept together, and can be put back into the head in their proper locations.**

7. If the hydraulic lifters are removed from the valve lifter guide, store them in the straight up position.

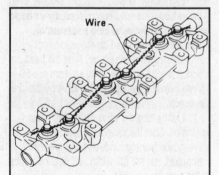

FIG. 107 Using a wire to secure the hydraulic lifter in the valve lifter guide — VG30E engine

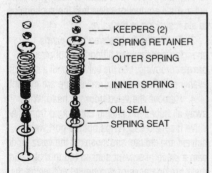

FIG. 108 View of the valve components. Only the VG30E engine has double valve springs

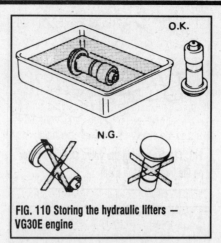

FIG. 110 Storing the hydraulic lifters — VG30E engine

➡ **If the hydraulic lifters are allowed to lay on their sides, air may enter the lifter, causing it to be spongy. It is a good idea to soak them oil to keep air from entering them. DO NOT disassemble the hydraulic lifter.**

To install:

8. Using a power wire brush, clean the deposits from the valve.

9. Inspect the valve for cracks, warpage and seating condition; if necessary, recondition them.

10. Slide the valve into it's correct position. Assemble the spring seat, the inner spring, the outer spring and the valve spring retainer onto the cylinder head.

➡ **Before final installation of a valve, it should be lapped into position.**

11. Using the valve spring compressor, compress the valve spring assembly; then, install the valve (collets) keepers.

12. Slowly, release the valve spring compressor, making sure the valve (collets) keepers have engaged with the valve stem.

13. Install the other valves in the same manner.

14. After the other valves have been installed, install valve lifter guide and rocker arm assembly. Torque the rocker arm assembly-to-cylinder head bolts to 13–16 ft. lbs. (18–22 Nm).

15. Install the cylinder head to the engine.

VE30DE Engine

◆ SEE FIG. 109

1. Remove the cylinder head(s) from the engine.

2. Remove the camshaft bracket-to-cylinder head bolts and the brackets, camshafts and rocker arms.

3. Using the valve spring compressor, compress the valve springs and remove the

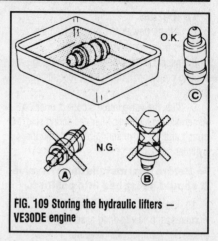

FIG. 109 Storing the hydraulic lifters — VE30DE engine

valve (collet) keepers; a small magnet is very helpful for removing the keepers and spring seats.

➡ **Valve spring compressors are available at most auto parts and auto tool shops.**

4. Remove the valve spring compressor, the valve spring retainer, the spring and the spring seat.

5. Remove the hydraulic lifters from the cylinder head and store them in the straight up position.

➡ **If the hydraulic lifters are allowed to lay on their sides, air may enter the lifter, causing it to be spongy. It is a good idea to soak them oil to keep air from entering them. DO NOT disassemble the hydraulic lifter.**

6. Slide the valve out from the other side of the cylinder head.

➡ **Since it is very important that each valve and its spring, retainer, spring seat and keepers is reassembled in its original location, you must keep these parts in order. The best way to do this is to cut 24 holes in a piece of heavy cardboard or wood. Label each hole with the cylinder number and either IN or EX, corresponding to the location of each valve in the head. As you remove each valve, insert it into the holder, and assemble the seats, springs, keepers and retainers to the stem on the labeled side of the holder. This way each valve and its attending parts are kept together, and can be put back into the head in their proper locations.**

To install:

7. Using a power wire brush, clean the deposits from the valve.

8. Inspect the valve for cracks, warpage and seating condition; if necessary, recondition them.

9. Slide the valve into it's correct position. Assemble the hydraulic lifter, the spring seat, the spring and the valve spring retainer onto the cylinder head.

➡ **Before final installation of a valve, it should be lapped into position.**

10. Using the valve spring compressor, compress the valve spring assembly; then, install the valve (collets) keepers.

11. Slowly, release the valve spring compressor, making sure the valve (collets) keepers have engaged with the valve stem.

12. Install the other valves in the same manner.

13. After the other valves have been installed, install the rocker arms, the camshafts and the camshaft brackets. Torque the camshaft brackets-to-cylinder head bolts to 6.7–8.7 ft. lbs. (9.0–11.0 Nm).

14. Install the cylinder head to the engine.

INSPECTION

◆ SEE FIGS. 111 AND 112

Before the valves can be properly inspected, the stem, lower end of the stem and the entire valve face and head must be cleaned. An old valve works well for clipping carbon from the valve head, and a wire brush, gasket scraper or putty knife can be used for cleaning the valve face and the area between the face and lower stem. Do not scratch the valve face during cleaning. Clean the entire stem with a rag soaked in thinners to remove all varnish and gum.

Thorough inspection of the valves requires the use of a micrometer and a dial indicator is needed to measure the inside diameter of the valve guides. If these instruments are not available to you, the valves and head can be taken to a reputable machine shop for inspection. Refer to the Valve Specifications chart for valve stem and stem-to-guide specifications.

If the above instruments are at your disposal, measure the diameter of each valve stem at the locations illustrated. Jot these measurements down. Using the dial indicator, measure the inside diameter of the valve guides at their bottom, top and midpoint 90° apart. Jot these measurements down also. Subtract the valve stem measurement from the valve guide inside measurement; if the clearance exceeds that

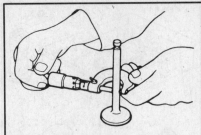

FIG. 111 Measuring the valve stem diameter on the center of the stem

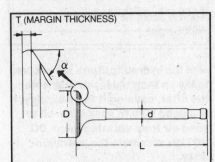

FIG. 112 Critical valve dimensions. When the valve head has been worn down to 0.020 in. in margin thickness (T), replace the valve. Grinding allowance for the valve stem tip is 0.008 in. or less

listed in the specifications chart under Stem-to-Guide Clearance, replace the valve(s). Stem-to-guide clearance can also be checked at a machine shop, where a dial indicator would be used.

Check the top of each valve stem for pitting and unusual wear due to improper rocker adjustment, etc. The stem tip can be ground flat if it is worn, but no more than 0.5mm can be removed; if this limit must be exceeded to make the tip flat and square, then the valve must be replaced. If the valve stem tips are ground, make sure you fix the valve securely into a jig designed for this purpose, so the tip contacts the grinding wheel squarely at exactly 90°. Most machine shops that handle automotive work are equipped for this job.

REFACING

◆ SEE FIG. 113

Valve refacing should only be handled by a reputable machine shop, as the experience and equipment needed to do the job are beyond that of the average owner/mechanic. During the course of a normal valve job, refacing is necessary when simply lapping the valves into their seats will not correct the seat and face wear. When the valves are reground

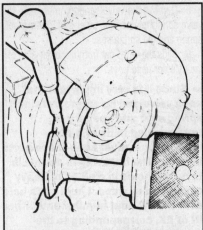

FIG. 113 Valve refacing should be handled by an engine specialist or machinist

(resurfaced), the valve seats must also be recut, again requiring special equipment and experience.

VALVE LAPPING

◆ SEE FIG. 124

The valves must be lapped into their seats after resurfacing, to ensure proper sealing. Even if the values have not been refaced, they should be lapped into the head before reassembly.

Set the cylinder head on the workbench, combustion chamber side up. Rest the head on wooden blocks on either end, so there are 50–75mm between the tops of the valve guides and the bench.

1. Lightly lube the valve stem with clean engine oil. Coat the valve seat completely with valve grinding compound. Use just enough compound that the full width and circumference of the seat are covered.

2. Install the valve in its proper location in the head. Attach the suction cup end of the valve lapping tool to the valve head. It usually helps to put a small amount of saliva into the suction cup to aid it sticking to the valve.

3. Rotate the tool between the palms, changing position and lifting the tool often to prevent grooving. Lap the valve in until a smooth, evenly polished seat and valve face are evident.

4. Remove the valve from the head. Wipe away all traces of grinding compound from the valve face and seat. Wipe out the port with a solvent soaked rag, and swab out the valve guide with a piece of solvent soaked rag to make sure there are no traces of compound grit inside the guide. This cleaning is very important, as the engine will ingest any grit remaining when started.

5. Proceed through the remaining valves, one at a time. Make sure the valve faces, seats,

FIG. 124 Lapping the valves

cylinder ports and valve guides are clean before reassembling the valve train.

Valve Stem Seals

REPLACEMENT

Cylinder Head Installed

VG30E ENGINE
▶ SEE FIGS. 114-119

1. Disconnect the negative battery cable.
2. Remove the rocker arm cover, the rocker arm assembly and the valve lifter guide.
3. Rotate the crankshaft to bring the piston, of the cylinder being worked on, to the top of it's travel; this will prevent the valve from falling into the cylinder.
4. Install the valve spring compressor KV10110600 (J–33966) so it is fastened to the top of the cylinder head.
5. Compress the valve spring assembly and remove the valve (collet) keepers.
6. Release the valve spring pressure. Remove the valve spring compressor.
7. Remove the valve spring retainer, the outer spring, the inner spring and the spring seat.
8. Use the oil seal removal tool KV101107900 to remove the intake valve oil seal.
9. Use pliers to remove the exhaust valve oil seal.

To install:

10. Lubricate the new oil seal with engine oil.

➡ **Before installing a new oil seal, be sure to install the spring seal first.**

11. Use the oil seal installation tool KV10107501 to install the intake valve oil seal.

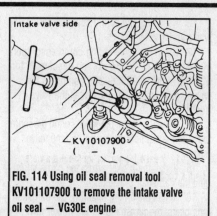

FIG. 114 Using oil seal removal tool KV101107900 to remove the intake valve oil seal — VG30E engine

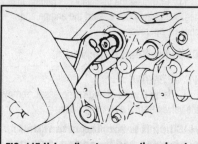

FIG. 115 Using pliers to remove the exhaust valve oil seal — VG30E engine

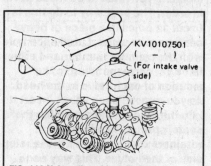

FIG. 116 Using oil seal installation tool KV10107501 to install the intake valve oil seal — VG30E engine

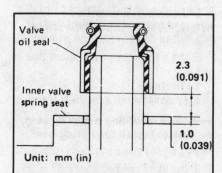

FIG. 117 Cross-sectional view of an installed oil seal — VG30E engine

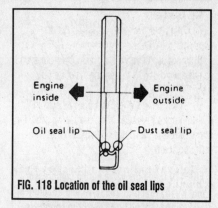

FIG. 118 Location of the oil seal lips

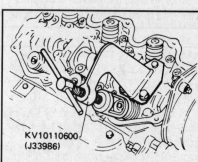

FIG. 119 Using valve spring compressor tool KV10110600 (J-33986) to compress valve spring assembly — VG30E engine

12. Install the exhaust valve oil seal by hand.
13. Assemble the inner spring, the outer spring and spring retainer over the valve.
14. Install the valve spring compressor tool KV10110600 (J–33986) and compress valve spring assembly.
15. Install the valve (collet) keepers and release the spring pressure; be sure the keepers are seated on the valve stem.
16. Install the valve lifter guide and the rocker arm assembly. Install the rocker arm covers.
17. Connect the negative battery cable. Start the engine and check the operation.

VE30DE ENGINE
▶ SEE FIGS. 120–122

1. Disconnect the negative battery cable.
2. Remove the rocker arm cover(s) and the timing chains from the camshafts.
3. Remove the camshaft sprocket(s)-to-camshaft(s) bolt(s).
4. Rotate the crankshaft to bring the piston to the TDC of it's compression stroke, of the cylinder being worked on, to the top of it's travel; this will prevent the valve from falling into the cylinder.
5. Remove the camshaft bracket(s), the camshaft(s) and the rocker arms.
6. Using the valve spring compressor tool KV10116200 (J–26336–A) and attachment tool KV10115900 (J–26336–20), compress the

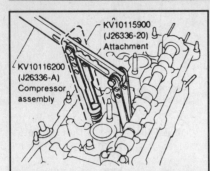

FIG. 120 Using the valve spring compressor tool KV10116200 (J-26336-A) and attachment tool KV10115900 (J-26336-20) to compress the valve spring assembly — VE30DE engine

FIG. 121 Using oil seal removal tool J-36467 or equivalent to remove the oil seals — VE30DE engine

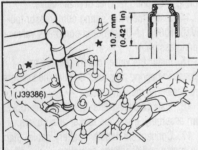

FIG. 122 Using the oil seal installation tool J-39386 or equivalent to install the new oil seals — VE30DE engine

valve spring assembly and remove the valve (collet) keepers.

7. Slowly, release the valve spring pressure and remove the valve spring compressor.

8. Remove the valve spring retainer, the spring and the spring seat.

9. Using oil seal removal tool J-36467 or equivalent, remove the oil seal(s).

To install:

10. Lubricate the new oil seals with engine oil.

11. Using the oil seal installation tool J-39386 or equivalent, install the new oil seal(s).

12. Assemble the spring seat, the spring, the valve spring retainer.

13. Using the valve spring compressor tool KV10116200 (J-26336-A) and attachment tool KV10115900 (J-26336-20), compress the valve spring assembly and install the valve (collet) keepers.

14. Slowly, release the valve spring pressure; be sure the keepers are seated on the valve stem.

15. Install the rocker arms, the camshaft(s) and the camshaft brackets.

16. Install the timing chain(s), the camshaft sprockets–to–camshaft and the rocker arm cover.

17. Complete the installation, connect the negative battery cable, start the engine and check it operation.

Cylinder Head Removed

VG30E ENGINE

1. Using a valve spring compressor, remove the valves from the cylinder head.

➡ **Since it is very important that each valve and its spring, retainer, spring seat and keepers is reassembled in its original location, you must keep these parts in order. The best way to do this is to cut 12 holes in a piece of heavy cardboard or wood. Label each hole with the cylinder number and either IN or EX, corresponding to the location of each valve in the head. As you remove each valve, insert it into the holder, and assemble the seats, springs, keepers and retainers to the stem on the labeled side of the holder. This way each valve and its attending parts are kept together, and can be put back into the head in their proper locations.**

2. Use the oil seal removal tool KV101107900 to remove the intake valve oil seal.

3. Use pliers to remove the exhaust valve oil seal.

To install:

4. Lubricate the new oil seal with engine oil.

➡ **Before installing a new oil seal, be sure to install the spring seal first.**

5. Use the oil seal installation tool KV10107501 to install the intake valve oil seal.

6. Install the exhaust valve oil seal by hand.

7. Using a valve spring compressor, install the valves into the cylinder head.

VE30DE ENGINE

➡ SEE FIG. 123

1. Using a spark plug and a washer, install it into the spark plug hole on the combustion chamber.

2. Remove the camshaft bracket-to-cylinder head bolts and the brackets, camshaft(s) and rocker arms.

3. Remove the hydraulic lifters from the cylinder head and store them in the straight up position.

➡ **If the hydraulic lifters are allowed to lay on their sides, air may enter the lifter, causing it to be spongy. It is a good idea to soak them oil to keep air from entering them. DO NOT disassemble the hydraulic lifter.**

4. Using the valve spring compressor tool KV10116200 (J-26336-A) and attachment tool KV10115900 (J-26336-20), compress the valve spring assembly and remove the valve (collet) keepers.

5. Slowly, release the valve spring pressure and remove the valve spring compressor.

6. Remove the valve spring retainer, the spring and the spring seat.

7. Using oil seal removal tool J-36467 or equivalent, remove the oil seal(s).

To install:

8. Lubricate the new oil seals with engine oil.

9. Using the oil seal installation tool J-39386 or equivalent, install the new oil seal(s).

10. Assemble the hydraulic lifter, the spring seat, the spring, the valve spring retainer.

11. Using the valve spring compressor tool KV10116200 (J-26336-A) and attachment tool KV10115900 (J-26336-20), compress the valve spring assembly and install the valve (collet) keepers.

12. Slowly, release the valve spring pressure; be sure the keepers are seated on the valve stem.

13. Install the rocker arms, the camshaft(s) and the camshaft brackets.

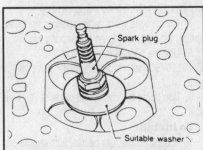

FIG. 123 Using a spark plug and a washer to secure the valves — VE30DE engine

Valve Springs

REMOVAL & INSTALLATION

Cylinder Head Installed

VG30E ENGINE

1. Disconnect the negative battery cable.
2. Remove the rocker arm cover, the rocker arm assembly and the valve lifter guide.
3. Rotate the crankshaft to bring the piston, of the cylinder being worked on, to the top of it's travel; this will prevent the valve from falling into the cylinder.
4. Install the valve spring compressor KV10110600 (J–33966) so it is fastened to the top of the cylinder head.
5. Compress the valve spring assembly and remove the valve (collet) keepers.
6. Release the valve spring pressure. Remove the valve spring compressor.
7. Remove the valve spring retainer, the outer spring and the inner spring.

To install:

8. Assemble the inner spring, the outer spring and spring retainer over the valve.
9. Install the valve spring compressor tool KV10110600 (J–33986) and compress valve spring assembly.
10. Install the valve (collet) keepers and release the spring pressure; be sure the keepers are seated on the valve stem.
11. Install the valve lifter guide and the rocker arm assembly. Install the rocker arm covers.
12. Connect the negative battery cable. Start the engine and check the operation.

VE30DE ENGINE

1. Disconnect the negative battery cable.
2. Remove the rocker arm cover(s) and the timing chains from the camshafts.
3. Remove the camshaft sprocket(s)–to-camshaft(s) bolt(s).
4. Rotate the crankshaft to bring the piston to the TDC of it's compression stroke, of the cylinder being worked on, to the top of it's travel; this will prevent the valve from falling into the cylinder.
5. Remove the camshaft bracket(s), the camshaft(s) and the rocker arms.
6. Using the valve spring compressor tool KV10116200 (J–26336–A) and attachment tool KV10115900 (J–26336–20), compress the valve spring assembly and remove the valve (collet) keepers.
7. Slowly, release the valve spring pressure and remove the valve spring compressor.
8. Remove the valve spring retainer and the spring.

To install:

9. Assemble the spring and the valve spring retainer.
10. Using the valve spring compressor tool KV10116200 (J–26336–A) and attachment tool KV10115900 (J–26336–20), compress the valve spring assembly and install the valve (collet) keepers.
11. Slowly, release the valve spring pressure; be sure the keepers are seated on the valve stem.
12. Install the rocker arms, the camshaft(s) and the camshaft brackets.
13. Install the timing chain(s), the camshaft sprockets-to-camshaft and the rocker arm cover.
14. Complete the installation, connect the negative battery cable, start the engine and check it operation.

Cylinder Head Removed

VG30E ENGINE

1. Using a valve spring compressor, compress the valve spring assembly.
2. Remove the valve keepers, the retainer and the valve springs from the cylinder head.
3. To install, use a valve spring compressor and compress the valve spring assembly.
4. Install the valve springs, the retainer and the keepers.
5. Slowly, release the spring compressor's pressure, making sure the keepers are in position on the valve lands.

VE30DE ENGINE

1. Using a spark plug and a washer, install it into the spark plug hole on the combustion chamber.
2. Remove the camshaft bracket-to-cylinder head bolts and the brackets, camshaft(s) and rocker arms.
3. Remove the hydraulic lifters from the cylinder head and store them in the straight up position.

➡ **If the hydraulic lifters are allowed to lay on their sides, air may enter the lifter, causing it to be spongy. It is a good idea to soak them oil to keep air from entering them. DO NOT disassemble the hydraulic lifter.**

4. Using the valve spring compressor tool KV10116200 (J–26336–A) and attachment tool KV10115900 (J–26336–20), compress the valve spring assembly and remove the valve (collet) keepers.
5. Slowly, release the valve spring pressure and remove the valve spring compressor.
6. Remove the valve spring retainer and the spring.

To install:

7. Assemble the hydraulic lifter, the spring seat and the spring.
8. Using the valve spring compressor tool KV10116200 (J–26336–A) and attachment tool KV10115900 (J–26336–20), compress the valve spring assembly and install the valve (collet) keepers.
9. Slowly, release the valve spring pressure; be sure the keepers are seated on the valve stem.
10. Install the rocker arms, the camshaft(s) and the camshaft brackets.

INSPECTION

VG30E Engine

◆ SEE FIG. 125 AND 126
1. Remove the spring from the cylinder head.
2. Using a tri-square, check the valve spring for squareness; the squareness should be:
• Outer spring — Less than 0.087 in. (2.2mm)
• Inner spring — Less than 0.075 in. (1.9mm)
3. If the squareness exceeds the specifications, replace the spring(s).
4. Using a spring pressure gauge, measure the valve spring pressure; the valve spring pressure should be:
• Outer spring   Normal — 117.7 lbs. (523.7 N) at 1.181 in. (30.0mm)   Minimum — 104.1 lbs. (462.9 N) at 1.181 in. (30.0mm)
• Inner spring   Normal — 57.3 lbs. (255.0 N) at 0.984 in. (25.0mm)   Minimum — 50.7 lbs. (225.6 N) at 0.984 in. (25.0mm)
5. If the spring(s) exceed the limits, replace it.
6. Install the springs onto the cylinder head.

VE30DE Engine

1. Remove the spring from the cylinder head.
2. Using a tri-square, check the valve spring for squareness; the squareness should be less than 0.079 in. (2.0mm)
3. If the squareness exceeds the specifications, replace the spring.
4. Using a spring pressure gauge, measure the valve spring pressure; the valve spring pressure should be:
• Normal — 120.4 lbs. (535.5 N) at 1.059 in. (26.9mm)
• Maximum — 107.4 lbs. (477.6 N) at 1.059 in. (26.9mm)
5. If the spring exceed the limit, replace it.
6. Install the spring into the cylinder head.

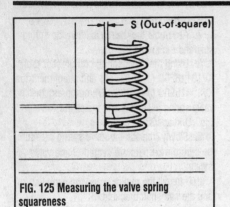
FIG. 125 Measuring the valve spring squareness

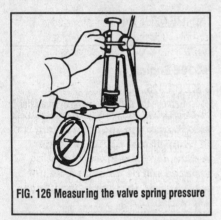
FIG. 126 Measuring the valve spring pressure

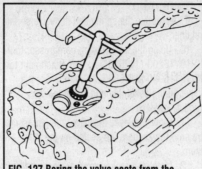
FIG. 127 Boring the valve seats from the cylinder head

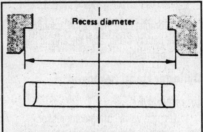
FIG. 128 View of the valve seat and the cylinder head recess

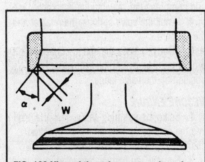
FIG. 129 View of the valve seat angle and valve contact surface "W"

Valve Seats

REMOVAL & INSTALLATION

♦ SEE FIGS. 127–129

Check the valve seat inserts for any evidence of pitting or excessive wear at the valve contact surface. The valve seats can be replaced. Because the cylinder head must be machined to accept the new seat inserts, consult an engine specialist or machinist about this work.

➡ **When repairing a valve seat, first check the valve and guide; if wear is evident here, replace the valve and/or guide, then correct the valve seat.**

1. Remove the valve from the cylinder head.
2. Using a valve seat cutting tool, bore out the old seat until it collapses.

➡ **The machine depth stop should be set so the boring cannot continue beyond the bottom face of the seat recess in the cylinder head.**

3. Ream the cylinder head recess to install a 0.020 in. (0.5mm) oversize valve seat.

To install:

4. Using an oil bath, heat the cylinder head to 302–320°F (150–160°C) for VG30E engine or 230–266°F (110–130°C) for VE30DE engine.
5. Press fit the new valve seat into the cylinder head until it seats.
6. After cooling the cylinder head, grind or cut the seat to specifications:
- VG30E engine   Seat face angle
  Intake valve — 45°
  Exhaust valve — 45°
Valve-to-seat contacting width "W"
  Intake valve — 0.0689 in. (1.75mm)
  Exhaust valve — 0.067 in. (1.7mm)
- VE30DE engine   Seat face angle
  Intake valve — 44°53'–45°07'
  Exhaust valve — 44°53'–45°07'
  Valve-to-seat contacting width "W"
  Intake valve — 0.0417–0.0528 in. (1.06–1.34mm)

Exhaust valve — 0.050–0.061 in. (1.27–1.55mm)

7. After cutting, lap the valve to the seat.
8. Install the valve to the cylinder head.

Valve Guide

INSPECTION

1. Remove the cylinder head from the engine.
2. Mount a dial indicator at a right angle to the valve stem and measure the valve deflection; the valve deflection should be less than 0.0079 in. (0.20mm).
3. If the valve deflection is in excess, perform the following procedures:
   a. Remove the valve from the cylinder head.
   b. Using a micrometer, measure the valve stem diameter in 3 positions: top, center and bottom.
   c. Using a internal dial micrometer, measure the valve guide diameter in 3 positions: top, center and bottom.
4. The valve guide clearance should be:
- VG30E engine   Normal clearance
     Intake — 0.0008–0.0021 in. (0.020–0.053mm)
     Exhaust — 0.0016–0.0029 in. (0.040–0.073mm)
     Maximum clearance Intake — 0.0039 in. (0.10mm)
     Exhaust — 0.0039 in. (0.10mm)
- VE30DE engine Maximum clearance
     Intake — 0.0031 in. (0.08mm)
     Exhaust — 0.0040 in. (0.10mm)
5. If the valve guide is defective, replace it.

REMOVAL & INSTALLATION

♦ SEE FIG. 130

1. Remove the valve assembly(s) from the cylinder head.
2. Using an oil bath, heat the cylinder head to
- VG30E engine — 302–320°F (150–160°C)
- VE30DE engine — 230–266°F (110–130°C)
3. Using a valve guide drift and a hammer, drive the guide(s) from the cylinder head.

To install:

4. Using a valve guide reamer, ream the cylinder head to accept the new valve guides:
- VG30E engine Intake — 0.4400–0.4408 in. (11.175–11.196mm)
     Exhaust — 0.4793–0.4802 in. (12.175–12.196mm)

• VE30DE engine Intake — 0.4006–0.4014 in. (10.175–10.196mm)

Exhaust — 0.4006–0.4014 in. (10.175–10.196mm)

5. Using an oil bath, heat the cylinder head to:
• VG30E engine — 302–320°F (150–160°C)
• VE30DE engine — 230–266°F (110–130°C)

6. Using a valve guide drift and a hammer, drive the valve guide(s) into the cylinder head until the guides project above the cylinder head:

VG30E engine — 0.520–0.528 in. (13.2–13.4mm).

VE30DE engine — 0.535–0.543 in. (13.6–13.8mm).

7. Ream the new valve guide bores to:
• VG30E engine Intake — 0.2756–0.2763 in. (7.000–7.018mm)

Exhaust — 0.3150–0.3157 in. (8.000–8.018mm)
• VE30DE engine Intake — 0.2362–0.2369 in. (6.000–6.018mm)

Exhaust — 0.2362–0.2369 in. (6.000–6.018mm)

8. Install the valve assembly(s) into the cylinder head.

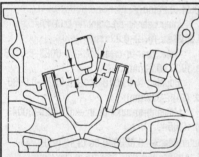

FIG. 130 Installing the valve guide into the cylinder head

Valve Lifters

REMOVAL & INSTALLATION

VG30E Engine

1. Disconnect the negative battery cable.
2. Remove the rocker arm cover and the rocker arm assembly.
3. Remove the valve lifters from the valve lifter guide.

➡ **When removing the valve lifters, it is a good idea to soak them in container of engine oil; this will keep air from entering the lifters.**

To install:
4. Install the valve lifters into the valve lifter guide.

5. Install the rocker arm assembly and the rocker arm cover.
6. Connect the negative battery cable. Start the engine and check the operation.

VE30DE Engine

1. Disconnect the negative battery cable.
2. Remove the rocker arm cover(s) and the timing chains from the camshafts.
3. Remove the camshaft sprocket(s)-to-camshaft(s) bolt(s).
4. Remove the camshaft bracket(s), the camshaft(s) and the rocker arms.
5. Lift the valve lifters from the cylinder head.

➡ **When removing the valve lifters, it is a good idea to soak them in container of engine oil; this will keep air from entering the lifters.**

To install:
6. Install the valve lifter into the cylinder head.
7. Install the rocker arms, the camshaft(s) and the camshaft brackets.
8. Install the timing chain(s), the camshaft sprockets-to-camshaft and the rocker arm cover.
9. Complete the installation, connect the negative battery cable, start the engine and check it operation.

Oil Pan

REMOVAL & INSTALLATION

VG30E Engine

◆ SEE FIGS. 131 AND 132

1. Raise and safely support the vehicle.
2. Connect a lifting device to the engine and apply upward pressure to take the engine weight off the supports or support the engine by using crankshaft damper.
3. Remove the oil pan plug and drain the oil into a container.

✳✳ CAUTION

The EPA warns that prolonged contact with used engine oil may cause a number of skin disorders, including cancer! You should make every effort to minimize your exposure to used engine oil. Protective gloves should be worn when changing the oil. Wash your hands and any other exposed skin areas as soon as possible after

exposure to used engine oil. Soap and water or waterless hand cleaner should be used.

4. Remove the under covers from under the engine.
5. On the 1985–88 models, remove the exhaust front tube fixing nuts. On the 1989–92 models, remove the exhaust pipe-to-exhaust manifold bolts and lower the exhaust pipe.
6. Remove the engine mount insulator-to-crossmember nuts and bolts.
7. Remove the center crossmember-to-chassis bolts and the crossmember.
8. Remove the oil pan-to-engine bolts, in sequence. Using the oil pan removal tool KV10111100 or equivalent, separate the oil pan from the engine.

✳✳ WARNING

Do not drive the seal cutter into the oil pump or rear oil seal retainer portion, for the aluminum mating surfaces will be damaged. Do not use a prybar, for the oil pan flange will be deformed.

9. Clean all the sealing surfaces.

To install:
10. Apply sealant to the 4 joints on the lower surface of the block. Apply sealant to the corresponding areas of the oil pan gasket on both upper and lower surfaces.
11. Using a new oil pan gasket, install the oil pan and torque the oil pan-to-engine bolts, by reversing the removal sequence, to 4.6–6.1 ft. lbs. (6.3–8.3 Nm) for 1985–88 or 5.1–5.8 ft. lbs. (7–8 Nm) for 1989–92.
12. Install the exhaust pipe connection.
13. Install the center crossmember. Torque the center crossmember-to-chassis nuts/bolts to 29–36 ft. lbs. (39–49 Nm) for 1985–88 or 57–72 ft. lbs. (77–98 Nm) for 1989–92 and engine mount-to-crossmember nuts/bolts to 29–36 ft. lbs. (39–49 Nm) for 1985–88 or 57–72 ft. lbs. (77–98 Nm) for 1989–92.
14. Install the under covers to the engine. After 30 minutes of gasket curing time, refill the oil pan with the specified quantity of clean oil. Operate the engine and check for leaks.

VE30DE Engine

1. Raise and safely support the vehicle.
2. Connect a lifting device to the engine and apply upward pressure to take the engine weight off the supports or support the engine by using crankshaft damper.
3. Remove the oil pan plug and drain the oil into a container.

The EPA warns that prolonged contact with used engine oil may cause a number of skin disorders, including cancer! You should make every effort to minimize your exposure to used engine oil. Protective gloves should be worn when changing the oil. Wash your hands and any other exposed skin areas as soon as possible after exposure to used engine oil. Soap and water or waterless hand cleaner should be used.

4. Remove the under covers from under the engine.

5. Remove the front exhaust pipe-to-exhaust manifold bolts and support; remove the front exhaust pipe.

6. Remove the engine mount insulator-to-crossmember nuts and bolts.

7. Remove the center crossmember-to-chassis bolts and the crossmember.

8. Remove the oil pan-to-engine bolts, in sequence. Using the oil pan removal tool KV10111100 or equivalent, separate the oil pan from the engine.

✳✳ WARNING

Do not drive the seal cutter into the oil pump or rear oil seal retainer portion, for the aluminum mating surfaces will be damaged. Do not use a prybar, for the oil pan flange will be deformed.

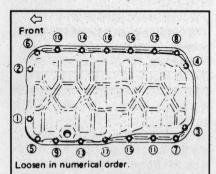

Loosen in numerical order.

FIG. 131 Removing the oil pan-to-engine bolts in numerical order — VG30E engine

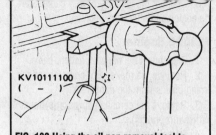

KV10111100

FIG. 132 Using the oil pan removal tool to separate the oil pan from the engine

9. Clean all the sealing surfaces.

To install:

10. Apply sealant to the 4 joints on the lower surface of the block. Apply sealant to the corresponding areas of the oil pan gasket on both upper and lower surfaces.

11. Using a new oil pan gasket, install the oil pan and torque the oil pan-to-engine bolts, by reversing the removal sequence, to 4.6–6.1 ft. lbs. (6.3–8.3 Nm).

12. Install the exhaust pipe connection.

13. Install the center crossmember. Torque the center crossmember-to-chassis nuts/bolts to 57–72 ft. lbs. (77–98 Nm) and engine mount-to-crossmember nuts/bolts to 57–72 ft. lbs. (77–98 Nm).

14. Install the under covers to the engine. After 30 minutes of gasket curing time, refill the oil pan with the specified quantity of clean oil. Operate the engine and check for leaks.

Oil Pump

REMOVAL

VG30E Engine

▶ SEE FIG. 133

1. Remove all accessory drive belts and the alternator.

2. Remove the timing (cam) belt covers and remove the timing belt.

3. Unbolt the engine from its mounts and raise the engine up from the unibody.

4. Drain the engine oil and remove the oil pan.

5. Remove the oil pump assembly-to-engine bolts, along with the oil strainer, and remove the assembly from the engine.

VE30DE Engine

▶ SEE FIG. 134

The oil pump is an integral part of the front cover.

2. Remove the cylinder heads.

3. Unbolt the engine from its mounts and raise the engine up from the unibody.

4. Remove the crankshaft damper-to-crankshaft bolt and the damper.

5. Drain the engine oil and remove the oil pan.

6. Remove the oil strainer-to-engine bolt, oil strainer-to-oil pump bolts and the strainer.

7. Remove the front cover-to-engine bolts and the front cover.

8. Remove the oil pump assembly-to-engine bolts, along with the oil strainer, and remove the assembly from the engine.

9. Clean the gasket mating surfaces.

INSPECTION

VG30E Engine

▶ SEE FIGS. 135–137

1. Using a feeler gauge, check the following clearances:

Body-to-outer gear — 0.0043–0.0079 in. (0.11–0.20mm)

Inner gear-to-crescent — 0.0047–0.0091 in. (0.12–0.23mm)

Outer gear-to-crescent — 0.0083–0.0126 in. (0.21–0.32mm)

Housing-to-inner gear — 0.0020–0.0035 in. (0.05–0.09mm)

Housing-to-outer gear — 0.0020–0.0043 in. (0.05–0.11mm)

outer gear — 0.0020–0.0043 in. (0.05–0.11mm)

2. If any clearances are exceeded, replace the gear set or the entire oil pump assembly.

3. Inspect the regulator valve by performing the following procedures:

a. Check the regulator valve components for wear and/or damage.

b. Check the valve's sliding surface and valve spring.

c. Lubricate the regulator valve with engine oil and make sure it falls smoothly into the valve hole by it's own weight.

d. If damaged, replace the regulator valve set or the oil pump assembly.

4. Inspect the oil pressure relief valve by performing the following procedures:

a. Push the oil pressure relief valve ball and check for movement, cracks and breaks.

b. If replacement is necessary, pry the valve from the housing and install a new valve by tapping it into place.

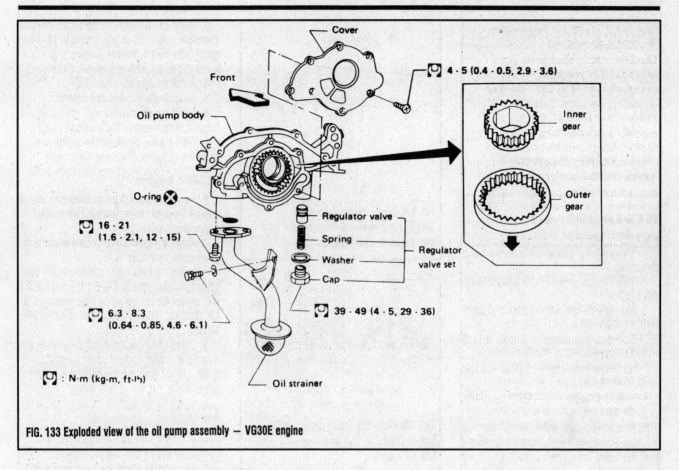

FIG. 133 Exploded view of the oil pump assembly — VG30E engine

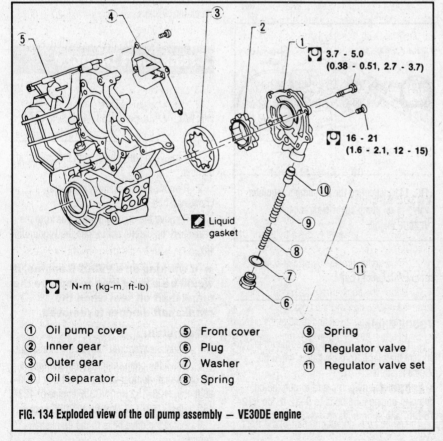

(1) Oil pump cover
(2) Inner gear
(3) Outer gear
(4) Oil separator
(5) Front cover
(6) Plug
(7) Washer
(8) Spring
(9) Spring
(10) Regulator valve
(11) Regulator valve set

FIG. 134 Exploded view of the oil pump assembly — VE30DE engine

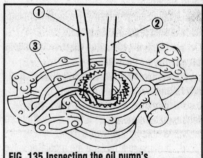

FIG. 135 Inspecting the oil pump's body-to-outer gear, inner gear-to-crescent and outer gear-to-crescent clearances — VG30E engine

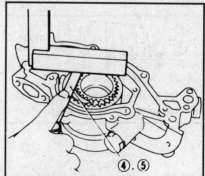

FIG. 136 Inspecting the oil pump's housing-to-inner gear and housing-to-outer gear clearances — VG30E engine

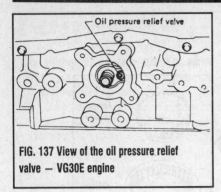

FIG. 137 View of the oil pressure relief valve — VG30E engine

VE30DE Engine

♦ SEE FIGS. 138–141

1. Using a feeler gauge, check the following clearances:

Body-to-outer gear — 0.0043–0.0079 in. (0.11–0.20mm)

Inner gear-to-crescent — 0.0047–0.0091 in. (0.12–0.23mm)

Outer gear-to-crescent — 0.0083–0.0126 in. (0.21–0.32mm)

Housing-to-inner gear — 0.0020–0.0035 in. (0.05–0.09mm)

Housing-to-outer gear — 0.0020–0.0043 in. (0.05–0.11mm)

2. If the inner gear-to-outer gear tip clearance is exceeded, replace the gear set; if any other gear clearances are exceeded, replace the front cover assembly.

3. Inspect the regulator valve by performing the following procedures:

a. Check the regulator valve components for wear and/or damage.

b. Check the valve's sliding surface and valve spring.

c. Lubricate the regulator valve with engine oil and make sure it falls smoothly into the valve hole by it's own weight.

d. If damaged, replace the regulator valve set or the oil pump assembly.

e. Using micrometers, check the regulator valve-to-oil pump cover clearance; the clearance should be 0.0016–0.0038 in. (0.040–0.097mm).

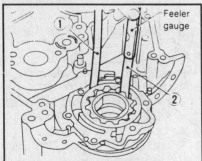

FIG. 138 Inspecting the oil pump's body-to-outer gear and inner gear-to-outer gear tip clearances — VE30DE engine

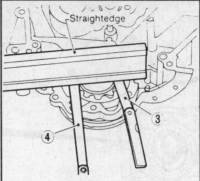

FIG. 139 Inspecting the oil pump's body-to-inner gear and body-to-outer gear clearances — VE30DE engine

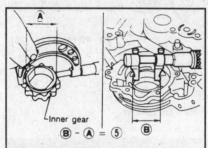

FIG. 140 Inspecting the oil pump's inner gear-to-brazed portion clearance — VE30DE engine

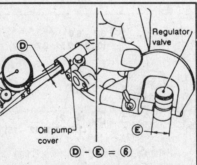

FIG. 141 Inspecting the oil pump's regulator valve-to-oil pump cover clearance — VE30DE engine

INSTALLATION

VG30E Engine

1. Pack the oil pump full of petroleum jelly to prevent the pump from cavitating when the engine is started.

2. Install the oil pump and torque the oil pump-to-engine long bolts to 9–12 ft. lbs. (12–16 Nm) and short bolts to 4.3–5.1 ft. lbs. (6–7 Nm).

3. Using a new O-ring, install the strainer and torque the strainer-to-oil pump bolts to 12–15 ft. lbs. (16–21 Nm) and the strainer-to-engine bolt to 4.6–6.1 ft. lbs. (6.3–8.3 Nm).

4. Install the oil pan.

5. Install the timing belt and covers.

6. Install the alternator and all drive belts. Reconnect the negative battery cable.

7. Start engine, check ignition timing and check for oil leaks.

VE30DE Engine

1. Pack the oil pump full of petroleum jelly to prevent the pump from cavitating when the engine is started.

2. Apply a bead of liquid sealant to the front cover mating surfaces.

3. Install the front cover and torque the front cover-to-engine bolts to 4.6–6.1 ft. lbs. (6.3–8.3 Nm) except for bolt above oil filter housing and 12–15 ft. lbs. (16–21 Nm) for bolt above oil filter housing.

4. Using a new gasket, install the strainer and torque the strainer-to-front cover bolts to 12–15 ft. lbs. (16–21 Nm) and the strainer-to-engine bolt to 4.6–6.1 ft. lbs. (6.3–8.3 Nm).

5. Install the oil pan.

6. Install the cylinder heads.

7. Install the alternator and all drive belts. Reconnect the negative battery cable.

8. Start engine, check ignition timing and check for oil leaks.

Crankshaft Damper

REMOVAL & INSTALLATION

1. Remove the drive belts from the crankshaft damper.

2. Remove the crankshaft damper-to-crankshaft bolt.

3. Remove the crankshaft damper from the crankshaft; be careful not to lose the Woodruff® key.

➡ **If working on a VE30DE engine, it would be a good idea to replace the crankshaft oil seal when the crankshaft damper is removed.**

To install:

4. Install the Woodruff® key to the crankshaft.

5. Install the crankshaft damper and torque the crankshaft damper-to-crankshaft bolt to 90–98 ft. lbs. (123–132 Nm) VG30E engine or 123–130 ft. lbs. (167–177 Nm) for VE30DE engine.

6. Install the drive belts to the crankshaft damper.

Timing Belt Cover and Seal

REMOVAL & INSTALLATION

VG30E Engine

1. Raise vehicle and safely support.

2. Remove the engine under covers and drain engine coolant from the radiator; be careful not to allow coolant to contact drive belts.

3. Remove the front right side wheel and tire assembly. Remove the engine side cover.

4. Remove the engine coolant reservoir tank and radiator hoses.

5. Remove the A.S.C.D. (speed control device) actuator.

6. Remove all the drive belts from the engine. When removing the power steering drive belt, loosen the idler pulley from the right side wheel housing.

7. Remove the idler bracket of the compressor drive belt.

8. Remove the crankshaft damper and the Woodruff® key. Remove the timing belt covers.

9. Using a prybar, pry the oil seal from the oil pump; be careful not to scratch the crankshaft or oil pump housing sealing surface.

To install:

10. Using a new oil seal, lubricate it with engine oil, and press it into the oil pump housing; be careful not to tear the sealing lip.

11. Install lower and upper timing belt covers.

12. Install crankshaft damper and idler bracket of the compressor drive belt. Tighten the crankshaft pulley bolt to 90–98 ft. lbs. (123–132 Nm).

13. Install the drive belts. Clean and regap the spark plugs, if necessary, then install in the cylinder head.

14. Install the coolant reservoir tank, radiator hoses, A.S.C.D. actutator.

15. Install the right front wheel. Install engine under cover and side covers.

16. Refill the cooling system. Check ignition timing and road test for proper operation.

Timing Chain Cover and Seal

REMOVAL & INSTALLATION

VE30DE Engine

The timing chain (front) cover is an integral part of the oil pump housing.

1. Refer to the "Oil Pump, Removal and Installation" procedures and remove the timing chain cover.

2. Using a small prybar, pry the oil seal from the timing chain cover; be careful not to scratch the timing chain cover sealing surface.

3. Using a new oil seal, lubricate it with engine oil and press it into the timing chain cover.

4. Install the timing chain cover; be careful not to tear the oil seal's sealing lip on the crankshaft.

Timing Belt

REMOVAL & INSTALLATION

VG30E Engine

♦ SEE FIGS. 142 AND 143

1985–87

1. Raise and safely support the vehicle.

2. Remove the engine under covers and drain engine coolant from the radiator; be careful not to allow coolant to contact drive belts.

3. Remove the front right side wheel and tire assembly. Remove the engine side cover.

4. From the right side of the vehicle, remove the following items:

   a. The injector cooling fan duct for 1985–86 models.

   b. The engine coolant reservoir tank and radiator hoses.

   c. The A.S.C.D. (speed control device) actuator.

5. Remove all the drive belts from the engine. When removing the power steering drive belt, loosen the idler pulley from the right side wheel housing.

6. Rotate the crankshaft to position the No. 1 cylinder at the TDC of it's compression stroke.

7. Remove the idler bracket of the compressor drive belt and crankshaft pulley.

8. Remove the timing belt covers.

➡ **Make sure the punch marks on the camshaft sprockets align with the punch marks on the rear timing belt cover and the punch mark on the crankshaft sprocket aligns with the punch mark on the oil pump.**

9. Loosen the timing belt idler pulley bolt. Using a hexagon wrench, rotate the idler pulley to release it's tension on the timing belt and tighten the idler pulley bolt.

10. Remove the rocker covers. Loosen the rocker shaft securing bolts so rockers will no longer bear on the cam lobes. Remove all spark plugs.

11. Remove the timing belt.

➡ **Be careful not to bend the new belt installing it. Timing belts are designed to flex only the way they turn around the pulleys.**

To install:

➡ **After removing timing belt, do not rotate crankshaft and camshaft separately, because valves will hit piston heads.**

12. Make sure all pulleys and the belt are free of oil and water. Install the timing belt, aligning the arrow on the timing belt forward. Align the white lines on the timing belt with the punch marks on all 3 pulleys.

13. Loosen the tensioner locknut to allow spring tension to tension the belt. Then, using the hexagon wrench, turn the tensioner first clockwise, then counterclockwise in 2–3 cycles. This will seat the belt. Now, torque the tensioner locknut to 32–43 ft. lbs. (43–58 Nm).

14. Tighten rocker shaft bolts alternately in 3 stages. Before tightening each pair of bolts, turn the engine over so the affected rocker will not touch its cam lobe. Final torque is 13–16 ft. lbs. (18–22 Nm). Install the rocker covers.

15. Install lower and upper timing belt covers.

16. Install crankshaft pulley and idler bracket of the compressor drive belt. Tighten the crankshaft pulley bolt to 90–98 ft. lbs. (123–132 Nm).

17. Install the drive belts. Clean and regap the spark plugs, if necessary, then install in the cylinder head.

18. Install the coolant reservoir tank, radiator hoses, A.S.C.D. actuator. Install the injector cooling fan duct for 1985–86 models.

19. Install the right front wheel. Install engine under cover and side covers.

20. Refill the cooling system. Check ignition timing and road test for proper operation.

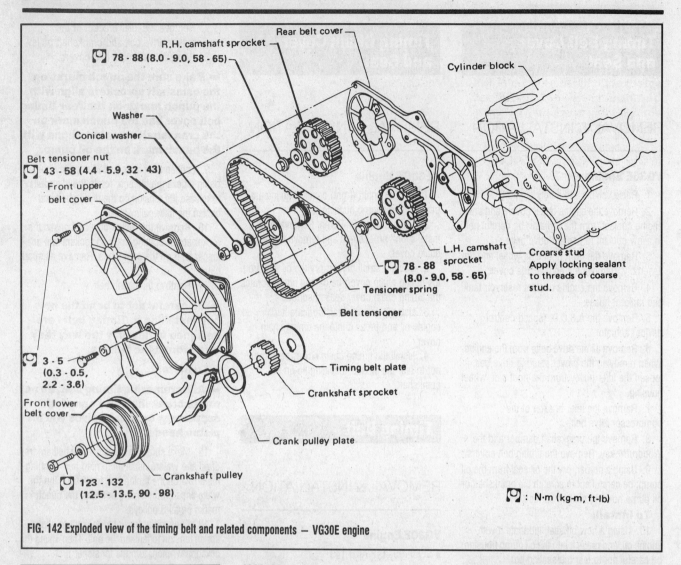

R.H. camshaft sprocket
🔧 78 - 88 (8.0 - 9.0, 58 - 65)

Rear belt cover

Cylinder block

Washer

Conical washer

Belt tensioner nut
🔧 43 - 58 (4.4 - 5.9, 32 - 43)

Front upper belt cover

L.H. camshaft sprocket
🔧 78 - 88 (8.0 - 9.0, 58 - 65)

Coarse stud
Apply locking sealant to threads of coarse stud.

Tensioner spring

Belt tensioner

🔧 3 - 5 (0.3 - 0.5, 2.2 - 3.6)

Timing belt plate

Crankshaft sprocket

Front lower belt cover

Crank pulley plate

Crankshaft pulley
🔧 123 - 132 (12.5 - 13.5, 90 - 98)

🔧 : N·m (kg-m, ft-lb)

FIG. 142 Exploded view of the timing belt and related components — VG30E engine

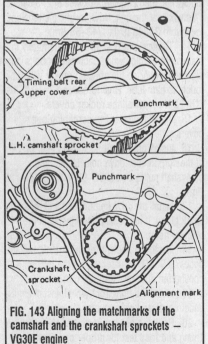

Timing belt rear upper cover

Punchmark

L.H. camshaft sprocket

Punchmark

Crankshaft sprocket

Alignment mark

FIG. 143 Aligning the matchmarks of the camshaft and the crankshaft sprockets — VG30E engine

1988–92

▶ SEE FIGS. 144 AND 145

1. Raise and safely support the vehicle.

2. Remove the engine under covers and drain engine coolant from the radiator; be careful not to allow coolant to contact drive belts.

3. Remove the front right side wheel and tire assembly. Remove the engine side cover.

4. Remove all the drive belts from the engine.

5. Rotate the crankshaft to position the No. 1 cylinder at the TDC of it's compression stroke.

6. Remove the upper radiator hose and the water inlet hose. Remove the water pump pulley.

7. Remove the idler bracket of the compressor drive belt and crankshaft pulley.

8. Remove the upper and lower timing belt covers.

➡ **Make sure the punch marks on the camshaft sprockets align with the punch marks on the rear timing belt cover and the punch mark on the crankshaft sprocket aligns with the punch mark on the oil pump.**

9. Loosen the timing belt idler pulley bolt. Using a hexagon wrench, rotate the idler pulley to release it's tension and remove the timing belt.

➡ **Be careful not to bend the new belt installing it. Timing belts are designed to flex only the way they turn around the pulleys.**

To install:

➡ **After removing timing belt, do not rotate crankshaft and camshaft separately, because valves will hit piston heads.**

10. Confirm that No. 1 cylinder is at TDC on its compression stroke. Install tensioner and tensioner spring. If stud is removed apply locking sealant to threads before installing.

11. Swing tensioner fully clockwise with hexagon wrench and temporarily tighten locknut.

12. Set timing belt, align the arrow on the timing belt forward. Align the white lines on the timing belt with the punch marks on all 3 pulleys.

➡ **There are 133 total timing belt teeth. If timing belt is installed correctly there will be 40 teeth between left and right camshaft sprocket timing marks. There will be 43 teeth between left camshaft sprocket and crankshaft sprocket timing marks.**

13. Loosen tensioner locknut, keeping tensioner steady with a hexagon wrench.

14. Swing tensioner 70–80° clockwise with hexagon wrench and temporarily tighten locknut.

15. Install all the spark plugs. Turn crankshaft clockwise 2–3 times, then slowly set No. 1 cylinder at TDC on its compression stroke.

16. Push middle of timing belt between right camshaft sprocket and tensioner pulley with a force of 22 lbs. (98 N).

17. Loosen tensioner locknut, keeping tensioner steady with a hexagon wrench.

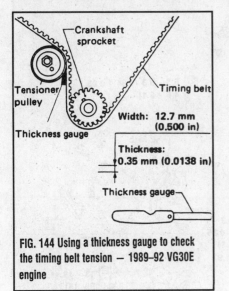

FIG. 144 Using a thickness gauge to check the timing belt tension — 1989–92 VG30E engine

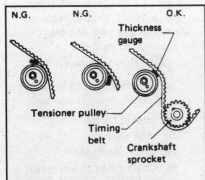

FIG. 145 Positioning the thickness gauge correctly to adjust the timing belt tension — VG30E engine

18. Using a feeler gauge or equivalent, which is 0.0138 in. (0.35mm) thick and 0.500 in. (13mm) wide, set gauge at the bottom of tensioner pulley and timing belt. Turn crankshaft clockwise and position the gauge completely between tensioner pulley and timing belt. The timing belt will move about 2.5 teeth.

19. Tighten tensioner locknut, keeping tensioner steady with a hexagon wrench.

20. Turn crankshaft clockwise or counterclockwise and remove the gauge.

21. Rotate the engine 3 times, then set No. 1 at TDC on its compression stroke.

22. Check timing belt deflection on 1988 model year only. Timing belt deflection is 13.0–14.5mm at 22 lbs. of pressure. If it is out of specified range, readjust the timing belt.

Timing Chain

REMOVAL & INSTALLATION

VE30DE Engine

◆ SEE FIGS. 146-159

1. Release the fuel system pressure. Disconnect the negative battery cable.

2. Raise and safely support the vehicle. Remove the under covers from the vehicle.

3. Remove the front right wheel and engine side cover.

4. Drain the cooling system by removing the engine drain plugs and opening the radiator drain cock.

5. Remove the radiator.

6. Remove the air duct from the intake manifold.

7. Remove the blow-by pipe.

8. Remove the vacuum hoses, the fuel lines, electrical connectors and etc., that may be in the way.

9. From the right rear of the engine, remove the EGR valve-to-exhaust manifold tube.

10. Remove the intake manifold collector supports.

11. Remove the following hoses:
   • Pressure regulator vacuum hose
   • Throttle chamber water hoses
   • Canister purge hose
   • Blow-by hose

12. Remove the intake manifold collector.

13. Remove the ignition coils and the spark plugs.

14. Remove the IAA unit and heater pipe. Remove the fuel injector rail assembly.

15. From the front of the intake manifold, remove the right VTC solenoid valve.

16. Remove the intake manifold.

17. Remove the drive belts, the air conditioning compressor and the alternator.

18. Remove the air conditioning compressor bracket and the alternator bracket.

19. Remove the idler pulley bracket and the dipstick tube.

20. Remove the left exhaust manifold. Remove the power steering pump and it's bracket.

21. Remove the right exhaust manifold. Remove the rocker arm covers.

22. Working between the intake and exhaust camshafts, of each cylinder head, remove the upper timing chain guides.

23. Rotate the crankshaft to position the No. 1 cylinder on TDC of it's compression stroke.

24. Remove the crank angle sensor. Remove the timing chain tensioners from each upper timing chain.

25. Using a backup wrench to secure the intake camshaft, remove the intake camshaft sprocket-to-camshaft bolts, the VTC assemblies and the intake camshaft sprockets.

26. Remove the both cylinder heads. Remove the water pipe.

27. Remove the water pump pulley and the water pump.

28. Remove the oil pan, the crankshaft pulley, the oil strainer and the oil filter bracket.

29. Remove the front cover, the alternator adjusting bar and the upper timing chains.

30. Remove the lower timing chain guides, the idler sprockets and the lower timing chain.

31. Inspect the timing chains for cracks and/or excessive wear at the roller links; if necessary, replace the timing chain(s).

To install:

31. Install the crankshaft sprocket on the crankshaft.

32. Make sure the No. 1 cylinder is at the TDC of it's compression stroke.

33. Install the right idler sprocket and timing chain guides.

34. Position the lower timing chain on the right idler sprocket by aligning the mating mark on the right idler sprocket with the silver mating mark on the lower timing chain.

35. Install the left idler sprocket with the lower timing chain; align the mating marks on the lower timing chain with the mating marks on the left idler sprocket and crankshaft sprocket. Install the chain guide and the chain tensioner.

36. Position the upper timing chains on the idler sprockets by aligning the mating marks on the idler sprockets with the gold mating marks on the upper timing chains.

37. Install the oil pump drive spacer, the front cover and the alternator adjusting bar by performing the following procedures:

   a. Remove all traces of sealant from the mating surfaces of the front cover and the engine block.

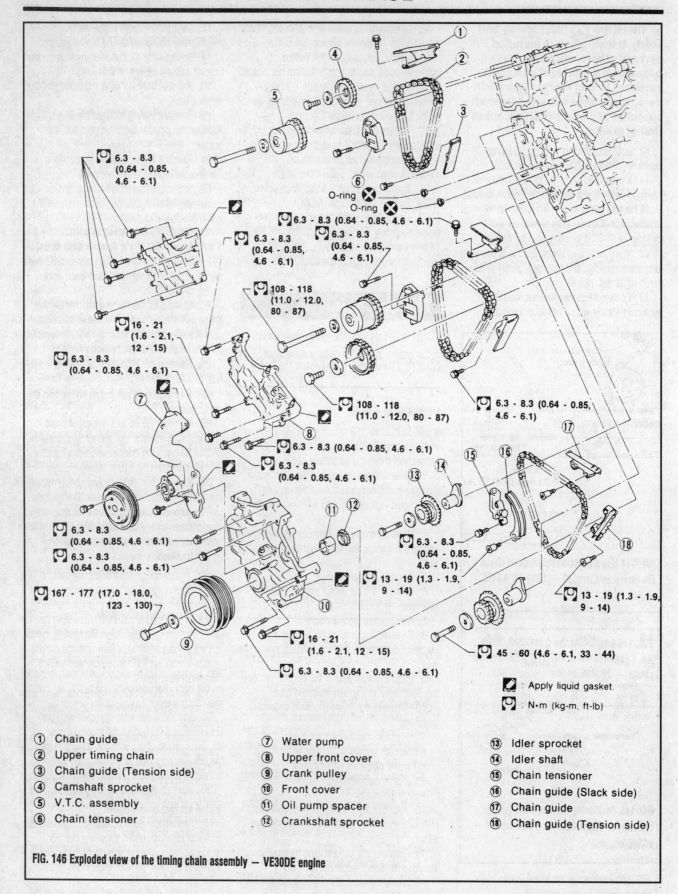

6.3 - 8.3 (0.64 - 0.85, 4.6 - 6.1)

6.3 - 8.3 (0.64 - 0.85, 4.6 - 6.1)

O-ring

O-ring

6.3 - 8.3 (0.64 - 0.85, 4.6 - 6.1)

6.3 - 8.3 (0.64 - 0.85, 4.6 - 6.1)

108 - 118 (11.0 - 12.0, 80 - 87)

16 - 21 (1.6 - 2.1, 12 - 15)

6.3 - 8.3 (0.64 - 0.85, 4.6 - 6.1)

108 - 118 (11.0 - 12.0, 80 - 87)

6.3 - 8.3 (0.64 - 0.85, 4.6 - 6.1)

6.3 - 8.3 (0.64 - 0.85, 4.6 - 6.1)

6.3 - 8.3 (0.64 - 0.85, 4.6 - 6.1)

6.3 - 8.3 (0.64 - 0.85, 4.6 - 6.1)

13 - 19 (1.3 - 1.9, 9 - 14)

167 - 177 (17.0 - 18.0, 123 - 130)

16 - 21 (1.6 - 2.1, 12 - 15)

6.3 - 8.3 (0.64 - 0.85, 4.6 - 6.1)

45 - 60 (4.6 - 6.1, 33 - 44)

13 - 19 (1.3 - 1.9, 9 - 14)

: Apply liquid gasket.

: N•m (kg-m, ft-lb)

① Chain guide
② Upper timing chain
③ Chain guide (Tension side)
④ Camshaft sprocket
⑤ V.T.C. assembly
⑥ Chain tensioner

⑦ Water pump
⑧ Upper front cover
⑨ Crank pulley
⑩ Front cover
⑪ Oil pump spacer
⑫ Crankshaft sprocket

⑬ Idler sprocket
⑭ Idler shaft
⑮ Chain tensioner
⑯ Chain guide (Slack side)
⑰ Chain guide
⑱ Chain guide (Tension side)

FIG. 146 Exploded view of the timing chain assembly — VE30DE engine

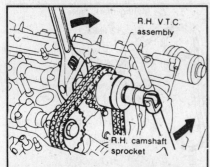

FIG. 147 Removing the camshaft sprocket and the VTC assembly — VE30DE engine

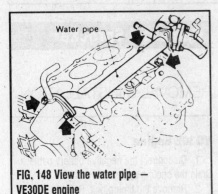

FIG. 148 View the water pipe — VE30DE engine

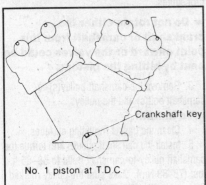

FIG. 149 Positioning the crankshaft of the No. 1 piston is set at TDC of it's compression stroke — VE30DE engine

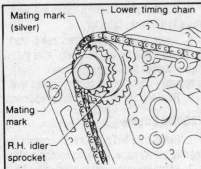

FIG. 150 Positioning the lower timing chain on the right side idler sprocket — VE30DE engine

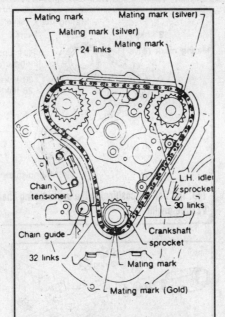

FIG. 151 Positioning the lower timing chain on the idler sprockets and the crankshaft sprocket — VE30DE engine

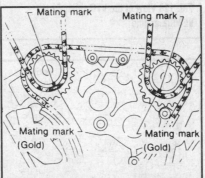

FIG. 152 Positioning the upper timing chains on the idler sprockets — VE30DE engine

b. Using liquid sealant, apply a continuous bead to the mating surface of the front cover.

c. Wipe excessive sealant from the cylinder head mounting surfaces.

38. Install the oil filter bracket, the oil strainer, the crankshaft pulley and the oil pan.

39. Make sure the No. 1 cylinder is on the TDC of it's compression stroke.

40. Install the water pump by performing the following procedures:

a. Remove all traces of sealant from the mating surface of the water pump.

b. Remove all traces of sealant from the mating surface of the engine.

c. Using liquid sealant, apply a continuous bead to the mating surface of the water pump.

41. Install the water pump pulley. Install the water pipe by performing the following procedures:

a. Torque bolt **a** and **b** finger-tight.

b. Torque bolt **c** to 12–15 ft. lbs. (16–21 Nm).

c. Torque bolt **a** to 2.2–6.5 ft. lbs. (3–9 Nm).

d. Torque bolt **b** to 12–15 ft. lbs. (16–21 Nm).

e. Torque bolt **a** to 12–15 ft. lbs. (16–21 Nm).

42. Rotate the crankshaft counterclockwise, until the No. 1 piston is set at approx. 120° before TDC on the compression stroke, to prevent interference of the valves and pistons.

43. Install the cylinder heads.

44. Install the camshafts, the camshaft brackets and the rocker arms. Position the right side exhaust camshaft at about 10 o'clock position and the left side exhaust camshaft at about 12 o'clock position.

45. Install the right side VTC assembly and the right camshaft sprocket. Align the mating marks on the right upper timing chain with the mating marks on the right VTC assembly and the right camshaft sprocket.

46. Install the right timing chain tensioner. Before installing the chain tensioner, press-in sleeve until the hook can be engaged on the pin; make sure the hook used to retain the chain tensioner is released.

➡ **There are 2 types of chain tensioners; be careful not to install the left chain tensioner onto the right cylinder head.**

47. Rotate the crankshaft clockwise to set the No. 1 piston at the TDC of it's compression stroke.

48. Install the left side VTC assembly and the left camshaft sprocket. Align the mating marks on the left upper timing chain with the mating marks on the left VTC assembly and the left camshaft sprocket.

49. Install the left chain tensioner; make sure the upper timing chains are in the correct positions.

50. Install the crank angle sensor; make sure the position of the camshaft and rotor position of the crank angle sensor are aligned.

51. Install the upper front covers. Install the upper chain guides on both cylinder heads. Install the rocker arm covers.

52. Install any parts removed in the reverse order of removal. When installing the VTC solenoid valve, always use new O-rings and lubricate the O-rings with engine oil.

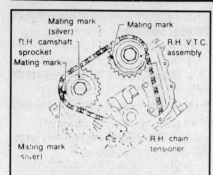

FIG. 153 Positioning the right upper timing chain with the mating marks on the right VTC assembly and the right camshaft sprocket — VE30DE engine

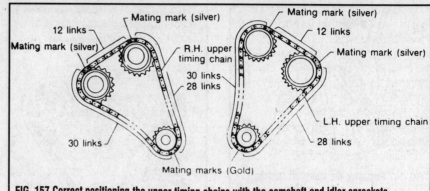

FIG. 157 Correct positioning the upper timing chains with the camshaft and idler sprockets — VE30DE engine

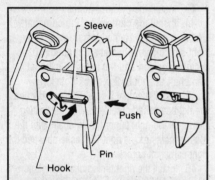

FIG. 154 View of the pin positions on the upper timing chain tensioners — VE30DE engine

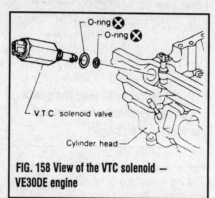

FIG. 158 View of the VTC solenoid — VE30DE engine

Camshaft Sprocket

REMOVAL & INSTALLATION

VG30E Engine

1. Disconnect the negative battery cable. Drain the cooling system.
2. Remove the timing belt. Refer to the Timing Belt, Removal and Installation procedures.

➡ **Do not rotate either the crankshaft or camshaft from this point onward or the valves could be bent by hitting the pistons.**

3. Remove the camshaft pulley(s)-to-camshaft bolt(s) and the pulleys.
   To install:
4. Clean the gasket mounting surfaces.
5. Install the camshaft pulleys and torque the camshaft pulley-to-camshaft bolts to 58–65 ft. lbs. (78–88 Nm). Make sure the pulley marked R3 goes on the right and that marked L3 goes on the left.
6. Align the timing marks, if necessary, and then install the timing belt and adjust the belt tension.
7. Connect all the vacuum hoses and water hoses to the intake collector.
8. Connect the negative battery cable. Start the engine check the engine timing. After the engine reaches the normal operating temperature check for the correct coolant level.
9. Road test the vehicle for proper operation.

VE30DE Engine

1. Release the fuel pressure. Disconnect the negative battery cable. Drain the cooling system.
2. Rotate the crankshaft to position the No. 1 piston on TDC of it's compression stroke.

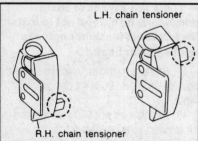

FIG. 155 View of the right and left upper timing chain tensioners — VE30DE engine

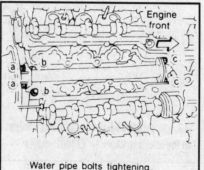

Water pipe bolts tightening procedure
1) Tighten a and b bolts to finger tight
2) Tighten c bolts to 16 to 21 N·m (1.6 to 2.1 kg-m. 12 to 15 ft-lb)
3) Tighten a bolts to 3 to 9 N·m (0.3 to 0.9 kg-m. 2.2 to 6.5 ft-lb)
4) Tighten b bolts to 16 to 21 N·m (1.6 to 2.1 kg-m. 12 to 15 ft-lb)
3) Tighten a bolts to 16 to 21 N·m (1.6 to 2.1 kg-m. 12 to 15 ft-lb)

FIG. 159 View of the water pipe and torque procedure — VE30DE engine

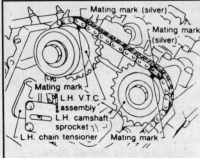

FIG. 156 Positioning the upper left timing chain with the mating marks on the left VTC assembly and the left camshaft sprocket — VE30DE engine

3. Disconnect all the electrical connectors, vacuum hoses and water hoses connected to the intake manifold collector.

4. The crank angle sensor is located in the rear of the left cylinder head, mark it's position, disconnect the electrical connector from it and remove it.

5. Remove the intake manifold collector. Refer to the section Intake Manifold Removal and Installation for correct bolt removal sequence.

6. Remove the upper timing chain(s). Refer to the Timing Chain, Removal and Installation procedures.

➡ **Do not rotate either the crankshaft or camshaft from this point onward or the valves could be bent by hitting the pistons.**

7. Remove the camshaft sprockets-to-camshafts bolts and the camshaft sprockets.

To install:

8. Clean the gasket mounting surfaces.

9. Position the right exhaust camshaft key at about 10 o'clock position and the left camshaft key at about 12 o'clock position.

10. Install the upper timing chains and sprockets; torque the timing chain sprocket-to-camshaft bolts to 80–87 ft. lbs. (108–118 Nm).

11. Install the intake manifold collector.

12. Align and install the crank angle sensor to the rear of the left cylinder head, connect the electrical connector to it.

13. Connect all the electrical connectors, vacuum hoses and water hoses to the intake manifold collector. Refill the cooling system.

14. Connect the negative battery cable. Start the engine check the engine timing. After the engine reaches the normal operating temperature check for the correct coolant level.

15. Road test the vehicle for proper operation.

Camshaft and Bearings

REMOVAL & INSTALLATION

VG30E Engine

1. Remove the timing belt. Refer to the Timing Belt Removal and Installation procedure.

2. Drain the coolant by removing drain plug on the cylinder block.

3. Remove the collector assembly and intake manifold. Refer to Intake Manifold Removal and Installation procedure.

4. Remove the cylinder head from the engine. Refer to Cylinder Head Removal and Installation.

5. With cylinder head mounted on a suitable workbench, remove the rocker shafts with rocker arms. Bolts should be loosened in 2–3 steps.

6. Remove hydraulic valve lifters and lifter guide.

7. Hold hydraulic valve lifters with wire so they will not drop from lifter guide.

8. Remove the camshaft front oil seal and slide camshaft out the front of the cylinder head assembly.

To install:

9. Install camshaft, locate plate, cylinder head rear cover and front oil seal. Set camshaft knock pin at 12:00 o'clock position. Install cylinder head with new gasket to engine. Refer to the Cylinder Head Removal and Installation procedure.

10. Install valve lifter guide assembly. Assemble valve lifters in their original position. After installing them in the correct location remove the wire holding them in lifter guide.

11. Install rocker shafts in correct position with rocker arms. Tighten bolts in 2–3 stages to 13–16 ft. lbs. Before tightening, be sure to set camshaft lobe at the position where lobe is not lifted or the valve closed. You can set each cylinder one at a time or follow the procedure below (timing belt must be installed in the correct position):

a. Set No. 1 piston at TDC on its compression stroke and tighten rocker shaft bolts for No. 2, No. 4 and No. 6 cylinders.

b. Set No. 4 piston at TDC on its compression stroke and tighten rocker shaft bolts for No. 1, No. 3 and No. 5 cylinders.

c. Torque specification for the rocker shaft retaining bolts is 13–16 ft. lbs.

12. Install the intake manifold and collector assembly. Refer to Intake Manifold Removal and Installation procedure.

13. Install rear timing belt cover and camshaft sprocket. The left and right camshaft sprockets are different parts. Install the correct sprocket in the correct position.

14. Install the timing belt. Refer to Timing Belt Removal and Installation procedure.

INSPECTION

◆ SEE FIGS. 160-165

VG30E Engine

1. Visually check the camshaft for scratches, seizures and/or wear; if necessary, replace the camshaft.

2. To check the camshaft runout, perform the following procedures:

a. Position camshaft in a set of "V" blocks.

b. Mount a dial indicator so it contacts the camshaft at a 90° angle to the bearing surfaces.

➡ **Engine specialists and most machine shops are equipment with the testing equipment.**

c. Measure the cam bearing journal runout. The maximum (limit) runout is 0.004 in. (0.01mm). If the runout exceeds the limit replace the camshaft.

3. To check the camshaft lobe height, use a micrometer to check cam (lobe) height, making

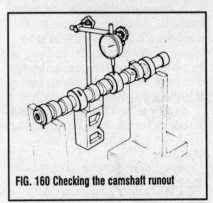

FIG. 160 Checking the camshaft runout

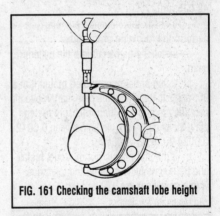

FIG. 161 Checking the camshaft lobe height

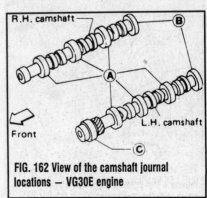

FIG. 162 View of the camshaft journal locations — VG30E engine

sure the anvil and the spindle of the micrometer are positioned directly on the heel and tip of the cam lobe.

• Standard cam height — 1.5566–1.5641 in. (39.537–39.727mm)

• Cam wear limit — 0.0059 in. (0.15mm)

4. To check the camshaft journals and bearing saddles, perform the following procedures:

a. Using a micrometer, measure the camshaft bearing journals:

• A — 1.8472–1.8480 in. (46.920–46.940mm)

• B — 1.6701–1.6709 in. (42.420–42.440mm)

• C — 1.8866–1.8874 in. (47.920–47.940mm)

b. If the measurements are less than the limits listed, the camshaft will have to be replaced, since the camshafts in all of the engines covered in this guide run directly on the cylinder head surface; no actual bearings or bushings are used, so no oversize bearings or bushings are available.

c. Using an internal micrometer, measure the cylinder head camshaft bearing journals:

• A — 1.8504–1.8514 in. (47.000–47.025mm)

• B — 1.6732–1.6742 in. (42.500–42.525mm)

• C — 1.8898–1.8907 in. (48.000–48.025mm)

5. To check the camshaft end play, perform the following procedures:

a. Install the camshaft into the cylinder head.

b. Using a dial micrometer, mount it at a 90° angle to the end of the camshaft. Move the camshaft in and out, then, measure the end play; the end play should be between 0.0012–0.0024 in. (0.03–0.06mm).

c. If the end play is out of range, install another locate plate to bring the tolerance within specifications.

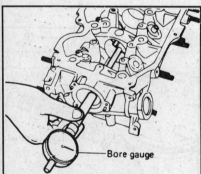

FIG. 163 Using an internal micrometer to measure the cylinder head camshaft journals — VG30E engine — VE30DE engine is similar

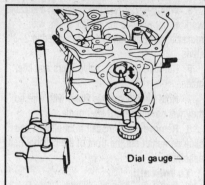

FIG. 164 Checking the camshaft end play — VG30E engine — VE30DE engine is similar

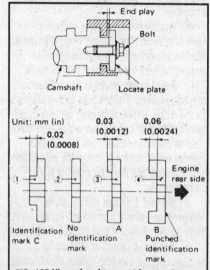

FIG. 165 View of replacement locate plates to adjust end play — VG30E engine

VE30DE Engine

1. Visually check the camshaft for scratches, seizures and/or wear; if necessary, replace the camshaft.

2. To check the camshaft runout, perform the following procedures:

a. Position camshaft in a set of "V" blocks.

b. Mount a dial indicator so it contacts the camshaft at a 90° angle to the bearing surfaces.

➡ **Engine specialists and most machine shops are equipment with the testing equipment.**

c. Measure the cam bearing journal runout. The maximum (limit) runout is 0.002 in. (0.05mm). If the runout exceeds the limit replace the camshaft.

3. To check the camshaft lobe height, use a micrometer to check cam (lobe) height, making sure the anvil and the spindle of the micrometer

are positioned directly on the heel and tip of the cam lobe.

Standard camheight — 1.4834–1.4909 in. (37.678–37.686mm)

Cam wear limit — 0.002 in. (0.05mm)

4. To check the camshaft journals and bearing saddles, perform the following procedures:

a. Using a micrometer, measure the camshaft bearing journals; it should be 1.0211–1.0218 in. (25.935–25.955mm).

b. If the measurements are less than the limits listed, the camshaft will have to be replaced, since the camshafts in all of the engines covered in this guide run directly on the cylinder head surface; no actual bearings or bushings are used, so no oversize bearings or bushings are available.

c. Using an internal micrometer, measure the cylinder head camshaft bearing journals; it should be 1.4834–1.4909 in. (37.678–37.868mm)

5. To check the camshaft end play, perform the following procedures:

a. Install the camshaft into the cylinder head.

b. Using a dial micrometer, mount it at a 90° angle to the end of the camshaft. Move the camshaft in and out, then, measure the end play; the end play should be between 0.0028–0.0058 in. (0.070–0.148mm).

c. If the end play is beyond 0.0079 in. (0.20mm), replace the camshaft.

Pistons and Connecting Rods

REMOVAL

◆ SEE FIGS. 166-168

1. Remove the engine and place it on a work stand.

2. Remove the cylinder head and the oil pan.

3. Remove any carbon buildup from the cylinder wall at the top end of the piston travel with a ridge reamer tool.

4. Position the piston to be removed at the bottom of its stroke so the connecting rod bearing cap can be reached easily from under the engine.

5. Remove the connecting rod bearing cap nuts and remove the cap and lower half of the bearing. Cover the rod bolts with lengths of rubber tubing or hose to protect the cylinder walls when the rod and piston assembly is driven out.

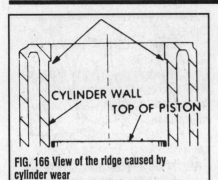

FIG. 166 View of the ridge caused by cylinder wear

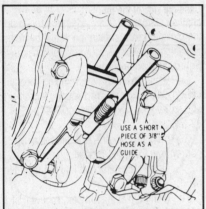

FIG. 167 Install lengths of rubber tubing on the rod bolts before removing the piston assemblies; this will protect the cylinder walls from damage

FIG. 168 Tap out the piston assemblies with a wooden hammer handle. Note tubing covering rod bolts (arrow)

6. Push the piston and connecting rod up and out of the cylinder block with a length of wood. Use care not to scratch the cylinder wall with the connecting rod or the wooden tool.

7. Keep all of the components from each cylinder together and install them in the cylinder from which they were removed.

CLEANING AND INSPECTION

Pistons

▶ SEE FIGS. 169-172

1. Refer to the Piston Ring Replacement and remove the piston rings.

2. Scrap the carbon from the piston top; do not scratch the piston in any way during cleaning.

3. Using a broken piston ring or ring cleaning tool, clean out the piston ring grooves.

4. Clean the entire piston with solvent and a brush; DO NOT use a wire brush.

5. To check the piston ring side clearance, perform the following procedures:

   a. Once the piston is thoroughly cleaned, slide a piston ring into it's groove and check the side clearance with a feeler gauge. Make sure you insert the gauge between the ring and its lower land (lower edge of the groove), because any wear that occurs forms a step at the inner portion of the lower land.

   b. If the piston grooves have worn to the extent that relatively high steps exist on the lower land, the piston should be replaced, because these will interfere with the operation of the new rings and ring clearances will be excessive.

   c. Piston rings are not furnished in oversize widths to compensate for ring groove wear.

6. Measure the piston diameter with a micrometer; since this micrometer may not be part of your tool kit as it is necessarily large, you may have to have the pistons checked at a machine shop. Take the measurements at right angles to the wrist pin center line, about an inch down the piston skirt from the top.

Piston Pin

1. Make sure the piston is free of wear, scratches and or scoring; if necessary, replace the piston pin, piston and/or connecting rod.

2. Using a micrometer, measure the piston pin diameter.

Piston Ring End Gap

▶ SEE FIG. 173

➡ **Piston ring end gap should be checked while the rings are removed from the pistons. Incorrect end gap indicates that the wrong size rings are being used; ring breakage could occur.**

1. Compress the piston rings to be used in a cylinder, one at a time, into that cylinder.

2. Squirt clean oil into the cylinder, so the rings and the top 50mm of cylinder wall are coated.

3. Using an inverted piston, press the rings approximately 25mm below the deck of the block.

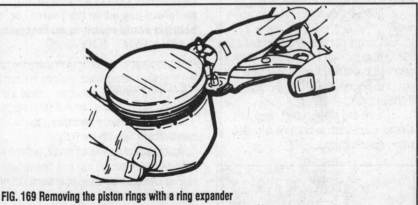

FIG. 169 Removing the piston rings with a ring expander

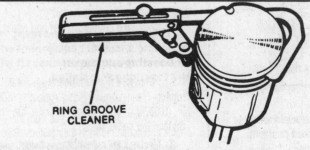

FIG. 170 Use a ring groove cleaner to properly clean the ring groove

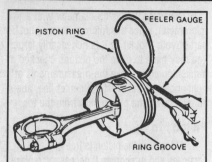

FIG. 171 Measuring piston ring side clearance

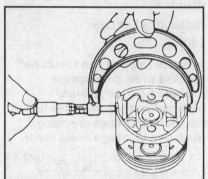

FIG. 172 Measuring the piston diameter. Check diameter on the piston pin axis and 90° from the axis

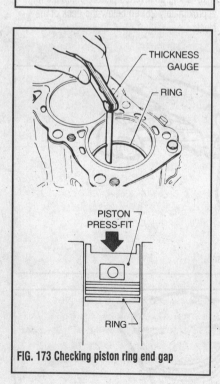

FIG. 173 Checking piston ring end gap

4. Measure the ring end gap with a feeler gauge and compare to the Ring Gap chart in this Section; replace the ring if necessary.

Connecting Rod

♦ SEE FIGS. 174 AND 175

1. To check the connecting rod side clearance, perform the following procedures:

   a. The connecting rods are to be installed in the engine.

   b. Determine the clearance between the connecting rod sides and the crankshaft using a feeler gauge.

➡ **If clearance is below the minimum tolerance, check with a machinist about machining the rod to provide adequate clearance. If clearance is excessive, substitute an unworn rod and recheck; if clearance is still outside specifications, the crankshaft must be welded and reground or replaced.**

2. To check connecting rod big end bearing clearances, perform the following procedures:

   a. Remove the rod bearing caps one at a time.

   b. Using a clean, dry shop rag, thoroughly clean all oil from the crank journal and bearing insert in the cap.

➡ **The Plastigage® gauging material you will be using to check clearances with is soluble in oil; therefore any oil on the journal or bearing could result in an incorrect reading.**

   c. Lay a strip of Plastigage® along the full length of the bearing insert or along the crank journal if the engine is out of the vehicle and inverted.

   d. Reinstall the cap and torque to specifications listed in the Torque Specifications chart.

   e. Remove the rod cap and determine bearing clearance by comparing the width of the now flattened Plastigage® to the scale on the Plastigage® envelope. Journal taper is determined by comparing the width of the Plastigage® strip near its ends.

   f. Rotate the crankshaft 90° and retest, to determine journal eccentricity.

➡ **Do not rotate the crankshaft with the Plastigage® installed.**

3. The connecting rods can be further inspected when they are removed from the engine and separated from their pistons. Rod alignment (straightness and squareness) must be checked by a machinist, as the rod must be

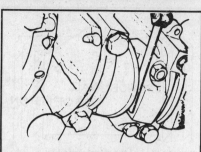

FIG. 174 Checking connecting rod side clearance. Make sure the feeler gauge is between the shoulder of the crank journal and the side of the rod

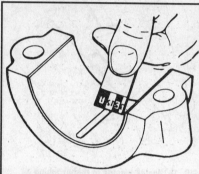

FIG. 175 Checking connecting rod bearing clearance with Plastigage®

set in a special fixture. Many machine shops also perform a Magna fluxing service, which is a process that shows up any tiny cracks that you may be unable to see.

Cylinder Bore

♦ SEE FIGS. 176–178

1. Place a rag over the crankshaft journals.

2. Wipe out each cylinder with a clean, solvent soaked rag.

3. Visually inspect the cylinder bores for roughness, scoring or scuffing; also check the bores by feel.

4. To measure the cylinder bore, perform the following procedures:

   a. Measure the cylinder bore diameter with an inside micrometer or a telescope gauge and micrometer.

   b. Measure the bore at points parallel and perpendicular to the engine centerline at the top (below the ridge) and bottom of the bore.

   c. Subtract the bottom measurements from the top to determine cylinder taper.

5. Compare the piston diameter to the bore diameter of each cylinder; the difference is the piston clearance. If the clearance is greater than that specified in the Piston and Ring Specifications chart, have the cylinders honed or rebored and replace the pistons with an

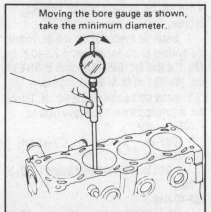

FIG. 176 Checking cylinder bore diameter with a telescoping gauge

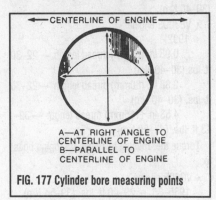

A—AT RIGHT ANGLE TO CENTERLINE OF ENGINE
B—PARALLEL TO CENTERLINE OF ENGINE

FIG. 177 Cylinder bore measuring points

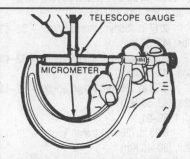

FIG. 178 Measure the telescope gauge with a mircometer to determine cylinder bore diameter

oversize set. Piston clearance can also be checked by inverting a piston into an oiled cylinder and sliding in a feeler gauge between the 2.

➡ **When any one cylinder needs boring, all cylinders must be bored.**

6. To check ring endgap, perform the following procedures:

   a. Insert a compression ring into the cylinder.

   b. Lightly oil the cylinder bore and push the ring down into the cylinder with a piston, to the bottom of its travel.

c. Measure the ring endgap with a feeler gauge. If the gap is not within specification, replace the ring; DO NOT file the ring ends.

PISTON PIN REPLACEMENT

♦ SEE FIGS. 179 AND 180

1. Using a oil bath, heat the piston/connection rod assembly to 140–158°F (60–70°C).

2. Using a shop press, press the piston pin from the piston assembly.

➡ **If may be necessary to take the piston/connecting rod assemblies to an engine specialist or machinist for piston pin removal.**

3. To install, lubricate the piston pin with engine and press it into the piston/connection assembly; make sure it is centered in the piston.

PISTON RING REPLACEMENT

1. Remove the piston rings from the piston.

2. On the piston, clean the piston ring grooves.

3. Using engine oil, lubricate the the pistons and rings.

4. Install the rings on the piston, lowest ring first, using a piston ring expander.

➡ **There is a high risk of breaking or distorting the rings or scratching the piston, if the rings are installed by hand or other means.**

5. Position the rings on the piston as illustrated; spacing of the various piston ring gaps is crucial to proper oil retention and even cylinder wear. When installing new rings, refer to the installation diagram furnished with the new parts.

ROD BEARING REPLACEMENT

If the bearing insert and crank journal appear intact and are within tolerances, no further service is required and the bearing caps can be reinstalled; remove Plastigage® before installation. If clearances are not within tolerances, the bearing inserts in both the connecting rod and rod cap must be replaced with undersize inserts and/or the crankshaft must be reground.

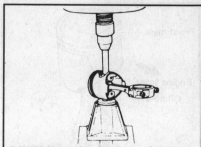

FIG. 179 Piston pins must be pressed in and out with a special press

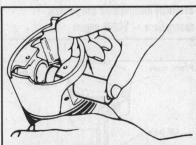

FIG. 180 Piston pin-to-piston fit should be such that the pin can be slid in smoothly by hand at room temperature

1. Install the bearing insert halves, by pressing them into the bearing caps and connecting rods. Make sure the tab in each insert fits into the notch in each rod and cap.

2. Lube the face of each insert with engine oil prior to installing each rod into the engine.

IDENTIFICATION AND POSITIONING

♦ SEE FIGS. 181-183

The pistons are marked with a punch mark or notch in the piston head. When installed in the engine the punch mark or notch is to face the front of the engine.

The connecting rods are installed in the engine with the oil hole facing the right side of the engine.

➡ **It is advisable to number the pistons, connecting rods and bearing caps in some manner so they can be reinstalled in the same cylinder, facing in the same direction from which they are removed.**

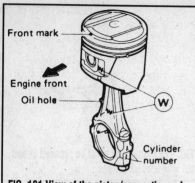

FIG. 181 View of the piston/connecting rod assembly identification and position descriptions — VG30E engine

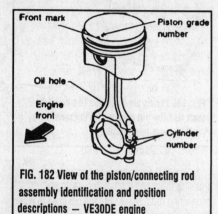

FIG. 182 View of the piston/connecting rod assembly identification and position descriptions — VE30DE engine

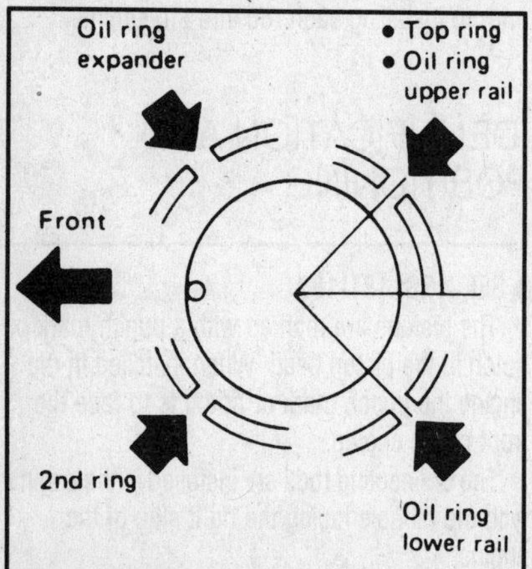

FIG. 183 Position of the piston rings on the piston

INSTALLATION

1. Coat the bearing face of the connecting rod and the outer face of the pistons with engine oil.

2. Install the piston/connecting rod assemblies by using the correct placement of the pistons/connecting rod assemblies and piston rings.

3. Turn the crankshaft until the rod journal of the particular cylinder you are working on, is brought to the TDC position.

4. With the piston and rings clamped in a ring compressor, the punched or notch mark on the head of the piston toward the front of the engine and the oil hole side of the connecting rod toward the right side of the engine, push the piston and connecting rod assembly into the cylinder bore until the big bearing end of the connecting rod contacts and is seated on the rod journal of the crankshaft. Use care not to scratch the cylinder wall with the connecting rod.

5. Push down farther on the piston and turn the crankshaft while the connecting rod rides around on the crankshaft rod journal. Turn the crankshaft until the crankshaft rod journal is at Bottom Dead Center (BDC).

6. Align the mark on the connecting rod bearing cap with that on the connecting rod and tighten the bearing cap bolts:
   • VG30E engine 1985–87 — 33–40 ft. lbs. (44–54 Nm)
   1988–92   1st step — 10–12 ft. lbs. (14–16 Nm)
             2nd step — 28–33 ft. lbs. (38–44 Nm)
   • VE30DE engine 1st step — 10–12 ft. lbs. (14–16 Nm)   2nd step — 43–48 ft. lbs. (59–65 Nm)

7. Install all of the piston/connecting rod assemblies.

8. Install the oil strainer, pickup tube and oil pan.

9. Install the cylinder head.

10. Install engine assembly in vehicle.

11. Check all fluid levels and road test.

Rear Main Oil Seal

REMOVAL & INSTALLATION

Oil Seal Retainer Removed

1. Remove the transaxle. Refer to Section 7 for procedure.

2. Remove the flywheel.

3. Remove the rear oil seal retainer.

4. Using a prybar, pry the oil seal from the retainer.

5. Liberally apply clean engine oil to the new oil seal and carefully install it into the retainer.

6. Using a new gasket, install the rear oil seal retainer onto the engine. Torque the bolts to 4.0–5.3 ft. lbs. (5.4–7.2 Nm) for 1985–88 engines or 4.6–6.1 ft. lbs. (6.3–8.3 Nm) for 1989–92 engines.

7. Install the flywheel in the vehicle. Torque the flywheel-to-crankshaft bolts to 72–80 ft. lbs. (98–108 Nm) for 1985–88 engines or 61–69 ft. lbs. (83–93 Nm) for 1989–92 engines.

8. Install the transaxle in the vehicle. Torque the: automatic transaxle-to-engine bolts to:
   • VG30E engine
      1985–88 — 22–36 ft. lbs. (39–49 Nm)
      1989–92
         0.98 in. (25mm) thread length — 22–30 ft. lbs. (30–40 Nm)
         1.77 in. (45mm) thread length — 29–36 ft. lbs. (39–49 Nm)
         2.36 in. (60mm) thread length — 22–30 ft. lbs. (30–40 Nm)
   • VE30DE engine
      1992
         0.98 in. (25mm) thread length — 22–30 ft. lbs. (30–40 Nm)
         2.36 in. (60mm) thread length — 22–30 ft. lbs. (30–40 Nm)
         4.53 in. (115mm) thread length — 32–43 ft. lbs. (43–58 Nm)

   Torque the: manual transaxle-to-engine bolts to:
   • VG30E engine
      1985–86 — 29–40 ft. lbs. (39–54 Nm)
      1987–88 0.98 in. (25mm) thread length — 22–30 ft. lbs. (30–40 Nm)
         2.17 in. (55mm) thread length — 32–43 ft. lbs. (43–58 Nm)
         2.36 in. (60mm) thread length — 32–43 ft. lbs. (43–58 Nm)
         2.56 in. (66mm) thread length — 32–43 ft. lbs. (43–58 Nm)
      1989–91
         0.98 in. (25mm) thread length — 22–30 ft. lbs. (30–40 Nm)
         2.17 in. (55mm) thread length — 32–43 ft. lbs. (43–58 Nm)
         2.56 in. (66mm) thread length — 32–43 ft. lbs. (43–58 Nm)
   • VE30DE engine
      1992
         0.98 in. (25mm) thread length — 22–30 ft. lbs. (30–40 Nm)
         1.10 in. (28mm) thread length — 22–30 ft. lbs. (30–40 Nm)
         2.24 in. (57mm) thread length — 29–36 ft. lbs. (39–49 Nm)
         2.52 in. (64mm) thread length — 29–36 ft. lbs. (39–49 Nm)

Oil Seal Retainer Installed

1. Remove the transaxle. Refer to Section 7 for procedure.

2. Remove the flywheel.

3. Using a prybar, pry the oil seal from the retainer.

4. Liberally apply clean engine oil to the new oil seal.

5. Using an oil seal installation tool, drive the new oil seal into the retainer until it seats.

6. Install the flywheel in the vehicle. Torque the flywheel-to-crankshaft bolts to 72–80 ft. lbs. (98–108 Nm) for 1985–88 engines or 61–69 ft. lbs. (83–93 Nm) for 1989–92 engines.

7. Install the transaxle in the vehicle. Torque the: automatic transaxle-to-engine bolts to:
- VG30E engine 1985–88 — 22–36 ft. lbs. (39–49 Nm)

  1989–92 0.98 in. (25mm) thread length — 22–30 ft. lbs. (30–40 Nm)

  1.77 in. (45mm) thread length — 29–36 ft. lbs. (39–49 Nm)

  2.36 in. (60mm) thread length — 22–30 ft. lbs. (30–40 Nm)
- VE30DE engine 1992 0.98 in. (25mm) thread length — 22–30 ft. lbs. (30–40 Nm)

  2.36 in. (60mm) thread length — 22–30 ft. lbs. (30–40 Nm)

  4.53 in. (115mm) thread length — 32–43 ft. lbs. (43–58 Nm)

Torque the: manual transaxle-to-engine bolts to:
- VG30E engine 1985–86 — 29–40 ft. lbs. (39–54 Nm)

  1987–88 0.98 in. (25mm) thread length — 22–30 ft. lbs. (30–40 Nm)

  2.17 in. (55mm) thread length — 32–43 ft. lbs. (43–58 Nm)

  2.36 in. (60mm) thread length — 32–43 ft. lbs. (43–58 Nm)

  2.56 in. (65mm) thread length — 32–43 ft. lbs. (43–58 Nm)

  1989–91 0.98 in. (25mm) thread length — 22–30 ft. lbs. (30–40 Nm)

  2.17 in. (55mm) thread length — 32–43 ft. lbs. (43–58 Nm)

  2.56 in. (65mm) thread length — 32–43 ft. lbs. (43–58 Nm)
- VE30DE engine 1992 0.98 in. (25mm) thread length — 22–30 ft. lbs. (30–40 Nm)

  1.10 in. (28mm) thread length — 22–30 ft. lbs. (30–40 Nm)

  2.24 in. (57mm) thread length — 29–36 ft. lbs. (39–49 Nm)

  2.52 in. (64mm) thread length — 29–36 ft. lbs. (39–49 Nm)

Crankshaft and Main Bearings

REMOVAL & INSTALLATION

♦ SEE FIGS. 184-189

➡ **Before removing the crankshaft, check main bearing clearances as described under Main Bearing Clearance Check below.**

1. Remove the piston and connecting rod assemblies following the procedure in this Section.

2. Check crankshaft thrust clearance (end play) before removing the crank from the block. Using a prybar, pry the crankshaft the extent of its travel forward and measure thrust clearance at the center main bearing (No. 4 bearing) with a feeler gauge. Pry the crankshaft the extent of its rearward travel, and measure the other side of the bearing. If clearance is greater than specified, the thrust washers must be replaced (see Main Bearing Replacement, below).

3. Remove the main bearing beam-to-engine bolts and the beam.

4. Remove the crankshaft from the block. Remove the crankshaft main bearings.

5. Follow the crankshaft inspection, main bearing clearance checking and replacement procedures below before reinstalling the crankshaft.

To install:

6. Using new crankshaft main bearings, install the upper portion into the cylinder block; make the sure the oil are aligned with the block and the bearing offsets are engaged with the notches in the block.

7. Lubricate the crankshaft with engine oil and install it into the block.

8. Using new crankshaft main bearings, install the lower portion into the main bearing beam; make the sure the bearing offsets are engaged with the notches in the beam.

9. Install the main bearing beam and torque the main bearing beam-to-engine bolts, in 2–3 steps, to 67–74 ft. lbs. (90–100 Nm).

10. Complete the installation by reversing the removal procedures.

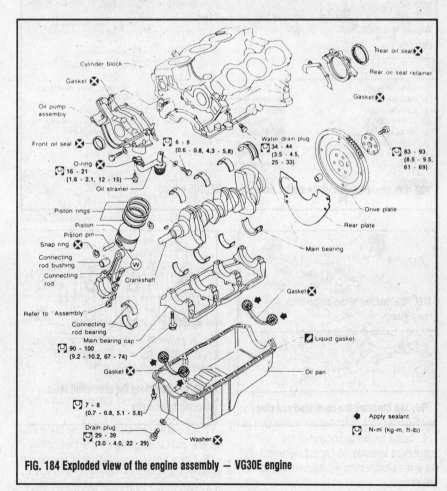

FIG. 184 Exploded view of the engine assembly — VG30E engine

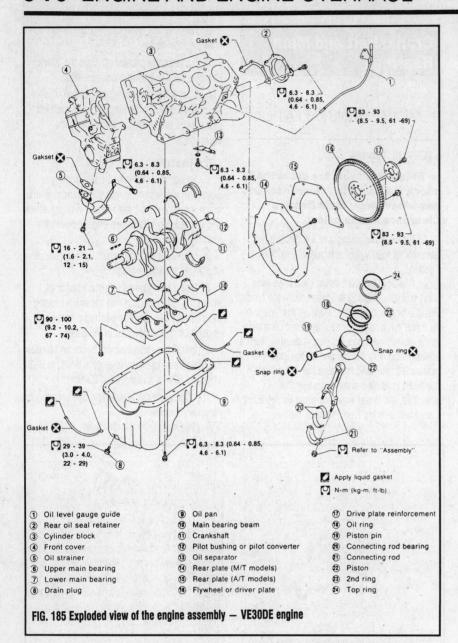

FIG. 185 Exploded view of the engine assembly — VE30DE engine

① Oil level gauge guide	⑨ Oil pan	⑰ Drive plate reinforcement
② Rear oil seal retainer	⑩ Main bearing beam	⑱ Oil ring
③ Cylinder block	⑪ Crankshaft	⑲ Piston pin
④ Front cover	⑫ Pilot bushing or pilot converter	⑳ Connecting rod bearing
⑤ Oil strainer	⑬ Oil separator	㉑ Connecting rod
⑥ Upper main bearing	⑭ Rear plate (M/T models)	㉒ Piston
⑦ Lower main bearing	⑮ Rear plate (A/T models)	㉓ 2nd ring
⑧ Drain plug	⑯ Flywheel or driver plate	㉔ Top ring

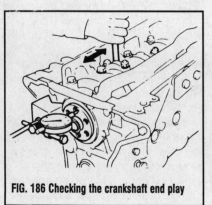

FIG. 186 Checking the crankshaft end play

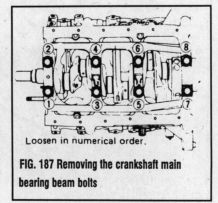

Loosen in numerical order.

FIG. 187 Removing the crankshaft main bearing beam bolts

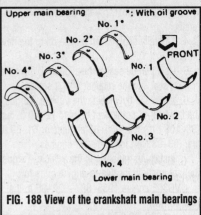

FIG. 188 View of the crankshaft main bearings

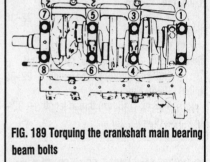

FIG. 189 Torquing the crankshaft main bearing beam bolts

INSPECTION

Crankshaft

♦ SEE FIGS. 190 AND 191

Crankshaft inspection and servicing should be handled exclusively by a reputable machinist, as most of the necessary procedures require a dial indicator and fixing jig, a large micrometer, and machine tools such as a crankshaft grinder. While at the machine shop, the crankshaft should be thoroughly cleaned (especially the oil passages); magna fluxed (to check for minute cracks) and the following checks made: Main journal diameter, crank pin (connecting rod journal) diameter, taper and out-of-round, and runout. Wear, beyond specification limits, in any of these areas means the crankshaft must be reground or replaced.

1. Check the crankshaft main and pin journals for scoring, wear and/or cracks.

2. Using a micrometer, measure the journals for taper and out-of-round; both should be less than 0.002 in. (0.005mm).

3. Using a dial micrometer, inspect the crankshaft journals for runout; it should be less than 0.0039 in. (0.10mm).

4. If any of the check do not meet specifications, machine the crankshaft and have bearings matched to it.

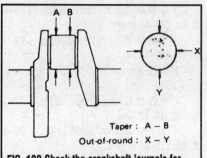

FIG. 190 Check the crankshaft journals for out-of-round and taper

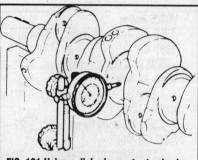

FIG. 191 Using a dial micrometer to check for crankshaft journal runout

Crankshaft journal grade number	Main journal grade number 0	1	2
0	0	1	2
1	1	2	3
2	2	3	4

FIG. 195 Crankshaft main bearing grade number chart

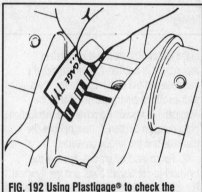

FIG. 192 Using Plastigage® to check the crankshaft main bearing clearance

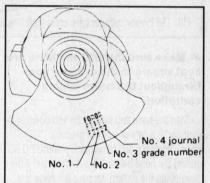

FIG. 194 Location of the grade number of each main journal bearing on the crankshaft

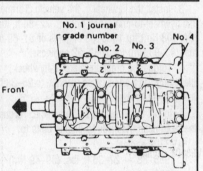

FIG. 193 Location of the grade number of each main journal bearing on the cylinder block

Main Bearing Clearance Check

♦ SEE FIG. 192-195

Checking man bearing clearances is done in the same manner as checking connecting rod big end clearances.

1. With the crankshaft installed, remove the main bearing beam. Clean all oil from the bearing insert in the cap and from the crankshaft journal, as the Plastigage® material is oil soluble.

2. Lay a strip of Plastigage® along the full width of the main bearing(s).

3. Install the bearing beam and torque to specification. Tighten bearing caps gradually in 2–3 stages.

➡ **Do not rotate the crankshaft with the Plastigage® installed.**

4. Remove the bearing beam and determine bearing clearance by comparing the width of the now flattened Plastigage® with the scale on the Plastigage® envelope. Journal taper is determined by comparing the width of the Plastigage® strip near its ends. Rotate the crankshaft 90° and retest, to determine journal eccentricity.

5. Repeat the above for the remaining bearings. If the bearing journal and insert appear in good shape (with no unusual wear visible) and are within tolerances, no further main bearing service is required. If unusual wear is evident and/or the clearances are outside specifications, the bearings must be replaced and the cause of their wear found.

6. If the crankshaft is reused, measure the main bearing clearances and select thickness of the main bearings.

7. If the crankshaft is replaced with a new one, it is necessary to select the thickness of the main bearings as follows:

a. Grade number of each cylinder block main journal is punched on the respective cylinder block.

b. Grade number of each crankshaft main journal is punched on the respective crankshaft.

c. Select the main bearing with the suitable thickness according to the table.

Cylinder Block

♦ SEE FIG. 196

Most inspection and service work on the cylinder block should be handled by a machinist or professional engine rebuilding shop. Included in this work are bearing alignment checks, line boring, deck resurfacing, hot-tanking and cylinder honing or boring. A block that has been checked and properly serviced will last much longer than one which has not had the proper attention when the opportunity was there for it.

Cylinder deglazing (honing) can, however, be performed by the owner/mechanic who is careful and takes his or her time. The cylinder bores become glazed during normal operation as the rings continually ride up and down against them. This shiny glaze must be removed in order for a new set of piston rings to be able to properly seat themselves.

Cylinder hones are available at most auto tool stores and parts jobbers. With the piston and rod assemblies removed from the block, cover the crankshaft completely with a rag or cover to keep grit from the hone and cylinder material off of it. Chuck a hone into a variable speed power drill (preferable here to a constant speed drill), and insert it into the cylinder.

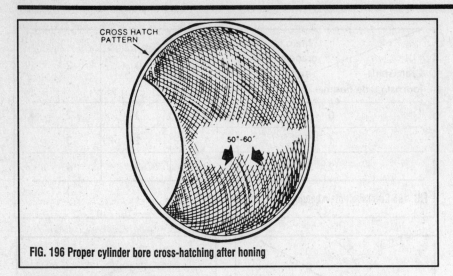
CROSS HATCH PATTERN

50°–60°

FIG. 196 Proper cylinder bore cross-hatching after honing

➡ **Make sure the drill and hone are kept square to the cylinder bore throughout the entire honing operation.**

Start the hone and move it up and down in the cylinder at a rate which will produce approximately a 60° crosshatch pattern. DO NOT extend the hone below the cylinder bore! After developing the pattern, remove the hone and recheck piston fit. Wash the cylinders with a detergent and water solution to remove the hone and cylinder grit. Wipe the bores out several times with a clean rag soaked in clean engine oil. Remove the cover from the crankshaft, and check closely to see that no grit has found its way onto the crankshaft.

Flywheel and Ring Gear

REMOVAL & INSTALLATION

1. If equipped with a manual transaxle, refer to the Clutch Removal and Installation procedures in Section 7, then remove the transaxle and the clutch assembly. If equipped with an automatic transaxle, refer to the Automatic Transaxle Removal and Installation procedures in Section 7, then remove the transaxle and the torque converter.

2. For manual transaxles, remove the flywheel-to-crankshaft bolts and the flywheel. For automatic transaxles, remove the driveplate-to-crankshaft bolts and the driveplate.

To install:

3. Install the flywheel in the vehicle. Torque the flywheel-to-crankshaft bolts to 72–80 ft. lbs. (98–108 Nm) for 1985–88 engines or 61–69 ft. lbs. (83–93 Nm) for 1989–92 engines.

4. Torque the pressure plate-to-flywheel place bolts, in a criss-cross manner, to 25–33 ft. lbs. (34–44 Nm).

5. Install the transaxle in the vehicle. Torque the: automatic transaxle-to-engine bolts to:
  • VG30E engine
    1985–88 — 22–36 ft. lbs. (39–49 Nm)
    1989–92
      0.98 in. (25mm) thread length — 22–30 ft. lbs. (30–40 Nm)

1.77 in. (55mm) thread length — 29–36 ft. lbs. (39–49 Nm)
      2.36 in. (60mm) thread length — 22–30 ft. lbs. (30–40 Nm)
  • VE30DE engine
    1992
      0.98 in. (25mm) thread length — 22–30 ft. lbs. (30–40 Nm)
      2.36 in. (60mm) thread length — 22–30 ft. lbs. (30–40 Nm)
      4.53 in. (115mm) thread length — 32–43 ft. lbs. (43–58 Nm)
Torque the: manual transaxle-to-engine bolts to:
  • VG30E engine
    1985–86 — 29–40 ft. lbs. (39–54 Nm)
    1987–88
      0.98 in. (25mm) thread length — 22–30 ft. lbs. (30–40 Nm)
      2.17 in. (55mm) thread length — 32–43 ft. lbs. (43–58 Nm)
      2.36 in. (60mm) thread length — 32–43 ft. lbs. (43–58 Nm)
      2.56 in. (65mm) thread length — 32–43 ft. lbs. (43–58 Nm)
    1989–91
      0.98 in. (25mm) thread length — 22–30 ft. lbs. (30–40 Nm)
      2.17 in. (55mm) thread length — 32–43 ft. lbs. (43–58 Nm)
      2.56 in. (65mm) thread length — 32–43 ft. lbs. (43–58 Nm)
  • VE30DE engine
    1992
      0.98 in. (25mm) thread length — 22–30 ft. lbs. (30–40 Nm)
      1.10 in. (28mm) thread length — 22–30 ft. lbs. (30–40 Nm)
      2.24 in. (57mm) thread length — 29–36 ft. lbs. (39–49 Nm)
      2.52 in. (64mm) thread length — 29–36 ft. lbs. (39–49 Nm)

EXHAUST SYSTEM

♦ SEE FIGS. 197 AND 198

Safety Precautions

For a number of reasons, exhaust system work can be dangerous. Always observe the following precautions:
  1. Raise and safely support the vehicle.

2. Wear safety goggles to protect your eyes from metal chips that may fly free while working on the exhaust system.
  3. If you are using a torch be careful not to come close to any fuel lines.
  4. Always use the proper tool for the job.

Special Tools

A number of special exhaust tools can be rented or bought from a local auto parts store. It may also be quite helpful to use solvents designed to loosen rusted nuts or bolts. Remember that these products are often flammable, apply only to parts after they are cool.

Front Pipe

REMOVAL & INSTALLATION

1. Raise and safely support the vehicle.
2. Remove the exhaust pipe clamps and any front exhaust pipe shield.
3. Soak the exhaust manifold front pipe mounting studs with penetrating oil. Remove attaching nuts and gasket from the manifold.

➡ **If the studs snap off, while removing the front pipe the manifold will have to be removed and the stud will have to be drill out and the hole tapped.**

4. Remove any exhaust pipe mounting hanger or bracket.
5. Remove front pipe from the catalytic converter.
6. Install the front pipe on the manifold with seal, if equipped.

To install:

7. Install the pipe on the catalytic converter. Assemble all parts loosely and position pipe to insure proper clearance from body of vehicle.
8. Tighten mounting studs, bracket bolts on exhaust clamps.
9. Install exhaust pipe shield.
10. Start engine and check for exhaust leaks.

Catalytic Converter

REMOVAL & INSTALLATION

1. Raise and safely support the vehicle.
2. Remove the converter lower shield.
3. Disconnect converter from front pipe.
4. Disconnect converter from center pipe.

➡ **Assemble all parts loosely and position converter before tightening the exhaust clamps.**

5. Remove catalytic converter.
6. To install reverse the removal procedures. Always use new clamps and exhaust seals, start engine and check for leaks.

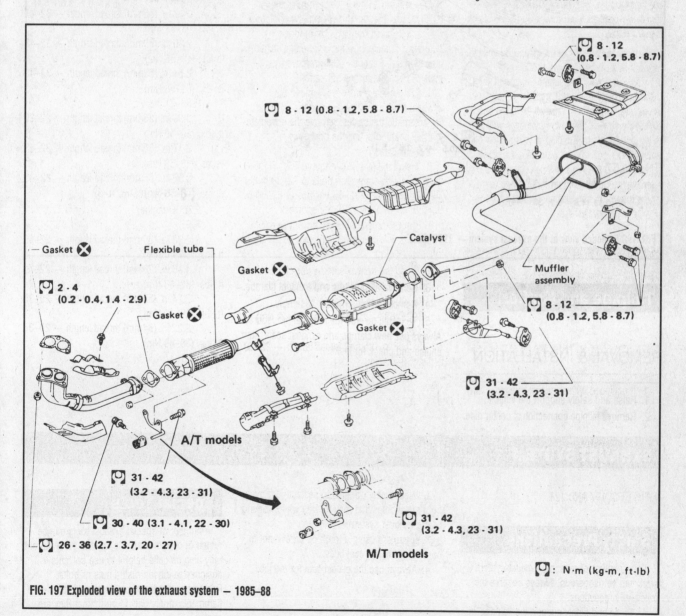

FIG. 197 Exploded view of the exhaust system — 1985–88

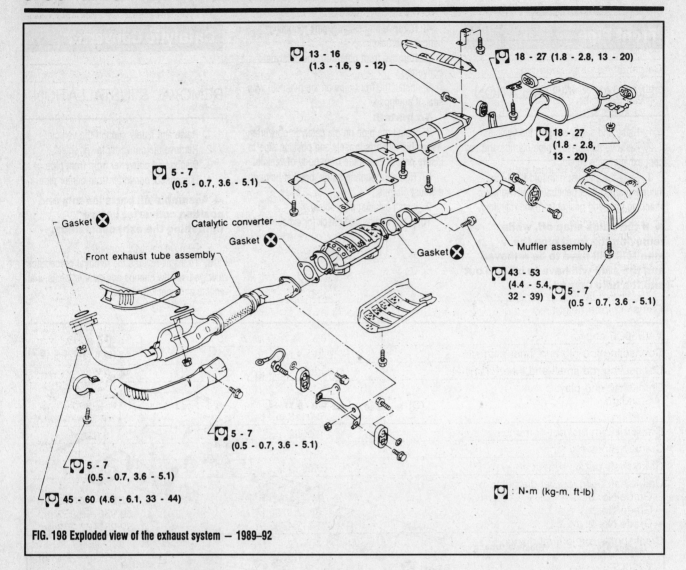

FIG. 198 Exploded view of the exhaust system — 1989–92

Tailpipe and Muffler

REMOVAL & INSTALLATION

1. Raise and safely support the vehicle.
2. Remove tailpipe connection at center pipe.
3. Remove all brackets and exhaust clamps.
4. Remove tailpipe/muffler assembly.
5. To install reverse the removal procedures. Always use new clamps and exhaust seals, start engine and check for leaks.

ENGINE SPECIFICATIONS

Component	U.S.	Metric
Camshaft bearing clearance	0.0018–0.0034 in.	0.045–0.086mm
Camshaft bearing journals		
VG30E engine		
Journal A	1.8472–1.8480 in.	46.920–46.940mm
Journal B	1.6701–1.6709 in.	42.420–42.440mm
Journal C	1.8866–1.8874 in.	47.920–47.940mm
VD30E engine	1.0211–1.0218 in.	25.935–25.955mm
Camshaft bearing journal runout		
VG30E engine		
Standard	0.0016 in.	0.04mm
Maximum	0.004 in.	0.01mm
VE30DE engine		
Standard	0.0008 in.	0.02mm
Maximum	0.002 in.	0.05mm
Camshaft end play		
VG30E engine	0.0012–0.0024 in.	0.03–0.06mm
VE30DE engine	0.0028–0.0058 in.	0.070–0.148mm
Camshaft lobe height		
VG30E engine	1.5566–1.5641 in.	39.537–39.727mm
VE30DE engine	1.4834–1.4909 in.	37.678–37.686mm
Connecting rod big end inner diameter	2.0866–2.0871 in.	53.000–53.013mm
Connecting rod small end inner diameter	0.9835–0.9843 in.	24.980–25.000mm
Crankshaft end play		
Standard	0.0020–0.0067 in.	0.050–0.170mm
Limit	0.0118 in.	0.30mm
Crankshaft journal out-of-round	0.0002 in.	0.005mm
Crankshaft journal taper	0.0002 in.	0.005mm
Crankshaft journal runout	0.0039 in.	0.10mm
Crankshaft main journal diameter		
Grade No. 0	2.790–2.4793 in.	62.967–62.975mm
Grade No. 1	2.4787–2.4790 in.	62.959–62.967mm
Grade No. 2	2.4784–2.4787 in.	62.951–62.959mm
Crankshaft's rod journal diameter		
VG30E engine	1.9667–1.9675 in.	49.955–49.974mm
VE30DE engine		
Grade No. 0	1.9672–1.9675 in.	49.968–49.974mm
Grade No. 1	1.9670–1.9672 in.	49.962–49.968mm
Grade No. 2	1.9667–1.9670 in.	49.955–49.962mm
Cylinder block (cylinder head) flatness		
Standard	0.0012 in.	0.03mm
Limit	0.0039 in.	0.10mm
Cylinder block main bearing diameter		
Grade No. 0	2.6238–2.6242 in.	66.645–66.654mm
Grade No. 1	2.6242–2.6245 in.	66.654–66.663mm
Grade No. 2	2.6245–2.6249 in.	66.663–66.672mm
Cylinder bore inner diameter		
Grade No. 1	3.4252–3.4256 in.	87.000–87.010mm
Grade No. 2	3.4256–3.4260 in.	87.010–87.020mm
Grade No. 3	3.4260–3.4264 in.	87.020–87.030mm
Cylinder head camshaft bearing journals:		
VG30E engine		
Journal A	1.8504–1.8514 in.	47.000–47.025mm
Journal B	1.6732–1.6742 in.	42.500–42.525mm
Journal C	1.8898–1.8907 in.	48.000–48.025mm
VE30DE engine	1.0236–1.0244 in.	26.000–26.021mm
Cylinder head warpage	Max. 0.004 in.	Max. 0.10mm
Hydraulic lifter outer diameter		
VG30E engine	0.6278–0.6282 in.	15.947–15.957mm
VE30DE engine	0.6685–0.6690 in.	16.980–16.993mm

ENGINE SPECIFICATIONS

Component	U.S.	Metric
Hydraulic lifter guide inside diameter		
VG30E engine	0.6299–0.6304 in.	16.000–16.013mm
VE30DE engine	0.6693–0.6701 in.	17.000–17.020mm
Hysraulic lifter clearance		
VG30E engine	0.0017–0.0026 in.	0.043–0.066mm
VE30DE engine	0.0003–0.0016 in.	0.007–0.040mm
Oil pump clearances		
VG30E Engine		
Body-to-outer gear	0.0043–0.0079 in.	0.11–0.20mm
Inner gear-to-crescent	0.0047–0.0091 in.	0.12–0.23mm
Outer gear-to-crescent	0.0083–0.0126 in.	0.21–0.32mm
Housing-to-inner gear	0.0020–0.0035 in.	0.05–0.09mm
Housing-to-outer gear	0.0020–0.0043 in.	0.05–0.11mm
VE30DE Engine		
Body-to-outer gear	0.0045–0.0079 in.	0.114–0.200mm
Inner gear-to-outer gear tip	Max. 0.0071 in.	Max. 0.18mm
Body-to-inner gear	0.0020–0.0043 in.	0.05–0.11mm
Body-to-outer gear	0.0020–0.0043 in.	0.05–0.11mm
Inner gear-to-brazed portion	0.0018–0.0036 in.	0.045–0.091mm
Oil pump regulator valve-to-oil pump cover clearance	0.0016–0.0038 in.	0.040–0.097mm
Piston pin diameter		
VG30E engine	0.8256–0.8261 in.	20.971–20.984mm
VE30DE engine	0.8657–0.8662 in.	21.989–22.001mm
Piston pin bushing inner diameter		
VG30E engine	0.8261–0.8265 in.	20.982–20.994mm
VE30DE engine	0.8661–0.8666 in.	22.000–22.012mm
Piston pin bushing-to-rod bearing clearance	0.0002–0.0007 in.	0.005–0.017mm
Piston pin-to-piston interference fit	0–0.0002 in.	0–0.004mm
Piston-to-cylinder clearance	0.0006–0.0014 in.	0.015–0.035mm
Piston pin hole diameter		
VG30E engine	0.8255–0.8260 in.	20.969–20.981mm
VE30DE engine	0.8656–0.8661 in.	21.987–21.999mm
Piston skirt diameter		
VG30E engine		
Grade No. 1	3.4238–3.4242 in.	86.965–86.975mm
Grade No. 2	3.4242–3.4246 in.	86.975–86.985mm
Grade No. 3	3.4246–3.4250 in.	86.985–86.995mm
VE30DE engine		
Grade No. 1	3.4242–3.4246 in.	86.975–86.985mm
Grade No. 2	3.4246–3.4250 in.	86.985–86.995mm
Grade No. 3	3.4250–3.4254 in.	86.995–87.005mm
Rocker arm inner diameter		
VG30E engine	0.7089–0.7098 in.	18.007–18.028
Rocker arm-to-rocker shaft clearance		
VG30E engine	0.0003–0.0019 in.	0.007–0.049mm
Rocker arm shaft (rocker arm) diameter		
VG30E engine	0.7082–0.7087 in.	17.988–18.000mm

ENGINE SPECIFICATIONS

Component	U.S.	Metric
Valve guide clearance		
VG30E engine		
Normal clearance		
Intake valve guide	0.0008–0.0021 in.	0.020–0.053mm
Exhaust valve guide	0.0016–0.0029 in.	0.040–0.073mm
Maximum clearance		
Intake valve guide	0.0039 in.	0.10mm
Exhaust valve guide	0.0039 in.	0.10mm
VE30DE engine		
Maximum clearance		
Intake valve guide	0.0031 in.	0.08mm
Exhaust valve guide	0.0040 in.	(0.10mm
Valve-to-guide deflection	0.0079 in.	0.20mm
Valve guide in head projection		
VG30E engine	0.520–0.528 in.	13.2–13.4mm
VE30DE engine	0.535–0.543 in.	13.6–13.8mm
Valve guide reaming		
VG30E engine		
Intake valve guide	0.2756–0.2763 in.	7.000–7.018mm
Exhaust valve guide	0.3150–0.3157 in.	8.000–8.018mm
VE30DE engine		
Intake valve guide	0.2362–0.2369 in.	6.000–6.018mm
Exhaust valve guide	0.2362–0.2369 in.	6.000–6.018mm
Valve head diameter		
VG30E engine		
Intake	1.654–1.661 in.	42.0–42.2mm
Exhaust	1.378–1.386 in.	35.0–35.2mm
VE30DE engine		
Intake	1.378–1.386 in.	35.0–35.2mm
Exhaust 1.201–1.209 in.	30.5–30.7mm	
Valve length		
VG30E engine		
Intake	4.933–4.957 in.	125.3–125.9mm
Exhaust	4.890–4.913 in.	124.2–124.8mm
VE30DE engine		
Intake	4.3405–4.3602 in.	110.25–110.75mm
Exhaust 4.0335–4.0531 in.	102.45–102.95mm	
Valve-to-lifter clearance	0.0 in.	0.0mm
Valve seats		
VG30E engine		
Seat face angle		
Intake valve	45°	45°
Exhaust valve	45°	45°
Valve-to-seat contacting width "W"		
Intake valve	0.0689 in.	1.75mm
Exhaust valve	0.067 in.	1.7mm
VE30DE engine		
Seat face angle		
Intake valve	44°53'–45°07'	44°53'–45°07'
Exhaust valve	44°53'–45°07'	44°53'–45°07'
Valve-to-seat contacting width "W"		
Intake valve	0.0417–0.0528 in.	1.06–1.34mm
Exhaust valve	0.050–0.061 in.	1.27–1.55mm
Valve spring free height		
VG30E engine		
Inner	1.736 in.	44.1mm
Outer	2.016 in.	51.2mm
VE30DE engine	1.7768 in.	45.13mm

ENGINE SPECIFICATIONS

Component	U.S.	Metric
Valve spring pressure		
VG30E engine		
Inner	57.3 lbs. @ 0.984 in.	255.0 N @ 25.0mm
Outer	117.7 lbs. @ 1.181 in.	523.7 N @ 30.0mm
VE30DE engine	120.4 lbs. @ 1.059 in.	535.5 @ 26.9mm
Valve spring squareness		
VG30E engine		
Outer spring	Max. 0.087 in.	Max. 2.2mm
Inner spring	Max. 0.075 in.	Max. 1.9mm
VE30DE engine	1.059 in.	26.9mm
Valve stem diameter		
VG30E engine		
Intake	0.2742–0.2748 in.	6.965–6.980mm
Exhaust	0.3136–0.3138 in.	7.965–7.970mm
VE30DE engine		
Intake	0.2352–0.2354 in.	5.975–5.980mm
Exhaust 0.2344–0.2346 in.	5.955–5.960mm	

Troubleshooting Basic Charging System Problems

Problem	Cause	Solution
Noisy alternator	• Loose mountings • Loose drive pulley • Worn bearings • Brush noise • Internal circuits shorted (High pitched whine)	• Tighten mounting bolts • Tighten pulley • Replace alternator • Replace alternator • Replace alternator
Squeal when starting engine or accelerating	• Glazed or loose belt	• Replace or adjust belt
Indicator light remains on or ammeter indicates discharge (engine running)	• Broken fan belt • Broken or disconnected wires • Internal alternator problems • Defective voltage regulator	• Install belt • Repair or connect wiring • Replace alternator • Replace voltage regulator
Car light bulbs continually burn out—battery needs water continually	• Alternator/regulator overcharging	• Replace voltage regulator/alternator
Car lights flare on acceleration	• Battery low • Internal alternator/regulator problems	• Charge or replace battery • Replace alternator/regulator
Low voltage output (alternator light flickers continually or ammeter needle wanders)	• Loose or worn belt • Dirty or corroded connections • Internal alternator/regulator problems	• Replace or adjust belt • Clean or replace connections • Replace alternator or regulator

Troubleshooting Basic Starting System Problems

Problem	Cause	Solution
Starter motor rotates engine slowly	• Battery charge low or battery defective	• Charge or replace battery
	• Defective circuit between battery and starter motor	• Clean and tighten, or replace cables
	• Low load current	• Bench-test starter motor. Inspect for worn brushes and weak brush springs.
	• High load current	• Bench-test starter motor. Check engine for friction, drag or coolant in cylinders. Check ring gear-to-pinion gear clearance.
Starter motor will not rotate engine	• Battery charge low or battery defective	• Charge or replace battery
	• Faulty solenoid	• Check solenoid ground. Repair or replace as necessary.
	• Damage drive pinion gear or ring gear	• Replace damaged gear(s)
	• Starter motor engagement weak	• Bench-test starter motor
	• Starter motor rotates slowly with high load current	• Inspect drive yoke pull-down and point gap, check for worn end bushings, check ring gear clearance
	• Engine seized	• Repair engine
Starter motor drive will not engage (solenoid known to be good)	• Defective contact point assembly	• Repair or replace contact point assembly
	• Inadequate contact point assembly ground	• Repair connection at ground screw
	• Defective hold-in coil	• Replace field winding assembly
Starter motor drive will not disengage	• Starter motor loose on flywheel housing	• Tighten mounting bolts
	• Worn drive end busing	• Replace bushing
	• Damaged ring gear teeth	• Replace ring gear or driveplate
	• Drive yoke return spring broken or missing	• Replace spring
Starter motor drive disengages prematurely	• Weak drive assembly thrust spring	• Replace drive mechanism
	• Hold-in coil defective	• Replace field winding assembly
Low load current	• Worn brushes	• Replace brushes
	• Weak brush springs	• Replace springs

Troubleshooting Engine Mechanical Problems

Problem	Cause	Solution
External oil leaks	• Fuel pump gasket broken or improperly seated	• Replace gasket
	• Cylinder head cover RTV sealant broken or improperly seated	• Replace sealant; inspect cylinder head cover sealant flange and cylinder head sealant surface for distortion and cracks
	• Oil filler cap leaking or missing	• Replace cap
External oil leaks	• Oil filter gasket broken or improperly seated	• Replace oil filter
	• Oil pan side gasket broken, improperly seated or opening in RTV sealant	• Replace gasket or repair opening in sealant; inspect oil pan gasket flange for distortion
	• Oil pan front oil seal broken or improperly seated	• Replace seal; inspect timing case cover and oil pan seal flange for distortion
	• Oil pan rear oil seal broken or improperly seated	• Replace seal; inspect oil pan rear oil seal flange; inspect rear main bearing cap for cracks, plugged oil return channels, or distortion in seal groove
	• Timing case cover oil seal broken or improperly seated	• Replace seal
	• Excess oil pressure because of restricted PCV valve	• Replace PCV valve
	• Oil pan drain plug loose or has stripped threads	• Repair as necessary and tighten
	• Rear oil gallery plug loose	• Use appropriate sealant on gallery plug and tighten
	• Rear camshaft plug loose or improperly seated	• Seat camshaft plug or replace and seal, as necessary
	• Distributor base gasket damaged	• Replace gasket
Excessive oil consumption	• Oil level too high	• Drain oil to specified level
	• Oil with wrong viscosity being used	• Replace with specified oil
	• PCV valve stuck closed	• Replace PCV valve
	• Valve stem oil deflectors (or seals) are damaged, missing, or incorrect type	• Replace valve stem oil deflectors
	• Valve stems or valve guides worn	• Measure stem-to-guide clearance and repair as necessary
	• Poorly fitted or missing valve cover baffles	• Replace valve cover
	• Piston rings broken or missing	• Replace broken or missing rings
	• Scuffed piston	• Replace piston
	• Incorrect piston ring gap	• Measure ring gap, repair as necessary
	• Piston rings sticking or excessively loose in grooves	• Measure ring side clearance, repair as necessary
	• Compression rings installed upside down	• Repair as necessary
	• Cylinder walls worn, scored, or glazed	• Repair as necessary

Troubleshooting Engine Mechanical Problems (cont.)

Problem	Cause	Solution
	• Piston ring gaps not properly staggered	• Repair as necessary
	• Excessive main or connecting rod bearing clearance	• Measure bearing clearance, repair as necessary
No oil pressure	• Low oil level	• Add oil to correct level
	• Oil pressure gauge, warning lamp or sending unit inaccurate	• Replace oil pressure gauge or warning lamp
	• Oil pump malfunction	• Replace oil pump
	• Oil pressure relief valve sticking	• Remove and inspect oil pressure relief valve assembly
	• Oil passages on pressure side of pump obstructed	• Inspect oil passages for obstruction
	• Oil pickup screen or tube obstructed	• Inspect oil pickup for obstruction
	• Loose oil inlet tube	• Tighten or seal inlet tube
Low oil pressure	• Low oil level	• Add oil to correct level
	• Inaccurate gauge, warning lamp or sending unit	• Replace oil pressure gauge or warning lamp
	• Oil excessively thin because of dilution, poor quality, or improper grade	• Drain and refill crankcase with recommended oil
	• Excessive oil temperature	• Correct cause of overheating engine
	• Oil pressure relief spring weak or sticking	• Remove and inspect oil pressure relief valve assembly
	• Oil inlet tube and screen assembly has restriction or air leak	• Remove and inspect oil inlet tube and screen assembly. (Fill inlet tube with lacquer thinner to locate leaks.)
	• Excessive oil pump clearance	• Measure clearances
	• Excessive main, rod, or camshaft bearing clearance	• Measure bearing clearances, repair as necessary
High oil pressure	• Improper oil viscosity	• Drain and refill crankcase with correct viscosity oil
	• Oil pressure gauge or sending unit inaccurate	• Replace oil pressure gauge
	• Oil pressure relief valve sticking closed	• Remove and inspect oil pressure relief valve assembly
Main bearing noise	• Insufficient oil supply	• Inspect for low oil level and low oil pressure
	• Main bearing clearance excessive	• Measure main bearing clearance, repair as necessary
	• Bearing insert missing	• Replace missing insert
	• Crankshaft end play excessive	• Measure end play, repair as necessary
	• Improperly tightened main bearing cap bolts	• Tighten bolts with specified torque
	• Loose flywheel or drive plate	• Tighten flywheel or drive plate attaching bolts
	• Loose or damaged vibration damper	• Repair as necessary

Troubleshooting Engine Mechanical Problems (cont.)

Problem	Cause	Solution
Connecting rod bearing noise	• Insufficient oil supply	• Inspect for low oil level and low oil pressure
	• Carbon build-up on piston	• Remove carbon from piston crown
	• Bearing clearance excessive or bearing missing	• Measure clearance, repair as necessary
	• Crankshaft connecting rod journal out-of-round	• Measure journal dimensions, repair or replace as necessary
	• Misaligned connecting rod or cap	• Repair as necessary
	• Connecting rod bolts tightened improperly	• Tighten bolts with specified torque
Piston noise	• Piston-to-cylinder wall clearance excessive (scuffed piston)	• Measure clearance and examine piston
	• Cylinder walls excessively tapered or out-of-round	• Measure cylinder wall dimensions, rebore cylinder
	• Piston ring broken	• Replace all rings on piston
	• Loose or seized piston pin	• Measure piston-to-pin clearance, repair as necessary
	• Connecting rods misaligned	• Measure rod alignment, straighten or replace
	• Piston ring side clearance excessively loose or tight	• Measure ring side clearance, repair as necessary
	• Carbon build-up on piston is excessive	• Remove carbon from piston
Valve actuating component noise	• Insufficient oil supply	• Check for: (a) Low oil level (b) Low oil pressure (c) Plugged push rods (d) Wrong hydraulic tappets (e) Restricted oil gallery (f) Excessive tappet to bore clearance
	• Push rods worn or bent	• Replace worn or bent push rods
	• Rocker arms or pivots worn	• Replace worn rocker arms or pivots
	• Foreign objects or chips in hydraulic tappets	• Clean tappets
	• Excessive tappet leak-down	• Replace valve tappet
	• Tappet face worn	• Replace tappet; inspect corresponding cam lobe for wear
	• Broken or cocked valve springs	• Properly seat cocked springs; replace broken springs
	• Stem-to-guide clearance excessive	• Measure stem-to-guide clearance, repair as required
	• Valve bent	• Replace valve
	• Loose rocker arms	• Tighten bolts with specified torque
	• Valve seat runout excessive	• Regrind valve seat/valves
	• Missing valve lock	• Install valve lock
	• Push rod rubbing or contacting cylinder head	• Remove cylinder head and remove obstruction in head
	• Excessive engine oil (four-cylinder engine)	• Correct oil level

Troubleshooting the Cooling System

Problem	Cause	Solution
High temperature gauge indication—overheating	• Coolant level low	• Replenish coolant
	• Fan belt loose	• Adjust fan belt tension
	• Radiator hose(s) collapsed	• Replace hose(s)
	• Radiator airflow blocked	• Remove restriction (bug screen, fog lamps, etc.)
	• Faulty radiator cap	• Replace radiator cap
	• Ignition timing incorrect	• Adjust ignition timing
	• Idle speed low	• Adjust idle speed
	• Air trapped in cooling system	• Purge air
	• Heavy traffic driving	• Operate at fast idle in neutral intermittently to cool engine
	• Incorrect cooling system component(s) installed	• Install proper component(s)
	• Faulty thermostat	• Replace thermostat
	• Water pump shaft broken or impeller loose	• Replace water pump
	• Radiator tubes clogged	• Flush radiator
	• Cooling system clogged	• Flush system
	• Casting flash in cooling passages	• Repair or replace as necessary. Flash may be visible by removing cooling system components or removing core plugs.
	• Brakes dragging	• Repair brakes
	• Excessive engine friction	• Repair engine
	• Antifreeze concentration over 68%	• Lower antifreeze concentration percentage
	• Missing air seals	• Replace air seals
	• Faulty gauge or sending unit	• Repair or replace faulty component
	• Loss of coolant flow caused by leakage or foaming	• Repair or replace leaking component, replace coolant
	• Viscous fan drive failed	• Replace unit
Low temperature indication—undercooling	• Thermostat stuck open	• Replace thermostat
	• Faulty gauge or sending unit	• Repair or replace faulty component
Coolant loss—boilover	• Overfilled cooling system	• Reduce coolant level to proper specification
	• Quick shutdown after hard (hot) run	• Allow engine to run at fast idle prior to shutdown
	• Air in system resulting in occasional "burping" of coolant	• Purge system
	• Insufficient antifreeze allowing coolant boiling point to be too low	• Add antifreeze to raise boiling point
	• Antifreeze deteriorated because of age or contamination	• Replace coolant
	• Leaks due to loose hose clamps, loose nuts, bolts, drain plugs, faulty hoses, or defective radiator	• Pressure test system to locate source of leak(s) then repair as necessary

Troubleshooting the Cooling System (cont.)

Problem	Cause	Solution
Coolant loss—boilover	• Faulty head gasket • Cracked head, manifold, or block • Faulty radiator cap	• Replace head gasket • Replace as necessary • Replace cap
Coolant entry into crankcase or cylinder(s)	• Faulty head gasket • Crack in head, manifold or block	• Replace head gasket • Replace as necessary
Coolant recovery system inoperative	• Coolant level low • Leak in system • Pressure cap not tight or seal missing, or leaking • Pressure cap defective • Overflow tube clogged or leaking • Recovery bottle vent restricted	• Replenish coolant to FULL mark • Pressure test to isolate leak and repair as necessary • Repair as necessary • Replace cap • Repair as necessary • Remove restriction
Noise	• Fan contacting shroud • Loose water pump impeller • Glazed fan belt • Loose fan belt • Rough surface on drive pulley • Water pump bearing worn • Belt alignment	• Reposition shroud and inspect engine mounts • Replace pump • Apply silicone or replace belt • Adjust fan belt tension • Replace pulley • Remove belt to isolate. Replace pump. • Check pulley alignment. Repair as necessary.
No coolant flow through heater core	• Restricted return inlet in water pump • Heater hose collapsed or restricted • Restricted heater core • Restricted outlet in thermostat housing • Intake manifold bypass hole in cylinder head restricted • Faulty heater control valve • Intake manifold coolant passage restricted	• Remove restriction • Remove restriction or replace hose • Remove restriction or replace core • Remove flash or restriction • Remove restriction • Replace valve • Remove restriction or replace intake manifold

NOTE: *Immediately after shutdown, the engine enters a condition known as heat soak. This is caused by the cooling system being inoperative while engine temperature is still high. If coolant temperature rises above boiling point, expansion and pressure may push some coolant out of the radiator overflow tube. If this does not occur frequently it is considered normal.*

4

EMISSION
CONTROLS

AIR POLLUTION

The earth's atmosphere, at or near sea level, consists of 78% nitrogen, 21% oxygen and 1% other gases, approximately. If it were possible to remain in this state, 100% clean air would result. However, many varied causes allow other gases and particulates to mix with the clean air, causing the air to become unclean or polluted.

Certain of these pollutants are visible while others are invisible, with each having the capability of causing distress to the eyes, ears, throat, skin and respiratory system. Should these pollutants be concentrated in a specific area and under the right conditions, death could result due to the displacement or chemical change of the oxygen content in the air. These pollutants can cause much damage to the environment and to the many man made objects that are exposed to the elements.

To better understand the causes of air pollution, the pollutants can be categorized into 3 separate types, natural, industrial and automotive.

Natural Pollutants

Natural pollution has been present on earth before man appeared and is still a factor to be considered when discussing air pollution, although it causes only a small percentage of the present overall pollution problem existing in our country. It is the direct result of decaying organic matter, wind born smoke and particulates from such natural events as plains and forest fires (ignited by heat or lightning), volcanic ash, sand and dust which can spread over a large area of the countryside.

Such a phenomenon of natural pollution has been recent volcanic eruptions, with the resulting plume of smoke, steam and volcanic ash blotting out the sun's rays as it spreads and rises higher into the atmosphere, where the upper air currents catch and carry the smoke and ash, while condensing the steam back into water vapor. As the water vapor, smoke and ash traveled on their journey, the smoke dissipates into the atmosphere while the ash and moisture settle back to earth in a trail hundred of miles long. In many cases, lives are lost and millions of dollars of property damage result, and ironically, man can only stand by and watch it happen.

Industrial Pollution

Industrial pollution is caused primarily by industrial processes, the burning of coal, oil and natural gas, which in turn produces smoke and fumes. Because the burning fuels contain much sulfur, the principal ingredients of smoke and fumes are sulfur dioxide (SO_2) and particulate matter. This type of pollutant occurs most severely during still, damp and cool weather, such as at night. Even in its less severe form, this pollutant is not confined to just cities. Because of air movements, the pollutants move for miles over the surrounding countryside, leaving in its path a barren and unhealthy environment for all living things.

Working with Federal, State and Local mandated rules, regulations and by carefully monitoring the emissions, industries have greatly reduced the amount of pollutant emitted from their industrial sources, striving to obtain an acceptable level. Because of the mandated industrial emission clean up, many land areas and streams in and around the cities that were formerly barren of vegetation and life, have now begun to move back in the direction of nature's intended balance.

Automotive Pollutants

The third major source of air pollution is the automotive emissions. The emissions from the internal combustion engine were not an appreciable problem years ago because of the small number of registered vehicles and the nation's small highway system. However, during the early 1950's, the trend of the American people was to move from the cities to the surrounding suburbs. This caused an immediate problem in the transportation areas because the majority of the suburbs were not afforded mass transit conveniences. This lack of transportation created an attractive market for the automobile manufacturers, which resulted in a dramatic increase in the number of vehicles produced and sold, along with a marked increase in highway construction between cities and the suburbs. Multi-vehicle families emerged with much emphasis placed on the individual vehicle per family member. As the increase in vehicle ownership and usage occurred, so did the pollutant levels in and around the cities, as the suburbanites drove daily to their businesses and employment in the city and its fringe area, returning at the end of the day to their homes in the suburbs.

It was noted that a fog and smoke type haze was being formed and at times, remained in suspension over the cities and did not quickly dissipate. At first this "smog", derived from the words "smoke" and "fog", was thought to result from industrial pollution but it was determined that the automobile emissions were largely to blame. It was discovered that as normal automobile emissions were exposed to sunlight for a period of time, complex chemical reactions would take place.

It was found the smog was a photo chemical layer and was developed when certain oxides of nitrogen (NOx) and unburned hydrocarbons (HC) from the automobile emissions were exposed to sunlight and was more severe when the smog would remain stagnant over an area in which a warm layer of air would settle over the top of a cooler air mass at ground level, trapping and holding the automobile emissions, instead of the emissions being dispersed and diluted through normal air flows. This type of air stagnation was given the name "Temperature Inversion".

Temperature Inversion

In normal weather situations, the surface air is warmed by the heat radiating from the earth's surface and the sun's rays and will rise upward, into the atmosphere, to be cooled through a convection type heat expands with the cooler upper air. As the warm air rises, the surface pollutants are carried upward and dissipated into the atmosphere.

When a temperature inversion occurs, we find the higher air is no longer cooler but warmer than the surface air, causing the cooler surface air to become trapped and unable to move. This warm air blanket can extend from above ground level to a few hundred or even a few thousand feet into the air. As the surface air is trapped, so are the pollutants, causing a severe smog condition. Should this stagnant air mass extend to a few thousand feet high, enough air movement with the inversion takes place to allow the smog layer to rise above ground level but the pollutants still cannot dissipate. This inversion can remain for days over an area, with only the smog level rising or lowering from ground level to a few hundred feet high. Meanwhile, the pollutant levels increases, causing eye irritation, respirator problems, reduced visibility, plant damage and in some cases, cancer type diseases.

This inversion phenomenon was first noted in the Los Angeles, California area. The city lies in a basin type of terrain and during certain weather conditions, a cold air mass is held in the basin while a warmer air mass covers it like a lid.

Because this type of condition was first documented as prevalent in the Los Angeles area, this type of smog was named Los Angeles Smog, although it occurs in other areas where a large concentration of automobiles are used and the air remains stagnant for any length of time.

Internal Combustion Engine Pollutants

Consider the internal combustion engine as a machine in which raw materials must be placed so a finished product comes out. As in any machine operation, a certain amount of wasted material is formed. When we relate this to the internal combustion engine, we find that by putting in air and fuel, we obtain power from this

mixture during the combustion process to drive the vehicle. The by-product or waste of this power is, in part, heat and exhaust gases with which we must concern ourselves.

HEAT TRANSFER

The heat from the combustion process can rise to over 4000°F (2204°C). The dissipation of this heat is controlled by a ram air effect, the use of cooling fans to cause air flow and having a liquid coolant solution surrounding the combustion area and transferring the heat of combustion through the cylinder walls and into the coolant. The coolant is then directed to a thin-finned, multi-tubed radiator, from which the excess heat is transferred to the outside air by 1 or all of the 3 heat transfer methods, conduction, convection or radiation.

The cooling of the combustion area is an important part in the control of exhaust

emissions. To understand the behavior of the combustion and transfer of its heat, consider the air/fuel charge. It is ignited and the flame front burns progressively across the combustion chamber until the burning charge reaches the cylinder walls. Some of the fuel in contact with the walls is not hot enough to burn, thereby snuffing out or Quenching the combustion process. This leaves unburned fuel in the combustion chamber. This unburned fuel is then forced out of the cylinder along with the exhaust gases and into the exhaust system.

Many attempts have been made to minimize the amount of unburned fuel in the combustion chambers due to the snuffing out or "Quenching", by increasing the coolant temperature and lessening the contact area of the coolant around the combustion area. Design limitations within the combustion chambers prevent the complete burning of the air/fuel charge, so a certain amount of the unburned fuel is still expelled into the exhaust system, regardless of modifications to the engine.

EXHAUST EMISSIONS

Composition Of The Exhaust Gases

The exhaust gases emitted into the atmosphere are a combination of burned and unburned fuel. To understand the exhaust emission and its composition review some basic chemistry.

When the air/fuel mixture is introduced into the engine, we are mixing air, composed of nitrogen (78%), oxygen (21%) and other gases (1%) with the fuel, which is 100% hydrocarbons (HC), in a semi-controlled ratio. As the combustion process is accomplished, power is produced to move the vehicle while the heat of combustion is transferred to the cooling system. The exhaust gases are then composed of nitrogen, a diatomic gas (N_2), the same as was introduced in the engine, carbon dioxide ($CO2$), the same gas that is used in beverage carbonation and water vapor (H_2O). The nitrogen (N_2), for the most part passes through the engine unchanged, while the oxygen (O_2) reacts (burns) with the hydrocarbons (HC) and produces the carbon dioxide (CO_2) and the water vapors (H_2O). If this chemical process would be the only

process to take place, the exhaust emissions would be harmless. However, during the combustion process, other pollutants are formed and are considered dangerous. These pollutants are carbon monoxide (CO), hydrocarbons (HC), oxides of nitrogen (NOx) oxides of sulfur (SOx) and engine particulates.

Lead (Pb), is considered 1 of the particulates and is present in the exhaust gases whenever leaded fuels are used. Lead (Pb) does not dissipate easily. Levels can be high along roadways when it is emitted from vehicles and can pose a health threat. Since the increased usage of unleaded gasoline and the phasing out of leaded gasoline for fuel, this pollutant is gradually diminishing. While not considered a major threat lead is still considered a dangerous pollutant.

HYDROCARBONS

Hydrocarbons (HC) are essentially unburned fuel that have not been successfully burned during the combustion process or have escaped into the atmosphere through fuel evaporation. The main sources of incomplete combustion are

rich air/fuel mixtures, low engine temperatures and improper spark timing. The main sources of hydrocarbon emission through fuel evaporation come from the vehicle's fuel tank and carburetor bowl.

To reduce combustion hydrocarbon emission, engine modifications were made to minimize dead space and surface area in the combustion chamber. In addition the air/fuel mixture was made more lean through improved carburetion, fuel injection and by the addition of external controls to aid in further combustion of the hydrocarbons outside the engine. Two such methods were the addition of an air injection system, to inject fresh air into the exhaust manifolds and the installation of a catalytic converter, a unit that is able to burn traces of hydrocarbons without affecting the internal combustion process or fuel economy.

To control hydrocarbon emissions through fuel evaporation, modifications were made to the fuel tank and carburetor bowl to allow storage of the fuel vapors during periods of engine shutdown, and at specific times during engine operation, to purge and burn these same vapors by blending them with the air/fuel mixture.

CARBON MONOXIDE

Carbon monoxide is formed when not enough oxygen is present during the combustion process to convert carbon (C) to carbon dioxide (CO_2). An increase in the carbon monoxide (CO) emission is normally accompanied by an increase in the hydrocarbon (HC) emission because of the lack of oxygen to completely burn all of the fuel mixture.

Carbon monoxide (CO) also increases the rate at which the photo chemical smog is formed by speeding up the conversion of nitric oxide (NO) to nitrogen dioxide (NO_2). To accomplish this, carbon monoxide (CO) combines with oxygen (O_2) and nitrogen dioxide (NO_2) to produce carbon dioxide (CO_2) and nitrogen dioxide (NO_2). ($CO + O_2 + NO = CO_2 + NO_2$).

The dangers of carbon monoxide, which is an odorless, colorless toxic gas are many. When carbon monoxide is inhaled into the lungs and passed into the blood stream, oxygen is replaced by the carbon monoxide in the red blood cells, causing a reduction in the amount of oxygen being supplied to the many parts of the body. This lack of oxygen causes headaches, lack of coordination, reduced mental alertness and should the carbon monoxide concentration be high enough, death could result.

NITROGEN

Normally, nitrogen is an inert gas. When heated to approximately 2500°F (1371°C) through the combustion process, this gas becomes active and causes an increase in the nitric oxide (NOx) emission.

Oxides of nitrogen (NOx) are composed of approximately 97–98% nitric oxide (NO2). Nitric oxide is a colorless gas but when it is passed into the atmosphere, it combines with oxygen and forms nitrogen dioxide (NO2). The nitrogen dioxide then combines with chemically active hydrocarbons (HC) and when in the presence of sunlight, causes the formation of photo chemical smog.

OZONE

To further complicate matters, some of the nitrogen dioxide (NO_2) is broken apart by the sunlight to form nitric oxide and oxygen. (NO_2 + sunlight = NO + O). This single atom of oxygen then combines with diatomic (meaning 2 atoms) oxygen (O_2) to form ozone (O_3). Ozone is 1 of the smells associated with smog. It has a pungent and offensive odor, irritates the eyes and lung tissues, affects the growth of plant life and causes rapid deterioration of rubber products. Ozone can be formed by sunlight as well as electrical discharge into the air.

The most common discharge area on the automobile engine is the secondary ignition electrical system, especially when inferior quality spark plug cables are used. As the surge of high voltage is routed through the secondary cable, the circuit builds up an electrical field around the wire, acting upon the oxygen in the surrounding air to form the ozone. The faint glow along the cable with the engine running that may be visible on a dark night, is called the "corona discharge." It is the result of the electrical field passing from a high along the cable, to a low in the surrounding air, which forms the ozone gas. The combination of corona and ozone has been a major cause of cable deterioration. Recently, different types and better quality insulating materials have lengthened the life of the electrical cables.

Although ozone at ground level can be harmful, ozone is beneficial to the earth's inhabitants. By having a concentrated ozone layer called the 'ozonosphere', between 10 and 20 miles (16–32km) up in the atmosphere much of the ultra violet radiation from the sun's rays are absorbed and screened. If this ozone layer were not present, much of the earth's surface would be burned, dried and unfit for human life.

There is much discussion concerning the ozone layer and its density. A feeling exists that this protective layer of ozone is slowly diminishing and corrective action must be directed to this problem. Much experimenting is presently being conducted to determine if a problem exists and if so, the short and long term effects of the problem and how it can be remedied.

OXIDES OF SULFUR

Oxides of sulfur (SOx) were initially ignored in the exhaust system emissions, since the sulfur content of gasoline as a fuel is less than $\frac{1}{10}$ of 1%. Because of this small amount, it was felt that it contributed very little to the overall pollution problem. However, because of the difficulty in solving the sulfur emissions in industrial pollutions and the introduction of catalytic converter to the automobile exhaust systems, a change was mandated. The automobile exhaust system, when equipped with a catalytic converter, changes the sulfur dioxide (SO_2) into the sulfur trioxide (SO_3).

When this combines with water vapors (H_2O), a sulfuric acid mist (H_2SO_4) is formed and is a very difficult pollutant to handle and is extremely corrosive. This sulfuric acid mist that is formed, is the same mist that rises from the vents of an automobile storage battery when an active chemical reaction takes place within the battery cells.

When a large concentration of vehicles equipped with catalytic converters are operating in an area, this acid mist will rise and be distributed over a large ground area causing land, plant, crop, paints and building damage.

PARTICULATE MATTER

A certain amount of particulate matter is present in the burning of any fuel, with carbon constituting the largest percentage of the particulates. In gasoline, the remaining percentage of particulates is the burned remains of the various other compounds used in its manufacture. When a gasoline engine is in good internal condition, the particulate emissions are low but as the engine wears internally, the particulate emissions increase. By visually inspecting the tail pipe emissions, a determination can be made as to where an engine defect may exist. An engine with light gray smoke emitting from the tail pipe normally indicates an increase in the oil consumption through burning due to internal engine wear. Black smoke would indicate a defective fuel delivery system, causing the engine to operate in a rich mode. Regardless of the color of the smoke, the internal part of the engine or the fuel delivery system should be repaired to a "like new" condition to prevent excess particulate emissions.

Diesel and turbine engines emit a darkened plume of smoke from the exhaust system because of the type of fuel used. Emission control regulations are mandated for this type of emission and more stringent measures are being used to prevent excess emission of the particulate matter. Electronic components are being introduced to control the injection of the fuel at precisely the proper time of piston travel, to achieve the optimum in fuel ignition and fuel usage. Other particulate after-burning components are being tested to achieve a cleaner particular emission.

Good grades of engine lubricating oils should be used, meeting the manufacturers specification. "Cut-rate" oils can contribute to the particulate emission problem because of their low "flash" or ignition temperature point.

Such oils burn prematurely during the combustion process causing emissions of particulate matter.

The cooling system is an important factor in the reduction of particulate matter. With the cooling system operating at a temperature specified by the manufacturer, the optimum of combustion will occur. The cooling system must be maintained in the same manner as the engine oiling system, as each system is required to perform properly in order for the engine to operate efficiently for a long time.

Other Automobile Emission Sources

Before emission controls were mandated on the internal combustion engines, other sources of engine pollutants were discovered, along with the exhaust emission. It was determined the engine combustion exhaust produced 60% of the total emission pollutants, fuel evaporation from the fuel tank and carburetor vents produced 20%, with the another 20% being produced through the crankcase as a by-product of the combustion process.

CRANKCASE EMISSIONS

Crankcase emissions are made up of water, acids, unburned fuel, oil fumes and particulates. The emissions are classified as hydrocarbons (HC) and are formed by the small amount of unburned, compressed air/fuel mixture entering the crankcase from the combustion area during the compression and power strokes, between the cylinder walls and piston rings. The head of the compression and combustion help to form the remaining crankcase emissions.

Since the first engines, crankcase emissions were allowed to go into the air through a road draft tube, mounted on the lower side of the engine block. Fresh air came in through an open oil filler cap or breather. The air passed through the crankcase mixing with blow-by gases. The motion of the vehicle and the air blowing past the open end of the road draft tube caused a low pressure area at the end of the tube. Crankcase emissions were simply drawn out of the road draft tube into the air.

To control the crankcase emission, the road draft tube was deleted. A hose and/or tubing was routed from the crankcase to the intake manifold so the blow-by emission could be burned with the air/fuel mixture. However, it was found that intake manifold vacuum, used to draw the crankcase emissions into the manifold, would vary in strength at the wrong time and not allow the proper emission flow. A regulating type valve was needed to control the flow of air through the crankcase.

Testing, showed the removal of the blow-by gases from the crankcase as quickly as possible, was most important to the longevity of the engine. Should large accumulations of blow-by gases remain and condense, dilution of the engine oil would occur to form water, soots, resins, acids and lead salts, resulting in the formation of sludge and varnishes. This condensation of the blow-by gases occur more frequently on vehicles used in numerous starting and stopping conditions, excessive idling and when the engine is not allowed to attain normal operating temperature through short runs. The crankcase purge control or PCV system will be described in detail later in this section.

FUEL EVAPORATIVE EMISSIONS

Gasoline fuel is a major source of pollution, before and after it is burned in the automobile engine. From the time the fuel is refined, stored, pumped and transported, again stored until it is pumped into the fuel tank of the vehicle, the gasoline gives off unburned hydrocarbons (HC)

into the atmosphere. Through redesigning of the storage areas and venting systems, the pollution factor has been diminished but not eliminated, from the refinery standpoint. However, the automobile still remained the primary source of vaporized, unburned hydrocarbon (HC) emissions.

Fuel pumped form an underground storage tank is cool but when exposed to a warner ambient temperature, will expand. Before controls were mandated, an owner would fill the fuel tank with fuel from an underground storage tank and park the vehicle for some time in warm area, such as a parking lot. As the fuel would warm, it would expand and should no provisions or area be provided for the expansion, the fuel would spill out the filler neck and onto the ground, causing hydrocarbon (HC) pollution and creating a severe fire hazard. To correct this condition, the vehicle manufacturers added overflow plumbing and/or gasoline tanks with built in expansion areas or domes.

However, this did not control the fuel vapor emission from the fuel tank and the carburetor bowl. It was determined that most of the fuel evaporation occurred when the vehicle was stationary and the engine not operating. Most vehicles carry 5–25 gallons (19–95 liters) of gasoline. Should a large concentration of vehicles be parked in one area, such as a large parking lot, excessive fuel vapor emissions would take place, increasing as the temperature increases.

To prevent the vapor emission from escaping into the atmosphere, the fuel system is designed to trap the fuel vapors while the vehicle is stationary, by sealing the fuel system from the atmosphere. A storage system is used to collect and hold the fuel vapors from the carburetor and the fuel tank when the engine is not operating. When the engine is started, the storage system is then purged of the fuel vapors, which are drawn into the engine and burned with the air/fuel mixture.

The components of the fuel evaporative system will be described in detail later in this section.

EMISSION CONTROLS

There are 3 sources of automotive pollutants: Crankcase fumes, exhaust gases and gasoline evaporation. The pollutants formed from these substances fall into 3 categories: unburnt Hydrocarbons (HC), Carbon Monoxide (CO) and Oxides of Nitrogen (NOx). The equipment that is used to limit these pollutants is commonly called emission control equipment.

Crankcase Ventilation System

OPERATION

◆ SEE FIGS. 1 AND 2

The crankcase emission control equipment consists of a Positive Crankcase Ventilation (PCV) valve, a closed oil filler cap and hoses to connect this equipment.

When the engine is running, a small portion of the gases which are formed in the combustion chamber during combustion leak by the piston rings and enter the crankcase. Since these gases are under pressure they tend to escape from the crankcase and enter into the atmosphere. If these gases were allowed to remain in the crankcase for any length of time, they would contaminate the engine oil and cause sludge to build up. If the gases are allowed to escape into the atmosphere, they would pollute the air, as

they contain unburned hydrocarbons. The crankcase emission control equipment recycles these gases back into the engine combustion chamber where they are burned.

Crankcase gases are recycled in the following manner: while the engine is running, clean filtered air is drawn into the crankcase through the air filter and then through a hose leading to the rocker cover. As the air passes through the crankcase, it picks up the combustion gases and carries them out of the crankcase, up through the PCV valve and into the intake manifold. After they enter the intake manifold, they are drawn into the combustion chamber and burned.

The most critical component in the system is the PCV valve. This vacuum controlled valve regulates the amount of gases which are recycled into the combustion changer. At low engine speeds the valve is partially closed, limiting the flow of gases into the intake manifold. As engine speed increases, the valve opens to admit greater quantities of the gases into the intake manifold. If the valve should become blocked or plugged, the gases will be prevented from escaping from the crankcase by

the normal route. Since these gases are under pressure, they will find their own way out of the crankcase. This alternate route is usually a weak oil seal or gasket in the engine. As the gas escapes by the gasket, it also creates an oil leak. Besides causing oil leaks, a clogged PCV valve also allows these gases to remain in the crankcase for an extended period of time, promoting the formation of sludge in the engine.

TESTING

PCV Valve

Check the PCV system hoses and connections, to see that there are no leaks. Then replace or tighten, as necessary.

With the engine running at idle, remove the ventilation hose from the PCV valve. If the valve is working properly, a hissing noise will be heard as air passes through it and a strong vacuum should be felt when a finger is placed over the valve inlet. Refer to the illustrations.

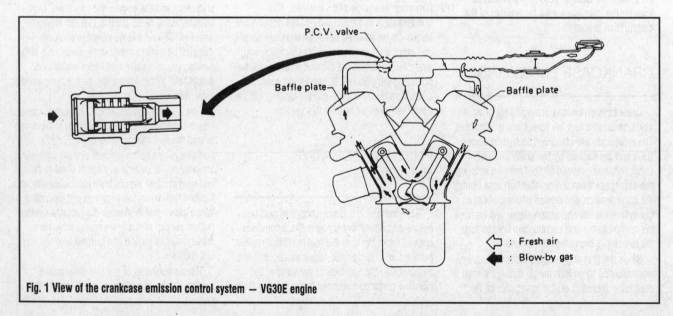

Fig. 1 View of the crankcase emission control system — VG30E engine

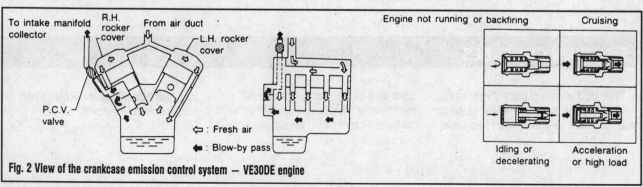

Fig. 2 View of the crankcase emission control system — VE30DE engine

To check the valve, remove it and blow through both of its ends. When blowing from the side which goes toward the intake manifold, very little air should pass through it. When blowing from the crankcase (valve cover) side, air should pass through freely. Replace the valve with a new one, if the valve fails to function as outlined.

➡ **Do not attempt to clean or adjust the valve. Replace it with a new one.**

PCV Filter

Replace the PCV filter inside the air cleaner when you replace the PCV valve or more frequently, if operating in dusty or smoggy conditions.

REMOVAL & INSTALLATION

To remove the PCV valve, simply loosen the hose clamp and remove the valve from the manifold-to-crankcase hose and intake manifold. Install the PCV valve in the reverse order of removal.

Disconnect all hoses and clean with compressed air. If any hose cannot be freed of obstructions, replace it.

Evaporative Emission Controls

OPERATION

▸ SEE FIGS. 3-8

When raw fuel evaporates, the vapors contain hydrocarbons. To prevent these fumes from escaping into the atmosphere, the fuel evaporative emission control system was developed.

The system consists of a sealed fuel tank, a vapor/liquid separator, a vapor vent line, a carbon canister, a vacuum signal line and a canister purge line.

In operation, fuel vapors and/or liquid are routed to the liquid/vapor separator or check valve where liquid fuel is directed back into the fuel tank as fuel vapors flow into the charcoal filled canister. The charcoal absorbs and stores the fuel vapors when the engine is not running or is at idle. When the air intakes are opened, vacuum from above the throttle valves is routed through a vacuum signal line to the purge control valve on the canister. The control valve opens and allows the fuel vapors to be drawn from the canister through a purge line and into the intake manifold and the combustion chambers.

INSPECTION AND SERVICE

Hoses

Check the hoses for proper connections and damage. Replace as necessary.

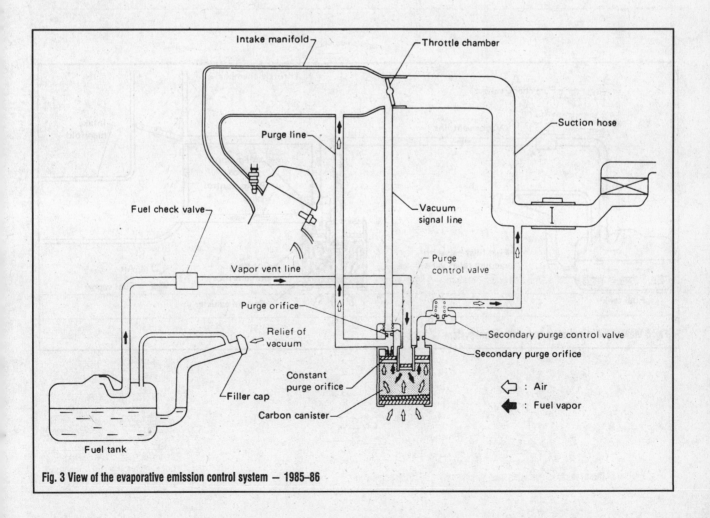

Fig. 3 View of the evaporative emission control system — 1985–86

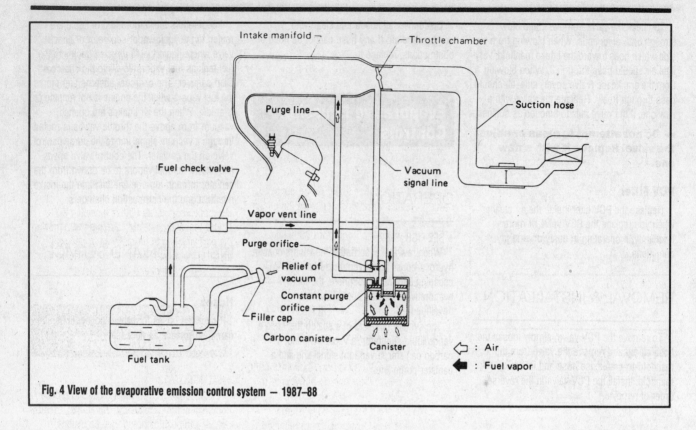

Fig. 4 View of the evaporative emission control system — 1987–88

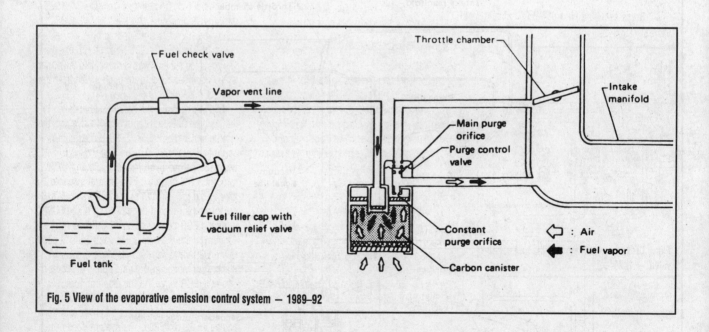

Fig. 5 View of the evaporative emission control system — 1989–92

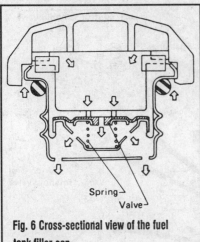

Fig. 6 Cross-sectional view of the fuel tank filler cap

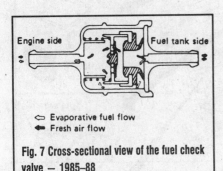

⟲ Evaporative fuel flow
⬅ Fresh air flow

Fig. 7 Cross-sectional view of the fuel check valve — 1985–88

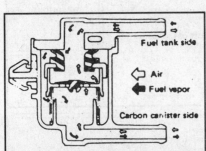

Fig. 8 Cross-sectional view of the fuel check valve — 1989–92

Purge Control Valve(s)

♦ SEE FIGS. 3-5

1. To check the operation of the carbon canister purge control valve, perform the following procedures:

a. Disconnect the rubber hose between the top of the canister control valve and the intake manifold at the intake manifold.

b. Blow into the hose from the intake manifold side of the valve; if air can be blown into the valve, replace it.

c. Disconnect the lower purge control valve-to-intake manifold hose from the intake manifold.

d. Blow into the hose from the intake manifold side of the valve; air should be able to be blown into the valve. If not, replace it.

2. To check the operation of the secondary purge control valve, used on 1985–86 models, perform the following procedures:

a. Disconnect the rubber hose between the top of the secondary purge control valve and the intake duct at the intake duct.

b. Blow into the hose from the intake duct side of the valve; if air can be blown into the valve, replace it.

c. Disconnect the secondary purge control valve hose from the carbon canister.

d. Blow into the hose from the carbon canister side of the valve; air should be able to be blown into the valve. If not, replace it.

Carbon Canister

♦ SEE FIGS. 3-5

The carbon canister has an air filter in the bottom of the canister. The filter element should be checked once a year or every 12,000 miles; more frequently if the vehicle is operated in dusty areas. Replace the filter by pulling it out of the bottom of the canister and installing a new one.

Fuel Cap

♦ SEE FIG. 6

1. Wipe the valve housing clean.

2. Suck air through the cap.

3. A slight resistance indicates that the valve is in good condition. Resistance should disappear when the valve clicks.

4. If the valve is clogged or if no resistance is felt, replace the fuel cap.

Fuel Check Valve

♦ SEE FIGS. 7 AND 8

Blow air through the connector on the tank side. A considerable resistance should be felt and a portion of air flow should be directed toward the canister.

REMOVAL & INSTALLATION

Removal and installation of the various evaporative emission control system components consists of disconnecting the hoses, loosening retaining screws and removing the part which is to be replaced or checked. Install in the reverse order. When replacing hose, make sure it is fuel and vapor resistant.

Exhaust Gas Recirculation (EGR)

♦ SEE FIGS. 9-13

Exhaust gas recirculation is used to reduce combustion temperatures in the engine, thereby reducing the oxides of nitrogen emissions.

An EGR valve is mounted on the right rear side of the upper intake manifold collector for 1985–88 the VG30E engine and the 1992 VE30DE engine or the rear center of the upper intake manifold collector for 1989–92 VG30E engine. The recycled exhaust gas is drawn into the upper intake manifold collector through a tube from the exhaust manifold to the EGR valve.

An EGR control solenoid valve is installed in the vacuum line between the EGR valve and the throttle valve housing; its OFF/ON operation is controlled by the ECM. When the engine is warmed and operating between idle and 2700 rpm, the ECM turns the EGR control solenoid **ON** to cut the vacuum to the EGR valve. When the engine is running over 2700 rpm, the ECM turns the EGR control solenoid **OFF** to supply vacuum to the EGR valve. As vacuum is applied to the EGR valve vacuum diaphragm, the diaphragm moves against the spring pressure to open the EGR valve. As the diaphragm moves up, it opens the exhaust gas metering valve which allows exhaust gas to be pulled into the engine intake manifold. The system does not operate when the engine is idling because the exhaust gas recirculation would cause a rough idle.

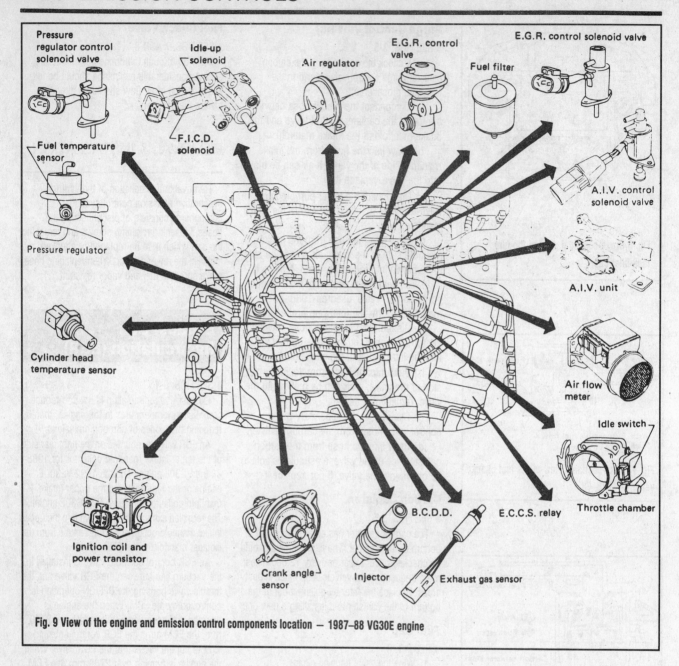

Fig. 9 View of the engine and emission control components location — 1987–88 VG30E engine

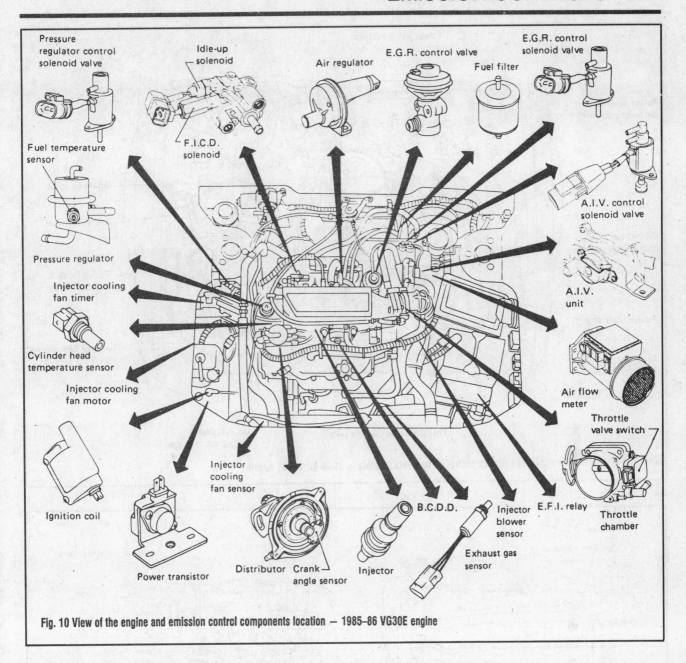

Pressure regulator control solenoid valve

Idle-up solenoid

Air regulator

E.G.R. control valve

Fuel filter

E.G.R. control solenoid valve

F.I.C.D. solenoid

Fuel temperature sensor

A.I.V. control solenoid valve

Pressure regulator

A.I.V. unit

Injector cooling fan timer

Cylinder head temperature sensor

Air flow meter

Injector cooling fan motor

Throttle valve switch

Ignition coil

Injector cooling fan sensor

B.C.D.D.

Injector blower sensor

E.F.I. relay

Throttle chamber

Power transistor

Distributor

Crank angle sensor

Injector

Exhaust gas sensor

Fig. 10 View of the engine and emission control components location — 1985–86 VG30E engine

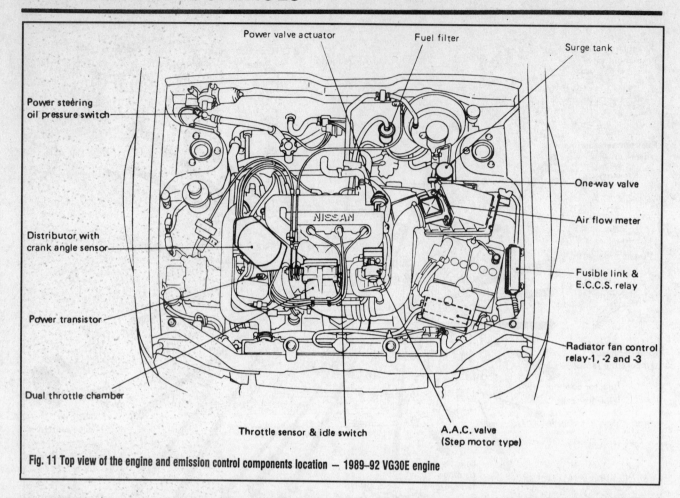

Fig. 11 Top view of the engine and emission control components location — 1989–92 VG30E engine

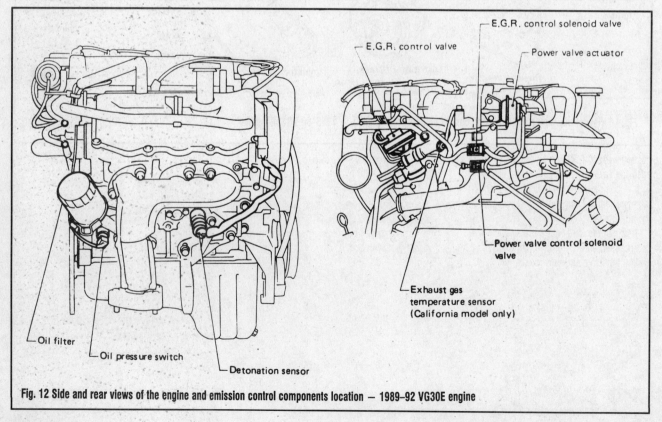

Fig. 12 Side and rear views of the engine and emission control components location — 1989–92 VG30E engine

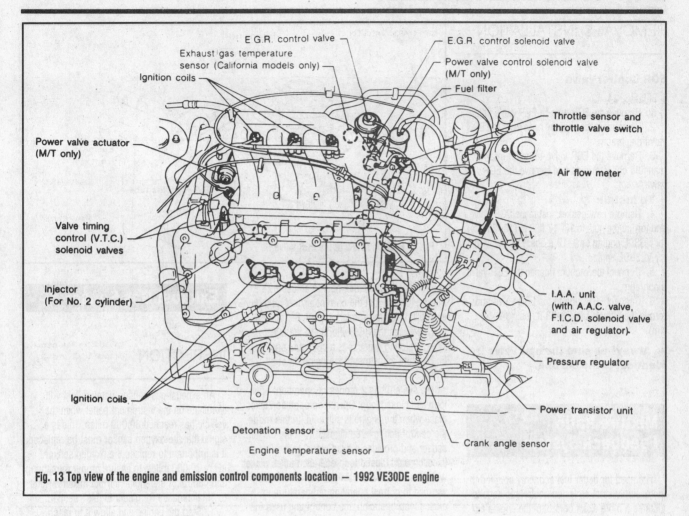

Fig. 13 Top view of the engine and emission control components location — 1992 VE30DE engine

Labels:
- E.G.R. control valve
- Exhaust gas temperature sensor (California models only)
- Ignition coils
- Power valve actuator (M/T only)
- Valve timing control (V.T.C.) solenoid valves
- Injector (For No. 2 cylinder)
- Ignition coils
- Detonation sensor
- Engine temperature sensor
- E.G.R. control solenoid valve
- Power valve control solenoid valve (M/T only)
- Fuel filter
- Throttle sensor and throttle valve switch
- Air flow meter
- I.A.A. unit (with A.A.C. valve, F.I.C.D. solenoid valve and air regulator)
- Pressure regulator
- Power transistor unit
- Crank angle sensor

TESTING

♦ SEE FIG. 15

1. Remove the EGR valve.

2. Using a vacuum source, apply enough vacuum, about 4.72 in. Hg, to the diaphragm to open the valve.

3. Check the valve for damage, such as warpage, cracks and excessive wear around the valve and seat.

4. Clean the seat with a brush and compressed air and remove any deposits from around the valve and port (seat).

5. To check the operation of the EGR control solenoid valve, perform the following procedures:

a. Remove the valve and apply vacuum to the intake manifold port of the valve. The valve should not allow vacuum to pass through the EGR valve port; it should pass through the upper port of the valve.

b. Connect 12 volt to the electrical harness connector terminals; it should pass through the EGR valve port of the valve.

c. If the valve does not respond correctly to the test, replace it.

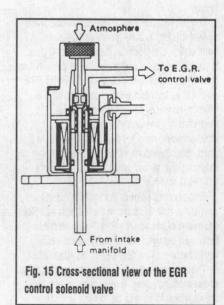

Labels:
- Atmosphere
- To E.G.R. control valve
- From intake manifold

Fig. 15 Cross-sectional view of the EGR control solenoid valve

REMOVAL & INSTALLATION

EGR Control Valve

♦ SEE FIG. 14

1. Remove the EGR tube-to-EGR valve fitting.
2. Disconnect the vacuum hose from the EGR valve diaphragm.
3. Remove the EGR valve-to-upper intake manifold collector nuts and remove the EGR valve.

To install:

4. Using a new gasket, install the EGR valve and torque the nuts to 13–17 ft. lbs. (18–23 Nm) for VG30E engine or 9–12 ft. lbs. (13–16 Nm) for VE30DE engine.
5. Connect the vacuum hose to the EGR valve diaphragm.
6. Connect EGR tube to the EGR valve and torque the fitting(s) to 25–33 ft. lbs. (34–44 Nm).

➡ **Always be sure the new valve is identical to the old one.**

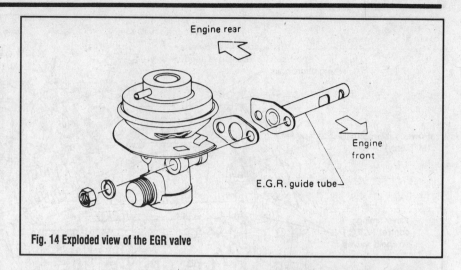

Fig. 14 Exploded view of the EGR valve

Mixture Ratio Feedback System

The need for better fuel economy coupled to increasingly strict emission control regulations dictates a more exact control of the engine air/fuel mixture. Nissan has developed a Mixture Ratio Feedback System in response to these needs.

The principle of the system is to control the air/fuel mixture exactly, so more complete combustion can occur in the engine, and more thorough oxidation and reduction of the exhaust gases can occur in the catalytic converter. The object is to maintain a stoichiometric air/fuel mixture, which is chemically correct for theoretically complete combustion. The stoichiometric ratio is 14.7:1 (air to fuel). At that point, the converter's efficiency is greatest in oxidizing and reducing HC, CO and NOx into CO_2, H_2O and N_2.

Components used in the system include an oxygen sensor, installed in the exhaust manifold upstream of the converter, a 3-way oxidation reduction catalytic converter, an electronic control unit and the fuel injection system itself.

The oxygen sensor reads the oxygen content of the exhaust gases. It generates an electric signal which is sent to the control unit. The control unit then decides how to adjust the mixture to keep it at the correct air/fuel ratio. For example, if the mixture is too lean, the control unit increases the fuel metering to the injectors. The monitoring process is a continual one, so fine mixture adjustments are going on at all times.

The system has 2 modes of operation: open loop and closed loop. Open loop operation takes place when the engine is still cold. In this mode, the control unit ignores signals from the oxygen sensor and provides a fixed signal to the fuel injection unit. Closed loop operation takes place when the engine and catalytic converter have warmed to normal operating temperature. In closed loop operation, the control unit uses the oxygen sensor signals to adjust the mixture. The burned mixture's oxygen content is read by the oxygen sensor, which continues to signal the control unit, and so on. Thus, the closed loop mode is an interdependent system of information feedback.

Mixture is, of course, not readily adjustable in this system. All system adjustments require the use of a CO meter. Thus, they should be entrusted to a qualified dealer with access to the equipment and special training in the system's repair. The only regularly scheduled maintenance is replacement of the oxygen sensor at 30,000 mile intervals.

It should be noted that proper operation of the system is entirely dependent on the oxygen sensor. Thus, if the sensor is not replaced at the correct interval or if the sensor fails during normal operation, the engine fuel mixture will be incorrect, resulting in poor fuel economy, starting problems or stumbling and stalling of the engine when warm.

Exhaust Gas Sensor

INSPECTION

An exhaust gas sensor warning light will illuminate on the instrument panel when the vehicle has reached 30,000 miles. This is a signal that the oxygen sensor must be replaced. It is important to replace the oxygen sensor every 30,000 miles, to ensure proper monitoring and control of the engine air/fuel mixture. Refer to "Maintenance Reminder Lights" section.

1. Start the engine and allow it to reach normal operating temperature.
2. Run the engine at approximately 2000 rpm under no load. Block the front wheels and set the parking brake.
3. An inspection lamp has been provided on the bottom of the control unit, which is located in the passenger compartment on the driver's side kick panel, next to the clutch or brake pedal. If the oxygen sensor is operating correctly, the inspection lamp will go on and off more than 5 times in 10 seconds. The inspection lamp can be more easily seen with the aid of a mirror.
4. If the lamp does not go ON and OFF as specified, the system is not operating correctly. Check the battery, ignition system, engine oil and coolant levels, all fuses, the fuel injection wiring harness connectors, all vacuum hoses, the oil filler cap and dipstick for proper seating and the valve clearance and engine compression. If all of these parts are in good order and the inspection lamp still does not go ON and OFF at least 5 times in 10 seconds, the oxygen sensor is probably faulty. However, the possibility exists that the malfunction could be in the fuel injection control unit. The system should be tested by a qualified dealer with specific training in the Mixture Ratio Feedback System.

REMOVAL & INSTALLATION

◆ SEE FIGS. 9–10 AND 33

1. Disconnect the negative battery cable and the sensor electrical lead. Unscrew the sensor from the exhaust manifold.

2. Coat the threads of the replacement sensor with a nickel base anti-seize compound. Do not use other types of compounds, since they may electrically insulate the sensor. Do not get compound on sensor housing. Install the sensor into the manifold. Installation torque for the sensor is about 18–25 ft. lbs. on 1985–88 or 30–37 ft. lbs. on 1989–92. Connect the electrical lead. Be careful handling the electrical lead. It is easily damaged.

3. Reconnect the battery cable.

The oxygen sensor is installed in the exhaust manifold for 1985–88 or exhaust pipe for 1989–92 and is removed in the same manner as a spark plug. Exercise care when handling the sensor do not drop or handle the sensor roughly. Care should be used not to get compound on the sensor itself.

Maintenance Reminder Lights

RESETTING

USA Models

On models with a sensor relay, reset the relay by pushing the button. Reset relay at 30,000 and 60,000 miles. At 90,000 miles, locate and disconnect warning light wire connector.

On models without sensor light relay and Canada models locate and disconnect the single warning light harness connector. The reminder light will no longer function.

WARNING LIGHT CONNECTOR LOCATIONS

◆ SEE FIGS. 30-32

On 1985–86 models, disconnect the warning lamp harness connector at the left of the brake pedal, after 90,000 miles. The sensor relay is located is located at the lower left side of the instrument panel.

On 1987 model, disconnect the warning lamp harness connector at the left of the brake pedal, after 90,000 miles. The sensor relay is located at the lower right side of the instrument panel.

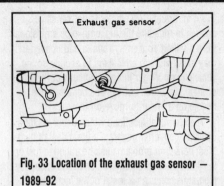

Fig. 33 Location of the exhaust gas sensor — 1989–92

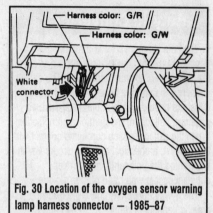

Fig. 30 Location of the oxygen sensor warning lamp harness connector — 1985–87

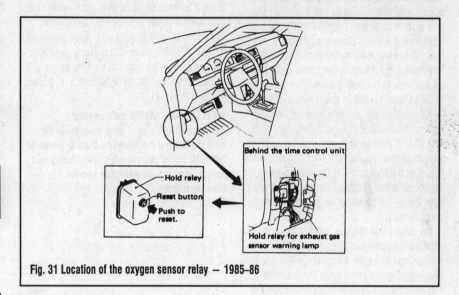

Fig. 31 Location of the oxygen sensor relay — 1985–86

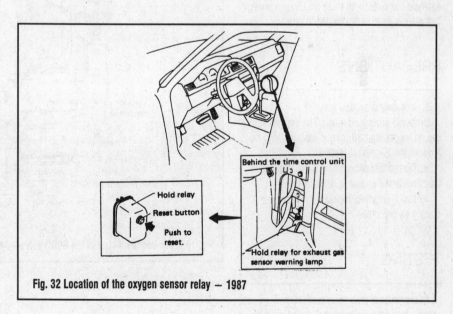

Fig. 32 Location of the oxygen sensor relay — 1987

Catalytic Converter

The catalytic converter is a muffler like container built into the exhaust system to aid in the reduction of exhaust emissions. The catalyst element consists of a honeycomb monolithic substrate coated with a noble metal such as platinum, palladium, rhodium or a combination. When the exhaust gases come into contact with the catalyst, a chemical reaction occurs which will reduce the pollutants into harmless substances like water and carbon dioxide.

The 3-way converter, unlike the oxidizing type, is capable of reducing HC, CO and NOx emissions; all at the same time. In theory, it seems impossible to reduce all 3 pollutants in one system since the reduction of HC and CO requires the addition of oxygen, while the reduction of NOx calls for the removal of oxygen. In actuality, the 3 way system really can reduce all 3 pollutants but only if the amount of oxygen in the exhaust system is precisely controlled.

All models have an oxygen sensor warning light on the dashboard, which illuminates at the first 30,000 mile interval, signaling the need for oxygen sensor replacement. The oxygen sensor is part of the Mixture Ratio Feedback System, described in this section. The Feedback System uses the 3-way converter as one of its major components.

No regular maintenance is required for the catalytic converter system, except for periodic replacement of the Air Induction System filter(s). Filter replacement procedures are in Section 1. The Air Induction System is used to supply the catalytic converter with fresh air. Oxygen present in the air is used in the oxidation process.

PRECAUTIONS

1. Use only unleaded fuel.
2. Avoid prolonged idling. The engine should run on longer than 20 min. at curb idle and no longer than 10 min. at fast idle.
3. Do not disconnect any of the spark plug leads while the engine is running.
4. Make engine compression checks as quickly as possible.

TESTING

At the present time there is no known way to reliably test catalytic converter operation in the field. The only reliable test is a 12 hour and 40 min. soak test (CVS) which must be done in a laboratory.

An infrared HC/CO tester is not sensitive enough to measure the higher tailpipe emissions from a failing converter. Thus, a bad converter may allow enough emissions to escape so the vehicle is no longer in compliance with Federal or state standards but will still not cause the needle on a tester to move off 0.

The chemical reactions which occur inside a catalytic converter generate a great deal of heat. Most converter problems can be traced to fuel or ignition system problems which cause unusually high emissions. As a result of the increased intensity of the chemical reactions, the converter literally burns itself up.

A completely failed converter might cause a tester to show a slight reading. As a result, it is occasionally possible to detect one of these.

As long as you avoid severe overheating and the use of leaded fuels, it is reasonably safe to assume that the converter is working properly. If you are in doubt, take the vehicle to a diagnostic center that has a tester.

➡ **If the catalytic converter becomes blocked the engine will not run. The converter has 5 year or 50,000 mile warranty; contact your local Nissan dealer for more information.**

Boost Controlled Deceleration Device (BCDD)

1985–88

◆ SEE FIG. 16

The Boost Controlled Deceleration Device (BCDD) is used to reduce hydrocarbon emissions during coasting conditions.

High manifold vacuum during coasting prevents the complete combustion of the air/fuel mixture because of the reduced amount of air. This condition will result in a large amount of HC emission. Enriching the air/fuel mixture for a short time (during the high vacuum condition) will reduce the emission of the HC.

However, enriching the air/fuel mixture with only the mixture adjusting screw will cause poor engine idle or invite an increase in the Carbon Monoxide (CO) content of the exhaust gases. The BCDD consists of an independent system that kicks in when the engine is coasting and enriches the air/fuel mixture, which reduces the hydrocarbon content of the exhaust gases. This is accomplished without adversely affecting engine idle and the carbon monoxide content of the exhaust gases.

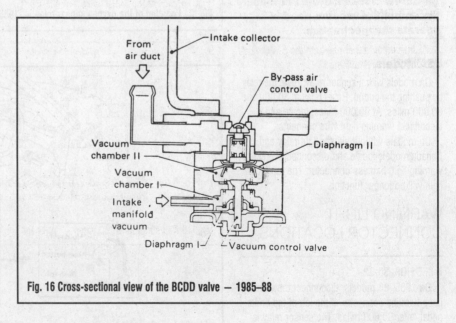

Fig. 16 Cross-sectional view of the BCDD valve — 1985–88

ADJUSTMENT

▶ SEE FIGS. 17-19

Normally, the BCDD does not need adjustment. However, if the need should arise because of suspected malfunction of the system, proceed as follows:

1. Using a "T" connecter, install a quick response vacuum gauge in the BCDD valve-to-intake manifold hose.

2. Start and warm the engine until it reaches normal operating temperature.

3. Observe the vacuum gauge while racing the engine; vacuum should increase sharply, then decrease sharply and level off at a predetermined set pressure for a speed other than idle or an idling pressure for idle speed.

4. If the valve does not react as described, adjust the valve's operating pressure.

5. Pry the rubber cap from the end of the BCDD valve.

6. While racing the engine, turn the adjusting screw until a set pressure of 22.44 ± 0.79 in. Hg (76.0 ± 2.7 kPa) of vacuum is obtained.

➡ **Turning the screw ¼ of a turn in either direction will change the operation pressure about 0.79 in. Hg (2.7 kPa). Turning the screw counterclockwise will increase the amount of vacuum needed to operate the mechanism. Turning the screw clockwise will decrease the amount of vacuum needed to operate the mechanism.**

7. Install the rubber cap onto the BCDD valve after the system is adjusted.

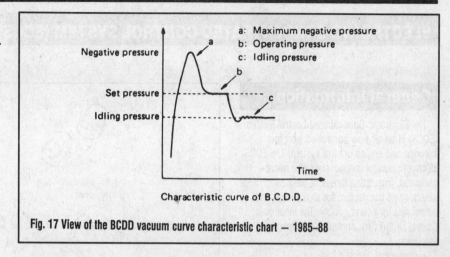

a: Maximum negative pressure
b: Operating pressure
c: Idling pressure

Fig. 17 View of the BCDD vacuum curve characteristic chart — 1985–88

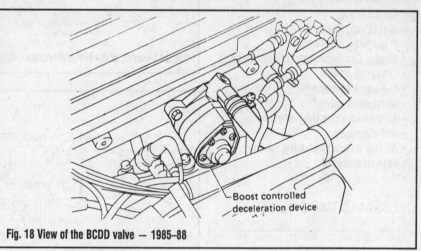

Fig. 18 View of the BCDD valve — 1985–88

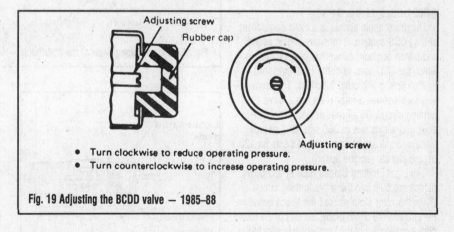

- Turn clockwise to reduce operating pressure.
- Turn counterclockwise to increase operating pressure.

Fig. 19 Adjusting the BCDD valve — 1985–88

ELECTRONIC CONCENTRATED CONTROL SYSTEM (ECCS)

General Information

The Electronic Concentrated Control System (ECCS) is an air flow controlled, port fuel injection and engine control system. The ECCS electronic control unit consists of a micro-computer, inspection lamps, a diagnostic mode selector and connectors for signal input and output and for power supply. The Electronic Control Unit (ECU), controls the following functions:

• Amount of injected fuel
• Ignition timing
• Mixture ratio feedback
• Pressure regulator control
• Exhaust Gas Recirculation (EGR) operation
• Idle speed control
• Fuel pump operation
• Air regulator control
• Air Injection Valve (AIV) operation
• Self-diagnostics
• Air flow meter self-cleaning control
• Fail safe system

SYSTEM COMPONENTS

Crank Angle Sensor

♦ SEE FIGS. 9-11, 13, 34-37

The crank angle sensor is a basic component of the ECCS system. It monitors engine speed and piston position, as well as sending signals, which the ECU uses to control fuel injection, ignition timing and other functions. The crank angle sensor has a rotor plate and a wave forming circuit. On all models, the rotor plate is equipped with a row of 360 slits for 1 degree signals (crank angle) and a row of 6 slits for 120 degree signals (engine speed).

The Light Emitting Diodes (LED's) and photo diodes are built into the wave forming circuit. When the rotor plate passes the space between the LED and the photo diode, the slits of the rotor plate continually cut the light which is sent to the photo diode from the LED. This generates rough shaped pulses which are converted into ON/OFF pulses by the wave forming circuit and then sent to the ECU.

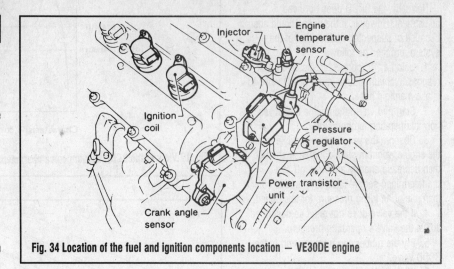

Fig. 34 Location of the fuel and ignition components location — VE30DE engine

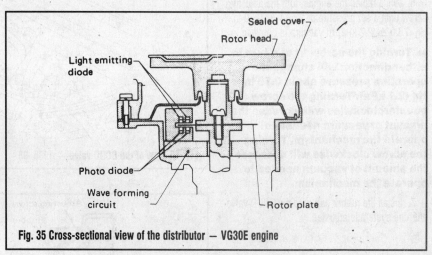

Fig. 35 Cross-sectional view of the distributor — VG30E engine

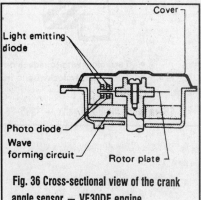

Fig. 36 Cross-sectional view of the crank angle sensor — VE30DE engine

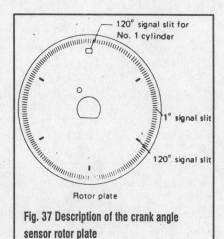

Fig. 37 Description of the crank angle sensor rotor plate

Cylinder Head Temperature Sensor

♦ SEE FIGS. 9, 10, 13 AND 34

The cylinder head temperature sensor, built into the front of the cylinder head for 1985–88 or on top of the water inlet housing for 1989–92, monitors changes in cylinder head temperature and transmits a signal to the ECU. The temperature sensing unit employs a thermistor which is sensitive to the change in temperature, with electrical resistance decreasing as temperature rises.

Air Flow Meter

♦ SEE FIGS. 9, 10, 11 AND 13

The air flow meter measures the mass flow rate of intake air. The volume of air entering the engine is measured by the use of a hot wire placed in the intake air stream. The control unit sends current to the wire to maintain it at a preset temperature. As the intake air moves past the wire, it removes heat and the control unit must increase the voltage to the wire to maintain it at the preset temperature. By measuring the amount of current necessary to maintain the temperature of the wire in the air stream, the ECU knows exactly how much air is entering the engine. A self-cleaning system briefly heats the hot air wire to approximately 1832°F (1000°C) after engine shutdown to burn off any dust or contaminants on the wire.

Throttle Valve Switch

♦ SEE FIGS. 9–13, 38 AND 39

A throttle valve switch is attached to the throttle chamber and operates in response to accelerator pedal movement. The switch has an idle contact and a full throttle contact. The idle contact closes when the throttle valve is positioned at idle and opens when it is in any other position.

Fuel Injector

♦ SEE FIGS. 40 AND 41

The fuel injectors, connected to a fuel rail and installed directly in front of the intake valve port, are small, precision solenoid valves. As the ECU sends an injection signal to each injector, the coil built into the injector pulls the needle valve back and fuel is injected through the nozzle and into the intake manifold. The amount of fuel injected is dependent on how long the signal is (pulse duration); the longer the signal, the more fuel delivered.

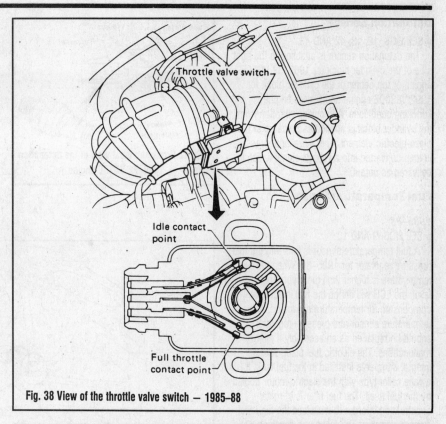

Fig. 38 View of the throttle valve switch — 1985–88

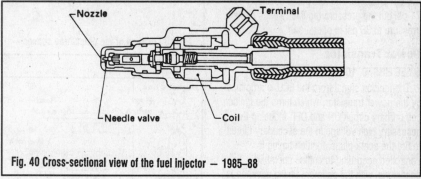

Fig. 40 Cross-sectional view of the fuel injector — 1985–88

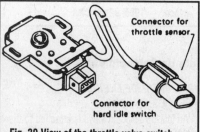

Fig. 39 View of the throttle valve switch — 1989–92

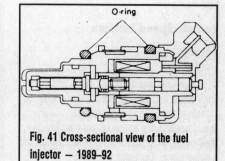

Fig. 41 Cross-sectional view of the fuel injector — 1989–92

Detonation Sensor

♦ SEE FIGS. 12, 13, 42 AND 43

The detonation sensor is attached to the right side of the cylinder block for 1989–92 VG30E engine or top center of the cylinder block for 1992 VE30DE engine and senses engine knocking conditions. A knocking vibration from the cylinder block is applied as pressure to the piezo-electric element. This vibrational pressure is then converted into a voltage signal which is delivered as output.

Fuel Temperature Sensor

1985–88

♦ SEE FIGS. 9 AND 10

A fuel temperature sensor is built into the fuel pressure regulator for 1985–88. When the fuel temperature is higher than the preprogrammed level, the ECU will enrich the fuel injected to compensate for temperature expansion. The temperature sensor and pressure regulator should be replaced as an assembly if either malfunctions. The electric fuel pump with an integral damper is installed in the fuel tank. It is a vane roller type with the electric motor cooled by the fuel itself. The fuel filter is of metal construction in order to withstand the high fuel system pressure. The fuel pump develops 61–71 psi but the pressure regulator keeps system pressure at 36 psi in operation.

Power Transistor

♦ SEE FIGS. 9, 10, 34 AND 44

The ignition signal from the ECU is amplified by the power transistor, which turns the ignition coil primary circuit ON and OFF, inducing the necessary high voltage in the secondary circuit to fire the spark plugs. Ignition timing is controlled according to engine operating conditions, with the optimum timing advance for each driving condition preprogrammed into the ECU memory.

Vehicle Speed Sensors

1989–92 Vehicles

♦ SEE FIG. 45

The vehicle speed sensors are mounted at each wheel and provide individual wheel speed signals to the ECU. On conventional speedometers, the speed sensor consists of a reed switch which transforms vehicle speed into a pulse signal. On digital electronic speedometers, the speed sensor consists of an LED, photo diode, shutter and wave forming circuit. It operates on the same principle as the crank angle sensor.

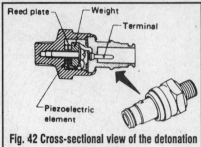

Fig. 42 Cross-sectional view of the detonation sensor — 1989–92 VG30E engine

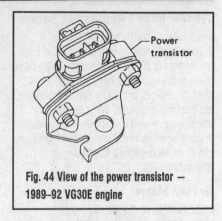

Fig. 44 View of the power transistor — 1989–92 VG30E engine

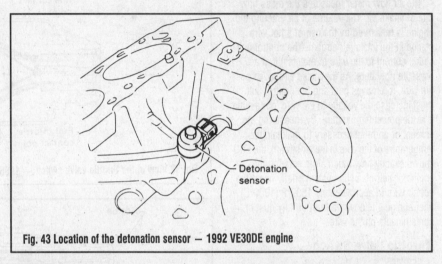

Fig. 43 Location of the detonation sensor — 1992 VE30DE engine

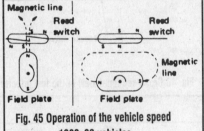

Fig. 45 Operation of the vehicle speed sensor — 1989–92 vehicles

Idle-Up Solenoid Valve

1985–88 VG30E ENGINE

♦ SEE FIGS. 9 AND 10

An idle-up solenoid valve is attached to the intake collector to stabilize idle speed when the engine load is heavy because of electrical load, power steering load, etc. An air regulator provides an air bypass when the engine is cold in order to increase idle speed during warmup (fast idle). A bimetal, heater and rotary shutter are built into the air regulator. When bimetal temperature is low, the air bypass port is open. As the engine starts and electric current flows through a heater, the bimetal begins to rotate the

shutter to close off the air bypass port. The air passage remains closed until the engine is stopped and the bimetal temperature drops.

Air Injection Valve (AIV)

1985–88 VG30E ENGINE

♦ SEE FIGS. 28 AND 29

The Air Injection Valve (AIV) sends secondary air to the exhaust manifold, utilizing a vacuum caused by exhaust pulsation in the exhaust manifold. When the exhaust pressure is below atmospheric pressure (negative pressure), secondary air is sent to the exhaust manifold. When the exhaust pressure is above atmospheric pressure, the reed valves prevent secondary air from being sent to the air cleaner. The AIV control solenoid valve cuts the intake manifold vacuum signal for AIV control. The solenoid valve actuates in response to the ON/OFF signal from the ECU. When the solenoid is OFF, the vacuum signal from the intake manifold is cut. As the control unit outputs an on signal, the coil pulls the plunger downward and feeds the vacuum signal to the AIV control valve.

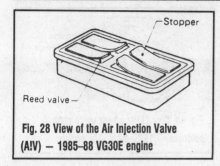

Fig. 28 View of the Air Injection Valve (AIV) — 1985–88 VG30E engine

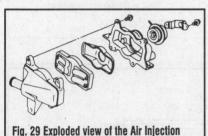

Fig. 29 Exploded view of the Air Injection Valve (AIV) — 1985–88 VG30E engine

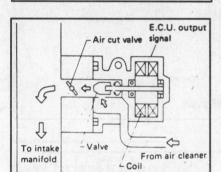

Fig. 20 Cross-sectional view of the Auxiliary Air Control (ACC) valve — 1985–92 VG30E engine

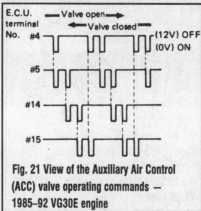
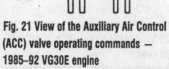

Fig. 21 View of the Auxiliary Air Control (ACC) valve operating commands — 1985–92 VG30E engine

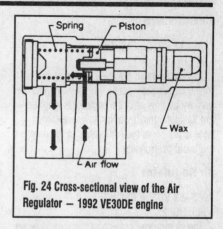

Fig. 24 Cross-sectional view of the Air Regulator — 1992 VE30DE engine

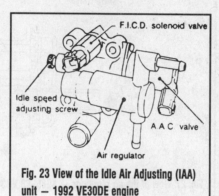

Fig. 23 View of the Idle Air Adjusting (IAA) unit — 1992 VE30DE engine

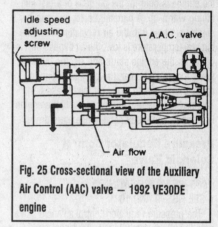

Fig. 25 Cross-sectional view of the Auxiliary Air Control (AAC) valve — 1992 VE30DE engine

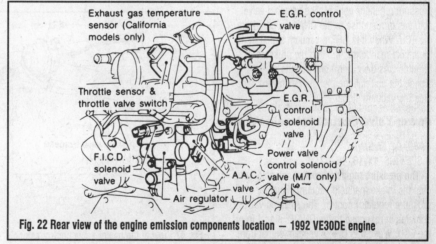

Fig. 22 Rear view of the engine emission components location — 1992 VE30DE engine

Electronic Control Unit (ECU)

The ECU consists of a microcomputer, inspection lamps, a diagnostic mode selector, and connectors for signal input and output, and for power supply. The unit controls engine operation.

Auxiliary Air Control (AAC) Valve

1989–92 VG30E ENGINE

♦ SEE FIGS. 20 AND 21

The Auxiliary Air Control (AAC) valve is used for centralized control of the auxiliary air supply; it controls the quantity of air entering the engine to enhance emissions quality.

The valve is operated by a step motor. The motor has 4 winding phases that are operated by the ECU to turn the motor winding ON and OFF, in sequence. Each time the AAC valve opens or closes, to change the auxiliary air quantity, an ON pulse is issued. When no change in the air quantity is needed, the valve remains at a certain opening: no pulse signal is issued.

Idle Air Adjusting (IAA) Unit

1992 VE30DE ENGINE

♦ SEE FIGS. 22-25

The Idle Air Adjusting (IAA) unit is made up of the Auxiliary Air Control (AAC) valve, the Fast Idle Control Device (FIDC) solenoid, the Air Regulator and the idle adjusting screw. It receives the signal from the ECU and controls the idle speed at the preset valve.

The air regulator provides an air bypass when the engine is cold for fast idle during warm-up.

The regulator consists of wax, a piston and spring. When the engine temperature is low, the air bypass port opens. When the engine temperature is high, the wax expands and moves the piston up to close the air bypass port; the idle speed decreases.

The Fast Idle Control Device (FIDC) solenoid supplies additional air, when the air conditioner switch is ON.

The Auxiliary Air Control (AAC) valve is controlled by the ECU, using an ON/OFF pulse, to provide a larger amount of air to the engine.

Air Cut Valve

1989–92 VG30E ENGINE
♦ SEE FIG. 26

The air cut valve gradually closes as the engine temperature rises. The valve restricts the auxiliary air flow after the engine has warmed and limits the maximum air flow, even when there is trouble in the AAC valve, so the engine can avoid overrunning.

Air Regulator

1985–88 VG30E ENGINE
♦ SEE FIG. 27

The air regulator provides an air bypass when the engine is cold for the purpose of a fast idle during warm-up. A bimetal, heater and rotary shutter are built into the air regulator. When the bimetal temperature is low, the air bypass port is open. As the engine starts and electric current flows through a heater, the bimetal begins to rotate the shutter to close off the bypass port. The air passage remains closed until the engine is stopped and the bimetal temperature drops.

Pressure Regulator Control Solenoid Valve

1985–88 VG30E ENGINE
♦ SEE FIGS. 9 AND 10

The pressure regulator control solenoid valve cuts the intake manifold vacuum signal for pressure regulator control. The solenoid valve actuates in response to the ON/OFF signal from the ECU. When it is OFF, a vacuum signal from the intake manifold is fed into the pressure regulator. As the control unit outputs an ON signal, the coil pull the plunger downward and cuts the vacuum signal.

Power Valve Control Solenoid Valve

1989–92 ENGINES
♦ SEE FIGS. 11-13, 46–47

The pressure regulator control solenoid valve cuts the intake manifold vacuum signal for pressure regulator control. The solenoid valve actuates in response to the ON/OFF signal from the ECU. When it is OFF, a vacuum signal from the intake manifold is cut. As the control unit outputs an ON signal, the coil pull the plunger downward and feeds vacuum to the power valve actuator.

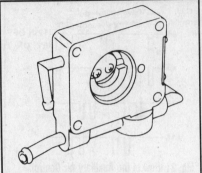

Fig. 26 View of the air cut valve — 1989–92 VG30E engine

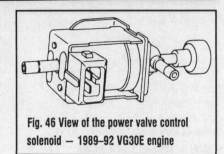

Fig. 46 View of the power valve control solenoid — 1989–92 VG30E engine

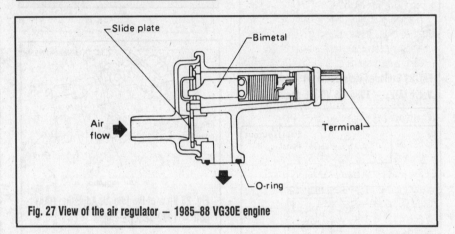

Fig. 27 View of the air regulator — 1985–88 VG30E engine

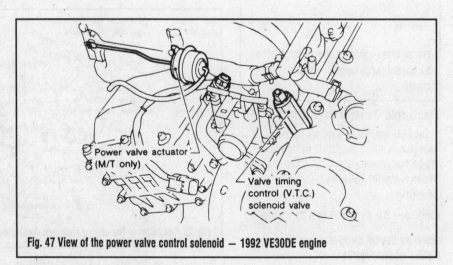

Fig. 47 View of the power valve control solenoid — 1992 VE30DE engine

Power Valve

1989–92

◆ SEE FIGS. 11-13, AND 47-49

The power valve is used to control the suction passage of the power valve control system. If is set in the fully closed or fully opened position by the power valve actuator, which is operated by the vacuum stored in the surge tank. The vacuum in the surge tank is controlled by the power valve control solenoid valve.

Power Steering Oil Pressure Switch

1989–92

◆ SEE FIGS. 11–12, 50–51

The power steering oil pressure switch is attached to the power steering high-pressure tube and detects the power steering load, sending a load signal to the ECU. The ECU then sends an idle-up signal to the AAC valve.

Exhaust Gas Temperature Sensor (California)

1989–92

◆ SEE FIGS. 12, 13, 22 AND 52

The EGR temperature sensor monitors exhaust gas temperature and transmits a signal to the ECU. The temperature sensing unit employs a thermistor which is sensitive to changes in temperature. Electric resistance of the thermistor decreases in response to a rise in temperature.

SYSTEM OPERATION

In operation, the on-board computer (control unit) calculates the basic injection pulse width by processing signals from the crank angle sensor and air flow meter. Receiving signals from each sensor which detects various engine operating conditions, the computer adds various enrichments (which are preprogrammed) to the basic injection amount. In this manner, the optimum amount of fuel is delivered through the injectors. The fuel is enriched when starting, during warm-up, when accelerating when cylinder head temperature is high and when operating under a heavy load. The fuel is leaned during deceleration according to the closing rate of the throttle valve. Fuel shut-off is accomplished during deceleration, when vehicle speed exceeds 137 mph, or when engine speed exceeds 6400 rpm for about 500 revolutions.

The mixture ratio feedback system (closed loop control) is designed to control the air/fuel mixture precisely to the stoichiometric or optimum point so that the 3-way catalytic converter can minimize CO, HC and NOx

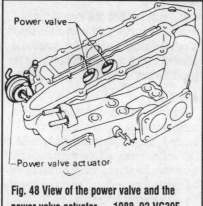

Fig. 48 View of the power valve and the power valve actuator — 1988–92 VG30E engine

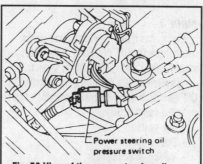

Fig. 50 View of the power steering oil pressure switch location — 1989–92 VG30E engine

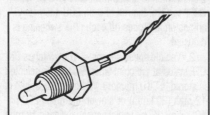

Fig. 52 View of the exhaust gas temperature sensor (California) — 1989–92

emissions simultaneously. The optimum air/fuel fuel mixture is 14.7:1. This system uses an exhaust gas (oxygen) sensor located in the exhaust manifold to give an indication of whether the fuel mixture is richer or leaner than the stoichiometric point. The control unit adjusts the injection pulse width according to the sensor voltage so the mixture ratio will be within the narrow window around the stoichiometric fuel ratio. The system goes into closed loop as soon as the oxygen sensor heats up enough to register. The system will operate under open loop when starting the engine, when the engine temperature is cold, when exhaust gas sensor temperature is cold, when driving at high speeds or under heavy load, at idle (after mixture ratio learning is completed), during deceleration, if the

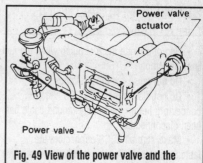

Fig. 49 View of the power valve and the power valve actuator — 1992 VE30DE engine

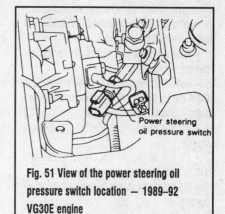

Fig. 51 View of the power steering oil pressure switch location — 1989–92 VG30E engine

exhaust gas sensor malfunctions, or when the exhaust gas sensor monitors a rich condition for more than 10 seconds and during deceleration.

Ignition timing is controlled in response to engine operating conditions. The optimum ignition timing in each driving condition is preprogrammed in the computer. The signal from the control unit is transmitted to the power transistor and controls ignition timing. The idle speed is also controlled according to engine operating conditions, temperature and gear position. On manual transmission models, if battery voltage is less than 12 volts for a few seconds, a higher idle speed will be maintained by the control unit to improve charging function.

There is a fail-safe system built into the ECCS control unit. If the output voltage of the air flow meter is extremely low, the ECU will substitute a preprogrammed value for the air flow meter signal and allow the vehicle to be driven as long as the engine speed is kept below 2000 rpm. If the cylinder head temperature sensor circuit is open, the control unit clamps the warmup enrichment at a certain amount. This amount is almost the same as that when the cylinder head temperature is between 68–176°F (20–80°C). If the fuel pump circuit malfunctions, the fuel pump relay comes on until the engine stops. This allows the fuel pump to receive power from the relay.

SERVICE PRECAUTIONS

• Do not operate the fuel pump when the fuel lines are empty.

• Do not reuse fuel hose clamps.

• Do not disconnect the ECCS harness connectors before the battery ground cable has been disconnected.

• Make sure all ECCS connectors are fastened securely. A poor connection can cause an extremely high surge voltage in the coil and condenser and result in damage to integrated circuits.

• Keep the ECCS harness at least 4 in. (102mm) away from adjacent harnesses to prevent an ECCS system malfunction due to external electronic "noise."

• Keep all parts and harnesses dry during service.

• Before attempting to remove any parts, turn OFF the ignition switch and disconnect the battery ground cable.

• Always use a 12 volt battery as a power source.

• Do not attempt to disconnect the battery cables with the engine running.

• Do not depress the accelerator pedal when starting.

• Do not rev up the engine immediately after starting or just prior to shutdown.

• Do not attempt to disassemble the ECCS control unit under any circumstances.

• If a battery cable is disconnected, the memory will return to the ROM (programmed) values. Engine operation may vary slightly, but this is not an indication of a problem. Do not replace parts because of a slight variation.

• If installing a 2-way or CB radio, keep the antenna as far as possible away from the electronic control unit. Keep the antenna feeder line at least 8 in. (203mm) away from the ECCS harness and do not let the 2 run parallel for a long distance. Be sure to ground the radio to the vehicle body.

Diagnosis and Testing

SELF-DIAGNOSTIC SYSTEM

The self-diagnostic function is useful for diagnosing malfunctions in major sensors and actuators of the ECCS system. There are 5 modes in self-diagnostics

MODE 1

During closed loop operation, the green inspection lamp turns ON when a lean condition is detected and OFF when a rich condition is detected. During open loop operation, the red inspection lamp stays OFF.

MODE 2

The green inspection lamp function is the same as in Mode 1. During closed loop operation, the red inspection lamp turns ON and OFF simultaneously with the green inspection lamp when the mixture ratio is controlled within the specified value. During open loop operation, the red inspection lamp stays OFF.

MODE 3

This mode is the same as the former self-diagnosis mode.

MODE 4

During this mode, the inspection lamps monitor the ON/OFF condition of the idle switch, starter switch and vehicle speed sensor.

In switches ON/OFF diagnosis system, ON/OFF operation of the following switches can be detected continuously:

• Idle switch
• Starter switch
• Vehicle speed sensor

1. Idle switch and starter switch — the switches ON/OFF status at the point when Mode IV is selected is stored in ECU memory. When either switch is turned from ON to OFF or OFF to ON, the red LED on ECU alternately comes on and goes off each time switching is detected.

2. Vehicle speed sensor — The switches ON/OFF status at the point when Mode IV is selected is stored in ECU memory. When vehicle speed is 12 mph (20 km/h) or slower, the green LED on ECU is off. When vehicle speed exceeds 12 mph (20 km/h), the green LED on ECU comes ON.

MODE 5

The moment a malfunction is detected, the display will be presented immediately by flashing the inspection lamps during the driving test.

In real time diagnosis, if any of the following items are judged to be faulty, a malfunction is indicated immediately:

• Crank angle sensor
• Ignition signal
• Air flow meter output signal
• Fuel pump (some models)

Consequently, this diagnosis is a very effective measure to diagnose whether the above systems cause the malfunction or not, during driving test. Compared with self-diagnosis, real time diagnosis is very sensitive, and can detect malfunctioning conditions in a moment. Further,

items regarded to be malfunctions in this diagnosis are not stored in ECU memory.

To switch the modes, turn the ignition switch ON, then turn the diagnostic mode selector on the control unit fully clockwise and wait for the inspection lamps to flash. Count the number of flashes until the inspection lamps have flashed the number of the desired mode, then immediately turn the diagnostic mode selector fully counterclockwise.

➡ When the ignition switch is turned OFF during diagnosis in each mode, and then turned back on again after the power to the control unit has dropped off completely, the diagnosis will automatically return to Mode 1.

The stored memory will be lost if the battery terminal is disconnected, or Mode 4 is selected after selecting Mode 3. However, if the diagnostic mode selector is kept turned fully clockwise, it will continue to change in the order of Mode 1, 2, 3, etc., and in this case, the stored memory will not be erased.

In Mode 3, the control unit constantly monitors the function of sensors and actuators regardless of ignition key position. If a malfunction occurs, the information is stored in the control unit and can be retrieved from the memory by turning ON the diagnostic mode selector on the side of the control unit. When activated, the malfunction is indicated by flashing a red and green LED (also located on the control unit). Since all the self-diagnostic results are stored in the control unit memory, even intermittent malfunctions can be diagnosed. A malfunctioning part's group is indicated by the number of both red and green LED's flashing. First, the red LED flashes and the green flashes follow. The red LED refers to the number of tens, while the green refers to the number of units. If the red LED flashes twice and the green LED flashes once, a Code 21 is being displayed. All malfunctions are classified by their trouble code number.

The diagnostic result is retained in the control unit memory until the starter is operated 50 times after a diagnostic item is judged to be malfunctioning. The diagnostic result will then be canceled automatically. If a diagnostic item which has been judged malfunctioning and stored in memory is again judged to be malfunctioning before the starter is operated 50 times, the second result will replace the previous one and stored in the memory until the starter is operated 50 more times.

In Mode 5 (real time diagnosis), if the crank angle sensor, ignition signal or air flow meter output signal are judged to be malfunctioning, the malfunction will be indicated immediately.

This diagnosis is very effective for determining whether these systems are causing a malfunction during the driving test. Compared with self-diagnosis, real time diagnosis is very sensitive and can detect malfunctioning conditions immediately. However, malfunctioning items in this diagnosis mode are not stored in memory.

TESTING PRECAUTIONS

• Before connecting or disconnecting control unit ECU harness connectors, make sure the ignition switch is **OFF** and the negative battery cable is disconnected to avoid the possibility of damage to the control unit.

• When performing ECU input/output signal diagnosis, remove the pin terminal retainer from the 20 and 16-pin connectors to make it easier to insert tester probes into the connector.

• When connecting or disconnecting pin connectors from the ECU, take care not to bend or break any pin terminals. Check that there are no bends or breaks on ECU pin terminals before attempting any connections.

• Before replacing any ECU, perform the ECU input/output signal diagnosis to make sure the ECU is functioning properly or not.

• After performing the Electronic Control System Inspection, perform the ECCS self-diagnosis and driving test.

• When measuring supply voltage of ECU controlled components with a circuit tester, separate one tester probe from another. If the 2 tester probes accidentally make contact with each other during measurement, a short circuit will result and damage the power transistor in the ECU.

VACUUM DIAGRAMS

CHECKING IDLE SPEED AND IGNITION TIMING — VG30E ENGINE

PREPARATION

1. Make sure that the following parts are in good order.
   - Battery
   - Ignition system
   - Engine oil and coolant levels
   - Fuses
   - E.C.U. S.M.J. harness connector
   - Vacuum hoses
   - Air intake system (Oil filler cap, oil level gauge, etc.)
   - Fuel pressure
   - Engine compression
   - E.G.R. control valve operation
   - Throttle valve
2. On air conditioner equipped models, checks should be carried out while the air conditioner is "OFF".

3. On automatic transaxle equipped models, when checking idle rpm, ignition timing and mixture ratio, checks should be carried out while shift lever is in "N" position.
4. When measuring "CO" percentage, insert probe more than 40 cm (15.7 in) into tail pipe.
5. Turn off headlamps, heater blower, rear defogger.
6. Keep front wheels pointed straight ahead.
7. Make the check after the radiator fan has stopped.

WARNING:
Apply parking brake and block both front and rear wheels with chocks.

Overall inspection sequence

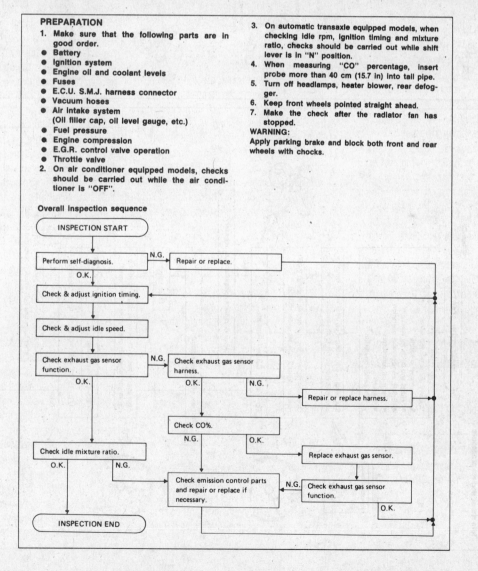

CHECKING IDLE SPEED AND IGNITION TIMING — VG30E ENGINE, CONT.

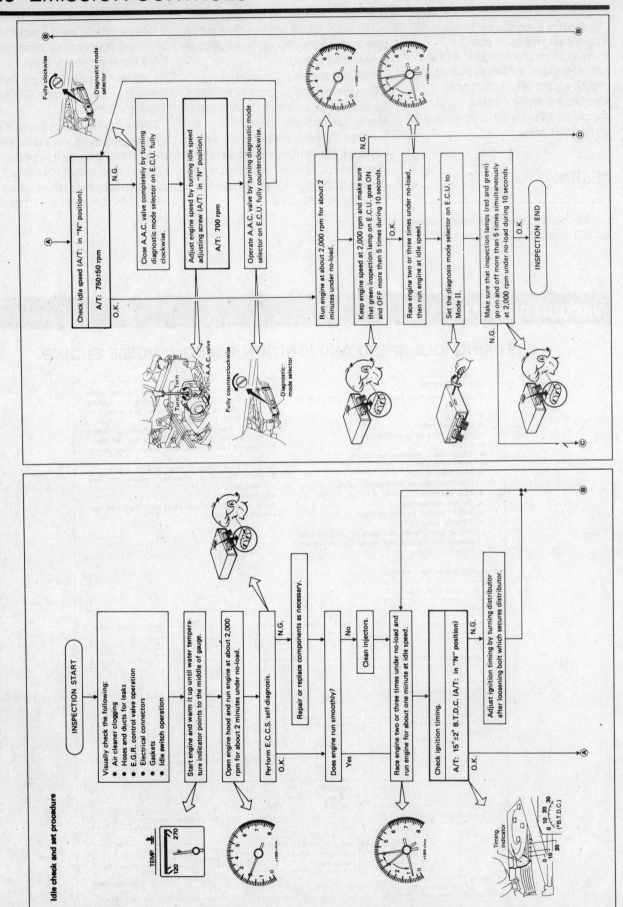

Idle check and set procedure

INSPECTION START

Visually check the following:
• Air cleaner clogging
• Hoses and ducts for leaks
• E.G.R. control valve operation
• Electrical connectors
• Gaskets
• Idle switch operation

Start engine and warm it up until water temperature indicator points to the middle of gauge.

Open engine hood and run engine at about 2,000 rpm for about 2 minutes under no-load.

Perform E.C.C.S. self-diagnosis. — N.G. → Repair or replace components as necessary.

O.K.

Does engine run smoothly? — No → Clean injectors.

Yes

Race engine two or three times under no-load and run engine for about one minute at idle speed.

Check ignition timing.
A/T: 15°±2° B.T.D.C. (A/T: in "N" position) — N.G. → Adjust ignition timing by turning distributor after loosening bolt which secures distributor.

O.K.

Check idle speed (A/T: in "N" position).
A/T: 750±50 rpm — N.G. → Close A.A.C. valve completely by turning diagnostic mode selector on E.C.U. fully clockwise.

O.K.

Adjust engine speed by turning idle speed adjusting screw (A/T: in "N" position).
A/T: 700 rpm

Operate A.A.C. valve by turning diagnostic mode selector on E.C.U. fully counterclockwise.

Run engine at about 2,000 rpm for about 2 minutes under no-load.

Keep engine speed at 2,000 rpm and make sure that green inspection lamp on E.C.U. goes ON and OFF more than 5 times during 10 seconds. — N.G.

O.K.

Race engine two or three times under no-load, then run engine at idle speed.

Set the diagnosis mode selector on E.C.U. to Mode II.

Make sure that inspection lamps (red and green) go on and off more than 5 times simultaneously at 2,000 rpm under no-load during 10 seconds. — N.G.

O.K.

INSPECTION END

Fully clockwise
Diagnostic mode selector

A.A.C. valve
Turn Turn

Fully counterclockwise
Diagnostic mode selector

Timing indicator
(°B.T.D.C.)

CHECKING IDLE SPEED AND IGNITION TIMING – VG30E ENGINE, CONT.

Ⓔ

Check CO%.

Idle CO: 0.2 - 8.0%

After checking CO%,
1) Disconnect the resistor from terminals of engine temperature sensor harness connector.
2) Connect engine temperature sensor harness connector to engine temperature sensor.

O.K. → Replace exhaust gas sensor.

N.G.

Run engine at 2,000 rpm and make sure that green inspection lamp on E.C.U. goes ON and OFF more than 5 times during 10 seconds.

O.K. → Ⓑ

N.G. →

Connect exhaust gas sensor harness connector to exhaust gas sensor.

Check fuel pressure regulator.

Check air flow meter and its circuit.

Check injector and its circuit.
Clean or replace if necessary.

Check engine temperature sensor and its circuit.

Ⓒ

Ⓑ

Ⓓ

Check exhaust gas sensor harness:
1) Turn off engine and disconnect battery ground cable.
2) Disconnect E.C.U. S.M.J. harness connector from E.C.U.
3) Disconnect exhaust gas sensor harness connector and connect main harness side terminal for exhaust gas sensor to ground with a jumper wire.
4) Check for continuity between terminal No. 29 of E.C.U. S.M.J. harness connector and body ground

Continuity exists .... O.K.
Continuity does not exist .... N.G.

N.G. → Repair or replace harness.

O.K. →

Connect S.M.J. harness connector to E.C.U.

1) Disconnect engine temperature sensor harness connector.
2) Connect a resistor (2.5 kΩ) between terminals of engine temperature sensor harness connector.
3) Disconnect a jumper wire connected to exhaust gas sensor harness connector (main harness side).

Connect battery ground cable, start engine and warm it up until water temperature indicator points to middle of gauge.

Race engine two or three times under no-load, then run engine at idle.

Ⓔ

Ⓒ

Exhaust gas sensor harness connector

Engine temperature sensor harness connector

2.5 kΩ resistor

TEMP 120 270

×1000 r/min

SELF-DIAGNOSIS – VG30E ENGINE

Self-diagnosis
CHECK ENGINE LIGHT

A check engine light has been adopted. This light blinks under the following conditions:

Condition	California model	Non-California model
	Light illuminates when any one of conditions 1), 2), 3) and 4) is satisfied.	Light illuminates when any one of conditions 1), 2) and 4) is satisfied.

1) When ignition switch is turned "ON" (for bulb check).
2) When systems related to emission performance malfunction in Mode I (with engine running).
   - **This check engine light always illuminates and is synchronous with red L.E.D.**
3) When a malfunction is detected regarding the following self-diagnostic items:

Malfunction	Self-diagnosis code No.
Air flow meter circuit	12
Engine temperature sensor circuit	13
Vehicle speed sensor circuit	14
E.C.U. (E.C.C.S. control unit)	31
E.G.R. function	32
Exhaust gas sensor circuit	33
Exhaust gas temperature sensor circuit	35
Throttle sensor circuit	43
Injector leak	45
Injector circuit	51

- The check engine light will turn off when normal operation is resumed. Mode III memory must be cleared as the contents remain stored.
4) When crank angle sensor or C.P.U. of E.C.U. malfunctions and fail-safe system operates during engine rotation.

E.C.U. L.E.D.
In the E.C.U., Green and Red L.E.D.'s have been adopted to monitor the self-diagnostic functions.

SEF257L

Analog meter

Check engine light

Digital meter

Check engine light

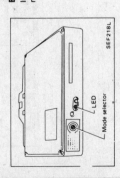

SEF218L

LED

Mode selector

Self-diagnosis (Cont'd)
HOW TO SWITCH MODES

- Turn ignition switch "ON". (Do not start engine.)

BULB CHECK

(Turn diagnostic mode selector on E.C.U. fully clockwise.)

Read the number of flashes.

Flashing N times

Once — Twice — Three times — Four times — Five times

(Turn diagnostic mode selector fully counterclockwise.)

Mode I — EXHAUST GAS SENSOR MONITOR

Mode II — MIXTURE RATIO FEEDBACK CONTROL MONITOR

Mode III — SELF-DIAGNOSTIC MODE

Mode IV — SWITCHES ON/OFF DIAGNOSTIC MODE

Mode V — REAL-TIME DIAGNOSTIC MODE

*1 While the diagnostic mode selector is kept turned fully clockwise, it will continue to change in the order of Mode I → II → III → IV → V → I ...

*2 The malfunction code is erased from the backup memory of the E.C.U.
- Return the diagnostic mode selector to the original position so as not to disturb the idle speed.

SELF-DIAGNOSIS — MODE III — VG30E ENGINE

Self-diagnosis — Mode III
Self-diagnostic mode

The E.C.U. constantly monitors the function of these sensors and actuators, regardless of ignition key position. If a malfunction occurs, the information is stored in the E.C.U. and can be retrieved from the memory by turning on the diagnostic mode selector, located on the side of the E.C.U. When activated, the malfunction is indicated by flashing a red and a green L.E.D. (Light Emitting Diode), also located on the E.C.U. Since all the self-diagnostic results are stored in the E.C.U.'s memory even intermittent malfunctions can be diagnosed.

A malfunction is indicated by the number of both red and green flashing L.E.D.s. First, the red L.E.D. flashes and the green flashes follow. The red L.E.D. corresponds to units of ten and the green L.E.D. corresponds to units of one. For example, when the red L.E.D. flashes once and the green L.E.D. flashes twice, this signifies the number "12", showing that the air flow meter signal is malfunctioning. All problems are classified by code numbers in this way.

- When the engine fails to start, crank it two or more seconds before beginning self-diagnosis.
- Read out self-diagnostic results first and then erase the malfunction records which are stored in the ECU memory. If it is erased, the self-diagnosis function for intermittent malfunctions will be lost.

Code No. 12

SEF056L

DISPLAY CODE TABLE

Code No.	Detected items	California	Non-California
11	Crank angle sensor ciruit	X	X
12	Air flow meter circuit	X	X
13	Engine temperature sensor circuit	X	X
14	Vehicle speed sensor circuit	X	X
21	Ignition signal missing in primary coil	X	X
22	Fuel pump signal	X	X
31	E.C.U. (E.C.C.S. control unit)	X	X
32	E.G.R. function	X	—
33	Exhaust gas sensor circuit	X	X
34	Detonation sensor circuit	X	X
35	Exhaust gas temperature sensor circuit	X	—
43	Throttle sensor circuit	X	X
45	Injector leak	X	—
51	Injector circuit	X	X
54	A/T control circuit	X	X
55	No malfunction in the above circuit	X	X

X: Available —: Not available

HOW TO ERASE SELF-DIAGNOSITC RESULTS

The malfunction code is erased from the backup memory of the E.C.U. by the following:

- when the battery terminal is disconnected, the malfunction code will be lost from the backup memory within 24 hours.
- when mode IV is selected after selecting mode III.

SELF-DIAGNOSIS — MODE I — VG30E ENGINE

Self-diagnosis — Mode I
Exhaust gas sensor monitor

This mode checks the exhaust gas sensor for proper functioning. The operation of the E.C.U. L.E.D. in this mode differs with mixture ratio control conditions as follows:

Mode	L.E.D.	Engine stopped (Ignition switch "ON")	Engine running	
			Open loop condition	Closed loop condition
Mode	Green	ON	*Remains ON or OFF	Blinks
Mode II	Red	ON	Except for California model — For California model • ON: a. when the CHECK ENGINE LIGHT ITEMS are stored in the E.C.U. b. when fail-safe system is operating • OFF: except for the above conditions	

*: Maintains conditions just before switching to open loop

EXHAUST GAS SENSOR FUNCTION CHECK

If the number of L.E.D. blinks is less than that specified, replace the exhaust gas sensor.

If the L.E.D. does not blink, check exhaust gas sensor circuit.

SELF-DIAGNOSIS — MODE II — VG30E ENGINE

Self-diagnosis — Mode II
Mixture ratio feedback control monitor

This mode checks, through the E.C.U. L.E.D., optimum control of the mixture ratio. The operation of the L.E.D., as shown below, differs with the control conditions of the mixture ratio (for example, richer or leaner mixture ratios, etc., which are controlled by the E.C.U.).

Mode	L.E.D.	Engine stopped (Ignition switch "ON")	Engine running	
			Open loop condition	Closed loop condition
				Blinks
				Compensating mixture ratio
				More than 5% rich / Between 5% lean and 5% rich / More
Mode	Green	ON	*Remains ON or OFF	
Mode II	Red	OFF	*Remains ON or OFF	Synchronized with green L.E.D. / Remains ON

*: Maintains conditions just before switching to open loop

If the red L.E.D. remains on or off during the closed-loop operation, the mixture ratio may not be controlled properly. Using the following procedures, check the related components or adjust the mixture ratio.

SELF-DIAGNOSIS — MODE III — VG30E ENGINE, CONT.

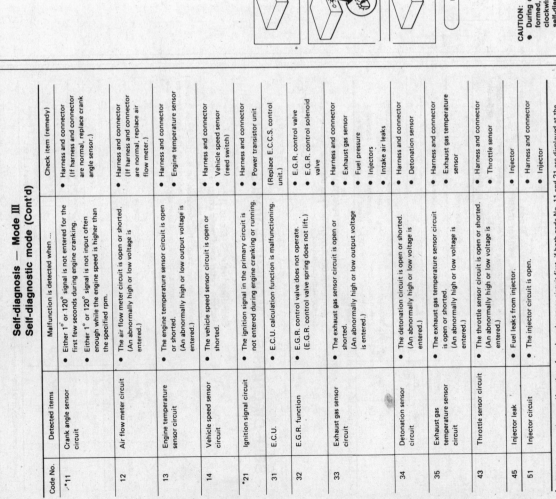

Self-diagnosis — Mode III
Self-diagnostic mode (Cont'd)

Code No.	Detected items	Malfunction is detected when ...	Check item (remedy)
*11	Crank angle sensor circuit	• Either 1° or 120° signal is not entered for the first few seconds during engine cranking. • Either 1° or 120° signal is not input often enough while the engine speed is higher than the specified rpm.	• Harness and connector (If harness and connector are normal, replace crank angle sensor.)
12	Air flow meter circuit	• The air flow meter circuit is open or shorted. (An abnormally high or low voltage is entered.)	• Harness and connector (If harness and connector are normal, replace air flow meter.)
13	Engine temperature sensor circuit	• The engine temperature sensor circuit is open or shorted. (An abnormally high or low output voltage is entered.)	• Harness and connector • Engine temperature sensor
14	Vehicle speed sensor circuit	• The vehicle speed sensor circuit is open or shorted.	• Harness and connector • Vehicle speed sensor (reed switch)
*21	Ignition signal circuit	• The ignition signal in the primary circuit is not entered during engine cranking or running.	• Harness and connector • Power transistor unit
31	E.C.U.	• E.C.U. calculation function is malfunctioning.	• (Replace E.C.C.S. control unit.)
32	E.G.R. function	• E.G.R. control valve does not operate. (E.G.R. control valve spring does not lift.)	• E.G.R. control valve • E.G.R. control solenoid valve
33	Exhaust gas sensor circuit	• The exhaust gas sensor circuit is open or shorted. (An abnormally high or low output voltage is entered.)	• Harness and connector • Exhaust gas sensor • Fuel pressure • Injectors • Intake air leaks
34	Detonation sensor circuit	• The detonation circuit is open or shorted. (An abnormally high or low voltage is entered.)	• Harness and connector • Detonation sensor
35	Exhaust gas temperature sensor circuit	• The exhaust gas temperature sensor circuit is open or shorted. (An abnormally high or low voltage is entered.)	• Harness and connector • Exhaust gas temperature sensor
43	Throttle sensor circuit	• The throttle sensor circuit is open or shorted. (An abnormally high or low voltage is entered.)	• Harness and connector • Throttle sensor
45	Injector leak	• Fuel leaks from injector.	• Injector
51	Injector circuit	• The injector circuit is open.	• Harness and connector • Injector

*: Check items causing a malfunction of crank angle sensor circuit first, if both code No. 11 and 21 are displayed at the same time.

SELF-DIAGNOSIS — MODE IV — VG30E ENGINE

Self-diagnosis — Mode IV
Switches ON/OFF diagnostic mode

In switches ON/OFF diagnostic system, ON/OFF operation of the following switches can be detected continuously.
- Idle switch
- Starter switch
- Vehicle speed sensor

(1) Idle switch & Starter switch

The switches ON/OFF status in Mode IV is stored in E.C.U. memory. When either switch is turned from "ON" to "OFF" or "OFF" to "ON", the red L.E.D. on E.C.U. alternately comes on and goes off each time switching is performed.

(2) Vehicle Speed Sensor

The switches ON/OFF status in Mode IV is selected is stored in E.C.U. memory. The green L.E.D. on E.C.U. remains off when vehicle speed is 20 km/h (12 MPH) or below, and comes ON at higher speeds.

Self-diagnosis — Mode IV
Switches ON/OFF diagnostic mode (Cont'd)
PROCEDURE

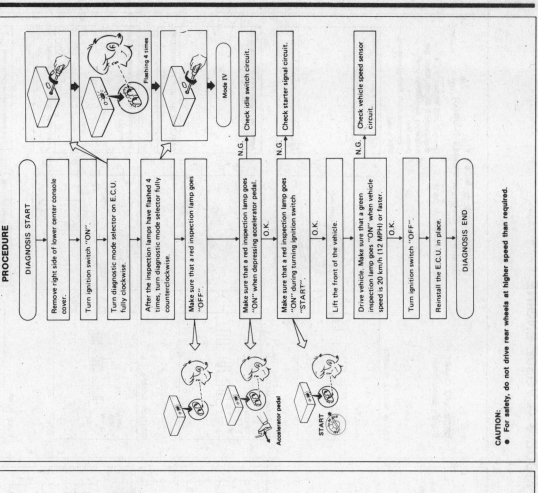

DIAGNOSIS START

↓

Remove right side of lower center console cover.

↓

Turn ignition switch "ON".

↓

Turn diagnostic mode selector on E.C.U. fully clockwise.

↓

After the inspection lamps have flashed 4 times, turn diagnostic mode selector fully counterclockwise.

↓

Make sure that a red inspection lamp goes "OFF".

↓

Make sure that a red inspection lamp goes "ON" when depressing accelerator pedal. — N.G. → Check idle switch circuit.

↓ O.K.

Make sure that a red inspection lamp goes "ON" during turning ignition switch "START". — N.G. → Check starter signal circuit.

↓ O.K.

Lift the front of the vehicle.

↓

Drive vehicle. Make sure that a green inspection lamp goes "ON" when vehicle speed is 20 km/h (12 MPH) or faster. — N.G. → Check vehicle speed sensor circuit.

↓ O.K.

Turn ignition switch "OFF".

↓

Reinstall the E.C.U. in place.

↓

DIAGNOSIS END

Flashing 4 times

Mode IV

Accelerator pedal

START

CAUTION:
- For safety, do not drive rear wheels at higher speed than required.

SELF-DIAGNOSIS — MODE V — VG30E ENGINE

Self-diagnosis — Mode V
Real-time diagnostic mode

In real-time diagnosis, if the following items are judged to be working incorrectly, a malfunction will be indicated immediately.
- Crank angle sensor (120° signal & 1° signal) output signal
- Ignition signal
- Air flow meter output signal
- Fuel pump

Consequently, this diagnosis very effectively determines whether the above systems cause the malfunction, during driving test. Compared with self-diagnosis, real-time diagnosis is very sensitive and can detect malfunctions instantly. However, items regarded as malfunctions in this diagnosis are not stored in E.C.U. memory.

PROCEDURE

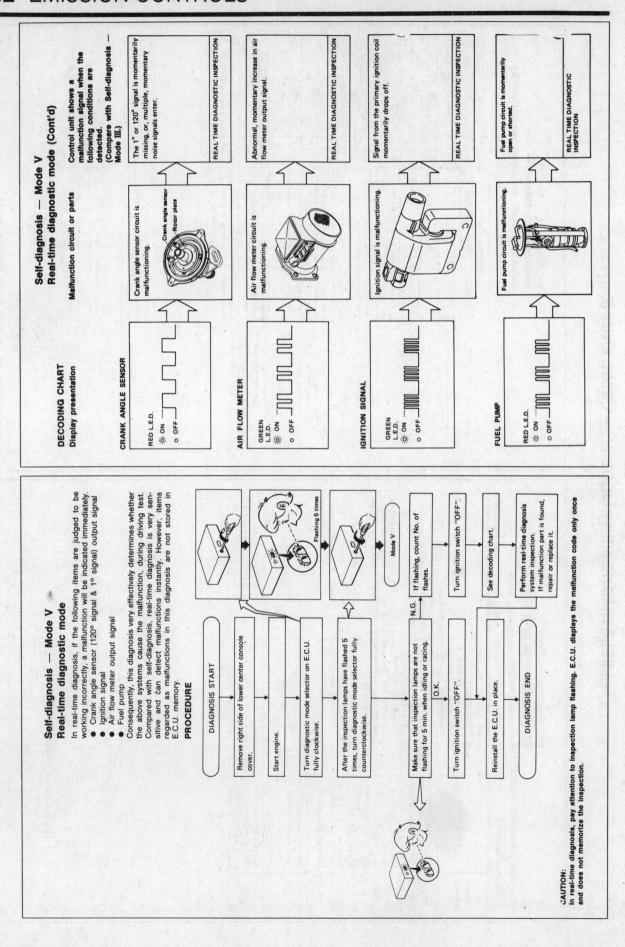

DIAGNOSIS START

Remove right side of lower center console cover.

Start engine.

Turn diagnostic mode selector on E.C.U. fully clockwise.

After the inspection lamps have flashed 5 times, turn diagnostic mode selector fully counterclockwise.

Flashing 5 times

Mode V

Make sure that inspection lamps are not flashing for 5 min. when idling or racing.

N.G. → If flashing, count No. of flashes.

Turn ignition switch "OFF".

See decoding chart.

Perform real-time diagnosis system inspection. If malfunction part is found, repair or replace it.

O.K.

Turn ignition switch "OFF".

Reinstall the E.C.U. in place.

DIAGNOSIS END

CAUTION:
In real-time diagnosis, pay attention to inspection lamp flashing. E.C.U. displays the malfunction code only once and does not memorize the inspection.

Self-diagnosis — Mode V
Real-time diagnostic mode (Cont'd)

DECODING CHART

Display presentation | **Malfunction circuit or parts** |

Control unit shows a malfunction signal when the following conditions are detected.
(Compare with Self-diagnosis — Mode III.)

CRANK ANGLE SENSOR

RED L.E.D.
☀ ON
○ OFF

Crank angle sensor circuit is malfunctioning.

Crank angle sensor
Rotor plate

The 1° or 120° signal is momentarily missing, or, multiple, momentary noise signals enter.

REAL TIME DIAGNOSTIC INSPECTION

AIR FLOW METER

GREEN L.E.D.
☀ ON
○ OFF

Air flow meter circuit is malfunctioning.

Abnormal, momentary increase in air flow meter output signal.

REAL TIME DIAGNOSTIC INSPECTION

IGNITION SIGNAL

GREEN L.E.D.
☀ ON
○ OFF

Ignition signal is malfunctioning.

Signal from the primary ignition coil momentarily drops off.

REAL TIME DIAGNOSTIC INSPECTION

FUEL PUMP

RED L.E.D.
☀ ON
○ OFF

Fuel pump circuit is malfunctioning.

Fuel pump circuit is momentarily open or shorted.

REAL TIME DIAGNOSTIC INSPECTION

SELF-DIAGNOSIS — MODE V — VG30E ENGINE, CONT.

REAL-TIME DIAGNOSTIC INSPECTION

Crank Angle Sensor

Self-diagnosis — Mode V
Real-time diagnostic mode (Cont'd)

X: Available
—: Not available

Check sequence	Check items	Check conditions	Check parts			If malfunction, perform the following items.
			Crank angle sensor harness connector	Sensor & actuator	E.C.U. S.M.J. harness connector	
1	Tap and wiggle harness connector or component during real-time diagnosis.	During real-time diagnosis	X	X	X	Go to check item 2.
2	Check harness continuity at connector.	Engine stopped	X	—	—	Go to check item 3.
3	Disconnect harness connector, and then check dust adhesion to harness connector.	Engine stopped	X	—	X	Clean terminal surface.
4	Check pin terminal bend.	Engine stopped	—	—	X	Take out bend.
5	Reconnect harness connector and then recheck harness continuity at connector.	Engine stopped	X	—	—	Replace terminal.
6	Tap and wiggle harness connector or component during real-time diagnosis.	During real-time diagnosis	X	X	X	If malfunction codes are displayed during real-time diagnosis, replace terminal.

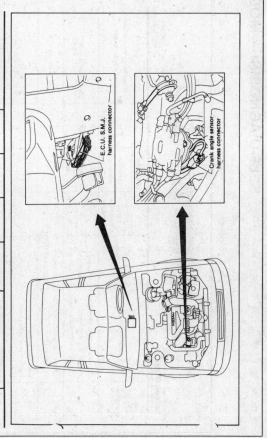

E.C.U. S.M.J. harness connector

Crank angle sensor harness connector

Air Flow Meter

Self-diagnosis — Mode V
Real-time diagnostic mode (Cont'd)

X: Available
—: Not available

Check sequence	Check items	Check conditions	Check parts			If malfunction, perform the following items.
			Air flow meter harness connector	Sensor & actuator	E.C.U. S.M.J. harness connector	
1	Tap and wiggle harness connector or component during real-time diagnosis.	During real-time diagnosis	X	X	X	Go to check item 2.
2	Check harness continuity at connector.	Engine stopped	X	—	—	Go to check item 3.
3	Disconnect harness connector, and then check dust adhesion to harness connector.	Engine stopped	X	—	X	Clean terminal surface.
4	Check pin terminal bend.	Engine stopped	—	—	X	Take out bend.
5	Reconnect harness connector and then recheck harness continuity at connector.	Engine stopped	X	—	—	Replace terminal.
6	Tap and wiggle harness connector or component during real-time diagnosis.	During real-time diagnosis	X	X	X	If malfunction codes are displayed during real-time diagnosis, replace terminal.

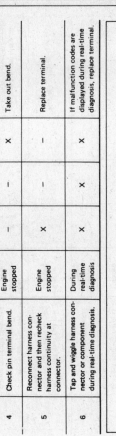

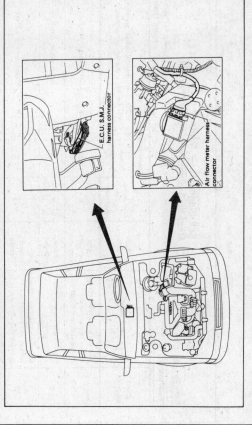

E.C.U. S.M.J. harness connector

Air flow meter harness connector

SELF-DIAGNOSIS — MODE V — VG30E ENGINE, CONT.

Self-diagnosis — Mode V
Real-time diagnostic mode (Cont'd)

Ignition Signal

X: Available
–: Not available

Check sequence	Check items	Check conditions	Ignition signal harness connector	Sensor & actuator	E.C.U. S.M.J. harness connector	If malfunction, perform the following items.
			Check parts			
1	Tap and wiggle harness connector or component during real-time diagnosis.	During real-time diagnosis	X	X	X	Go to check item 2.
2	Check harness continuity at connector.	Engine stopped	X	X	–	Go to check item 3.
3	Disconnect harness connector, and then check dust adhesion to harness connector.	Engine stopped	X	–	X	Clean terminal surface.
4	Check pin terminal bend.	Engine stopped	–	–	X	Take out bend.
5	Reconnect harness connector and then recheck harness continuity at connector.	Engine stopped	X	–	–	Replace terminal.
6	Tap and wiggle harness connector or component during real-time diagnosis.	During real-time diagnosis	X	X	X	If malfunction codes are displayed during real-time diagnosis, replace terminal.

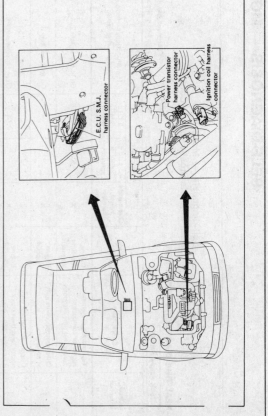

E.C.U. S.M.J. harness connector

Power transistor harness connector

Ignition coil harness connector

Self-diagnosis — Mode V
Real-time diagnostic mode (Cont'd)

Fuel pump

X: Available
–: Not available

Check sequence	Check items	Check conditions	Fuel pump harness connector	Sensor & actuator	E.C.U. S.M.J. harness connector	If malfunction, perform the following items.
			Check parts			
1	Tap and wiggle harness connector or component during real-time diagnosis.	During real-time diagnosis	X	X	X	Go to check item 2.
2	Check harness continuity at connector.	Engine stopped	X	–	–	Go to check item 3.
3	Disconnect harness connector, and then check dust adhesion to harness connector.	Engine stopped	X	–	X	Clean terminal surface.
4	Check pin terminal bend.	Engine stopped	–	–	X	Take out bend.
5	Reconnect harness connector and then recheck harness continuity at connector.	Engine stopped	X	–	–	Replace terminal.
6	Tap and wiggle harness connector or component during real-time diagnosis.	During real-time diagnosis	X	X	X	If malfunction codes are displayed during real-time diagnosis, replace terminal.

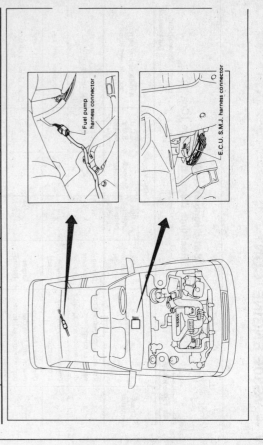

Fuel pump harness connector

E.C.U. S.M.J. harness connector

BASIC INSPECTION DIAGNOSTIC CHART – VG30E ENGINE

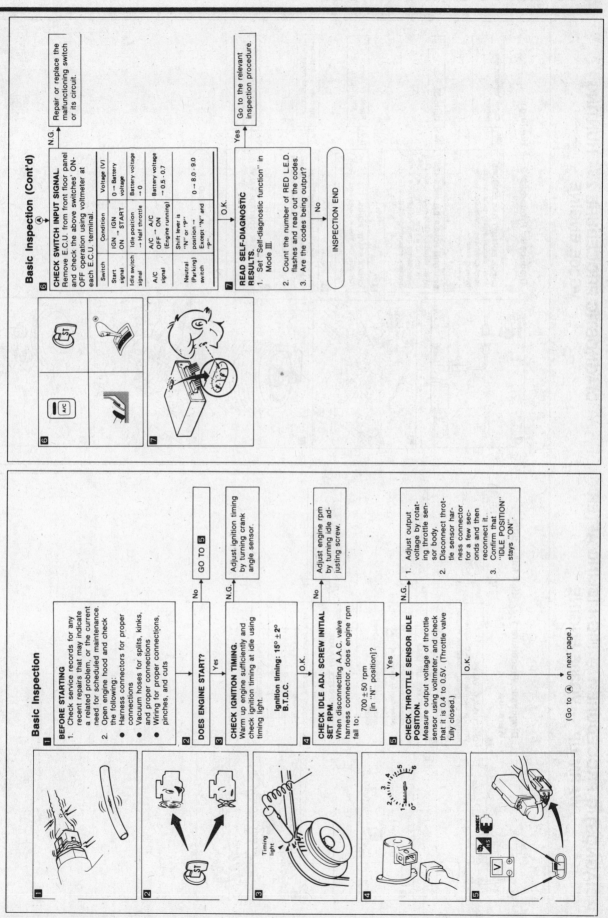

Basic Inspection (Cont'd)

6 CHECK SWITCH INPUT SIGNAL.
Remove E.C.U. from front floor panel and check the above switches' ON-OFF operation using voltmeter at each E.C.U. terminal.

Switch	Condition	Voltage (V)
Start signal	IGN → IGN ON → START	0 → Battery voltage
Idle switch signal	Idle position → Half throttle	Battery voltage → 0
A/C signal	A/C A/C OFF → ON (Engine running)	Battery voltage → 0.5 - 0.7
Neutral (Parking) switch	Shift lever is "N" or "P" position → Except "N" and "P"	0 → 8.0 - 9.0

N.G. → Repair or replace the malfunctioning switch or its circuit.

O.K.

7 READ SELF-DIAGNOSTIC RESULTS.
1. Set "Self-diagnostic function" in Mode III
2. Count the number of RED L.E.D. flashes and read out the codes.
3. Are the codes being output?

Yes → Go to the relevant inspection procedure.

No

INSPECTION END

Basic Inspection

1 BEFORE STARTING
1. Check service records for any recent repairs that may indicate a related problem, or the current need for scheduled maintenance.
2. Open engine hood and check the following:
   - Harness connectors for proper connections
   - Vacuum hoses for splits, kinks, and proper connections
   - Wiring for proper connections, pinches, and cuts

2 DOES ENGINE START?

No → GO TO 5

Yes

3 CHECK IGNITION TIMING.
Warm up engine sufficiently and check ignition timing at idle using timing light.

Ignition timing: 15° ±2° B.T.D.C.

N.G. → Adjust ignition timing by turning crank angle sensor.

O.K.

4 CHECK IDLE ADJ. SCREW INITIAL SET RPM.
When disconnecting A.A.C. valve harness connector, does engine rpm fall to;

700 ± 50 rpm [in "N" position]?

No → Adjust engine rpm by turning idle adjusting screw.

Yes

5 CHECK THROTTLE SENSOR IDLE POSITION.
Measure output voltage of throttle sensor using voltmeter, and check that it is 0.4 to 0.5V. (Throttle valve fully closed.)

N.G. →
1. Adjust output voltage by rotating throttle sensor body.
2. Disconnect throttle sensor harness connector for a few seconds and then reconnect it.
3. Confirm that "IDLE POSITION" stays "ON".

O.K.

→ (Go to Ⓐ on next page.)

(Go to next page.)

DIAGNOSTIC PROCEDURE 2 — HUNTING — VG30E ENGINE

Diagnostic Procedure 2 — Hunting

1 CHECK EXHAUST GAS SENSORS. When disconnecting exhaust gas sensor harness connector, is the hunting fixed?

Yes → Check exhaust gas sensor.

No ↓

2 PERFORM POWER BALANCE TEST. When disconnecting each spark plug cord one at a time, is there any cylinder which does not produce a momentary engine speed drop?

No → Go to **4**

Yes ↓

3 CHECK SPARK PLUGS. Remove the spark plugs and check for fouling, etc.

N.G. → Repair or replace spark plug(s).

O.K. ↓

4 CHECK FOR INTAKE AIR LEAK. When pinching blow-by hose (lowering the blow-by air supply), does the engine speed rise?

Yes → Discover air leak location and repair.

No ↓

5 CHECK E.G.R. CONTROL VALVE. Check E.G.R. control valve for sticking.

N.G. → Repair or replace.

O.K. ↓

INSPECTION END

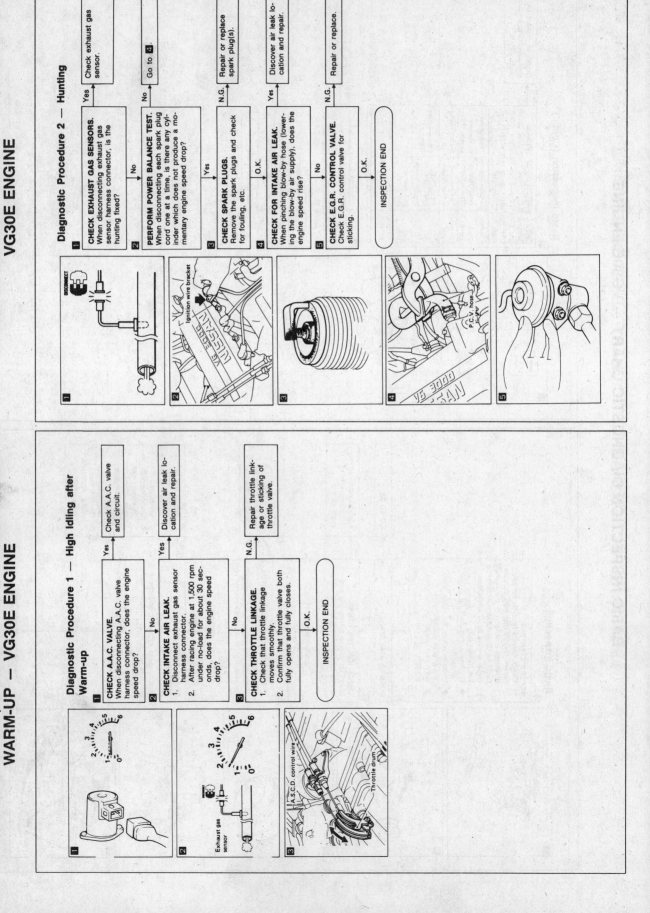

DIAGNOSTIC PROCEDURE 1 — HIGH IDLING AFTER WARM-UP — VG30E ENGINE

Diagnostic Procedure 1 — High Idling after Warm-up

1 CHECK A.A.C. VALVE. When disconnecting A.A.C. valve harness connector, does the engine speed drop?

Yes → Check A.A.C. valve and circuit.

No ↓

2 CHECK INTAKE AIR LEAK.
1. Disconnect exhaust gas sensor harness connector.
2. After racing engine at 1,500 rpm under no-load for about 30 seconds, does the engine speed drop?

Yes → Discover air leak location and repair.

No ↓

3 CHECK THROTTLE LINKAGE.
1. Check that throttle linkage moves smoothly.
2. Confirm that throttle valve both fully opens and fully closes.

N.G. → Repair throttle linkage or sticking of throttle valve.

O.K. ↓

INSPECTION END

DIAGNOSTIC PROCEDURE 3 — UNSTABLE IDLE — VG30E ENGINE

Diagnostic Procedure 3 — Unstable Idle (Cont'd)

7 CHECK EXHAUST GAS SENSOR.
1. Set "Self-diagnostic function" in Mode I
2. Maintaining engine at 2,000 rpm under no-load, check to make sure that GREEN LED on the E.C.U. goes ON and OFF more than 5 times during 10 seconds.

→ N.G. → Replace exhaust gas sensor.

→ O.K.

8 CHECK FOR INTAKE AIR LEAK.
When pinching blow-by hose (lowering the blow-by air supply), does the engine speed rise?

→ Yes → Discover air leak location and repair.

→ No

9 CHECK IDLE ADJ. SCREW CLOGGING.
1. Set Self-diagnostic mode selector to fully clockwise position.
2. Can you set engine rpm as follows by turning idle adjusting screw?
   700 ±50 rpm
   [in "N" position]

→ No → Check for IAS clogging or throttle valve clogging.

→ Yes

10 CHECK COMPRESSION PRESSURE.
• Check compression pressure.
   Standard: kPa (kg/cm², psi)/300 rpm
   1,196 (12.2, 173)
   Minimum: kPa (kg/cm², psi)/300 rpm
   883 (9.0, 128)
   Difference between each cylinder: kPa (kg/cm², psi)/300 rpm
   98 (1.0, 14)

→ N.G. → Check pistons, piston rings, valves, valve seats and cylinder head gaskets.

→ O.K.

11 CHECK E.C.U. HARNESS CONNECTOR.
Check the E.C.U. pin terminals for damage or poor connection of E.C.U. harness connector.

→ N.G. → Repair or replace.

→ O.K.

12 TRY A KNOWN GOOD E.C.U.

→ INSPECTION END

Diagnostic Procedure 3 — Unstable Idle

1 CHECK E.G.R. CONTROL VALVE.
Check E.G.R. control valve for sticking.

→ N.G. → Repair or replace.

→ O.K.

2 PERFORM POWER BALANCE TEST.
When disconnecting each injector harness connector one at a time, is there any cylinder which does not produce a momentary engine speed drop?

→ No → Go to 6

→ Yes

3 CHECK INJECTOR.
1. Remove crank angle sensor from engine. (Harness connector should remain connected.)
2. Turn ignition switch ON. (Do not start engine.)
3. When rotating crank angle sensor main shaft, does each injector make an operating sound?

→ No → Check injector(s) and circuit(s).

→ Yes

4 CHECK IGNITION SPARK.
1. Disconnect spark plug cord.
2. Connect a known good spark plug to the spark plug cord.
3. Place end of spark plug against a suitable ground and crank engine.
4. Check for spark.

→ N.G. → Check ignition coil, ignition wire, power transistor unit and their circuits.

→ O.K.

5 CHECK SPARK PLUGS.
Remove the spark plugs and check for fouling, etc.

→ N.G. → Repair or replace spark plug(s).

→ O.K.

6 CHECK FUEL PRESSURE.
1. Release fuel pressure to zero.
2. Install fuel pressure gauge and check fuel pressure.
   At idle:
   Approx. 250.1 kPa
   (2.55 kg/cm², 36.3 psi)

→ N.G. → Check fuel pump and circuit.

→ O.K.

(Go to Ⓐ on next page.)

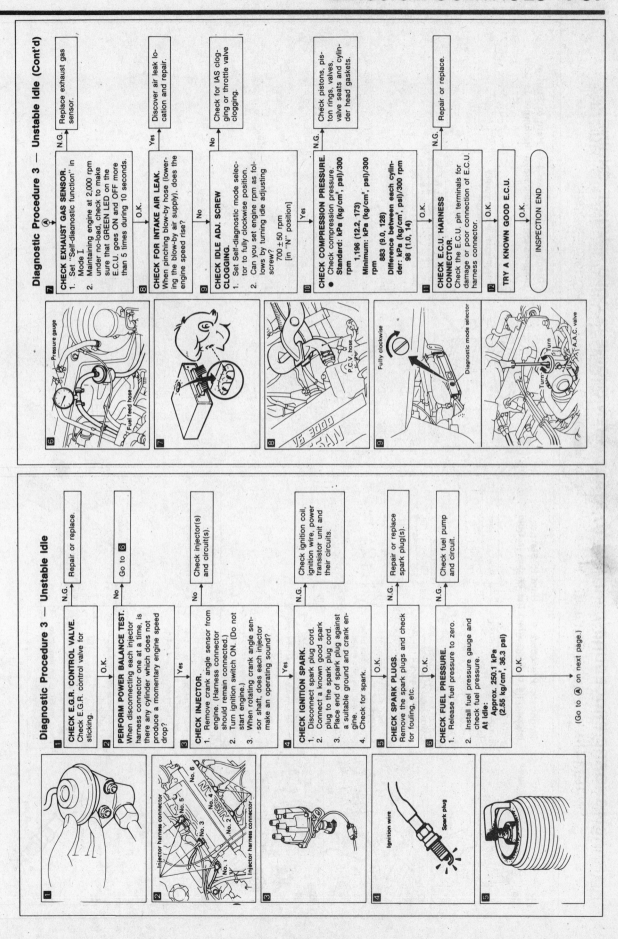

DIAGNOSTIC PROCEDURE 4 — HARD TO START WHEN ENGINE IS COLD — VG30E ENGINE

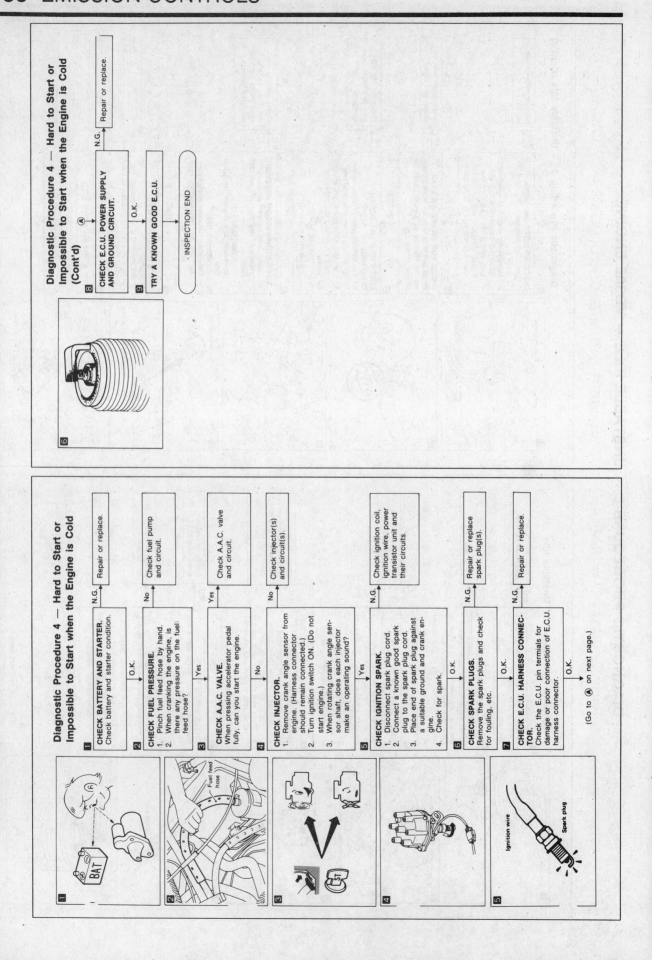

Diagnostic Procedure 4 — Hard to Start or Impossible to Start when the Engine is Cold

1. **CHECK BATTERY AND STARTER.**
   Check battery and starter condition.
   N.G. → Repair or replace.
   O.K. ↓

2. **CHECK FUEL PRESSURE.**
   1. Pinch fuel feed hose by hand.
   2. When cranking the engine, is there any pressure on the fuel feed hose?
   No → Check fuel pump and circuit.
   Yes ↓

3. **CHECK A.A.C. VALVE.**
   When pressing accelerator pedal fully, can you start the engine.
   Yes → Check A.A.C. valve and circuit.
   No ↓

4. **CHECK INJECTOR.**
   1. Remove crank angle sensor from engine. (Harness connector should remain connected.)
   2. Turn ignition switch ON. (Do not start engine.)
   3. When rotating crank angle sensor shaft, does each injector make an operating sound?
   No → Check injector(s) and circuit(s).
   Yes ↓

5. **CHECK IGNITION SPARK.**
   1. Disconnect spark plug cord.
   2. Connect a known good spark plug to the spark plug cord.
   3. Place end of spark plug against a suitable ground and crank engine.
   4. Check for spark.
   N.G. → Check ignition coil, ignition wire, power transistor unit and their circuits.
   O.K. ↓

6. **CHECK SPARK PLUGS.**
   Remove the spark plugs and check for fouling, etc.
   N.G. → Repair or replace spark plug(s).
   O.K. ↓

7. **CHECK E.C.U. HARNESS CONNEC-TOR.**
   Check the E.C.U. pin termials for damage or poor connection of E.C.U. harness connector.
   N.G. → Repair or replace.
   O.K. ↓

   (Go to Ⓐ on next page.)

Fuel feed hose

Ignition wire

Spark plug

Diagnostic Procedure 4 — Hard to Start or Impossible to Start when the Engine is Cold (Cont'd)

Ⓐ

8. **CHECK E.C.U. POWER SUPPLY AND GROUND CIRCUIT.**
   N.G. → Repair or replace.
   O.K. ↓

9. **TRY A KNOWN GOOD E.C.U.**

   → INSPECTION END

DIAGNOSTIC PROCEDURE 6 — HARD TO START UNDER NORMAL CONDITIONS — VG30E ENGINE

Diagnostic Procedure 6 — Hard to Start or Impossible to Start under Normal Conditions

1. **CHECK BATTERY AND STARTER.** Check battery and starter operation.
   - N.G. → Repair or replace.
   - O.K. →

2. **CHECK FUEL PRESSURE.**
   1. Pinch fuel feed hose by hand.
   2. When cranking the engine, is there any pressure on the fuel feed hose?
   - No → Check fuel pump and circuit.
   - Yes →

3. **CHECK INJECTOR FOR LEAKAGE.** When pressing accelerator pedal fully, can you start the engine.
   - Yes → Check injector(s) for leakage.
   - No →

4. **CHECK INJECTOR.**
   1. Remove crank angle sensor from engine. (Harness connector should remain connected.)
   2. Turn ignition switch ON. (Do not start engine.)
   3. When rotating crank angle sensor shaft, does each injector make an operating sound?
   - No → Check injectors and circuits.
   - Yes →

5. **CHECK IGNITION SPARK.**
   1. Disconnect spark plug cord.
   2. Connect a known good spark plug to the spark plug cord.
   3. Place end of spark plug against a suitable ground and crank engine.
   4. Check for spark.
   - N.G. → Check ignition coil, ignition wire, power transistor unit and circuits.
   - O.K. →

6. **CHECK SPARK PLUGS.** Remove the spark plugs and check for fouling, etc.
   - N.G. → Repair or replace spark plug(s).
   - O.K. →

7. **CHECK E.G.R. CONTROL VALVE.** Check E.G.R. control valve for sticking.
   - N.G. → Repair or replace.
   - O.K. → (Go to Ⓐ on next page.)

DIAGNOSTIC PROCEDURE 5 — HARD TO START WHEN ENGINE IS HOT — VG30E ENGINE

Diagnostic Procedure 5 — Hard to Start or Impossible to Start when the Engine is Hot

1. **CHECK FUEL PRESSURE.**
   1. Pinch fuel feed hose by hand.
   2. When cranking the engine, is there any pressure on the fuel feed hose?
   - No → Check fuel pump and circuit.
   - Yes →

2. **CHECK FUEL VAPOR.**
   1. Disconnect fuel pressure regulator vacuum hose and plug hose.
   2. Can you start engine?
   - Yes → Check fuel properties.
   - No →

3. **CHECK INJECTOR.**
   1. Remove crank angle sensor from engine. (Harness connector should remain connected.)
   2. Turn ignition switch ON. (Do not start engine.)
   3. When rotating crank angle sensor shaft, does each injector make an operating sound?
   - No → Check injector(s) and circuit(s).
   - Yes →

4. **CHECK IGNITION SPARK.**
   1. Disconnect spark plug cord.
   2. Connect a known good spark plug to the spark plug cord.
   3. Place end of spark plug against a suitable ground and crank engine.
   4. Check for spark.
   - N.G. → Check ignition coil, ignition wire, power transistor unit and circuits.
   - O.K. →

5. **CHECK E.C.U. HARNESS CONNECTOR.** Check the E.C.U. pin terminals for damage or poor connection of E.C.U. harness connector.
   - N.G. → Repair or replace.
   - O.K. →

6. **CHECK E.C.U. POWER SUPPLY AND GROUND CIRCUIT.**
   - N.G. → Repair or replace.
   - O.K. →

7. **TRY A KNOWN GOOD E.C.U.**
   - INSPECTION END

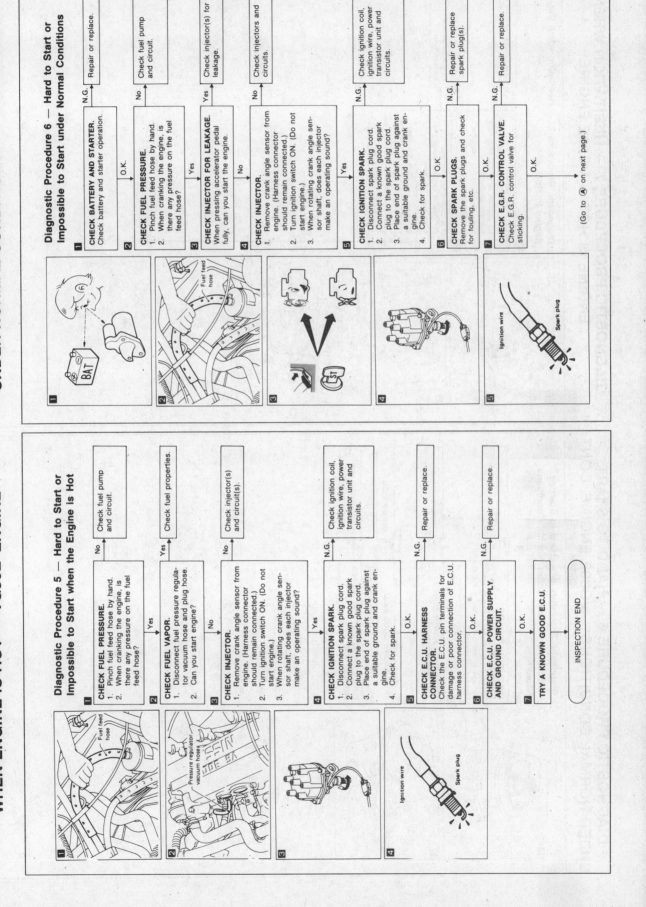

DIAGNOSTIC PROCEDURE 7 — HESITATION WHEN ENGINE IS HOT — VG30E ENGINE

Diagnostic Procedure 7 — Hesitation when the Engine is Hot

1 CHECK FUEL VAPOR.
1. Disconnect fuel pressure regulator vacuum hose and plug hose.
2. Perform cruise test.
3. Does the hesitation disappear?

Yes → Check fuel properties.

No ↓

2 CHECK CANISTER PURGE.
1. Disconnect canister purge line hose and plug hose.
2. Perform cruise test.
3. Does the hesitation disappear?

Yes → Check purge and vacuum lines.

No ↓

INSPECTION END

DIAGNOSTIC PROCEDURE 6 — HARD TO START UNDER NORMAL CONDITIONS — VG30E ENGINE, CONT.

Diagnostic Procedure 6 — Hard to Start or Impossible to Start under Normal Conditions (Cont'd)

Ⓐ ↓

8 CHECK E.C.U. HARNESS CONNECTOR.
Check the E.C.U. pin terminals for damage or poor connection of E.C.U. harness connector.

N.G. → Repair or replace.

O.K. ↓

9 CHECK E.C.U. POWER SUPPLY AND GROUND CIRCUIT.

N.G. → Repair or replace.

O.K. ↓

10 TRY A KNOWN GOOD E.C.U.

Trouble is fixed. → Replace E.C.U.

Trouble is not fixed. ↓

11 CHECK TIMING BELT FOR PROPER INSTALLATION.

N.G. → Replace timing belt.

O.K. ↓

INSPECTION END

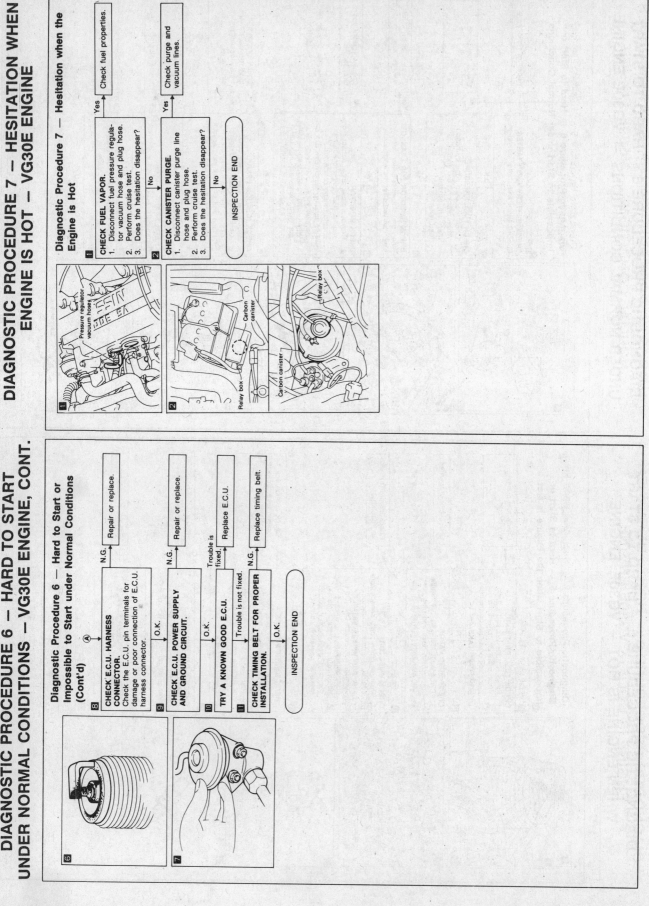

DIAGNOSTIC PROCEDURE 9 — HESITATION UNDER NORMAL CONDITIONS — VG30E ENGINE

Diagnostic Procedure 9 — Hesitation under Normal Conditions

1. CHECK SPARK PLUGS.
Remove spark plugs and check for fouling, etc.

→ N.G. → Repair or replace spark plug(s).

→ O.K.

2. CHECK EXHAUST GAS SENSOR.
1. Set "Self-diagnostic function" in Mode I.
2. Maintaining engine at 2,000 rpm under no-load, check that GREEN LED on the E.C.U. goes ON and OFF more than 5 times during 10 seconds.

→ Yes → Replace exhaust gas sensor.

→ No

3. CHECK CANISTER PURGE.
1. Disconnect canister purge line hose and plug hose.
2. Perform cruise test.
3. Does the hesitation disappear?

→ Yes → Check purge and vacuum lines.

→ No

4. CHECK FOR INTAKE AIR LEAK.
When pinching blow-by hose (lowering the blow-by air supply), does the engine speed rise?

→ Yes → Discover air leak location and repair.

→ No

INSPECTION END

[1]

[2]

[3] Relay box, Carbon canister

[4] Relay box, Carbon canister, P.C.V. hose, VG 3000 NISSAN

DIAGNOSTIC PROCEDURE 8 — HESITATION WHEN ENGINE IS COLD — VG30E ENGINE

Diagnostic Procedure 8 — Hesitation when the Engine is Cold

1. CHECK SPARK PLUGS.
Remove spark plugs and check for fouling, etc.

→ N.G. → Repair or replace spark plug(s).

→ O.K.

2. CHECK FOR INTAKE AIR LEAK.
When pinching blow-by hose (lowering the blow-by air supply), does the engine speed rise?

→ Yes → Discover air leak location and repair.

→ No

3. TRY A KNOWN GOOD AIR FLOW METER.

→ Trouble is fixed. → Replace air flow meter.

→ Trouble is not fixed.

4. CHECK FOR INTAKE VALVE DEPOSITS.
If there are deposits on intake valves, remove them.

INSPECTION END

[1]

[2] P.C.V. hose, VG 3000 NISSAN

DIAGNOSTIC PROCEDURE 10 — ENGINE STALLS WHEN TURNING — VG30E ENGINE

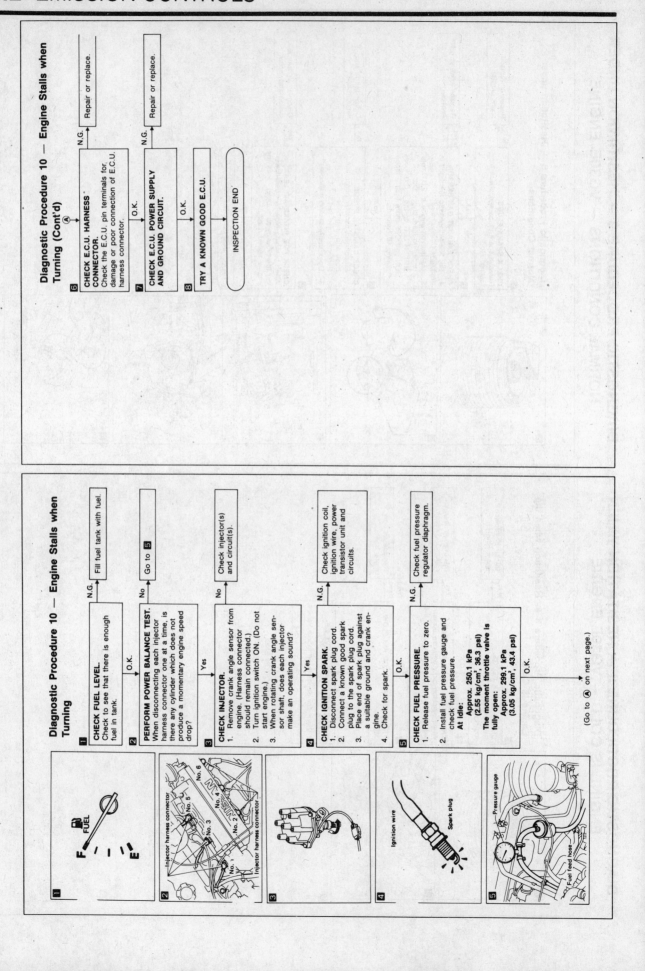

Diagnostic Procedure 10 — Engine Stalls when Turning

1 CHECK FUEL LEVEL.
Check to see that there is enough fuel in tank.
→ N.G. → Fill fuel tank with fuel.
↓ O.K.

2 PERFORM POWER BALANCE TEST.
When disconnecting each injector harness connector one at a time, is there any cylinder which does not produce a momentary engine speed drop?
→ No → Go to **5**
↓ Yes

3 CHECK INJECTOR.
1. Remove crank angle sensor from engine. (Harness connector should remain connected.)
2. Turn ignition switch ON. (Do not start engine.)
3. When rotating crank angle sensor main shaft, does each injector make an operating sound?
→ No → Check injector(s) and circuit(s).
↓ Yes

4 CHECK IGNITION SPARK.
1. Disconnect spark plug cord.
2. Connect a known good spark plug to the spark plug cord.
3. Place end of spark plug against a suitable ground and crank engine.
4. Check for spark.
→ N.G. → Check ignition coil, ignition wire, power transistor unit and circuits.
↓ O.K.

5 CHECK FUEL PRESSURE.
1. Release fuel pressure to zero.
2. Install fuel pressure gauge and check fuel pressure.
At Idle:
Approx. 250.1 kPa (2.55 kg/cm², 36.3 psi)
The moment throttle valve is fully open:
Approx. 299.1 kPa (3.05 kg/cm², 43.4 psi)
→ N.G. → Check fuel pressure regulator diaphragm.
↓ O.K.

(Go to Ⓐ on next page.)

Diagnostic Procedure 10 — Engine Stalls when Turning (Cont'd)
Ⓐ

6 CHECK E.C.U. HARNESS CONNECTOR.
Check the E.C.U. pin terminals for damage or poor connection of E.C.U. harness connector.
→ N.G. → Repair or replace.
↓ O.K.

7 CHECK E.C.U. POWER SUPPLY AND GROUND CIRCUIT.
→ N.G. → Repair or replace.
↓ O.K.

8 TRY A KNOWN GOOD E.C.U.

INSPECTION END

1 FUEL F — E

2 No. 6 No. 5 No. 4 No. 3 No. 2 No. 1 Injector harness connector

3 Ignition wire Spark plug

4 Ignition wire Spark plug

5 Pressure gauge Fuel feed hose

DIAGNOSTIC PROCEDURE 11 — ENGINE STALLS WHEN ENGINE IS HOT — VG30E ENGINE

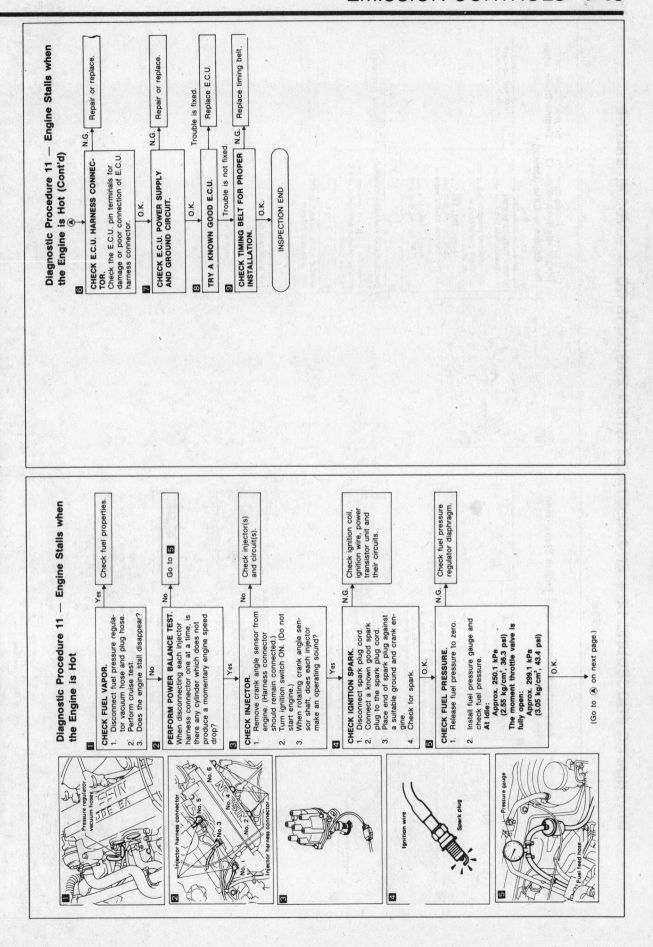

Diagnostic Procedure 11 — Engine Stalls when the Engine is Hot

1 CHECK FUEL VAPOR.
1. Disconnect fuel pressure regulator vacuum hose and plug hose.
2. Perform cruise test.
3. Does the engine stall disappear?

→ Yes → Check fuel properties.

→ No

2 PERFORM POWER BALANCE TEST.
When disconnecting each injector harness connector one at a time, is there any cylinder which does not produce a momentary engine speed drop?

→ No → Go to 5

→ Yes

3 CHECK INJECTOR.
1. Remove crank angle sensor from engine. (Harness connector should remain connected.)
2. Turn ignition switch ON. (Do not start engine.)
3. When rotating crank angle sensor shaft, does each injector make an operating sound?

→ No → Check injector(s) and circuit(s).

→ Yes

4 CHECK IGNITION SPARK.
1. Disconnect spark plug cord.
2. Connect a known good spark plug to the spark plug cord.
3. Place end of spark plug against a suitable ground and crank engine.
4. Check for spark.

→ N.G. → Check ignition coil, ignition wire, power transistor unit and their circuits.

→ O.K.

5 CHECK FUEL PRESSURE.
1. Release fuel pressure to zero.
2. Install fuel pressure gauge and check fuel pressure.
   At idle:
   Approx. 250.1 kPa
   (2.55 kg/cm², 36.3 psi)
   The moment throttle valve is fully open:
   Approx. 299.1 kPa
   (3.05 kg/cm², 43.4 psi)

→ N.G. → Check fuel pressure regulator diaphragm.

→ O.K.

(Go to Ⓐ on next page.)

Diagnostic Procedure 11 — Engine Stalls when the Engine is Hot (Cont'd)

Ⓐ

6 CHECK E.C.U. HARNESS CONNECTOR.
Check the E.C.U. pin terminals for damage or poor connection of E.C.U. harness connector.

→ N.G. → Repair or replace.

→ O.K.

7 CHECK E.C.U. POWER SUPPLY AND GROUND CIRCUIT.

→ N.G. → Repair or replace.

→ O.K.

Trouble is fixed.

8 TRY A KNOWN GOOD E.C.U. → Replace E.C.U.

Trouble is not fixed.

9 CHECK TIMING BELT FOR PROPER INSTALLATION.

→ N.G. → Replace timing belt.

→ O.K.

INSPECTION END

DIAGNOSTIC PROCEDURE 12 — ENGINE STALLS WHEN ENGINE IS COLD — VG30E ENGINE

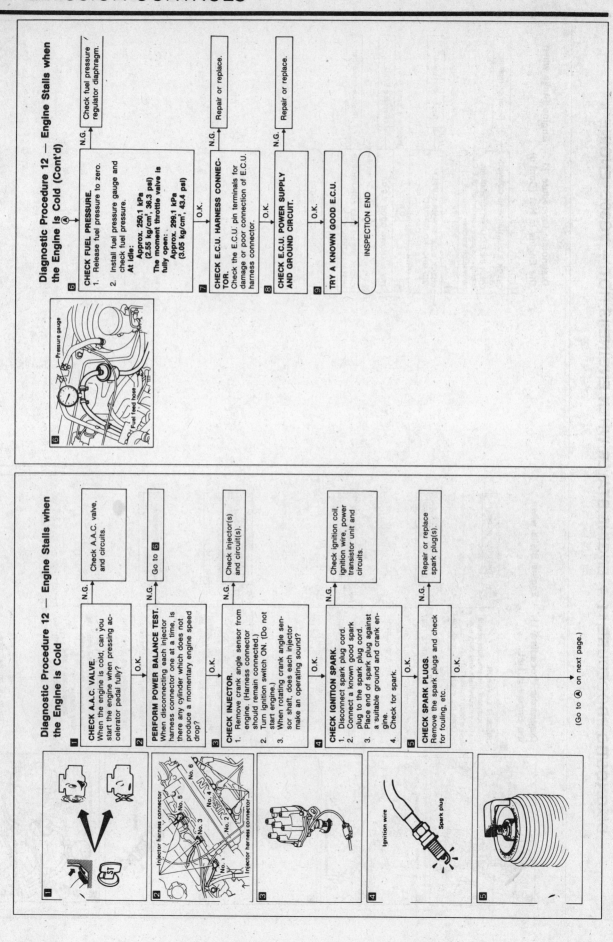

Diagnostic Procedure 12 — Engine Stalls when the Engine is Cold (Cont'd)

6 **CHECK FUEL PRESSURE.**
1. Release fuel pressure to zero.
2. Install fuel pressure gauge and check fuel pressure.
   At idle:
   Approx. 250.1 kPa
   (2.55 kg/cm², 36.3 psi)
   The moment throttle valve is fully open:
   Approx. 299.1 kPa
   (3.05 kg/cm², 43.4 psi)

→ N.G. → Check fuel pressure regulator diaphragm.

↓ O.K.

7 **CHECK E.C.U. HARNESS CONNECTOR.**
Check the E.C.U. pin terminals for damage or poor connection of E.C.U. harness connector.

→ N.G. → Repair or replace.

↓ O.K.

8 **CHECK E.C.U. POWER SUPPLY AND GROUND CIRCUIT.**

→ N.G. → Repair or replace.

↓ O.K.

9 **TRY A KNOWN GOOD E.C.U.**

↓

INSPECTION END

6 Pressure gauge — Fuel feed hose

Diagnostic Procedure 12 — Engine Stalls when the Engine is Cold

1 **CHECK A.A.C. VALVE.**
When the engine is cold, can you start the engine when pressing accelerator pedal fully?

→ N.G. → Check A.A.C. valve, and circuits.

↓ O.K.

2 **PERFORM POWER BALANCE TEST.**
When disconnecting each injector harness connector one at a time, is there any cylinder which does not produce a momentary engine speed drop?

→ N.G. → Go to 6

↓ O.K.

3 **CHECK INJECTOR.**
1. Remove crank angle sensor from engine. (Harness connector should remain connected.)
2. Turn ignition switch ON. (Do not start engine.)
3. When rotating crank angle sensor shaft, does each injector make an operating sound?

→ N.G. → Check injector(s) and circuit(s).

↓ O.K.

4 **CHECK IGNITION SPARK.**
1. Disconnect spark plug cord.
2. Connect a known good spark plug to the spark plug cord.
3. Place end of spark plug against a suitable ground and crank engine.
4. Check for spark.

→ N.G. → Check ignition coil, ignition wire, power transistor unit and circuits.

↓ O.K.

5 **CHECK SPARK PLUGS.**
Remove the spark plugs and check for fouling, etc.

→ N.G. → Repair or replace spark plug(s).

↓ O.K.

(Go to Ⓐ on next page.)

1

2 Injector harness connector — No. 6, No. 5, No. 4, No. 3, No. 2, No. 1 — Injector harness connector

3

4 Ignition wire — Spark plug

5

DIAGNOSTIC PROCEDURE 13 — ENGINE STALLS WHEN STEPPING ON ACCELERATOR MOMENTARILY — VG30E ENGINE

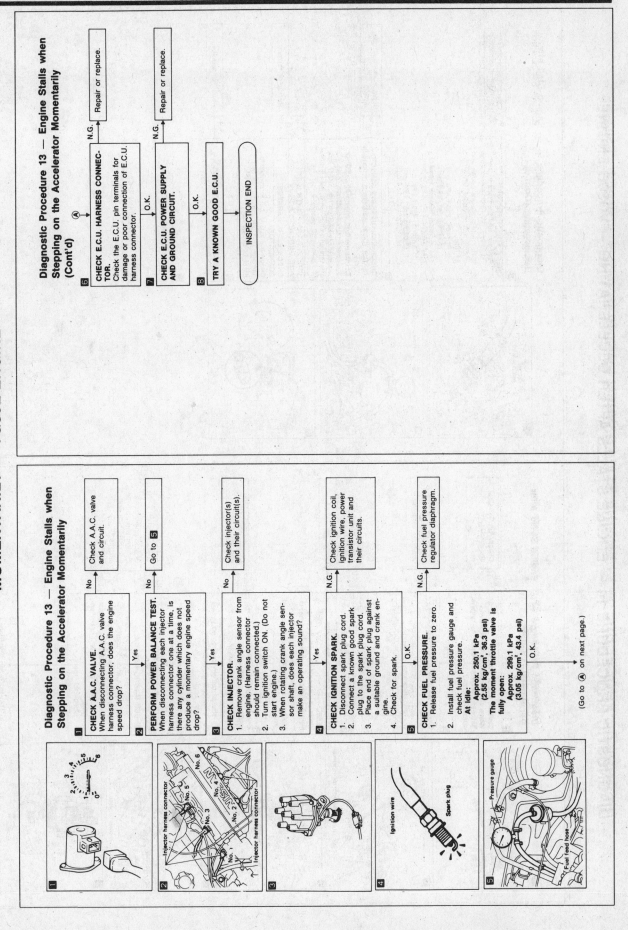

Diagnostic Procedure 13 — Engine Stalls when Stepping on the Accelerator Momentarily

1 **CHECK A.A.C. VALVE.**
When disconnecting A.A.C. valve harness connector, does the engine speed drop?

→ No → Check A.A.C. valve and circuit.

↓ Yes

2 **PERFORM POWER BALANCE TEST.**
When disconnecting each injector harness connector one at a time, is there any cylinder which does not produce a momentary engine speed drop?

→ No → Go to 5

↓ Yes

3 **CHECK INJECTOR.**
1. Remove crank angle sensor from engine. (Harness connector should remain connected.)
2. Turn ignition switch ON. (Do not start engine.)
3. When rotating crank angle sensor shaft, does each injector make an operating sound?

→ No → Check injector(s) and their circuit(s).

↓ Yes

4 **CHECK IGNITION SPARK.**
1. Disconnect spark plug cord.
2. Connect a known good spark plug to the spark plug cord.
3. Place end of spark plug against a suitable ground and crank engine.
4. Check for spark.

→ N.G. → Check ignition coil, ignition wire, power transistor unit and their circuits.

↓ O.K.

5 **CHECK FUEL PRESSURE.**
1. Release fuel pressure to zero.
2. Install fuel pressure gauge and check fuel pressure.
   At idle:
   **Approx. 250.1 kPa
   (2.55 kg/cm², 36.3 psi)**
   The moment throttle valve is fully open:
   **Approx. 299.1 kPa
   (3.05 kg/cm², 43.4 psi)**

→ N.G. → Check fuel pressure regulator diaphragm.

↓ O.K.

(Go to Ⓐ on next page.)

Diagnostic Procedure 13 — Engine Stalls when Stepping on the Accelerator Momentarily (Cont'd)

Ⓐ

6 **CHECK E.C.U. HARNESS CONNECTOR.**
Check the E.C.U. pin terminals for damage or poor connection of E.C.U. harness connector.

→ N.G. → Repair or replace.

↓ O.K.

7 **CHECK E.C.U. POWER SUPPLY AND GROUND CIRCUIT.**

→ N.G. → Repair or replace.

↓ O.K.

8 **TRY A KNOWN GOOD E.C.U.**

↓

INSPECTION END

1 (gauge)

2 No. 5, No. 6, No. 4, No. 3, No. 2, No. 1, Injector harness connector

3 (distributor)

4 Ignition wire, Spark plug

5 Pressure gauge, Fuel feed hose

DIAGNOSTIC PROCEDURE 14 — ENGINE STALLS AFTER DECELERATING — VG30E ENGINE

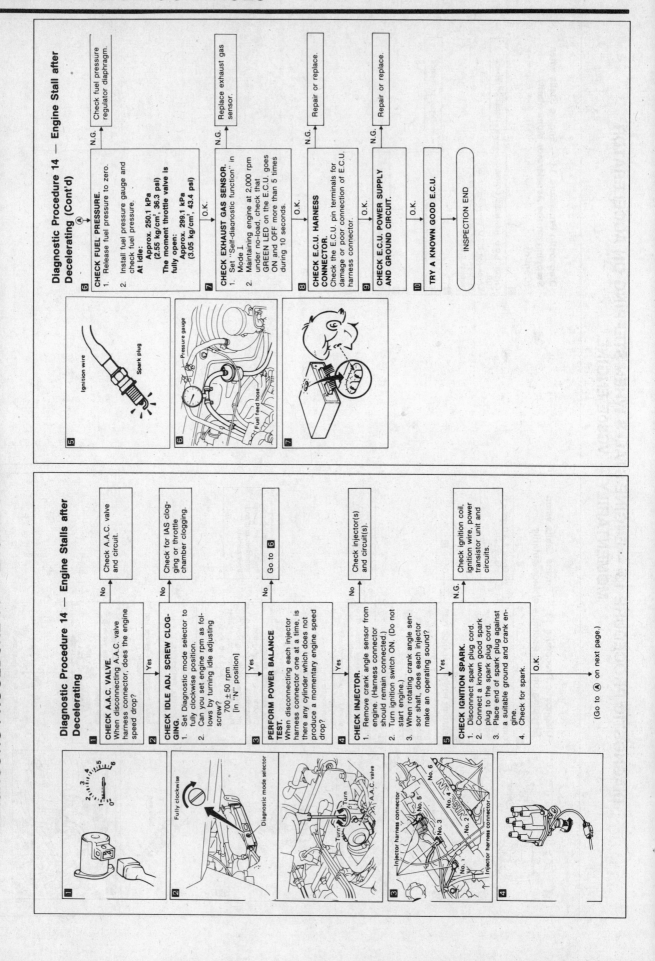

Diagnostic Procedure 14 — Engine Stall after Decelerating (Cont'd)

6 CHECK FUEL PRESSURE.
1. Release fuel pressure to zero.
2. Install fuel pressure gauge and check fuel pressure.
At idle:
Approx. 250.1 kPa
(2.55 kg/cm², 36.3 psi)
The moment throttle valve is fully open:
Approx. 299.1 kPa
(3.05 kg/cm², 43.4 psi)

N.G. → Check fuel pressure regulator diaphragm.

O.K.

7 CHECK EXHAUST GAS SENSOR.
1. Set "Self-diagnosis function" in Mode I.
2. Maintaining engine at 2,000 rpm under no-load, check that GREEN LED on the E.C.U. goes ON and OFF more than 5 times during 10 seconds.

N.G. → Replace exhaust gas sensor.

O.K.

8 CHECK E.C.U. HARNESS CONNECTOR.
Check the E.C.U. pin terminals for damage or poor connection of E.C.U. harness connector.

N.G. → Repair or replace.

O.K.

9 CHECK E.C.U. POWER SUPPLY AND GROUND CIRCUIT.

N.G. → Repair or replace.

O.K.

10 TRY A KNOWN GOOD E.C.U.

(INSPECTION END)

5 Ignition wire / Spark plug

6 Pressure gauge / Fuel feed hose

7

Diagnostic Procedure 14 — Engine Stalls after Decelerating

1 CHECK A.A.C. VALVE.
When disconnecting A.A.C. valve harness connector, does the engine speed drop?

No → Check A.A.C. valve and circuit.

Yes

2 CHECK IDLE ADJ. SCREW CLOGGING.
1. Set Diagnostic mode selector to fully clockwise position.
2. Can you set engine rpm as follows by turning idle adjusting screw?
700 ± 50 rpm
[in "N" position]

No → Check for IAS clogging or throttle chamber clogging.

Yes

3 PERFORM POWER BALANCE TEST.
When disconnecting each injector harness connector one at a time, is there any cylinder which does not produce a momentary engine speed drop?

No → Go to 6

Yes

4 CHECK INJECTOR.
1. Remove crank angle sensor from engine. (Harness connector should remain connected.)
2. Turn ignition switch ON. (Do not start engine.)
3. When rotating crank angle sensor shaft, does each injector make an operating sound?

No → Check injector(s) and circuit(s).

Yes

5 CHECK IGNITION SPARK.
1. Disconnect spark plug cord.
2. Connect a known good spark plug to the spark plug cord.
3. Place end of spark plug against a suitable ground and crank engine.
4. Check for spark.

N.G. → Check ignition coil, ignition wire, power transistor unit and circuits.

O.K. → Ⓐ on next page.

(Go to Ⓐ on next page.)

1 Fully clockwise / Diagnostic mode selector

2 Turn / Turn / A.A.C. valve

3 Injector harness connector / No. 6 / No. 5 / No. 4 / No. 3 / No. 2 / No. 1 / Injector harness connector

4

DIAGNOSTIC PROCEDURE 15 — ENGINE STALLS WHEN ACCELERATING OR CRUISING — VG30E ENGINE

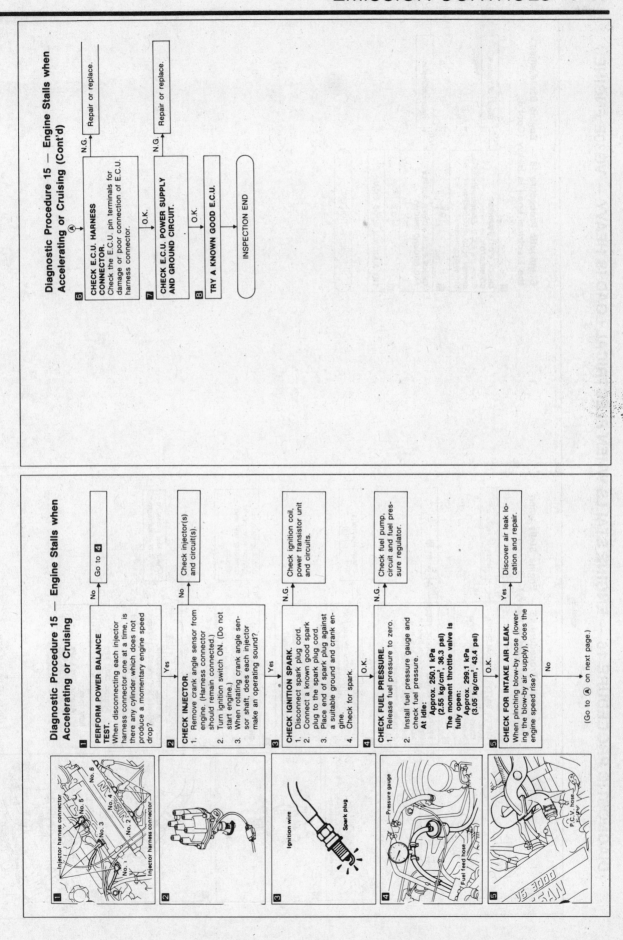

Diagnostic Procedure 15 — Engine Stalls when Accelerating or Cruising (Cont'd)

6 **CHECK E.C.U. HARNESS CONNECTOR.**
Check the E.C.U. pin terminals for damage or poor connection of E.C.U. harness connector.

→ N.G. → Repair or replace.

→ O.K.

7 **CHECK E.C.U. POWER SUPPLY AND GROUND CIRCUIT.**

→ N.G. → Repair or replace.

→ O.K.

8 **TRY A KNOWN GOOD E.C.U.**

INSPECTION END

Diagnostic Procedure 15 — Engine Stalls when Accelerating or Cruising

1 **PERFORM POWER BALANCE TEST.**
When disconnecting each injector harness connector one at a time, is there any cylinder which does not produce a momentary engine speed drop?

→ No → Go to 4

→ Yes

2 **CHECK INJECTOR.**
1. Remove crank angle sensor from engine. (Harness connector should remain connected.)
2. Turn ignition switch ON. (Do not start engine.)
3. When rotating crank angle sensor shaft, does each injector make an operating sound?

→ No → Check injector(s) and circuit(s).

→ Yes

3 **CHECK IGNITION SPARK.**
1. Disconnect spark plug cord.
2. Connect a known good spark plug to the spark plug cord.
3. Place end of spark plug against a suitable ground and crank engine.
4. Check for spark.

→ N.G. → Check ignition coil, power transistor unit and circuits.

→ O.K.

4 **CHECK FUEL PRESSURE.**
1. Release fuel pressure to zero.
2. Install fuel pressure gauge and check fuel pressure.
At idle:
Approx. 250.1 kPa
(2.55 kg/cm², 36.3 psi)
The moment throttle valve is fully open:
Approx. 299.1 kPa
(3.05 kg/cm², 43.4 psi)

→ N.G. → Check fuel pump, circuit and fuel pressure regulator.

→ O.K.

5 **CHECK FOR INTAKE AIR LEAK.**
When pinching blow-by hose (lowering the blow-by air supply), does the engine speed rise?

→ Yes → Discover air leak location and repair.

→ No

(Go to Ⓐ on next page.)

DIAGNOSTIC PROCEDURE 16 — ENGINE STALLS WHEN ELECTRICAL LOAD IS HEAVY — VG30E ENGINE

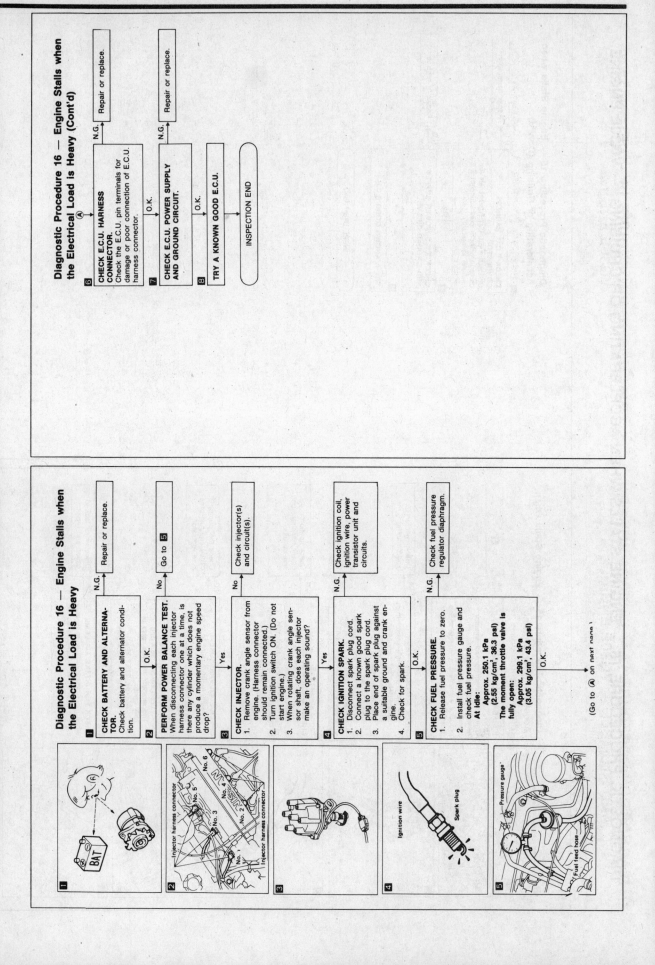

Diagnostic Procedure 16 — Engine Stalls when the Electrical Load is Heavy

1 CHECK BATTERY AND ALTERNATOR.
Check battery and alternator condition.
→ N.G. → Repair or replace.
→ O.K. →

2 PERFORM POWER BALANCE TEST.
When disconnecting each injector harness connector one at a time, is there any cylinder which does not produce a momentary engine speed drop?
→ No → Go to **5**
→ Yes →

3 CHECK INJECTOR.
1. Remove crank angle sensor from engine. (Harness connector should remain connected.)
2. Turn ignition switch ON. (Do not start engine.)
3. When rotating crank angle sensor shaft, does each injector make an operating sound?
→ No → Check injector(s) and circuit(s).
→ Yes →

4 CHECK IGNITION SPARK.
1. Disconnect spark plug cord.
2. Connect a known good spark plug to the spark plug cord.
3. Place end of spark plug against a suitable ground and crank engine.
4. Check for spark.
→ N.G. → Check ignition coil, ignition wire, power transistor unit and circuits.
→ O.K. →

5 CHECK FUEL PRESSURE.
1. Release fuel pressure to zero.
2. Install fuel pressure gauge and check fuel pressure.
At idle:
Approx. 250.1 kPa
(2.55 kg/cm², 36.3 psi)
The moment throttle valve is fully open:
Approx. 299.1 kPa
(3.05 kg/cm², 43.4 psi)
→ N.G. → Check fuel pressure regulator diaphragm.
→ O.K. →

(Go to Ⓐ on next page.)

Diagnostic Procedure 16 — Engine Stalls when the Electrical Load is Heavy (Cont'd)

Ⓐ

6 CHECK E.C.U. HARNESS CONNECTOR.
Check the E.C.U. pin terminals for damage or poor connection of E.C.U. harness connector.
→ N.G. → Repair or replace.
→ O.K. →

7 CHECK E.C.U. POWER SUPPLY AND GROUND CIRCUIT.
→ N.G. → Repair or replace.
→ O.K. →

8 TRY A KNOWN GOOD E.C.U.

INSPECTION END

DIAGNOSTIC PROCEDURE 18 — DETONATION VG30E ENGINE

Diagnostic Procedure 18 — Detonation

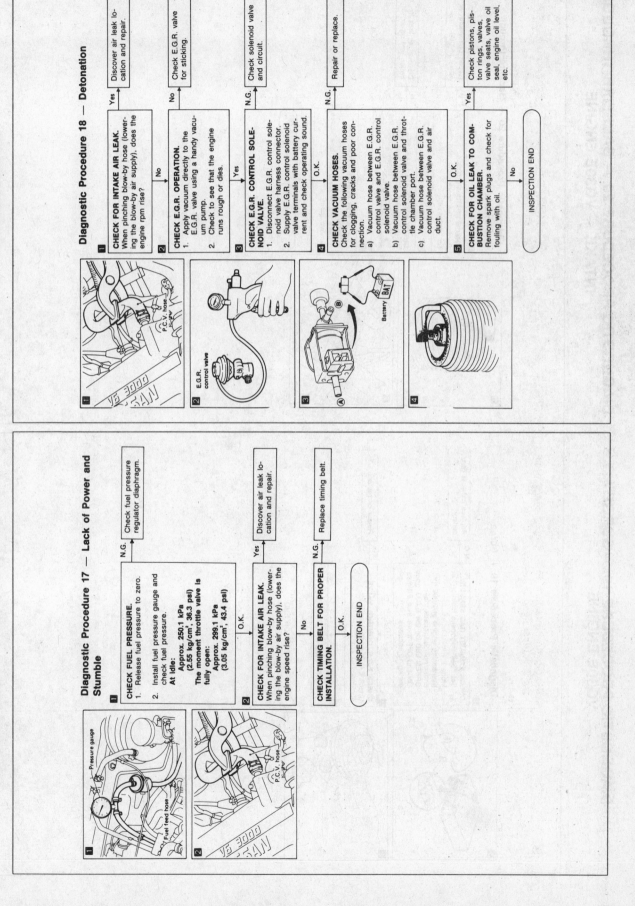

1 CHECK FOR INTAKE AIR LEAK.
When pinching blow-by hose (lowering the blow-by air supply), does the engine rpm rise?

Yes → Discover air leak location and repair.

No ↓

2 CHECK E.G.R. OPERATION.
1. Apply vacuum directly to the E.G.R. valve using a handy vacuum pump.
2. Check to see that the engine runs rough or dies.

No → Check E.G.R. valve for sticking.

Yes ↓

3 CHECK E.G.R. CONTROL SOLENOID VALVE.
1. Disconnect E.G.R. control solenoid valve harness connector.
2. Supply E.G.R. control solenoid valve terminals with battery current and check operating sound.

N.G. → Check solenoid valve and circuit.

O.K. ↓

4 CHECK VACUUM HOSES.
Check the following vacuum hoses for clogging, cracks and poor connection.
a) Vacuum hose between E.G.R. control valve and E.G.R. control solenoid valve.
b) Vacuum hose between E.G.R. control solenoid valve and throttle chamber port.
c) Vacuum hose between E.G.R. control solenoid valve and air duct.

N.G. → Repair or replace.

O.K. ↓

5 CHECK FOR OIL LEAK TO COMBUSTION CHAMBER.
Remove spark plugs and check for fouling with oil.

Yes → Check pistons, piston rings, valves, valve seats, valve oil seal, engine oil level, etc.

No ↓

INSPECTION END

DIAGNOSTIC PROCEDURE 17 — LACK OF POWER AND STUMBLE — VG30E ENGINE

Diagnostic Procedure 17 — Lack of Power and Stumble

1 CHECK FUEL PRESSURE.
1. Release fuel pressure to zero.
2. Install fuel pressure gauge and check fuel pressure.
At idle:
Approx. 250.1 kPa
(2.55 kg/cm², 36.3 psi)
The moment throttle valve is fully open:
Approx. 299.1 kPa
(3.05 kg/cm², 43.4 psi)

N.G. → Check fuel pressure regulator diaphragm.

O.K. ↓

2 CHECK FOR INTAKE AIR LEAK.
When pinching blow-by hose (lowering the blow-by air supply), does the engine speed rise?

Yes → Discover air leak location and repair.

No ↓

CHECK TIMING BELT FOR PROPER INSTALLATION.

N.G. → Replace timing belt.

O.K. ↓

INSPECTION END

DIAGNOSTIC PROCEDURE 20 — BACKFIRE THROUGH INTAKE — VG30E ENGINE

Diagnostic Procedure 20 — Backfire through the Intake

1 CHECK SPARK PLUGS.
Remove the spark plugs and check for fouling, etc.

→ N.G. → Repair or replace spark plug(s).

↓ O.K.

2 CHECK INTAKE AIR LEAK.
When pinching blow-by hose (lowering the blow-by air supply), does the engine speed rise?

→ Yes → Discover air leak location and repair.

↓ No

3 CHECK FOR INTAKE VALVE DEPOSITS.
If there are deposits on intake valves, remove them.

↓

INSPECTION END

DIAGNOSTIC PROCEDURE 19 — SURGE VG30E ENGINE

Diagnostic Procedure 19 — Surge

1 CHECK EXHAUST GAS SENSOR.
1. Set "Self-diagnostic function" in Mode I.
2. Maintaining engine at 2,000 rpm under no-load, check that GREEN LED on the E.C.U. goes ON and OFF more than 5 times during 10 seconds.

→ N.G. → Replace exhaust gas sensor.

↓ O.K.

2 CHECK E.G.R. CONTROL VALVE.
Check E.G.R. control valve for sticking.

→ N.G. → Repair or replace.

↓ O.K.

3 TRY A KNOWN GOOD E.C.U.

↓ O.K.

INSPECTION END

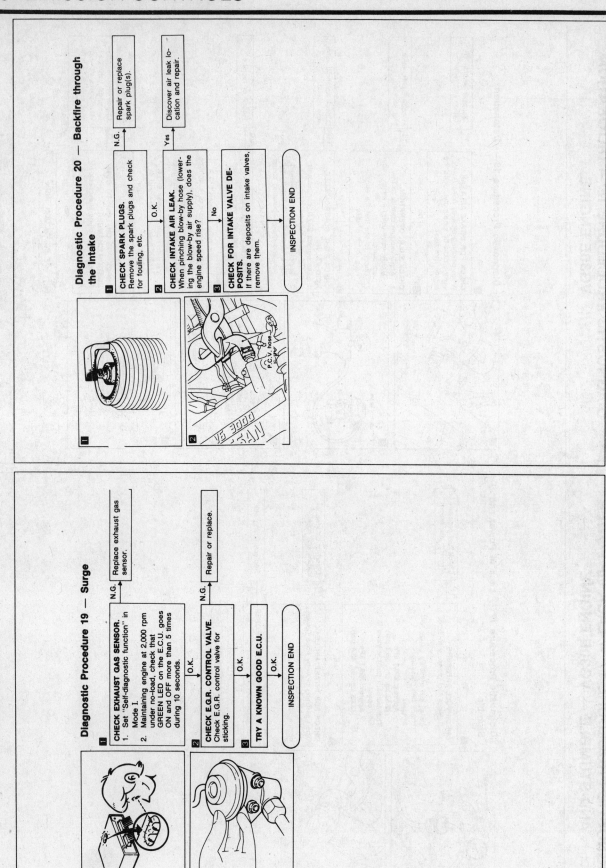

DIAGNOSTIC PROCEDURE 21 — BACKFIRE THROUGH EXHAUST — VG30E ENGINE

DIAGNOSTIC PROCEDURE 22 — MAIN POWER SUPPLY AND GROUND CIRCUIT — VG30E ENGINE

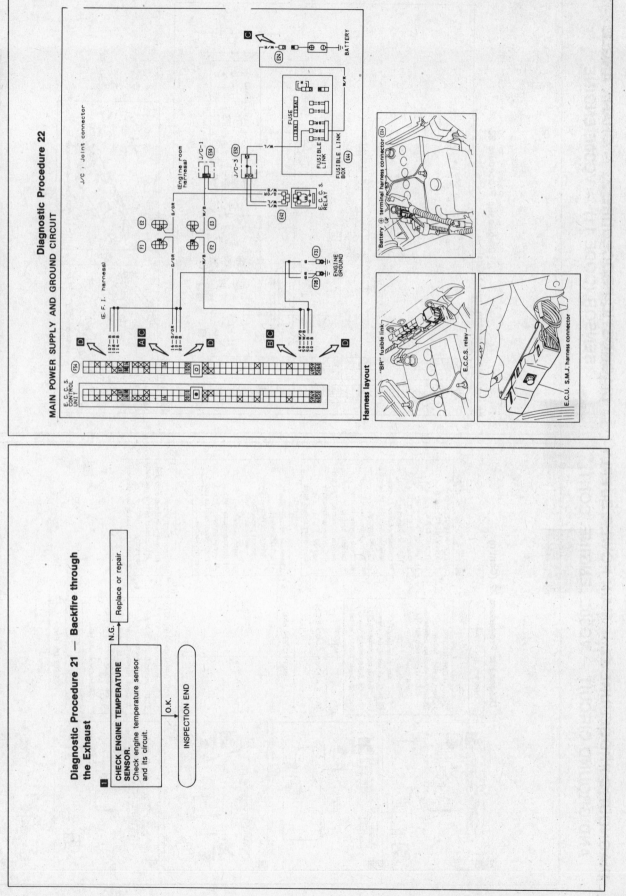

Diagnostic Procedure 22

MAIN POWER SUPPLY AND GROUND CIRCUIT

Diagnostic Procedure 21 — Backfire through the Exhaust

CHECK ENGINE TEMPERATURE SENSOR.
Check engine temperature sensor and its circuit.

O.K. → INSPECTION END

N.G. → Replace or repair.

DIAGNOSTIC PROCEDURE 23 – CRANK ANGLE SENSOR (CODE 11) – VG30E ENGINE

DIAGNOSTIC PROCEDURE 22 – MAIN POWER SUPPLY AND GROUND CIRCUIT – VG30E ENGINE, CONT.

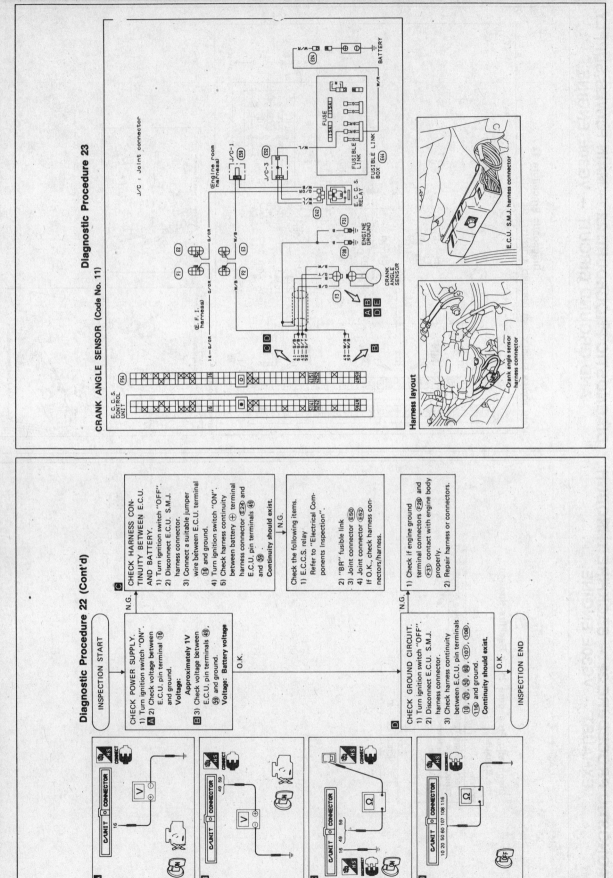

DIAGNOSTIC PROCEDURE 23 — CRANK ANGLE SENSOR (CODE 11) — VG30E ENGINE, CONT.

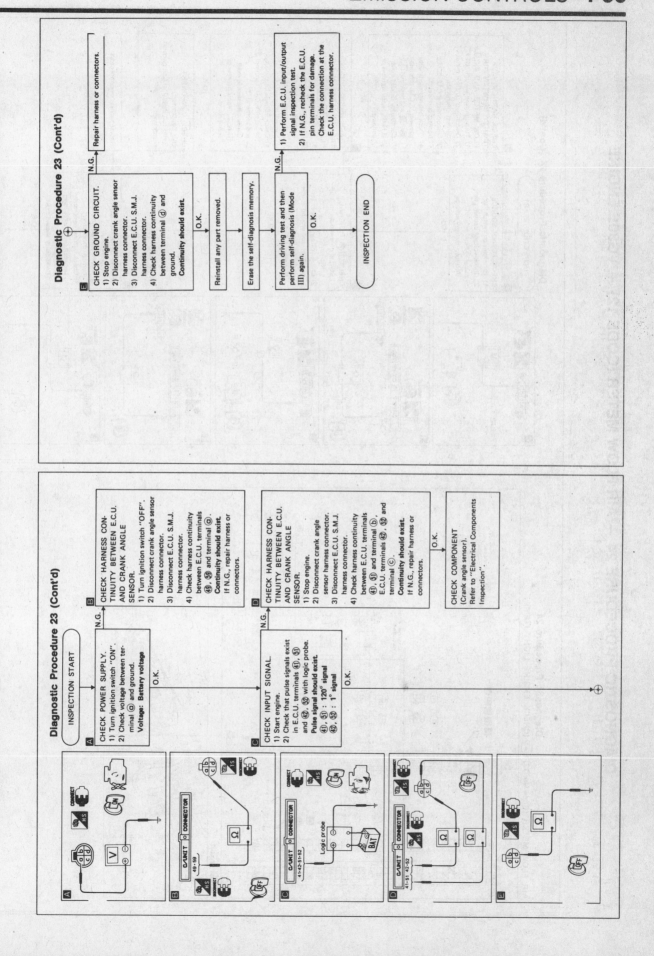

Diagnostic Procedure 23 (Cont'd)

INSPECTION START

A CHECK POWER SUPPLY.
1) Turn ignition switch "ON".
2) Check voltage between terminal ⓐ and ground.
Voltage: Battery voltage

N.G. →

B CHECK HARNESS CONTINUITY BETWEEN E.C.U. AND CRANK ANGLE SENSOR.
1) Turn ignition switch "OFF".
2) Disconnect crank angle sensor harness connector.
3) Disconnect E.C.U. S.M.J. harness connector.
4) Check harness continuity between E.C.U. terminals ⑭, ㊾ and terminal ⓐ.
Continuity should exist.
If N.G., repair harness or connectors.

O.K.

C CHECK INPUT SIGNAL.
1) Start engine.
2) Check that pulse signals exist in E.C.U. terminals ㊶, ㊿ and ㊷, ㊾ with logic probe.
Pulse signal should exist.
㊶, ㊿ : 120° signal
㊷, ㊾ : 1° signal

N.G. →

D CHECK HARNESS CONTINUITY BETWEEN E.C.U. AND CRANK ANGLE SENSOR.
1) Stop engine.
2) Disconnect crank angle sensor harness connector.
3) Disconnect E.C.U. S.M.J. harness connector.
4) Check harness continuity between E.C.U. terminals ㊶, ㊿ and terminal ⓑ, E.C.U. terminals ㊷, ㊾ and terminal ⓒ.
Continuity should exist.
If N.G., repair harness or connectors.

O.K.

CHECK COMPONENT
(Crank angle sensor).
Refer to "Electrical Components Inspection".

O.K. → ⊕

Diagnostic Procedure 23 (Cont'd)

⊕

E CHECK GROUND CIRCUIT.
1) Stop engine.
2) Disconnect crank angle sensor harness connector.
3) Disconnect E.C.U. S.M.J. harness connector.
4) Check harness continuity between terminal ⓓ and ground.
Continuity should exist.

N.G. → Repair harness or connectors.

O.K.

Reinstall any part removed.

Erase the self-diagnosis memory.

Perform driving test and then perform self-diagnosis (Mode III) again.

N.G. → 1) Perform E.C.U. input/output signal inspection test.
2) If N.G., recheck the E.C.U. pin terminals for damage. Check the connection at the E.C.U. harness connector.

O.K.

INSPECTION END

DIAGNOSTIC PROCEDURE 24 — AIR FLOW METER (CODE 12) — VG30E ENGINE

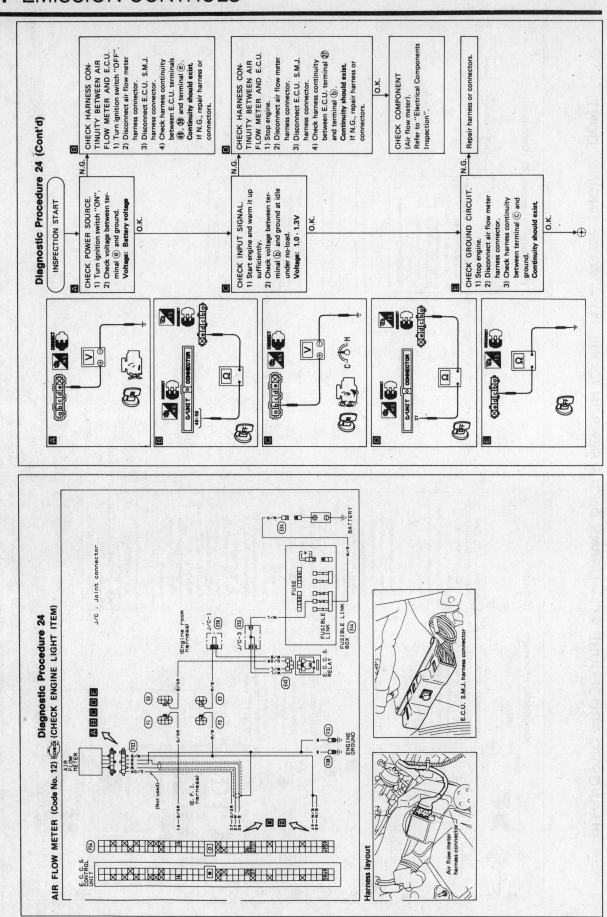

AIR FLOW METER (Code No. 12) [CHECK] (CHECK ENGINE LIGHT ITEM)

Diagnostic Procedure 24

Diagnostic Procedure 24 (Cont'd)

INSPECTION START

A CHECK POWER SOURCE.
1) Turn ignition switch "ON".
2) Check voltage between terminal ⓔ and ground.
   Voltage: Battery voltage

B CHECK HARNESS CONTINUITY BETWEEN AIR FLOW METER AND E.C.U.
1) Turn ignition switch "OFF".
2) Disconnect air flow meter harness connector.
3) Disconnect E.C.U. S.M.J. harness connector.
4) Check harness continuity between E.C.U. terminals ㊾, ㊿ and terminal ⓔ.
   Continuity should exist.
   If N.G., repair harness or connectors.

C CHECK INPUT SIGNAL.
1) Start engine and warm it up sufficiently.
2) Check voltage between terminal ⓑ and ground at idle under no-load.
   Voltage: 1.0 - 1.3V

D CHECK HARNESS CONTINUITY BETWEEN AIR FLOW METER AND E.C.U.
1) Stop engine.
2) Disconnect air flow meter harness connector.
3) Disconnect E.C.U. S.M.J. harness connector.
4) Check harness continuity between E.C.U. terminal ㉗ and terminal ⓑ.
   Continuity should exist.
   If N.G., repair harness or connectors.

CHECK COMPONENT
(Air flow meter).
Refer to "Electrical Components Inspection".

E CHECK GROUND CIRCUIT.
1) Stop engine.
2) Disconnect air flow meter harness connector.
3) Check harness continuity between terminal ⓒ and ground.
   Continuity should exist.

Repair harness or connectors.

Harness layout

J/C : Joint connector

DIAGNOSTIC PROCEDURE 24 — AIR FLOW METER (CODE 12) — VG30E ENGINE, CONT.

DIAGNOSTIC PROCEDURE 25 — ENGINE TEMPERATURE SENSOR (CODE 13) — VG30E ENGINE

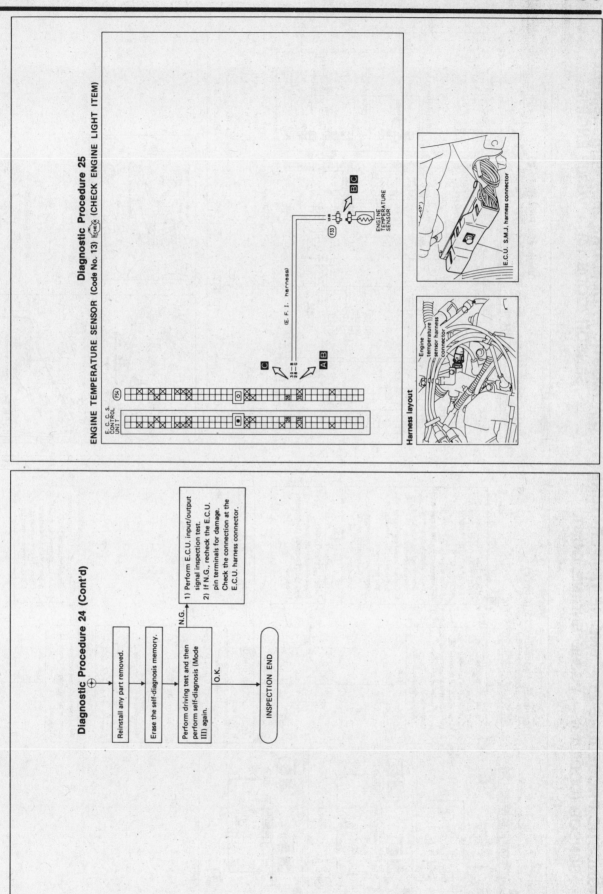

DIAGNOSTIC PROCEDURE 26 – VEHICLE SPEED SENSOR (CODE 14) – VG30E ENGINE

Diagnostic Procedure 26

VEHICLE SPEED SENSOR (Code No. 14) (Switch ON/OFF diagnosis)
(CHECK ENGINE LIGHT ITEM)

(DM): Digital type combination meter
(NM): Needle type combination meter

Harness layout

DIAGNOSTIC PROCEDURE 25 – ENGINE TEMPERATURE SENSOR (CODE 13) – VG30E ENGINE, CONT.

Diagnostic Procedure 25 (Cont'd)

INSPECTION START

A
CHECK INPUT SIGNAL.
1) Start engine.
2) Make sure that voltage between E.C.U. terminal ㉘ and ground changes during engine warm-up.
Cold → Hot:
Approximately 5 – 0V

O.K. →

B
N.G. → CHECK HARNESS CONTINUITY BETWEEN ENGINE TEMPERATURE SENSOR AND E.C.U.
1) Stop engine.
2) Disconnect engine temperature sensor harness connector.
3) Disconnect E.C.U. S.M.J. harness connector.
4) Check harness continuity between E.C.U. terminal ㉘ and terminal ⓖ.
Continuity should exist.
If N.G., repair harness or connectors.

O.K. →

CHECK COMPONENT
(Engine temperature sensor).
Refer to "Electrical Components Inspection".

C
CHECK GROUND CIRCUIT.
1) Stop engine.
2) Disconnect engine temperature sensor harness connector.
3) Disconnect E.C.U. S.M.J. harness connector.
4) Check harness continuity between E.C.U. terminal ㉚ and terminal ⓑ.

N.G. → Repair harness or connectors.

O.K. ↓

Reinstall any part removed.

↓

Erase the self-diagnosis memory.

↓

Perform driving test and then perform self-diagnosis (Mode III) again.

N.G. → 1) Perform E.C.U. input/output signal inspection test.
2) If N.G., recheck the E.C.U. pin terminals for damage.
Check the connection at the E.C.U. harness connector.

O.K. ↓

INSPECTION END

DIAGNOSTIC PROCEDURE 27 — IGNITION SIGNAL (CODE 21) — VG30E ENGINE

Diagnostic Procedure 27

IGNITION SIGNAL (Code No. 21)

Harness layout

Power transistor harness connector
E.C.U. S.M.J. harness connector
Ignition coil harness connector
Resistor and condenser harness connector

DIAGNOSTIC PROCEDURE 26 — VEHICLE SPEED SENSOR (CODE 14) — VG30E ENGINE, CONT.

Diagnostic Procedure 26 (Cont'd)

INSPECTION START

↓

Make sure that speedometer in combination meter operates properly.

— N.G. → Check power supply and ground circuit for instrument panel. (See EL section.) If N.G., repair harness or connectors. → CHECK COMPONENT (Vehicle speed sensor). Refer to "Electrical Components Inspection".

O.K. ↓

A CHECK INPUT SIGNAL.
1) Jack up front wheels.
2) Disconnect E.C.U. S.M.J. harness connector.
3) Check resistance between E.C.U. terminal ㊳ and ground. With transmission in neutral, turn both front wheels. Continuity should be intermittent.

— N.G. → **B** CHECK HARNESS CONTINUITY BETWEEN COMBINATION METER AND E.C.U.
1) Remove combination meter from instrument panel.
2) Disconnect combination meter harness connectors ⑯ and ⑲.
3) Check harness continuity between E.C.U. terminal ㊳ and terminal ⑥. Continuity should exist.
⑯: Digital meter
⑲: Needle meter

O.K. ↓

Reinstall any part removed.

↓

Erase the self-diagnosis memory.

↓

Perform switch ON/OFF diagnosis (Mode IV).

— N.G. → 1) Perform E.C.U. input/output signal inspection test.
2) If N.G., recheck the E.C.U. pin terminals for damage. Check the connection at the E.C.U. harness connector.

O.K. ↓

INSPECTION END

A C.UNIT CONNECTOR 53

B Needle meter — Digital meter — C.UNIT CONNECTOR 53

DIAGNOSTIC PROCEDURE 27 — IGNITION SIGNAL (CODE 21) — VG30E ENGINE, CONT.

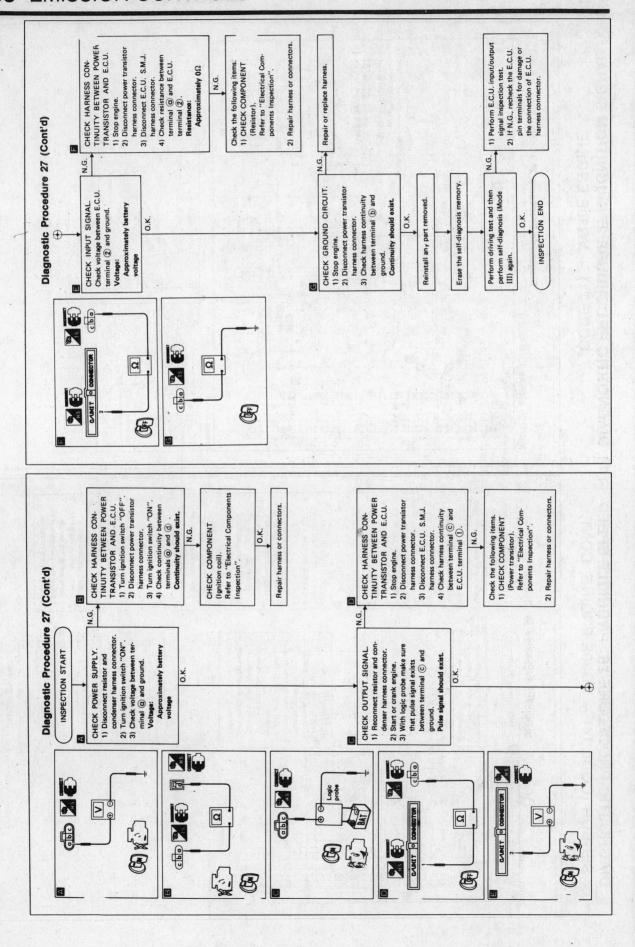

DIAGNOSTIC PROCEDURE 28 — FUEL PUMP (CODE 22) — VG30E ENGINE

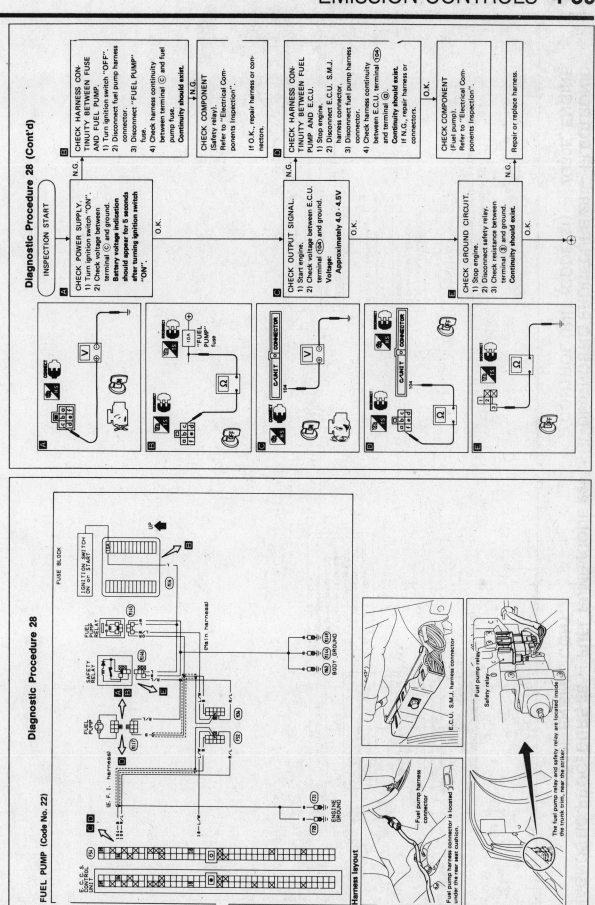

Diagnostic Procedure 28 (Cont'd)

INSPECTION START

A CHECK POWER SUPPLY.
1) Turn ignition switch "ON".
2) Check voltage between terminal ⓒ and ground.
Battery voltage indication should appear for 5 seconds after turning ignition switch "ON".

N.G. → **B** CHECK HARNESS CONTINUITY BETWEEN FUSE AND FUEL PUMP.
1) Turn ignition switch "OFF".
2) Disconnect fuel pump harness connector.
3) Disconnect "FUEL PUMP" fuse.
4) Check harness continuity between terminal ⓒ and fuel pump fuse.
Continuity should exist.

N.G. → CHECK COMPONENT (Safety relay).
Refer to "Electrical Components Inspection".

If O.K., repair harness or connectors.

O.K. ↓

C CHECK OUTPUT SIGNAL.
1) Start engine.
2) Check voltage between E.C.U. terminal ⑩④ and ground.
Voltage: Approximately 4.0 - 4.5V

N.G. → **D** CHECK HARNESS CONTINUITY BETWEEN FUEL PUMP AND E.C.U.
1) Stop engine.
2) Disconnect E.C.U. S.M.J. harness connector.
3) Disconnect fuel pump harness connector.
4) Check harness continuity between E.C.U. terminal ⑩④ and terminal ⓓ.
Continuity should exist.
If N.G., repair harness or connectors.

O.K. → CHECK COMPONENT (Fuel pump).
Refer to "Electrical Components Inspection".

O.K. ↓

E CHECK GROUND CIRCUIT.
1) Stop engine.
2) Disconnect safety relay.
3) Check resistance between terminal ⑨ and ground.
Continuity should exist.

N.G. → Repair or replace harness.

O.K. → ⊕

Diagnostic Procedure 28

FUEL PUMP (Code No. 22)

Harness layout

Fuel pump harness connector is located under the rear seat cushion.

E.C.U. S.M.J. harness connector

Fuel pump harness connector

Fuel pump relay

Safety relay

The fuel pump relay and safety relay are located inside the trunk trim, near the striker.

DIAGNOSTIC PROCEDURE 29 — ELECTRONIC CONTROL UNIT (CODE 31) — VG30E ENGINE

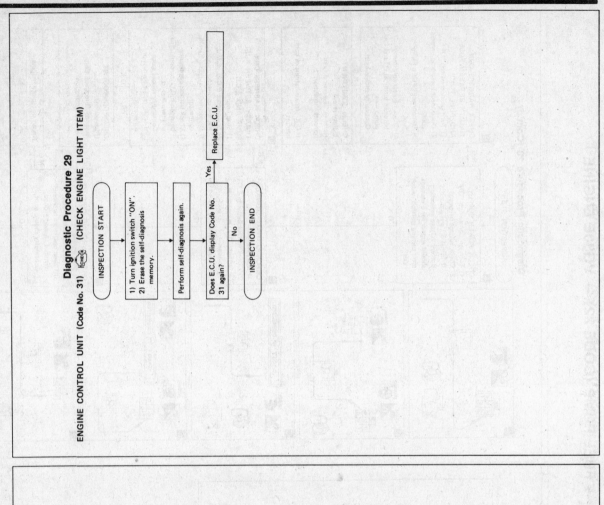

ENGINE CONTROL UNIT (Code No. 31) (CHECK ENGINE LIGHT ITEM)

Diagnostic Procedure 29

INSPECTION START

1) Turn ignition switch "ON".
2) Erase the self-diagnosis memory.

Perform self-diagnosis again.

Does E.C.U. display Code No. 31 again? — Yes → Replace E.C.U.

No

INSPECTION END

DIAGNOSTIC PROCEDURE 28 — FUEL PUMP (CODE 22) VG30E ENGINE, CONT.

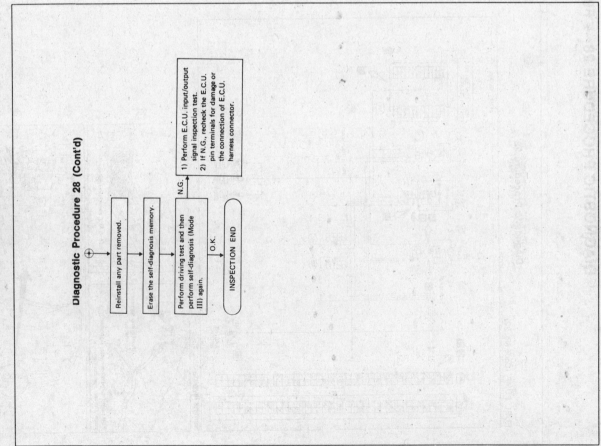

Diagnostic Procedure 28 (Cont'd)

Reinstall any part removed.

Erase the self-diagnosis memory.

Perform driving test and then perform self-diagnosis again. (Mode III)

O.K. → INSPECTION END

N.G.

1) Perform E.C.U. input/output signal inspection test.
2) If N.G., recheck the E.C.U. pin terminals for damage or the connection of E.C.U. harness connector.

DIAGNOSTIC PROCEDURE 30 — EGR FUNCTION (CODE 32) — VG30E ENGINE

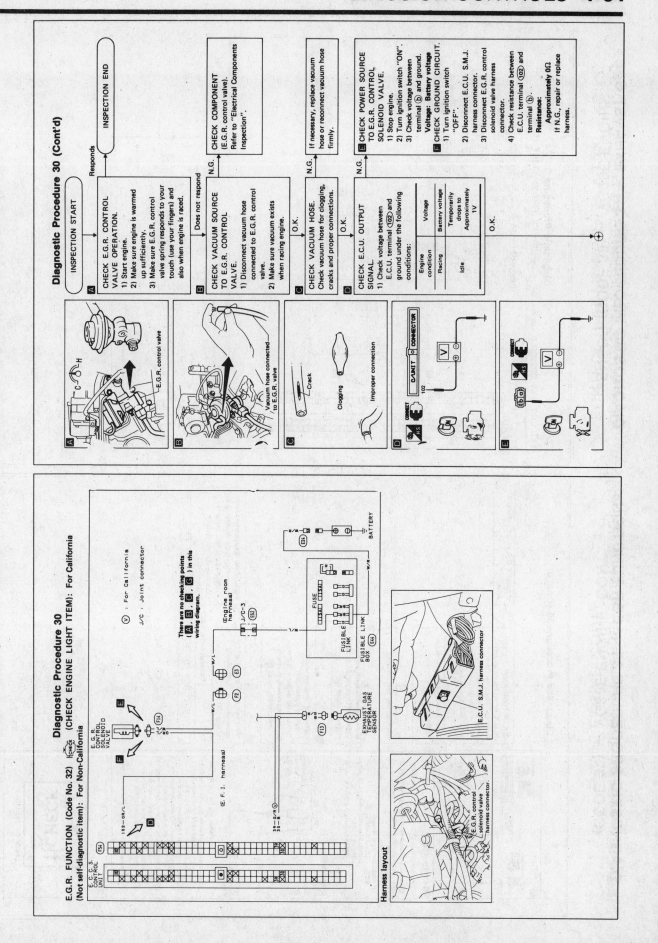

Diagnostic Procedure 30 (Cont'd)

INSPECTION START

A CHECK E.G.R. CONTROL VALVE OPERATION.
1) Start engine.
2) Make sure engine is warmed up sufficiently.
3) Make sure E.G.R. control valve spring responds to your touch (use your fingers) and also when engine is raced.

Responds → INSPECTION END

Does not respond →

B CHECK VACUUM SOURCE TO E.G.R. CONTROL VALVE.
1) Disconnect vacuum hose connected to E.G.R. control valve.
2) Make sure vacuum exists when racing engine.

N.G. → CHECK COMPONENT (E.G.R. control valve). Refer to "Electrical Components Inspection".

O.K. →

C CHECK VACUUM HOSE. Check vacuum hose for clogging, cracks and proper connections.

N.G. → If necessary, replace vacuum hose or reconnect vacuum hose firmly.

O.K. →

D CHECK E.C.U. OUTPUT SIGNAL.
1) Check voltage between E.C.U. terminal ⑩ and ground under the following conditions:

Engine condition	Voltage
Idle	Battery voltage
Racing	Temporarily drops to Approximately 1V

N.G. →

O.K. →

E CHECK POWER SOURCE TO E.G.R. CONTROL SOLENOID VALVE.
1) Stop engine.
2) Turn ignition switch "ON".
3) Check voltage between terminal ⓑ and ground.
Voltage: Battery voltage

F CHECK GROUND CIRCUIT.
1) Turn ignition switch "OFF".
2) Disconnect E.C.U. S.M.J. harness connector.
3) Disconnect E.G.R. control solenoid valve harness connector.
4) Check resistance between E.C.U. terminal ⑩ and terminal ⓑ.
Resistance: Approximately 0Ω
If N.G., repair or replace harness.

Vacuum hose connected to E.G.R. valve

Crack

Clogging

Improper connection

Diagnostic Procedure 30

E.G.R. FUNCTION (Code No. 32) 〈CHECK ENGINE LIGHT ITEM〉: For California
(Not self-diagnostic item): For Non-California

Ⓥ : For California
J/C : Joint connector

There are no checking points (Ⓐ, Ⓑ, Ⓒ, Ⓖ) in this wiring diagram.

E.G.R. CONTROL SOLENOID VALVE

E.F.I. harness

E.C.C.S. CONTROL UNIT

Engine room harness

BATTERY

FUSE

FUSIBLE LINK

FUSIBLE LINK BOX

EXHAUST GAS TEMPERATURE SENSOR

E.C.U. S.M.J. harness connector

E.G.R. control solenoid valve harness connector

Harness layout

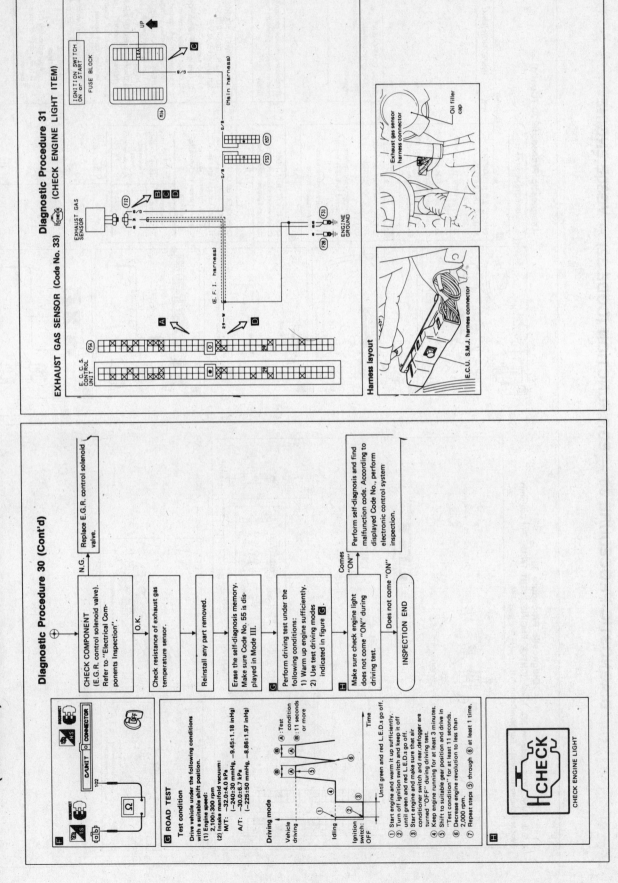

DIAGNOSTIC PROCEDURE 31 – EXHAUST GAS SENSOR (CODE 33) – VG30E ENGINE

Diagnostic Procedure 31

EXHAUST GAS SENSOR (Code No. 33) (CHECK ENGINE LIGHT ITEM)

Harness layout

DIAGNOSTIC PROCEDURE 30 – EGR FUNCTION (CODE 32) – VG30E ENGINE, CONT.

Diagnostic Procedure 30 (Cont'd)

CHECK COMPONENT
(E.G.R. control solenoid valve).
Refer to "Electrical Components Inspection".

N.G. → Replace E.G.R. control solenoid valve.

O.K.

Check resistance of exhaust gas temperature sensor.

Reinstall any part removed.

Erase the self-diagnosis memory. Make sure Code No. 55 is displayed in Mode III.

[G] Perform driving test under the following conditions:
1) Warm up engine sufficiently.
2) Use test driving modes indicated in figure [G].

[H] Make sure check engine light does not come "ON" during driving test.

Comes "ON" → Perform self-diagnosis and find malfunction code. According to displayed Code No., perform electronic control system inspection.

Does not come "ON"

INSPECTION END

[G] ROAD TEST

Test condition

Drive vehicle under the following conditions with a suitable shift position.

(1) Engine speed:
    2,100±300 rpm
(2) Intake manifold vacuum:
    M/T: −32.0±4.0 kPa
    (−240±30 mmHg, −9.45±1.18 inHg)
    A/T: −30.0±6.7 kPa
    (−225±50 mmHg, −8.86±1.97 inHg)

Driving mode

Ⓐ: Test condition
Ⓑ: 11 seconds or more

① Start engine and warm it up sufficiently.
② Turn off ignition switch and keep it off until green and red L.E.D.s go off.
③ Start engine and make sure that air conditioner switch and rear defogger are turned "OFF" during driving test.
④ Keep engine running for at least 3 minutes.
⑤ Shift to suitable gear position and drive in "Test condition" for at least 11 seconds.
⑥ Decrease engine revolution to less than 2,000 rpm.
⑦ Repeat steps ⑤ through ⑥ at least 1 time.

Until green and red L.E.D.s go off.

[H]

CHECK CHECK ENGINE LIGHT

DIAGNOSTIC PROCEDURE 32 — DETONATION SENSOR (CODE 34) — VG30E ENGINE

Diagnostic Procedure 32

DETONATION SENSOR (Code No. 34)

DIAGNOSTIC PROCEDURE 31 — EXHAUST GAS SENSOR (CODE 33) — VG30E ENGINE, CONT.

Diagnostic Procedure 31 (Cont'd)

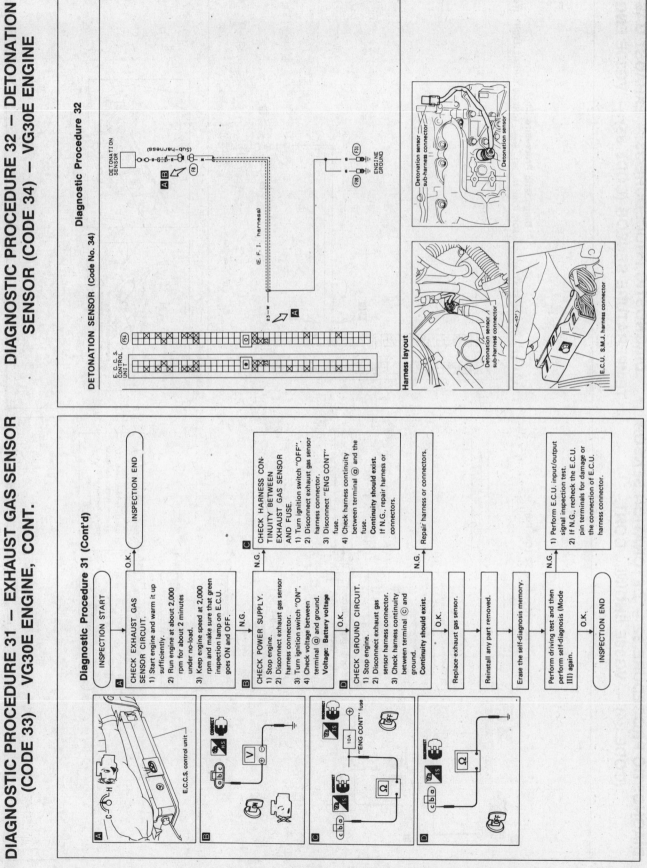

DIAGNOSTIC PROCEDURE 33 — EXHAUST GAS TEMPERATURE SENSOR (CODE 35) — VG30E ENGINE

DIAGNOSTIC PROCEDURE 32 — DETONATION SENSOR (CODE 34) — VG30E ENGINE, CONT.

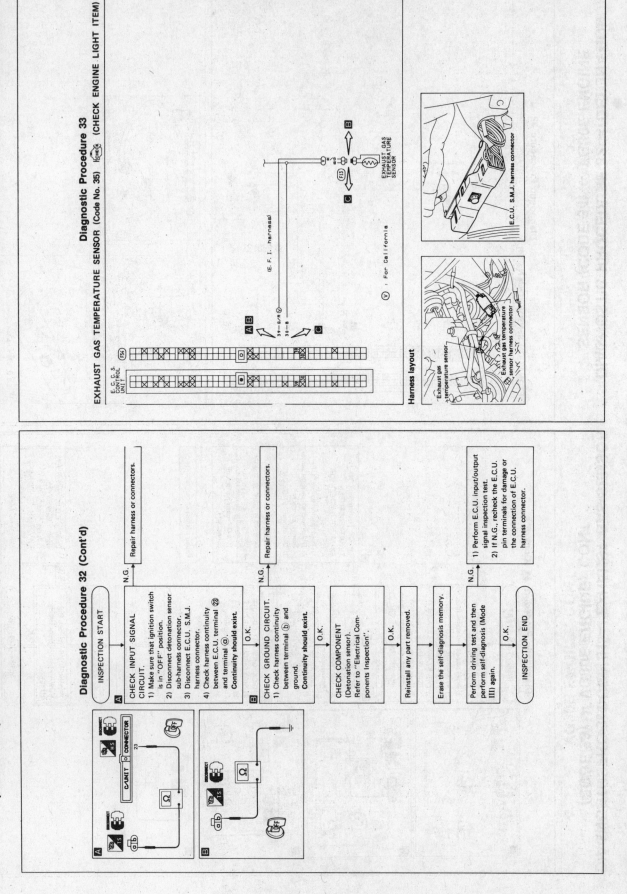

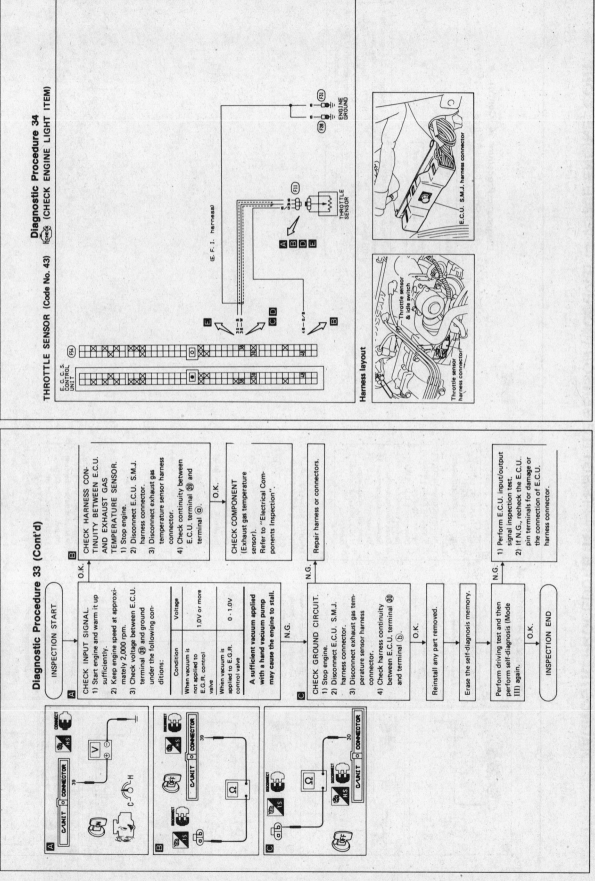

DIAGNOSTIC PROCEDURE 34 — THROTTLE SENSOR (CODE 43) — VG30E ENGINE

DIAGNOSTIC PROCEDURE 33 — EXHAUST GAS TEMPERATURE SENSOR (CODE 35) — VG30E ENGINE, CONT.

DIAGNOSTIC PROCEDURE 34 — THROTTLE SENSOR (CODE 43) — VG30E ENGINE, CONT.

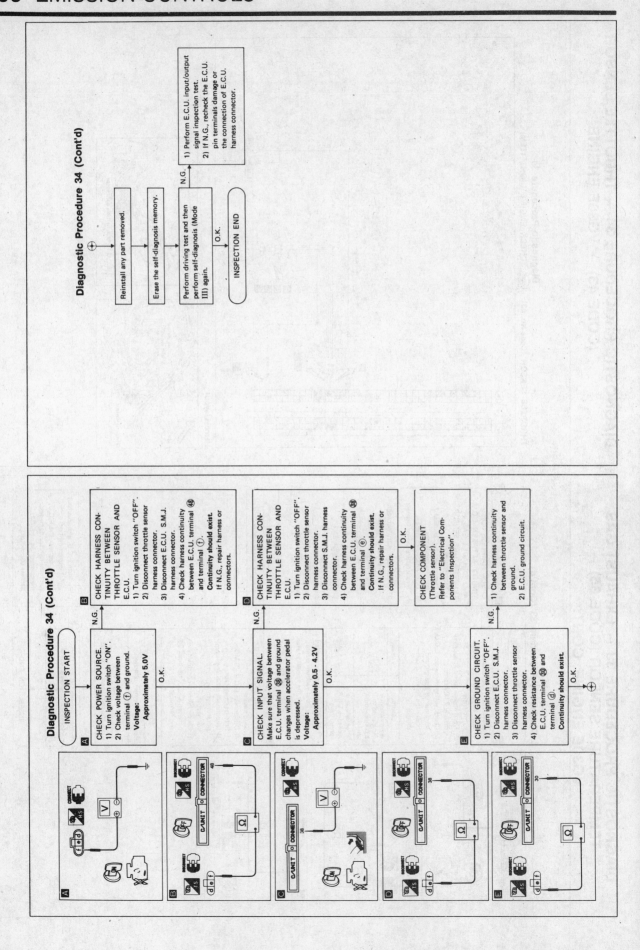

Diagnostic Procedure 34 (Cont'd)

Reinstall any part removed.

Erase the self-diagnosis memory.

Perform driving test and then perform self-diagnosis (Mode III) again.

INSPECTION END

N.G. 1) Perform E.C.U. input/output signal inspection test.
2) If N.G., recheck the E.C.U. pin terminals damage or the connection of E.C.U. harness connector.

O.K.

Diagnostic Procedure 34

INSPECTION START

Ⓐ CHECK POWER SOURCE.
1) Turn ignition switch "ON".
2) Check voltage between terminal ⓕ and ground.
Voltage:
Approximately 5.0V

N.G. **Ⓑ** CHECK HARNESS CONTINUITY BETWEEN THROTTLE SENSOR AND E.C.U.
1) Turn ignition switch "OFF".
2) Disconnect throttle sensor harness connector.
3) Disconnect E.C.U. S.M.J. harness connector.
4) Check harness continuity between E.C.U. terminal ㊽ and terminal ⓕ.
Continuity should exist.
If N.G., repair harness or connectors.

O.K.

Ⓒ CHECK INPUT SIGNAL.
Make sure that voltage between E.C.U. terminal ㉚ and ground changes when accelerator pedal is depressed.
Voltage:
Approximately 0.5 - 4.2V

N.G. **Ⓓ** CHECK HARNESS CONTINUITY BETWEEN THROTTLE SENSOR AND E.C.U.
1) Turn ignition switch "OFF".
2) Disconnect throttle sensor harness connector.
3) Disconnect S.M.J. harness connector.
4) Check harness continuity between E.C.U. terminal ㉚ and terminal ⓔ.
Continuity should exist.
If N.G., repair harness or connectors.

O.K. CHECK COMPONENT
(Throttle sensor).
Refer to "Electrical Components Inspection".

O.K.

Ⓔ CHECK GROUND CIRCUIT.
1) Turn ignition switch "OFF".
2) Disconnect E.C.U. S.M.J. harness connector.
3) Disconnect throttle sensor harness connector.
4) Check resistance between E.C.U. terminal ㉚ and terminal ⓓ.
Continuity should exist.

N.G. 1) Check harness continuity between throttle sensor and ground.
2) E.C.U. ground circuit.

O.K.

DIAGNOSTIC PROCEDURE 35 — INJECTOR LEAK (CODE 45) — VG30E ENGINE

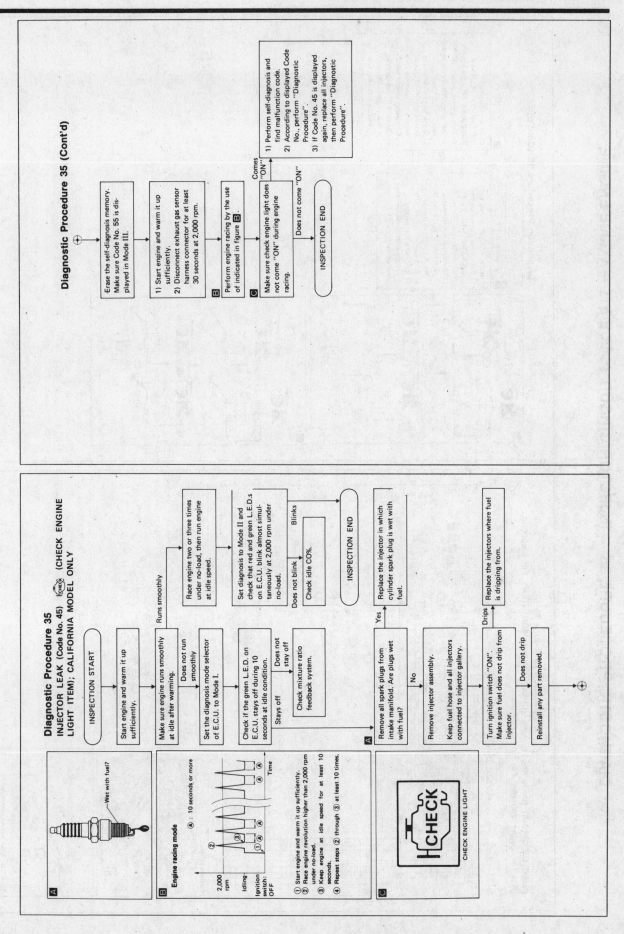

DIAGNOSTIC PROCEDURE 36 – INJECTOR CIRCUIT (CODE 51) – VG30E ENGINE

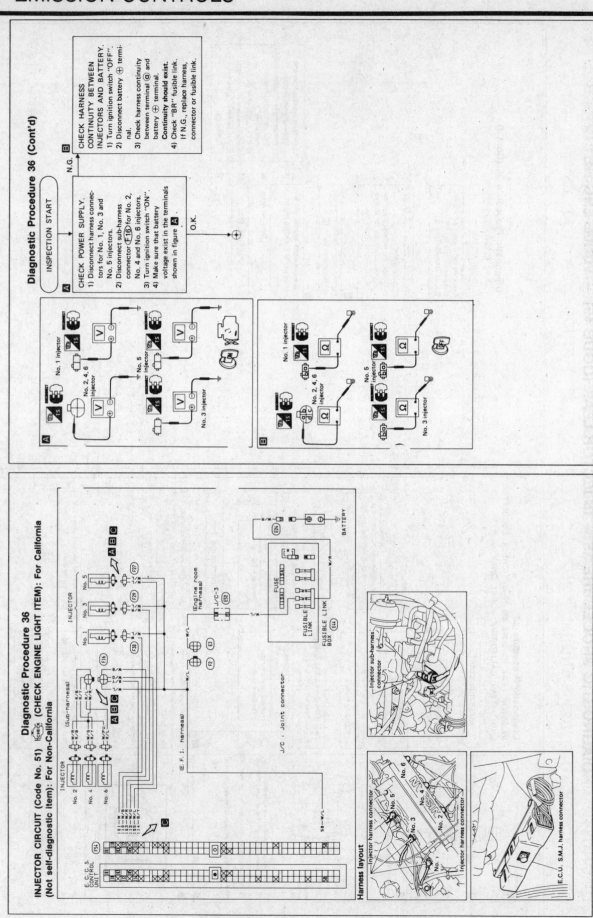

Diagnostic Procedure 36 (Cont'd)

INSPECTION START

A CHECK POWER SUPPLY.
1) Disconnect harness connectors for No. 1, No. 3 and No. 5 injectors.
2) Disconnect sub-harness connector (F16) for No. 2, No. 4 and No. 6 injectors.
3) Turn ignition switch "ON".
4) Make sure that battery voltage exist in the terminals shown in figure **A**.

O.K. →

N.G.

B CHECK HARNESS CONTINUITY BETWEEN INJECTORS AND BATTERY.
1) Turn ignition switch "OFF".
2) Disconnect battery ⊕ terminal.
3) Check harness continuity between terminal ⓐ and battery ⊕ terminal. **Continuity should exist.**
4) Check "BR" fusible link. If N.G, replace harness, connector or fusible link.

INJECTOR CIRCUIT (Code No. 51) ⓒₑ꜀ₖ (CHECK ENGINE LIGHT ITEM): For California
(Not self-diagnostic item): For Non-California

Diagnostic Procedure 36

Harness layout

DIAGNOSTIC PROCEDURE 36 – INJECTOR CIRCUIT (CODE 51) – VG30E ENGINE, CONT.

DIAGNOSTIC PROCEDURE 37 – A/T CONTROL (CODE 54) – VG30E ENGINE

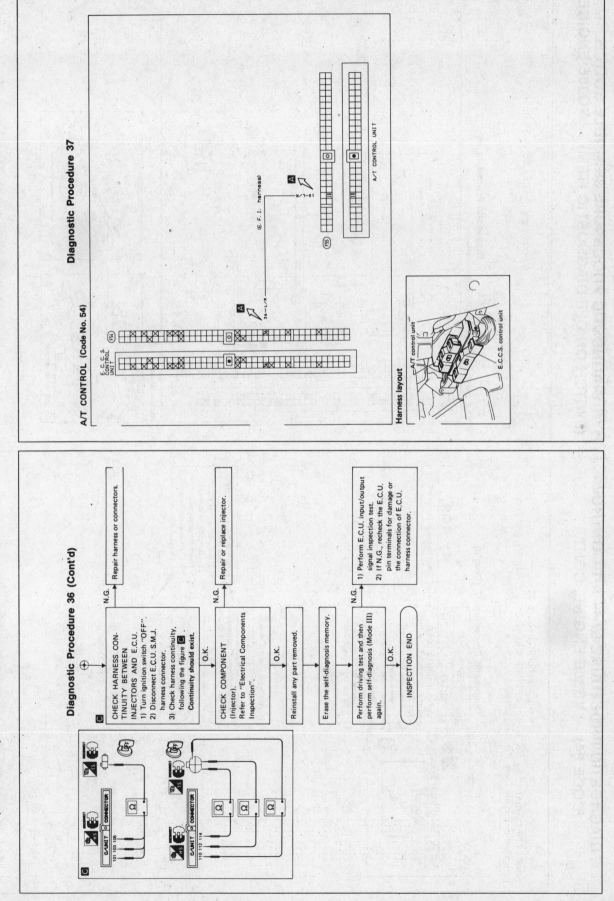

Diagnostic Procedure 36 (Cont'd)

C

CHECK HARNESS CONTINUITY BETWEEN INJECTORS AND E.C.U.
1) Turn ignition switch "OFF".
2) Disconnect E.C.U. S.M.J. harness connector.
3) Check harness continuity, following the figure C. Continuity should exist.

N.G. → Repair harness or connectors.

O.K.

CHECK COMPONENT (Injector).
Refer to "Electrical Components Inspection".

N.G. → Repair or replace injector.

O.K.

Reinstall any part removed.

Erase the self-diagnosis memory.

Perform driving test and then perform self-diagnosis (Mode III) again.

N.G. →
1) Perform E.C.U. input/output signal inspection test.
2) If N.G., recheck the E.C.U. pin terminals for damage or the connection of E.C.U. harness connector.

O.K.

INSPECTION END

Diagnostic Procedure 37

A/T CONTROL (Code No. 54)

E.C.C.S. CONTROL UNIT

(E.F.I. harness)

A/T CONTROL UNIT

Harness layout

A/T control unit

E.C.C.S. control unit

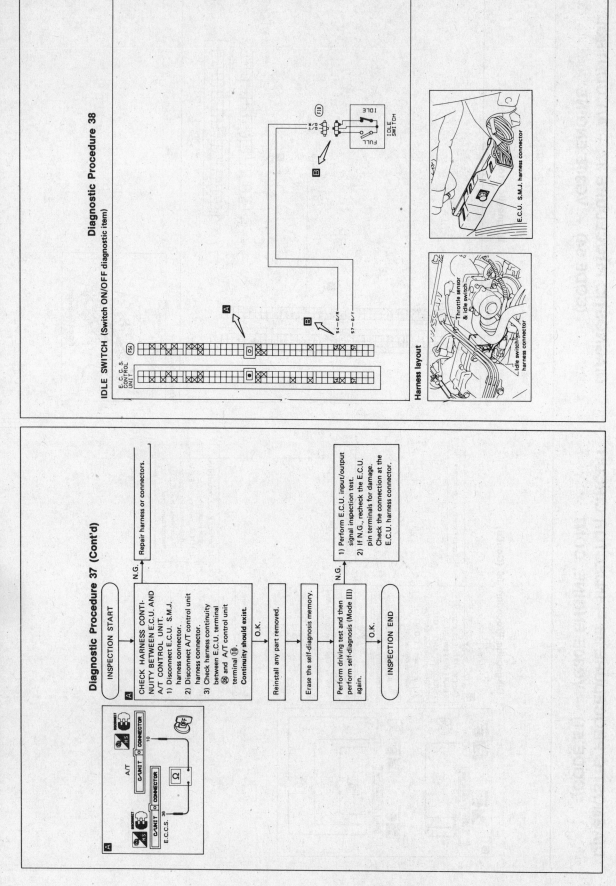

DIAGNOSTIC PROCEDURE 38 — IDLE SWITCH (SWITCH ON/OFF DIAGNOSTIC ITEM) — VG30E ENGINE

Diagnostic Procedure 38

IDLE SWITCH (Switch ON/OFF diagnostic item)

Harness layout

DIAGNOSTIC PROCEDURE 37 — A/T CONTROL (CODE 54) — VG30E ENGINE, CONT.

Diagnostic Procedure 37 (Cont'd)

INSPECTION START

CHECK HARNESS CONTI-NUITY BETWEEN E.C.U. AND A/T CONTROL UNIT.
1) Disconnect E.C.U. S.M.J. harness connector.
2) Disconnect A/T control unit harness connector.
3) Check harness continuity between E.C.U. terminal ㊱ and A/T control unit terminal ⑩.
Continuity should exist.

N.G. → Repair harness or connectors.

O.K.

Reinstall any part removed.

Erase the self-diagnosis memory.

Perform driving test and then perform self-diagnosis (Mode III) again.

N.G. → 1) Perform E.C.U. input/output signal inspection test.
2) If N.G., recheck the E.C.U. pin terminals for damage. Check the connection at the E.C.U. harness connector.

O.K.

INSPECTION END

A/T

E.C.C.S.

DIAGNOSTIC PROCEDURE 39 — START SIGNAL (SWITCH ON/OFF DIAGNOSIS) — VG30E ENGINE

DIAGNOSTIC PROCEDURE 38 — IDLE SWITCH (SWITCH ON/OFF DIAGNOSTIC ITEM) — VG30E ENGINE, CONT.

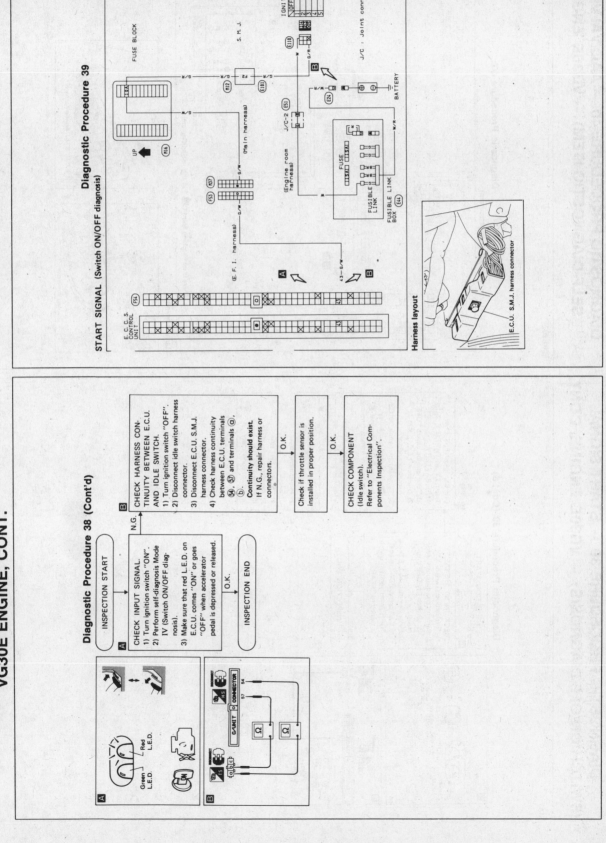

START SIGNAL (Switch ON/OFF diagnosis)

Diagnostic Procedure 39

Harness layout

E.C.U. S.M.J. harness connector

Diagnostic Procedure 38 (Cont'd)

INSPECTION START

A CHECK INPUT SIGNAL.
1) Turn ignition switch "ON".
2) Perform self-diagnosis Mode IV (Switch ON/OFF diagnosis).
3) Make sure that red L.E.D. on E.C.U. comes "ON" or goes "OFF" when accelerator pedal is depressed or released.

O.K. → INSPECTION END

N.G. →

B CHECK HARNESS CONTINUITY BETWEEN E.C.U. AND IDLE SWITCH.
1) Turn ignition switch "OFF".
2) Disconnect idle switch harness connector.
3) Disconnect E.C.U. S.M.J. harness connector.
4) Check harness continuity between E.C.U. terminals 54, 57 and terminals ⓐ, ⓑ.

Continuity should exist.
If N.G., repair harness or connectors.

O.K. → Check if throttle sensor is installed in proper position.

O.K. → CHECK COMPONENT (Idle switch). Refer to "Electrical Components Inspection".

DIAGNOSTIC PROCEDURE 40 — AAC VALVE (NOT SELF-DIAGNOSTIC ITEM) — VG30E ENGINE

DIAGNOSTIC PROCEDURE 39 — START SIGNAL (SWITCH ON/OFF DIAGNOSIS) — VG30E ENGINE, CONT.

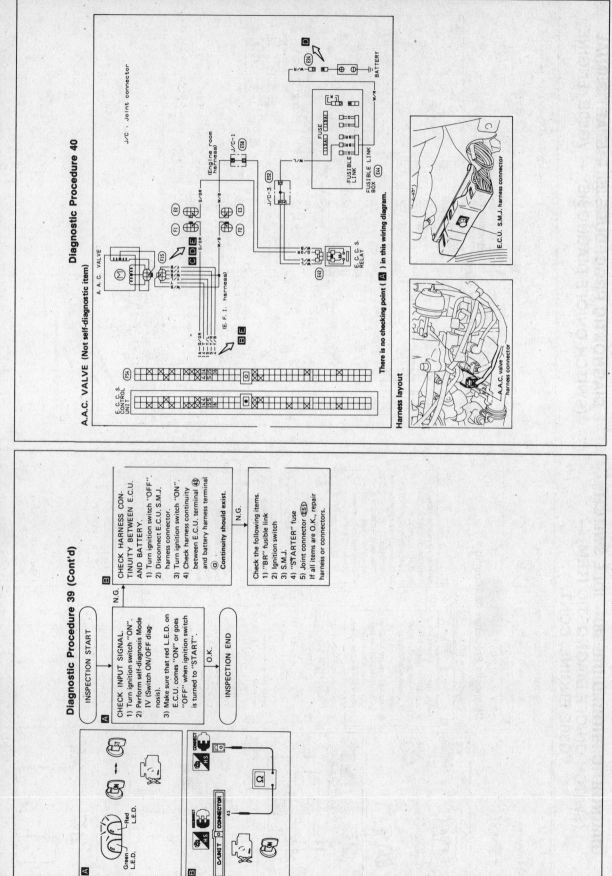

A.A.C. VALVE (Not self-diagnostic item)

Diagnostic Procedure 40

J/C : Joint connector

There is no checking point (A) in this wiring diagram.

Harness layout

E.C.U. S.M.J. harness connector

A.A.C. valve harness connector

Diagnostic Procedure 39 (Cont'd)

INSPECTION START

A CHECK INPUT SIGNAL.
1) Turn ignition switch "ON".
2) Perform self-diagnosis Mode IV (Switch ON/OFF diagnosis).
3) Make sure that red L.E.D. on E.C.U. comes "ON", or goes "OFF" when ignition switch is turned to "START".

O.K. → INSPECTION END

N.G. →

B CHECK HARNESS CONTINUITY BETWEEN E.C.U. AND BATTERY.
1) Turn ignition switch "OFF".
2) Disconnect E.C.U. S.M.J. harness connector.
3) Turn ignition switch "ON".
4) Check harness continuity between E.C.U. terminal 43 and battery harness terminal G.

Continuity should exist.

N.G. →

Check the following items.
1) "BR" fusible link
2) Ignition switch
3) S.M.J.
4) "STARTER" fuse
5) Joint connector (J1)
If all items are O.K., repair harness or connectors.

Green L.E.D.   Red L.E.D.

DIAGNOSTIC PROCEDURE 40 – AAC VALVE (NOT SELF-DIAGNOSTIC ITEM) – VG30E ENGINE, CONT.

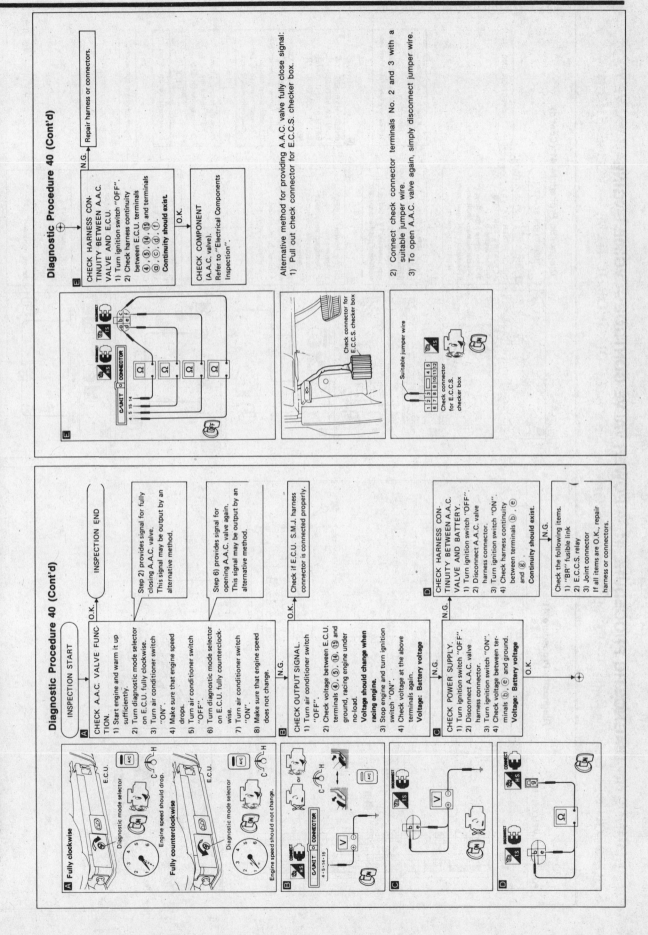

Diagnostic Procedure 40 (Cont'd)

INSPECTION START

A CHECK A.A.C. VALVE FUNCTION.
1) Start engine and warm it up sufficiently.
2) Turn diagnostic mode selector on E.C.U. fully clockwise.
3) Turn air conditioner switch "ON".
4) Make sure that engine speed drops.
5) Turn air conditioner switch "OFF".
6) Turn diagnostic mode selector on E.C.U. fully counterclockwise.
7) Turn air conditioner switch "ON".
8) Make sure that engine speed does not change.

O.K. → INSPECTION END

Step 2) provides signal for fully closing A.A.C. valve.
This signal may be output by an alternative method.

Step 6) provides signal for opening A.A.C. valve again.
This signal may be output by an alternative method.

Check if E.C.U. S.M.J. harness connector is connected properly.

N.G. → **B** CHECK OUTPUT SIGNAL.
1) Turn air conditioner switch "OFF".
2) Check voltage between E.C.U. terminals ④, ⑤, ⑭, ⑮ and ground, racing engine under no-load.
Voltage should change when racing engine.
3) Stop engine and turn ignition switch "ON".
4) Check voltage at the above terminals again.
Voltage: Battery voltage

O.K. →

N.G. → **C** CHECK POWER SUPPLY.
1) Turn ignition switch "OFF".
2) Disconnect A.A.C. valve harness connector.
3) Turn ignition switch "ON".
4) Check voltage between terminals ⓑ, ⓔ and ground.
Voltage: Battery voltage

O.K. →

N.G. → **D** CHECK HARNESS CONTINUITY BETWEEN A.A.C. VALVE AND BATTERY.
1) Turn ignition switch "OFF".
2) Disconnect A.A.C. valve harness connector.
3) Turn ignition switch "ON".
4) Check harness continuity between terminals ⓑ, ⓔ and ⓖ
Continuity should exist.

N.G. → Check the following items.
1) "BR" fusible link
2) E.C.C.S. relay
3) Joint connector
If all items are O.K., repair harness or connectors.

Diagnostic Procedure 40 (Cont'd)

E CHECK HARNESS CONTINUITY BETWEEN A.A.C. VALVE AND E.C.U.
1) Turn ignition switch "OFF".
2) Check harness continuity between E.C.U. terminals ④, ⑤, ⑭, ⑮ and terminals ⓖ, ⓒ, ⓓ, ⓕ.
Continuity should exist.

N.G. → Repair harness or connectors.

O.K. → CHECK COMPONENT (A.A.C. valve).
Refer to "Electrical Components Inspection".

Alternative method for providing A.A.C. valve fully close signal:
1) Pull out check connector for E.C.C.S. checker box.
2) Connect check connector terminals No. 2 and 3 with a suitable jumper wire.
3) To open A.A.C. valve again, simply disconnect jumper wire.

Check connector for E.C.C.S. checker box

Suitable jumper wire

Check connector for E.C.C.S. checker box

DIAGNOSTIC PROCEDURE 41 — POWER VALVE CONTROL — VG30E ENGINE

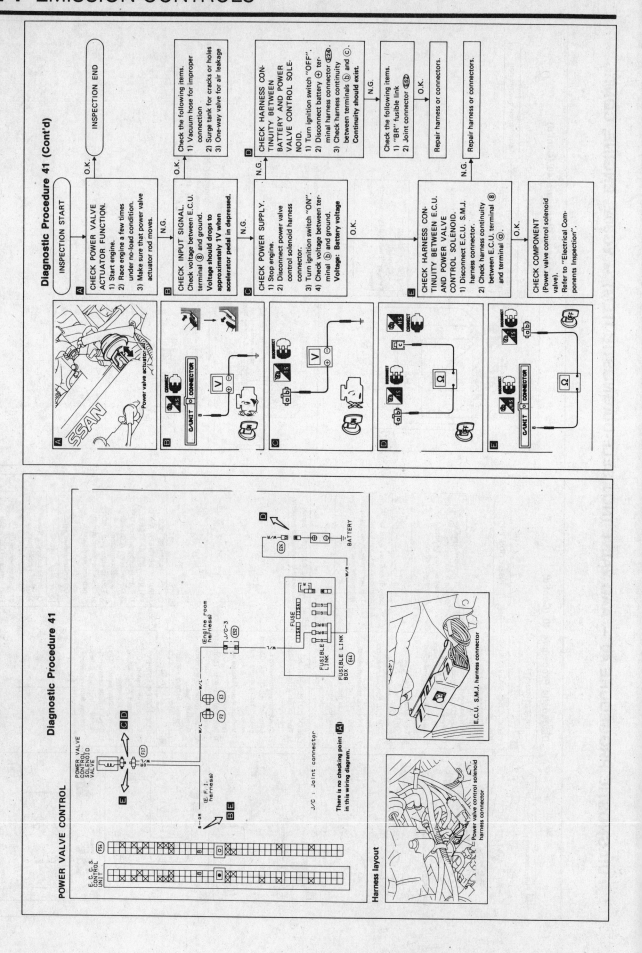

Diagnostic Procedure 41

INSPECTION START

A CHECK POWER VALVE ACTUATOR FUNCTION.
1) Start engine.
2) Race engine a few times under no-load condition.
3) Make sure that power valve actuator rod moves.

O.K. → INSPECTION END

N.G.

B CHECK INPUT SIGNAL.
Check voltage between E.C.U. terminal ⑧ and ground.
Voltage should drops to approximately 1V when accelerator pedal in depressed.

O.K. → Check the following items.
1) Vacuum hose for improper connection
2) Surge tank for cracks or holes
3) One-way valve for air leakage

N.G.

C CHECK POWER SUPPLY.
1) Stop engine.
2) Disconnect power valve control solenoid harness connector.
3) Turn ignition switch "ON".
4) Check voltage between terminal ⓑ and ground.
Voltage: Battery voltage

N.G. → **D** CHECK HARNESS CONTINUITY BETWEEN BATTERY AND POWER VALVE CONTROL SOLENOID.
1) Turn ignition switch "OFF".
2) Disconnect battery ⊕ terminal harness connector E23 and ⓒ.
3) Check harness continuity between terminals ⓑ and ⓒ. Continuity should exist.

N.G. → Check the following items.
1) "BR" fusible link
2) Joint connector E52

O.K. → Repair harness or connectors.

O.K.

E CHECK HARNESS CONTINUITY BETWEEN E.C.U. AND POWER VALVE CONTROL SOLENOID.
1) Disconnect E.C.U. S.M.J. harness connector.
2) Check harness continuity between E.C.U. terminal ⑧ and terminal ⓐ.

N.G. → Repair harness or connectors.

O.K.

CHECK COMPONENT
(Power valve control solenoid valve).
Refer to "Electrical Components Inspection".

A Power valve actuator

B C·UNIT CONNECTOR

POWER VALVE CONTROL

E.C.C.S. CONTROL UNIT

POWER VALVE CONTROL SOLENOID VALVE

(E.F.I. harness)

J/C: Joint connector

There is no checking point ⓐ in this wiring diagram.

(Engine room harness)

FUSE

FUSIBLE LINK

FUSIBLE LINK BOX

BATTERY

E.C.U. S.M.J. harness connector

Power valve control solenoid harness connector

Harness layout

DIAGNOSTIC PROCEDURE 42 — RADIATOR FAN CONTROL — VG30E ENGINE

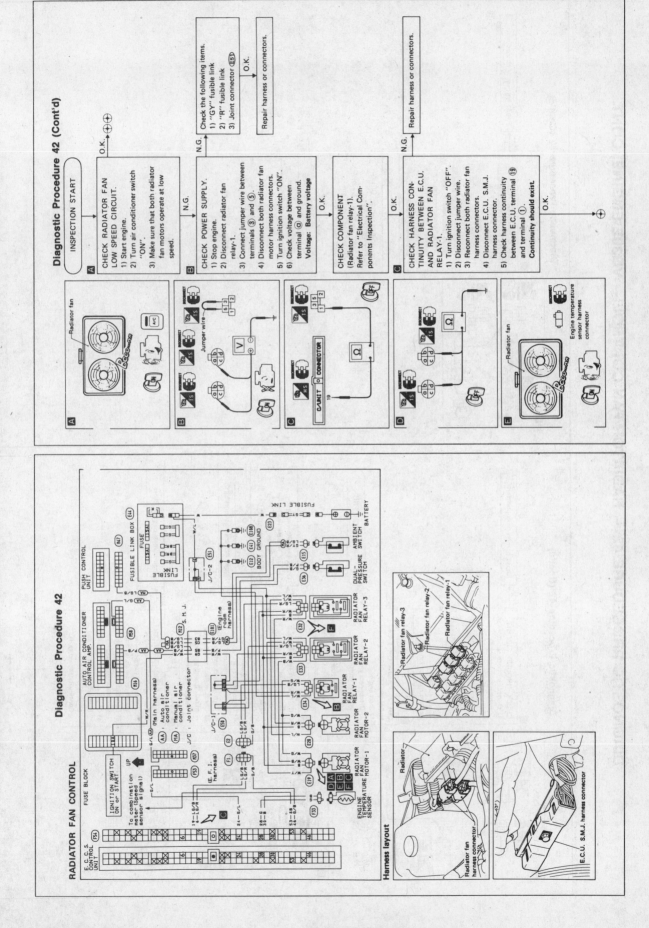

Diagnostic Procedure 42 (Cont'd)

INSPECTION START

A CHECK RADIATOR FAN LOW SPEED CIRCUIT.
1) Start engine.
2) Turn air conditioner switch "ON".
3) Make sure that both radiator fan motors operate at low speed.

O.K. → ⊕

N.G.

B CHECK POWER SUPPLY.
1) Stop engine.
2) Disconnect radiator fan relay-1.
3) Connect jumper wire between terminals ③ and ⑤.
4) Disconnect both radiator fan motor harness connectors.
5) Turn ignition switch "ON".
6) Check voltage between terminal ⓐ and ground.
   Voltage: Battery voltage

N.G. → Check the following items.
1) "GY" fusible link
2) "R" fusible link
3) Joint connector (E51)

O.K. → Repair harness or connectors.

O.K.

C CHECK COMPONENT
(Radiator fan relay-1).
Refer to "Electrical Components Inspection".

O.K.

C CHECK HARNESS CONTINUITY BETWEEN E.C.U. AND RADIATOR FAN RELAY-1.
1) Turn ignition switch "OFF".
2) Disconnect jumper wire.
3) Reconnect both radiator fan harness connectors.
4) Disconnect E.C.U. S.M.J. harness connector.
5) Check harness continuity between E.C.U. terminal ⑲ and terminal ①.
   Continuity should exist.

N.G. → Repair harness or connectors.

O.K. → ⊕

RADIATOR FAN CONTROL

Harness layout

DIAGNOSTIC PROCEDURE 42 — RADIATOR FAN CONTROL — VG30E ENGINE, CONT.

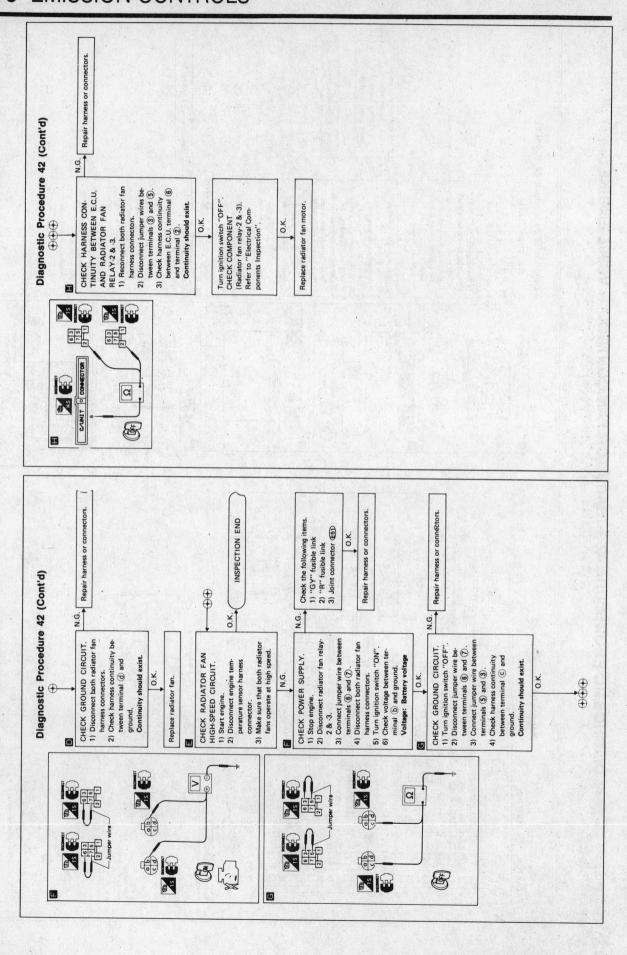

Diagnostic Procedure 42 (Cont'd)

H CHECK HARNESS CONTINUITY BETWEEN E.C.U. AND RADIATOR FAN RELAY-2 & -3.
1) Reconnect both radiator fan harness connectors.
2) Disconnect jumper wires between terminals ③ and ⑤.
3) Check harness continuity between E.C.U. terminal ⑥ and terminal ②.
Continuity should exist.

N.G. → Repair harness or connectors.

O.K. ↓

Turn ignition switch "OFF".
CHECK COMPONENT
(Radiator fan relay-2 & -3).
Refer to "Electrical Components Inspection".

O.K. ↓

Replace radiator fan motor.

Diagnostic Procedure 42 (Cont'd)

D CHECK GROUND CIRCUIT.
1) Disconnect both radiator fan harness connectors.
2) Check harness continuity between terminal ⓓ and ground.
Continuity should exist.

N.G. → Repair harness or connectors.

O.K. ↓

Replace radiator fan.

E CHECK RADIATOR FAN HIGH-SPEED CIRCUIT.
1) Start engine.
2) Disconnect engine temperature sensor harness connector.
3) Make sure that both radiator fans operate at high speed.

O.K. → INSPECTION END

N.G. ↓

F CHECK POWER SUPPLY.
1) Stop engine.
2) Disconnect radiator fan relay-2 & -3.
3) Connect jumper wire between terminals ⑥ and ⑦.
4) Disconnect both radiator fan harness connectors.
5) Turn ignition switch "ON".
6) Check voltage between terminal ⓑ and ground.
Voltage: Battery voltage

N.G. → Check the following items.
1) "GY" fusible link
2) "R" fusible link
3) Joint connector (E5)

O.K. → Repair harness or connectors.

O.K. ↓

G CHECK GROUND CIRCUIT.
1) Turn ignition switch "OFF".
2) Disconnect jumper wire between terminals ⑥ and ⑦.
3) Connect jumper wire between terminals ⑤ and ③.
4) Check harness continuity between terminal ⓒ and ground.
Continuity should exist.

N.G. → Repair harness or connectors.

O.K. ↓

DIAGNOSTIC PROCEDURE 43 — FAIL SAFE SYSTEM FOR CRANK ANGLE SENSOR AND CPU OF ECU — VG30E ENGINE

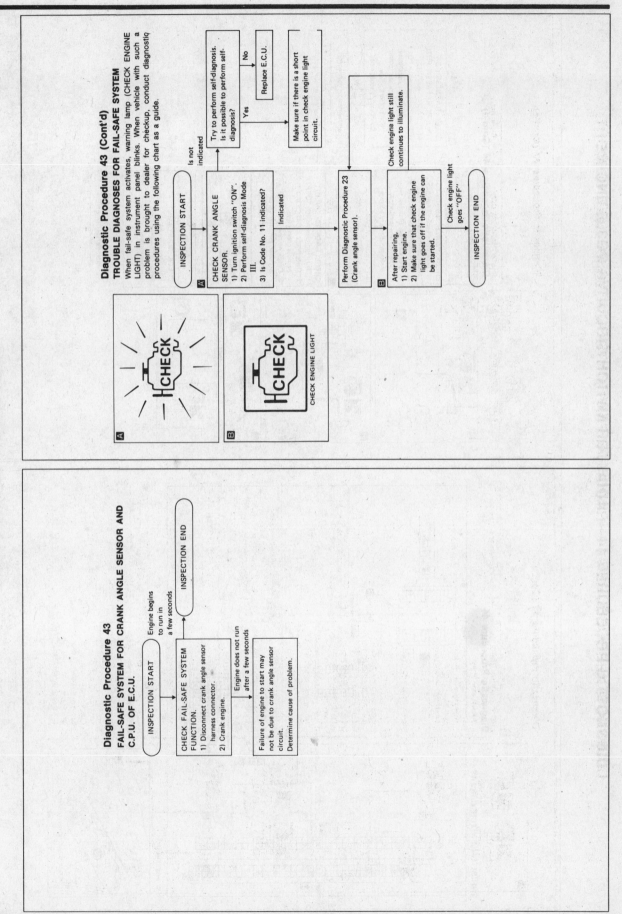

Diagnostic Procedure 43
FAIL-SAFE SYSTEM FOR CRANK ANGLE SENSOR AND C.P.U. OF E.C.U.

INSPECTION START

CHECK FAIL-SAFE SYSTEM FUNCTION.
1) Disconnect crank angle sensor harness connector.
2) Crank engine.

Engine begins to run in a few seconds → INSPECTION END

Engine does not run after a few seconds

Failure of engine to start may not be due to crank angle sensor circuit.
Determine cause of problem.

Diagnostic Procedure 43 (Cont'd)
TROUBLE DIAGNOSES FOR FAIL-SAFE SYSTEM

When fail-safe system activates, warning lamp (CHECK ENGINE LIGHT) in instrument panel blinks. When vehicle with such a problem is brought to dealer for checkup, conduct diagnostiq procedures using the following chart as a guide.

INSPECTION START

A | CHECK CRANK ANGLE SENSOR.
1) Turn ignition switch "ON".
2) Perform self-diagnosis Mode III.
3) Is Code No. 11 indicated?

Is not indicated → Try to perform self-diagnosis. Is it possible to perform self-diagnosis?
No → Replace E.C.U.
Yes → Make sure if there is a short point in check engine light circuit.

Indicated → Perform Diagnostic Procedure 23 (Crank angle sensor).

B | After repairing,
1) Start engine.
2) Make sure that check engine light goes off if the engine can be started.

Check engine light still continues to illuminate.

Check engine light goes "OFF".

INSPECTION END

CHECK ENGINE LIGHT

DIAGNOSTIC PROCEDURE 44 – INHIBITOR SWITCH CIRCUIT – VG30E ENGINE

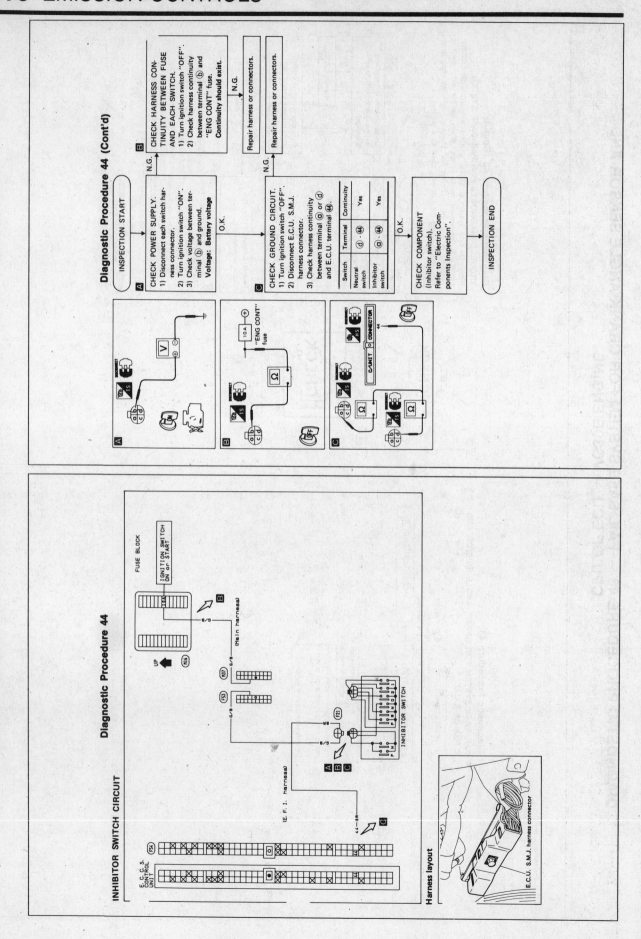

Diagnostic Procedure 44 (Cont'd)

INSPECTION START

A CHECK POWER SUPPLY.
1) Disconnect each switch harness connector.
2) Turn ignition switch "ON".
3) Check voltage between terminal ⓑ and ground.
Voltage: Battery voltage

B CHECK HARNESS CONTINUITY BETWEEN FUSE AND EACH SWITCH.
1) Turn ignition switch "OFF".
2) Check harness continuity between terminal ⓑ and "ENG CONT" fuse.
Continuity should exist.

N.G. → Repair harness or connectors.

C CHECK GROUND CIRCUIT.
1) Turn ignition switch "OFF".
2) Disconnect E.C.U. S.M.J. harness connector.
3) Check harness continuity between terminal ⓒ or ⓓ and E.C.U. terminal ㊹.

Switch	Terminal	Continuity
Neutral switch	ⓓ - ㊹	Yes
Inhibitor switch	ⓖ - ㊹	Yes

N.G. → Repair harness or connectors.

CHECK COMPONENT (Inhibitor switch). Refer to "Electric Components Inspection".

INSPECTION END

Diagnostic Procedure 44

INHIBITOR SWITCH CIRCUIT

Harness layout

INSPECTING ECU TERMINALS WITH CONNECTORS CONNECTED — VG30E ENGINE

E.C.U. Inspection table

Electrical Components Inspection (Cont'd)

*Data are reference values.

TERMINAL NO.	ITEM	CONDITION	*DATA
1	Ignition signal	Engine is running. — Idle speed	0.4 - 0.6V
		Engine is running. — Engine speed is 4,000 rpm.	1.9 - 2.1V
2	Ignition check	Engine is running. — Idle speed	BATTERY VOLTAGE (11 - 14V)
4, 5, 14, 15	A.A.C. valve	Engine is running. — Racing condition	Voltage briefly decreases from battery voltage (11 - 14V).
6	Radiator fan (High speed)	Engine is running. — Radiator fan is not operating.	BATTERY VOLTAGE (11 - 14V)
		Engine is running. — Radiator fan is operating.	0.7 - 0.8V
8	Power valve control solenoid valve	Engine is running. — Idle speed	BATTERY VOLTAGE (11 - 14V)
		Engine is running. — Racing (up to 4,000 rpm) quickly	0.7 - 0.8V
9	Air conditioner relay	Engine is running. — Air conditioner switch "OFF".	BATTERY VOLTAGE (11 - 14V)
		Engine is running. — Air conditioner switch "ON".	0.7 - 0.8V
16	E.C.U. power source (Self-shutoff)	Engine is running. — Idle speed	0.8 - 1.0V
		Engine is not running. — For a few seconds after turning ignition switch "OFF".	BATTERY VOLTAGE (11 - 14V)
18	Fuel pump relay	Engine is running. — Normal condition	BATTERY VOLTAGE (11 - 14V)
		Engine is running. — Abnormal condition [Fuel pump voltage control circuit (E.C.U. terminal No. 104) is inoperative.]	0.7 - 0.8V

Electrical Components Inspection (Cont'd)

*Data are reference values.

TERMINAL NO.	ITEM	CONDITION	*DATA
19	Radiator fan (Low speed)	Engine is running. — Radiator fan is not operating.	BATTERY VOLTAGE (11 - 14V)
		Engine is running. — Radiator fan is operating.	0.7 - 0.8V
23	Detonation sensor	Engine is running.	3.0 - 4.0V
25	Electric load signal	Engine is running. — Electric load signal is "OFF".	BATTERY VOLTAGE (11 - 14V)
		Engine is running. — Electric load signal (Rear defogger switch) is "ON".	0.1 - 0.3V
27	Air flow meter	Engine is running. (Warm-up condition) — Idle speed	1.0 - 1.3V
		Engine is running. (Warm-up condition) — Engine speed is 3,000 rpm.	1.8 - 2.0V
28	Engine temperature sensor	Engine is running.	0 - 5.0V Output voltage varies with engine temperature.
34	Power steering oil pressure switch	Engine is running. — Steering wheel stays straight.	8.0 - 9.0V
		Engine is running. — Steering wheel is turned.	0 - 0.2V
38	Throttle sensor	Ignition switch "ON"	0.5 - 4.2V Output voltage varies with throttle valve opening angle.
39	Exhaust gas temperature sensor	Engine is running. (Warm-up condition) — Idle speed	1.0V or more
		Engine is running. (Warm-up condition) — E.G.R. system is operating.	0 - 1.0V

INSPECTING ECU TERMINALS WITH CONNECTORS CONNECTED – VG30E ENGINE, CONT.

Electrical Components Inspection (Cont'd)

*Data are reference values.

TERMINAL NO.	ITEM	CONDITION	*DATA
41, 51	Crank angle sensor (Reference signal)	Engine is running. — Do not run engine at high speed under no-load.	0.2 - 0.4V Output voltage slightly varies with engine speed.
42, 52	Crank angle sensor (Position signal)	Engine is running. — Do not run engine at high speed under no-load.	2.5 - 2.7V Output voltage slightly varies with engine speed.
43	Start signal	Ignition switch "ON"	0V
		Ignition switch "START"	BATTERY VOLTAGE (11 - 14V)
44	Inhibitor switch	Ignition switch "ON" — Gear position is "N" or "P" (A/T model).	BATTERY VOLTAGE (11 - 14 V)
		Ignition switch "ON" — Except the above conditions	0V
45	Ignition switch	Ignition switch "ON" — Engine stopped	BATTERY VOLTAGE (11 - 14V)
46	Air conditioner switch	Engine is running. — Air conditioner switch "OFF"	8.0 - 9.0V
		Engine is running. — Air conditioner switch "ON"	0.5 - 0.7V
48	Power source for sensors	Ignition switch "ON" — Engine stopped	Approximately 5.0V
49	Battery source	Ignition switch "ON" — Engine stopped	BATTERY VOLTAGE (11 - 14V)
53	Vehicle speed sensor	Ignition switch "ON" — Engine stopped — While rotating front wheel by hand	0 or 7.0 - 9.0V

Electrical Components Inspection (Cont'd)

*Data are reference values.

TERMINAL NO.	ITEM	CONDITION	*DATA
54	Idle switch	Ignition switch "ON" — Accelerator pedal is fully released (engine stopped).	9.0 - 10.0V
		Ignition switch "ON" — Accelerator pedal is depressed (engine stopped).	0V
57	Power source for idle switch	Ignition switch "ON" — Engine stopped	8.0 - 9.0V
59	Power supply	Ignition switch "ON" — Idle speed	BATTERY VOLTAGE (11 - 14V)
101, 103, 105, 110, 112, 114	Injectors	Ignition switch "OFF"	BATTERY VOLTAGE (11 - 14V)
102	E.G.R. control solenoid valve	Engine is running. (Warm-up condition) — Idle speed — Engine speed is approximately 3,400 rpm or more.	0.7 - 0.8V
		Engine is running. (Warm-up condition) — Engine speed is between idle and approximately 3,400 rpm.	BATTERY VOLTAGE (11 - 14V)
104	Fuel pump voltage control	Ignition switch "ON" — 5 seconds after turning ignition switch "ON"	BATTERY VOLTAGE (11 - 14V)
		Engine is running. — 30 seconds after engine begins to run.	4.0 - 4.5V
		Engine is running. — Racing (up to 4,000 rpm)	2.0 - 4.5V

E.C.U. S.M.J. HARNESS CONNECTOR TERMINAL LAYOUT

H.S.

CHECKING IDLE SPEED AND IGNITION TIMING — VE30DE ENGINE

Direct Ignition System

CHECKING IDLE SPEED AND IGNITION TIMING

Idle speed

Check idle speed in "DATA MONITOR" mode with CONSULT.

```
★MONITOR  ☆NO FAIL   □
CAS·RPM (POS)   750rpm



        RECORD
```
SEF698L

Ignition timing

Any of the following three methods may be used, however, methods "A" and "B" give more reliable results and are preferable.

● **Method A (With S.S.T.)**

1. Disconnect No. 1 ignition coil harness connector.

No. 1 ignition coil

Engine front

SEF699L

2. Connect S.S.T. and clamp wire with timing light as shown.
3. Check ignition timing.

Tool

Tool

Tool

Timing light

SEF701L

Align direction marks on S.S.T. and timing light clamp if aligning mark is punched.

KV10900010
(J36777-1)

(J39387)

Align

SEF702L

● **Method B (Without S.S.T.)**

1. Remove No. 1 ignition coil.

No. 1 ignition coil

Engine front

SEF699L

Direct Ignition System (Cont'd)

2. Connect No. 1 ignition coil and No. 1 spark plug with suitable high-tension wire as shown, and attach timing light clamp to this wire.
3. Check ignition timing.

Suitable high-tension wire

Timing light

No. 1 ignition coil

SEF700L

4. For above procedures, enlarge suitable high-tension wire end with insulating tape as shown.

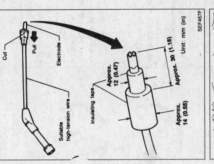

Cut

Pull

Electrode

Suitable high-tension wire

Insulating tape

Approx. 12 (0.47)

Approx. 14 (0.55)

Approx. 30 (1.18)

Unit: mm (in)

SEF467F

● **Method C (Without S.S.T.)**

Clamp wire as shown.

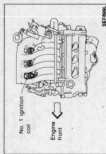

Timing light

Loop wire

SEF703L

INSPECTION AND ADJUSTMENT — VE30DE ENGINE

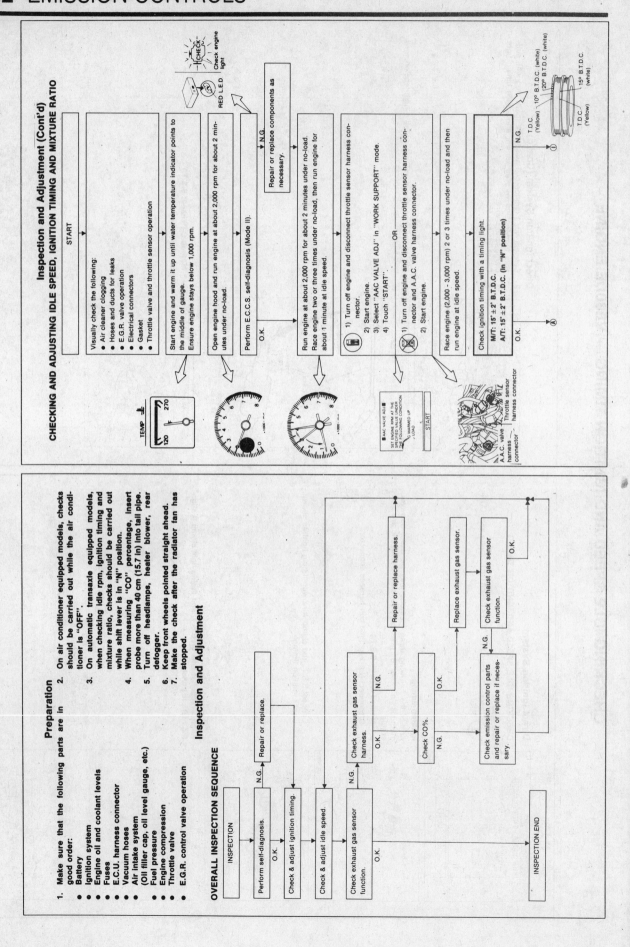

Preparation

1. Make sure that the following parts are in good order:
   - Battery
   - Ignition system
   - Engine oil and coolant levels
   - Fuses
   - E.C.U. harness connector
   - Vacuum hoses
   - Air intake system
   - (Oil filler cap, oil level gauge, etc.)
   - Fuel pressure
   - Engine compression
   - Throttle valve
   - E.G.R. control valve operation

2. On air conditioner equipped models, checks should be carried out while the air conditioner is "OFF".
3. On automatic transaxle equipped models, when checking idle rpm, ignition timing and mixture ratio, checks should be carried out while shift lever is in "N" position.
4. When measuring "CO" percentage, insert probe more than 40 cm (15.7 in) into tail pipe.
5. Turn off headlamps, heater blower, rear defogger.
6. Keep front wheels pointed straight ahead.
7. Make the check after the radiator fan has stopped.

Inspection and Adjustment

OVERALL INSPECTION SEQUENCE

INSPECTION
↓
Perform self-diagnosis. → N.G. → Repair or replace.
↓ O.K.
Check & adjust ignition timing.
↓
Check & adjust idle speed.
↓
Check exhaust gas sensor function. → N.G. → Check exhaust gas sensor harness. → O.K. → Check CO%. → N.G. → Check emission control parts and repair or replace if necessary.
  ↓ N.G.   ↓ O.K.
  Repair or replace harness.   Check exhaust gas sensor function. → N.G. → Replace exhaust gas sensor.
                                                            ↓ O.K.
INSPECTION END

CHECKING AND ADJUSTING IDLE SPEED, IGNITION TIMING AND MIXTURE RATIO

Inspection and Adjustment (Cont'd)

START
↓
Visually check the following:
- Air cleaner clogging
- Hoses and ducts for leaks
- E.G.R. valve operation
- Electrical connectors
- Gasket
- Throttle valve and throttle sensor operation
↓
Start engine and warm it up until water temperature indicator points to the middle of gauge.
Ensure engine stays below 1,000 rpm.
↓
Open engine hood and run engine at about 2,000 rpm for about 2 minutes under no-load.
↓
Perform E.C.C.S. self-diagnosis (Mode II). → N.G. → Repair or replace components as necessary.
↓ O.K.
Run engine at about 2,000 rpm for about 2 minutes under no-load. Race engine two or three times under no-load, then run engine for about 1 minute at idle speed.
↓
1) Turn off engine and disconnect throttle sensor harness connector.
2) Start engine.
3) Select "AAC VALVE ADJ" in "WORK SUPPORT" mode.
4) Touch "START".

OR

1) Turn off engine and disconnect throttle sensor harness connector and A.A.C. valve harness connector.
2) Start engine.
↓
Race engine (2,000 - 3,000 rpm) 2 or 3 times under no-load and then run engine at idle speed.
↓
Check ignition timing with a timing light.
M/T: 15° ± 2° B.T.D.C.
A/T: 15° ± 2° B.T.D.C. (In "N" position) → N.G.
↓ O.K.
Ⓐ

RED L.E.D. — Check engine light

■ AAC VALVE ADJ ■
SET ENGINE RPM AT THE SPECIFIED VALUE UNDER THE FOLLOWING CONDITION.
● WARMED UP
● NO LOAD
START

A.A.C. valve harness connector — Throttle sensor harness connector

T.D.C. 10° B.T.D.C. (Yellow) (white)
20° B.T.D.C. (white)
T.D.C. 15° B.T.D.C. (Yellow) (white)

INSPECTION AND ADJUSTMENT — VE30DE ENGINE, CONT.

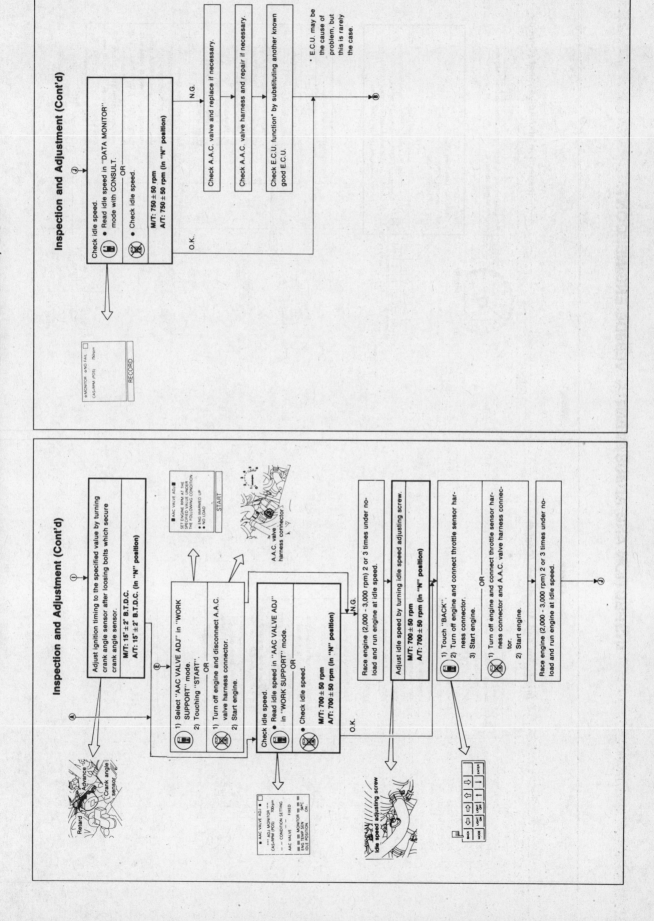

Inspection and Adjustment (Cont'd)

Check idle speed.
- Read idle speed in "DATA MONITOR" mode with CONSULT.
  OR
- Check idle speed.

M/T: 750 ± 50 rpm
A/T: 750 ± 50 rpm (in "N" position)

N.G. →

Check A.A.C. valve and replace if necessary.

Check A.A.C. valve harness and repair if necessary.

Check E.C.U. function* by substituting another known good E.C.U.

- E.C.U. may be the cause of problem, but this is rarely the case.

O.K.

RECORD

⊕ MONITOR ☆ NO FAIL   750rpm
CAS·RPM (POS)

Inspection and Adjustment (Cont'd)

Adjust ignition timing to the specified value by turning crank angle sensor after loosing bolts which secure crank angle sensor.

M/T: 15° ± 2° B.T.D.C.
A/T: 15° ± 2° B.T.D.C. (in "N" position)

Retard   Advance
Crank angle sensor

1) Select "AAC VALVE ADJ" in "WORK SUPPORT" mode.
2) Touching "START".
  OR
1) Turn off engine and disconnect A.A.C. valve harness connector.
2) Start engine.

■ AAC VALVE ADJ ■
SET ENGINE RPM AT THE SPECIFIED VALUE UNDER THE FOLLOWING CONDITION.
- ENG WARMED UP
- NO LOAD

START

A.A.C. valve harness connector

Check idle speed.
- Read idle speed in "AAC VALVE ADJ" in "WORK SUPPORT" mode.
  OR
- Check idle speed.

M/T: 700 ± 50 rpm
A/T: 700 ± 50 rpm (in "N" position)

■ AAC VALVE ADJ ■
···· ADJ MONITOR
CAS·RPM (POS)   700rpm
─ CONDITION SETTING ─
AAC VALVE   FIXED
■ MONITOR ■
ENG TEMP SEN   94°C
IDLE POSITION   ON

N.G.

Race engine (2,000 - 3,000 rpm) 2 or 3 times under no-load and run engine at idle speed.

Adjust idle speed by turning idle speed adjusting screw.

M/T: 700 ± 50 rpm
A/T: 700 ± 50 rpm (in "N" position)

1) Touch "BACK".
2) Turn off engine and connect throttle sensor harness connector.
3) Start engine.
  OR
1) Turn off engine and connect throttle sensor harness connector and A.A.C. valve harness connector.
2) Start engine.

idle speed adjusting screw

Race engine (2,000 - 3,000 rpm) 2 or 3 times under no-load and run engine at idle speed.

O.K.

ENTER
LIGHT LIGHT
COPY   ON OFF
MODE   LIGHT LIGHT
BACK

INSPECTION AND ADJUSTMENT — VE30DE ENGINE, CONT.

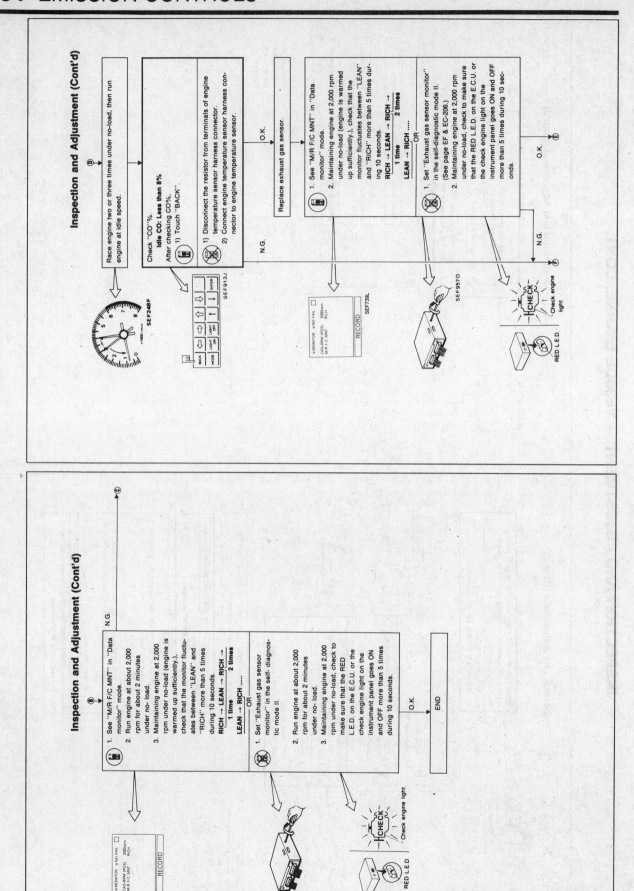

Inspection and Adjustment (Cont'd)

Race engine two or three times under no-load, then run engine at idle speed.

SEF248F

Check "CO"%.
Idle CO: Less than 8%
After checking CO%,
1) Touch "BACK".

SEF913J

1) Disconnect the resistor from terminals of engine temperature sensor harness connector.
2) Connect engine temperature sensor harness connector to engine temperature sensor.

O.K.

Replace exhaust gas sensor.

N.G.

SEF39L

1. See "M/R F/C MNT" in "Data monitor" mode.
2. Maintaining engine at 2,000 rpm under no-load (engine is warmed up sufficiently.), check that the monitor fluctuates between "LEAN" and "RICH" more than 5 times during 10 seconds.

RICH → LEAN → RICH →
1 time   2 times
LEAN → RICH .....
.... OR

SEF957D

1. Set "Exhaust gas sensor monitor" in the self-diagnostic mode II.
(See page EF & EC-206.)
2. Maintaining engine at 2,000 rpm under no-load, check to make sure that the RED L.E.D. on the E.C.U. or the check engine light on the instrument panel goes ON and OFF more than 5 times during 10 seconds.

RED L.E.D.

Check engine light

O.K.

N.G.

Inspection and Adjustment (Cont'd)

N.G.

1. See "M/R F/C MNT" in "Data monitor" mode.
2. Run engine at about 2,000 rpm for about 2 minutes under no-load.
3. Maintaining engine at 2,000 rpm under no-load (engine is warmed up sufficiently.), check that the monitor fluctuates between "LEAN" and "RICH" more than 5 times during 10 seconds.

RICH → LEAN → RICH →
1 time   2 times
LEAN → RICH .....
.... OR

1. Set "Exhaust gas sensor monitor" in the self- diagnostic mode II.
2. Run engine at about 2,000 rpm for about 2 minutes under no-load.
3. Maintaining engine at 2,000 rpm under no-load, check to make sure that the RED L.E.D. on the E.C.U. or the check engine light on the instrument panel goes ON and OFF more than 5 times during 10 seconds.

O.K.

END

RECORD

RED L.E.D.

Check engine light

INSPECTION AND ADJUSTMENT – VE30DE ENGINE, CONT.

Inspection and Adjustment (Cont'd)

Connect exhaust gas sensor harness connector to exhaust gas sensor.

↓

Check fuel pressure regulator.

↓

Check air flow meter and its circuit.

↓

Check injector and its circuit.

Clean or replace if necessary.

↓

Check engine temperature sensor and its circuit.

↓

Check E.C.U. function* by substituting another known good E.C.U.

→ (E)

*: E.C.U. may be the cause of a problem, but this is rarely the case.

Inspection and Adjustment (Cont'd)

(C)

Check exhaust gas sensor harness:
1) Turn off engine and disconnect battery ground cable.
2) Disconnect E.C.U. S.M.J. harness connector from E.C.U.
3) Disconnect exhaust gas sensor harness connector and connect main harness side terminal for exhaust gas sensor to ground with a jumper wire.
4) Check for continuity between terminal No. 29 of E.C.U. S.M.J. harness connector and body ground.

Continuity exists. .... O.K.
Continuity does not exist. .... N.G.

N.G. → Repair or replace harness.

O.K. →

Connect E.C.U. S.M.J. harness connector to control unit.

↓

1) Connect battery ground cable.
2) Select "ENG TEMPERATURE" in "ACTIVE TEST" mode.
3) Set "ENGINE TEMP" to 20°C (68°F) by touching "Qu" and "Od" and "UP", "DOWN"

OR

1) Disconnect engine temperature sensor harness connector.
2) Connect a resistor (2.5 kΩ) between terminals of engine temperature sensor harness connector.
3) Connect battery ground cable.

↓

Start engine and warm it up until water temperature indicator points to middle of gauge.

→ (D)

(E)

Exhaust gas sensor harness connector

CAUNIT CONNECTOR 29

ACTIVE TEST   20°C
ENGINE TEMP
CAS=RPM (POS)   0rpm
INJ PULSE   0.7msec
IGN TIMING   17BTDC
QU UP DWN OD

Engine temperature sensor harness connector

2.5 kΩ resistor

TEMP
120   270

SELF-DIAGNOSIS — VE30DE ENGINE

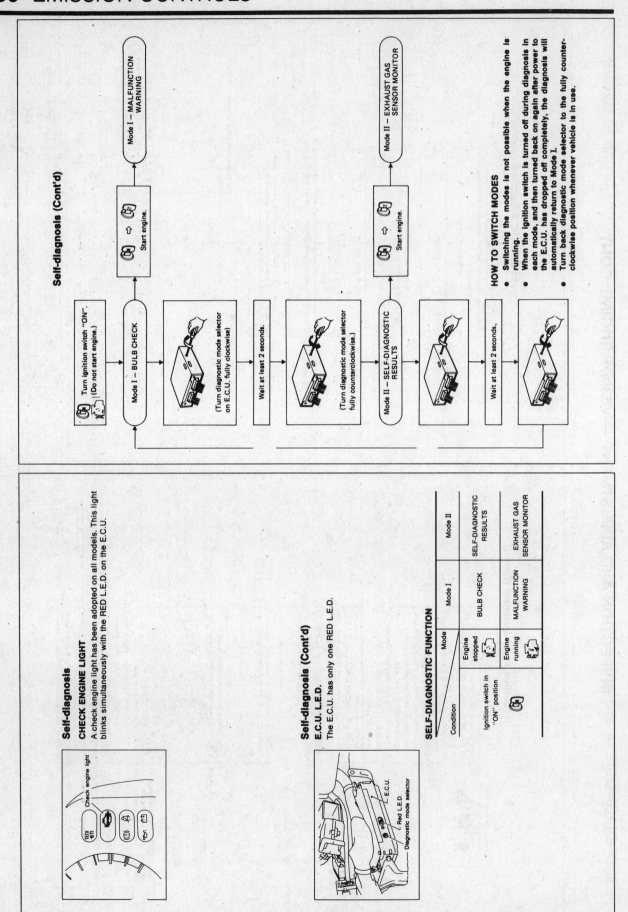

Self-diagnosis

CHECK ENGINE LIGHT

A check engine light has been adopted on all models. This light blinks simultaneously with the RED L.E.D. on the E.C.U.

Check engine light

Self-diagnosis (Cont'd)

E.C.U. L.E.D.

The E.C.U. has only one RED L.E.D.

E.C.U.

Red L.E.D.

Diagnostic mode selector

SELF-DIAGNOSTIC FUNCTION

Condition \ Mode		Mode I	Mode II
Ignition switch in "ON" position	Engine stopped	BULB CHECK	SELF-DIAGNOSTIC RESULTS
	Engine running	MALFUNCTION WARNING	EXHAUST GAS SENSOR MONITOR

Self-diagnosis (Cont'd)

Turn ignition switch "ON". (Do not start engine.)

Mode I — BULB CHECK

(Turn diagnostic mode selector on E.C.U. fully clockwise.)

Wait at least 2 seconds.

(Turn diagnostic mode selector fully counterclockwise.)

Mode II — SELF-DIAGNOSTIC RESULTS

Wait at least 2 seconds.

Start engine. → Mode I — MALFUNCTION WARNING

Start engine. → Mode II — EXHAUST GAS SENSOR MONITOR

HOW TO SWITCH MODES

- Switching the modes is not possible when the engine is running.
- When the ignition switch is turned off during diagnosis in each mode, and then turned back on again after power to the E.C.U. has dropped off completely, the diagnosis will automatically return to Mode I.
- Turn back diagnostic mode selector to the fully counter-clockwise position whenever vehicle is in use.

SELF-DIAGNOSIS — MODE I — VE30DE ENGINE

Self-diagnosis — Mode I

MODE I — BULB CHECK

In this mode, the RED L.E.D. in the E.C.U. and the CHECK ENGINE LIGHT in the instrument panel stay "ON". If either remain "OFF", check the bulb in the CHECK ENGINE LIGHT or the RED L.E.D.

MODE I — MALFUNCTION WARNING

FOR CALIFORNIA MODEL

CHECK ENGINE LIGHT and RED L.E.D.	Condition
ON	When the following malfunction (check engine light item) is detected or the E.C.U.'s C.P.U. is malfunctioning.
OFF	O.K.

Code No.	Malfunction
12	Air flow meter circuit
13	Engine temperature sensor circuit
14	Vehicle speed sensor circuit
31	E.C.U. (E.C.C.S. control unit)
32	E.G.R. function
33	Exhaust gas sensor circuit
35	Exhaust gas temperature sensor circuit
43	Throttle sensor circuit
45	Injector leak
51	Injector circuit

- **These Code Numbers are clarified in Mode II — SELF-DIAGNOSTIC RESULTS.**
- **The RED L.E.D. and the CHECK ENGINE LIGHT will turn off when normal condition is detected. At this time, the Mode II — SELF-DIAGNOSTIC RESULTS memory must be cleared as the contents remain stored.**

FOR NON-CALIFORNIA MODEL

CHECK ENGINE LIGHT and RED L.E.D.	Condition
ON	When the E.C.U.'s C.P.U. is malfunctioning.
OFF	O.K.

SELF-DIAGNOSIS — MODE II — VE30DE ENGINE

Self-diagnosis — Mode II (Self-diagnostic results)

DESCRIPTION

In this mode, a malfunction code is indicated by the number of flashes from the RED L.E.D. or the CHECK ENGINE LIGHT as shown below:

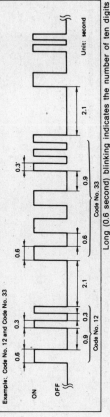

Example: Code No. 12 and Code No. 33

Unit: second

Long (0.6 second) blinking indicates the number of ten digits and short (0.3 second) blinking indicates the number of single digits.

For example, the red L.E.D. flashes once for 0.6 seconds and then it flashes twice for 0.3 seconds. This indicates the number "12" and refers to a malfunction in the air flow meter. In this way, all the problems are classified by their code numbers. The diagnostic results will remain in E.C.U. memory.

Display code table

Code No.	Detected items	California model	Non-California model
11*	Crank angle sensor circuit	X	X
12 🔧	Air flow meter circuit	X	X
13 🔧	Engine temperature sensor circuit	X	X
14 🔧	Vehicle speed sensor circuit	X	X
21*	Ignition signal circuit	X	X
31 🔧	E.C.U.	X	X
32 🔧	E.G.R. function	X	—
33 🔧	Exhaust gas sensor circuit	X	X
34 🔧	Detonation sensor circuit	X	X
35 🔧	Exhaust gas temperature sensor circuit	X	—
43 🔧	Throttle sensor circuit	X	—
45 🔧	Injector leak	X	—
51 🔧	Injector circuit	X	X
54	Signal circuit from A/T control unit to E.C.U. (A/T only)	X	X
55	No malfunction in the above circuits	X	X

X: Available
—: Not available
🔧 : Check engine light item

Check items causing a malfunction of crank angle sensor circuit first. If both code No. 11 and 21 are displayed at the same time.

SELF-DIAGNOSIS — MODE II — VE30DE ENGINE

Self-diagnosis — Mode II (Self-diagnostic results) (Cont'd)

Code No.	Detected items	Malfunction is detected when	Check item (remedy)
*11	Crank angle sensor circuit	• Either 1° or 120° signal is not entered for the first few seconds during engine cranking. • Either 1° or 120° signal is not input often enough while the engine speed is higher than the specified rpm.	• Harness and connector (If harness and connector are normal, replace crank angle sensor.)
12	Air flow meter circuit	• The air flow meter circuit is open or shorted. (An abnormally high or low voltage is entered.)	• Harness and connector (If harness and connector are normal, replace air flow meter.)
13	Engine temperature sensor circuit	• The engine temperature sensor circuit is open or shorted. (An abnormally high or low output voltage is entered.)	• Harness and connector • Engine temperature sensor
14	Vehicle speed sensor circuit	• The vehicle speed sensor circuit is open or shorted.	• Harness and connector • Vehicle speed sensor (reed switch)
*21	Ignition signal circuit	• The ignition signal in the primary circuit is not entered during engine cranking or running.	• Harness and connector • Power transistor unit
31	E.C.U.	• E.C.U. calculation function is malfunctioning.	• (Replace E.C.C.S. control unit.)
32	E.G.R. function	• E.G.R. control valve does not operate. (E.G.R. control valve spring does not lift.)	• E.G.R. control valve • E.G.R. control solenoid valve
33	Exhaust gas sensor circuit	• The exhaust gas sensor circuit is open or shorted. (An abnormally high or low output voltage is entered.)	• Harness and connector • Exhaust gas sensor • Fuel pressure • Injectors • Intake air leaks
34	Detonation sensor circuit	• The detonation circuit is open or shorted. (An abnormally high or low voltage is entered.)	• Harness and connector • Detonation sensor
35	Exhaust gas temperature sensor circuit	• The exhaust gas temperature sensor circuit is open or shorted. (An abnormally high or low voltage is entered.)	• Harness and connector • Exhaust gas temperature sensor
43	Throttle sensor circuit	• The throttle sensor circuit is open or shorted. (An abnormally high or low voltage is entered.)	• Harness and connector • Throttle sensor
45	Injector leak	• Fuel leaks from injector.	• Injector
51	Injector circuit	• The injector circuit is open.	• Harness and connector • Injector
54	Signal circuit from A/T control unit to E.C.U. (A/T only)	• The A/T communication line is open or shorted.	• Harness and connector

*: Check items causing a malfunction of crank angle sensor circuit first, if both code No. 11 and 21 are displayed at the same time.

Self-diagnosis — Mode II (Self-diagnostic results) (Cont'd)

HOW TO ERASE SELF-DIAGNOSTIC RESULTS

The malfunction code is erased from the backup memory on the E.C.U. when the diagnostic mode is changed from Mode II to Mode I. (Refer to "HOW TO SWITCH MODES.")

• When the battery terminal is disconnected, the malfunction code will be lost from the backup memory within 24 hours.
• Before starting self-diagnosis, do not erase the stored memory before beginning self-diagnosis.

Self-diagnosis — Mode II (Exhaust gas sensor monitor)

DESCRIPTION

In this mode, the CHECK ENGINE LIGHT and RED L.E.D. display the condition of the fuel mixture (lean or rich) which is monitored by the exhaust gas sensor.

CHECK ENGINE LIGHT and RED L.E.D.	Fuel mixture condition in the exhaust gas	Air fuel ratio feedback control condition
ON	Lean	Closed loop control
OFF	Rich	Closed loop control
*Remains ON or OFF	Any condition	Open loop control

*: Maintains conditions just before switching to open loop.

HOW TO CHECK EXHAUST GAS SENSOR

1. Set Mode II. (Refer to "HOW TO SWITCH MODES.")
2. Start engine and warm it up until engine coolant temperature indicator points to the middle of the gauge.
3. Run engine at about 2,000 rpm for about 2 minutes under no-load conditions.
4. Make sure RED L.E.D. or CHECK ENGINE LIGHT goes ON and OFF more than 5 times every 10 seconds; measured at 2,000 rpm under no-load.

EMISSION CONTROLS 4-89

CONSULT INSPECTION PROCEDURE — VE30DE ENGINE

E.C.C.S. COMPONENT PARTS APPLICATION — Consult (Cont'd)

E.C.C.S. COMPONENT PARTS	WORK SUPPORT	SELF-DIAGNOSTIC RESULTS	DATA MONITOR	ACTIVE TEST	FUNCTION TEST
INPUT					
Crank angle sensor		X	X		
Air flow meter		X	X		
Engine temperature sensor		X	X	X	
Exhaust gas sensor		X	X		
Vehicle speed sensor		X	X		X
Throttle sensor	X	X	X		X
Exhaust gas temperature sensor*		X			
Detonation sensor		X			
Ignition switch (start signal)			X		X
Air conditioner switch			X		
Neutral switch			X		X
Power steering oil pressure switch			X		X
Battery			X		
A/T signal		X			
Injectors		X	X	X	X
Power transistors (ignition timing)		X (ignition signal)		X	X
OUTPUT					
A.A.C. valve	X		X	X	X
Valve timing control solenoid valve			X	X	X
E.G.R. control solenoid valve			X	X	X
Power valve control solenoid valve**			X		X
Air conditioner relay			X		
Fuel pump relay	X		X	X	X
Radiator fan			X	X	X

*: The E.C.C.S. component part marked * is applicable to vehicles for California only.
**: M/T models only
X: Applicable

CONSULT INSPECTION PROCEDURE

Consult

CONSULT INSPECTION PROCEDURE

1. Turn off ignition switch.
2. Connect "CONSULT" to diagnostic connector. (Diagnostic connector is located in left dash side panel.)

Diagnostic connector for CONSULT

CONSULT

SEF392I

Consult (Cont'd)

3. Turn on ignition switch.
4. Touch "START".

NISSAN
CONSULT

☐ START
☐ SUB MODE

SEF642L

5. Touch "ENGINE".

SELECT SYSTEM
☐ ENGINE
☐ A/T

SEF226L

6. Perform each diagnostic mode according to the inspection sheet as follows:

For further information, see the CONSULT Operation Manual.

SELECT DIAG MODE
☐ WORK SUPPORT
☐ SELF-DIAG RESULTS
☐ DATA MONITOR
☐ ACTIVE TEST
☐ ECU PART NUMBER
☐ FUNCTION TEST

CONSULT INSPECTION PROCEDURE – VE30DE ENGINE, CONT.

Consult (Cont'd)

FUNCTION

Diagnostic mode	Function
Work support	This mode enables a technician to adjust some devices faster and more accurately by following the indications on the CONSULT unit.
Self-diagnostic results	Self-diagnostic results can be read and erased quickly.
Date monitor	Input/Output data in the control unit can be read.
Active test	Mode in which CONSULT drives some actuators apart from the control units and also shifts some parameters in a specified range.
E.C.U. part number	E.C.U. part number can be read.
Function test	Conducted by CONSULT instead of a technician to determine whether each system is "OK" or "NG".

WORK SUPPORT MODE

WORK ITEM	CONDITION	USAGE
THROTTLE SENSOR ADJUSTMENT	CHECK THE THROTTLE SENSOR SIGNAL. ADJUST IT TO THE SPECIFIED VALUE BY ROTATING THE SENSOR BODY UNDER THE FOLLOWING CONDITIONS. • IGN SW "ON" • ENG NOT RUNNING • ACC PEDAL NOT PRESSED	When adjusting throttle sensor initial position,
AAC VALVE ADJUSTMENT	SET ENGINE RPM AT THE SPECIFIED VALUE UNDER THE FOLLOWING CONDITIONS. • ENGINE WARMED UP • NO-LOAD	When adjusting idle speed,
FUEL PRESSURE RELEASE	FUEL PUMP WILL STOP BY TOUCHING "START" DURING IDLING. CRANK A FEW TIMES AFTER ENGINE STALLS.	When releasing fuel pressure from fuel line,

Consult (Cont'd)

SELF-DIAGNOSTIC RESULTS MODE

DIAGNOSTIC ITEM	DIAGNOSTIC ITEM IS DETECTED WHEN ...	CHECK ITEM (REMEDY)
CRANK ANGLE SENSOR*	• Either 1° or 120° signal is not entered for the first few seconds during engine cranking. • Either 1° or 120° signal is not input often enough while the engine speed is higher than the specified rpm.	• Harness and connector (If harness and connector are normal, replace crank angle sensor.)
AIR FLOW METER	• The air flow meter circuit is open or shorted. (An abnormally high or low voltage is entered.)	• Harness and connector (If harness and connector are normal, replace air flow meter.)
ENGINE TEMP SENSOR	• The engine temperature sensor circuit is open or shorted. (An abnormally high or low output voltage is entered.)	• Harness and connector • Engine temperature sensor
CAR SPEED SENSOR	• The vehicle speed sensor circuit is open or shorted.	• Harness and connector • Vehicle speed sensor (reed switch)
IGNITION SIGNAL—PRIMARY*	• The ignition signal in primary circuit is not entered during engine cranking or running.	• Harness and connector • Power transistor unit
CONTROL UNIT	• E.C.U. calculation function is malfunctioning.	• (Replace E.C.C.S. control unit.)
E.G.R. SYSTEM**	• E.G.R. control valve does not operate. (E.G.R. control valve spring does not lift.)	• E.G.R. control valve • E.G.R. control solenoid valve
EXH GAS SENSOR	• The exhaust gas sensor circuit is open or shorted. (An abnormally high or low output voltage is entered.)	• Harness and connector • Exhaust gas sensor • Fuel pressure • Injectors • Intake air leaks
DETONATION SENSOR	• The detonation circuit is open or shorted. (An abnormally high or low voltage is entered.)	• Harness and connector • Detonation sensor
EXHAUST GAS TEMP SENSOR**	• The exhaust gas temperature sensor circuit is open or shorted. (An abnormally high or low voltage is entered.)	• Harness and connector • Exhaust gas temperature sensor
THROTTLE SENSOR	• The throttle sensor circuit is open or shorted. (An abnormally high or low voltage is entered.)	• Harness and connector • Throttle sensor
INJECTOR FUEL LEAK**	• Fuel leaks from injector.	• Injector
INJECTOR OPEN**	• The injector circuit is open.	• Injector
A/T COMM LINE	• The A/T communication line is open or shorted.	• Harness and connector

*: Check items causing a malfunction of crank angle sensor circuit first, if both "CRANK ANGLE SENSOR" and "IGN SIGNAL—PRIMARY" are displayed at the same time.
: The diagnostic item marked "" is applicable to vehicles for California only.

CONSULT INSPECTION PROCEDURE — VE30DE ENGINE, CONT.

Consult (Cont'd)

DATA MONITOR MODE

Remarks:
- The monitor item marked "*" is applicable to vehicles for California only.
- The monitor item marked "**" is applicable to M/T models only.
- Specification data are reference values.
- Specification data are out-put/in-put values which are detected or supplied by E.C.U. at the connector.
- Specification data may not be directly related to their components signals/values/operations.
  ie. Adjust ignition timing with a timing light before monitoring IGN TIMING, because the monitor may show the specification data in spite of the ignition timing being not adjusted to the specification data. This IGN TIMING monitors the calculated data by E.C.U. according to the input signals from crank angle sensor and other ignition timing related sensors.

MONITOR ITEM	CONDITION	SPECIFICATION	CHECK ITEM WHEN OUTSIDE SPEC.
CAS·RPM (POS) CAS·RPM (REF)	• Tachometer: Connect • Run engine and compare tachometer indication with the CONSULT value.	Almost the same speed as the CONSULT value.	• Harness and connector • Crank angle sensor
AIR FLOW MTR	• Engine: After warming up, idle the engine • A/C switch "OFF" • No-load	Idle: 0.8 - 1.5V; 2,000 rpm: 1.4 - 1.8V	• Harness and connector • Air flow meter
ENG TEMP SEN	• Engine: After warming up	More than 70°C (158°F)	• Harness and connector • Engine temperature sensor
EXH GAS SEN	• Engine: After warming up	0 - 0.3V ↔ 0.6 - 1.0V LEAN ↔ RICH	• Harness and connector • Exhaust gas sensor • Intake air leaks • Injectors
M/R F/C MNT	• Maintaining engine speed at 2,000 rpm	Changes more than 5 times during 10 seconds.	
CAR SPEED SEN	• Turn drive wheels and compare speedometer indication with the CONSULT value	Almost the same speed as the CONSULT value	• Harness and connector • Vehicle speed sensor
BATTERY VOLT	• Ignition switch: ON (Engine stopped)	11 - 14V	• Battery • E.C.U. power supply circuit
THROTTLE SEN	• Ignition switch: ON (Engine stopped)	Throttle valve fully closed: 0.4 - 0.5V; Throttle valve fully opened: Approx. 4.0V	• Harness and connector • Throttle sensor • Throttle sensor adjustment
EGR TEMP SEN*	• Engine: After warming up	Less than 4.5V	• Harness and connector • Exhaust gas temperature sensor
START SIGNAL	• Ignition switch: ON → START	OFF → ON	• Harness and connector • Starter switch
IDLE POSITION	• Ignition switch: ON (Engine stopped)	Throttle valve: Idle position: ON; Throttle valve: Slightly open: OFF	• Harness and connector • Throttle sensor • Throttle sensor adjustment
AIR COND SIG	• Engine: After warming up, idle the engine	A/C switch "OFF": OFF; A/C switch "ON": ON	• Harness and connector • Air conditioner switch

Consult (Cont'd)

MONITOR ITEM	CONDITION	SPECIFICATION	CHECK ITEM WHEN OUTSIDE SPEC.
NEUTRAL SW	• Ignition switch: ON	Shift lever "P" or "N": ON; Except above: OFF	• Harness and connector • Neutral switch
PW/ST SIGNAL	• Engine: After warming up, idle the engine	Steering wheel in neutral (forward direction): OFF; The steering wheel is turned: ON	• Harness and connector • Power steering oil pressure switch
INJ PULSE	• Engine: After warming up • A/C switch "OFF" • Shift lever "N" • No-load	Idle: 2.0 - 3.0 msec.; 2,000 rpm: 1.8 - 2.8 msec.	• Harness and connector • Injector • Air flow meter • Intake air system
IGN TIMING	ditto	Idle: 15° B.T.D.C.; 2,000 rpm: More than 25° B.T.D.C.	• Harness and connector • Crank angle sensor
AAC VALVE	ditto	Idle: 15 - 40%; 2,000 rpm: —	• Harness and connector • A.A.C. valve
FUEL PUMP RLY	• Ignition switch is turned to ON (Operates for 5 seconds • Engine running and cranking • When engine is stopped (stops in 1.5 seconds) • Except as shown above	ON; OFF	• Harness and connector • Fuel pump relay
RADIATOR FAN	• After warming up engine, idle the engine. • A/C switch "OFF"	Engine temperature is 94°C (201°F) or less: OFF; Engine temperature is between 95°C (203°F) and 104°C (219°F): LOW; Engine temperature is 105°C (221°F) or more: HIGH	• Harness and connector • Radiator fan relay • Radiator fan
A/F ALPHA	• Engine: After warming up	Maintaining engine speed at 2,000 rpm	75 - 125% • Injectors • Air flow meter • Exhaust gas sensor • Canister purge line • Intake air system
AIR COND RLY	• Air conditioner switch OFF → ON	OFF → ON	• Harness and connector • Air conditioner switch • Air conditioner relay
EGR CONT S/V	• Engine: After warming up • A/C switch "OFF" • Shift lever "N" • No-load	Idle: ON; 2,000 rpm: OFF	• Harness and connector • E.G.R. control solenoid valve

CONSULT INSPECTION PROCEDURE – VE30DE ENGINE, CONT.

Consult (Cont'd)

ACTIVE TEST MODE

TEST ITEM	CONDITION	JUDGEMENT	CHECK ITEM (REMEDY)
FUEL INJECTION TEST	• Engine: Return to the original trouble condition. • Change the amount of fuel injection with the CONSULT.	If trouble symptom disappears, see CHECK ITEM.	• Harness and connector • Fuel injectors • Exhaust gas sensors
AAC/V OPENING TEST	• Engine: After warming up, idle the engine. • Change the AAC valve opening percent with the CONSULT.	Engine speed changes according to the opening percent.	• Harness and connector • AAC valve
ENGINE TEMP TEST	• Engine: Return to the original trouble condition. • Change the engine coolant temperature with the CONSULT.	If trouble symptom disappears, see CHECK ITEM.	• Harness and connector • Engine temperature sensor • Fuel injectors
IGN TIMING TEST	• Engine: Return to the original trouble condition. • Timing light: Set. • Retard the ignition timing with the CONSULT.	If trouble symptom disappears, see CHECK ITEM.	• Adjust initial ignition timing
POWER BALANCE TEST	• Engine: After warming up, idle the engine. • A/C switch "OFF". • Shift lever "N". • Cut off each injector signal one at a time with the CONSULT.	Engine runs rough or dies.	• Harness and connector • Compression • Injectors • Power transistor • Spark plugs • Ignition coils
RADIATOR FAN TEST	• Ignition switch: ON. • Turn the radiator fan "ON" and "OFF" with the CONSULT.	Radiator fan moves and stops.	• Harness and connector • Radiator fan motor
FUEL PUMP RLY TEST	• Ignition switch: ON (Engine stopped). • Turn the fuel pump relay "ON" and "OFF" with the CONSULT and listen to operating sound.	Fuel pump relay makes the operating sound.	• Harness and connector • Fuel pump relay
EGR CONT SOL/V TEST VIAS SOL/V TEST (Power valve)* VALVE TIM SOL TEST	• Ignition switch: ON. • Turn solenoid valve "ON" and "OFF" with the CONSULT and listen to operating sound.	Each solenoid valve makes an operating sound.	• Harness and connector • Solenoid valve
SELF-LEARN CONT TEST	• In this test, the coefficient of self-learning control mixture ratio returns to the original coefficient by touching "CLEAR" on the screen.		

*: M/T models only

Consult (Cont'd)

MONITOR ITEM	CONDITION	SPECIFICATION	CHECK ITEM WHEN OUTSIDE SPEC.
VALVE TIM SOL	• Jack up front wheel. • Engine: After warming up.	• Idle → OFF • Shift select lever to any range except "N" or "P" range. • Quickly depress accelerator pedal, then quickly release it. → OFF → ON → OFF	• Harness and connector • Valve timing control solenoid valve
VIAS S/V**	• Engine: After warming up	• Idle → OFF • Quickly depress accelerator pedal, then quickly release it → OFF → ON → OFF	• Harness and connector • Power valve control solenoid valve

BASIC INSPECTION DIAGNOSTIC CHART – VE30DE ENGINE

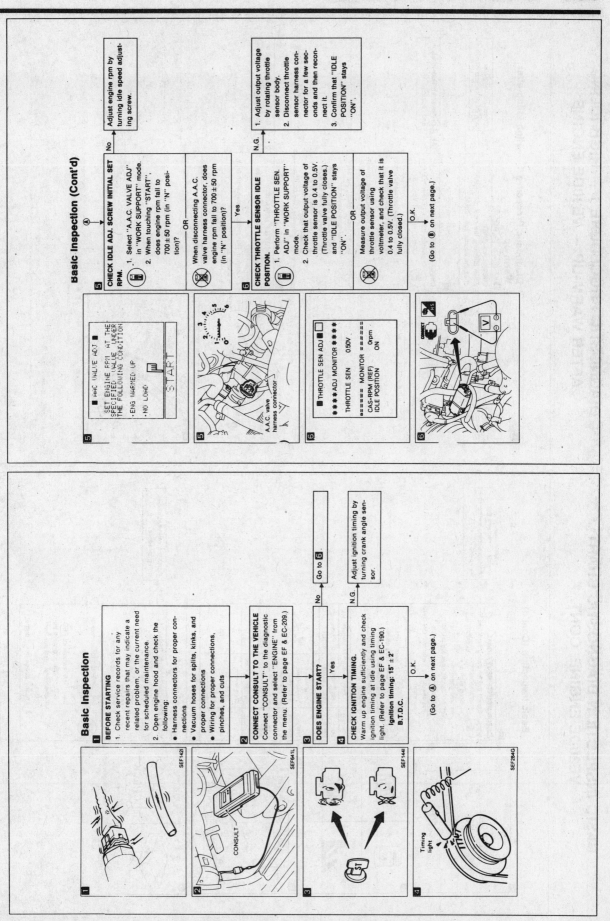

Basic Inspection

1 BEFORE STARTING

1. Check service records for any recent repairs that may indicate a related problem, or the current need for scheduled maintenance.

2. Open engine hood and check the following:

- Harness connectors for proper connections
- Vacuum hoses for splits, kinks, and proper connections
- Wiring for proper connections, pinches, and cuts

SEF142I

2 CONNECT CONSULT TO THE VEHICLE

Connect "CONSULT" to the diagnostic connector and select "ENGINE" from the menu. (Refer to page EF & EC-209.)

SEF641L

3 DOES ENGINE START?

→ No → Go to 6.

Yes

4 CHECK IGNITION TIMING.

Warm up engine sufficiently and check ignition timing at idle using timing light. (Refer to page EF & EC-190.)

Ignition timing: 15° ± 2°
B.T.D.C.

→ N.G. → Adjust ignition timing by turning crank angle sensor.

O.K.

(Go to Ⓐ on next page.)

SEF144I

Timing light

SEF284G

Basic Inspection (Cont'd)

Ⓐ

5 CHECK IDLE ADJ. SCREW INITIAL SET RPM.

1. Select "A.A.C. VALVE ADJ" in "WORK SUPPORT" mode.
2. When touching "START", does engine rpm fall to 700 ± 50 rpm (in "N" position)?

– OR –

When disconnecting A.A.C. valve harness connector, does engine rpm fall to 700 ± 50 rpm (in "N" position)?

→ No → Adjust engine rpm by turning idle speed adjusting screw.

Yes

5 ■ AAC VALVE ADJ ■
SET ENGINE RPM AT THE SPECIFIED VALUE UNDER THE FOLLOWING CONDITION.
• ENG WARMED UP
• NO LOAD

【START】

5 A.A.C. valve harness connector

6 CHECK THROTTLE SENSOR IDLE POSITION.

1. Perform "THROTTLE SEN. ADJ" in "WORK SUPPORT" mode.
2. Check that output voltage of throttle sensor is 0.4 to 0.5V. (Throttle valve fully closes.) and "IDLE POSITION" stays "ON".

– OR –

Measure output voltage of throttle sensor using voltmeter, and check that it is 0.4 to 0.5V. (Throttle valve fully closed.)

→ N.G. → 1. Adjust output voltage by rotating throttle sensor body.
2. Disconnect throttle sensor harness connector for a few seconds and then reconnect it.
3. Confirm that "IDLE POSITION" stays "ON".

O.K.

(Go to Ⓑ on next page.)

6 ■ THROTTLE SEN ADJ ■
■■■■ADJ MONITOR■■■■
THROTTLE SEN   0.50V
■=====MONITOR=====■
CAS-RPM (REF)   0rpm
IDLE POSITION   ON

6 CONNECT
Ⓥ

DIAGNOSTIC PROCEDURE 1 — HIGH IDLING AFTER WARM-UP — VE30DE ENGINE

Diagnostic Procedure 1 — High Idling after Warm-up

1 CHECK I.A.A. UNIT.
When pinching the I.A.A. unit hose, does the engine speed drop?
→ Yes → Check air regulator, A.A.C. valve and circuit.
→ No

2 CHECK INTAKE AIR LEAK.
1. Select "SELF-LEARNING CONT" in "ACTIVE TEST" mode.
2. Clear the self-learning control coefficient by touching "CLEAR".
3. Does the engine speed drop?
   OR
1. Disconnect exhaust gas sensor harness connector.
2. After racing engine at 1,500 rpm under no load for about 30 seconds, does the engine speed drop?
→ Yes → Discover air leak location and repair.
→ No

3 CHECK THROTTLE LINKAGE.
1. Check that throttle linkage moves smoothly.
2. Confirm that throttle valve both fully opens and fully closes.
→ N.G. → Repair throttle linkage or sticking of throttle valve.
→ O.K.

INSPECTION END

```
■ ACTIVE TEST        100%
SELF-LEARN
CONTROL
= = MONITOR = = =
CAS-RPM (POS)      787rpm
ENG TEMP SEN        95°C
EXH GAS SEN        0.02V
A/F ALPHA           98%
          CLEAR
```

Exhaust gas sensor

BASIC INSPECTION DIAGNOSTIC CHART VE30DE ENGINE, CONT.

Basic Inspection (Cont'd)

7 CHECK SWITCH INPUT SIGNAL.
Select the following switches in "DATA MONITOR" mode.
a) Start signal,
b) Idle position,
c) Air conditioner signal,
d) Neutral (Parking) switch,
and check the switches' ON-OFF operation.
OR
Remove E.C.U. from front floor panel and check the above switches' ON-OFF operation using voltmeter at each E.C.U. terminal.

Switch	Condition	Voltage (V)
Start signal	IGN IGN ON → START	0 → Battery voltage
Idle position	Engine warmed up sufficiently Idle position → Depress the accelerator pedal.	0.4 - 0.5 Approx. 4.0
A/C signal	A/C A/C OFF → ON (Engine running)	Battery voltage → Approx. 0.2
Neutral (Parking) switch	Shift lever is "N" or "P" position → Except "N" and "P".	0 → 4.0 - 5.0

→ N.G. → Repair or replace the malfunctioning switch or its circuit.
→ O.K.

8 READ SELF-DIAGNOSTIC RESULTS.
1. Perform "SELF-DIAG RESULTS" mode.
2. Read out self-diagnostic results.
3. Is a failure detected?
   OR
1. Set "Self-diagnostic results mode" in Mode II.
2. Count the number of RED L.E.D. or check engine light flashes and read out the codes.
3. Are the codes being output?
→ Yes → Go to the relevant inspection procedure.
→ No

INSPECTION END

```
☆ MONITOR  ☆ NO FAIL
START SIGNAL        OFF
IDLE POSITION        ON
AIR COND SIG        OFF
NEUTRAL SW           ON
            RECORD
```

```
■ SELF-DIAG RESULTS
FAILURE DETECTED    TIME
• NO SELF-DIAGNOSTIC
  FAILURE INDICATED
FURTHER TESTING MAY
BE REQUIRED **
   ERASE   PRINT
```

CHECK — Check engine light

RED L.E.D.

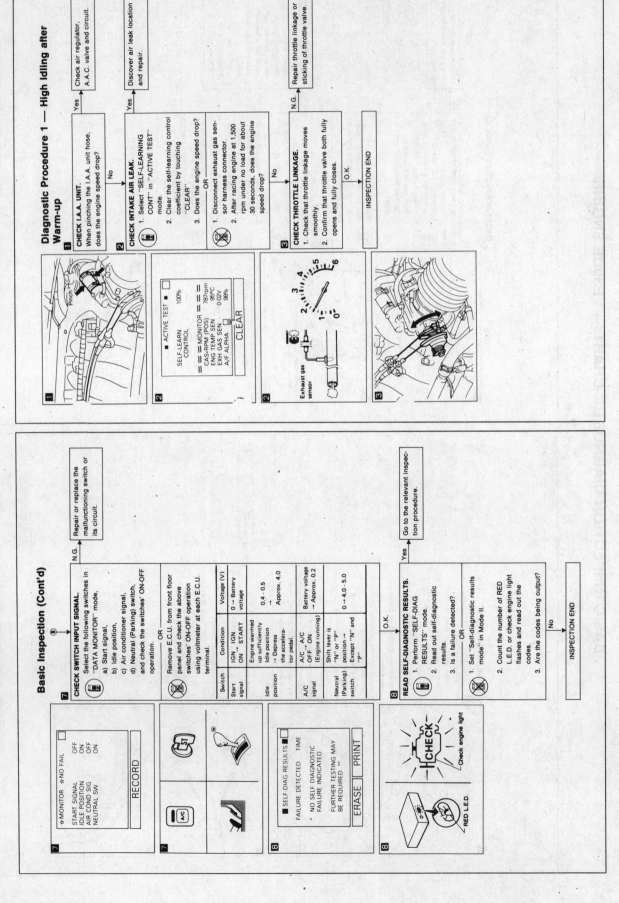

DIAGNOSTIC PROCEDURE 2 — HUNTING — VE30DE ENGINE

Diagnostic Procedure 2 — Hunting (Cont'd)

4 CHECK FOR INTAKE AIR LEAK.
When pinching blow-by hose (lowering the blow-by air supply), does the engine speed rise?

Yes → Discover air leak location and repair.

No →

5 CHECK E.G.R. CONTROL VALVE.
Check E.G.R. control valve for sticking.

N.G. → Repair or replace.

O.K. →

INSPECTION END

Diagnostic Procedure 2 — Hunting

1 CHECK EXHAUST GAS SENSOR.
When disconnecting exhaust gas sensor harness connector, is the hunting fixed?

Yes → Check exhaust gas sensor.

No →

2 PERFORM POWER BALANCE TEST.
1. Perform "POWER BALANCE" in "ACTIVE TEST" mode.
2. Is there any cylinder which does not produce a momentary engine speed drop?

OR

When disconnecting each ignition coil harness connector one at a time, is there any cylinder which does not produce a momentary engine speed drop?

No → Go to **4**.

Yes →

3 CHECK SPARK PLUGS.
Remove the spark plugs and check for fouling, etc.

N.G. → Repair or replace spark plug(s).

O.K. →

(Go to Ⓐ on next page.)

ACTIVE TEST ■
···· POWER BALANCE ····
MONITOR
CAS·RPM (POS)   700rpm
AIR FLOW MTR   1.11V
AAC VALVE   22%

| 1 | 2 | 3 | 4 |
| 5 | 6 | | |

TEST START

Ignition coil harness connector

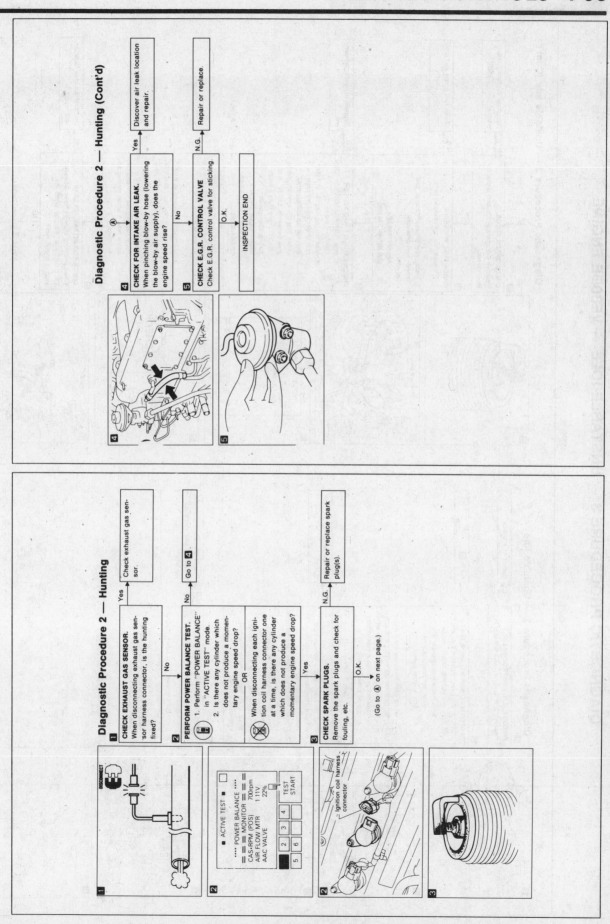

DIAGNOSTIC PROCEDURE 3 — UNSTABLE IDLE — VE30DE ENGINE

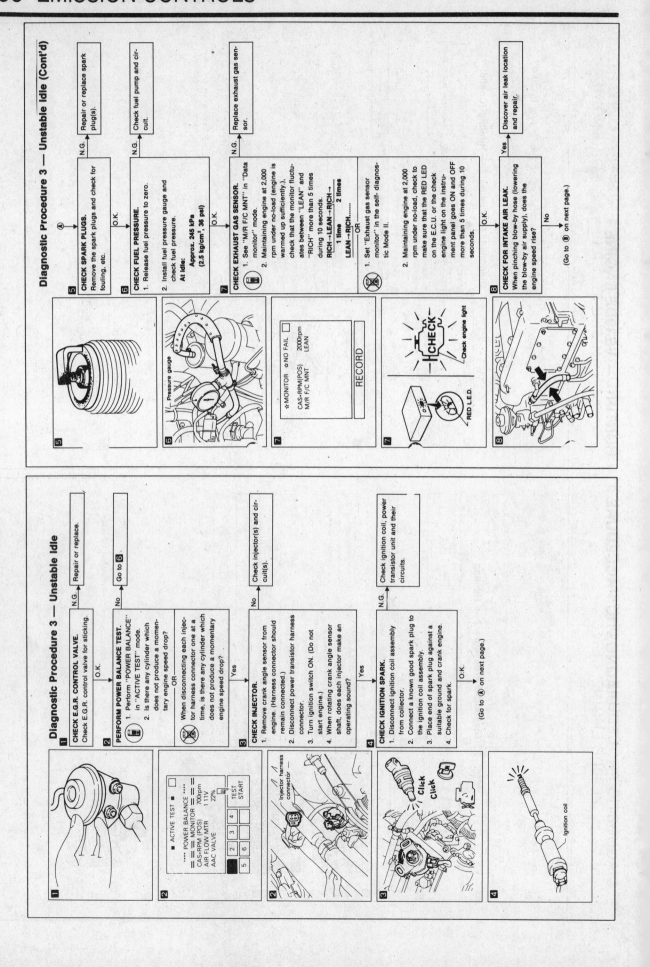

Diagnostic Procedure 3 — Unstable Idle (Cont'd)

5 CHECK SPARK PLUGS.
Remove the spark plugs and check for fouling, etc.

→ N.G. → Repair or replace spark plug(s).

O.K. ↓

6 CHECK FUEL PRESSURE.
1. Release fuel pressure to zero.
2. Install fuel pressure gauge and check fuel pressure.

At idle:
Approx. 245 kPa
(2.5 kg/cm², 36 psi)

→ N.G. → Check fuel pump and circuit.

O.K. ↓

7 CHECK EXHAUST GAS SENSOR.
1. See "M/R F/C MNT" in "Data monitor" mode.
2. Maintaining engine at 2,000 rpm under no-load (engine is warmed up sufficiently.), check that the monitor fluctuates between "LEAN" and "RICH" more than 5 times during 10 seconds.
RICH→LEAN→RICH→
  1 time   2 times
LEAN→RICH......
OR
Set "Exhaust gas sensor monitor" in the self-diagnostic Mode II.
Maintaining engine at 2,000 rpm under no-load, check to make sure that the RED LED on the E.C.U. or the check engine light on the instrument panel goes ON and OFF more than 5 times during 10 seconds.

→ N.G. → Replace exhaust gas sensor.

O.K. ↓

8 CHECK FOR INTAKE AIR LEAK.
When pinching blow-by hose (lowering the blow-by air supply), does the engine speed rise?

→ Yes → Discover air leak location and repair.

No ↓

(Go to ⓑ on next page.)

Diagnostic Procedure 3 — Unstable Idle

1 CHECK E.G.R. CONTROL VALVE.
Check E.G.R. control valve for sticking.

→ N.G. → Repair or replace.

O.K. ↓

2 PERFORM POWER BALANCE TEST.
1. Perform "POWER BALANCE" in "ACTIVE TEST" mode.
2. Is there any cylinder which does not produce a momentary engine speed drop?
OR
When disconnecting each injector harness connector one at a time, is there any cylinder which does not produce a momentary engine speed drop?

→ No → Go to 6

Yes ↓

3 CHECK INJECTOR.
1. Remove crank angle sensor from engine. (Harness connector should remain connected.)
2. Disconnect power transistor harness connector.
3. Turn ignition switch ON. (Do not start engine.)
4. When rotating crank angle sensor shaft, does each injector make an operating sound?

→ No → Check injector(s) and circuit(s).

Yes ↓

4 CHECK IGNITION SPARK.
1. Disconnect ignition coil assembly from collector.
2. Connect a known good spark plug to the ignition coil assembly.
3. Place end of spark plug against a suitable ground and crank engine.
4. Check for spark.

→ N.G. → Check ignition coil, power transistor unit and their circuits.

O.K. ↓

(Go to ⓐ on next page.)

DIAGNOSTIC PROCEDURE 4 – HARD TO START WHEN ENGINE IS COLD – VE30DE ENGINE

Diagnostic Procedure 4 — Hard to Start or Impossible to Start when the Engine is Cold

1 CHECK BATTERY AND STARTER.
Check battery and starter condition.

→ N.G. → Repair or replace.

O.K. ↓

2 CHECK FUEL PRESSURE.
1. Pinch fuel feed hose with fingers.
2. When cranking the engine, is there any pressure on the fuel feed hose?

→ No → Check fuel pump and circuit.

Yes ↓

3 CHECK AIR REGULATOR AND A.A.C. VALVE.
When pressing accelerator pedal fully, can you start the engine.

→ Yes → Check A.A.C. valve, air regulator and circuit.

No ↓

4 CHECK INJECTOR.
1. Remove crank angle sensor from engine. (Harness connector should remain connected.)
2. Disconnect power transistor harness connector.
3. Turn ignition switch ON. (Do not start engine.)
4. When rotating crank angle sensor shaft, does each injector make an operating sound?

→ No → Check injector(s) and circuit(s).

Yes ↓

5 CHECK IGNITION SPARK.
1. Disconnect ignition coil assembly from collector.
2. Connect a known good spark plug to the ignition coil assembly.
3. Place end of spark plug against a suitable ground and crank engine.
4. Check for spark.

→ N.G. → Check ignition coil, power transistor unit and their circuits.

O.K. ↓

(Go to Ⓐ on next page.)

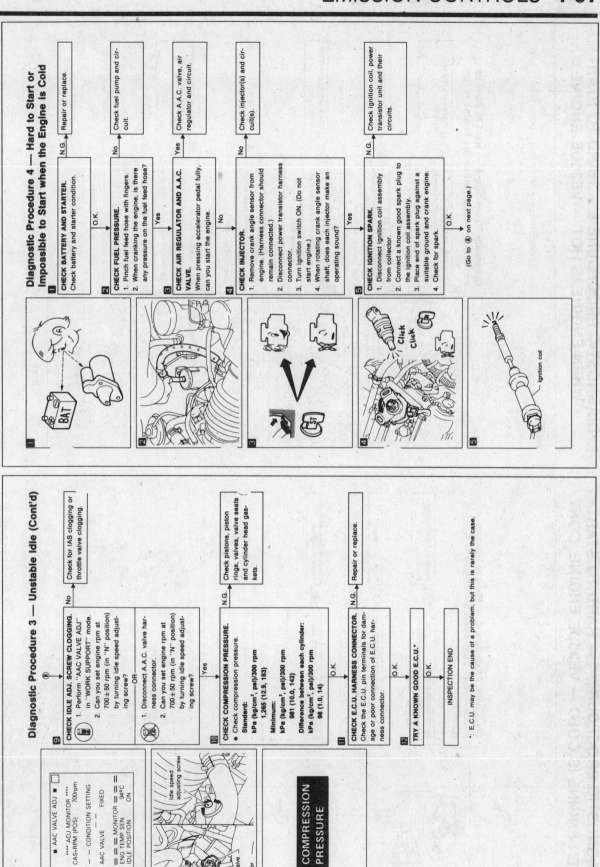

Ignition coil

DIAGNOSTIC PROCEDURE 3 – UNSTABLE IDLE VE30DE ENGINE, CONT.

Diagnostic Procedure 3 — Unstable Idle (Cont'd)

Ⓑ ↓

9 CHECK IDLE ADJ. SCREW CLOGGING.
1. Perform "AAC VALVE ADJ" in "WORK SUPPORT" mode.
2. Can you set engine rpm at 700±50 rpm (in "N" position) by turning idle speed adjusting screw?
— OR —
1. Disconnect A.A.C. valve harness connector.
2. Can you set engine rpm at 700±50 rpm (in "N" position) by turning idle speed adjusting screw?

→ No → Check for IAS clogging or throttle valve clogging.

Yes ↓

10 CHECK COMPRESSION PRESSURE.
● Check compression pressure.
Standard:
kPa (kg/cm², psi)/300 rpm
1,265 (12.9, 183)
Minimum:
kPa (kg/cm², psi)/300 rpm
981 (10.0, 142)
Difference between each cylinder:
kPa (kg/cm², psi)/300 rpm
98 (1.0, 14)

→ N.G. → Check pistons, piston rings, valves, valve seats and cylinder head gaskets.

O.K. ↓

11 CHECK E.C.U. HARNESS CONNECTOR.
Check the E.C.U. pin terminals for damage or poor connection of E.C.U. harness connector.

→ N.G. → Repair or replace.

O.K. ↓

12 TRY A KNOWN GOOD E.C.U.*

O.K. ↓

INSPECTION END

*: E.C.U. may be the cause of a problem, but this is rarely the case.

■ AAC VALVE ADJ ■ □
······ ADJ MONITOR ······
CAS·RPM (POS) 700rpm
— — CONDITION SETTING — —
AAC VALVE ····· FIXED
== = MONITOR = == ==
ENG TEMP SEN   94°C
IDLE POSITION   ON

Idle speed adjusting screw

A.A.C. valve harness connector

COMPRESSION PRESSURE

DIAGNOSTIC PROCEDURE 5 — HARD TO START WHEN ENGINE IS HOT — VE30DE ENGINE

DIAGNOSTIC PROCEDURE 4 — HARD TO START WHEN ENGINE IS COLD — VE30DE ENGINE, CONT.

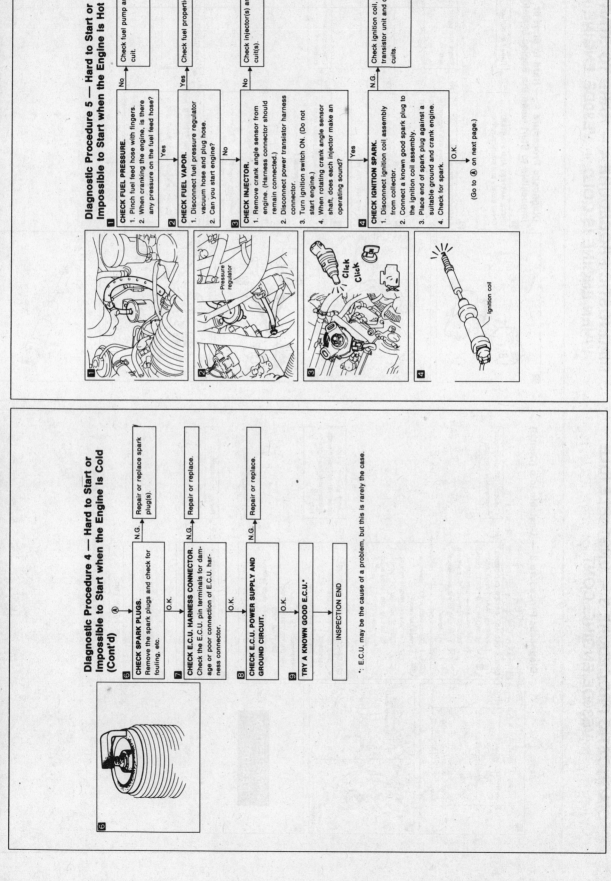

Diagnostic Procedure 5 — Hard to Start or Impossible to Start when the Engine Is Hot

1 CHECK FUEL PRESSURE.
1. Pinch fuel feed hose with fingers.
2. When cranking the engine, is there any pressure on the fuel feed hose?
   - No → Check fuel pump and circuit.
   - Yes ↓

2 CHECK FUEL VAPOR.
1. Disconnect fuel pressure regulator vacuum hose and plug hose.
2. Can you start engine?
   - Yes → Check fuel properties.
   - No ↓

3 CHECK INJECTOR.
1. Remove crank angle sensor from engine. (Harness connector should remain connected.)
2. Disconnect power transistor harness connector.
3. Turn ignition switch ON. (Do not start engine.)
4. When rotating crank angle sensor shaft, does each injector make an operating sound?
   - No → Check injector(s) and circuit(s).
   - Yes ↓

4 CHECK IGNITION SPARK.
1. Disconnect ignition coil assembly from collector.
2. Connect a known good spark plug to the ignition coil assembly.
3. Place end of spark plug against a suitable ground and crank engine.
4. Check for spark.
   - N.G. → Check ignition coil, power transistor unit and circuits.
   - O.K. → (Go to Ⓐ on next page.)

Pressure regulator

Click Click

Ignition coil

Diagnostic Procedure 4 — Hard to Start or Impossible to Start when the Engine Is Cold (Cont'd)

Ⓐ

6 CHECK SPARK PLUGS.
Remove the spark plugs and check for fouling, etc.
   - N.G. → Repair or replace spark plug(s).
   - O.K. ↓

7 CHECK E.C.U. HARNESS CONNECTOR.
Check the E.C.U. pin terminals for damage or poor connection of E.C.U. harness connector.
   - N.G. → Repair or replace.
   - O.K. ↓

8 CHECK E.C.U. POWER SUPPLY AND GROUND CIRCUIT.
   - N.G. → Repair or replace.
   - O.K. ↓

9 TRY A KNOWN GOOD E.C.U.*

INSPECTION END

*: E.C.U. may be the cause of a problem, but this is rarely the case.

DIAGNOSTIC PROCEDURE 6 — HARD TO START UNDER NORMAL CONDITIONS — VE30DE ENGINE

Diagnostic Procedure 6 — Hard to Start or Impossible to Start under Normal Conditions

1. **CHECK BATTERY AND STARTER.**
   Check battery and starter operation.
   → N.G. → Repair or replace.
   → O.K.

2. **CHECK FUEL PRESSURE.**
   1. Pinch fuel feed hose with fingers.
   2. When cranking the engine, is there any pressure on the fuel feed hose?
   → No → Check fuel pump and circuit.
   → Yes

3. **CHECK INJECTOR FOR LEAKAGE.**
   When pressing accelerator pedal fully, can you start the engine.
   → Yes → Check injector(s) for leakage.
   → No

4. **CHECK INJECTOR.**
   1. Remove crank angle sensor from engine. (Harness connector should remain connected.)
   2. Disconnect power transistor harness connector.
   3. Turn ignition switch ON. (Do not start engine.)
   4. When rotating crank angle sensor shaft, does each injector make an operating sound?
   → No → Check injectors and circuits.
   → Yes

5. **CHECK IGNITION SPARK.**
   1. Disconnect ignition coil assembly from collector.
   2. Connect a known good spark plug to the ignition coil assembly.
   3. Place end of spark plug against a suitable ground and crank engine.
   4. Check for spark.
   → N.G. → Check ignition coil, power transistor unit and circuits.
   → O.K.
   (Go to Ⓐ on next page.)

Ignition coil

Click Click

BAT

ST

DIAGNOSTIC PROCEDURE 5 — HARD TO START WHEN ENGINE IS HOT — VE30DE ENGINE, CONT.

Diagnostic Procedure 5 — Hard to Start or Impossible to Start when the Engine is Hot (Cont'd)

Ⓐ

5. **CHECK E.C.U. HARNESS CONNECTOR.**
   Check the E.C.U. pin terminals for damage or poor connection of E.C.U. harness connector.
   → N.G. → Repair or replace.
   → O.K.

6. **CHECK E.C.U. POWER SUPPLY AND GROUND CIRCUIT.**
   → N.G. → Repair or replace.
   → O.K.

7. **TRY A KNOWN GOOD E.C.U.***

   INSPECTION END

*: E.C.U. may be the cause of a problem, but this is rarely the case.

DIAGNOSTIC PROCEDURE 7 – HESITATION WHEN ENGINE IS HOT – VE30DE ENGINE

Diagnostic Procedure 7 — Hesitation when the Engine Is Hot

1 | **CHECK FUEL VAPOR.**
1. Disconnect fuel pressure regulator vacuum hose and plug hose.
2. Perform cruise test.
3. Does the hesitation disappear? → Yes → Check fuel properties.

No ↓

2 | **CHECK CANISTER PURGE.**
1. Disconnect canister purge line hose and plug hose.
2. Perform cruise test.
3. Does the hesitation disappear? → Yes → Check purge and vacuum lines.

No ↓

3 | **CHECK FOR INTAKE AIR LEAK.**
When pinching blow-by hose (lowering the blow-by air supply), does the engine speed rise? → Yes → Discover air leak location and repair.

No ↓

INSPECTION END

DIAGNOSTIC PROCEDURE 6 – HARD TO START UNDER NORMAL CONDITIONS – VE30DE ENGINE

Diagnostic Procedure 6 — Hard to Start or Impossible to Start under Normal Conditions (Cont'd)

Ⓐ

6 | **CHECK SPARK PLUGS.**
Remove the spark plugs and check for fouling, etc. → N.G. → Repair or replace spark plug(s).

O.K. ↓

7 | **CHECK E.G.R. CONTROL VALVE.**
Check E.G.R. control valve for sticking. → N.G. → Repair or replace.

O.K. ↓

8 | **CHECK E.C.U. HARNESS CONNECTOR.**
Check the E.C.U. pin terminals for damage or poor connection of E.C.U. harness connector. → N.G. → Repair or replace.

O.K. ↓

9 | **CHECK E.C.U. POWER SUPPLY AND GROUND CIRCUIT.** → N.G. → Repair or replace.

O.K. ↓

10 | **TRY A KNOWN GOOD E.C.U.***

Trouble is fixed. → Replace E.C.U.

Trouble is not fixed. ↓

INSPECTION END

*: E.C.U. may be the cause of a problem, but this is rarely the case.

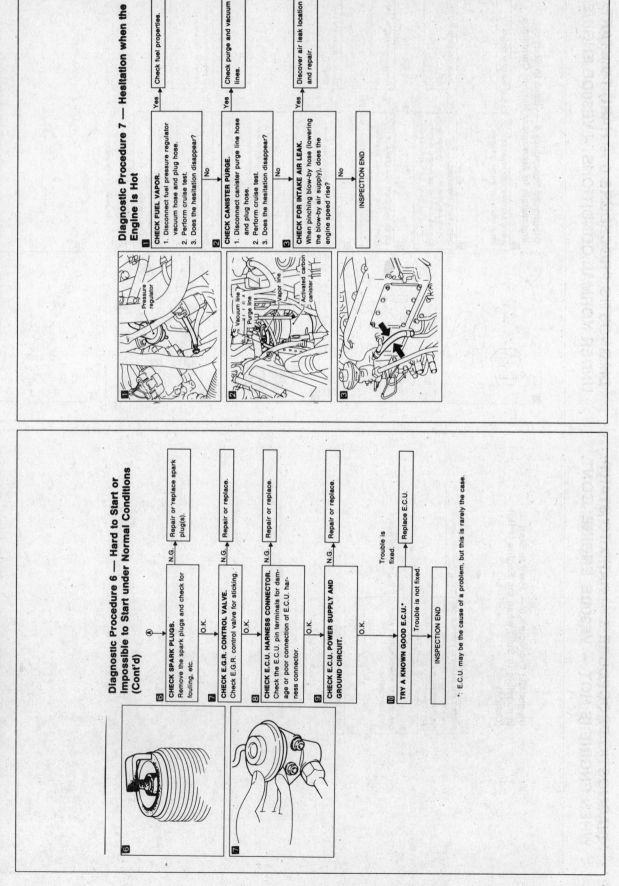

DIAGNOSTIC PROCEDURE 9 — HESITATION UNDER NORMAL CONDITIONS — VE30DE ENGINE

Diagnostic Procedure 9 — Hesitation under Normal Conditions

1 CHECK SPARK PLUGS.
Remove spark plugs and check for fouling, etc.

N.G. → Repair or replace spark plug(s).

O.K. ↓

2 CHECK EXHAUST GAS SENSOR.
1. See "M/R F/C MNT" in "DATA MONITOR" mode.
2. Maintaining engine at 2,000 rpm under no-load (with engine warmed up sufficiently.), check to make sure that the monitor fluctuates between "LEAN" and "RICH" more than 5 times during 10 seconds.

RICH→LEAN→RICH→
1 time   2 times
LEAN→RICH.......

OR

1. Set "Exhaust gas sensor monitor" in the self-diagnostic Mode II.
2. Maintaining engine at 2,000 rpm under no load, check that the RED LED on the E.C.U. or the check engine light on the instrument panel goes ON and OFF more than 5 times during 10 seconds.

Yes → Replace exhaust gas sensor.

No ↓

3 CHECK CANISTER PURGE.
1. Disconnect canister purge line hose and plug hose.
2. Perform cruise test.
3. Does the hesitation disappear?

Yes → Check purge and vacuum lines.

No ↓

4 CHECK FOR INTAKE AIR LEAK.
When pinching blow-by hose (lowering the blow-by air supply), does the engine speed rise?

Yes → Discover air leak location and repair.

No ↓

INSPECTION END

DIAGNOSTIC PROCEDURE 8 — HESITATION WHEN ENGINE IS COLD — VE30DE ENGINE

Diagnostic Procedure 8 — Hesitation when the Engine Is Cold

1 CHECK SPARK PLUGS.
Remove spark plugs and check for fouling, etc.

N.G. → Repair or replace spark plug(s).

O.K. ↓

2 CHECK FOR INTAKE AIR LEAK.
When pinching blow-by hose (lowering the blow-by air supply), does the engine speed rise?

Yes → Discover air leak location and repair.

No ↓

3 TRY A KNOWN GOOD AIR FLOW METER.

Trouble is fixed → Replace air flow meter.

Trouble is not fixed ↓

4 CHECK FOR INTAKE VALVE DEPOSITS.
If there are deposits on intake valves, remove them.

INSPECTION END

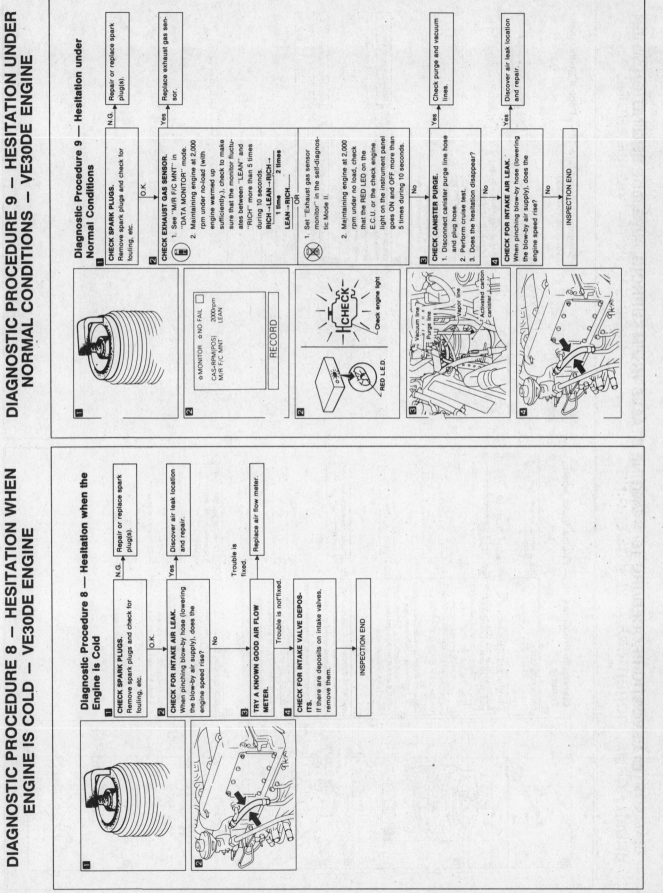

RECORD

☆ MONITOR ☆ NO FAIL ☐ 2000rpm
CAS·RPM(POS) LEAN
M/R F/C MNT

CHECK

Check engine light

RED L.E.D.

Vacuum line
Purge line
Vapor line
Activated carbon canister

DIAGNOSTIC PROCEDURE 10 — ENGINE STALLS WHEN TURNING — VE30DE ENGINE

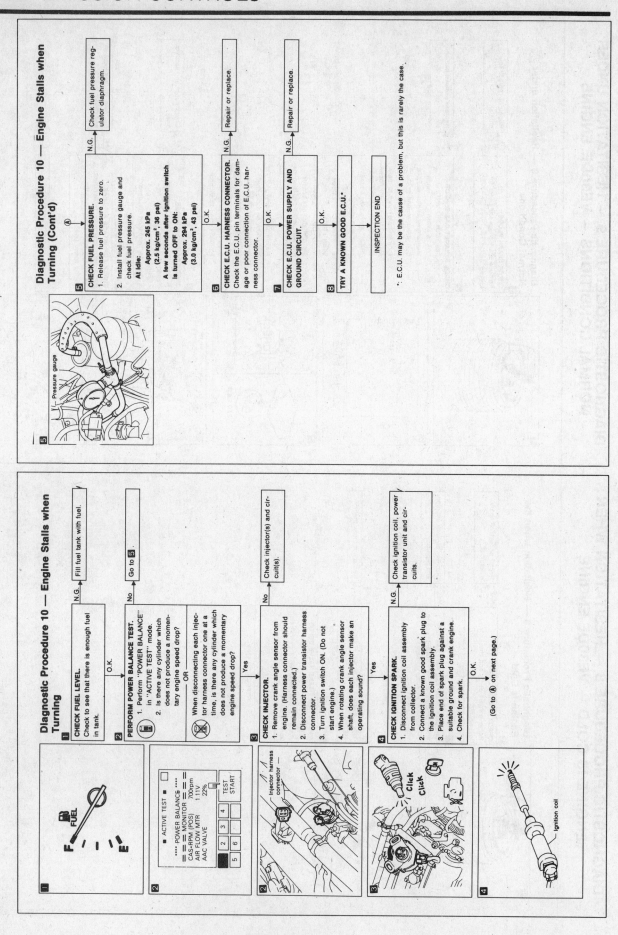

Diagnostic Procedure 10 — Engine Stalls when Turning

1 CHECK FUEL LEVEL.
Check to see that there is enough fuel in tank.

→ N.G. → Fill fuel tank with fuel.

↓ O.K.

2 PERFORM POWER BALANCE TEST.
1. Perform "POWER BALANCE" in "ACTIVE TEST" mode.
2. Is there any cylinder which does not produce a momentary engine speed drop?
OR
When disconnecting each injector harness connector one at a time, is there any cylinder which does not produce a momentary engine speed drop?

→ No → Go to 5.

```
■ ACTIVE TEST ■
···· POWER BALANCE ····
▬ ▬ MONITOR ▬ ▬
CAS-RPM (POS)    700rpm
AIR FLOW MTR     1.11V
AAC VALVE        22%
   2   3   4     TEST
   5   6         START
```

↓ Yes

3 CHECK INJECTOR.
1. Remove crank angle sensor from engine. (Harness connector should remain connected.)
2. Disconnect power transistor harness connector.
3. Turn ignition switch ON. (Do not start engine.)
4. When rotating crank angle sensor shaft, does each injector make an operating sound?

→ No → Check injector(s) and circuit(s).

Injector harness connector

↓ Yes

4 CHECK IGNITION SPARK.
1. Disconnect ignition coil assembly from collector.
2. Connect a known good spark plug to the ignition coil assembly.
3. Place end of spark plug against a suitable ground and crank engine.
4. Check for spark.

→ N.G. → Check ignition coil, power transistor unit and circuits.

Click Click

Ignition coil

↓ O.K.

(Go to Ⓐ on next page.)

Diagnostic Procedure 10 — Engine Stalls when Turning (Cont'd)

Ⓐ
↓

5 CHECK FUEL PRESSURE.
1. Release fuel pressure to zero.
2. Install fuel pressure gauge and check fuel pressure.
At idle:
Approx. 245 kPa
(2.5 kg/cm², 36 psi)
A few seconds after ignition switch is turned OFF to ON:
Approx. 294 kPa
(3.0 kg/cm², 43 psi)

Pressure gauge

→ N.G. → Check fuel pressure regulator diaphragm.

↓ O.K.

6 CHECK E.C.U. HARNESS CONNECTOR.
Check the E.C.U. pin terminals for damage or poor connection of E.C.U. harness connector.

→ N.G. → Repair or replace.

↓ O.K.

7 CHECK E.C.U. POWER SUPPLY AND GROUND CIRCUIT.

→ N.G. → Repair or replace.

↓ O.K.

8 TRY A KNOWN GOOD E.C.U.*

↓

INSPECTION END

*: E.C.U. may be the cause of a problem, but this is rarely the case.

DIAGNOSTIC PROCEDURE 11 — ENGINE STALLS WHEN ENGINE IS HOT — VE30DE ENGINE

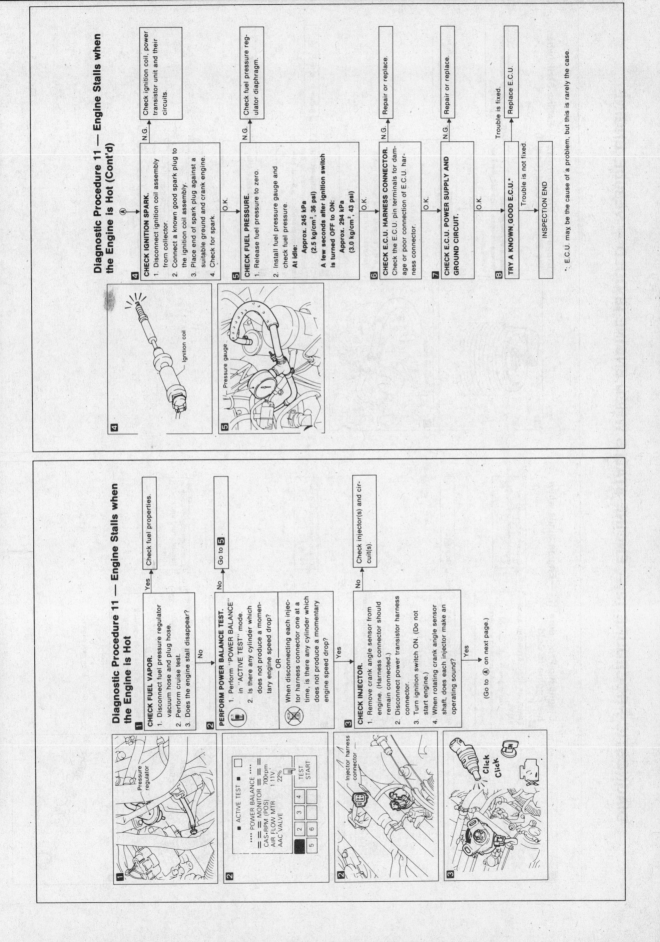

Diagnostic Procedure 11 — Engine Stalls when the Engine is Hot

1 CHECK FUEL VAPOR.
1. Disconnect fuel pressure regulator vacuum hose and plug hose.
2. Perform cruise test.
3. Does the engine stall disappear?

Yes → Check fuel properties.

No

2 PERFORM POWER BALANCE TEST.
1. Perform "POWER BALANCE" in "ACTIVE TEST" mode.
2. Is there any cylinder which does not produce a momentary engine speed drop?

OR

When disconnecting each injector harness connector one at a time, is there any cylinder which does not produce a momentary engine speed drop?

No → Go to **5**

Yes

3 CHECK INJECTOR.
1. Remove crank angle sensor from engine. (Harness connector should remain connected.)
2. Disconnect power transistor harness connector.
3. Turn ignition switch ON. (Do not start engine.)
4. When rotating crank angle sensor shaft, does each injector make an operating sound?

No → Check injector(s) and circuit(s).

Yes

(Go to Ⓐ on next page.)

Diagnostic Procedure 11 — Engine Stalls when the Engine is Hot (Cont'd)

Ⓐ

4 CHECK IGNITION SPARK.
1. Disconnect ignition coil assembly from collector.
2. Connect a known good spark plug to the ignition coil assembly.
3. Place end of spark plug against a suitable ground and crank engine.
4. Check for spark.

N.G. → Check ignition coil, power transistor unit and their circuits.

O.K.

5 CHECK FUEL PRESSURE.
1. Release fuel pressure to zero.
2. Install fuel pressure gauge and check fuel pressure.

At idle:
Approx. 245 kPa
(2.5 kg/cm², 36 psi)
A few seconds after ignition switch is turned OFF to ON:
Approx. 294 kPa
(3.0 kg/cm², 43 psi)

N.G. → Check fuel pressure regulator diaphragm.

O.K.

6 CHECK E.C.U. HARNESS CONNECTOR.
Check the E.C.U. pin terminals for damage or poor connection of E.C.U. harness connector.

N.G. → Repair or replace.

O.K.

7 CHECK E.C.U. POWER SUPPLY AND GROUND CIRCUIT.

N.G. → Repair or replace.

O.K.

8 TRY A KNOWN GOOD E.C.U.*

Trouble is fixed. → Replace E.C.U.

Trouble is not fixed.

INSPECTION END

*: E.C.U. may be the cause of a problem, but this is rarely the case.

DIAGNOSTIC PROCEDURE 12 — ENGINE STALLS WHEN ENGINE IS COLD — VE30DE ENGINE

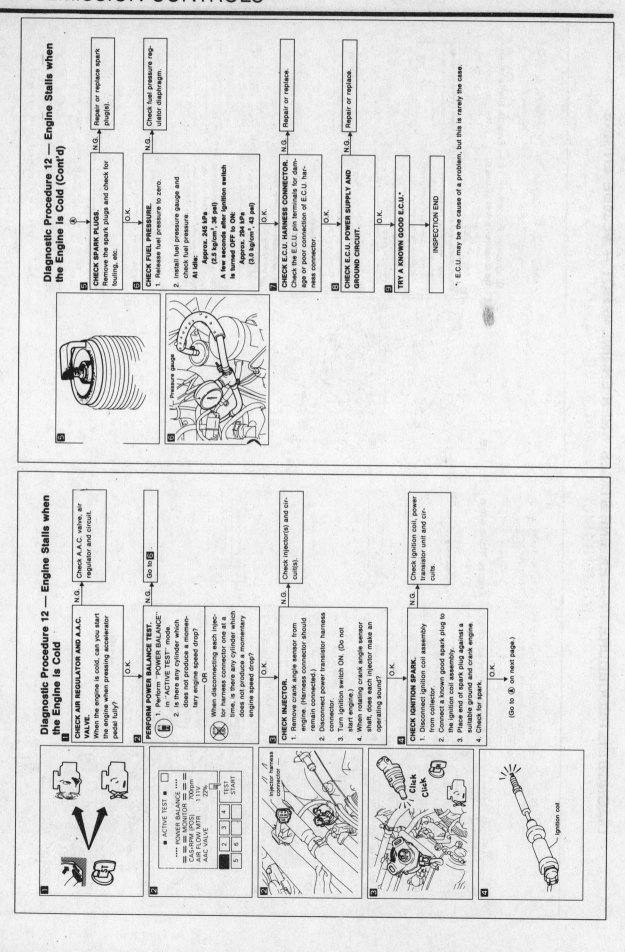

Diagnostic Procedure 12 — Engine Stalls when the Engine is Cold

1 CHECK AIR REGULATOR AND A.A.C. VALVE.
When the engine is cold, can you start the engine when pressing accelerator pedal fully?
N.G. → Check A.A.C. valve, air regulator and circuit.
O.K. ↓

2 PERFORM POWER BALANCE TEST.
1. Perform "POWER BALANCE" in "ACTIVE TEST" mode.
2. Is there any cylinder which does not produce a momentary engine speed drop?
— OR —
When disconnecting each injector harness connector one at a time, is there any cylinder which does not produce a momentary engine speed drop?
N.G. → Go to 6
O.K. ↓

ACTIVE TEST
POWER BALANCE
MONITOR
CAS·RPM (POS) 700rpm
AIR FLOW MTR 111V
AAC VALVE 22%
TEST START

3 CHECK INJECTOR.
1. Remove crank angle sensor from engine. (Harness connector should remain connected.)
2. Disconnect power transistor harness connector.
3. Turn ignition switch ON. (Do not start engine.)
4. When rotating crank angle sensor shaft, does each injector make an operating sound?
N.G. → Check injector(s) and circuit(s).
O.K. ↓

Injector harness connector

4 CHECK IGNITION SPARK.
1. Disconnect ignition coil assembly from collector.
2. Connect a known good spark plug to the ignition coil assembly.
3. Place end of spark plug against a suitable ground and crank engine.
4. Check for spark.
N.G. → Check ignition coil, power transistor unit and circuits.
O.K. ↓
(Go to Ⓐ on next page.)

Click Click

Ignition coil

Diagnostic Procedure 12 — Engine Stalls when the Engine is Cold (Cont'd)

Ⓐ ↓

5 CHECK SPARK PLUGS.
Remove the spark plugs and check for fouling, etc.
N.G. → Repair or replace spark plug(s).
O.K. ↓

6 CHECK FUEL PRESSURE.
1. Release fuel pressure to zero.
2. Install fuel pressure gauge and check fuel pressure.
At idle:
Approx. 245 kPa (2.5 kg/cm², 36 psi)
A few seconds after ignition switch is turned OFF to ON:
Approx. 294 kPa (3.0 kg/cm², 43 psi)
N.G. → Check fuel pressure regulator diaphragm.
O.K. ↓

Pressure gauge

7 CHECK E.C.U. HARNESS CONNECTOR.
Check the E.C.U. pin terminals for damage or poor connection of E.C.U. harness connector.
N.G. → Repair or replace.
O.K. ↓

8 CHECK E.C.U. POWER SUPPLY AND GROUND CIRCUIT.
N.G. → Repair or replace.
O.K. ↓

9 TRY A KNOWN GOOD E.C.U.*
↓
INSPECTION END

*: E.C.U. may be the cause of a problem, but this is rarely the case.

DIAGNOSTIC PROCEDURE 13 — ENGINE STALLS WHEN STEPPING ON ACCELERATOR MOMENTARILY — VE30DE ENGINE

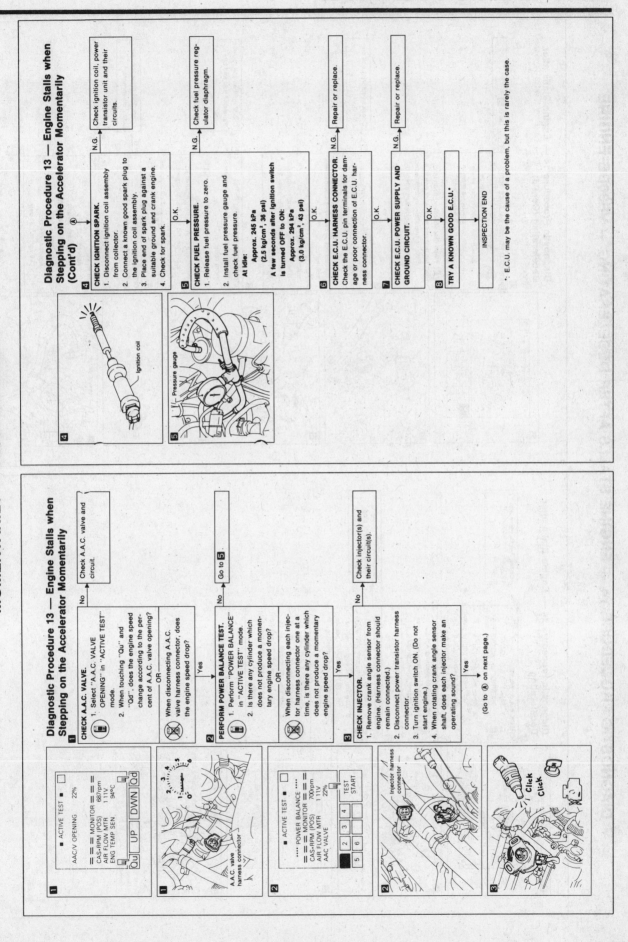

Diagnostic Procedure 13 — Engine Stalls when Stepping on the Accelerator Momentarily

1 CHECK A.A.C. VALVE.
1. Select "A.A.C. VALVE OPENING" in "ACTIVE TEST" mode.
2. When touching "Qu" and "Qd", does the engine speed change according to the percent of A.A.C. valve opening?
   OR
   When disconnecting A.A.C. valve harness connector, does the engine speed drop?

No → Check A.A.C. valve and circuit.

Yes ↓

2 PERFORM POWER BALANCE TEST.
1. Perform "POWER BALANCE" in "ACTIVE TEST" mode.
2. Is there any cylinder which does not produce a momentary engine speed drop?
   OR
   When disconnecting each injector harness connector one at a time, is there any cylinder which does not produce a momentary engine speed drop?

No → Go to **5**

Yes ↓

3 CHECK INJECTOR.
1. Remove crank angle sensor from engine. (Harness connector should remain connected.)
2. Disconnect power transistor harness connector.
3. Turn ignition switch ON. (Do not start engine.)
4. When rotating crank angle sensor shaft, does each injector make an operating sound?

No → Check injector(s) and their circuit(s).

Yes ↓

(Go to Ⓐ on next page.)

Diagnostic Procedure 13 — Engine Stalls when Stepping on the Accelerator Momentarily (Cont'd)

Ⓐ

4 CHECK IGNITION SPARK.
1. Disconnect ignition coil assembly from collector.
2. Connect a known good spark plug to the ignition coil assembly.
3. Place end of spark plug against a suitable ground and crank engine.
4. Check for spark.

N.G. → Check ignition coil, power transistor unit and their circuits.

O.K. ↓

5 CHECK FUEL PRESSURE.
1. Release fuel pressure to zero.
2. Install fuel pressure gauge and check fuel pressure.
   At idle:
   Approx. 245 kPa
   (2.5 kg/cm², 36 psi)
   A few seconds after ignition switch is turned OFF to ON:
   Approx. 294 kPa
   (3.0 kg/cm², 43 psi)

N.G. → Check fuel pressure regulator diaphragm.

O.K. ↓

6 CHECK E.C.U. HARNESS CONNECTOR.
Check the E.C.U. pin terminals for damage or poor connection of E.C.U. harness connector.

N.G. → Repair or replace.

O.K. ↓

7 CHECK E.C.U. POWER SUPPLY AND GROUND CIRCUIT.

N.G. → Repair or replace.

O.K. ↓

8 TRY A KNOWN GOOD E.C.U.*

INSPECTION END

*: E.C.U. may be the cause of a problem, but this is rarely the case.

DIAGNOSTIC PROCEDURE 14 — ENGINE STALLS AFTER DECELERATING — VE30DE ENGINE

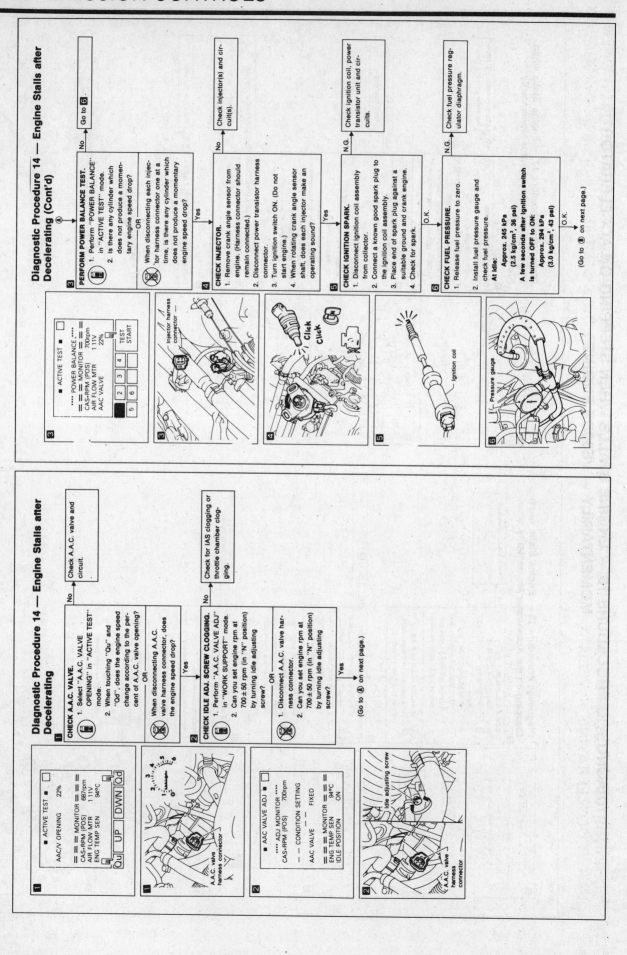

Diagnostic Procedure 14 — Engine Stalls after Decelerating

1 CHECK A.A.C. VALVE.
1. Select "A.A.C. VALVE OPENING" in "ACTIVE TEST" mode.
2. When touching "Ou" and "Od", does the engine speed change according to the percent of A.A.C. valve opening?

OR

When disconnecting A.A.C. valve harness connector, does the engine speed drop?

No → Check A.A.C. valve and circuit.

Yes

2 CHECK IDLE ADJ. SCREW CLOGGING.
1. Perform "A.A.C. VALVE ADJ" in "WORK SUPPORT" mode.
2. Can you set engine rpm at 700±50 rpm (in "N" position) by turning idle adjusting screw?

OR

1. Disconnect A.A.C. valve harness connector.
2. Can you set engine rpm at 700±50 rpm (in "N" position) by turning idle adjusting screw?

No → Check for IAS clogging or throttle chamber clogging.

Yes

(Go to Ⓐ on next page.)

Diagnostic Procedure 14 — Engine Stalls after Decelerating (Cont'd)

Ⓐ → Go to ⑥

3 PERFORM POWER BALANCE TEST.
1. Perform "POWER BALANCE" in "ACTIVE TEST" mode.
2. Is there any cylinder which does not produce a momentary engine speed drop?

OR

When disconnecting each injector harness connector one at a time, is there any cylinder which does not produce a momentary engine speed drop?

No → Check injector(s) and circuit(s).

Yes

4 CHECK INJECTOR.
1. Remove crank angle sensor from engine. (Harness connector should remain connected.)
2. Disconnect power transistor harness connector.
3. Turn ignition switch ON. (Do not start engine.)
4. When rotating crank angle sensor shaft, does each injector make an operating sound?

No → Check ignition coil, power transistor unit and circuits.

Yes

5 CHECK IGNITION SPARK.
1. Disconnect ignition coil assembly from collector.
2. Connect a known good spark plug to the ignition coil assembly.
3. Place end of spark plug against a suitable ground and crank engine.
4. Check for spark.

N.G. → Check ignition coil, power transistor unit and circuits.

O.K.

6 CHECK FUEL PRESSURE.
1. Release fuel pressure to zero.
2. Install fuel pressure gauge and check fuel pressure.

At idle:
Approx. 245 kPa
(2.5 kg/cm², 36 psi)

A few seconds after ignition switch is turned OFF to ON:
Approx. 294 kPa
(3.0 kg/cm², 43 psi)

N.G. → Check fuel pressure regulator diaphragm.

O.K.

(Go to Ⓑ on next page.)

DIAGNOSTIC PROCEDURE 15 — ENGINE STALLS WHEN ACCELERATING OR CRUISING — VE30DE ENGINE

Diagnostic Procedure 15 — Engine Stalls when Accelerating or Cruising

1 PERFORM POWER BALANCE TEST.
1. Perform "POWER BALANCE" in "ACTIVE TEST" mode.
2. Is there any cylinder which does not produce a momentary engine speed drop?

OR

When disconnecting each injector harness connector one at a time, is there any cylinder which does not produce a momentary engine speed drop?

→ No → Go to **4**

| Yes ↓

2 CHECK INJECTOR.
1. Remove crank angle sensor from engine. (Harness connector should remain connected.)
2. Disconnect power transistor harness connector.
3. Turn ignition switch ON. (Do not start engine.)
4. When rotating crank angle sensor shaft, does each injector make an operating sound?

→ No → Check injector(s) and circuit(s).

| Yes ↓

3 CHECK IGNITION SPARK.
1. Disconnect ignition coil assembly from collector.
2. Connect a known good spark plug to the ignition coil assembly.
3. Place end of spark plug against a suitable ground and crank engine.
4. Check for spark.

→ N.G. → Check ignition coil, power transistor unit and circuits.

| O.K.

(Go to Ⓐ on next page.)

1
■ ACTIVE TEST ■
‥‥ POWER BALANCE ‥‥
‥‥ MONITOR ‥‥
CAS-RPM (POS)   700rpm
AIR FLOW MTR   1.11V
AAC VALVE   22%

| 2 | 3 | 4 |
| 5 | 6 |

TEST START

1 Injector harness connector

2 Click Click

3 Ignition coil

DIAGNOSTIC PROCEDURE 14 — ENGINE STALLS AFTER DECELERATING — VE30DE ENGINE, CONT.

Diagnostic Procedure 14 — Engine Stalls after Decelerating (Cont'd)

Ⓑ ↓

7 CHECK EXHAUST GAS SENSOR.
1. See "M/R F/C MNT" in "DATA MONITOR" mode.
2. Maintaining engine at 2,000 rpm under no-load (with engine warmed up sufficiently), check to make sure that the monitor fluctuates between "LEAN" and "RICH" more than 5 times during 10 seconds.

RICH→LEAN→RICH→
1 time

LEAN→RICH→.......
2 times

OR

1. Set "Exhaust gas sensor monitor" in the self- diagnostic Mode II.
2. Maintaining engine at 2,000 rpm under no load, check that the RED LED on the E.C.U. or the check engine light on the instrument panel goes ON and OFF more than 5 times during 10 seconds.

→ N.G. → Replace exhaust gas sensor.

| O.K.

8 CHECK E.C.U. HARNESS CONNECTOR.
Check the E.C.U. pin terminals for damage or poor connection of E.C.U. harness connector.

→ N.G. → Repair or replace.

| O.K.

9 CHECK E.C.U. POWER SUPPLY AND GROUND CIRCUIT.

→ N.G. → Repair or replace.

| O.K.

10 TRY A KNOWN GOOD E.C.U.*

↓

INSPECTION END

* E.C.U. may be the cause of a problem, but this is rarely the case.

7
☆ MONITOR ☆ NO FAIL
CAS-RPM(POS)   2000rpm
M/R F/C MNT   LEAN

RECORD

7 CHECK
Check engine light

RED L.E.D.

DIAGNOSTIC PROCEDURE 16 — ENGINE STALLS WHEN ELECTRICAL LOAD IS HEAVY VE30DE ENGINE

Diagnostic Procedure 16 — Engine Stalls when the Electrical Load Is Heavy

1 CHECK BATTERY AND ALTERNATOR.
Check battery and alternator condition.

→ N.G. → Repair or replace.

O.K.

2 PERFORM POWER BALANCE TEST.
1. Perform "POWER BALANCE" in "ACTIVE TEST" mode.
2. Is there any cylinder which does not produce a momentary engine speed drop?

OR

When disconnecting each injector harness connector one at a time, is there any cylinder which does not produce a momentary engine speed drop?

→ No → Go to **5**

Yes

3 CHECK INJECTOR.
1. Remove crank angle sensor from engine. (Harness connector should remain connected.)
2. Disconnect power transistor harness connector.
3. Turn ignition switch ON. (Do not start engine.)
4. While rotating crank angle sensor shaft, does each injector make an operating sound?

→ No → Check injector(s) and circuit(s).

Yes

4 CHECK IGNITION SPARK.
1. Disconnect ignition coil assembly from collector.
2. Connect a known good spark plug to the ignition coil assembly.
3. Place end of spark plug against a suitable ground and crank engine.
4. Check for spark.

→ N.G. → Check ignition coil, power transistor unit and circuits.

O.K.

(Go to Ⓐ on next page.)

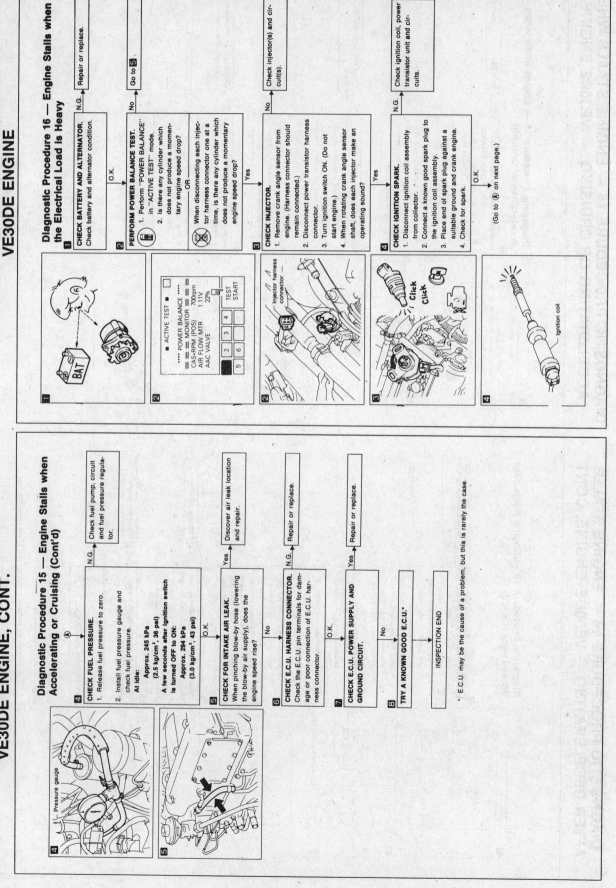

1

2
- ■ ACTIVE TEST ■
- ···· POWER BALANCE ····
- CAS•RPM (POS)   700rpm
- AIR FLOW MTR   111V
- AAC VALVE   22%

		4
1	2	3	
	5	6	

TEST START

2 Injector harness connector

3 Click Click

4 Ignition coil

DIAGNOSTIC PROCEDURE 15 — ENGINE STALLS WHEN ACCELERATING OR CRUISING VE30DE ENGINE, CONT.

Diagnostic Procedure 15 — Engine Stalls when Accelerating or Cruising (Cont'd)

Ⓐ

4 CHECK FUEL PRESSURE.
1. Release fuel pressure to zero.
2. Install fuel pressure gauge and check fuel pressure.
At idle:
   Approx. 245 kPa
   (2.5 kg/cm², 36 psi)
A few seconds after ignition switch is turned OFF to ON:
   Approx. 294 kPa
   (3.0 kg/cm², 43 psi)

→ N.G. → Check fuel pump, circuit and fuel pressure regulator.

O.K.

5 CHECK FOR INTAKE AIR LEAK.
When pinching blow-by hose (lowering the blow-by air supply), does the engine speed rise?

→ Yes → Discover air leak location and repair.

No

6 CHECK E.C.U. HARNESS CONNECTOR.
Check the E.C.U. pin terminals for damage or poor connection of E.C.U. harness connector.

→ N.G. → Repair or replace.

O.K.

7 CHECK E.C.U. POWER SUPPLY AND GROUND CIRCUIT.

→ No → Repair or replace.

Yes

8 TRY A KNOWN GOOD E.C.U.*

INSPECTION END

* E.C.U. may be the cause of a problem, but this is rarely the case.

4 Pressure gauge

5

DIAGNOSTIC PROCEDURE 17 — LACK OF POWER AND STUMBLE — VE30DE ENGINE

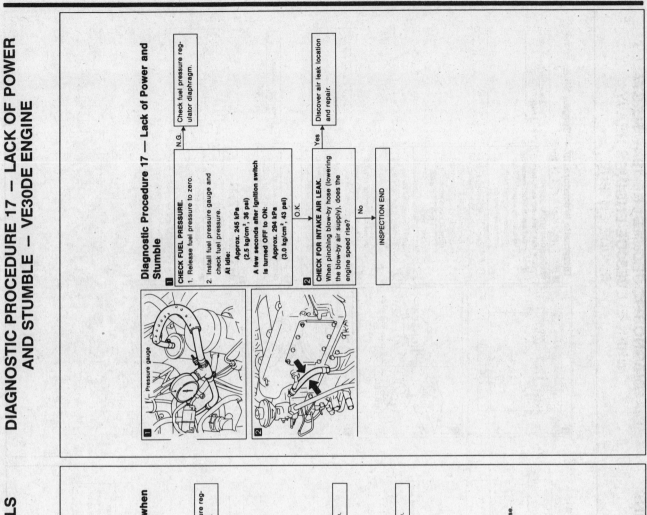

Diagnostic Procedure 17 — Lack of Power and Stumble

1 **CHECK FUEL PRESSURE.**
1. Release fuel pressure to zero.
2. Install fuel pressure gauge and check fuel pressure.

At Idle:
Approx. 245 kPa
(2.5 kg/cm², 36 psi)

A few seconds after ignition switch is turned OFF to ON:
Approx. 294 kPa
(3.0 kg/cm², 43 psi)

N.G. → Check fuel pressure regulator diaphragm.

O.K.

2 **CHECK FOR INTAKE AIR LEAK.**
When pinching blow-by hose (lowering the blow-by air supply), does the engine speed rise?

Yes → Discover air leak location and repair.

No

INSPECTION END

1 Pressure gauge

2

DIAGNOSTIC PROCEDURE 16 — ENGINE STALLS WHEN ELECTRICAL LOAD IS HEAVY — VE30DE ENGINE, CONT.

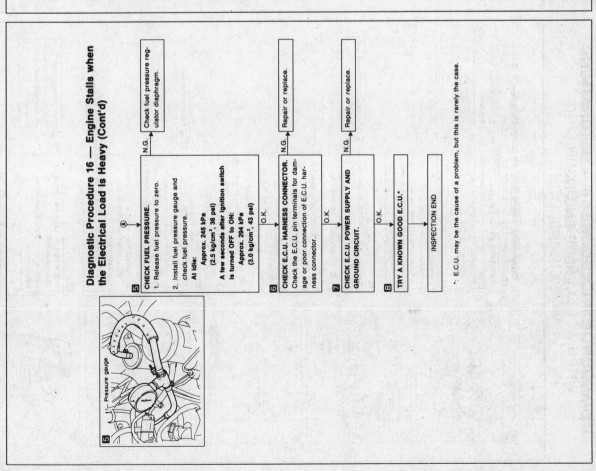

Diagnostic Procedure 16 — Engine Stalls when the Electrical Load is Heavy (Cont'd)

Ⓐ

5 **CHECK FUEL PRESSURE.**
1. Release fuel pressure to zero.
2. Install fuel pressure gauge and check fuel pressure.

At Idle:
Approx. 245 kPa
(2.5 kg/cm², 36 psi)

A few seconds after ignition switch is turned OFF to ON:
Approx. 294 kPa
(3.0 kg/cm², 43 psi)

N.G. → Check fuel pressure regulator diaphragm.

O.K.

6 **CHECK E.C.U. HARNESS CONNECTOR.**
Check the E.C.U. pin terminals for damage or poor connection of E.C.U. harness connector.

N.G. → Repair or replace.

O.K.

7 **CHECK E.C.U. POWER SUPPLY AND GROUND CIRCUIT.**

N.G. → Repair or replace.

O.K.

8 **TRY A KNOWN GOOD E.C.U.***

INSPECTION END

5 Pressure gauge

*: E.C.U. may be the cause of a problem, but this is rarely the case.

DIAGNOSTIC PROCEDURE 19 — SURGE VE30DE ENGINE

Diagnostic Procedure 19 — Surge

1 CHECK EXHAUST GAS SENSOR.
1. See "M/R F/C MNT" in "DATA MONITOR" mode.
2. Maintaining engine at 2,000 rpm under no-load (with engine warmed up sufficiently.), check to make sure that the monitor fluctuates between "LEAN" and "RICH" more than 5 times during 10 seconds.

   RICH→LEAN→RICH→
   1 time   2 times
   LEAN→RICH→
   — OR —

1. Set "Exhaust gas sensor monitor" in the self-diagnostic Mode II.
2. Maintaining engine at 2,000 rpm under no load, check that the RED LED on the E.C.U. or the check engine light on the instrument panel goes ON and OFF more than 5 times during 10 seconds.

   N.G. → Replace exhaust gas sensor(s).

   O.K.

2 CHECK E.G.R. CONTROL VALVE.
Check E.G.R. control valve for sticking.

   N.G. → Repair or replace.

   O.K.

3 TRY A KNOWN GOOD E.C.U.

   O.K.

   INSPECTION END

DIAGNOSTIC PROCEDURE 18 — DETONATION VE30DE ENGINE

Diagnostic Procedure 18 — Detonation

1 CHECK FOR INTAKE AIR LEAK.
When pinching blow-by hose (lowering the blow-by air supply), does the engine rpm rise?

   Yes → Discover air leak location and repair.

   No

2 CHECK E.G.R. OPERATION.
1. Apply vacuum directly to the E.G.R. valve using a handy vacuum pump.
2. Check to see that the engine runs rough or dies.

   No → Check E.G.R. valve for sticking.

   Yes

3 CHECK E.G.R. CONTROL SOLENOID VALVE.
1. Select "E.G.R. CONT SOL VALVE" in "ACTIVE TEST" mode.
2. Turn E.G.R. control solenoid valve ON and OFF.
3. Check operating sound.
   — OR —
1. Disconnect E.G.R. control solenoid valve harness connector.
2. Supply E.G.R. control solenoid valve terminals with battery current and check operating sound.

   N.G. → Check solenoid valve and circuit.

   O.K.

4 CHECK VACUUM HOSES.
Check the following vacuum hoses for clogging, cracks and poor connection.
a) Vacuum hose between E.G.R. control valve and E.G.R. control solenoid valve.
b) Vacuum hose between E.G.R. control solenoid valve and throttle chamber port.
c) Vacuum hose between E.G.R. control solenoid valve and air duct.

   N.G. → Repair or replace.

   O.K.

5 CHECK FOR OIL LEAK TO COMBUSTION CHAMBER.
Remove spark plugs and check for fouling with oil.

   Yes → Check pistons, piston rings, valves, valve seats, valve oil seal, engine oil level, etc.

   No

   INSPECTION END

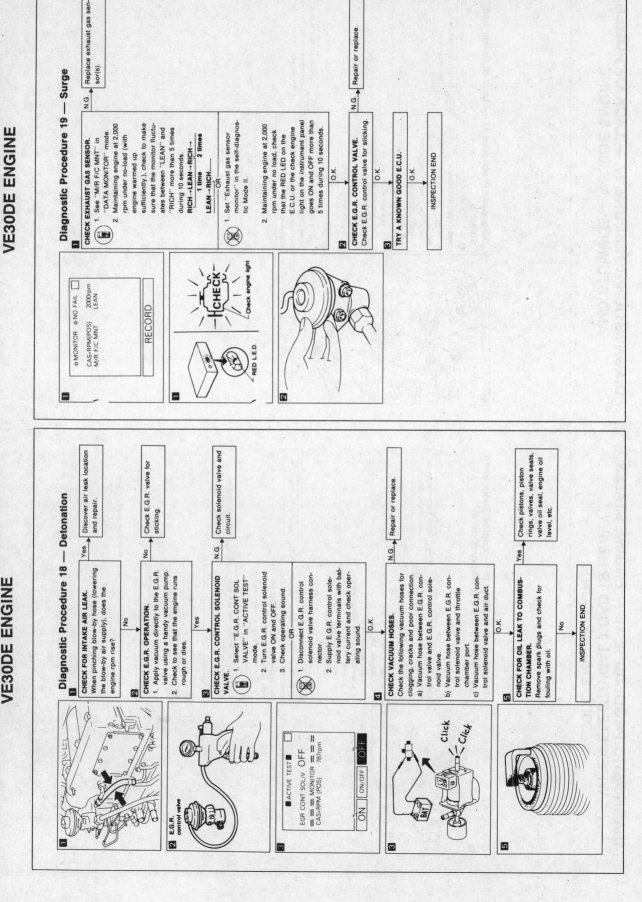

☆ MONITOR ☆ NO FAIL □
CAS-RPM(POS)   2000rpm
M/R F/C MNT   LEAN

RECORD

CHECK — Check engine light
RED L.E.D.

E.G.R. control valve

■ ACTIVE TEST ■
EGR CONT SOL/V OFF
= = = MONITOR = = =
CAS-RPM (POS)   787rpm
ON ON/OFF OFF

Click Click
BAT

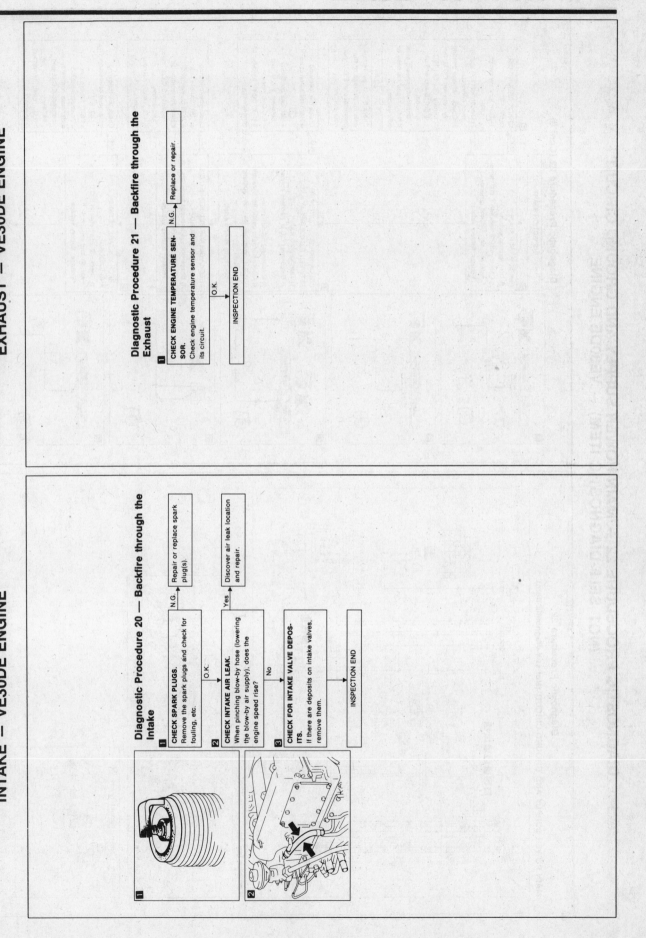

DIAGNOSTIC PROCEDURE 21 — BACKFIRE THROUGH EXHAUST — VE30DE ENGINE

Diagnostic Procedure 21 — Backfire through the Exhaust

1. CHECK ENGINE TEMPERATURE SENSOR.
Check engine temperature sensor and its circuit.

N.G. → Replace or repair.

O.K. → INSPECTION END

DIAGNOSTIC PROCEDURE 20 — BACKFIRE THROUGH INTAKE — VE30DE ENGINE

Diagnostic Procedure 20 — Backfire through the Intake

1. CHECK SPARK PLUGS.
Remove the spark plugs and check for fouling, etc.

N.G. → Repair or replace spark plug(s).

O.K. ↓

2. CHECK INTAKE AIR LEAK.
When pinching blow-by hose (lowering the blow-by air supply), does the engine speed rise?

Yes → Discover air leak location and repair.

No ↓

3. CHECK FOR INTAKE VALVE DEPOSITS.
If there are deposits on intake valves, remove them.

↓

INSPECTION END

DIAGNOSTIC PROCEDURE 22 — MAIN POWER SUPPLY AND GROUND CIRCUIT (NOT SELF-DIAGNOSTIC ITEM) — VE30DE ENGINE

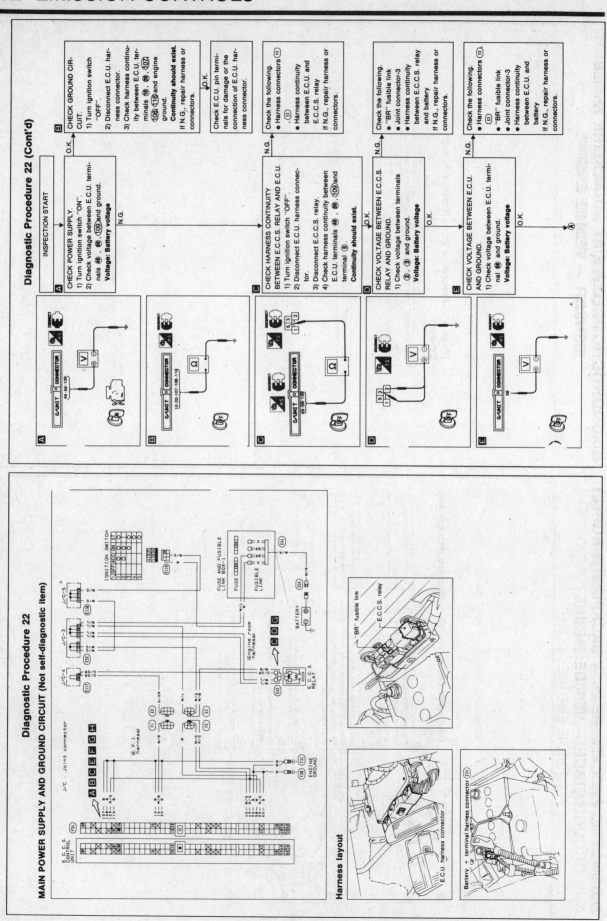

DIAGNOSTIC PROCEDURE 23 — CRANK ANGLE SENSOR — VE30DE ENGINE

Diagnostic Procedure 23

CRANK ANGLE SENSOR (Code No. 11)

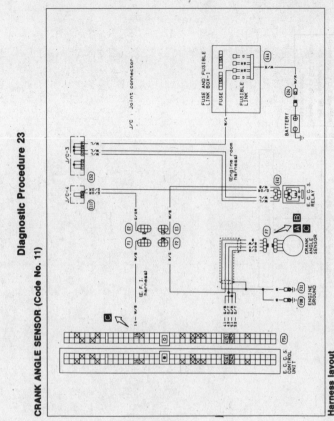

Harness layout

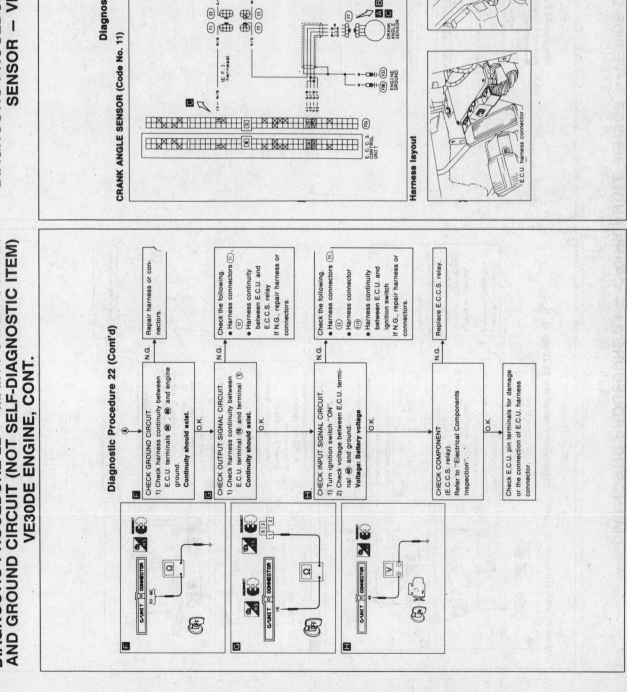

DIAGNOSTIC PROCEDURE 22 — MAIN POWER SUPPLY AND GROUND CIRCUIT (NOT SELF-DIAGNOSTIC ITEM) VE30DE ENGINE, CONT.

Diagnostic Procedure 22 (Cont'd)

Ⓐ

F CHECK GROUND CIRCUIT.
1) Check harness continuity between E.C.U. terminals ㊿ , ㊿ and engine ground.
Continuity should exist.

— N.G. → Repair harness or connectors.

O.K.

G CHECK OUTPUT SIGNAL CIRCUIT.
1) Check harness continuity between E.C.U. terminal ⑯ and terminal ①.
Continuity should exist.

— N.G. → Check the following.
● Harness connectors Ⓕ⑪
Ⓕ②
● Harness continuity between E.C.U. and E.C.C.S. relay
If N.G., repair harness or connectors.

O.K.

H CHECK INPUT SIGNAL CIRCUIT.
1) Turn ignition switch "ON".
2) Check voltage between E.C.U. terminal ㊽ and ground.
Voltage: Battery voltage

— N.G. → Check the following.
● Harness connectors Ⓕ②
Ⓕ③
● Harness connector
● Harness continuity between E.C.U. and ignition switch
If N.G., repair harness or connectors.

O.K.

CHECK COMPONENT
(E.C.C.S. relay).
Refer to "Electrical Components Inspection".

— N.G. → Replace E.C.C.S. relay.

O.K.

Check E.C.U. pin terminals for damage or the connection of E.C.U. harness connector.

DIAGNOSTIC PROCEDURE 23 – CRANK ANGLE SENSOR – VE30DE ENGINE, CONT.

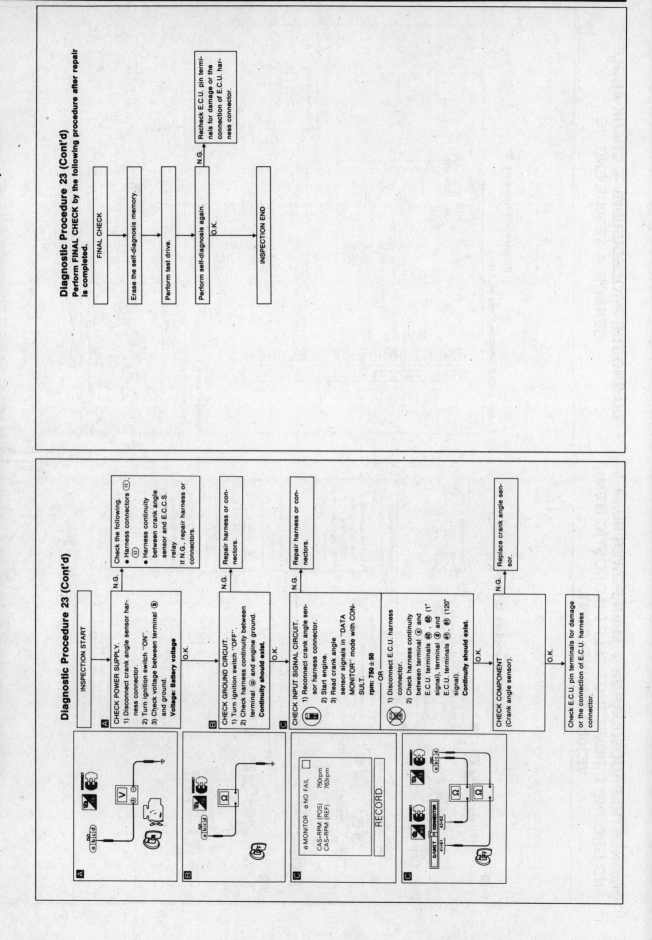

Diagnostic Procedure 23 (Cont'd)

INSPECTION START

A CHECK POWER SUPPLY.
1) Disconnect crank angle sensor harness connector.
2) Turn ignition switch "ON".
3) Check voltage between terminal ① and ground.
Voltage: Battery voltage

→ N.G. → Check the following.
- Harness connectors ®
- ® Harness continuity between crank angle sensor and E.C.C.S. relay
If N.G., repair harness or connectors.

O.K. ↓

B CHECK GROUND CIRCUIT.
1) Turn ignition switch "OFF".
2) Check harness continuity between terminal ② and engine ground.
Continuity should exist.

→ N.G. → Repair harness or connectors.

O.K. ↓

C CHECK INPUT SIGNAL CIRCUIT.
1) Reconnect crank angle sensor harness connector.
2) Start engine.
3) Read crank angle sensor signals in "DATA MONITOR" mode with CONSULT.
rpm: 750 ± 50
OR
1) Disconnect E.C.U. harness connector.
2) Check harness continuity between terminal ① and E.C.U. terminals ④, ㉟ (1° signal), terminals ③ and E.C.U. terminals ㉟, ㉟ (120° signal).
Continuity should exist.

→ N.G. → Repair harness or connectors.

O.K. ↓

CHECK COMPONENT (Crank angle sensor).

→ N.G. → Replace crank angle sensor.

O.K. ↓

Check E.C.U. pin terminals for damage or the connection of E.C.U. harness connector.

Diagnostic Procedure 23 (Cont'd)
Perform FINAL CHECK by the following procedure after repair is completed.

FINAL CHECK
↓
Erase the self-diagnosis memory.
↓
Perform test drive.
↓
Perform self-diagnosis again.

→ N.G. → Recheck E.C.U. pin terminals for damage or the connection of E.C.U. harness connector.

O.K. ↓

INSPECTION END

A

B

C ☆MONITOR ☆NO FAIL
CAS-RPM (POS)   750rpm
CAS-RPM (REF)   763rpm

RECORD

C C·UNIT CONNECTOR
41•45   42•52

DIAGNOSTIC PROCEDURE 24 — AIR FLOW METER — VE30DE ENGINE

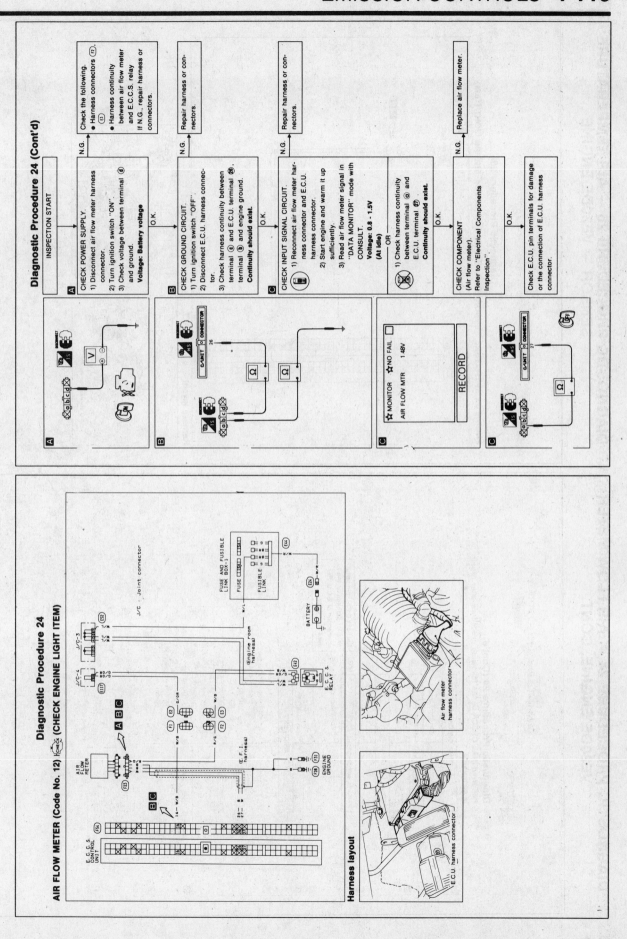

Diagnostic Procedure 24 (Cont'd)

INSPECTION START

A CHECK POWER SUPPLY.
1) Disconnect air flow meter harness connector.
2) Turn ignition switch "ON".
3) Check voltage between terminal ⓔ and ground.
Voltage: Battery voltage

N.G. → Check the following.
● Harness connectors ⑫
● Harness continuity between air flow meter and E.C.C.S. relay
If N.G., repair harness or connectors.

O.K. ↓

B CHECK GROUND CIRCUIT.
1) Turn ignition switch "OFF".
2) Disconnect E.C.U. harness connector.
3) Check harness continuity between terminal ⓓ and E.C.U. terminal ㉖, terminal ⓑ and engine ground.
Continuity should exist.

N.G. → Repair harness or connectors.

O.K. ↓

C CHECK INPUT SIGNAL CIRCUIT.
1) Reconnect air flow meter harness connector and E.C.U. harness connector.
2) Start engine and warm it up sufficiently.
3) Read air flow meter signal in "DATA MONITOR" mode with CONSULT.
Voltage: 0.8 - 1.5V
(At Idle)

OR

1) Check harness continuity between terminal ⓒ and E.C.U. terminal ㉗.
Continuity should exist.

N.G. → Repair harness or connectors.

O.K. ↓

CHECK COMPONENT
(Air flow meter).
Refer to "Electrical Components Inspection".

O.K. ↓

Check E.C.U. pin terminals for damage or the connection of E.C.U. harness connector.

N.G. → Replace air flow meter.

A

B

C MONITOR ✩ NO FAIL
AIR FLOW MTR   1.48V

RECORD

C

Diagnostic Procedure 24

AIR FLOW METER (Code No. 12) (CHECK ENGINE LIGHT ITEM)

Harness layout

DIAGNOSTIC PROCEDURE 25 — AIR TEMPERATURE SENSOR — VE30DE ENGINE

Diagnostic Procedure 25

ENGINE TEMPERATURE SENSOR (Code No. 13) (CHECK ENGINE LIGHT ITEM)

DIAGNOSTIC PROCEDURE 24 — AIR FLOW METER VE30DE ENGINE, CONT.

Diagnostic Procedure 24 (Cont'd)

Perform FINAL CHECK by the following procedure after repair is completed.

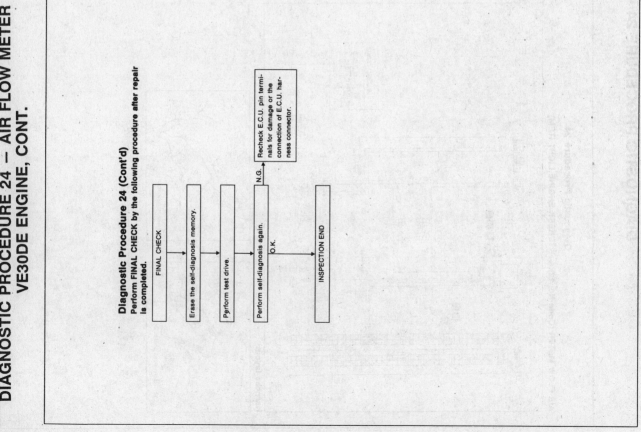

FINAL CHECK

Erase the self-diagnosis memory.

Perform test drive.

Perform self-diagnosis again. — N.G. → Recheck E.C.U. pin terminals for damage or the connection of E.C.U. harness connector.

O.K.

INSPECTION END

DIAGNOSTIC PROCEDURE 25 — AIR TEMPERATURE SENSOR — VE30DE ENGINE, CONT.

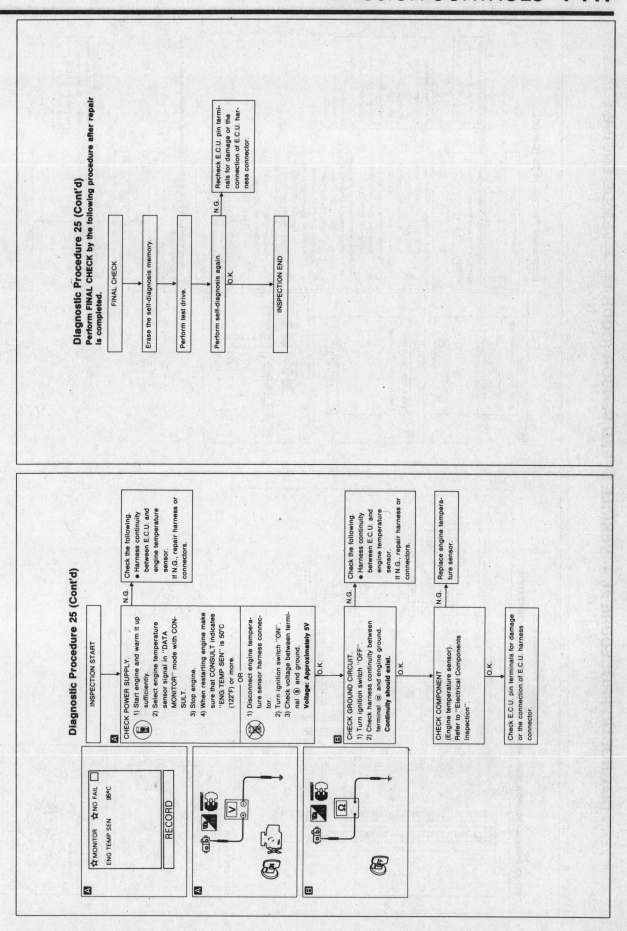

Diagnostic Procedure 25 (Cont'd)
Perform FINAL CHECK by the following procedure after repair is completed.

FINAL CHECK

↓

Erase the self-diagnosis memory.

↓

Perform test drive.

↓

Perform self-diagnosis again. → N.G. → Recheck E.C.U. pin terminals for damage or the connection of E.C.U. harness connector.

↓ O.K.

INSPECTION END

Diagnostic Procedure 25 (Cont'd)

INSPECTION START

↓

Ⓐ CHECK POWER SUPPLY.
1) Start engine and warm it up sufficiently.
2) Select engine temperature sensor signal in "DATA MONITOR" mode with CONSULT.
3) Stop engine.
4) When restarting engine make sure that CONSULT indicates "ENG TEMP SEN" is 50°C (122°F) or more.
OR
1) Disconnect engine temperature sensor harness connector.
2) Turn ignition switch "ON".
3) Check voltage between terminal ⓐ and ground.
Voltage: Approximately 5V

→ N.G. → Check the following.
● Harness continuity between E.C.U. and engine temperature sensor.
If N.G., repair harness or connectors.

↓ O.K.

Ⓑ CHECK GROUND CIRCUIT.
1) Turn ignition switch "OFF".
2) Check harness continuity between terminal ⓑ and engine ground.
Continuity should exist.

→ N.G. → Check the following.
● Harness continuity between E.C.U. and engine temperature sensor.
If N.G., repair harness or connectors.

↓ O.K.

CHECK COMPONENT
(Engine temperature sensor).
Refer to "Electrical Components Inspection".

→ N.G. → Replace engine temperature sensor.

↓ O.K.

Check E.C.U. pin terminals for damage or the connection of E.C.U. harness connector.

Ⓐ ☆ MONITOR ☆ NO FAIL

ENG TEMP SEN   95°C

RECORD

Ⓐ (test setup with voltmeter V)

Ⓑ (test setup with ohmmeter Ω)

DIAGNOSTIC PROCEDURE 26 — VEHICLE SPEED SENSOR (CODE 14) — VE30DE ENGINE

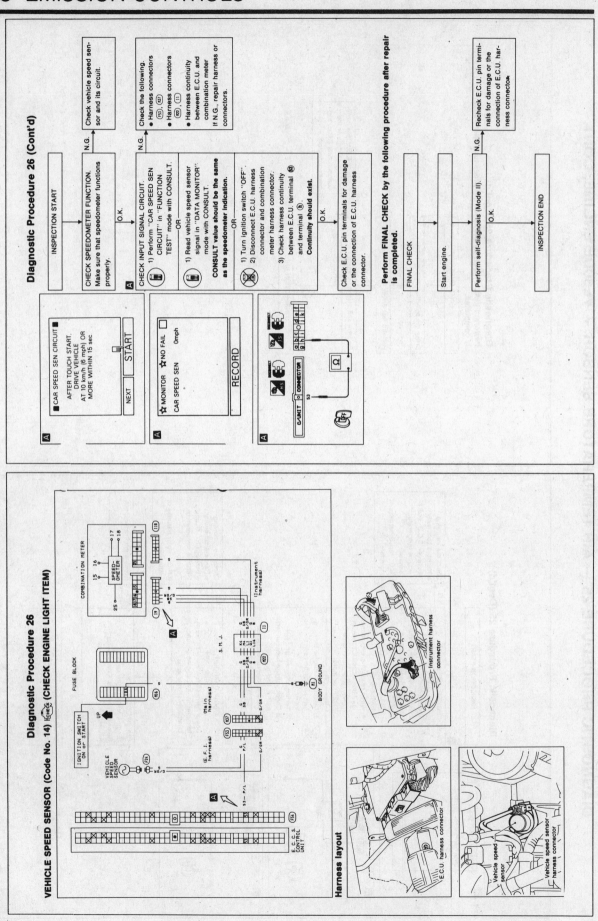

Diagnostic Procedure 26 (Cont'd)

INSPECTION START

CHECK SPEEDOMETER FUNCTION.
Make sure that speedometer functions properly.

N.G. → Check vehicle speed sensor and its circuit.

O.K.

CHECK INPUT SIGNAL CIRCUIT.
1) Perform "CAR SPEED SEN CIRCUIT" in "FUNCTION TEST" mode with CONSULT.

OR

1) Read vehicle speed sensor signal in "DATA MONITOR" mode with CONSULT.
CONSULT value should be the same as the speedometer indication.

OR

1) Turn ignition switch "OFF".
2) Disconnect E.C.U. harness connector and combination meter harness connector.
3) Check harness continuity between E.C.U. terminal and terminal.
Continuity should exist.

N.G. → Check the following.
● Harness connectors
● Harness connectors
● Harness continuity between E.C.U. and combination meter
If N.G., repair harness or connectors.

O.K.

Check E.C.U. pin terminals for damage or the connection of E.C.U. harness connector.

Perform FINAL CHECK by the following procedure after repair **is completed.**

FINAL CHECK

Start engine.

Perform self-diagnosis (Mode II).

N.G. → Recheck E.C.U. pin terminals for damage or the connection of E.C.U. harness connector.

O.K.

INSPECTION END

Diagnostic Procedure 26

VEHICLE SPEED SENSOR (Code No. 14) (CHECK ENGINE LIGHT ITEM)

Harness layout

DIAGNOSTIC PROCEDURE 27 — IGNITION SIGNAL (CODE 21) — VE30DE ENGINE

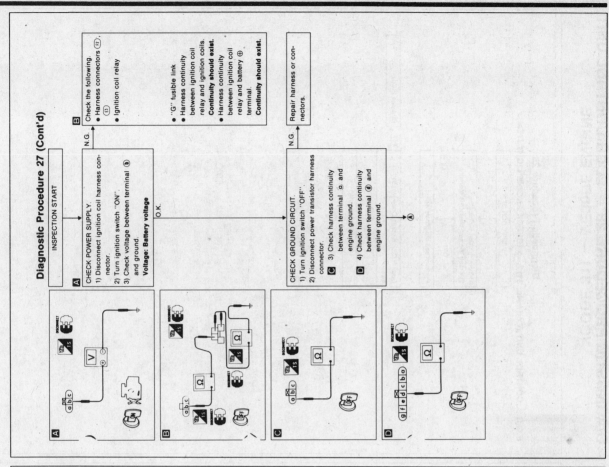

Diagnostic Procedure 27 (Cont'd)

INSPECTION START

A CHECK POWER SUPPLY.
1) Disconnect ignition coil harness connector.
2) Turn ignition switch "ON".
3) Check voltage between terminal ⓑ and ground.
Voltage: Battery voltage

N.G. → **B** Check the following.
● Harness connectors ⑫
● Ignition coil relay
● "G" fusible link
● Harness continuity between ignition coil relay and ignition coils. **Continuity should exist.**
● Harness continuity between ignition coil relay and battery ⊕ terminal. **Continuity should exist.**

O.K. ↓

CHECK GROUND CIRCUIT.
1) Turn ignition switch "OFF".
2) Disconnect power transistor harness connector.
C 3) Check harness continuity between terminal ⓖ and engine ground.
D 4) Check harness continuity between terminal ⓓ and engine ground.

N.G. → Repair harness or connectors.

O.K. → Ⓐ

Diagnostic Procedure 27

IGNITION SIGNAL (Code No. 21)

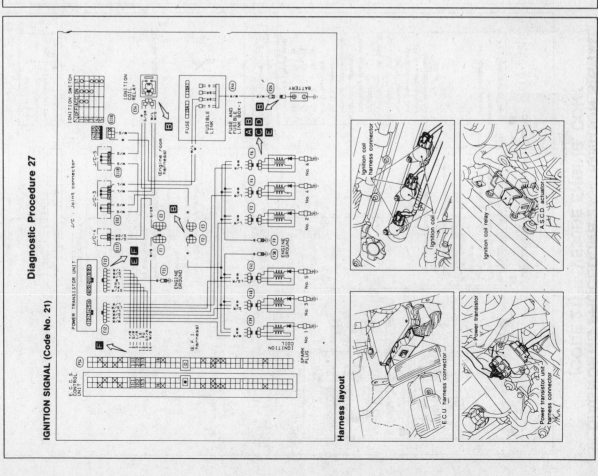

Harness layout

DIAGNOSTIC PROCEDURE 28 – ECCS CONTROL UNIT (CODE 31) – VE30DE ENGINE

DIAGNOSTIC PROCEDURE 27 – IGNITION SIGNAL (CODE 21) – VE30DE ENGINE, CONT.

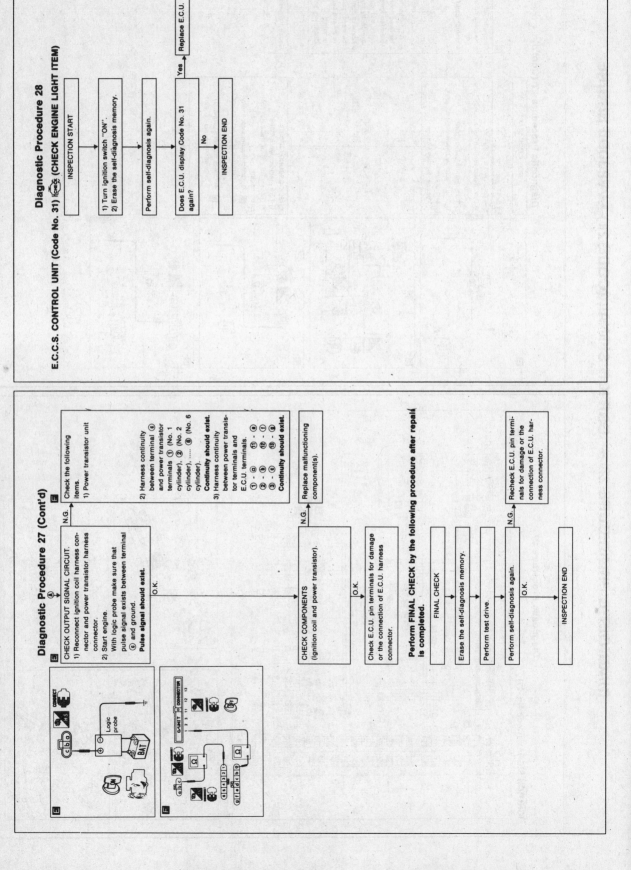

Diagnostic Procedure 28

E.C.C.S. CONTROL UNIT (Code No. 31) [CHECK ENGINE LIGHT ITEM]

INSPECTION START

1) Turn ignition switch "ON".
2) Erase the self-diagnosis memory.

Perform self-diagnosis again.

Does E.C.U. display Code No. 31 again? — Yes → Replace E.C.U.

No

INSPECTION END

Diagnostic Procedure 27 (Cont'd)

E | CHECK OUTPUT SIGNAL CIRCUIT.
1) Reconnect ignition coil harness connector and power transistor harness connector.
2) Start engine.
With logic probe make sure that pulse signal exists between terminal ⓔ and ground.
Pulse signal should exist.

N.G. → Check the following items.
1) Power transistor unit

2) Harness continuity between terminal ⓔ and power transistor terminals ① (No. 1 cylinder), ② (No. 2 cylinder), ... ⑥ (No. 6 cylinder).
Continuity should exist.
3) Harness continuity between power transistor terminals and E.C.U. terminals.
① – ⑫   ⑪ – ⑪
② – ⑩   ⑫ – ⑩
② – ⑥   ⑬ – ①
Continuity should exist.

O.K.

CHECK COMPONENTS (Ignition coil and power transistor). — N.G. → Replace malfunctioning component(s).

O.K.

Check E.C.U. pin terminals for damage or the connection of E.C.U. harness connector.

Perform FINAL CHECK by the following procedure after repair is completed.

FINAL CHECK

Erase the self-diagnosis memory.

Perform test drive.

Perform self-diagnosis again. — N.G. → Recheck E.C.U. pin terminals for damage or the connection of E.C.U. harness connector.

O.K.

INSPECTION END

DIAGNOSTIC PROCEDURE 29 — EGR FUNCTION (CODE 32) — VE30DE ENGINE

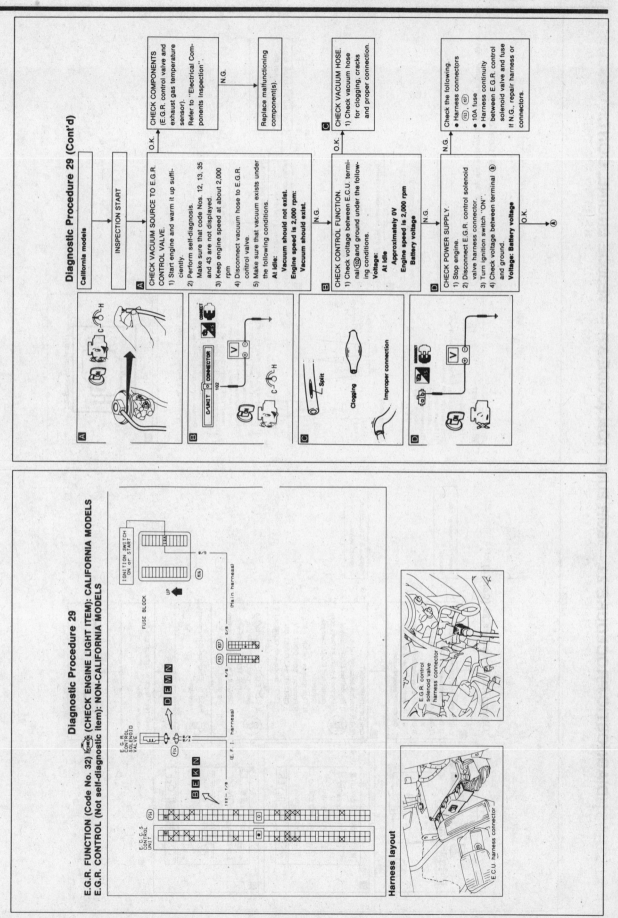

Diagnostic Procedure 29 (Cont'd)

California models

INSPECTION START

A
CHECK VACUUM SOURCE TO E.G.R. CONTROL VALVE.
1) Start engine and warm it up sufficiently.
2) Perform self-diagnosis.
 Make sure that code Nos. 12, 13, 35 and 43 are not displayed.
3) Keep engine speed at about 2,000 rpm.
4) Disconnect vacuum hose to E.G.R. control valve.
5) Make sure that vacuum exists under the following conditions.
At idle:
 Vacuum should not exist.
Engine speed is 2,000 rpm:
 Vacuum should exist.

N.G. → **B**

O.K. → CHECK COMPONENTS
(E.G.R. control valve and exhaust gas temperature sensor).
Refer to "Electrical Components inspection".

N.G. → Replace malfunctioning component(s).

B
CHECK CONTROL FUNCTION.
1) Check voltage between E.C.U. terminal ⑩ and ground under the following conditions.
Voltage:
 At idle
 Approximately 0V
 Engine speed is 2,000 rpm
 Battery voltage

N.G. → **D**

O.K. → **C** CHECK VACUUM HOSE.
1) Check vacuum hose for clogging, cracks and proper connection.

D
CHECK POWER SUPPLY.
1) Stop engine.
2) Disconnect E.G.R. control solenoid valve harness connector.
3) Turn ignition switch "ON".
4) Check voltage between terminal ⓐ and ground.
Voltage: Battery voltage

N.G. → Check the following.
● Harness connectors
● 10A fuse
● Harness continuity between E.G.R. control solenoid valve and fuse
If N.G., repair harness or connectors.

O.K. → Ⓐ

E.G.R. FUNCTION (Code No. 32) (CHECK ENGINE LIGHT ITEM): **CALIFORNIA MODELS**
E.G.R. CONTROL (Not self-diagnostic item): **NON-CALIFORNIA MODELS**

Diagnostic Procedure 29

Harness layout

DIAGNOSTIC PROCEDURE 29 — EGR FUNCTION (CODE 32) — VE30DE ENGINE, CONT.

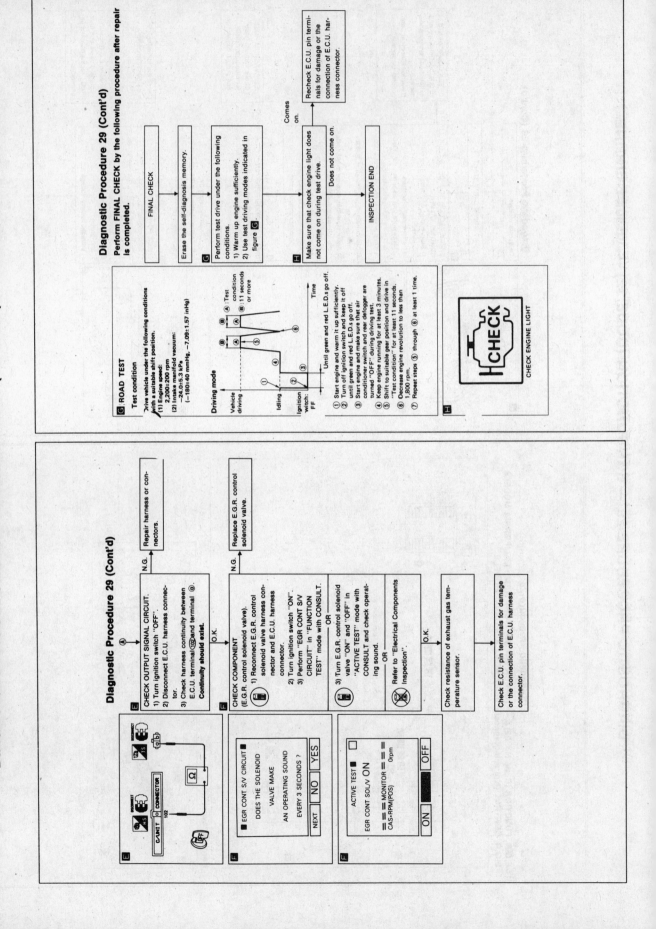

Diagnostic Procedure 29 (Cont'd)

E CHECK OUTPUT SIGNAL CIRCUIT.
1) Turn ignition switch "OFF".
2) Disconnect E.C.U. harness connector.
3) Check harness continuity between E.C.U. terminal ⑩ and terminal ⑭.
Continuity should exist.

N.G. → Repair harness or connectors.

O.K.

F CHECK COMPONENT
(E.G.R. control solenoid valve).
1) Reconnect E.G.R. control solenoid valve harness connector and E.C.U. harness connector.
2) Turn ignition switch "ON".
3) Perform "EGR CONT S/V CIRCUIT" in "FUNCTION TEST" mode with CONSULT.

OR

3) Turn E.G.R. control solenoid valve "ON" and "OFF" in "ACTIVE TEST" mode with CONSULT and check operating sound.

OR

Refer to "Electrical Components Inspection".

N.G. → Replace E.G.R. control solenoid valve.

O.K.

Check resistance of exhaust gas temperature sensor.

Check E.C.U. pin terminals for damage or the connection of E.C.U. harness connector.

E CONNECT / DISCONNECT
CANIT CONNECTOR 102

F ■ EGR CONT S/V CIRCUIT ■
DOES THE SOLENOID
VALVE MAKE
AN OPERATING SOUND
EVERY 3 SECONDS ?
NEXT | NO | YES

F ☐ ACTIVE TEST ☐
EGR CONT SOL/v ON
══ ══ MONITOR ══ ══
CAS-RPM(POS)   0rpm
ON | OFF

Diagnostic Procedure 29 (Cont'd)

Perform FINAL CHECK by the following procedure after repair is completed.

FINAL CHECK

Erase the self-diagnosis memory.

G Perform test drive under the following conditions.
1) Warm up engine sufficiently.
2) Use test driving modes indicated in figure G.

H Make sure that check engine light does not come on during test drive.

Comes on. → Recheck E.C.U. pin terminals for damage or the connection of E.C.U. harness connector.

Does not come on.

INSPECTION END

G ROAD TEST

Test condition

Drive vehicle under the following conditions with a suitable shift position.
(1) Engine speed:
2,200±200 rpm
(2) Intake manifold vacuum:
−24.0±5.3 kPa
(−180±40 mmHg, −7.09±1.57 inHg)

Ⓐ : Test condition
Ⓑ : 11 seconds or more

Driving mode

Vehicle driving
Idling
Ignition switch: FF

Until green and red L.E.D.s go off.

① Start engine and warm it up sufficiently.
② Turn off ignition switch and keep it off until green and red L.E.D.s go off.
③ Start engine and make sure that air conditioner switch and rear defogger are turned "OFF" during driving test.
④ Keep engine running for at least 3 minutes.
⑤ Shift to suitable gear position and drive in "Test condition" for at least 11 seconds.
⑥ Decrease engine revolution to less than 1,800 rpm.
⑦ Repeat steps ⑤ through ⑥ at least 1 time.

H

CHECK ENGINE LIGHT

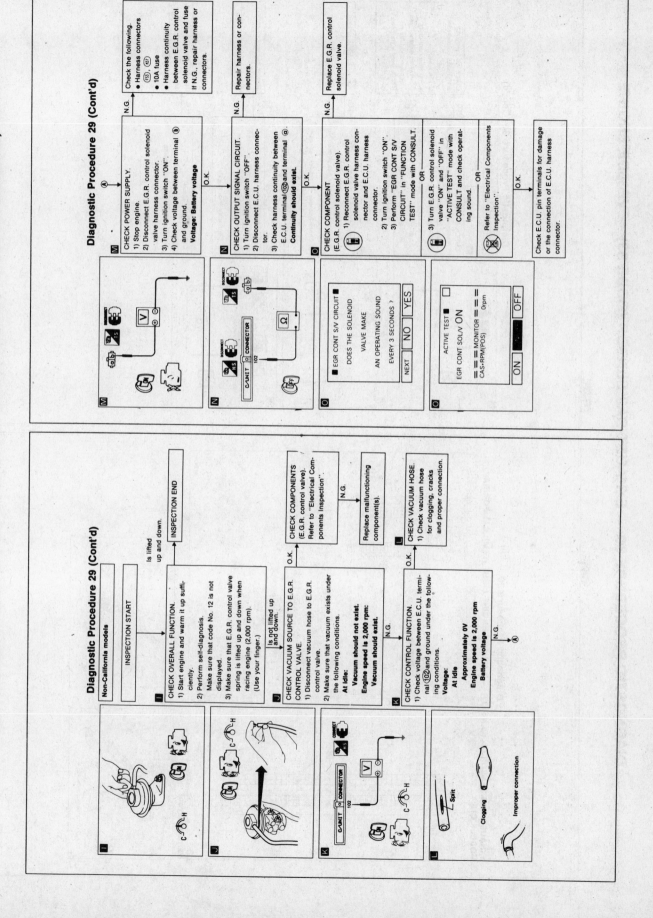

Diagnostic Procedure 29 (Cont'd)

Non-California models

INSPECTION START

I — CHECK OVERALL FUNCTION.
1) Start engine and warm it up sufficiently.
2) Perform self-diagnosis.
Make sure that code No. 12 is not displayed.
3) Make sure that E.G.R. control valve spring is lifted up and down when racing engine (2,000 rpm).
(Use your finger.)

Is lifted up and down. → INSPECTION END

Is not lifted up and down. ↓

J — CHECK VACUUM SOURCE TO E.G.R. CONTROL VALVE.
1) Disconnect vacuum hose to E.G.R. control valve.
2) Make sure that vacuum exists under the following conditions.
At idle:
Vacuum should not exist.
Engine speed is 2,000 rpm:
Vacuum should exist.

N.G. → **CHECK COMPONENTS**
(E.G.R. control valve).
Refer to "Electrical Components Inspection".

O.K. → Replace malfunctioning component(s).

K — CHECK CONTROL FUNCTION.
1) Check voltage between E.C.U. terminal ⑩② and ground under the following conditions.
Voltage:
At idle
Approximately 0V
Engine speed is 2,000 rpm
Battery voltage

O.K. → **L — CHECK VACUUM HOSE.**
1) Check vacuum hose for clogging, cracks and proper connection.

N.G. → Ⓐ

Diagnostic Procedure 29 (Cont'd)

Ⓐ

M — CHECK POWER SUPPLY.
1) Stop engine.
2) Disconnect E.G.R. control solenoid valve harness connector.
3) Turn ignition switch "ON".
4) Check voltage between terminal ⓑ and ground.
Voltage: Battery voltage

N.G. → Check the following.
● Harness connectors
   ⑤⑤ ⑧⑦
● 10A fuse
● Harness continuity between E.G.R. control solenoid valve and fuse
If N.G., repair harness or connectors.

O.K. ↓

N — CHECK OUTPUT SIGNAL CIRCUIT.
1) Turn ignition switch "OFF".
2) Disconnect E.C.U. harness connector.
3) Check harness continuity between E.C.U. terminal ⑩② and terminal ⓒ.
Continuity should exist.

N.G. → Repair harness or connectors.

O.K. ↓

O — CHECK COMPONENT
(E.G.R. control solenoid valve).
1) Reconnect E.G.R. control solenoid valve harness connector and E.C.U. harness connector.
2) Turn ignition switch "ON".
3) Perform "EGR CONT S/V CIRCUIT" in "FUNCTION TEST" mode with CONSULT.
   OR
3) Turn E.G.R. control solenoid valve "ON" and "OFF" in "ACTIVE TEST" mode with CONSULT and check operating sound.
   OR
   Refer to "Electrical Components Inspection".

N.G. → Replace E.G.R. control solenoid valve.

O.K. ↓

Check E.C.U. pin terminals for damage or the connection of E.C.U. harness connector.

■ EGR CONT S/V CIRCUIT ■
DOES THE SOLENOID
VALVE MAKE
AN OPERATING SOUND
EVERY 3 SECONDS ?
NEXT | NO | YES

ACTIVE TEST
EGR CONT SOL/v ON
═ ═ MONITOR ═ ═ ═
CAS-RPM(POS)   0rpm
ON
OFF

Split
Clogging
Improper connection

DIAGNOSTIC PROCEDURE 30 — EXHAUST GAS SENSOR (CODE 33) — VE30DE ENGINE

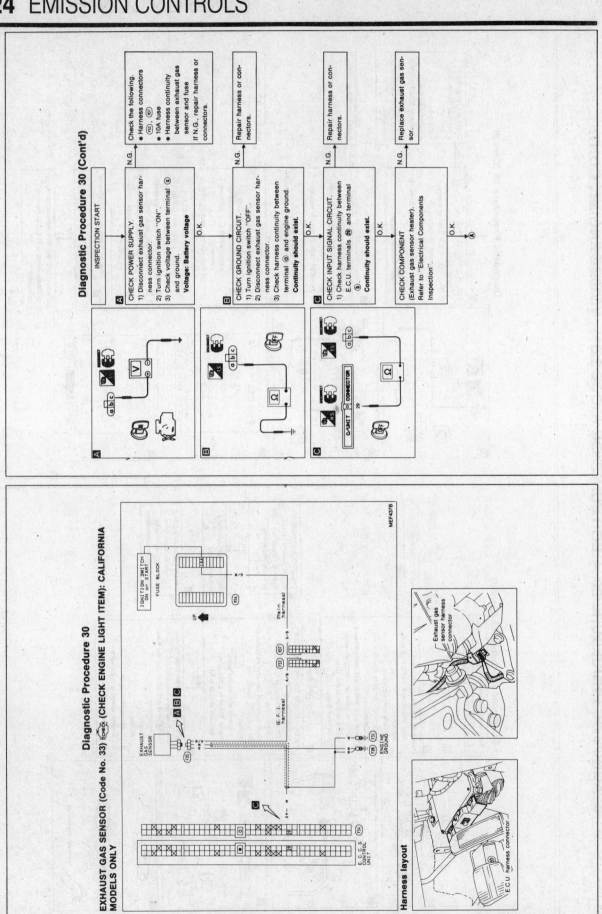

Diagnostic Procedure 30 (Cont'd)

INSPECTION START

A CHECK POWER SUPPLY.
1) Disconnect exhaust gas sensor harness connector.
2) Turn ignition switch "ON".
3) Check voltage between terminal ⓒ and ground.
Voltage: Battery voltage

N.G. → Check the following.
- Harness connectors ⑬ ⑰
- 10A fuse
- Harness continuity between exhaust gas sensor and fuse
If N.G., repair harness or connectors.

O.K. ↓

B CHECK GROUND CIRCUIT.
1) Turn ignition switch "OFF".
2) Disconnect exhaust gas sensor harness connector.
3) Check harness continuity between terminal ⓐ and engine ground.
Continuity should exist.

N.G. → Repair harness or connectors.

O.K. ↓

C CHECK INPUT SIGNAL CIRCUIT.
1) Check harness continuity between E.C.U. terminals ㉘ and terminal ⓑ.
Continuity should exist.

N.G. → Repair harness or connectors.

O.K. ↓

CHECK COMPONENT
(Exhaust gas sensor heater).
Refer to "Electrical Components Inspection".

N.G. → Replace exhaust gas sensor.

O.K. → Ⓐ

MEF437B

Diagnostic Procedure 30

EXHAUST GAS SENSOR (Code No. 33) (CHECK ENGINE LIGHT ITEM): CALIFORNIA MODELS ONLY

Harness layout

DIAGNOSTIC PROCEDURE 30 — EXHAUST GAS SENSOR (CODE 33) — VE30DE ENGINE, CONT.

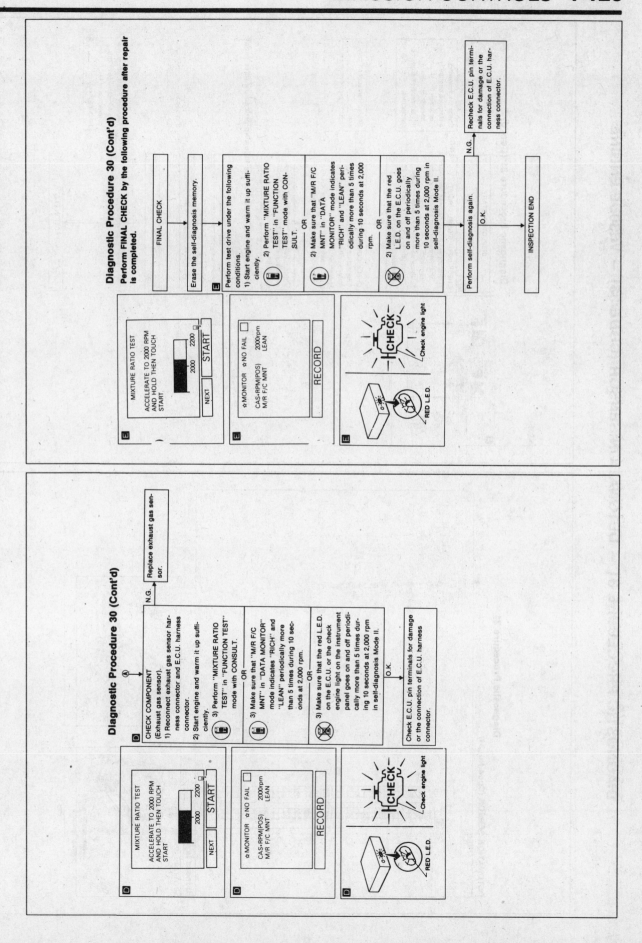

Diagnostic Procedure 30 (Cont'd)

Perform FINAL CHECK by the following procedure after repair is completed.

FINAL CHECK

↓

Erase the self-diagnosis memory.

↓

E Perform test drive under the following conditions.

1) Start engine and warm it up sufficiently.

2) Perform "MIXTURE RATIO TEST" in "FUNCTION TEST" mode with CONSULT.

OR

2) Make sure that "M/R F/C MNT" in "DATA MONITOR" mode indicates "RICH" and "LEAN" periodically more than 5 times during 10 seconds at 2,000 rpm.

OR

2) Make sure that the red L.E.D. on the E.C.U. goes on and off periodically more than 5 times during 10 seconds at 2,000 rpm in self-diagnosis Mode II.

↓

Perform self-diagnosis again.

→ N.G. → Recheck E.C.U. pin terminals for damage or the connection of E.C.U. harness connector.

↓ O.K.

INSPECTION END

E MIXTURE RATIO TEST

ACCELERATE TO 2000 RPM AND HOLD THEN TOUCH START

2000   2200

NEXT   START

E ☆MONITOR ☆NO FAIL

CAS-RPM(POS)   2000rpm
M/R F/C MNT   LEAN

RECORD

E CHECK — Check engine light

RED L.E.D.

Diagnostic Procedure 30 (Cont'd)

Ⓐ

D CHECK COMPONENT (Exhaust gas sensor).

1) Reconnect exhaust gas sensor harness connector and E.C.U. harness connector.

2) Start engine and warm it up sufficiently.

3) Perform "MIXTURE RATIO TEST" in "FUNCTION TEST" mode with CONSULT.

OR

3) Make sure that "M/R F/C MNT" in "DATA MONITOR" mode indicates "RICH" and "LEAN" periodically more than 5 times during 10 seconds at 2,000 rpm.

OR

3) Make sure that the red L.E.D. on the E.C.U. or the check engine light on the instrument panel goes on and off periodically more than 5 times during 10 seconds at 2,000 rpm in self-diagnosis Mode II.

→ N.G. → Replace exhaust gas sensor.

↓ O.K.

Check E.C.U. pin terminals for damage or the connection of E.C.U. harness connector.

D MIXTURE RATIO TEST

ACCELERATE TO 2000 RPM AND HOLD THEN TOUCH START

2000   2200

NEXT   START

D ☆MONITOR ☆NO FAIL

CAS-RPM(POS)   2000rpm
M/R F/C MNT   LEAN

RECORD

D CHECK — Check engine light

RED L.E.D.

DIAGNOSTIC PROCEDURE 31 — DETONATION SENSOR (CODE 33) — VE30DE ENGINE

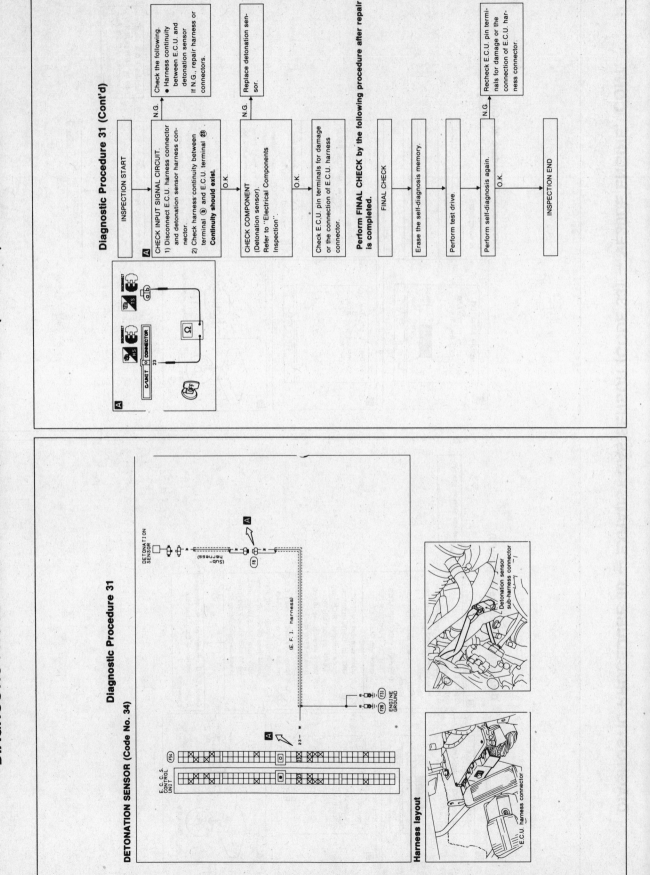

Diagnostic Procedure 31 (Cont'd)

INSPECTION START

A CHECK INPUT SIGNAL CIRCUIT.
1) Disconnect E.C.U. harness connector and detonation sensor harness connector.
2) Check harness continuity between terminal ⑪ and E.C.U. terminal ㉓ **Continuity should exist.**

N.G. → Check the following.
● Harness continuity between E.C.U. and detonation sensor
If N.G., repair harness or connectors.

O.K.

CHECK COMPONENT
(Detonation sensor).
Refer to "Electrical Components Inspection".

N.G. → Replace detonation sensor.

O.K.

Check E.C.U. pin terminals for damage or the connection of E.C.U. harness connector.

Perform FINAL CHECK by the following procedure after repair is completed.

FINAL CHECK

Erase the self-diagnosis memory.

Perform test drive.

Perform self-diagnosis again.

N.G. → Recheck E.C.U. pin terminals for damage or the connection of E.C.U. harness connector.

O.K.

INSPECTION END

Diagnostic Procedure 31

DETONATION SENSOR (Code No. 34)

Harness layout

DIAGNOSTIC PROCEDURE 32 — EXHAUST GAS TEMPERATURE SENSOR (CODE 33) — VE30DE ENGINE

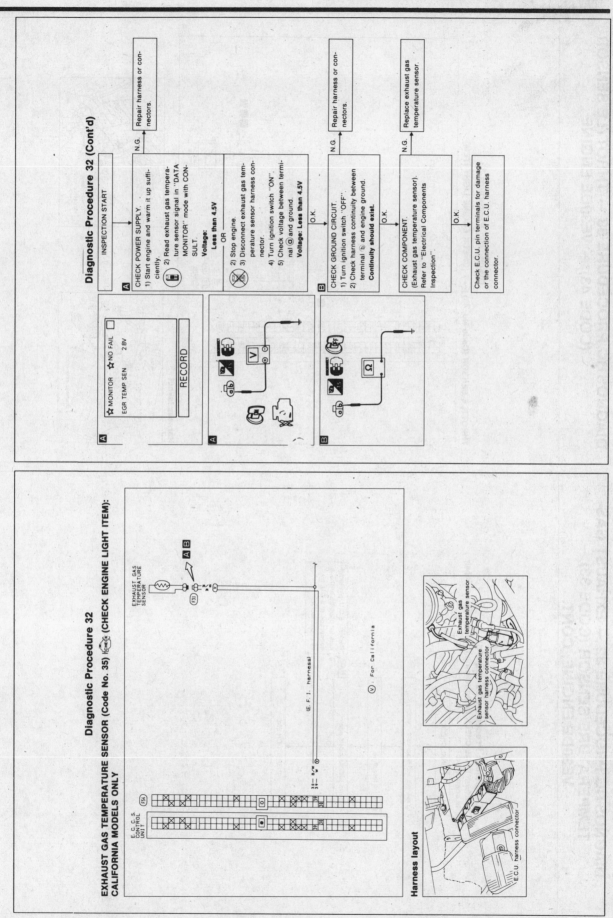

Diagnostic Procedure 32 (Cont'd)

INSPECTION START

A

CHECK POWER SUPPLY.
1) Start engine and warm it up sufficiently.
2) Read exhaust gas temperature sensor signal in "DATA MONITOR" mode with CONSULT.

Voltage:
Less than 4.5V

— OR —

2) Stop engine.
3) Disconnect exhaust gas temperature sensor harness connector.
4) Turn ignition switch "ON".
5) Check voltage between terminal ⓐ and ground.
Voltage: Less than 4.5V

N.G. → Repair harness or connectors.

O.K.

B

CHECK GROUND CIRCUIT.
1) Turn ignition switch "OFF".
2) Check harness continuity between terminal ⓑ and engine ground.
Continuity should exist.

N.G. → Repair harness or connectors.

O.K.

CHECK COMPONENT
(Exhaust gas temperature sensor).
Refer to "Electrical Components Inspection".

N.G. → Replace exhaust gas temperature sensor.

O.K.

Check E.C.U. pin terminals for damage or the connection of E.C.U. harness connector.

A

☆ MONITOR ☆NO FAIL

EGR TEMP SEN   2.8V

RECORD

A

B

EXHAUST GAS TEMPERATURE SENSOR (Code No. 35) (CHECK ENGINE LIGHT ITEM): CALIFORNIA MODELS ONLY

Diagnostic Procedure 32

EXHAUST GAS TEMPERATURE SENSOR

Ⓐ Ⓑ

(E.F.I. harness)

Ⓥ : For California

E.C.C.S. CONTROL UNIT

39 — B/W
39 — W

Harness layout

Exhaust gas temperature sensor

Exhaust gas temperature sensor harness connector

E.C.U. harness connector

DIAGNOSTIC PROCEDURE 33 — THROTTLE SENSOR (CODE 43) — VE30DE ENGINE

Diagnostic Procedure 33

THROTTLE SENSOR (Code No. 43) [CHECK] (CHECK ENGINE LIGHT ITEM)

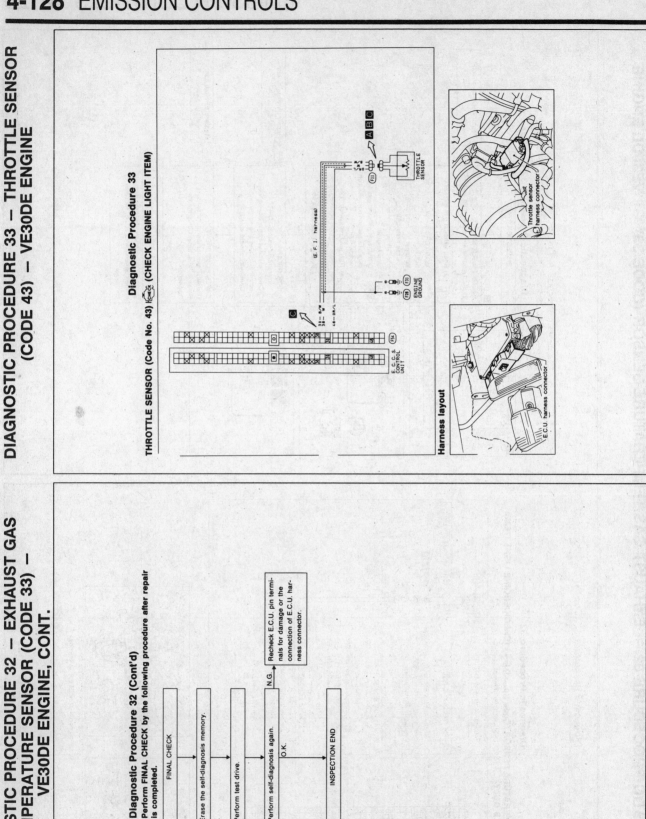

Harness layout

DIAGNOSTIC PROCEDURE 32 — EXHAUST GAS TEMPERATURE SENSOR (CODE 33) — VE30DE ENGINE, CONT.

Diagnostic Procedure 32 (Cont'd)

Perform FINAL CHECK by the following procedure after repair is completed.

FINAL CHECK

↓

Erase the self-diagnosis memory.

↓

Perform test drive.

↓

Perform self-diagnosis again. —N.G.→ Recheck E.C.U. pin terminals for damage or the connection of E.C.U. harness connector.

O.K.

↓

INSPECTION END

DIAGNOSTIC PROCEDURE 33 — THROTTLE SENSOR (CODE 43) — VE30DE ENGINE, CONT.

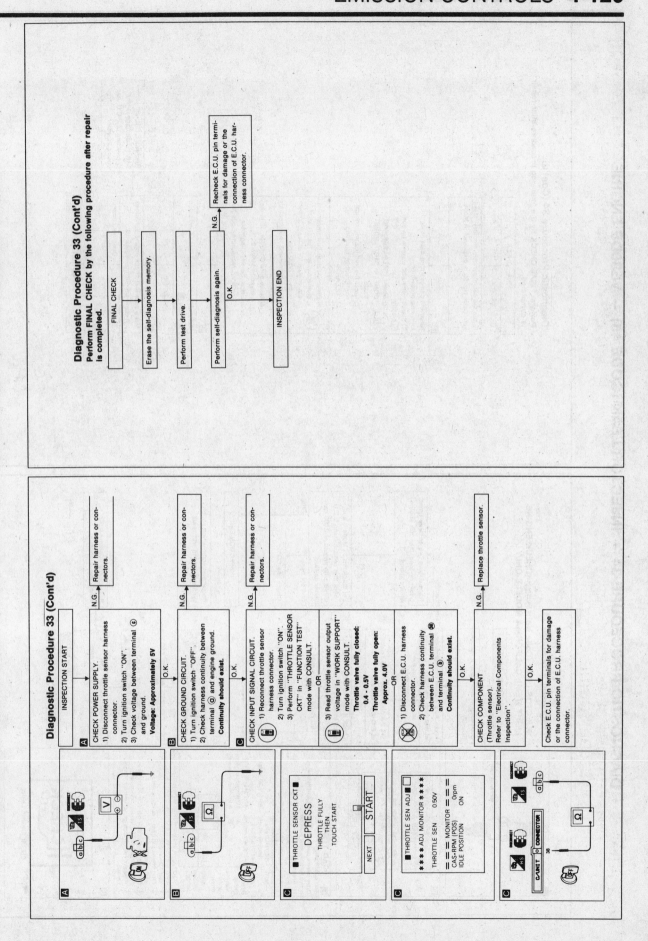

Diagnostic Procedure 33 (Cont'd)

INSPECTION START

A CHECK POWER SUPPLY.
1) Disconnect throttle sensor harness connector.
2) Turn ignition switch "ON".
3) Check voltage between terminal ⓒ and ground.
Voltage: Approximately 5V

→ N.G. → Repair harness or connectors.

O.K.

B CHECK GROUND CIRCUIT.
1) Turn ignition switch "OFF".
2) Check harness continuity between terminal ⓖ and engine ground.
Continuity should exist.

→ N.G. → Repair harness or connectors.

O.K.

C CHECK INPUT SIGNAL CIRCUIT.
1) Reconnect throttle sensor harness connector.
2) Turn ignition switch "ON"
3) Perform "THROTTLE SENSOR CKT" in "FUNCTION TEST" mode with CONSULT.
OR
3) Read throttle sensor output voltage in "WORK SUPPORT" mode with CONSULT.
Throttle valve fully closed:
0.4 - 0.5V
Throttle valve fully open:
Approx. 4.0V
OR
1) Disconnect E.C.U. harness connector.
2) Check harness continuity between E.C.U. terminal ㉟ and terminal ⓑ.
Continuity should exist.

→ N.G. → Repair harness or connectors.

O.K.

CHECK COMPONENT
(Throttle sensor).
Refer to "Electrical Components Inspection".

→ N.G. → Replace throttle sensor.

O.K.

Check E.C.U. pin terminals for damage or the connection of E.C.U. harness connector.

Diagnostic Procedure 33 (Cont'd)
Perform FINAL CHECK by the following procedure after repair is completed.

FINAL CHECK

Erase the self-diagnosis memory.

Perform test drive.

Perform self-diagnosis again.

→ N.G. → Recheck E.C.U. pin terminals for damage or the connection of E.C.U. harness connector.

O.K.

INSPECTION END

A ■ THROTTLE SENSOR CKT ■
DEPRESS
THROTTLE FULLY
THEN
TOUCH START
NEXT | START

C ■ THROTTLE SEN ADJ ■
★★★★ADJ MONITOR ★★★★
THROTTLE SEN   0.50V
= = = MONITOR = =
CAS·RPM (POS)   0rpm
IDLE POSITION   ON

C CONSULT CONNECTOR 38

DIAGNOSTIC PROCEDURE 34 – INJECTOR LEAK (CODE 45) – VE30DE ENGINE

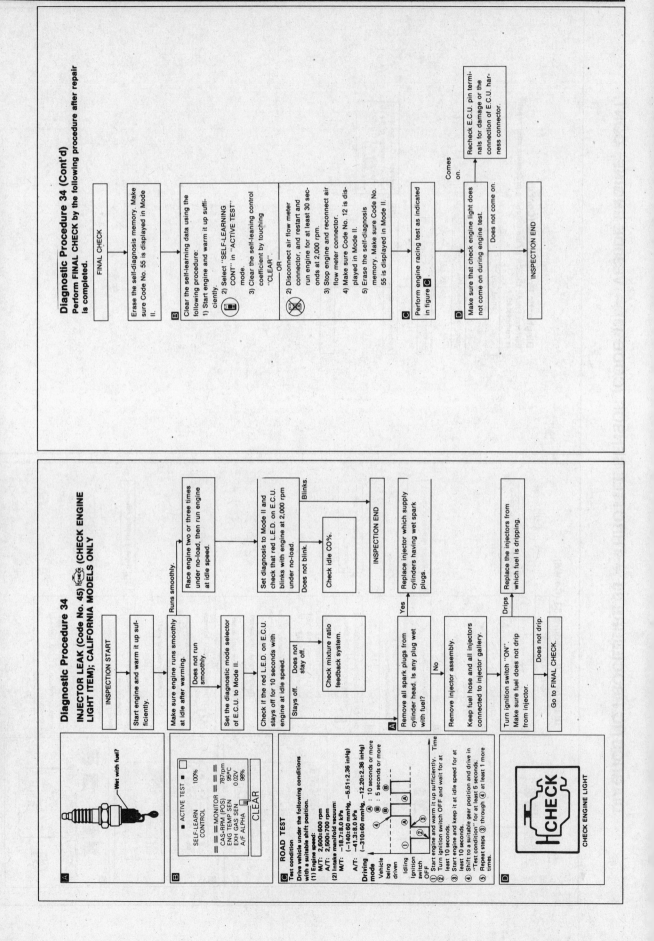

Diagnostic Procedure 34

INJECTOR LEAK (Code No. 45) [CHECK] (CHECK ENGINE LIGHT ITEM); CALIFORNIA MODELS ONLY

INSPECTION START

Start engine and warm it up sufficiently.

Make sure engine runs smoothly at idle after warming. — Runs smoothly. → Race engine two or three times under no-load, then run engine at idle speed. → Set diagnosis to Mode II and check that red L.E.D. on E.C.U. blinks with engine at 2,000 rpm under no-load. — Blinks. → Check idle CO%. → **INSPECTION END**

Does not run smoothly. — Does not blink.

Set the diagnostic mode selector of E.C.U. to Mode II.

Check if the red L.E.D. on E.C.U. stays off for 10 seconds with engine at idle speed. — Stays off. → Does not stay off. → Check mixture ratio feedback system.

A

Remove all spark plugs from cylinder head. Is any plug wet with fuel? — Yes → Replace injector which supply cylinders having wet spark plugs.

No

Remove injector assembly.

Keep fuel hose and all injectors connected to injector gallery.

Turn ignition switch "ON". Make sure fuel does not drip from injector. — Drips → Replace the injectors from which fuel is dripping.

Does not drip.

Go to FINAL CHECK.

A
Wet with fuel?

B
■ SELF-LEARN
CONTROL   100%

≡ ≡ =MONITOR= ≡ ≡
CAS-RPM (POS)   787rpm
ENG TEMP SEN   95°C
EXH GAS SEN   0.02V
A/F ALPHA   98%

■ ACTIVE TEST ■ □

CLEAR

C
ROAD TEST
Test condition
Drive vehicle under the following conditions with a suitable shift position.
(1) Engine speed:
    M/T: 2,800±600 rpm
    A/T: 2,500±700 rpm
(2) Intake manifold vacuum:
    M/T: -18.7±8.0 kPa
          (-140±60 mmHg, -5.51±2.36 inHg)
    A/T: -41.3±8.0 kPa
          (-310±50 mmHg, -12.20±2.36 inHg)
Driving mode
Ⓐ : 10 seconds or more
Ⓑ : 5 seconds or more

① Start engine and warm it up sufficiently.
② Turn ignition switch OFF and wait for at least 10 seconds.
③ Start engine and keep it at idle speed for at least 10 seconds.
④ Shift to a suitable gear position and drive in "Test condition" for at least 5 seconds.
⑤ Repeat steps ③ through ④ at least 1 more times.

D
[CHECK] CHECK
CHECK ENGINE LIGHT

Diagnostic Procedure 34 (Cont'd)

Perform FINAL CHECK by the following procedure after repair is completed.

FINAL CHECK

Erase the self-diagnosis memory. Make sure Code No. 55 is displayed in Mode II.

B
Clear the self-learning data using the following procedure.
1) Start engine and warm it up sufficiently.
2) Select "SELF-LEARNING CONT" in "ACTIVE TEST" mode.
3) Clear the self-learning control coefficient by touching "CLEAR".
— OR —
2) Disconnect air flow meter connector, and restart and run engine for at least 30 seconds at 2,000 rpm.
3) Stop engine and reconnect air flow meter connector.
4) Make sure Code No. 12 is displayed in Mode II.
5) Erase the self-diagnosis memory. Make sure Code No. 55 is displayed in Mode II.

C
Perform engine racing test as indicated in figure C

D
Make sure that check engine light does not come on during engine test. — Comes on. → Recheck E.C.U. pin terminals for damage or the connection of E.C.U. harness connector.

Does not come on.

INSPECTION END

DIAGNOSTIC PROCEDURE 35 — INJECTOR CIRCUIT (CODE 51) — VE30DE ENGINE

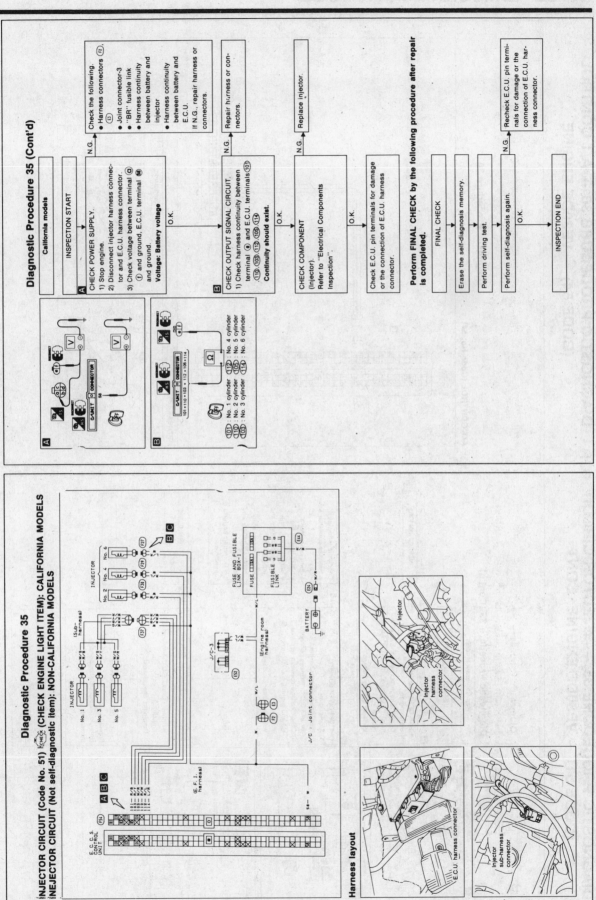

INJECTOR CIRCUIT (Code No. 51) [CHECK] (CHECK ENGINE LIGHT ITEM): CALIFORNIA MODELS
INJECTOR CIRCUIT (Not self-diagnostic item): NON-CALIFORNIA MODELS

DIAGNOSTIC PROCEDURE 36 — A/T CONTROL (CODE 54) — VE30DE ENGINE

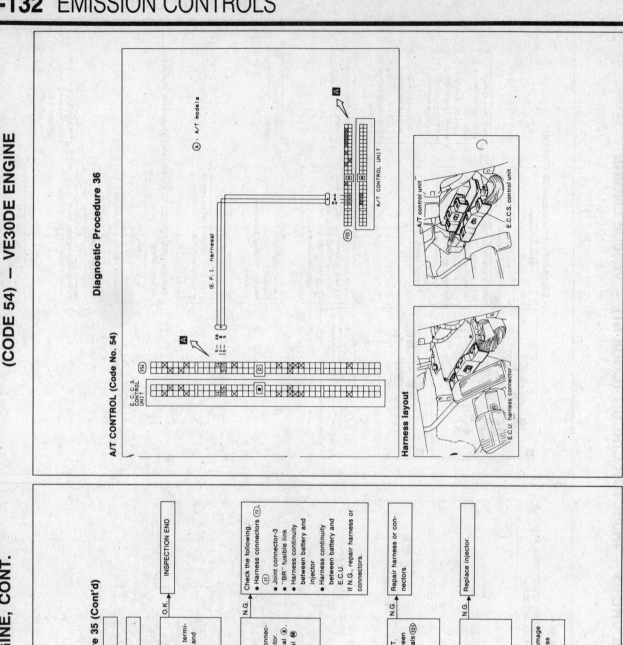

DIAGNOSTIC PROCEDURE 35 — INJECTOR CIRCUIT (CODE 51) — VE30DE ENGINE, CONT.

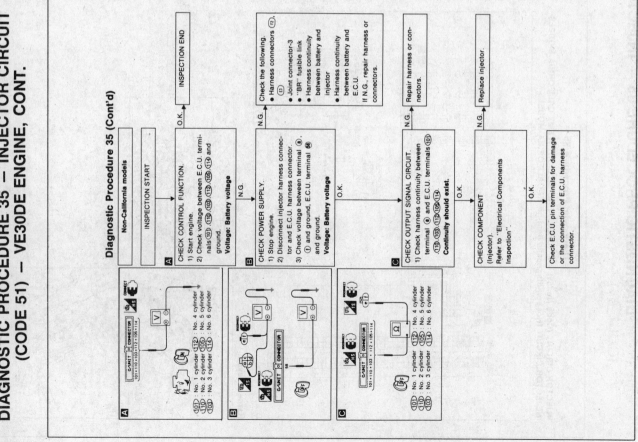

DIAGNOSTIC PROCEDURE 37 — THROTTLE VALVE SWITCH (NOT SELF-DIAGNOSTIC ITEM) VE30DE ENGINE

Diagnostic Procedure 37

THROTTLE VALVE SWITCH (Not self-diagnostic item)

(E.F.I. harness)

51— B/YL
52— B/OR

A

E. C. C. S.
CONTROL
UNIT

IDLE

THROTTLE VALVE
SWITCH

B C

B/YL
B/OR

Idle switch
harness connector

E.C.U. harness connector

Harness layout

DIAGNOSTIC PROCEDURE 36 — A/T CONTROL (CODE 54) — VE30DE ENGINE, CONT.

Diagnostic Procedure 36 (Cont'd)

INSPECTION START

A

CHECK INPUT SIGNAL CIRCUIT.
1) Turn ignition switch "OFF".
2) Disconnect E.C.U. harness connector
   and A/T control unit harness connector.
3) Check harness continuity between
   E.C.U. terminal ⑨ and terminal ⑱.
   E.C.U. terminal ⑩ and terminal ⑪.
   E.C.U. terminal ⑯ and terminal ⑰.
   Continuity should exist.

N.G. → Check the following.
● Harness continuity
  between E.C.U. and A/T
  control unit
  If N.G., repair harness or
  connectors.

O.K.

Check E.C.U. pin terminals for damage
or the connection of E.C.U. harness
connector.

**Perform FINAL CHECK by the following procedure after repair
is completed.**

FINAL CHECK

Erase the self-diagnosis memory.

Perform test drive.

Perform self-diagnosis again.

N.G. → Recheck E.C.U. pin terminals for damage or the
connection of E.C.U. har-
ness connector.

O.K.

INSPECTION END

A

A/T CONT. CONNECTOR

CONT. CONNECTOR

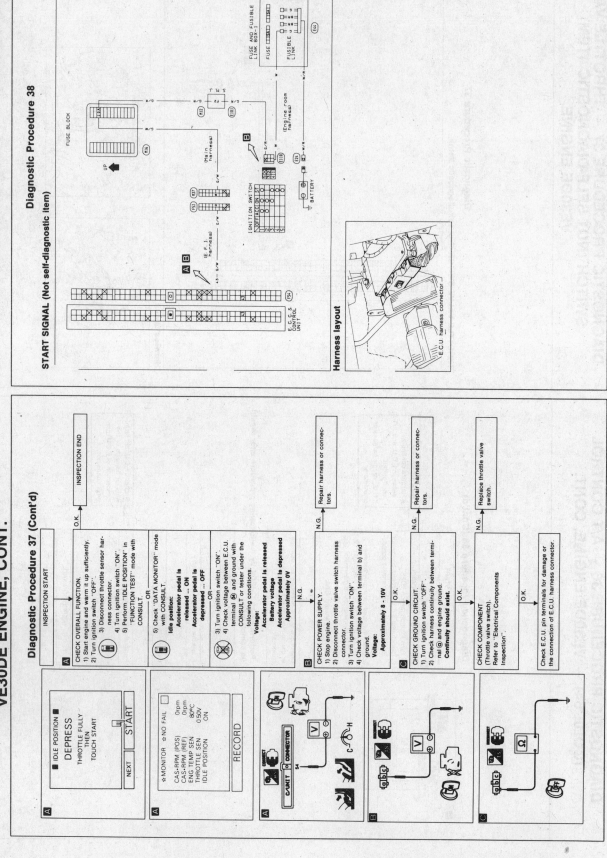

DIAGNOSTIC PROCEDURE 38 — START SIGNAL (NOT SELF-DIAGNOSTIC ITEM) — VE30DE ENGINE

Diagnostic Procedure 38

START SIGNAL (Not self-diagnostic item)

FUSE AND FUSIBLE LINK BOX-1

Harness layout

E.C.U. harness connector

DIAGNOSTIC PROCEDURE 37 — THROTTLE VALVE SWITCH (NOT SELF-DIAGNOSTIC ITEM) VE30DE ENGINE, CONT.

Diagnostic Procedure 37 (Cont'd)

INSPECTION START

A CHECK OVERALL FUNCTION.
1) Start engine and warm it up sufficiently.
2) Turn ignition switch "OFF".
3) Disconnect throttle sensor harness connector.
4) Turn ignition switch "ON".
5) Perform "IDLE POSITION" in "FUNCTION TEST" mode with CONSULT.
  OR
5) Check "DATA MONITOR" mode with CONSULT.
Idle position:
  Accelerator pedal is released ... ON
  Accelerator pedal is depressed ... OFF
  OR
3) Turn ignition switch "ON".
4) Check voltage between E.C.U. terminal ⑭ and ground with CONSULT or tester under the following conditions.
Voltage:
  Accelerator pedal is released
    Battery voltage
  Accelerator pedal is depressed
    Approximately 0V

O.K. → INSPECTION END

N.G.

B CHECK POWER SUPPLY.
1) Stop engine.
2) Disconnect throttle valve switch harness connector.
3) Turn ignition switch "ON".
4) Check voltage between terminal b and ground.
Voltage:
  Approximately 8 - 10V

N.G. → Repair harness or connectors.

O.K.

C CHECK GROUND CIRCUIT.
1) Turn ignition switch "OFF".
2) Check harness continuity between terminal ⓐ and engine ground.
Continuity should exist.

N.G. → Repair harness or connectors.

O.K.

CHECK COMPONENT
(Throttle valve switch).
Refer to "Electrical Components Inspection".

N.G. → Replace throttle valve switch.

O.K.

Check E.C.U. pin terminals for damage or the connection of E.C.U. harness connector.

IDLE POSITION
■ DEPRESS
THROTTLE FULLY
THEN
TOUCH START
NEXT   START

☆MONITOR ☆NO FAIL
CAS·RPM (POS)   0rpm
CAS·RPM (REF)   0rpm
ENG TEMP SEN   80°C
THROTTLE SEN   0.50V
IDLE POSITION   ON
RECORD

DIAGNOSTIC PROCEDURE 39 — POWER STEERING OIL PRESSURE SWITCH (NOT SELF-DIAGNOSTIC ITEM) VE30DE ENGINE

DIAGNOSTIC PROCEDURE 38 — START SIGNAL (NOT SELF-DIAGNOSTIC ITEM) — VE30DE ENGINE

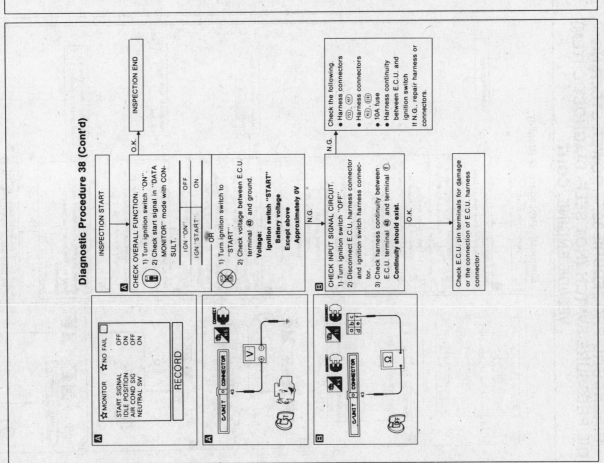

Diagnostic Procedure 39

POWER STEERING OIL PRESSURE SWITCH (Not self-diagnostic item)

POWER STEERING OIL PRESSURE SWITCH

(E.F.I. harness)

E.C.C.S. CONTROL UNIT

Harness layout

Power steering oil pressure switch harness connector

E.C.U harness connector

Diagnostic Procedure 38 (Cont'd)

INSPECTION START

A CHECK OVERALL FUNCTION.
1) Turn ignition switch "ON".
2) Check start signal in "DATA MONITOR" mode with CONSULT.

	IGN "ON"	OFF
	IGN "START"	ON

OR

1) Turn ignition switch to "START".
2) Check voltage between E.C.U. terminal ㊸ and ground.
Voltage:
Ignition switch "START"
Battery voltage
Except above
Approximately 0V

O.K. → INSPECTION END

N.G.

B CHECK INPUT SIGNAL CIRCUIT.
1) Turn ignition switch "OFF".
2) Disconnect E.C.U. harness connector and ignition switch harness connector.
3) Check harness continuity between E.C.U. terminal ㊸ and terminal Ⓛ.
Continuity should exist.

N.G. → Check the following.
● Harness connectors ㊲, ㊼
● Harness connectors ㊺, ㊼
● 10A fuse
● Harness continuity between E.C.U. and ignition switch
If N.G., repair harness or connectors.

O.K. → Check E.C.U. pin terminals for damage or the connection of E.C.U. harness connector.

A MONITOR ☆NO FAIL ☐
START SIGNAL OFF
IDLE POSITION ON
AIR COND SIG OFF
NEUTRAL SW ON

RECORD

A C/UNIT CONNECTOR 43

B C/UNIT CONNECTOR 43

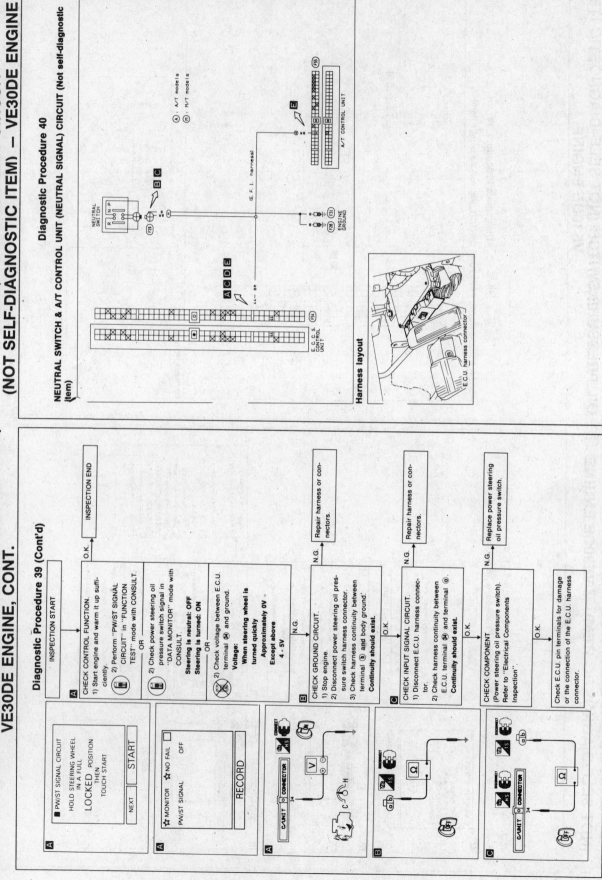

DIAGNOSTIC PROCEDURE 40 — NEUTRAL SWITCH AND A/T CONTROL UNIT CIRCUIT (NOT SELF-DIAGNOSTIC ITEM) — VE30DE ENGINE

Diagnostic Procedure 40

NEUTRAL SWITCH & A/T CONTROL UNIT (NEUTRAL SIGNAL) CIRCUIT (Not self-diagnostic item)

DIAGNOSTIC PROCEDURE 39 — POWER STEERING OIL PRESSURE SWITCH (NOT SELF- DIAGNOSTIC ITEM) VE30DE ENGINE, CONT.

Diagnostic Procedure 39 (Cont'd)

DIAGNOSTIC PROCEDURE 40 — NEUTRAL SWITCH AND A/T CONTROL UNIT CIRCUIT (NOT SELF-DIAGNOSTIC ITEM) — VE30DE ENGINE, CONT.

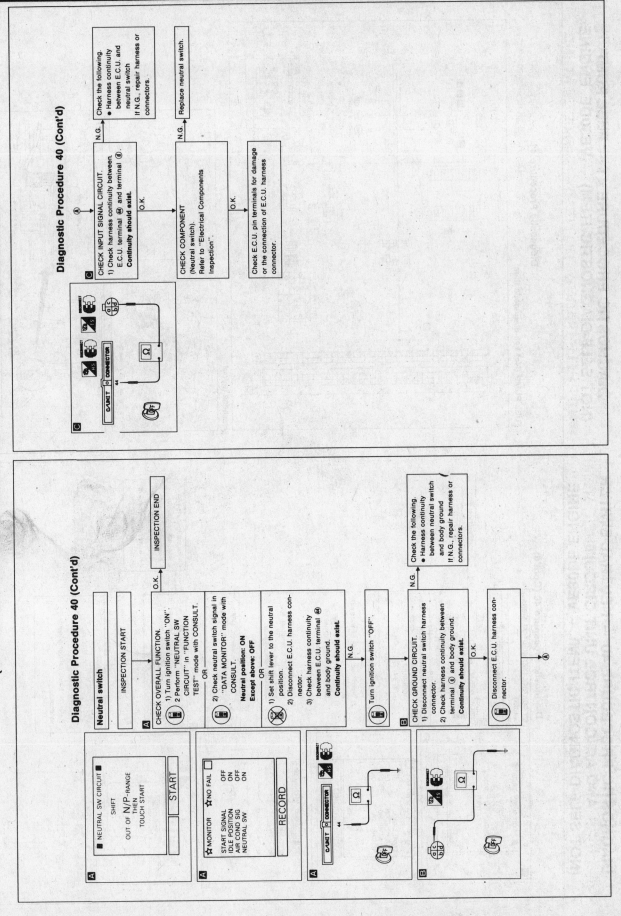

Diagnostic Procedure 40 (Cont'd)

Neutral switch

INSPECTION START

A CHECK OVERALL FUNCTION.
1) Turn ignition switch "ON".
2 Perform "NEUTRAL SW CIRCUIT" in "FUNCTION TEST" mode with CONSULT.

— OR —

2) Check neutral switch signal in "DATA MONITOR" mode with CONSULT.
Neutral position: ON
Except above: OFF

— OR —

1) Set shift lever to the neutral position.
2) Disconnect E.C.U. harness connector.
3) Check harness continuity between E.C.U. terminal ㊽ and body ground.
Continuity should exist.

O.K. → INSPECTION END

N.G. →

B Turn ignition switch "OFF".

CHECK GROUND CIRCUIT.
1) Disconnect neutral switch harness connector.
2) Check harness continuity between terminal ⓒ and body ground.
Continuity should exist.

N.G. → Check the following.
● Harness continuity between neutral switch and body ground
If N.G., repair harness or connectors.

O.K. →

Disconnect E.C.U. harness connector.

→ Ⓐ

Diagnostic Procedure 40 (Cont'd)

Ⓐ

C CHECK INPUT SIGNAL CIRCUIT.
1) Check harness continuity between E.C.U. terminal ㊽ and terminal ⓓ.
Continuity should exist.

N.G. → Check the following.
● Harness continuity between E.C.U. and neutral switch
If N.G., repair harness or connectors.

O.K. →

CHECK COMPONENT (Neutral switch).
Refer to "Electrical Components Inspection".

N.G. → Replace neutral switch.

O.K. →

Check E.C.U. pin terminals for damage or the connection of E.C.U. harness connector.

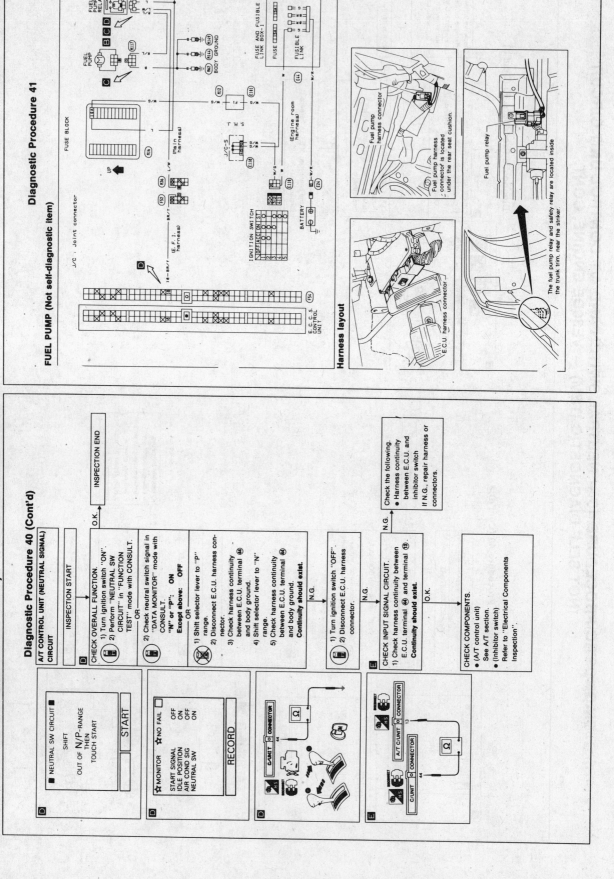

DIAGNOSTIC PROCEDURE 41 — FUEL PUMP (NOT SELF-DIAGNOSTIC ITEM) — VE30DE ENGINE

Diagnostic Procedure 41

FUEL PUMP (Not self-diagnostic item)

Harness layout

DIAGNOSTIC PROCEDURE 40 — NEUTRAL SWITCH AND A/T CONTROL UNIT CIRCUIT (NOT SELF-DIAGNOSTIC ITEM) — VE30DE ENGINE

Diagnostic Procedure 40 (Cont'd)

A/T CONTROL UNIT (NEUTRAL SIGNAL) CIRCUIT

DIAGNOSTIC PROCEDURE 41 – FUEL PUMP (NOT SELF-DIAGNOSTIC ITEM) – VE30DE ENGINE, CONT.

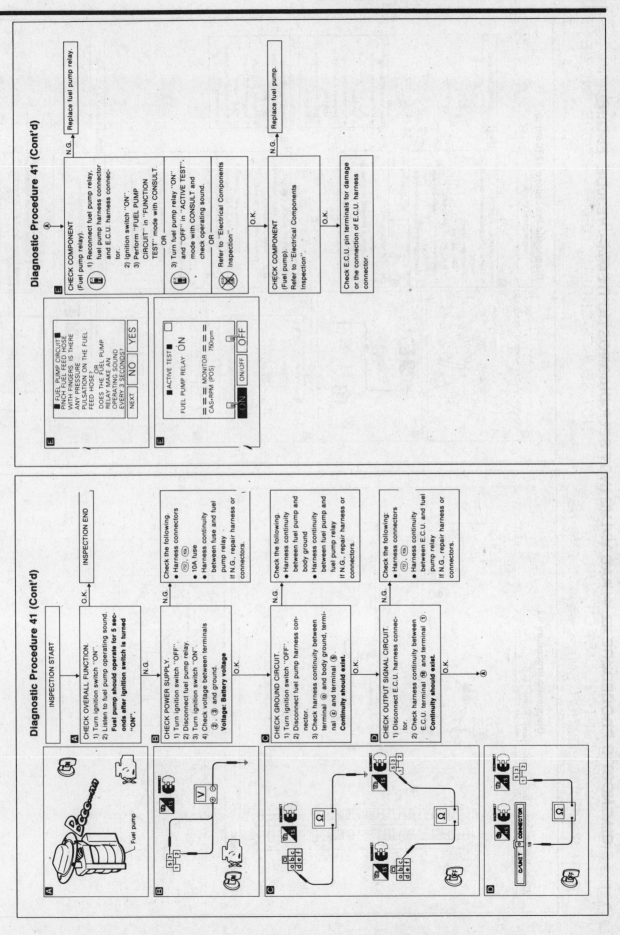

Diagnostic Procedure 41 (Cont'd)

INSPECTION START

A CHECK OVERALL FUNCTION.
1) Turn ignition switch "ON".
2) Listen to fuel pump operating sound.
Fuel pump should operate for 5 seconds after ignition switch is turned "ON".

O.K. → **INSPECTION END**

N.G. ↓

B CHECK POWER SUPPLY.
1) Turn ignition switch "OFF".
2) Disconnect fuel pump relay.
3) Turn ignition switch "ON".
4) Check voltage between terminals ②, ③ and ground.
Voltage: Battery voltage

N.G. → Check the following.
● Harness connectors
● 10A fuse
● Harness continuity between fuse and fuel pump relay
If N.G., repair harness or connectors.

O.K. ↓

C CHECK GROUND CIRCUIT.
1) Turn ignition switch "OFF".
2) Disconnect fuel pump harness connector.
3) Check harness continuity between terminal ④ and body ground, terminal ④ and terminal ⑤.
Continuity should exist.

N.G. → Check the following.
● Harness continuity between fuel pump and body ground
● Harness continuity between fuel pump and fuel pump relay
If N.G., repair harness or connectors.

O.K. ↓

D CHECK OUTPUT SIGNAL CIRCUIT.
1) Disconnect E.C.U. harness connector.
2) Check harness continuity between E.C.U. terminal ⑱ and terminal ①.
Continuity should exist.

N.G. → Check the following:
● Harness connectors
● Harness continuity between E.C.U. and fuel pump relay
If N.G., repair harness or connectors.

O.K. → Ⓐ

Diagnostic Procedure 41 (Cont'd)

Ⓐ

E CHECK COMPONENT
(Fuel pump relay).
1) Reconnect fuel pump relay, fuel pump harness connector and E.C.U. harness connector.
2) Ignition switch "ON".
3) Perform "FUEL PUMP CIRCUIT" in "FUNCTION TEST" mode with CONSULT.
OR
3) Turn fuel pump relay "ON" and "OFF" in "ACTIVE TEST" mode with CONSULT and check operating sound.
OR
Refer to "Electrical Components Inspection".

N.G. → Replace fuel pump relay.

O.K. ↓

E ■ FUEL PUMP CIRCUIT ■
PINCH FUEL FEED HOSE
WITH FINGERS. IS THERE
ANY PRESSURE
PULSATION ON THE FUEL
FEED HOSE?
DOES THE FUEL PUMP
RELAY MAKE AN
OPERATING SOUND
EVERY 3 SECONDS?

| NEXT | NO | YES |

E ■ ACTIVE TEST ■ ▢
FUEL PUMP RELAY ON

=== == MONITOR == ==
CAS·RPM (POS)   750rpm

| ON | ON/OFF | OFF |

E CHECK COMPONENT
(Fuel pump).
Refer to "Electrical Components Inspection".

N.G. → Replace fuel pump.

O.K. ↓

Check E.C.U. pin terminals for damage or the connection of E.C.U. harness connector.

DIAGNOSTIC PROCEDURE 42 — AAC VALVE (NOT SELF-DIAGNOSTIC ITEM) — VE30DE ENGINE

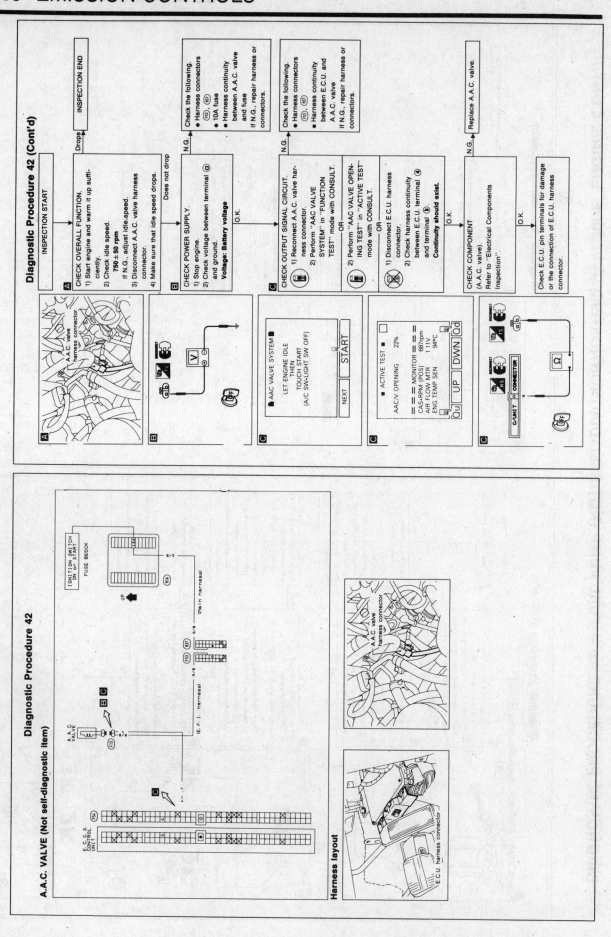

Diagnostic Procedure 42 (Cont'd)

INSPECTION START

A CHECK OVERALL FUNCTION.
1) Start engine and warm it up sufficiently.
2) Check idle speed.
 750 ± 50 rpm
 If N.G., adjust idle speed.
3) Disconnect A.A.C. valve harness connector.
4) Make sure that idle speed drops.

Does not drop

B CHECK POWER SUPPLY.
1) Stop engine.
2) Check voltage between terminal ⓐ and ground.
 Voltage: Battery voltage

O.K.

C CHECK OUTPUT SIGNAL CIRCUIT.
1) Reconnect A.A.C. valve harness connector.
2) Perform "AAC VALVE SYSTEM" in "FUNCTION TEST" mode with CONSULT.
 OR
2) Perform "AAC VALVE OPENING TEST" in "ACTIVE TEST" mode with CONSULT.
 OR
1) Disconnect E.C.U. harness connector.
2) Check harness continuity between E.C.U. terminal ④ and terminal ⓑ.
 Continuity should exist.

O.K.

CHECK COMPONENT (A.A.C. valve).
Refer to "Electrical Components Inspection".

O.K.

Check E.C.U. pin terminals for damage or the connection of E.C.U. harness connector.

Drops → **INSPECTION END**

N.G. → Check the following.
● Harness connectors
● 10A fuse
● Harness continuity between A.A.C. valve and fuse
If N.G., repair harness or connectors.

N.G. → Check the following.
● Harness connectors
● Harness continuity between E.C.U. and A.A.C. valve
If N.G., repair harness or connectors.

N.G. → Replace A.A.C. valve.

B
LET ENGINE IDLE
THEN
TOUCH START
(A/C SW-LIGHT SW OFF)
AAC VALVE SYSTEM ■
NEXT START

C
ACTIVE TEST ■
AAC/V OPENING 22%
MONITOR
CAS·RPM (POS) 687rpm
AIR FLOW MTR 1.11V
ENG TEMP SEN 94°C
Qu UP DWN Qd

Diagnostic Procedure 42

A.A.C. VALVE (Not self-diagnostic item)

IGNITION SWITCH ON or START
FUSE BLOCK
UP

A.A.C. VALVE
B C
(E.F.I. harness)
(main harness)
C

E.C.C.S. CONTROL UNIT

Harness layout

DIAGNOSTIC PROCEDURE 43 — POWER VALVE CONTROL (NOT SELF-DIAGNOSTIC ITEM) — VE30DE ENGINE

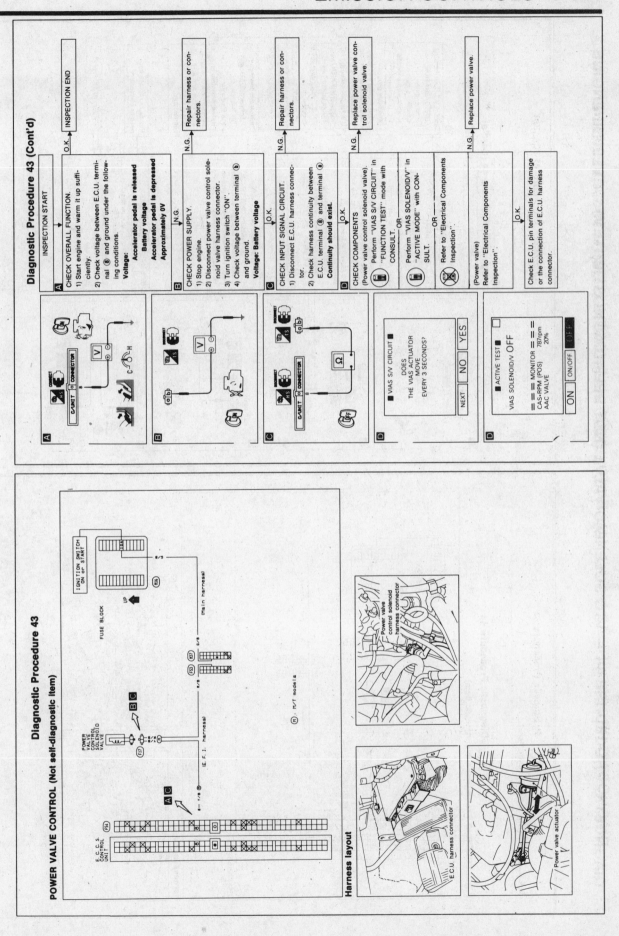

POWER VALVE CONTROL (Not self-diagnostic item)

Diagnostic Procedure 43 (Cont'd)

INSPECTION START

A CHECK OVERALL FUNCTION.
1) Start engine and warm it up sufficiently.
2) Check voltage between E.C.U. terminal ⑧ and ground under the following conditions.

Voltage:
Accelerator pedal is released
Battery voltage
Accelerator pedal is depressed
Approximately 0V

O.K. → INSPECTION END

N.G. ↓

B CHECK POWER SUPPLY.
1) Stop engine.
2) Disconnect power valve control solenoid valve harness connector.
3) Turn ignition switch "ON".
4) Check voltage between terminal ⓑ and ground.
Voltage: Battery voltage

N.G. → Repair harness or connectors.

O.K. ↓

C CHECK INPUT SIGNAL CIRCUIT.
1) Disconnect E.C.U. harness connector.
2) Check harness continuity between E.C.U. terminal ⑧ and terminal ⓑ.
Continuity should exist.

N.G. → Repair harness or connectors.

O.K. ↓

D CHECK COMPONENTS
(Power valve control solenoid valve.)
• Perform "VIAS S/V CIRCUIT" in "FUNCTION TEST" mode with CONSULT.
OR
• Perform "VIAS SOLENOID/V" in "ACTIVE MODE" with CONSULT.
OR
• Refer to "Electrical Components Inspection".

N.G. → Replace power valve control solenoid valve.

O.K. ↓

(Power valve)
Refer to "Electrical Components Inspection".

N.G. → Replace power valve.

O.K. ↓

Check E.C.U. pin terminals for damage or the connection of E.C.U. harness connector.

D VIAS S/V CIRCUIT
DOES THE VIAS ACTUATOR MOVE EVERY 3 SECONDS?
NEXT   NO   YES

D ACTIVE TEST
VIAS SOLENOID/v OFF
≡ ≡ ≡ MONITOR ≡ ≡ ≡
CAS•RPM (POS)   787rpm
AAC VALVE   20%
ON   ON/OFF   OFF

Harness layout

Diagnostic Procedure 43

Power valve control solenoid harness connector

E.C.U. harness connector

Power valve actuator

DIAGNOSTIC PROCEDURE 44 — VTC SOLENOID VALVE (NOT SELF-DIAGNOSTIC ITEM) — VE30DE ENGINE

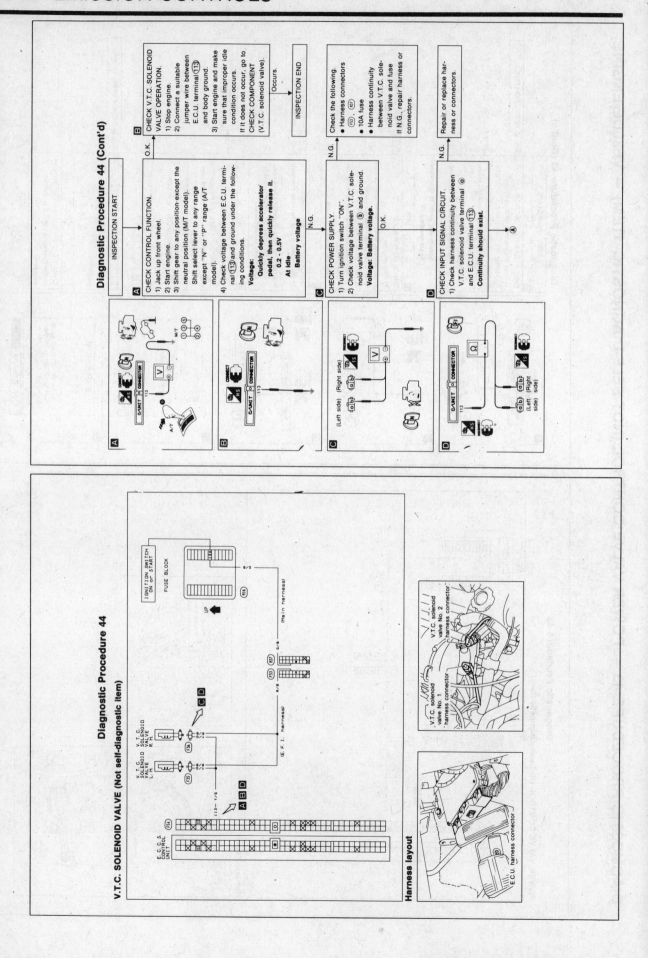

Diagnostic Procedure 44 (Cont'd)

INSPECTION START

A CHECK CONTROL FUNCTION.
1) Jack up front wheel.
2) Start engine.
3) Shift gear to any position except the neutral position (M/T model).
   Shift select lever to any range except "N" or "P" range (A/T model).
4) Check voltage between E.C.U. terminal ⑪⑬ and ground under the following conditions:
   Voltage:
   Quickly depress accelerator pedal, then quickly release it.
   0.2 - 0.5V
   At idle
   Battery voltage

O.K. → **B** CHECK V.T.C. SOLENOID VALVE OPERATION.
1) Stop engine.
2) Connect a suitable jumper wire between E.C.U. terminal ⑪⑬ and body ground.
3) Start engine and make sure that improper idle condition occurs.
If it does not occur, go to CHECK COMPONENT (V.T.C. solenoid valve).

Occurs. → INSPECTION END

N.G. ↓

C CHECK POWER SUPPLY.
1) Turn ignition switch "ON".
2) Check voltage between V.T.C. solenoid valve terminal ① and ground.
   Voltage: Battery voltage.

N.G. → Check the following.
• Harness connectors ⑤⑤, ⑭⑦
• 10A fuse
• Harness continuity between V.T.C. solenoid valve and fuse
If N.G., repair harness or connectors.

O.K. ↓

D CHECK INPUT SIGNAL CIRCUIT.
1) Check harness continuity between V.T.C. solenoid valve terminal ② and E.C.U. terminal ⑪⑬.
   Continuity should exist.

N.G. → Repair or replace harness or connectors.

A ↓

Diagnostic Procedure 44

V.T.C. SOLENOID VALVE (Not self-diagnostic item)

Harness layout

DIAGNOSTIC PROCEDURE 45 — RADIATOR FAN CONTROL (NOT SELF-DIAGNOSTIC ITEM) VE30DE ENGINE

Diagnostic Procedure 45

RADIATOR FAN CONTROL (Not self-diagnostic item)

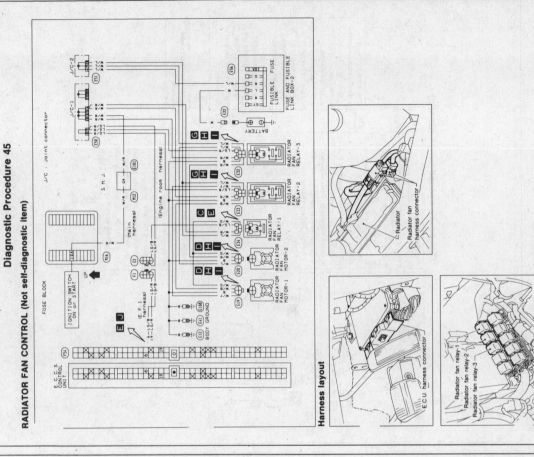

Harness layout

DIAGNOSTIC PROCEDURE 44 — VTC SOLENOID VALVE (NOT SELF-DIAGNOSTIC ITEM) VE30DE ENGINE, CONT.

Diagnostic Procedure 44 (Cont'd)

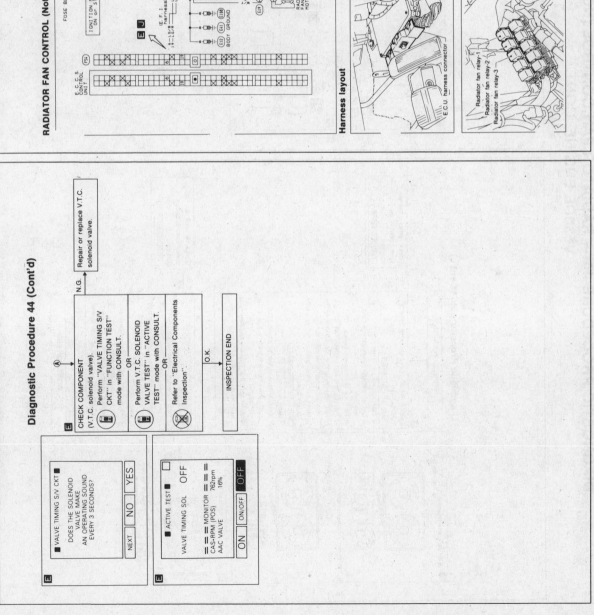

CHECK COMPONENT
(V.T.C. solenoid valve).
Perform "VALVE TIMING S/V CKT" in "FUNCTION TEST" mode with CONSULT.

OR

Perform V.T.C. SOLENOID VALVE TEST" in "ACTIVE TEST" mode with CONSULT.

OR

Refer to "Electrical Components Inspection".

N.G. → Repair or replace V.T.C. solenoid valve.

O.K.

INSPECTION END

VALVE TIMING S/V CKT
DOES THE SOLENOID VALVE MAKE AN OPERATING SOUND EVERY 3 SECONDS?

NEXT   NO   YES

ACTIVE TEST
VALVE TIMING SOL   OFF
═══ MONITOR ═══
CAS-RPM (POS)   762rpm
AAC VALVE   16%

ON   ON/OFF   OFF

DIAGNOSTIC PROCEDURE 45 — RADIATOR FAN CONTROL (NOT SELF-DIAGNOSTIC ITEM) VE30DE ENGINE, CONT.

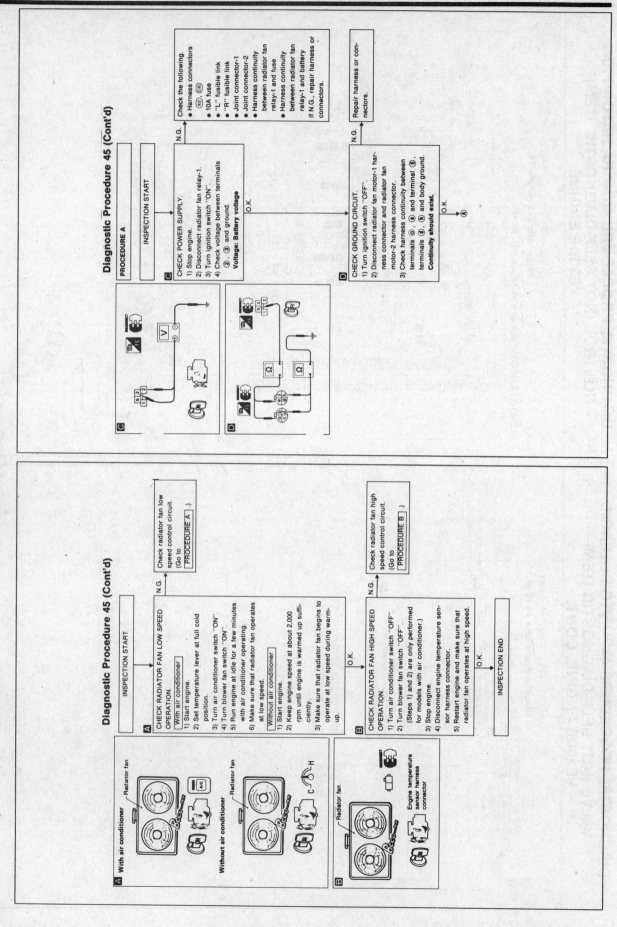

Diagnostic Procedure 45 (Cont'd)

INSPECTION START

A CHECK RADIATOR FAN LOW SPEED OPERATION.

With air conditioner
1) Start engine.
2) Set temperature lever at full cold position.
3) Turn air conditioner switch "ON".
4) Turn blower fan switch "ON".
5) Run engine at idle for a few minutes with air conditioner operating.
6) Make sure that radiator fan operates at low speed.

Without air conditioner
1) Start engine.
2) Keep engine speed at about 2,000 rpm until engine is warmed up sufficiently.
3) Make sure that radiator fan begins to operate at low speed during warm-up.

N.G. → Check radiator fan low speed control circuit. (Go to PROCEDURE A .)

O.K. ↓

B CHECK RADIATOR FAN HIGH SPEED OPERATION.
1) Turn air conditioner switch "OFF".
2) Turn blower fan switch "OFF". (Steps 1) and 2) are only performed for models with air conditioner.)
3) Stop engine.
4) Disconnect engine temperature sensor harness connector.
5) Restart engine and make sure that radiator fan operates at high speed.

N.G. → Check radiator fan high speed control circuit. (Go to PROCEDURE B .)

O.K. ↓

INSPECTION END

A With air conditioner
Radiator fan

Without air conditioner
Radiator fan

B Radiator fan

Engine temperature sensor harness connector

Diagnostic Procedure 45 (Cont'd)

PROCEDURE A

INSPECTION START

C CHECK POWER SUPPLY.
1) Stop engine.
2) Disconnect radiator fan relay-1.
3) Turn ignition switch "ON".
4) Check voltage between terminals ②, ③ and ground.
Voltage: Battery voltage

N.G. → Check the following.
• Harness connectors (M2), (E11)
• 10A fuse
• "L" fusible link
• "R" fusible link
• Joint connector-1
• Joint connector-2
• Harness continuity between radiator fan relay-1 and fuse
• Harness continuity between radiator fan relay-1 and battery
If N.G., repair harness or connectors.

O.K. →

D CHECK GROUND CIRCUIT.
1) Turn ignition switch "OFF".
2) Disconnect radiator fan motor-1 harness connector and radiator fan motor-2 harness connector.
3) Check harness continuity between terminals ⓐ, ① and terminal ⑤, terminals ④, ① and body ground.
Continuity should exist.

N.G. → Repair harness or connectors.

O.K. → (A)

DIAGNOSTIC PROCEDURE 45 — RADIATOR FAN CONTROL (NOT SELF-DIAGNOSTIC ITEM) VE30DE ENGINE, CONT.

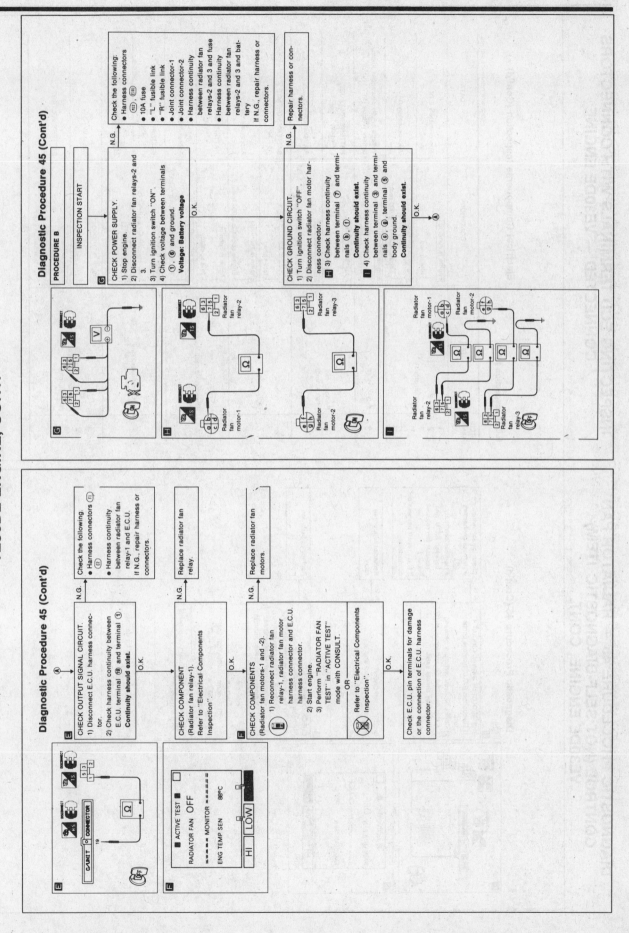

Diagnostic Procedure 45 (Cont'd)

PROCEDURE B

INSPECTION START

G CHECK POWER SUPPLY.
1) Stop engine.
2) Disconnect radiator fan relays-2 and 3.
3) Turn ignition switch "ON".
4) Check voltage between terminals ① , ⑧ and ground.
Voltage: Battery voltage

N.G. → Check the following:
- Harness connectors ⑩ ⑪
- 10A fuse
- "L" fusible link
- "R" fusible link
- Joint connector-1
- Joint connector-2
- Harness continuity between radiator fan relays-2 and 3 and fuse
- Harness continuity between radiator fan relays-2 and 3 and battery
If N.G., repair harness or connectors.

O.K. ↓

H CHECK GROUND CIRCUIT.
1) Turn ignition switch "OFF".
2) Disconnect radiator fan motor harness connector.
3) Check harness continuity between terminal ⑦ and terminals ⑩, ①.
Continuity should exist.
4) Check harness continuity between terminal ③ and terminals ⑥, ①, terminal ⑤ and body ground.
Continuity should exist.

N.G. → Repair harness or connectors.

O.K. → (A)

E CHECK OUTPUT SIGNAL CIRCUIT.
1) Disconnect E.C.U. harness connector.
2) Check harness continuity between E.C.U. terminal ⑲ and terminal ①.
Continuity should exist.

N.G. → Check the following:
- Harness connectors ⑪
- Harness continuity between radiator fan relay-1 and E.C.U.
If N.G., repair harness or connectors.

O.K. ↓

CHECK COMPONENT
(Radiator fan relay-1).
Refer to "Electrical Components Inspection".

N.G. → Replace radiator fan relay.

O.K. ↓

F CHECK COMPONENTS
(Radiator fan motors-1 and -2).
1) Reconnect radiator fan relay-1, radiator fan motor harness connector and E.C.U. harness connector.
2) Start engine.
3) Perform "RADIATOR FAN TEST" in "ACTIVE TEST" mode with CONSULT.
— OR —
Refer to "Electrical Components Inspection".

N.G. → Replace radiator fan motors.

O.K. ↓

Check E.C.U. pin terminals for damage or the connection of E.C.U. harness connector.

ACTIVE TEST ■
RADIATOR FAN OFF
===== MONITOR =====
ENG TEMP SEN   88°C
HI   LOW

DIAGNOSTIC PROCEDURE 45 — RADIATOR FAN CONTROL (NOT SELF-DIAGNOSTIC ITEM) VE30DE ENGINE, CONT.

Diagnostic Procedure 45 (Cont'd)

(A) →

CHECK OUTPUT SIGNAL CIRCUIT.
1) Disconnect E.C.U. harness connector.
2) Check harness continuity between E.C.U. terminal ⑥ and terminal ②. **Continuity should exist.**

→ N.G. → Check the following.
- Harness connectors (F₁) (F)
- Harness continuity between E.C.U. and radiator fan relays-2 and 3

If N.G., repair harness or connectors.

→ O.K.

CHECK COMPONENT
(Radiator fan relays-2 and 3).
Refer to "Electrical Components Inspection".

→ N.G. → Replace radiator fan relay.

→ O.K.

CHECK COMPONENTS
(Radiator fan motors-1 and -2).
1) Reconnect radiator fan relay-2, radiator fan motor harness connector, engine temperature sensor harness connector and E.C.U. harness connector.
2) Start engine.
3) Perform "RADIATOR FAN TEST" in "ACTIVE TEST" mode with CONSULT.
— OR —
Refer to "Electrical Components Inspection".

→ N.G. → Replace radiator fan motors.

→ O.K.

Check E.C.U. pin terminals for damage or the connection of E.C.U. harness connector.

```
■ ACTIVE TEST ■        □
RADIATOR FAN   OFF
===== MONITOR =====
ENG TEMP SEN    88°C

HI
LOW
```

INSPECTING ECU TERMINALS WITH CONNECTORS CONNECTED — VE30DE ENGINE

E.C.U. inspection table

Electrical Components Inspection (Cont'd)

*Data are reference values.

TERMINAL NO.	ITEM	CONDITION	*DATA
1, 2, 3, 11, 12, 13	Ignition signal	Engine is running. / Idle speed	Approximately 0.1V
		Engine is running. / Engine speed is 2,000 rpm.	Approximately 0.1V
4	A.A.C. valve	Engine is running. / Racing condition	Voltage briefly decreases from battery voltage (11 - 14V).
		Engine is running.	BATTERY VOLTAGE (11 - 14V)
6	Radiator fan (High speed)	Engine is running. / Radiator fan is not operating.	Approximately 0V
		Engine is running. / Radiator fan is operating.	BATTERY VOLTAGE (11 - 14V)
7	Tachometer	Engine is running. / Idle speed	Approximately 2.5V
		Engine is running. / Engine speed is 2,000 rpm.	BATTERY VOLTAGE (11 - 14V)
8	Power valve control solenoid valve	Engine is running. / Idle speed	Approximately 0V
		Engine is running. / Racing (up to 4,000 rpm) quickly	BATTERY VOLTAGE (11 - 14V)
9	Air conditioner relay	Engine is running. / Air conditioner switch "OFF"	BATTERY VOLTAGE (11 - 14V)
		Engine is running. / Air conditioner switch "ON"	Approximately 0V
16	E.C.U. power source (Self-shutoff)	Engine is running. / Idle speed	0.8 - 1.0V
		Engine is running. / For a few seconds after turning ignition switch "OFF"	BATTERY VOLTAGE (11 - 14V)

INSPECTING ECU TERMINALS WITH CONNECTORS CONNECTED – VE30DE ENGINE, CONT.

Electrical Components Inspection (Cont'd)

*Data are reference values.

TERMINAL NO.	ITEM	CONDITION	*DATA
18	Fuel pump relay	Ignition switch "ON" / For 5 seconds after turning ignition switch "ON"	0.7 - 0.9V
		Engine is running. / 5 seconds after turning ignition switch "ON"	BATTERY VOLTAGE (11 - 14V)
19	Radiator fan (Low speed)	Engine is running. / Radiator fan is not operating.	BATTERY VOLTAGE (11 - 14V)
		Engine is running. / Radiator fan is operating.	Approximately 0V
23	Detonation sensor	Engine is running.	2.0 - 3.0V
27	Air flow meter	Engine is running. (Warm-up condition) / Idle speed.	0.8 - 1.5V
		Engine is running. (Warm-up condition) / Engine speed is 3,000 rpm.	1.4 - 2.0V
28	Engine temperature sensor	Engine is running.	0 - 5.0V Output voltage varies with engine temperature.
29	Exhaust gas sensor	Engine is running. / After warming up sufficiently and engine speed is 2,000 rpm.	0 ↔ Approximately 0V
34	Power steering oil pressure switch	Engine is running. / Steering wheel stays straight.	4.0 - 5.0V
		Engine is running. / Steering wheel is turned.	Approximately 0V
38	Throttle sensor	Ignition switch "ON"	0.4 - 4.0V Output voltage varies with throttle valve opening angle.

Electrical Components Inspection (Cont'd)

*Data are reference values.

TERMINAL NO.	ITEM	CONDITION	*DATA
39	Exhaust gas temperature sensor	Engine is running. (Warm-up condition) / Idle speed.	1.0V or more
		Engine is running. (Warm-up condition) / E.G.R. system is operating.	0 - 1.0V
41 51	Crank angle sensor (Reference signal)	Engine is running. / Do not run engine at high speed under no-load.	1.0 - 1.5V Output voltage slightly varies with engine speed.
42 52	Crank angle sensor (Position signal)	Engine is running. / Do not run engine at high speed under no-load.	2.3 - 2.6V Output voltage slightly varies with engine speed.
43	Start signal	Ignition switch "ON"	0V
		Ignition switch "START"	BATTERY VOLTAGE (11 - 14V)
44	Neutral switch (M/T models) Inhibitor switch (A/T models)	Ignition switch "ON" / Gear position is "Neutral" (M/T models) Gear position is "N" or "P" (A/T models)	0V
45	Ignition switch	Ignition switch "ON" / Except the above conditions	4.0 - 5.0V
		Ignition switch "ON" / Engine stopped	BATTERY VOLTAGE (11 - 14V)
46	Air conditioner switch	Engine is running. / Air conditioner switch "OFF"	BATTERY VOLTAGE (11 - 14V)
		Engine is running. / Air conditioner switch "ON"	Approximately 0.2V
48	Power source for sensors	Ignition switch "ON" / Engine stopped	Approximately 5.0V
49	Battery source	Ignition switch "ON" / Engine stopped	BATTERY VOLTAGE (11 - 14V)

INSPECTING ECU TERMINALS WITH CONNECTORS CONNECTED – VE30DE ENGINE, CONT.

Electrical Components Inspection (Cont'd)

*Data are reference values.

TER-MINAL NO.	ITEM	CONDITION	*DATA
53	Vehicle speed sensor	Ignition switch "ON" / Engine stopped / While rotating front wheel by hand	0 or 7.0 - 9.0V
54	Throttle valve switch (Idle position)	Ignition switch "ON" / Accelerator pedal is fully released (engine stopped).	8.0 - 10.0V
		Ignition switch "ON" / Accelerator pedal is depressed (engine stopped).	0V
57	Power source for throttle valve switch	Ignition switch "ON" / Engine stopped	8.0 - 10.0V
58	Battery	Ignition switch "OFF"	BATTERY VOLTAGE (11 - 14V)
59	Power supply	Ignition switch "ON" / Idle speed	BATTERY VOLTAGE (11 - 14V)
101 103 105 110 112 114	Injectors	Ignition switch "OFF"	BATTERY VOLTAGE (11 - 14V)
		Engine is running. (Warm-up condition) / Idle speed. Engine speed is approximately 2,700 rpm or more (M/T models) 3,200 rpm or more (A/T models)	Approximately 0V
102	E.G.R. control solenoid valve	Engine is running. (Warm-up condition) / Engine speed is between idle and approximately 2,700 rpm or more (M/T models) 3,200 rpm or more (A/T models)	BATTERY VOLTAGE (11 - 14V)

Electrical Components Inspection (Cont'd)

*Data are reference values.

TER-MINAL NO.	ITEM	CONDITION	*DATA
113	Valve timing control solenoid valve	Engine is running. / Idle speed	BATTERY VOLTAGE (11 - 14V)
		Engine is running. / Quickly depress accelerator pedal, then quickly release it.	0.2 - 0.5V

E.C.U. S.M.J. HARNESS CONNECTOR TERMINAL LAYOUT

5

FUEL
SYSTEM

Fuel Injection Systems 5-2

FUEL INJECTION SYSTEM

➡ **This Section pertains to the removal, installation and adjustment of fuel system related components. For comprehensive diagnostic and testing of the emission and fuel systems, refer to Section 4.**

Description of System

The Electronic Fuel Injection (EFI) systems use various types of sensors to convert engine operating conditions into electronic signals. The generated information is fed into an Electronic Control Unit (ECU), where it is analyzed, then calculated electrical signals are then sent to the various equipment, to control idle speed, timing and amount of fuel being injected into the engine.

Relieving Fuel System Pressure

♦ SEE FIGS. 1–6

1. On the 1985 models, remove the rear seat.
2. Start the engine.
3. On the 1985 models, disconnect the fuel pump electrical connector, located on the left side of the vehicle. On the 1986–92 models, remove the fuel pump fuse from the fuse block.

➡ **If using the CONSULT diagnostic tester on the 1992 VE30DE engine, place it in the WORK SUPPORT mode and depress the START button, with the engine idling, to release the fuel pressure.**

4. After the engine stalls, try to restart the engine; if the engine will not start, the fuel pressure has been released.
5. Turn the ignition switch **OFF**. On the 1985 models, reconnect the electrical connector and replace the rear seat. On the 1986–92 models, reinstall the fuel pump fuse into the fuse block.

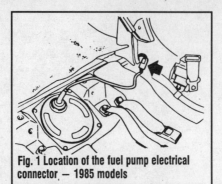

Fig. 1 Location of the fuel pump electrical connector — 1985 models

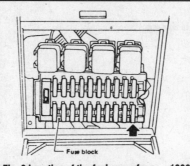

Fig. 2 Location of the fuel pump fuse — 1986 models

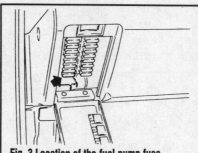

Fig. 3 Location of the fuel pump fuse — 1987–88 models

Fig. 4 Location of the fuel pump fuse — 1989–91 models

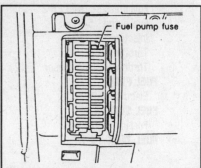

Fig. 5 Location of the fuel pump fuse — 1992 models

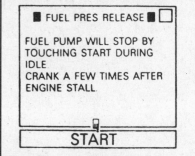

```
■ FUEL PRES RELEASE ■ □

FUEL PUMP WILL STOP BY
TOUCHING START DURING
IDLE
CRANK A FEW TIMES AFTER
ENGINE STALL.



        START
```

Fig. 6 View of the CONSULT diagnostic tester START button — 1992 models

Electric Fuel Pump

REMOVAL & INSTALLATION

♦ SEE FIGS. 7 AND 8

1. Refer to "Relieving Fuel System Pressure" procedures, in this section, and release the fuel pressure. Reducing the fuel pressure to zero is a very important step for correct removal of the electric fuel pump.
2. Disconnect the negative battery cable.
3. If necessary, remove the rear seat. Open the trunk lid, disconnect the fuel gauge electrical connector and remove the fuel tank inspection cover.

➡ **If vehicle has no fuel tank inspection cover the fuel tank must be lowered or removed to gain access to the in-tank fuel pump.**

4. Disconnect the fuel outlet and the return hoses. Remove the fuel tank, if necessary; refer to the Fuel Tank, Removal And Installation procedure in this section.

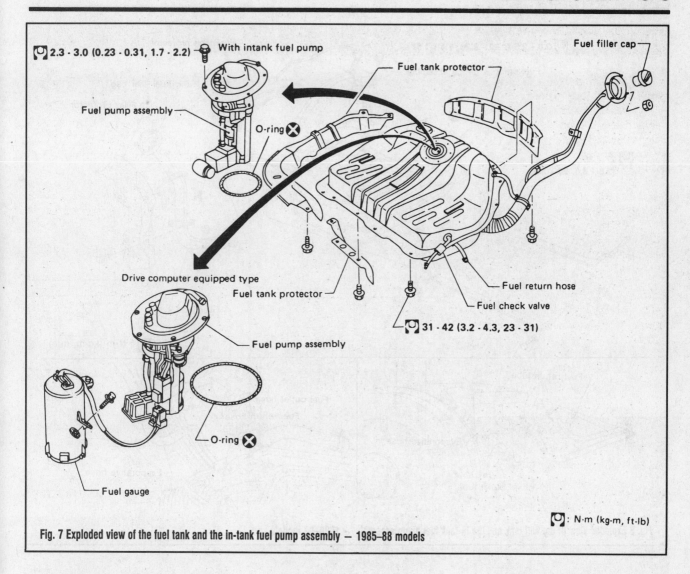

2.3 - 3.0 (0.23 - 0.31, 1.7 - 2.2)   With intank fuel pump

Fuel filler cap

Fuel tank protector

Fuel pump assembly

O-ring ⊗

Drive computer equipped type

Fuel tank protector

Fuel pump assembly

Fuel return hose

Fuel check valve

31 - 42 (3.2 - 4.3, 23 - 31)

O-ring ⊗

Fuel gauge

: N·m (kg-m, ft-lb)

Fig. 7 Exploded view of the fuel tank and the in-tank fuel pump assembly — 1985–88 models

5. Remove the fuel pump assembly-to-fuel tank bolts and lift the fuel pump assembly from the fuel tank. Discard the O-ring. Plug the fuel tank opening with a clean rag, to prevent dirt from entering the system.

➡ **When removing or installing the fuel pump assembly, be careful not to damage or deform it. Install a new O-ring.**

To install:

6. Using a new O-ring, install fuel pump assembly into the fuel tank.

7. Install the fuel pump assembly-to-fuel tank bolts and torque the bolts to 1.7–2.2 ft. lbs. (2.3–3.0 Nm) for 1985–88 or 1.4–1.9 ft. lbs. (2.0–2.5 Nm) for 1989–92. Install the fuel tank if removed, refer to the Fuel Tank, Removal And Installation procedure in this section.

8. Reconnect the fuel lines and the electrical connector.

9. Install the fuel tank inspection cover.

10. Connect battery cable, start engine and check for fuel leaks.

➡ **On some models, the "Check Engine Light" will stay ON after installation is completed. The memory code in the control unit must be erased. To erase the code, disconnect the battery cable for 10 seconds then reconnect after installation of fuel pump.**

TESTING

◆ SEE FIGS. 9-13

1. To inspect the electrical condition of the fuel pump, perform the following procedures:

    a. Turn the ignition switch **OFF**.

    b. In the trunk, disconnect the fuel pump electrical connector.

c. Using an ohmmeter, set on the lowest scale, connect the probes to terminals **a** and **c**. The resistance should be 0.5 ohms; if not, replace the fuel pump.

d. If the fuel pump resistance is OK, reconnect the fuel pump electrical connector.

2. Release the fuel pressure. Connect a fuel pressure gauge between the fuel filter outlet and fuel feed tube.

3. Start the engine and read the pressure; it should be:

VG30E engine 1985–88 30 psi (206 kPa) — At idle

37 psi (255 kPa) — At the moment the accelerator is fully depressed

1989–92 36.3 psi (250.1 kPa) — At idle

43.4 psi (299.1 kPa) — Disconnected fuel pressure valve vacuum hose   VE30DE engine 36 psi (245 kPa) — At idle

43 psi (294 kPa) — Disconnected fuel pressure valve vacuum hose.

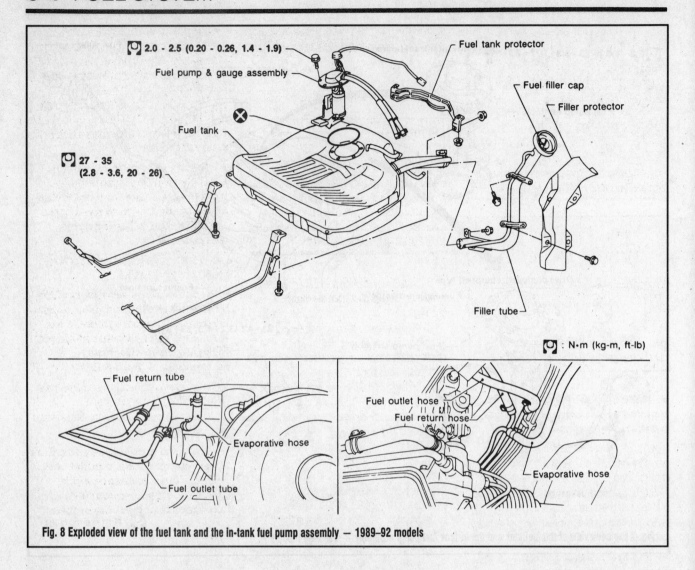

2.0 - 2.5 (0.20 - 0.26, 1.4 - 1.9)

Fuel pump & gauge assembly

Fuel tank protector

Fuel filler cap

Filler protector

Fuel tank

27 - 35 (2.8 - 3.6, 20 - 26)

Filler tube

: N·m (kg-m, ft-lb)

Fuel return tube

Evaporative hose

Fuel outlet tube

Fuel outlet hose

Fuel return hose

Evaporative hose

Fig. 8 Exploded view of the fuel tank and the in-tank fuel pump assembly — 1989–92 models

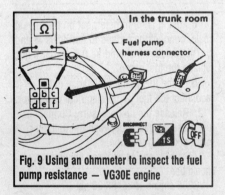

In the trunk room

Fuel pump harness connector

Fig. 9 Using an ohmmeter to inspect the fuel pump resistance — VG30E engine

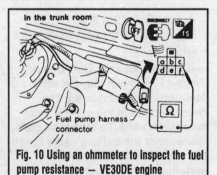

In the trunk room

Fuel pump harness connector

Fig. 10 Using an ohmmeter to inspect the fuel pump resistance — VE30DE engine

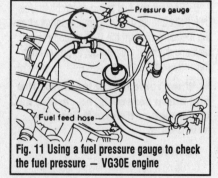

Pressure gauge

Fuel feed hose

Fig. 11 Using a fuel pressure gauge to check the fuel pressure — VG30E engine

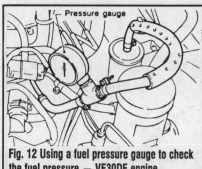

Fig. 12 Using a fuel pressure gauge to check the fuel pressure — VE30DE engine

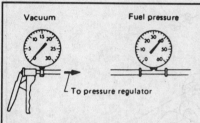

Fig. 13 Using a variable vacuum source to check the fuel pump pressure

➡ **Make sure the fuel filter is not blocked before replacing any fuel system components.**

4. Stop the engine. Disconnect the fuel pressure regulator vacuum hose from the intake manifold and plug the intake manifold opening.

5. Using a variable vacuum source, connect it to the fuel pressure regulator.

6. Start the engine and read the fuel pressure gauge as the vacuum is changed.

➡ **The fuel pressure should decrease as the vacuum increases; if not, replace the fuel pressure regulator.**

7. If pressure is not as specified, replace the pressure regulator and repeat the test. If the pressure is still incorrect, check for clogged or deformed fuel lines, then replace the fuel pump.

Throttle Body

REMOVAL & INSTALLATION

◆ SEE FIGS. 14–16

✳✳ CAUTION

Never smoke when working around gasoline! Avoid all sources of sparks or ignition. Gasoline vapors are EXTREMELY volatile!

1. Disconnect the negative battery cable and remove the intake duct from the throttle chamber.

2. Disconnect the vacuum hoses and the electrical harness connector from the throttle chamber. Disconnect the accelerator cable from the throttle chamber.

3. On the 1989–92 VG30E and 1992 VE30DE engines, remove the dual intake duct to the throttle body bolts, remove the duct and discard the gasket.

4. Remove the mounting bolts and the throttle chamber from the intake manifold.

To install:

5. Use a new gasket and reverse the removal procedures. Torque the throttle chamber-to-intake manifold collector bolts, using 2 steps, to:

    a. Step 1 — 6.5–8.0 ft. lbs. (9–11 Nm)
    b. Step 2 — 13–16 ft. lbs. (18–22 Nm)

6. On the 1989–92 VG30E and 1992 VE30DE engines, use a new gasket and install the dual intake duct to the throttle body and torque the dual intake duct-to-throttle body bolts to 13–16 ft. lbs. (18–22 Nm).

7. Install and/or adjust the throttle cable, if necessary. On the VE30DE engine, torque the throttle body-to-intake manifold collector bolts in the proper sequence.

➡ **Check the throttle for smooth operation and make sure the bypass port is free from obstacles and is clean. Check to make sure the idle speed adjusting screw moves smoothly.**

8. Connect the electrical connector and the hoses to the throttle body.

➡ **Because of the sensitivity of the air flow meter, there cannot be any air leaks in the fuel system. Even the smallest leak could unbalance the system and affect the performance of the vehicle.**

9. Connect the air duct to the throttle body. Connect the negative battery cable.

10. Start the engine. Check for air leaks and engine operation.

➡ **During every check, pay attention to hose connections, dipstick and oil filler cap for evidence of air leaks. Should you encounter any, take steps to correct the problem.**

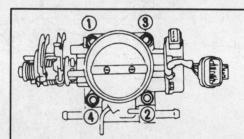

Tighten in numerical order. Throttle chamber bolts tightening procedure
1) Tighten all bolts to 9 to 11 N·m (0.9 to 1.1 kg-m, 6.5 to 8.0 ft-lb).
2) Tighten all bolts to 18 to 22 N·m (1.8 to 2.2 kg-m, 13 to 16 ft-lb)

Fig. 16 View of the throttle body torquing sequence — 1992 VE30DE engine

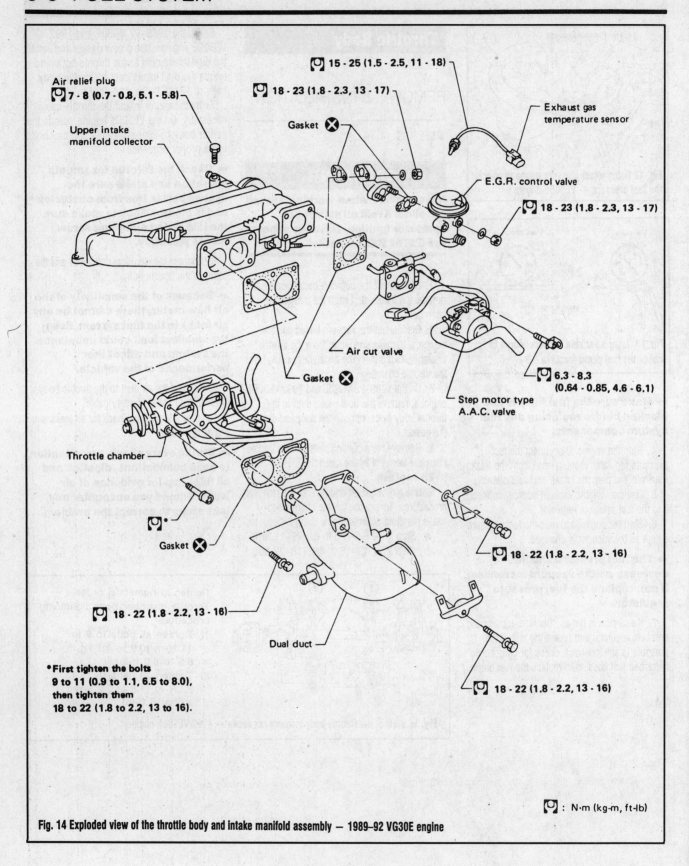

Air relief plug
⊙ 7 - 8 (0.7 - 0.8, 5.1 - 5.8)

⊙ 15 - 25 (1.5 - 2.5, 11 - 18)

⊙ 18 - 23 (1.8 - 2.3, 13 - 17)

Upper intake
manifold collector

Gasket ⊗

Exhaust gas
temperature sensor

E.G.R. control valve

⊙ 18 - 23 (1.8 - 2.3, 13 - 17)

Air cut valve

Gasket ⊗

⊙ 6.3 - 8.3
(0.64 - 0.85, 4.6 - 6.1)

Step motor type
A.A.C. valve

Throttle chamber

⊙ *

Gasket ⊗

⊙ 18 - 22 (1.8 - 2.2, 13 - 16)

⊙ 18 - 22 (1.8 - 2.2, 13 - 16)

Dual duct

⊙ 18 - 22 (1.8 - 2.2, 13 - 16)

*First tighten the bolts
9 to 11 (0.9 to 1.1, 6.5 to 8.0),
then tighten them
18 to 22 (1.8 to 2.2, 13 to 16).

⊙ : N·m (kg-m, ft-lb)

Fig. 14 Exploded view of the throttle body and intake manifold assembly — 1989–92 VG30E engine

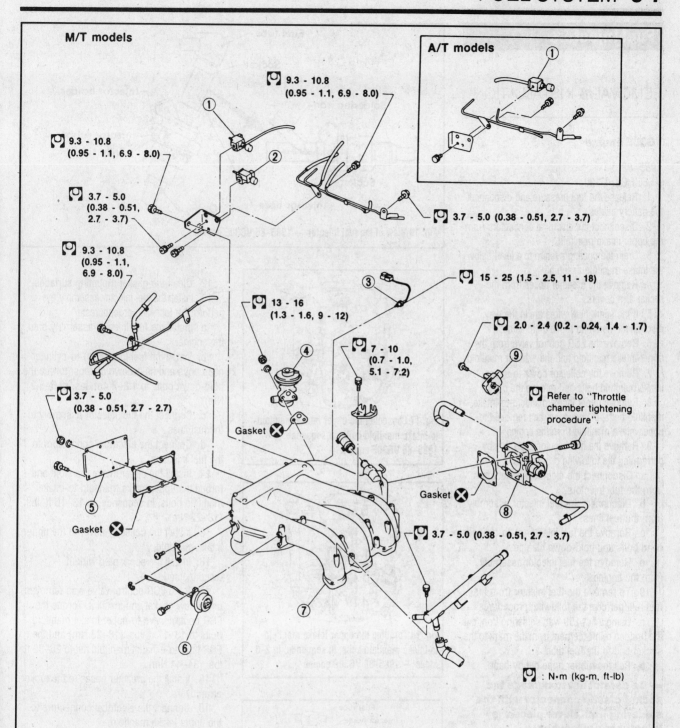

M/T models

A/T models

9.3 - 10.8 (0.95 - 1.1, 6.9 - 8.0)

9.3 - 10.8 (0.95 - 1.1, 6.9 - 8.0)

3.7 - 5.0 (0.38 - 0.51, 2.7 - 3.7)

9.3 - 10.8 (0.95 - 1.1, 6.9 - 8.0)

3.7 - 5.0 (0.38 - 0.51, 2.7 - 3.7)

15 - 25 (1.5 - 2.5, 11 - 18)

13 - 16 (1.3 - 1.6, 9 - 12)

2.0 - 2.4 (0.2 - 0.24, 1.4 - 1.7)

7 - 10 (0.7 - 1.0, 5.1 - 7.2)

Refer to "Throttle chamber tightening procedure".

3.7 - 5.0 (0.38 - 0.51, 2.7 - 2.7)

Gasket

Gasket

Gasket

3.7 - 5.0 (0.38 - 0.51, 2.7 - 3.7)

: N•m (kg-m, ft-lb)

① E.G.R. control solenoid valve
② Power valve control solenoid valve (M/T only)
③ Exhaust gas temperature sensor
④ E.G.R. control valve
⑤ Intake manifold collector cover (M/T only)
⑥ Power valve actuator (M/T only)
⑦ Intake manifold collector
⑧ Throttle chamber
⑨ Throttle sensor

Fig. 15 Exploded view of the throttle body and intake manifold assembly — 1992 VE30DE engine

Fuel Injectors

REMOVAL & INSTALLATION

VG30E engine

1985–88
♦ SEE FIGS. 17-20

1. Release the fuel pressure and disconnect the battery cables.

2. Disconnect the electrical connectors from the upper intake manifold.

3. Drain the cooling system to a level below the intake manifold assembly.

4. Remove the breather hoses from the rocker arm covers.

5. If the spark plug wires are in the way, disconnect them and move them aside.

6. Remove the EGR control valve from the upper intake manifold and the exhaust manifold.

7. Remove the collector cover-to-upper intake manifold bolts and remove the cover.

8. Remove upper intake manifold-to-intake manifold bolts, in sequence, and remove the upper intake manifold from the engine.

9. Remove the fuel injector assembly by performing the following procedures:

    a. Disconnect the electrical connectors from the fuel injectors.

    b. Disconnect the fuel injector assembly from the fuel lines.

    c. Remove the fuel injector(s)-to-cylinder head bolts and hold-down clamps.

    d. Remove the fuel injector assembly from the engine.

10. To remove the fuel injector from the fuel rail, perform the following procedures:

    a. Using a hot 150 watt soldering iron, cut the braided reinforcement from the mark to the socket end to the fuel tube.

    b. Pull the rubber hose out by hand.

➡ Be careful not to damage the socket plastic connector with the soldering iron. Never place the injector in a vise when disconnecting the rubber hose.

To install:

11. To install the fuel injector to the fuel rail, perform the following procedures:

    a. Clean the injector tail piece and the fuel tube end.

    b. Using fuel, wet the inside of the new rubber hose.

    c. Push the end of the rubber hose, with the hose sockets, onto the injector tail piece and the fuel tube end by hand, as far as it will go.

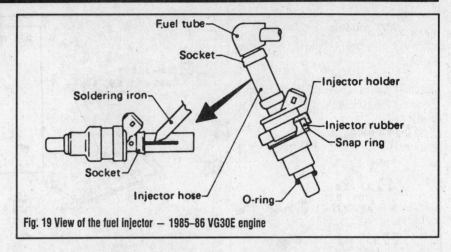

Fig. 19 View of the fuel injector — 1985–86 VG30E engine

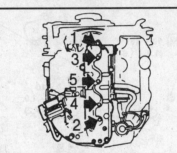

Fig. 17 Loosening the upper intake manifold-to-intake manifold bolts, in sequence — 1985–88 VG30E engine

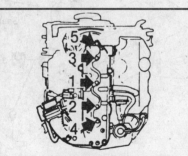

Fig. 18 Torquing the upper intake manifold-to-intake manifold bolts, in sequence, in 2–3 steps — 1985–88 VG30E engine

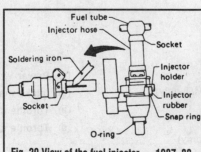

Fig. 20 View of the fuel injector — 1987–88 VG30E engine

12. Clean the gasket mounting surfaces.

13. Install the fuel injector assembly by perform the following procedures:

    a. Install the fuel injector assembly onto the engine.

    b. Install the fuel injector(s)-to-cylinder head bolts and hold-down clamps; torque the hold-down bolts to 1.8–2.4 ft. lbs. (2.5–3.2 Nm).

    c. Connect the fuel injector assembly to the fuel lines.

    d. Connect the electrical connectors to the fuel injectors.

14. Install the upper intake manifold and torque the upper intake manifold-to-intake manifold bolts, in sequence, to 13–16 ft. lbs. (18–22 Nm).

15. Install the collector cover to the upper intake manifold.

16. Install the spark plug wire, if disconnected.

17. If the EGR control valve was removed, use a new gasket and install it. Torque the EGR control valve-to-upper intake manifold bolts to 13–17 ft. lbs. (18–23 Nm) and the EGR tube-to-exhaust manifold nut to 25–33 ft. lbs. (34–44 Nm).

18. Install the breather hoses to the rocker arm covers.

19. Connect the electrical connectors to the upper intake manifold.

20. Refill the cooling system.

21. Connect the negative battery cable.

22. Start the engine and check for leaks.

1989–92
♦ SEE FIGS. 21–26

1. Disconnect the negative battery cable and relieve the fuel pressure.

2. Disconnect the air intake duct from the dual duct housing.

3. Disconnect the electrical connectors from the throttle body, the step motor AAC valve and the exhaust gas temperature sensor.

4. Disconnect and label the hoses from the rocker arm cover, the throttle body, the step motor AAC valve, the EGR control valve and the air cut valve.

5. If the spark plug wires are in the way, disconnect them and move them aside. Disconnect the accelerator cable from the throttle body.

6. Remove the upper intake manifold collector-to-intake manifold bolts, in sequence, and lift the assembly from the intake manifold. Discard the gasket.

7. Remove the lower intake manifold collector-to-intake manifold bolts, in sequence, and lift the assembly from the intake manifold. Discard the gasket.

8. Remove the fuel injector assembly by performing the following procedures:

   a. Disconnect the electrical connectors from the fuel injectors.

   b. Disconnect the fuel injector assembly from the fuel lines.

   c. Remove the fuel rail-to-cylinder head bolts.

   d. Remove the fuel rail assembly from the engine.

9. To remove the fuel injector from the fuel rail, remove the fuel injector-to-fuel rail bolts and the fuel injector from the fuel rail; discard the O-ring.

To install:

10. To install the fuel injector to the fuel rail, perform the following procedures:

   a. Install a new O-ring onto the fuel injector.

   b. Wet the new O-ring with fuel and press the injector into the fuel rail.

   c. Install the bolts and tighten the fuel injector retainer.

11. Clean the gasket mounting surfaces.

12. Install the fuel injector assembly by performing the following procedures:

   a. Install the fuel rail assembly to the engine.

   b. Install the fuel rail-to-cylinder head bolts and torque the bolts to 1.8–2.4 ft. lbs. (2.5–3.2 Nm).

   c. Connect the fuel injector assembly to the fuel lines.

   d. Connect the electrical connectors to the fuel injectors.

13. Use a new gasket and install the lower intake manifold collector; torque the lower intake manifold collector-to-intake manifold bolts, in 2–3 steps, in sequence, to 13–16 ft. lbs. (18–22 Nm).

14. Use a new gasket and install the upper intake manifold collector-to-intake manifold; torque the bolts to 5.1–5.8 ft. lbs. (7–8 Nm).

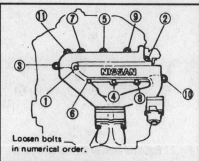

Fig. 21 Loosening the upper intake manifold collector bolts, in sequence — 1989–92 VG30E engine

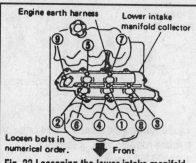

Fig. 22 Loosening the lower intake manifold collector bolts, in sequence — 1989–92 VG30E engine

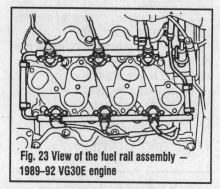

Fig. 23 View of the fuel rail assembly — 1989–92 VG30E engine

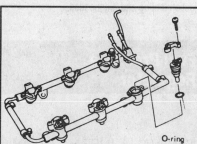

Fig. 24 Replacing the fuel injector in the fuel rail — 1989–92 VG30E engine

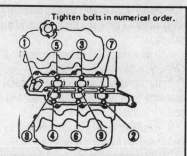

Fig. 25 Torquing the lower intake manifold collector bolts, in sequence — 1989–92 VG30E engine

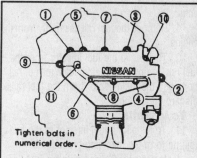

Fig. 26 Torquing the upper intake manifold collector-to-intake manifold bolts, in sequence — 1989–92 VG30E engine

15. Connect the spark plug wire, if disconnected. Connect the accelerator cable to the throttle body.

16. Connect the hoses to the rocker arm cover, the throttle body, the step motor AAC valve, the EGR control valve and the air cut valve.

17. Connect the electrical connectors to the throttle body, the step motor AAC valve and the exhaust gas temperature sensor.

18. Connect the negative battery cable.

19. Start the engine and check for leaks.

VE30DE Engine

◆ SEE FIG. 27 AND 28

1. Disconnect the negative battery cable.

2. Disconnect the electrical connectors from the throttle position sensor, the exhaust gas temperature sensor and/or etc.

3. Label and disconnect the hoses from the throttle body, the EGR valve, the EGR control solenoid valve, the intake manifold collector, the power valve control solenoid valve (if equipped with a manual transaxle) and the power valve actuator (if equipped with a manual transaxle).

4. Disconnect the accelerator cable from the throttle body.

5. Remove the intake manifold collector support-to-intake manifold collector and the intake manifold collector support-to-cylinder head bolts and the supports.

6. Remove the intake manifold collector-to-intake manifold bolts and the intake manifold collector.

7. If necessary, disconnect the electrical connectors from the ignition coils.

8. If necessary, disconnect the electrical connector from the crank angle sensor and the power transistor.

9. Remove the fuel injector assembly by performing the following procedures:

a. Disconnect the electrical connectors from the fuel injectors.

b. Disconnect the fuel injector assembly from the fuel lines.

c. Remove the fuel rail-to-cylinder head bolts.

d. Remove the fuel rail assembly from the engine.

10. To remove the fuel injector from the fuel rail, remove the fuel injector-to-fuel rail bolts and the fuel injector from the fuel rail; discard the O-rings.

To install:

11. To install the fuel injector to the fuel rail, perform the following procedures:

a. Install new O-rings onto the fuel injector.

b. Wet the new O-rings with fuel and press the injector into the fuel rail.

c. Install the bolts and tighten the fuel injector retainer.

12. Clean the gasket mounting surfaces.

13. Install the fuel injector assembly by performing the following procedures:

a. Install the fuel rail assembly to the engine.

b. Install the fuel rail-to-cylinder head bolts and torque the bolts to 12–14 ft. lbs. (16–20 Nm).

c. Connect the fuel injector assembly to the fuel lines.

d. Connect the electrical connectors to the fuel injectors.

14. Connect the electrical connectors to the ignition coils, if disconnected.

15. Using a new gasket, install the intake manifold collector and torque the intake manifold collector-to-intake manifold bolts, in sequence, to 13–16 ft. lbs. (18–22 Nm).

16. Install the intake manifold collector support and torque the bolts to 12–15 ft. lbs. (16–21 Nm).

17. Connect the accelerator cable to the throttle body.

18. Connect the hoses to the throttle body, the EGR valve, the EGR control solenoid valve, the intake manifold collector, the power valve control solenoid valve (if equipped with a manual transaxle) and the power valve actuator (if equipped with a manual transaxle).

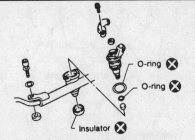

Fig. 27 Exploded view of the fuel injector to fuel rail assembly — 1992 VE30DE engine

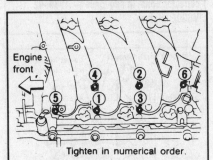

Fig. 28 Torquing the intake manifold collector-to-intake manifold bolts, in sequence — 1992 VE30DE engine

19. If disconnected, connect the electrical connectors to the crank angle sensor and the power transistor.

20. If disconnected, connect the electrical connectors to the ignition coils.

21. Connect the electrical connectors from the throttle position sensor, the exhaust gas temperature sensor and/or etc.

22. Connect the negative battery cable.

23. Start the engine and check for leaks.

INJECTOR TESTING

Refer to Section 4 for all electronic fuel injection testing and diagnostics.

Fuel Pressure Regulator

REMOVAL & INSTALLATION

VG30E Engine

1985–88
♦ SEE FIG. 29

The pressure regulator is always located on

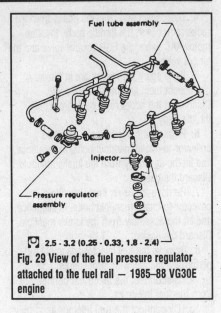

2.5 - 3.2 (0.25 - 0.33, 1.8 - 2.4)

Fig. 29 View of the fuel pressure regulator attached to the fuel rail — 1985–88 VG30E engine

the fuel return side of the fuel injection rail and is positioned at the front of the fuel rail, on top of the intake manifold.

※※ CAUTION

Never smoke when working around gasoline! Avoid all sources of sparks or ignition. Gasoline vapors are EXTREMELY volatile!

1. Release the fuel system pressure and disconnect the vacuum hose.

2. Remove the fuel pressure regulator hose clamps.

3. Separate the fuel pressure regulator from the hoses.

4. Remove the fuel pressure regulator-to-engine bolt.

To install:

5. Connect the fuel pressure regulator to the fuel rail hoses and the fuel return line hose.

6. Using new hose clamps, secure the fuel hoses to the fuel pressure regulator. Connect the vacuum hose to the fuel pressure regulator.

7. Install the fuel pressure regulator-to-engine bolt.

8. Start the engine and check for leaks.

1989–92
♦ SEE FIGS. 21 – 26

The pressure regulator is always located on the fuel return side of the fuel injection rail and is attached to the right rear of the fuel rail assembly, at the right rear corner of the intake manifold.

1. Disconnect the negative battery cable and relieve the fuel pressure.

2. Disconnect the air intake duct from the dual duct housing.

3. Disconnect the electrical connectors from the throttle body, the step motor AAC valve and the exhaust gas temperature sensor.

4. Disconnect and label the hoses from the rocker arm cover, the throttle body, the step motor AAC valve, the EGR control valve and the air cut valve.

5. If the spark plug wires are in the way, disconnect them and move them aside. Disconnect the accelerator cable from the throttle body.

6. Remove the upper intake manifold collector-to-intake manifold bolts, in sequence, and lift the assembly from the intake manifold. Discard the gasket.

7. Remove the lower intake manifold collector-to-intake manifold bolts, in sequence, and lift the assembly from the intake manifold. Discard the gasket.

8. Remove the fuel injector assembly by performing the following procedures:

   a. Disconnect the electrical connectors from the fuel injectors.

   b. Disconnect the fuel injector assembly from the fuel lines.

   c. Remove the fuel rail-to-cylinder head bolts.

   d. Remove the fuel rail assembly from the engine.

9. Remove the fuel pressure regulator from the fuel rail assembly.

To install:

10. To install the fuel pressure regulator to the fuel rail.

11. Clean the gasket mounting surfaces.

12. Install the fuel injector assembly by performing the following procedures:

   a. Install the fuel rail assembly to the engine.

   b. Install the fuel rail-to-cylinder head bolts and torque the bolts to 1.8–2.4 ft. lbs. (2.5–3.2 Nm).

   c. Connect the fuel injector assembly to the fuel lines.

   d. Connect the electrical connectors to the fuel injectors.

13. Use a new gasket and install the lower intake manifold collector; torque the lower

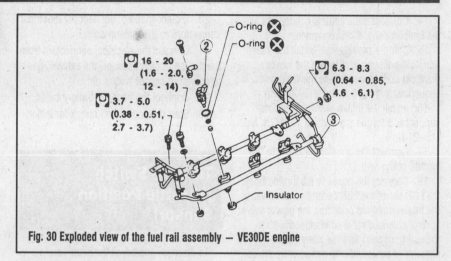

Fig. 30 Exploded view of the fuel rail assembly — VE30DE engine

intake manifold collector-to-intake manifold bolts, in 2–3 steps, in sequence, to 13–16 ft. lbs. (18–22 Nm).

14. Use a new gasket and install the upper intake manifold collector-to-intake manifold; torque the bolts to 5.1–5.8 ft. lbs. (7–8 Nm).

15. Connect the spark plug wire, if disconnected. Connect the accelerator cable to the throttle body.

16. Connect the hoses to the rocker arm cover, the throttle body, the step motor AAC valve, the EGR control valve and the air cut valve.

17. Connect the electrical connectors to the throttle body, the step motor AAC valve and the exhaust gas temperature sensor.

18. Connect the negative battery cable.

19. Start the engine and check for leaks.

VE30DE Engine

▶ SEE FIG. 27–28 AND 30

The pressure regulator is always located on the fuel return side of the fuel injection rail and is attached to the left rear of the fuel rail assembly, at the left rear corner of the intake manifold.

1. Disconnect the negative battery cable.

2. Disconnect the electrical connectors from the throttle position sensor, the exhaust gas temperature sensor and/or etc.

3. Label and disconnect the hoses from the throttle body, the EGR valve, the EGR control solenoid valve, the intake manifold collector, the power valve control solenoid valve (if equipped

with a manual transaxle) and the power valve actuator (if equipped with a manual transaxle).

4. Disconnect the accelerator cable from the throttle body.

5. Remove the intake manifold collector support-to-intake manifold collector and the intake manifold collector support-to-cylinder head bolts and the supports.

6. Remove the intake manifold collector-to-intake manifold bolts and the intake manifold collector.

7. If necessary, disconnect the electrical connectors from the ignition coils.

8. If necessary, disconnect the electrical connector from the crank angle sensor and the power transistor.

9. Remove the fuel injector assembly by performing the following procedures:

   a. Disconnect the electrical connectors from the fuel injectors.

   b. Disconnect the fuel injector assembly from the fuel lines.

   c. Remove the fuel rail-to-cylinder head bolts.

   d. Remove the fuel rail assembly from the engine.

10. Remove the fuel pressure regulator from the fuel rail.

To install:

11. Install the fuel pressure regulator to the fuel rail assembly.

12. Clean the gasket mounting surfaces.

13. Install the fuel injector assembly by performing the following procedures:

   a. Install the fuel rail assembly to the engine.

   b. Install the fuel rail-to-cylinder head bolts and torque the bolts to 12–14 ft. lbs. (16–20 Nm).

   c. Connect the fuel injector assembly to the fuel lines.

   d. Connect the electrical connectors to the fuel injectors.

14. Connect the electrical connectors to the ignition coils, if disconnected.

15. Using a new gasket, install the intake manifold collector and torque the intake manifold collector-to-intake manifold bolts, in sequence, to 13–16 ft. lbs. (18–22 Nm).

16. Install the intake manifold collector support and torque the bolts to 12–15 ft. lbs. (16–21 Nm).

17. Connect the accelerator cable to the throttle body.

18. Connect the hoses to the throttle body, the EGR valve, the EGR control solenoid valve, the intake manifold collector, the power valve control solenoid valve (if equipped with a manual transaxle) and the power valve actuator (if equipped with a manual transaxle).

19. If disconnected, connect the electrical connectors to the crank angle sensor and the power transistor.

20. If disconnected, connect the electrical connectors to the ignition coils.

21. Connect the electrical connectors from the throttle position sensor, the exhaust gas temperature sensor and/or etc.

22. Connect the negative battery cable.

23. Start the engine and check for leaks.

Throttle Switch (Throttle Position Sensor)

To diagnose and adjust the throttle switch (sensor), refer to the "Electronic Engine Controls" section in Section 4. The procedure can be found in the diagnostic charts.

Air Flow Meter

The air flow meter measures the quantity of intake air and sends a signal to the ECU so the base injector pulse width can be determined. The air meter is provided with a flap in the air passage. As the air flows through the passage, the flap rotates and its angle of rotation signals the ECU. The sensor is located between the air cleaner and intake manifold.

To diagnose the air flow sensor, refer to the "Electronic Engine Controls" section in Section 4. The procedure can be found in the diagnostic charts.

FUEL TANK

REMOVAL & INSTALLATION

◆ SEE FIGS. 7 AND 8

1. Remove the battery ground cable and drain the fuel from the fuel tank.

2. If necessary, remove the back seat.

3. Raise and safely support the vehicle.

4. Disconnect all hoses, lines and the electrical connection from the gas tank assembly.

5. Disconnect the fuel filler hose at the gas tank.

6. Remove the fuel tank protector-to-fuel tank bolts and the fuel tank protector-to-chassis bolts; then remove the fuel tank protector(s).

7. On the 1985–88 models, remove the fuel tank-to-chassis bolts and lower the fuel tank. On the 1989–92 models, remove the rear fuel tank strap-to-chassis bolts, swing the straps downward and lower the tank assembly from the vehicle.

To Install:

8. Raise the fuel tank into position and support it.

9. On the 1985–88 models, torque the fuel tank-to-chassis bolts to 23–31 ft. lbs. (31–42

Nm). On the 1989–92 models, swing the fuel tank straps upward and torque the rear fuel tank strap-to-chassis bolts to 20–26 ft. lbs. (27–35 Nm).

10. Install the fuel tank protector(s) to the fuel tank and/or the chassis.

11. Reconnect the fuel filler hose at the fuel tank with a new hose clamp.

12. Connect all hoses, lines and the electrical connection to the gas tank assembly. Always use new hose clamps to prevent leaks.

13. If the rear seat was removed, install it.

14. Refill the gas tank. Reconnect the battery ground cable.

15. Check the operation of the fuel pump.

TORQUE SPECIFICATIONS

Component	English	Metric
Dual intake duct-to-throttle body bolts		
1989–92	13–16 ft. lbs.	18–22 Nm
EGR control valve-to-upper intake manifold bolts		
VG30E engine		
1985–88	13–17 ft. lbs.	18–23 Nm
EGR tube-to-exhaust manifold nut		
VG30E engine		
1985–88	25–33 ft. lbs.	34–44 Nm
Fuel injector-to-cylinder head bolts	1.8–2.4 ft. lbs.	2.5–3.2 Nm
Fuel injector hold-down clamps bolts		
VG30E engine		
1985–88	1.8–2.4 ft. lbs.	2.5–3.2 Nm
Fuel pump assembly-to-fuel tank bolts		
1985–88	1.7–2.2 ft. lbs.	2.3–3.0 Nm
1989–92	1.4–1.9 ft. lbs.	2.0–2.5 Nm
Fuel rail-to-cylinder head bolts		
VG30E engine		
1989–92	1.8–2.4 ft. lbs.	2.5–3.2 Nm
VE30DE engine		
1992	12–14 ft. lbs.	16–20 Nm
Fuel tank-to-chassis bolts		
1985–88	23–31 ft. lbs.	31–42 Nm
1989–92	20–26 ft. lbs.	27–35 Nm
Intake manifold collector-to-intake manifold bolts		
VE30DE engine		
1992	13–16 ft. lbs.	18–22 Nm
Intake manifold collector support bolts		
VE30DE engine		
1992	12–15 ft. lbs.	16–21 Nm
Lower intake manifold collector-to-intake manifold bolts		
1989–92	13–16 ft. lbs.	18–22 Nm
Throttle chamber-to-intake manifold collector bolts		
Step 1	6.5–8.0 ft. lbs.	9–11 Nm
Step 2	13–16 ft. lbs.	18–22 Nm
Upper intake manifold collector-to-intake manifold bolts		
VG30E engine		
1989–92	5.1–5.8 ft. lbs.	7–8 Nm
Upper intake manifold-to-intake manifold bolts		
VG30E engine		
1985–88	13–16 ft. lbs.	18–22 Nm

E.C.U.
- Do not disassemble E.C.C.S. control unit (E.C.U.).
- Do not turn diagnosis mode selector forcibly.
- If a battery terminal is disconnected, the memory will return to the ROM value. The E.C.C.S. will now start to self-control at its initial value. Engine operation can vary slightly when the terminal is disconnected. However, this is not an indication of a problem. Do not replace parts because of a slight variation.

WIRELESS EQUIPMENT
- When installing C.B. ham radio or a mobile phone, be sure to observe the following as it may adversely affect electronic control systems depending on its installation location.
1) Keep the antenna as far as possible away from the electronic control units.
2) Keep the antenna feeder line more than 20 cm (7.9 in) away from the harness of electronic controls. Do not let them run parallel for a long distance.
3) Adjust the antenna and feeder line so that the standing-wave ratio can be kept smaller.
4) Be sure to ground the radio to vehicle body.

BATTERY
- Always use a 12 volt battery as power source.
- Do not attempt to disconnect battery cables while engine is running.

INJECTOR
- Do not disconnect injector harness connectors with engine running.
- Do not apply battery power directly to injectors.

E.C.C.S. PARTS HANDLING
- Handle air flow meter carefully to avoid damage.
- Do not disassemble air flow meter.
- Do not clean air flow meter with any type of detergent.
- Do not disassemble auxiliary air control valve.
- Even a slight leak in the air intake system can cause serious problems.
- Do not shock or jar the crank angle sensor.

WHEN STARTING
- Do not depress accelerator pedal when starting.
- Immediately after starting, do not rev up engine unnecessarily.
- Do not rev up engine just prior to shutdown.

FUEL PUMP
- Do not operate fuel pump when there is no fuel in lines.
- Tighten fuel hose clamps to the specified torque.

E.C.C.S. HARNESS HANDLING
- Securely connect E.C.C.S. harness connectors.
  A poor connection can cause an extremely high (surge) voltage to develop in coil and condenser, thus resulting in damage to ICs.
- Keep E.C.C.S. harness at least 10 cm (3.9 in) away from adjacent harnesses, to prevent an E.C.C.S. system malfunction due to receiving external noise, degraded operation of ICs, etc.
- Keep E.C.C.S. parts and harnesses dry.
- Before removing parts, turn off ignition switch and then disconnect battery ground cable.

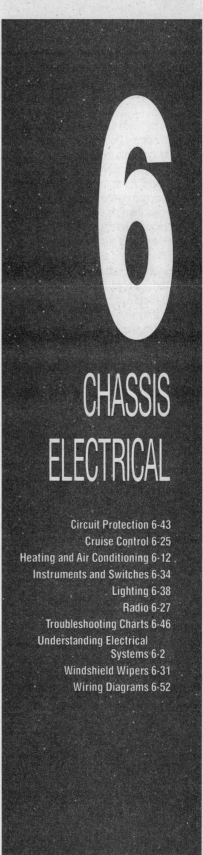

6

CHASSIS ELECTRICAL

BASIC ELECTRICITY

At the rate which both import and domestic manufacturers are incorporating electronic control systems into their production lines, it won't be long before every new vehicle is equipped with one or more on-board computer. These electronic components (with no moving parts) should theoretically last the life of the vehicle, provided nothing external happens to damage the circuits or memory chips.

While it is true that electronic components should never wear out, in the real world malfunctions do occur. It is also true that any computer-based system is extremely sensitive to electrical voltages and cannot tolerate careless or haphazard testing or service procedures. An inexperienced individual can literally do major damage looking for a minor problem by using the wrong kind of test equipment or connecting test leads or connectors with the ignition switch ON. When selecting test equipment, make sure the manufacturers instructions state that the tester is compatible with whatever type of electronic control system is being serviced. Read all instructions carefully and double check all test points before installing probes or making any test connections.

The following section outlines basic diagnosis techniques for dealing with computerized automotive control systems. Along with a general explanation of the various types of test equipment available to aid in servicing modern electronic automotive systems, basic repair techniques for wiring harnesses and connectors is given. Read the basic information before attempting any repairs or testing on any computerized system, to provide the background of information necessary to avoid the most common and obvious mistakes that can cost both time and money. Although the replacement and testing procedures are simple in themselves, the systems are not, and unless one has a thorough understanding of all components and their function within a particular computerized control system, the logical test sequence these systems demand cannot be followed. Minor malfunctions can make a big difference, so it is important to know how each component affects the operation of the overall electronic system to find the ultimate cause of a problem without replacing good components unnecessarily. It is not enough to use the correct test equipment; the test equipment must be used correctly.

Safety Precautions

❊ CAUTION

Whenever working on or around any computer based microprocessor control system, always observe these general precautions to prevent the possibility of personal injury or damage to electronic components.

• Never install or remove battery cables with the key ON or the engine running. Jumper cables should be connected with the key OFF to avoid power surges that can damage electronic control units. Engines equipped with computer controlled systems should avoid both giving and getting jump starts due to the possibility of serious damage to components from arcing in the engine compartment when connections are made with the ignition ON.

• Always remove the battery cables before charging the battery. Never use a high output charger on an installed battery or attempt to use any type of "hot shot" (24 volt) starting aid.

• Exercise care when inserting test probes into connectors to insure good connections without damaging the connector or spreading the pins. Always probe connectors from the rear (wire) side, NOT the pin side, to avoid accidental shorting of terminals during test procedures.

• Never remove or attach wiring harness connectors with the ignition switch ON, especially to an electronic control unit.

• Do not drop any components during service procedures and never apply 12 volts directly to any component (like a solenoid or relay) unless instructed specifically to do so. Some component electrical windings are designed to safely handle only 4 or 5 volts and can be destroyed in seconds if 12 volts are applied directly to the connector.

• Remove the electronic control unit if the vehicle is to be placed in an environment where temperatures exceed approximately 176°F (80°C), such as a paint spray booth or when arc or gas welding near the control unit location in the car.

• When possible use a flashlight instead of a drop light.

• Do not allow extension cords for power tools or drop lights to lie on or across any of the vehicle wiring.

• NEVER use an external power supply to retain component memory when working on the instrument panel or inside the car, if the car is equipped with an air bag.

• Leave electronic components in the package until you are ready to install them and never touch the connector pins.

• Touch the metal of the car often when servicing electronic components to remove and static charge that may build on your body. This charge will damage electronic components if you touch them.

ORGANIZED TROUBLESHOOTING

When diagnosing a specific problem, organized troubleshooting is a must. The complexity of a modern automobile demands that you approach any problem in a logical, organized manner. There are certain troubleshooting techniques that are standard:

1. Establish when the problem occurs. Does the problem appear only under certain conditions? Were there any noises, odors, or other unusual symptoms?

2. Isolate the problem area. To do this, make some simple tests and observations; then eliminate the systems that are working properly. Check for obvious problems such as broken wires, dirty connections or split or disconnected vacuum hoses. Always check the obvious before assuming something complicated is the cause.

3. Test for problems systematically to determine the cause once the problem area is isolated. Are all the components functioning properly? Is there power going to electrical switches and motors? Is there vacuum at vacuum switches and/or actuators? Is there a mechanical problem such as bent linkage or loose mounting screws? Doing careful, systematic checks will often turn up most causes on the first inspection without wasting time checking components that have little or no relationship to the problem.

4. Test all repairs after the work is done to make sure that the problem is fixed. Some causes can be traced to more than one component, so a careful verification of repair work is important to pick up additional malfunctions that may cause a problem to reappear or a different problem to arise. A blown fuse, for example, is a simple problem that may require more than another fuse to repair. If you

don't look for a problem that caused a fuse to blow, for example, a shorted wire may go undetected.

Experience has shown that most problems tend to be the result of a fairly simple and obvious cause, such as loose or corroded connectors or air leaks in the intake system; making careful inspection of components during testing essential to quick and accurate troubleshooting. Special, hand held computerized testers designed specifically for diagnosing the EEC-IV system are available from a variety of aftermarket sources, as well as from the vehicle manufacturer, but care should be taken that any test equipment being used is designed to diagnose that particular computer controlled system accurately without damaging the control unit (ECU) or components being tested.

➡ **Pinpointing the exact cause of trouble in an electrical system can sometimes only be accomplished by the use of special test equipment. The following describes commonly used test equipment and explains how to put it to best use in diagnosis. In addition to the information covered below, the manufacturer's instructions booklet provided with the tester should be read and clearly understood before attempting any test procedures.**

TEST EQUIPMENT

Jumper Wires

Jumper wires are simple, yet extremely valuable, pieces of test equipment. Jumper wires are merely wires that are used to bypass sections of a circuit. The simplest type of jumper wire is merely a length of multistrand wire with an alligator clip at each end. Jumper wires are usually fabricated from lengths of standard automotive wire and whatever type of connector (alligator clip, spade connector or pin connector) that is required for the particular vehicle being tested. The well equipped tool box will have several different styles of jumper wires in several different lengths. Some jumper wires are made with three or more terminals coming from a common splice for special purpose testing. In cramped, hard-to-reach areas it is advisable to have insulated boots over the jumper wire terminals in order to prevent accidental grounding, sparks, and possible fire, especially when testing fuel system components.

Jumper wires are used primarily to locate open electrical circuits, on either the ground (−) side of the circuit or on the hot (+) side. If an electrical component fails to operate, connect the jumper wire between the component and a good ground. If the component operates only with the jumper installed, the ground circuit is open. If the ground circuit is good, but the component does not operate, the circuit between the power feed and component is open. You can sometimes connect the jumper wire directly from the battery to the hot terminal of the component, but first make sure the component uses 12 volts in operation. Some electrical components, such as fuel injectors, are designed to operate on about 4 volts and running 12 volts directly to the injector terminals can burn out the wiring. By inserting an inline fuse holder between a set of test leads, a fused jumper wire can be used for bypassing open circuits. Use a 5 amp fuse to provide protection against voltage spikes. When in doubt, use a voltmeter to check the voltage input to the component and measure how much voltage is being applied normally. By moving the jumper wire successively back from the lamp toward the power source, you can isolate the area of the circuit where the open is located. When the component stops functioning, or the power is cut off, the open is in the segment of wire between the jumper and the point previously tested.

✳✳✳ CAUTION

Never use jumpers made from wire that is of lighter gauge than used in the circuit under test. If the jumper wire is of too small gauge, it may overheat and possibly melt. Never use jumpers to bypass high resistance loads (such as motors) in a circuit. Bypassing resistances, in effect, creates a short circuit which may, in turn, cause damage and fire. Never use a jumper for anything other than temporary bypassing of components in a circuit.

12 Volt Test Light

The 12 volt test light is used to check circuits and components while electrical current is flowing through them. It is used for voltage and ground tests. Twelve volt test lights come in different styles but all have three main parts; a ground clip, a probe, and a light. The most commonly used 12 volt test lights have pick-type probes. To use a 12 volt test light, connect the ground clip to a good ground and probe wherever necessary with the pick. The pick should be sharp so that it can penetrate wire insulation to make contact with the wire, without making a large hole in the insulation. The wrap-around light is handy in hard to reach areas or where it is difficult to support a wire to push a probe pick into it. To use the wrap around light, hook the wire to probed with the hook and pull the trigger. A small pick will be forced through the wire insulation into the wire core.

✳✳✳ CAUTION

Do not use a test light to probe electronic ignition spark plug or coil wires. Never use a pick-type test light to probe wiring on computer controlled systems unless specifically instructed to do so. Any wire insulation that is pierced by the test light probe should be taped and sealed with silicone after testing.

Like the jumper wire, the 12 volt test light is used to isolate opens in circuits. But, whereas the jumper wire is used to bypass the open to operate the load, the 12 volt test light is used to locate the presence of voltage in a circuit. If the test light glows, you know that there is power up to that point; if the 12 volt test light does not glow when its probe is inserted into the wire or connector, you know that there is an open circuit (no power). Move the test light in successive steps back toward the power source until the light in the handle does glow. When it does glow, the open is between the probe and point previously probed.

➡ **The test light does not detect that 12 volts (or any particular amount of voltage) is present; it only detects that some voltage is present. It is advisable before using the test light to touch its terminals across the battery posts to make sure the light is operating properly.**

Self-Powered Test Light

The self-powered test light usually contains a 1.5 volt penlight battery. One type of self-powered test light is similar in design to the 12 volt test light. This type has both the battery and the light in the handle and pick-type probe tip. The second type has the light toward the open tip, so that the light illuminates the contact point. The self-powered test light is dual purpose piece of test equipment. It can be used to test for either open or short circuits when power is isolated from the circuit (continuity test). A powered test light should not be used on any computer controlled system or component unless specifically instructed to do so. Many engine sensors can be destroyed by even this small amount of voltage applied directly to the terminals.

Open Circuit Testing

To use the self-powered test light to check for open circuits, first isolate the circuit from the vehicle's 12 volt power source by disconnecting the battery or wiring harness connector. Connect the test light ground clip to a good ground and probe sections of the circuit sequentially with the test light. (start from either end of the circuit). If the light is out, the open is between the probe and the circuit ground. If the light is on, the open is between the probe and end of the circuit toward the power source.

Short Circuit Testing

By isolating the circuit both from power and from ground, and using a self-powered test light, you can check for shorts to ground in the circuit. Isolate the circuit from power and ground. Connect the test light ground clip to a good ground and probe any easy-to-reach test point in the circuit. If the light comes on, there is a short somewhere in the circuit. To isolate the short, probe a test point at either end of the isolated circuit (the light should be on). Leave the test light probe connected and open connectors, switches, remove parts, etc., sequentially, until the light goes out. When the light goes out, the short is between the last circuit component opened and the previous circuit opened.

➡ **The 1.5 volt battery in the test light does not provide much current. A weak battery may not provide enough power to illuminate the test light even when a complete circuit is made (especially if there are high resistances in the circuit). Always make sure that the test battery is strong. To check the battery, briefly touch the ground clip to the probe; if the light glows brightly the battery is strong enough for testing. Never use a self-powered test light to perform checks for opens or shorts when power is applied to the electrical system under test. The 12 volt vehicle power will quickly burn out the 1.5 volt light bulb in the test light.**

Voltmeter

A voltmeter is used to measure voltage at any point in a circuit, or to measure the voltage drop across any part of a circuit. It can also be used to check continuity in a wire or circuit by indicating current flow from one end to the other. Voltmeters usually have various scales on the meter dial and a selector switch to allow the selection of different voltages. The voltmeter has a positive and a negative lead. To avoid damage to the meter, always connect the negative lead to the negative (–) side of circuit (to ground or nearest the ground side of the circuit) and connect the positive lead to the positive (+) side of the circuit (to the power source or the nearest power source). Note that the negative voltmeter lead will always be black and that the positive voltmeter will always be some color other than black (usually red). Depending on how the voltmeter is connected into the circuit, it has several uses.

voltmeter can be connected either in parallel or in series with a circuit and it has a very high resistance to current flow. When connected in parallel, only a small amount of current will flow through the voltmeter current path; the rest will flow through the normal circuit current path and the circuit will work normally. When the voltmeter is connected in series with a circuit, only a small amount of current can flow through the circuit. The circuit will not work properly, but the voltmeter reading will show if the circuit is complete or not.

Available Voltage Measurement

Set the voltmeter selector switch to the 20V position and connect the meter negative lead to the negative post of the battery. Connect the positive meter lead to the positive post of the battery and turn the ignition switch ON to provide a load. Read the voltage on the meter or digital display. A well charged battery should register over 12 volts. If the meter reads below 11.5 volts, the battery power may be insufficient to operate the electrical system properly. This test determines voltage available from the battery and should be the first step in any electrical trouble diagnosis procedure. Many electrical problems, especially on computer controlled systems, can be caused by a low state of charge in the battery. Excessive corrosion at the battery cable terminals can cause a poor contact that will prevent proper charging and full battery current flow.

Normal battery voltage is 12 volts when fully charged. When the battery is supplying current to one or more circuits it is said to be "under load". When everything is off the electrical system is under a "no-load" condition. A fully charged battery may show about 12.5 volts at no load; will drop to 12 volts under medium load; and will drop even lower under heavy load. If the battery is partially discharged the voltage decrease under heavy load may be excessive, even though the battery shows 12 volts or more at no load. When allowed to discharge further, the battery's available voltage under load will decrease more severely. For this reason, it is important that the battery be fully charged during all testing procedures to avoid errors in diagnosis and incorrect test results.

Voltage Drop

When current flows through a resistance, the voltage beyond the resistance is reduced (the larger the current, the greater the reduction in voltage). When no current is flowing, there is no voltage drop because there is no current flow. All points in the circuit which are connected to the power source are at the same voltage as the power source. The total voltage drop always equals the total source voltage. In a long circuit with many connectors, a series of small, unwanted voltage drops due to corrosion at the connectors can add up to a total loss of voltage which impairs the operation of the normal loads in the circuit.

INDIRECT COMPUTATION OF VOLTAGE DROPS

1. Set the voltmeter selector switch to the 20 volt position.
2. Connect the meter negative lead to a good ground.
3. Probe all resistances in the circuit with the positive meter lead.
4. Operate the circuit in all modes and observe the voltage readings.

DIRECT MEASUREMENT OF VOLTAGE DROPS

1. Set the voltmeter switch to the 20 volt position.
2. Connect the voltmeter negative lead to the ground side of the resistance load to be measured.
3. Connect the positive lead to the positive side of the resistance or load to be measured.
4. Read the voltage drop directly on the 20 volt scale.

Too high a voltage indicates too high a resistance. If, for example, a blower motor runs too slowly, you can determine if there is too high a resistance in the resistor pack. By taking voltage drop readings in all parts of the circuit, you can isolate the problem. Too low a voltage drop indicates too low a resistance. If, for example, a blower motor runs too fast in the MED and/or LOW position, the problem can be isolated in the resistor pack by taking voltage drop readings in all parts of the circuit to locate a possibly shorted resistor. The maximum allowable voltage drop under load is critical, especially if there is more than one high resistance problem in a circuit because all voltage drops are cumulative. A small drop is normal due to the resistance of the conductors.

HIGH RESISTANCE TESTING

1. Set the voltmeter selector switch to the 4 volt position.

2. Connect the voltmeter positive lead to the positive post of the battery.

3. Turn on the headlights and heater blower to provide a load.

4. Probe various points in the circuit with the negative voltmeter lead.

5. Read the voltage drop on the 4 volt scale. Some average maximum allowable voltage drops are:

    FUSE PANEL — 7 volts
    IGNITION SWITCH — 5 volts
    HEADLIGHT SWITCH — 7 volts
    IGNITION COIL (+) — 5 volts
    ANY OTHER LOAD — 1.3 volts

➡ Voltage drops are all measured while a load is operating; without current flow, there will be no voltage drop.

Ohmmeter

The ohmmeter is designed to read resistance (ohms) in a circuit or component. Although there are several different styles of ohmmeters, all will usually have a selector switch which permits the measurement of different ranges of resistance (usually the selector switch allows the multiplication of the meter reading by 10, 100, 1,000, and 10,000). A calibration knob allows the meter to be set at zero for accurate measurement. Since all ohmmeters are powered by an internal battery (usually 9 volts), the ohmmeter can be used as a self-powered test light. When the ohmmeter is connected, current from the ohmmeter flows through the circuit or component being tested. Since the ohmmeter's internal resistance and voltage are known values, the amount of current flow through the meter depends on the resistance of the circuit or component being tested.

The ohmmeter can be used to perform continuity test for opens or shorts (either by observation of the meter needle or as a self-powered test light), and to read actual resistance in a circuit. It should be noted that the ohmmeter is used to check the resistance of a component or wire while there is no voltage applied to the circuit. Current flow from an outside voltage source (such as the vehicle battery) can damage the ohmmeter, so the circuit or component should be isolated from the vehicle electrical

system before any testing is done. Since the ohmmeter uses its own voltage source, either lead can be connected to any test point.

➡ When checking diodes or other solid state components, the ohmmeter leads can only be connected one way in order to measure current flow in a single direction. Make sure the positive (+) and negative (–) terminal connections are as described in the test procedures to verify the one-way diode operation.

In using the meter for making continuity checks, do not be concerned with the actual resistance readings. Zero resistance, or any resistance readings, indicate continuity in the circuit. Infinite resistance indicates an open in the circuit. A high resistance reading where there should be none indicates a problem in the circuit. Checks for short circuits are made in the same manner as checks for open circuits except that the circuit must be isolated from both power and normal ground. Infinite resistance indicates no continuity to ground, while zero resistance indicates a dead short to ground.

RESISTANCE MEASUREMENT

The batteries in an ohmmeter will weaken with age and temperature, so the ohmmeter must be calibrated or "zeroed" before taking measurements. To zero the meter, place the selector switch in its lowest range and touch the two ohmmeter leads together. Turn the calibration knob until the meter needle is exactly on zero.

➡ All analog (needle) type ohmmeters must be zeroed before use, but some digital ohmmeter models are automatically calibrated when the switch is turned on. Self-calibrating digital ohmmeters do not have an adjusting knob, but its a good idea to check for a zero readout before use by touching the leads together. All computer controlled systems require the use of a digital ohmmeter with at least 10 mega-ohms impedance for testing. Before any test procedures are attempted, make sure the ohmmeter used is compatible with the electrical system or damage to the on-board computer could result.

To measure resistance, first isolate the circuit from the vehicle power source by disconnecting the battery cables or the harness connector. Make sure the key is OFF when disconnecting any components or the battery. Where

necessary, also isolate at least one side of the circuit to be checked to avoid reading parallel resistances. Parallel circuit resistances will always give a lower reading than the actual resistance of either of the branches. When measuring the resistance of parallel circuits, the total resistance will always be lower than the smallest resistance in the circuit. Connect the meter leads to both sides of the circuit (wire or component) and read the actual measured ohms on the meter scale. Make sure the selector switch is set to the proper ohm scale for the circuit being tested to avoid misreading the ohmmeter test value.

Never use an ohmmeter with power applied to the circuit. Like the self-powered test light, the ohmmeter is designed to operate on its own power supply. The normal 12 volt automotive electrical system current could damage the meter!

Ammeters

An ammeter measures the amount of current flowing through a circuit in units called amperes or amps. Amperes are units of electron flow which indicate how fast the electrons are flowing through the circuit. Since Ohms Law dictates that current flow in a circuit is equal to the circuit voltage divided by the total circuit resistance, increasing voltage also increases the current level (amps). Likewise, any decrease in resistance will increase the amount of amps in a circuit. At normal operating voltage, most circuits have a characteristic amount of amperes, called "current draw" which can be measured using an ammeter. By referring to a specified current draw rating, measuring the amperes, and comparing the two values, one can determine what is happening within the circuit to aid in diagnosis. An open circuit, for example, will not allow any current to flow so the ammeter reading will be zero. More current flows through a heavily loaded circuit or when the charging system is operating.

An ammeter is always connected in series with the circuit being tested. All of the current that normally flows through the circuit must also flow through the ammeter; if there is any other path for the current to follow, the ammeter reading will not be accurate. The ammeter itself has very little resistance to current flow and therefore will not affect the circuit, but it will measure current draw only when the circuit is closed and electricity is flowing. Excessive current draw can blow fuses and drain the battery, while a reduced current draw can cause motors to run slowly, lights to dim and other components to not operate properly. The ammeter can help diagnose these conditions by locating the cause of the high or low reading.

Multimeters

Different combinations of test meters can be built into a single unit designed for specific tests. Some of the more common combination test devices are known as Volt/Amp testers, Tach/Dwell meters, or Digital Multimeters. The Volt/Amp tester is used for charging system, starting system or battery tests and consists of a voltmeter, an ammeter and a variable resistance carbon pile. The voltmeter will usually have at least two ranges for use with 6, 12 and 24 volt systems. The ammeter also has more than one range for testing various levels of battery loads and starter current draw and the carbon pile can be adjusted to offer different amounts of resistance. The Volt/Amp tester has heavy leads to carry large amounts of current and many later models have an inductive ammeter pickup that clamps around the wire to simplify test connections. On some models, the ammeter also has a zero-center scale to allow testing of charging and starting systems without switching leads or polarity. A digital multimeter is a voltmeter, ammeter and ohmmeter combined in an instrument which gives a digital readout. These are often used when testing solid state circuits because of their high input impedance (usually 10 megohms or more).

The tach/dwell meter combines a tachometer and a dwell (cam angle) meter and is a specialized kind of voltmeter. The tachometer scale is marked to show engine speed in rpm and the dwell scale is marked to show degrees of distributor shaft rotation. In most electronic ignition systems, dwell is determined by the control unit, but the dwell meter can also be used to check the duty cycle (operation) of some electronic engine control systems. Some tach/dwell meters are powered by an internal battery, while others take their power from the car battery in use. The battery powered testers usually require calibration much like an ohmmeter before testing.

Special Test Equipment

A variety of diagnostic tools are available to help troubleshoot and repair computerized engine control systems. The most sophisticated of these devices are the console type engine analyzers that usually occupy a garage service bay, but there are several types of aftermarket electronic testers available that will allow quick circuit tests of the engine control system by plugging directly into a special connector located in the engine compartment or under the dashboard. Several tool and equipment manufacturers offer simple, hand held testers that measure various circuit voltage levels on command to check all system components for proper operation. Although these testers usually cost about $300–500, consider that the average computer control unit (or ECM) can cost just as much and the money saved by not replacing perfectly good sensors or components in an attempt to correct a problem could justify the purchase price of a special diagnostic tester the first time it's used.

These computerized testers can allow quick and easy test measurements while the engine is operating or while the car is being driven. In addition, the on-board computer memory can be read to access any stored trouble codes; in effect allowing the computer to tell you where it hurts and aid trouble diagnosis by pinpointing exactly which circuit or component is malfunctioning. In the same manner, repairs can be tested to make sure the problem has been corrected. The biggest advantage these special testers have is their relatively easy hookups that minimize or eliminate the chances of making the wrong connections and getting false voltage readings or damaging the computer accidentally.

➡ **It should be remembered that these testers check voltage levels in circuits; they don't detect mechanical problems or failed components if the circuit voltage falls within the preprogrammed limits stored in the tester PROM unit. Also, most of the hand held testes are designed to work only on one or two systems made by a specific manufacturer.**

A variety of aftermarket testers are available to help diagnose different computerized control systems. Owatonna Tool Company (OTC), for example, markets a device called the OTC Monitor which plugs directly into the assembly line diagnostic link (ALDL). The OTC tester makes diagnosis a simple matter of pressing the correct buttons and, by changing the internal PROM or inserting a different diagnosis cartridge, it will work on any model from full size to subcompact, over a wide range of years. An adapter is supplied with the tester to allow connection to all types of ALDL links, regardless of the number of pin terminals used. By inserting an updated PROM into the OTC tester, it can be easily updated to diagnose any new modifications of computerized control systems.

Wiring Harnesses

The average automobile contains about 1/2 mile of wiring, with hundreds of individual connections. To protect the many wires from damage and to keep them from becoming a confusing tangle, they are organized into bundles, enclosed in plastic or taped together and called wire harnesses. Different wiring harnesses serve different parts of the vehicle. Individual wires are color coded to help trace them through a harness where sections are hidden from view.

A loose or corroded connection or a replacement wire that is too small for the circuit will add extra resistance and an additional voltage drop to the circuit. A ten percent voltage drop can result in slow or erratic motor operation, for example, even though the circuit is complete. Automotive wiring or circuit conductors can be in any one of three forms:

1. Single strand wire
2. Multistrand wire
3. Printed circuitry

Single strand wire has a solid metal core and is usually used inside such components as alternators, motors, relays and other devices. Multistrand wire has a core made of many small strands of wire twisted together into a single conductor. Most of the wiring in an automotive electrical system is made up of multistrand wire, either as a single conductor or grouped together in a harness. All wiring is color coded on the insulator, either as a solid color or as a colored wire with an identification stripe. A printed circuit is a thin film of copper or other conductor that is printed on an insulator backing. Occasionally, a printed circuit is sandwiched between two sheets of plastic for more protection and flexibility. A complete printed circuit, consisting of conductors, insulating material and connectors for lamps or other components is called a printed circuit board. Printed circuitry is used in place of individual wires or harnesses in places where space is limited, such as behind instrument panels.

Wire Gauge

Since computer controlled automotive electrical systems are very sensitive to changes in resistance, the selection of properly sized wires is critical when systems are repaired. The wire gauge number is an expression of the cross section area of the conductor. The most common system for expressing wire size is the American Wire Gauge (AWG) system.

Wire cross section area is measured in circular mils. A mil is 1/1000 in. (0.001 in. [0.0254mm]); a circular mil is the area of a circle one mil in diameter. For example, a conductor $1/4$ in. (6mm) in diameter is 0.250 in. or 250 mils. The circular mil cross section area of the wire is 250 squared (250^2)or 62,500 circular mils. Imported car models usually use metric wire gauge designations, which is simply the cross section area of the conductor in square millimeters (mm^2).

Gauge numbers are assigned to conductors of various cross section areas. As gauge number increases, area decreases and the conductor becomes smaller. A 5 gauge conductor is smaller than a 1 gauge conductor and a 10 gauge is smaller than a 5 gauge. As the cross section area of a conductor decreases, resistance increases and so does the gauge number. A conductor with a higher gauge number will carry less current than a conductor with a lower gauge number.

➡ **Gauge wire size refers to the size of the conductor, not the size of the complete wire. It is possible to have two wires of the same gauge with different diameters because one may have thicker insulation than the other.**

12 volt automotive electrical systems generally use 10, 12, 14, 16 and 18 gauge wire. Main power distribution circuits and larger accessories usually use 10 and 12 gauge wire. Battery cables are usually 4 or 6 gauge, although 1 and 2 gauge wires are occasionally used. Wire length must also be considered when making repairs to a circuit. As conductor length increases, so does resistance. An 18 gauge wire, for example, can carry a 10 amp load for 10 feet without excessive voltage drop; however if a 15 foot wire is required for the same 10 amp load, it must be a 16 gauge wire.

An electrical schematic shows the electrical current paths when a circuit is operating properly. It is essential to understand how a circuit works before trying to figure out why it doesn't. Schematics break the entire electrical system down into individual circuits and show only one particular circuit. In a schematic, no attempt is made to represent wiring and components as they physically appear on the vehicle; switches and other components are shown as simply as possible. Face views of harness connectors show the cavity or terminal locations in all multi-pin connectors to help locate test points.

If you need to backprobe a connector while it is on the component, the order of the terminals must be mentally reversed. The wire color code can help in this situation, as well as a keyway, lock tab or other reference mark.

➡ **Wiring diagrams are not included in this book. As trucks have become more complex and available with longer option lists, wiring diagrams have grown in size and complexity. It has become almost impossible to provide a readable reproduction of a wiring diagram in a book this size. Information on ordering wiring diagrams from the vehicle manufacturer can be found in the owner's manual.**

WIRING REPAIR

Soldering is a quick, efficient method of joining metals permanently. Everyone who has the occasion to make wiring repairs should know how to solder. Electrical connections that are soldered are far less likely to come apart and will conduct electricity much better than connections that are only "pig-tailed" together. The most popular (and preferred) method of soldering is with an electrical soldering gun. Soldering irons are available in many sizes and wattage ratings. Irons with higher wattage ratings deliver higher temperatures and recover lost heat faster. A small soldering iron rated for no more than 50 watts is recommended, especially on electrical systems where excess heat can damage the components being soldered.

There are three ingredients necessary for successful soldering; proper flux, good solder and sufficient heat. A soldering flux is necessary to clean the metal of tarnish, prepare it for soldering and to enable the solder to spread into tiny crevices. When soldering, always use a resin flux or resin core solder which is non-corrosive and will not attract moisture once the job is finished. Other types of flux (acid core) will leave a residue that will attract moisture and cause the wires to corrode. Tin is a unique metal with a low melting point. In a molten state, it dissolves and alloys easily with many metals. Solder is made by mixing tin with lead. The most common proportions are 40/60, 50/50 and 60/40, with the percentage of tin listed first. Low priced solders usually contain less tin, making them very difficult for a beginner to use because more heat is required to melt the solder. A common solder is 40/60 which is well suited for all-around general use, but 60/40 melts easier, has more tin for a better joint and is preferred for electrical work.

Soldering Techniques

Successful soldering requires that the metals to be joined be heated to a temperature that will melt the solder—usually 360–460°F (182–

238°C). Contrary to popular belief, the purpose of the soldering iron is not to melt the solder itself, but to heat the parts being soldered to a temperature high enough to melt the solder when it is touched to the work. Melting flux-cored solder on the soldering iron will usually destroy the effectiveness of the flux.

➡ **Soldering tips are made of copper for good heat conductivity, but must be "tinned" regularly for quick transference of heat to the project and to prevent the solder from sticking to the iron. To "tin" the iron, simply heat it and touch the flux-cored solder to the tip; the solder will flow over the hot tip. Wipe the excess off with a clean rag, but be careful as the iron will be hot.**

After some use, the tip may become pitted. If so, simply dress the tip smooth with a smooth file and "tin" the tip again. An old saying holds that "metals well cleaned are half soldered." Flux-cored solder will remove oxides but rust, bits of insulation and oil or grease must be removed with a wire brush or emery cloth. For maximum strength in soldered parts, the joint must start off clean and tight. Weak joints will result in gaps too wide for the solder to bridge.

If a separate soldering flux is used, it should be brushed or swabbed on only those areas that are to be soldered. Most solders contain a core of flux and separate fluxing is unnecessary. Hold the work to be soldered firmly. It is best to solder on a wooden board, because a metal vise will only rob the piece to be soldered of heat and make it difficult to melt the solder. Hold the soldering tip with the broadest face against the work to be soldered. Apply solder under the tip close to the work, using enough solder to give a heavy film between the iron and the piece being soldered, while moving slowly and making sure the solder melts properly. Keep the work level or the solder will run to the lowest part and favor the thicker parts, because these require more heat to melt the solder. If the soldering tip overheats (the solder coating on the face of the tip burns up), it should be retinned. Once the soldering is completed, let the soldered joint stand until cool. Tape and seal all soldered wire splices after the repair has cooled.

Wire Harness and Connectors

The on-board computer (ECM) wire harness electrically connects the control unit to the various solenoids, switches and sensors used by the control system. Most connectors in the engine compartment or otherwise exposed to the elements are protected against moisture and dirt which could create oxidation and deposits on the terminals. This protection is important because of the very low voltage and current levels used by the computer and sensors. All connectors have a lock which secures the male and female terminals together, with a secondary lock holding the seal and terminal into the connector. Both terminal locks must be released when disconnecting ECM connectors.

These special connectors are weather-proof and all repairs require the use of a special terminal and the tool required to service it. This tool is used to remove the pin and sleeve terminals. If removal is attempted with an ordinary pick, there is a good chance that the terminal will be bent or deformed. Unlike standard blade type terminals, these terminals cannot be straightened once they are bent. Make certain that the connectors are properly seated and all of the sealing rings in place when connecting leads. On some models, a hinge-type flap provides a backup or secondary locking feature for the terminals. Most secondary locks are used to improve the connector reliability by retaining the terminals if the small terminal lock tangs are not positioned properly.

Molded-on connectors require complete replacement of the connection. This means splicing a new connector assembly into the harness. All splices in on-board computer systems should be soldered to insure proper contact. Use care when probing the connections or replacing terminals in them as it is possible to short between opposite terminals. If this happens to the wrong terminal pair, it is possible to damage certain components. Always use jumper wires between connectors for circuit checking and never probe through weatherproof seals.

Open circuits are often difficult to locate by sight because corrosion or terminal misalignment are hidden by the connectors. Merely wiggling a connector on a sensor or in the wiring harness may correct the open circuit condition. This should always be considered when an open circuit or a failed sensor is indicated. Intermittent problems may also be caused by oxidized or loose connections. When using a circuit tester for diagnosis, always probe connections from the wire side. Be careful not to damage sealed connectors with test probes.

All wiring harnesses should be replaced with identical parts, using the same gauge wire and connectors. When signal wires are spliced into a harness, use wire with high temperature insulation only. With the low voltage and current levels found in the system, it is important that the best possible connection at all wire splices be made by soldering the splices together. It is seldom necessary to replace a complete

harness. If replacement is necessary, pay close attention to insure proper harness routing. Secure the harness with suitable plastic wire clamps to prevent vibrations from causing the harness to wear in spots or contact any hot components.

➡ **Weatherproof connectors cannot be replaced with standard connectors. Instructions are provided with replacement connector and terminal packages. Some wire harnesses have mounting indicators (usually pieces of colored tape) to mark where the harness is to be secured.**

In making wiring repairs, it's important that you always replace damaged wires with wires that are the same gauge as the wire being replaced. The heavier the wire, the smaller the gauge number. Wires are color-coded to aid in identification and whenever possible the same color coded wire should be used for replacement. A wire stripping and crimping tool is necessary to install solderless terminal connectors. Test all crimps by pulling on the wires; it should not be possible to pull the wires out of a good crimp.

Wires which are open, exposed or otherwise damaged are repaired by simple splicing. Where possible, if the wiring harness is accessible and the damaged place in the wire can be located, it is best to open the harness and check for all possible damage. In an inaccessible harness, the wire must be bypassed with a new insert, usually taped to the outside of the old harness.

When replacing fusible links, be sure to use fusible link wire, NOT ordinary automotive wire. Make sure the fusible segment is of the same gauge and construction as the one being replaced and double the stripped end when crimping the terminal connector for a good contact. The melted (open) fusible link segment of the wiring harness should be cut off as close to the harness as possible, then a new segment spliced in as described. In the case of a damaged fusible link that feeds two harness wires, the harness connections should be replaced with two fusible link wires so that each circuit will have its own separate protection.

➡ **Most of the problems caused in the wiring harness are due to bad ground connections. Always check all vehicle ground connections for corrosion or looseness before performing any power feed checks to eliminate the chance of a bad ground affecting the circuit.**

Repairing Hard Shell Connectors

Unlike molded connectors, the terminal contacts in hard shell connectors can be replaced. Weatherproof hard-shell connectors with the leads molded into the shell have non-replaceable terminal ends. Replacement usually involves the use of a special terminal removal tool that depress the locking tangs (barbs) on the connector terminal and allow the connector to be removed from the rear of the shell. The connector shell should be replaced if it shows any evidence of burning, melting, cracks, or breaks. Replace individual terminals that are burnt, corroded, distorted or loose.

➡ **The insulation crimp must be tight to prevent the insulation from sliding back on the wire when the wire is pulled. The insulation must be visibly compressed under the crimp tabs, and the ends of the crimp should be turned in for a firm grip on the insulation.**

The wire crimp must be made with all wire strands inside the crimp. The terminal must be fully compressed on the wire strands with the ends of the crimp tabs turned in to make a firm grip on the wire. Check all connections with an ohmmeter to insure a good contact. There should be no measurable resistance between the wire and the terminal when connected.

Mechanical Test Equipment

Vacuum Gauge

Most gauges are graduated in inches of mercury (in.Hg), although a device called a manometer reads vacuum in inches of water (in. H_2O). The normal vacuum reading usually varies between 18 and 22 in.Hg at sea level. To test engine vacuum, the vacuum gauge must be connected to a source of manifold vacuum. Many engines have a plug in the intake manifold which can be removed and replaced with an adapter fitting. Connect the vacuum gauge to the fitting with a suitable rubber hose or, if no manifold plug is available, connect the vacuum gauge to any device using manifold vacuum, such as EGR valves, etc. The vacuum gauge can be used to determine if enough vacuum is reaching a component to allow its actuation.

Hand Vacuum Pump

Small, hand-held vacuum pumps come in a variety of designs. Most have a built-in vacuum gauge and allow the component to be tested without removing it from the vehicle. Operate the pump lever or plunger to apply the correct amount of vacuum required for the test specified in the diagnosis routines. The level of vacuum in inches of Mercury (in.Hg) is indicated on the pump gauge. For some testing, an additional vacuum gauge may be necessary.

Intake manifold vacuum is used to operate various systems and devices on late model vehicles. To correctly diagnose and solve problems in vacuum control systems, a vacuum source is necessary for testing. In some cases, vacuum can be taken from the intake manifold

when the engine is running, but vacuum is normally provided by a hand vacuum pump. These hand vacuum pumps have a built-in vacuum gauge that allow testing while the device is still attached to the component. For some tests, an additional vacuum gauge may be necessary.

HEATER

Heater Assembly

REMOVAL & INSTALLATION

♦ SEE FIGS. 1 AND 2

➡ No factory removal and installation procedures are given; use this procedure as a guide.

Refer to the exploded view of each heater system. You may be able to skip several of the following steps if only certain components of the heater assembly need service.

1. Disconnect the negative battery cable. Set the TEMP lever to the **HOT** position and drain the coolant.

✳✳✳ CAUTION

When draining the coolant, keep in mind that cats and dogs are attracted by the ethylene glycol antifreeze, and are quite likely to drink any that is left in an uncovered container or in puddles on the ground. This will prove fatal in sufficient quantity. Always drain the coolant into a sealable container. Coolant should be reused unless it is contaminated or several years old.

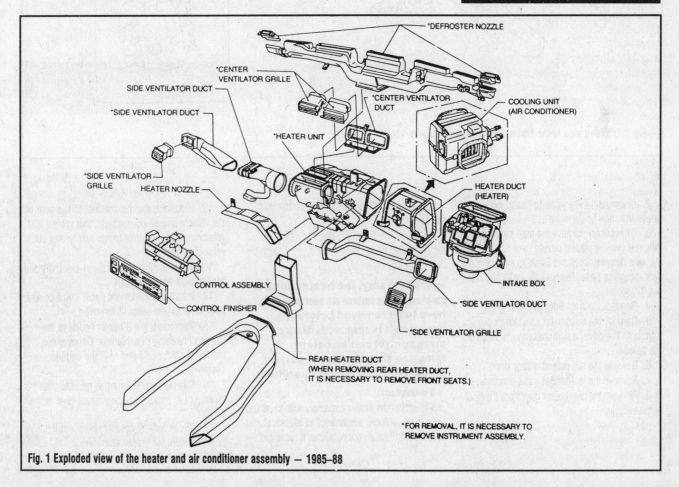

Fig. 1 Exploded view of the heater and air conditioner assembly — 1985–88

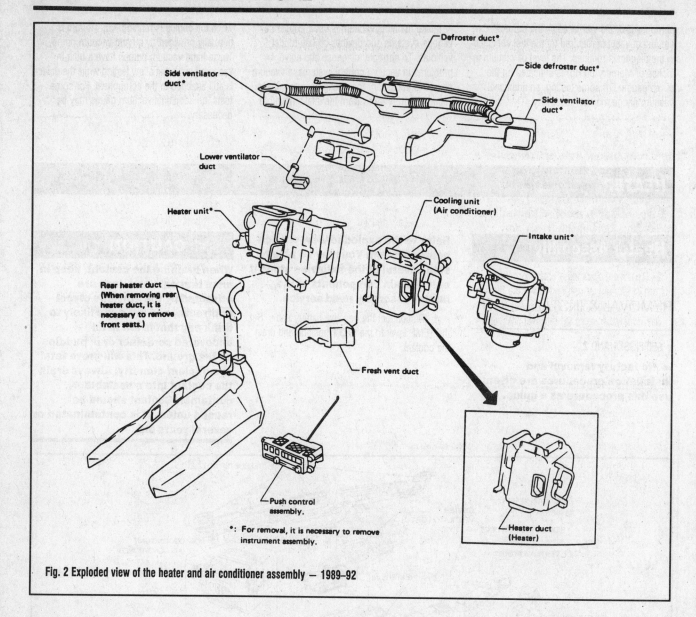

Side ventilator duct*

Defroster duct*

Side defroster duct*

Side ventilator duct*

Lower ventilator duct

Heater unit*

Cooling unit (Air conditioner)

Intake unit*

Rear heater duct (When removing rear heater duct, it is necessary to remove front seats.)

Fresh vent duct

Push control assembly.

Heater duct (Heater)

*: For removal, it is necessary to remove instrument assembly.

Fig. 2 Exploded view of the heater and air conditioner assembly — 1989–92

2. Disconnect the engine-to-heater core hoses from the heater core of the heater unit.

3. If necessary, remove the front seats. To do this, remove the plastic covers over the ends of the seat runners, front and back, to expose the seat mounting bolts. Remove the bolts and lift out the seats.

4. Remove the front floor carpets.

5. Remove the instrument panel lower covers from both the driver's and passenger's sides of the vehicle.

6. Remove the left side ventilator duct.

7. Remove the instrument panel assembly.

8. Remove the rear heater duct from the floor of the vehicle.

9. Label and disconnect the wire harness connectors.

10. Remove the heater unit mounting fasteners and lift out the heater together with the heater control assembly.

➡ **If necessary, the heater control cables and control assembly may have to be removed before the heater unit is removed. Always mark control cables before removing them to ensure correct adjustment and proper operation.**

To install:

11. Install the heater assembly with retaining bolts in the vehicle. Reconnect all electrical and heater control cable connections, if removed.

12. Install the rear heater duct to the floor of the vehicle and all components that were removed to gain access to the rear heater duct retaining bolts.

13. Install the instrument panel assembly and the left side ventilator duct.

14. Install the instrument panel lower covers, floor carpets and seats, if removed.

15. Reconnect the 2 heater hoses to the heater core using new clamps. Connect the battery ground cable and refill the cooling system.

16. Run the engine for a few minutes with the heater ON to make sure the coolant level is correct.

17. Check for any coolant leaks and the heater system for proper operation.

Blower Motor

REMOVAL & INSTALLATION

◆ SEE FIGS. 1 AND 2

➡ **It may be necessary to remove the glove box assembly to gain clearance for the blower motor removal and installation. The blower motor is located behind the glove box, facing the floor.**

1. Disconnect the electrical harness from the blower motor.

2. Remove the retaining bolts from the bottom of the blower unit and lower the blower motor from the case.

3. To install, reverse the removal procedures.

Heater Core

REMOVAL & INSTALLATION

◆ SEE FIGS. 1 AND 2

1. Remove the heater assembly. Loosen the clips and screws and remove the center ventilation cover and heater control assembly.

2. Remove the screws securing the door shafts.

3. Remove the clips securing the left and right heater cases, and then separate the cases. Remove the heater core.

4. To install, reverse the removal procedures.

Control Panel

REMOVAL & INSTALLATION

Push Control Unit

◆ SEE FIG. 3

1. Disconnect the negative battery cable. From the center of the dash, remove the cluster lid **C**.

2. Remove the radio.

3. Remove the 4 push control unit-to-dash screws and the push control unit.

4. Disconnect the temperature control cable from the push control unit.

5. Remove the fresh air vent door cable assembly from the push control unit.

6. Disconnect the electrical harness connector from the push control unit.

7. Remove the push control unit.

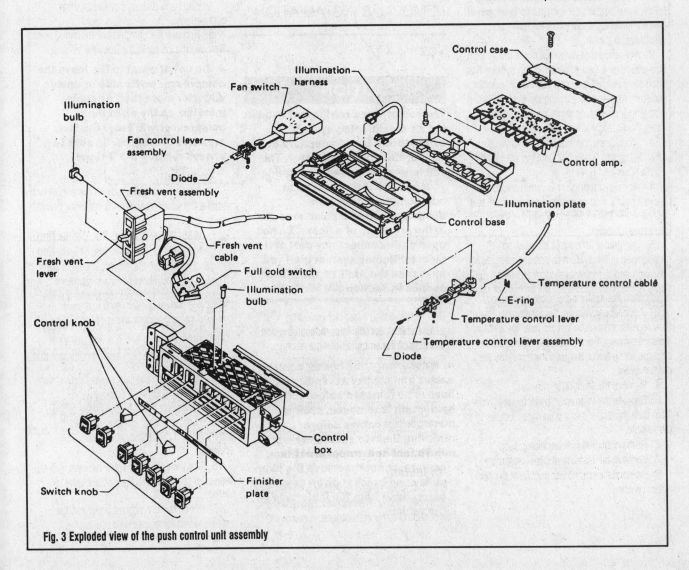

Fig. 3 Exploded view of the push control unit assembly

To install:

8. Install the push control unit.

9. Connect the electrical harness connector to the push control unit.

10. Install the fresh air vent door cable assembly to the push control unit.

11. Connect the temperature control cable to the push control unit.

12. Install push control unit and tighten the 4 push control unit-to-dash screws.

13. Install the radio.

14. At the center of the dash, install the cluster lid **C**. Connect the negative battery cable.

Manual Control

1. Disconnect the negative battery cable.

2. Remove control cables by unfastening clamps at door levers.

3. Remove the center finish panel screws and pull bezel out. Later models also have metal retaining clips. Refer to the "instrument panel" in section 10.

4. Disconnect electrical connector and remove heater control head assembly mounting bolts. Remove ground wire from intake box, if equipped.

5. Remove heater control head assembly.

To install:

6. Install the heater control and reconnect the control cables and electrical connectors.

7. Install the center finish panel and check operation.

8. Connect the negative battery cable.

AIR CONDITIONER

Special Precautions

1. All refrigerant service work must be done with the proper recycling equipment. Carefully follow the manufacturer's instructions for use of that equipment. Do not allow the freon to discharge to the air.

2. Any amount of water will make the system less effective. When any part of the system has been removed, plug or cap the lines to prevent moisture from the air entering the system. When installing a new component, do not uncap the fittings until ready to attach the lines.

3. When assembling a fitting, always use a new O-ring and lightly lubricate the fitting with compressor oil.

4. When a compressor is removed, do not leave it on it's side or upside down for more than 10 minutes. The oil may leak into the low pressure chamber.

5. The proper amount of oil must be maintained in the system to prevent compressor damage and to maintain system efficiency. Be sure to measure and adjust the amount of oil removed or added to the system, especially when replacing the compressor.

Compressor

REMOVAL & INSTALLATION

♦ SEE FIGS. 4–7

❄ CAUTION

The compressed refrigerant used in the air conditioning system expands into the atmosphere at a temperature of –2°F or lower. This will freeze any surface, including your eyes, that it contacts. In addition, the refrigerant decomposes into a poisonous gas in the presence of a flame. Do not open or disconnect any part of the air conditioning system until you have read the SAFETY WARNINGS section in Section 1.

1. Refer to Section 1 for discharging and charging of the air conditioning system. Discharge the air conditioning system.

2. Disconnect the negative battery cable.

3. Remove all the necessary equipment in order to gain access to the compressor mounting bolts.

4. Remove the compressor drive belt.

➡ **To facilitate removal of the compressor belt, remove the idler pulley and bracket as an assembly beforehand from the underside of the vehicle.**

5. Discharge the air conditioning system.

6. Remove the refrigerant line(s) to compressor connector bolts. Disconnect and plug the refrigerant lines with a clean shop towel.

7. Label and disconnect all electrical connections.

8. Remove the compressor mounting bolts. Remove the compressor from the vehicle.

➡ **Do not attempt to the leave the compressor on its side or upside down for more than a couple minutes, as the oil in the compressor will enter the low pressure chambers. Be sure to always replace the O-rings.**

To install:

9. Install the compressor on the engine and torque the compressor-to-compressor bracket bolts to:

    1985–90 — 37–50 ft. lbs. (50–68 Nm)

    1991–92 — 33–44 ft. lbs. (45–60 Nm)

10. Connect all the electrical connections. Unplug and reconnect all refrigerant lines connector to the compressor and torque the bolts to:

    1985–88 — 9–10 ft. lbs. (12–14 Nm)

    1989–92 — 5.8–8.0 ft. lbs. (8–11 Nm)

11. Install all the necessary equipment that was removed.

12. Install and adjust the drive belt.

13. Connect the negative battery cable.

14. Evacuate and charge the system as required. Make sure the oil level is correct for the compressor.

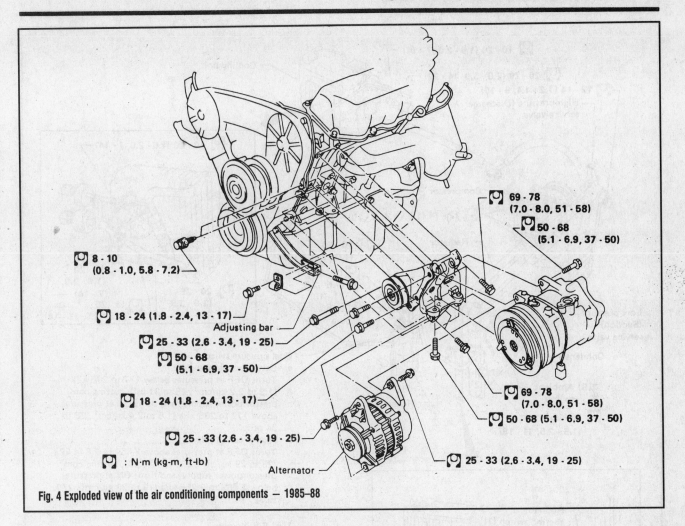

8 - 10
(0.8 - 1.0, 5.8 - 7.2)

18 - 24 (1.8 - 2.4, 13 - 17)

Adjusting bar

25 - 33 (2.6 - 3.4, 19 - 25)

50 - 68
(5.1 - 6.9, 37 - 50)

18 - 24 (1.8 - 2.4, 13 - 17)

25 - 33 (2.6 - 3.4, 19 - 25)

: N·m (kg-m, ft-lb)

Alternator

69 - 78
(7.0 - 8.0, 51 - 58)

50 - 68
(5.1 - 6.9, 37 - 50)

69 - 78
(7.0 - 8.0, 51 - 58)

50 - 68 (5.1 - 6.9, 37 - 50)

25 - 33 (2.6 - 3.4, 19 - 25)

Fig. 4 Exploded view of the air conditioning components — 1985–88

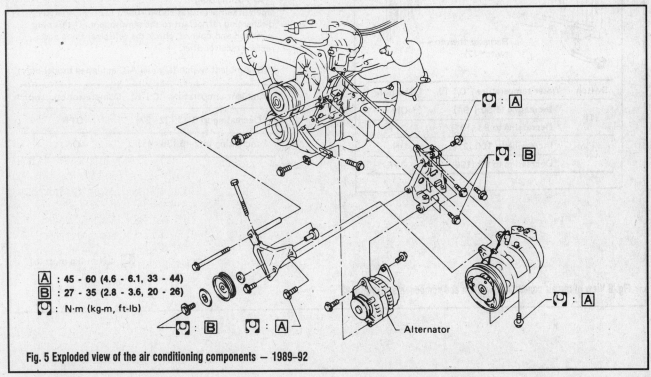

Ⓐ : 45 - 60 (4.6 - 6.1, 33 - 44)
Ⓑ : 27 - 35 (2.8 - 3.6, 20 - 26)
: N·m (kg-m, ft-lb)

: Ⓑ   : Ⓐ

: Ⓐ

: Ⓑ

: Ⓐ

Alternator

Fig. 5 Exploded view of the air conditioning components — 1989–92

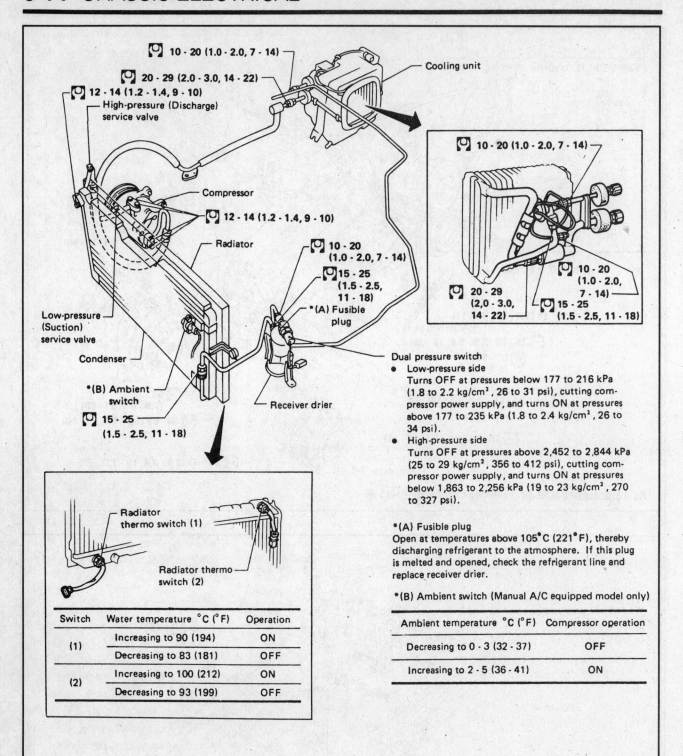

10 - 20 (1.0 - 2.0, 7 - 14)

20 - 29 (2.0 - 3.0, 14 - 22)

12 - 14 (1.2 - 1.4, 9 - 10)
High-pressure (Discharge)
service valve

Cooling unit

Compressor

12 - 14 (1.2 - 1.4, 9 - 10)

Radiator

10 - 20
(1.0 - 2.0, 7 - 14)

15 - 25
(1.5 - 2.5,
11 - 18)

*(A) Fusible
plug

Low-pressure
(Suction)
service valve

Condenser

*(B) Ambient
switch

15 - 25
(1.5 - 2.5, 11 - 18)

Receiver drier

10 - 20 (1.0 - 2.0, 7 - 14)

20 - 29
(2.0 - 3.0,
14 - 22)

10 - 20
(1.0 - 2.0,
7 - 14)

15 - 25
(1.5 - 2.5, 11 - 18)

Radiator
thermo switch (1)

Radiator thermo
switch (2)

Dual pressure switch
- Low-pressure side
  Turns OFF at pressures below 177 to 216 kPa
  (1.8 to 2.2 kg/cm², 26 to 31 psi), cutting compressor power supply, and turns ON at pressures
  above 177 to 235 kPa (1.8 to 2.4 kg/cm², 26 to
  34 psi).
- High-pressure side
  Turns OFF at pressures above 2,452 to 2,844 kPa
  (25 to 29 kg/cm², 356 to 412 psi), cutting compressor power supply, and turns ON at pressures
  below 1,863 to 2,256 kPa (19 to 23 kg/cm², 270
  to 327 psi).

*(A) Fusible plug
Open at temperatures above 105°C (221°F), thereby
discharging refrigerant to the atmosphere. If this plug
is melted and opened, check the refrigerant line and
replace receiver drier.

*(B) Ambient switch (Manual A/C equipped model only)

Switch	Water temperature °C (°F)	Operation
(1)	Increasing to 90 (194)	ON
	Decreasing to 83 (181)	OFF
(2)	Increasing to 100 (212)	ON
	Decreasing to 93 (199)	OFF

Ambient temperature °C (°F)	Compressor operation
Decreasing to 0 - 3 (32 - 37)	OFF
Increasing to 2 - 5 (36 - 41)	ON

: N·m (kg-m, ft-lb)

Fig. 6 View of the air conditioning system and components — 1985–88

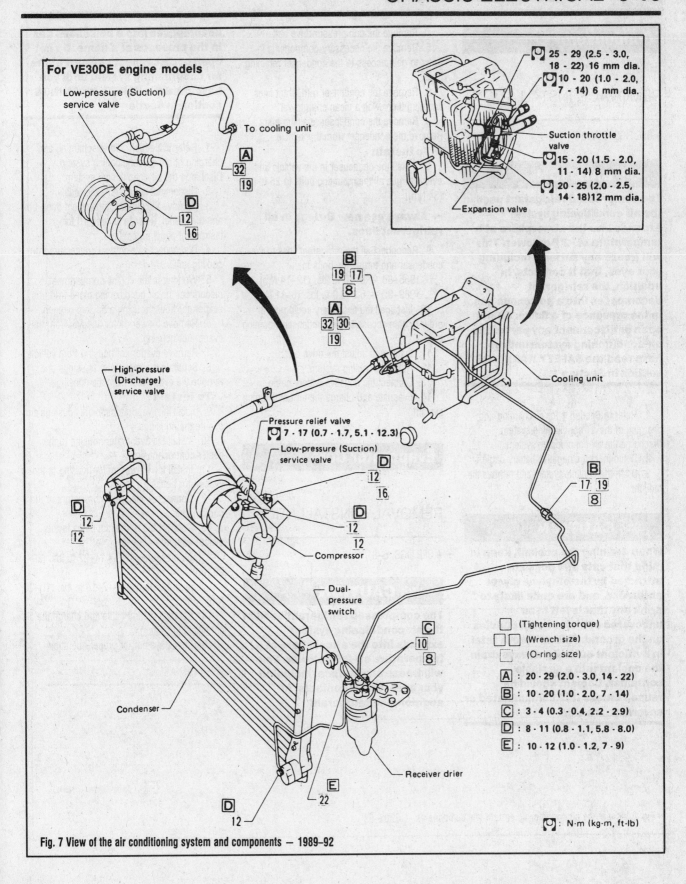

For VE30DE engine models

Low-pressure (Suction)
service valve

To cooling unit

[A]
[32]
[19]

[D]
[12]
[16]

25 - 29 (2.5 - 3.0,
18 - 22) 16 mm dia.

10 - 20 (1.0 - 2.0,
7 - 14) 6 mm dia.

Suction throttle
valve

15 - 20 (1.5 - 2.0,
11 - 14) 8 mm dia.

20 - 25 (2.0 - 2.5,
14 - 18) 12 mm dia.

Expansion valve

[B]
[19] [17]
[8]

[A]
[32] [30]
[19]

Cooling unit

High-pressure
(Discharge)
service valve

Pressure relief valve
7 - 17 (0.7 - 1.7, 5.1 - 12.3)

Low-pressure (Suction)
service valve

[D]
[12]
[16]

[B]
[17] [19]
[8]

[D]
[12]
[12]

[D]
[12]
[12]

Compressor

Dual-
pressure
switch

[C]
[10]
[8]

Condenser

Receiver drier

[E]
[22]

[D]
[12]

(Tightening torque)

(Wrench size)

(O-ring size)

[A] : 20 - 29 (2.0 - 3.0, 14 - 22)

[B] : 10 - 20 (1.0 - 2.0, 7 - 14)

[C] : 3 - 4 (0.3 - 0.4, 2.2 - 2.9)

[D] : 8 - 11 (0.8 - 1.1, 5.8 - 8.0)

[E] : 10 - 12 (1.0 - 1.2, 7 - 9)

: N·m (kg-m, ft-lb)

Fig. 7 View of the air conditioning system and components — 1989–92

Condenser

REMOVAL & INSTALLATION

♦ SEE FIGS. 6 AND 7

> ❄❄ **CAUTION**
>
> **The compressed refrigerant used in the air conditioning system expands into the atmosphere at a temperature of –2°F or lower. This will freeze any surface, including your eyes, that it contacts. In addition, the refrigerant decomposes into a poisonous gas in the presence of a flame. Do not open or disconnect any part of the air conditioning system until you have read the SAFETY WARNINGS section in Section 1.**

1. Refer to Section 1 for discharging and charging of the air conditioning system. Discharge the air conditioning system.
2. Disconnect the negative battery cable.
3. Drain the cooling system and remove the radiator.

> ❄❄ **CAUTION**
>
> **When draining the coolant, keep in mind that cats and dogs are attracted by the ethylene glycol antifreeze, and are quite likely to drink any that is left in an uncovered container or in puddles on the ground. This will prove fatal in sufficient quantity. Always drain the coolant into a sealable container. Coolant should be reused unless it is contaminated or several years old.**

4. Remove the compressor drive belt.
5. Remove the necessary components in order to gain access to the condenser retaining bolts.
6. Remove the condenser refrigerant lines and plug them with a clean shop towel.
7. Remove the condenser retaining bolts. Remove the condenser from the vehicle.

To install:

8. Install the condenser in the vehicle and evenly torque all the mounting bolts to 25 ft. lbs. (34 Nm).

➡ **Always use new O-rings in all refrigerant lines.**

9. Reconnect all the refrigerant lines to the condenser and torque the bolts to:

    1985–88 — 9–10 ft. lbs. (12–14 Nm)
    1989–92 — 5.8–8.0 ft. lbs. (8–11 Nm)
10. Install all the necessary equipment in order to gain access to the condenser mounting bolts.
11. Install and adjust the drive belt.
12. Refill the cooling system.
13. Connect the negative battery cable.
14. Evacuate and charge the air conditioning system.

Evaporator Core

REMOVAL & INSTALLATION

♦ SEE FIGS. 6–8

> ❄❄ **CAUTION**
>
> **The compressed refrigerant used in the air conditioning system expands into the atmosphere at a temperature of –2°F or lower. This will freeze any surface, including your eyes, that it contacts. In addition, the refrigerant decomposes into a poisonous gas in the presence of a flame. Do not open or disconnect any part of the air conditioning system until you have read the SAFETY WARNINGS section in Section 1.**

1. Refer to Section 1 for discharging and charging of the air conditioning system. Discharge the air conditioning system.
2. Disconnect negative battery cable.
3. Remove the glove compartment door, box and trim panel. Refer to section 10 for instrument panel procedures.
4. Disconnect all electrical connectors from cooling unit.
5. Working in the engine compartment, disconnect the air conditioning pipes from the evaporator housing using a backup wrench.
6. Remove blower motor housing from the evaporator housing.
7. Remove evaporator housing from vehicle.
8. Separate the evaporator housings and remove the evaporator from the housings.

To install:

9. Install the evaporator into the housings and secure the housings.
10. Install the evaporator housing to the heater control housing.
11. Install the blower motor housing to the evaporator housing.
12. Connect all electrical connectors to the cooling unit.
13. Connect the refrigerant pipes to the evaporator and torque to:

    High pressure pipe — 14–22 ft. lbs. (20–29 Nm)

    Low pressure pipe — 7–14 ft. lbs. (10–20 Nm)
14. Connect battery cable and charge the air conditioning system.
15. Check system for proper operation.

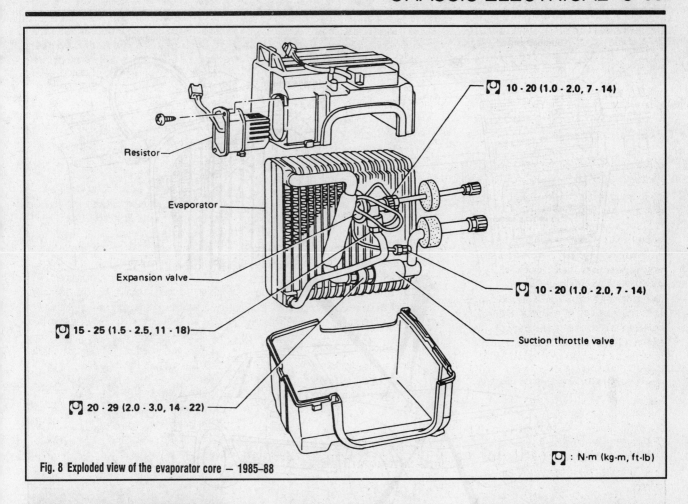

Resistor

Evaporator

Expansion valve

10 - 20 (1.0 - 2.0, 7 - 14)

10 - 20 (1.0 - 2.0, 7 - 14)

Suction throttle valve

15 - 25 (1.5 - 2.5, 11 - 18)

20 - 29 (2.0 - 3.0, 14 - 22)

[Q] : N·m (kg-m, ft-lb)

Fig. 8 Exploded view of the evaporator core — 1985–88

Receiver/Drier

REMOVAL & INSTALLATION

▶ SEE FIGS. 6 AND 7

The receiver/drier is a round soup can looking unit, located next to the condenser. The receiver/drier removes moisture from the air conditioning system. If the system has been exposed to atmosphere for a period of time, replace the receiver/drier. The unit will only hold a specific amount of moisture.

➡ **The receiver/drier is equipped with a fusible plug located at the top of the assembly. The plug will melt at 221°F (105°C), discharging the refrigerant to atmosphere. If the plug is melted or opened, check for an overheating condition and replace the receiver/drier.**

1. Refer to Section 1 for discharging and charging of the air conditioning system. Properly discharge the system into freon recovery equipment.

2. Disconnect the pressure switch.

3. Disconnect the freon lines and cap them to prevent moisture from entering the system.

4. Unbolt and remove the receiver/drier.

5. Installation is the reverse of removal. Be sure to use new O-rings and gaskets. Always evacuate, recharge and leak test as outlined in Section 1.

Expansion Valve

REMOVAL & INSTALLATION

▶ SEE FIGS. 6 AND 7

The expansion valve is located in the evaporator housing. The evaporator, which is between the blower and the heater, can be removed without removing the heater core.

1. Refer to Section 1 for discharging and charging of the air conditioning system. Properly discharge the system using freon recovery equipment.

2. Disconnect and plug the evaporator line fittings at the firewall.

3. Remove the blower motor housing; remove the glove compartment to make this easier.

4. Remove the evaporator housing.

5. Installation is the reverse of removal. Make sure the seals between the housings are in good condition, replace as necessary. Always use new O-rings on the freon line fittings.

6. Always evacuate, recharge and leak test as outlined in Section 1.

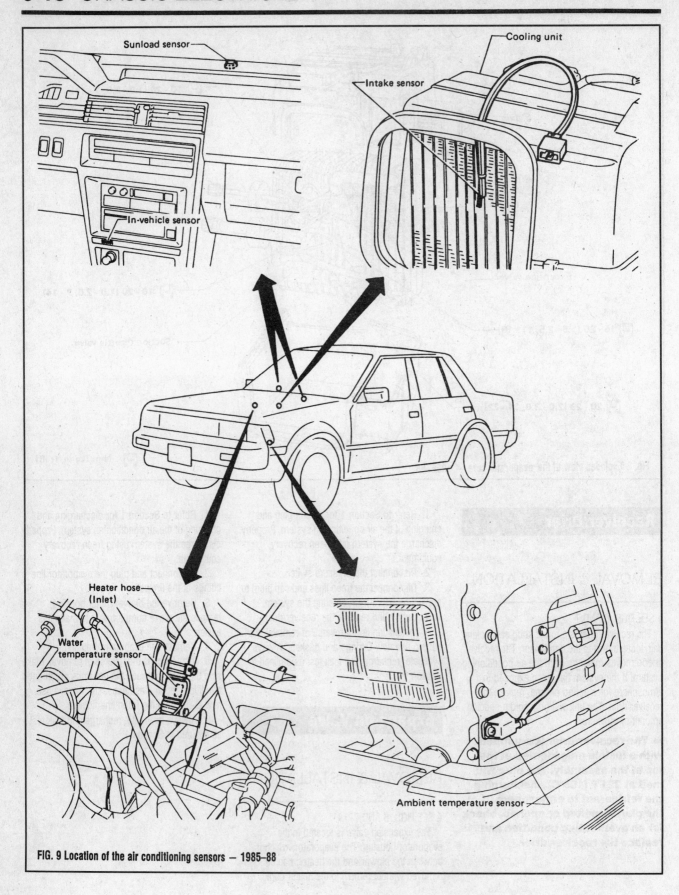

Sunload sensor

In-vehicle sensor

Cooling unit

Intake sensor

Heater hose (Inlet)

Water temperature sensor

Ambient temperature sensor

FIG. 9 Location of the air conditioning sensors — 1985–88

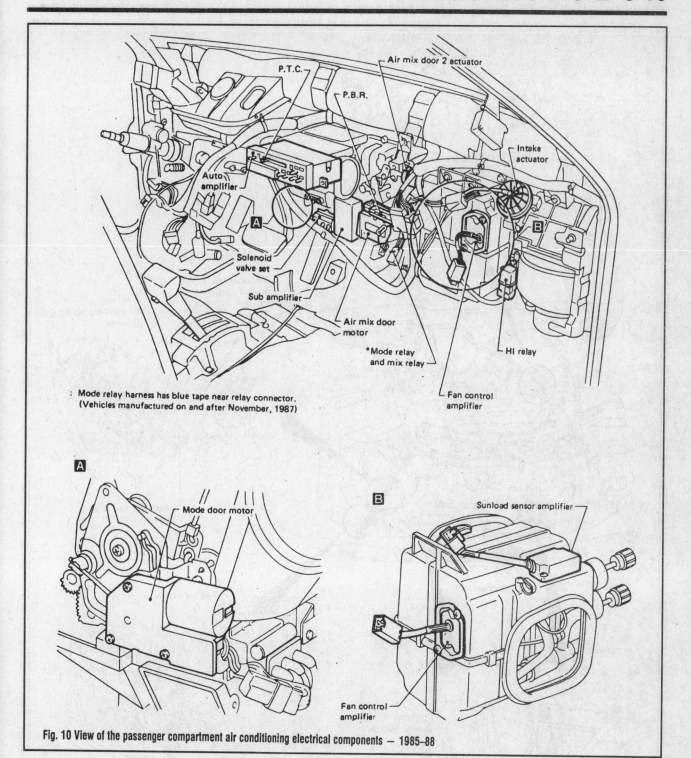

P.T.C.

P.B.R.

Air mix door 2 actuator

Intake actuator

Auto amplifier

A

Solenoid valve set

Sub amplifier

B

Air mix door motor

*Mode relay and mix relay

HI relay

Fan control amplifier

: Mode relay harness has blue tape near relay connector.
(Vehicles manufactured on and after November, 1987)

A

Mode door motor

B

Sunload sensor amplifier

Fan control amplifier

Fig. 10 View of the passenger compartment air conditioning electrical components — 1985–88

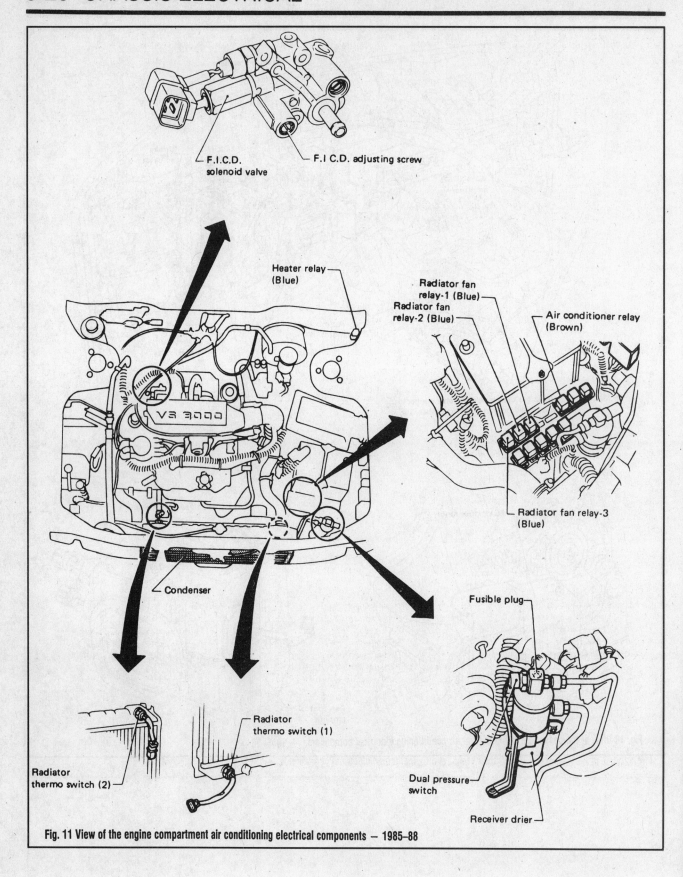

- F.I.C.D. solenoid valve
- F.I C.D. adjusting screw
- Heater relay (Blue)
- Radiator fan relay-1 (Blue)
- Radiator fan relay-2 (Blue)
- Air conditioner relay (Brown)
- Radiator fan relay-3 (Blue)
- Condenser
- Fusible plug
- Radiator thermo switch (1)
- Radiator thermo switch (2)
- Dual pressure switch
- Receiver drier

Fig. 11 View of the engine compartment air conditioning electrical components — 1985–88

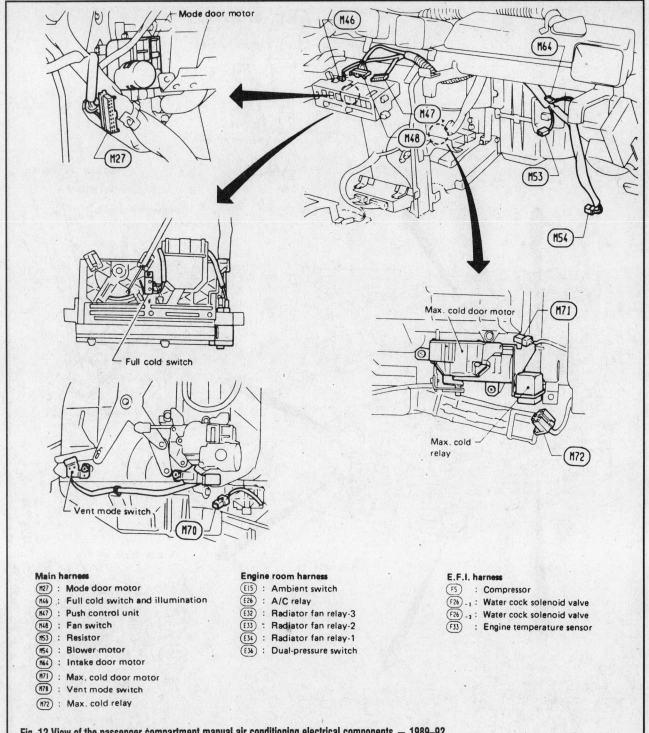

Main harness

- (M27) : Mode door motor
- (M46) : Full cold switch and illumination
- (M47) : Push control unit
- (M48) : Fan switch
- (M53) : Resistor
- (M54) : Blower motor
- (M64) : Intake door motor
- (M71) : Max. cold door motor
- (M70) : Vent mode switch
- (M72) : Max. cold relay

Engine room harness

- (E15) : Ambient switch
- (E26) : A/C relay
- (E32) : Radiator fan relay-3
- (E33) : Radiator fan relay-2
- (E34) : Radiator fan relay-1
- (E36) : Dual-pressure switch

E.F.I. harness

- (F5) : Compressor
- (F26)₋₁ : Water cock solenoid valve
- (F26)₋₂ : Water cock solenoid valve
- (F33) : Engine temperature sensor

Fig. 12 View of the passenger compartment manual air conditioning electrical components — 1989–92

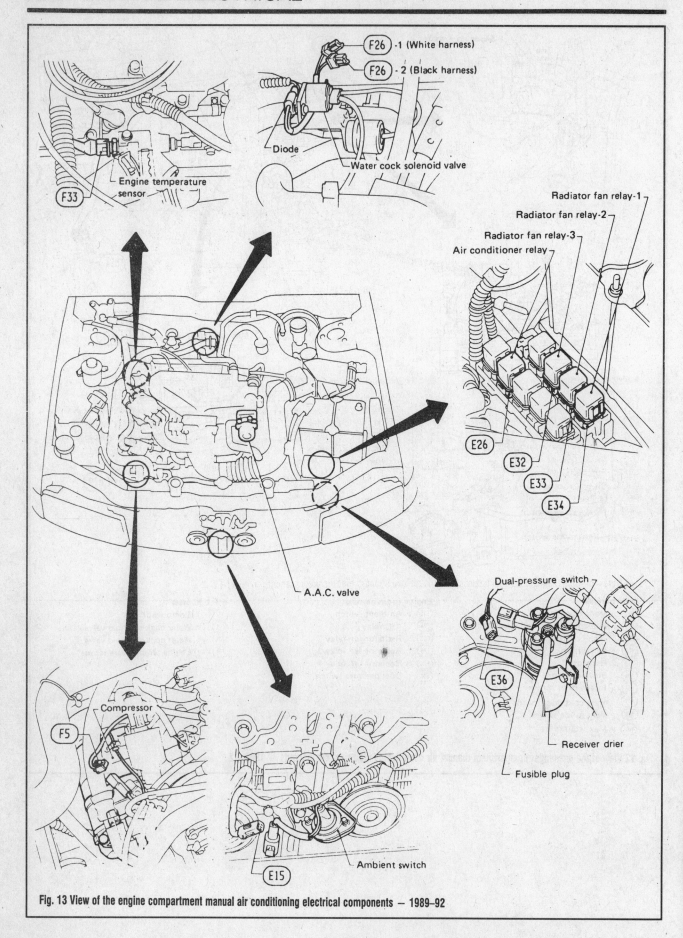

F26 -1 (White harness)

F26 -2 (Black harness)

Diode

Water cock solenoid valve

Engine temperature sensor

F33

Radiator fan relay-1

Radiator fan relay-2

Radiator fan relay-3

Air conditioner relay

E26

E32

E33

E34

A.A.C. valve

Dual-pressure switch

E36

Receiver drier

Fusible plug

Compressor

F5

E15

Ambient switch

Fig. 13 View of the engine compartment manual air conditioning electrical components – 1989–92

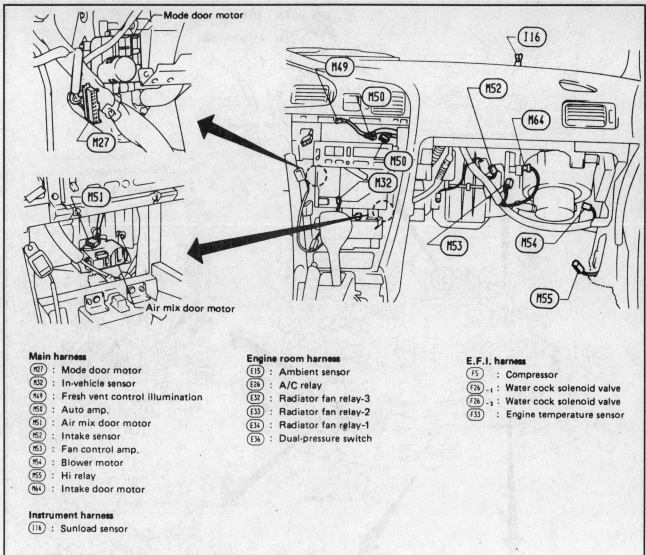

Main harness

- M27 : Mode door motor
- M32 : In-vehicle sensor
- M49 : Fresh vent control illumination
- M50 : Auto amp.
- M51 : Air mix door motor
- M52 : Intake sensor
- M53 : Fan control amp.
- M54 : Blower motor
- M55 : Hi relay
- M64 : Intake door motor

Instrument harness

- I16 : Sunload sensor

Engine room harness

- E15 : Ambient sensor
- E26 : A/C relay
- E32 : Radiator fan relay-3
- E33 : Radiator fan relay-2
- E34 : Radiator fan relay-1
- E36 : Dual-pressure switch

E.F.I. harness

- F5 : Compressor
- F26 -1 : Water cock solenoid valve
- F26 -2 : Water cock solenoid valve
- F33 : Engine temperature sensor

Fig. 14 View of the passenger compartment automatic air conditioning electrical components — 1989–92

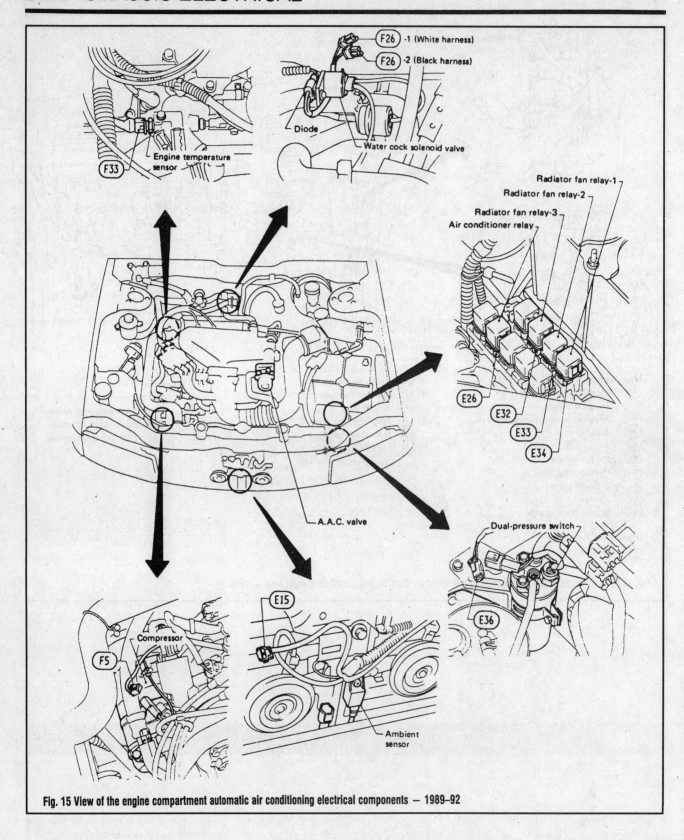

Fig. 15 View of the engine compartment automatic air conditioning electrical components — 1989–92

Refrigerant Lines

REMOVAL & INSTALLATION

♦ SEE FIGS. 6 AND 7

❊❊❊ CAUTION

The compressed refrigerant used in the air conditioning system expands into the atmosphere at a temperature of –2°F or lower. This will freeze any surface, including your eyes, that it contacts. In addition, the refrigerant decomposes into a poisonous gas in the presence of a flame. Do not open or disconnect any part of the air conditioning system until you have read the SAFETY WARNINGS section in Section 1.

1. Refer to Section 1 for discharging and charging of the air conditioning system. Discharge the air conditioning system.

2. Use a flare nut and backup wrench to loosen the air conditioning pipe fittings. If the fitting does not loosen on the first attempt, soak the area with refrigerant oil and let stand for 15 minutes. Slowly loosen the fitting. If the fitting binds, retighten. Go back and forth while lubricating until the fitting loosens.

3. Remove the refrigerant pipe from the vehicle.

➡ Always plug all open refrigerant pipes to prevent moisture from entering the system. An air tight system is good, moisture in the system is BAD.

To install:

4. Install the refrigerant pipe with new O-rings lubricated with refrigerant oil only. Do not any other type of oil; this will contaminate the air conditioning system.

5. After inserting the pipe into the union until the O-ring is no longer visible, torque the high pressure fittings to 14–22 ft. lbs. (20–29 Nm) and the low pressure fittings to 7–14 ft. lbs. (10–20 Nm).

6. After the system has been serviced: evacuate, recharge and leak test the air conditioning system as outlined in Section 1.

Dual Pressure Switch

The dual pressure switch has 2 functions. The first is to turn the air conditioning compressor OFF when the refrigerant level is low. The second is to turn the compressor OFF when the refrigerant high side pressure is too high. Either condition can cause damage to the system. The switch is located on top of the receiver/drier.

The pressure switch will turn the compressor OFF, if the cooling fan is defective.

REMOVAL & INSTALLATION

♦ SEE FIGS. 6 AND 7

❊❊❊ CAUTION

The compressed refrigerant used in the air conditioning system expands into the atmosphere at a temperature of –2°F or lower. This will freeze any surface, including your eyes, that it contacts. In addition, the refrigerant decomposes into a poisonous gas in the presence of a flame. Do not open or disconnect any part of the air conditioning system until you have read the SAFETY WARNINGS section in Section 1.

1. Refer to Section 1 for discharging and charging of the air conditioning system. Discharge the air conditioning system.

2. Disconnect the electrical connector.

3. Remove the switch from the high side pipe of the receiver/drier. Use a wrench to prevent the component from twisting.

4. To install, apply thread sealing tape to the pressure switch and torque to 7–9 ft. lbs. (10–12 Nm).

Pressure Relief Valve

♦ SEE FIG. 7

The air conditioning system is protected by a pressure relief valve, located on the end of the high side hose near the compressor. When the refrigerant pressure reaches an abnormal level of 540 psi (3727 kPa), the release port automatically opens and releases refrigerant to the atmosphere.

CRUISE CONTROL

♦ SEE FIGS. 16–18

General Description

Nissan refers to their cruise control as the Automatic Speed Control Device (ASCD) system. The ASCD system maintains a desired speed of the vehicle under normal driving conditions. The cruise control system's main parts are the control switches, control unit, actuator, speed sensor, vacuum pump, vacuum pump relay, vacuum switch, vacuum tank, electrical release switches and electrical harness.

➡ The use of the speed control is not recommended when driving conditions do not permit maintaining a constant speed, such as in heavy traffic or on roads that are winding, icy, snow covered or slippery.

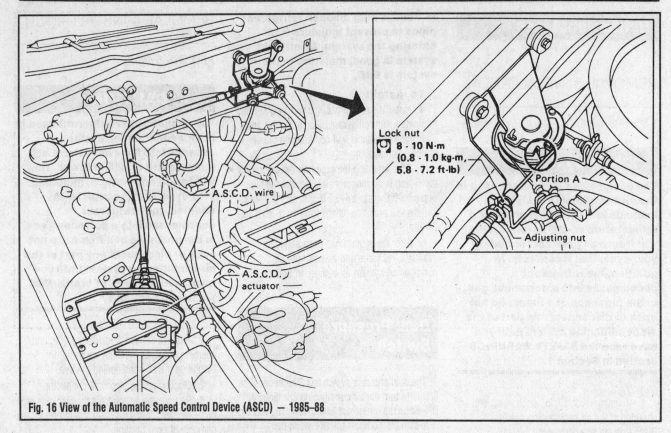

Fig. 16 View of the Automatic Speed Control Device (ASCD) — 1985–88

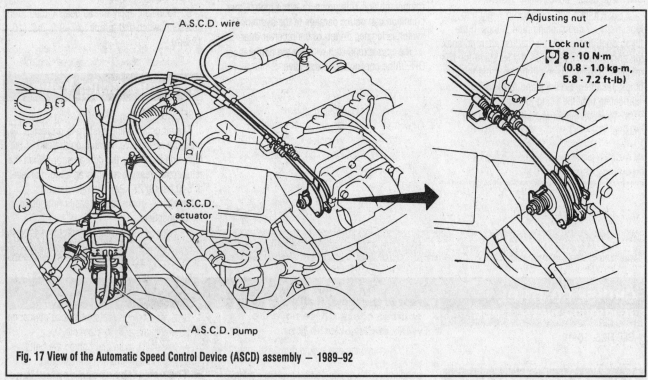

Fig. 17 View of the Automatic Speed Control Device (ASCD) assembly — 1989–92

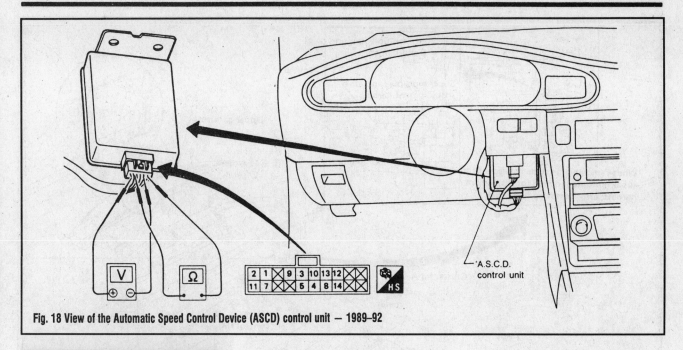

Fig. 18 View of the Automatic Speed Control Device (ASCD) control unit — 1989–92

Diagnosis and Testing

SERVICE PRECAUTIONS

❊ CAUTION

If equipped with an air bag system, the system must be fully disabled before performing repairs, following all safety precautions. Failure to disarm the system could result in personal injury and/or property damage.

• Never disconnect any electrical connection with the ignition switch **ON** unless instructed to do so in a test.

• Always wear a grounded wrist static strap when servicing any control module or component labeled with a Electrostatic Discharge (ESD) sensitive device symbol.

• Avoid touching module connector pins.

• Leave new components and modules in the shipping package until ready to install them.

• Always touch a vehicle ground after sliding across a vehicle seat or walking across vinyl or carpeted floors to avoid static charge damage.

• Never allow welding cables to lie on, near or across any vehicle electrical wiring.

• Do not allow extension cords for power tools or drop lights to lie on, near or across any vehicle electrical wiring.

• Do not operate the cruise control or the engine with the drive wheels off the ground unless specifically instructed to do so by a test procedure.

ADJUSTMENT

◆ SEE FIGS. 16 AND 17

1. Loosen the Automatic Speed Control Device (ASCD) locknuts.

2. Adjust the locknut until the throttle just starts to open.

3. Back off the adjusting locknut 1/2–1 turn.

4. Tighten the locknuts to 5.8–7.2 ft. lbs. (8–10 Nm).

ENTERTAINMENT SYSTEMS

Radio/Cassette Deck

REMOVAL & INSTALLATION

1985–88

◆ SEE FIGS. 19–21

➡ **An auxiliary fuse is located in the** rear of the radio. If all other power sources check OK, remove the radio and check the fuse.

1. Remove the ash tray and the ash tray bracket.

2. Remove the lower instrument panel cover.

3. Remove the instrument cluster lid-C.

4. Remove the radio mounting bolts and the radio.

5. Disconnect the electrical harness connector and the antenna plug from the radio.

To install:

6. Connect the electrical harness connector and the antenna plug to the radio.

7. Install the radio and tighten the bolts.

8. Install the instrument cluster lid-C.

9. Install the lower instrument panel cover.

10. Install the ash tray and the ash tray bracket.

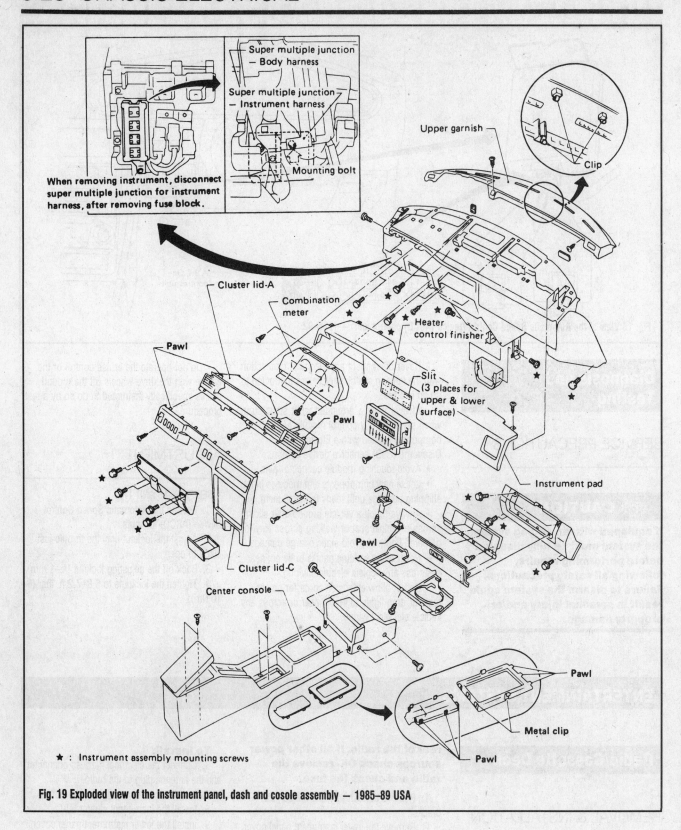

Super multiple junction
— Body harness

Super multiple junction
— Instrument harness

Mounting bolt

When removing instrument, disconnect super multiple junction for instrument harness, after removing fuse block.

Upper garnish

Clip

Cluster lid-A

Combination meter

Heater control finisher

Slit (3 places for upper & lower surface)

Pawl

Pawl

Instrument pad

Pawl

Cluster lid-C

Center console

Pawl

Metal clip

Pawl

★ : Instrument assembly mounting screws

Fig. 19 Exploded view of the instrument panel, dash and console assembly — 1985–89 USA

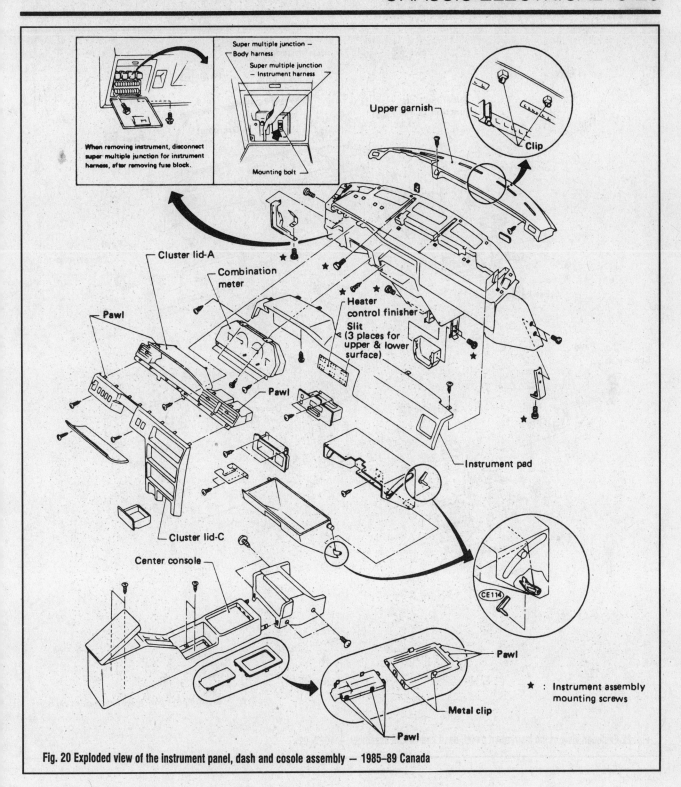

Super multiple junction —
Body harness

Super multiple junction —
Instrument harness

When removing instrument, disconnect
super multiple junction for instrument
harness, after removing fuse block.

Mounting bolt

Upper garnish

Clip

Cluster lid-A

Combination
meter

Pawl

Heater
control finisher

Slit
(3 places for
upper & lower
surface)

Pawl

Instrument pad

Cluster lid-C

Center console

CE114

Pawl

Metal clip

Pawl

★ : Instrument assembly
mounting screws

Fig. 20 Exploded view of the instrument panel, dash and cosole assembly — 1985–89 Canada

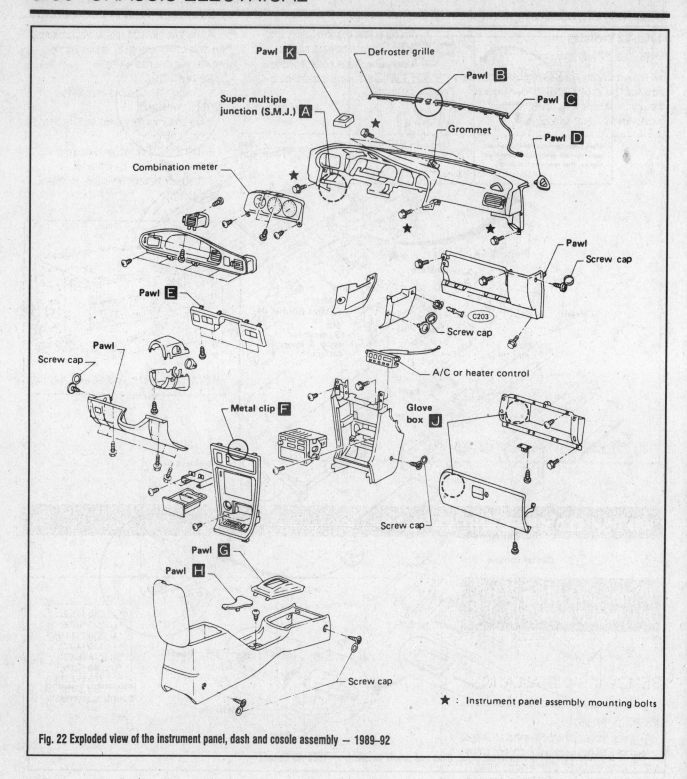

Pawl **K**
Defroster grille
Pawl **B**
Super multiple junction (S.M.J.) **A**
Pawl **C**
Grommet
Pawl **D**
Combination meter
Pawl
Screw cap
Pawl **E**
C203
Screw cap
Pawl
Screw cap
A/C or heater control
Metal clip **F**
Glove box **J**
Screw cap
Pawl **G**
Pawl **H**
Screw cap
★ : Instrument panel assembly mounting bolts

Fig. 22 Exploded view of the instrument panel, dash and cosole assembly — 1989–92

1989–92 Vehicles

♦ SEE FIGS. 22 AND 23

➡ **An auxiliary fuse is located in the rear of the radio. If all other power sources check OK, remove the radio and check the fuse.**

1. Disconnect the negative battery cable.
2. Remove the ash tray and bracket.
3. Remove the cluster center trim panel screws. Pull the trim panel straight out to disengage the clips.

4. Remove the radio retaining bolts and pull the radio out far enough to disconnect the antenna and electrical wiring.

To Install:

5. Position the radio and connect the electrical connectors.
6. Install the retaining bolts and torque to 24 inch lbs. (1.36 Nm).
7. Install the center cluster trim panel.
8. Install the ash tray and bracket.
9. Connect the negative battery cable and check operation.

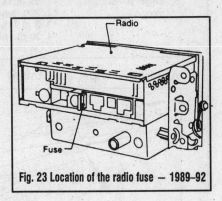

Fig. 23 Location of the radio fuse — 1989–92

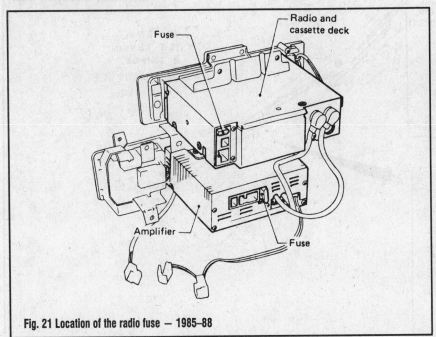

Fig. 21 Location of the radio fuse — 1985–88

WINDSHIELD WIPER AND WASHERS

Windshield Wiper Blade and Arm

REMOVAL & INSTALLATION

♦ SEE FIGS. 24 AND 25

1. Some models have covers that are hinged to the arm. Pull these upward at the end of the arm opposite the blade. Other models have covers that fit over the end of the linkage shaft and the arm; simply pull these off. If necessary, turn the ignition switch on and turn the wipers on and then off again to bring them to the full park position.

2. Hold the wiper arm against the torque and loosen the nut which attaches the arm to the linkage shaft with a socket wrench. Remove the nut.

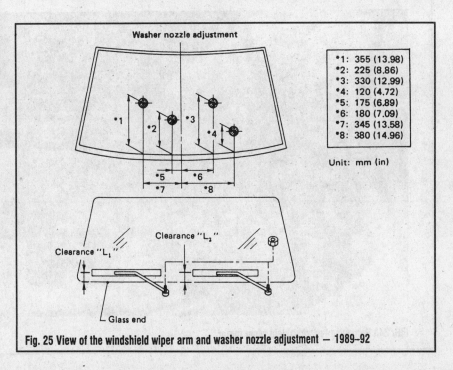

*1:	355 (13.98)
*2:	225 (8.86)
*3:	330 (12.99)
*4:	120 (4.72)
*5:	175 (6.89)
*6:	180 (7.09)
*7:	345 (13.58)
*8:	380 (14.96)

Unit: mm (in)

Fig. 25 View of the windshield wiper arm and washer nozzle adjustment — 1989–92

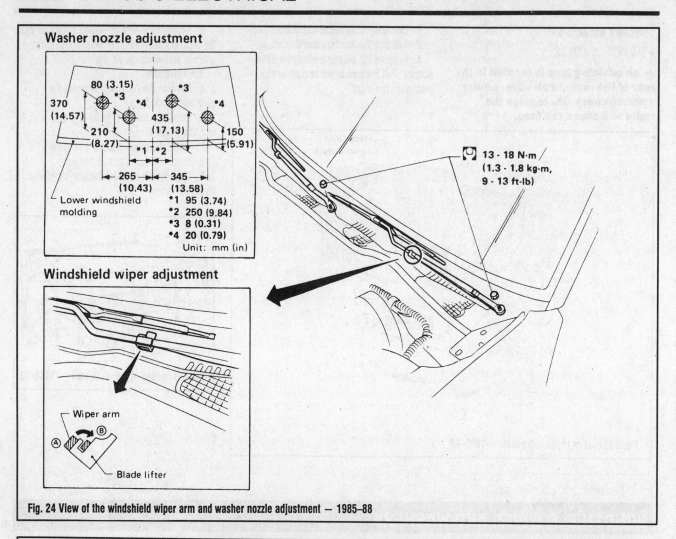

Fig. 24 View of the windshield wiper arm and washer nozzle adjustment — 1985–88

FIG. 24A Removing the windshield wiper motor

3. Note or measure the distance between the blade and the lower edge of the windshield — this is usually about 1 in. (25mm). The blade is usually parallel with the bottom of the windshield. Then, turn the arm outward on its hinges so its spring pressure is removed from the lower end. Pull the lower end of the arm straight off the splines on the shaft.

To install:

4. First, align the wiper blade with the bottom of the windshield at the proper clearance. Then, install the end of the arm over the end of the shaft, turning it slightly, if necessary, in either direction so the splines will engage.

5. Install the attaching nut. Hold the arm to minimize torque on the driveshaft and torque the nut to:

    1985–88 — 9–13 ft. lbs. (13–18 Nm)
    1989–92 — 12–17 ft. lbs. (17–23 Nm)

6. Install decorative caps or covers.

Windshield Motor and Linkage

REMOVAL & INSTALLATION

1. Disconnect the battery ground cable. The wiper motor and linkage are accessible from under the hood. Raise the wiper blade from the windshield and remove the retaining nut. Remove the wiper blades and arms.

2. Remove the nuts holding the wiper pivots to the body. Remove the screws holding the wiper motor to the firewall.

3. Disconnect the wiper motor wiring connector and remove the cowl air intake grille.

4. Disconnect the wiper motor from the linkage and remove the linkage assembly through the cowl top.

5. Installation is the reverse of removal.

➡ **If the wipers do not park correctly, adjust the position of the automatic stop cover of the wiper motor, if equipped.**

Rear Wiper Motor

REMOVAL & INSTALLATION

Station Wagon

♦ SEE FIG. 26

➡ **To perform this procedure, you will need a soft material used to seal the plastic water shields used in vehicle doors and tailgates.**

1. Disconnect the negative battery cable. Bend the wiper arm to raise the wiper blade off the rear window glass. Then, remove the attaching nut and washers; then, work the wiper arm off the motor shaft.

2. Remove the attaching screws and remove the tailgate inner finish panel. Carefully peel the plastic water shield off the sealer.

3. Disconnect the electrical connector at the motor. Remove the motor mounting bolts and remove the motor.

4. Install the motor in reverse of the removal procedure. Torque the rear window wiper arm-to-motor nut to 9–13 ft. lbs. (13–18 Nm).

5. Before installing the water shield, run a fresh ring of sealer around the outer edge.

Windshield Washer Fluid Reservoir

REMOVAL & INSTALLATION

Front and Rear

♦ SEE FIGS. 24–27

1. Disconnect the negative battery cable and reservoir electrical connector.

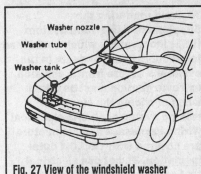

Fig. 27 View of the windshield washer reservoir and nozzle system — 1989–92

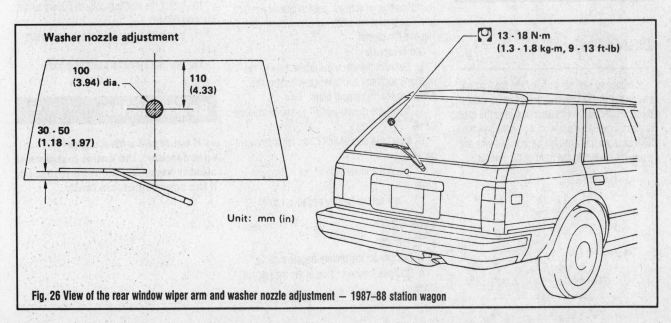

Fig. 26 View of the rear window wiper arm and washer nozzle adjustment — 1987–88 station wagon

2. Disconnect the fluid tube from the washer motor. If the tube is too tight to remove, do not force. Heat the tube with a heat gun if the tube has no extra slack or cut the tube at the motor end.

3. Remove the reservoir retaining bolts and slide out of the bracket.

4. Installation is the reverse of removal. Apply petroleum jelly to the motor nipple before installing the washer tube.

Windshield Washer Motor

REMOVAL & INSTALLATION

Front and Rear

▶ SEE FIG. 27

Remove the washer reservoir/motor

assembly from the vehicle and drain into a suitable container. Pull the motor from the rubber grommet. If having difficulty, lubricate the grommet with penetrating oil and try again. Apply petroleum jelly to install the motor.

INSTRUMENTS AND SWITCHES

❊❊❊ CAUTION

To avoid rendering the Supplemental Restraint System (SRS) inoperative, which could lead to personal injury or death in the event of a severe frontal collision, extreme caution must be taken when servicing the electrical related systems. All SRS electrical wiring harnesses and connectors are covered with YELLOW outer insulation. Do not use electrical test equipment on any circuit related to the SRS (air bag).

Air Bag

DISARMING

If equipped with an air bag, turn the ignition switch OFF. The negative battery cable must be disconnected and wait 10 minutes after the cable is disconnected before working on the system. SRS sensors must always be installed with the arrow marks facing the front of the vehicle.

Instrument Cluster

REMOVAL & INSTALLATION

1985–88

▶ SEE FIGS. 19 AND 20

1. Disconnect the battery negative cable.
2. Remove the lower side of the instrument cover.
3. Remove the cluster lid "C"-to-instrument panel screws and remove the cluster lid "C".
4. Remove the cluster lid "A"-to-instrument panel screws and remove the cluster lid "A".
5. Remove the instrument cluster-to-instrument panel screws, pull the cluster forward and disconnect the electrical connectors; then, remove the cluster.

To install:

6. Connect the electrical connectors to the instrument cluster and install the instrument cluster to the instrument panel.
7. Install the cluster lid "A" to the instrument panel.
8. Install the cluster lid "C" to the instrument panel.
9. Install the lower side of the instrument cover.
10. Connect the battery negative cable.

1989–92

▶ SEE FIG. 22

1. Disconnect the battery negative cable.
2. Remove the lower side of the instrument cover.

3. Remove the steering column covers from the steering column.
4. Remove the lower instrument cluster cover.
5. Remove the instrument cluster cover-to-instrument panel screws and remove the cluster cover.
6. Remove the instrument cluster-to-instrument panel screws, pull the cluster forward and disconnect the electrical connectors; then, remove the cluster.

To install:

7. Connect the electrical connectors to the instrument cluster and install the instrument cluster to the instrument panel.
8. Install the instrument cluster cover to the instrument cluster.
9. Install the lower instrument cluster cover.
10. Install the steering column covers to the steering column.
11. Install the lower side of the instrument cover.
12. Connect the battery negative cable.

Speedometer

➡ **If equipped with a digital speedometer, the entire instrument cluster assembly must be replaced, if the speedometer is faulty.**

REMOVAL & INSTALLATION

Analog (Needle Type) Speedometers

1. Disconnect the negative battery cable.
2. Remove the cluster.
3. Disconnect the speedometer cable and remove the speedometer fasteners.
4. Carefully remove the speedometer from the cluster. Be careful not to damage the printed circuit board.
5. To install, reverse the removal procedures.

Speedometer Cable

REMOVAL & INSTALLATION

1. Remove any lower dash covers that may be in the way and disconnect the speedometer cable from the back of the speedometer.

➡ **It may be necessary to remove the Instrument cluster to gain access to the cable.**

2. Pull the cable from the cable housing. If the cable is broken, the other 1/2 of the cable will have to be removed from the transaxle end. Remove the cable-to-transaxle hold-down bolt and remove the cable from the transaxle.

To Install:

3. Lubricate the cable with graphite powder (sold as speedometer cable lubricant) and feed the cable into the housing. It is best to start as the speedometer end and feed the cable towards the transaxle.
4. Check the speedometer cable operation.

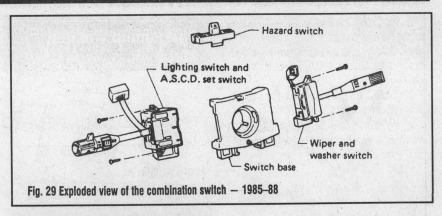

Fig. 29 Exploded view of the combination switch — 1985–88

Windshield Wiper Switch

REMOVAL & INSTALLATION

♦ SEE FIGS. 28–31

The wiper switch can be removed without removing the combination switch from the steering column.

1. Remove the steering column cover.
2. Disconnect the wiper switch electrical connector.
3. Remove the wiper switch-to-combination switch retaining screws.
4. To install, reverse the removal procedures.

Rear Window Wiper Switch

REMOVAL & INSTALLATION

1. Remove the instrument cluster.
2. Remove the nut that attaches the combination switch to the dash.
3. Disconnect the electrical connectors from the rear of the switch, then remove it.
4. Installation is the reverse of the removal procedure.

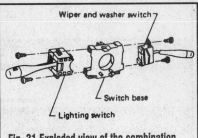

Fig. 31 Exploded view of the combination switch — 1989–92

Headlight Switch

REMOVAL & INSTALLATION

♦ SEE FIGS. 28–31

The headlight switch can be removed without removing the combination switch from the steering column.

1. Remove the steering column cover.
2. Disconnect the headlight switch electrical connector.
3. Remove the headlight switch to combination switch retaining screws.
4. To install, reverse the removal procedures.

Ignition Switch

Ignition switch removal and installation procedures are covered in Section 8; Suspension and Steering.

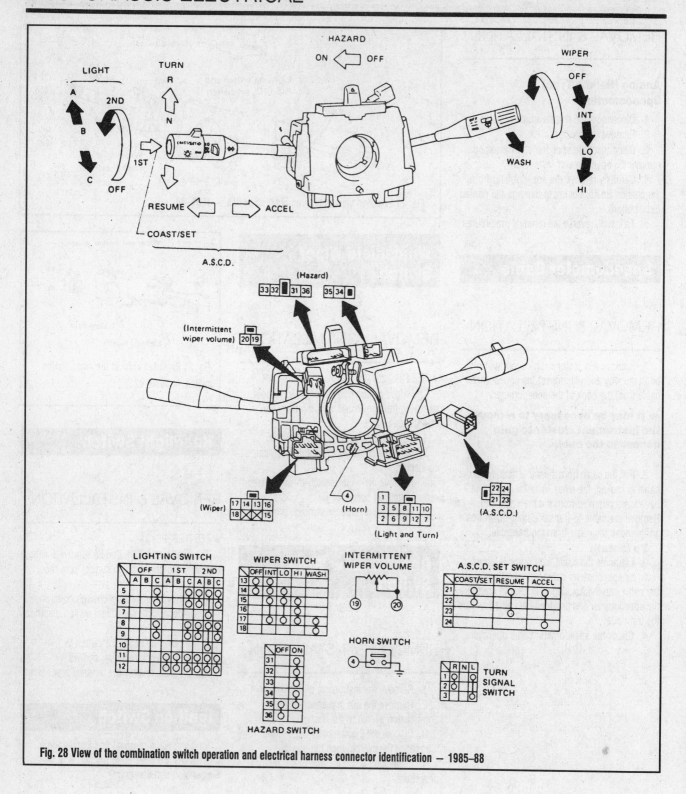

Fig. 28 View of the combination switch operation and electrical harness connector identification — 1985–88

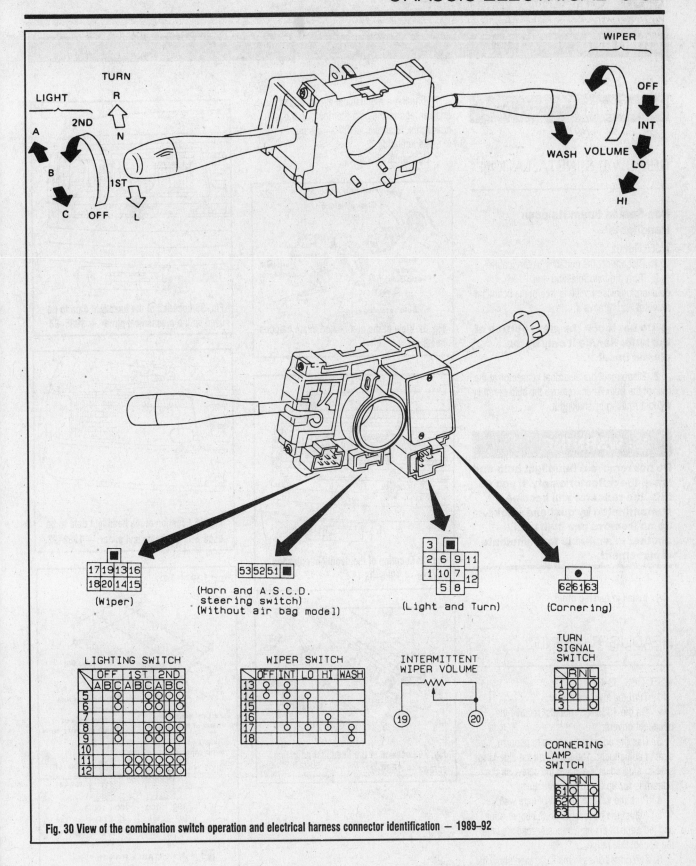

Fig. 30 View of the combination switch operation and electrical harness connector identification — 1989–92

LIGHTING

Headlights

REMOVAL & INSTALLATION

Non-Sealed Beam Halogen Headlights

⏵ SEE FIG. 32

1. Disconnect the negative battery cable.
2. Turn the bulb retaining ring counterclockwise until it is free of the headlight reflector and remove it.

➡ **Do not touch the glass portion of the bulb. Handle it only by the plastic base!**

3. Disconnect the electrical connector at the rear of the bulb. Then, remove the bulb carefully without rotating or shaking it.

❄ WARNING

Do not remove a headlight bulb and leave the reflector empty. If you do this, the reflector will become contaminated by dust and smoke. Do not remove one bulb until another is available for immediate replacement.

4. Install in reverse order.

HEADLIGHT AIMING

⏵ SEE FIGS. 33–37

1. Turn the low beam **ON**.
2. On the 1985–88 models, remove the headlight covers.
3. Use the adjusting screws to perform aiming adjustment. The screw on the side is for side-to-side adjustment and the screw on the bottom is for up and down adjustment.
4. Park the vehicle in front of bare wall.
5. Adjust the headlights so the upper edge and left edge of the high intensity zone are within the acceptable range.
6. The dotted lines in the illustration show the center of the headlights. "H" equals horizontal center line of headlights and "WL" equals the distance between each headlight center.

7. If using a mechanical aimer, adjust the adapter legs to the data stamped on the headlights. Example: 4H2V — means:
Vertical side: 2
Horizontal side: 4

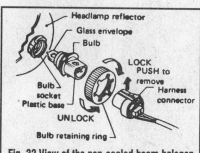

Fig. 32 View of the non-sealed beam halogen headlight

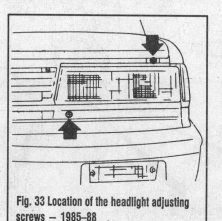

Fig. 33 Location of the headlight adjusting screws — 1985–88

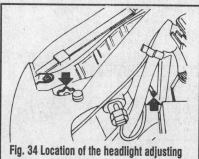

Fig. 34 Location of the headlight adjusting screws — 1989–92

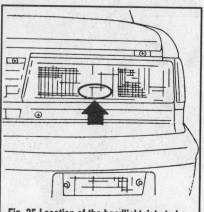

Fig. 35 Location of the headlight data to be used with a mechanical aimer — 1985–88

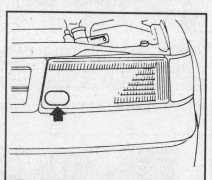

Fig. 36 Location of the headlight data to be used with a mechanical aimer — 1989–92

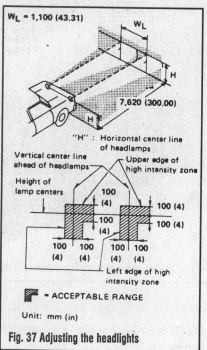

Fig. 37 Adjusting the headlights

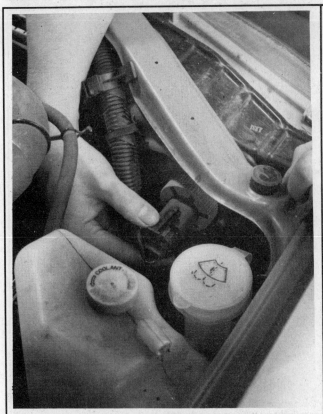

FIG. 32A Location of the halogen beam headlight on the 1991 Maxima

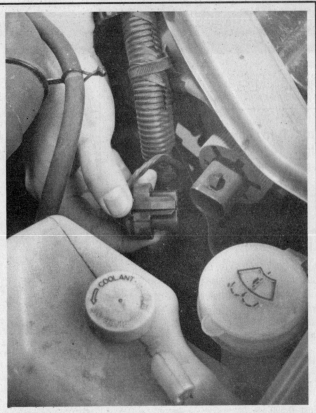

FIG. 32B Disconnecting the electrical connector from the halogen beam headlight on the 1991 Maxima

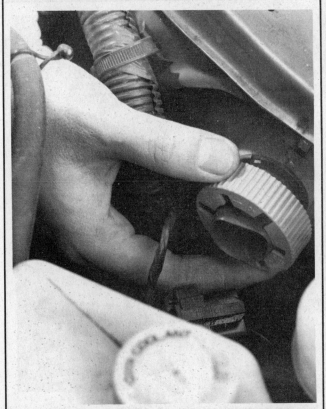

FIG. 32C Removing the halogen beam headlight retainer on the 1991 Maxima

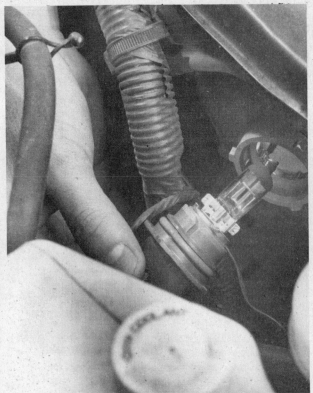

FIG. 32D Removing the halogen beam headlight on the 1991 Maxima

Signal and Marker Lights

REMOVAL & INSTALLATION

Front Turn Signal and Parking Lights

▶ SEE FIGS. 38–40

1. Remove turn signal/parking light lens with retaining screws.

➡ Combine 40(A), 40(B) & 40(C) into 1 piece of art)

2. Slightly depress the bulb and turn it counterclockwise to release it.

3. To install the bulb carefully push down and turn bulb clockwise at the same time.

4. Install the turn signal/parking light lens with retaining screws.

Side Marker Lights

▶ SEE FIGS. 38–40

1. Remove side marker light lens with retaining screws.

2. Turn the bulb socket counterclockwise to release it from lens.

3. Pull bulb straight out.

4. To install bulb carefully push straight in.

5. Turn the bulb socket clockwise to install it in lens.

6. Install side marker light lens with retaining screws.

Rear Turn Signal, Brake and Parking Lights

▶ SEE FIGS. 38–40

1. Remove rear trim panel in rear of vehicle if necessary to gain access to the bulb socket.

2. Slightly depress the bulb and turn it counterclockwise to release it.

3. To install the bulb carefully push down and turn bulb clockwise at the same time.

4. Install trim panel if necessary.

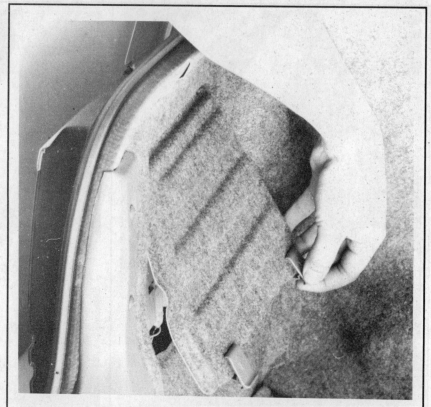

FIG. 38A Removing the rear light assembly cover on the 1991 Maxima

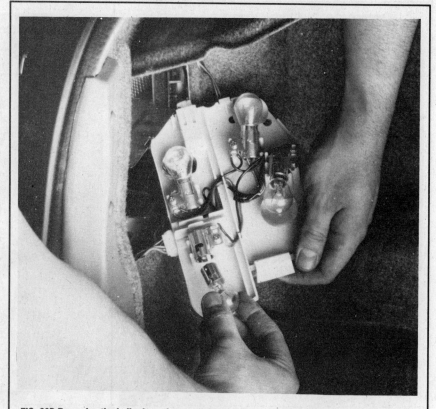

FIG. 38B Removing the bulbs from the rear light assemby on the 1991 Maxima

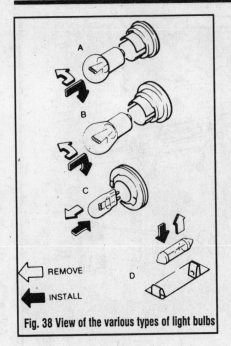

REMOVE

INSTALL

Fig. 38 View of the various types of light bulbs

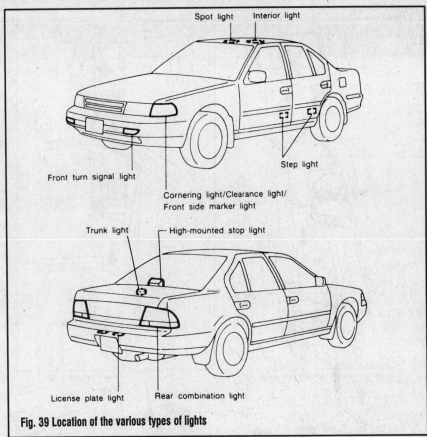

Spot light   Interior light

Front turn signal light

Step light

Cornering light/Clearance light/
Front side marker light

Trunk light   High-mounted stop light

License plate light   Rear combination light

Fig. 39 Location of the various types of lights

LIGHT BULB CHART

Item	Wattage (W)	Bulb No.
Cornering/Front clearance	27/8	1157
Front turn signal light	27	1156 NA
Front side marker light	3.8	194
Rear combination light		
Turn signal	27	1156
Stop/Tail	27/8	1157
Back-up	27	1156
Rear side marker light	3.8	194
License plate light	7.5 or 8	89 (7.5W) or 67 (8W)
High-mounted stop light	18	921
Interior light	10	
Spot light	10	
Step light	3.4	158
Trunk light	3.4	158

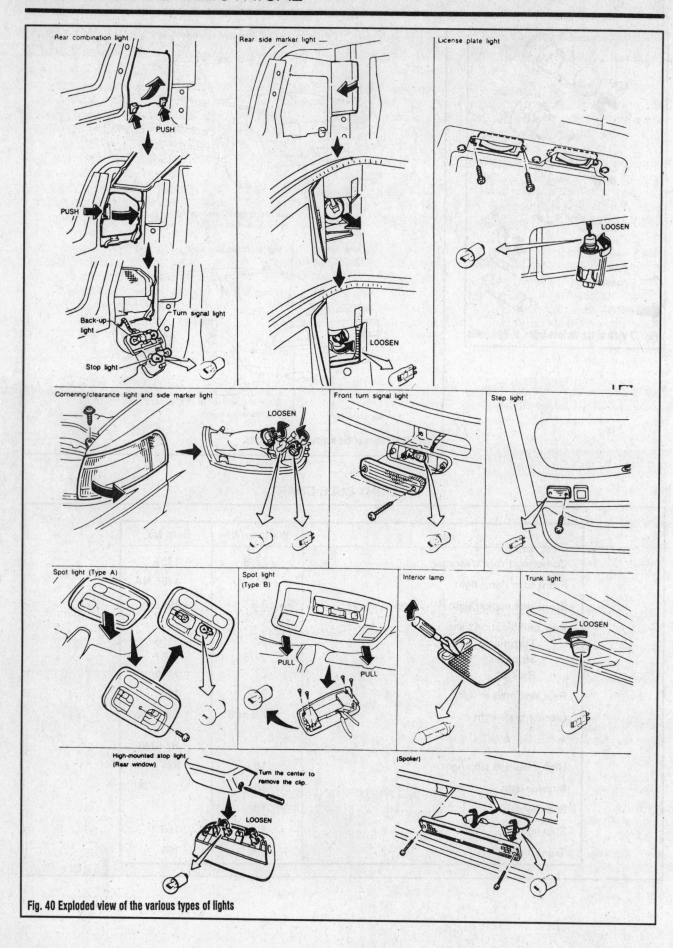

Fig. 40 Exploded view of the various types of lights

TRAILER WIRING

Wiring the vehicle for towing is fairly easy. There are a number of good wiring kits available and these should be used, rather than trying to design your own. All trailers will need brake lights and turn signals as well as tail lights and side marker lights. Most states require extra marker lights for overwide trailers. Also, most states have recently required back-up lights for trailers, and most trailer manufacturers have been building trailers with back-up lights for several years.

Never allow the trailer load to exceed 1000 lbs. (454 kg); the trailer load equals the trailer weight plus its cargo weight. Towing loads greater than specified or use of improper towing equipment could adversely affect the vehicle handling, braking and/or performance.

Keep the tongue load between 9–11 percent of the total trailer load. If the tongue load becomes excessive, rearrange the cargo to allow for proper tongue load.

Determine the equipment on your trailer and buy the wiring kit necessary. The kit will contain all the wires needed, plus a plug adapter set which included the female plug, mounted on the bumper or hitch, and the male plug, wired into or plugged into the trailer harness.

When installing the kit, follow the manufacturer's instructions. The color coding of the wires is standard throughout the industry.

One point to note, most imported vehicles, have separate turn signals. The signals operate with the same bulb. For those vehicles with separate turn signals, you can purchase an

isolation unit so the brake lights won't blink whenever the turn signals are operated or you can go to your local electronics supply house and buy 4 diodes to wire in series with the brake and turn signal bulbs. Diodes will isolate the brake and turn signals. The choice is yours. The isolation units are simple and quick to install but far more expensive than the diodes. The diodes, however, require more work to install properly, since they require the cutting of each bulb's wire and soldering in place of the diode.

One final point, the best kits are those with a spring loaded cover on the vehicle mounted socket. This cover prevents dirt and moisture from corroding the terminals. Never let the vehicle socket hang loosely. Always mount it securely to the bumper or hitch.

CIRCUIT PROTECTION

Fuses

REPLACEMENT

▶ SEE FIGS. 41 AND 42

The fuses can be easily inspected to see if they are blown. Simply pull the fuse from the block, inspect it and replace it with a new one, if necessary.

➡ **When replacing a blown fuse, be certain to replace it with one of the correct amperage.**

Fusible Links

▶ SEE FIG. 43

A fusible link(s) is a protective device used in an electrical circuit. When current increases beyond a certain amperage, the fusible metal wire of the link melts, thus breaking the electrical circuit and preventing further damage to the other components and wiring. Whenever a fusible link is melted because of a short circuit, correct the cause before installing a new link. All fusible links are the plug in kind.

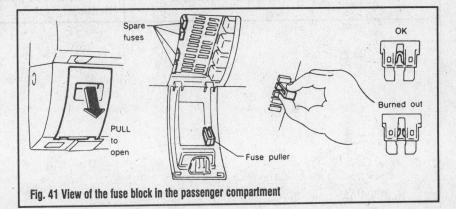

Fig. 41 View of the fuse block in the passenger compartment

REPLACEMENT

▶ SEE FIG. 43

To replace them, simply unplug the bad link and insert the new one.

Flashers

To replace the flasher carefully pull it from the electrical connector. If necessary remove any component that restricts removal.

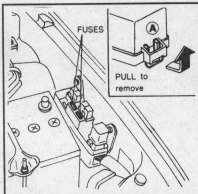

Fig. 42 View of the fuse block in the engine compartment

FIG. 41A View of the in-vehicle fuse panel on the 1991 Maxima

FIG. 41B View of the underhood fusible link, fuse and relay box on the 1991 Maxima

FIG. 41C View of the underhood relay box on the 1991 Maxima

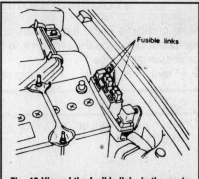

Fig. 43 View of the fusible links in the engine compartment

Troubleshooting Basic Turn Signal and Flasher Problems

Most problems in the turn signals or flasher system can be reduced to defective flashers or bulbs, which are easily replaced. Occasionally, problems in the turn signals are traced to the switch in the steering column, which will require professional service.

F = Front   R = Rear   • = Lights off   o = Lights on

Problem		Solution
One turn signal light on one side doesn't work		• Check and/or replace bulb • Check for corrosion in socket. Clean contacts. • Check for poor ground at socket
Turn signal flashes too fast or too slow		• Check any bulb on the side flashing too fast. A heavy-duty bulb is probably installed in place of a regular bulb. • Check the bulb flashing too slow. A standard bulb was probably installed in place of a heavy-duty bulb. • Check for loose connections or corrosion at the bulb socket
Indicator lights don't work in either direction		• Check if the turn signals are working • Check the dash indicator lights • Check the flasher by substitution
Turn signals light, but do not flash		• Replace the flasher
No turn signals light on either side		• Check the fuse. Replace if defective. • Check the flasher by substitution • Check for open circuit, short circuit or poor ground
Both turn signals on one side don't work		• Check for bad bulbs • Check for bad ground in both housings

One indicator light doesn't light		• On systems with 1 dash indicator: See if the lights work on the same side. Often the filaments have been reversed in systems combining stoplights with taillights and turn signals.
		  Check the flasher by substitution
		• On systems with 2 indicators: Check the bulbs on the same side
		  Check the indicator light bulb
		  Check the flasher by substitution

Troubleshooting Basic Lighting Problems

Problem	Cause	Solution
Lights		
One or more lights don't work, but others do	• Defective bulb(s) • Blown fuse(s) • Dirty fuse clips or light sockets • Poor ground circuit	• Replace bulb(s) • Replace fuse(s) • Clean connections • Run ground wire from light socket housing to car frame
Lights burn out quickly	• Incorrect voltage regulator setting or defective regulator • Poor battery/alternator connections	• Replace voltage regulator • Check battery/alternator connections
Lights go dim	• Low/discharged battery • Alternator not charging • Corroded sockets or connections • Low voltage output	• Check battery • Check drive belt tension; repair or replace alternator • Clean bulb and socket contacts and connections • Replace voltage regulator
Lights flicker	• Loose connection • Poor ground • Circuit breaker operating (short circuit)	• Tighten all connections • Run ground wire from light housing to car frame • Check connections and look for bare wires
Lights "flare"—Some flare is normal on acceleration—if excessive, see "Lights Burn Out Quickly"	• High voltage setting	• Replace voltage regulator
Lights glare—approaching drivers are blinded	• Lights adjusted too high • Rear springs or shocks sagging • Rear tires soft	• Have headlights aimed • Check rear springs/shocks • Check/correct rear tire pressure
Turn Signals		
Turn signals don't work in either direction	• Blown fuse • Defective flasher • Loose connection	• Replace fuse • Replace flasher • Check/tighten all connections
Right (or left) turn signal only won't work	• Bulb burned out • Right (or left) indicator bulb burned out • Short circuit	• Replace bulb • Check/replace indicator bulb • Check/repair wiring
Flasher rate too slow or too fast	• Incorrect wattage bulb • Incorrect flasher	• Flasher bulb • Replace flasher (use a variable load flasher if you pull a trailer)
Indicator lights do not flash (burn steadily)	• Burned out bulb • Defective flasher	• Replace bulb • Replace flasher
Indicator lights do not light at all	• Burned out indicator bulb • Defective flasher	• Replace indicator bulb • Replace flasher

Troubleshooting Basic Dash Gauge Problems

Problem	Cause	Solution
Coolant Temperature Gauge		
Gauge reads erratically or not at all	• Loose or dirty connections • Defective sending unit	• Clean/tighten connections • Bi-metal gauge: remove the wire from the sending unit. Ground the wire for an instant. If the gauge registers, replace the sending unit.
	• Defective gauge	• Magnetic gauge: disconnect the wire at the sending unit. With ignition ON gauge should register COLD. Ground the wire; gauge should register HOT.
Ammeter Gauge—Turn Headlights ON (do not start engine). Note reaction		
Ammeter shows charge Ammeter shows discharge Ammeter does not move	• Connections reversed on gauge • Ammeter is OK • Loose connections or faulty wiring • Defective gauge	• Reinstall connections • Nothing • Check/correct wiring • Replace gauge
Oil Pressure Gauge		
Gauge does not register or is inaccurate	• On mechanical gauge, Bourdon tube may be bent or kinked	• Check tube for kinks or bends preventing oil from reaching the gauge
	• Low oil pressure	• Remove sending unit. Idle the engine briefly. If no oil flows from sending unit hole, problem is in engine.
	• Defective gauge	• Remove the wire from the sending unit and ground it for an instant with the ignition ON. A good gauge will go to the top of the scale.
	• Defective wiring	• Check the wiring to the gauge. If it's OK and the gauge doesn't register when grounded, replace the gauge.
	• Defective sending unit	• If the wiring is OK and the gauge functions when grounded, replace the sending unit
All Gauges		
All gauges do not operate	• Blown fuse • Defective instrument regulator	• Replace fuse • Replace instrument voltage regulator
All gauges read low or erratically	• Defective or dirty instrument voltage regulator	• Clean contacts or replace
All gauges pegged	• Loss of ground between instrument voltage regulator and car • Defective instrument regulator	• Check ground • Replace regulator

Troubleshooting Basic Dash Gauge Problems

Problem	Cause	Solution
Warning Lights		
Light(s) do not come on when ignition is ON, but engine is not started	• Defective bulb • Defective wire • Defective sending unit	• Replace bulb • Check wire from light to sending unit • Disconnect the wire from the sending unit and ground it. Replace the sending unit if the light comes on with the ignition ON.
Light comes on with engine running	• Problem in individual system • Defective sending unit	• Check system • Check sending unit (see above)

Troubleshooting the Heater

Problem	Cause	Solution
Blower motor will not turn at any speed	• Blown fuse • Loose connection • Defective ground • Faulty switch • Faulty motor • Faulty resistor	• Replace fuse • Inspect and tighten • Clean and tighten • Replace switch • Replace motor • Replace resistor
Blower motor turns at one speed only	• Faulty switch • Faulty resistor	• Replace switch • Replace resistor
Blower motor turns but does not circulate air	• Intake blocked • Fan not secured to the motor shaft	• Clean intake • Tighten security
Heater will not heat	• Coolant does not reach proper temperature • Heater core blocked internally • Heater core air-bound • Blend-air door not in proper position	• Check and replace thermostat if necessary • Flush or replace core if necessary • Purge air from core • Adjust cable
Heater will not defrost	• Control cable adjustment incorrect • Defroster hose damaged	• Adjust control cable • Replace defroster hose

Troubleshooting Basic Windshield Wiper Problems

Problem	Cause	Solution
Electric Wipers		
Wipers do not operate—Wiper motor heats up or hums	• Internal motor defect • Bent or damaged linkage • Arms improperly installed on linking pivots	• Replace motor • Repair or replace linkage • Position linkage in park and reinstall wiper arms
Electric Wipers		
Wipers do not operate—No current to motor	• Fuse or circuit breaker blown • Loose, open or broken wiring • Defective switch • Defective or corroded terminals • No ground circuit for motor or switch	• Replace fuse or circuit breaker • Repair wiring and connections • Replace switch • Replace or clean terminals • Repair ground circuits
Wipers do not operate—Motor runs	• Linkage disconnected or broken	• Connect wiper linkage or replace broken linkage
Vacuum Wipers		
Wipers do not operate	• Control switch or cable inoperative • Loss of engine vacuum to wiper motor (broken hoses, low engine vacuum, defective vacuum/fuel pump) • Linkage broken or disconnected • Defective wiper motor	• Repair or replace switch or cable • Check vacuum lines, engine vacuum and fuel pump • Repair linkage • Replace wiper motor
Wipers stop on engine acceleration	• Leaking vacuum hoses • Dry windshield • Oversize wiper blades • Defective vacuum/fuel pump	• Repair or replace hoses • Wet windshield with washers • Replace with proper size wiper blades • Replace pump

TORQUE SPECIFICATIONS

Component	English	Metric
Condenser mounting bolts	25 ft. lbs.	34 Nm
Compressor-to-compressor bracket bolts:		
1985–90	37–50 ft. lbs.	50–68 Nm
1991–92	33–44 ft. lbs.	45–60 Nm
Cruise control cable locknuts	5.8–7.2 ft. lbs.	8–10 Nm
Pressure switch-to-receiver/drier	7–9 ft. lbs.	10–12 Nm
Rear window wiper arm-to-motor nut	9–13 ft. lbs.	13–18 Nm
Refrigerant lines connector-to-compressor:		
1985–88	9–10 ft. lbs.	12–14 Nm
1989–92	5.8–8.0 ft. lbs.	8–11 Nm
Refrigerant pipes-to-evaporator:		
High pressure pipe	14–22 ft. lbs.	20–29 Nm
Low pressure pipe	7–14 ft. lbs.	10–20 Nm
Windshield wiper arm-to-linkage nut:		
1985–88	9–13 ft. lbs.	13–18 Nm
1989–92	12–17 ft. lbs.	17–23 Nm

WIRING DIAGRAMS

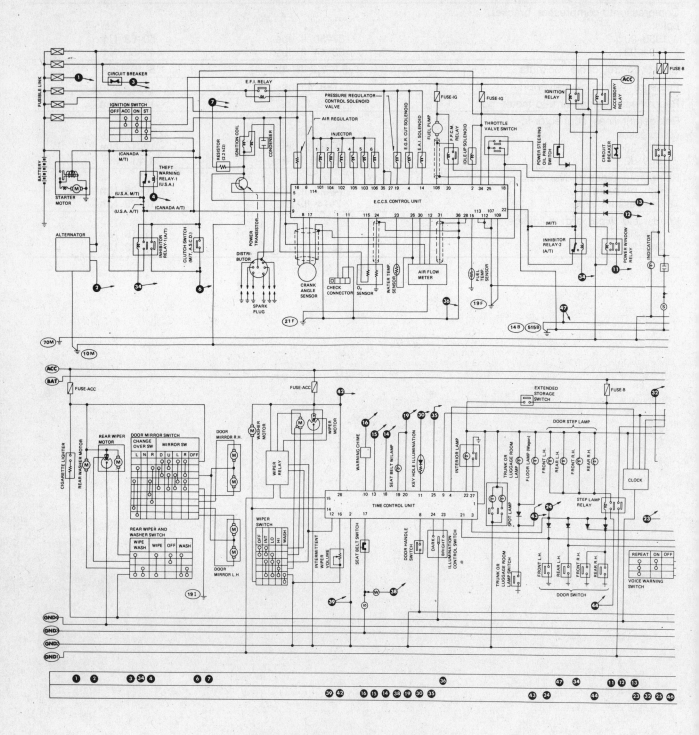

w1. 1985 Maxima wiring schematic — needle type meter

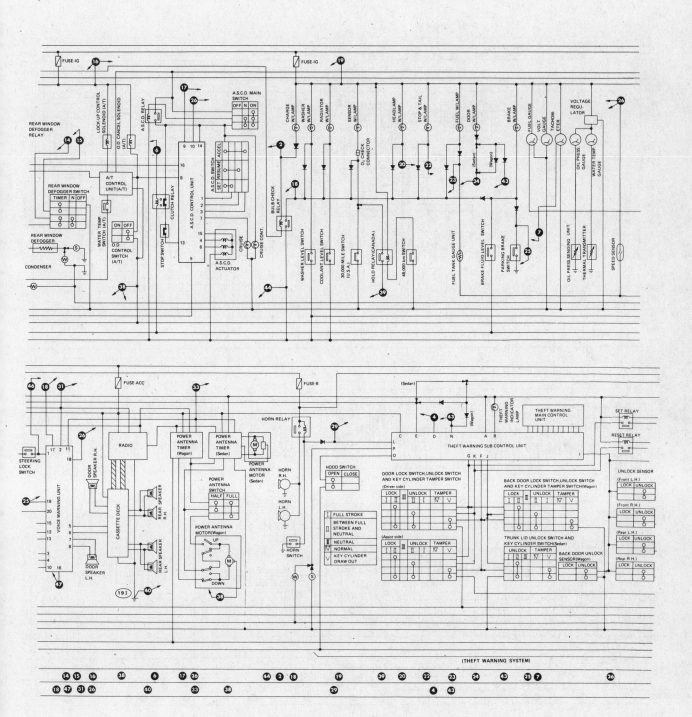

w1. 1985 Maxima wiring schematic — needle type meter

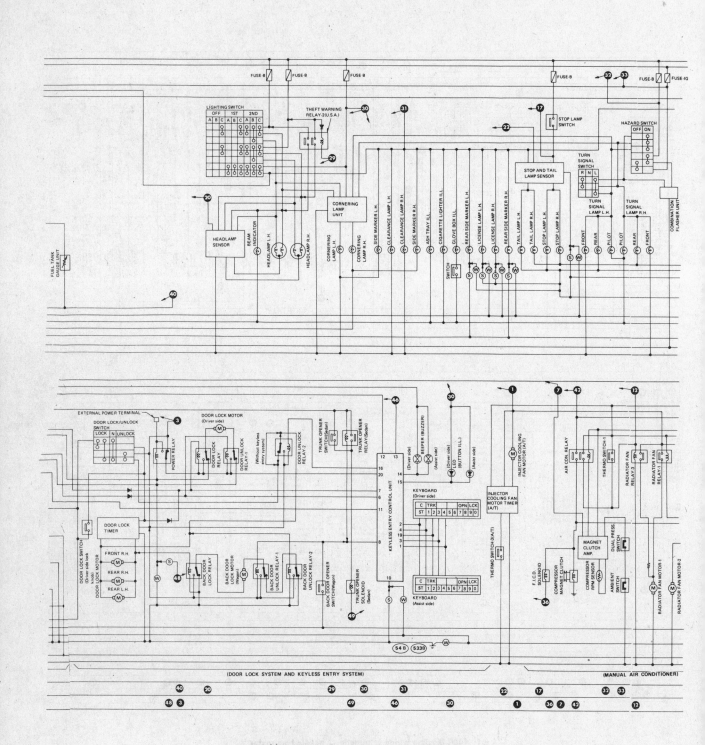

w1. 1985 Maxima wiring schematic — needle type meter

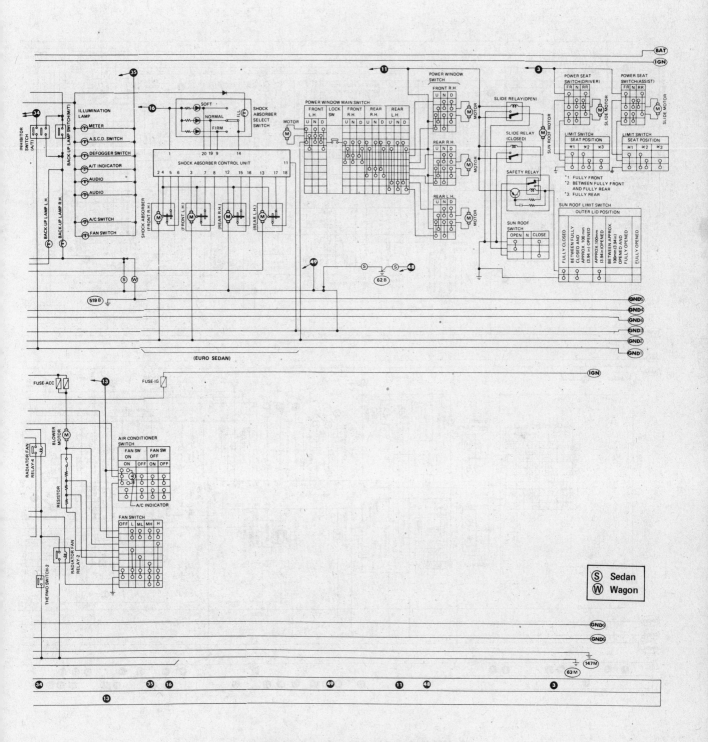

w1. 1985 Maxima wiring schematic — needle type meter

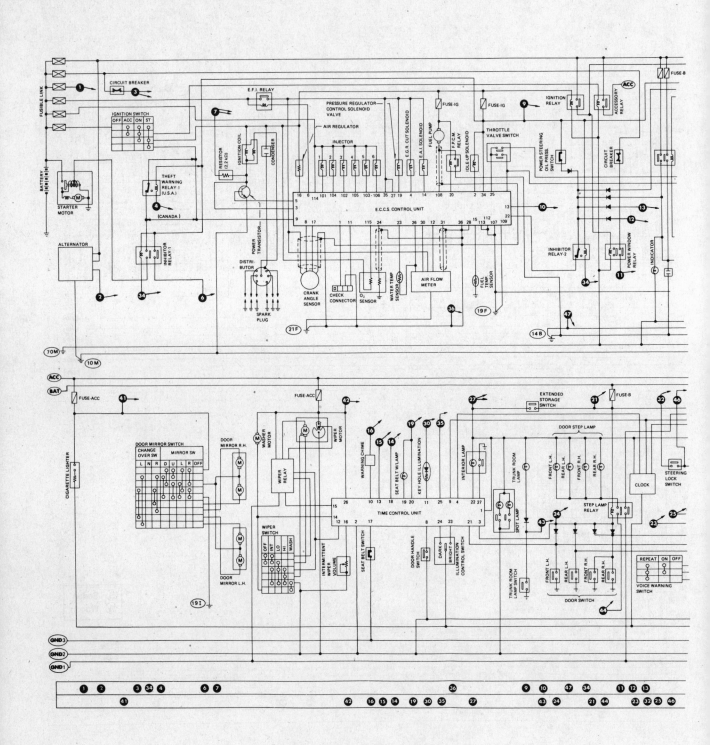

w2. 1985 Maxima wiring schematic — digital type meter

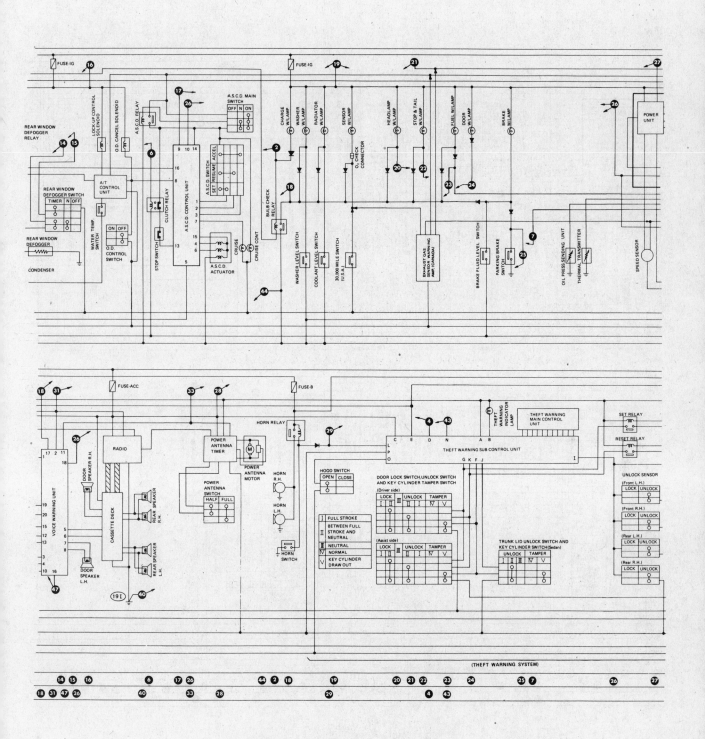

w2. 1985 Maxima wiring schematic — digital type meter

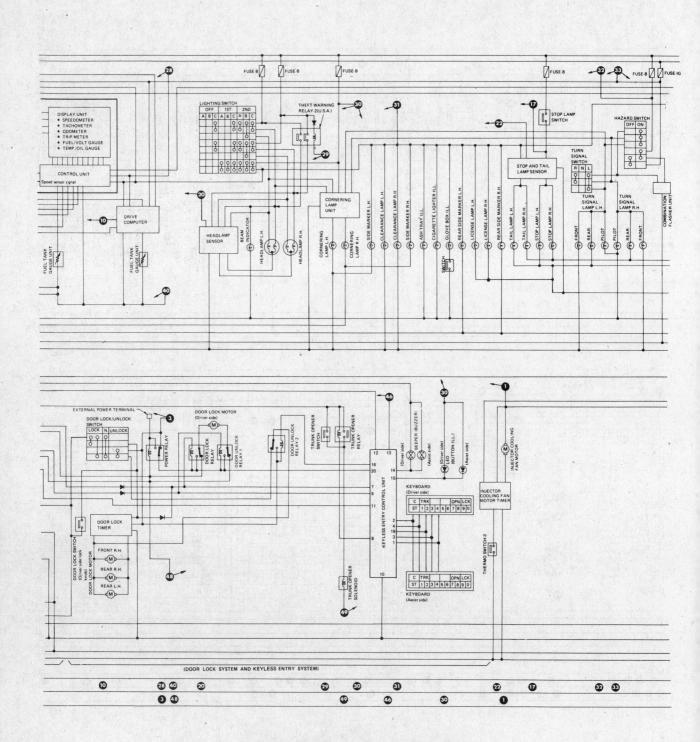

w2. 1985 Maxima wiring schematic — digital type meter

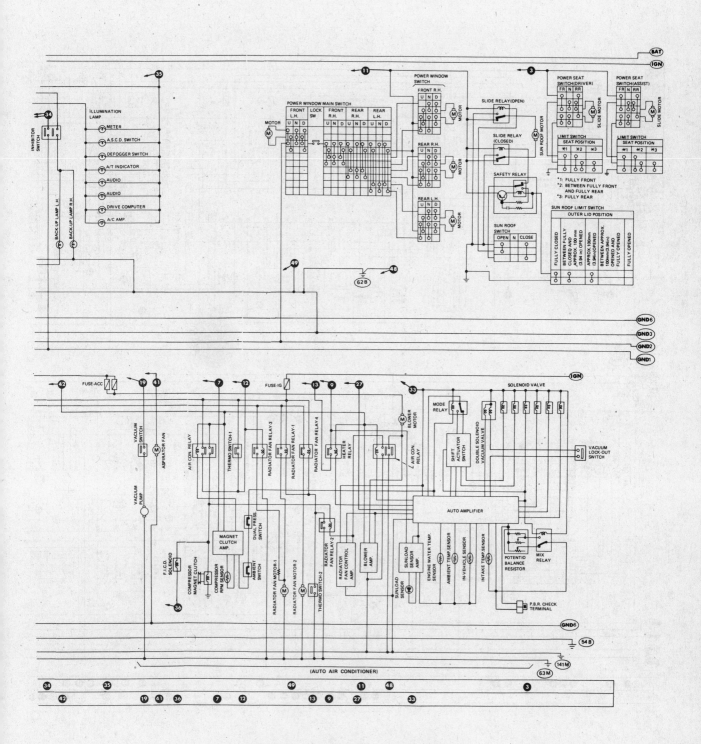

w2. 1985 Maxima wiring schematic — digital type meter

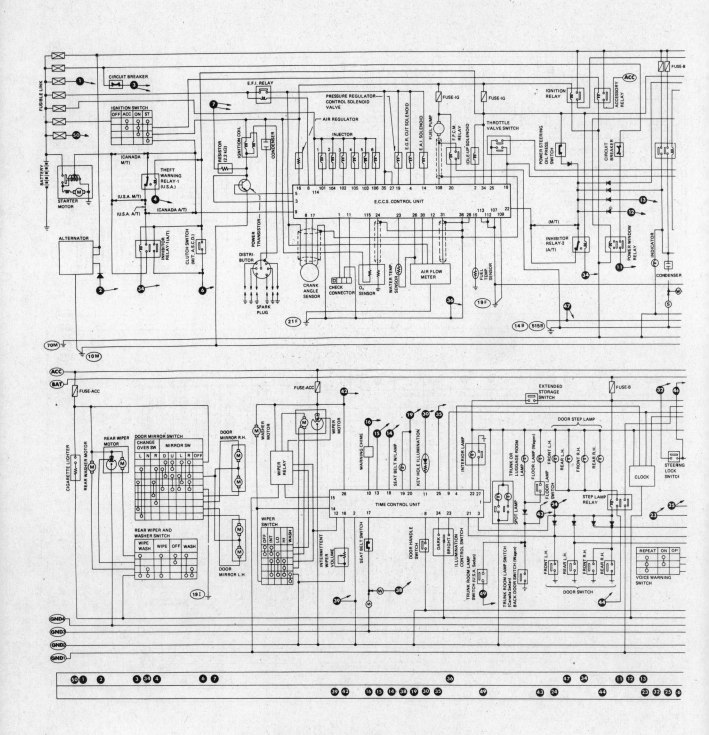

w3. 1986 Maxima wiring schematic — needle type meter

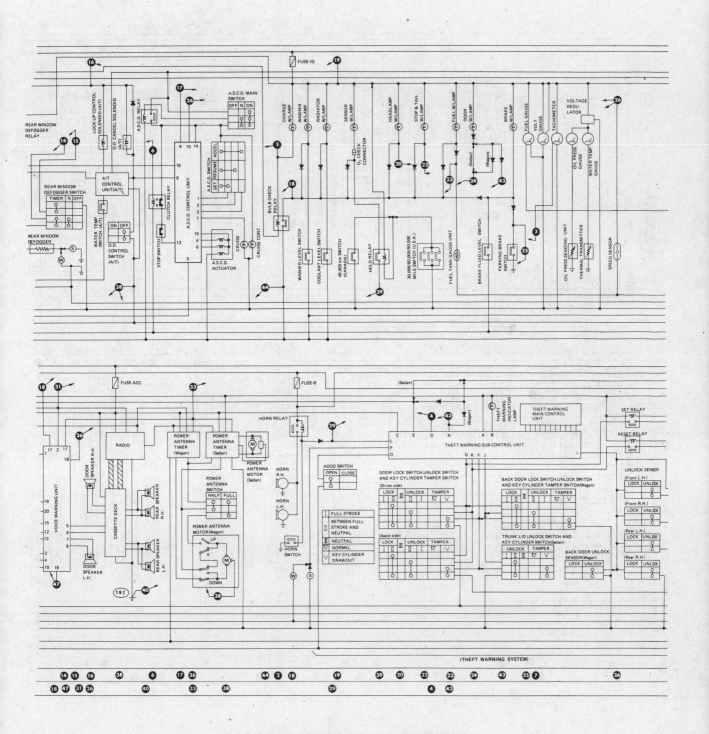

w3. 1986 Maxima wiring schematic — needle type meter

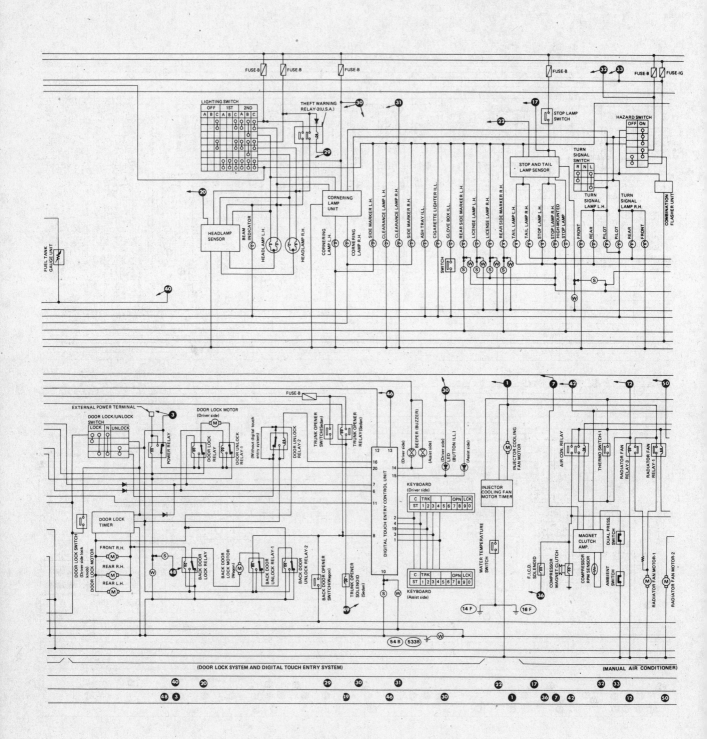

w3. 1986 Maxima wiring schematic — needle type meter

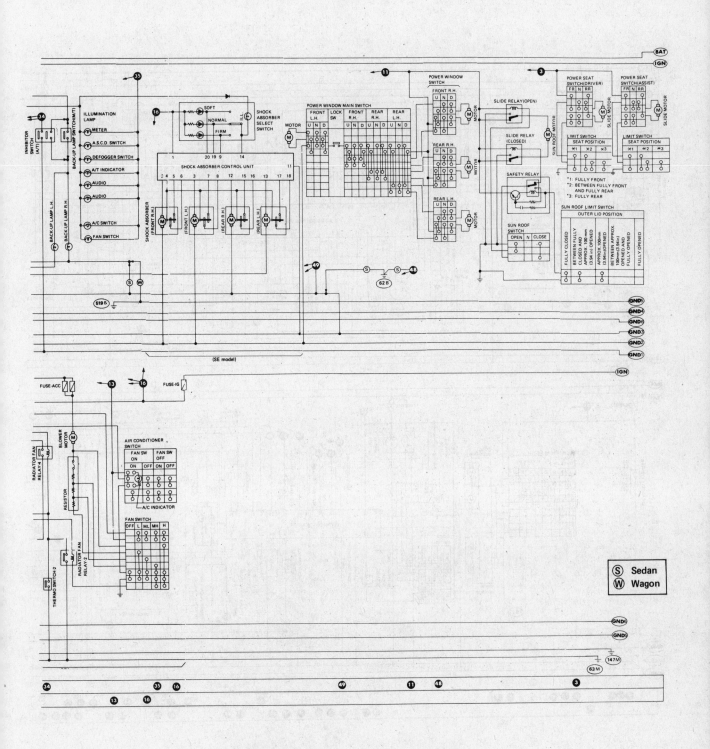

w3. 1986 Maxima wiring schematic — needle type meter

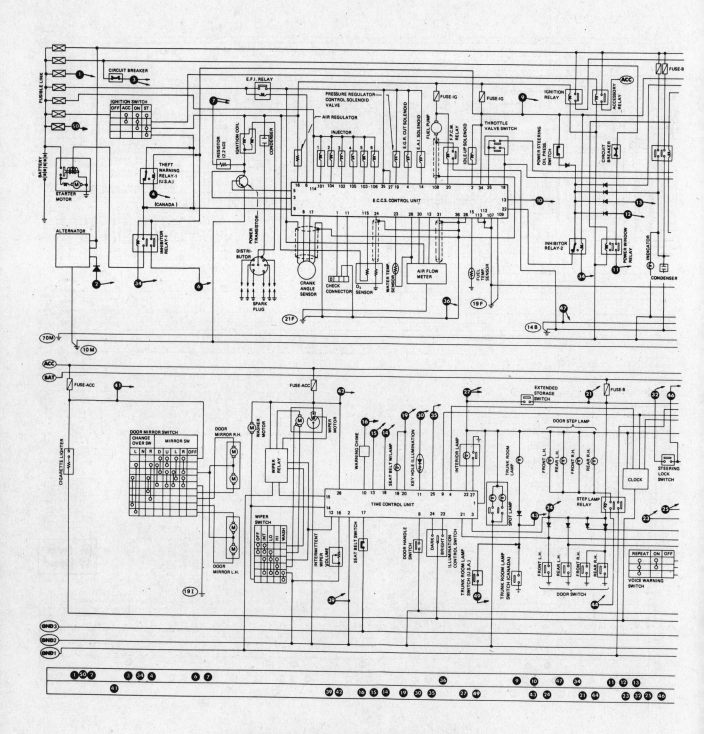

w4. 1986 Maxima wiring schematic — digital type meter

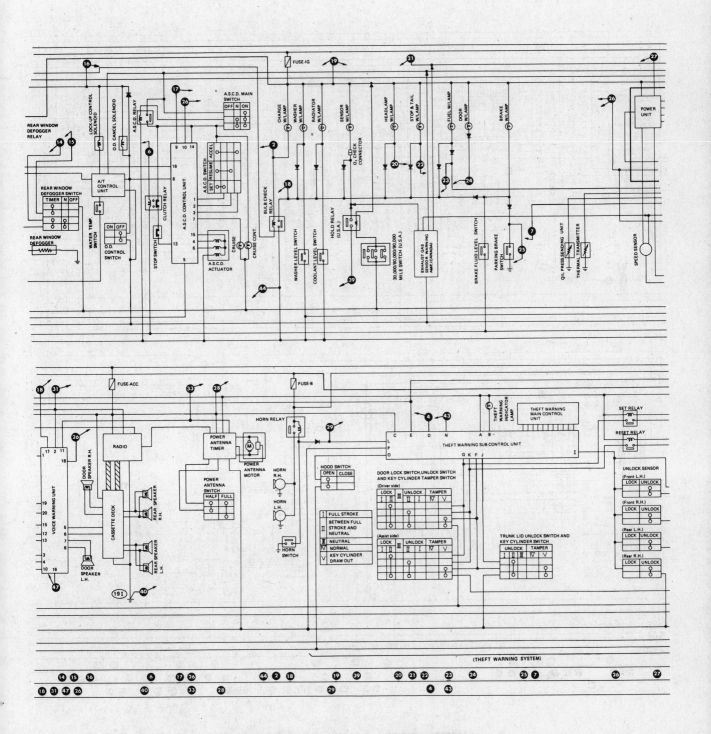

w4. 1986 Maxima wiring schematic — digital type meter

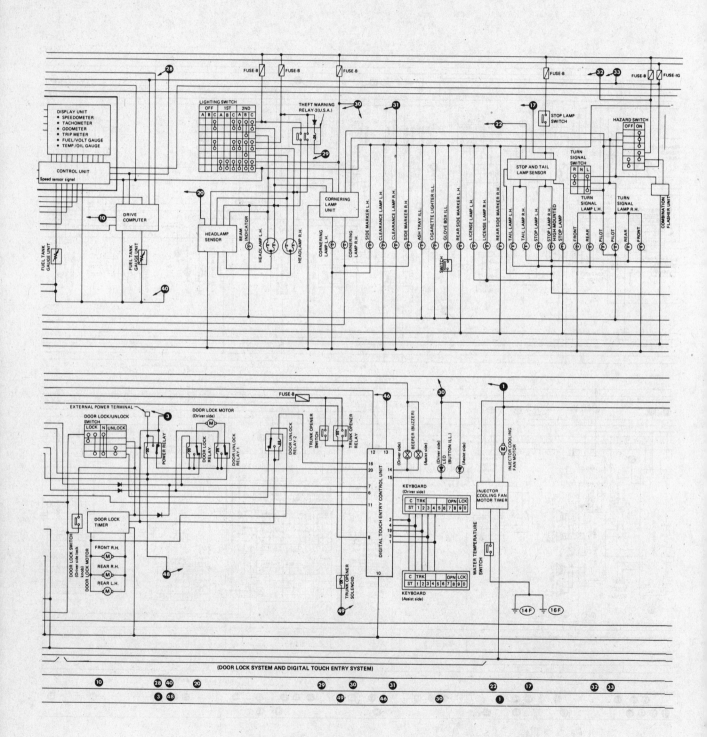

w4. 1986 Maxima wiring schematic — digital type meter

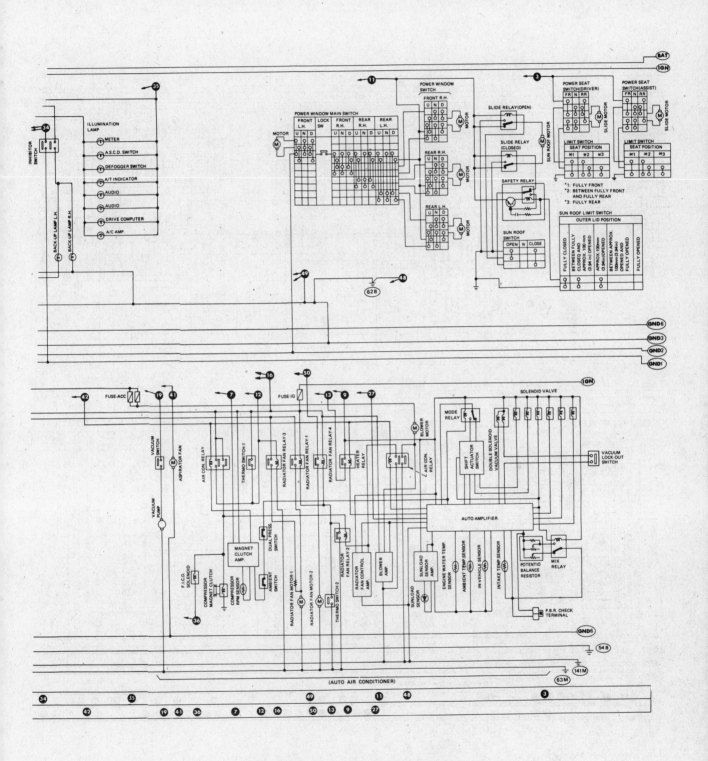

w4. 1986 Maxima wiring schematic — digital type meter

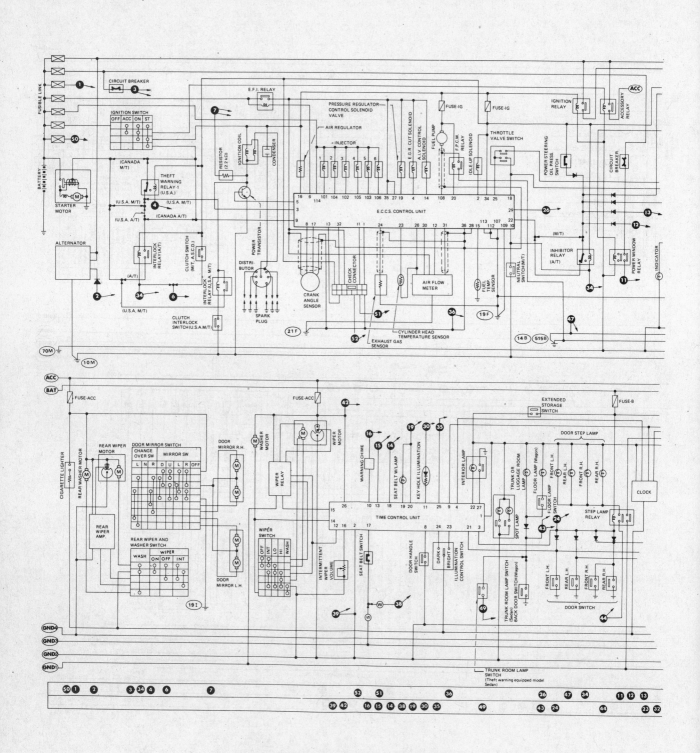

w5. 1987 Maxima wiring schematic — needle type meter

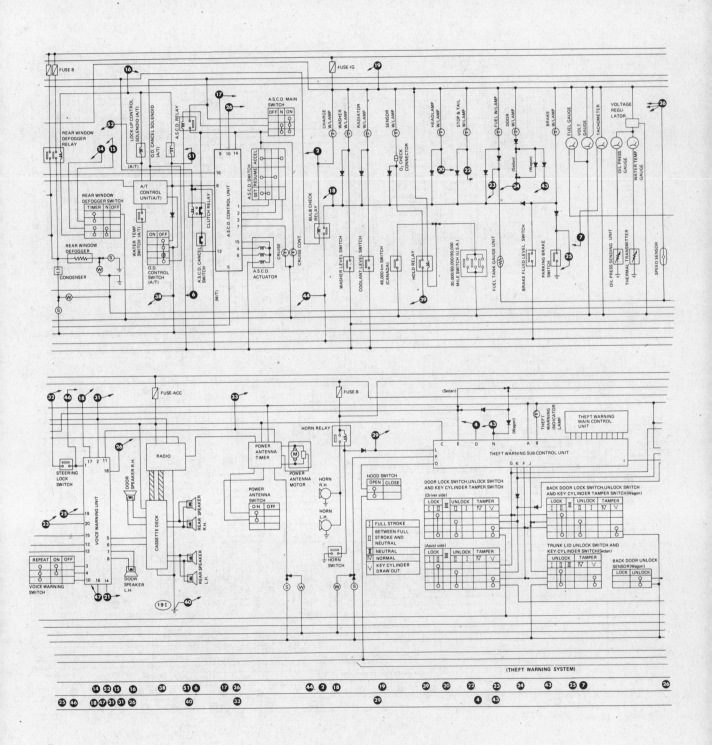

w5. 1987 Maxima wiring schematic — needle type meter

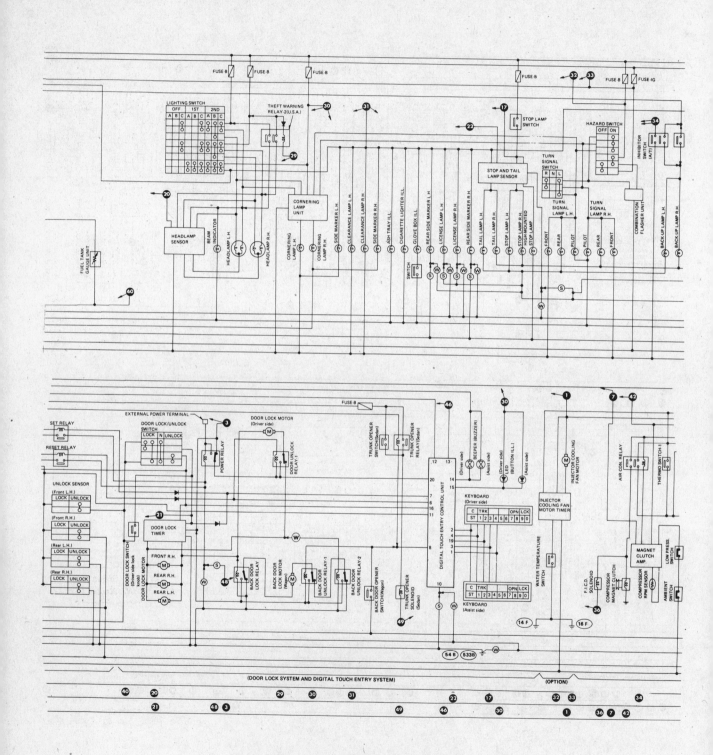

w5. 1987 Maxima wiring schematic — needle type meter

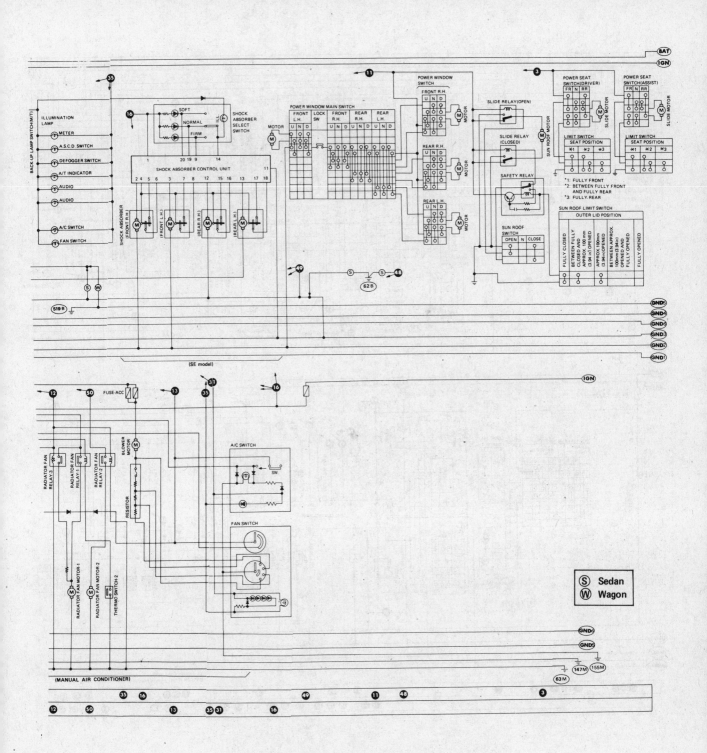

w5. 1987 Maxima wiring schematic — needle type meter

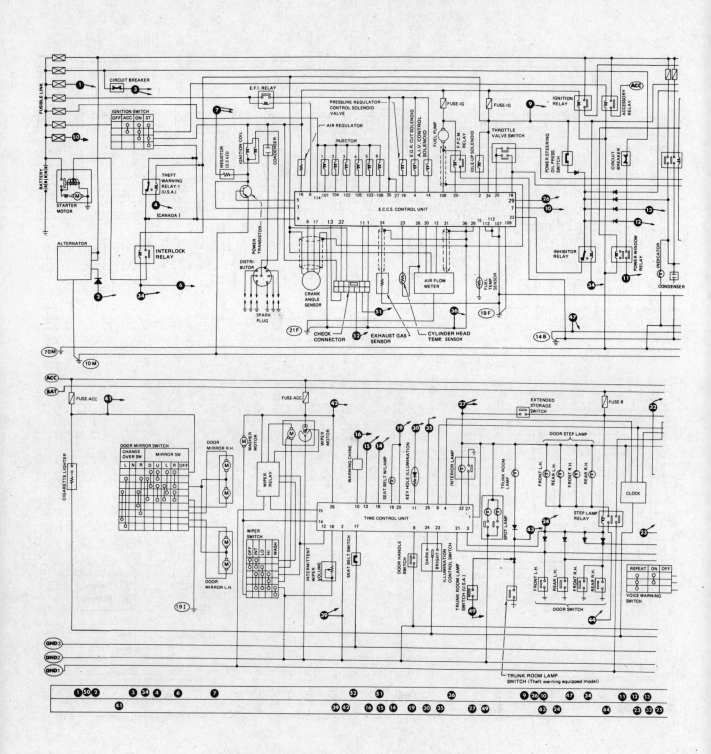

w6. 1987 Maxima wiring schematic — digital type meter

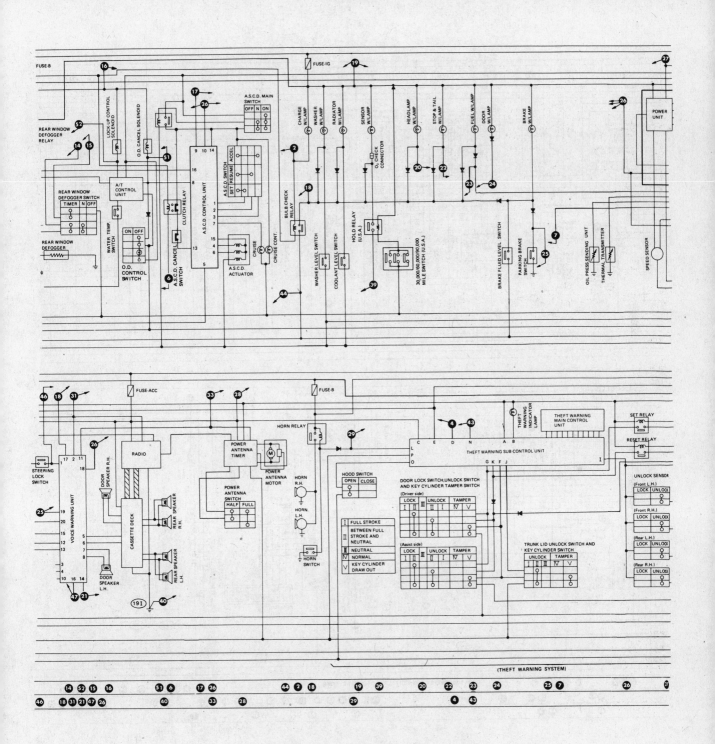

w6. **1987 Maxima wiring schematic — digital type meter**

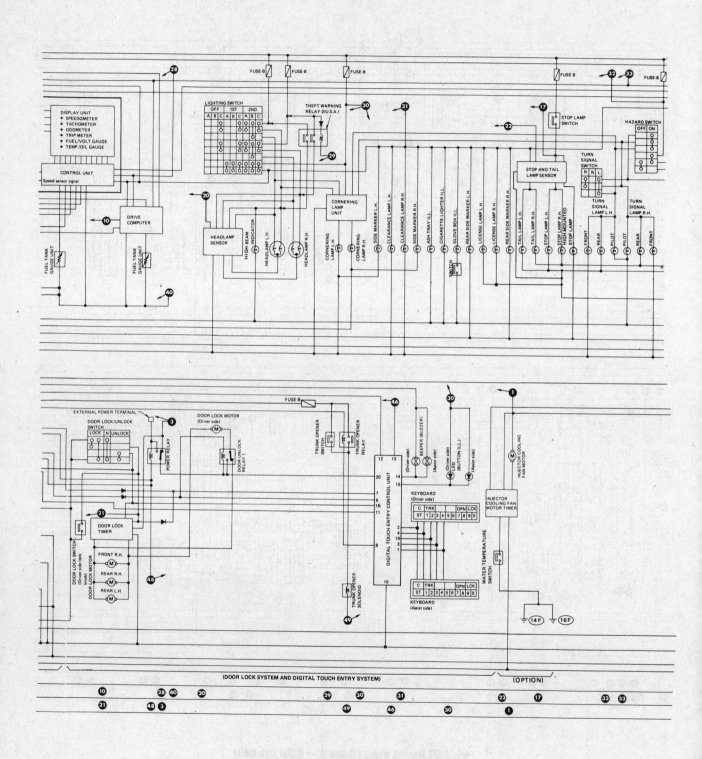

w6. 1987 Maxima wiring schematic — digital type meter

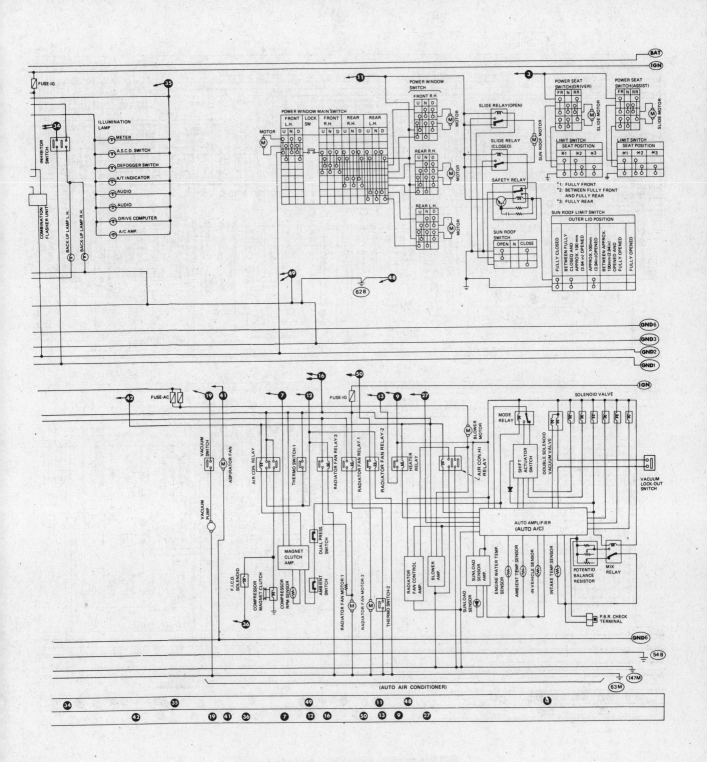

w6. **1987 Maxima wiring schematic — digital type meter**

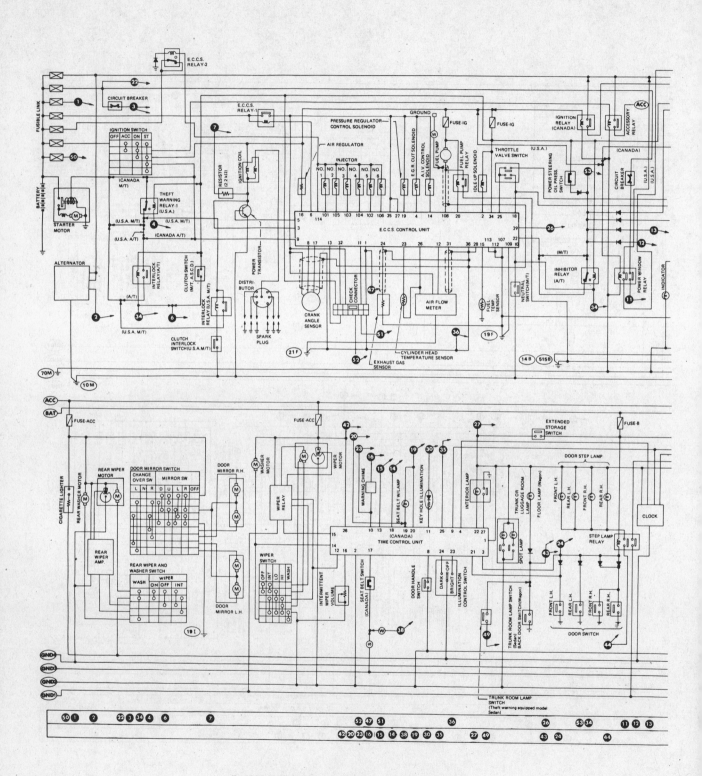

w7. 1988 Maxima wiring schematic — needle type meter

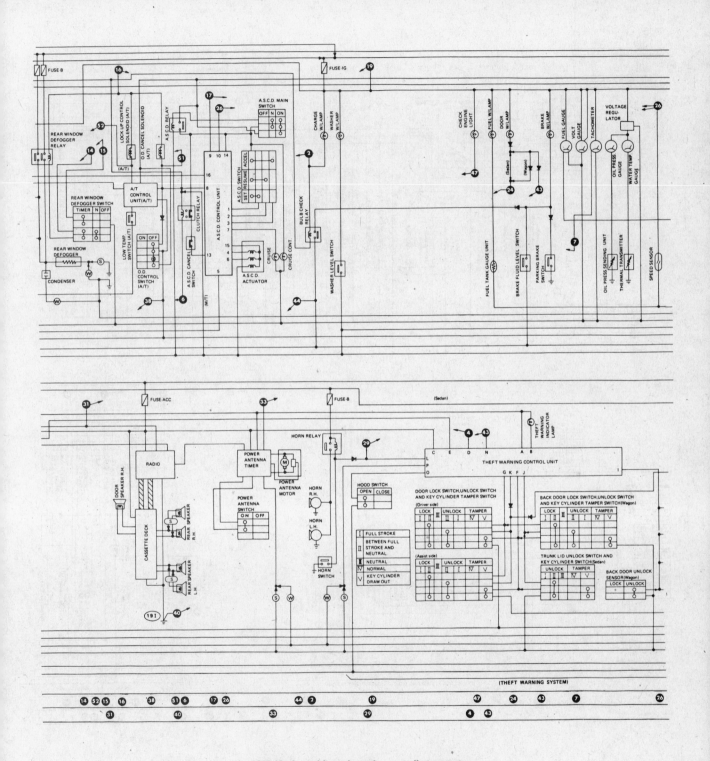

w7. 1988 Maxima wiring schematic — needle type meter

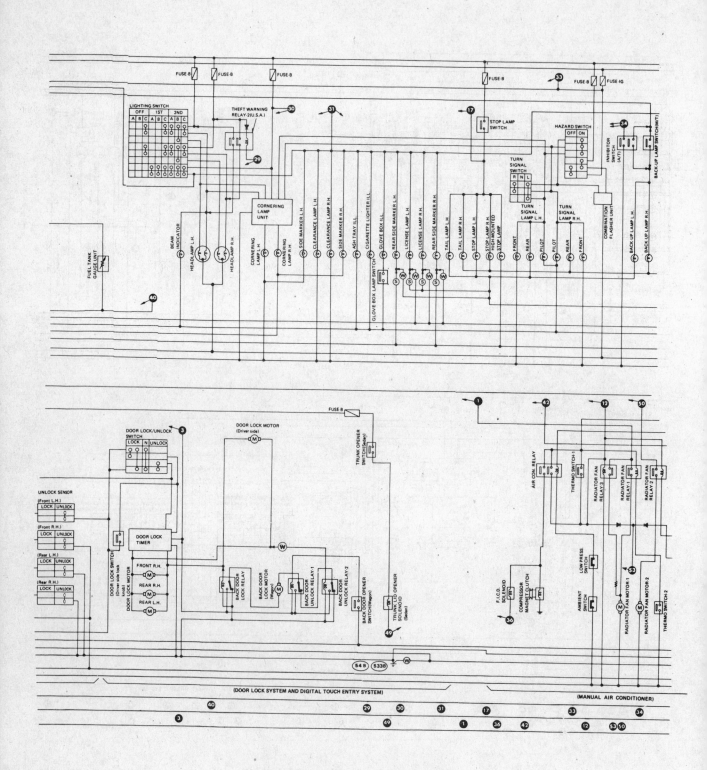

w7. 1988 Maxima wiring schematic — needle type meter

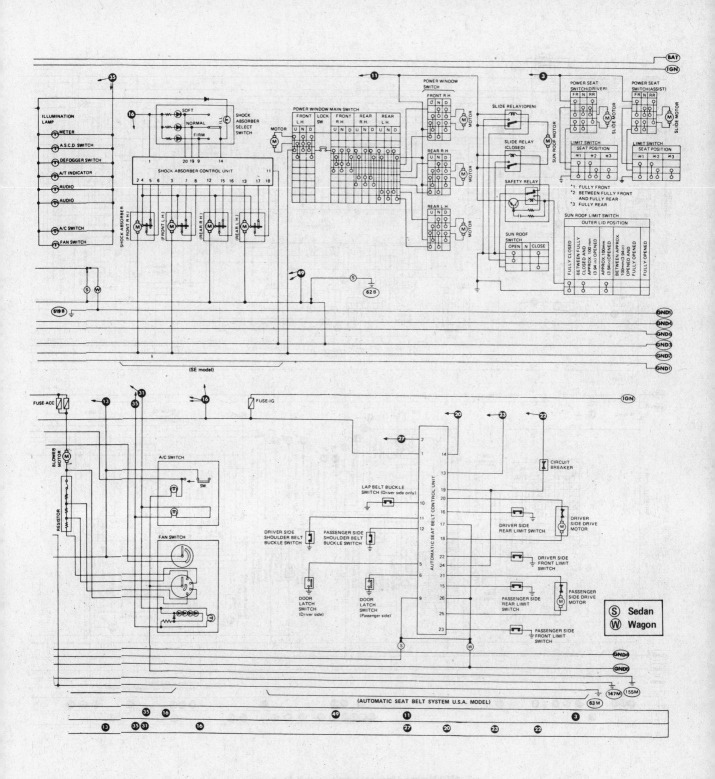

w7. 1988 Maxima wiring schematic — needle type meter

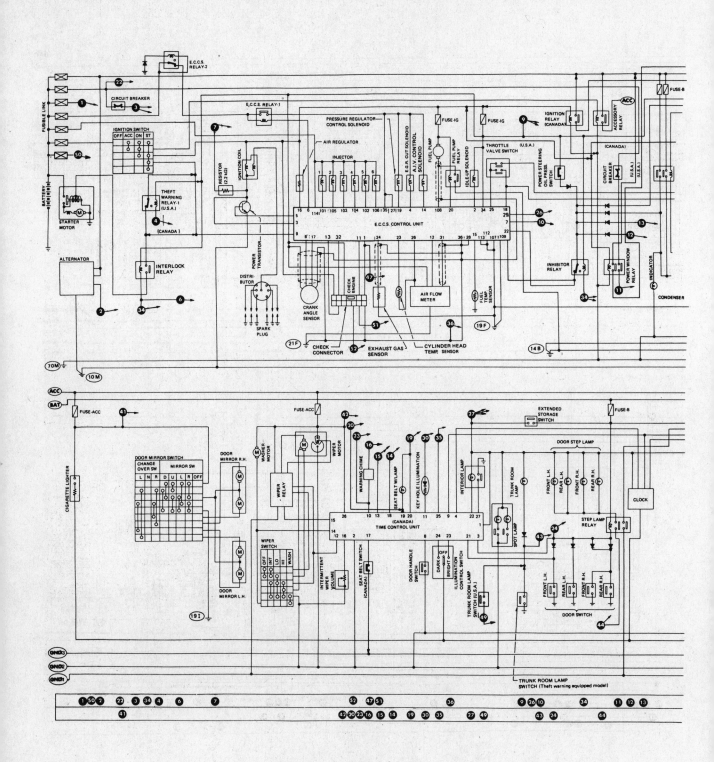

w8. 1988 Maxima wiring schematic — digital type meter

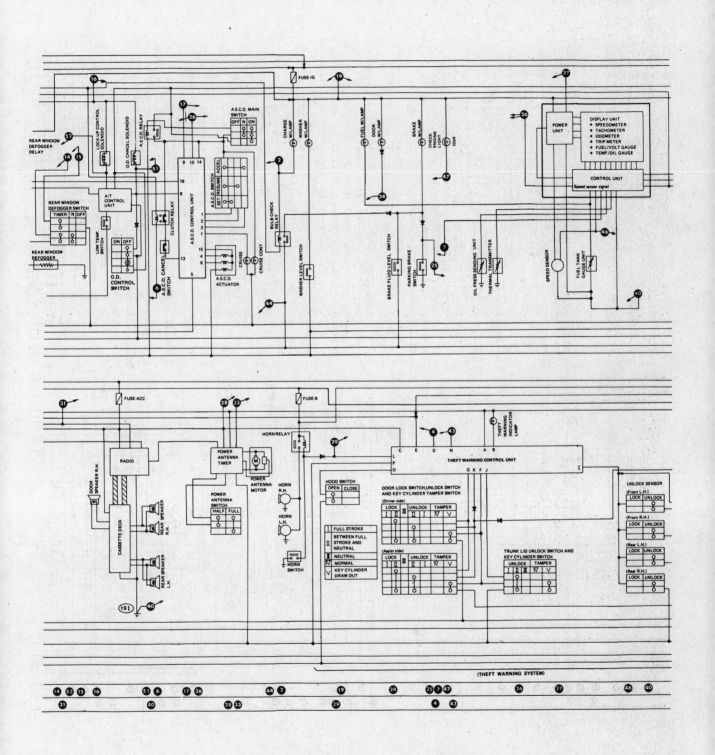

w8. 1988 Maxima wiring schematic — digital type meter

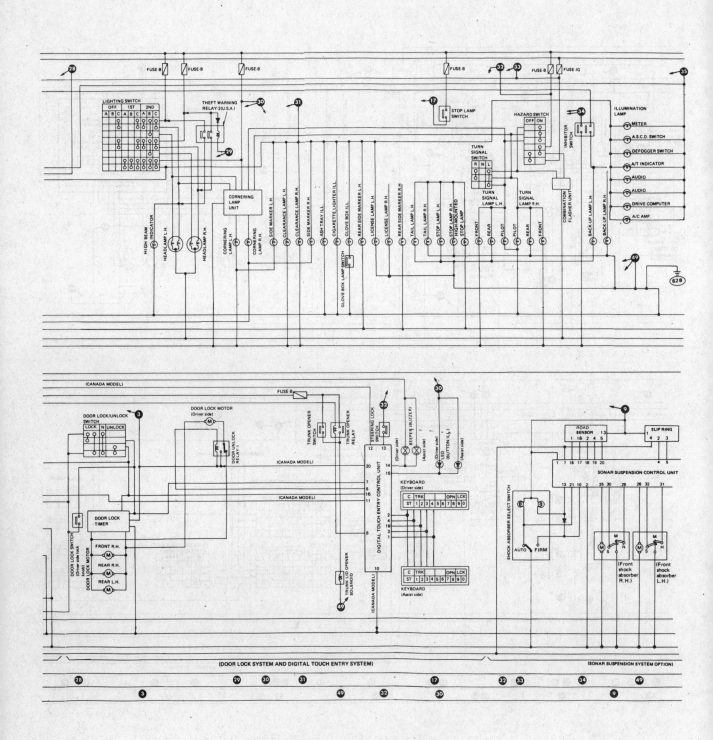

w8. **1988 Maxima wiring schematic — digital type meter**

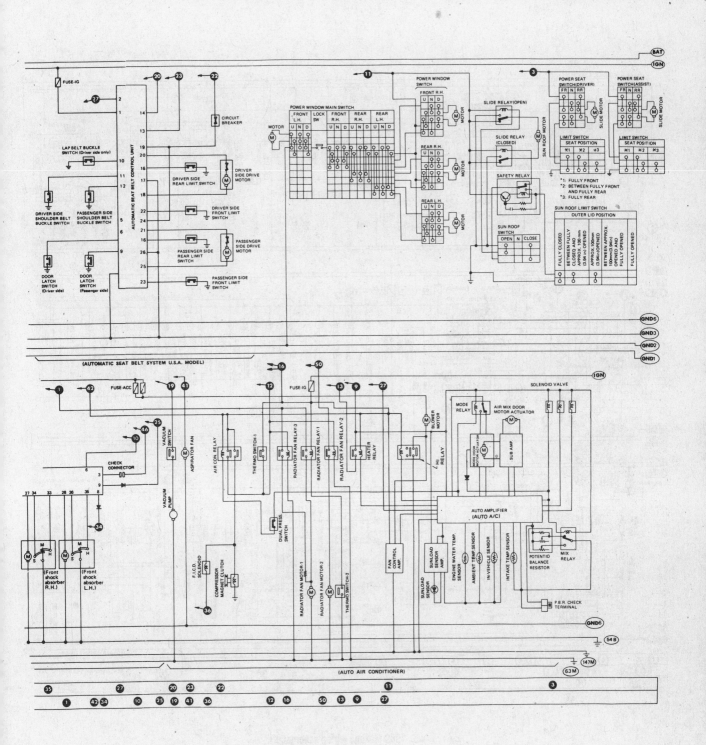

w8. 1988 Maxima wiring schematic — digital type meter

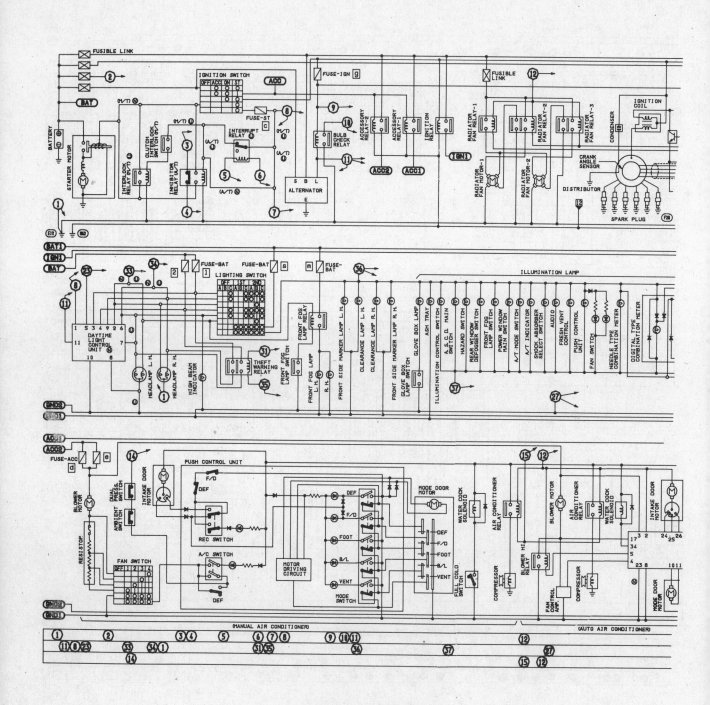

w9. 1989 Maxima wiring schematic

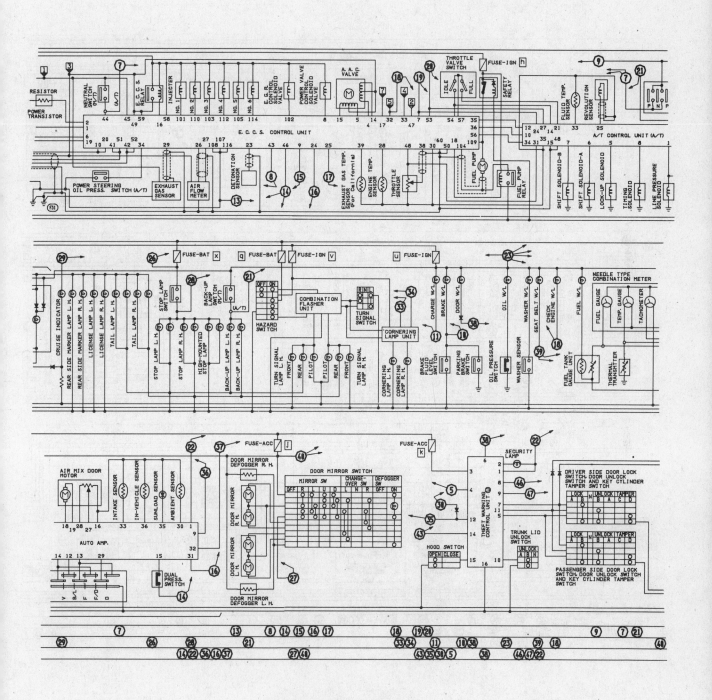

w9. 1989 Maxima wiring schematic

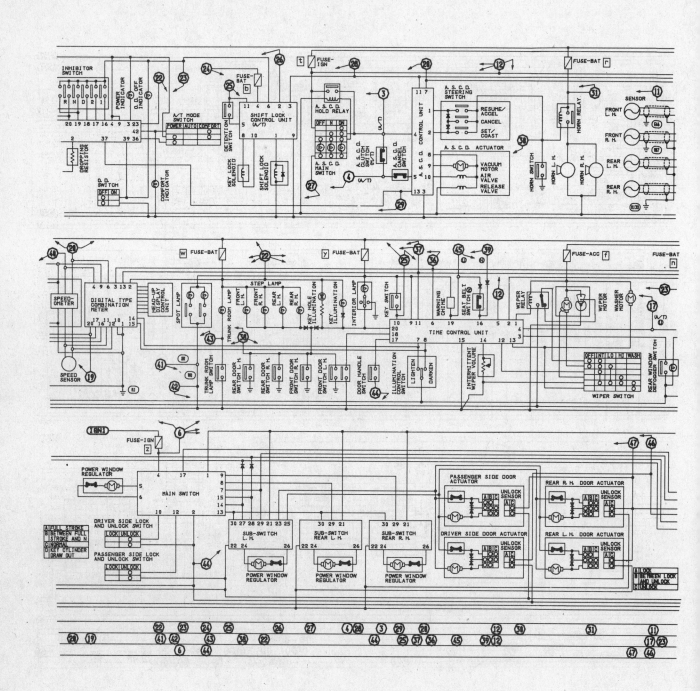

w9. 1989 Maxima wiring schematic

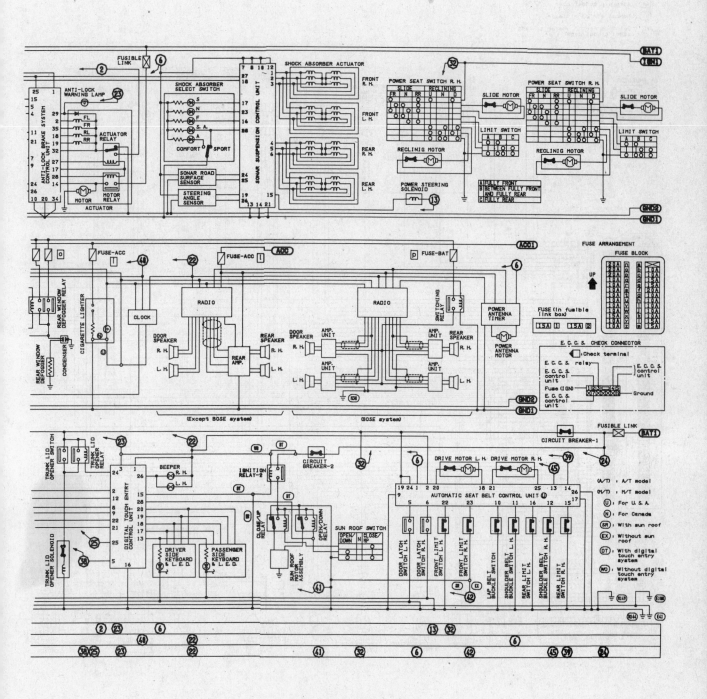

w9. 1989 Maxima wiring schematic

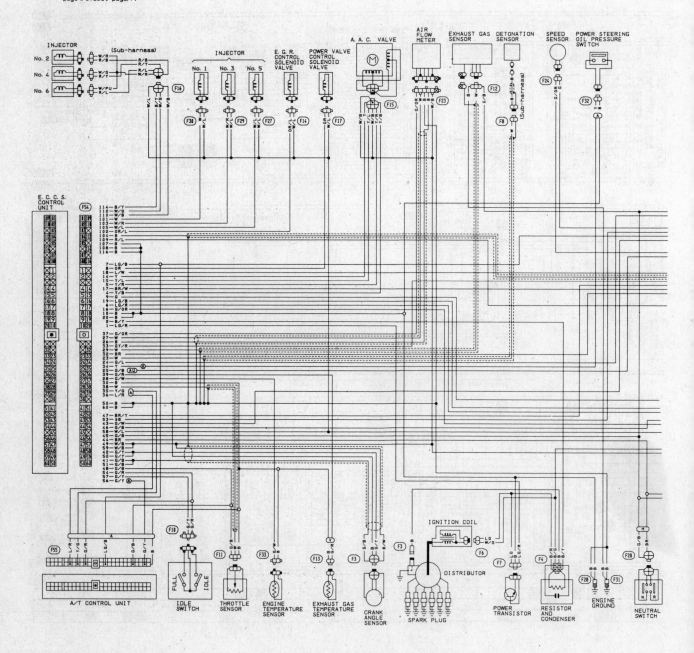

w10. 1989 Maxima E.C.C.S. wiring schematic

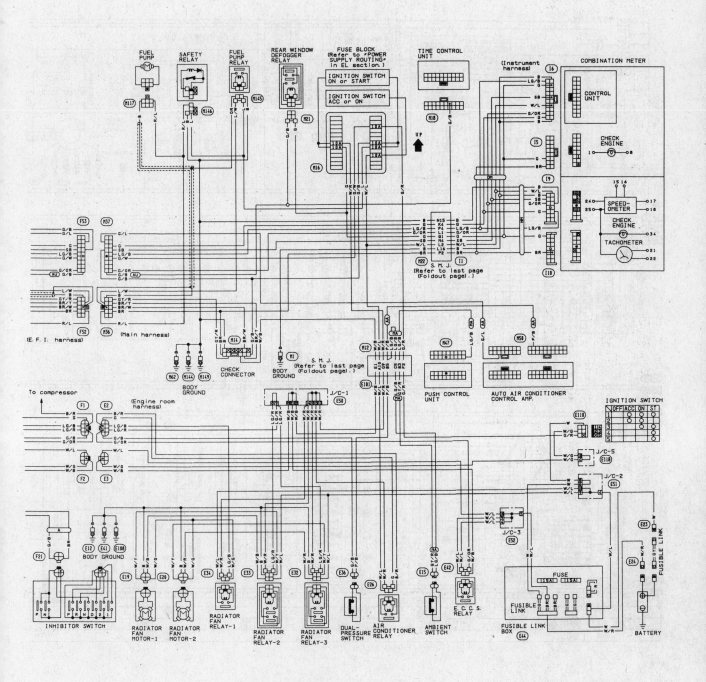

w10. 1989 Maxima E.C.C.S. wiring schematic

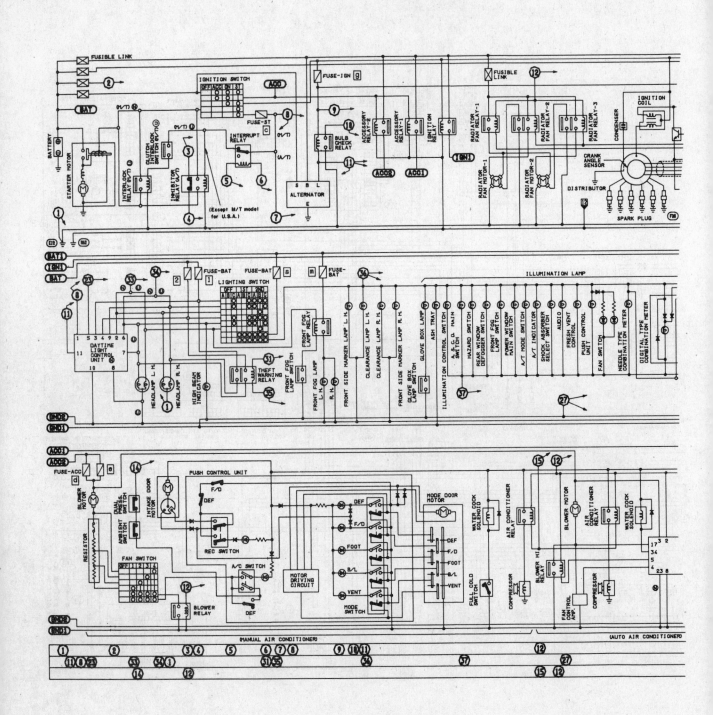

w11. 1990 Maxima wiring schematic

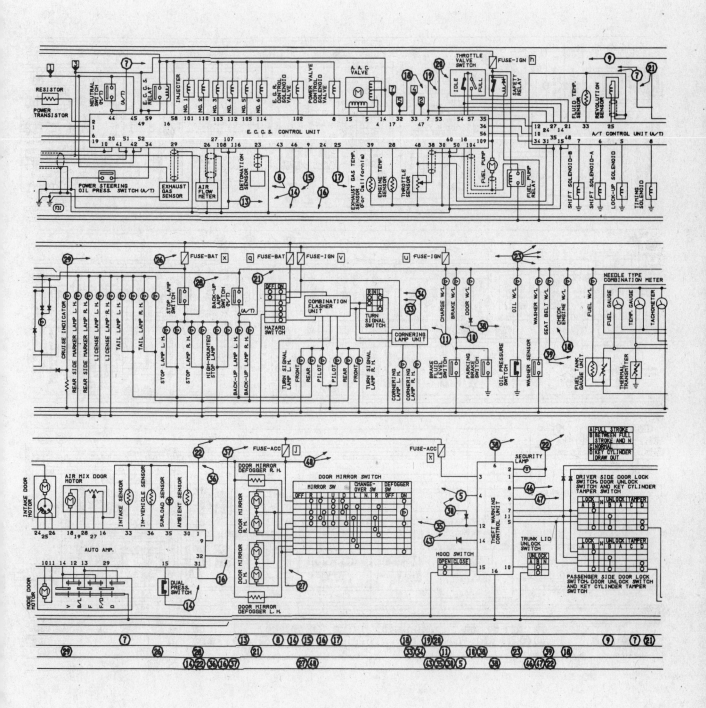

w11. 1990 Maxima wiring schematic

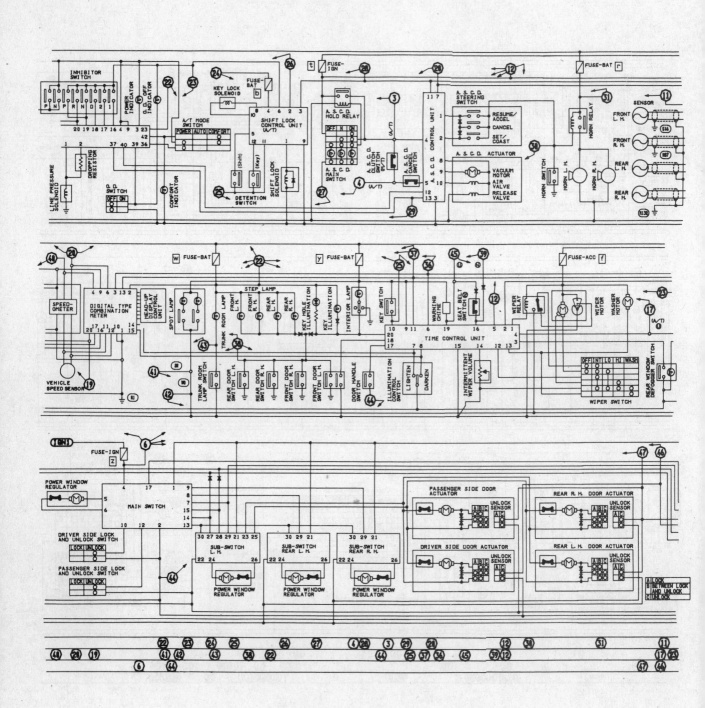

w11. 1990 Maxima wiring schematic

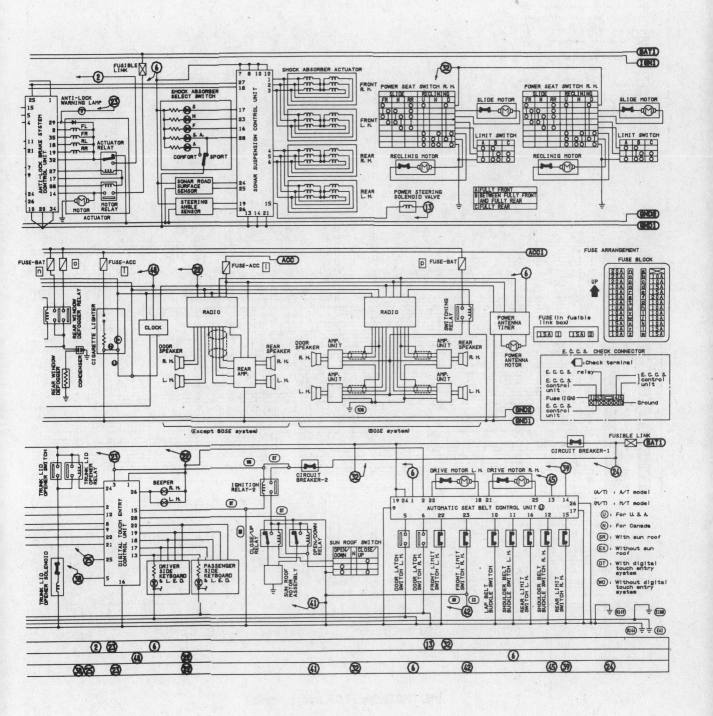

w11. 1990 Maxima wiring schematic

A : A/T model
M : M/T model
V : For California
AU : A/T model for U.S.A.
DM : Digital type combination meter
NM : Needle type combination meter
AA : Auto air conditioner
MA : Manual air conditioner
J/C : Joint connector (Refer to last page (Foldout page).)

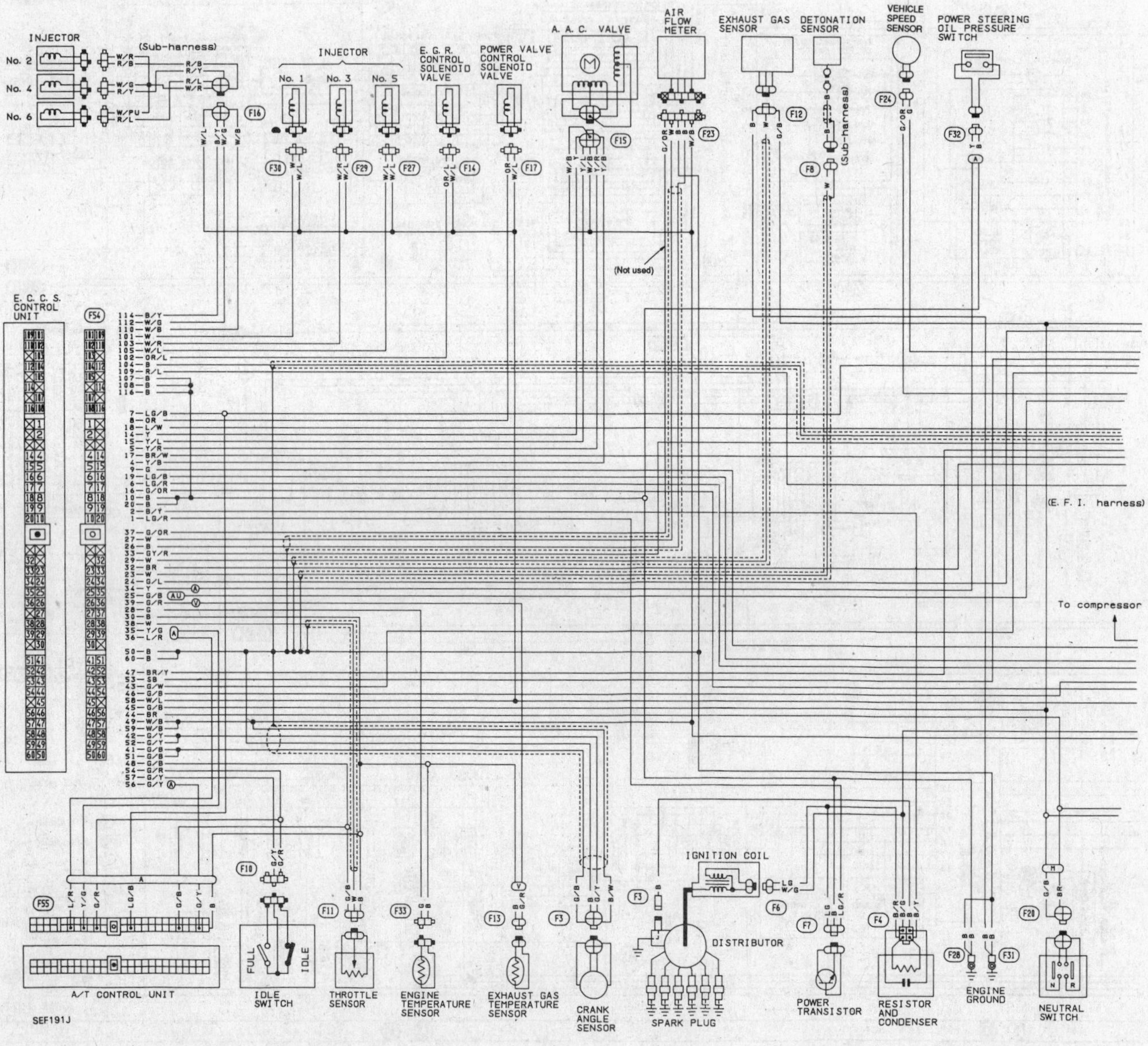

w12. 1990 Maxima E.C.C.S. wiring schematic

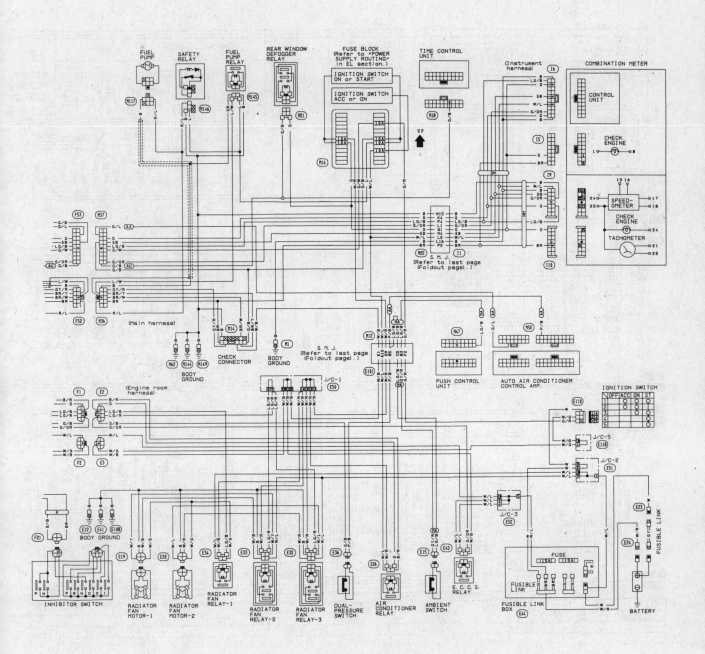

w12. 1990 Maxima E.C.C.S. wiring schematic

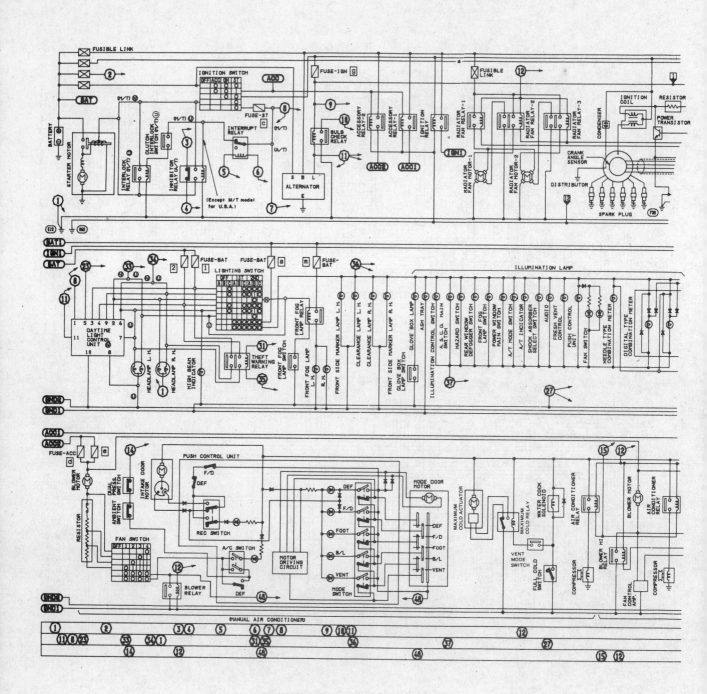

w13. 1991 Maxima wiring schematic

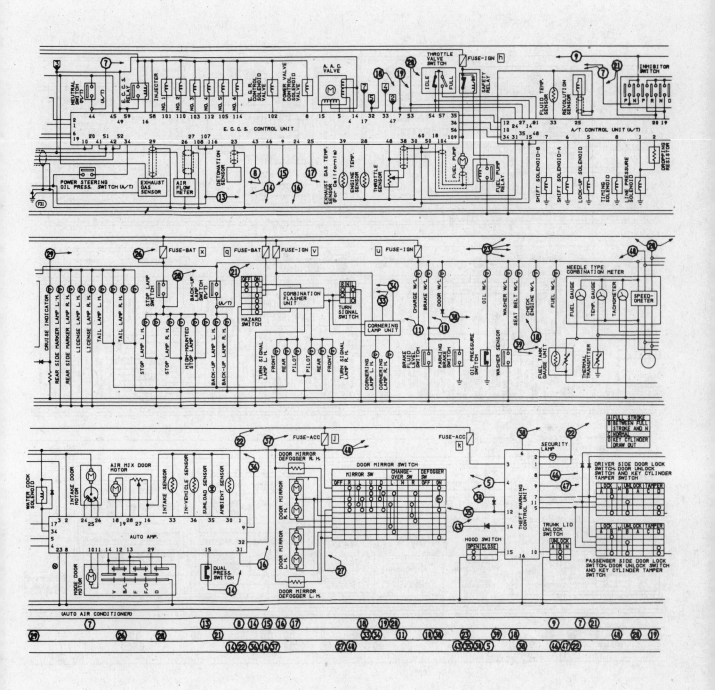

w13. 1991 Maxima wiring schematic

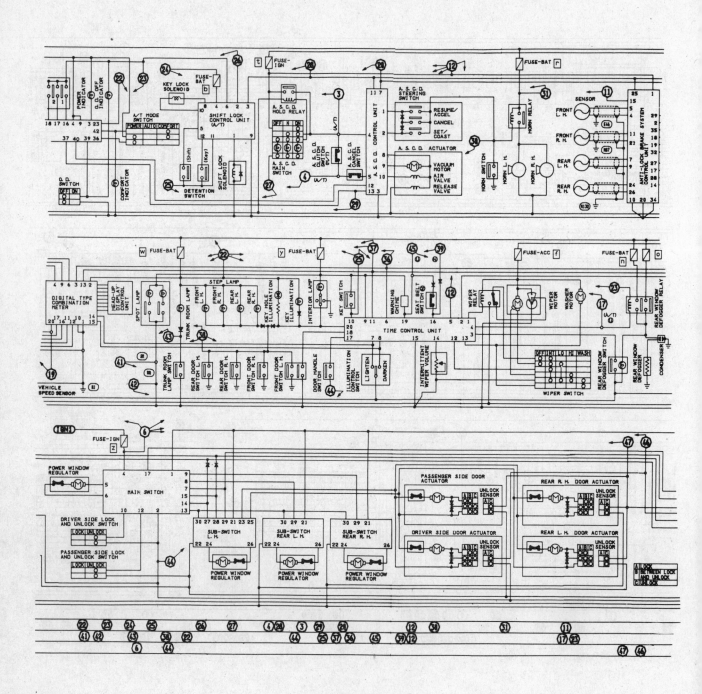

w13. 1991 Maxima wiring schematic

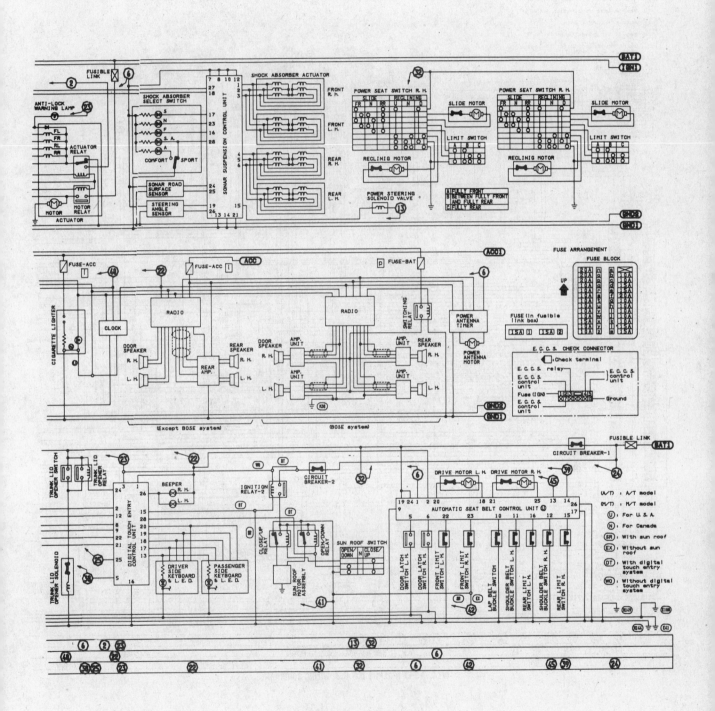

w13. 1991 Maxima wiring schematic

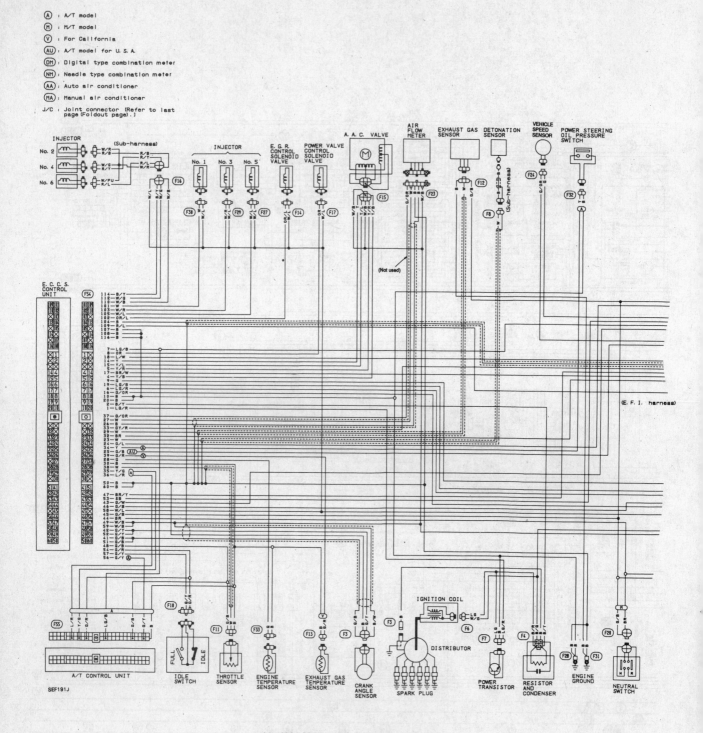

w14. 1991 Maxima E.C.C.S. wiring schematic

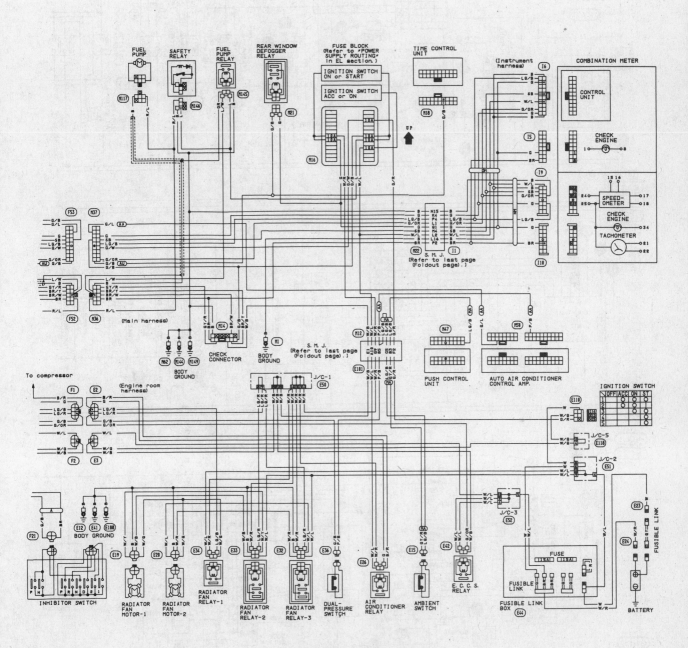

w14. 1991 Maxima E.C.C.S. wiring schematic

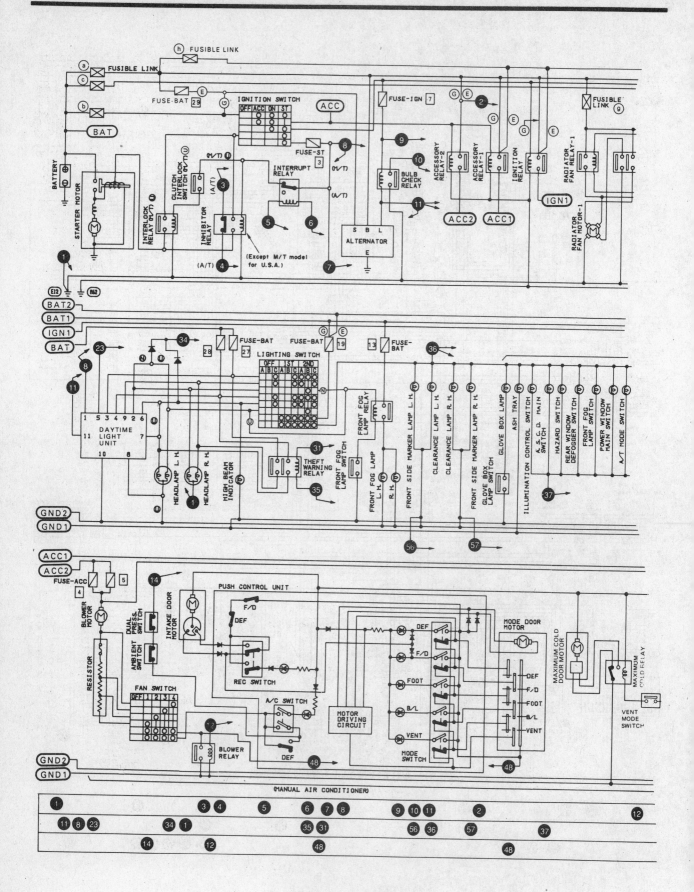

w15. 1992 Maxima wiring schematic

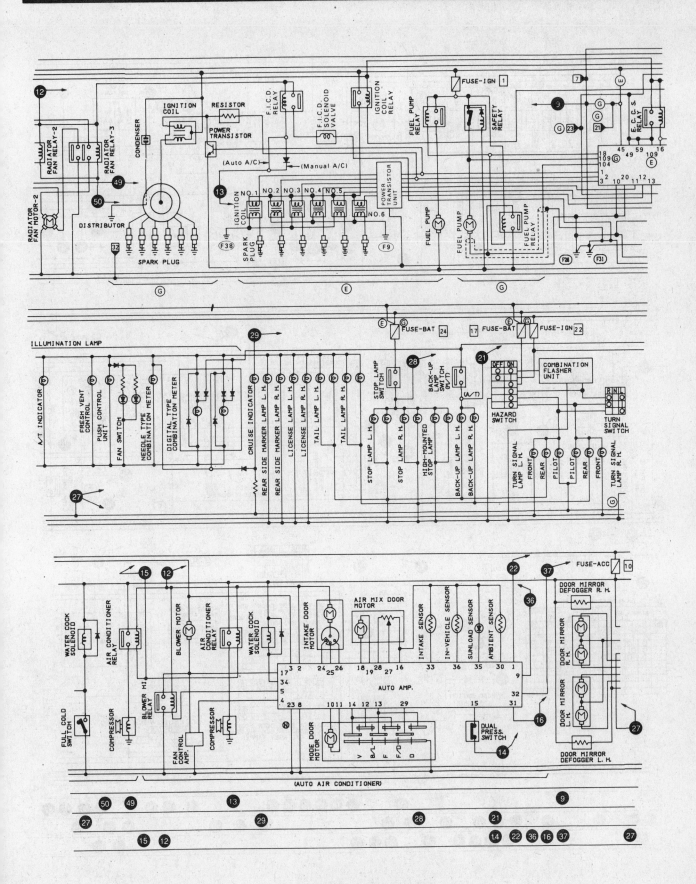

w15. 1992 Maxima wiring schematic

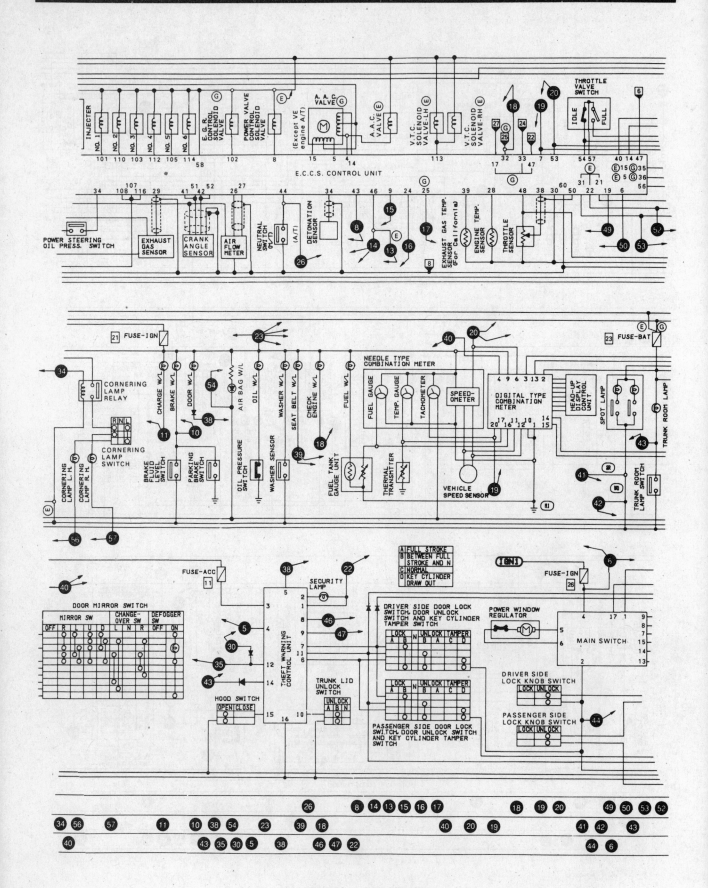

w15. 1992 Maxima wiring schematic

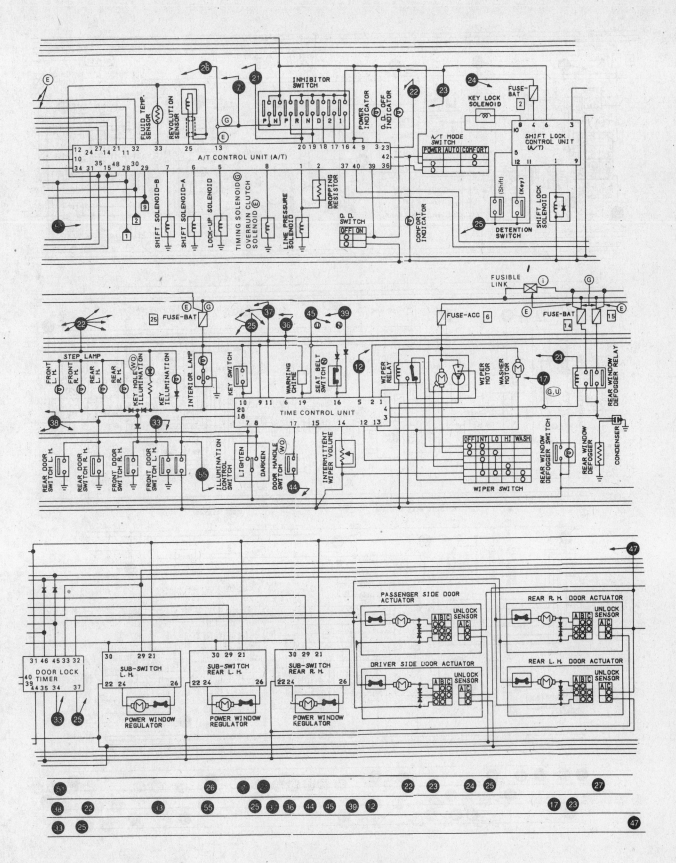

w15. 1992 Maxima wiring schematic

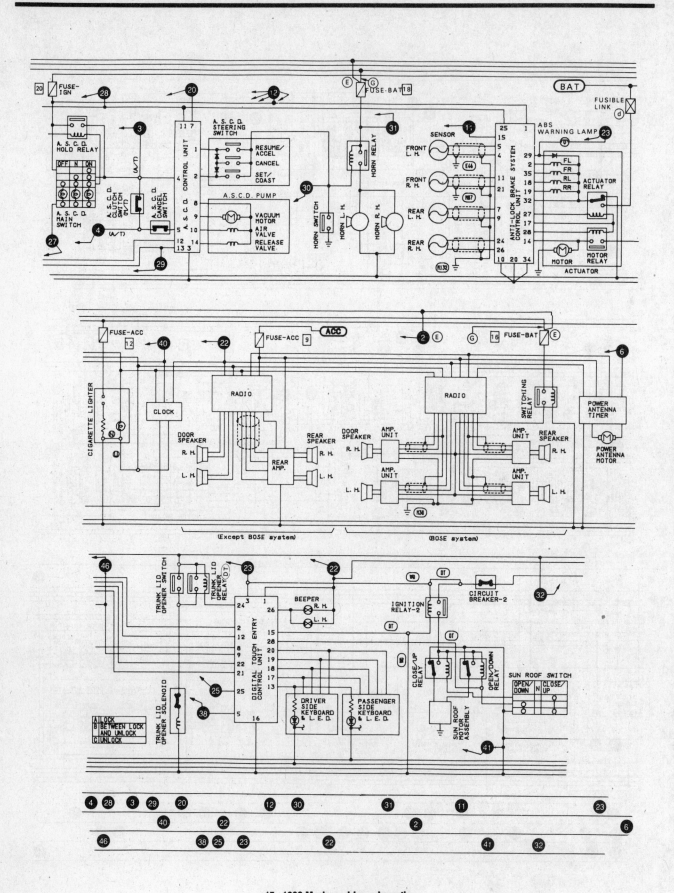

w15. 1992 Maxima wiring schematic

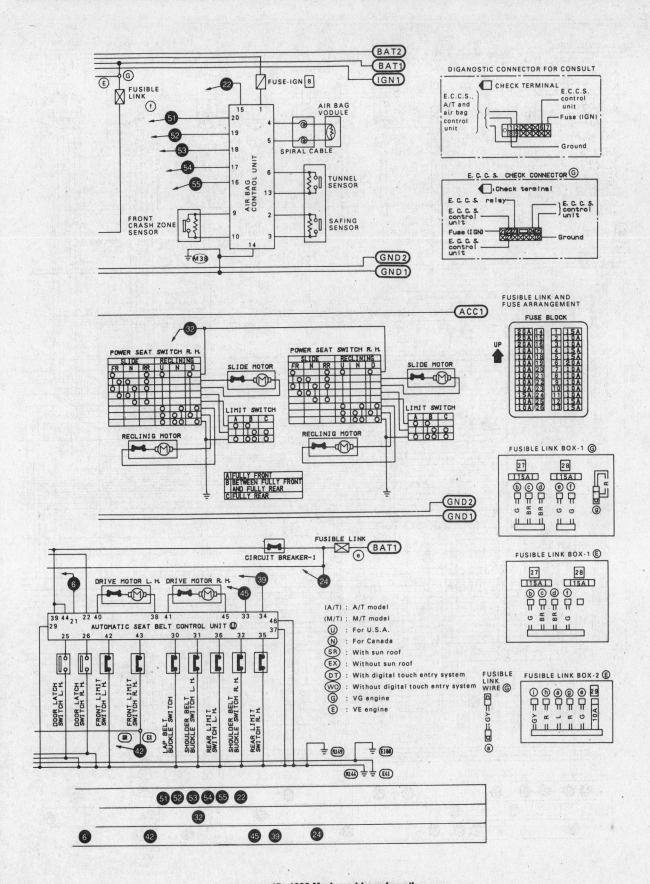

w15. 1992 Maxima wiring schematic

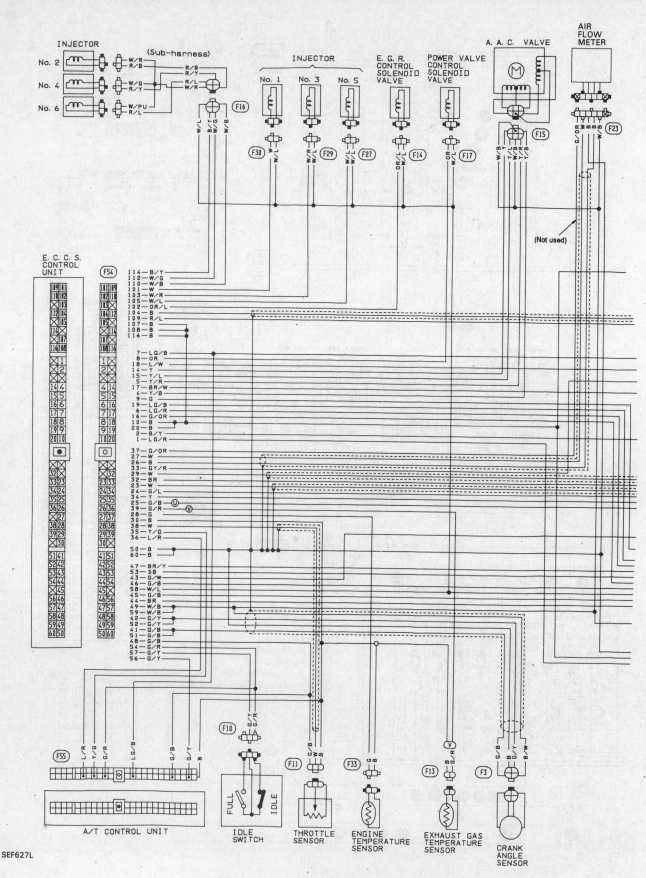

SEF627L

w16. 1992 Maxima E.C.C.S. wiring schematic — VG30e T engine

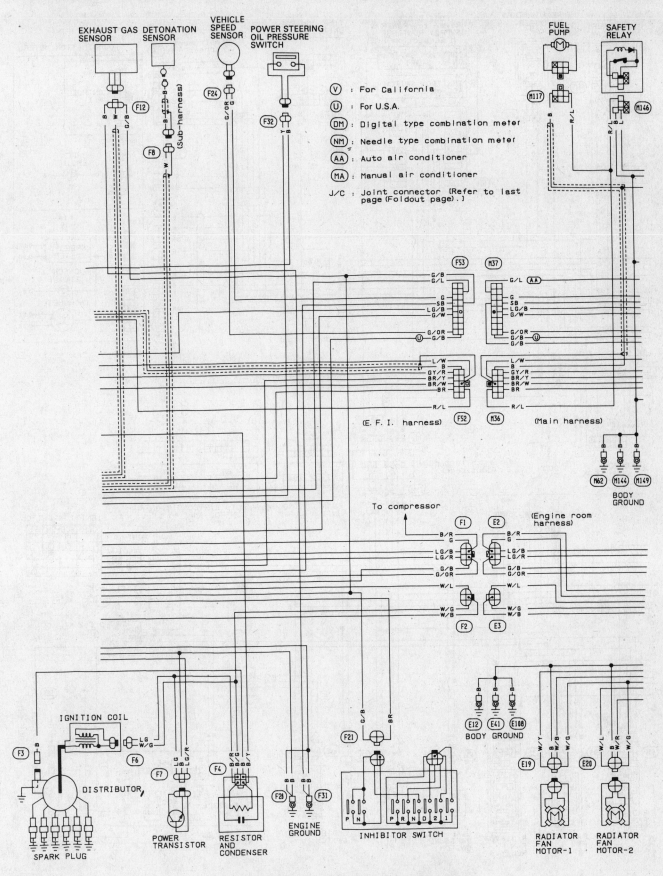

w16. 1992 Maxima E.C.C.S. wiring schematic – VG30e T engine

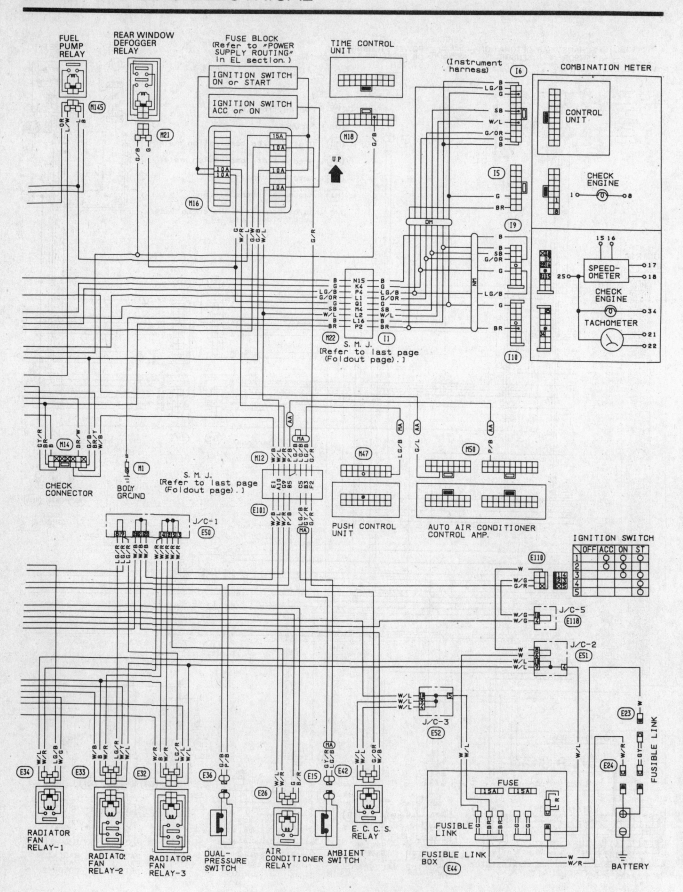

w16. 1992 Maxima E.C.C.S. wiring schematic — VG30e T engine

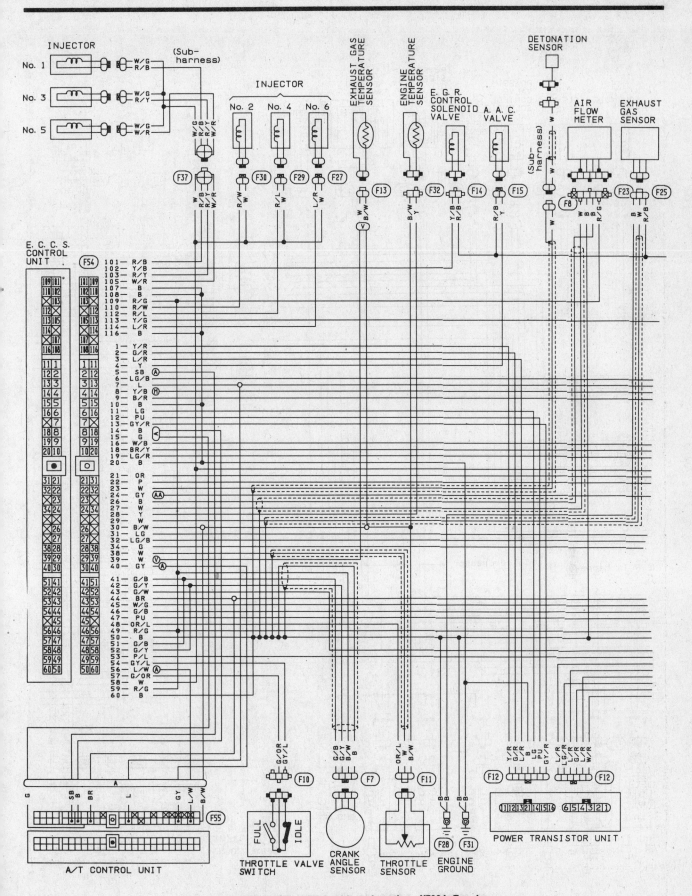

w17. 1992 Maxima E.C.C.S. wiring schematic – VE30de T engine

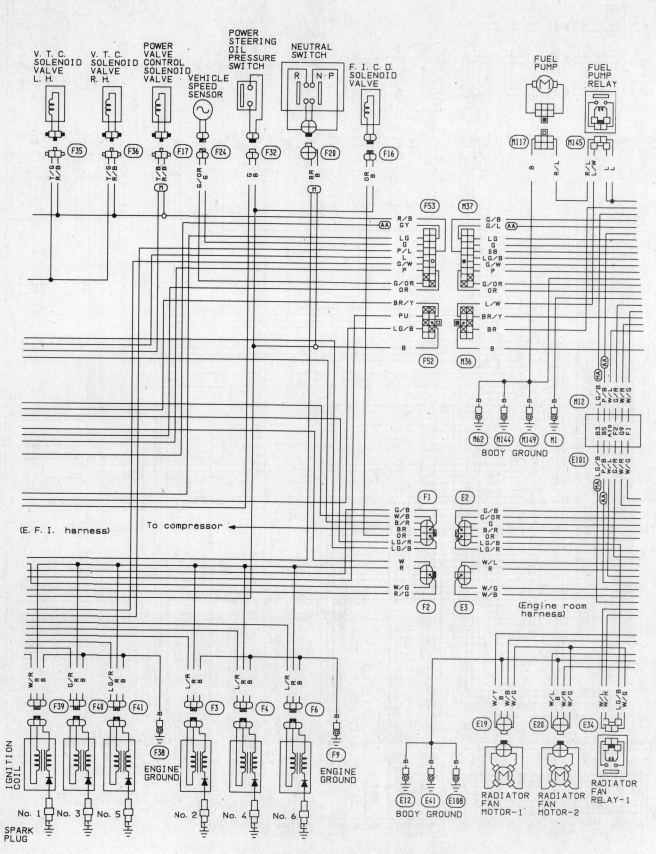

w17. 1992 Maxima E.C.C.S. wiring schematic — VE30de T engine

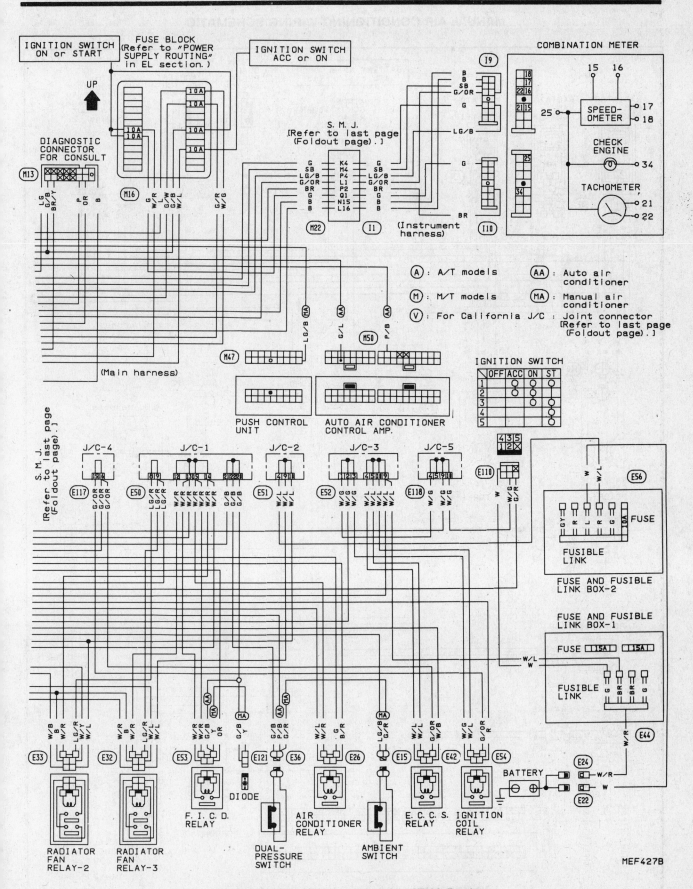

w17. 1992 Maxima E.C.C.S. wiring schematic — VE30de T engine

MEF427B

MANUAL AIR CONDITIONING WIRING SCHEMATIC

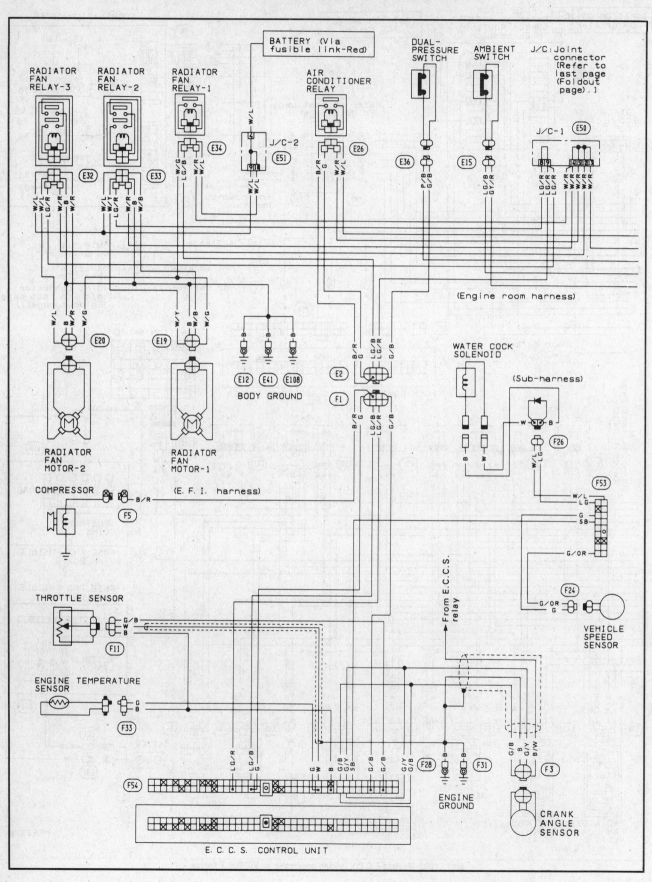

MANUAL AIR CONDITIONING WIRING SCHEMATIC, CONT'D

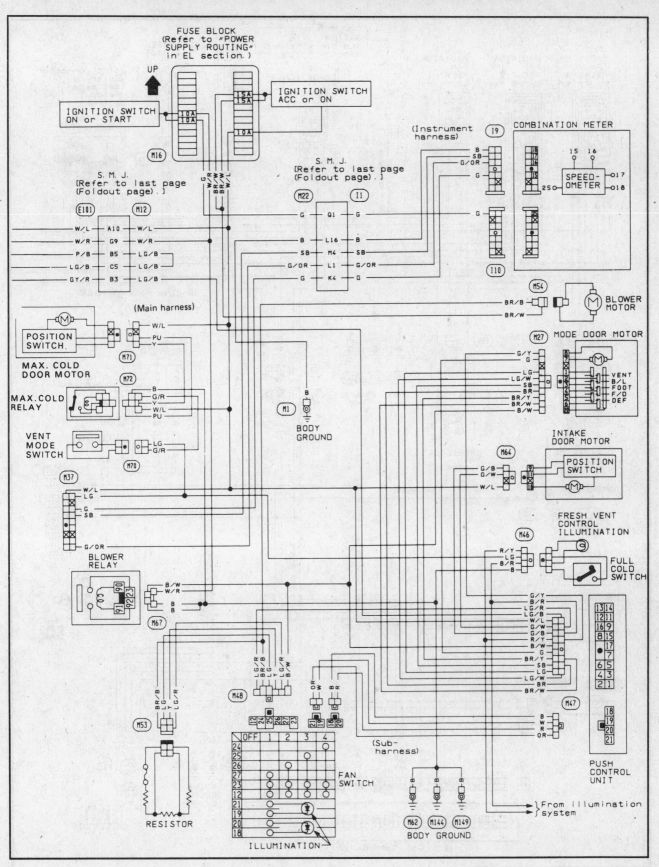

AUTOMATIC AIR CONDITIONING WIRING SCHEMATIC

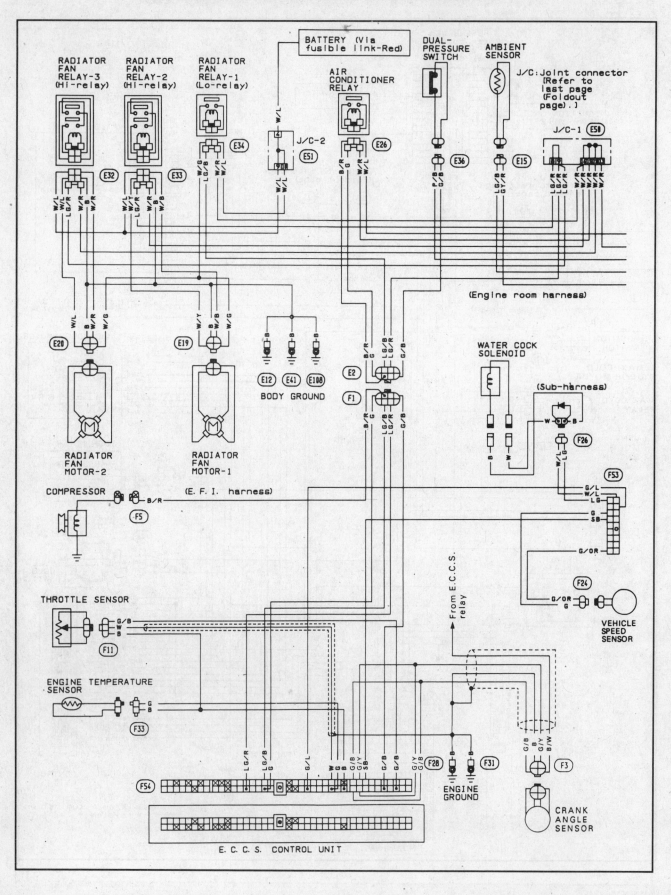

AUTOMATIC AIR CONDITIONING WIRING SCHEMATIC, CONT'D

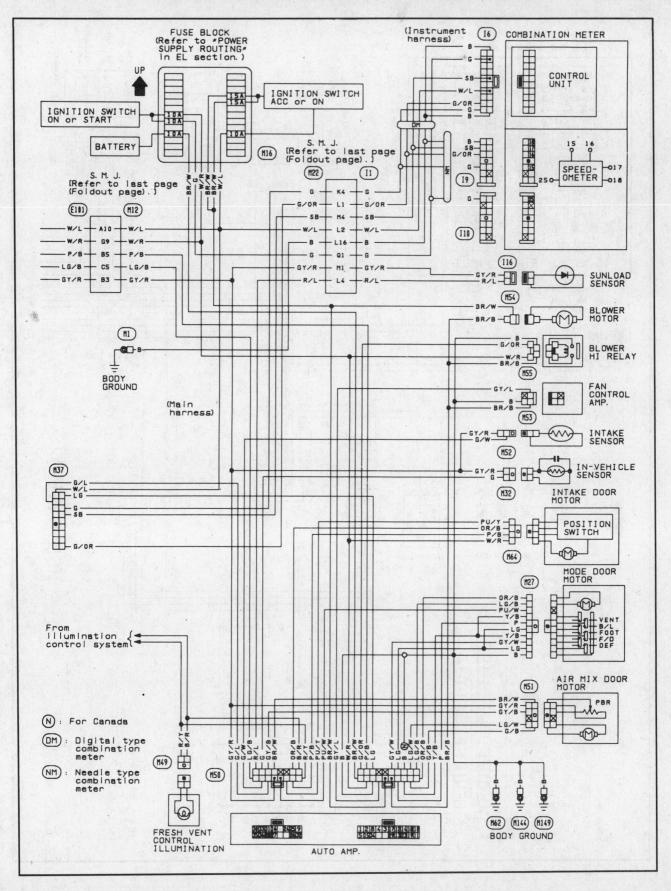

AUTOMATIC SPEED CONTROL DEVICE WIRING SCHEMATIC — VG30E ENGINE

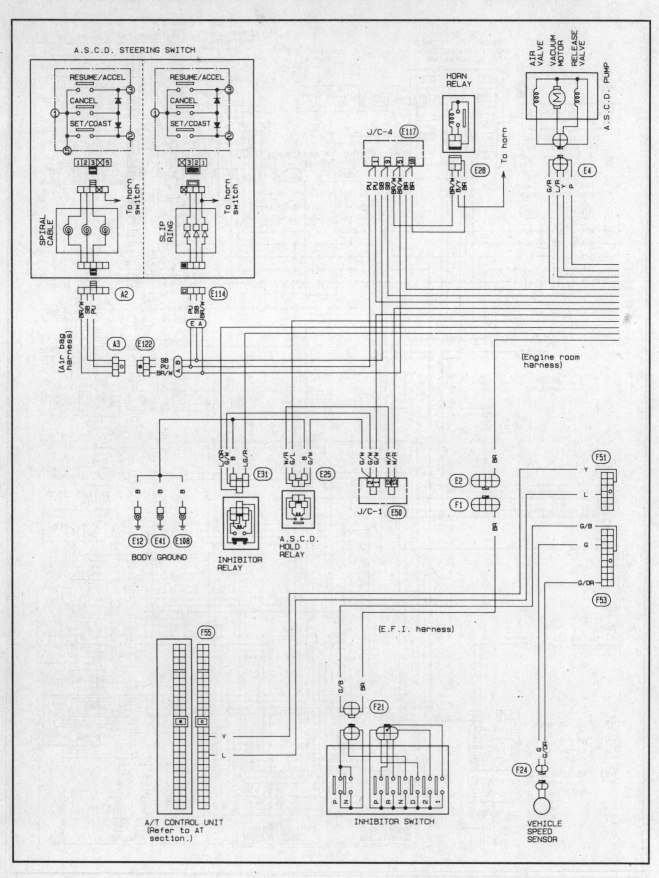

AUTOMATIC SPEED CONTROL DEVICE WIRING SCHEMATIC — VG30E ENGINE, CONT'D

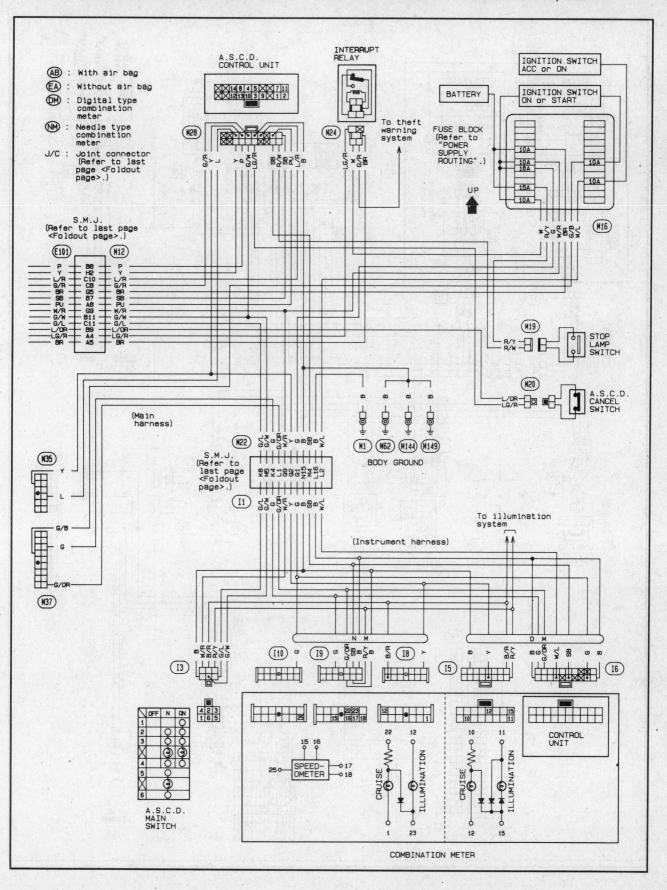

AUTOMATIC SPEED CONTROL DEVICE WIRING SCHEMATIC — VE30DE ENGINE

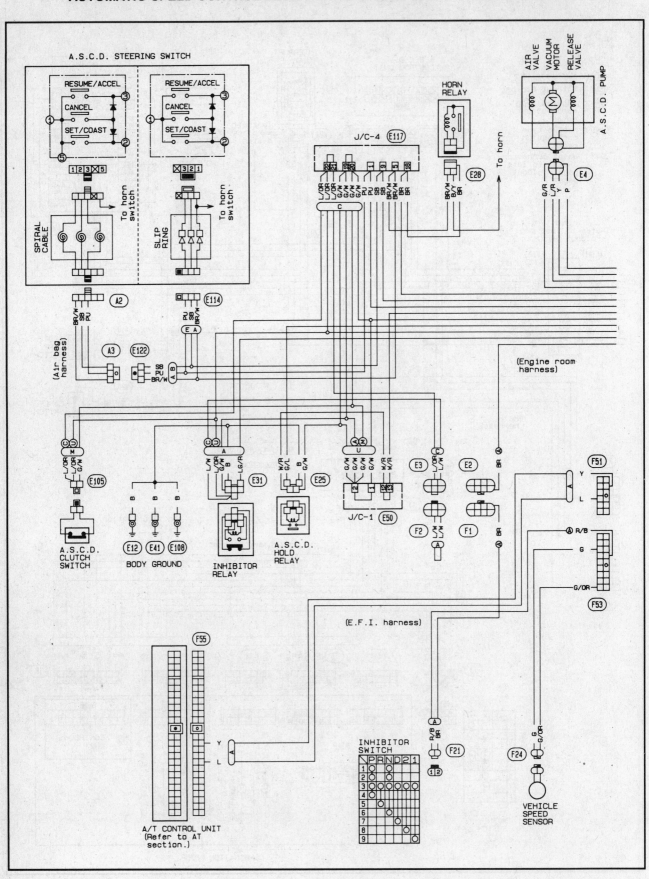

AUTOMATIC SPEED CONTROL DEVICE WIRING SCHEMATIC — VE30DE ENGINE, CONT'D

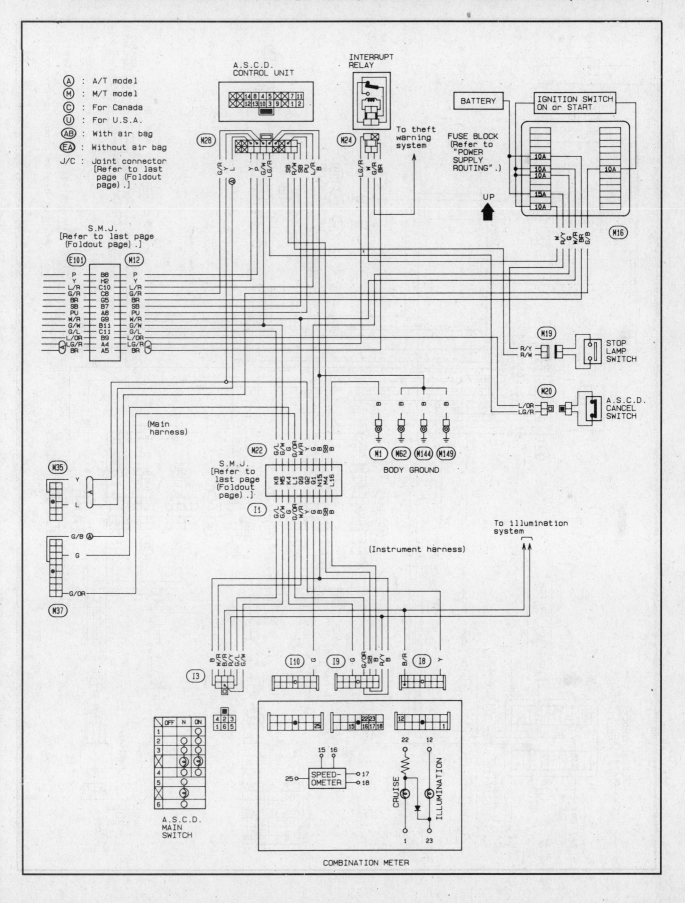

COMBINATION METER

RADIO WIRING SCHEMATIC — BOSE SYSTEM

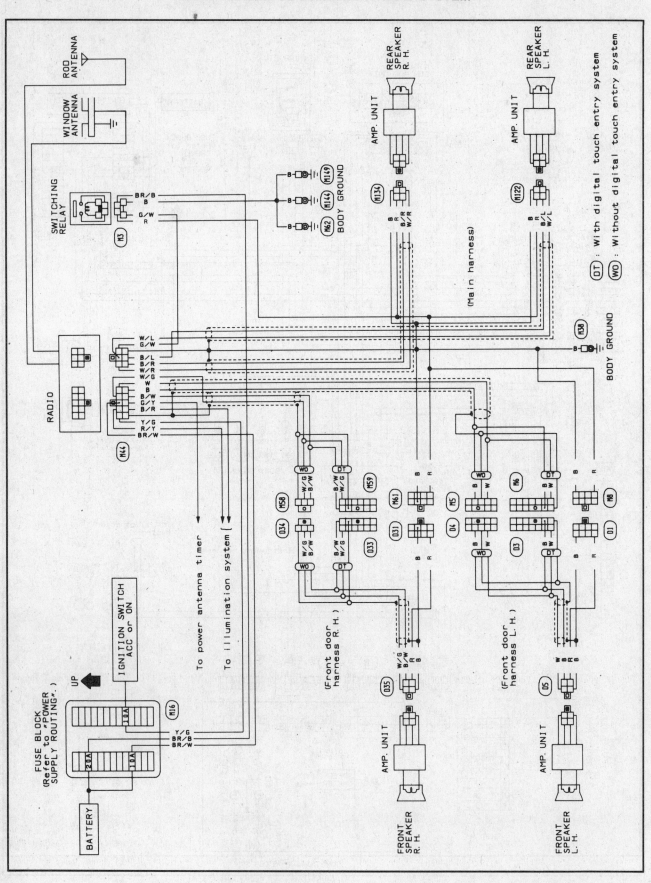

RADIO WIRING SCHEMATIC — EXCEPT BOSE SYSTEM

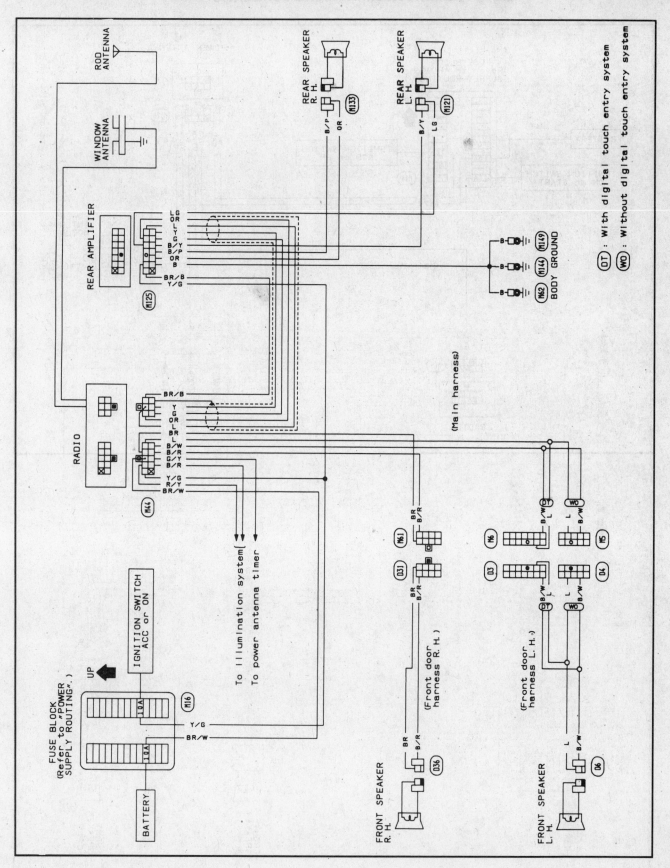

POWER ANTENNA WIRING SCHEMATIC

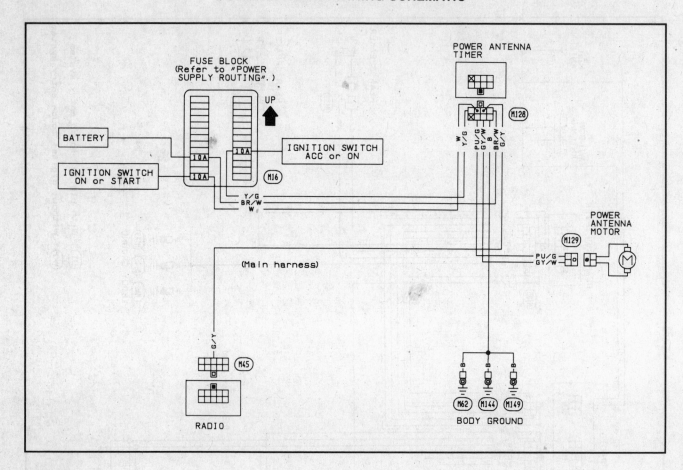

WINDSHIELD WIPER AND WASHER WIRING SCHEMATIC

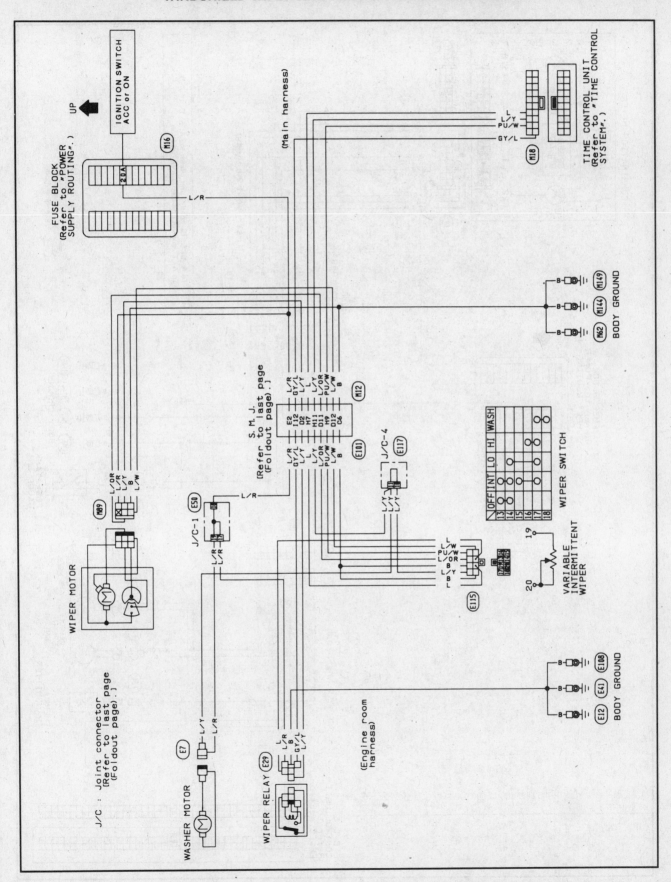

INSTRUMENT CLUSTER WIRING SCHEMATIC — NEEDLE TYPE

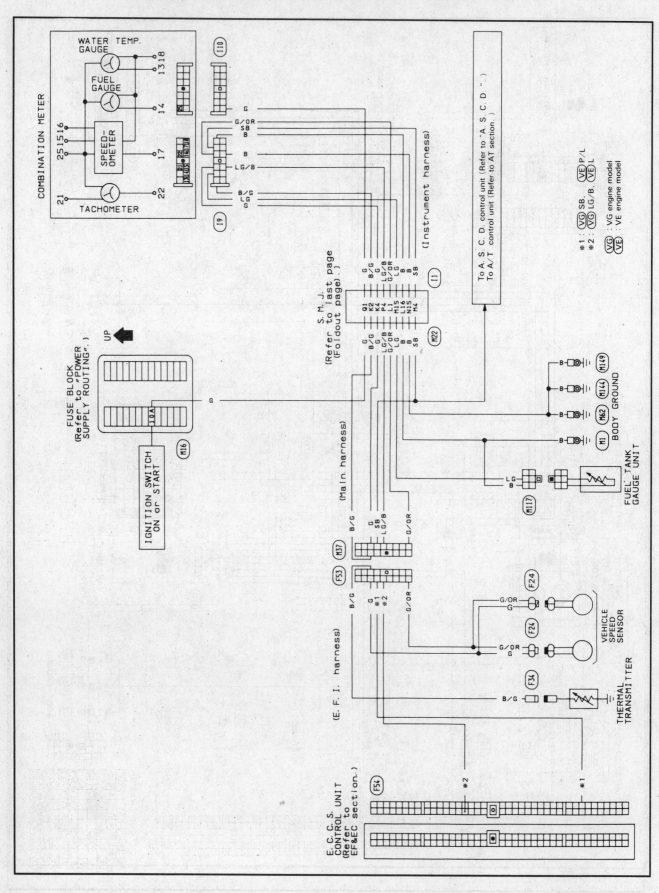

INSTRUMENT CLUSTER WIRING SCHEMATIC — DIGITAL TYPE

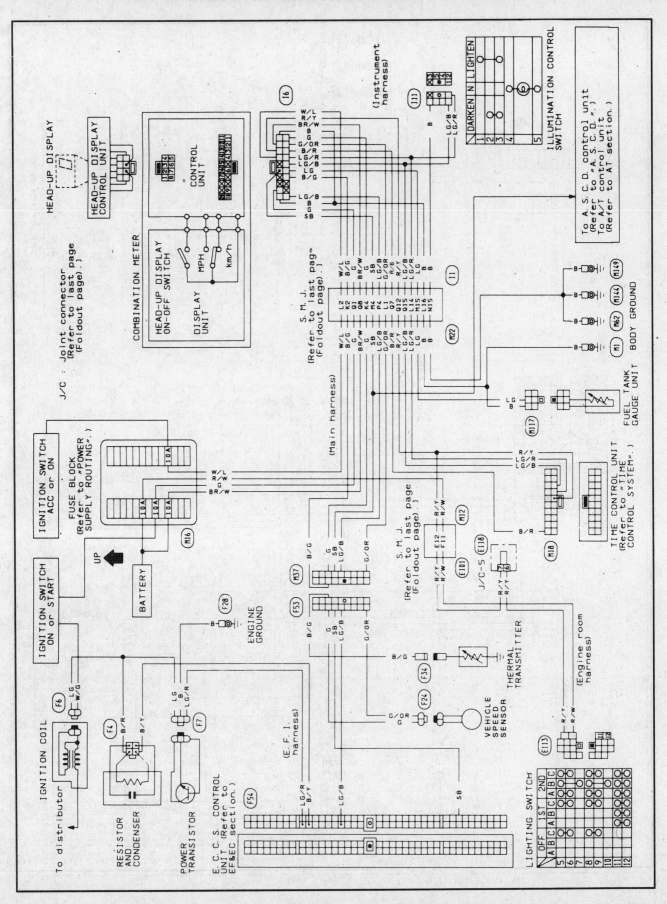

HEADLIGHT WIRING SCHEMATIC — USA

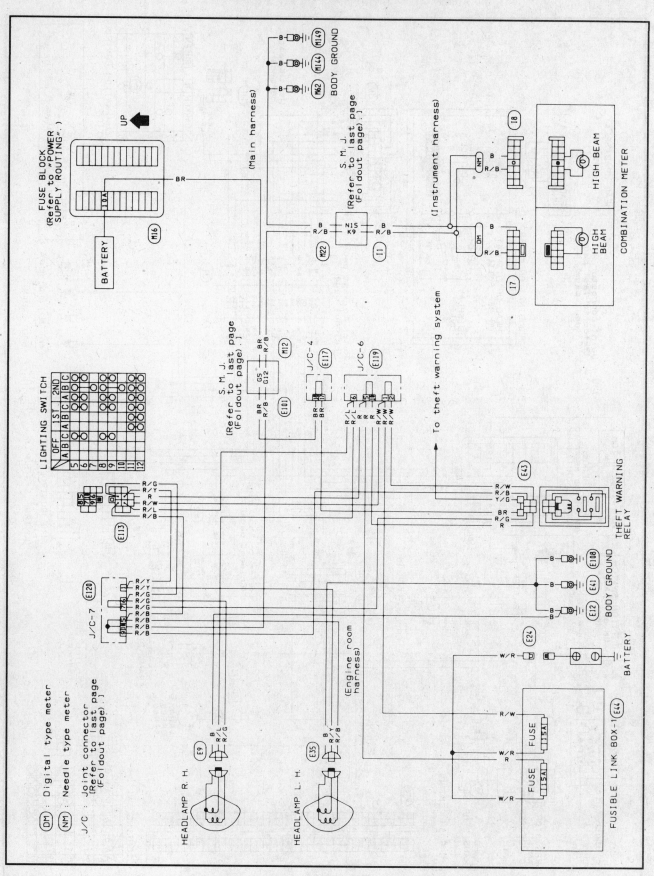

HEADLIGHT WIRING SCHEMATIC — CANADA

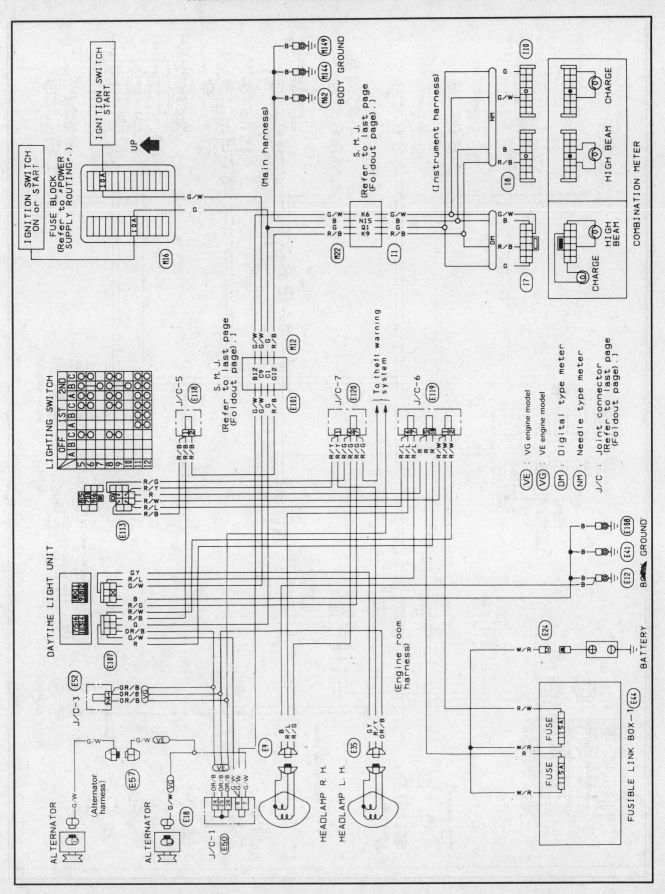

LICENSE, TAIL AND STOP LIGHTS WIRING SCHEMATIC

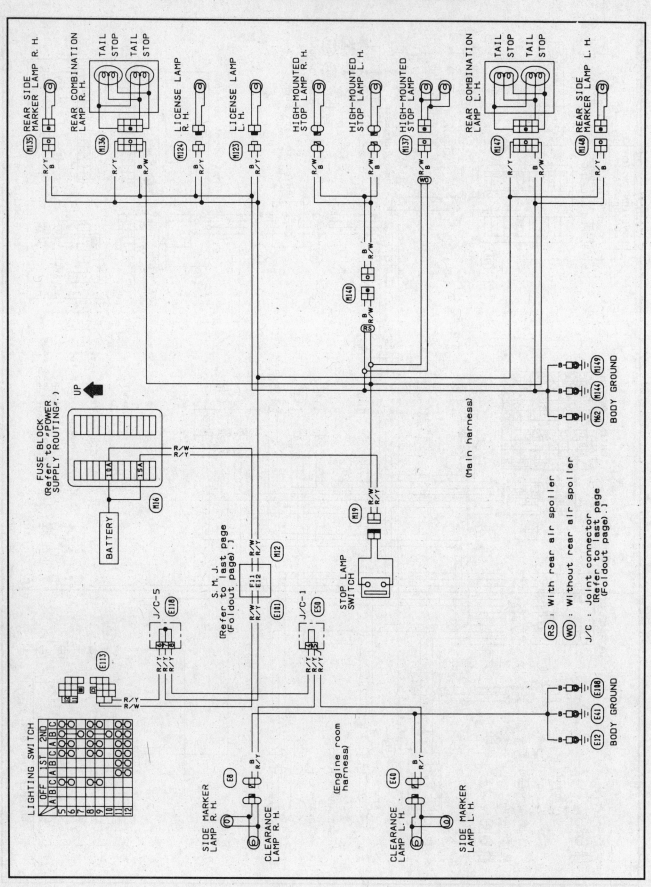

BACKUP LIGHTS WIRING SCHEMATIC

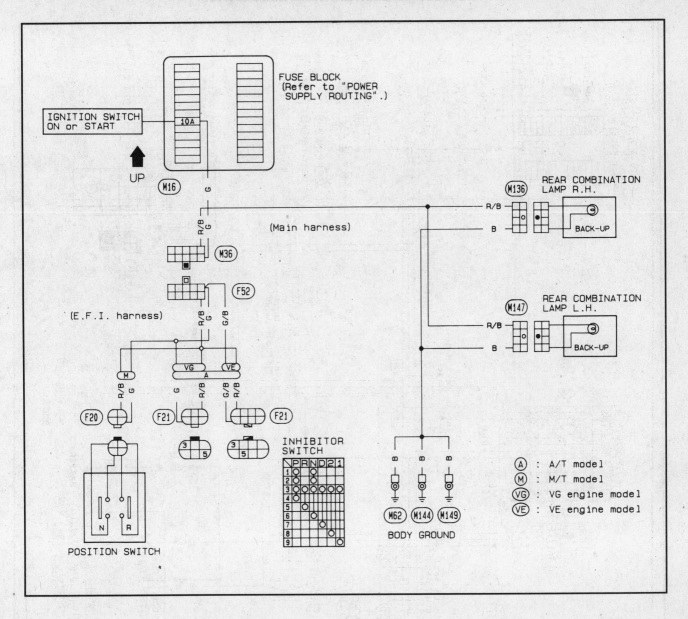

FRONT FOG LIGHTS WIRING SCHEMATIC

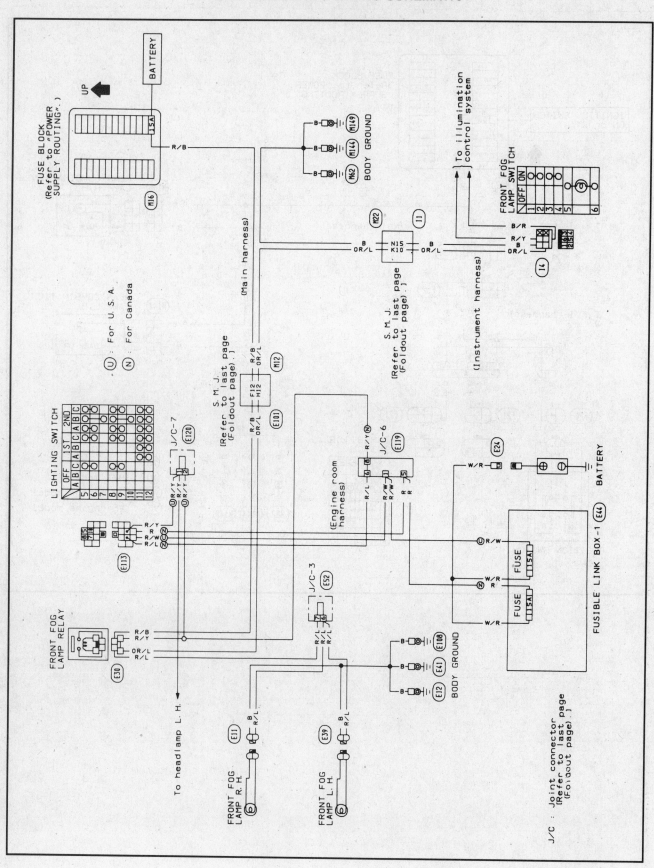

TURN SIGNAL AND HAZARD WARNING LIGHTS WIRING SCHEMATIC

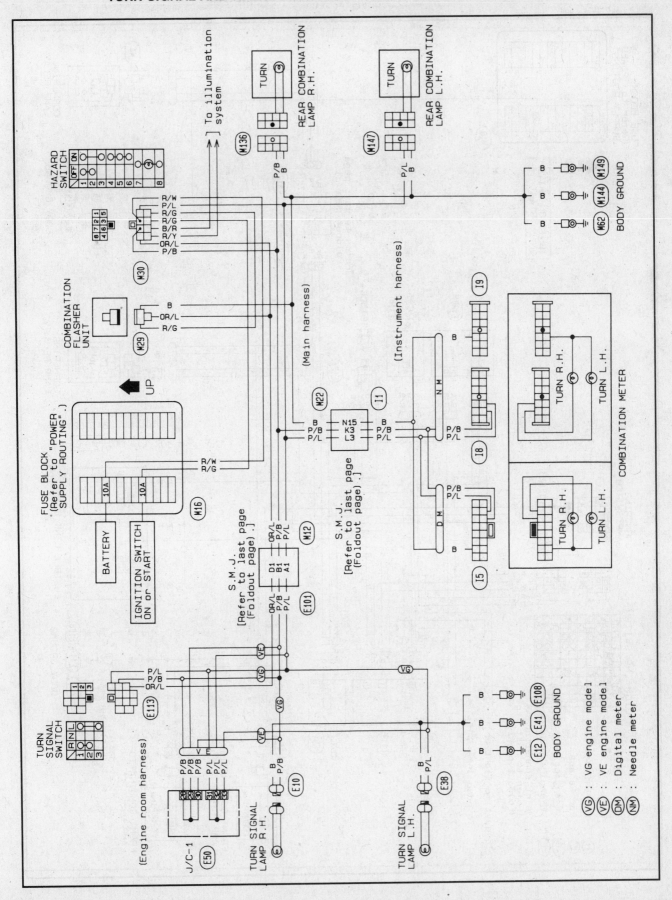

CORNERING LIGHTS WIRING SCHEMATIC

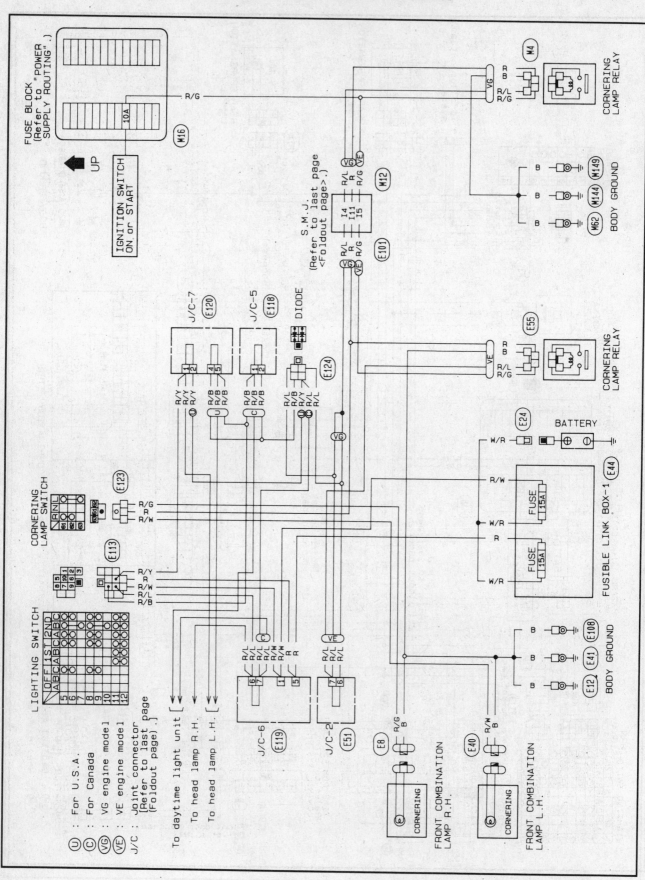

INTERIOR ILLUMINATION LIGHTS WIRING SCHEMATIC — DIGITAL TYPE

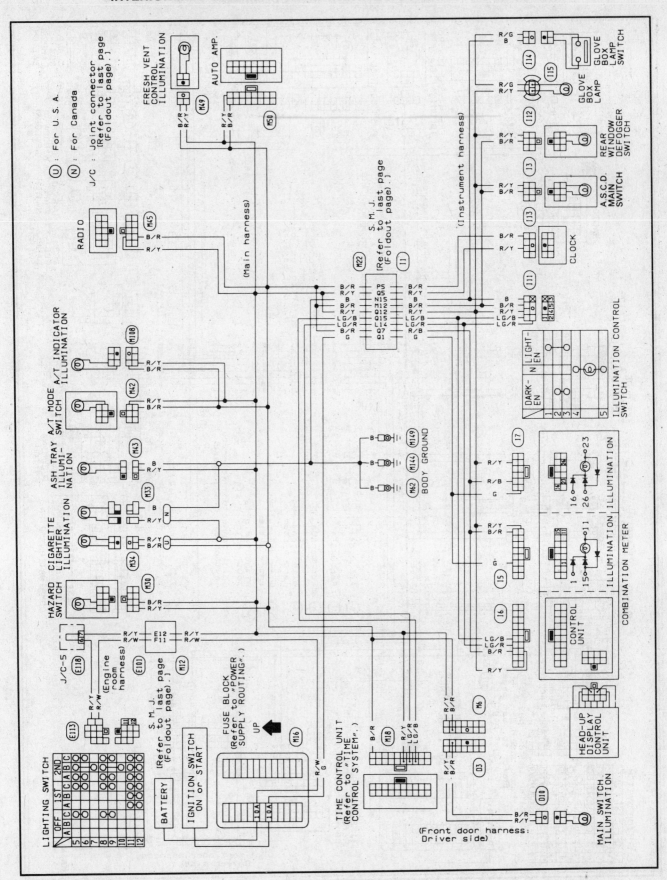

INTERIOR ILLUMINATION LIGHTS WIRING SCHEMATIC — NEEDLE TYPE

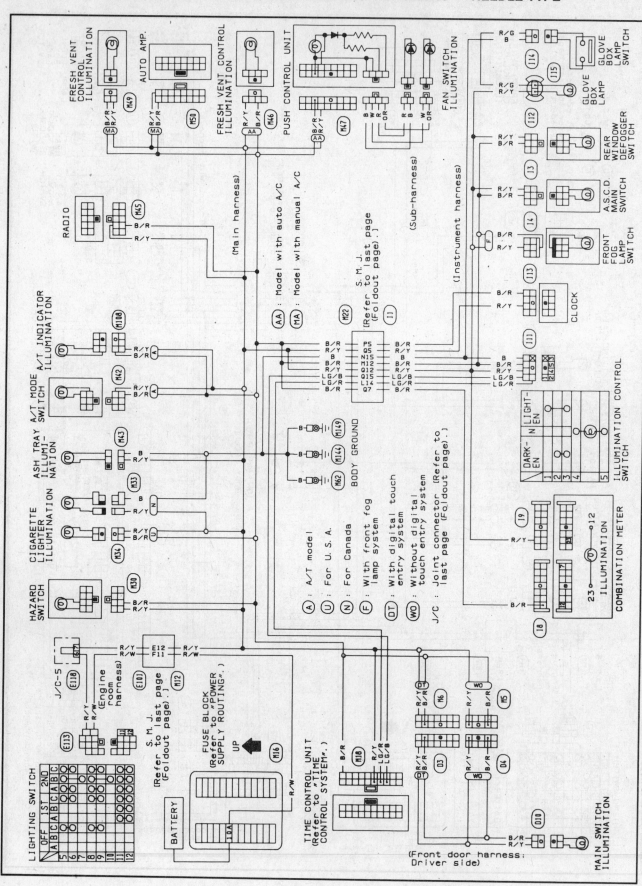

INTERIOR SPOT, STEP AND TRUNK LIGHTS WIRING SCHEMATIC

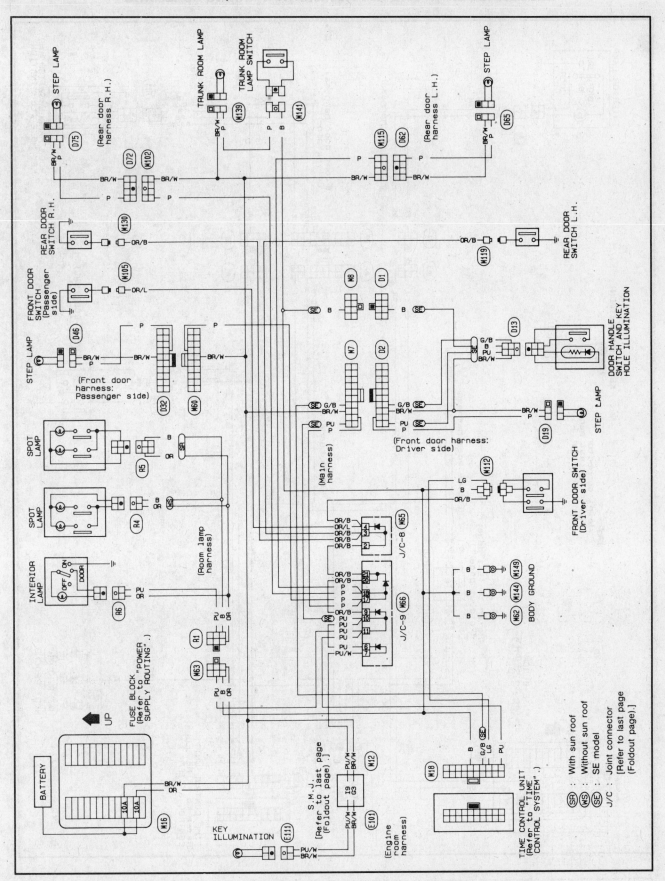

ILLUMINATED ENTRY AND KEY ILLUMINATION WIRING SCHEMATIC

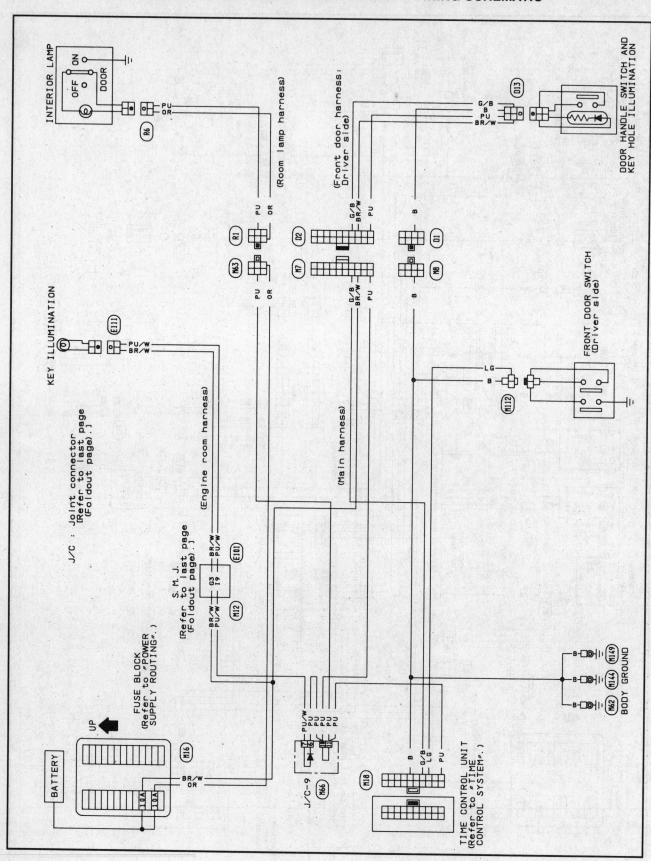

WARNING LIGHTS WIRING SCHEMATIC — DIGITAL TYPE

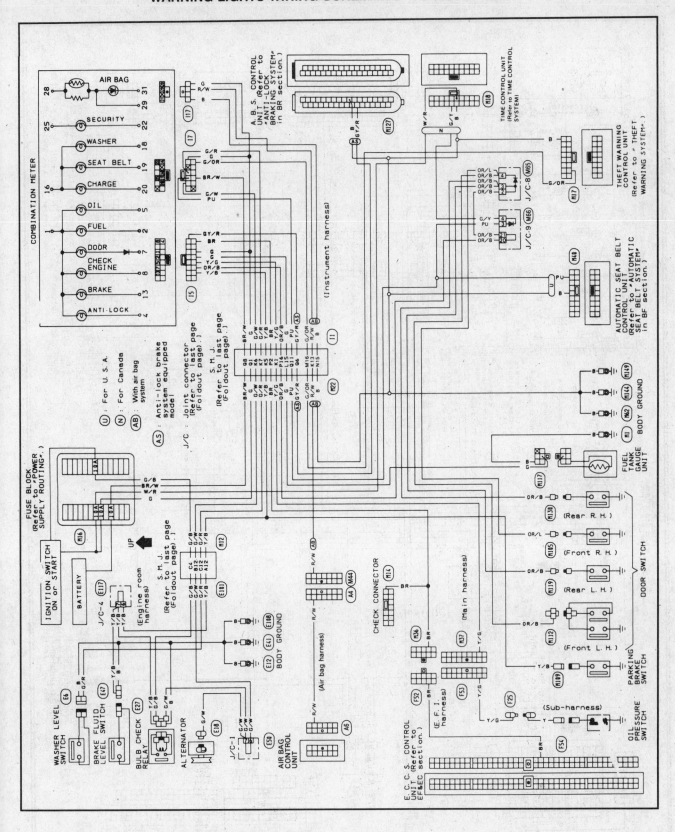

WARNING LIGHTS WIRING SCHEMATIC — NEEDLE TYPE

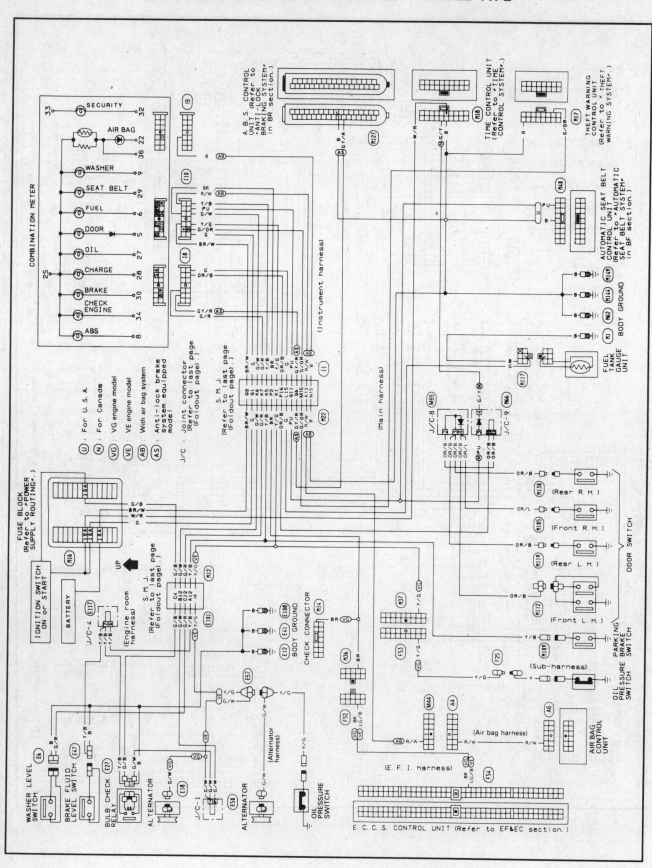

WARNING CHIME WIRING SCHEMATIC

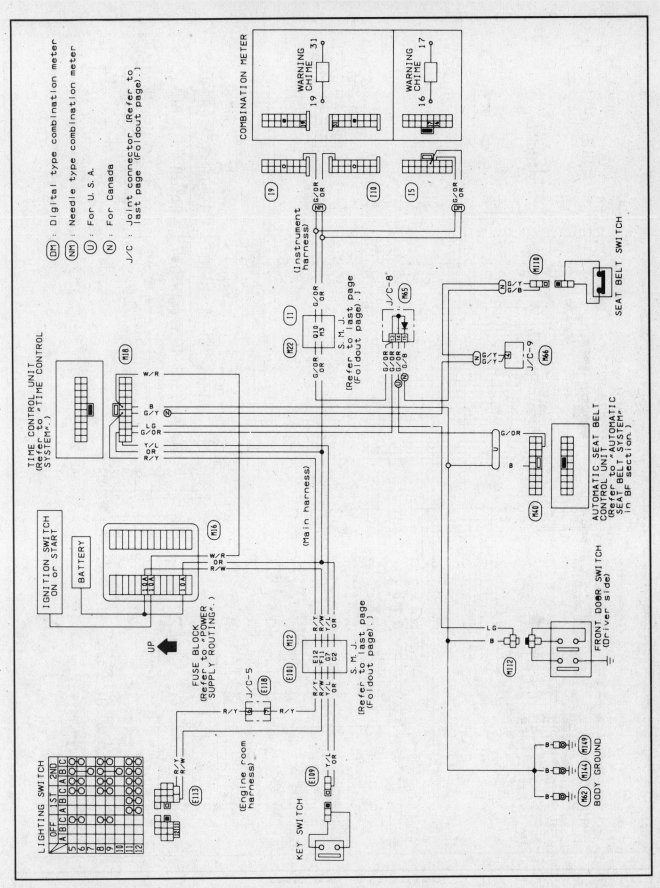

TIME CONTROL SYSTEM WIRING SCHEMATIC

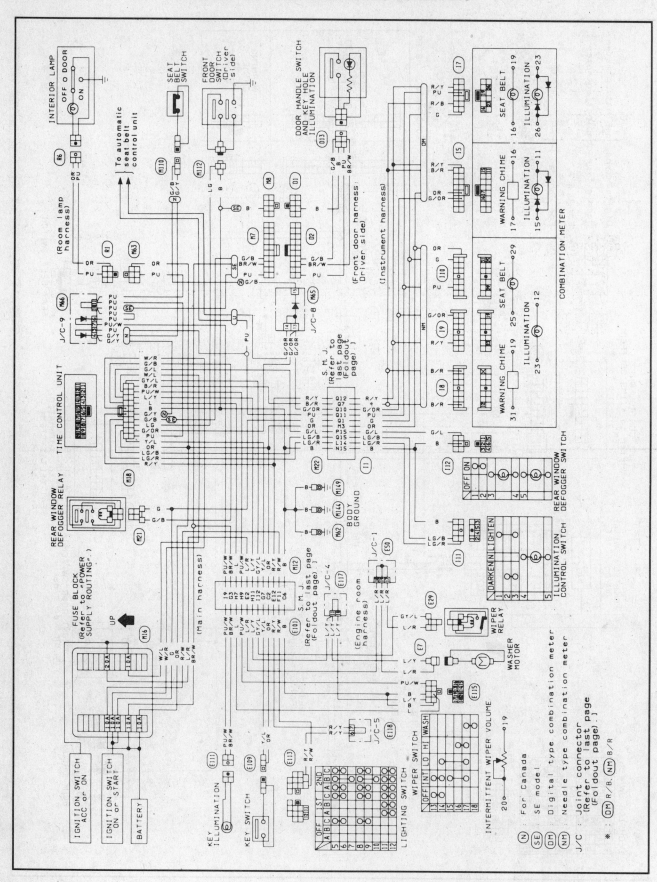

REAR WINDOW DEFOGGER WIRING SCHEMATIC

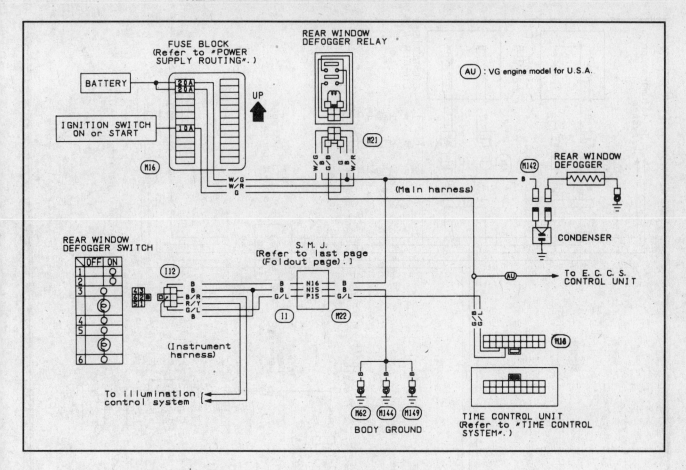

HORN, CIGARETTE LIGHTER, CLOCK WIRING SCHEMATIC

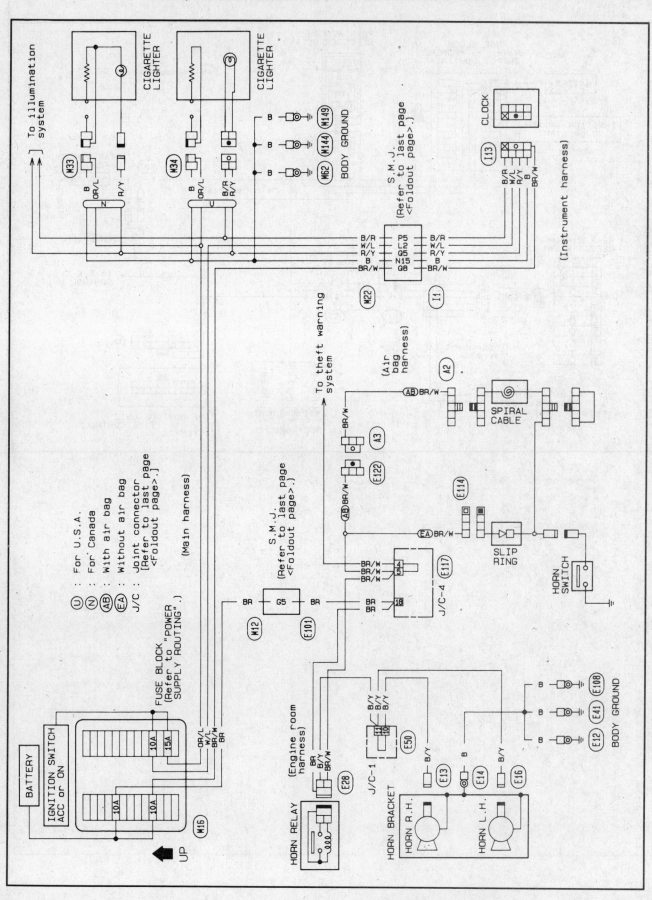

THEFT WARNING SYSTEM WIRING SCHEMATIC

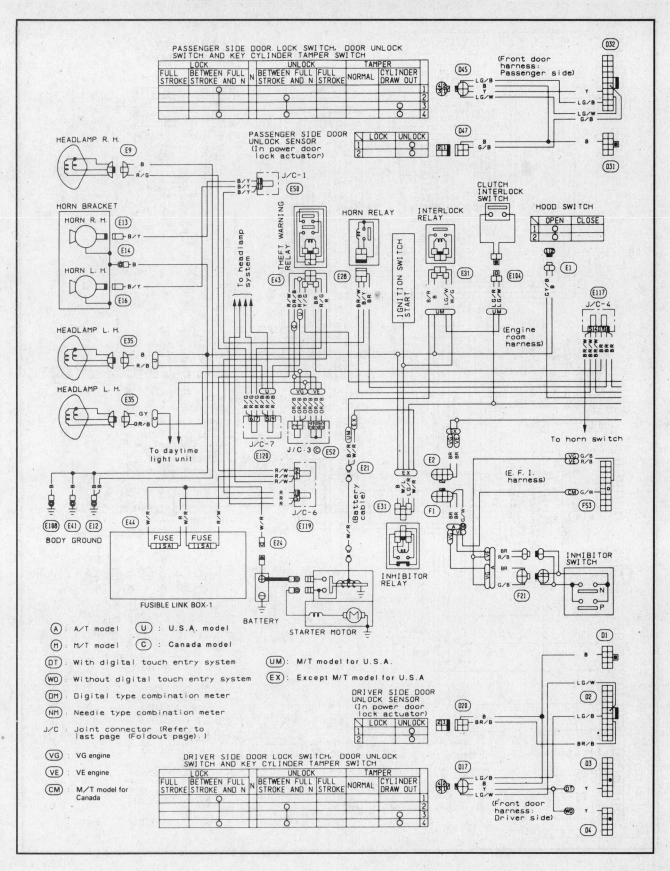

THEFT WARNING SYSTEM WIRING SCHEMATIC, CONT'D

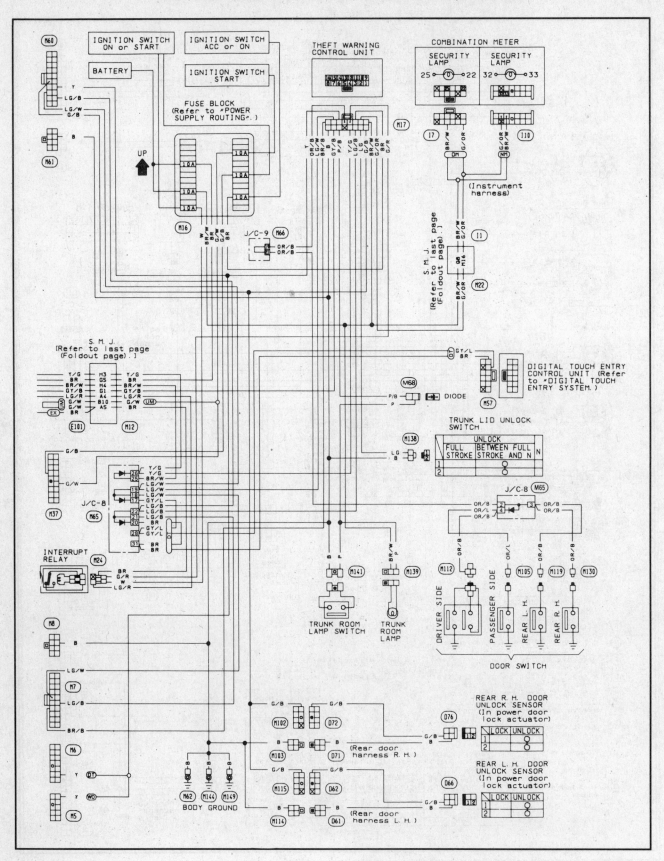

DIGITAL TOUCH ENTRY SYSTEM WIRING SCHEMATIC

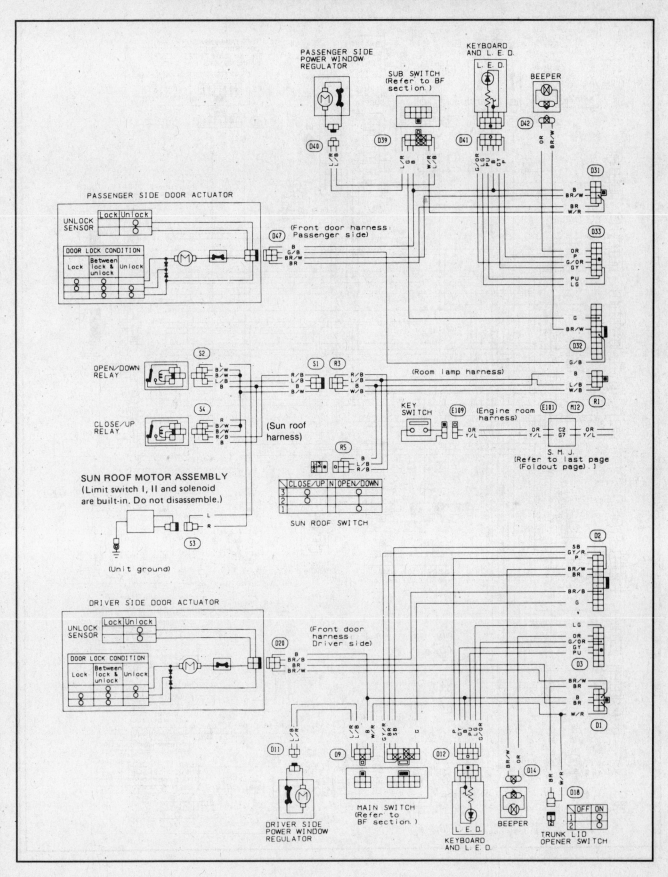

DIGITAL TOUCH ENTRY SYSTEM WIRING SCHEMATIC, CONT'D

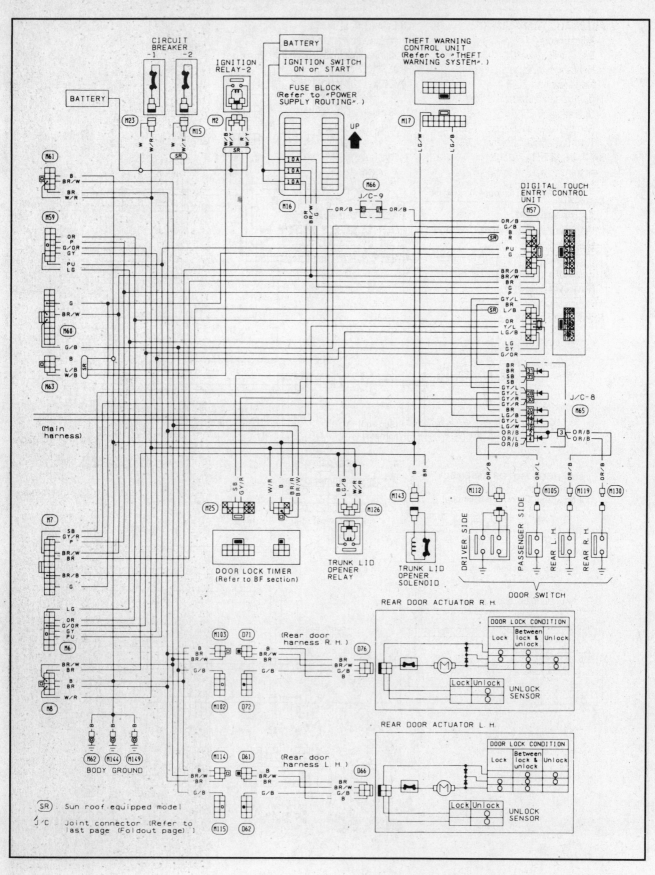

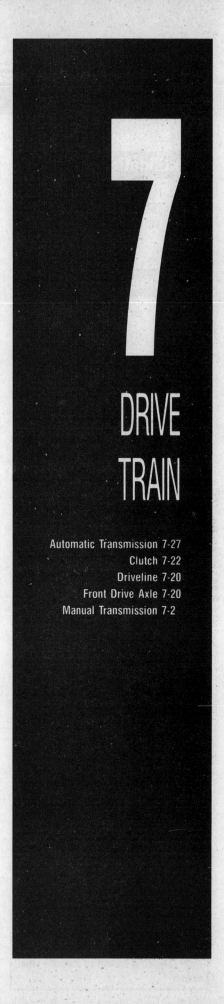

7

DRIVE TRAIN

MANUAL TRANSAXLE

Identification

◆ SEE FIG. 1

The manual transaxle serial number label is stamped on the upper part of the transaxle housing.

Adjustments

CLUTCH SWITCH

1985–88

◆ SEE FIGS. 2 AND 3

1. Adjust the clutch pedal height with the clutch switch.

2. Adjust the clutch pedal free-play with the push rod: Clutch pedal height "H" — 6.73–7.13 in. (171–181mm)   Clutch pedal free-play "A" — 0.04–0.12 in. (1.0–3.0mm)

3. Fully depress the clutch pedal and adjust the clearance "C" between the clutch pedal stopper rubber and threaded end of clutch interlock switch; the clearance should be 0.039–0.079 in. (1.0–2.0mm).

1989–92

◆ SEE FIG. 4–6

1. Adjust the clutch pedal height with the A.S.C.D. cancel switch; the pedal height "H" should be 6.50–6.89 in. (165–175mm).

2. Adjust the clutch pedal free-play with the push rod; the clutch pedal free-play "A" should be 0.039–0.118 in. (1.0–3.0mm).

3. On the USA models, fully depress the clutch pedal and adjust the clearance "C" between the clutch pedal stopper rubber and threaded end of clutch interlock switch; the clearance should be 0.004–0.039 in. (0.1–1.0mm).

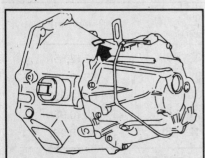

Fig. 1 Location of the manual transaxle serial number

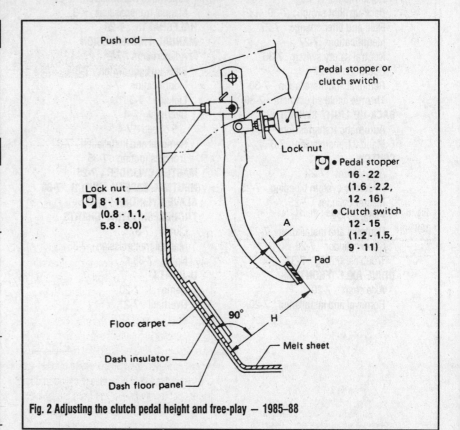

Fig. 2 Adjusting the clutch pedal height and free-play — 1985–88

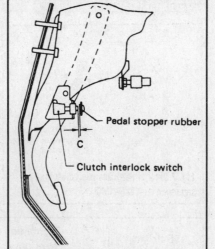

Fig. 3 Adjusting the clutch pedal stopper clearance — 1985–88

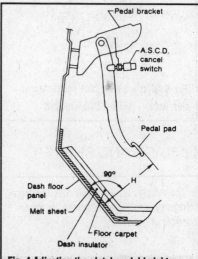

Fig. 4 Adjusting the clutch pedal height — 1989–92

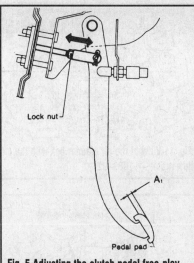

Fig. 5 Adjusting the clutch pedal free-play — 1989-92

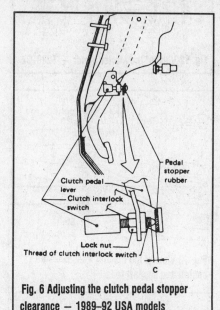

Fig. 6 Adjusting the clutch pedal stopper clearance — 1989-92 USA models

LINKAGE AND SHIFTER

The vehicles are equipped with an integral linkage system. No adjustments are either possible or necessary.

Back-Up Light Switch

REMOVAL & INSTALLATION

1. Raise and safely support the vehicle.

2. Disconnect the electrical connections.

3. Remove switch from transaxle housing, when removing place drain pan under transaxle to catch fluid.

4. To install reverse removal procedures.

Transaxle

REMOVAL & INSTALLATION

1985–88

◆ SEE FIGS. 7 AND 8

1. Remove the battery and battery bracket.

2. Remove the air cleaner and the air flow meter.

3. Raise and safely support the vehicle so there is clearance to remove the transaxle from underneath. Securely support the engine via the oil pan using a cushioning wooden block and a floor jack.

4. Drain the fluid from the transaxle.

5. Remove both driveshafts from the transaxle as described later in this Section. Securely support the transaxle with another jack.

6. Remove the clutch release cylinder; do not disconnect the hydraulic line from the cylinder.

7. Disconnect the speedometer cable.

8. Remove the transaxle-to-engine bolts. Remove the transaxle from the vehicle by sliding the transaxle input shaft out of the clutch,

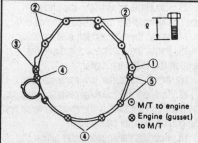

Fig. 7 View of the transaxle bolt torque sequence — 1985–1988

lowering the rear of the transaxle and then lowering the transaxle from the vehicle.

To install:

9. Install the transaxle in the correct position. Torque the transaxle-to-engine bolts.

10. Connect the speedometer cable.

11. Install the clutch release cylinder.

12. Securely support the transaxle. Install the driveshafts.

13. Refill the transaxle with the required amount of approved fluid; the oil fill capacity is 5.0 qts. (4.7L). Connect the speedometer cable.

14. Install the air flow meter and the air cleaner.

15. Remove the battery and battery bracket.

16. Road test the vehicle for proper shift operation.

1989–91

◆ SEE FIGS. 9 AND 10

1. Remove the battery and battery bracket.

2. Remove the air cleaner and the air flow meter.

3. Raise and safely support the vehicle so there is clearance to remove the transaxle from underneath. Securely support the engine via the oil pan using a cushioning wooden block and a floor jack.

4. Drain the fluid from the transaxle.

5. Remove both driveshafts from the transaxle as described later in this Section. Securely support the transaxle with another jack.

6. Remove the clutch release cylinder; do not disconnect the hydraulic line from the cylinder.

7. Disconnect electrical harness connector from the speed sensor and the position switch.

8. Remove the transaxle-to-engine bolts. Remove the transaxle from the vehicle by sliding the transaxle input shaft out of the clutch, lowering the rear of the transaxle and then lowering the transaxle from of the vehicle.

To install:

9. Install the transaxle in the correct position. Torque the transaxle-to-engine bolts.

10. Connect electrical harness connector from the speed sensor and the position switch.

11. Install the clutch release cylinder.

Bolt No.	Tightening torque N·m (kg·m, ft-lb)	ℓ mm (in)
1	43 - 58 (4.4 - 5.9, 32 - 43)	65 (2.56)
2	43 - 58 (4.4 - 5.9, 32 - 43)	55 (2.17)
3	43 - 58 (4.4 - 5.9, 32 - 43)	60 (2.36)
4	30 - 40 (3.1 - 4.1, 22 - 30)	25 (0.98)
5	16 - 21 (1.6 - 2.1, 12 - 15)	25 (0.98)

Fig. 8 Manual transaxle bolt length and torque chart — 1985–88

Bolt No.	Tightening torque N·m (kg-m, ft-lb)	ℓ mm (in)
1	16 - 21 (1.6 - 2.1, 12 - 15)	25 (0.98)
2	30 - 40 (3.1 - 4.1, 22 - 30)	28 (1.10)
3	39 - 49 (4.0 - 5.0, 29 - 36)	57 (2.24)
4	39 - 49 (4.0 - 5.0, 29 - 36)	57 (2.24)
5	39 - 49 (4.0 - 5.0, 29 - 36)	64 (2.52)
6	30 - 40 (3.1 - 4.1, 22 - 30)	25 (0.98)
Front gusset to engine	30 - 40 (3.1 - 4.1, 22 - 30)	25 (0.98)
Rear gusset to engine	30 - 40 (3.1 - 4.1, 22 - 30)	25 (0.98)

Fig. 10 Manual transaxle bolt length and torque chart — 1989–9288

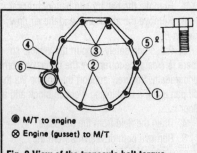

● M/T to engine

⊗ Engine (gusset) to M/T

Fig. 9 View of the transaxle bolt torque sequence — 1989–1992

12. Securely support the transaxle. Install the driveshafts.

13. Refill the transaxle with the required amount of approved fluid; the oil fill capacity is 5.0 qts. (4.7L). Connect the speedometer cable.

14. Install the air flow meter and the air cleaner.

15. Remove the battery and battery bracket.

16. Road test the vehicle for proper shift operation.

1992

▶ SEE FIGS. 9-13

1. Remove the battery and battery bracket.

2. Remove the air cleaner box with the air flow meter.

3. Raise and safely support the vehicle so there is clearance to remove the transaxle from underneath. Securely support the engine via the oil pan using a cushioning wooden block and a floor jack.

4. Drain the fluid from the transaxle.

5. Remove both driveshafts from the transaxle as described later in this Section. Securely support the transaxle with another jack.

6. Remove the clutch release cylinder; do not disconnect the hydraulic line from the cylinder. Remove the clutch hose clamp.

7. Disconnect the speedometer pinion and position switch connectors.

8. Disconnect electrical harness connector from the back-up light switch, the neutral switch and the ground harness connectors.

9. Remove the starter from the transaxle.

10. Remove the shift control rod and the support rod from the transaxle.

11. Remove the rear and left side mounts.

12. Remove the transaxle-to-engine bolts. Remove the transaxle from the vehicle by sliding the transaxle input shaft out of the clutch, lowering the rear of the transaxle and then lowering the transaxle from of the vehicle.

To install:

13. Install the transaxle in the correct position. Torque the transaxle-to-engine bolts.

14. Install the rear and left side mounts.

15. Install the shift control rod and the support rod to the transaxle.

16. Install the starter to the transaxle.

17. Connect electrical harness connector to the back-up light switch, the neutral switch and the ground harness connectors.

18. Connect the speedometer pinion and position switch connectors.

19. Install the hydraulic clutch release cylinder hose clamp. Install the clutch release cylinder.

20. Securely support the transaxle. Install the driveshafts.

21. Refill the transaxle with the required amount of approved fluid; the oil fill capacity is 5.0 qts. (4.7L). Connect the speedometer cable.

22. Install the air flow meter and the air cleaner.

23. Remove the battery and battery bracket.

24. Road test the vehicle for proper shift operation.

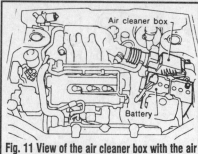

Fig. 11 View of the air cleaner box with the air flow meter — 1989–92

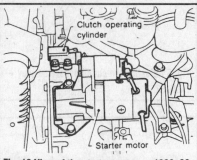

Fig. 12 View of the starter motor — 1989–92

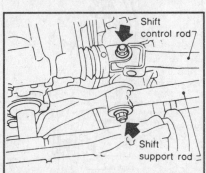

Fig. 13 View of the manual transaxle shift control and support rods

OVERHAUL

Model RS5F50A

DISASSEMBLY OF TRANSAXLE

▶ SEE FIGS. 14-18 AND 20-22

1. Drain the oil from the transaxle.

2. Before removing the transaxle case, remove the bolts and plugs.

3. Tap on the case lightly with a rubber mallet and then lift off the transaxle case.

4. With a rubber mallet, remove the position switch from the case.

5. Mesh the 4th gear and then remove the reverse idler shaft and the reverse idler gear.

6. Remove the reverse arm shaft and the reverse level assembly.

7. Remove the 5th/reverse check plug, spring and ball.

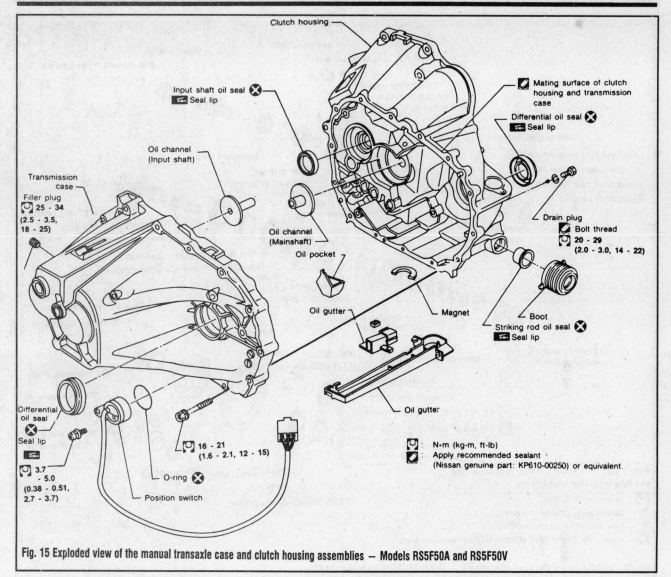

Fig. 15 Exploded view of the manual transaxle case and clutch housing assemblies — Models RS5F50A and RS5F50V

8. Remove the stopper rings and retaining pins from the 5th/reverse and 3rd/4th fork rods.

9. Remove the 5th/reverse and 3rd/4th fork rods. Then remove the forks and brackets.

10. Remove both the input and mainshafts with the 1st/2nd fork and fork rod as a set.

11. Remove the final drive assembly.

12. Remove the reverse check assembly.

13. With a hammer and punch, remove the retaining pin and detach the selector.

14. To make it easier to remove the retaining pin which hods the striking lever to the striking rod, remove the drain plug.

15. With a hammer and punch remove the retaining pin and then withdraw the striking level and striking rod.

Gears and Shafts

ENDPLAY MEASUREMENT

♦ SEE FIG. 14

Before disassembly of the input shaft or the main shaft, measure the gear endplay to insure

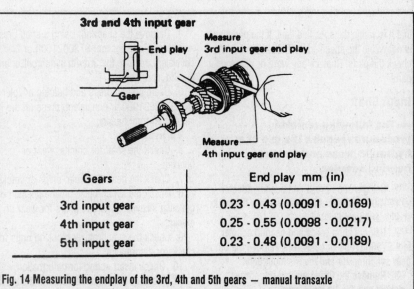

Gears	End play mm (in)
3rd input gear	0.23 - 0.43 (0.0091 - 0.0169)
4th input gear	0.25 - 0.55 (0.0098 - 0.0217)
5th input gear	0.23 - 0.48 (0.0091 - 0.0189)

Fig. 14 Measuring the endplay of the 3rd, 4th and 5th gears — manual transaxle

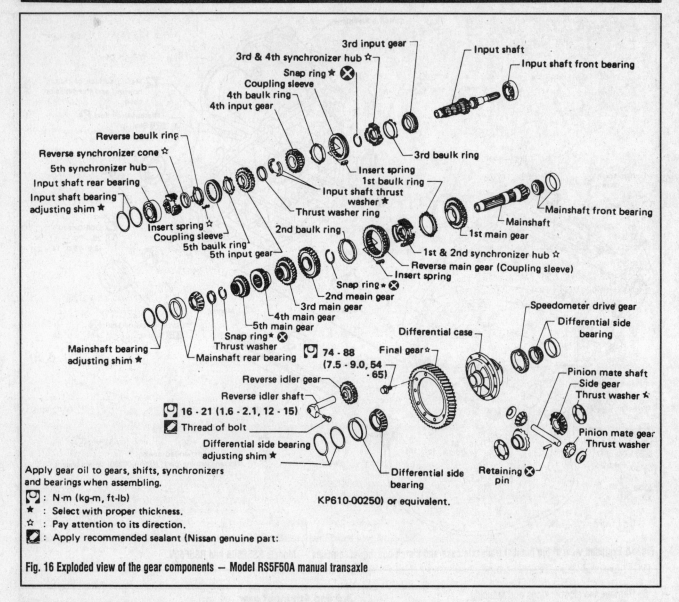

Apply gear oil to gears, shifts, synchronizers and bearings when assembling.

- 🔧 : N·m (kg-m, ft-lb)
- ★ : Select with proper thickness.
- ☆ : Pay attention to its direction.
- 🔩 : Apply recommended sealant (Nissan genuine part:

KP610-00250) or equivalent.

Fig. 16 Exploded view of the gear components — Model RS5F50A manual transaxle

that it is within the specified limit. If the end play is not within the specified limit, disassemble and check the parts. Replace any worn or damaged parts.

Input Shaft

➡ **The following removal procedures require the use of a hydraulic press and various bearing adapter.**

1. Using a shop press and bearing adapter tool ST30031000 or equivalent, remove the input shaft rear bearing.

2. Using a shop press and bearing adapter tool ST30021000 or equivalent, remove the 5th gear synchronizer and the 5th input gear.

3. Remove the thrust washer ring, thrust washers and the 4th input gear.

4. Remove the snapring. Using a shop press and bearing adapter tool ST30021000 or equivalent, remove the 3rd/4th synchronizer and the 3rd input gear.

5. Using a shop press and bearing adapter tool ST30031000 or equivalent, press off the input shaft front bearing.

To inspect:

6. Check the shaft for cracks, wear or bending.

7. Check the gears for wear, chips or cracks.

8. Check the synchronizer spline position of coupling sleeves, hubs and gears for wear or cracks.

9. Check the synchronizer blocking rings for cracks or deformation.

10. Check insert spring for deformation.

11. Measure the distance between the block rings and 3rd/5th input gears. The maximum limit is 0.028 in. (0.7mm); standard measurement is 0.0394–0.0531 in. (1.0–1.35mm).

12. Check that the bearing rolls freely.

13. Inspect the bearing for noise, cracks, pitting and wear.

To assemble:

14. Place the inserts in the 3 grooves on the coupling sleeve of the 3rd/4th synchronizer and the 5th synchronizer. Lubricate the 3rd input gear inner surface with gear oil, then install the 3rd input gear and 3rd balk ring.

15. Press the 3rd/4th synchronizer hub together, pay attention to its direction.

16. Install the snapring of the proper thickness that will minimize the clearance of the groove in the input shaft. The allowable groove clearance should be 0–0.004 in. (0–0.100mm).

17. Lubricate the 4th input gear with gear oil, then install the 4th input gear, thrust washers and thrust washer ring. The thrust washers should be selected to minimize clearance of the groove in the input shaft. The allowable groove clearance should be 0–0.0024 in. (0–0.06mm).

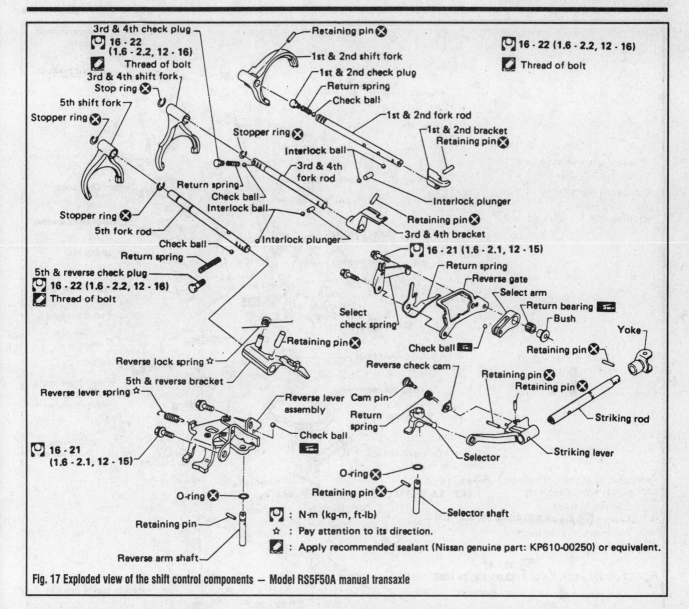

Fig. 17 Exploded view of the shift control components — Model RS5F50A manual transaxle

18. Lubricate the inner surface of 5th gear with gear oil, then install 5th gear.

19. Press on the 5th gear synchronizer.

20. Install the input shaft front and rear bearing.

21. Measure the gear endplay and correct as required.

Mainshaft

▸ SEE FIG. 19

➡ **The following removal procedures require the use of a shop press and various bearing adapters.**

1. Using a shop press and bearing adapter, remove the mainshaft rear bearing.

2. Remove the thrust washer and snapring.

3. Using a shop press and bearing adapter, remove the 5th and 4th main gears.

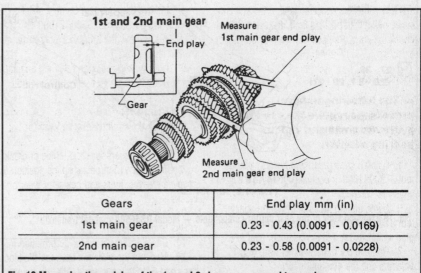

Gears	End play mm (in)
1st main gear	0.23 – 0.43 (0.0091 – 0.0169)
2nd main gear	0.23 – 0.58 (0.0091 – 0.0228)

Fig. 19 Measuring the endplay of the 1sr and 2nd gears — manual transaxle

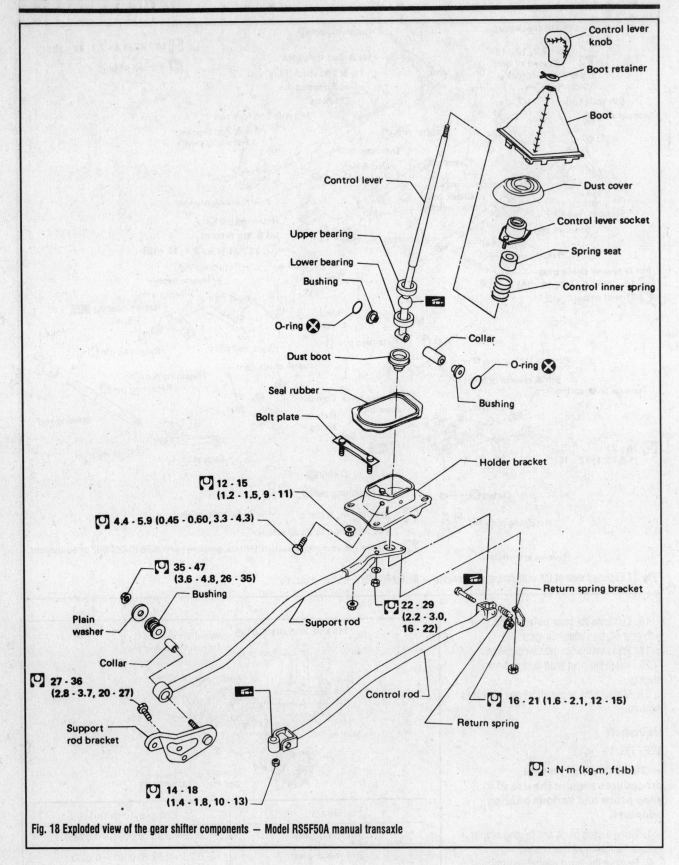

Control lever knob

Boot retainer

Boot

Control lever

Dust cover

Upper bearing

Control lever socket

Lower bearing

Spring seat

Bushing

Control inner spring

O-ring

Collar

Dust boot

O-ring

Seal rubber

Bushing

Bolt plate

Holder bracket

12 - 15 (1.2 - 1.5, 9 - 11)

4.4 - 5.9 (0.45 - 0.60, 3.3 - 4.3)

35 - 47 (3.6 - 4.8, 26 - 35)

Bushing

Return spring bracket

Plain washer

22 - 29 (2.2 - 3.0, 16 - 22)

Support rod

Collar

27 - 36 (2.8 - 3.7, 20 - 27)

Control rod

16 - 21 (1.6 - 2.1, 12 - 15)

Return spring

Support rod bracket

: N·m (kg-m, ft-lb)

14 - 18 (1.4 - 1.8, 10 - 13)

Fig. 18 Exploded view of the gear shifter components — Model RS5F50A manual transaxle

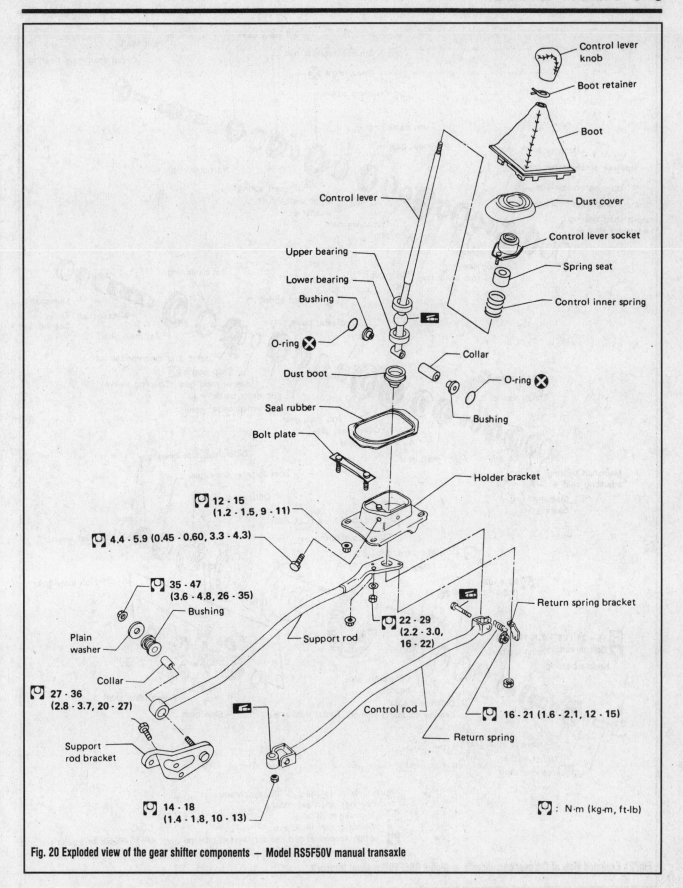

Fig. 20 Exploded view of the gear shifter components — Model RS5F50V manual transaxle

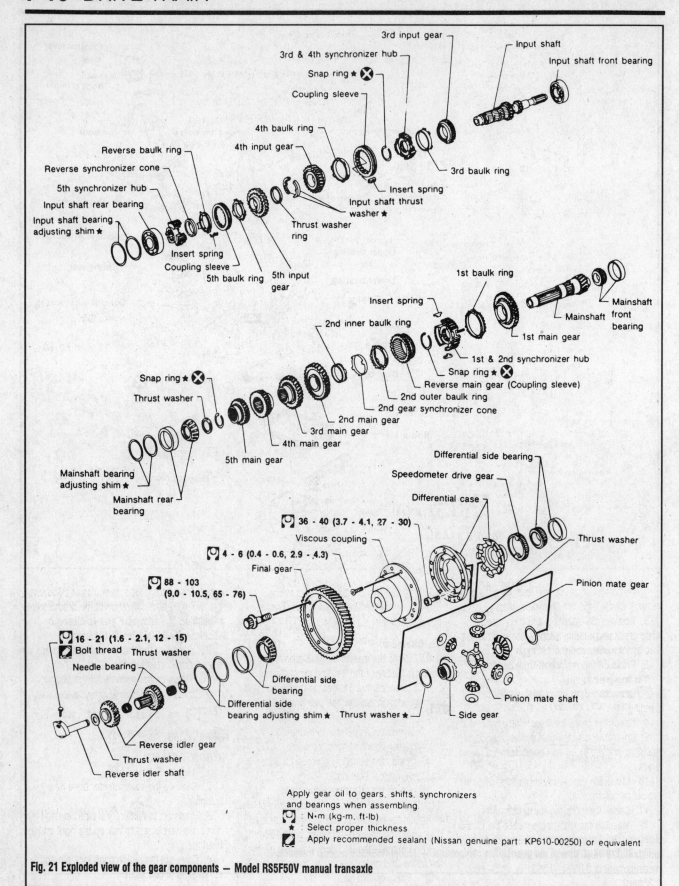

Fig. 21 Exploded view of the gear components — Model RS5F50V manual transaxle

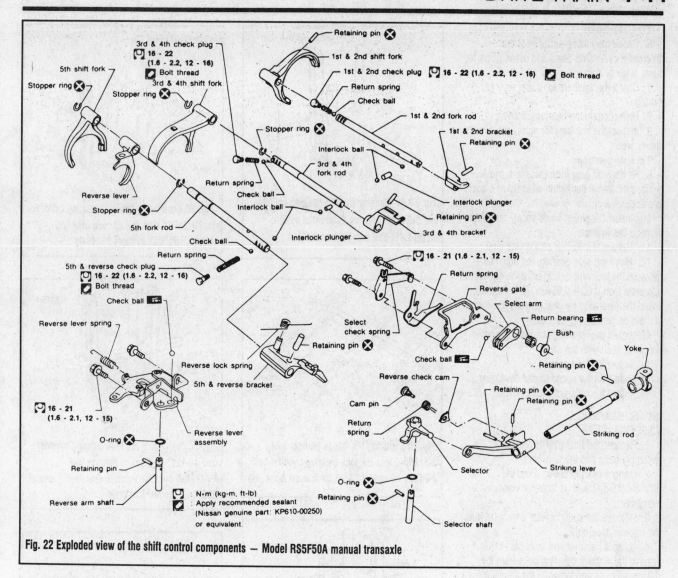

Fig. 22 Exploded view of the shift control components — Model RS5F50A manual transaxle

4. Using a shop press and bearing adapter, remove the 3rd and the 2nd main gears.

5. Remove the snapring and then using a shop press and bearing adapter, remove the 1st/2nd synchronizer and the 1st main gear.

6. Press off the mainshaft front bearing.

To inspect:

7. Check the shaft for cracks, wear or bending.

8. Check the gears for wear, chips or cracks.

9. Check the synchronizer spline position of coupling sleeves, hubs and gears for wear or cracks.

10. Check the synchronizer blocking rings for cracks or deformation.

11. Check insert spring for deformation.

12. Measure the distance between the block rings and 3rd/5th input gears. The maximum limit is 0.028 in. (0.7mm); standard measurement is 0.0394–0.0531 in. (1.0–1.35mm).

13. Check that the bearing rolls freely.

14. Inspect the bearing for noise, cracks, pitting and wear.

To assemble:

15. Place the inserts in the 3 grooves on the coupling sleeve of the 1st/2nd synchronizer.

16. Lubricate the 1st gear inner surface with gear oil, then install the 1st gear and 1st balk ring.

17. Press the 1st/2nd synchronizer hub together, pay attention to its direction.

18. Install the coupling sleeve with 3 inserts and the 2nd gear balk ring.

19. Install the snapring of the proper thickness that will minimize the clearance of the groove in the mainshaft. The allowable groove clearance should be 0–0.004 in. (0–0.100mm).

20. Lubricate the 2nd gear with gear oil, then install the 2nd gear.

21. Press on 3rd gear.

22. Press on 4th gear.

23. Press on 5th gear.

24. Install the snapring of proper thickness that will minimize clearance of the groove in the mainshaft. The allowable groove clearance should be 0–0.0059 in. (0–0.15mm).

25. Press on the thrust washer and press on the mainshaft rear bearing.

26. Press on the mainshaft front bearing.

27. Measure the gear endplay as the final check.

Final Drive Assembly

MODEL RS5F50A

1. Remove the final gear.

2. Remove the speedometer drive gear by cutting it.

3. Press out the differential side bearing inner races. Be careful not to mix up the right and left bearing.

4. Drive out the pinion shaft lock pin and remove the pinion shaft.

To inspect:

5. Check the mating surfaces of the differential case, side gears and pinion gears for burrs, wear or damage.

6. Check the washers for burrs, wear or damage.

7. Make certain the bearing roll freely.

8. Inspect the bearings for noise, pits, cracks and/or wear.

To assemble:

9. Fit the side gear thrust washers and side gears, then install the pinion washers and gears in place.

10. Install the pinion shaft, taking care not to damage the washers.

11. Set a dial indicator on the side gear.

12. Move the side gear up and down to measure the indicator deflection. If the deflection is greater than 0.004–0.008 in. (0.1–0.2mm), adjust the clearance by changing the thickness of the side gear thrust washers.

13. Install the retaining pin, making certain the pin is flush with the case.

14. Install the final gear.

15. Install a new speedometer drive gear.

16. Install the differential side bearing.

MODEL RS5F50V

♦ SEE FIGS. 23-28

1. Remove the final gear-to-viscous assembly bolts and the final gear.

2. Using a bearing puller, press the differential side bearings from the viscous assembly.

3. Remove the speedometer drive gear from the viscous assembly.

4. Using a hammer and an impact driver, remove the viscous coupling bolts from the differential case and separate the coupling from case.

5. Matchmark the differential cases, then remove differential cases bolts and separate the cases.

6. Remove the pinion mate shaft with gears from the differential case.

To inspect:

7. Check the mating surfaces of the differential case, viscous coupling, side gears and pinion mate gears.

8. Check the washers for wear.

9. Check the viscous coupling for cracks and the silicone oil for leakage.

10. Make sure the bearings roll freely and are free of noise, cracks, pitting or wear.

➡ **When replacing the taper roller bearing, replace the outer and inner race as a set.**

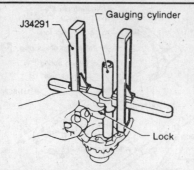

Fig. 23 Positioning the lock gauging cylinder tool J-34291 onto the differential case — model RS5F50V manual transaxle

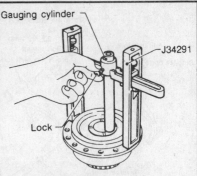

Fig. 26 Positioning the lock gauging cylinder tool J-34291 onto the viscous coupling — model RS5F50V manual transaxle

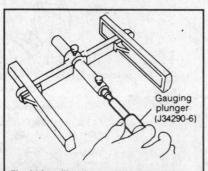

Fig. 24 Installing the gauge plunger tool J-34290-6 into the lock gauging cylinder tool J-34291 — model RS5F50V manual transaxle

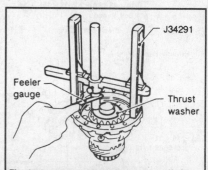

Fig. 27 Positioning the lock gauging cylinder tool J-34291 and gauge plunger tool J-34290-6 onto the viscous coupling — model RS5F50V manual transaxle

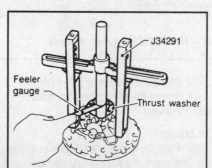

Fig. 25 Positioning the lock gauging cylinder tool J-34291 and gauge plunger tool J-34290-6 onto the differential case — model RS5F50V manual transaxle

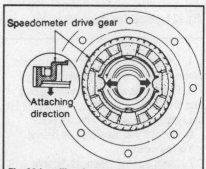

Fig. 28 Installing the speedometer drive gear onto the differential gear — model RS5F50V manual transaxle

To assemble:

11. Measure the clearance between the side gear and the differential case with washers, using the following procedures:

a. Set the gauging tool J–34291 or equivalent, on the differential case and lock the gauging cylinder in place with the set screw.

b. Install the gauging plunger tool J–34290–6 or equivalent, into the cylinder.

c. Install the pinion mate gears and side gear with the thrust washer on the differential case.

d. Set the tool and allow the gauging plunger to rest on the side gear thrust washer.

e. Measure the gap between the plunger and the cylinder; the measurement should give exact clearance between the side gear and the differential case with washers; the standard clearance is 0.044–0.008 in. (0.1–0.2mm).

f. If the clearance is not within specifications, adjust the clearance by changing the thickness of the side gear thrust washer.

12. Measure the clearance between the side gear and the viscous coupling with washers, using the following procedures:

a. Place the side gear and thrust washer on the pinion mate gears, installed on the differential case.

b. Measure dimension **X** in at least 4 places.

c. Set the gauging tool J–34291 or equivalent, on the viscous coupling and lock the gauging cylinder in place with the set screw.

d. Install the gauging plunger tool J–34290–6 or equivalent, into the cylinder.

e. Install the pinion mate gears and side gear with the original washers on the differential case. Align the paint marks.

f. Tighten the differential case bolts.

g. Set the tool and allow the gauging plunger to rest on the side gear thrust washer.

h. Measure the gap between the plunger and the cylinder; the measurement should give exact clearance between the side gear and the differential case with washers; the standard clearance is 0.044–0.008 in. (0.1–0.2mm).

i. If the clearance is not within specifications, adjust the clearance by changing the thickness of the side gear thrust washer.

13. Install the viscous coupling.

14. Install the speedometer drive gear onto the differential case; be sure to align the projection of the speedometer drive gear with the groove of the differential case.

15. Using a shop press and bearing installer tool KV38100300 or equivalent, press the differential side bearing onto the differential case.

16. Using a shop press and bearing installer tool ST30613000 or equivalent, press the differential side bearing onto the viscous coupling.

17. Install the final gear onto the final drive assembly and torque the final gear-to-final drive assembly bolts in a criss-cross pattern to 65–76 ft. lbs. (88–103 Nm).

ASSEMBLY OF TRANSAXLE

1. With a pin punch, install the striking lever and select rod.

2. Install the select shifter and retaining pin.

3. Install the reverse gate assembly.

4. Install the final drive assembly.

5. Install the input shaft and the mainshaft with the 1st and 2nd shift fork assembly.

➡ **Be careful not to damage the input shaft oil seal during installation.**

6. Install the interlock balls and plunger.

7. Install the 3rd/4th shift fork and bracket, then install the 3rd/4th shift rod, circular clip and retaining pin.

8. Install the interlock balls.

9. Install the 5th shift fork and bracket, then install the shift rod, circular clip and retaining pin.

10. Install the 5th/reverse check plug, spring and ball.

11. Lubricate the check ball with multi-purpose grease and install the reverse lever assembly.

12. Install the reverse arm shaft and retaining pin.

13. Mesh 4th gear. Then install the reverse idler gear and shaft, paying attention to the direction of the tapped hole.

14. Place the U-shaped magnet on the clutch housing.

➡ **To aid in the installation of the transaxle case, place the shift selector in the 1st/2nd shift bracket or between the 1st/2nd bracket and the 3rd/4th bracket.**

15. Apply sealant to the mating surface of the transaxle case and install it.

16. Install the position switch.

17. Apply sealant to the threads of the check plugs. Install the balls, springs and plugs.

18. After assembly, check that the transaxle can be shifted into each gear smoothly.

19. Using a torque wrench, measure the driveshaft turning torque; it should be 78–191 inch lbs. (8.8–21.6 Nm).

AVAILABLE SNAPRING SELECTION

Item	Part Number	Thickness in. (mm)
Synchronizer hubs	32269-03E00	0.0787 (2.00)
	32269-03E01	0.0807 (2.05)
	32269-03E02	0.0827 (2.10)
	32269-03E03	0.0768 (1.95)
Mainshaft 5th gear	32348-05E00	0.0768 (1.95)
	32348-05E01	0.0807 (2.05)
	32348-05E02	0.0846 (2.15)
	32348-05E03	0.0886 (2.25)

INPUT SHAFT SIDE ADJUSTING SHIM SELECTION

Dial Gauge Deflection in. (mm)	Suitable Shim(s) in. (mm)
0.0256-0.0272 (0.65-0.69)	0.0252 (0.64)
0.0272-0.0287 (0.69-0.73)	0.0268 (0.68)
0.0287-0.0303 (0.73-0.77)	0.0283 (0.72)
0.0303-0.0319 (0.77-0.81)	0.0299 (0.76)
0.0319-0.0335 (0.81-0.85)	0.0315 (0.80)
0.0335-0.0350 (0.85-0.89)	0.0157 + 0.0173 (0.40 + 0.44)
0.0350-0.0366 (0.89-0.93)	0.0173 + 0.0173 (0.44 + 0.44)
0.0366-0.0382 (0.93-0.97)	0.0173 + 0.0189 (0.44 + 0.48)
0.0382-0.0398 (0.97-1.01)	0.0189 + 0.0189 (0.48 + 0.48)
0.0398-0.0413 (1.01-1.05)	0.0189 + 0.0205 (0.48 + 0.52)
0.0413-0.0429 (1.05-1.09)	0.0205 + 0.0205 (0.52 + 0.52)
0.0429-0.0445 (1.09-1.13)	0.0205 + 0.0220 (0.52 + 0.56)
0.0445-0.0461 (1.13-1.17)	0.0220 + 0.0220 (0.56 + 0.56)
0.0461-0.0476 (1.17-1.21)	0.0220 + 0.0236 (0.56 + 0.60)
0.0476-0.0492 (1.21-1.25)	0.0236 + 0.0236 (0.60 + 0.60)
0.0492-0.0508 (1.25-1.29)	0.0236 + 0.0252 (0.60 + 0.64)
0.0508-0.0524 (1.29-1.33)	0.0252 + 0.0252 (0.64 + 6.64)
0.0524-0.0539 (1.33-1.37)	0.0252 + 0.0268 (0.64 + 0.68)
0.0539-0.0555 (1.37-1.41)	0.0268 + 0.0268 (0.68 + 0.68)
0.0555-0.0571 (1.41-1.45)	0.0268 + 0.0283 (0.68 + 0.72)
0.0571-0.0587 (1.45-1.49)	0.0283 + 0.0283 (0.72 + 0.72)
0.0587-0.0602 (1.49-1.53)	0.0283 + 0.0299 (0.72 + 0.76)
0.0602-0.0618 (1.53-1.57)	0.0299 + 0.0299 (0.76 + 0.76)
0.0618-0.0634 (1.57-1.61)	0.0299 + 0.0315 (0.76 + 0.80)
0.0634-0.0650 (1.61-1.65)	0.0315 + 0.0315 (0.80 + 0.80)
0.0650-0.0665 (1.65-1.69)	0.0173 + 0.0472 (0.44 + 1.20)

AVAILABLE THRUST WASHER SELECTION

Item	Part Number	Thickness in. (mm)
Input Shaft	32278-03E01	0.1772 (4.500)
	32278-03E02	0.1781 (4.525)
	32278-03E03	0.1791 (4.550)
	32278-03E04	0.1801 (4.575)
Differential side gear	38424-E3000	0.0295-0.0315 (0.75-0.80)
	38424-E3001	0.0315-0.0335 (0.80-0.85)
	38424-E3002	0.0335-0.0354 (0.85-0.90)
	38424-E3003	0.0354-0.0374 (0.90-0.95)

BEARING PRELOAD AND ENDPLAY

Item	in. (mm)
Mainshaft bearing preload	0.0098-0.0122 (0.25-0.31)
Input shaft endplay	−0.0024-0 (−0.06-0)
Differential side bearing preload	0.0157-0.0181 (0.40-0.46)

CLEARANCE SPECIFICATIONS

Item	in. (mm)
Input shaft	0-0.0024 (0-0.06)
Differential side gear	0-0.008 (0-0.2)
Block ring to gear standard	0.0394-0.0531 (1.0-1.35)
Block ring to gear wear limit	0.028 (0.7)

INPUT SHAFT BEARING ADJUSTING SHIMS

Part Number	Thickness in. (mm)
32225-08E00	0.0157 (0.40)
32225-08E01	0.0173 (0.44)
32225-08E02	0.0189 (0.48)
32225-08E03	0.0205 (0.52)
32225-08E04	0.0220 (0.56)
32225-08E05	0.0236 (0.60)
32225-08E06	0.0252 (0.64)
32225-08E07	0.0268 (0.68)
32225-08E08	0.0283 (0.72)
32225-08E09	0.0299 (0.76)
32225-08E10	0.0315 (0.80)
32225-08E11	0.0472 (1.20)

DIFFERENTIAL SIDE BEARING ADJUSTING SHIMS

Part Number	Thickness in. (mm)
38453-03E11	0.0157 (0.40)
38453-03E00	0.0173 (0.44)
38453-03E01	0.0189 (0.48)
38453-03E12	0.0205 (0.52)
38453-03E02	0.0220 (0.56)
38453-03E03	0.0236 (0.60)
38453-03E04	0.0252 (0.64)
38453-03E05	0.0268 (0.68)
38453-03E06	0.0283 (0.72)
38453-03E07	0.0299 (0.76)
38453-03E08	0.0315 (0.80)
38453-03E13	0.0472 (1.20)

MAINSHAFT BEARING ADJUSTING SHIMS

Part Number	Thickness in. (mm)
32139-03E11	0.0157 (0.40)
32139-03E00	0.0173 (0.44)
32139-03E01	0.0189 (0.48)
32139-03E12	0.0205 (0.52)
32139-03E02	0.0220 (0.56)
32139-03E03	0.0236 (0.60)
32139-03E04	0.0252 (0.64)
32139-03E05	0.0268 (0.68)
32139-03E06	0.0283 (0.72)
32139-03E07	0.0299 (0.76)
32139-03E08	0.0315 (0.80)
32139-03E13	0.0472 (1.20)

DIFFERENTIAL SIDE BEARING ADJUSTING SHIMS

Dial Indicator Deflection in. (mm)	Suitable Shim(s) in. (mm)
0.0185-0.0201 (0.47-0.51)	0.0173 + 0.0189 (0.44 + 0.48)
0.0201-0.0217 (0.51-0.55)	0.0189 + 0.0189 (0.48 + 0.48)
0.0217-0.0232 (0.55-0.59)	0.0189 + 0.0205 (0.48 + 0.52)
0.0232-0.0248 (0.59-0.63)	0.0205 + 0.0205 (0.52 + 0.52)
0.0248-0.0264 (0.63-0.67)	0.0205 + 0.0220 (0.52 + 0.56)
0.0264-0.0280 (0.67-0.71)	0.0220 + 0.0220 (0.56 + 0.56)
0.0280-0.0295 (0.71-0.75)	0.0220 + 0.0236 (0.56 + 0.60)
0.0295-0.0311 (0.75-0.79)	0.0236 + 0.0236 (0.60 + 0.60)
0.0311-0.0327 (0.79-0.83)	0.0236 + 0.0252 (0.60 + 0.64)
0.0327-0.0343 (0.83-0.87)	0.0252 + 0.0252 (0.64 + 0.64)
0.0343-0.0358 (0.87-0.91)	0.0252 + 0.0268 (0.64 + 0.68)
0.0358-0.0374 (0.91-0.95)	0.0268 + 0.0268 (0.68 + 0.68)
0.0374-0.0390 (0.95-0.99)	0.0268 + 0.0283 (0.68 + 0.72)
0.0390-0.0406 (0.99-1.03)	0.0283 + 0.0283 (0.72 + 0.72)
0.0406-0.0421 (1.03-1.07)	0.0283 + 0.0299 (0.72 + 0.76)
0.0421-0.0437 (1.07-1.11)	0.0299 + 0.0299 (0.76 + 0.76)
0.0437-0.0453 (1.11-1.15)	0.0299 + 0.0315 (0.76 + 0.80)
0.0453-0.0469 (1.15-1.19)	0.0315 + 0.0315 (0.80 + 0.80)
0.0469-0.0484 (1.19-1.23)	0.0173 + 0.0472 (0.44 + 1.20)
0.0484-0.0500 (1.23-1.27)	0.0189 + 0.0472 (0.48 + 1.20)
0.0500-0.0516 (1.27-1.31)	0.0205 + 0.0472 (0.52 + 1.20)

GEAR ENDPLAY

Position	Endplay in. (mm)
Main 1st gear	0.0091-0.0169 (0.23-0.43)
Main 2nd gear	0.0091-0.0228 (0.23-0.58)
Input 3rd gear	0.0091-0.0169 (0.23-0.43)
Input 4th gear	0.0098-0.0217 (0.25-0.55)
Input 5th gear	0.0091-0.0189 (0.23-0.48)

SNAPRING CLEARANCE

Measured	in. (mm)
3rd/4th synchronizer hub	0-0.10 (0-0.0039)
1st/2nd synchronizer hub	0-0.10 (0-0.0039)
Mainshaft 5th gear	0-0.15 (0-0.0059)

TORQUE SPECIFICATIONS

	ft. lbs.	Nm
Transaxle installation		
Engine rear plate to transaxle	12-15	16-21
Transaxle to engine	29-40	39-54
Gusset to transaxle	12-15	16-21
Gusset to engine	22-30	30-40
Engine mounting to transaxle	32-43	48-58
Speedometer pinion	2.7-3.7	3.7-5.0
Starter	22-27	30-36
Transaxle gear control installation		
Control rod to bracket—2WD	4.3-5.8	6-8
Control rod to bracket—4WD	8-10	11-14
Support rod to transaxle—2WD	22-24	30-32
Support rod to transaxle—4WD	6.7-8.7	9.1-11.8
Control bracket to body—2WD	5.8-8.0	8-11
Control bracket to body—4WD	6.7-8.7	9.1-11.8

TORQUE SPECIFICATIONS CONT'D

	ft. lbs.	Nm
Gear assembly		
Clutch housing to transmission case	12-15	16-21
Reverse lever assembly securing bolt	12-15	16-21
5th/Reverse check plug	12-16	16-22
1st/2nd check plug	12-16	16-22
3rd/4th check plug	12-16	16-22
Reverse gate securing bolt	12-15	16-21
Final gear to differential case	54-65	74-88
Filler plug (4WD)	23-31	31-42
Drain plug	11-14	15-20
Position switch securing bolt	2.7-3.7	3.7-5.0

SPECIAL TOOLS

(Kent-Moore) Tool name	Description
ST30600000 (J25863-01) Drift	
ST22452000 (–) Drift	
ST30621000 (J25742-5) Drift	
ST30611000 (J25742-1) Drift	
ST30720000 (–) Drift	
(J34290) Shim selecting tool set	
(J34305) Snap ring remover and installer	
KV38106500 (J34284) Preload adapter	
KV32101000 (J25689-A) Pin punch	
ST22730000 (J25681) Puller	

SPECIAL TOOLS CONT'D

(Kent-Moore)	Description
ST30031000 (J22912-01) Puller	
ST30021000 (J22912-01) Puller	
ST3306S001 (—) Diff. side bearing puller set ① ST33051001 Puller ② ST33061000 (J8107-2) Adapter	
ST33290001 (J34286) Puller	
ST33400001 (J26082) Drift	

Halfshaft

REMOVAL & INSTALLATION

♦ SEE FIGS. 29, 30 AND 31

1. Raise and safely support the vehicle with the front wheels hanging freely.

2. Remove the wheel(s). Remove the brake caliper assembly. The brake hose does not need to be disconnected from the caliper. Be careful not to depress the brake pedal or the piston will pop out. Do not twist the brake hose.

3. Pull out the cotter pin from the castellated nut on the wheel hub and then remove the wheel bearing locknut.

➡ Cover the boots with a shop towel or waste cloth so not to damage them when removing the halfshaft.

4. Separate the halfshaft from the steering knuckle by tapping it with a block of wood and a mallet.

➡ It may be necessary to loosen (do not remove) the strut-to-chassis nuts to gain clearance for steering knuckle removal from the halfshaft.

5. Remove the tie rod-to-steering knuckle ball joint. Remove the 3 lower ball joint-to-lower control arm nuts/bolts and then pull the arm down.

➡ Always use a new nut when replacing the tie rod ball joint.

6. Using a prybar, reach through the engine right crossmember and carefully pry the right side inner CV-joint from the transaxle support bearing flange.

7. Using a block of wood on an hydraulic floor jack, support the engine under the oil pan.

8. If necessary, remove the support bearing bracket from the engine and then withdraw the right halfshaft.

9. Carefully insert a small prybar between the left CV-joint inner flange and the transaxle case mounting surface and pry the halfshaft out of the case. Withdraw the shaft from the steering knuckle and remove it.

To install:

10. When installing the shafts into the transaxle, use a new oil seal and then install an alignment tool, KV38106700 for the left side or KV38106800 for the right side, along the inner circumference of the oil seal.

11. Insert the halfshaft into the transaxle, align the serrations and then remove the alignment tool.

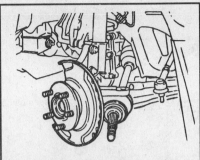

Fig. 29 Separating the halfshaft from the steering knuckle

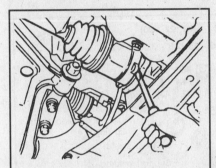

Fig. 30 Separating the right halfshaft from the transaxle

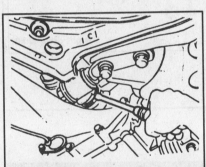

Fig. 31 Separating the left halfshaft from the manual transaxle

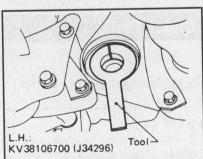

L.H.: KV38106700 (J34296) Tool

Fig. 32 Using halfshaft installation tool KV38106700 to install the left halfshaft into the transaxle

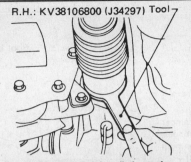

R.H.: KV38106800 (J34297) Tool

Fig. 33 Using halfshaft installation tool KV38106800 to install the right halfshaft into the transaxle

12. Push the halfshaft, then press-fit the circular clip on the shaft into the clip groove on the side gear.

➡ **After insertion, attempt to pull the flange out of the side joint to make sure the circular clip is properly seated in the side gear and will not come out.**

13. Install support bearing bracket bolts and tighten the bolts. Insert the halfshaft in the steering knuckle. Tighten the strut mounting bolts to 23–31 ft. lbs. (31–42 Nm) for 1985–88 or 29–40 ft. lbs. (39–54 Nm) for 1989–92, if loosened.

14. Connect the lower ball joint and tie rod end in the correct position. Torque the lower ball joint-to-control arm nuts to 56–80 ft. lbs. (76–109 Nm) and the tie rod end-to-steering knuckle nut to 22–29 ft. lbs. (29–39 Nm).

15. Install the caliper assembly and the wheel bearing locknut. Tighten the nut to 174–231 ft. lbs. (235–314 Nm).

16. Install a new cotter pin on the wheel hub and install the wheel.

17. If the brake hose was disconnected, bleed the brake system. Road test the vehicle for proper operation.

CV-JOINT OVERHAUL

Transaxle Side

♦ SEE FIGS. 34

1. Remove boot bands.
2. Before separating the joint assembly, matchmark slide joint housing and inner race.
3. Pry off snapring **A** and pull out the slide joint housing.

➡ **Cover driveshaft serration with tape so not to damage the boot.**

4. Place matchmarks on the inner race and the halfshaft.
5. Pry off snapring **C**. Remove the ball cage, the inner race and the balls as a unit.
6. Pry off snapring **B** and remove the boot.

To install:

7. Install the boot and a new snapring **B**.
8. Install the ball cage, the inner race and the balls as a unit. Install a new snapring **C**.
9. Align the inner race and halfshaft matchmarks, then, install the slide joint housing.
10. Install a new snapring **A**. Install the boot and secure with bands.

Wheel Side

➡ **The joint on the wheel side cannot be disassembled.**

1. Matchmark the halfshaft and the joint assembly.
2. Separate joint assembly with suitable tool.
3. Remove boot bands.

To install:

4. Install boot with new boot bands.
5. Align matchmarks and lightly tap joint assembly onto the shaft.
6. Pack halfshaft with grease.
7. Lock both boot band clamps.

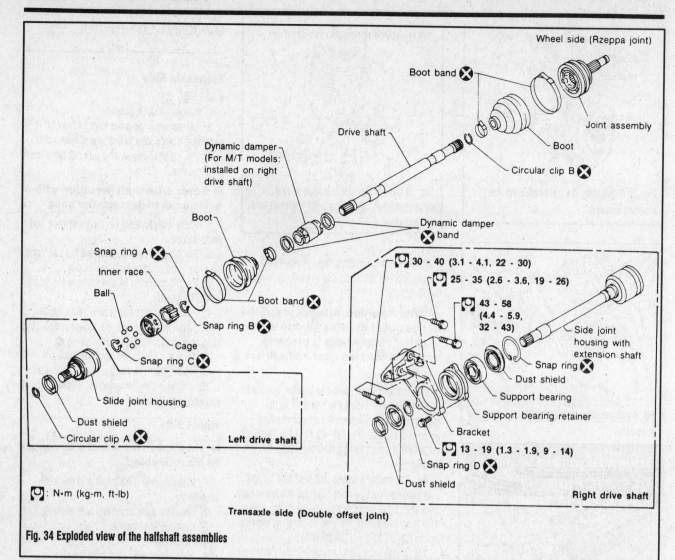

Wheel side (Rzeppa joint)

Boot band ✖

Joint assembly

Drive shaft

Boot

Dynamic damper
(For M/T models:
installed on right
drive shaft)

Circular clip B ✖

Boot

Dynamic damper ✖ band

Snap ring A ✖

Inner race

Ball

Boot band ✖

Snap ring B ✖

Cage

Snap ring C ✖

Slide joint housing

Dust shield

Circular clip A ✖

Left drive shaft

🔧 30 - 40 (3.1 - 4.1, 22 - 30)

🔧 25 - 35 (2.6 - 3.6, 19 - 26)

🔧 43 - 58
(4.4 - 5.9,
32 - 43)

Side joint
housing with
extension shaft

Snap ring ✖

Dust shield

Support bearing

Support bearing retainer

Bracket

🔧 13 - 19 (1.3 - 1.9, 9 - 14)

Snap ring D ✖

Dust shield

Right drive shaft

🔧 : N•m (kg-m, ft-lb)

Transaxle side (Double offset joint)

Fig. 34 Exploded view of the halfshaft assemblies

CLUTCH

❄ CAUTION

The clutch driven disc contains asbestos, which has been determined to be a cancer causing agent. Never clean clutch surface with compressed air! Avoid inhaling any dust from any clutch surface! When cleaning clutch surfaces, use a commercially available brake cleaning fluid.

Adjustments

PEDAL HEIGHT AND FREE-PLAY

◆ SEE FIGS. 2-6

All models have a hydraulically operated clutch. Pedal height is usually adjusted with a stopper limiting the upward travel of the pedal. Pedal free-play is adjusted at the master cylinder pushrod.

Clutch Pedal

REMOVAL & INSTALLATION

◆ SEE FIG. 36

1. Remove the clutch master cylinder pushrod-to-clutch pedal clevis pin.
2. Remove the clutch pedal-to-bracket fulcrum pin nut and the fulcrum pin.
3. Remove the clutch pedal from the vehicle.
4. To install, reverse the removal procedures. Check and/or adjust the clutch pedal height and free-play.

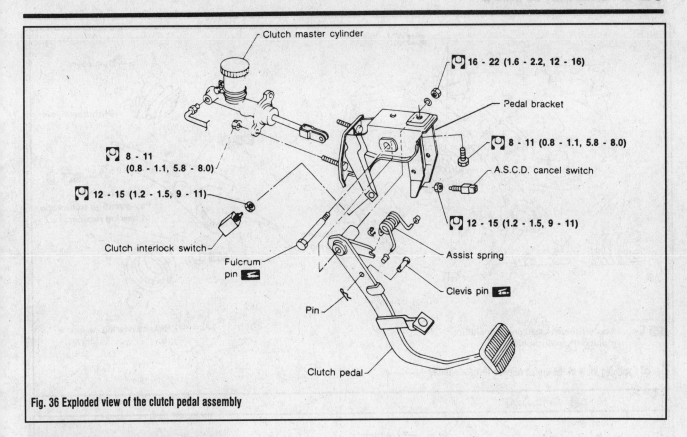

Fig. 36 Exploded view of the clutch pedal assembly

Driven Disc and Pressure Plate

REMOVAL & INSTALLATION

♦ SEE FIGS. 37-43

1. Remove the transaxle from the engine as detailed earlier in this Section.

2. Insert a clutch aligning bar or similar tool all the way into the clutch disc hub. This must be done so as to support the weight of the clutch disc during removal. Mark the clutch assembly-to-flywheel relationship with paint or a center punch so the clutch assembly can be assembled in the same position from which it is removed.

3. Loosen the bolts in sequence, a turn at a time. Remove the bolts.

4. Remove the pressure plate and clutch disc.

5. Remove the release mechanism from the transaxle housing. Apply lithium based molybdenum disulfide grease to the bearing sleeve inside groove, the contact point of the withdrawal lever and bearing sleeve, the contact surface of the lever ball pin and lever. Replace the release mechanism.

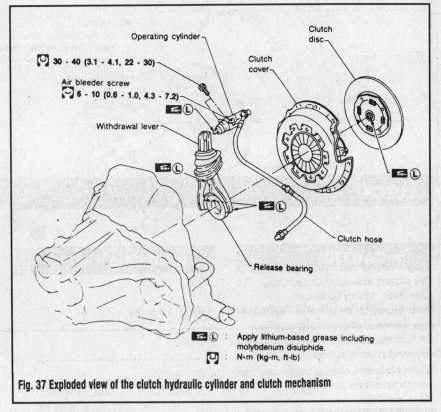

Fig. 37 Exploded view of the clutch hydraulic cylinder and clutch mechanism

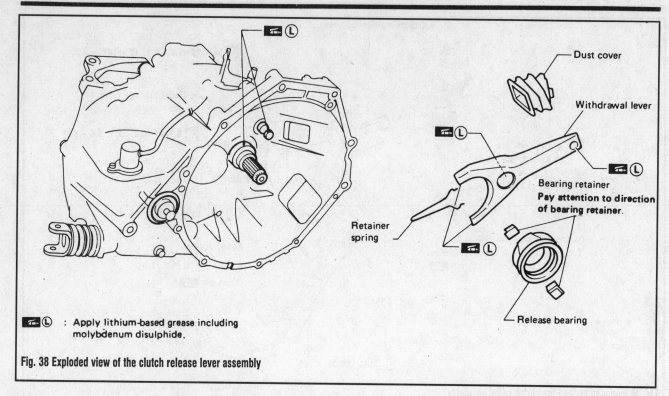

: Apply lithium-based grease including molybdenum disulphide.

Fig. 38 Exploded view of the clutch release lever assembly

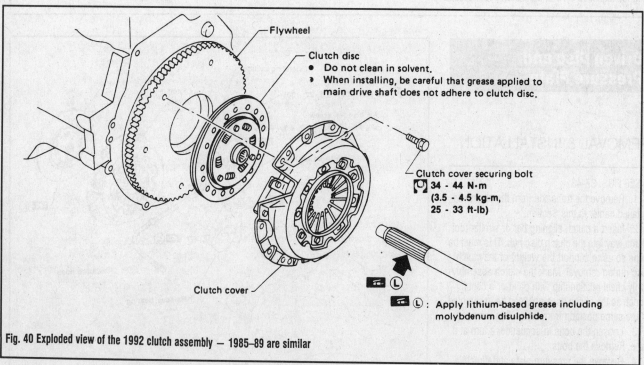

Fig. 40 Exploded view of the 1992 clutch assembly — 1985–89 are similar

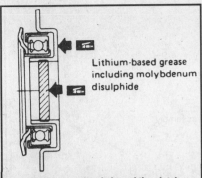

Fig. 39 Cross-sectional view of the clutch release bearing and lubrication points

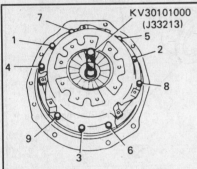

Fig. 41 View of the clutch pressure plate bolt torquing sequence

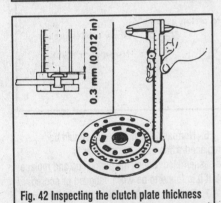

Fig. 42 Inspecting the clutch plate thickness

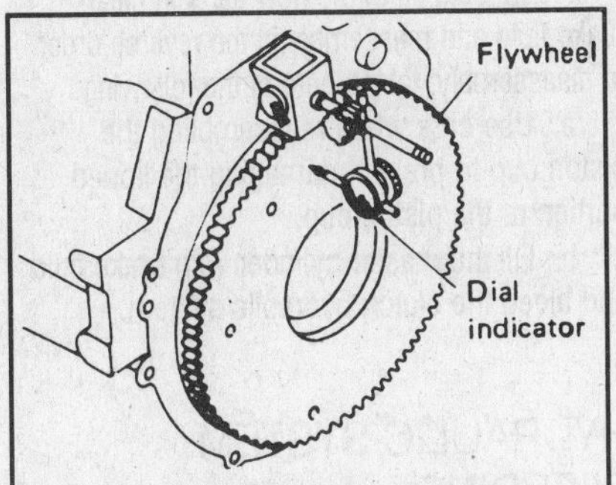

Fig. 43 Inspecting the flywheel runout

To inspect:

6. Inspect the pressure plate for wear, scoring, etc., and reface or replace, as necessary. Measure the thickness of the clutch plate lining; if the it is worn to a minimum of 0.012 in. (0.3mm), replace the clutch plate.

7. Inspect the release bearing and replace as necessary. Apply a small amount of grease to the transaxle input shaft splines. Install the disc on the splines and slide back and forth a few times. Remove the disc and remove excess grease on hub. Be sure no grease contacts the disc or pressure plate.

8. Using a dial indicator, mount it to the engine and inspect the flywheel runout; if the runout exceeds 0.0059 in. (0.15mm), replace it.

To install:

9. Install the disc, aligning it with a splined dummy shaft.

10. Install the pressure plate and torque the bolts to 16–22 ft. lbs. (22–29 Nm) for 1985–91 or 25–33 ft. lbs. (34–44 Nm) for 1992.

11. Remove the dummy shaft.

12. Replace the transaxle.

Clutch Master Cylinder

REMOVAL & INSTALLATION

▶ SEE FIG. 36

1. Disconnect the clutch pedal arm from the pushrod.

2. Disconnect the clutch hydraulic line from the master cylinder.

➡ **Take precautions to keep brake fluid from coming in contact with any painted surfaces.**

3. Remove the master cylinder-to-chassis nuts and remove the master cylinder and pushrod toward the engine compartment side.

To install:

4. Install the master cylinder and torque the master cylinder-to-chassis nuts or bolts to 5.8–8.0 ft. lbs. (8–11 Nm).

5. Connect the pushrod to the clutch pedal.

6. Connect the clutch hydraulic line to the clutch master cylinder.

7. Bleed the clutch hydraulic system.

OVERHAUL

▶ SEE FIG. 44

1. Remove the master cylinder from the vehicle.

2. Drain the clutch fluid from the master cylinder reservoir.

3. Remove the boot and circlip and remove the pushrod.

4. Remove the stopper, piston, cup and return spring.

To assemble:

5. Clean all of the parts in clean brake fluid.

6. Check the master cylinder and piston for wear, corrosion and scores and replace the parts as necessary. Light scoring and glaze can be removed with crocus cloth soaked in brake fluid.

7. Generally, the cup seal should be replaced each time the master cylinder is disassembled. Check the cup and replace it, if it is worn, fatigued or damaged.

8. Check the clutch fluid reservoir, filler cap, dust cover and the pipe for distortion and damage and replace the parts as necessary.

9. Lubricate all new parts with clean brake fluid.

10. Reassemble the master cylinder parts in the reverse order of disassembly; be careful not to damage the cup seal lipped portions.

11. Install the clutch master cylinder onto the vehicle.

12. Check and/or adjust the height of the clutch pedal.

13. Fill the master cylinder and clutch fluid reservoir and then bleed the clutch hydraulic system.

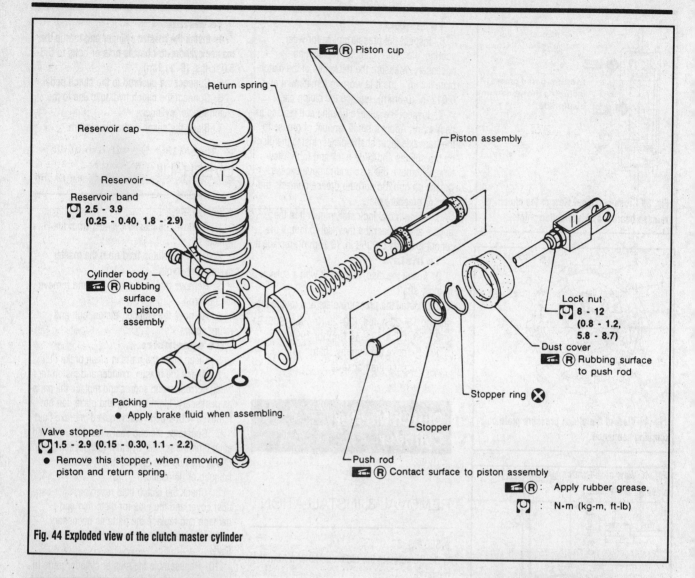

Fig. 44 Exploded view of the clutch master cylinder

Labels in figure:
- Piston cup ■Ⓡ
- Return spring
- Piston assembly
- Reservoir cap
- Reservoir
- Reservoir band ⟨⟩ 2.5 - 3.9 (0.25 - 0.40, 1.8 - 2.9)
- Cylinder body ■Ⓡ Rubbing surface to piston assembly
- Lock nut ⟨⟩ 8 - 12 (0.8 - 1.2, 5.8 - 8.7)
- Dust cover ■Ⓡ Rubbing surface to push rod
- Packing ● Apply brake fluid when assembling.
- Stopper ring ⊗
- Stopper
- Push rod ■Ⓡ Contact surface to piston assembly
- Valve stopper ⟨⟩ 1.5 - 2.9 (0.15 - 0.30, 1.1 - 2.2) ● Remove this stopper, when removing piston and return spring.
- ■Ⓡ : Apply rubber grease.
- ⟨⟩ : N·m (kg-m, ft-lb)

Clutch Slave Cylinder

REMOVAL & INSTALLATION

▶ SEE FIG. 37

1. Remove the slave cylinder attaching bolts and the pushrod from the release fork.
2. Disconnect the flexible fluid hose from the slave cylinder and remove the unit from the vehicle.

To Install:

3. Install the slave cylinder in the reverse order of removal and torque the slave cylinder mounting bolts to 22–30 ft. lbs. (30–40 Nm).
4. Connect the clutch hydraulic line to the clutch slave cylinder.
5. Bleed the clutch hydraulic system.

OVERHAUL

▶ SEE FIG. 45

1. Remove the slave cylinder from the vehicle.
2. Remove the pushrod and boot.
3. Force out the piston by blowing compressed air into the slave cylinder at the hose connection.

✿✿✿ CAUTION

Be careful not to apply excess air pressure to avoid possible injury.

4. Clean all of the parts in clean brake fluid.

To assemble:

5. Check and replace the slave cylinder bore and piston, if wear or severe scoring exists. Light scoring and glaze can be removed with crocus cloth soaked in brake fluid.

6. Normally, the piston cup should be replaced when the slave cylinder is disassembled. Check the piston cup and replace it, if it is found to be worn, fatigued or scored.

7. Replace the rubber boot, if it is cracked or broken.

8. Lubricate all of the new parts in clean brake fluid and reassemble in the reverse order of disassembly, taking note of the following:

  a. Use care when reassembling the piston cup to prevent damaging the lipped portion of the piston cup.

  b. Fill the master cylinder with brake fluid and bleed the clutch hydraulic system.

HYDRAULIC SYSTEM BLEEDING

▶ SEE FIG. 46

1. Check and fill the clutch fluid reservoir to the specified level, as necessary.

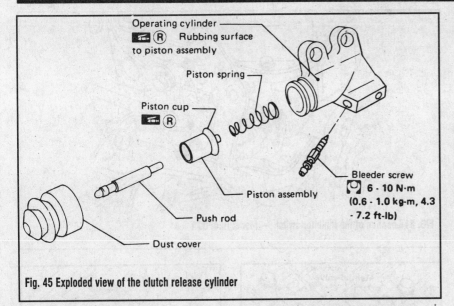

Fig. 45 Exploded view of the clutch release cylinder

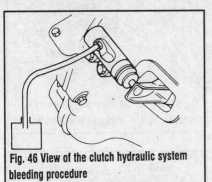

Fig. 46 View of the clutch hydraulic system bleeding procedure

➡ **Take precautionary measures to prevent the brake fluid from getting on any painted surfaces.**

3. Pump the clutch pedal SLOWLY several times, hold it down and loosen the bleeder screw.

4. Tighten the bleeder screw and release the clutch pedal gradually.

➡ **Repeat this operation until air bubbles disappear from the brake fluid being expelled out through the bleeder screw.**

5. Repeat until all evidence of air bubbles completely disappears from the brake fluid being pumped out through the tube.

6. When the air is completely removed, securely tighten the bleeder screw and replace the dust cap.

7. Check and refill the master cylinder reservoir, as necessary.

8. Depress the clutch pedal several times to check the operation of the clutch and check for leaks.

➡ **During the bleeding process, continue to check and replenish the reservoir to prevent the fluid level from getting lower than 1/2 the specified level.**

2. Remove the dust cap from the bleeder screw on the clutch slave cylinder and connect a tube to the bleeder screw and insert the other end of the tube into a clean glass or metal container.

AUTOMATIC TRANSAXLE

Identification

♦ SEE FIGS. 47 AND 48

The automatic transaxle serial number label is attached to the upper portion of the automatic transaxle oil pan for models RL4F02A and RE4F02A or to the upper right side of the transaxle for model RE4F02V.

Fig. 48 Location of the transaxle serial number — model RE4F02V

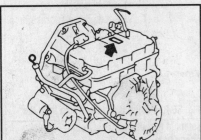

Fig. 47 Location of the transaxle serial number — models RL4F02A and RE4F02A

Control Valve Assembly

REMOVAL & INSTALLATION

Model RL4F02A

♦ SEE FIGS. 49 AND 50

1. Remove the battery and its bracket.

2. Remove the air cleaner, the air flow meter, the air damper and the solenoid valves, all as an assembly; be careful not to damage the air flow meter.

3. Disconnect the control cable and the throttle wire. Remove the throttle lever.

4. Remove the control cylinder.

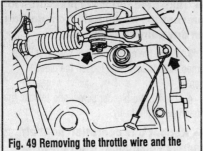

Fig. 49 Removing the throttle wire and the throttle lever — Model RL4F02A transaxle

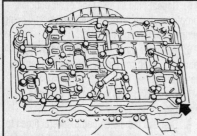

Fig. 50 Installing the control valve assembly bolts — Model RL4F02A transaxle

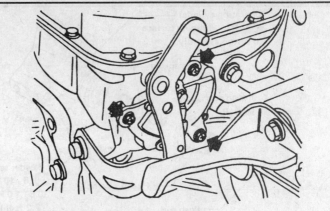

FIG. 51 Location of the inhibitor switch — Model RE4F02A

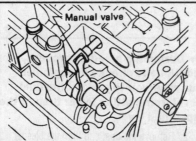

Fig. 52 View of the control valve assembly's manual valve — Model RE4F02A transaxle

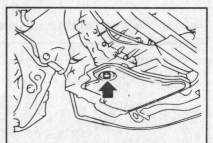

Fig. 53 Remove the drain plug to drain the transaxle fluid — Model RE4F04V transaxle

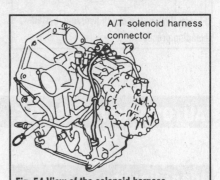

Fig. 54 View of the solenoid harness connector — Model RE4F04V transaxle

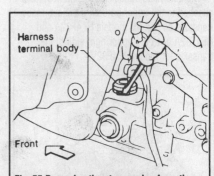

Fig. 55 Removing the stopper ring from the solenoid harness terminal body — Model RE4F04V transaxle

5. Disconnect the electrical harness connector from the control valve assembly.

6. Remove the control valve assembly-to-transaxle bolts and remove the assembly; be careful not to drop the manual valve out of the valve body.

7. Disassemble, inspect and assemble the control valve assembly.

To install:

8. Set the manual shaft in **N**, then align the manual plate with the groove in the manual valve of the control valve assembly.

9. Install the control valve assembly and torque the assembly-to-transaxle bolts to 5.1–6.5 ft. lbs. (7–9 Nm) for non-arrowed bolts or 2.7–3.7 ft. lbs. (3.7–5.0 Nm) for arrowed bolts.

10. Connect the electrical harness connector to the control valve assembly.

11. Install the control cylinder.

12. Install the throttle lever. Connect the control cable and the throttle wire.

13. Install the air cleaner, the air flow meter, the air damper and the solenoid valves, all as an assembly.

14. Install the battery and its bracket.

15. Check and/or refill the transaxle to the correct level.

Model RE4F02A

♦ SEE FIGS. 51 AND 52

1. Remove the air cleaner, the battery and its bracket.

2. Remove the control valve cover-to-transaxle bolts and the cover.

➥ **If the cover sticks, bump it with a soft hammer to break it loose.**

3. Disconnect the electrical harness connectors from the control valve assembly.

4. Remove the control valve-to-transaxle bolts and lift the control valve assembly from the transaxle; be careful not to drop the manual valve out the the valve body.

To install:

5. Using a putty knife, clean the gasket mounting surfaces.

6. Install the control valve assembly into the transaxle and torque the assembly-to-transaxle screws to 5.1–6.5 ft. lbs. (7–9 Nm) for non-arrowed bolts or 2.7–3.7 ft. lbs. (3.7–5.0 Nm) for arrowed bolts.

7. Connect the electrical connectors to the control valve assembly.

8. Using a new gasket and sealant, install the control valve cover and torque the cover-to-transaxle bolts to 3.6–5.1 ft. lbs. (5–7 Nm).

9. Check and/or refill the transaxle to the correct level.

Model RE4F04V

♦ SEE FIGS. 53-58

1. Raise and safely support the vehicle.

2. Remove the drain plug and drain the fluid from the transaxle.

3. Remove the oil pan and gasket.

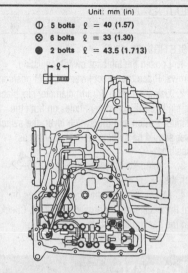

Unit: mm (in)

① 5 bolts ℓ = 40 (1.57)
⊗ 6 bolts ℓ = 33 (1.30)
● 2 bolts ℓ = 43.5 (1.713)

Fig. 56 View of the control valve assembly bolts — Model RE4F04V transaxle

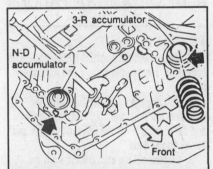

Fig. 57 Using compressed air to remove the 3-R and N-D accumulators — Model RE4F04V transaxle

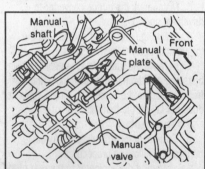

Fig. 58 Positioning the manual shaft in neutral and aligning the manual plate with the groove in the manual valve — Model RE4F04V transaxle

4. Disconnect the solenoid harness connector from the top of the transaxle.

5. Using a small prybar, remove the stopper ring from the solenoid harness terminal body.

6. Push on the terminal body to remove the solenoid harness from the transaxle case.

7. Remove the control valve assembly-to-transaxle bolts and the control assembly; be careful not to drop the manual valve, the tube connector, the tubes and the 3-R accumulator return spring.

8. If necessary, disassemble and inspect the control valve assembly.

9. If necessary, use compressed air to remove the 3-R and N-D accumulators; be sure to hold each piston with a rag to prevent damaging the part.

To install:

10. If the 3-R and N-D accumulators were removed, install them.

11. If the control valve assembly was disassembled, reassemble it.

12. Install the control valve assembly to the transaxle.

13. Position the manual shaft in neutral and align the manual plate with the groove in the manual valve.

14. Press on the solenoid harness to install it into the transaxle case.

15. Install the stopper ring into the solenoid harness terminal body.

16. Connect the solenoid harness connector to the top of the transaxle.

17. Using a new gasket, install the oil pan. Refill the transaxle.

Revolution Sensor

REMOVAL & INSTALLATION

Model RE4F04V

♦ SEE FIG. 59

1. Remove the revolution sensor-to-transaxle cover.

2. Remove the revolution sensor from the transaxle.

3. To install, use a new gasket and sealant and reverse the removal procedures.

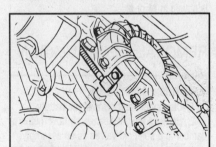

Fig. 59 View of the revolution sensor cover — Model RE4F04V transaxle

Differential Side Oil Seal

REMOVAL & INSTALLATION

♦ SEE FIGS. 60 AND 61

1. Raise and safely support the vehicle.

2. Remove the left halfshaft from the transaxle.

3. Using the seal removal tool J-34286 or equivalent, remove the oil seal from the transaxle.

To install:

4. Lubricate the oil seal surface with automatic transmission fluid.

5. Using an oil seal drift, drive the new oil seal into the transaxle.

6. Install the left halfshaft into the transaxle.

Adjustments

SHIFT SELECTOR

♦ SEE FIG. 62

1. Move the selector from the **P** to the **1** range; you should be able to feel the detents in each range.

➡ **If the detents cannot be felt or the pointer indicating the range is improperly aligned, the control cable needs to be adjusted.**

2. Place the selector lever in the **P** range.

3. Connect the control cable end to the manual lever in the transaxle unit and tighten the control cable bolts.

4. Move the selector lever from **P** to **1** range; make sure the selector lever can move smoothly and without any sliding noise.

5. Place the selector lever in the **P** range again.

6. Make sure the control lever locks in the **P** range.

7. Raise and safely support the vehicle.

8. Loosen the control lever locknuts.

9. Turn locknut **X** until it touches the select rod end while holding the select rod horizontal and tighten locknut **Y**.

10. Move the selector lever from **P** to **1** range; make sure the selector lever can move smoothly and without any sliding noise.

11. Apply grease to the contacting areas of the selector lever and the select rod.

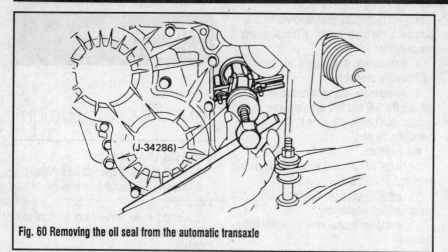

Fig. 60 Removing the oil seal from the automatic transaxle

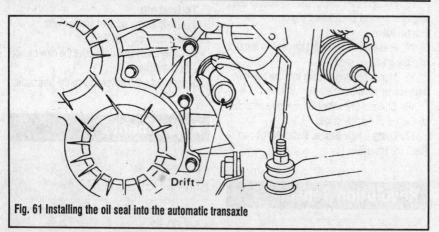

Fig. 61 Installing the oil seal into the automatic transaxle

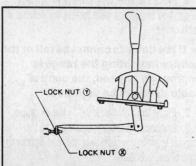

Fig. 62 View of the shifter selector adjusting locknuts — automatic transaxle

THROTTLE CABLE

♦ SEE FIG. 63

The throttle cable is operated via a cam on the throttle shaft of the injection unit. The adjustment is located on the side of the air intake plenum.

1. Loosen the 2 locknuts that position the cable. Open the throttle lever and hold it at the fully open position.

2. Back off both locknuts. Slide the outer cable as far as it will go away from the throttle cam.

3. Turn the nut, on the side away from the throttle, until it just starts to hold. Then, back it off ³/₄–1¹/₄ revolutions. Tighten the nut on the throttle side to lock this position securely.

Inhibitor Switch

The inhibitor switch allows the backup lights to work when the transaxle is placed in **R** range and acts as a neutral switch, by allowing the current to pass to the starter when the transaxle is placed in **N** or **P**.

REMOVAL & INSTALLATION

♦ SEE FIGS. 64 AND 65

1. Disconnect and remove the battery.

2. Remove the air cleaner, air flow meter, air damper and solenoid valves as an assembly.

3. Remove the control cable end from the unit.

4. Disconnect the electrical harness. Remove the inhibitor switch retaining bolts and the inhibitor switch.

5. To install, reverse the removal procedures and adjust the switch.

ADJUSTMENT

♦ SEE FIGS. 66–68

1. Loosen the inhibitor switch adjusting screws. Place the select lever in the **N** position.

2. Using a 0.16 in. (4mm) diameter pin, place the pin into the adjustment holes on both the inhibitor switch and the switch lever; the switch lever should be as near vertical position as possible.

3. Tighten the adjusting screws to 16–22 inch lbs.

4. Make sure while holding the brakes on, that the engine will start only in **P** or **N**. Check that the backup lights turn ON only in **R**.

Transaxle

REMOVAL & INSTALLATION

♦ SEE FIGS. 69–72

1. Disconnect the negative battery cables. If necessary, remove the battery and the battery tray.

2. Remove the oil cooler lines from the transaxle and drain the fluid from the transaxle and the radiator. Plug the transaxle fittings and the oil cooler lines.

3. Disconnect the shift linkage from the transaxle. If equipped, disconnect the electrical harness connector from the transaxle.

4. Refer to Section 3 and remove the engine and transaxle as an assembly.

5. Matchmark the torque converter-to-driveplate position.

6. Rotate the crankshaft and remove the torque converter-to-flywheel bolts.

7. Remove the transaxle assembly-to-engine bolts and pull the transaxle assembly rearward from the engine; be careful the torque converter does not fall off the transaxle's shaft.

To inspect:

8. To inspect the driveplate for runout, perform the following procedures:

   a. Mount a dial indicator to the rear of the engine and zero the indicator.

   b. Rotate the crankshaft and measure the runout at various positions on the driveplate.

   c. The runout should be less than 0.020 in. (0.5mm); if not, replace the driveplate and ring gear.

9. Using a straight-edge and a ruler, measure the torque converter-to-transaxle recessed depth, it should be:

• 1985–88 — 0.689–0.787 in. (17.5–20.0mm)

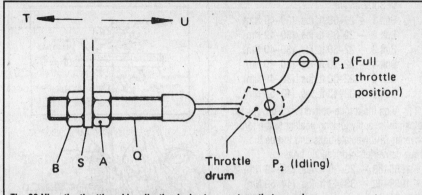

Fig. 63 View the throttle cable adjusting locknuts — automatic transaxle

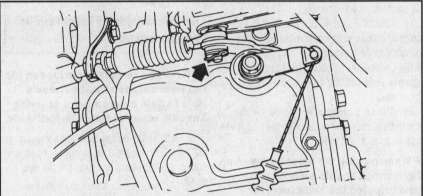

Fig. 64 View of the inhibitor switch control cable end — 1985-91 automatic transaxle

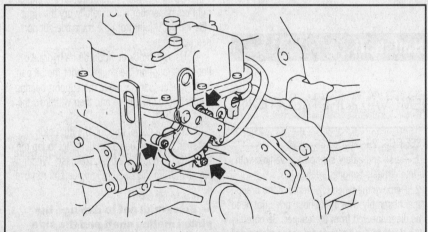

Fig. 65 View of the inhibitor switch — 1985-91 vehicles with an automatic transaxle

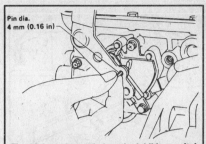

Fig. 66 Inserting a pin into the inhibitor switch adjustment holes — 1985-91 vehicles with an automatic transaxle

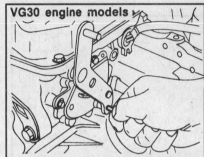

Fig. 67 Inserting a pin into the inhibitor switch adjustment holes — 1992 vehicles with a VG30E engine and an automatic transaxle

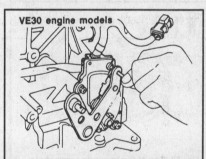

Fig. 68 Inserting a pin into the inhibitor switch adjustment holes — 1992 vehicles with a VE30DE engine and an automatic transaxle

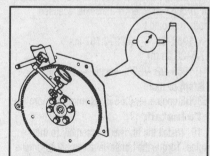

Fig. 69 Using a dial indicator to inspect the driveplate runout

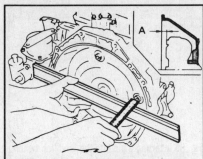

Fig. 70 Using a straight-edge and a ruler to measure the torque converter-to-transaxle recess.

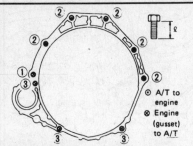

Fig. 71 View of the transaxle assembly-to-engine bolt No. identifications — 1989–92 VG30E engine

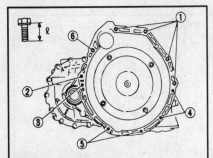

Fig. 72 View of the transaxle assembly-to-engine bolt No. identifications — 1992 VE30DE engine

9. Using a straight-edge and a ruler, measure the torque converter-to-transaxle recessed depth, it should be:
- 1985–88 — 0.689–0.787 in. (17.5–20.0mm)
- 1989–92: VG30E engine — 0.71 in. (18mm) or more

VE30DE engine — 0.55 in. (14mm) or more

To install:

10. Install the transaxle assembly to the engine. Torque the transaxle assembly-to-engine bolts, as follows:
- 1985–88 — 29–36 ft. lbs. (39–49 Nm)
- 1989–92: VG30E engine:
  - Bolt 1 — 22–30 ft. lbs. (30–40 Nm)
  - Bolt 2 — 29–36 ft. lbs. (39–49 Nm)
  - Bolt 3 — 22–30 ft. lbs. (30–40 Nm)

VE30DE engine:
- Bolt 1 — 29–36 ft. lbs. (39–49 Nm)
- Bolt 2 — 29–36 ft. lbs. (39–49 Nm)
- Bolt 3 — 22–30 ft. lbs. (30–40 Nm)
- Bolt 4 — 22–30 ft. lbs. (30–40 Nm)
- Bolt 5 — 22–30 ft. lbs. (30–40 Nm)
- Bolt 6 — 32–43 ft. lbs. (43–58 Nm)

11. Align the torque converter-to-driveplate matchmarks, apply locking sealant to the torque converter-to-driveplate bolts and torque the torque converter-to-driveplate bolts to:
- 1985–88 — 29–36 ft. lbs. (39–49 Nm)
- 1989–92 — 33–43 ft. lbs. (44–59 Nm)

12. Rotate the crankshaft several revolutions to make sure the transaxle rotates freely.

13. Refer to Section 3 and install the engine and transaxle as an assembly.

14. Adjust the neutral safety switch. If equipped with an electrical harness connector, connect it to the transaxle.

15. Connect the oil cooler lines to the transaxle. Refill with the correct fluid to the proper level.

16. With the parking brake applied and the engine idling, move the selector lever through **N** to **D**, to **2**, to **1** and to **R**.

➡ **When moving the selector lever, a slight shock should be felt by the hand gripping the selector lever each time the transaxle is shifted.**

17. Test drive the vehicle and check its operation.

Halfshaft

REMOVAL & INSTALLATION

◆ SEE FIGS. 29–31 AND 35

1. Raise and safely support the vehicle with the front wheels hanging freely.

2. Remove the wheel(s). Remove the brake caliper assembly. The brake hose does not need to be disconnected from the caliper. Be careful not to depress the brake pedal or the piston will pop out. Do not twist the brake hose.

3. Pull out the cotter pin from the castellated nut on the wheel hub and then remove the wheel bearing locknut.

➡ **Cover the boots with a shop towel or waste cloth so not to damage them when removing the halfshaft.**

4. Separate the halfshaft from the steering knuckle by tapping it with a block of wood and a mallet.

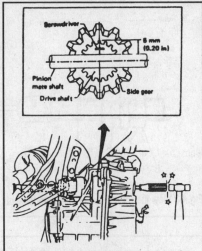

Fig. 35 Removing the left halfshaft from the automatic transaxle

➡ **It may be necessary to loosen (do not remove) the strut-to-chassis nuts to gain clearance for steering knuckle removal from the halfshaft.**

5. Remove the tie rod-to-steering knuckle ball joint. Remove the 3 lower ball joint-to-lower control arm nuts/bolts and then pull the arm down.

➡ **Always use a new nut when replacing the tie rod ball joint.**

6. Using a prybar, reach through the engine right crossmember and carefully pry the right side inner CV-joint from the transaxle support bearing flange.

7. Using a block of wood on an hydraulic floor jack, support the engine under the oil pan.

8. If necessary, remove the support bearing bracket from the engine and then withdraw the right halfshaft.

9. Insert a dowel through the right side halfshaft hole and use a small mallet to tap the left halfshaft out of the transaxle case. Withdraw the shaft from the steering knuckle and remove it.

➡ **Be careful not to damage the pinion mating shaft and the side gear while tapping the left halfshaft out of the transaxle case.**

To install:

10. When installing the shafts into the transaxle, use a new oil seal and then install an alignment tool, KV38106700 for the left side or KV38106800 for the right side, along the inner circumference of the oil seal.

11. Insert the halfshaft into the transaxle, align the serrations and then remove the alignment tool.

12. Push the halfshaft, then press-fit the circular clip on the shaft into the clip groove on the side gear.

➡ **After insertion, attempt to pull the flange out of the side joint to make sure the circular clip is properly seated in the side gear and will not come out.**

13. Install support bearing bracket bolts and tighten the bolts. Insert the halfshaft in the steering knuckle. Tighten the strut mounting bolts to 23–31 ft. lbs. (31–42 Nm) for 1985–88 or 29–40 ft. lbs. (39–54 Nm) for 1989–92, if loosened.

14. Connect the lower ball joint and tie rod end in the correct position. torque the lower ball joint-to-control arm nuts to 56–80 ft. lbs. (76–109 Nm) and the tie rod end-to-steering knuckle nut to 22–29 ft. lbs. (29–39 Nm).

15. Install the caliper assembly and the wheel bearing locknut. Tighten the nut to 174–231 ft. lbs. (235–314 Nm).

16. Install a new cotter pin on the wheel hub and install the wheel.

17. If the brake hose was disconnected, bleed the brake system. Road test the vehicle for proper operation.

CV-JOINT OVERHAUL

Transaxle Side

◆ SEE FIG. 34

1. Remove boot bands.

2. Before separating the joint assembly, matchmark slide joint housing and inner race.

3. Pry off snapring **A** and pull out the slide joint housing.

➡ **Cover driveshaft serration with tape so not to damage the boot.**

4. Place matchmarks on the inner race and the halfshaft.

5. Pry off snapring **C**. Remove the ball cage, the inner race and the balls as a unit.

6. Pry off snapring **B** and remove the boot.

To Install:

7. Install the boot and a new snapring **B**.

8. Install the ball cage, the inner race and the balls as a unit. Install a new snapring **C**.

9. Align the inner race and halfshaft matchmarks, then, install the slide joint housing.

10. Install a new snapring **A**. Install the boot and secure with bands.

Wheel Side

➡ **The joint on the wheel side cannot be disassembled.**

1. Matchmark the halfshaft and the joint assembly.

2. Separate joint assembly with suitable tool.

3. Remove boot bands.

To Install:

4. Install boot with new boot bands.

5. Align matchmarks and lightly tap joint assembly onto the shaft.

6. Pack halfshaft with grease.

7. Lock both boot band clamps.

TORQUE SPECIFICATIONS

Component	English	Metric
Automatic transaxle assembly-to-engine bolts		
1985–88	29–36 ft. lbs.	39–49 Nm
1989–92:		
VG30E engine:		
Bolt 1	22–30 ft. lbs.	30–40 Nm
Bolt 2	29–36 ft. lbs.	39–49 Nm
Bolt 3	22–30 ft. lbs.	30–40 Nm
VE30DE engine:		
Bolt 1	29–36 ft. lbs.	39–49 Nm
Bolt 2	29–36 ft. lbs.	39–49 Nm
Bolt 3	22–30 ft. lbs.	30–40 Nm
Bolt 4	22–30 ft. lbs.	30–40 Nm
Bolt 5	22–30 ft. lbs.	30–40 Nm
Bolt 6	32–43 ft. lbs.	43–58 Nm
Clutch master cylinder-to-chassis nuts/ bolts	5.8–8.0 ft. lbs.	8–11 Nm
Clutch pressure plate bolts		
1985–91	16–22 ft. lbs.	22–29 Nm
1992	25–33 ft. lbs.	34–44 Nm
Clutch slave cylinder bolts	22–30 ft. lbs.	30–40 Nm
Control valve assembly-to-transaxle bolts		
Model RL4F02A		
Non-arrowed bolts	5.1–6.5 ft. lbs.	7–9 Nm
Arrowed bolts	2.7–3.7 ft. lbs.	3.7–5.0 Nm
Model RE4F02A		
Non-arrowed bolts	5.1–6.5 ft. lbs.	7–9 Nm
Arrowed bolts	2.7–3.7 ft. lbs.	3.7–5.0 Nm
Control valve cover-to-transaxle bolts		
Model RE4F02A	3.6–5.1 ft. lbs.	5–7 Nm
Final gear-to-final drive assembly bolts	65–76 ft. lbs.	88–103 Nm
Lower ball joint-to-control arm nuts	56–80 ft. lbs.	76–109 Nm
Strut mounting bolts:		
1985–88	23–31 ft. lbs.	31–42 Nm
1989–92	29–40 ft. lbs.	39–54 Nm
Tie rod end-to-steering knuckle nut	22–29 ft. lbs.	29–39 Nm
Torque converter-to-driveplate bolts:		
1985–88	29–36 ft. lbs.	39–49 Nm
1989–92	33–43 ft. lbs.	44–59 Nm
Wheel bearing locknut	174–231 ft. lbs.	235–314 Nm

Troubleshooting the Manual Transmission

Problem	Cause	Solution
Transmission shifts hard	• Clutch adjustment incorrect • Clutch linkage or cable binding • Shift rail binding	• Adjust clutch • Lubricate or repair as necessary • Check for mispositioned selector arm roll pin, loose cover bolts, worn shift rail bores, worn shift rail, distorted oil seal, or extension housing not aligned with case. Repair as necessary.
	• Internal bind in transmission caused by shift forks, selector plates, or synchronizer assemblies • Clutch housing misalignment • Incorrect lubricant • Block rings and/or cone seats worn	• Remove, dissemble and inspect transmission. Replace worn or damaged components as necessary. • Check runout at rear face of clutch housing • Drain and refill transmission • Blocking ring to gear clutch tooth face clearance must be 0.030 inch or greater. If clearance is correct it may still be necessary to inspect blocking rings and cone seats for excessive wear. Repair as necessary.
Gear clash when shifting from one gear to another	• Clutch adjustment incorrect • Clutch linkage or cable binding • Clutch housing misalignment • Lubricant level low or incorrect lubricant • Gearshift components, or synchronizer assemblies worn or damaged	• Adjust clutch • Lubricate or repair as necessary • Check runout at rear of clutch housing • Drain and refill transmission and check for lubricant leaks if level was low. Repair as necessary. • Remove, disassemble and inspect transmission. Replace worn or damaged components as necessary.
Transmission noisy	• Lubricant level low or incorrect lubricant • Clutch housing-to-engine, or transmission-to-clutch housing bolts loose • Dirt, chips, foreign material in transmission • Gearshift mechanism, transmission gears, or bearing components worn or damaged • Clutch housing misalignment	• Drain and refill transmission. If lubricant level was low, check for leaks and repair as necessary. • Check and correct bolt torque as necessary • Drain, flush, and refill transmission • Remove, disassemble and inspect transmission. Replace worn or damaged components as necessary. • Check runout at rear face of clutch housing

Troubleshooting the Manual Transmission

Problem	Cause	Solution
Jumps out of gear	• Clutch housing misalignment	• Check runout at rear face of clutch housing
	• Gearshift lever loose	• Check lever for worn fork. Tighten loose attaching bolts.
	• Offset lever nylon insert worn or lever attaching nut loose	• Remove gearshift lever and check for loose offset lever nut or worn insert. Repair or replace as necessary.
	• Gearshift mechanism, shift forks, selector plates, interlock plate, selector arm, shift rail, detent plugs, springs or shift cover worn or damaged	• Remove, disassemble and inspect transmission cover assembly. Replace worn or damaged components as necessary.
	• Clutch shaft or roller bearings worn or damaged	• Replace clutch shaft or roller bearings as necessary
Jumps out of gear (cont.)	• Gear teeth worn or tapered, synchronizer assemblies worn or damaged, excessive end play caused by worn thrust washers or output shaft gears	• Remove, disassemble, and inspect transmission. Replace worn or damaged components as necessary.
	• Pilot bushing worn	• Replace pilot bushing
Will not shift into one gear	• Gearshift selector plates, interlock plate, or selector arm, worn, damaged, or incorrectly assembled	• Remove, disassemble, and inspect transmission cover assembly. Repair or replace components as necessary.
	• Shift rail detent plunger worn, spring broken, or plug loose	• Tighten plug or replace worn or damaged components as necessary
	• Gearshift lever worn or damaged	• Replace gearshift lever
	• Synchronizer sleeves or hubs, damaged or worn	• Remove, disassemble and inspect transmission. Replace worn or damaged components.
Locked in one gear—cannot be shifted out	• Shift rail(s) worn or broken, shifter fork bent, setscrew loose, center detent plug missing or worn	• Inspect and replace worn or damaged parts
	• Broken gear teeth on countershaft gear, clutch shaft, or reverse idler gear	• Inspect and replace damaged part
	Gearshift lever broken or worn, shift mechanism in cover incorrectly assembled or broken, worn damaged gear train components	• Disassemble transmission. Replace damaged parts or assemble correctly.

Troubleshooting Basic Clutch Problems

Problem	Cause
Excessive clutch noise	Throwout bearing noises are more audible at the lower end of pedal travel. The usual causes are: • Riding the clutch • Too little pedal free-play • Lack of bearing lubrication A bad clutch shaft pilot bearing will make a high pitched squeal, when the clutch is disengaged and the transmission is in gear or within the first 2″ of pedal travel. The bearing must be replaced. Noise from the clutch linkage is a clicking or snapping that can be heard or felt as the pedal is moved completely up or down. This usually requires lubrication. Transmitted engine noises are amplified by the clutch housing and heard in the passenger compartment. They are usually the result of insufficient pedal free-play and can be changed by manipulating the clutch pedal.
Clutch slips (the car does not move as it should when the clutch is engaged)	This is usually most noticeable when pulling away from a standing start. A severe test is to start the engine, apply the brakes, shift into high gear and SLOWLY release the clutch pedal. A healthy clutch will stall the engine. If it slips it may be due to: • A worn pressure plate or clutch plate • Oil soaked clutch plate • Insufficient pedal free-play
Clutch drags or fails to release	The clutch disc and some transmission gears spin briefly after clutch disengagement. Under normal conditions in average temperatures, 3 seconds is maximum spin-time. Failure to release properly can be caused by: • Too light transmission lubricant or low lubricant level • Improperly adjusted clutch linkage
Low clutch life	Low clutch life is usually a result of poor driving habits or heavy duty use. Riding the clutch, pulling heavy loads, holding the car on a grade with the clutch instead of the brakes and rapid clutch engagement all contribute to low clutch life.

Troubleshooting Basic Automatic Transmission Problems

Problem	Cause	Solution
Fluid leakage	• Defective pan gasket	• Replace gasket or tighten pan bolts
	• Loose filler tube	• Tighten tube nut
	• Loose extension housing to transmission case	• Tighten bolts
	• Converter housing area leakage	• Have transmission checked professionally
Fluid flows out the oil filler tube	• High fluid level	• Check and correct fluid level
	• Breather vent clogged	• Open breather vent
	• Clogged oil filter or screen	• Replace filter or clean screen (change fluid also)
	• Internal fluid leakage	• Have transmission checked professionally
Transmission overheats (this is usually accompanied by a strong burned odor to the fluid)	• Low fluid level	• Check and correct fluid level
	• Fluid cooler lines clogged	• Drain and refill transmission. If this doesn't cure the problem, have cooler lines cleared or replaced.
	• Heavy pulling or hauling with insufficient cooling	• Install a transmission oil cooler
	• Faulty oil pump, internal slippage	• Have transmission checked professionally
Buzzing or whining noise	• Low fluid level	• Check and correct fluid level
	• Defective torque converter, scored gears	• Have transmission checked professionally
No forward or reverse gears or slippage in one or more gears	• Low fluid level	• Check and correct fluid level
	• Defective vacuum or linkage controls, internal clutch or band failure	• Have unit checked professionally
Delayed or erratic shift	• Low fluid level	• Check and correct fluid level
	• Broken vacuum lines	• Repair or replace lines
	• Internal malfunction	• Have transmission checked professionally

Lockup Torque Converter Service Diagnosis

Problem	Cause	Solution

No lockup	• Faulty oil pump
	• Sticking governor valve
	• Valve body malfunction
	  (a) Stuck switch valve
	  (b) Stuck lockup valve
	  (c) Stuck fail-safe valve
	• Failed locking clutch
	• Leaking turbine hub seal
	• Faulty input shaft or seal ring
		• Replace oil pump
		• Repair or replace as necessary
		• Repair or replace valve body or its internal components as necessary
		
		• Replace torque converter
		• Replace torque converter
		• Repair or replace as necessary

Will not unlock	• Sticking governor valve
	• Valve body malfunction
	  (a) Stuck switch valve
	  (b) Stuck lockup valve
	  (c) Stuck fail-safe valve
		• Repair or replace as necessary
		• Repair or replace valve body or its internal components as necessary

Stays locked up at too low a speed in direct	• Sticking governor valve
	• Valve body malfunction
	  (a) Stuck switch valve
	  (b) Stuck lockup valve
	  (c) Stuck fail-safe valve
		• Repair or replace as necessary
		• Repair or replace valve body or its internal components as necessary

Locks up or drags in low or second	• Faulty oil pump
	• Valve body malfunction
	  (a) Stuck switch valve
	  (b) Stuck fail-safe valve
		• Replace oil pump
		• Repair or replace valve body or its internal components as necessary

Sluggish or stalls in reverse	• Faulty oil pump
	• Plugged cooler, cooler lines or fittings
	• Valve body malfunction
	  (a) Stuck switch valve
	  (b) Faulty input shaft or seal ring
		• Replace oil pump as necessary
		• Flush or replace cooler and flush lines and fittings
		• Repair or replace valve body or its internal components as necessary

Loud chatter during lockup engagement (cold)	• Faulty torque converter • Failed locking clutch • Leaking turbine hub seal	• Replace torque converter • Replace torque converter • Replace torque converter
Vibration or shudder during lockup engagement	• Faulty oil pump • Valve body malfunction • Faulty torque converter • Engine needs tune-up	• Repair or replace oil pump as necessary • Repair or replace valve body or its internal components as necessary • Replace torque converter • Tune engine
Vibration after lockup engagement	• Faulty torque converter • Exhaust system strikes underbody • Engine needs tune-up • Throttle linkage misadjusted	• Replace torque converter • Align exhaust system • Tune engine • Adjust throttle linkage

Lockup Torque Converter Service Diagnosis

Problem	Cause	Solution
Vibration when revved in neutral Overheating: oil blows out of dip stick tube or pump seal	• Torque converter out of balance • Plugged cooler, cooler lines or fittings • Stuck switch valve	• Replace torque converter • Flush or replace cooler and flush lines and fittings • Repair switch valve in valve body or replace valve body
Shudder after lockup engagement	• Faulty oil pump • Plugged cooler, cooler lines or fittings • Valve body malfunction • Faulty torque converter • Fail locking clutch • Exhaust system strikes underbody • Engine needs tune-up • Throttle linkage misadjusted	• Replace oil pump • Flush or replace cooler and flush lines and fittings • Repair or replace valve body or its internal components as necessary • Replace torque converter • Replace torque converter • Align exhaust system • Tune engine • Adjust throttle linkage

Transmission Fluid Indications

The appearance and odor of the transmission fluid can give valuable clues to the overall condition of the transmission. Always note the appearance of the fluid when you check the fluid level or change the fluid. Rub a small amount of fluid between your fingers to feel for grit and smell the fluid on the dipstick.

If the fluid appears:	It indicates:
Clear and red colored	• Normal operation
Discolored (extremely dark red or brownish) or smells burned	• Band or clutch pack failure, usually caused by an overheated transmission. Hauling very heavy loads with insufficient power or failure to change the fluid, often result in overheating. Do not confuse this appearance with newer fluids that have a darker red color and a strong odor (though not a burned odor).
Foamy or aerated (light in color and full of bubbles)	• The level is too high (gear train is churning oil) • An internal air leak (air is mixing with the fluid). Have the transmission checked professionally.
Solid residue in the fluid	• Defective bands, clutch pack or bearings. Bits of band material or metal abrasives are clinging to the dipstick. Have the transmission checked professionally.
Varnish coating on the dipstick	• The transmission fluid is overheating

8

SUSPENSION AND STEERING

WHEELS

Wheels

REMOVAL & INSTALLATION

1. If using a lug wrench, loosen the lug nuts before raising the vehicle.
2. Raise and safely support the vehicle.
3. Remove the lug nuts and wheel from the vehicle.

To install:

4. Install the wheel and hand tighten the lug nuts until they are snug.
5. Lower the vehicle and torque the lug nuts to 58–72 ft. lbs. (78–98 Nm) for 1985–86 or 72–87 ft. lbs. (98–118 Nm) for 1987–92.

Wheel Lug Studs

REMOVAL & INSTALLATION

Front

1. Raise and safely support the vehicle.
2. Remove the front wheel.
3. Remove the front brake caliper and support it with a wire; do not disconnect the brake hose from the caliper.
4. Remove the brake caliper support from the steering knuckle. Remove the brake rotor.
5. Rotate the wheel hub so the damaged wheel stud is positioned with the open position of the steering knuckle.
6. Using a drift punch and a hammer, drive the damaged wheel stud from the wheel hub.

To install:

7. Install the new lug bolt and draw the new wheel stud into place, using the wheel nut and a stack of washers.

8. Install the brake rotor and the caliper support onto the steering knuckle.
9. Install the front brake caliper assembly onto the caliper support.
10. Install the wheel and torque the lug nuts to 58–72 ft. lbs. (78–98 Nm) for 1985–86 or 72–87 ft. lbs. (98–118 Nm) for 1987–92.
11. Road test the vehicle.

Rear

DRUM BRAKES

1. Raise the vehicle and support safely.
2. Remove the wheel.
3. Remove the brake drum from the vehicle, as outlined in Section 9.
4. Remove the grease cap, cotter pin, hub nut, washer and wheel hub; be sure to plug the wheel bearing opening with a clean cloth to keep dirt out of the bearing.
5. Using a press or a hammer and a drift punch, drive the damaged lug bolt(s) from the wheel hub.

To install:

6. Using a lug nut and a stack of washers, draw the lug bolt(s) into the wheel hub.
7. Install the wheel hub, the washer and the hub nut. Torque the wheel bearing hub nut to 137–188 ft. lbs. (186–255 Nm).
8. Install the brake drum onto the wheel hub as outlined in Section 9.
9. Install the wheel and torque the lug nuts to 72–87 ft. lbs. (98–118 Nm).
10. Lower the vehicle and road test.

REAR DISC BRAKES

1985–88

1. Raise and safely support the vehicle.
2. Remove the rear wheel.
3. Remove the caliper and the caliper support; be sure to support the caliper on a wire.

4. Remove the center bearing cap, cotter pin, adjusting cap, hub nut, washer and outside wheel bearing.
5. Remove the rotor/wheel hub assembly from the vehicle. Drive the lug bolt out with a hammer and drift punch or a shop press.

To install:

6. Install the new lug bolt and draw the new wheel stud into place, using the wheel nut and a stack of washers.
7. Install the rotor/wheel hub assembly onto the vehicle and torque the hub nut to 6.5–8.7 ft. lbs. (9–12 Nm) for 1985–86 or 18–25 ft. lbs. (25–34 Nm) for 1987–88.
8. Install a new cotter pin, grease cap, rear wheel, lug nuts and lower the vehicle.
9. Torque the lug nuts to 58–72 ft. lbs. (78–98 Nm) for 1985–86 or 72–87 ft. lbs. (98–118 Nm) for 1987–88.
10. Road test the vehicle.

1989–92

1. Raise and safely support the vehicle.
2. Remove the rear wheel.
3. Remove the caliper and brake rotor as outlined in Section 9.
4. Remove the wheel lug bolt by tapping through with a hammer if there is enough clearance to remove the stud. If not, remove the center bearing cap, cotter pin and hub nut.
5. Remove the wheel hub from the vehicle. Drive the lug bolt out with a hammer and drift punch or a shop press.

To install:

6. Install the new lug bolt and draw the new wheel stud into place, using the wheel nut and a stack of washers.
7. If the wheel hub was removed, install it onto the vehicle and torque the hub nut to 137–188 ft. lbs. (186–255 Nm).
8. Install a new cotter pin, grease cap, rear wheel, lug nuts and lower the vehicle.
9. Torque the lug nuts to 72–87 ft. lbs. (98–118 Nm).
10. Road test the vehicle.

FRONT SUSPENSION

MacPherson Strut

REMOVAL & INSTALLATION

♦ SEE FIGS. 1–5

1. Disconnect the negative battery cable. If equipped with adjustable struts, disconnect the sub-harness connector at the strut tower.
2. Raise and safely support the vehicle.
3. Remove the wheel. Mark the position of the strut-to-steering knuckle location.
4. Detach the brake tube from the strut.
5. Support the control arm.
6. Remove the strut-to-steering knuckle bolts.

➡ **On the 1989–92 models equipped with adjustable struts, remove the shock absorber actuator-to-plate bolts and separate the actuator from the plate; the plate is located on top of the strut.**

7. Support the strut and remove the 3 upper strut-to-chassis nuts. Remove the strut from the vehicle.

To install:

8. Install the strut assembly onto the vehicle and torque the following:
Strut-to-body nuts:
1985–88 — 23–31 ft. lbs. (31–42 Nm)
1989–92 — 29–40 ft. lbs. (39–54 Nm)
Strut-to-knuckle bolts:
1985–88 — 82–91 ft. lbs. (112–124 Nm)
1989–92 — 116–123 ft. lbs. (157–167 Nm)
9. If equipped with a shock absorber actuator for 1989–92, install the actuator and torque the actuator-to-plate bolts to 2.2–2.8 ft. lbs. (2.9–3.8 Nm).
10. If brake hose was disconnected from the brake caliper, bleed brakes and install the wheel.
11. Connect the negative battery cable and the adjustable strut electrical connectors, if equipped.

STRUT CARTRIDGE REPLACEMENT

♦ SEE FIGS. 3-9

✳✳ CAUTION

The coil springs are under considerable tension and can exert enough force to cause serious injury. Disassemble the struts only using the proper tools and use extreme caution.

Coil springs must be removed with the aid of a coil spring compressor. If you don't have one, don't try to improvise by using something else: you could risk injury. The Nissan coil spring compressor is special tool HT71730000, which is a totally different unit. These are the recommended compressors, although they are probably not the only spring compressors which will work. Always follow manufacturer's instructions when operating a spring compressor.

1. Remove the strut assembly from the vehicle and secure assembly in a vise.
2. Attach the spring compressor to the spring, leaving the top few coils free.
3. Remove the dust cap from the top of the strut to expose the center nut, if a dust cap is provided.
4. Compress the spring just far enough to permit the strut insulator to be turned by hand. Remove the self locking center nut.
5. Take out the strut insulator, strut bearing, oil seal, upper spring seat and bound bumper rubber from the top of the strut. Note their sequence of removal and be sure to assemble them in the same order.
6. Remove the spring with the spring compressor still attached.

To assemble:

7. Reassemble the strut assembly and observe the following:
   a. Make sure you assemble the unit with the shock absorber piston rod fully extended.
   b. When assembling, take care that the rubber spring seats, both top and bottom, and the spring are positioned in their grooves before releasing the spring.

8. Torque the strut locknut to 51–65 ft. lbs. (69–88 Nm) for 1985–88 or 30–39 ft. lbs. (41–53 Nm) for 1989–92.

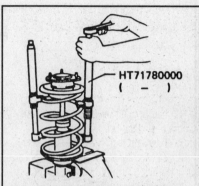

Fig. 6 Using the coil spring compressor to contract and secure the strut coil spring

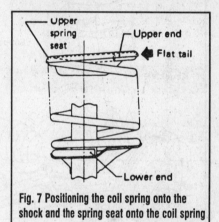

Fig. 7 Positioning the coil spring onto the shock and the spring seat onto the coil spring

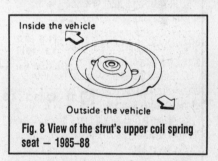

Fig. 8 View of the strut's upper coil spring seat — 1985–88

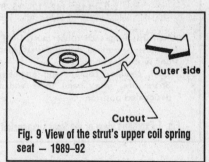

Fig. 9 View of the strut's upper coil spring seat — 1989–92

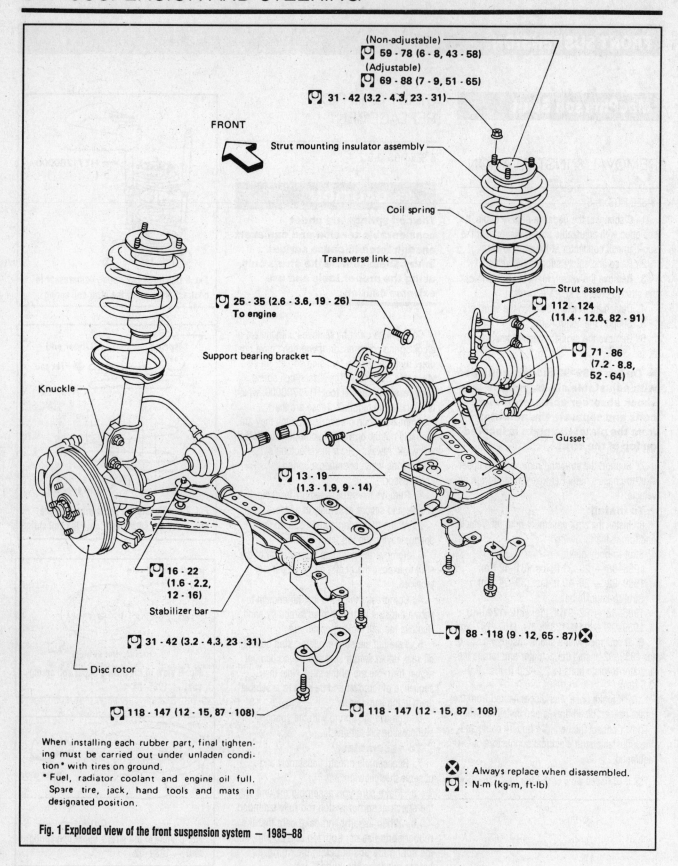

(Non-adjustable)
59 - 78 (6 - 8, 43 - 58)
(Adjustable)
69 - 88 (7 - 9, 51 - 65)

31 - 42 (3.2 - 4.3, 23 - 31)

FRONT

Strut mounting insulator assembly

Coil spring

Transverse link

25 - 35 (2.6 - 3.6, 19 - 26)
To engine

Strut assembly

112 - 124 (11.4 - 12.6, 82 - 91)

71 - 86 (7.2 - 8.8, 52 - 64)

Support bearing bracket

Knuckle

Gusset

13 - 19 (1.3 - 1.9, 9 - 14)

16 - 22 (1.6 - 2.2, 12 - 16)

Stabilizer bar

31 - 42 (3.2 - 4.3, 23 - 31)

88 - 118 (9 - 12, 65 - 87)

Disc rotor

118 - 147 (12 - 15, 87 - 108)

118 - 147 (12 - 15, 87 - 108)

When installing each rubber part, final tightening must be carried out under unladen condition* with tires on ground.
* Fuel, radiator coolant and engine oil full. Spare tire, jack, hand tools and mats in designated position.

⊗ : Always replace when disassembled.
🔧 : N·m (kg-m, ft-lb)

Fig. 1 Exploded view of the front suspension system — 1985-88

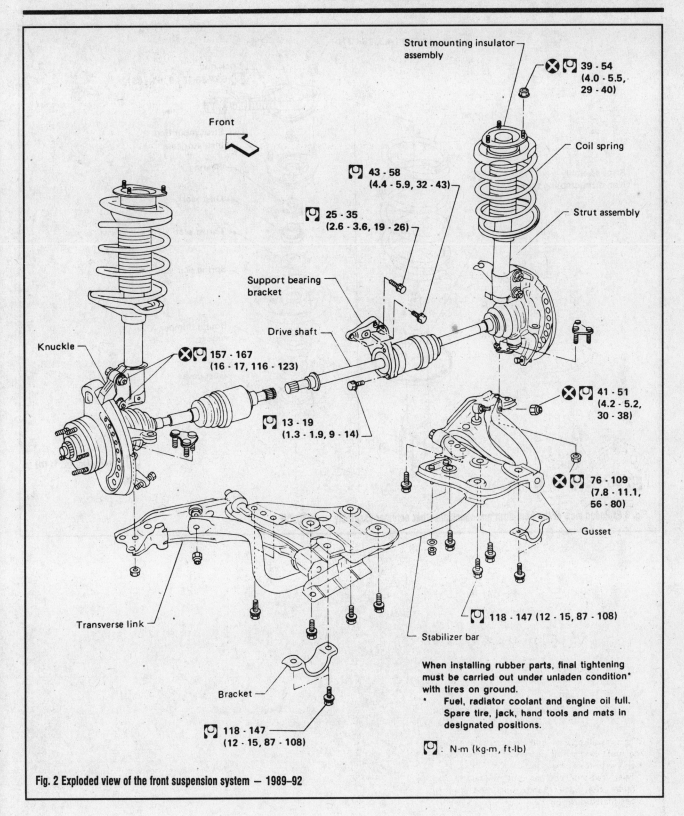

Strut mounting insulator assembly

⊗ 🔧 39 - 54
(4.0 - 5.5,
29 - 40)

Front

🔧 43 - 58
(4.4 - 5.9, 32 - 43)

Coil spring

🔧 25 - 35
(2.6 - 3.6, 19 - 26)

Strut assembly

Support bearing bracket

Drive shaft

Knuckle

⊗ 🔧 157 - 167
(16 - 17, 116 - 123)

⊗ 🔧 41 - 51
(4.2 - 5.2,
30 - 38)

🔧 13 - 19
(1.3 - 1.9, 9 - 14)

⊗ 🔧 76 - 109
(7.8 - 11.1,
56 - 80)

Gusset

🔧 118 - 147 (12 - 15, 87 - 108)

Transverse link

Stabilizer bar

When installing rubber parts, final tightening must be carried out under unladen condition* with tires on ground.

* Fuel, radiator coolant and engine oil full. Spare tire, jack, hand tools and mats in designated positions.

Bracket

🔧 118 - 147
(12 - 15, 87 - 108)

🔧 : N·m (kg-m, ft-lb)

Fig. 2 Exploded view of the front suspension system — 1989–92

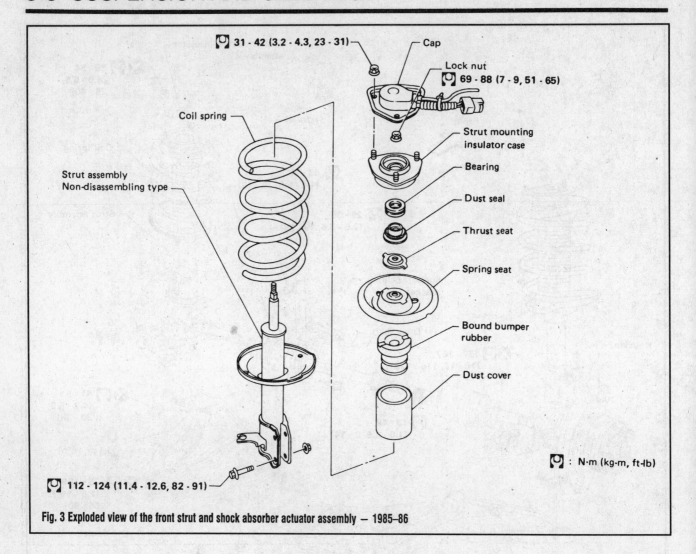

31 - 42 (3.2 - 4.3, 23 - 31)

Cap

Lock nut
69 - 88 (7 - 9, 51 - 65)

Coil spring

Strut mounting
insulator case

Bearing

Dust seal

Strut assembly
Non-disassembling type

Thrust seat

Spring seat

Bound bumper
rubber

Dust cover

: N·m (kg-m, ft-lb)

112 - 124 (11.4 - 12.6, 82 - 91)

Fig. 3 Exploded view of the front strut and shock absorber actuator assembly — 1985–86

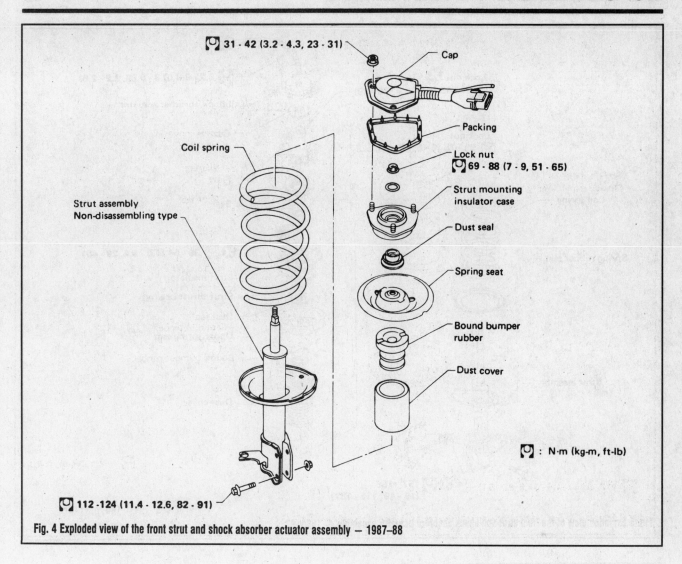

Fig. 4 Exploded view of the front strut and shock absorber actuator assembly — 1987–88

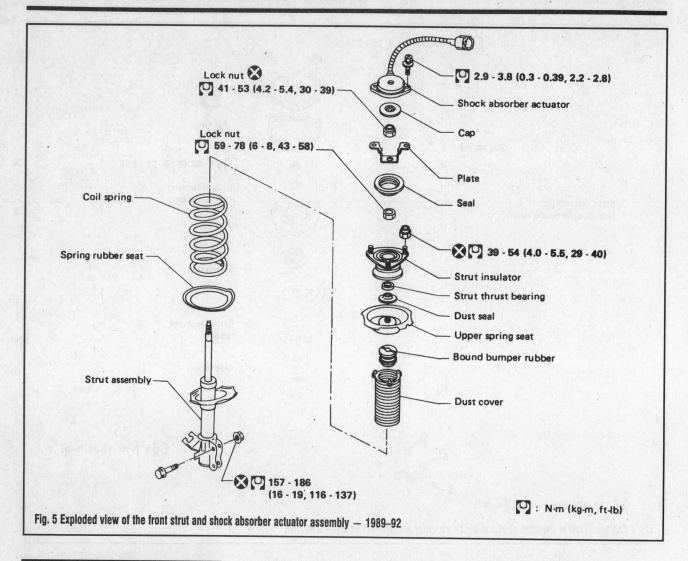

Lock nut ✕
🔧 41 - 53 (4.2 - 5.4, 30 - 39)

🔧 2.9 - 3.8 (0.3 - 0.39, 2.2 - 2.8)

Shock absorber actuator

Cap

Lock nut
🔧 59 - 78 (6 - 8, 43 - 58)

Plate

Seal

Coil spring

Spring rubber seat

✕ 🔧 39 - 54 (4.0 - 5.5, 29 - 40)

Strut insulator

Strut thrust bearing

Dust seal

Upper spring seat

Bound bumper rubber

Strut assembly

Dust cover

✕ 🔧 157 - 186
(16 - 19, 116 - 137)

🔧 : N·m (kg-m, ft-lb)

Fig. 5 Exploded view of the front strut and shock absorber actuator assembly — 1989–92

Ball Joint

INSPECTION

Hand Method

The lower ball joint should be replaced when play becomes excessive. Nissan does not publish specifications on just what constitutes excessive play, relying instead on a method of determining the force (in inch pounds) required to keep the ball joint turning. This method is not very helpful to the backyard mechanic since it involves removing the ball joint, which is what we are trying to avoid in the first place. An effective way to determine ball joint play is to raise the vehicle until the wheel is just a couple of inches off the ground and the ball joint is unloaded (meaning you can't raise directly under the ball joint). Place a long bar under the tire and move the wheel and tire assembly up and down.

Keep one hand on top of the tire while you are doing this. If there is over ¼ in. of play at the top of the tire, the ball joint is probably bad. This is assuming that the wheel bearings are in good shape and properly adjusted. As a double check on this, have someone watch the ball joint while you move the tire up and down with the bar. If you can see considerably play, besides feeling play at the top of the wheel, the ball joint needs replacing.

Dial Indicator Method

♦ SEE FIG. 10

1. Raise and safely support the vehicle.
2. Clamp a dial indicator to the control arm and place the tip of the dial on the lower edge of the brake caliper.
3. Zero the indicator.
4. Make sure the front wheels are straight-ahead and the brake pedal is fully depressed.
5. Insert a long prybar between the control arm and the inner rim of the wheel.

6. Push down and release the prybar and observe the reading (deflection) on the dial indicator. Take several readings and use the maximum dial indicator deflection as the ball joint vertical endplay. Make sure to 0 the indicator after each reading. If the reading is not within specifications, replace the control arm or the ball joint. Ball joint vertical endplay specifications are as follows:

1985–88 — 0.004–0.039 in. (0.1–1.0mm) or less

1989–92 — 0 in. (0mm)

REMOVAL & INSTALLATION

♦ SEE FIGS. 11–13

1. Raise and safely support the vehicle.
2. Refer to the Drive Axle, Removal and Installation procedures, in Section 7 and remove the drive axle.
3. Loosen but not remove the strut-to-chassis nuts.

4. Remove the lower ball joint-to-control arm bolt/nut assembly. Remove the ball joint cotter pin and nut.

5. Using the Ball Joint Remover tool HT72520000, separate the ball joint from the control arm.

To install:

6. Install the ball joint in the control arm and tighten the ball joint-to-steering knuckle nut to 52–64 ft. lbs. (71–86 Nm) and the ball joint-to-control arm bolt assembly/nuts to 56–80 ft. lbs. (76–109 Nm).

7. Install the drive axle.

8. To complete the installation, reverse the removal procedures.

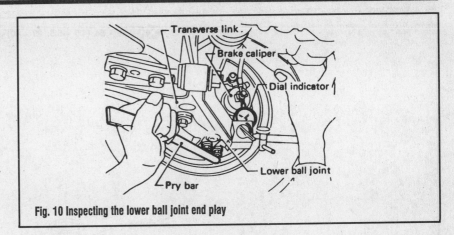

Fig. 10 Inspecting the lower ball joint end play

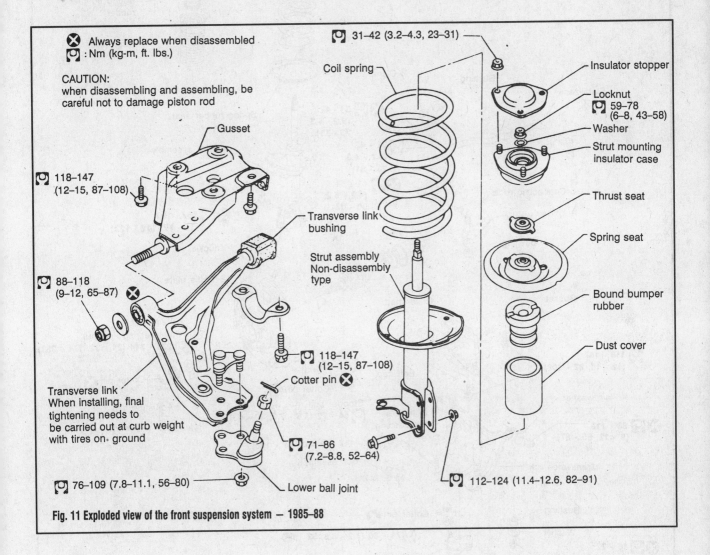

Fig. 11 Exploded view of the front suspension system — 1985–88

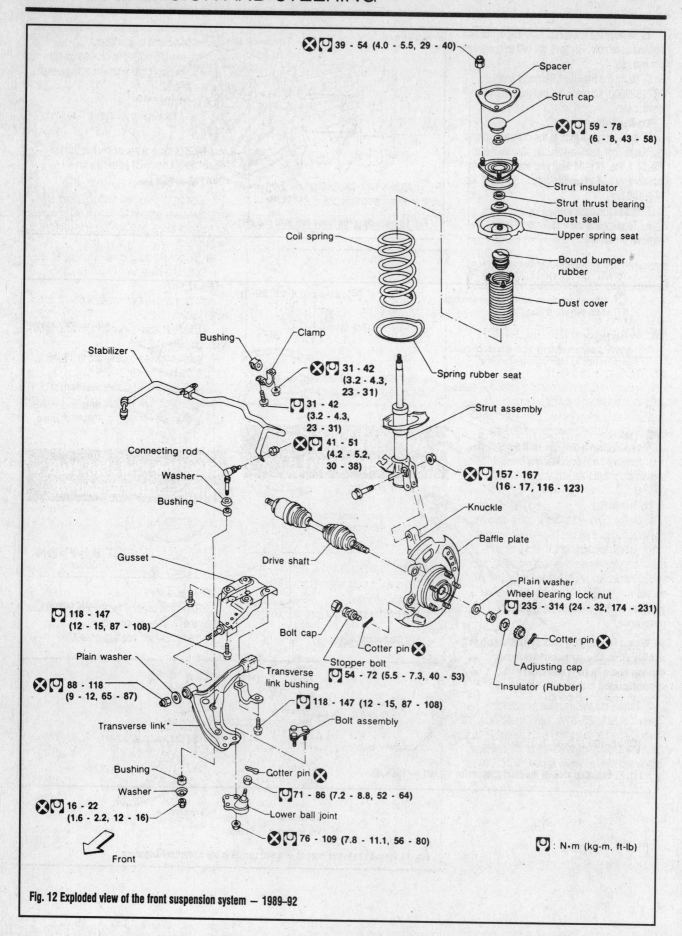

Fig. 12 Exploded view of the front suspension system — 1989–92

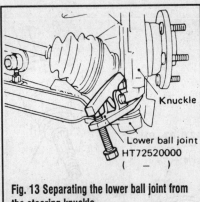

Fig. 13 Separating the lower ball joint from the steering knuckle

Stabilizer Bar

REMOVAL & INSTALLATION

◆ SEE FIGS. 1, 2, 15 AND 16

1. Raise and safely support the vehicle.
2. On the 1985–88 models, remove the stabilizer bar-to-lower control arm mounting nuts. On the 1989–92 models, remove the stabilizer bar-to-stabilizer ball joint socket nuts.
3. Remove the 4 stabilizer bar bracket-to-chassis bolts and then pull the bar from the vehicle.

To install:

4. On the 1989–92 models, make sure the stabilizer ball joint socket is positioned properly.
5. Install the stabilizer bar and mounting brackets. Never fully tighten the mounting bolts unless the vehicle is resting on the ground with normal weight upon the wheels. Be sure the stabilizer bar ball joint socket is properly positioned.

➡ **When installing the stabilizer bar, make sure the paint mark and clamp face is in their correct directions.**

6. Torque the stabilizer bar bracket-to-chassis bolts to 23–31 ft. lbs. (31–42 Nm) and the stabilizer bar-to-control arm nuts to 12–16 ft. lbs. (16–22 Nm) for 1985–88 or the stabilizer bar-to-stabilizer ball joint socket nuts to 30–38 ft. lbs. (40–51 Nm) for 1989–92.

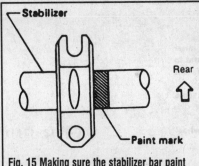

Fig. 15 Making sure the stabilizer bar paint mark and the clamp face are in their correct directions

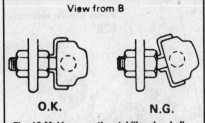

Fig. 16 Making sure the stabilizer bar ball joint socket is properly positioned

Lower Control Arm (Transverse Link)

REMOVAL & INSTALLATION

◆ SEE FIGS. 11, 12 AND 14

1. Raise and safely support the vehicle.
2. Remove the wheel.
3. Remove the lower ball joint-to-control arm bolts.
4. Remove the stabilizer bar.

5. Remove the control arm-to-chassis bolts and the control arm-to-gusset nut.
6. Remove the gusset-to-chassis bolts.
7. Remove the control arm and the gusset from the vehicle.

To install:

8. Install the lower control arm onto the vehicle.

➡ **Always use a new nut when installing the ball joint to the control arm.**

9. Tighten all bolts and nuts until they are snug enough to support the weight of the vehicle but not quite fully tight. Then, lower the vehicle to the ground.
10. Torque the bolts in numerical order to:
    Gusset-to-body bolts to 87–108 ft. lbs. (118–147 Nm)
    Control arm-to-gusset nut to 65–87 ft. lbs. (88–118 Nm)
    Lower ball joint-to-control arm nuts to 56–80 ft. lbs. (76–109 Nm)
    Stabilizer bar-to-control arm to 12–16 ft. lbs. (16–22 Nm) for 1985–88
    Stabilizer bar-to-stabilizer ball joint socket nuts to 30–38 ft. lbs. (40–51 Nm) for 1989–92
11. Install the wheel.

Steering Knuckle, Hub and Bearing Assembly

REMOVAL & INSTALLATION

◆ SEE FIGS. 17–19

1. Raise and support the front of the vehicle safely and remove the wheels.
2. Remove wheel bearing locknut.

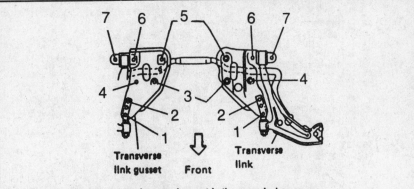

Fig. 14 Torque the lower control arm and gusset in the numerical sequence

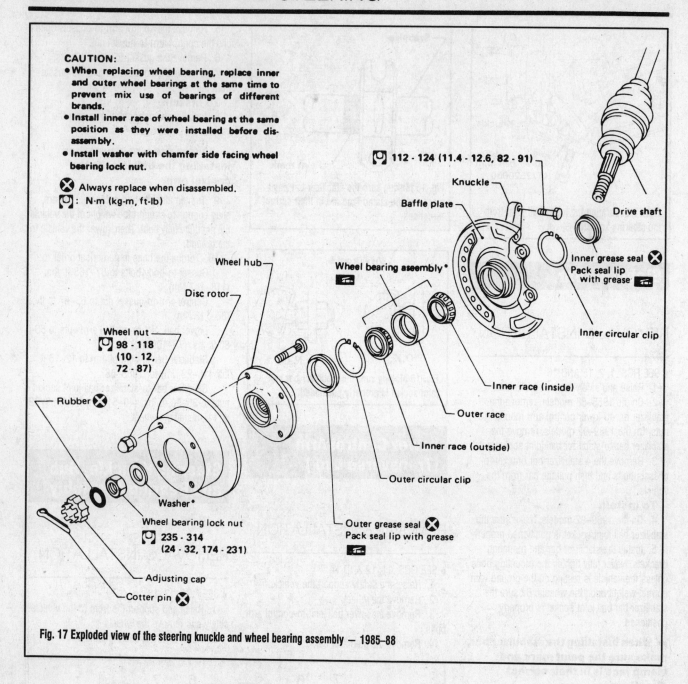

CAUTION:
- When replacing wheel bearing, replace inner and outer wheel bearings at the same time to prevent mix use of bearings of different brands.
- Install inner race of wheel bearing at the same position as they were installed before disassembly.
- Install washer with chamfer side facing wheel bearing lock nut.

⊗ Always replace when disassembled.

⊙ : N·m (kg-m, ft-lb)

112 - 124 (11.4 - 12.6, 82 - 91)

Knuckle

Baffle plate

Drive shaft

Inner grease seal ⊗
Pack seal lip with grease

Inner circular clip

Wheel hub

Wheel bearing assembly *

Disc rotor

Wheel nut
98 - 118
(10 - 12, 72 - 87)

Rubber ⊗

Inner race (inside)

Outer race

Inner race (outside)

Outer circular clip

Washer *

Wheel bearing lock nut
235 - 314
(24 - 32, 174 - 231)

Outer grease seal ⊗
Pack seal lip with grease

Adjusting cap

Cotter pin ⊗

Fig. 17 Exploded view of the steering knuckle and wheel bearing assembly — 1985–88

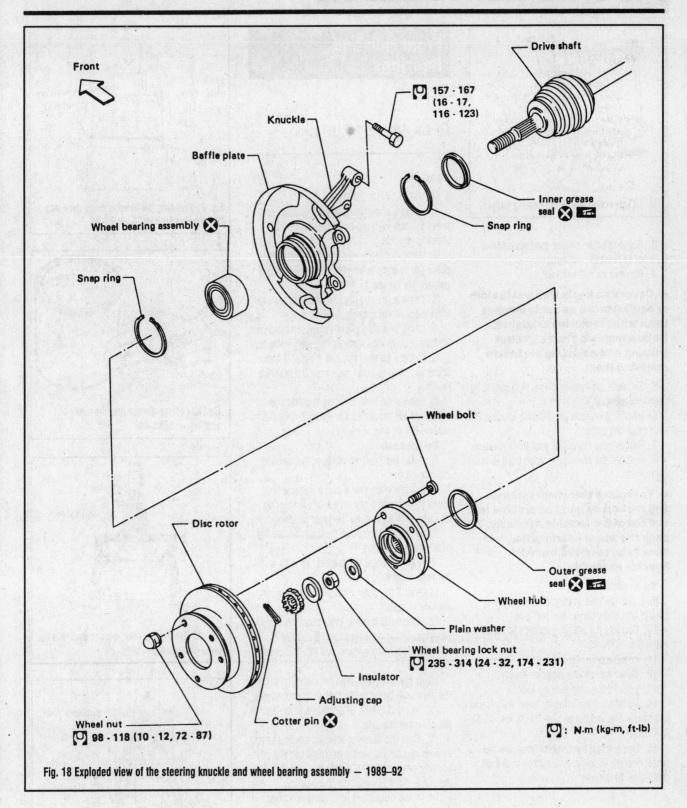

Front

Knuckle

Baffle plate

Wheel bearing assembly ⊗

Snap ring

157 - 167 (16 - 17, 116 - 123)

Drive shaft

Inner grease seal ⊗

Snap ring

Wheel bolt

Disc rotor

Outer grease seal ⊗

Wheel hub

Plain washer

Wheel bearing lock nut
235 - 314 (24 - 32, 174 - 231)

Insulator

Adjusting cap

Cotter pin ⊗

Wheel nut
98 - 118 (10 - 12, 72 - 87)

: N·m (kg-m, ft-lb)

Fig. 18 Exploded view of the steering knuckle and wheel bearing assembly — 1989-92

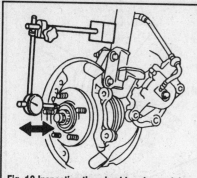

Fig. 19 Inspecting the wheel bearing endplay

3. Remove brake caliper assembly. Make sure not to twist the brake hose.

4. Remove tie rod ball joint.

➡ **Cover axle boots with waste cloth or equivalent so as not to damage them when removing driveshaft. Make a matching mark on strut housing and adjusting pin before removing them.**

5. Separate the halfshaft from the knuckle by slightly tapping it.

6. Mark and remove the steering knuckle-to-strut mounting bolts.

7. Remove the lower ball joint from knuckle.

8. Remove the steering knuckle from lower control arm.

➡ **To replace the wheel bearings and races they must be pressed in and out of the knuckle assembly. To pack the wheel bearings they will have to be removed from the knuckle assembly.**

To install:

9. Install the steering knuckle to the lower control arm and connect the ball joint.

10. Connect the steering knuckle to the strut and to the halfshaft.

11. Install the tie rod ball joint.

12. Install the brake caliper assembly.

13. Install the wheel bearing locknut

14. Install the front wheels, lower the vehicle and torque hub locknut to 174–231 ft. lbs. (235–314 Nm).

15. Using a dial micrometer, measure the wheel bearing endplay; it should be less than 0.0020 in. (0.05mm).

Front Hub and Bearings

REMOVAL & Installation

1985–88

◆ SEE FIGS. 17-18, 20-24, 31-37

1. Using a shop press and a suitable tool, press the hub with the inner race from the steering knuckle.

2. Using a shop press and a suitable tool, press the bearing inner race from the hub and remove the grease seal.

3. Using a prybar, pry the inner grease seal from the steering knuckle.

4. Using snapring pliers to remove the inner and outer snaprings from the steering knuckle.

5. Using a shop press and a suitable tool, press the bearing outer race from the steering knuckle.

6. Inspect the hub, steering knuckle and snaprings for cracks and/or wear; if necessary, replace the damaged part(s).

To install:

7. Install the inner snapring in the steering knuckle groove.

8. Using a shop press and a suitable tool, press the bearing outer race into the steering knuckle, until it seats on the inner snapring.

9. Using multi-purpose grease lubricate the new wheel bearings.

10. Pack the new grease seal lip with multi-purpose grease.

11. Install the outer snapring in the steering knuckle groove.

12. Install the bearing inner races on the bearings. Using a hammer and a suitable tool, drive the new outer grease seal into the steering knuckle.

13. If the driveshaft was not removed from the transaxle, perform the following procedures:

  a. Apply 3.5 tons of pressure to the hub in the steering knuckle.

  b. Spin the steering knuckle several turns, in both directions, and then measure the bearing preload; if the preload is not 0.4–4.0 lbs. (2.0–15.7 N), replace the bearing.

14. If the driveshaft was removed from the transaxle, perform the following procedures:

  a. Install the driveshaft into the hub and torque the hub locknut to 174–231 ft. lbs. (235–314 Nm).

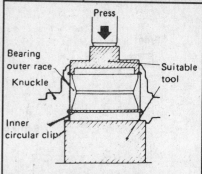

Fig. 31 Pressing the bearing outer race into the steering knuckle — 1985–88

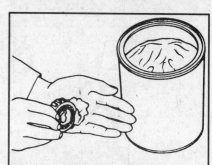

Fig. 32 Forcing grease into the new bearing — 1985–88

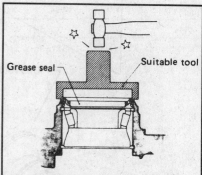

Fig. 33 Driving the outer grease seal into the steering knuckle — 1985–88

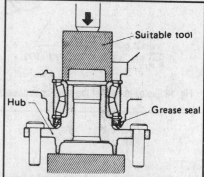

Fig. 34 Pressing the hub into the steering knuckle, when the driveshaft is not removed from the transaxle — 1985–88

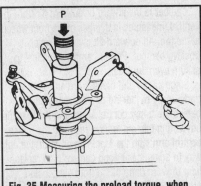

Fig. 35 Measuring the preload torque, when the driveshaft is not removed from the transaxle — 1985–88

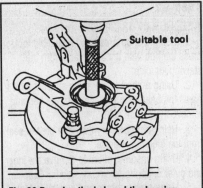

Fig. 20 Pressing the hub and the bearing inner race from the steering knuckle

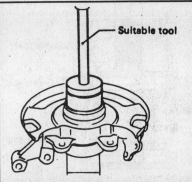

Fig. 24 Pressing the bearing outer race from the steering knuckle

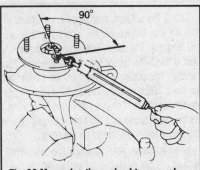

Fig. 36 Measuring the preload torque, when the driveshaft is removed from the transaxle — 1985–88

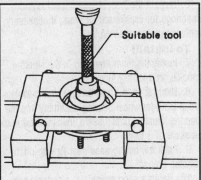

Fig. 21 Pressing the bearing inner race from the hub

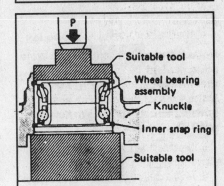

Fig. 25 Pressing the new wheel bearing assembly into the steering knuckle — 1989–92

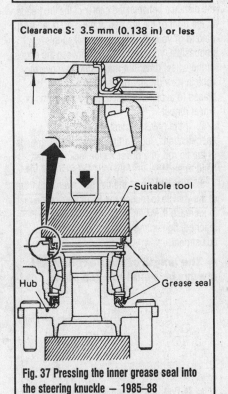

Fig. 37 Pressing the inner grease seal into the steering knuckle — 1985–88

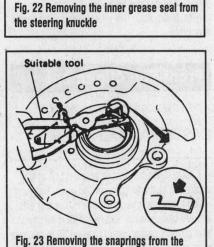

Fig. 22 Removing the inner grease seal from the steering knuckle

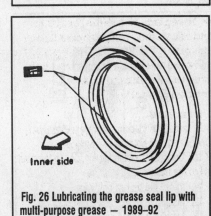

Fig. 26 Lubricating the grease seal lip with multi-purpose grease — 1989–92

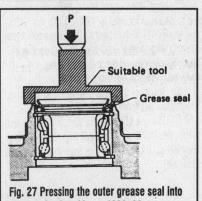

Fig. 27 Pressing the outer grease seal into the steering knuckle — 1989–92

Fig. 23 Removing the snaprings from the steering knuckle

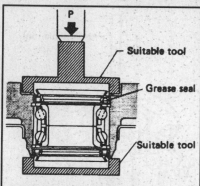

Fig. 28 Pressing the inner grease seal into the steering knuckle — 1989–92

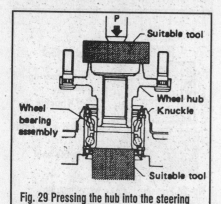

Fig. 29 Pressing the hub into the steering knuckle — 1989–92

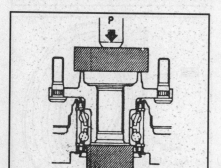

Fig. 30 Increasing the press load to check the wheel bearing operation — 1989–92

b. Spin the steering knuckle several turns, in both directions, and then measure the bearing preload; if the preload is not 1.1–10.1 lbs., replace the bearing.

15. Remove the hub locknut and remove the driveshaft from the hub.

16. Using a shop press and a suitable tool, press the inner grease seal into the steering knuckle so its clearance is less than 0.138 in. (3.5mm).

1989–92

▶ SEE FIGS. 17-18, 20-30

1. Using a shop press and a suitable tool, press the hub with the inner race from the steering knuckle.

2. Using a shop press and a suitable tool, press the bearing inner race from the hub and remove the grease seal.

3. Using a prybar, pry the inner grease seal from the steering knuckle.

4. Using snapring pliers to remove the inner and outer snaprings from the steering knuckle.

5. Using a shop press and a suitable tool, press the bearing outer race from the steering knuckle.

6. Inspect the hub, steering knuckle and snaprings for cracks and/or wear; if necessary, replace the damaged part(s).

To install:

7. Install the inner snapring in the steering knuckle groove.

8. Using a shop press and a suitable tool, press the new wheel bearing assembly into the steering knuckle, until it seats, using a maximum pressure of 3 tons.

9. Pack the new grease seal lip with multi-purpose grease.

10. Using a shop press and a suitable tool, press the new outer grease seal into the steering knuckle.

11. Using a shop press and a suitable tool, press the new inner grease seal into the steering knuckle.

12. Using a shop press and a suitable tool, press the hub into the steering knuckle, until it seats, using a maximum pressure of 3 tons; be careful not to damage the grease seal.

13. To check the bearing operation, perform the following procedures:

a. Increase the press pressure to 3.5–5.0 tons.

b. Spin the steering knuckle, several turns, in both directions.

c. Make sure the wheel bearings operate smoothly.

Front End Alignment

CASTER AND CAMBER

Caster is the forward or rearward tilt of the upper end of the kingpin, or the upper ball joint, which results in a slight tilt of the steering axis forward or backward. Rearward tilt is referred to as a positive caster, while forward tilt is referred to as negative caster.

Camber is the inward or outward tilt from the vertical, measured in degrees of the front wheels at the top. An outward tilt gives the wheel positive camber. Proper camber is critical to assure even tire wear.

Since caster and camber are adjusted traditionally by adding or subtracting shims behind the upper control arms, and the Nissans covered in this guide have replaced the upper control arm with the MacPherson strut, the only way to adjust caster and camber is to replace bent or worn parts of the front suspension.

TOE

Toe is the amount, measured in a fraction of an inch, that the wheels are closer together at one end than the other. Toe-in means that the front wheels are closer together at the front than the rear. Toe-out means the rears are closer than the front. Nissans are adjusted to have a slight amount of toe-in. Toe-in is adjusted by turning the tie rod, which has a right hand thread on one end and a left hand thread on the other.

You can check your vehicle's toe-in yourself without special equipment if you make careful measurements. The wheels must be straight ahead.

1. Toe-in can be determined by measuring the distance between the center of the tire treads, at the front of the tire and at the rear. If the tread pattern of your vehicle's tires makes this impossible, you can measure between the edges of the wheel rims, but make sure to move the vehicle forward and measure in a couple of places to avoid errors caused by bent rims or wheel runout.

2. If the measurement is not within specifications, loosen the locknuts at both ends of the tie rod (the driver's side locknut is left hand threaded).

3. Turn the top of the tie rod toward the front of the vehicle to reduce toe-in, or toward the rear to increase it. When the correct dimension is reached, tighten the locknuts and check the adjustment.

➡ **The length of the tie rods must always be equal to each other.**

WHEEL ALIGNMENT

Year	Model	Caster Range (deg.)	Caster Preferred Setting (deg.)	Camber Range (deg.)	Camber Preferred Setting (deg.)	Toe-in (in.)	Steering Axis Inclination (deg.)
1985	Maxima	1¼P–2¾P	2P	①	②	③	13¾P–15¼P
1986	Maxima	1¼P–2¾P	2P	①	②	③	13¾P–15¼P
1987	Maxima	1¼P–2¾P	2P	④	⑤	⑥	13⅚P–15⅓P
1988	Maxima	1¼P–2¾P	2P	④	⑤	⑥	13⅚P–15⅓P
1989	Maxima	½P–2P	1¼P	⑦	⑧	⑨	13⁷⁄₁₂P–15¹⁄₁₂P
1990	Maxima	½P–2P	1¼P	⑦	⑧	⑩	13⁷⁄₁₂P–15¹⁄₁₂P
1991	Maxima	½P–2P	1¼P	⑦	⑧	⑩	13⁷⁄₁₂P–15¹⁄₁₂P
1992	Maxima	½P–2P	1¼P	⑦	⑧	⑪	13⁷⁄₁₂P–15¹⁄₁₂P

N—Negative
P—Positive

① Front: ⁵⁄₁₂N–1¹⁄₁₂P
Rear:
Sedan: ½N–1P
Wagon: ⅓N–1⅙P
② Front: ⅔P
Rear:
Sedan: ¼P
Wagon: ⁵⁄₁₂P

③ Front: 0.04–0.12 in.
Rear:
Sedan: 0.24N–0.08N
Wagon: 0.28N–0.12N
④ Front: ⁵⁄₁₂N–1¹⁄₁₂P
Rear: 1⅙N–⅓N
⑤ Front: ⅔P
Rear: ⁵⁄₁₂N
⑥ Front: 0.04–0.12 in.
Rear: 0.08–0.24 in. toe-out

⑦ Front: 1N–½P
Rear: 1⅓N–⅙P
⑧ Front: ¼N
Rear: ⁷⁄₁₂N
⑨ Front: 0.04–0.12 in.
Rear: 0.04–0.12 in. toe-out
⑩ Front: 0.04–0.12 in.
Rear: 0–0.16 in. toe-out
⑪ Front: 0.04–0.12 in.
Rear: 0.12N–0.04N in.

REAR SUSPENSION

MacPherson Strut

REMOVAL & INSTALLATION

♦ SEE FIGS. 38–43

1. Remove the rear seat and the parcel shelf.
2. If equipped with an adjustable shock absorber, disconnect the electrical connector from the sonar unit.
3. On the 1985–88 models, remove the strut mounting cap from the strut. On the 1989–92 models, perform the following procedures:
   a. Remove the strut mounting cap from the strut.
   b. Remove the shock absorber actuator-to-actuator bracket bolts and the shock absorber actuator.
   c. If necessary, remove the actuator bracket-to-strut nut and the bracket.
4. Raise and safely support the vehicle; do not raise the vehicle at the parallel links or radius links. Remove the wheel(s).

5. Unclip the rear brake hydraulic line from the strut. Then, unbolt and remove the brake assembly, wheel bearings and backing plate.

➡ If equipped with disc brakes, suspend the brake caliper so the hydraulic line will not be stressed. If equipped with drum brakes, remove the entire brake assembly.

6. Remove the radius rod-to-strut bolt, stabilizer bar-to-radius rod bracket bolt, radius rod bracket-to-strut bolts and both parallel links-to-strut nut/bolt.
7. Support the strut from underneath. Remove the 3 strut-to-chassis nuts and lower the strut from the vehicle.

To install:
8. Install in the strut onto the vehicle. Install the brake assembly and the wheel(s).
9. Tighten all bolts sufficiently to safely support the vehicle; then, lower the vehicle to the ground.

10. Final torque the nuts and bolts, as follows:
   Upper strut-to-chassis nuts — 23–31 ft. lbs. (31–41 Nm)
   Radius rod bracket-to-strut bolts:
   1985–86 — 54–69 ft. lbs. (74–93 Nm)
   1987–92 — 43–58 ft. lbs. (59–78 Nm)
   Radius rod-to-bracket bolt — 65–80 ft. lbs. (88–108 Nm)
   Parallel links-to-strut nut/bolt — 65–87 ft. lbs. (88–118 Nm)
   Stabilizer bar-to-radius rod bracket bolt — 43–58 ft. lbs. (59–78 Nm)
11. Connect the brake line to the strut housing. If equipped, connect the electrical harness connector the shock absorber actuator.
12. If the brake line was disconnected, bleed the brake system.

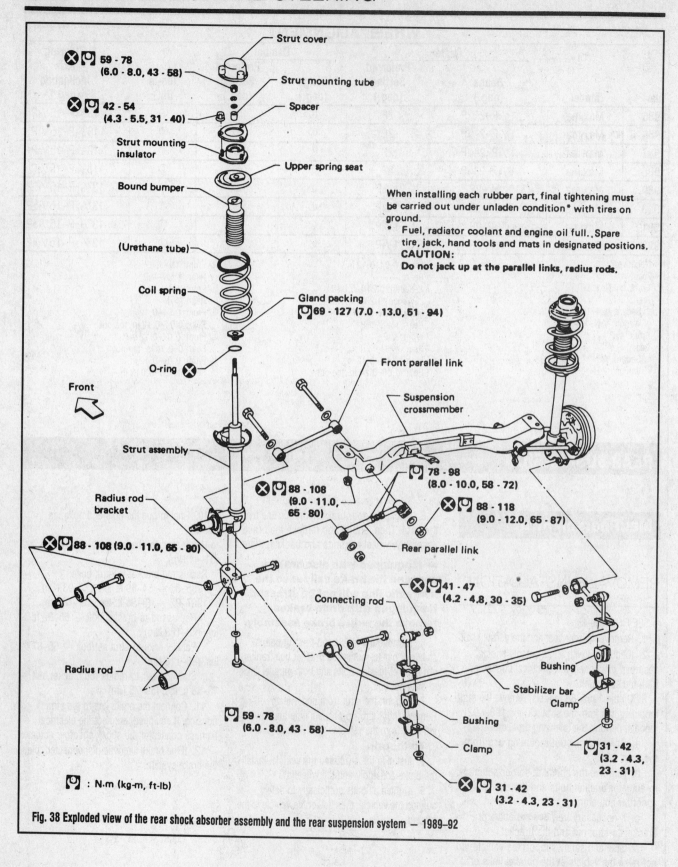

When installing each rubber part, final tightening must be carried out under unladen condition* with tires on ground.
* Fuel, radiator coolant and engine oil full. Spare tire, jack, hand tools and mats in designated positions.
CAUTION:
Do not jack up at the parallel links, radius rods.

Fig. 38 Exploded view of the rear shock absorber assembly and the rear suspension system — 1989–92

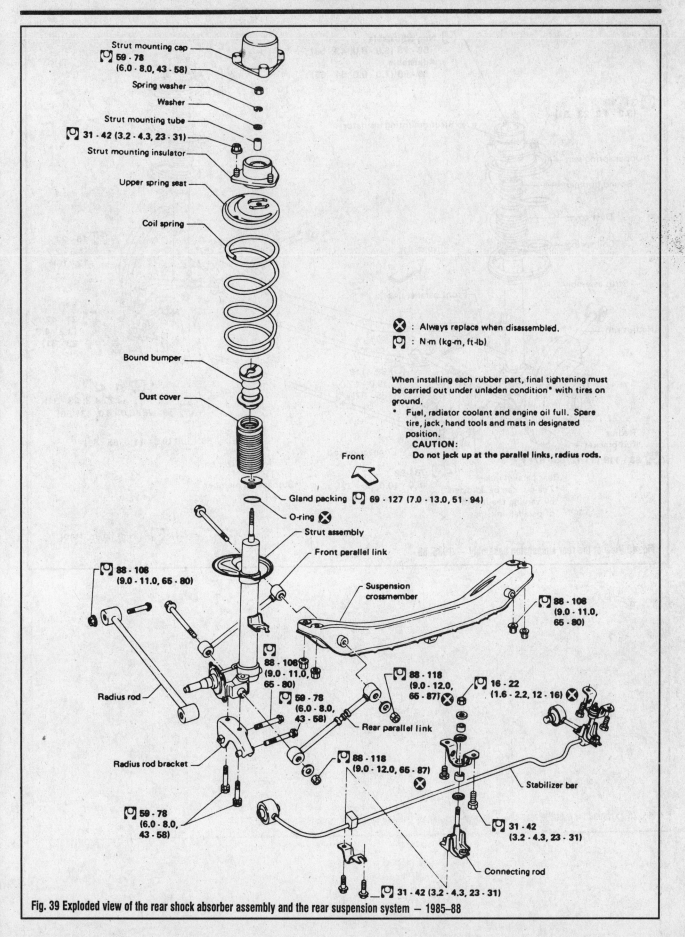

Strut mounting cap
59 - 78
(6.0 - 8.0, 43 - 58)

Spring washer

Washer

Strut mounting tube

31 - 42 (3.2 - 4.3, 23 - 31)

Strut mounting insulator

Upper spring seat

Coil spring

Bound bumper

Dust cover

⊗ : Always replace when disassembled.

: N·m (kg-m, ft-lb)

When installing each rubber part, final tightening must be carried out under unladen condition° with tires on ground.

° Fuel, radiator coolant and engine oil full. Spare tire, jack, hand tools and mats in designated position.
  CAUTION:
  Do not jack up at the parallel links, radius rods.

Front

Gland packing 69 - 127 (7.0 - 13.0, 51 - 94)

O-ring ⊗

Strut assembly

Front parallel link

Suspension crossmember

88 - 106 (9.0 - 11.0, 65 - 80)

88 - 106 (9.0 - 11.0, 65 - 80)

Radius rod

88 - 106 (9.0 - 11.0, 65 - 80)

59 - 78 (6.0 - 8.0, 43 - 58)

88 - 118 (9.0 - 12.0, 65 - 87)

16 - 22 (1.6 - 2.2, 12 - 16)

Rear parallel link

Radius rod bracket

88 - 118 (9.0 - 12.0, 65 - 87)

Stabilizer bar

59 - 78 (6.0 - 8.0, 43 - 58)

31 - 42 (3.2 - 4.3, 23 - 31)

Connecting rod

31 - 42 (3.2 - 4.3, 23 - 31)

Fig. 39 Exploded view of the rear shock absorber assembly and the rear suspension system — 1985–88

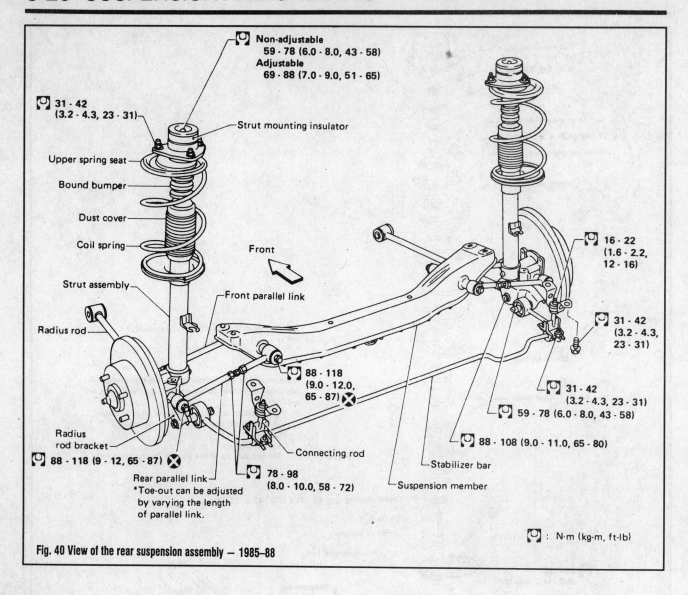

Non-adjustable
59 - 78 (6.0 - 8.0, 43 - 58)
Adjustable
69 - 88 (7.0 - 9.0, 51 - 65)

31 - 42
(3.2 - 4.3, 23 - 31)

Strut mounting insulator

Upper spring seat

Bound bumper

Dust cover

Coil spring

Front

Strut assembly

Front parallel link

Radius rod

16 - 22
(1.6 - 2.2,
12 - 16)

31 - 42
(3.2 - 4.3,
23 - 31)

88 - 118
(9.0 - 12.0,
65 - 87)

31 - 42
(3.2 - 4.3, 23 - 31)

59 - 78 (6.0 - 8.0, 43 - 58)

88 - 108 (9.0 - 11.0, 65 - 80)

Radius
rod bracket

88 - 118 (9 - 12, 65 - 87)

Connecting rod

Stabilizer bar

Suspension member

Rear parallel link
*Toe-out can be adjusted
by varying the length
of parallel link.

78 - 98
(8.0 - 10.0, 58 - 72)

: N·m (kg-m, ft-lb)

Fig. 40 View of the rear suspension assembly — 1985–88

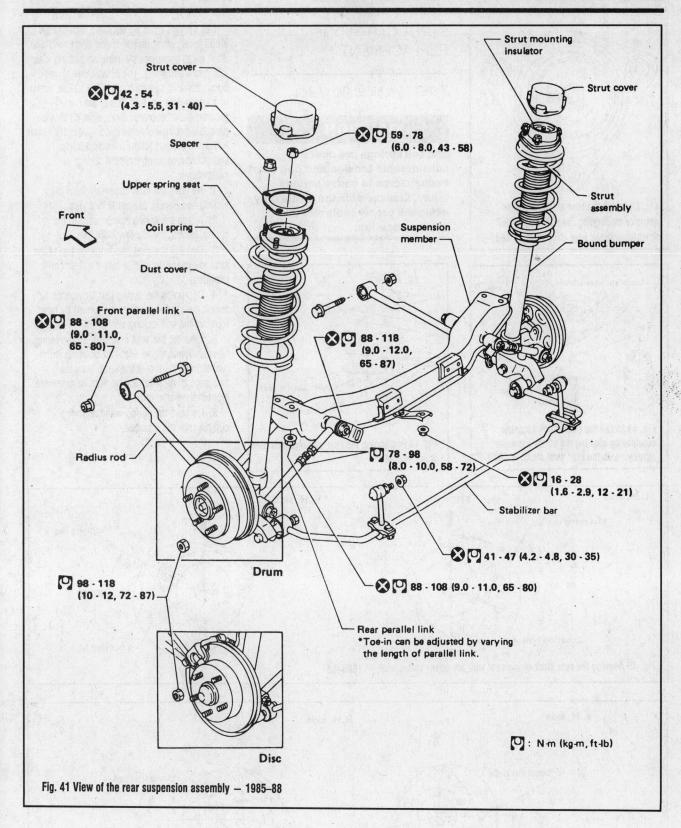

Fig. 41 View of the rear suspension assembly — 1985–88

Strut mounting insulator

Strut cover

Strut cover

⊗ 🔧 42 - 54 (4.3 - 5.5, 31 - 40)

⊗ 🔧 59 - 78 (6.0 - 8.0, 43 - 58)

Spacer

Upper spring seat

Strut assembly

Front

Coil spring

Suspension member

Bound bumper

Dust cover

Front parallel link

⊗ 🔧 88 - 108 (9.0 - 11.0, 65 - 80)

⊗ 🔧 88 - 118 (9.0 - 12.0, 65 - 87)

Radius rod

🔧 78 - 98 (8.0 - 10.0, 58 - 72)

⊗ 🔧 16 - 28 (1.6 - 2.9, 12 - 21)

Stabilizer bar

Drum

⊗ 🔧 41 - 47 (4.2 - 4.8, 30 - 35)

🔧 98 - 118 (10 - 12, 72 - 87)

⊗ 🔧 88 - 108 (9.0 - 11.0, 65 - 80)

Rear parallel link
*Toe-in can be adjusted by varying the length of parallel link.

🔧 : N·m (kg-m, ft-lb)

Disc

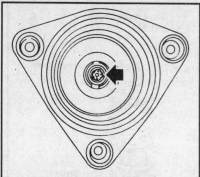

Fig. 42 Install the rear shock absorber actuator by aligning the shock absorber actuator with the rear strut stem — 1985–88

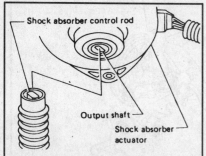

Fig. 43 Install the rear shock absorber actuator by aligning the shock absorber actuator with the rear strut stem — 1989–92

STRUT CARTRIDGE REPLACEMENT

◆ SEE FIGS. 6, 38, 39 AND 44–46

❄❄ CAUTION

The coil springs are under considerable tension and can exert enough force to cause serious injury. Disassemble the struts only using the proper tools and use extreme caution.

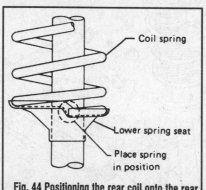

Fig. 44 Positioning the rear coil onto the rear shock absorber

Coil springs must be removed with the aid of a coil spring compressor. If you don't have one, don't try to improvise by using something else: you could risk injury. The Nissan coil spring compressor is special tool HT71730000, which is a totally different unit. These are the recommended compressors, although they are probably not the only spring compressors which will work. Always follow manufacturer's instructions when operating a spring compressor.

1. Remove the strut assembly from the vehicle and secure assembly in a vise.

2. Attach the spring compressor to the spring, leaving the top few coils free.

3. Remove the dust cap from the top of the strut to expose the center nut, if a dust cap is provided.

4. Compress the spring just far enough to permit the strut insulator to be turned by hand. Remove the self locking center nut.

5. Take out the strut insulator, strut bearing, oil seal, upper spring seat and bound bumper rubber from the top of the strut. Note their sequence of removal and be sure to assemble them in the same order.

6. Remove the spring with the spring compressor still attached.

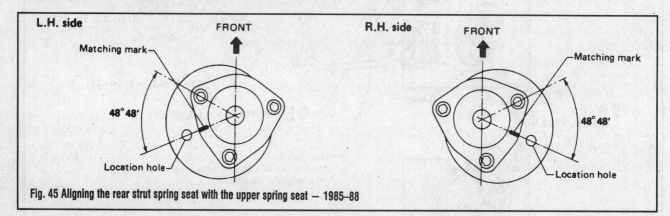

Fig. 45 Aligning the rear strut spring seat with the upper spring seat — 1985–88

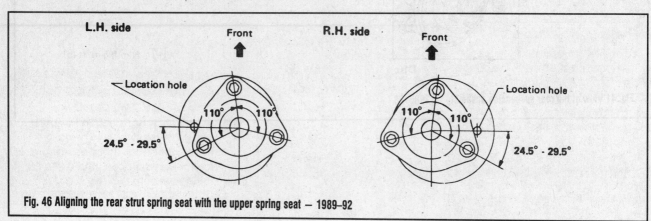

Fig. 46 Aligning the rear strut spring seat with the upper spring seat — 1989–92

To assemble:

7. Reassemble the strut assembly and observe the following:

a. Make sure you assemble the unit with the shock absorber piston rod fully extended.

b. When assembling, take care that the rubber spring seats, both top and bottom, and the spring are positioned in their grooves before releasing the spring.

8. Torque the strut locknut to 51–65 ft. lbs. (69–88 Nm) for 1985–88 or 43–58 ft. lbs. (59–78 Nm) for 1989–92.

Radius Rod

REMOVAL & INSTALLATION

◆ SEE FIGS. 38 AND 39

1. Raise and safely support the vehicle; do not raise the vehicle at the parallel links or radius links. If necessary, remove the wheel.

2. Remove the radius rod-to-strut nut/bolt.

3. Remove the radius rod-to-chassis nut/bolt and the radius rod.

To install:

4. Install in the radius rod onto the vehicle.

5. Tighten all bolts sufficiently to safely support the vehicle. If the wheel was removed, install it; then, lower the vehicle to the ground.

6. Final torque the nuts and bolts, as follows:
Radius rod-to-bracket nut/bolt — 65–80 ft. lbs. (88–108 Nm)
Radius rod-to-chassis nut/bolt — 65–80 ft. lbs. (88–108 Nm)

Parallel Link

REMOVAL & INSTALLATION

◆ SEE FIGS. 38 AND 39

1. Raise and safely support the vehicle; do not raise the vehicle at the parallel links or radius links. If necessary, remove the wheel.

2. Remove the parallel links-to-strut nut/bolt.

3. Remove the parallel links-to-suspension member nut/bolt and the parallel links.

To install:

4. Install in the parallel links onto the vehicle.

5. Tighten all bolts sufficiently to safely support the vehicle. If the wheel was removed, install it; then, lower the vehicle to the ground.

6. Final torque the nuts and bolts, as follows:
Parallel links-to-strut nut/bolt — 65–87 ft. lbs. (88–118 Nm)
Parallel links-to-suspension member nut/bolt — 65–87 ft. lbs. (88–118 Nm)

Stabilizer Bar

REMOVAL & INSTALLATION

◆ SEE FIGS. 38 AND 39

1. Raise and safely support the vehicle; do not raise the vehicle at the parallel links or radius links. If necessary, remove the wheels.

2. Remove the stabilizer bar-to-strut bolts.

3. Remove the stabilizer bar clamp-to-connecting rod nut/bolt and the stabilizer bar.

To install:

4. Install in the stabilizer bar onto the vehicle.

5. Tighten all bolts sufficiently to safely support the vehicle. If the wheels were removed, install them, then, lower the vehicle to the ground.

6. Final torque the nuts and bolts, as follows:
Stabilizer bar-to-radius rod bracket bolt — 43–58 ft. lbs. (59–78 Nm)
Stabilizer bar clamp-to-connecting rod nut/bolt — 43–58 ft. lbs. (59–78 Nm)

Rear Wheel Bearings

REMOVAL & INSTALLATION

1985–88

◆ SEE FIGS. 47-50

➡ After the rear wheel bearings have been removed or replaced or the rear axle has been reassembled be sure to adjust wheel bearing preload. Refer to the Adjustment procedure below.

1. Raise and safely support the vehicle.

2. Remove the rear wheels and the brake caliper assemblies.

➡ Brake hoses do not need to be disconnected from the brake caliper assemblies. Make sure the brake hoses are secure and do not let caliper assemblies hang unsupported from the vehicle. DO NOT depress brake pedal or piston will pop out.

3. Work off center hub cap by using thin tool. If necessary tap around it with a soft hammer while removing.

4. Pry out cotter pin and take off adjusting cap and wheel bearing locknut.

5. Remove wheel hub/disc brake rotor from spindle with bearings installed. Remove the outer bearing from the hub/disc brake rotor.

6. Remove inner bearing and grease seal from hub/disc brake rotor using long brass drift pin or equivalent.

7. If it is necessary to replace the bearing outer races, drive them out of the hub/disc brake rotor with a brass drift pin and mallet.

To install:

8. Install the outer bearing race with a tool, until it seats in the hub/disc brake rotor flush.

➡ The Nissan special tool number for this tool is KV401021S0.

9. Pack each wheel bearing with high temperature wheel bearing grease. Pack hub cap with the recommended wheel bearing grease up to shaded portions.

10. Install the inner bearing and grease seal (make sure the white nylon guide faces the spindle) in the proper position in the hub/disc brake rotor.

11. Install the wheel hub/disc brake rotor to the spindle.

12. Install the outer wheel bearing, lock washer, wheel bearing locknut, adjusting cap, cotter pin (always use a new cotter pin for installation), spread cotter pin then install the dust cap.

13. Install the brake caliper assemblies and bleed brakes, if necessary. Install the rear wheels.

1989–92

◆ SEE FIGS. 52 AND 53

✳ CAUTION

Since brake lining contains asbestos, A CARCINOGEN, don't use compressed air to remove brake dust from these parts. Use of compressed air can cause you to inhale asbestos fibers.

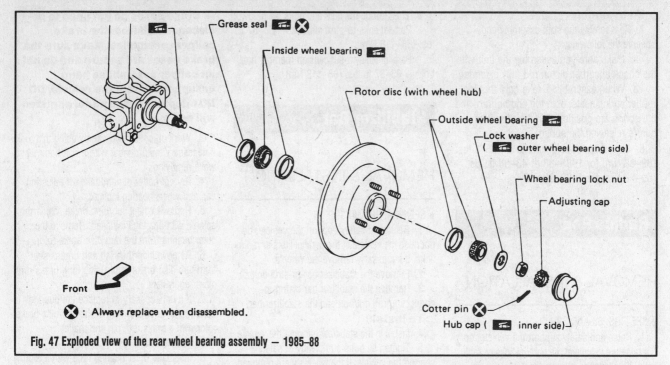

Fig. 47 Exploded view of the rear wheel bearing assembly — 1985–88

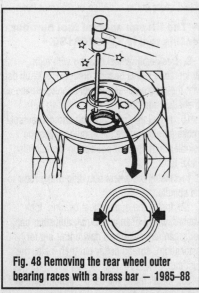

Fig. 48 Removing the rear wheel outer bearing races with a brass bar — 1985–88

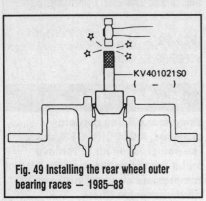

Fig. 49 Installing the rear wheel outer bearing races — 1985–88

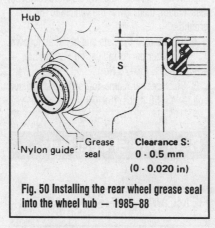

Fig. 50 Installing the rear wheel grease seal into the wheel hub — 1985–88

1. Raise and safely support the vehicle; secure it by via the body. Remove the rear wheel(s).

2. If equipped with disc brakes, perform the following procedures:

  a. Remove the brake caliper and hang by a piece of wire.

  b. Remove the brake caliper support.

  c. Remove the brake disc.

3. If equipped with drum brakes, perform the following procedures:

  a. Remove the brake drum.

  b. If necessary, remove the brake shoe assembly.

4. Remove the grease cap.

5. Remove the cotter pin and wheel bearing locknut, washer and the wheel hub bearing assembly.

→ The wheel hub bearing assembly is not repairable; it must be replaced, when defective.

To install:

6. Install the wheel hub bearing assembly, the washer and the wheel bearing locknut. Torque the wheel bearing locknut to 137–188 ft. lbs. (186–255 Nm).

7. Install a new cotter pin into the wheel bearing locknut.

8. Install a dial mircometer to the rear wheel hub bearing assembly and check the axial endplay; it should be less than 0.0020 in. (0.05mm).

9. Install the grease cap.

10. Install the brake assembly and the wheels.

WHEEL BEARING PRELOAD ADJUSTMENT

1985–88

◆ SEE FIG. 51

→ Before adjustment, thoroughly clean all parts to prevent dirt entry. Remove the brake caliper.

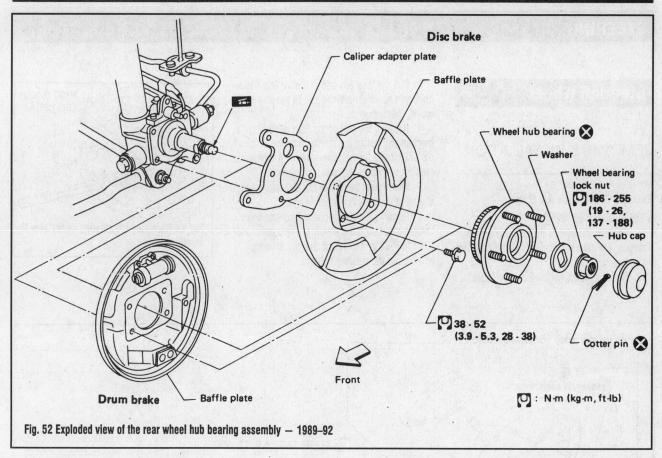

Fig. 52 Exploded view of the rear wheel hub bearing assembly — 1989–92

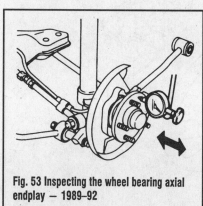

Fig. 53 Inspecting the wheel bearing axial endplay — 1989–92

1. Apply multi-purpose grease to the following parts:

   a. Threaded portion of the wheel spindle.

   b. Mating surfaces of the lock washer and outer wheel bearing.

   c. Inner hub cap.

   d. Grease seal lip.

2. Tighten the wheel bearing nut to 18–25 ft. lbs. (25–34 Nm).

3. Turn the wheel hub several times, in both directions, to seat the bearing correctly.

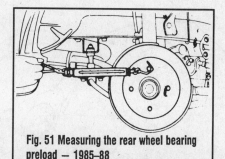

Fig. 51 Measuring the rear wheel bearing preload — 1985–88

4. Loosen the wheel bearing locknut until there is no preload and then tighten it to 6.5–8.7 ft. lbs. (9–12 Nm). Turn the wheel hub several times again and then retighten it to 6.5–8.7 ft. lbs. (9–12 Nm).

5. Install the adjusting cap and align any of its slots with the hole in the spindle.

➡ **If necessary, loosening the locknut as much as 15 degrees in order to align the spindle hole with one in the adjusting cap.**

6. Rotate the hub in both directions several times while measuring its starting torque and axial play. They should be as follows:

  • Axial play: 0

  • Wheel bearing preload (new grease seal) when measured at wheel hub bolt: 3.1 lbs. (13.7 N)

  • Wheel bearing preload (used grease seal) when measured at wheel hub bolt: 2.4 lbs. (10.8 N)

7. Correctly measure the rotation from the starting force toward the tangential direction against the hub bolt. The above figures do not allow for any "dragging" resistance. When measuring starting torque, confirm that no "dragging" exists. No wheel bearing axial play can exist at all.

8. Spread the cotter pin and install the inner hub cap.

Rear End Alignment

The rear camber is preset at the factory and cannot be adjusted; if the rear camber alignment is not within specifications, check the associated parts, then repair or replace them. The only adjustments that can be performed is rear toe-out.

STEERING

Steering Wheel

REMOVAL & INSTALLATION

Except 1992 With Air Bag

♦ SEE FIGS. 54, 55 AND 56

1. Position the wheels in the straight-ahead direction. The steering wheel should be right side up and level.

2. Disconnect the negative battery cable.

3. Pull out the horn pad. If the vehicle has a horn wire running from the pad to the steering wheel, disconnect it.

4. Remove the rest of the horn switching mechanism, noting the relative location of the parts. Remove the mechanism only if it hinders subsequent wheel removal procedures.

5. Matchmark the top of the steering column shaft and the steering wheel flange.

6. Remove the steering wheel-to-steering column nut. Using the steering wheel puller tool ST27180001 or equivalent, pull the steering wheel from the steering column.

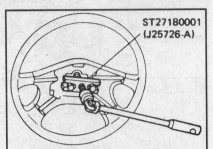

Fig. 55 Removing the steering wheel from the steering column

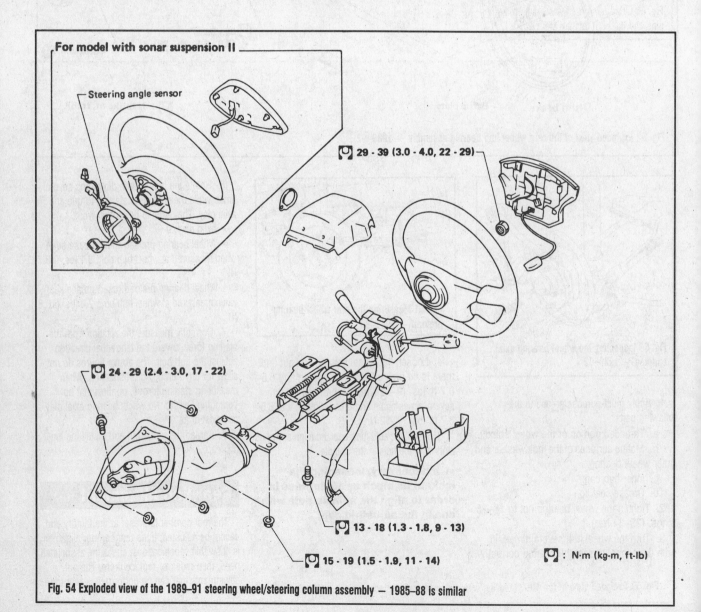

Fig. 54 Exploded view of the 1989–91 steering wheel/steering column assembly — 1985–88 is similar

➡ **Do not strike the shaft with a hammer, which may cause the column to collapse.**

To install:

7. Apply multi-purpose grease to the entire surface of the turn signal cancel pin (both portions) and the horn contact slip ring.

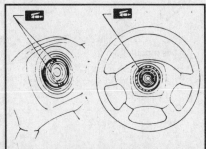

Fig. 56 Lubricating the turn signal canceling pins and the horn contact slip ring

8. Install the steering wheel by aligning the matchmarks. Do not drive or hammer the steering wheel into place or you may cause the collapsible steering column to collapse, in which case you'll have to buy a whole new steering column unit.

9. Tighten the steering wheel-to-steering column nut to 22–29 ft. lbs. (29–39 Nm).

10. Install the horn pad. Connect the negative battery cable.

1992 With Air Bag

♦ SEE FIGS. 57–59

1. Position the wheels in the straight-ahead direction. The steering wheel should be right side up and level.

2. Disconnect the negative battery cable.

✳✳ CAUTION

Wait 10 minutes after the battery cable has been disconnected, before attempting to work on the air bag unit. The air bag unit is still armed and can inflate, during the 10 minute period, and possibly causing bodily injury.

3. Remove the lower lid from the steering wheel and disconnect the air bag unit electrical connector.

4. Remove both side lids from the steering wheel.

5. Using a T50H Torx bit, remove the air bag-to-steering wheel bolts from both sides of the steering wheel; discard the bolts.

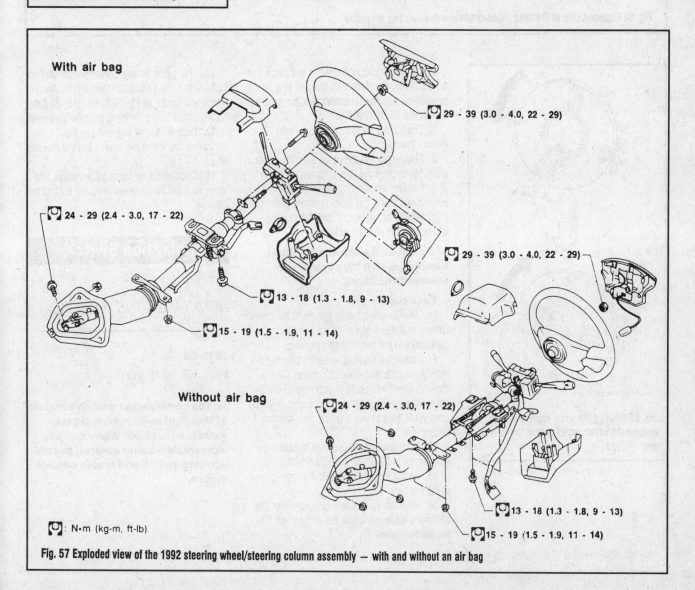

Fig. 57 Exploded view of the 1992 steering wheel/steering column assembly — with and without an air bag

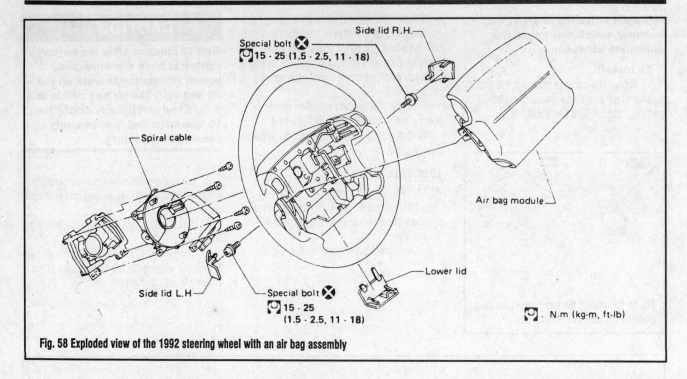

Side lid R.H.

Special bolt ⊗
☐ 15 - 25 (1.5 - 2.5, 11 - 18)

Spiral cable

Air bag module

Side lid L.H

Special bolt ⊗
☐ 15 - 25
(1.5 - 2.5, 11 - 18)

Lower lid

☐ . N·m (kg-m, ft-lb)

Fig. 58 Exploded view of the 1992 steering wheel with an air bag assembly

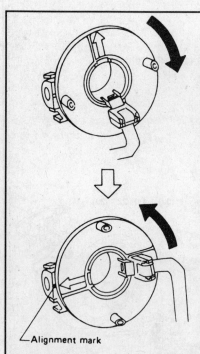

Alignment mark

Fig. 59 Aligning the spiral cable with the matchmark before installation of the air bag unit – 1992

6. Lift the air bag unit upward and place it in a safe, clean, dry place with the pad side facing upward; be sure the temperature in the area will not exceed 212°F (100°C).

7. Disconnect the horn connector and remove the nuts.

8. Matchmark the top of the steering column shaft and the steering wheel flange.

9. Remove the steering wheel-to-steering column nut. Using the steering wheel puller tool ST27180001 or equivalent, pull the steering wheel from the steering column.

➡ **Do not strike the shaft with a hammer, which may cause the column to collapse.**

To install:

10. Apply multi-purpose grease to the entire surface of the turn signal cancel pin (both portions) and the horn contact slip ring.

11. Install the steering wheel by aligning the matchmarks. Do not drive or hammer the steering wheel into place or you may cause the collapsible steering column to collapse, in which case you'll have to buy a whole new steering column unit.

12. Torque the steering wheel-to-steering column nut to 22–29 ft. lbs. (29–39 Nm).

13. Connect the horn electrical connector and install the nuts.

14. Align the spiral cable correctly with the alignment mark and install the air bag unit into the steering wheel.

15. Using new air bag-to-steering wheel Torx bolts, install them into both sides of the steering wheel and torque to 11–18 ft. lbs. (15–25 Nm).

16. Install both side lids to the steering wheel.

17. Connect the air bag unit electrical connector and install the lower lid to the steering wheel.

18. Connect the negative battery cable and make sure the air bag **red** indicator light turns ON.

Combination Switch

REMOVAL & INSTALLATION

1985–88

◆ SEE FIGS. 60, 61 AND 64

➡ **The combination switch consists of the: light switch, turn signal switch, windshield wiper switch, windshield washer control, hazard warning switch and cruise control switch.**

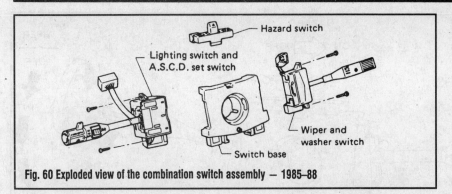

Fig. 60 Exploded view of the combination switch assembly — 1985–88

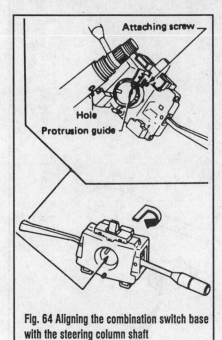

Fig. 64 Aligning the combination switch base with the steering column shaft

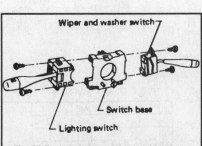

Fig. 62 Exploded view of the combination switch assembly — 1989–92

1. Disconnect the battery ground cable.
2. Remove the steering wheel. Observe the caution on the collapsible steering column.
3. Remove the steering column covers.
4. Disconnect the electrical plugs from the switch.

➡ **Individual stalk assemblies can be removed without removing the combination switch base assembly. Simply disconnect the electrical lead and remove the 2 stalk-to-base mounting screws.**

5. Remove the retaining screws and remove the switch.

To Install:

6. Install the combination switch in the proper position. The combination switch has a tab which must fit into a hole in the steering shaft in order for the system to return the switch to the neutral position after the turn has been made; be sure to align the tab and the hole when installing.
7. Install the steering column covers and steering wheel.
8. Reconnect the battery cable. Turn key to the **ON** position and check system for proper operation. Make sure the turn signals will cancel after the vehicle has made a turn.

1989–92

➧ SEE FIGS. 62–64

➡ **The combination switch consists of the: light switch, turn signal switch, windshield wiper switch, windshield washer control and hazard warning switch.**

1. Disconnect the battery ground cable.
2. Remove the steering wheel. Observe the caution on the collapsible steering column.
3. Remove the steering column covers.
4. Disconnect the electrical plugs from the switch.

➡ **Individual stalk assemblies can be removed without removing the combination switch base assembly. Simply disconnect the electrical lead and remove the 2 stalk-to-base mounting screws.**

5. Remove the retaining screws and remove the switch.

To Install:

6. Install the combination switch in the proper position. The combination switch has a tab which must fit into a hole in the steering shaft in order for the system to return the switch to the neutral position after the turn has been made; be sure to align the tab and the hole when installing.
7. Install the steering column covers and steering wheel.
8. Reconnect the battery cable. Turn key to the **ON** position and check system for proper operation. Make sure the turn signals will cancel after the vehicle has made a turn.

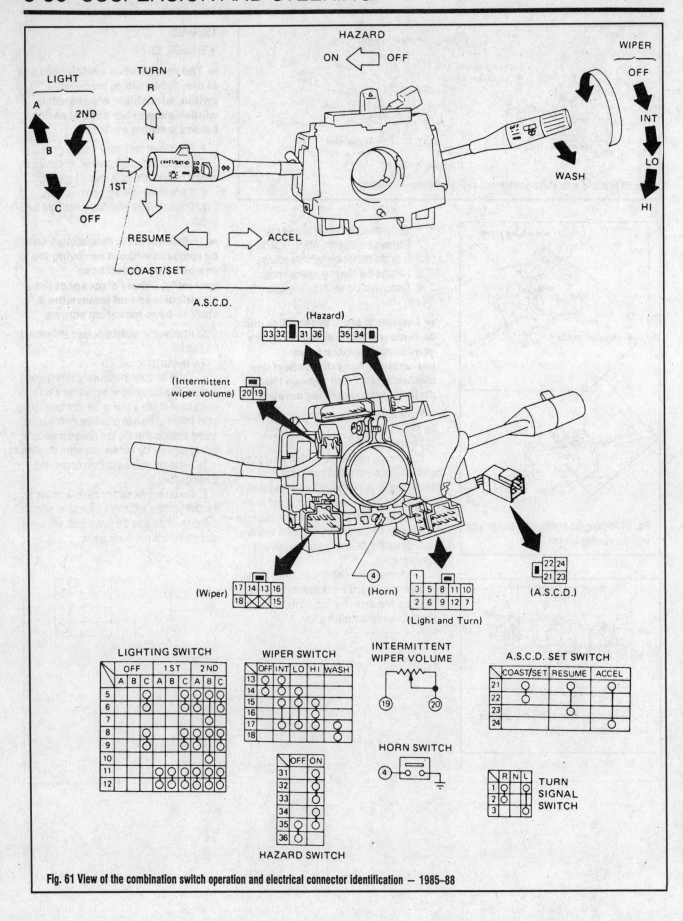

Fig. 61 View of the combination switch operation and electrical connector identification — 1985–88

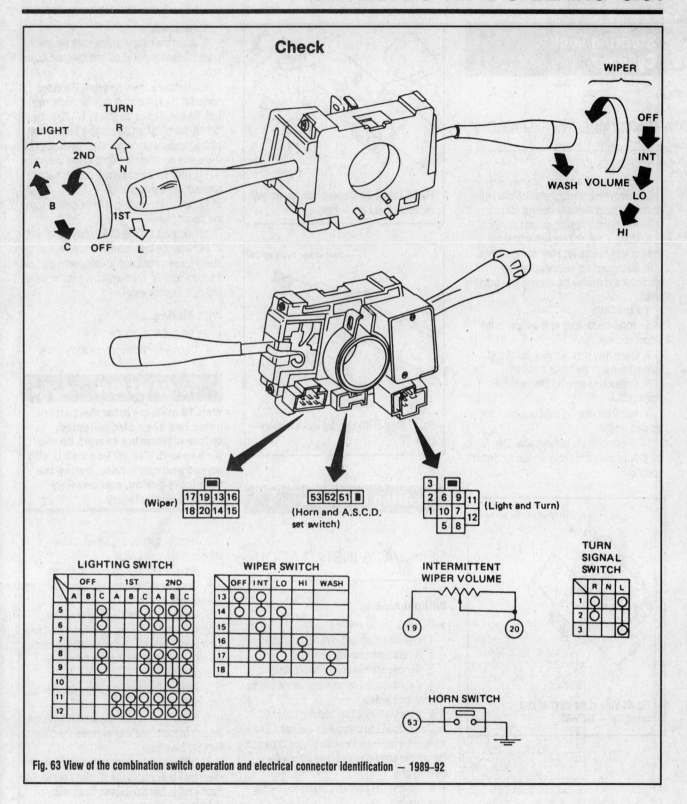

Check

Fig. 63 View of the combination switch operation and electrical connector identification — 1989–92

Steering Lock Cylinder

REMOVAL & INSTALLATION

◆ SEE FIGS. 65–67

1. Disconnect the battery ground cable.
2. Remove the steering wheel. Observe the caution on the collapsible steering column.
3. Remove the steering column covers.
4. Using a drill, drill the heads from the steering lock-to-steering shaft clamp screws.
5. Disconnect the electrical harness connector and remove the steering lock from the vehicle.

To install:

6. Install the steering lock cylinder in the proper position.
7. Using new shear screws, install and tighten them until the heads break off.
8. Connect the steering lock electrical connector.
9. Install the steering column covers and steering wheel.
10. Reconnect the battery cable. Turn key to the **ON** position and check system for proper operation.

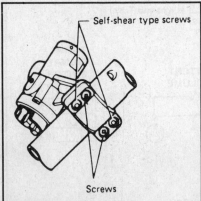

Fig. 65 View of the steering lock assembly — 1985–88

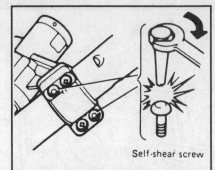

Fig. 66 Torque the steering lock screws until the heads break off — 1985–88

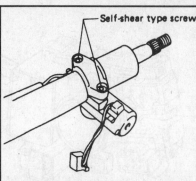

Fig. 67 View of the steering lock assembly — 1989–92

Steering Column

REMOVAL & INSTALLATION

Without Air Bag

◆ SEE FIGS. 54, 57 AND 69

1. Disconnect the negative battery cable.
2. Remove the steering wheel.
3. Remove the steering column covers.
4. Disconnect the combination switch and the steering lock wiring.
5. Remove most of the steering column support bracket and clamp nuts and bolts. Leave a few of the fasteners loosely installed to support the column while disconnecting it from the steering gear.
6. Remove the steering column-to-steering gear joint bolt.
7. Remove the temporarily installed column support bracket bolts and withdraw the column from the lower joint.
8. Withdraw the column spline shaft from the lower joint and remove the steering column. Be careful not to tear the column tube jacket insulator during removal.

To install:

9. Insert the column spline shaft into the lower joint and install all column fasteners finger-tight.

To install:

9. Insert the column spline shaft into the lower joint and install all column fasteners finger-tight.
10. Install the lower joint bolt. The cutout portion of the spline shaft must perfectly align with the bolt. Torque the bolt to 17–22 ft. lbs. (23–30 Nm). Tighten the steering bracket and clamp fasteners gradually. While tightening, make sure no stress is placed on the column.
11. Connect the combination switch and steering lock switch wiring.
12. Install the steering column covers. Install the steering wheel.
13. Connect the negative battery cable.
14. After the installation is complete, turn the steering wheel from stop-to-stop and make sure it turns smoothly. The number of turns to the left and right must be equal.

With Air Bag

◆ SEE FIGS. 57-59, 69-73

1. Disconnect the negative battery cable.

❄ CAUTION

Wait 10 minutes after the battery cable has been disconnected, before attempting to work on the air bag unit. The air bag unit is still armed and can inflate, during the 10 minute period, and possibly causing bodily injury.

2. Remove the steering wheel. Connect a stopper to the spiral cable.
3. Remove the steering column covers.
4. Disconnect the combination switch and the steering lock wiring.
5. Remove most of the steering column support bracket and clamp nuts and bolts. Leave a few of the fasteners loosely installed to support the column while disconnecting it from the steering gear.
6. Remove the steering column-to-steering gear joint bolt.
7. Remove the temporarily installed column support bracket bolts and withdraw the column from the lower joint.
8. Withdraw the column spline shaft from the lower joint and remove the steering column. Be careful not to tear the column tube jacket insulator during removal.

To install:

9. Insert the column spline shaft into the lower joint and install all column fasteners finger-tight.

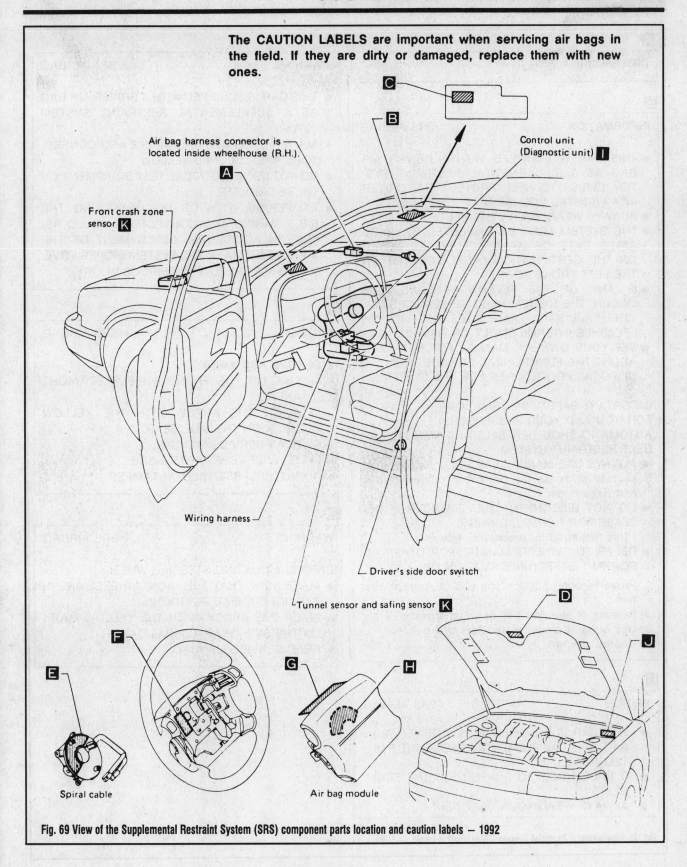

The **CAUTION LABELS** are important when servicing air bags in the field. If they are dirty or damaged, replace them with new ones.

C

B

Air bag harness connector is located inside wheelhouse (R.H.).

Control unit (Diagnostic unit) **I**

A

Front crash zone sensor **K**

Wiring harness

Driver's side door switch

D

Tunnel sensor and safing sensor **K**

J

F

E

Spiral cable

G

H

Air bag module

Fig. 69 View of the Supplemental Restraint System (SRS) component parts location and caution labels — 1992

A

DRIVER-AIRBAG

B

INFORMATION   SRS AIRBAG

- THIS CAR IS EQUIPPED WITH A DRIVER AIR BAG AS A SUPPLEMENTAL RESTRAINT SYSTEM (S.R.S.) TO HELP PROTECT THE DRIVER IN A FRONTAL COLLISION.
- ALWAYS WEAR YOUR SEAT BELT.
- THE SYSTEM MUST BE INSPECTED 10 YEARS AFTER DATE OF MANUFACTURE, AS NOTED ON THE CERTIFICATION LABEL LOCATED ON THE LEFT FRONT DOOR.
- IF ANY OF THE FOLLOWING CONDITIONS OCCUR, THE SYSTEM MUST BE SERVICED: THE "AIR BAG" LAMP DOES NOT GO ON, FLASHES INTERMITTENTLY OR REMAINS ON.
- SEE YOUR OWNER'S MANUAL FOR DETAILS ABOUT THE FUNCTIONING, SERVICE, AND DISPOSAL PROCEDURES FOR THE SYSTEM.

IMPORTANT SAFETY INFORMATION
FOR YOU AND YOUR PASSENGER
AUTOMATIC SHOULDER BELT AND MANUAL LAP BELT RESTRAINT SYSTEM

- ALWAYS USE MANUAL LAP BELT: Failure to do so may decrease the protection offered by the restraint system.
- DO NOT DISCONNECT THE EMERGENCY RELEASE FOR NORMAL DRIVING: This feature is for emergency use only.
- REFER TO OWNER'S MANUAL FOR OTHER IMPORTANT SAFETY INFORMATION ON:
1. Proper seating position and use of restraint system
2. Release of shoulder belt in an emergency
3. Use of hand crank for shoulder belt
4. Use by children

C

NOTICE   SRS AIRBAG

- THIS CAR IS EQUIPPED WITH A DRIVER AIR BAG AS A SUPPLEMENTAL RESTRAINT SYSTEM (S.R.S.)
- IT IS DESIGNED TO SUPPLEMENT THE SEAT BELT.
- ALWAYS WEAR YOUR SEAT BELT.

D

WARNING   SRS AIRBAG

- THIS CAR IS EQUIPPED WITH A DRIVER AIR BAG AS A SUPPLEMENTAL RESTRAINT SYSTEM (S.R.S.)
- ALL S.R.S. ELECTRICAL WIRING AND CONNECTORS ARE COLORED YELLOW.
- DO NOT USE ELECTRICAL TEST EQUIPMENT ON THESE CIRCUITS.
- TAMPERING WITH OR DISCONNECTING THE S.R.S. WIRING AND CONNECTORS COULD RESULT IN ACCIDENTAL DEPLOYMENT OF THE AIR BAG OR MAKE THE SYSTEM INOPERATIVE, WHICH MAY RESULT IN SERIOUS INJURY.

E

CAUTION   SRS AIRBAG

- BEFORE ASSEMBLY;
  — LINE UP THE FRONT WHEELS STRAIGHT AHEAD.
  — ALIGN THE ARROW WITH THE YELLOW MARK ON THE SIDE GEAR.
  — READ SERVICE MANUAL.
- NO SERVICEABLE PARTS INSIDE.
- DO NOT DISASSEMBLE OR TAMPER.

F

WARNING   SRS AIRBAG

BEFORE MOUNTING STEERING WHEEL;
- MAKE SURE THAT THE FRONT WHEELS ARE IN STRAIGHT-AHEAD POSITION.
- ALIGN THE ARROW WITH THE YELLOW MARK ON THE SIDE GEAR. (SPIRAL CABLE)
- READ SERVICE MANUAL.

Fig. 70 Supplemental Restraint System (SRS) caution labels — 1992

G

WARNING   SRS AIRBAG

- THIS AIR BAG MODULE CANNOT BE RE-PAIRED.
- USE DIAGNOSTIC INSTRUCTIONS TO DETERMINE IF THE UNIT IS OPERATIONAL.
- IF NOT OPERATIONAL, REPLACE AND DISPOSE OF THE ENTIRE UNIT AS DIRECTED IN THE INSTRUCTIONS.
- UNDER NO GIRCUMSTANCES SHOULD A DIAGNOSIS BE PERFORMED USING ELECTRICALLY POWERED TEST EQUIPMENT OR PROBING DEVICES.
- TAMPERING OR MISHANDLING CAN RESULT IN PERSONAL INJURY.
- STORE THE REMOVED AIR BAG MODULE WITH THE PAD SURFACE UP.
- FOR SPECIAL HANDLING OR STORAGE REFER TO SERVICE MANUAL.

H

DANGER POISON

- KEEP OUT OF THE REACH OF CHILDREN.
- CONTAINS SODIUM AZIDE AND POTASSIUM NITRATE.
- CONTENTS ARE POISONOUS AND EXTREMELY FLAMMABLE.
- CONTACT WITH ACID, WATER OR HEAVY METALS MAY PRODUCE HARMFUL AND IRRITATING GASES OR EXPLOSIVE COMPOUNDS.
- DO NOT DISMANTLE, INCINERATE, OR BRING INTO CONTACT WITH ELECTRICITY OR STORE AT TEMPERATURES EXCEEDING 200°F.
- FIRST AID: IF CONTENTS ARE SWALLOWED, INDUCE VOMITING;
  - FOR EYE CONTACT, FLUSH EYES WITH WATER FOR 15 MINUTES
  - IF GASES FROM ACID OR WATER CONTACT ARE INHALED, SEEK FRESH AIR
  - IN EVERY CASE, GET PROMPT MEDICAL ATTENTION
- FOR ADDITIONAL INFORMATION, SEE MATERIAL SAFETY DATA SHEET (MSDS) FOR THIS PRODUCT.

I

CAUTION SRS AIRBAG
- NO SERVICEABLE PARTS INSIDE.
- DO NOT DISASSEMBLE OR TAMPER.
- DO NOT DROP: KEEP DRY.
- WHILE REMOVED, STORE IN A CLEAN AND DRY AREA.
- IF WET CONDITION OCCURS, THIS UNIT MUST BE SERVICED.

J

CAUTION SRS AIRBAG

- TO AVOID DAMAGING THE S.R.S. SPIRAL CABLE, REMOVE THE STEERING WHEEL BEFORE REMOVING THE STEERING LOWER JOINT.

K

WARNING   SRS AIRBAG

- DO NOT DISASSEMBLE OR TAMPER.
- DISMANTLING AND INSTALLATION SHOULD ONLY BE PERFORMED BY TRAINED PERSONNEL.

Fig. 71 Supplemental Restraint System (SRS) caution labels — 1992, cont'd.

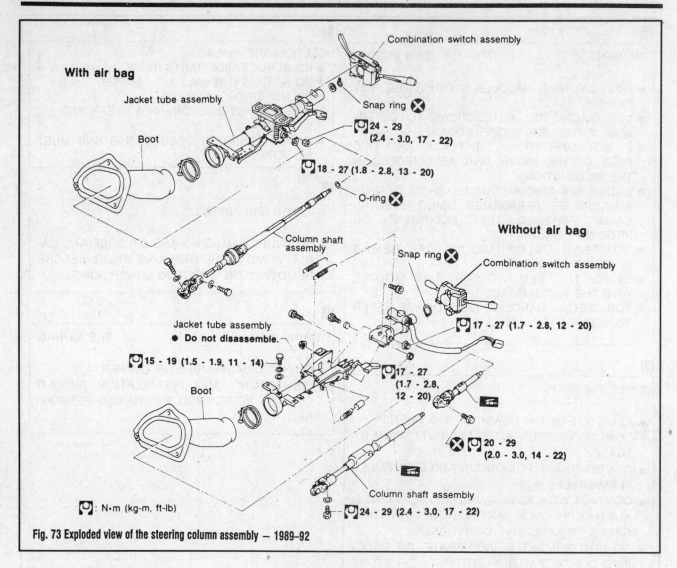

Fig. 73 Exploded view of the steering column assembly — 1989–92

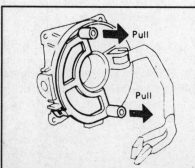

Fig. 72 Removing the stopper from the spiral cable — 1992 Supplemental Restraint System (SRS)

11. Connect the combination switch and steering lock switch wiring.

12. Install the steering column covers. Remove the stopper from the spiral cable and install the steering wheel.

13. Connect the negative battery cable and make sure the air bag **red** indicator light turns ON.

14. After the installation is complete, turn the steering wheel from stop-to-stop and make sure it turns smoothly. The number of turns to the left and right must be equal.

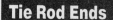

Tie Rod Ends

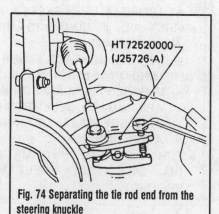

Fig. 74 Separating the tie rod end from the steering knuckle

10. Install the lower joint bolt. The cutout portion of the spline shaft must perfectly align with the bolt. Torque the bolt to 17–22 ft. lbs. (23–30 Nm). Tighten the steering bracket and clamp fasteners gradually. While tightening, make sure no stress is placed on the column.

REMOVAL & INSTALLATION

◆ SEE FIGS. 74–76
1. Raise and safely support the vehicle.

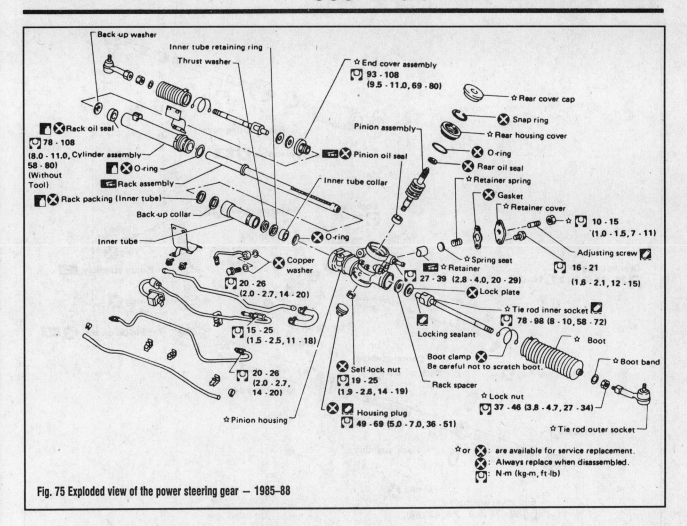

Fig. 75 Exploded view of the power steering gear — 1985–88

2. Locate the faulty tie rod end. It will have a lot of play in it and the dust cover will probably be ripped.

3. Remove the cotter key and nut from the tie rod stud. Note the position of the tie rod end in relation to the rest of the steering linkage.

4. Loosen the locknut holding the tie rod to the rest of the steering linkage.

5. Using the tie rod remover tool HT72520000 or equivalent, separate the tie rod steering knuckle.

6. Unscrew and remove the tie rod end, counting the number of turns it takes to completely free it.

To install:

7. Install the new tie rod end, turning it in exactly as far as you screwed out the old one. Make sure it is correctly positioned in relation to the rest of the steering linkage.

8. Install the tie rod ball joint to the steering knuckle and torque the:

Tie rod end-to-steering knuckle nut to 22–29 ft. lbs. (29–39 Nm)

Tie rod end-to-tie rod nut: 1985–88 — 27–34 ft. lbs. (37–46 Nm) 1989–92 — 58–72 ft. lbs. (78–98 Nm)

9. Install a new cotter pin. Before finally tightening the tie rod locknut or clamp, check and/or adjust the vehicle toe.

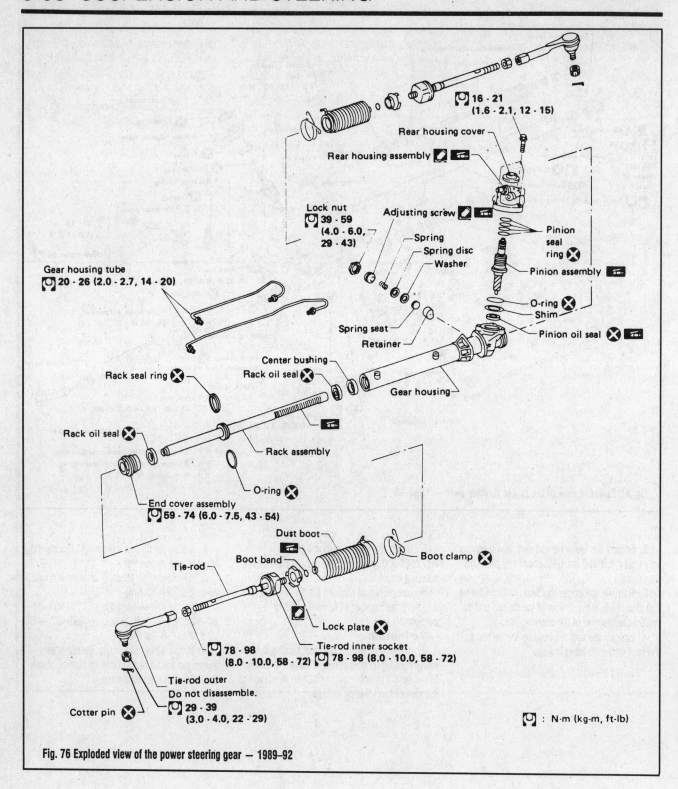

Fig. 76 Exploded view of the power steering gear — 1989–92

Power Steering Gear

REMOVAL & INSTALLATION

♦ SEE FIGS. 77 AND 78

1. Raise and safely support the vehicle. Remove the front wheels.

2. Disconnect the power steering hoses from the power steering gear and plug the hoses to prevent leakage.

3. Disconnect the tie rod ends from the steering knuckles.

4. Remove the lower steering column joint assembly from the steering gear pinion.

5. Remove the power steering gear and linkage assembly from the vehicle.

To install:

6. Install the power steering gear and linkage assembly into the vehicle.

7. Install the lower steering column joint assembly to the steering gear pinion and torque the bolt to 17–22 ft. lbs. (22–29 Nm).

8. Remove the power steering gear and linkage assembly to the vehicle and torque the clamp-to-chassis bolts to 54–72 ft. lbs. (73–97 Nm).

9. Install the tie rod ball joint to the steering knuckle and torque the tie rod end-to-steering knuckle nut to 22–29 ft. lbs. (29–39 Nm).

10. Connect the power steering hoses to the power steering gear.

11. Install the wheels and lower the vehicle.

12. Bleed the power steering system.

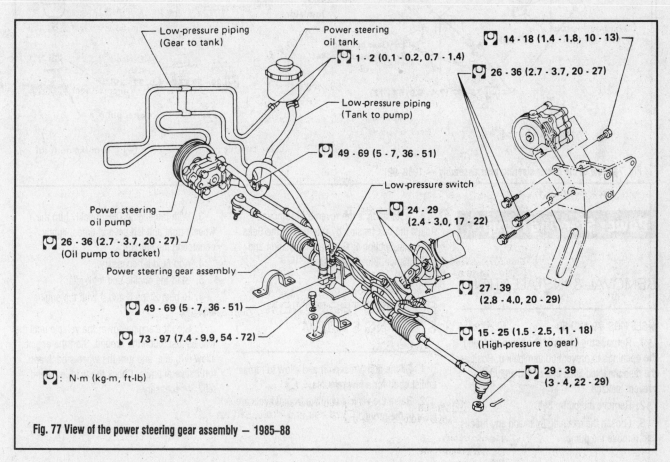

Fig. 77 View of the power steering gear assembly — 1985–88

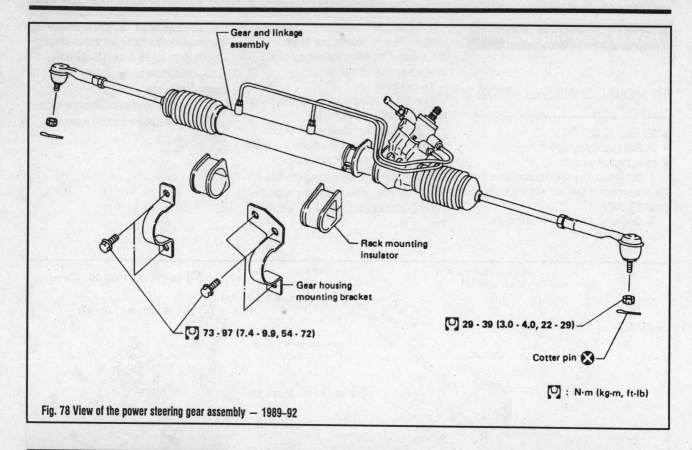

Gear and linkage assembly

Rack mounting insulator

Gear housing mounting bracket

🔧 73 - 97 (7.4 - 9.9, 54 - 72)

🔧 29 - 39 (3.0 - 4.0, 22 - 29)

Cotter pin ⊗

🔧 : N·m (kg-m, ft-lb)

Fig. 78 View of the power steering gear assembly — 1989–92

Power Steering Pump

REMOVAL & INSTALLATION

◆ SEE FIGS. 79 AND 80

1. Remove the hoses at the pump and plug the openings to prevent contamination. Position the disconnected lines in a raised attitude to prevent leakage.

2. Remove the pump belt.

3. Loosen the retaining bolts and any braces, and remove the pump.

4. Installation is the reverse of removal. Adjust the belt tension by referring to the Belts section in Section 1, General Information and Maintenance. Bleed the system.

BLEEDING THE POWER STEERING SYSTEM

1. Fill the pump reservoir and allow to remain undisturbed for a few minutes.

2. Raise the vehicle until the front wheels are clear of the ground.

3. With the engine OFF, quickly turn the wheels right and left several times, lightly contacting the stops.

4. Add fluid if necessary.

5. Start the engine and let it idle.

6. Repeat Steps 3 and 4 with the engine idling.

7. Stop the engine, lower the vehicle until the wheels just touch the ground. Start the engine, allow it to idle, and turn the wheels back and forth several times. Check the fluid level and refill, if necessary.

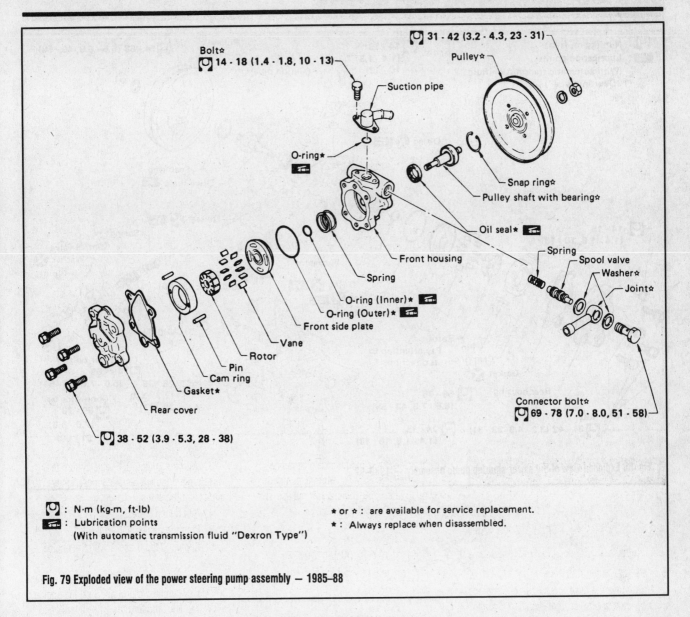

Fig. 79 Exploded view of the power steering pump assembly — 1985–88

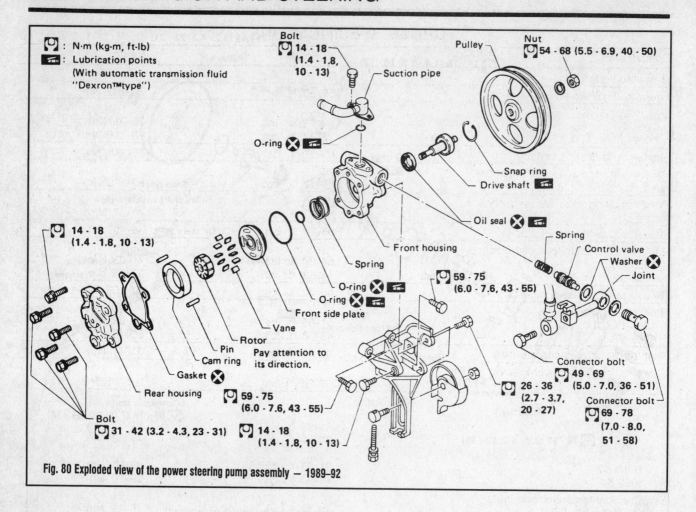

Fig. 80 Exploded view of the power steering pump assembly — 1989–92

TORQUE SPECIFICATIONS

Component	English	Metric
Air bag-to-steering wheel Torx bolts	11–18 ft. lbs.	15–25 Nm
Ball joint-to-control arm bolt assembly/nuts	56–80 ft. lbs.	76–109 Nm
Ball joint-to-steering knuckle nut	52–64 ft. lbs.	71–86 Nm
Control arm-to-gusset nut	65–87 ft. lbs.	88–118 Nm
Front strut-to-body nuts: 1985–88 1989–92	 23–31 ft. lbs. 29–40 ft. lbs.	 31–42 Nm 39–54 Nm
Front strut locknut Front 1985–88 1989–92	 51–65 ft. lbs. 30–39 ft. lbs.	 69–88 Nm 41–53 Nm

TORQUE SPECIFICATIONS

Component	English	Metric
Gusset-to-body bolts	87–108 ft. lbs.	118–147 Nm
Lower ball joint-to-control arm nuts	56–80 ft. lbs.	76–109 Nm
Lug nuts		
1985–86	58–72 ft. lbs.	78–98 Nm
1987–92	72–87 ft. lbs.	98–118 Nm
Parallel links-to-strut nut/bolt	65–87 ft. lbs.	88–118 Nm
Parallel links-to-suspension member nut/bolt	65–87 ft. lbs.	88–118 Nm
Power steering gear clamp-to-chassis bolts	54–72 ft. lbs.	73–97 Nm
Radius rod-to-bracket nut/bolt	65–80 ft. lbs.	88–108 Nm
Radius rod bracket-to-strut bolts:		
1985–86	54–69 ft. lbs.	74–93 Nm
1987–92	43–58 ft. lbs.	59–78 Nm
Radius rod-to-chassis nut/bolt	65–80 ft. lbs.	88–108 Nm
Rear strut locknut		
1985–88	51–65 ft. lbs.	69–88 Nm
1989–92	43–58 ft. lbs.	59–78 Nm
Rear upper strut-to-chassis nuts	23–31 ft. lbs.	31–41 Nm
Shock absorber actuator-to-plate bolts		
1989–92	2.2–2.8 ft. lbs.	2.9–3.8 Nm
Strut locknut		
Front		
1985–88	51–65 ft. lbs.	69–88 Nm
1989–92	30–39 ft. lbs.	41–53 Nm
Rear		
1985–88	51–65 ft. lbs.	69–88 Nm
1989–92	43–58 ft. lbs.	59–78 Nm
Stabilizer bar-to-control arm nuts		
1985–88	12–16 ft. lbs.	16–22 Nm
Stabilizer bar bracket-to-chassis bolts	23–31 ft. lbs.	31–42 Nm
Stabilizer bar-to-radius rod bracket bolt	43–58 ft. lbs.	59–78 Nm
Stabilizer bar-to-stabilizer ball joint socket nuts		
1989–92	30–38 ft. lbs.	40–51 Nm
Stabilizer bar clamp-to-connecting rod nut/bolt	43–58 ft. lbs.	59–78 Nm
Steering column-to-steering gear bolt	17–22 ft. lbs.	23–30 Nm
Steering wheel-to-steering column nut	22–29 ft. lbs.	29–39 Nm
Strut-to-steering knuckle bolts:		
1985–88	82–91 ft. lbs.	112–124 Nm
1989–92	116–123 ft. lbs.	157–167 Nm
Tie rod end-to-steering knuckle nut	22–29 ft. lbs.	29–39 Nm
Tie rod end-to-tie rod nut:		
1985–88	27–34 ft. lbs.	37–46 Nm
1989–92	58–72 ft. lbs.	78–98 Nm
Upper rear strut-to-chassis nuts	23–31 ft. lbs.	31–41 Nm
Wheel bearing hub nut		
Front wheel	174–231 ft. lbs.	235–314 Nm
Rear drum brake	137–188 ft. lbs.	186–255 Nm
Rear disc brake		
1985–86	6.5–8.7 ft. lbs.	9–12 Nm
1987–88	18–25 ft. lbs.	25–34 Nm
1989–92	137–188 ft. lbs.	186–255 Nm

Troubleshooting the Turn Signal Switch

Problem	Cause	Solution
Turn signal will not cancel	• Loose switch mounting screws • Switch or anchor bosses broken • Broken, missing or out of position detent, or cancelling spring	• Tighten screws • Replace switch • Reposition springs or replace switch as required
Turn signal difficult to operate	• Turn signal lever loose • Switch yoke broken or distorted • Loose or misplaced springs • Foreign parts and/or materials in switch • Switch mounted loosely	• Tighten mounting screws • Replace switch • Reposition springs or replace switch • Remove foreign parts and/or material • Tighten mounting screws
Turn signal will not indicate lane change	• Broken lane change pressure pad or spring hanger • Broken, missing or misplaced lane change spring • Jammed wires	• Replace switch • Replace or reposition as required • Loosen mounting screws, reposition wires and retighten screws
Turn signal will not stay in turn position	• Foreign material or loose parts impeding movement of switch yoke • Defective switch	• Remove material and/or parts • Replace switch
Hazard switch cannot be pulled out	• Foreign material between hazard support cancelling leg and yoke	• Remove foreign material. No foreign material impeding function of hazard switch—replace turn signal switch.
No turn signal lights	• Inoperative turn signal flasher • Defective or blown fuse • Loose chassis to column harness connector • Disconnect column to chassis connector. Connect new switch to chassis and operate switch by hand. If vehicle lights now operate normally, signal switch is inoperative • If vehicle lights do not operate, check chassis wiring for opens, grounds, etc.	• Replace turn signal flasher • Replace fuse • Connect securely • Replace signal switch • Repair chassis wiring as required

Troubleshooting the Turn Signal Switch (cont.)

Problem	Cause	Solution
Instrument panel turn indicator lights on but not flashing	• Burned out or damaged front or rear turn signal bulb • If vehicle lights do not operate, check light sockets for high resistance connections, the chassis wiring for opens, grounds, etc. • Inoperative flasher • Loose chassis to column harness connection • Inoperative turn signal switch • To determine if turn signal switch is defective, substitute new switch into circuit and operate switch by hand. If the vehicle's lights operate normally, signal switch is inoperative.	• Replace bulb • Repair chassis wiring as required • Replace flasher • Connect securely • Replace turn signal switch • Replace turn signal switch
Stop light not on when turn indicated	• Loose column to chassis connection • Disconnect column to chassis connector. Connect new switch into system without removing old.	• Connect securely • Replace signal switch
Stop light not on when turn indicated (cont.)	Operate switch by hand. If brake lights work with switch in the turn position, signal switch is defective. • If brake lights do not work, check connector to stop light sockets for grounds, opens, etc.	• Repair connector to stop light circuits using service manual as guide
Turn indicator panel lights not flashing	• Burned out bulbs • High resistance to ground at bulb socket • Opens, ground in wiring harness from front turn signal bulb socket to indicator lights	• Replace bulbs • Replace socket • Locate and repair as required
Turn signal lights flash very slowly	• High resistance ground at light sockets • Incorrect capacity turn signal flasher or bulb • If flashing rate is still extremely slow, check chassis wiring harness from the connector to light sockets for high resistance • Loose chassis to column harness connection • Disconnect column to chassis connector. Connect new switch into system without removing old. Operate switch by hand. If flashing occurs at normal rate, the signal switch is defective.	• Repair high resistance grounds at light sockets • Replace turn signal flasher or bulb • Locate and repair as required • Connect securely • Replace turn signal switch

Troubleshooting the Turn Signal Switch (cont.)

Problem	Cause	Solution
Hazard signal lights will not flash—turn signal functions normally	• Blow fuse • Inoperative hazard warning flasher • Loose chassis-to-column harness connection • Disconnect column to chassis connector. Connect new switch into system without removing old. Depress the hazard warning lights. If they now work normally, turn signal switch is defective. • If lights do not flash, check wiring harness "K" lead for open between hazard flasher and connector. If open, fuse block is defective	• Replace fuse • Replace hazard warning flasher in fuse panel • Conect securely • Replace turn signal switch • Repair or replace brown wire or connector as required

Troubleshooting the Power Steering Pump

Problem	Cause	Solution
Chirp noise in steering pump	• Loose belt	• Adjust belt tension to specification
Belt squeal (particularly noticeable at full wheel travel and stand still parking)	• Loose belt	• Adjust belt tension to specification
Growl noise in steering pump	• Excessive back pressure in hoses or steering gear caused by restriction	• Locate restriction and correct. Replace part if necessary.
Growl noise in steering pump (particularly noticeable at stand still parking)	• Scored pressure plates, thrust plate or rotor • Extreme wear of cam ring	• Replace parts and flush system • Replace parts
Groan noise in steering pump	• Low oil level • Air in the oil. Poor pressure hose connection.	• Fill reservoir to proper level • Tighten connector to specified torque. Bleed system by operating steering from right to left—full turn.
Rattle noise in steering pump	• Vanes not installed properly • Vanes sticking in rotor slots	• Install properly • Free up by removing burrs, varnish, or dirt
Swish noise in steering pump	• Defective flow control valve	• Replace part
Whine noise in steering pump	• Pump shaft bearing scored	• Replace housing and shaft. Flush system.

Troubleshooting the Power Steering Pump (cont.)

Problem	Cause	Solution
Hard steering or lack of assist	• Loose pump belt • Low oil level in reservoir **NOTE:** Low oil level will also result in excessive pump noise • Steering gear to column misalignment • Lower coupling flange rubbing against steering gear adjuster plug • Tires not properly inflated	• Adjust belt tension to specification • Fill to proper level. If excessively low, check all lines and joints for evidence of external leakage. Tighten loose connectors. • Align steering column • Loosen pinch bolt and assemble properly • Inflate to recommended pressure
Foaming milky power steering fluid, low fluid level and possible low pressure	• Air in the fluid, and loss of fluid due to internal pump leakage causing overflow	• Check for leaks and correct. Bleed system. Extremely cold temperatures will cause system aeriation should the oil level be low. If oil level is correct and pump still foams, remove pump from vehicle and separate reservoir from body. Check welsh plug and body for cracks. If plug is loose or body is cracked, replace body.
Low pump pressure	• Flow control valve stuck or inoperative • Pressure plate not flat against cam ring	• Remove burrs or dirt or replace. Flush system. • Correct
Momentary increase in effort when turning wheel fast to right or left	• Low oil level in pump • Pump belt slipping • High internal leakage	• Add power steering fluid as required • Tighten or replace belt • Check pump pressure.
Steering wheel surges or jerks when turning with engine running especially during parking	• Low oil level • Loose pump belt • Steering linkage hitting engine oil pan at full turn • Insufficient pump pressure	• Fill as required • Adjust tension to specification • Correct clearance • Check pump pressure. Replace flow control valve if defective.
Steering wheel surges or jerks when turning with engine running especially during parking (cont.)	• Sticking flow control valve	• Inspect for varnish or damage, replace if necessary
Excessive wheel kickback or loose steering	• Air in system	• Add oil to pump reservoir and bleed by operating steering. Check hose connectors for proper torque and adjust as required

Troubleshooting the Power Steering Pump (cont.)

Problem	Cause	Solution
Low pump pressure	• Extreme wear of cam ring	• Replace parts. Flush system.
	• Scored pressure plate, thrust plate, or rotor	• Replace parts. Flush system.
	• Vanes not installed properly	• Install properly
	• Vanes sticking in rotor slots	• Freeup by removing burrs, varnish, or dirt
	• Cracked or broken thrust or pressure plate	• Replace part

9

BRAKES

BRAKE OPERATING SYSTEM

Adjustments

DRUM TYPE BRAKES

1. Raise and support the rear of the vehicle on jackstands.
2. Remove the rubber cover from the backing plate.
3. Insert a brake adjusting tool through the hole in the brake backing plate. Turn the toothed adjusting nut to spread the brake shoes, making contact with the brake drum.
➡ **When adjusting the brake shoes, turn the wheel until considerable drag is felt.**

4. When considerable drag is felt, back off the adjusting nut a few notches, so the correct clearance is maintained between the brake drum and the brake shoes. Make sure the wheel rotates freely.

BRAKE PEDAL

♦ SEE FIGS. 1–3

1. Before adjusting the pedal, make sure the wheel brakes are correctly adjusted.
2. To adjust the pedal free height, perform the following procedure:
   a. Loosen the input rod locknut.
   b. Adjust the pedal free height to 7.24–7.64 in. (184–194mm) for 1985–88 or 6.26–6.65 in. (159–169mm) for 1989–92 with a manual transaxle or 6.65–7.05 in. (169–179mm) for 1989–92 with an automatic transaxle.
   c. Torque the locknut to 12–16 ft. lbs. (16–22 Nm); make sure the input rod tip stays inside the clevis.
3. To adjust the brake light and/or ASCD cancel switch(s)-to-pedal clearance, perform the following procedures:
   a. Disconnect the electrical connector from the brake light and/or ASCD cancel switch(s).
   b. Loosen the brake light switch and the ASCD cancel switch (1989–92) locknuts.
   c. Turn the switch(s) to adjust the clearance between the pedal stopper and the threaded end; the clearance should be 0.012–0.039 in. (0.3–1.0mm).

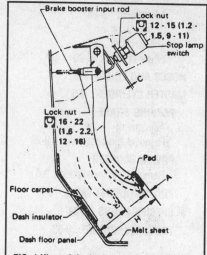

FIG. 1 View of the brake pedal adjustments — 1985–88

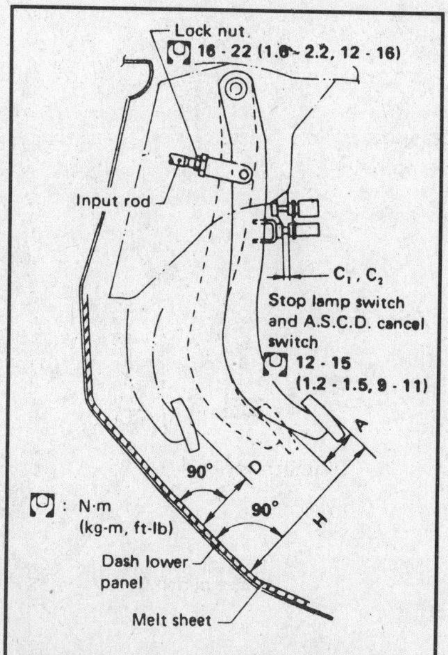

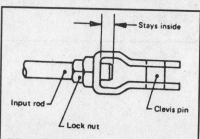

FIG. 2 View of the brake pedal adjustments — 1989–92

FIG. 3 Making sure the input rod stays inside the brake clevis when tightening the locknut

   d. Torque the brake light and/or ASCD cancel switch locknuts to 9–11 ft. lbs. (12–15 Nm).
   e. Connect the electrical connector to the brake light switch and/or the ASCD cancel switch.
4. Check the pedal free-play; it should be 0.04–0.12 in. (1–3mm). Make sure the brake light is OFF when the pedal is released.
5. Check the brake pedal depressed height with the engine running. If the height is under 3.94 in. (100mm) for 1985–88 or 3.54 in. (90mm) for 1989–92, check the system for leaks, accumulation of air or damage to the components, such as: master cylinder, wheel cylinder or etc.; make the necessary repairs.

Brake Light Switch

REMOVAL & INSTALLATION

1. Disconnect the negative battery terminal.
2. Disconnect the electrical connector from the brake light and/or ASCD cancel switch(s).
3. Loosen the brake light switch and/or the ASCD cancel switch (1989–92) locknuts.
4. Remove the brake light switch and/or the ASCD cancel switch (1989–92).

To Install:

5. Install the switch(s). Turn the switch(s) to adjust the clearance between the pedal stopper and the threaded end; the clearance should be 0.012–0.039 in. (0.3–1.0mm).
6. Torque the brake light and/or ASCD cancel switch locknuts to 9–11 ft. lbs. (12–15 Nm).
7. Connect the electrical connector to the brake light switch and/or the ASCD cancel switch. Make sure the brake light is OFF when the pedal is released.
8. Connect the negative battery cable.

Brake Pedal

REMOVAL & INSTALLATION

♦ SEE FIG. 4–6

1. Disconnect the negative battery cable.
2. Disconnect the input rod from the brake pedal.

3. On the 1985–88 models, remove the E-ring and return spring from the fulcrum bolt; discard the E-ring. On the 1989–92 models, remove the fulcrum bolt nut, washer and return spring.

4. Remove the fulcrum bolt and the brake pedal.

To install:

5. Install the brake pedal and the fulcrum bolt.

6. On the 1985–88 models, install the return spring and secure with a new E-ring. On the 1989–92 models, install the return spring, the washer and the nut; torque the nut to 12–16 ft. lbs. (16–22 Nm).

7. Install the input rod to the brake pedal and secure with the clevis pin.

8. Connect the negative battery cable.

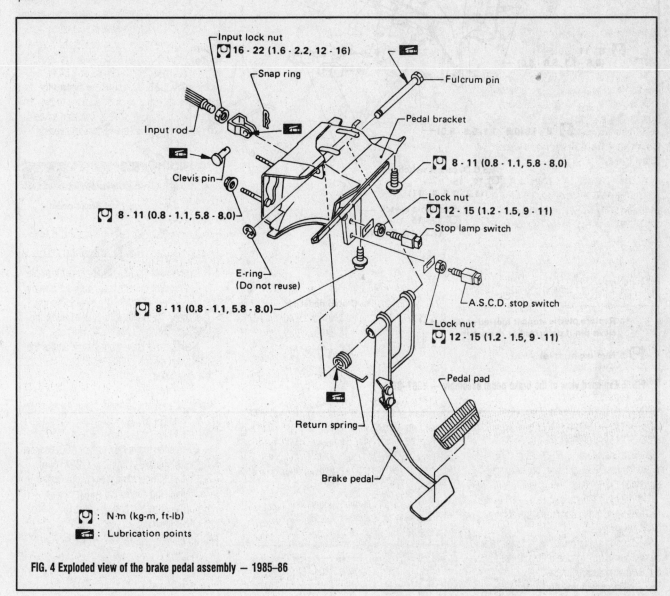

○ : N·m (kg-m, ft-lb)

◀▦ : Lubrication points

FIG. 4 Exploded view of the brake pedal assembly — 1985–86

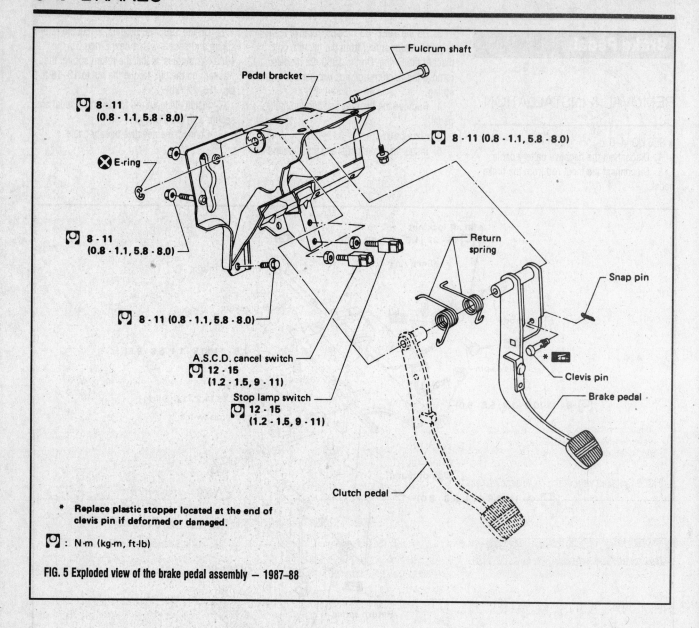

Fulcrum shaft

Pedal bracket

8 - 11 (0.8 - 1.1, 5.8 - 8.0)

8 - 11 (0.8 - 1.1, 5.8 - 8.0)

E-ring

Return spring

Snap pin

8 - 11 (0.8 - 1.1, 5.8 - 8.0)

Clevis pin

Brake pedal

8 - 11 (0.8 - 1.1, 5.8 - 8.0)

A.S.C.D. cancel switch
12 - 15 (1.2 - 1.5, 9 - 11)

Stop lamp switch
12 - 15 (1.2 - 1.5, 9 - 11)

Clutch pedal

* Replace plastic stopper located at the end of
clevis pin if deformed or damaged.

: N·m (kg-m, ft-lb)

FIG. 5 Exploded view of the brake pedal assembly — 1987–88

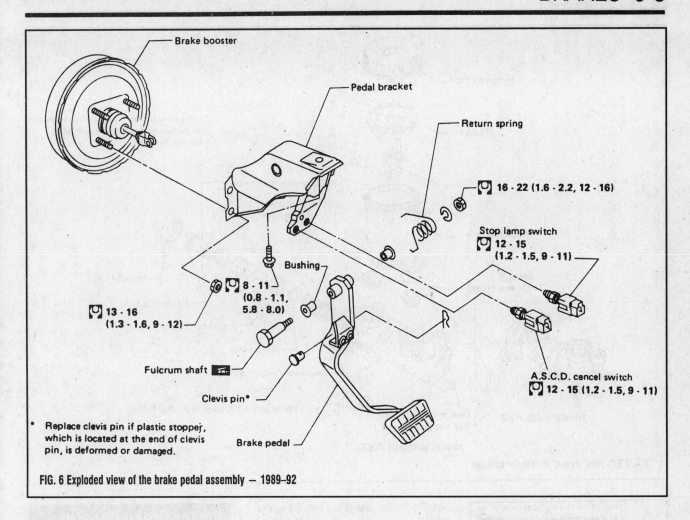

Brake booster

Pedal bracket

Return spring

16 - 22 (1.6 - 2.2, 12 - 16)

Stop lamp switch
12 - 15
(1.2 - 1.5, 9 - 11)

Bushing

8 - 11
(0.8 - 1.1,
5.8 - 8.0)

13 - 16
(1.3 - 1.6, 9 - 12)

A.S.C.D. cancel switch
12 - 15 (1.2 - 1.5, 9 - 11)

Fulcrum shaft

Clevis pin*

* Replace clevis pin if plastic stopper,
which is located at the end of clevis
pin, is deformed or damaged.

Brake pedal

FIG. 6 Exploded view of the brake pedal assembly — 1989–92

Master Cylinder

REMOVAL & INSTALLATION

♦ SEE FIG. 7

1. Disconnect the negative battery terminal and the electrical connector from the reservoir.

2. Clean the outside of the master cylinder thoroughly, particularly around the cap and fluid lines.

3. Disconnect the brake fluid tubes, then plug the openings to prevent dirt from entering the system.

4. Remove the master cylinder-to-power booster nuts and remove the master cylinder from the vehicle.

To install:

5. Bench bleed the master cylinder assembly before installation.

6. Install the master cylinder and torque the master cylinder-to-power booster nuts to 5.8–8.0 ft. lbs. (8–11 Nm).

7. Connect the brake lines.

8. Refill the reservoir with brake fluid and bleed the system. Adjust the brake system if necessary.

9. Connect the negative battery cable and the electrical to the bottom of the reservoir.

➡ **Ordinary brake fluid will boil and cause brake failure under the high temperatures developed in disc brake systems; use DOT 3 brake fiuid in the brake systems. The adjustable pushrod is used to adjust brake pedal free height.**

MASTER CYLINDER BLEEDING

1. Place the master cylinder in a vise.

2. Connect 2 lines to the fluid outlet orifices and into the reservoir.

3. Fill the reservoir with brake fluid.

4. Using a wooden dowel, depress the pushrod slowly, allowing the pistons to return. Do this several times until the air bubbles are all expelled.

5. Remove the bleeding tubes from the master cylinder, plug the outlets and install the caps.

OVERHAUL

♦ SEE FIG. 7–9

➡ **Use this service procedure and exploded view illustrations as a guide for overhaul of the master cylinder assembly. If in doubt about overhaul condition or service procedure REPLACE the complete assembly with a new master cylinder assembly.**

1. Remove the reservoir cap, the oil filter and the float from the reservoir.

2. Pull the reservoir from the master cylinder and discard the seals.

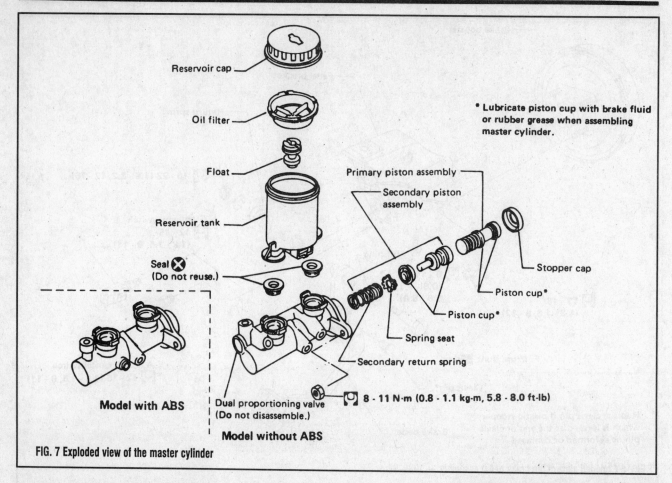

* Lubricate piston cup with brake fluid
or rubber grease when assembling
master cylinder.

Reservoir cap

Oil filter

Float

Reservoir tank

Primary piston assembly

Secondary piston
assembly

Seal ⊗
(Do not reuse.)

Stopper cap

Piston cup*

Piston cup*

Spring seat

Secondary return spring

Model with ABS

Dual proportioning valve
(Do not disassemble.)

8 - 11 N·m (0.8 - 1.1 kg-m, 5.8 - 8.0 ft-lb)

Model without ABS

FIG. 7 Exploded view of the master cylinder

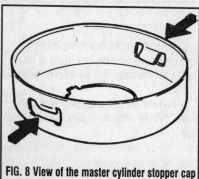

FIG. 8 View of the master cylinder stopper cap

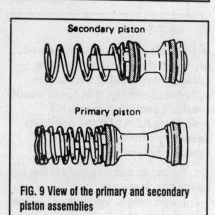

Secondary piston

Primary piston

FIG. 9 View of the primary and secondary
piston assemblies

3. Pry the the stopper cap from the master cylinder.

4. Dump the primary piston assembly and the secondary piston assembly from the master cylinder; be sure to pay attention to the direction of the parts.

5. Inspect the components for damage; if necessary, replace the damaged parts.

To install:

6. Clean all parts in clean brake fluid.

7. Install the secondary piston assembly and the primary piston assembly into the master cylinder.

➡ **If the stopper cap claw is deformed or damaged, replace it.**

8. Install the stopper cap to the master cylinder.

9. Using new seals, install the reservoir tank.

10. Into the reservoir, install the float, the oil filter and the reservoir cap.

Power Brake Booster

REMOVAL & INSTALLATION

◆ SEE FIG. 10

➡ **Make sure all vacuum lines and connectors are in good condition. A small vacuum leak will cause a big problem in the power brake system.**

1. Disconnect the negative battery cable. Remove the master cylinder mounting nuts and pull the master cylinder assembly (brake lines connected) away from the power booster.

2. Detach the vacuum line from the booster.

3. Detach the booster pushrod at the pedal clevis.

4. Unbolt the booster from under the dash and lift it out of the engine compartment.

To install:

5. Install the brake booster assembly to the vehicle; torque the booster-to-chassis nuts to 5.8–8 ft. lbs. (8–11 Nm) for 1985–90 or 9–12 ft. lbs. (13–16 Nm) for 1991–92.

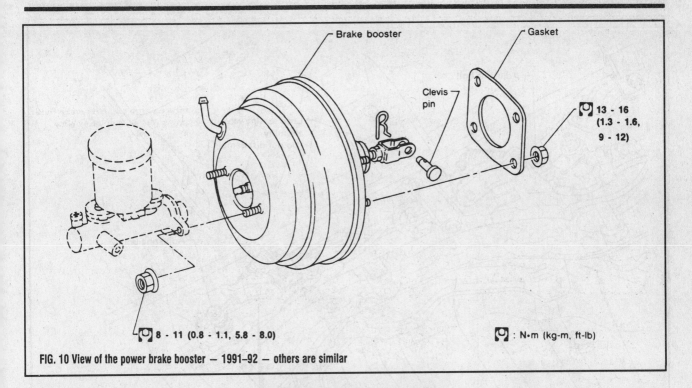

FIG. 10 View of the power brake booster — 1991–92 — others are similar

6. Install the master cylinder assembly and torque the master cylinder-to-power booster nuts to 5.8–8.0 ft. lbs. (8–11 Nm).

7. Connect the booster pushrod to the pedal clevis. Connect the vacuum lines to brake booster.

8. Connect the battery. Start the engine and check brake operation.

ADJUSTMENT

♦ SEE FIG. 11

1. Using a hand vacuum pump, apply 19.69 in. Hg (500mm Hg) of vacuum to the power booster.

2. Measure and/or adjust the push rod length to 0.4045–0.4144 in. (10.275–10.525mm).

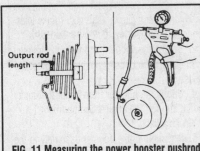

FIG. 11 Measuring the power booster pushrod length

Brake Proportioning Valve

REMOVAL & INSTALLATION

The master cylinders are equipped with integral dual proportioning valves that are not to be disassembled; if necessary, replace the master cylinder.

Twin Load Sensing Valve

♦ SEE FIG. 12

The twin load sensing valve is used on the 1989–92 vehicles

REMOVAL & INSTALLATION

1. If equipped with ABS, turn the ignition switch **OFF** and disconnect the electrical connectors from the ABS actuator.

2. Raise and safely support the vehicle.

3. Remove the brake tube(s) from the load sensing valve assembly(s); be sure to plug the openings to prevent dirt from entering the system.

4. Remove the load sensing valve-to-rear control arm bolt and the load sensing valve-to-chassis bolts and the load sensing valve.

To install:

5. If the load sensing valve is damaged, replace it with a new one.

6. Using multi-purpose grease, lubricate all rubbing areas of the load sensing valve.

7. Install the load sensing valve and torque the load sensing valve-to-chassis bolts to 25–29 ft. lbs. (34–39 Nm).

8. Torque the brake tube(s)-to-load sensing valve nut(s) to 12–14 ft. lbs. (17–20 Nm).

9. Check and/or adjust the load sensing valve.

ADJUSTMENT

♦ SEE FIGS. 13 AND 14

1. Raise and safely support the vehicle.

2. Place a person in the driver's seat and a 600 lb. (5,884 N) weight in the trunk.

3. Using the pressure gauge set KV991V0010 or equivalent, connect 1 gauge to the front brake air bleeder and 1 gauge to the rear brake air bleeder.

4. Bleed the air from the front and rear brake lines.

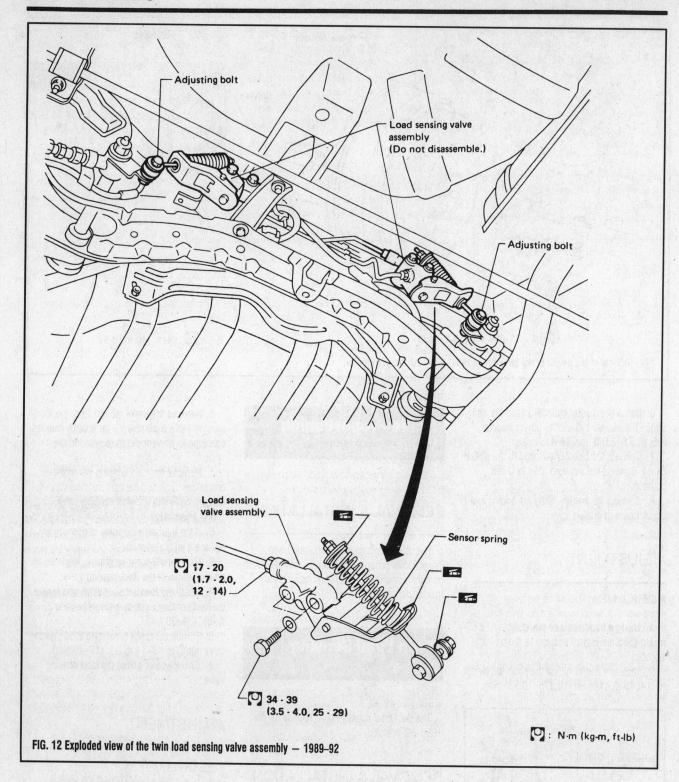

Adjusting bolt

Load sensing valve
assembly
(Do not disassemble.)

Adjusting bolt

Load sensing
valve assembly

Sensor spring

17 - 20
(1.7 - 2.0,
12 - 14)

34 - 39
(3.5 - 4.0, 25 - 29)

: N·m (kg-m, ft-lb)

FIG. 12 Exploded view of the twin load sensing valve assembly — 1989–92

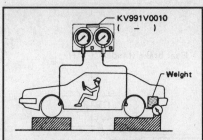

FIG. 13 Preparing the vehicle for inspection and adjustment of the twin load sensing valve — 1989–92

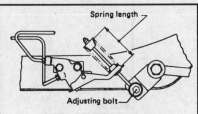

FIG. 14 Adjusting the load sensing valve spring length — 1989–92

5. Adjust the pressure gauge to raise the front brake pressure to 711 psi. (4,904 kPa) and check the rear brake pressure; the rear brake pressure should be 555–697 psi. (3,825–4,805 kPa).

6. Adjust the pressure gauge to raise the rear brake pressure to 1,422 psi. (9,807 kPa) and check the front brake pressure; the front brake pressure should be 739–939 psi. (5,100–6,473 kPa).

➡ **When raising the front brake pressure, depress the brake pedal slowly. Check the rear brake pressure 2 seconds after the front brake pressure reaches the specified valve.**

7. If the rear brake pressure is not within the specifications, use the adjusting bolt to adjust the sensor spring length.

8. Repeat Steps 5–7.

9. If the pressure is not within the specified range after the spring length is adjusted, replace the twin load sensing valve assembly.

Brake Hoses and Pipes

◆ SEE FIGS. 15–17

It is important to use quality brake hose intended specifically for the application. Hose of less than the best quality or hose not made to the specified length will tend to fatigue and may therefore create premature leakage and,

consequently, a potential for brake failure. Note also that brake hoses differs from one side of the car to the other and should therefore be ordered specifying the side on which it will be installed.

Make sure hose end mating surfaces are clean and free of nicks and burrs, which would prevent effective sealing. Use new copper seals on banjo fittings.

✳✳ CAUTION

When routing a brake hose to a vehicle, minimize hose twisting and bending upon installation!

REMOVAL & INSTALLATION

Front Brake Hose

✳✳ CAUTION

If working on a vehicle with an anti-lock braking system, be sure to turn the ignition switch OFF and disconnect the electrical connectors from the ABS actuator before attempting to open any brake line.

1. Place a drain pan under the hose connections. First, disconnect the hose where it connects to the body bracket and steel tube.

2. Unbolt the hose bracket from the strut assembly.

3. Remove the bolt to disconnect the banjo connection at the caliper.

To install:

4. Position the new hose, noting that the body bracket and the body end of the hose are keyed to prevent installation of the hose in the wrong direction. First attach the hose to the banjo connector on the caliper (torque connection).

5. Bolt the hose bracket located in the center of the hose to the strut, allowing the bracket to position the hose so it will not be twisted.

6. Attach the hose to the body bracket and steel brake tube.

7. Torque all connections. Bleed the system thoroughly, by referring to the correct bleeding procedure.

Rear Brake Hose

✳✳ CAUTION

If working on a vehicle with an anti-lock braking system, be sure to turn the ignition switch OFF and disconnect the electrical connectors from the ABS actuator before attempting to open any brake line.

1. Place a drain pan under the hose connections. Disconnect the double nut (using a primary wrench and a backup wrench) at the tube mounted on the floor pan. Then, disconnect the hose at the retaining clip.

2. Disconnect the hose at the trailing arm tube.

To install:

3. Install the new tube to the trailing arm connection first. Torque the connection.

4. Then, making sure it is not twisted, connect it to the tube on the floor pan. Again, torque the connection.

5. Bleed the system thoroughly, by referring to the correct bleeding procedure.

Caliper Hose-Rear Disc Brakes

✳✳ CAUTION

If working on a vehicle with an anti-lock braking system, be sure to turn the ignition switch OFF and disconnect the electrical connectors from the ABS actuator before attempting to open any brake line.

1. Place a drain pan under the hose connections. Disconnect the double nut (using a primary wrench and a backup wrench) at the tube mounted on the clip, located on the caliper-mounted bracket.

2. Disconnect the banjo connector by removing the through bolt.

To install:

3. Install the new hose by connecting the banjo connector first, using new copper seals and torquing the connection.

4. Making sure the hose is not twisted, make the connection to the tube, and torque the connection.

5. Secure the hose to the bracket with the retaining clip. Bleed the system thoroughly, by referring to the correct bleeding procedure.

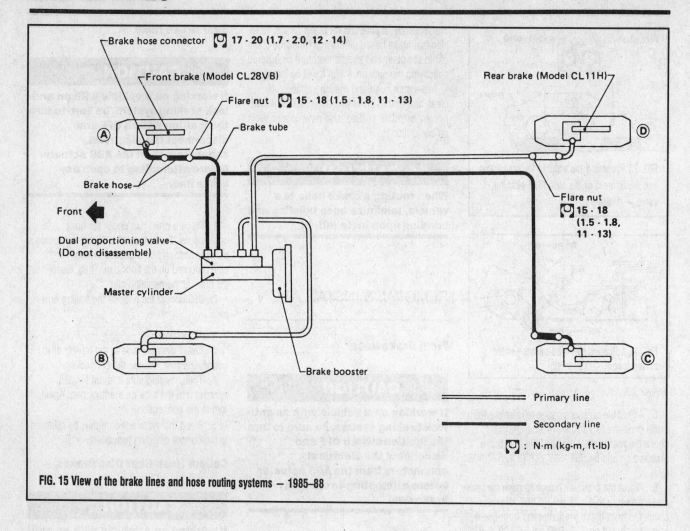

FIG. 15 View of the brake lines and hose routing systems — 1985–88

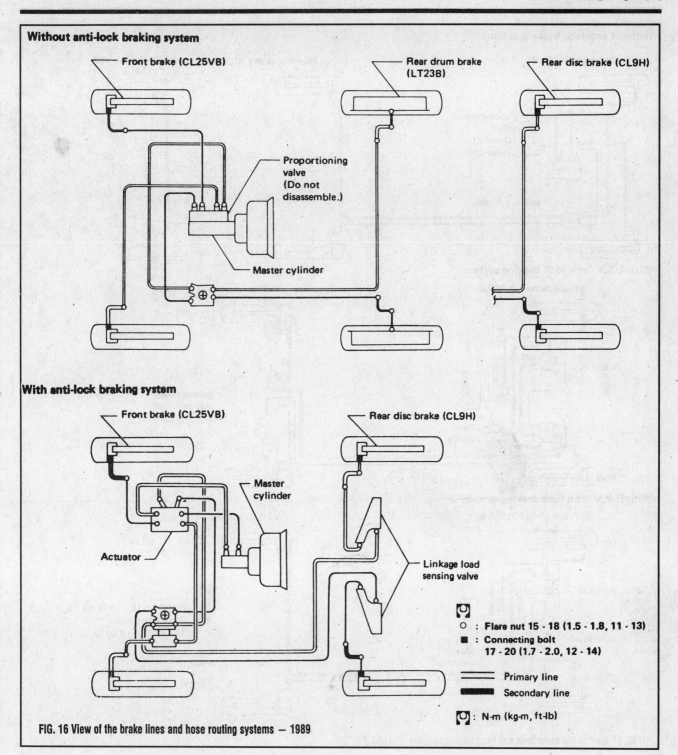

Without anti-lock braking system

Front brake (CL25VB)

Rear drum brake (LT23B)

Rear disc brake (CL9H)

Proportioning valve (Do not disassemble.)

Master cylinder

With anti-lock braking system

Front brake (CL25VB)

Rear disc brake (CL9H)

Master cylinder

Actuator

Linkage load sensing valve

○ : Flare nut 15 - 18 (1.5 - 1.8, 11 - 13)
■ : Connecting bolt 17 - 20 (1.7 - 2.0, 12 - 14)

Primary line
Secondary line

: N·m (kg-m, ft-lb)

FIG. 16 View of the brake lines and hose routing systems — 1989

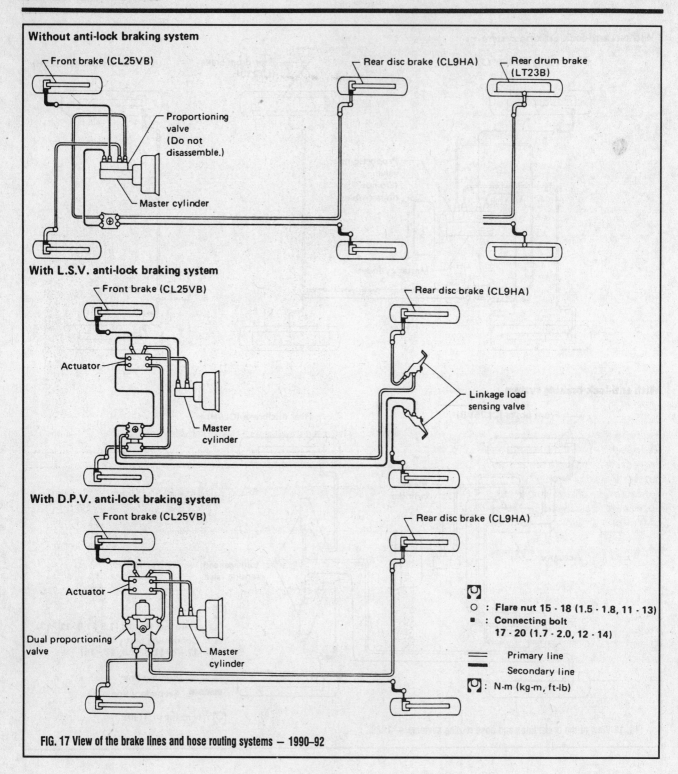

Without anti-lock braking system

Front brake (CL25VB)

Rear disc brake (CL9HA)

Rear drum brake (LT23B)

Proportioning valve (Do not disassemble.)

Master cylinder

With L.S.V. anti-lock braking system

Front brake (CL25VB)

Rear disc brake (CL9HA)

Actuator

Linkage load sensing valve

Master cylinder

With D.P.V. anti-lock braking system

Front brake (CL25VB)

Rear disc brake (CL9HA)

Actuator

Dual proportioning valve

Master cylinder

○ : Flare nut 15 - 18 (1.5 - 1.8, 11 - 13)
■ : Connecting bolt 17 - 20 (1.7 - 2.0, 12 - 14)

Primary line
Secondary line

: N·m (kg-m, ft-lb)

FIG. 17 View of the brake lines and hose routing systems — 1990–92

Brake System Bleeding

➡ **If vehicle is equipped with a Anti-Lock Brake System (ABS), refer to the bleeding procedures later in this section.**

The purpose of bleeding the brakes is to expel air trapped in the hydraulic system. The system must be bled whenever the pedal feels spongy, indicating that air, which is compressible, has entered the system. It must also be bled whenever the system has been opened or repaired. You will need a helper for this job.

Never reuse brake fluid which has been bled from the system.

BLEEDING PROCEDURE

♦ SEE FIG. 18

1. Clean all dirt from around the master cylinder reservoir caps. Remove the caps and fill the master cylinder to the proper level with clean, fresh brake fluid meeting DOT 3 specifications.

➡ **Brake fluid picks up moisture from the air, which reduces its effectiveness and causes brake line corrosion. Don't leave the master cylinder or the fluid container open any longer than necessary. Be careful not to spill brake fluid on painted surfaces. Wipe up any spilled fluid immediately and rinse the area with clear water.**

2. Clean all the bleeder screws. You may want to give each one a shot of penetrating solvent to loosen it. Seizure is a common problem with bleeder screws, which then break off, sometimes requiring replacement of the part to which they are attached.

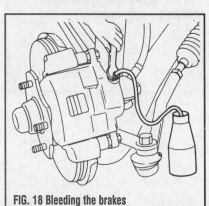

FIG. 18 Bleeding the brakes

FIG. 18A View of the rear drum brake wheel cylinder bleeding screw

FIG. 18B Bleeding the front wheel caliper

3. Attach a length of clear vinyl tubing to the bleeder screw on the left rear wheel cylinder or caliper. Insert the other end of the tube into a clear, clean jar 1/2 filled with brake fluid.

4. Have your helper SLOWLY depress the brake pedal. As this is done, open the bleeder (follow the correct bleeding order) screw 1/3–1/2 of a turn, and allow the fluid to run through the tube. Close the bleeder screw before the pedal reaches the end of its travel. Have your assistant slowly release the pedal. Repeat this process until no air bubbles appear in the expelled fluid.

5. Repeat the procedure on the other wheels in the following order:
   a. Right front caliper
   b. Right rear wheel cylinder or caliper
   c. Left front caliper

6. Be sure to check the fluid level in the master cylinder reservoirs often. Do not allow the reservoirs to run dry or the bleeding process will have to be repeated.

FRONT DISC BRAKES

☀ CAUTION

Brake shoes contain asbestos, which has been determined to be a cancer causing agent. Never clean the brake surfaces with compressed air! Avoid inhaling any dust from any brake surface! When cleaning brake surfaces, use a commercially available brake cleaning fluid.

Brake Pads

◆ SEE FIGS. 19 AND 20

REMOVAL & INSTALLATION

➡ **The front brake pads MUST ALWAYS be replaced as a complete set. Bleed the brake system only if necessary.**

Types CL28VB and CL25VB

1. Raise and safely support the vehicle. Remove the front wheel.

2. It may be necessary to use a C-clamp to compress the brake caliper piston to loosen the brake pads. Remove the pin (lower) bolt from the caliper.

3. Swing the caliper body upward on the upper bolt.

4. Remove the pad retainers and inner and outer shims.

➡ **Do not depress the brake pedal when the cylinder body is in the raised position or the piston will pop out. Avoid damaging the piston seal when removing/installing the pads and retainers.**

5. Remove the brake pads from the torque member.

To install:

6. Check the level of fluid in the master cylinder. If the fluid is near the maximum level, use a clean syringe to remove fluid until the level is down well below the lip of the reservoir.

7. Use a large C-clamp to press the caliper piston back into the caliper, to allow room for the installation of the thicker new pads.

8. Install the new pads, new shims and pad retainer(s).

9. Lower the brake caliper and torque the lower retaining bolt to 12–14 ft. lbs. (17–20 Nm) for 1985–88 or 16–23 ft. lbs. (22–31 Nm) for 1989–92. Torque the wheel nuts to 72–87 ft. lbs. (98–118 Nm).

10. Bleed and adjust the brakes, if necessary. Make sure you pump the brakes and get a hard pedal before driving the vehicle!

INSPECTION

1. Brake pad lining thickness can be checked without removing the pads.

2. When replacing pads, always check the surface of the rotors for scoring or wear.

3. Brake pad composite standard thickness is 0.433 in. (11.0mm). Brake pad composite wear limit is 0.079 in. (2.0mm).

4. The rotors should be removed for resurfacing if badly scored.

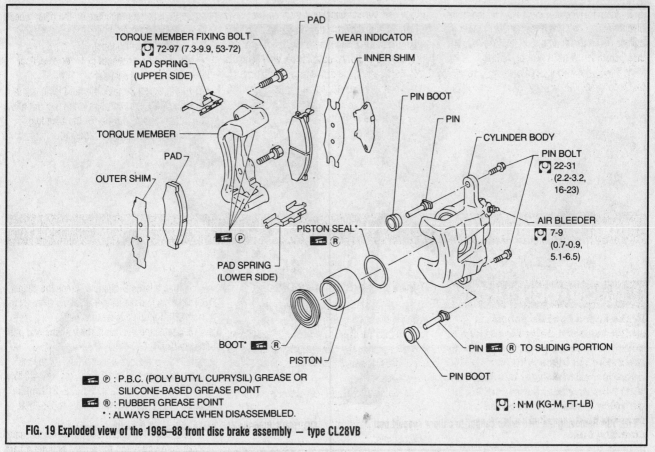

FIG. 19 Exploded view of the 1985–88 front disc brake assembly — type CL28VB

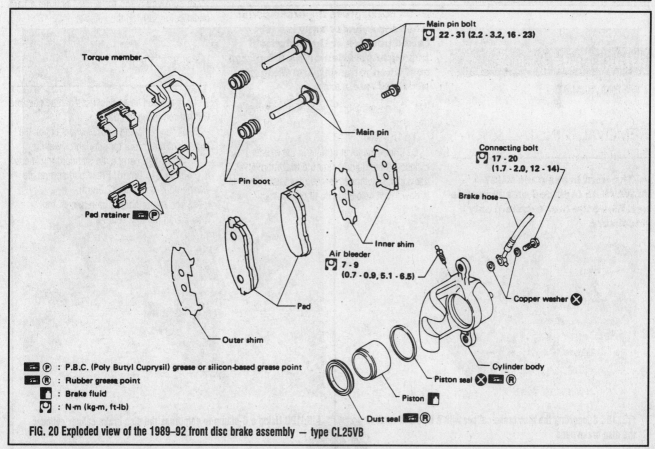

FIG. 20 Exploded view of the 1989–92 front disc brake assembly — type CL25VB

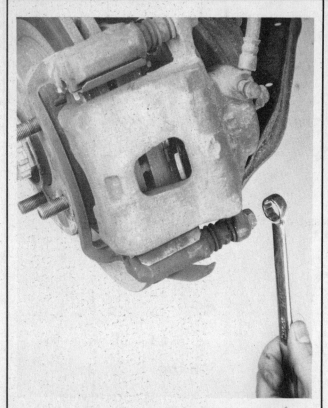

FIG. 19A Removing the disc brake caliper-to-caliper support bolt

FIG. 19B Lifting the disc brake caliper off the caliper support

FIG. 19C Supporting the disc brake caliper with a wire and removing the disc brake pads

FIG. 19D Using a C-clamp to compress the disc brake caliper cylinder

FIG. 19E Removing the disc brake pad shims from the caliper support

FIG. 19F View of the disc brake pads and shims

Brake Caliper

♦ SEE FIGS. 19 AND 20

REMOVAL & INSTALLATION

1. Refer to "Brake Pads Removal and Installation" procedure in this section and remove the brake pads.

2. Remove both guide pin bolts and brake hose connector; be sure to plug the openings to prevent dirt from entering the system.

3. Remove the caliper assembly from the vehicle.

To install:

4. Check the level of fluid in the master cylinder. If the fluid is near the maximum level, use a clean syringe to remove fluid until the level is down well below the lip of the reservoir.

5. Use a large C-clamp to press the caliper piston back into the caliper, to allow room for the installation of the thicker new pads.

6. Install the new pads, new shims and pad retainer(s).

7. Install the brake caliper and torque the caliper-to-torque member pin bolts to 12–14 ft. lbs. (17–20 Nm) for 1985–88 or 16–23 ft. lbs. (22–31 Nm) for 1989–92.

8. Using new copper washers, install the brake line to the brake caliper and torque the connecting bolt to 12–14 ft. lbs. (17–20 Nm). Torque the wheel nuts to 72–87 ft. lbs. (98–118 Nm).

9. Bleed and adjust the brakes, if necessary. Make sure you pump the brakes and get a hard pedal before driving the vehicle!

OVERHAUL

Types CL28VB and CL25VB

1. Remove the brake caliper from the vehicle.

2. Place a wooden block between the caliper piston and the pad retainer opposite it. Then, gently apply compressed air to the brake hose connection. This will remove the piston and dust seal. Note the direction in which the piston seal is installed.

To install:

3. Clean all parts in clean brake fluid. Inspect the inner cylinder bore for rust, scoring or mechanical wear. Remove minor imperfections with emery paper. Replace the caliper body, if the imperfections cannot be removed. Inspect the piston for such imperfections. If they exist, it must be replaced, as the surface is polished!

4. Inspect the lockpins, bolts, piston seal, bushings and pin seals for damage; replace all parts as necessary.

5. Insert the piston seal into the groove on the caliper body. Install the inner edge of the rubber boot into the piston groove and then install the piston. Work the edge of the rubber boot into the groove in the caliper body.

6. Install the caliper onto the vehicle. Refill the system with clean brake fluid and bleed it thoroughly. Make sure you pump the brakes and get a hard pedal before operating the vehicle.

Brake Disc (Rotor)

REMOVAL & INSTALLATION

1. Refer to the Caliper, Removal and Installation procedures, and remove the caliper. Using a wire, support the caliper assembly; do not disconnect the brake line from the caliper.

2. Remove the torque member-to-steering knuckle bolts and the torque member.

3. Remove the brake disc (rotor) from the wheel hub.

4. Inspect the disc for wear, cracks, runout and thickness; if necessary, replace the disc.

To install:

5. Install disc onto the wheel hub.

6. Install the torque member and torque the torque member-to-steering knuckle bolts to 53–72 ft. lbs. (72–97 Nm).

7. Use a large C-clamp to press the caliper piston back into the caliper, to allow room for the installation of the thicker new pads.

8. Install the new pads, new shims and pad retainer(s).

9. Lower the brake caliper and torque the lower retaining bolt to 12–14 ft. lbs. (17–20 Nm) for 1985–88 or 16–23 ft. lbs. (22–31 Nm) for 1989–92.

10. Check the level of fluid in the master cylinder. If the fluid is near the maximum level, use a clean syringe to remove fluid until the level is down well below the lip of the reservoir.

11. Torque the wheel nuts to 72–87 ft. lbs. (98–118 Nm).

12. Bleed and adjust the brakes, if necessary. Make sure you pump the brakes and get a hard pedal before driving the vehicle!

INSPECTION

◆ SEE FIGS. 21 AND 22

1. Check the brake rotor for roughness, cracks or chips; if necessary, replace the disc.

2. To inspect the disc runout, perform the following procedures:

   a. Secure the disc to the wheel hub with 2 nuts.

   b. Make sure the wheel bearing end play is within specifications.

   c. Using a dial indicator, rotate the wheel disc and check the disc runout; the runout should not exceed 0.0028 in. (0.07mm).

   d. If the runout exceeds specifications, move the disc to another position on the wheel hub and perform the dial indicator test.

   e. If the runout still exceeds specifications, machine the disc to specifications or replace it.

➡ **The rotor can be machined on a brake lathe; most auto parts stores**

have complete machine shop service. The rotors should be machined or replaced during every front disc brake pad replacement.

3. Using a micrometer, check the disc thickness at about 8 positions; if the thickness variation is greater than 0.0004 in. (0.01mm), replace or resurface the disc. The standard thickness if 0.866 in. (22.0mm); the repair limit thickness is 0.787 in. (20.0mm).

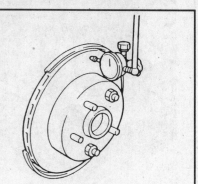

FIG. 21 Using a dial indicator to inspect the front wheel disc runout

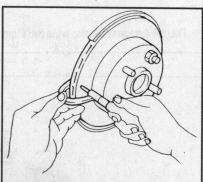

FIG. 22 Using a micrometer to check the front wheel disc thickness

REAR DISC BRAKES

❊ CAUTION

Brake shoes contain asbestos, which has been determined to be a cancer causing agent. Never clean the brake surfaces with compressed air! Avoid inhaling any dust from any brake surface! When cleaning brake surfaces, use a commercially available brake cleaning fluid.

Brake Pads

◆ SEE FIGS. 23-27

REMOVAL & INSTALLATION

➡ **All rear brake pads MUST ALWAYS be replaced as a complete set. Bleed the brake system only, if necessary.**

Types CL11H, CL9H and CL9HA

1. Raise and safely support the vehicle. Remove the rear wheel.

2. Remove the parking brake cable stay fixing bolt and the lock spring.

3. If necessary, use a C-clamp to compress the caliper piston to loosen the brake pads.

4. Remove the lower caliper-to-torque member pin bolt and raise the caliper.

5. Remove the pad retainers, the pads and the shims.

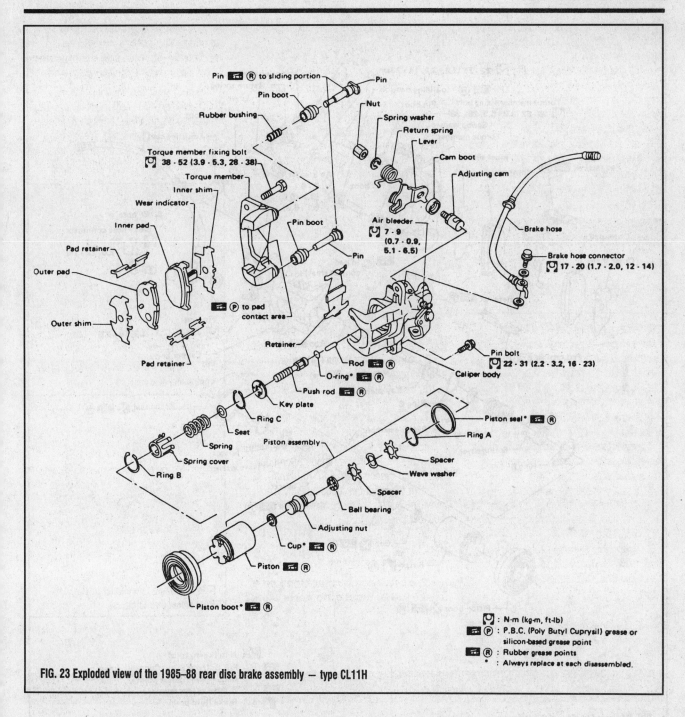

FIG. 23 Exploded view of the 1985–88 rear disc brake assembly — type CL11H

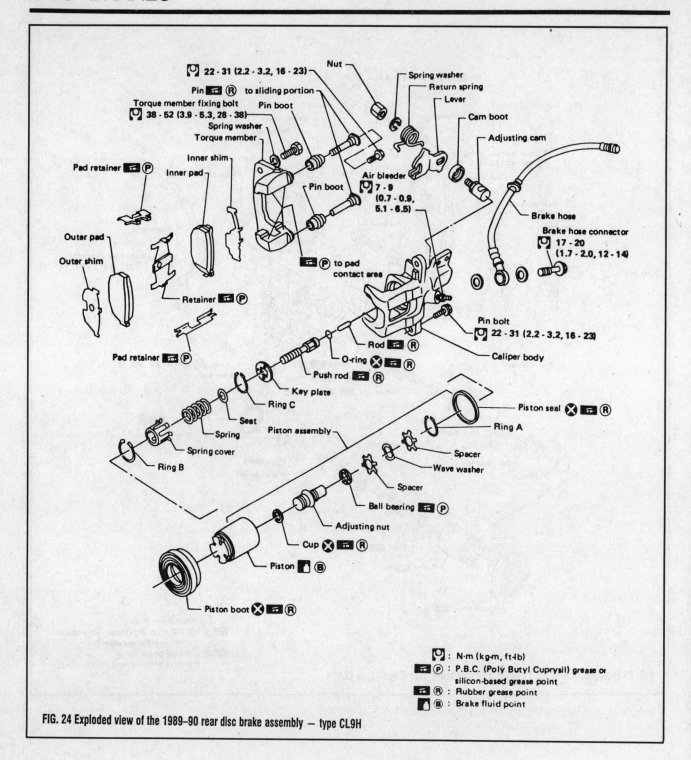

FIG. 24 Exploded view of the 1989–90 rear disc brake assembly — type CL9H

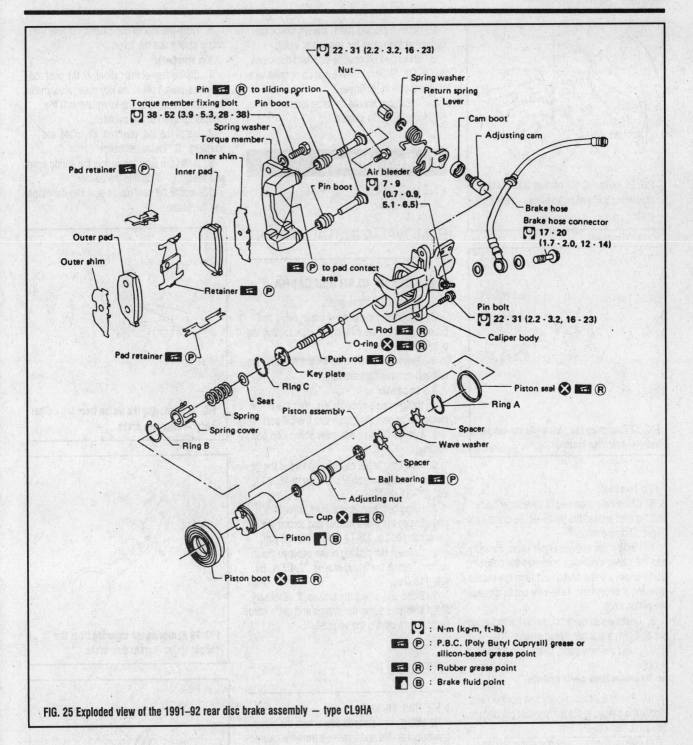

Nut 22 - 31 (2.2 - 3.2, 16 - 23)

Pin R **to sliding portion**
Torque member fixing bolt 38 - 52 (3.9 - 5.3, 28 - 38)
Pin boot
Spring washer
Torque member
Inner shim
Pad retainer P
Inner pad
Outer pad
Outer shim

Spring washer
Return spring
Lever
Cam boot
Adjusting cam

Air bleeder 7 - 9 (0.7 - 0.9, 5.1 - 6.5)

Pin boot

Brake hose
Brake hose connector 17 - 20 (1.7 - 2.0, 12 - 14)

P **to pad contact area**

Retainer P

Pad retainer P

Rod R
O-ring X R
Push rod R
Key plate
Ring C
Seat
Spring
Spring cover
Ring B

Pin bolt 22 - 31 (2.2 - 3.2, 16 - 23)
Caliper body

Piston seal X R
Ring A
Spacer
Wave washer
Spacer
Ball bearing P
Adjusting nut

Piston assembly

Cup X R
Piston B

Piston boot X R

N·m (kg-m, ft-lb)
P : P.B.C. (Poly Butyl Cuprysil) grease or silicon-based grease point
R : Rubber grease point
B : Brake fluid point

FIG. 25 Exploded view of the 1991–92 rear disc brake assembly — type CL9HA

FIG. 26 Removing the parking brake cable stay fixing bolt and lock spring — rear disc brake

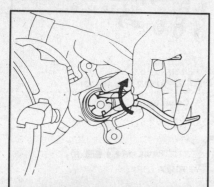

FIG. 27 Retracting the piston into the caliper body — rear disc brake

To install:

6. Clean the piston end of the caliper body and the area around the pin holes. Be careful not to get oil on the rotor.

7. Using a pair of needle nose pliers, carefully turn the piston clockwise back into the caliper body; remove some brake fluid from the master cylinder, if necessary. Take care not to damage the piston boot.

8. Coat the pad contact area on the mounting support with a silicone based grease.

9. Install the new pads, shims and the pad springs.

→ **Always use new shims.**

10. Swing the caliper body into position and torque the caliper-to-torque member pin bolts to 16–23 ft. lbs. (22–31 Nm).

11. Install the lock spring and the parking brake stay fixing bolt.

12. Replace the wheel, lower the vehicle and bleed the system, if necessary.

INSPECTION

1. Brake pad lining thickness can be checked without removing the pads.

2. When replacing pads, always check the surface of the rotors for scoring or wear.

3. Brake pad composite standard thickness is 0.354 in. (9.0mm). Brake pad composite wear limit is 0.079 in. (2.0mm).

4. The rotors should be removed for resurfacing if badly scored.

Brake Caliper

♦ SEE FIGS. 23-27

REMOVAL & INSTALLATION

Types CL11H, CL9H and CL9HA

1. Remove the brake pads.

2. Disconnect the parking brake cable and brake hose from the caliper; be sure to plug the openings.

3. Remove the caliper-to-torque member pin bolt and remove the caliper.

To install:

4. Using needle nosed pliers, turn the piston clockwise to seat the piston into the caliper.

5. Install the new pads, new shims and pad retainer(s).

6. Install the brake caliper and torque the caliper-to-torque member pin bolts to 16–23 ft. lbs. (22–31 Nm).

7. Using new copper washers, install the brake line to the brake caliper and torque the connecting bolt to 12–14 ft. lbs. (17–20 Nm).

8. Connect the parking brake cable to the caliper. Torque the wheel nuts to 72–87 ft. lbs. (98–118 Nm).

9. Bleed and adjust the brakes, if necessary. Make sure you pump the brakes and get a hard pedal before driving the vehicle!

OVERHAUL

♦ SEE FIGS. 28-36

1. Using needle nosed pliers, turn the piston counterclockwise and remove it from the caliper.

2. Using snapring pliers, remove snapring "A" from inside the piston.

3. Using snapring pliers, remove snapring "B" from inside the caliper; then remove the spring cover, the spring and the seat.

4. Using snapring pliers, remove snapring "C" from inside the caliper; then remove the key plate, pushrod and rod.

5. Using a small prybar, pry the piston seal from the outer edge of the caliper; be careful not to damage the cylinder body bore.

6. From the rear of the caliper, remove the return spring and the lever.

To install:

7. On the rear of the caliper, fit the pushrod into the square hole in the key plate; also, match the convex portion of the key plate with the concave portion of the cylinder.

8. Install the rod, pushrod, key plate and snapring "C" inside the caliper.

9. Install the seat, the spring, the spring cover and snapring "B" inside the caliper.

10. Install the new piston seal into the caliper and the piston.

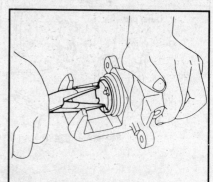

FIG. 28 Removing the piston from the caliper body — rear disc brake

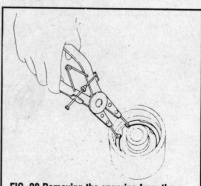

FIG. 29 Removing the snapring from the caliper piston — rear disc brake

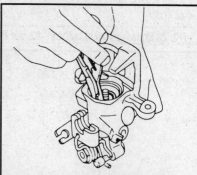

FIG. 30 Removing the snaprings from the caliper bore — rear disc brake

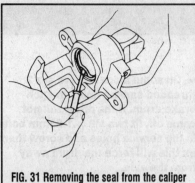

FIG. 31 Removing the seal from the caliper bore — rear disc brake

FIG. 32 Removing the return spring from the caliper — rear disc brake

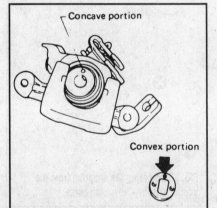

FIG. 33 View of the rear of the caliper — rear disc brake

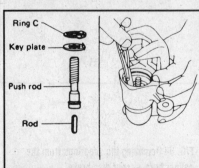

FIG. 34 View of the pushrod internal components of the caliper — rear disc brake

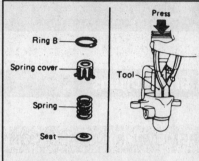

FIG. 35 View of the spring internal components of the caliper — rear disc brake

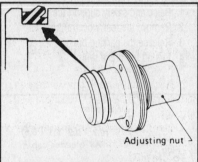

FIG. 36 View of the piston and seal of the caliper — rear disc brake

Brake Disc (Rotor)

REMOVAL & INSTALLATION

1. Refer to the Caliper, Removal and Installation procedures, and remove the caliper. Using a wire, support the caliper assembly; do not disconnect the brake line from the caliper.
2. Remove the torque member-to-strut bolts and the torque member.
3. Remove the brake disc (rotor) from the wheel hub.
4. Inspect the disc for wear, cracks, runout and thickness; if necessary, replace the disc.

To install:

5. Install disc onto the wheel hub.
6. Install the torque member and torque the torque member-to-strut bolts to 28–38 ft. lbs. (38–52 Nm).

7. Rotate the caliper piston back into the caliper, to allow room for the installation of the thicker new pads.
8. Install the new pads, new shims and pad retainer(s).
9. Lower the brake caliper and torque the caliper-to-torque member bolts to 16–23 ft. lbs. (22–31 Nm).
10. Check the level of fluid in the master cylinder. If the fluid is near the maximum level, use a clean syringe to remove fluid until the level is down well below the lip of the reservoir.
11. Torque the wheel nuts to 72–87 ft. lbs. (98–118 Nm).
12. Bleed and adjust the brakes, if necessary. Make sure you pump the brakes and get a hard pedal before driving the vehicle!

INSPECTION

♦ SEE FIGS. 21 AND 22
1. Check the brake rotor for roughness, cracks or chips; if necessary, replace the disc.
2. To inspect the disc runout, perform the following procedures:
    a. Secure the disc to the wheel hub with 2 nuts.
    b. Make sure the wheel bearing end play is within specifications.
    c. Using a dial indicator, rotate the wheel disc and check the disc runout; the runout should not exceed 0.0028 in. (0.07mm).
    d. If the runout exceeds specifications, move the disc to another position on the wheel hub and perform the dial indicator test.
    e. If the runout still exceeds specifications, machine the disc to specifications or replace it.

➡ **The rotor can be machined on a brake lathe; most auto parts stores have complete machine shop service. The rotors should be machined or replaced during every front disc brake pad replacement.**

3. Using a micrometer, check the disc thickness at about 8 positions; if the thickness variation is greater than 0.0004 in. (0.01mm), replace or resurface the disc. The standard thickness if 0.390 in. (10.0mm); the repair limit thickness is 0.315 in. (8.0mm).

REAR DRUM BRAKES

Brake Drums

REMOVAL & INSTALLATION

Type LT23B 1989–92

▶ SEE FIGS. 37 AND 38
1. Raise and safely support the vehicle.
2. Remove the rear wheel(s).
3. Release the parking brake.
4. Pull off the brake drums.

➡ **On some models there are 2 threaded service holes in each brake drum. If the drum will not come off, fit two M8 × 1.25mm bolts in the service holes and screw them in: this will force the drum away from the axle.**

5. If the drum cannot be easily removed, back off the brake adjustment.

➡ **Never depress the brake pedal while the brake drum is removed.**

6. Installation is the reverse of removal procedure.

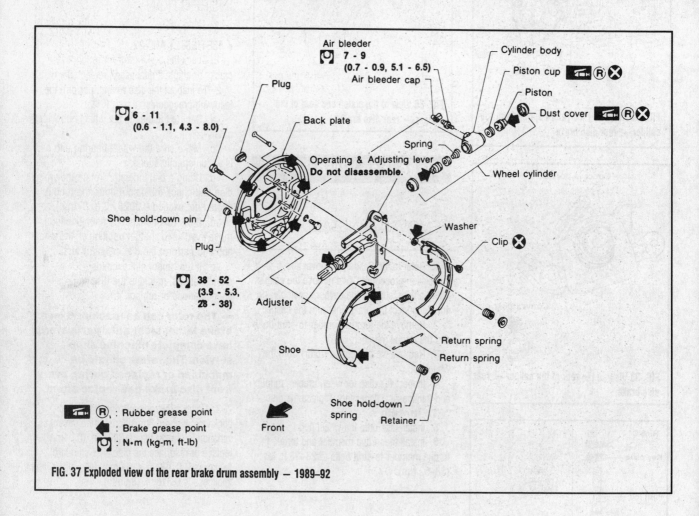

FIG. 37 Exploded view of the rear brake drum assembly — 1989–92

FIG. 37AA Using 2 M8 x 1.25 bolts to press the brake drum from the hub

FIG. 37A Cleaning and lubricating the rear brake shoe components

FIG. 37B Removing the brake shoe hold-down retainer and spring

FIG. 37C Removing the lower brake shoe retainer spring

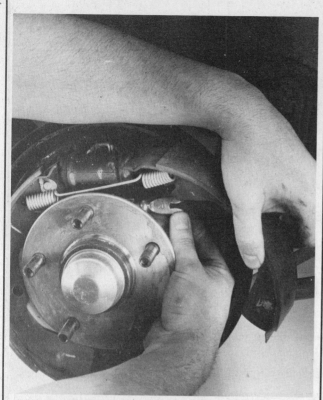

FIG. 37D Removing the brake shoe adjuster from the assembly

FIG. 37E Removing the brake shoe adjuster and upper retainer spring from the brake shoe assembly

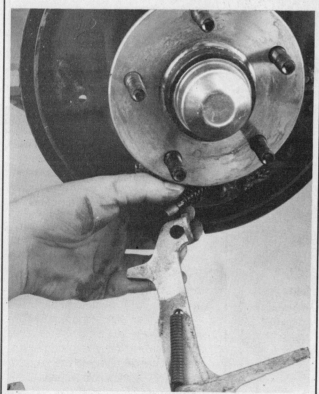

FIG. 37F Separating the parking brake lever from the parking brake cable on the rear brake shoe assemby

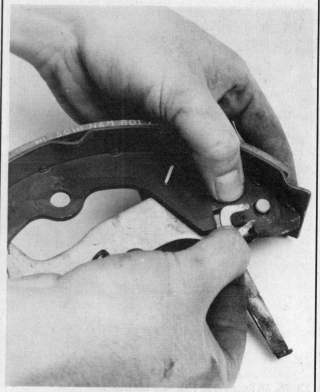

FIG. 37G View of the parking brake lever-to-rear brake shoe retaining clip

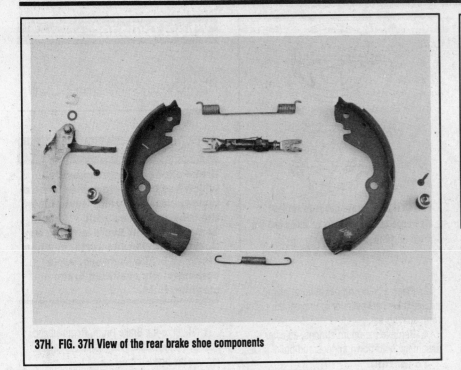

37H. FIG. 37H View of the rear brake shoe components

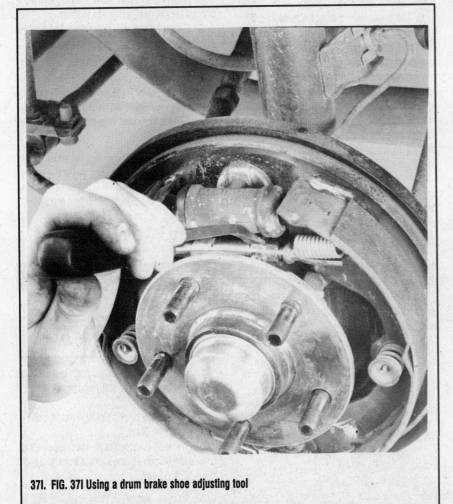

37I. FIG. 37I Using a drum brake shoe adjusting tool

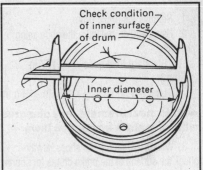

FIG. 38 Using 2 bolts to remove a tight brake drum — 1989–92

FIG. 39 Using a brake gauge to inspect the rear brake drum — 1989–92

INSPECTION

◆ SEE FIG. 39

1. After removing the brake drum, wipe out the accumulated dust with a damp cloth.

❋❋ CAUTION

Do not blow the brake dust out of the drums with compressed air or lung power. Brake linings contain asbestos, a known cancer causing substance. Dispose of the cloth after use.

2. Inspect the drum for cracks, deep grooves, roughness, scoring or out-of-roundness. Replace any brake drum which is cracked.

3. Smooth any slight scores by polishing the friction surface with the fine emery cloth or have the drum machined (trued) at a machine shop. Heavy or extensive scoring will cause excessive brake lining wear and should be removed from the brake drum through resurfacing.

4. Inspect the rear brake drum for the following:

   a. Standard inner diameter — 9.0 in. (228.6mm)

   b. Maximum inner diameter — 9.06 in. (230mm)

   c. Out-of-roundness — 0.0012 in. (0.03mm) or less

Brake Shoes

INSPECTION

1. Remove the brake drum.
2. Using a ruler, measure the shoe lining thickness:

   a. Standard thickness — 0.177 in. (4.5mm)

   b. Lining wear limit — 0.059 in. (1.5mm)

➡ **This measurement may disagree with your state inspection laws.**

3. When replacing brake shoes, always check the surface of the brake drums for scoring or wear. The brake drums should resurfaced or machined if badly scored.

REMOVAL & INSTALLATION

◆ SEE FIG. 37 AND 40

➡ **If you are not thoroughly familiar with the procedures involved in brake replacement, disassemble and assemble one side at a time, leaving the other wheel intact, as a reference. This will reduce the risk of assembling brakes incorrectly. Special brake tools are available to make this repair easier.**

1. Raise the vehicle and remove the wheels.
2. Release the parking brake. Remove the brake drum.

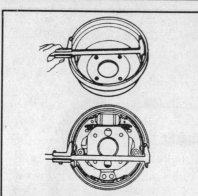

FIG. 40 Using a brake gauge to set the clearance between the brake shoes and the drum — 1989–92

3. Place a heavy rubber band or clamp around the wheel cylinder to prevent the piston from coming out.
4. Remove the return springs, adjuster assembly, hold-down springs and brake shoes.

To install:

5. Clean the backing plate and check the wheel cylinder for leaks.
6. The brake drums must be machined if scored or out of round.
7. Hook the return springs into the new shoes. The return spring ends should be between the shoes and the backing plate. The longer return spring must be adjacent to the wheel cylinder. A very thin film of lithium grease may be applied to the pivot points at the ends of the brake shoes. Grease the shoe locating buttons on the backing plate, also. Be careful not to get grease on the linings or drums.
8. Install the adjuster assembly (rotate nut until adjuster rod is at its shortest point) between brake shoes. Place one shoe in the adjuster and piston slots and pry the other shoe into position. Install hold-down springs.
9. Install the drums (adjust wheel bearings if necessary) and wheels. Adjust the brakes. Bleed the hydraulic system, if necessary.
10. Reconnect the handbrake, making sure it does not cause the shoes to drag when it is released.

Wheel Cylinder

REMOVAL & INSTALLATION

❊❊❊ CAUTION

Brake shoes contain asbestos, which has been determined to be a cancer causing agent. Never clean the brake surfaces with compressed air! Avoid inhaling any dust from any brake surface! When cleaning brake surfaces, use a commercially available brake cleaning fluid.

1. Refer to the Brake Drum, Removal and Installation procedures, in this section and remove the brake drum.
2. Disconnect the flare nut and the brake tube from the wheel cylinder, then plug the line to prevent dirt from entering the system.
3. Remove the brake shoes from the backing plate.
4. Remove the wheel cylinder-to-backing plate bolts and the wheel cylinder.

➡ **If the wheel cylinder is difficult to remove, bump it with a soft hammer to release it from the backing plate.**

To install:

5. Install the wheel cylinder assembly to the backing plate. Torque the wheel cylinder-to-backing plate bolts to 4.3–8.0 ft. lbs. (6–11 Nm).
6. Connect the brake line(s) and install the brake drum.
7. Bleed the brake system.

Brake Backing Plate

REMOVAL & INSTALLATION

1. Refer to the Wheel Cylinder, Removal and Installation procedures, and remove the wheel cylinder.
2. Remove the backing plate-to-strut bolts and the backing plate.
3. To install, reverse the removal procedures. Torque the backing plate-to-strut bolts to 28–38 ft. lbs. (38–52 Nm).

PARKING BRAKE

▶ SEE FIG. 41

Cables

REMOVAL & INSTALLATION

Left Cable

1. Remove the console and fully release the parking brake lever.
2. Back off on the adjusting nut to loosen the cable tension.
3. Working from under the vehicle, disconnect the cable at the equalizer.
4. Remove the cable lock plate from the rear suspension member.
5. Disconnect the cable from the rear brakes.
6. Disconnect the cable from the suspension arm.

7. Remove the cable.
8. Installation is the reverse of the removal procedure. Adjust the lever stroke.

Right Cable

1. Remove the console and fully release the parking brake lever.
2. Back off on the adjusting nut to loosen the cable tension.
3. Working from under the vehicle, disconnect the cable at the equalizer.
4. Remove the cable lock plate from the rear suspension member.
5. Disconnect the cable from the rear brakes.
6. Disconnect the cable from the suspension arm.
7. Remove the cable.
8. Installation is the reverse of the removal procedure. Adjust the lever stroke.

ADJUSTMENT

▶ SEE FIGS. 42 AND 43

1. Remove the console.
2. Pull up the hand brake lever with 44 lbs. of force and count the number of notches for full engagement:
   a. 1985–86: 7–8 notches
   b. 1987–88: 11–13 notches
   c. 1989–91: 9–11 notches
   d. 1992: 8–10 notches
3. Turn the parking brake adjusting nut at the control lever.
4. Check the adjustment and repeat as necessary.
5. Bend the parking brake warning light switchplate so the brake warning light turns ON when the ratchet at the parking brake lever is pulled and goes out when fully released.
6. After adjustment, install the console.

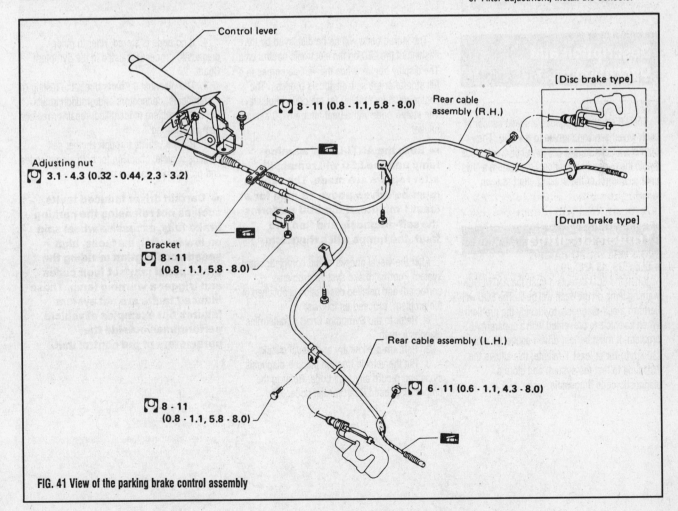

FIG. 41 View of the parking brake control assembly

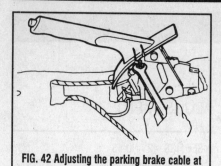

FIG. 42 Adjusting the parking brake cable at the control lever

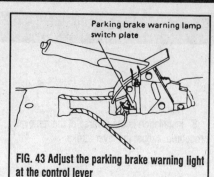

Parking brake warning lamp switch plate

FIG. 43 Adjust the parking brake warning light at the control lever

Parking Brake Lever

REMOVAL & INSTALLATION

1. Remove the console.
2. Raise and safely support the vehicle.
3. Disconnect the parking brake cables and the parking brake warning light connector from the control lever assembly.
4. Remove the control lever assembly-to-chassis bolts and the assembly.
5. To install, reverse the removal procedures. Torque the control lever assembly-to-chassis bolts to 5.8–8.0 ft. lbs. (8–11 Nm).
6. Install the parking brake cables and adjust the control lever.
7. Install the console.

ANTI-LOCK BRAKE SYSTEM

Description and Operation

◆ SEE FIG. 45

The ABS system employs a speed sensor at each wheel sending signals to the ECU. The control unit can trigger any or all of 4 solenoids within the hydraulic actuator. This system allows optimal control of the braking effort at each wheel.

Troubleshooting

◆ SEE FIGS. 48 AND 49

When the ECU detects a fault, the ANTI-LOCK warning lamp on the dash will be lit. The ECU will perform a self-diagnosis to identify the problem. When a vehicle is presented with a apparent ABS problem, it must be test driven above 19 mph (30 km/h) for at least 1 minute; this allows the ECU time to test the system and store a diagnostic code if possible.

The stored code will be be displayed by the flashing of the LED on the electronic control unit. The display begins when the vehicle comes to a full stop after the self-diagnosis process. The engine must be running for the code to display. The stored code will repeat after a 5-10 second pause.

➡ **Both the ANTI-LOCK warning lamp and the LED will remain lit after repairs are made. The vehicle must be driven above 19 mph for at least 1 minute. If the ECU performs the self-diagnosis and finds no fault, the lamps will extinguish.**

After the visual checks of the complete brake system, (normal brake system problems corrected) and detailed description is obtained of the problem, proceed as follows:

1. Refer to the Symptom Chart to determine diagnostic path.
2. Perform preliminary and visual checks.
3. Put the vehicle through the self-diagnosis cycle and record any fault code. Refer to the proper Diagnostic Chart for the code.

4. If no code is stored, refer to other diagnostic procedures listed in the Symptom Chart.
5. The diagnostic Charts direct the testing of components, connectors and ground circuits. Once the problem is identified, repair or replace items as needed.
6. Put the vehicle through another self-diagnosis cycle, checking for both stored codes and proper ABS performance.

➡ **Certain driver induced faults, such as not releasing the parking brake fully, excessive wheel spin on low traction surfaces, high speed acceleration or riding the brake pedal may set fault codes and trigger a warning lamp. These induced faults are not system failures but examples of vehicle performance outside the parameters of the control unit.**

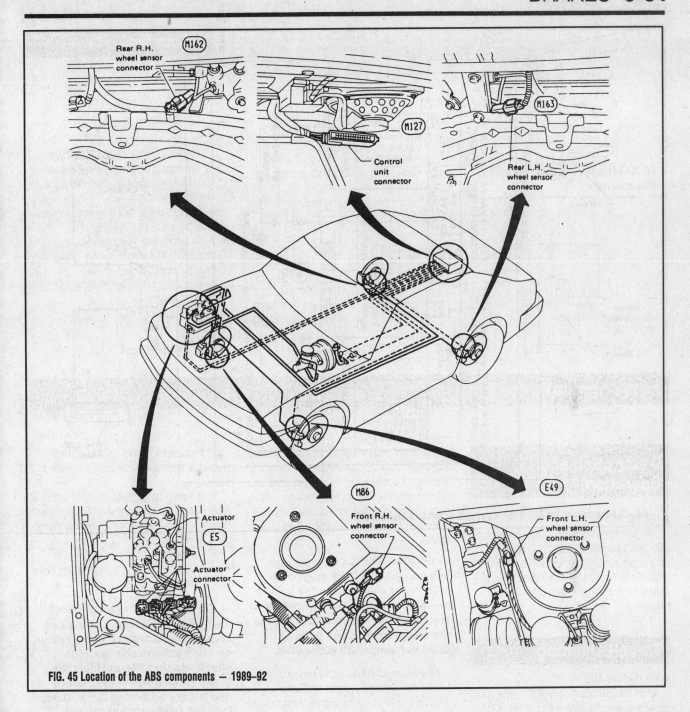

FIG. 45 Location of the ABS components — 1989–92

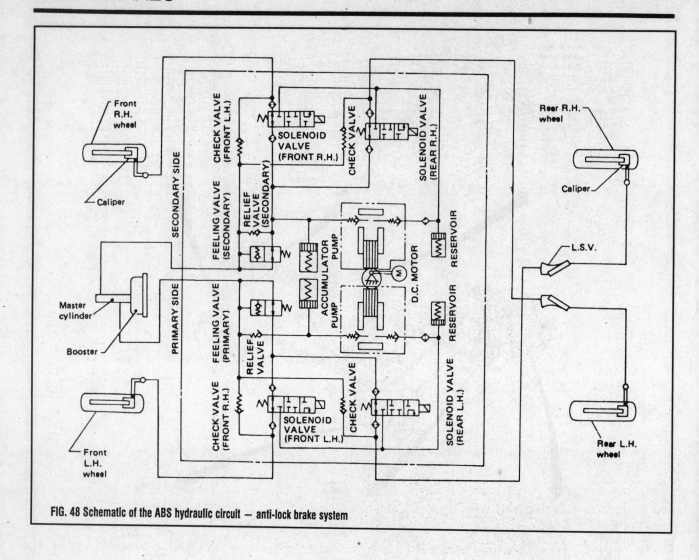

FIG. 48 Schematic of the ABS hydraulic circuit — anti-lock brake system

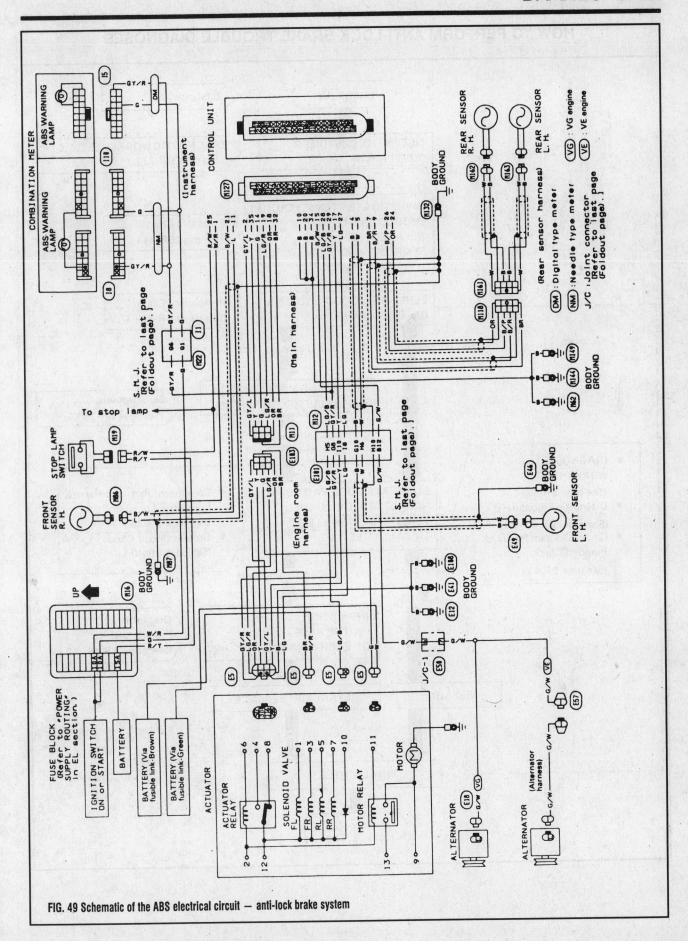

FIG. 49 Schematic of the ABS electrical circuit — anti-lock brake system

HOW TO PERFORM ANTI-LOCK BRAKE TROUBLE DIAGNOSES

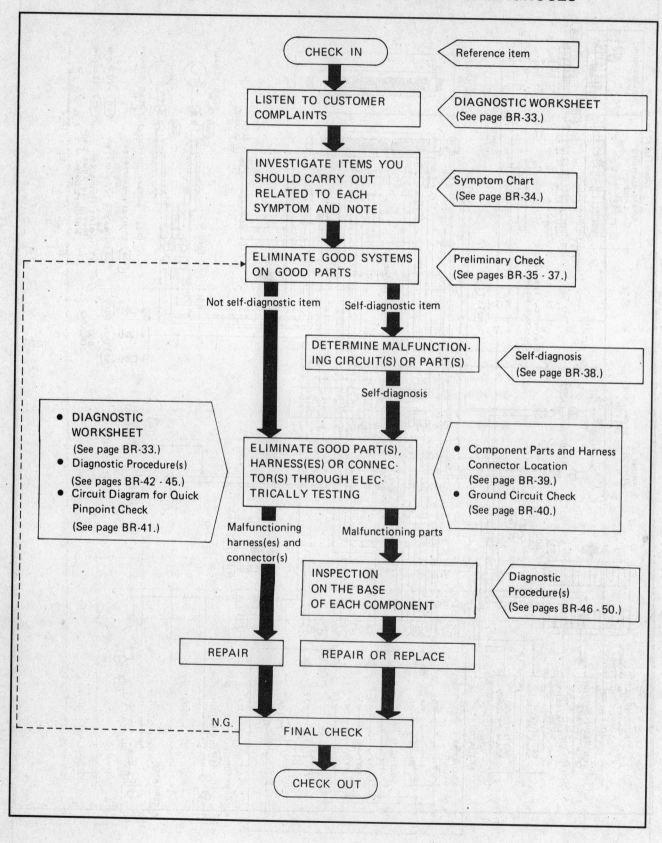

ANTI-LOCK BRAKE SYMPTOM CHART

PROCEDURE	REFERENCE PAGE		Pedal vibration & noise	Warning activates	Long stopping distance	Abnormal pedal action	ABS doesn't work	ABS works but warning activates	ABS works frequently
Electrical Components Inspection	BR-51	Actuator inspection					O		
Ground Circuit Check	BR-40	Motor ground					O		
Diagnostic Procedure (Select inspection with L.E.D. flashing No.)	BR-50	L.E.D. comes on continuously	O	O	O	O	O	O	
	BR-50	L.E.D. flashing 16	O	O	O	O	O	O	
	BR-49	L.E.D. flashing 10	O	O	O	O	O	O	
	BR-48	L.E.D. flashing 9	O	O	O	O	O	O	
	BR-47	L.E.D. flashing 5 - 8	O	O	O	O	O	O	
	BR-46	L.E.D. flashing 1 - 4	O	O	O	O	O	O	
Diagnostic Procedure	BR-45	Diagnostic Procedure 6							O
	BR-45	Diagnostic Procedure 5						O	
	BR-44	Diagnostic Procedure 4					O		
	BR-44	Diagnostic Procedure 3				O			
	BR-43	Diagnostic Procedure 2			O				
	BR-42	Diagnostic Procedure 1	O						
Preliminary Check	BR-37	Preliminary Check 4	O	O	O	O	O	O	
	BR-37	Preliminary Check 3	O	O					
	BR-36	Preliminary Check 2		O			O		O
	BR-35	Preliminary Check 1			O	O			O

ANTI-LOCK BRAKE TROUBLE DIAGNOSES — PRELIMINARY CHECK 1

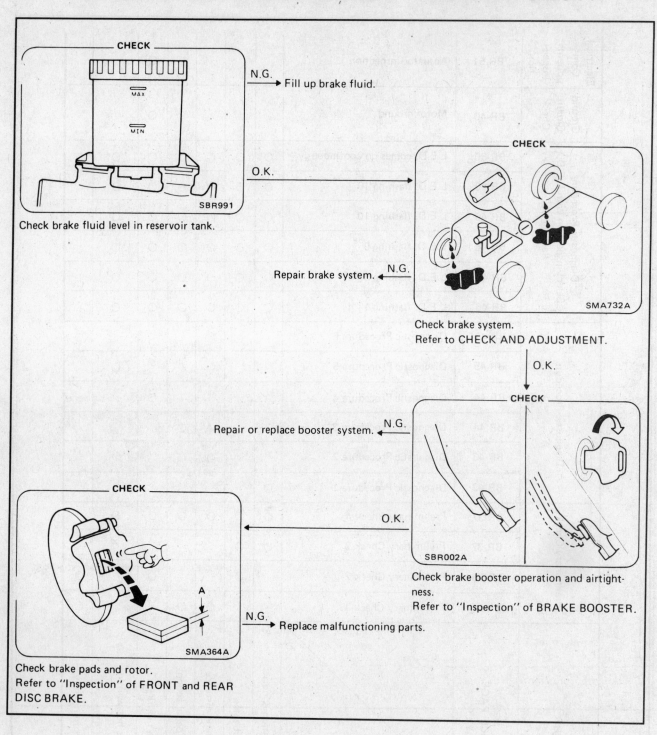

CHECK — N.G. → Fill up brake fluid.

Check brake fluid level in reservoir tank.

SBR991

O.K. →

CHECK

Repair brake system. ← N.G.

Check brake system.
Refer to CHECK AND ADJUSTMENT.

SMA732A

O.K. ↓

CHECK

Repair or replace booster system. ← N.G.

O.K. →

Check brake booster operation and airtight-ness.
Refer to "Inspection" of BRAKE BOOSTER.

SBR002A

CHECK

Check brake pads and rotor.
Refer to "Inspection" of FRONT and REAR DISC BRAKE.

SMA364A

N.G. → Replace malfunctioning parts.

ANTI-LOCK BRAKE TROUBLE DIAGNOSES — PRELIMINARY CHECK 2

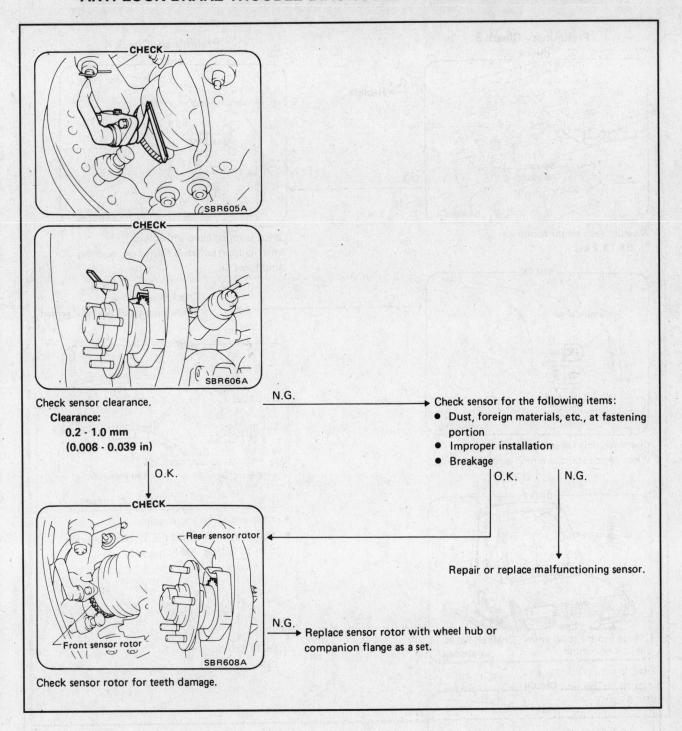

Check sensor clearance.
   Clearance:
      0.2 - 1.0 mm
      (0.008 - 0.039 in)

N.G. ──────────────────────▶ Check sensor for the following items:
      ● Dust, foreign materials, etc., at fastening portion
      ● Improper installation
      ● Breakage

O.K. ↓

O.K. │   N.G.

Repair or replace malfunctioning sensor.

Rear sensor rotor

Front sensor rotor

SBR608A

N.G. ──▶ Replace sensor rotor with wheel hub or companion flange as a set.

Check sensor rotor for teeth damage.

ANTI-LOCK BRAKE TROUBLE DIAGNOSES — PRELIMINARY CHECK 3 AND 4

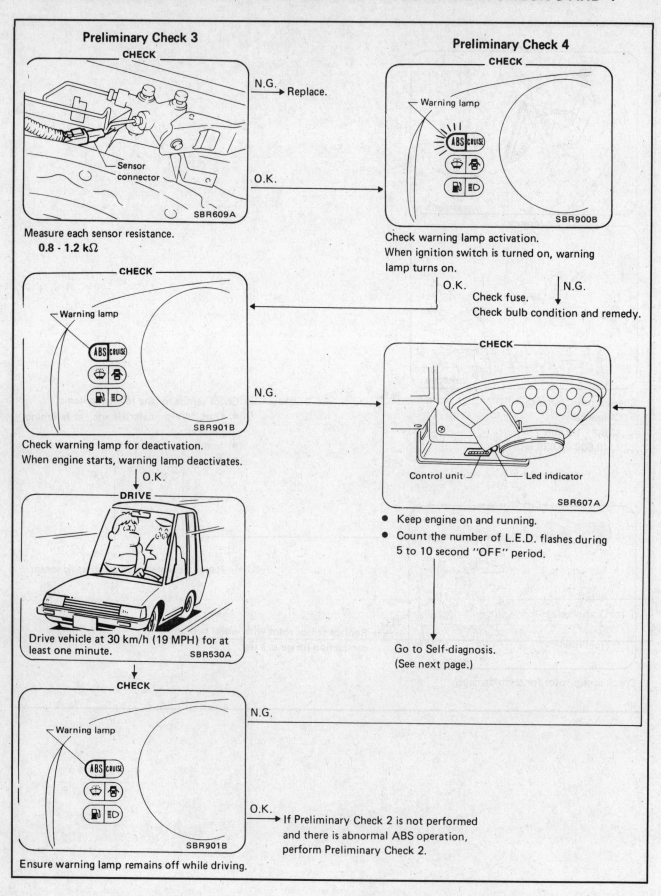

Preliminary Check 3

CHECK

SBR609A

Measure each sensor resistance.

0.8 - 1.2 kΩ

N.G. → Replace.

O.K. →

Sensor connector

Preliminary Check 4

CHECK

Warning lamp

ABS CRUISE

SBR900B

Check warning lamp activation.
When ignition switch is turned on, warning lamp turns on.

O.K.   N.G.

Check fuse.
Check bulb condition and remedy.

CHECK

Warning lamp

ABS CRUISE

SBR901B

Check warning lamp for deactivation.
When engine starts, warning lamp deactivates.

N.G. →

O.K.

DRIVE

Drive vehicle at 30 km/h (19 MPH) for at least one minute.

SBR530A

CHECK

Warning lamp

ABS CRUISE

SBR901B

Ensure warning lamp remains off while driving.

N.G.

O.K.
→ If Preliminary Check 2 is not performed and there is abnormal ABS operation, perform Preliminary Check 2.

CHECK

Control unit   Led indicator

SBR607A

- Keep engine on and running.
- Count the number of L.E.D. flashes during 5 to 10 second "OFF" period.

Go to Self-diagnosis.
(See next page.)

ANTI-LOCK BRAKE TROUBLE DIAGNOSES — FAULT CODES

No. of L.E.D. flashes	Malfunctioning part or unit
1	Left front actuator solenoid circuit
2	Right front actuator solenoid circuit
3	Right rear actuator solenoid circuit
4	Left rear actuator solenoid circuit
5	Left front wheel sensor circuit
6	Right front wheel sensor circuit
7	Right rear wheel sensor circuit
8	Left rear wheel sensor circuit
9	Motor and motor relay
10	Solenoid valve relay
16 or continuous	Control unit
Warning activates and L.E.D. "OFF"	Power supply or ground circuit for control unit

Example

Improper operation of left front rotor sensor circuit

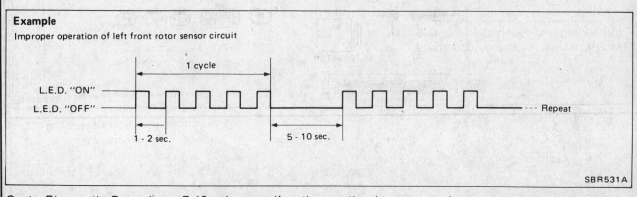

SBR531A

Go to Diagnostic Procedures 7-12, where malfunction portion is concerned.

ANTI-LOCK BRAKE TROUBLE DIAGNOSES — QUICK PINPOINT CIRCUIT CHECK

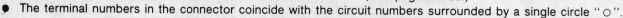

- The unit side connectors with a double circle "⬭" are connected to the harness side connectors shown in the "Component Parts and Harness Connector Location". (See page BR-39.)
- The terminal numbers in the connector coincide with the circuit numbers surrounded by a single circle "○".

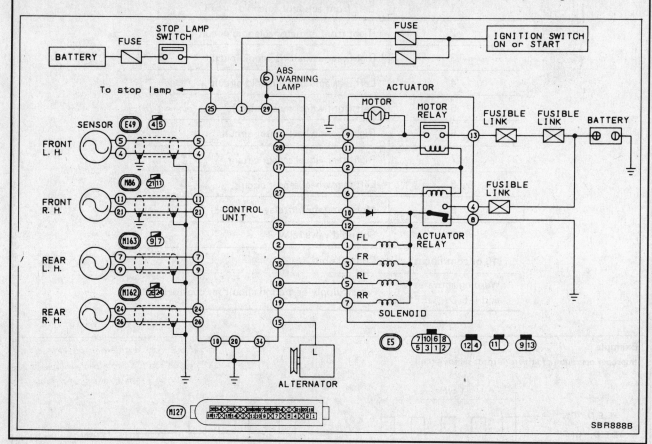

SBR888B

ANTI-LOCK BRAKE TROUBLE DIAGNOSES — DIAGNOSTIC PROCEDURE 1

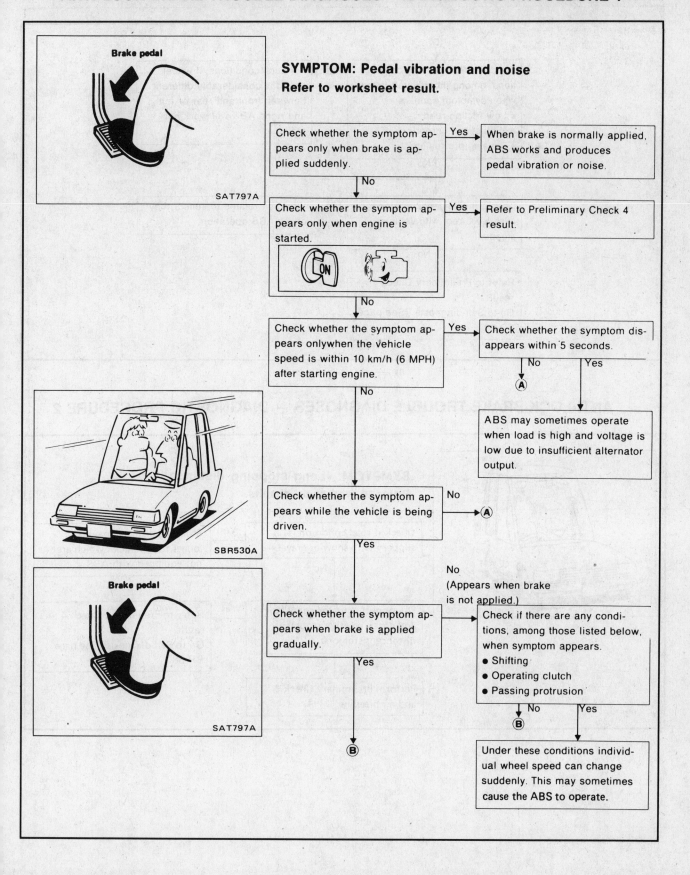

SYMPTOM: Pedal vibration and noise
Refer to worksheet result.

Brake pedal

SAT797A

Check whether the symptom appears only when brake is applied suddenly. —Yes→ When brake is normally applied, ABS works and produces pedal vibration or noise.

↓ No

Check whether the symptom appears only when engine is started. —Yes→ Refer to Preliminary Check 4 result.

ON

↓ No

Check whether the symptom appears onlywhen the vehicle speed is within 10 km/h (6 MPH) after starting engine. —Yes→ Check whether the symptom disappears within 5 seconds.

No — Ⓐ   Yes

↓ No

ABS may sometimes operate when load is high and voltage is low due to insufficient alternator output.

SBR530A

Check whether the symptom appears while the vehicle is being driven. —No→ Ⓐ

↓ Yes

Brake pedal

SAT797A

Check whether the symptom appears when brake is applied gradually.

No
(Appears when brake is not applied.)
→ Check if there are any conditions, among those listed below, when symptom appears.
● Shifting
● Operating clutch
● Passing protrusion

No — Ⓑ   Yes

↓ Yes

Ⓑ

Under these conditions individual wheel speed can change suddenly. This may sometimes cause the ABS to operate.

ANTI-LOCK BRAKE TROUBLE DIAGNOSES — DIAGNOSTIC PROCEDURE 1 (CONT'D)

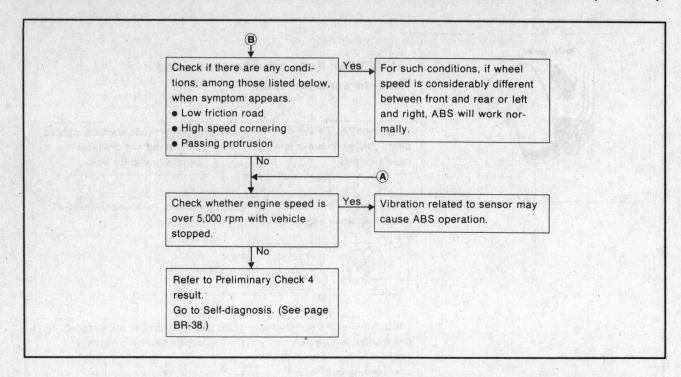

Ⓑ

Check if there are any conditions, among those listed below, when symptom appears.
- Low friction road
- High speed cornering
- Passing protrusion

→ Yes → For such conditions, if wheel speed is considerably different between front and rear or left and right, ABS will work normally.

↓ No

Ⓐ

Check whether engine speed is over 5,000 rpm with vehicle stopped.

→ Yes → Vibration related to sensor may cause ABS operation.

↓ No

Refer to Preliminary Check 4 result.
Go to Self-diagnosis. (See page BR-38.)

ANTI-LOCK BRAKE TROUBLE DIAGNOSES — DIAGNOSTIC PROCEDURE 2

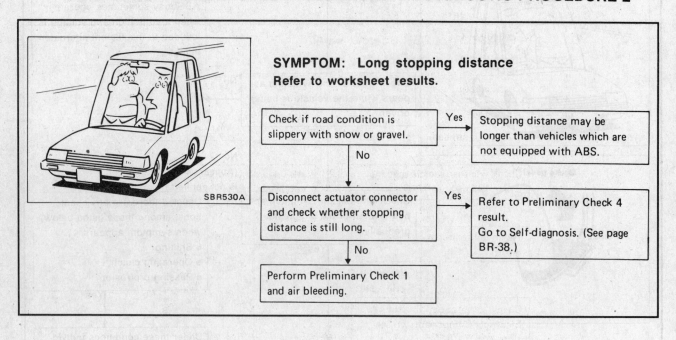

SBR530A

SYMPTOM: Long stopping distance
Refer to worksheet results.

Check if road condition is slippery with snow or gravel.

→ Yes → Stopping distance may be longer than vehicles which are not equipped with ABS.

↓ No

Disconnect actuator connector and check whether stopping distance is still long.

→ Yes → Refer to Preliminary Check 4 result.
Go to Self-diagnosis. (See page BR-38.)

↓ No

Perform Preliminary Check 1 and air bleeding.

ANTI-LOCK BRAKE TROUBLE DIAGNOSES — DIAGNOSTIC PROCEDURE 3

SYMPTOM: Abnormal pedal action
Refer to worksheet results.

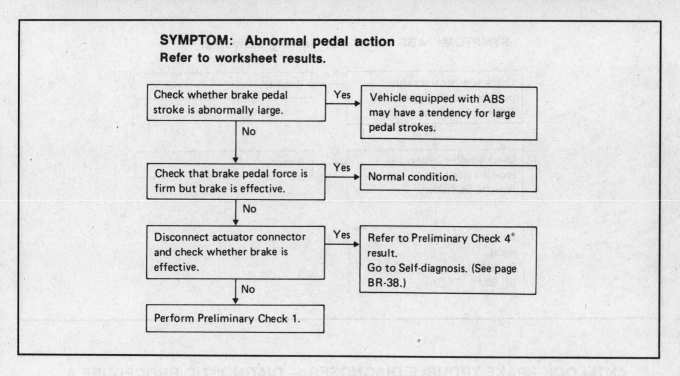

ANTI-LOCK BRAKE TROUBLE DIAGNOSES — DIAGNOSTIC PROCEDURE 4

SYMPTOM: ABS doesn't work.
Refer to worksheet results.

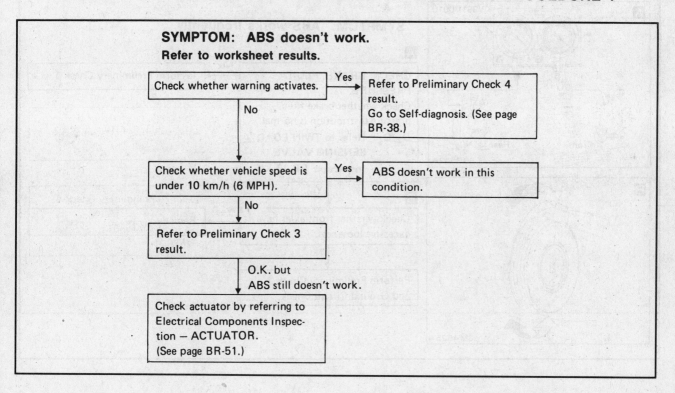

ANTI-LOCK BRAKE TROUBLE DIAGNOSES — DIAGNOSTIC PROCEDURE 5

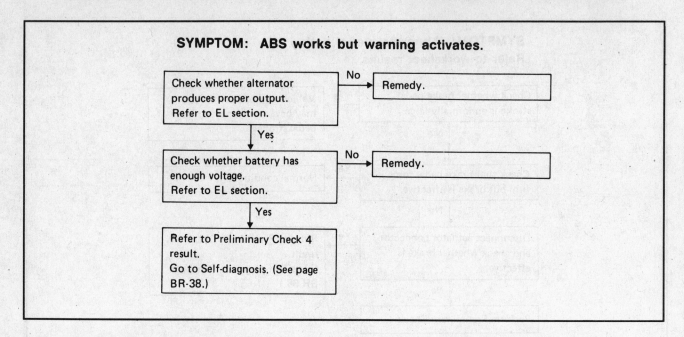

SYMPTOM: ABS works but warning activates.

Check whether alternator produces proper output.
Refer to EL section. → No → Remedy.

↓ Yes

Check whether battery has enough voltage.
Refer to EL section. → No → Remedy.

↓ Yes

Refer to Preliminary Check 4 result.
Go to Self-diagnosis. (See page BR-38.)

ANTI-LOCK BRAKE TROUBLE DIAGNOSES — DIAGNOSTIC PROCEDURE 6

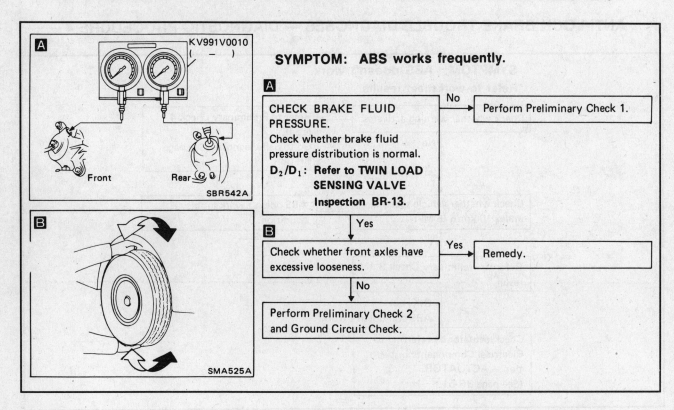

A

KV991V0010

Front   Rear

SBR542A

B

SMA525A

SYMPTOM: ABS works frequently.

A
CHECK BRAKE FLUID PRESSURE.
Check whether brake fluid pressure distribution is normal.
D_2/D_1: **Refer to TWIN LOAD SENSING VALVE Inspection BR-13.** → No → Perform Preliminary Check 1.

↓ Yes

B
Check whether front axles have excessive looseness. → Yes → Remedy.

↓ No

Perform Preliminary Check 2 and Ground Circuit Check.

ANTI-LOCK BRAKE TROUBLE DIAGNOSES — DIAGNOSTIC PROCEDURE 7

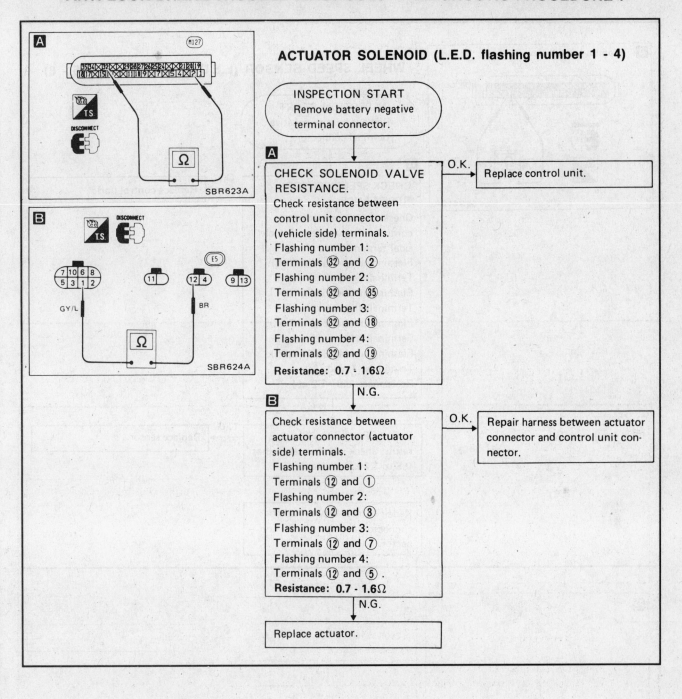

ACTUATOR SOLENOID (L.E.D. flashing number 1 - 4)

A SBR623A

B GY/L   BR   SBR624A

INSPECTION START
Remove battery negative terminal connector.

A
CHECK SOLENOID VALVE RESISTANCE.
Check resistance between control unit connector (vehicle side) terminals.
Flashing number 1:
Terminals ㉜ and ②
Flashing number 2:
Terminals ㉜ and ㉟
Flashing number 3:
Terminals ㉜ and ⑱
Flashing number 4:
Terminals ㉜ and ⑲
Resistance: 0.7 - 1.6Ω

→ O.K. → Replace control unit.

↓ N.G.

B
Check resistance between actuator connector (actuator side) terminals.
Flashing number 1:
Terminals ⑫ and ①
Flashing number 2:
Terminals ⑫ and ③
Flashing number 3:
Terminals ⑫ and ⑦
Flashing number 4:
Terminals ⑫ and ⑤ .
Resistance: 0.7 - 1.6Ω

→ O.K. → Repair harness between actuator connector and control unit connector.

↓ N.G.

Replace actuator.

ANTI-LOCK BRAKE TROUBLE DIAGNOSES — DIAGNOSTIC PROCEDURE 8

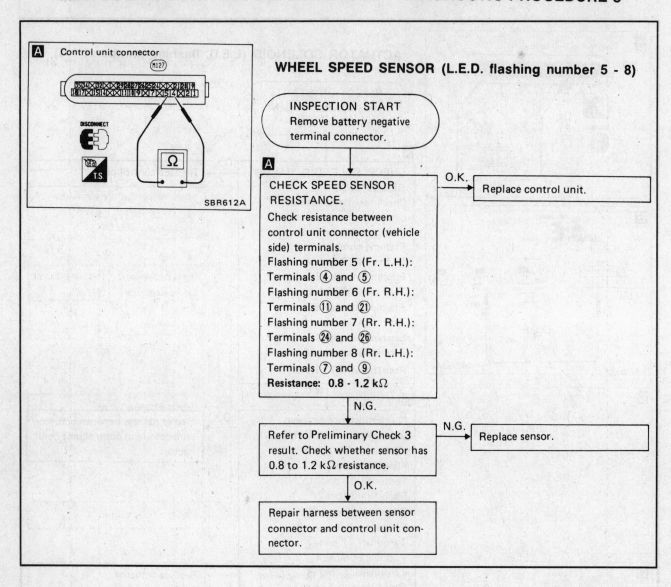

A Control unit connector

M127

DISCONNECT

T.S.

Ω

SBR612A

WHEEL SPEED SENSOR (L.E.D. flashing number 5 - 8)

INSPECTION START
Remove battery negative terminal connector.

A

↓

CHECK SPEED SENSOR RESISTANCE.
Check resistance between control unit connector (vehicle side) terminals.
Flashing number 5 (Fr. L.H.):
Terminals ④ and ⑤
Flashing number 6 (Fr. R.H.):
Terminals ⑪ and ㉑
Flashing number 7 (Rr. R.H.):
Terminals ㉔ and ㉖
Flashing number 8 (Rr. L.H.):
Terminals ⑦ and ⑨
Resistance: 0.8 - 1.2 kΩ

→ O.K. → Replace control unit.

↓ N.G.

Refer to Preliminary Check 3 result. Check whether sensor has 0.8 to 1.2 kΩ resistance.

→ N.G. → Replace sensor.

↓ O.K.

Repair harness between sensor connector and control unit connector.

ANTI-LOCK BRAKE TROUBLE DIAGNOSES — DIAGNOSTIC PROCEDURE 9

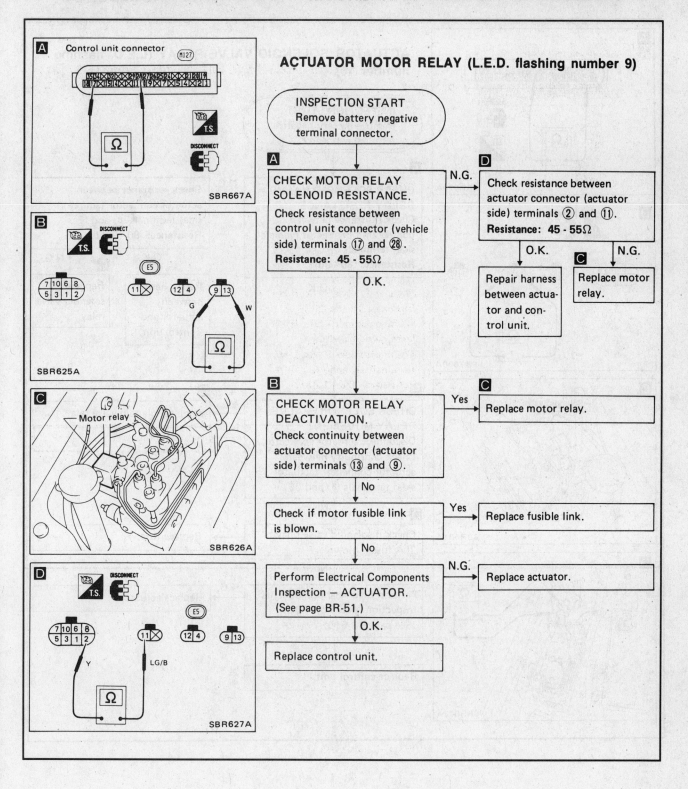

A Control unit connector

SBR667A

B

SBR625A

C Motor relay

SBR626A

D

SBR627A

ACTUATOR MOTOR RELAY (L.E.D. flashing number 9)

INSPECTION START
Remove battery negative terminal connector.

A
CHECK MOTOR RELAY SOLENOID RESISTANCE.
Check resistance between control unit connector (vehicle side) terminals ⑰ and ㉘.
Resistance: 45 - 55Ω

→ N.G. →

D
Check resistance between actuator connector (actuator side) terminals ② and ⑪.
Resistance: 45 - 55Ω

O.K. → Repair harness between actuator and control unit.

N.G. → **C** Replace motor relay.

O.K. ↓

B
CHECK MOTOR RELAY DEACTIVATION.
Check continuity between actuator connector (actuator side) terminals ⑬ and ⑨.

Yes → **C** Replace motor relay.

No ↓

Check if motor fusible link is blown.

Yes → Replace fusible link.

No ↓

Perform Electrical Components Inspection — ACTUATOR.
(See page BR-51.)

N.G. → Replace actuator.

O.K. ↓

Replace control unit.

ANTI-LOCK BRAKE TROUBLE DIAGNOSES — DIAGNOSTIC PROCEDURE 10

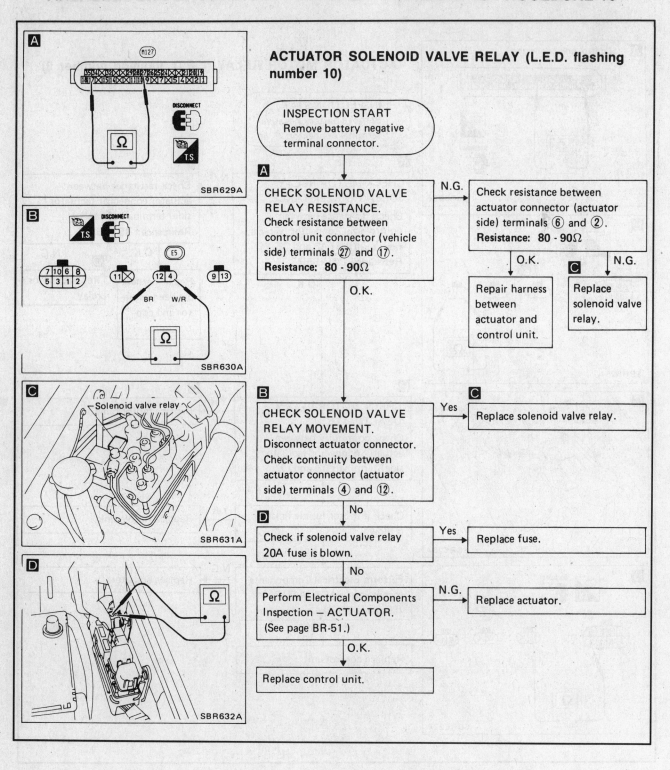

ACTUATOR SOLENOID VALVE RELAY (L.E.D. flashing number 10)

INSPECTION START
Remove battery negative terminal connector.

A CHECK SOLENOID VALVE RELAY RESISTANCE.
Check resistance between control unit connector (vehicle side) terminals ㉗ and ⑰.
Resistance: 80 - 90Ω

→ N.G. → Check resistance between actuator connector (actuator side) terminals ⑥ and ②.
Resistance: 80 - 90Ω

O.K. → Repair harness between actuator and control unit.

N.G. → **C** Replace solenoid valve relay.

O.K.

B CHECK SOLENOID VALVE RELAY MOVEMENT.
Disconnect actuator connector.
Check continuity between actuator connector (actuator side) terminals ④ and ⑫.

→ Yes → **C** Replace solenoid valve relay.

No

D Check if solenoid valve relay 20A fuse is blown.

→ Yes → Replace fuse.

No

Perform Electrical Components Inspection — ACTUATOR.
(See page BR-51.)

→ N.G. → Replace actuator.

O.K.

Replace control unit.

SBR629A

SBR630A

Solenoid valve relay

SBR631A

SBR632A

ANTI-LOCK BRAKE TROUBLE DIAGNOSES — DIAGNOSTIC PROCEDURE 11

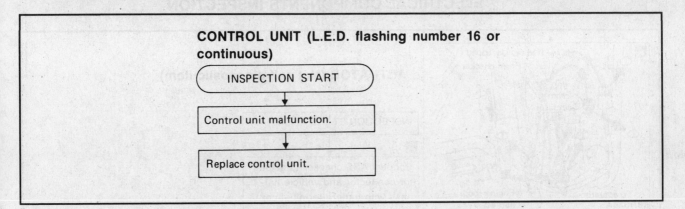

CONTROL UNIT (L.E.D. flashing number 16 or continuous)

INSPECTION START

↓

Control unit malfunction.

↓

Replace control unit.

ANTI-LOCK BRAKE TROUBLE DIAGNOSES — DIAGNOSTIC PROCEDURE 12

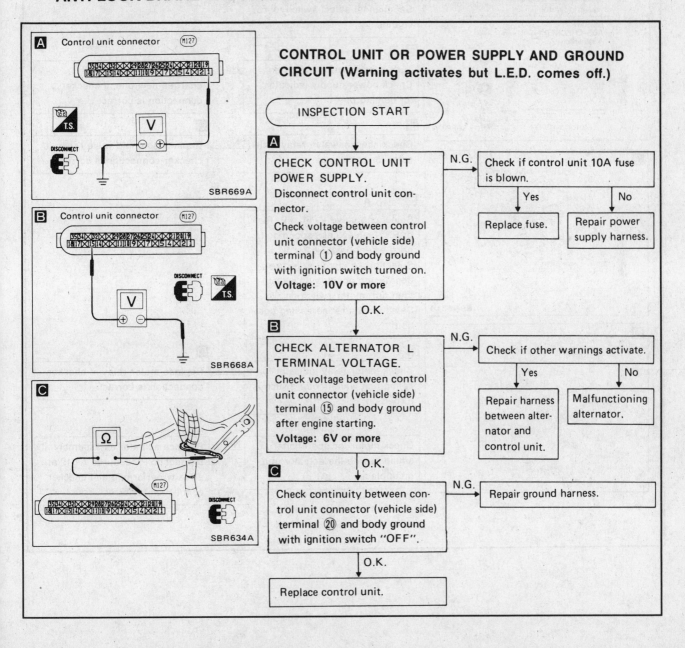

CONTROL UNIT OR POWER SUPPLY AND GROUND CIRCUIT (Warning activates but L.E.D. comes off.)

A Control unit connector (M127) SBR669A

B Control unit connector (M127) SBR668A

C (M127) SBR634A

INSPECTION START

A CHECK CONTROL UNIT POWER SUPPLY.
Disconnect control unit connector.
Check voltage between control unit connector (vehicle side) terminal ① and body ground with ignition switch turned on.
Voltage: 10V or more

— N.G. → Check if control unit 10A fuse is blown.
- Yes → Replace fuse.
- No → Repair power supply harness.

O.K. ↓

B CHECK ALTERNATOR L TERMINAL VOLTAGE.
Check voltage between control unit connector (vehicle side) terminal ⑮ and body ground after engine starting.
Voltage: 6V or more

— N.G. → Check if other warnings activate.
- Yes → Repair harness between alternator and control unit.
- No → Malfunctioning alternator.

O.K. ↓

C Check continuity between control unit connector (vehicle side) terminal ⑳ and body ground with ignition switch "OFF".

— N.G. → Repair ground harness.

O.K. ↓

Replace control unit.

ANTI-LOCK BRAKE TROUBLE DIAGNOSES — ELECTRICAL COMPONENTS INSPECTION

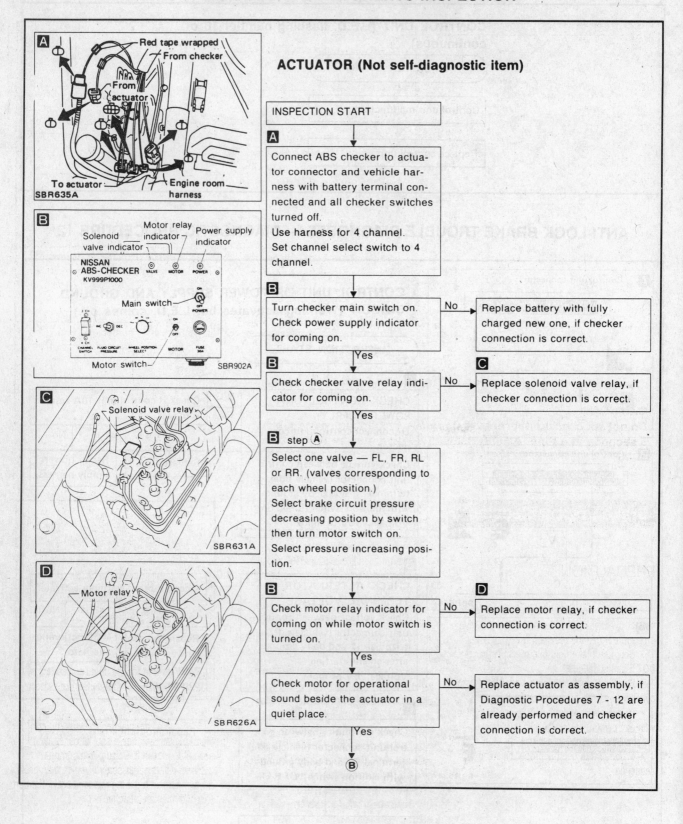

A

Red tape wrapped
From checker
From actuator
To actuator
Engine room harness

SBR635A

B

Solenoid valve indicator
Motor relay indicator
Power supply indicator

NISSAN
ABS-CHECKER
KV999P1000

VALVE   MOTOR   POWER

Main switch

POWER
ON
OFF

CHANNEL SWITCH
FLUID CIRCUIT PRESSURE
WHEEL POSITION SELECT
MOTOR
FUSE 30A

Motor switch

SBR902A

C

Solenoid valve relay

SBR631A

D

Motor relay

SBR626A

ACTUATOR (Not self-diagnostic item)

INSPECTION START

A
Connect ABS checker to actuator connector and vehicle harness with battery terminal connected and all checker switches turned off.
Use harness for 4 channel.
Set channel select switch to 4 channel.

B
Turn checker main switch on.
Check power supply indicator for coming on. → **No** → Replace battery with fully charged new one, if checker connection is correct.

↓ Yes

B
Check checker valve relay indicator for coming on. → **No** → **C** Replace solenoid valve relay, if checker connection is correct.

↓ Yes

B step Ⓐ
Select one valve — FL, FR, RL or RR. (valves corresponding to each wheel position.)
Select brake circuit pressure decreasing position by switch then turn motor switch on.
Select pressure increasing position.

B
Check motor relay indicator for coming on while motor switch is turned on. → **No** → **D** Replace motor relay, if checker connection is correct.

↓ Yes

Check motor for operational sound beside the actuator in a quiet place. → **No** → Replace actuator as assembly, if Diagnostic Procedures 7 - 12 are already performed and checker connection is correct.

↓ Yes

Ⓑ

ANTI-LOCK BRAKE TROUBLE DIAGNOSES —
ELECTRICAL COMPONENTS INSPECTION (CON'D)

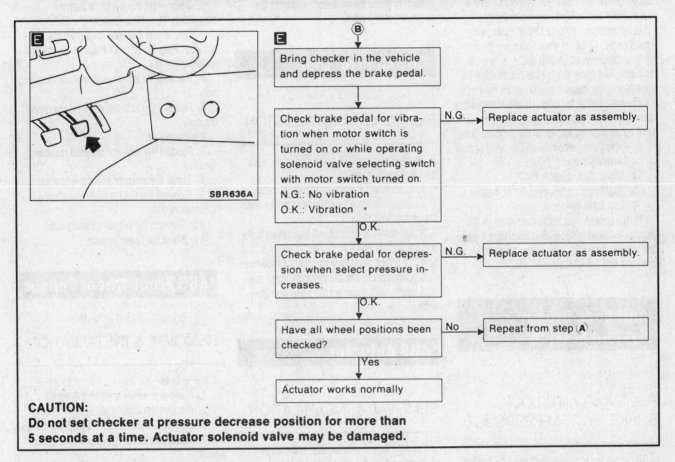

SBR636A

Ⓑ

Bring checker in the vehicle and depress the brake pedal.

Check brake pedal for vibration when motor switch is turned on or while operating solenoid valve selecting switch with motor switch turned on.
N.G.: No vibration
O.K.: Vibration

N.G. → Replace actuator as assembly.

O.K.

Check brake pedal for depression when select pressure increases.

N.G. → Replace actuator as assembly.

O.K.

Have all wheel positions been checked?

No → Repeat from step Ⓐ.

Yes

Actuator works normally

CAUTION:
Do not set checker at pressure decrease position for more than 5 seconds at a time. Actuator solenoid valve may be damaged.

Brake System Bleeding

PRECAUTIONS

• Carefully monitor the brake fluid level in the master cylinder at all times during the bleeding procedure. Keep the reservoir full at all times.
• Only use brake fluid that meets or exceeds DOT 3 specifications.
• Place a suitable container under the master cylinder to avoid spillage of brake fluid.
• Do not allow brake fluid to come in contact with any painted surface. Brake fluid makes excellent paint remover.
• Make sure to use the proper bleeding sequence.

BLEEDING PROCEDURE

♦ SEE FIGS. 18 AND 44
1. Turn the ignition switch **OFF** and disconnect the electrical connectors from the ABS actuator.
2. Clean all dirt from around the master cylinder reservoir caps. Remove the caps and fill the master cylinder to the proper level with clean, fresh brake fluid meeting DOT 3 specifications.

➡ **Brake fluid picks up moisture from the air, which reduces its effectiveness and causes brake line corrosion. Don't leave the master cylinder or the fluid container open any longer than necessary. Be careful not to spill brake fluid on painted surfaces. Wipe up any spilled fluid immediately and rinse the area with clear water.**

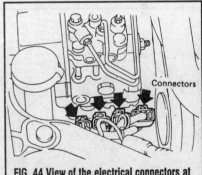

Connectors

FIG. 44 View of the electrical connectors at the ABS actuator — anti-lock brake system

3. Clean all the bleeder screws. You may want to give each one a shot of penetrating solvent to loosen it. Seizure is a common problem with bleeder screws, which then break off, sometimes requiring replacement of the part to which they are attached.

4. Attach a length of clear vinyl tubing to the bleeder screw on the left rear wheel cylinder or caliper. Insert the other end of the tube into a clear, clean jar ½ filled with brake fluid.

5. Have your helper SLOWLY depress the brake pedal. As this is done, open the bleeder (follow the correct bleeding order) screw ⅓–½ of a turn, and allow the fluid to run through the tube. Close the bleeder screw before the pedal reaches the end of its travel. Have your assistant slowly release the pedal. Repeat this process until no air bubbles appear in the expelled fluid.

6. Repeat the procedure on the other wheels in the following order:
   a. Right front caliper
   b. Right rear wheel cylinder or caliper
   c. Left front caliper

7. Be sure to check the fluid level in the master cylinder reservoirs often. Do not allow the reservoirs to run dry or the bleeding process will have to be repeated.

Anti-Lock Brake System Service

RELIEVING ANTI-LOCK BRAKE SYSTEM PRESSURE

To relieve the pressure from the ABS system, turn the ignition switch to the **OFF** position.

Disconnect the connectors from the ABS actuator. Wait a few minutes to allow for the system to bleed down, then disconnect the negative battery cable.

ABS Control Unit

REMOVAL & INSTALLATION

The ABS control unit is located in the trunk, next to the rear speaker.
1. Disconnect the negative battery cable.
2. Disconnect the electrical connector from the control unit.
3. Remove the control unit-to-chassis bolts and the control unit.
4. To install, reverse the removal procedures.
5. Connect the electrical connector to the ABS control unit. Connect the negative battery cable.

ABS Actuator

REMOVAL & INSTALLATION

The ABS Actuator is located in the engine compartment on the right front fender.

1. Relieve the pressure from the ABS system.
2. Disconnect the negative battery cable.
3. Disconnect the electrical harness connectors from the actuator.
4. Disconnect the fluid lines from the actuator. Plug the ends of the lines to prevent leakage.
5. Remove the actuator-to-bracket mounting nuts.
6. Remove the actuator from the mounting bracket.
   To install:
7. Position the actuator onto the mounting bracket.
8. Install the actuator mounting fasteners.
9. Connect the fluid lines and the harness connectors.
10. Connect the negative battery cable.
11. Bleed the brake system.

ABS Front Wheel Sensor

REMOVAL & INSTALLATION

♦ SEE FIG. 46
1. Raise and safely support the vehicle.
2. Remove the front wheels.
3. Disconnect the sensor harness connector.
4. Detach the sensor-to-steering knuckle bolts.
5. Unbolt the sensor from the rear of the steering knuckle.

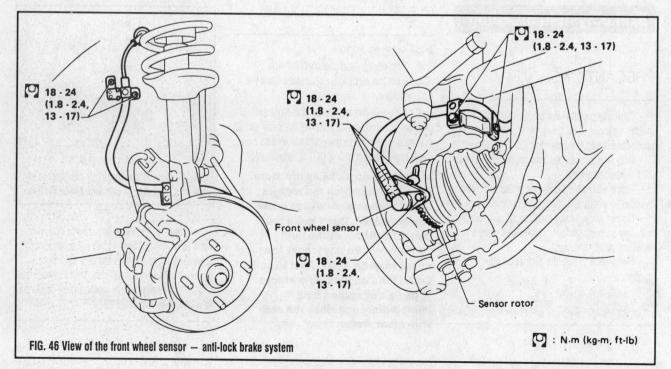

FIG. 46 View of the front wheel sensor — anti-lock brake system

6. Withdraw the sensor from the sensor rotor. Remove the sensor mounting brackets from the sensor wiring.

➡ **During removal and installation, take care not to damage the sensor or the teeth of the rotor.**

To install:

7. Transfer the mounting brackets to the new sensor. Insert the sensor through the opening in the the rear of the knuckle and engage the sensor with the rotor teeth.

8. Install the sensor mounting bolts. Check and adjust the sensor-to-rotor clearance. Once the clearance is set, tighten the sensor-to-steering knuckle bolts to 13–17 ft. lbs. (18–24 Nm).

9. Position and install the sensor mounting brackets. Make the sure the sensor wiring is routed properly.

10. Connect the sensor harness connector.

11. Mount the front wheels and lower the vehicle.

WHEEL SENSOR CLEARANCE ADJUSTMENT

1. Install the sensor.

2. Check the clearance between the edge of the sensor and rotor teeth using a feeler gauge; the clearance should be 0.008–0.039 in. (0.2–1.0mm).

3. To adjust the clearance, loosen the sensor mounting bolt(s) and move the sensor back and forth until the clearance is as specified.

4. Once the clearance is set, tighten the sensor mounting bolts to 13–17 ft. lbs. (18–24 Nm).

ABS Rear Wheel Sensor

REMOVAL & INSTALLATION

◆ SEE FIG. 47

1. Raise and safely support the vehicle.
2. Remove the rear wheels.
3. Disconnect the sensor harness connector.
4. Detach the sensor-to-mounting bracket bolt.
5. Remove the sensor mounting bolts.
6. Withdraw the sensor from the rear gusset.
7. Remove the sensor mounting brackets from the sensor wiring.

To install:

8. Transfer the mounting brackets to the new sensor.

9. Install the sensor. Check and adjust the sensor-to-rotor clearance. Once the clearance is set, tighten the sensor mounting bolt to 13–17 ft. lbs. (18–24 Nm).

10. Install the sensor mounting brackets. Make the sure the sensor wiring is routed properly.

11. Connect the sensor harness connector.

12. Mount the rear wheels and lower the vehicle.

WHEEL SENSOR CLEARANCE ADJUSTMENT

1. Install the rear wheel sensor.

2. Check the clearance between the edge of the sensor and rotor teeth using a feeler gauge; the clearance should be 0.008–0.039 in. (0.2–1.0mm).

3. To adjust the clearance, loosen the sensor bracket mounting bolts and move the bracket back and forth until the clearance is as specified.

4. Once the clearance is set, tighten the sensor mounting bracket bolt(s) to 13–17 ft. lbs. (18–24 Nm).

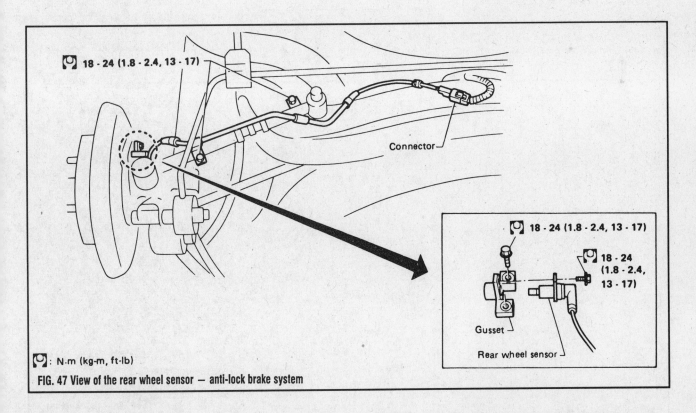

FIG. 47 View of the rear wheel sensor — anti-lock brake system

BRAKE SPECIFICATIONS
All measurements in inches unless noted

Year	Model	Master Cylinder Bore	Brake Disc Original Thickness	Brake Disc Minimum Thickness	Brake Disc Maximum Runout	Brake Drum Diameter Original Inside Diameter	Brake Drum Diameter Max. Wear Limit	Brake Drum Diameter Maximum Machine Diameter	Minimum Lining Thickness Front	Minimum Lining Thickness Rear
1985	Maxima	1.000	NA	①	0.0028	—	—	—	0.079	0.079
1986	Maxima	1.000	NA	①	0.0028	—	—	—	0.079	0.079
1987	Maxima	1.000	NA	①	0.0028	—	—	—	0.079	0.079
1988	Maxima	1.000	NA	①	0.0028	—	—	—	0.079	0.079
1989	Maxima	0.937 ④	⑦	②	0.0028	9.00	9.06	NA	0.079	③
1990	Maxima	0.937 ⑤	⑦	①	0.0028	9.00	9.06	NA	0.079	③
1991	Maxima	0.937 ⑤	⑦	①	0.0028	9.00	9.06	NA	0.079	③
1992	Maxima	⑥	⑦	②	0.0028	9.00	9.06	NA	0.079	③

NA—Not available
① Front: 0.787 in.
　Rear: 0.354 in.
② Front: 0.787 in.
　Rear: 0.315 in.

③ Disc: 0.079 in.
　Drum: 0.059 in.
④ 1.000 in. optional for GSE model
⑤ 1.000 in. optional for SE model with A.B.S.

⑥ 0.937 in.: without A.B.S.
　1.000 in.: with A.B.S.
⑦ Front: 0.870 in.
　Rear: 0.390 in.

Troubleshooting the Brake System

Problem	Cause	Solution
Low brake pedal (excessive pedal travel required for braking action.)	• Excessive clearance between rear linings and drums caused by inoperative automatic adjusters	• Make 10 to 15 alternate forward and reverse brake stops to adjust brakes. If brake pedal does not come up, repair or replace adjuster parts as necessary.
	• Worn rear brakelining	• Inspect and replace lining if worn beyond minimum thickness specification
	• Bent, distorted brakeshoes, front or rear	• Replace brakeshoes in axle sets
	• Air in hydraulic system	• Remove air from system. Refer to Brake Bleeding.
Low brake pedal (pedal may go to floor with steady pressure applied.)	• Fluid leak in hydraulic system	• Fill master cylinder to fill line; have helper apply brakes and check calipers, wheel cylinders, differential valve tubes, hoses and fittings for leaks. Repair or replace as necessary.
	• Air in hydraulic system	• Remove air from system. Refer to Brake Bleeding.
	• Incorrect or non-recommended brake fluid (fluid evaporates at below normal temp).	• Flush hydraulic system with clean brake fluid. Refill with correct-type fluid.
	• Master cylinder piston seals worn, or master cylinder bore is scored, worn or corroded	• Repair or replace master cylinder
Low brake pedal (pedal goes to floor on first application—o.k. on subsequent applications.)	• Disc brake pads sticking on abutment surfaces of anchor plate. Caused by a build-up of dirt, rust, or corrosion on abutment surfaces	• Clean abutment surfaces
Fading brake pedal (pedal height decreases with steady pressure applied.)	• Fluid leak in hydraulic system	• Fill master cylinder reservoirs to fill mark, have helper apply brakes, check calipers, wheel cylinders, differential valve, tubes, hoses, and fittings for fluid leaks. Repair or replace parts as necessary.
	• Master cylinder piston seals worn, or master cylinder bore is scored, worn or corroded	• Repair or replace master cylinder
Spongy brake pedal (pedal has abnormally soft, springy, spongy feel when depressed.)	• Air in hydraulic system	• Remove air from system. Refer to Brake Bleeding.
	• Brakeshoes bent or distorted	• Replace brakeshoes
	• Brakelining not yet seated with drums and rotors	• Burnish brakes
	• Rear drum brakes not properly adjusted	• Adjust brakes

Troubleshooting the Brake System (cont.)

Problem	Cause	Solution
Decreasing brake pedal travel (pedal travel required for braking action decreases and may be accompanied by a hard pedal.)	• Caliper or wheel cylinder pistons sticking or seized • Master cylinder compensator ports blocked (preventing fluid return to reservoirs) or pistons sticking or seized in master cylinder bore • Power brake unit binding internally	• Repair or replace the calipers, or wheel cylinders • Repair or replace the master cylinder • Test unit according to the following procedure: (a) Shift transmission into neutral and start engine (b) Increase engine speed to 1500 rpm, close throttle and fully depress brake pedal (c) Slow release brake pedal and stop engine (d) Have helper remove vacuum check valve and hose from power unit. Observe for backward movement of brake pedal. (e) If the pedal moves backward, the power unit has an internal bind—replace power unit
Grabbing brakes (severe reaction to brake pedal pressure.)	• Brakelining(s) contaminated by grease or brake fluid • Parking brake cables incorrectly adjusted or seized • Incorrect brakelining or lining loose on brakeshoes • Caliper anchor plate bolts loose • Rear brakeshoes binding on support plate ledges • Incorrect or missing power brake reaction disc • Rear brake support plates loose	• Determine and correct cause of contamination and replace brakeshoes in axle sets • Adjust cables. Replace seized cables. • Replace brakeshoes in axle sets • Tighten bolts • Clean and lubricate ledges. Replace support plate(s) if ledges are deeply grooved. Do not attempt to smooth ledges by grinding. • Install correct disc • Tighten mounting bolts
Chatter or shudder when brakes are applied (pedal pulsation and roughness may also occur.)	• Brakeshoes distorted, bent, contaminated, or worn • Caliper anchor plate or support plate loose • Excessive thickness variation of rotor(s)	• Replace brakeshoes in axle sets • Tighten mounting bolts • Refinish or replace rotors in axle sets
Noisy brakes (squealing, clicking, scraping sound when brakes are applied.)	• Bent, broken, distorted brakeshoes • Excessive rust on outer edge of rotor braking surface	• Replace brakeshoes in axle sets • Remove rust

Troubleshooting the Brake System (cont.)

Problem	Cause	Solution
Hard brake pedal (excessive pedal pressure required to stop vehicle. May be accompanied by brake fade.)	• Loose or leaking power brake unit vacuum hose • Incorrect or poor quality brake-lining • Bent, broken, distorted brakeshoes • Calipers binding or dragging on mounting pins. Rear brakeshoes dragging on support plate.	• Tighten connections or replace leaking hose • Replace with lining in axle sets • Replace brakeshoes • Replace mounting pins and bushings. Clean rust or burrs from rear brake support plate ledges and lubricate ledges with molydisulfide grease. **NOTE:** If ledges are deeply grooved or scored, do not attempt to sand or grind them smooth—replace support plate.
	• Caliper, wheel cylinder, or master cylinder pistons sticking or seized • Power brake unit vacuum check valve malfunction	• Repair or replace parts as necessary • Test valve according to the following procedure: (a) Start engine, increase engine speed to 1500 rpm, close throttle and immediately stop engine (b) Wait at least 90 seconds then depress brake pedal (c) If brakes are not vacuum assisted for 2 or more applications, check valve is faulty
	• Power brake unit has internal bind	• Test unit according to the following procedure: (a) With engine stopped, apply brakes several times to exhaust all vacuum in system (b) Shift transmission into neutral, depress brake pedal and start engine (c) If pedal height decreases with foot pressure and less pressure is required to hold pedal in applied position, power unit vacuum system is operating normally. Test power unit. If power unit exhibits a bind condition, replace the power unit.

Troubleshooting the Brake System (cont.)

Problem	Cause	Solution
Hard brake pedal (excessive pedal pressure required to stop vehicle. May be accompanied by brake fade.)	• Master cylinder compensator ports (at bottom of reservoirs) blocked by dirt, scale, rust, or have small burrs (blocked ports prevent fluid return to reservoirs). • Brake hoses, tubes, fittings clogged or restricted • Brake fluid contaminated with improper fluids (motor oil, transmission fluid, causing rubber components to swell and stick in bores • Low engine vacuum	• Repair or replace master cylinder **CAUTION:** Do not attempt to clean blocked ports with wire, pencils, or similar implements. Use compressed air only. • Use compressed air to check or unclog parts. Replace any damaged parts. • Replace all rubber components, combination valve and hoses. Flush entire brake system with DOT 3 brake fluid or equivalent. • Adjust or repair engine
Dragging brakes (slow or incomplete release of brakes)	• Brake pedal binding at pivot • Power brake unit has internal bind • Parking brake cables incorrrectly adjusted or seized • Rear brakeshoe return springs weak or broken • Automatic adjusters malfunctioning • Caliper, wheel cylinder or master cylinder pistons sticking or seized • Master cylinder compensating ports blocked (fluid does not return to reservoirs).	• Loosen and lubricate • Inspect for internal bind. Replace unit if internal bind exists. • Adjust cables. Replace seized cables. • Replace return springs. Replace brakeshoe if necessary in axle sets. • Repair or replace adjuster parts as required • Repair or replace parts as necessary • Use compressed air to clear ports. Do not use wire, pencils, or similar objects to open blocked ports.
Vehicle moves to one side when brakes are applied	• Incorrect front tire pressure • Worn or damaged wheel bearings • Brakelining on one side contaminated • Brakeshoes on one side bent, distorted, or lining loose on shoe • Support plate bent or loose on one side • Brakelining not yet seated with drums or rotors • Caliper anchor plate loose on one side • Caliper piston sticking or seized • Brakelinings water soaked • Loose suspension component attaching or mounting bolts • Brake combination valve failure	• Inflate to recommended cold (reduced load) inflation pressure • Replace worn or damaged bearings • Determine and correct cause of contamination and replace brakelining in axle sets • Replace brakeshoes in axle sets • Tighten or replace support plate • Burnish brakelining • Tighten anchor plate bolts • Repair or replace caliper • Drive vehicle with brakes lightly applied to dry linings • Tighten suspension bolts. Replace worn suspension components. • Replace combination valve

Troubleshooting the Brake System (cont.)

Problem	Cause	Solution
Noisy brakes (squealing, clicking, scraping sound when brakes are applied.) (cont.)	• Brakelining worn out—shoes contacting drum of rotor	• Replace brakeshoes and lining in axle sets. Refinish or replace drums or rotors.
	• Broken or loose holdown or return springs	• Replace parts as necessary
	• Rough or dry drum brake support plate ledges	• Lubricate support plate ledges
	• Cracked, grooved, or scored rotor(s) or drum(s)	• Replace rotor(s) or drum(s). Replace brakeshoes and lining in axle sets if necessary.
	• Incorrect brakelining and/or shoes (front or rear).	• Install specified shoe and lining assemblies
Pulsating brake pedal	• Out of round drums or excessive lateral runout in disc brake rotor(s)	• Refinish or replace drums, re-index rotors or replace

TORQUE SPECIFICATIONS

Component	English	Metric
ASCD cancel switch locknuts	9–11 ft. lbs.	12–15 Nm
Backing plate-to-strut bolts	28–38 ft. lbs.	38–52 Nm
Brake booster-to-chassis nuts		
1985–90	5.8–8 ft. lbs.	8–11 Nm
1991–92	9–12 ft. lbs.	13–16 Nm
Brake caliper-to-torque member bolt		
Front		
1985–88	12–14 ft. lbs.	17–20 Nm
1989–92	16–23 ft. lbs.	22–31 Nm
Rear	16–23 ft. lbs.	22–31 Nm
Brake light switch locknuts	9–11 ft. lbs.	12–15 Nm
Brake line-to-brake caliper bolt	12–14 ft. lbs.	17–20 Nm
Brake pedal fulcrum bolt	12–16 ft. lbs.	16–22 Nm
Brake tube(s)-to-load sensing valve nut(s)	12–14 ft. lbs.	17–20 Nm
Front wheel sensor-to-steering knuckle bolts	13–17 ft. lbs.	18–24 Nm
Load sensing valve-to-chassis bolts	25–29 ft. lbs.	34–39 Nm
Master cylinder-to-power booster nuts	5.8–8.0 ft. lbs.	8–11 Nm
Parking brake control lever assembly-to-chassis bolts	5.8–8.0 ft. lbs.	8–11 Nm
Rear wheel sensor bracket bolt(s)	13–17 ft. lbs.	18–24 Nm
Rear wheel sensor mounting bolt	13–17 ft. lbs.	18–24 Nm
Torque member-to-steering knuckle bolts	53–72 ft. lbs.	72–97 Nm
Torque member-to-rear strut bolts	28–38 ft. lbs.	38–52 Nm
Wheel cylinder-to-backing plate bolts	4.3–8.0 ft. lbs.	6–11 Nm
Wheel nuts	72–87 ft. lbs.	98–118 Nm

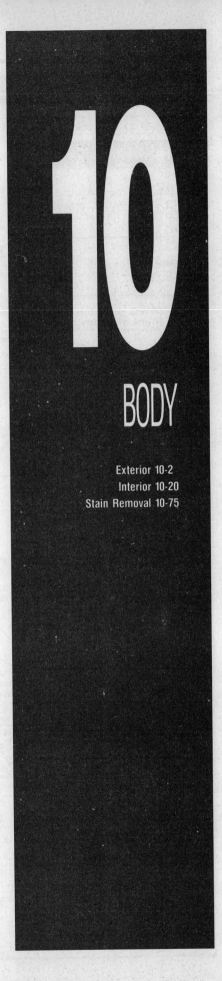

10

BODY

EXTERIOR

Doors

REMOVAL & INSTALLATION

Front and Rear

♦ SEE FIGS. 1–4

1. Place a jackstand under the door to support its weight.

→ **Place a rag between the lower edge of the door and jackstand to prevent damage to painted surface.**

2. Remove the inner panel from the door.

3. Disconnect the electrical connectors from inside the door. Pull the electrical harness from the door grommet.

4. Remove the door stop-to-chassis pin.

5. On the 1985–88 models, perform the following procedure:

   a. Remove the C-clips from the door hinge pins.

   b. Support the door.

   c. Remove the hinge pins from the door hinges.

   d. Remove the door; be careful not to loose hinge washers.

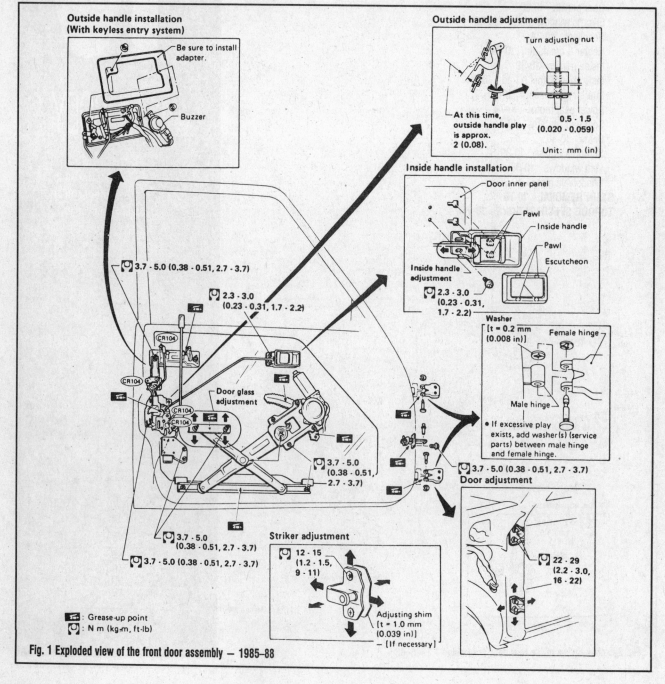

Fig. 1 Exploded view of the front door assembly — 1985–88

6. On the 1989–92 models, perform the following procedures:

a. Support the door.

b. Remove the door hinges-to-door bolts.

c. Remove the door.

To install:

7. On the 1985–88 models, perform the following procedures:

a. Coat the hinge link with multi-purpose grease.

b. Position the door onto the jackstands and support it.

c. Install the hinge washers and pins into the door hinges.

d. Secure the hinge pins with the C-clips.

8. On the 1989–92 models, perform the following procedures:

a. Coat the hinge link with multi-purpose grease.

b. Position the door onto the jackstands and support it.

c. Install the door hinge-to-door bolts and torque to 22–27 ft. lbs. (29–37 Nm).

9. Install the door stop-to-chassis pin.

10. Pull the electrical harness through the door grommet and connect the electrical connectors.

11. Install the inner door panel.

12. Check and/or adjust the door-to-body alignment.

ADJUSTMENT

Front and Rear

Proper door alignment can be obtained by

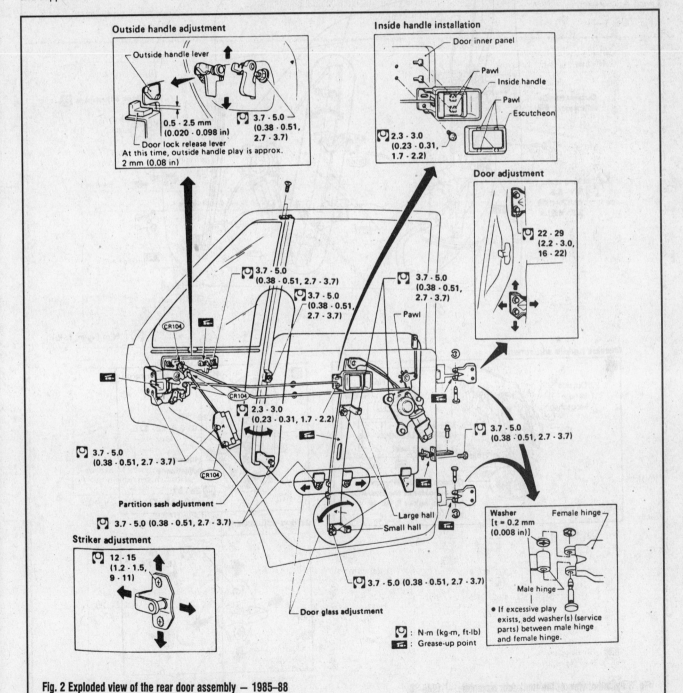

Fig. 2 Exploded view of the rear door assembly — 1985–88

adjusting the door hinge and door lock striker. The door hinge and striker can be moved up and down fore and aft in enlarged holes by loosening the attaching bolts.

➡ **The door should be adjusted for an even and parallel fit for the door opening and surrounding body panels.**

1. If the door striker bolts were loosened for adjustment, torque the door striker-to-chassis bolts to 9–12 ft. lbs. (13–16 Nm).

2. If the door hinge bolts were loosened for adjustment, torque the bolts to:
1985–88 — 16–22 ft. lbs. (22–29 Nm)
1989–92 — 22–27 ft. lbs. (29–37 Nm)

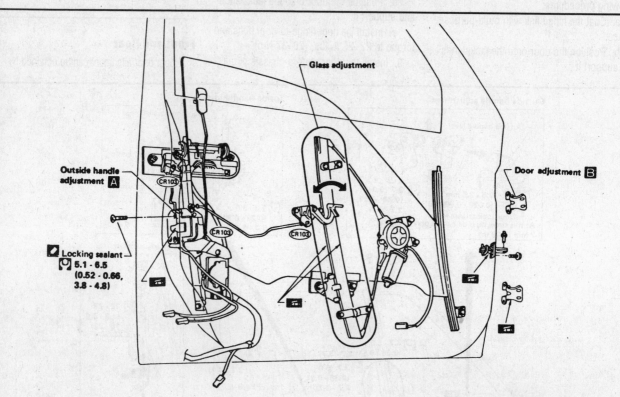

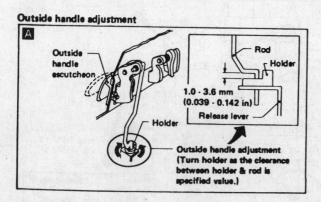

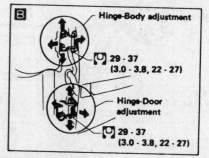

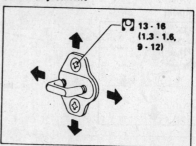

Fig. 3 Exploded view of the front door assembly — 1989–92

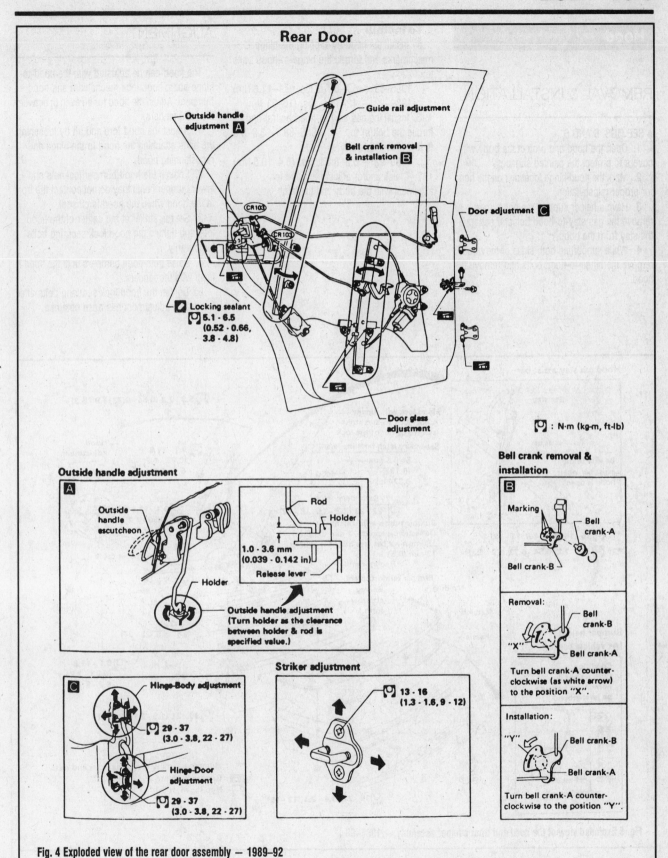

Rear Door

Outside handle adjustment **A**

Guide rail adjustment

Bell crank removal & installation **B**

Door adjustment **C**

CR103

CR103

Locking sealant
5.1 - 6.5
(0.52 - 0.66,
3.8 - 4.8)

Door glass adjustment

: N·m (kg-m, ft-lb)

Outside handle adjustment

A

Outside handle escutcheon

Holder

Rod

Holder

1.0 - 3.6 mm
(0.039 - 0.142 in)

Release lever

Outside handle adjustment
(Turn holder as the clearance
between holder & rod is
specified value.)

Bell crank removal & installation

B

Marking

Bell crank-A

Bell crank-B

Removal:

Bell crank-B

"X"

Bell crank-A

Turn bell crank-A counterclockwise (as white arrow)
to the position "X".

Installation:

"Y"

Bell crank-B

Bell crank-A

Turn bell crank-A counterclockwise to the position "Y".

C

Hinge-Body adjustment

29 - 37
(3.0 - 3.8, 22 - 27)

Hinge-Door adjustment

29 - 37
(3.0 - 3.8, 22 - 27)

Striker adjustment

13 - 16
(1.3 - 1.6, 9 - 12)

Fig. 4 Exploded view of the rear door assembly — 1989–92

Hood

REMOVAL & INSTALLATION

♦ SEE FIGS. 5 AND 6

1. Open the hood and protect the body with covers to protect the painted surfaces.

2. Mark the hood hinge locations on the hood for proper reinstallation.

3. Have a helper support the hood; then, remove the gas stay-to-hood bolt and separate the stay from the hood.

4. While supporting both sides of the hood, remove the hinge-to-hood bolts and remove the hood.

To Install:

5. Install the hood by aligning the hinge matchmarks and torque the hinge-to-hood bolts to:

1985–88 — 6.7–8.7 ft. lbs. (9.1–11.8 Nm)
1989–92 — 12–15 ft. lbs. (16–21 Nm)

6. Install the gas stay-to-hood bolt(s) and torque the bolt(s) to: 1985–88 — 3.9–5.3 ft. lbs. (5.3–7.2 Nm)

1989–92 — 6.2–8.0 ft. lbs. (8.4–10.8 Nm)

7. Check and/or adjust the hood for alignment with the body and the latch.

ALIGNMENT

The hood can be adjusted with the hood-to-hinge bolts, hood lock mechanism and hood bumpers. Adjust the hood for an even fit between the front fenders.

1. Adjust the hood fore and aft by loosening the bolts attaching the hood to the hinge and repositioning hood.

2. Loosen the hood bumper locknuts and lower bumpers until they do not contact the front of the hood when the hood is closed.

3. Set the striker at the center of the hood lock and tighten the hood lock securing bolts temporarily.

4. Raise both hood bumpers until the hood is flush with the fenders.

5. Tighten the hood lock securing bolts after the proper adjustment has been obtained.

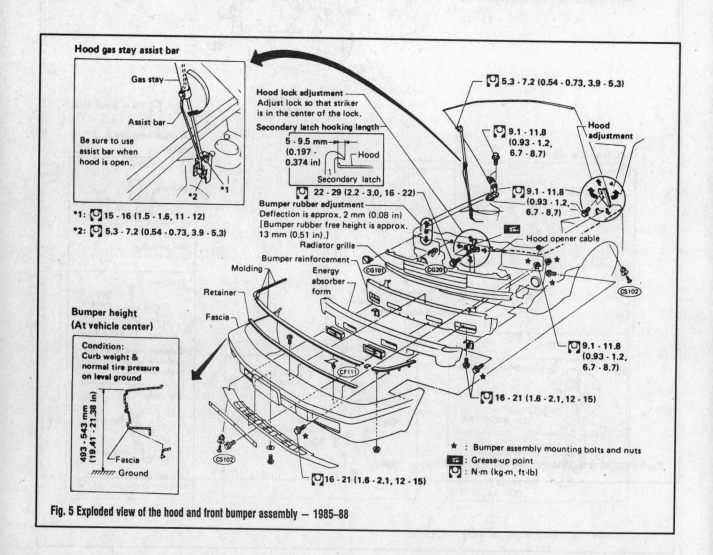

Fig. 5 Exploded view of the hood and front bumper assembly — 1985–88

Hood lock adjustment

- Adjust hood so that hood primary lock meshes at a position 1 to 1.5 mm (0.039 to 0.059 in) lower than fender.
- After hood lock adjustment, adjust bumper rubber.
- When securing hood lock, ensure it does not tilt. Striker must be positioned at the center of hood primary lock.
- After adjustment, ensure that hood primary and secondary lock operate properly.

Hood lock secondary latch hooking length

Bumper rubber adjustment

- Adjust so that hood is ligned with fender. At that time deflection is approx. 2 mm (0.08 in). [Bumper rubber free height is approx. 13 mm (0.51 in).]

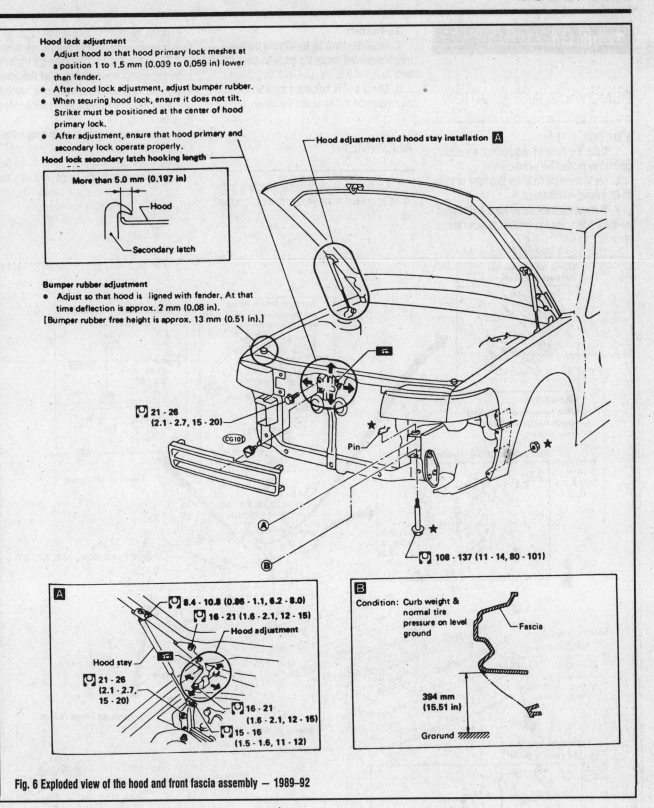

Fig. 6 Exploded view of the hood and front fascia assembly — 1989–92

Trunk Lid

REMOVAL & INSTALLATION

◆ SEE FIGS. 7–11

1. Open the trunk lid and position a cloth or cushion to protect the painted areas.

2. Mark the trunk lid hinge locations or trunk lid for proper reinstallation.

3. Support the trunk lid by hand and remove the trunk lid-to-hinge bolts; then, remove the trunk lid.

To install:

4. Install the trunk lid by aligning the hinge matchmarks and torque the hinge-to-trunk lid bolts to 3.3–4.0 ft. lbs. (4.4–5.4 Nm).

5. Check and/or adjust the trunk lid for alignment with the body and the striker.

ALIGNMENT

1. Loosen the trunk lid hinge attaching bolts until they are just loose enough to move the trunk lid.

2. Move the trunk lid fore and aft to obtain a flush fit between the trunk lid and the rear fender.

3. To obtain a snug fit between the trunk lid and weatherstrip, loosen the trunk lid lock striker attaching bolts enough to move the lid, working the striker up and down and from side to side as required.

4. After the adjustment is made torque the striker bolts to:

    1985–88 — 3.3–4.0 ft. lbs. (4.4–5.4 Nm)
    1989–92 — 3.8–4.8 ft. lbs. (5.1–6.5 Nm)

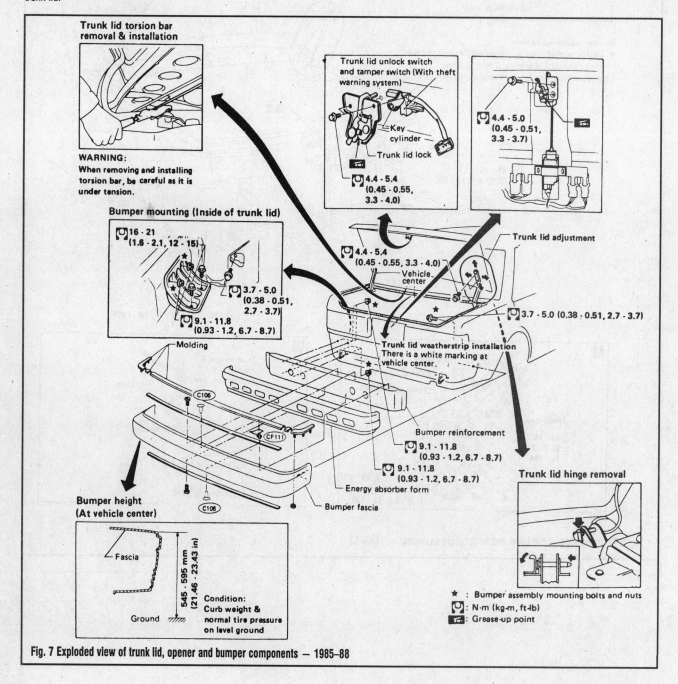

Fig. 7 Exploded view of trunk lid, opener and bumper components — 1985–88

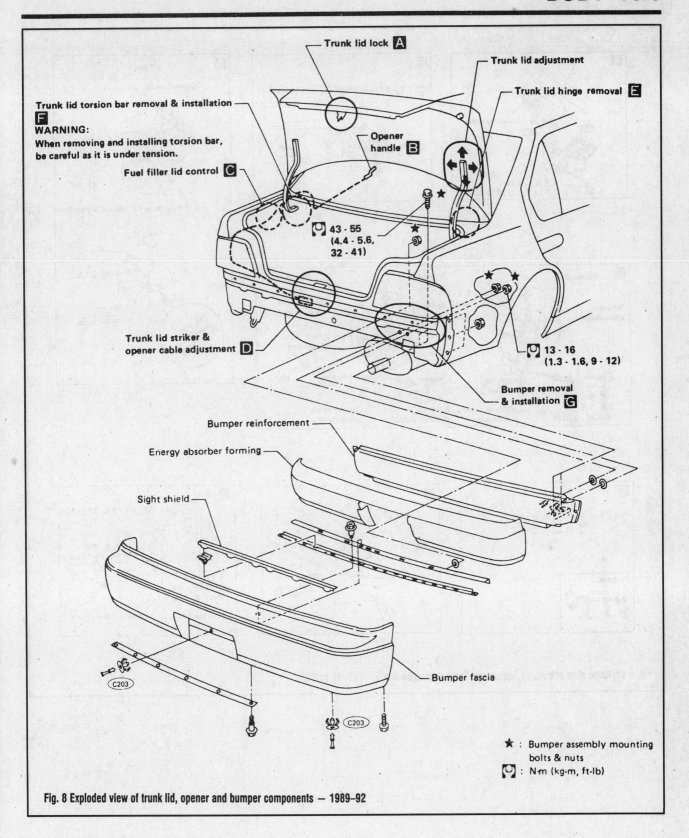

Trunk lid lock **A**

Trunk lid adjustment

Trunk lid hinge removal **E**

Trunk lid torsion bar removal & installation **F**

WARNING:
When removing and installing torsion bar, be careful as it is under tension.

Opener handle **B**

Fuel filler lid control **C**

43 - 55 (4.4 - 5.6, 32 - 41)

Trunk lid striker & opener cable adjustment **D**

13 - 16 (1.3 - 1.6, 9 - 12)

Bumper removal & installation **G**

Bumper reinforcement

Energy absorber forming

Sight shield

C203

C203

Bumper fascia

★ : Bumper assembly mounting bolts & nuts

: N·m (kg-m, ft-lb)

Fig. 8 Exploded view of trunk lid, opener and bumper components — 1989–92

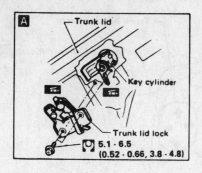

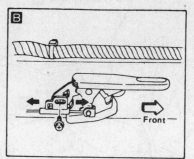

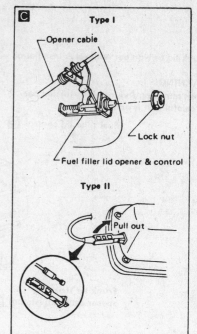

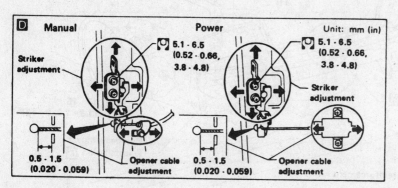

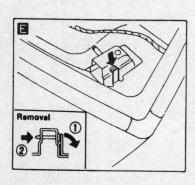

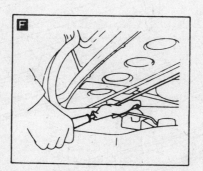

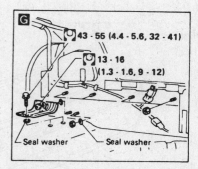

Fig. 9 Exploded view of trunk lid, opener and bumper components — 1989–92 cont'd

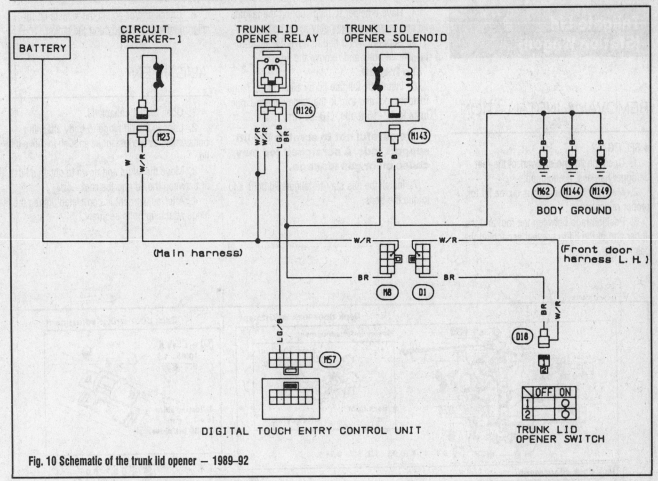

Fig. 10 Schematic of the trunk lid opener — 1989–92

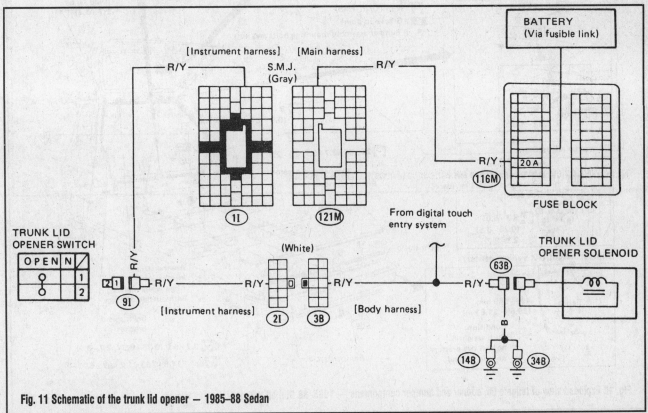

Fig. 11 Schematic of the trunk lid opener — 1985–88 Sedan

Tailgate Lid (Station Wagon)

REMOVAL & INSTALLATION

♦ SEE FIG. 12

1. Open the lid and disconnect the rear defogger harness, if equipped.

2. Mark the hinge locations on the lid for proper relocation.

3. Position rags between the roof and the upper end of the lid to prevent scratching the paint.

4. Have a helper to help support the tailgate lid and remove the gas stay-to-lid bolts.

5. Support the lid and remove the hinge-to-tailgate lid bolts and remove the lid.

To install:

6. Install the tailgate lid by aligning the hinge matchmarks and torque the tailgate lid-to-hinge bolts to 12–15 ft. lbs. (16–21 Nm).

➡ **Be careful not to scratch the lift support rods. A scratched rod may cause oil or gas leakage.**

7. Install the gas stay-to-tailgate lid bolts and torque the bolts.

8. Check and/or adjust the tailgate lid for alignment with the body and the striker.

ALIGNMENT

1. Open the hatchback lid.

2. Loosen the lid hinge to body attaching bolts until they are just loose enough to move the lid.

3. Move the lid up and down to obtain a flush fit between the lid and the roof.

4. After adjustment is completed tighten the hinge attaching bolts securely.

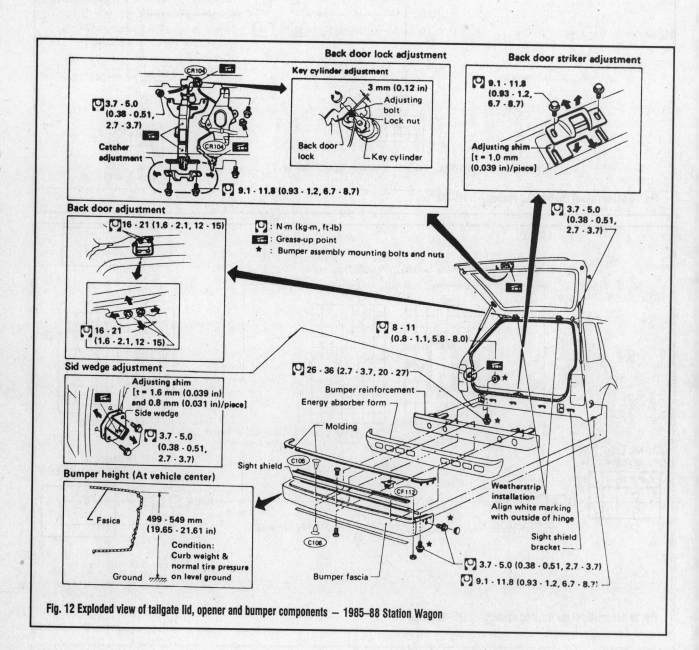

Fig. 12 Exploded view of tailgate lid, opener and bumper components — 1985–88 Station Wagon

Bumpers

REMOVAL & INSTALLATION

Front Bumper

♦ SEE FIGS. 5–6 AND 13

1. Disconnect the electrical connectors from bumper assembly, if equipped.

2. Remove bumper fascia-to-chassis bolts and bumper fascia.

3. Remove the energy absorber form-to-bumper reinforcement bolts and remove the energy absorber form.

4. Remove the bumper reinforcement-to-chassis nuts/bolts and the bumper reinforcement.

To install:

5. Torque the bumper reinforcement-to-chassis fasteners to:

Bolts: 1985–88 — 12–15 ft. lbs. (16–21 Nm)

1989–92 — 80–101 ft. lbs. (108–13 Nm)

Nuts 1985–88 — 6.7–8.7 ft. lbs. (9.1–11.8 Nm)

6. Install bumper absorber form to the bumper reinforcement.

7. Install the bumper fascia and tighten the bolts.

8. Connect the electrical connectors to the bumper assembly.

Rear Bumper

♦ SEE FIGS. 7–8 AND 12

1. Remove bumper fascia-to-chassis bolts and bumper fascia.

2. Remove the energy absorber form-to-bumper reinforcement bolts and remove the energy absorber form.

3. Remove the bumper reinforcement-to-chassis nuts/bolts and the bumper reinforcement.

To install:

4. Torque the bumper reinforcement-to-chassis fasteners to:

Bolts: 1985–88 Station Wagon — 20–27 ft. lbs. (26–36 Nm)

1989–92 — 80–101 ft. lbs. (108–137 Nm)

Nuts 1985–88 Sedan — 6.7–8.7 ft. lbs. (9.1–11.8 Nm)

Station Wagon — 5.8–8.0 ft. lbs. (8–11 Nm)

1989–92 — 9–12 ft. lbs. (13–16 Nm)

5. Install bumper absorber form to the bumper reinforcement.

6. Install the bumper fascia and tighten the bolts.

Grille

REMOVAL & INSTALLATION

♦ SEE FIGS. 5 AND 6

1. Remove radiator grille bracket bolts.

➡ **Some clips are used to hold the radiator grille assembly in place. The radiator grille assembly is made of plastic, thus never use excessive force to remove it.**

2. Remove radiator grille from the vehicle.

3. To install reverse the removal procedures.

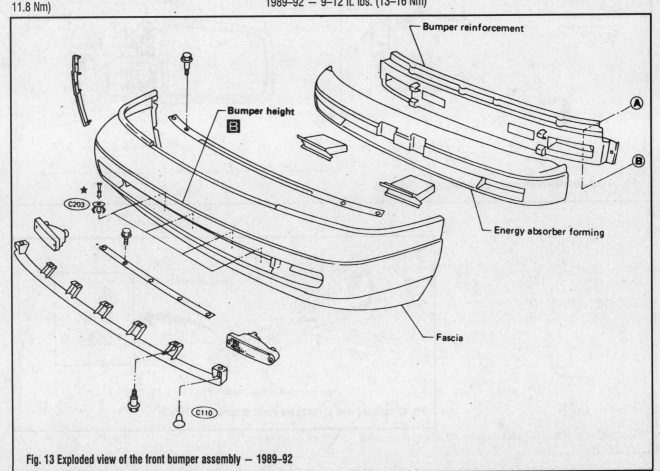

Fig. 13 Exploded view of the front bumper assembly — 1989–92

Outside Mirrors

REMOVAL & INSTALLATION

Power

♦ SEE FIGS. 14–16

1. Remove door corner finisher panel.
2. Remove mirror body attaching screws and remove mirror body.
3. Disconnect the electrical connection.

➡ **It may be necessary to remove the door trim panel to gain access to the electrical connection.**

4. To install, reverse the removal procedures and torque the power mirror-to-chassis bolts to 2.7–3.4 ft. lbs. (3.6–4.6 Nm).

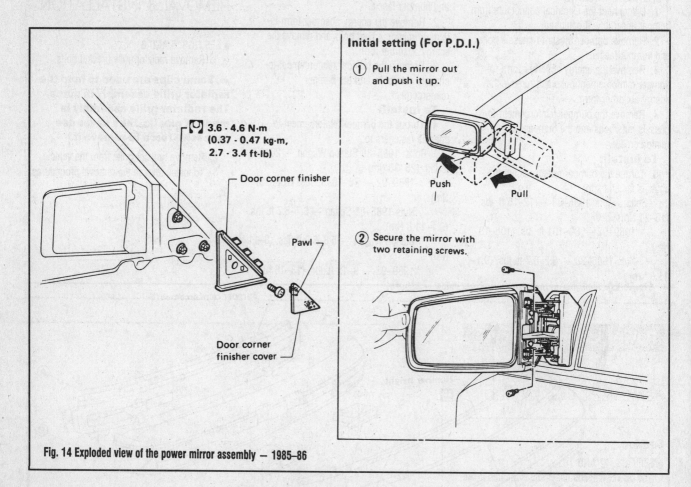

3.6 - 4.6 N·m
(0.37 - 0.47 kg-m,
2.7 - 3.4 ft-lb)

Door corner finisher

Pawl

Door corner finisher cover

Initial setting (For P.D.I.)

① Pull the mirror out and push it up.

Push   Pull

② Secure the mirror with two retaining screws.

Fig. 14 Exploded view of the power mirror assembly — 1985–86

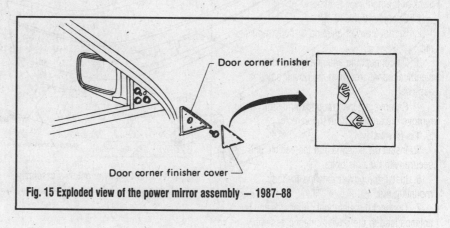

Door corner finisher

Door corner finisher cover

Fig. 15 Exploded view of the power mirror assembly — 1987–88

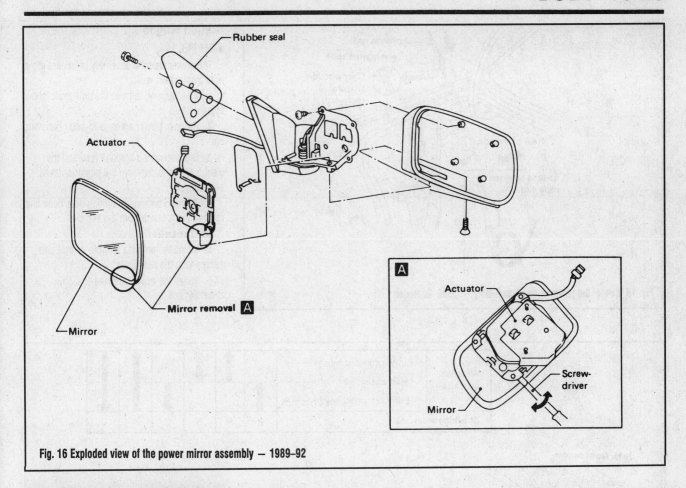

Fig. 16 Exploded view of the power mirror assembly — 1989–92

Power Antenna

REMOVAL & INSTALLATION

Sedan

♦ SEE FIGS. 17 AND 18

The power antenna assembly is located in the trunk at the right rear fender.

1. Open the trunk lid.
2. Remove power antenna-to-body mounting nut.
3. Disconnect the antenna lead and the electrical connector from the power antenna assembly.
4. Remove antenna mounting nuts/bolts and remove the antenna from the vehicle.

To install:

5. Install the antenna into the vehicle and secure with the nuts/bolts.
6. Install the power antenna-to-body mounting nut.
7. Connect the electrical connector and the antenna lead to the power antenna assembly.
8. Check the power antenna for proper operation.

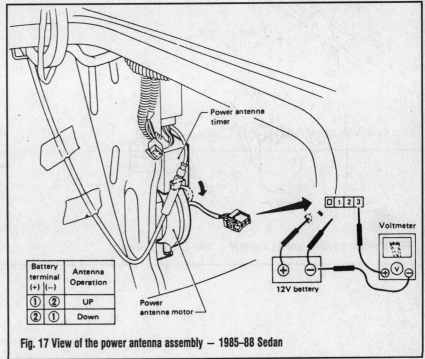

Battery terminal (+)	(−)	Antenna Operation
①	②	UP
②	①	Down

Fig. 17 View of the power antenna assembly — 1985–88 Sedan

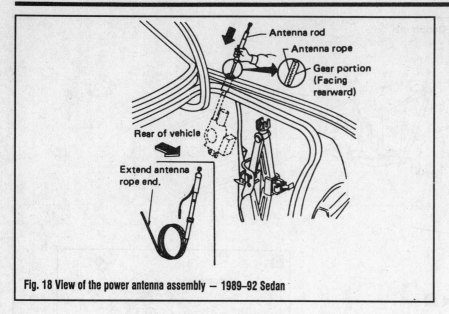

Fig. 18 View of the power antenna assembly — 1989–92 Sedan

Station Wagon

◆ SEE FIG. 19

The power antenna assembly is located at the right front wheel well.

1. If necessary, remove the right front fender splash shield.

2. Remove power antenna-to-body mounting nut.

3. Disconnect the antenna lead and the electrical connector from the power antenna assembly.

4. Remove antenna mounting nuts/bolts and remove the antenna from the vehicle.

To install:

5. Install the antenna into the vehicle and secure with the nuts/bolts.

6. Install the power antenna-to-body mounting nut.

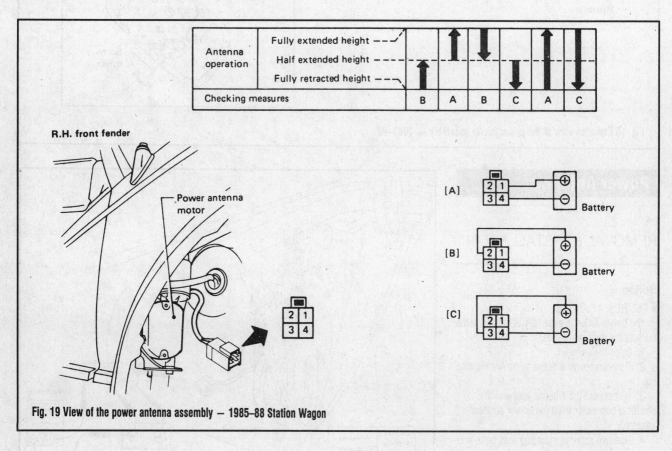

Antenna operation	Fully extended height						
	Half extended height						
	Fully retracted height						
Checking measures		B	A	B	C	A	C

Fig. 19 View of the power antenna assembly — 1985–88 Station Wagon

7. Connect the electrical connector and the antenna lead to the power antenna assembly.

8. If necessary, install the right front fender splash shield.

9. Check the power antenna for proper operation.

Power Sunroof

REMOVAL & INSTALLATION

◆ SEE FIGS. 20–23

Refer to the exploded view power sunroof assembly for the necessary removal and installation information.

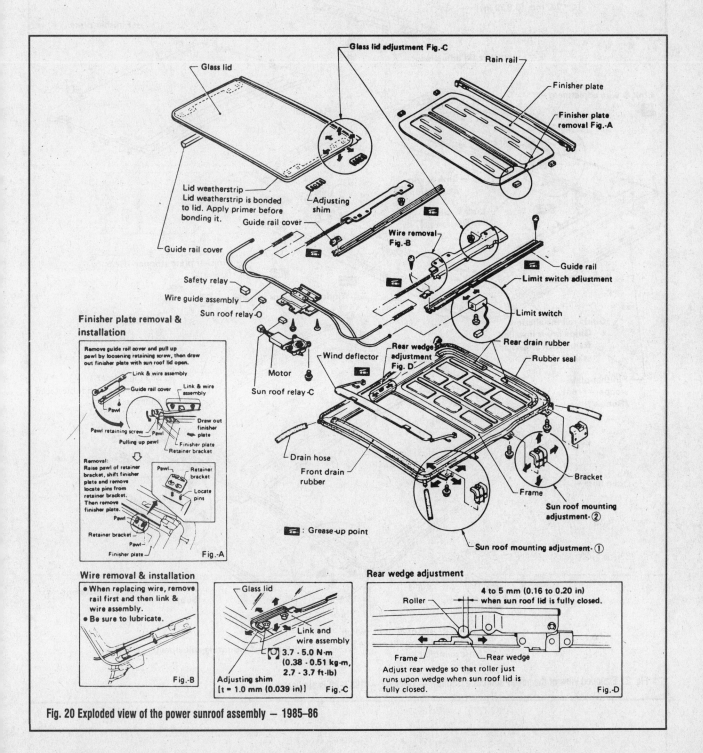

Fig. 20 Exploded view of the power sunroof assembly — 1985–86

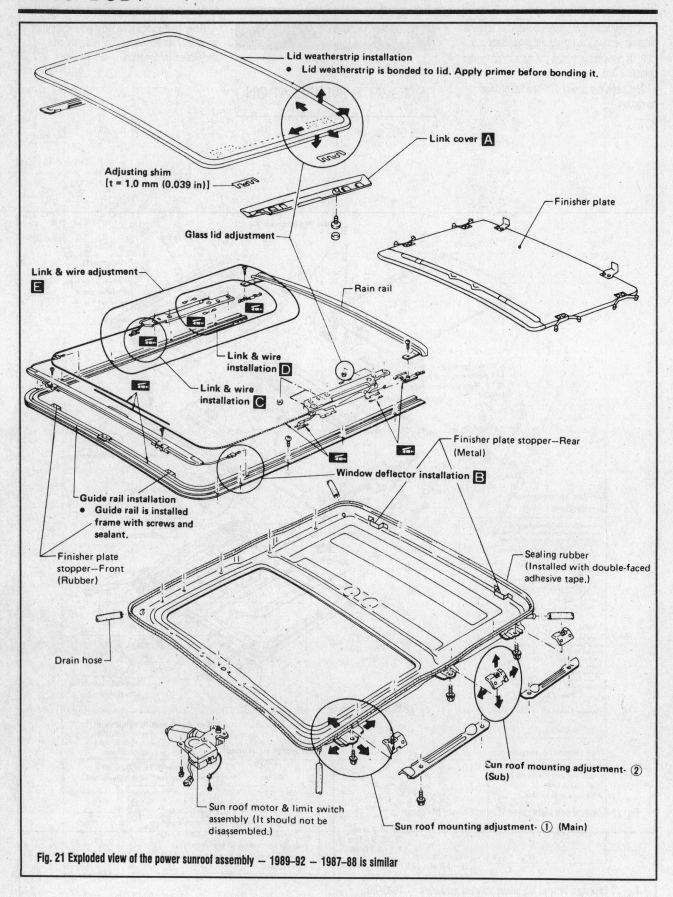

Lid weatherstrip installation
- Lid weatherstrip is bonded to lid. Apply primer before bonding it.

Link cover A

Adjusting shim
[t = 1.0 mm (0.039 in)]

Finisher plate

Glass lid adjustment

Link & wire adjustment
E

Rain rail

Link & wire
installation D

Link & wire
installation C

Finisher plate stopper—Rear
(Metal)

Window deflector installation B

Guide rail installation
- Guide rail is installed
frame with screws and
sealant.

Finisher plate
stopper—Front
(Rubber)

Sealing rubber
(Installed with double-faced
adhesive tape.)

Drain hose

Sun roof mounting adjustment- ②
(Sub)

Sun roof motor & limit switch
assembly (It should not be
disassembled.)

Sun roof mounting adjustment- ① (Main)

Fig. 21 Exploded view of the power sunroof assembly — 1989–92 — 1987–88 is similar

Link cover removal **A**

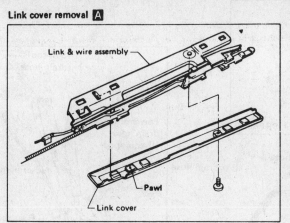

Link & wire assembly

Pawl

Link cover

Link & wire installation (Front portion – For deflector control) **C**

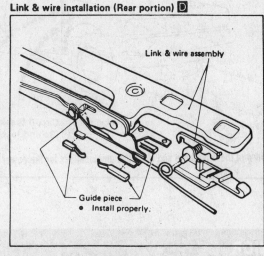

Link assembly

Guide rail

Wire assembly

Wind deflector installation **B**

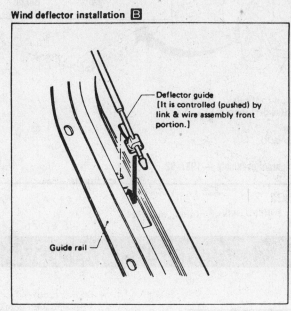

Deflector guide
(It is controlled (pushed) by link & wire assembly front portion.)

Guide rail

Link & wire installation (Rear portion) **D**

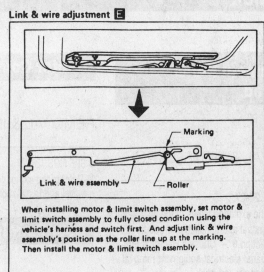

Link & wire assembly

Guide piece
• Install properly.

Link & wire adjustment **E**

Marking

Link & wire assembly

Roller

When installing motor & limit switch assembly, set motor & limit switch assembly to fully closed condition using the vehicle's harness and switch first. And adjust link & wire assembly's position as the roller line up at the marking. Then install the motor & limit switch assembly.

Fig. 22 Removal and installation information for the power sunroof assembly — 1987–92

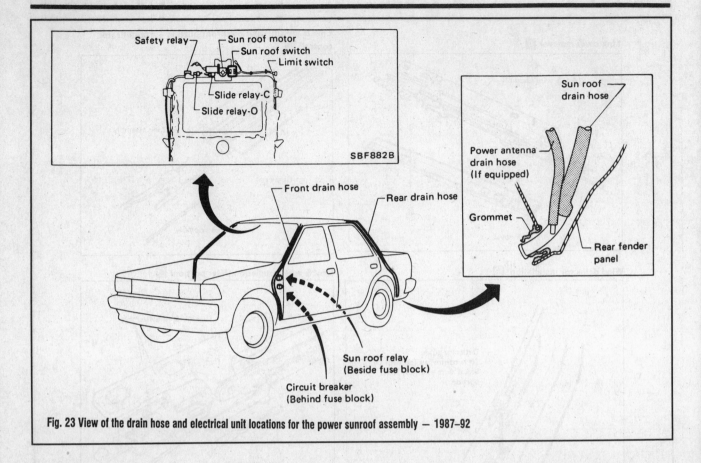

Fig. 23 View of the drain hose and electrical unit locations for the power sunroof assembly — 1987–92

INTERIOR

Instrument Panel and Pad

REMOVAL & INSTALLATION

◆ SEE FIGS. 24-27

Refer to the exploded views of the instrument panel for removal and installation procedures. Refer to "Section 6 — Chassis Electrical" for instrument panel electrical equipment removal and installation procedures.

Center Console

REMOVAL & INSTALLATION

◆ SEE FIGS. 24-27

Refer to the exploded views of the console for removal and installation procedures.

Door Panels

REMOVAL & INSTALLATION

Front and Rear

◆ SEE FIGS. 1-4, 28-32

1. Remove the arm rest, door inside handle escutcheon and door lock.

2. Remove the door finisher.
3. To install, reverse the removal procedures.

Interior Trim Panels

REMOVAL & INSTALLATION

Front and Rear

◆ SEE FIGS. 28-29, 31, 33–36

Refer to the exploded views of the interior trim panels for removal and installation procedures.

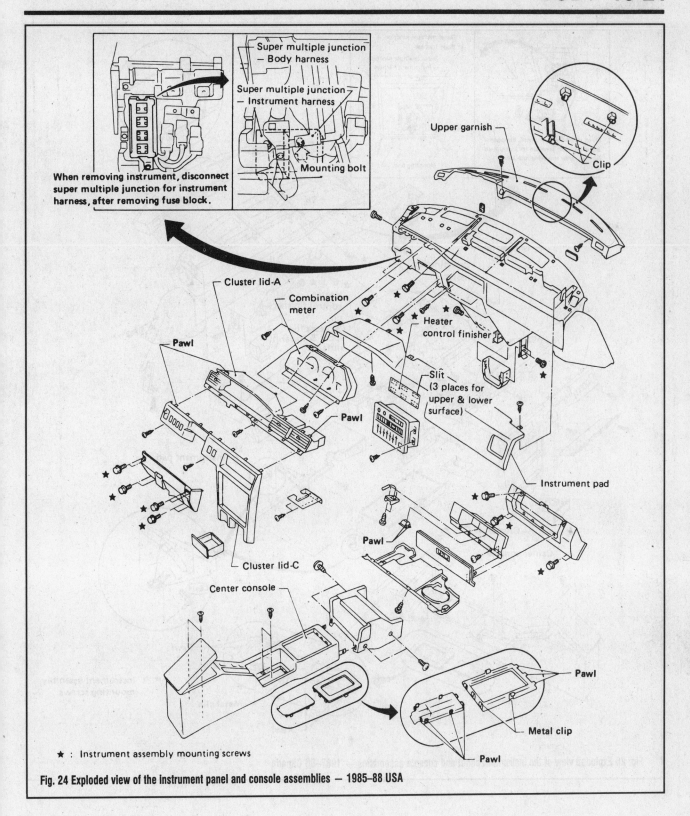

When removing instrument, disconnect super multiple junction for instrument harness, after removing fuse block.

Super multiple junction — Body harness

Super multiple junction — Instrument harness

Mounting bolt

Upper garnish

Clip

Cluster lid-A

Combination meter

Heater control finisher

Slit (3 places for upper & lower surface)

Pawl

Pawl

Pawl

Instrument pad

Pawl

Cluster lid-C

Center console

Pawl

Metal clip

Pawl

★ : Instrument assembly mounting screws

Fig. 24 Exploded view of the instrument panel and console assemblies — 1985–88 USA

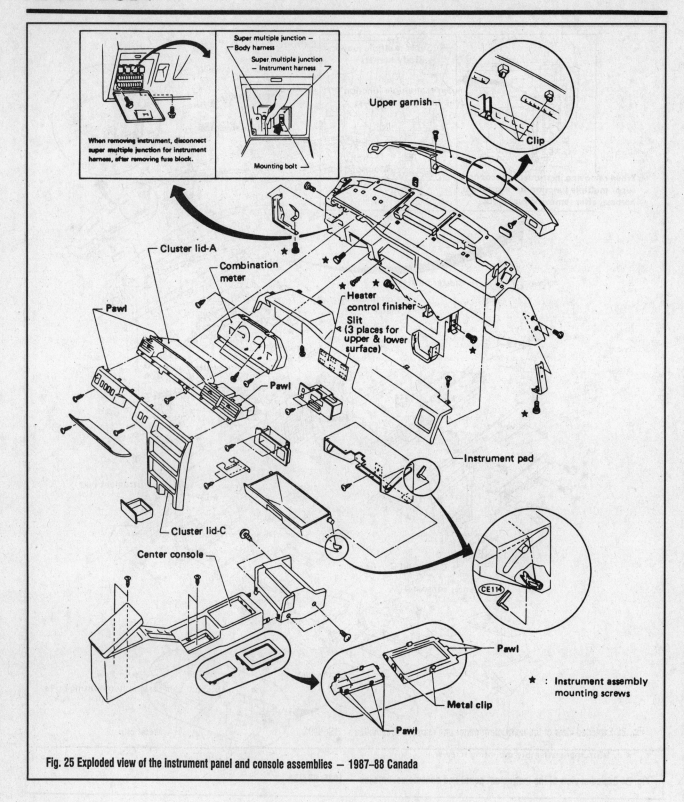

Super multiple junction —
Body harness

Super multiple junction
— Instrument harness

When removing instrument, disconnect
super multiple junction for instrument
harness, after removing fuse block.

Mounting bolt

Upper garnish

Clip

Cluster lid-A

Combination
meter

Heater
control finisher

Pawl

Slit
(3 places for
upper & lower
surface)

Pawl

Instrument pad

Cluster lid-C

Center console

CE114

Pawl

Metal clip

★ : Instrument assembly
mounting screws

Pawl

Fig. 25 Exploded view of the instrument panel and console assemblies — 1987–88 Canada

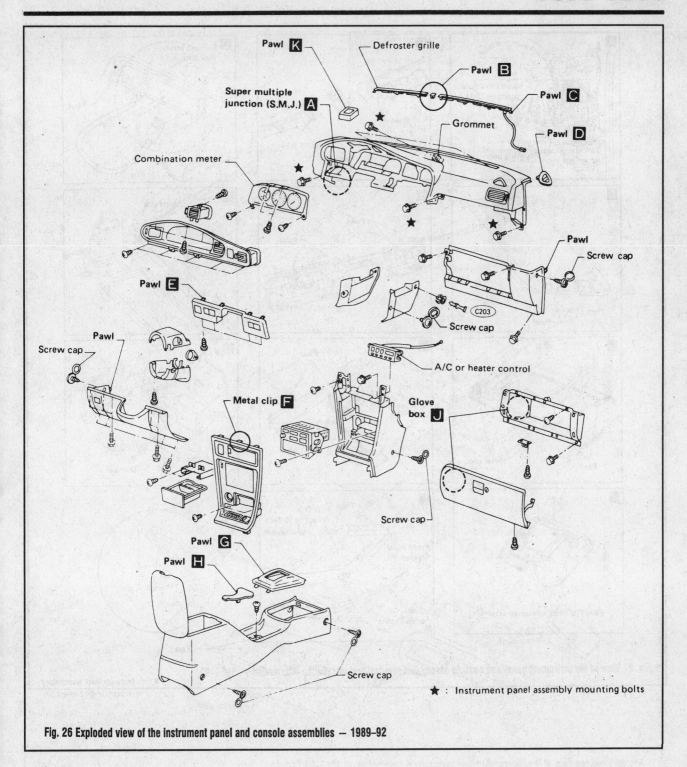

Fig. 26 Exploded view of the instrument panel and console assemblies — 1989–92

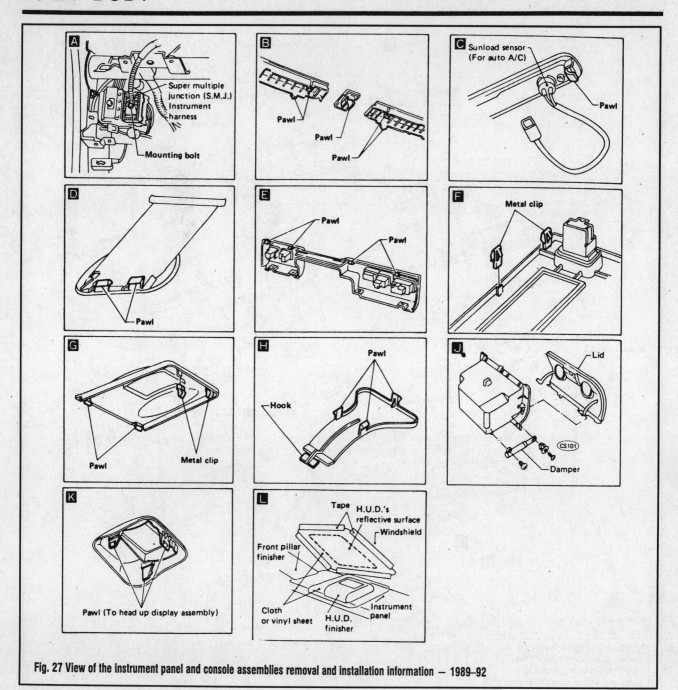

Fig. 27 View of the instrument panel and console assemblies removal and installation information — 1989–92

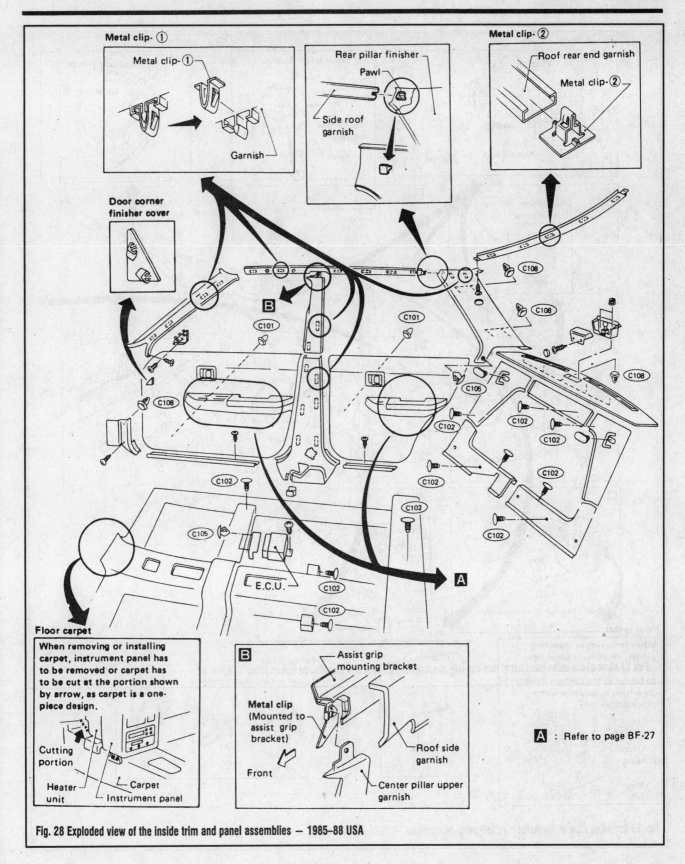

Metal clip-①

Metal clip-①

Garnish

Door corner finisher cover

Rear pillar finisher

Pawl

Side roof garnish

Metal clip-②

Roof rear end garnish

Metal clip-②

B

C101

C101

C108

C108

C108

C108

C105

C102

C102

C102

C102

C102

C102

C102

C102

C105

E.C.U.

C102

C102

A

Floor carpet

When removing or installing carpet, instrument panel has to be removed or carpet has to be cut at the portion shown by arrow, as carpet is a one-piece design.

Cutting portion

Heater unit

Carpet

Instrument panel

B

Assist grip mounting bracket

Metal clip (Mounted to assist grip bracket)

Front

Roof side garnish

Center pillar upper garnish

A : Refer to page BF-27

Fig. 28 Exploded view of the inside trim and panel assemblies — 1985–88 USA

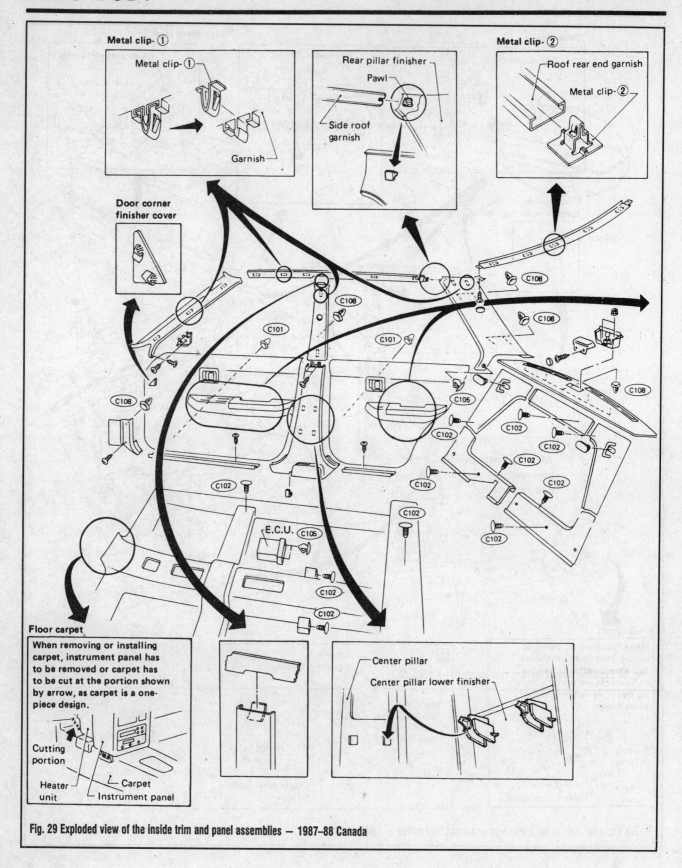

Metal clip- ①

Metal clip- ①

Garnish

Door corner
finisher cover

Rear pillar finisher

Pawl

Side roof
garnish

Metal clip- ②

Roof rear end garnish

Metal clip- ②

C108

C108

C108

C108

C101

C101

C108

C105

C102

C102

C102

C102

C108

C102

C102

C102

C102

C102

E.C.U.

C105

C102

C102

Floor carpet

When removing or installing
carpet, instrument panel has
to be removed or carpet has
to be cut at the portion shown
by arrow, as carpet is a one-
piece design.

Cutting
portion

Heater
unit

Carpet

Instrument panel

Center pillar

Center pillar lower finisher

Fig. 29 Exploded view of the inside trim and panel assemblies — 1987–88 Canada

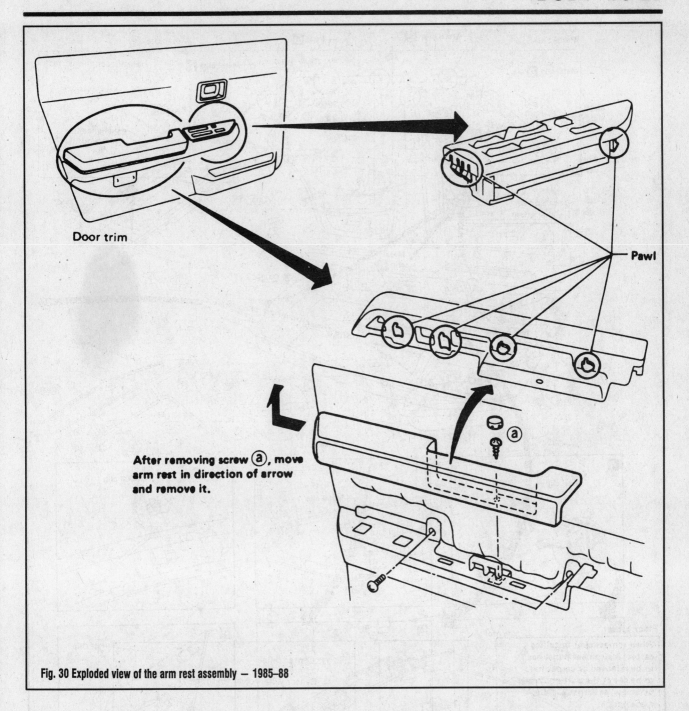

Door trim

Pawl

After removing screw ⓐ, move
arm rest in direction of arrow
and remove it.

ⓐ

Fig. 30 Exploded view of the arm rest assembly — 1985–88

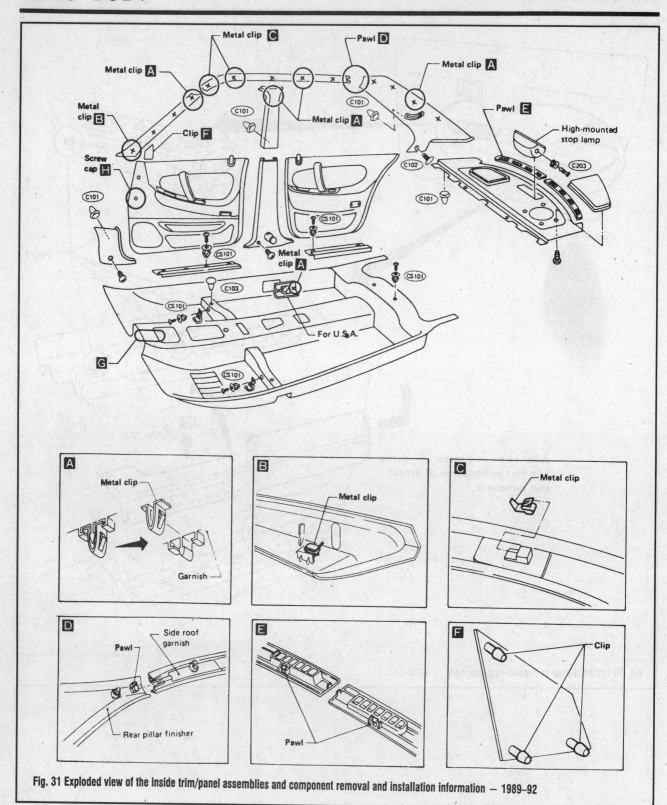

Fig. 31 Exploded view of the inside trim/panel assemblies and component removal and installation information — 1989–92

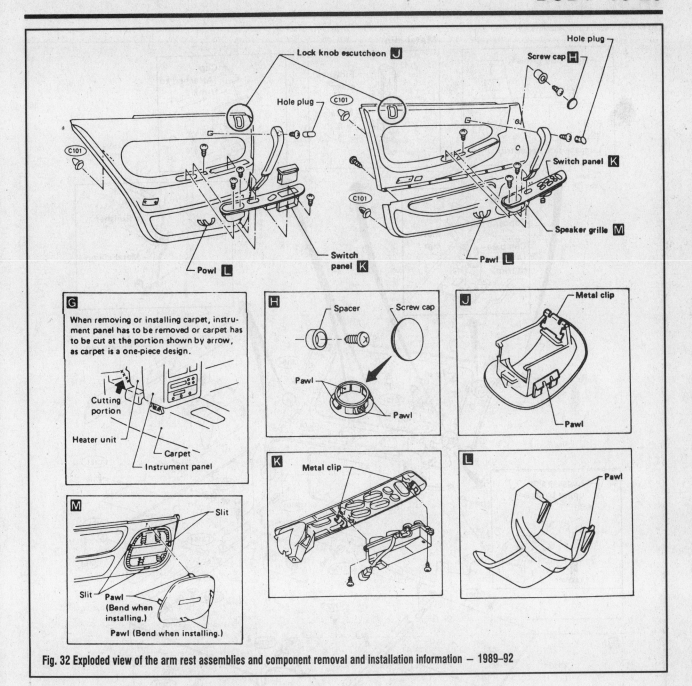

Fig. 32 Exploded view of the arm rest assemblies and component removal and installation information — 1989–92

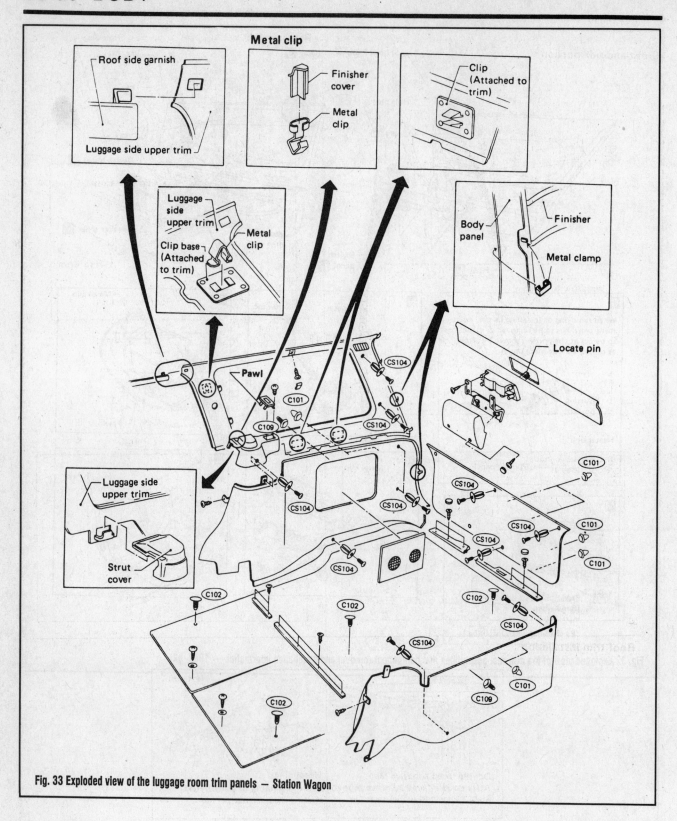

Metal clip

Roof side garnish

Luggage side upper trim

Finisher cover

Metal clip

Clip (Attached to trim)

Luggage side upper trim

Metal clip

Clip base (Attached to trim)

Body panel

Finisher

Metal clamp

Locate pin

Pawl

CS104

C101

C109

CS104

CS104

CS104

CS104

C101

CS104

CS104

C101

CS104

C101

Luggage side upper trim

Strut cover

C102

C102

CS104

C102

CS104

C102

CS104

C101

C102

CS104

C109

C101

Fig. 33 Exploded view of the luggage room trim panels — Station Wagon

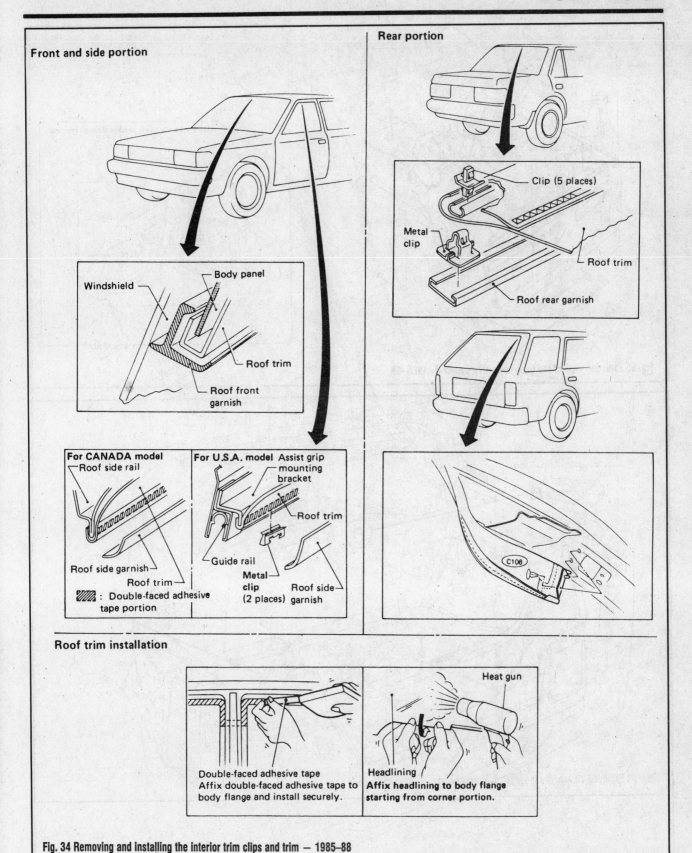

Front and side portion

Windshield

Body panel

Roof trim

Roof front garnish

For CANADA model
Roof side rail

Roof side garnish

Roof trim

▨ : Double-faced adhesive tape portion

For U.S.A. model
Assist grip mounting bracket

Roof trim

Guide rail

Metal clip (2 places)

Roof side garnish

Rear portion

Clip (5 places)

Metal clip

Roof trim

Roof rear garnish

C106

Roof trim installation

Double-faced adhesive tape
Affix double-faced adhesive tape to body flange and install securely.

Heat gun

Headling
Affix headling to body flange starting from corner portion.

Fig. 34 Removing and installing the interior trim clips and trim — 1985–88

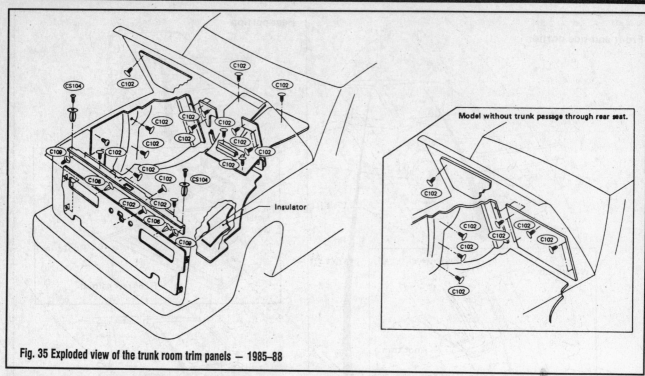

Fig. 35 Exploded view of the trunk room trim panels — 1985–88

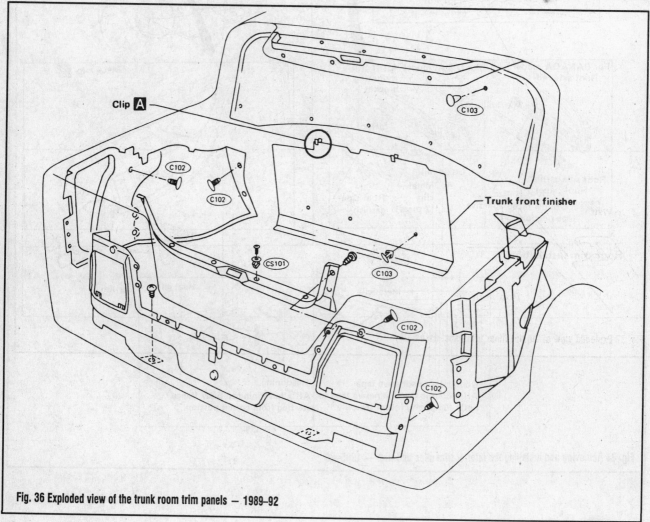

Fig. 36 Exploded view of the trunk room trim panels — 1989–92

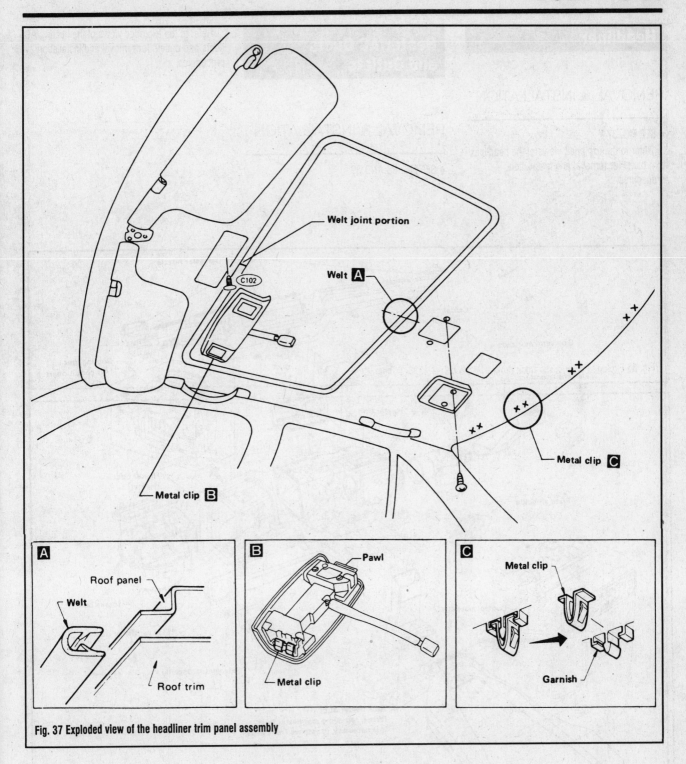

Welt joint portion

Welt **A**

C102

Metal clip **C**

Metal clip **B**

A
Roof panel
Welt
Roof trim

B
Pawl
Metal clip

C
Metal clip
Garnish

Fig. 37 Exploded view of the headliner trim panel assembly

REMOVAL & INSTALLATION

▶ SEE FIG. 37

Refer to the exploded views of the headliner trim panel for removal and installation procedures.

Heater/AC Ducts and Outlets

REMOVAL & INSTALLATION

▶ SEE FIG. 38 AND 39

Refer to the exploded views of the heating/AC ducts and outlets for removal and installation procedures.

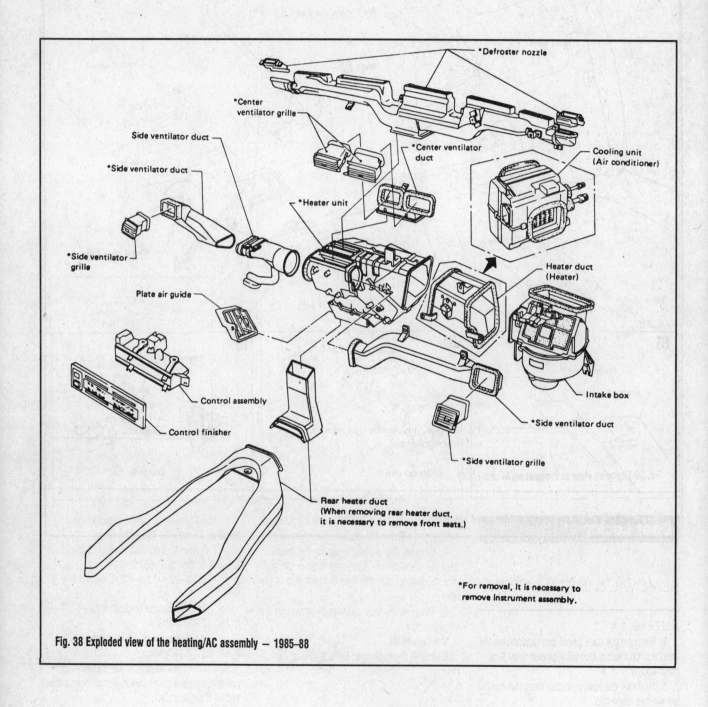

Fig. 38 Exploded view of the heating/AC assembly — 1985–88

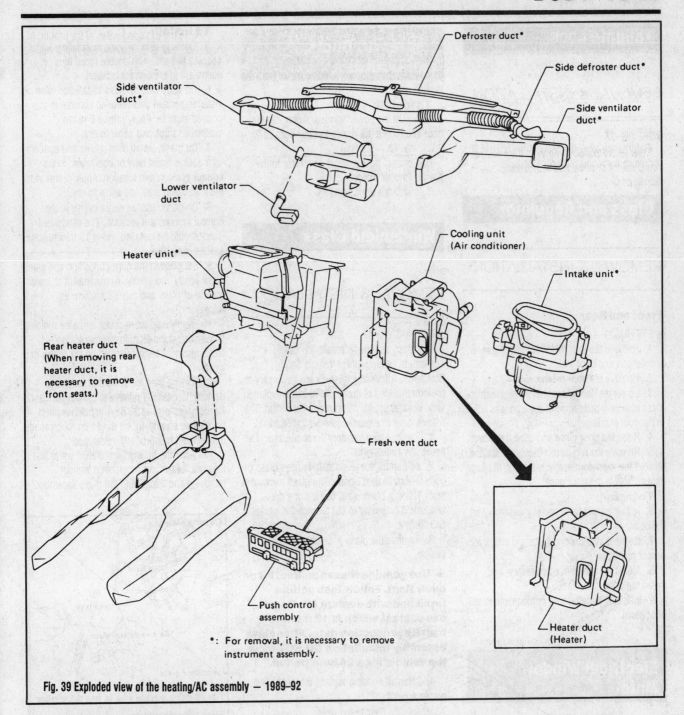

Fig. 39 Exploded view of the heating/AC assembly — 1989–92

Door Locks

REMOVAL & INSTALLATION

▶ SEE FIGS. 1-4

1. Remove the door panel and disconnect the electrical connector from the power door lock mechanism.

2. Remove the lock cylinder from the rod by turning the resin clip.

3. Loosen the nuts attaching the outside door handle and remove the outside door handle.

4. Remove the screws retaining the inside door handle and door lock, and remove the door lock assembly from the hole in the inside of the door.

5. Remove the lock cylinder by removing the retaining clip.

To install:

6. Install the lock cylinder and clip to the door.

7. Install the door lock assembly and handles. Torque the following items:

Power lock-to-door bolts: 1985–88 — 2.7–3.7 ft. lbs. (3.7–5.0 Nm)

1989–92 — 3.8–4.8 ft. lbs. (5.1–6.5 Nm)

Outside handle-to-door nuts — 2.7–3.7 ft. lbs. (3.7–5.0 Nm)

Inside handle-to-door screws — 1.7–2.2 ft. lbs. (2.3–3.0 Nm)

8. Connect the electrical connector to the power door lock mechanism. Install door panel and all attaching parts.

Tailgate Lock

REMOVAL & INSTALLATION

▶ SEE FIG. 12

Refer to the exploded view of the tailgate lid for removal and installation procedures.

Glass and Regulator

REMOVAL & INSTALLATION

Front and Rear

▶ SEE FIGS. 1–4

1. Remove the arm rest, door inside handle escutcheon and door lock.

2. Remove the door finisher.

3. Lower the door glass until the regulator-to-glass attaching bolts appear at the access holes in the door inside panel.

4. Raise the door glass and draw it upwards.

5. Remove the regulator attaching bolts and remove the regulator assembly through the large access hole in the door panel.

To install:

6. Install the window regulator assembly in the door.

7. Connect all mounting bolts and check for proper operation.

8. Adjust the window, if necessary, and install the door trim panel.

9. Install all the attaching components to the door panel.

Electrical Window Motor

REMOVAL & INSTALLATION

▶ SEE FIGS. 1–4

1. Remove the door panel.

2. Remove the power widow motor-to-door bolts

3. Remove all electrical connector.

4. Remove the power window motor from the vehicle.

To install:

5. Install the power window motor into the door and torque the motor-to-door bolts to 2.7–3.7 ft. lbs. (3.7–5.0 Nm).

6. Connect the electrical connector to the power window motor.

7. Install the door panel.

Windshield Glass

REMOVAL & INSTALLATION

▶ SEE FIGS. 40–42

The glass assembly installation has to conform to Federal Motor Vehicle Safety Standards. A few special tools are necessary to preform this kind of repair. Refer to the exploded view illustrations for necessary information. The following service procedures are recommend.

1. Remove all necessary components and all necessary molding(s).

2. Be careful not to scratch/damage glass or body — cut sealant bond using glass removal tools. Using a piano wire, pull it along the windshield boundary to cut through the gasket and sealant.

3. Remove the glass assembly from the vehicle.

➡ **Use genuine Nissan sealant kit or equivalent. Follow instructions furnished with sealant kit. Do not use sealant which is 12 months past its production date. After glass assembly installation DO NOT move the vehicle for a 24 hour period.**

4. Clean all bonding surface thoroughly with proper solvent.

To install:

5. On body side of glass installation, install spacers to panel with double faced tape or equivalent in the correct location.

6. On body side of glass installation, also install upper and side molding fastener in the correct location. Apply primer E to the installation track and allow to dry.

7. On glass, install dam rubber and spacers with double faced tape or equivalent, in the correct position and location. Apply primer A to the installation area and allow to dry.

8. On glass, apply sealant evenly in the correct amount and location. The windshield glass should be installed within 15 minutes after sealant is applied.

9. Set glass in the correct position and press glass lightly and evenly. Apply sealant to lower portion of glass and make it uniform as necessary.

10. Apply sealant to upper and side molding in the correct location. Install mouldings. Moldings must be installed so no excessive gap exists.

11. Drying time for sealant to reach the desired hardness is relative to temperature and humidity (as long as 20 days in cold weather) — the vehicle should not be driven on rough roads until sealant has properly vulcanized.

12. After the finished installation water test the area. Leaks can be repaired without removing and reinstalling the glass assembly.

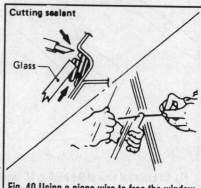

Fig. 40 Using a piano wire to free the window glass from the vehicle

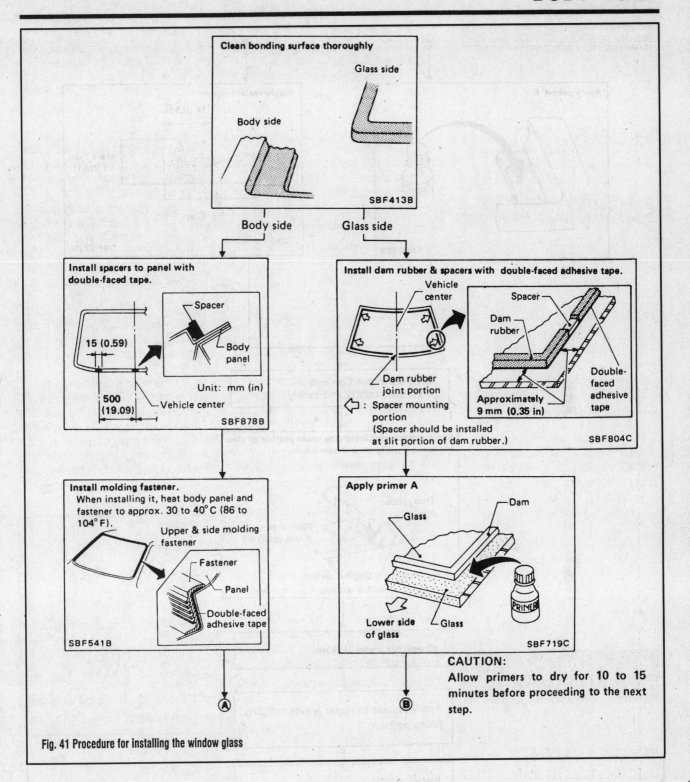

Clean bonding surface thoroughly

Glass side

Body side

Body side   Glass side

SBF413B

Install spacers to panel with double-faced tape.

Spacer

15 (0.59)

Body panel

Unit: mm (in)

500 (19.09)

Vehicle center

SBF878B

Install dam rubber & spacers with double-faced adhesive tape.

Vehicle center

Spacer

Dam rubber

Double-faced adhesive tape

Dam rubber joint portion

Approximately 9 mm (0.35 in)

⇦ : Spacer mounting portion
(Spacer should be installed at slit portion of dam rubber.)

SBF804C

Install molding fastener.
When installing it, heat body panel and fastener to approx. 30 to 40°C (86 to 104°F).

Upper & side molding fastener

Fastener

Panel

Double-faced adhesive tape

SBF541B

Apply primer A

Dam

Glass

Lower side of glass

Glass

SBF719C

Ⓐ

Ⓑ

CAUTION:
Allow primers to dry for 10 to 15 minutes before proceeding to the next step.

Fig. 41 Procedure for installing the window glass

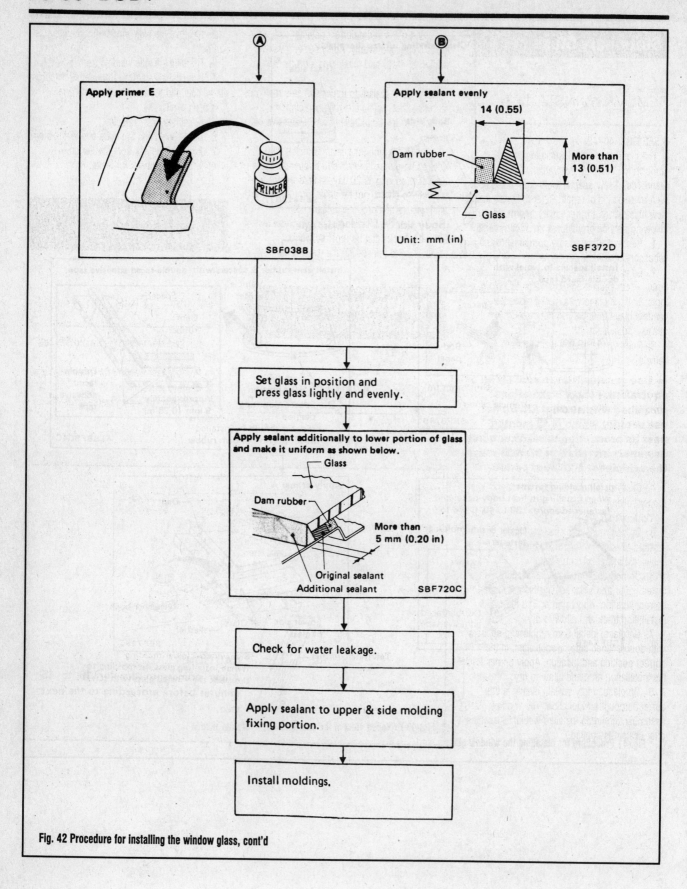

Fig. 42 Procedure for installing the window glass, cont'd

Stationary Glass

REMOVAL & INSTALLATION

▶ SEE FIGS. 40–42

The glass assembly installation has to conform to Federal Motor Vehicle Safety Standards. A few special tools are necessary to preform this kind of repair. Refer to the exploded view illustrations for necessary information. The following service procedures are recommend.

1. Remove all necessary components and all necessary molding(s).

2. Be careful not to scratch/damage glass or body — cut sealant bond using glass removal tools. Using a piano wire, pull it along the window glass boundary to cut through the gasket and sealant.

3. Remove the glass assembly from the vehicle.

➡ **Use genuine Nissan sealant kit or equivalent. Follow instructions furnished with sealant kit. Do not use sealant which is 12 months past its production date. After glass assembly installation DO NOT move the vehicle for a 24 hour period.**

4. Clean all bonding surface thoroughly with proper solvent.

To install:

5. On body side of glass installation, install spacers to panel with double faced tape or equivalent in the correct location.

6. On body side of glass installation, also install upper and side molding fastener in the correct location. Apply primer E to the installation track and allow to dry.

7. On glass, install dam rubber and spacers with double faced tape or equivalent, in the correct position and location. Apply primer A to the installation area and allow to dry.

8. On glass, apply sealant evenly in the correct amount and location. The window glass assembly should be installed within 15 minutes after sealant is applied.

9. Set glass in the correct position and press glass lightly and evenly. Apply sealant to lower portion of glass and make it uniform as necessary.

10. Apply sealant to upper and side molding in the correct location. Install mouldings. Moldings must be installed so no excessive gap exists.

11. Drying time for sealant to reach the desired hardness is relative to temperature and humidity (as long as 20 days in cold weather) — the vehicle should not be driven on rough roads until sealant has properly vulcanized.

12. After the finished installation water test the area. Leaks can be repaired without removing and reinstalling the glass assembly.

Side Window — Station Wagon

REMOVAL & INSTALLATION

▶ SEE FIG. 43

1. Remove the tail pillar finisher.

2. Remove the side window-to-vehicle nuts and bolts.

3. Remove the side window from the vehicle.

4. If necessary, remove the weatherstrip from the vehicle and replace it with a new one.

To install:

5. Install the side window.

6. Apply sealant to the bolts and install them.

7. After installation, spray water on the window seal and check for leaks.

Inside Rear View Mirror

REMOVAL & INSTALLATION

1. Remove rear view mirror mounting bolt cover.

2. Remove rear view mirror mounting bolts.

3. Remove mirror.

4. Installation is in the reverse order of removal.

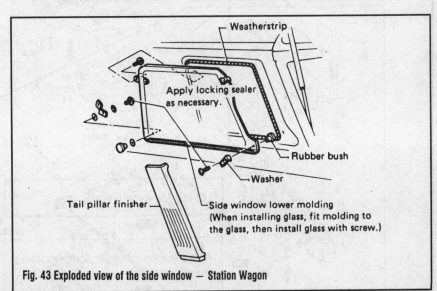

Fig. 43 Exploded view of the side window — Station Wagon

Seats

REMOVAL & INSTALLATION

Front

◆ SEE FIGS. 44–46

1. If equipped with power seats, disconnect the electrical connectors from the power seat motor.
2. Remove front seat-to-chassis bolts.
3. Remove front seat assembly.

To Install:

4. Install the front seat assembly.

5. Torque the front seat-to-chassis bolts to:
   1985–88 — 18–23 ft. lbs. (25–31 Nm)
   1989–92 — 32–41 ft. lbs. (43–55 Nm)

6. If equipped with power seats, connect the electrical connectors to the power seat motor.

7. If equipped with power seats, check the power seat motor operations.

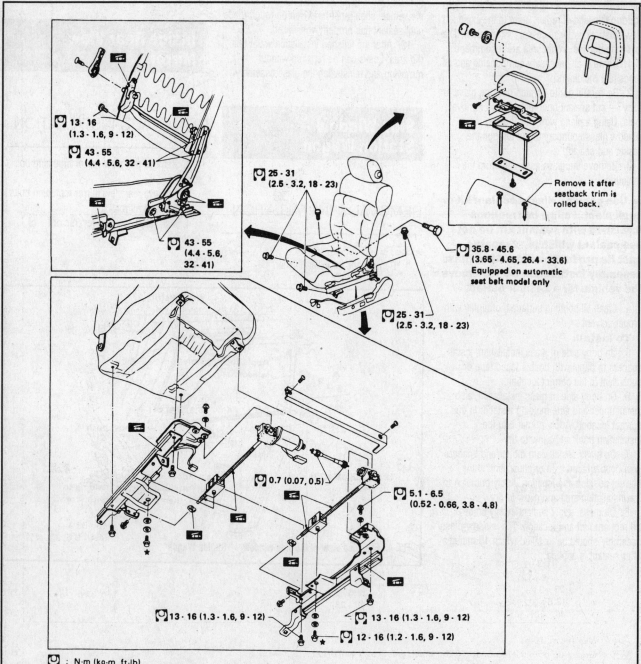

☒ : N·m (kg-m, ft-lb)

⬛ : Grease-up points (Do not apply too much grease as it will drip).

★ : If power seat does not operate because of a malfunction, remove the bolts marked ★ and set free the sliders, then remove seat mounting.

Fig. 45 Exploded view of the power operated front seat — 1985–88

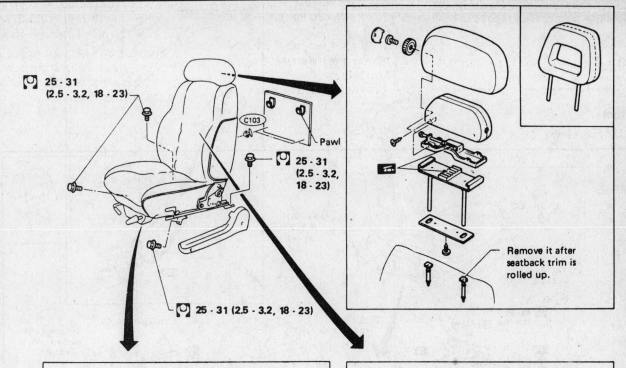

25 - 31
(2.5 - 3.2, 18 - 23)

C103

Pawl

25 - 31
(2.5 - 3.2,
18 - 23)

25 - 31 (2.5 - 3.2, 18 - 23)

Remove it after
seatback trim is
rolled up.

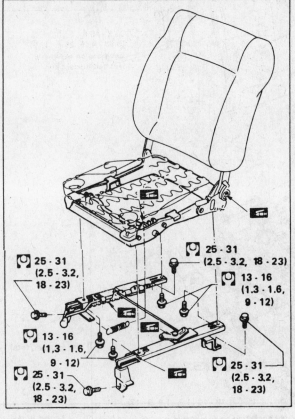

25 - 31
(2.5 - 3.2,
18 - 23)

25 - 31
(2.5 - 3.2, 18 - 23)

13 - 16
(1.3 - 1.6,
9 - 12)

13 - 16
(1.3 - 1.6,
9 - 12)

25 - 31
(2.5 - 3.2,
18 - 23)

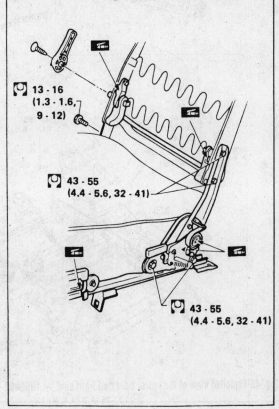

13 - 16
(1.3 - 1.6,
9 - 12)

43 - 55
(4.4 - 5.6, 32 - 41)

43 - 55
(4.4 - 5.6, 32 - 41)

: N·m (kg-m, ft-lb)

: Grease-up points (Do not apply too much grease as it will drip.)

Fig. 44 Exploded view of the manually operated front seat — 1985–88

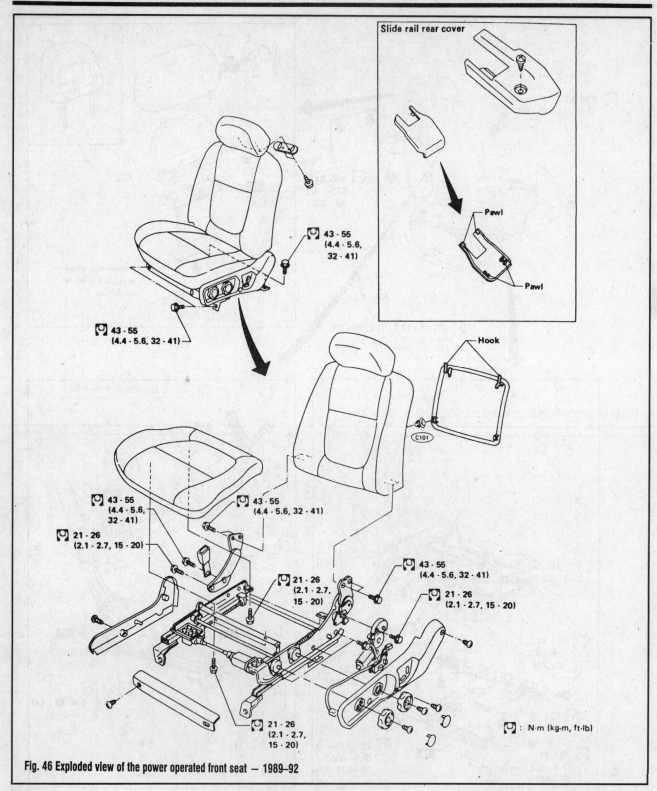

Fig. 46 Exploded view of the power operated front seat — 1989–92

Rear

SEDAN

▶ SEE FIGS. 47 AND 48

1. Remove upper rear seat back-to-chassis bolts and remove the upper rear seat back.

2. Remove rear seat back by tilting forward and pulling straight up.

3. Remove the lower seat cushion-to-chassis bolts and the lower seat cushion.

To install:

4. Install the lower seat cushion and torque the lower rear seat-to-chassis bolts to:

1985–88 — 3.8–4.8 ft. lbs. (5.1–6.5 Nm)

1989–92 — 15–20 ft. lbs. (21–26 Nm)

5. Install the upper rear seat back cushion and torque the upper rear seat back-to-chassis bolts to:

1985–88 — 3.8–4.8 ft. lbs. (5.1–6.5 Nm)

1989–92 — 15–20 ft. lbs. (21–26 Nm)

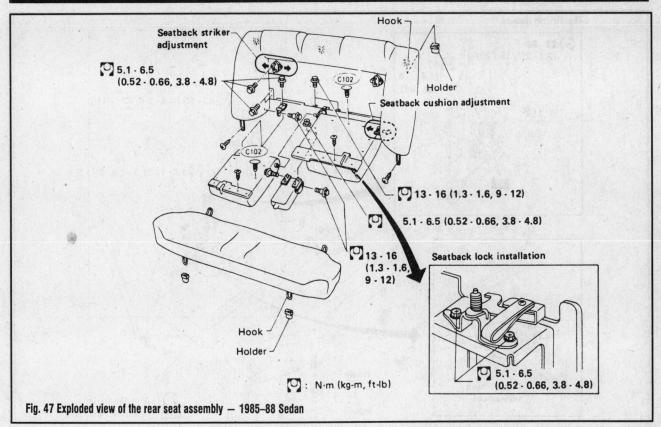

Fig. 47 Exploded view of the rear seat assembly — 1985–88 Sedan

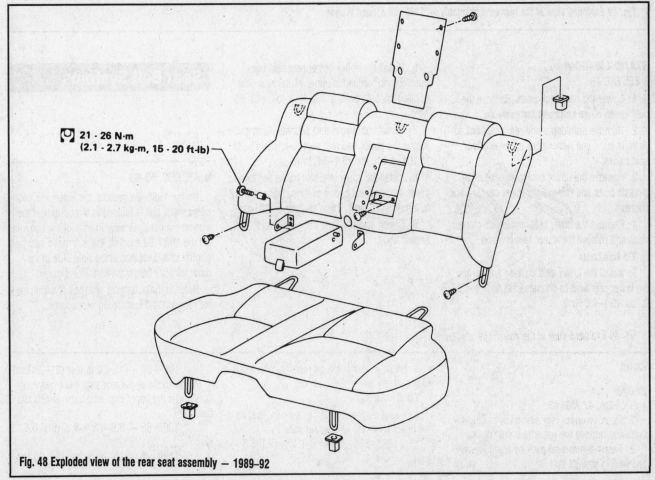

Fig. 48 Exploded view of the rear seat assembly — 1989–92

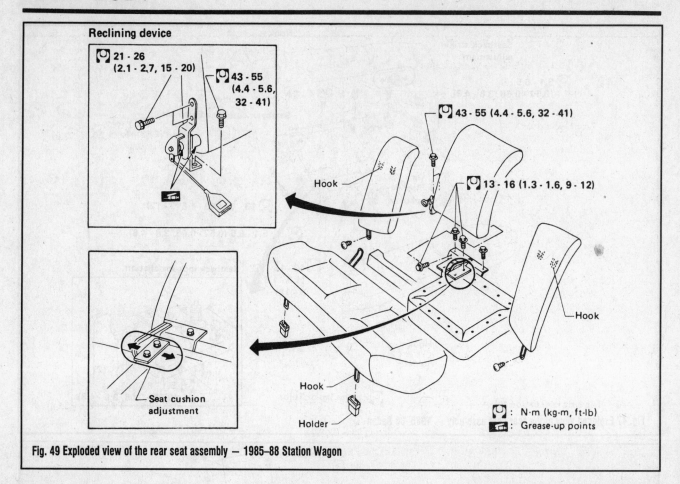

Fig. 49 Exploded view of the rear seat assembly — 1985–88 Station Wagon

STATION WAGON

♦ SEE FIG. 49

1. Lower the rear back seats. Remove the cushion-to-hinge bolts and the cushions.

2. Remove both upper end rear seat back-to-chassis bolts and remove the upper end rear seat backs.

3. Remove the upper center back seat-to-chassis bolts and remove the upper center back cushion.

4. Remove the lower seat cushion-to-chassis bolts and remove the lower seat cushion.

To install:

5. Install the lower seat cushion and torque the lower rear seat-to-chassis bolts to 3.8–4.8 ft. lbs. (5.1–6.5 Nm).

6. Install the upper center rear seat back cushion and torque the upper center rear seat back-to-chassis bolts to 32–41 ft. lbs. (43–55 Nm).

7. Install both upper end seat cushions and torque the upper end rear seat-to-chassis bolts to: 3.8–4.8 ft. lbs. (5.1–6.5 Nm).

8. Install the upper rear seat backs and torque the upper rear seat backs-to-hinge bolts to 9–12 ft. lbs. (13–16 Nm). Raise the rear seat backs.

9. Check and/or adjust the cushions, if necessary.

Seat Belt Systems

REMOVAL & INSTALLATION

♦ SEE FIGS. 50–53

On the 1985–88 models, the automatic seat belt control unit is located at the bottom of the instrument panel, directly in front of the console. On the 1989–92 models, the automatic seat belt control unit is located at the right side of the dash, directly below the instrument panel.

Refer to the automatic seat belt illustrations for removal and installation procedures.

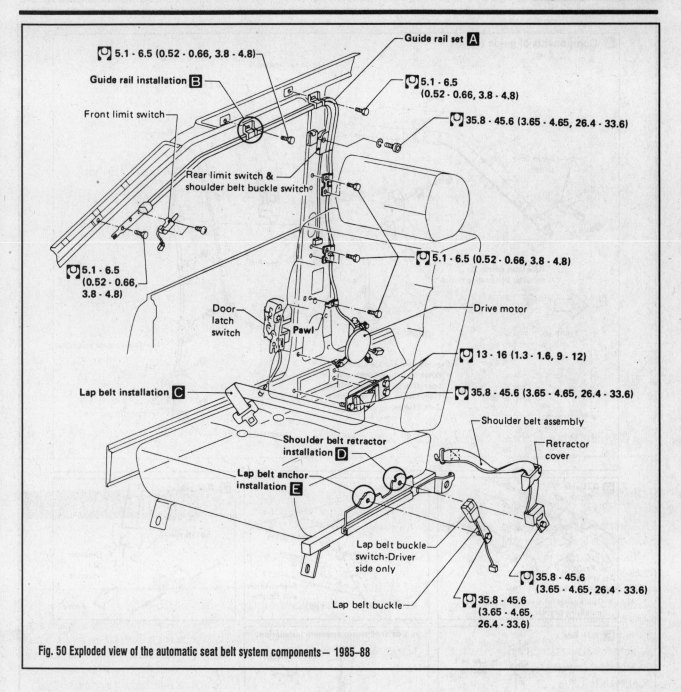

Guide rail set **A**

5.1 - 6.5 (0.52 - 0.66, 3.8 - 4.8)

Guide rail installation **B**

5.1 - 6.5
(0.52 - 0.66, 3.8 - 4.8)

35.8 - 45.6 (3.65 - 4.65, 26.4 - 33.6)

Front limit switch

Rear limit switch &
shoulder belt buckle switch

5.1 - 6.5 (0.52 - 0.66, 3.8 - 4.8)

5.1 - 6.5
(0.52 - 0.66,
3.8 - 4.8)

Door
latch
switch

Pawl

Drive motor

13 - 16 (1.3 - 1.6, 9 - 12)

Lap belt installation **C**

35.8 - 45.6 (3.65 - 4.65, 26.4 - 33.6)

Shoulder belt assembly

Shoulder belt retractor
installation **D**

Retractor
cover

Lap belt anchor
installation **E**

Lap belt buckle
switch-Driver
side only

35.8 - 45.6
(3.65 - 4.65, 26.4 - 33.6)

Lap belt buckle

35.8 - 45.6
(3.65 - 4.65,
26.4 - 33.6)

Fig. 50 Exploded view of the automatic seat belt system components — 1985–88

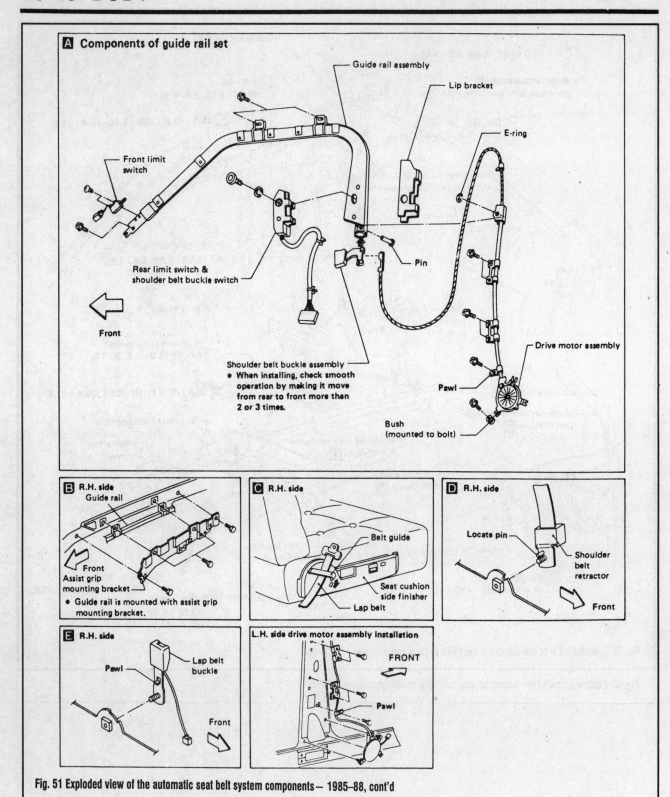

A Components of guide rail set

Guide rail assembly

Lip bracket

E-ring

Front limit switch

Rear limit switch & shoulder belt buckle switch

Front

Pin

Shoulder belt buckle assembly
● When installing, check smooth operation by making it move from rear to front more than 2 or 3 times.

Drive motor assembly

Pawl

Bush (mounted to bolt)

B R.H. side
Guide rail

Front

Assist grip mounting bracket
● Guide rail is mounted with assist grip mounting bracket.

C R.H. side

Belt guide

Seat cushion side finisher

Lap belt

D R.H. side

Locate pin

Shoulder belt retractor

Front

E R.H. side

Pawl

Lap belt buckle

Front

L.H. side drive motor assembly installation

FRONT

Pawl

Fig. 51 Exploded view of the automatic seat belt system components — 1985–88, cont'd

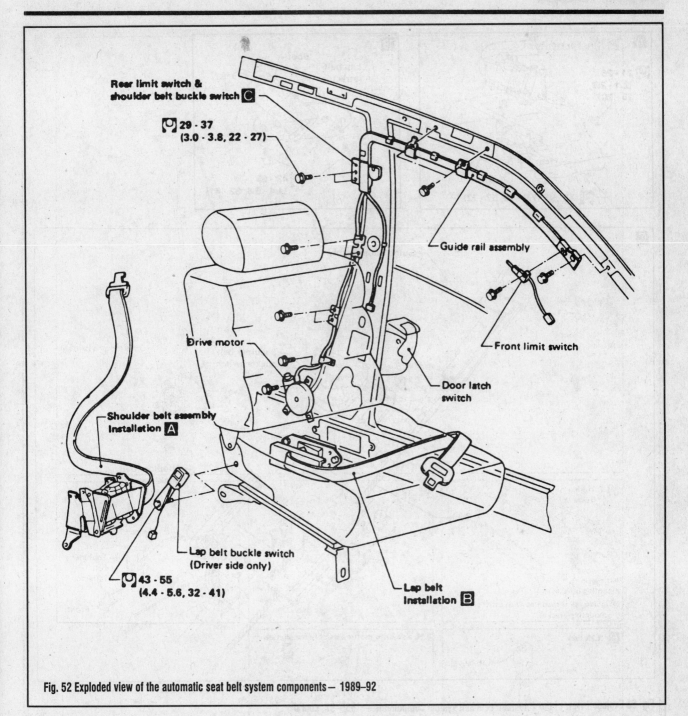

Rear limit switch &
shoulder belt buckle switch [C]

29 - 37
(3.0 - 3.8, 22 - 27)

Guide rail assembly

Drive motor

Front limit switch

Door latch
switch

Shoulder belt assembly
Installation [A]

Lap belt buckle switch
(Driver side only)

Lap belt
Installation [B]

43 - 55
(4.4 - 5.6, 32 - 41)

Fig. 52 Exploded view of the automatic seat belt system components — 1989–92

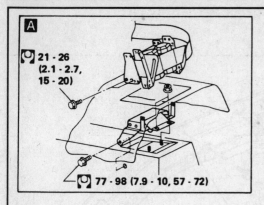

A

21 - 26
(2.1 - 2.7,
15 - 20)

77 - 98 (7.9 - 10, 57 - 72)

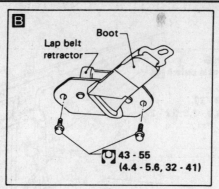

B

Boot

Lap belt
retractor

43 - 55
(4.4 - 5.6, 32 - 41)

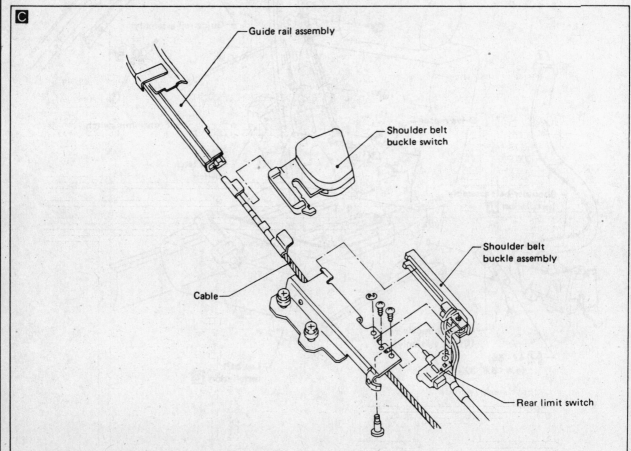

C

Guide rail assembly

Shoulder belt
buckle switch

Shoulder belt
buckle assembly

Cable

Rear limit switch

Fig. 53 Exploded view of the automatic seat belt system components — 1989–92, cont'd

AUTOMATIC SEAT BELT SYSTEM WIRING SCHEMATIC

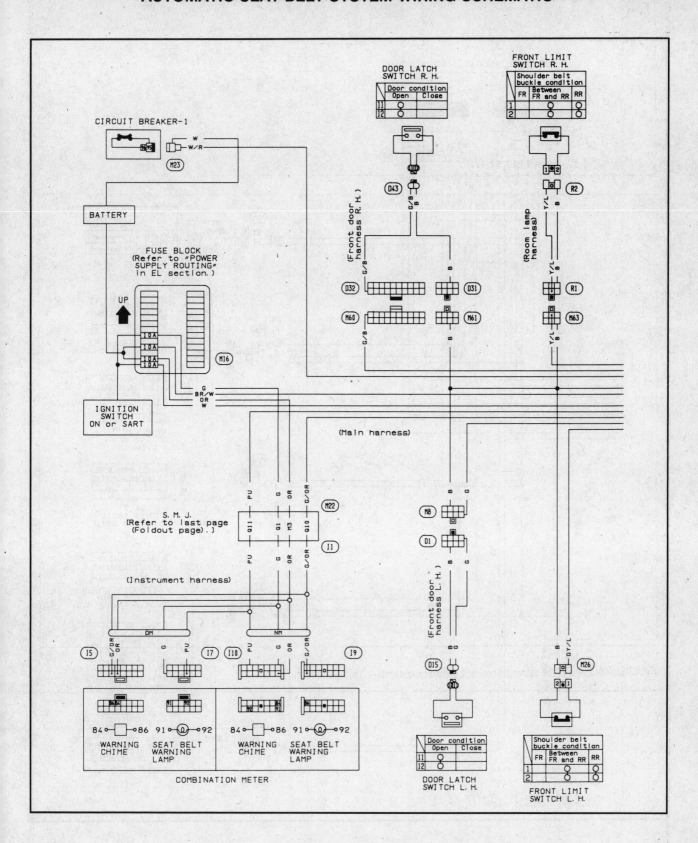

AUTOMATIC SEAT BELT SYSTEM WIRING SCHEMATIC — CONT'D

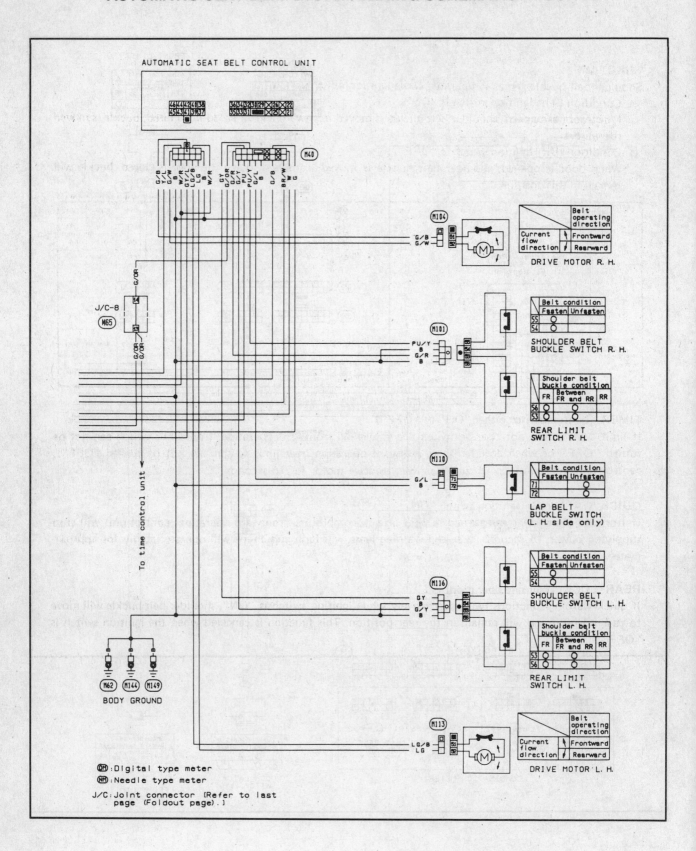

AUTOMATIC SEAT BELT SYSTEM DESCRIPTION

FUNCTION

Shoulder belt buckle is mainly operated while ignition switch is "ON".

Condition (A): Ignition switch is "ON".

When door is opened, shoulder belt buckle is moved frontward and when door is closed, buckle is moved rearward.

Condition (B): Ignition switch is "OFF".

When door is opened, shoulder belt buckle is moved frontward. When the door is closed, buckle will remain in this position.

(Voltage of output signal is approximate value.)

Input signal	Ignition switch	OFF	OFF	ON	ON	ON	ON	ON	ON	ON	ON	ON	OFF	OFF	OFF	OFF	OFF
	Door latch switch	OFF	ON	OFF	OFF	OFF	ON	ON	ON	OFF	OFF	OFF	OFF	ON	ON	ON	OFF
	Front limit switch	OFF	OFF	OFF	ON	ON	ON	ON	OFF	OFF	ON	ON	ON	ON	ON	OFF	OFF
	Rear limit switch	ON	ON	ON	ON	OFF	OFF	ON	ON	ON	ON	OFF	OFF	OFF	ON	ON	ON
Output signal	Drive motor power source for frontward operation	0V	0V	0V	0V	0V	12V	12V	0V	0V	0V	0V	0V	12V	12V	0V	0V
	Drive motor power source for rearward operation	0V	0V	12V	12V	0V	0V	0V	0V	12V	12V	0V	0V	0V	0V	0V	0V
Shoulder belt buckle	Function	Stop	Stop	Start to move	Moving	Stop	Start to move	Moving	Stop	Start to move	Moving	Stop	Stop	Start to move	Moving	Stop	Stop
	Position	Front	Front	Front	Between Front & Rear	Rear	Rear	Between Front & Rear	Front	Front	Between Front & Rear	Rear	Rear	Rear	Between Front & Rear	Front	Front

TIMER (Ignition switch either "ON" or "OFF")

If limit switch does not operate (when accomplishing frontward operation, front limit switch can not be turned "OFF" or when accomplishing rearward operation, rear limit switch can not be turned "OFF"), control unit will continue to supply power to drive motor for 15 seconds.

QUICK WARNING (Ignition switch "ON")

If front limit switch is not turned "OFF" after accomplishing frontward operation, control unit will stop supplying power 15 seconds later and warning lamp will flash and chime will operate rapidly for approximately 6 seconds.

REAR LOCK (Fail safe operation)

If quick warning functions twice successively while ignition switch is "ON", shoulder belt buckle will move to rear position and will remain in the rear position. This function is canceled when the ignition switch is "OFF".

AUTOMATIC SEAT BELT SYSTEM DESCRIPTION — CONT'D

WARNING

Priority	Warning item	Ignition switch	Indication of warning (Indicating time is approximate value.)		
1	Shoulder anchors are not at rear lock position.	ON	Lamp	ON / OFF — 1 sec. Continues flashing	
			Chime	ON / OFF	
		OFF → ON	Lamp	ON / OFF — 1 sec. Continues flashing	
			Chime	ON / OFF	
			Anchor	Not rear / Rear — 6 sec.	
			Lamp	ON / OFF — 6 sec.	
			Chime	ON / OFF	
			Anchor	Not rear / Rear — Within 6 sec.	
2	Shoulder belts are not fastened.	ON	Lamp	ON / OFF	
			Chime	ON / OFF	
			Belts	Not fastened / Fastened — 100 sec.	
			Lamp	ON / OFF	
			Chime	ON / OFF	
			Belts	Not fastened / Fastened — Within 6 sec.	
3	Driver side lap belt is not fastened.	OFF → ON	Lamp	ON / OFF	
			Chime	ON / OFF	
			Belts	Not fastened / Fastened — 6 sec.	
			Lamp	ON / OFF — 6 sec.	
			Chime	ON / OFF	
			Belts	Not fastened / Fastened — Within 6 sec.	
4	Normal (All belts are fastened and shoulder anchors are in rear lock position.)	OFF → ON	Lamp	ON / OFF	
			Chime	ON / OFF — 6 sec.	

AUTOMATIC SEAT BELT SYSTEM SYMPTOM CHART

Procedure	Reference page	Side	Component	No operation has made. (No warning indicated and no buckles movement performed)	Shoulder belt buckle in L.H. or R.H. side does not move.	Shoulder belt buckle moves frontwards only. (not rearwards)	Shoulder belt buckle moves rearwards only. (not frontwards)	Warnings indicate incorrectly or do not function.	Quick warning operates.
Electrical Components Inspection	BF-73	R.H. side	Motor	O	O				
	BF-73		Shoulder belt buckle switch	O				O	
	BF-73		Door latch switch	O		O	O		
	BF-73		Rear limit switch	O	O	O		O	
	BF-72		Front limit switch	O	O		O		O
	BF-73	L.H. side	Lap belt switch	O				O	
	BF-73		Motor	O	O				
	BF-73		Shoulder belt buckle switch	O				O	
	BF-73		Door latch switch	O		O	O		
	BF-73		Rear limit switch	O	O	O		O	
	BF-72		Front limit switch	O	O		O		O
	—		Warning chime	O				O	
	—		Warning lamp	O				O	
Diagnostic Procedure	BF-72		Procedure 8					O	
	BF-71		Procedure 7					O	
	BF-69		Procedure 6					O	
	BF-68		Procedure 5					O	
	BF-66		Procedure 4	O	O	O			
	BF-65		Procedure 3	O	O		O		O
	BF-64		Procedure 2			O	O		
	BF-61		Procedure 1	O	O				
Main Power Supply and Ground Circuit Check	BF-57		Procedure 2		O				
	BF-57		Procedure 1	O					
Preliminary Check	BF-55		Procedure 2					O	
	BF-54		Procedure 1		O	O	O		

AUTOMATIC SEAT BELT SYSTEM PRELIMINARY CHECK

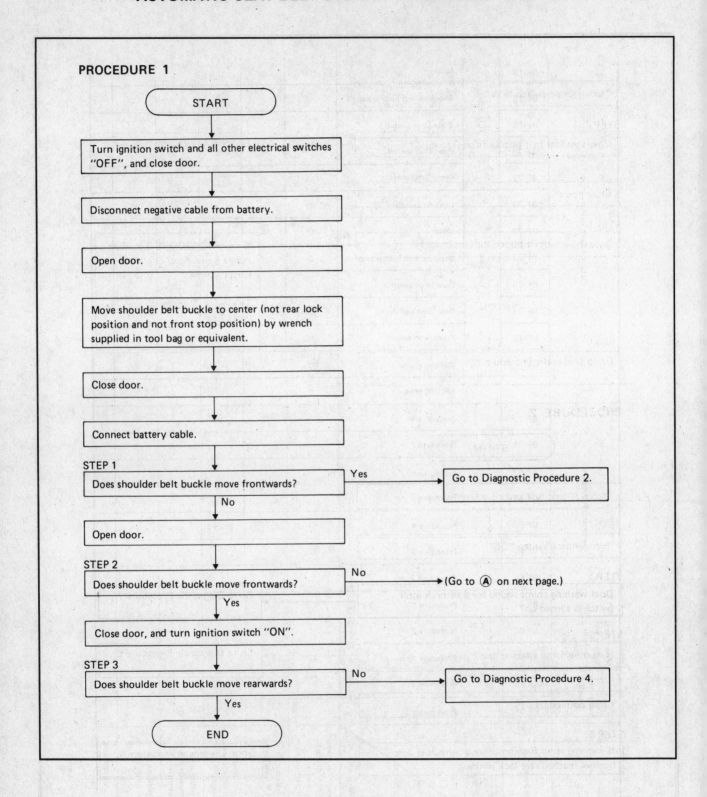

PROCEDURE 1

START

Turn ignition switch and all other electrical switches "OFF", and close door.

Disconnect negative cable from battery.

Open door.

Move shoulder belt buckle to center (not rear lock position and not front stop position) by wrench supplied in tool bag or equivalent.

Close door.

Connect battery cable.

STEP 1
Does shoulder belt buckle move frontwards? — Yes → Go to Diagnostic Procedure 2.

No

Open door.

STEP 2
Does shoulder belt buckle move frontwards? — No → (Go to Ⓐ on next page.)

Yes

Close door, and turn ignition switch "ON".

STEP 3
Does shoulder belt buckle move rearwards? — No → Go to Diagnostic Procedure 4.

Yes

END

AUTOMATIC SEAT BELT SYSTEM PRELIMINARY CHECK — CONT'D

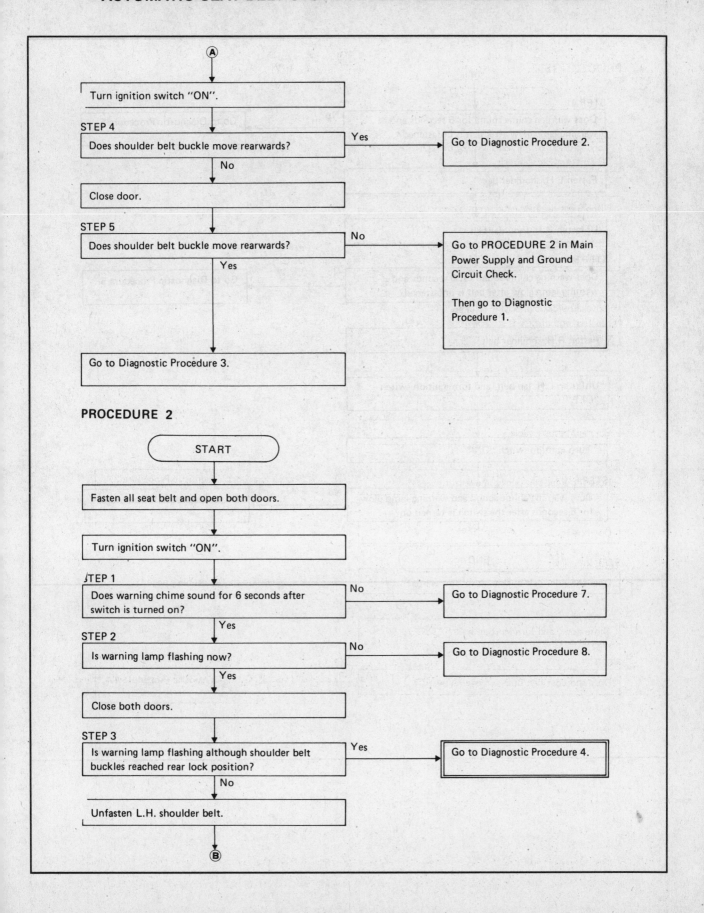

(A)

Turn ignition switch "ON".

STEP 4

Does shoulder belt buckle move rearwards? — Yes → Go to Diagnostic Procedure 2.

No

Close door.

STEP 5

Does shoulder belt buckle move rearwards? — No → Go to PROCEDURE 2 in Main Power Supply and Ground Circuit Check.

Then go to Diagnostic Procedure 1.

Yes

Go to Diagnostic Procedure 3.

PROCEDURE 2

START

Fasten all seat belt and open both doors.

Turn ignition switch "ON".

STEP 1

Does warning chime sound for 6 seconds after switch is turned on? — No → Go to Diagnostic Procedure 7.

Yes

STEP 2

Is warning lamp flashing now? — No → Go to Diagnostic Procedure 8.

Yes

Close both doors.

STEP 3

Is warning lamp flashing although shoulder belt buckles reached rear lock position? — Yes → Go to Diagnostic Procedure 4.

No

Unfasten L.H. shoulder belt.

(B)

AUTOMATIC SEAT BELT SYSTEM PRELIMINARY CHECK — CONT'D

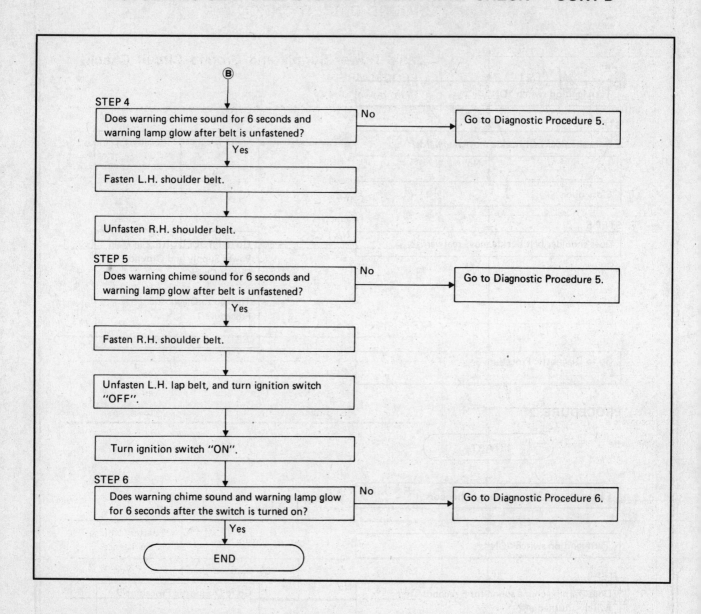

Ⓑ

STEP 4

Does warning chime sound for 6 seconds and warning lamp glow after belt is unfastened?

No → Go to Diagnostic Procedure 5.

Yes

Fasten L.H. shoulder belt.

Unfasten R.H. shoulder belt.

STEP 5

Does warning chime sound for 6 seconds and warning lamp glow after belt is unfastened?

No → Go to Diagnostic Procedure 5.

Yes

Fasten R.H. shoulder belt.

Unfasten L.H. lap belt, and turn ignition switch "OFF".

Turn ignition switch "ON".

STEP 6

Does warning chime sound and warning lamp glow for 6 seconds after the switch is turned on?

No → Go to Diagnostic Procedure 6.

Yes

END

AUTOMATIC SEAT BELT SYSTEM MAIN POWER SUPPLY AND GROUND CIRCUIT CHECK

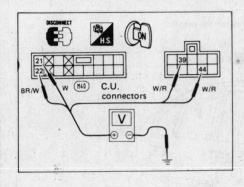

Main Power Supply and Ground Circuit Check
PROCEDURE 1
Main power supply

Terminals	Battery voltage existence condition	
	Ignition switch "ON"	Other than ignition switch "ON"
㉑ - Ground	Yes	No
㉒ - Ground	Yes	Yes
㉟ - Ground	Yes	Yes
㊹ - Ground	Yes	Yes

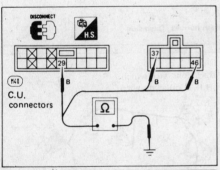

Ground circuit

Terminals	Continuity
㉙ - Ground	Yes
㊲ - Ground	Yes
㊻ - Ground	Yes

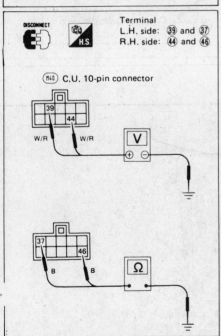

PROCEDURE 2
Power supply for motor drive

	Terminals	Battery voltage existence
L.H. side	㊴ - Ground	Yes
R.H. side	㊹ - Ground	Yes

Ground circuit for motor drive

	Terminals	Continuity
L.H. side	㊲ - Ground	Yes
R.H. side	㊻ - Ground	Yes

AUTOMATIC SEAT BELT SYSTEM HARNESS LAYOUT

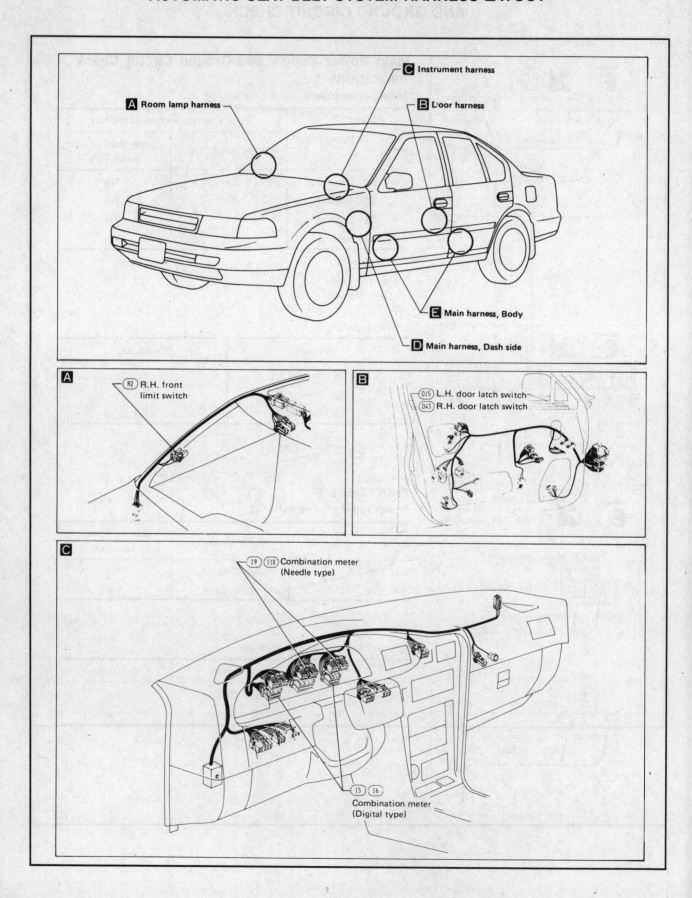

A Room lamp harness

C Instrument harness

B Door harness

E Main harness, Body

D Main harness, Dash side

A
R2 R.H. front limit switch

B
015 L.H. door latch switch
043 R.H. door latch switch

C
19 110 Combination meter (Needle type)

15 16 Combination meter (Digital type)

AUTOMATIC SEAT BELT SYSTEM HARNESS LAYOUT — CONT'D

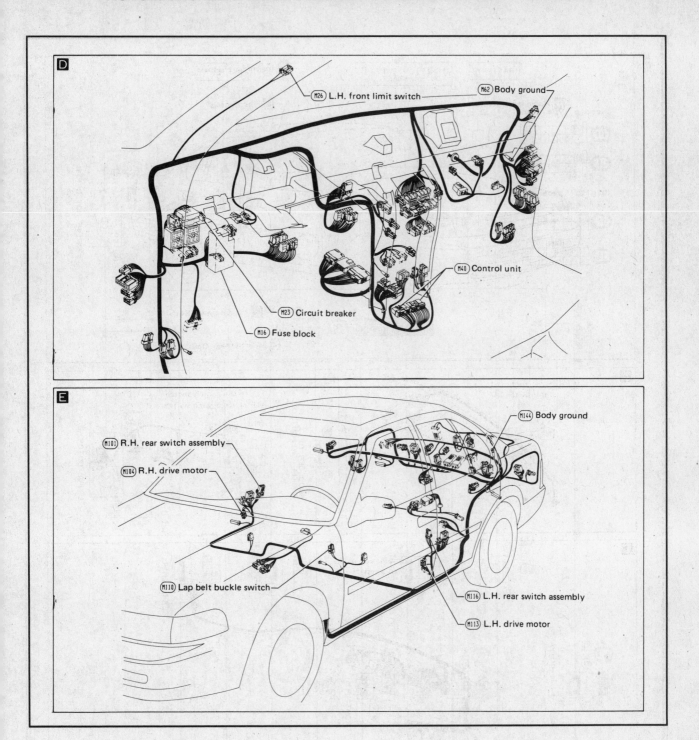

AUTOMATIC SEAT BELT SYSTEM QUICK PINPOINT CHECK

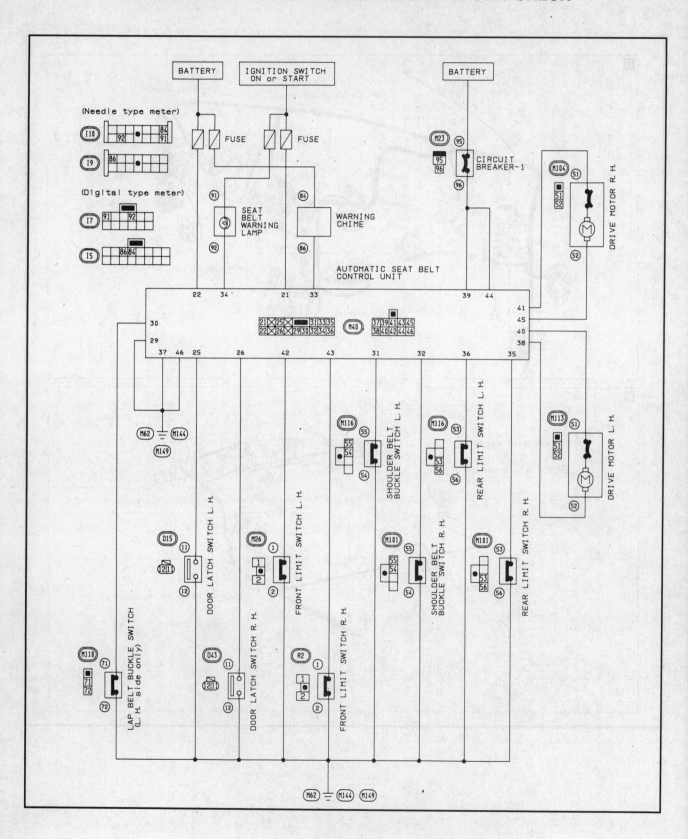

AUTOMATIC SEAT BELT SYSTEM DIAGNOSTIC PROCEDURES

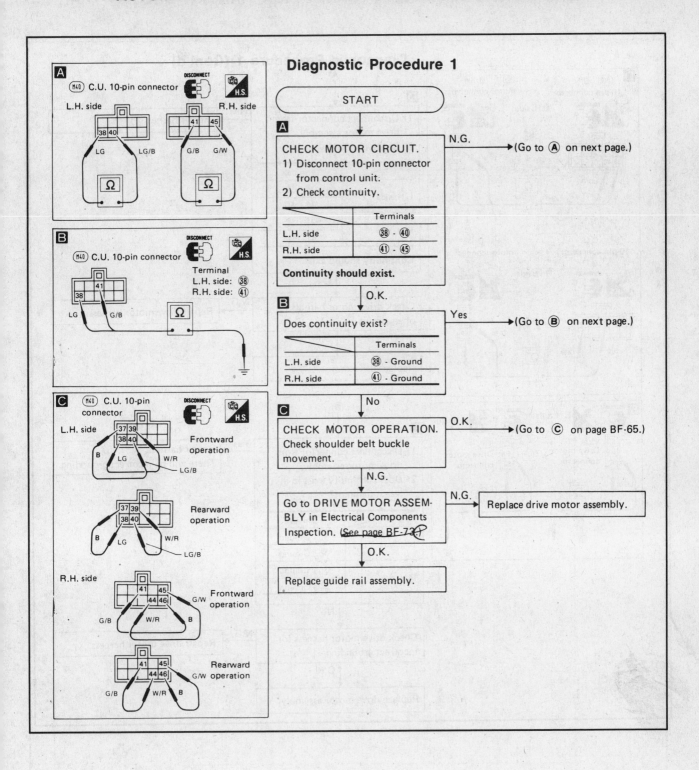

Diagnostic Procedure 1

START

A

CHECK MOTOR CIRCUIT.
1) Disconnect 10-pin connector from control unit.
2) Check continuity.

	Terminals
L.H. side	㊳ - ㊵
R.H. side	㊶ - ㊺

Continuity should exist.

N.G. → (Go to Ⓐ on next page.)

O.K.

B

Does continuity exist?

	Terminals
L.H. side	㊳ - Ground
R.H. side	㊶ - Ground

Yes → (Go to Ⓑ on next page.)

No

C

CHECK MOTOR OPERATION.
Check shoulder belt buckle movement.

O.K. → (Go to Ⓒ on page BF-65.)

N.G.

Go to DRIVE MOTOR ASSEMBLY in Electrical Components Inspection. (See page BF-73.)

N.G. → Replace drive motor assembly.

O.K.

Replace guide rail assembly.

A (M40) C.U. 10-pin connector   DISCONNECT   H.S.

L.H. side   R.H. side

38 40   41 45

LG   LG/B   G/B   G/W

Ω   Ω

B (M40) C.U. 10-pin connector   DISCONNECT   H.S.

Terminal
L.H. side: ㊳
R.H. side: ㊶

38   41

LG   G/B

Ω

C (M40) C.U. 10-pin connector   DISCONNECT   H.S.

L.H. side   37 39   Frontward operation
            38 40
B   LG   W/R
           LG/B

            37 39   Rearward operation
            38 40
B   LG   W/R
           LG/B

R.H. side
            41   45   Frontward operation
            44   46   G/W
G/B   W/R   B

            41   45   Rearward operation
            44   46   G/W
G/B   W/R   B

AUTOMATIC SEAT BELT SYSTEM DIAGNOSTIC PROCEDURES — CONT'D

Diagnostic Procedure 1 (Cont'd)

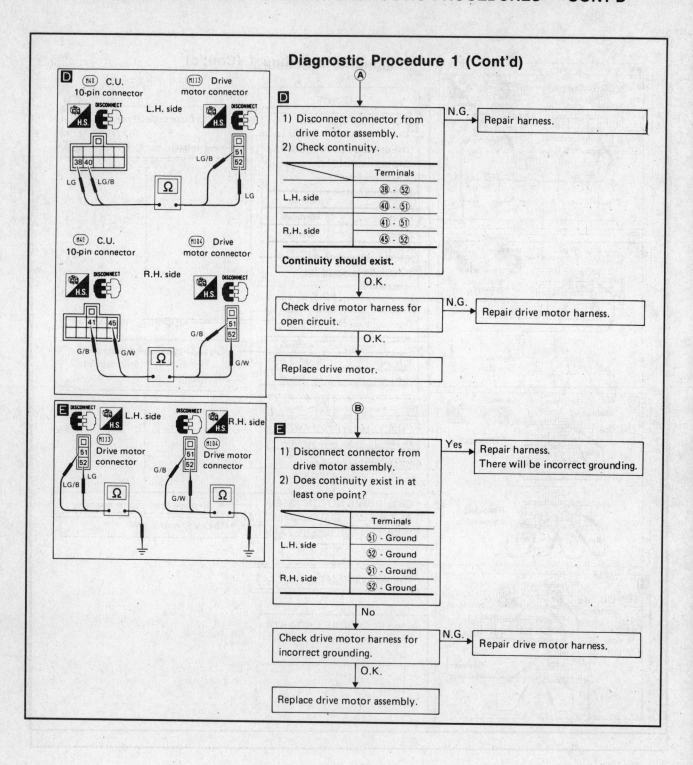

D

1) Disconnect connector from drive motor assembly.
2) Check continuity.

	Terminals
L.H. side	㊳ - ㊷
	㊵ - ㊿
R.H. side	㊶ - ㊿
	㊺ - ㊷

Continuity should exist.

→ N.G. → Repair harness.

↓ O.K.

Check drive motor harness for open circuit. → N.G. → Repair drive motor harness.

↓ O.K.

Replace drive motor.

E

1) Disconnect connector from drive motor assembly.
2) Does continuity exist in at least one point?

	Terminals
L.H. side	㊿ - Ground
	㊷ - Ground
R.H. side	㊿ - Ground
	㊷ - Ground

→ Yes → Repair harness. There will be incorrect grounding.

↓ No

Check drive motor harness for incorrect grounding. → N.G. → Repair drive motor harness.

↓ O.K.

Replace drive motor assembly.

AUTOMATIC SEAT BELT SYSTEM DIAGNOSTIC PROCEDURES — CONT'D

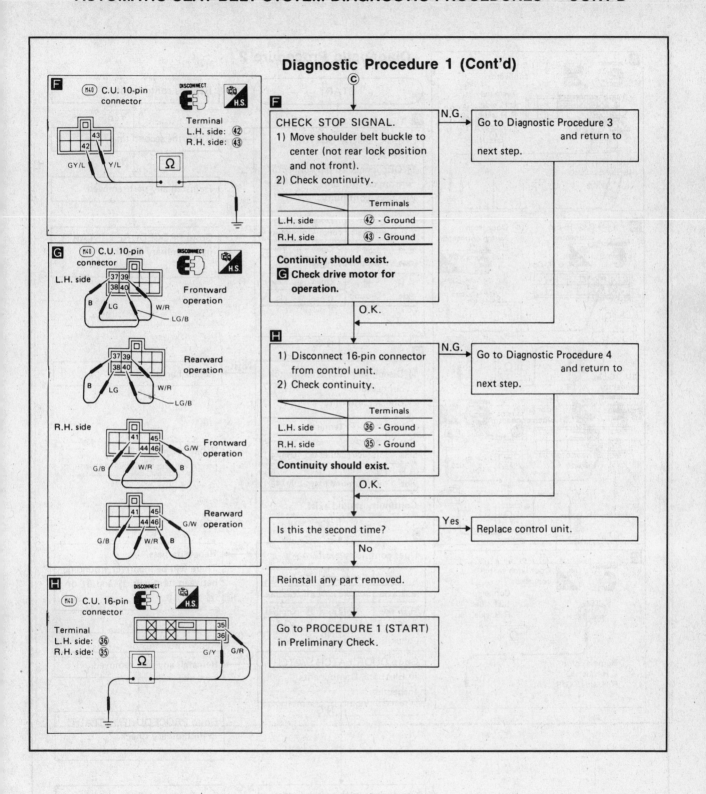

Diagnostic Procedure 1 (Cont'd)

F

CHECK STOP SIGNAL.
1) Move shoulder belt buckle to center (not rear lock position and not front).
2) Check continuity.

	Terminals
L.H. side	㊷ - Ground
R.H. side	㊸ - Ground

Continuity should exist.
G Check drive motor for operation.

N.G. → Go to Diagnostic Procedure 3 and return to next step.

O.K.

H

1) Disconnect 16-pin connector from control unit.
2) Check continuity.

	Terminals
L.H. side	㊱ - Ground
R.H. side	㉟ - Ground

Continuity should exist.

N.G. → Go to Diagnostic Procedure 4 and return to next step.

O.K.

Is this the second time? — Yes → Replace control unit.

No

Reinstall any part removed.

Go to PROCEDURE 1 (START) in Preliminary Check.

AUTOMATIC SEAT BELT SYSTEM DIAGNOSTIC PROCEDURES — CONT'D

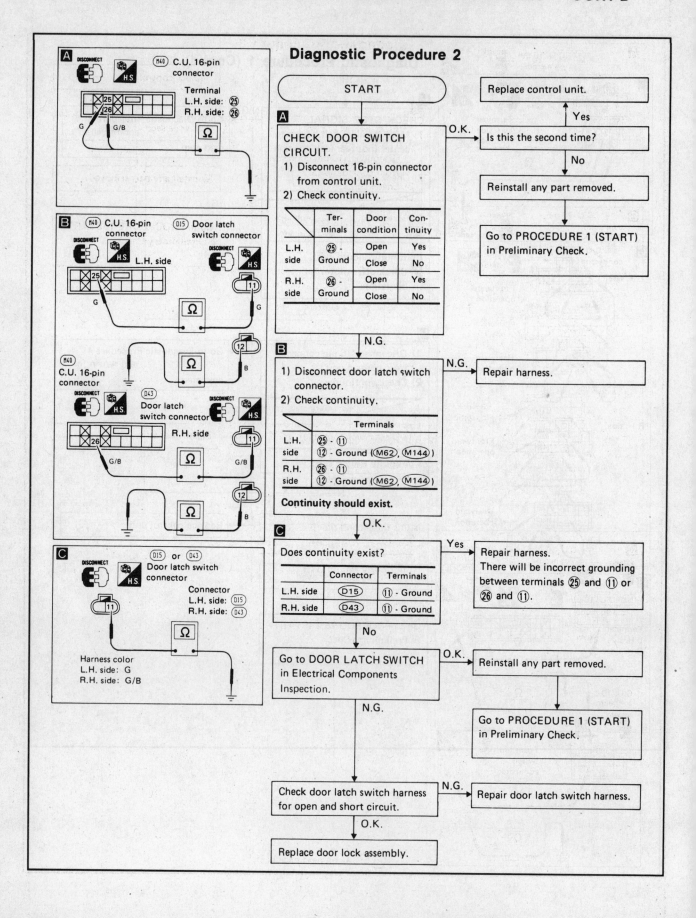

Diagnostic Procedure 2

A CHECK DOOR SWITCH CIRCUIT.
1) Disconnect 16-pin connector from control unit.
2) Check continuity.

	Terminals	Door condition	Continuity
L.H. side	25 - Ground	Open	Yes
		Close	No
R.H. side	26 - Ground	Open	Yes
		Close	No

O.K. → Is this the second time? — Yes → Replace control unit.

No → Reinstall any part removed. → Go to PROCEDURE 1 (START) in Preliminary Check.

N.G.

B 1) Disconnect door latch switch connector.
2) Check continuity.

	Terminals
L.H. side	25 - 11
	12 - Ground (M62, M144)
R.H. side	26 - 11
	12 - Ground (M62, M144)

Continuity should exist.

N.G. → Repair harness.

O.K.

C Does continuity exist?

	Connector	Terminals
L.H. side	D15	11 - Ground
R.H. side	D43	11 - Ground

Yes → Repair harness. There will be incorrect grounding between terminals 25 and 11 or 26 and 11.

No → Go to DOOR LATCH SWITCH in Electrical Components Inspection.

O.K. → Reinstall any part removed. → Go to PROCEDURE 1 (START) in Preliminary Check.

N.G.

Check door latch switch harness for open and short circuit.

N.G. → Repair door latch switch harness.

O.K.

Replace door lock assembly.

AUTOMATIC SEAT BELT SYSTEM DIAGNOSTIC PROCEDURES — CONT'D

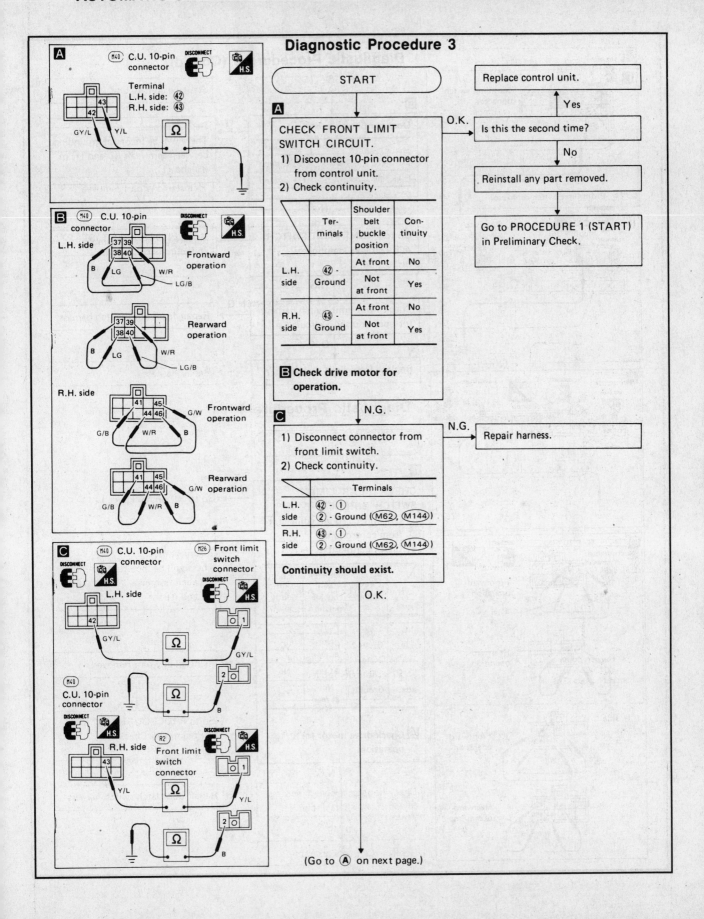

Diagnostic Procedure 3

START

A CHECK FRONT LIMIT SWITCH CIRCUIT.
1) Disconnect 10-pin connector from control unit.
2) Check continuity.

	Terminals	Shoulder belt buckle position	Continuity
L.H. side	42 - Ground	At front	No
		Not at front	Yes
R.H. side	43 - Ground	At front	No
		Not at front	Yes

B Check drive motor for operation.

N.G.

C
1) Disconnect connector from front limit switch.
2) Check continuity.

	Terminals
L.H. side	42 - 1
	2 - Ground (M62, M144)
R.H. side	43 - 1
	2 - Ground (M62, M144)

Continuity should exist.

O.K. ──→ (Go to A on next page.)

O.K. ──→ Is this the second time? ──Yes──→ Replace control unit.

No
↓

Reinstall any part removed.
↓

Go to PROCEDURE 1 (START) in Preliminary Check.

N.G. ──→ Repair harness.

A — (M40) C.U. 10-pin connector
Terminal
L.H. side: 42
R.H. side: 43
43 42 GY/L Y/L Ω

B — (M40) C.U. 10-pin connector
L.H. side
37 39 38 40
B LG W/R LG/B
Frontward operation

37 39 38 40
B LG W/R LG/B
Rearward operation

R.H. side
41 45 44 46
G/B W/R B G/W
Frontward operation

41 45 44 46
G/B W/R B G/W
Rearward operation

C — (M40) C.U. 10-pin connector (M26) Front limit switch connector
L.H. side
42 GY/L Ω
1 GY/L
2 B Ω

(M40) C.U. 10-pin connector
R.H. side (R2) Front limit switch connector
43 Y/L Ω
1 Y/L
2 B Ω

AUTOMATIC SEAT BELT SYSTEM DIAGNOSTIC PROCEDURES — CONT'D

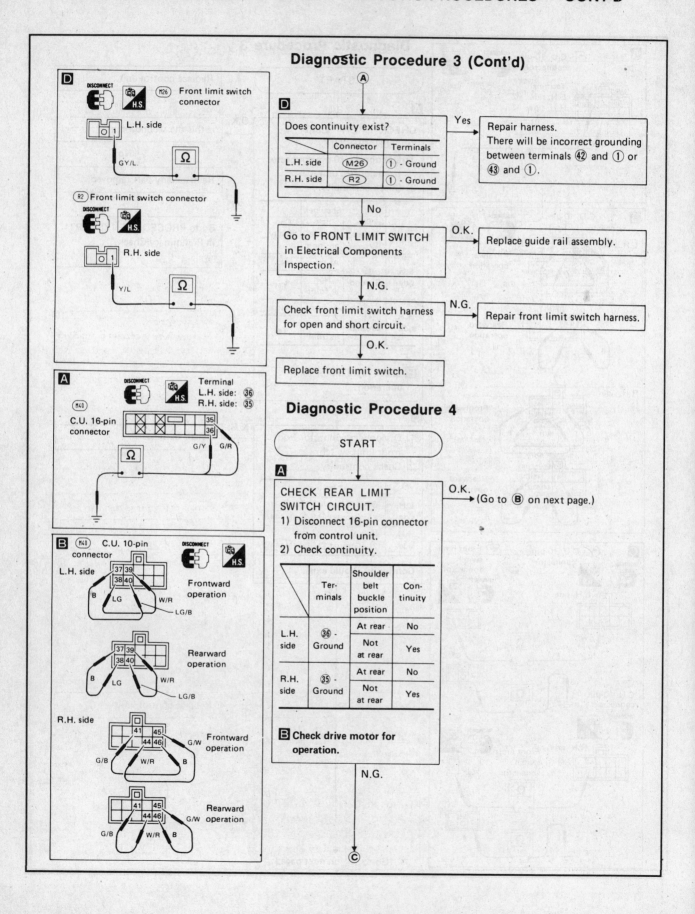

Diagnostic Procedure 3 (Cont'd)

D Does continuity exist?

	Connector	Terminals
L.H. side	M26	① - Ground
R.H. side	R2	① - Ground

Yes → Repair harness. There will be incorrect grounding between terminals ㊷ and ① or ㊸ and ①.

No ↓

Go to FRONT LIMIT SWITCH in Electrical Components Inspection.

O.K. → Replace guide rail assembly.

N.G. ↓

Check front limit switch harness for open and short circuit.

N.G. → Repair front limit switch harness.

O.K. ↓

Replace front limit switch.

Diagnostic Procedure 4

START

A CHECK REAR LIMIT SWITCH CIRCUIT.
1) Disconnect 16-pin connector from control unit.
2) Check continuity.

O.K. → (Go to Ⓑon next page.)

	Ter-minals	Shoulder belt buckle position	Con-tinuity
L.H. side	㊱ - Ground	At rear	No
		Not at rear	Yes
R.H. side	㉟ - Ground	At rear	No
		Not at rear	Yes

B Check drive motor for operation.

N.G. ↓

Ⓒ

AUTOMATIC SEAT BELT SYSTEM DIAGNOSTIC PROCEDURES — CONT'D

Diagnostic Procedure 4 (Cont'd)

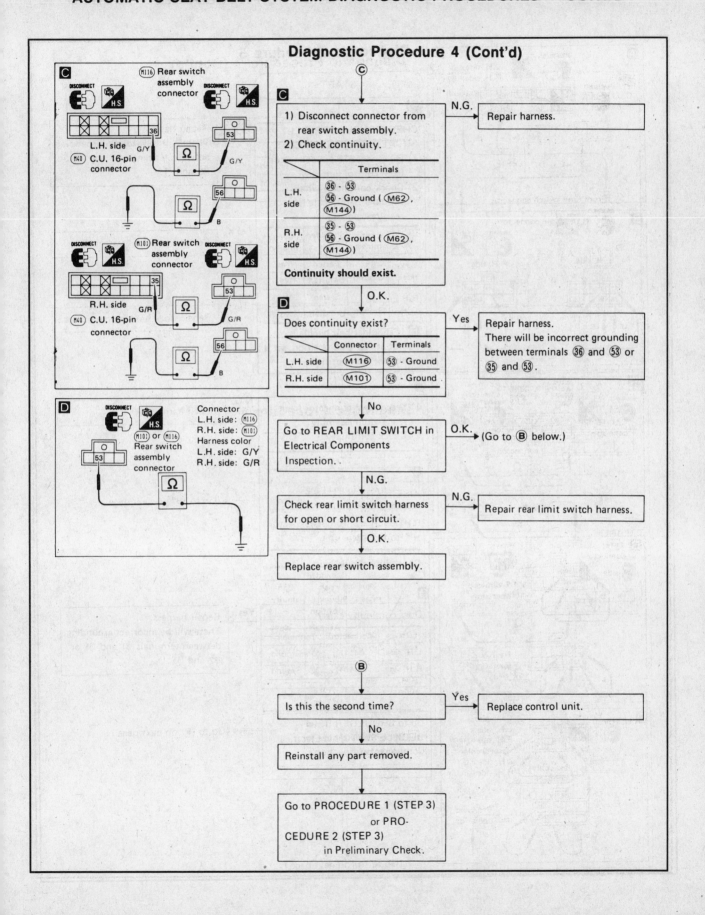

Ⓒ

Ⓒ
1) Disconnect connector from rear switch assembly.
2) Check continuity.

	Terminals
L.H. side	㊱ - ㊳ ㊵ - Ground (Ⓜ62 , Ⓜ144)
R.H. side	㉟ - ㊳ ㊵ - Ground (Ⓜ62 , Ⓜ144)

Continuity should exist.

N.G. → Repair harness.

O.K.

Ⓓ
Does continuity exist?

	Connector	Terminals
L.H. side	Ⓜ116	㊳ - Ground
R.H. side	Ⓜ101	㊳ - Ground

Yes → Repair harness.
There will be incorrect grounding between terminals ㊱ and ㊳ or ㉟ and ㊳.

No

Go to REAR LIMIT SWITCH in Electrical Components Inspection.

O.K. → (Go to Ⓑ below.)

N.G.

Check rear limit switch harness for open or short circuit.

N.G. → Repair rear limit switch harness.

O.K.

Replace rear switch assembly.

Ⓑ

Is this the second time?

Yes → Replace control unit.

No

Reinstall any part removed.

Go to PROCEDURE 1 (STEP 3) or PRO-CEDURE 2 (STEP 3) in Preliminary Check.

AUTOMATIC SEAT BELT SYSTEM DIAGNOSTIC PROCEDURES — CONT'D

Diagnostic Procedure 5

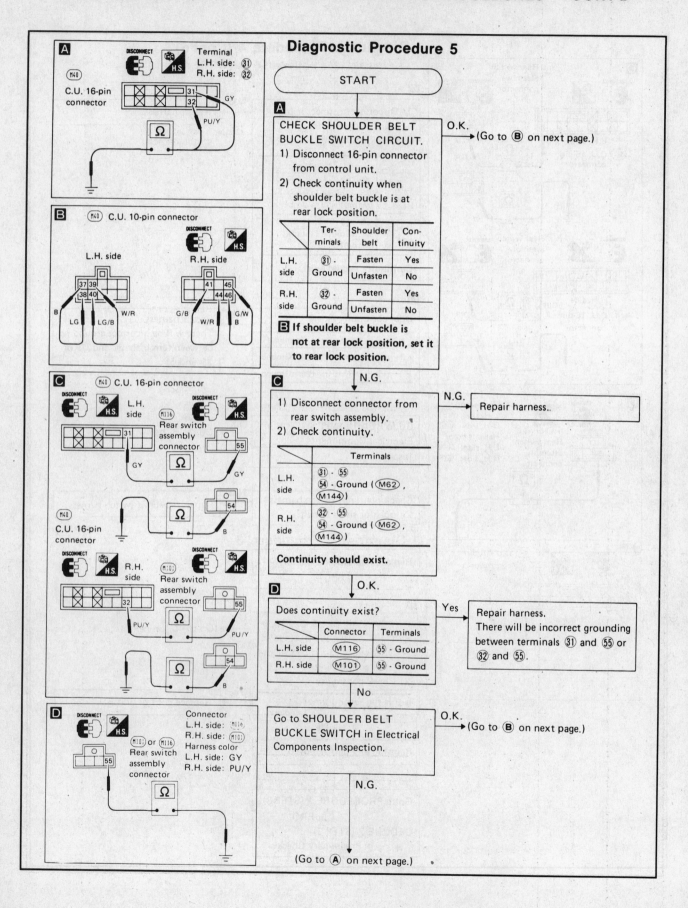

A CHECK SHOULDER BELT BUCKLE SWITCH CIRCUIT.
1) Disconnect 16-pin connector from control unit.
2) Check continuity when shoulder belt buckle is at rear lock position.

	Terminals	Shoulder belt	Continuity
L.H. side	③① - Ground	Fasten	Yes
		Unfasten	No
R.H. side	③② - Ground	Fasten	Yes
		Unfasten	No

B If shoulder belt buckle is not at rear lock position, set it to rear lock position.

O.K. → (Go to **B** on next page.)

N.G.

C
1) Disconnect connector from rear switch assembly.
2) Check continuity.

	Terminals
L.H. side	③① - ⑤⑤ ⑤④ - Ground (M62 , M144)
R.H. side	③② - ⑤⑤ ⑤④ - Ground (M62 , M144)

Continuity should exist.

N.G. → Repair harness..

O.K.

D Does continuity exist?

	Connector	Terminals
L.H. side	M116	⑤⑤ - Ground
R.H. side	M101	⑤⑤ - Ground

Yes → Repair harness. There will be incorrect grounding between terminals ③① and ⑤⑤ or ③② and ⑤⑤.

No

Go to SHOULDER BELT BUCKLE SWITCH in Electrical Components Inspection.

O.K. → (Go to **B** on next page.)

N.G.

(Go to **A** on next page.)

AUTOMATIC SEAT BELT SYSTEM DIAGNOSTIC PROCEDURES — CONT'D

Diagnostic Procedure 5 (Cont'd)

Ⓐ

Check shoulder belt buckle switch harness for open or short circuit. — N.G. → Repair shoulder belt buckle switch harness.

O.K.

Replace rear switch assembly.

Ⓑ

Is this the second time? — Yes → Replace control unit.

No

Reinstall any part removed.

Go to PROCEDURE 2 (STEP 4) in Preliminary Check.

Diagnostic Procedure 6

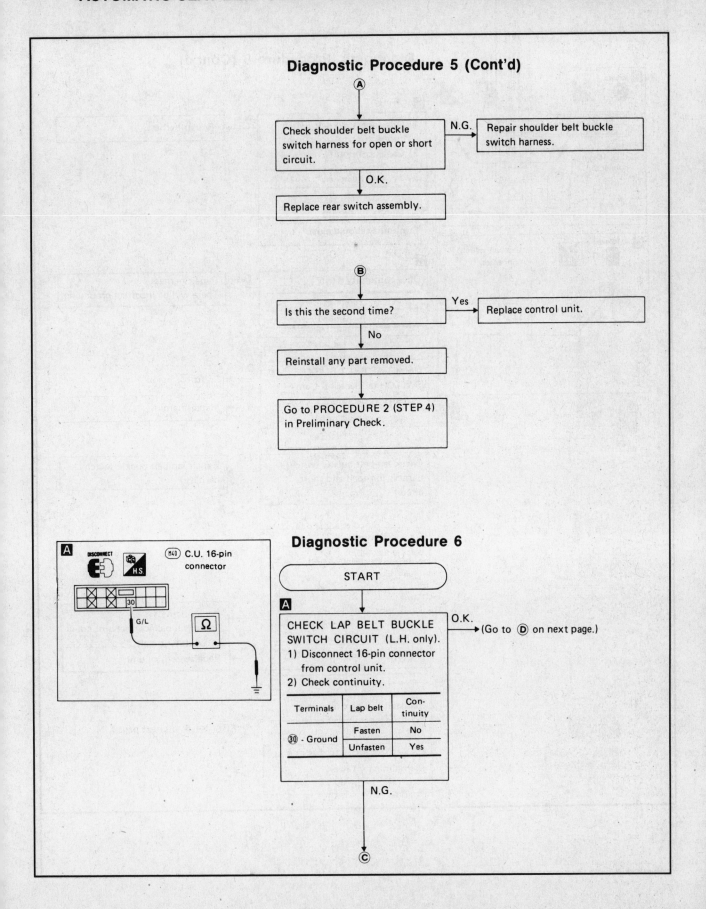

Ⓐ
(M40) C.U. 16-pin connector

30

G/L

Ω

START

Ⓐ

CHECK LAP BELT BUCKLE SWITCH CIRCUIT (L.H. only).
1) Disconnect 16-pin connector from control unit.
2) Check continuity.

O.K. → (Go to Ⓓ on next page.)

Terminals	Lap belt	Continuity
㉚ - Ground	Fasten	No
	Unfasten	Yes

N.G.

Ⓒ

AUTOMATIC SEAT BELT SYSTEM DIAGNOSTIC PROCEDURES — CONT'D

Diagnostic Procedure 6 (Cont'd)

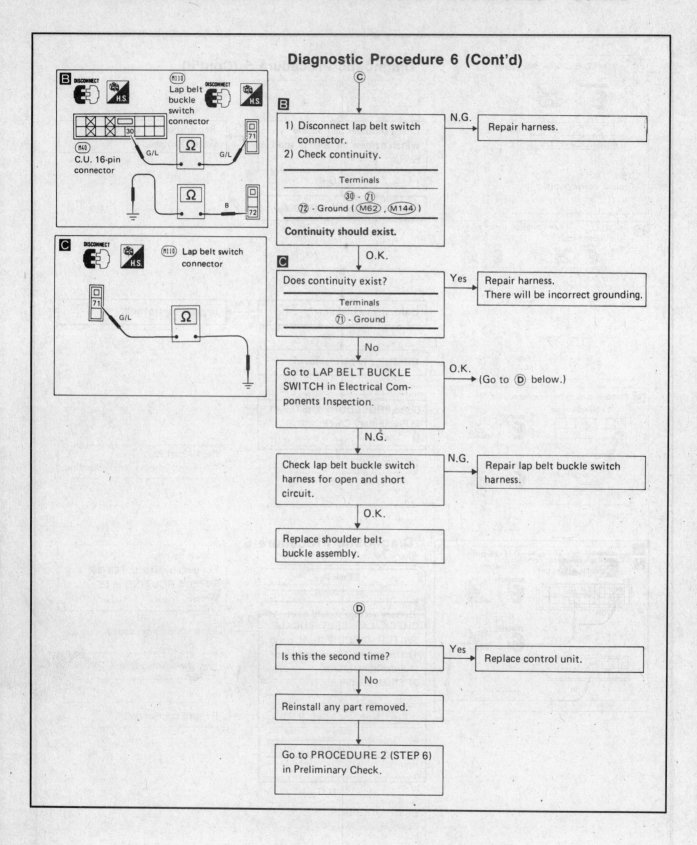

Ⓒ

B

1) Disconnect lap belt switch connector.
2) Check continuity.

Terminals
㉚ - ㉛
㉒ - Ground (Ⓜ62 , Ⓜ144)

Continuity should exist.

→ N.G. → Repair harness.

O.K.

C

Does continuity exist?

Terminals
㉛ - Ground

→ Yes → Repair harness. There will be incorrect grounding.

No

Go to LAP BELT BUCKLE SWITCH in Electrical Components Inspection.

→ O.K. → (Go to Ⓓ below.)

N.G.

Check lap belt buckle switch harness for open and short circuit.

→ N.G. → Repair lap belt buckle switch harness.

O.K.

Replace shoulder belt buckle assembly.

Ⓓ

Is this the second time?

→ Yes → Replace control unit.

No

Reinstall any part removed.

Go to PROCEDURE 2 (STEP 6) in Preliminary Check.

AUTOMATIC SEAT BELT SYSTEM DIAGNOSTIC PROCEDURES — CONT'D

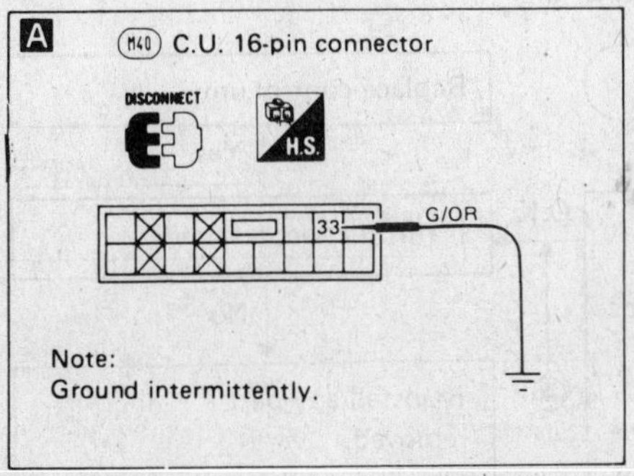
A
M40 C.U. 16-pin connector
DISCONNECT
H.S.
33
G/OR
Note:
Ground intermittently.

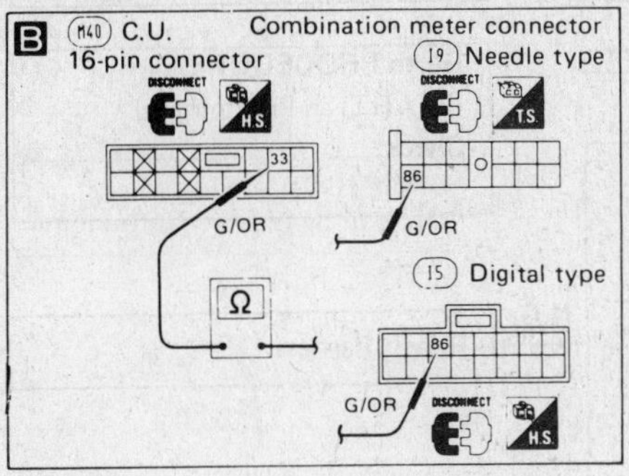
B
M40 C.U.
16-pin connector
Combination meter connector
19 Needle type
DISCONNECT
H.S
T.S
33
86
G/OR
G/OR
Ω
15 Digital type
86
G/OR
DISCONNECT
H.S

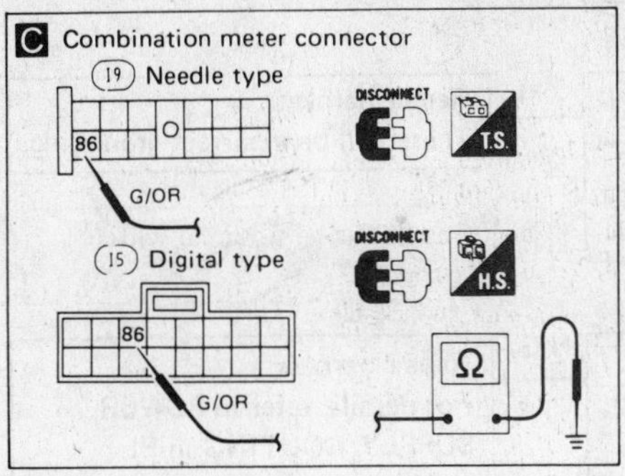
C
Combination meter connector
19 Needle type
DISCONNECT
T.S.
86
G/OR
15 Digital type
DISCONNECT
H.S.
86
G/OR
Ω

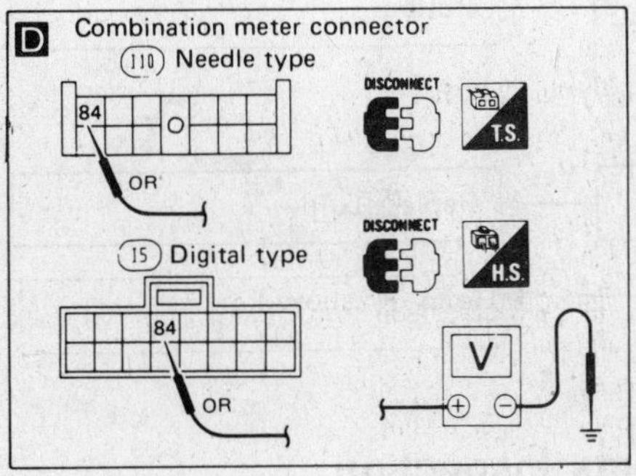
D
Combination meter connector
110 Needle type
DISCONNECT
T.S.
84
OR
15 Digital type
DISCONNECT
H.S.
84
OR
V

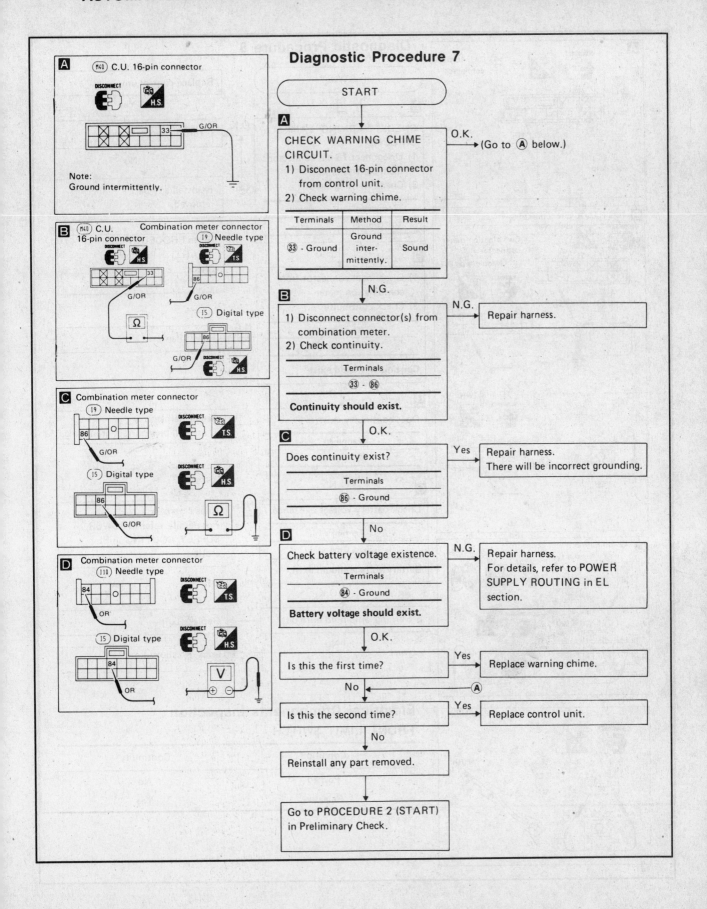

Diagnostic Procedure 7

START

A

CHECK WARNING CHIME CIRCUIT.
1) Disconnect 16-pin connector from control unit.
2) Check warning chime.

Terminals	Method	Result
㉝ - Ground	Ground inter-mittently.	Sound

O.K. → (Go to Ⓐ below.)

↓ N.G.

B

1) Disconnect connector(s) from combination meter.
2) Check continuity.

Terminals
㉝ - ㊻

Continuity should exist.

N.G. → Repair harness.

↓ O.K.

C

Does continuity exist?

Terminals
㊻ - Ground

Yes → Repair harness. There will be incorrect grounding.

↓ No

D

Check battery voltage existence.

Terminals
㊹ - Ground

Battery voltage should exist.

N.G. → Repair harness. For details, refer to POWER SUPPLY ROUTING in EL section.

↓ O.K.

Is this the first time?

Yes → Replace warning chime.

↓ No ← Ⓐ

Is this the second time?

Yes → Replace control unit.

↓ No

Reinstall any part removed.

↓

Go to PROCEDURE 2 (START) in Preliminary Check.

AUTOMATIC SEAT BELT SYSTEM DIAGNOSTIC PROCEDURES — CONT'D

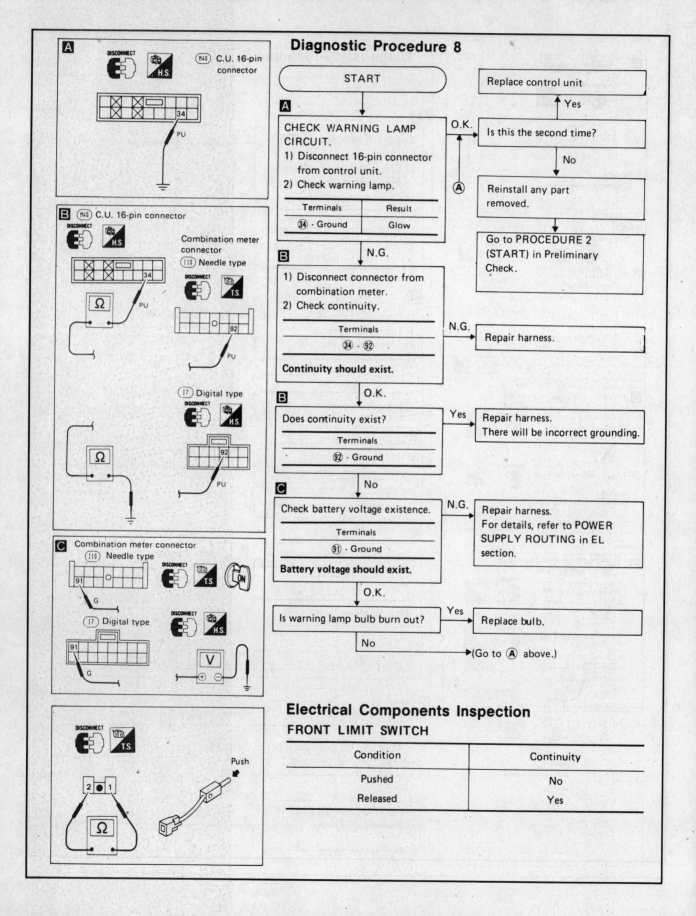

Diagnostic Procedure 8

START

A

CHECK WARNING LAMP CIRCUIT.
1) Disconnect 16-pin connector from control unit.
2) Check warning lamp.

Terminals	Result
34 - Ground	Glow

O.K. →

Replace control unit

↑ Yes

Is this the second time?

↓ No

Reinstall any part removed.

Go to PROCEDURE 2 (START) in Preliminary Check.

N.G.

B

1) Disconnect connector from combination meter.
2) Check continuity.

Terminals
34 - 92

Continuity should exist.

N.G. → Repair harness.

O.K.

B

Does continuity exist?

Terminals
92 - Ground

Yes → Repair harness. There will be incorrect grounding.

No

C

Check battery voltage existence.

Terminals
91 - Ground

Battery voltage should exist.

N.G. → Repair harness. For details, refer to POWER SUPPLY ROUTING in EL section.

O.K.

Is warning lamp bulb burn out?

Yes → Replace bulb.

No

→ (Go to Ⓐ above.)

Electrical Components Inspection
FRONT LIMIT SWITCH

Condition	Continuity
Pushed	No
Released	Yes

(A) C.U. 16-pin connector

34 PU

(B) C.U. 16-pin connector

Combination meter connector
Needle type
34 PU
92 PU

Digital type
92 PU

(C) Combination meter connector
Needle type
91 G

Digital type
91 G

Push
2 • 1

AUTOMATIC SEAT BELT SYSTEM ELECTRICAL COMPONENT INSPECTION

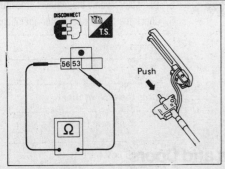

Electrical Components Inspection (Cont'd)
REAR LIMIT SWITCH

Condition	Continuity
Pushed	No
Released	Yes

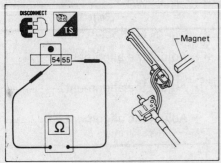

SHOULDER BELT BUCKLE SWITCH

Condition	Continuity
Move magnet toward buckle switch.	Yes
Move magnet away buckle switch.	No

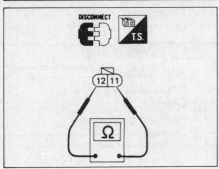

DOOR LATCH SWITCH
(Built-in door lock assembly)

Door condition	Continuity
Open	Yes
Closed	No

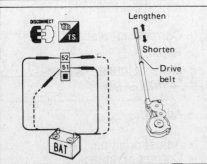

DRIVE MOTOR ASSEMBLY

Terminals		Drive belt operation
$\oplus$	$\ominus$	
52	51	Lengthen
51	52	Shorten

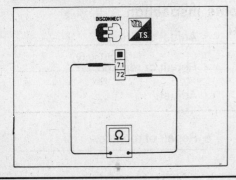

LAP BELT BUCKLE SWITCH
(Built-in lap belt buckle for L.H. side)

Condition	Continuity
Fastened	No
Unfastened	Yes

Power Seat Motor

REMOVAL & INSTALLATION

Front

♦ SEE FIGS. 45 AND 46

1. Remove front seat mounting bolts.
2. Remove front seat assembly.
3. Remove the power seat motor assembly frame-to-seat bolts and separate the frame from the seat.

4. Remove the power seat motor-to-frame bolts and remove the motor assembly from the frame.
5. To install, reverse the removal procedures.
6. Check the power seat motor operations.

Hood, Trunk Lid, Hatch Lid, Glass and Doors

Problem	Possible Cause	Correction
HOOD/TRUNK/HATCH LID		
Improper closure.	• Striker and latch not properly aligned.	• Adjust the alignment.
Difficulty locking and unlocking.	• Striker and latch not properly aligned.	• Adjust the alignment.
Uneven clearance with body panels.	• Incorrectly installed hood or trunk lid.	• Adjust the alignment.
WINDOW/WINDSHIELD GLASS		
Water leak through windshield.	• Defective seal.	• Fill sealant
	• Defective body flange.	• Correct.
Water leak through door window glass.	• Incorrect window glass installation.	• Adjust position.
	• Gap at upper window frame.	• Adjust position.
Water leak through quarter window.	• Defective seal.	• Replace seal.
	• Defective body flange.	• Correct.
Water leak through rear window.	• Defective seal.	• Replace seal.
	• Defective body flange.	• Correct.
FRONT/REAR DOORS		
Door window malfunction.	• Incorrect window glass installation.	• Adjust position.
	• Damaged or faulty regulator.	• Correct or replace.
Water leak through door edge.	• Cracked or faulty weatherstrip.	• Replace.
Water leak from door center.	• Drain hole clogged.	• Remove foreign objects.
	• Inadequate waterproof skeet contact or damage.	• Correct or replace.
Door hard to open.	• Incorrect latch or striker adjustment.	• Adjust.
Door does not open or close completely.	• Incorrect door installation.	• Adjust position.
	• Defective door check strap.	• Correct or replace.
	• Door check strap and hinge require grease.	• Apply grease.
Uneven gap between door and body.	• Incorrect door installation.	• Adjust position.
Wind noise around door.	• Improperly installed weatherstrip.	• Repair or replace.
	• Improper clearance between door glass and door weatherstrip.	• Adjust.
	• Deformed door.	• Repair or replace.

How to Remove Stains from Fabric Interior

For best results, spots and stains should be removed as soon as possible. Never use gasoline, lacquer thinner, acetone, nail polish remover or bleach. Use a 3' x 3" piece of cheesecloth. Squeeze most of the liquid from the fabric and wipe the stained fabric from the outside of the stain toward the center with a lifting motion. Turn the cheesecloth as soon as one side becomes soiled. When using water to remove a stain, be sure to wash the entire section after the spot has been removed to avoid water stains. Encrusted spots can be broken up with a dull knife and vacuumed before removing the stain.

Type of Stain	How to Remove It
Surface spots	Brush the spots out with a small hand brush or use a commercial preparation such as K2R to lift the stain.
Mildew	Clean around the mildew with warm suds. Rinse in cold water and soak the mildew area in a solution of 1 part table salt and 2 parts water. Wash with upholstery cleaner.
Water stains	Water stains in fabric materials can be removed with a solution made from 1 cup of table salt dissolved in 1 quart of water. Vigorously scrub the solution into the stain and rinse with clear water. Water stains in nylon or other synthetic fabrics should be removed with a commercial type spot remover.
Chewing gum, tar, crayons, shoe polish (greasy stains)	Do not use a cleaner that will soften gum or tar. Harden the deposit with an ice cube and scrape away as much as possible with a dull knife. Moisten the remainder with cleaning fluid and scrub clean.
Ice cream, candy	Most candy has a sugar base and can be removed with a cloth wrung out in warm water. Oily candy, after cleaning with warm water, should be cleaned with upholstery cleaner. Rinse with warm water and clean the remainder with cleaning fluid.
Wine, alcohol, egg, milk, soft drink (non-greasy stains)	Do not use soap. Scrub the stain with a cloth wrung out in warm water. Remove the remainder with cleaning fluid.
Grease, oil, lipstick, butter and related stains	Use a spot remover to avoid leaving a ring. Work from the outisde of the stain to the center and dry with a clean cloth when the spot is gone.
Headliners (cloth)	Mix a solution of warm water and foam upholstery cleaner to give thick suds. Use only foam—liquid may streak or spot. Clean the entire headliner in one operation using a circular motion with a natural sponge.
Headliner (vinyl)	Use a vinyl cleaner with a sponge and wipe clean with a dry cloth.
Seats and door panels	Mix 1 pint upholstery cleaner in 1 gallon of water. Do not soak the fabric around the buttons.
Leather or vinyl fabric	Use a multi-purpose cleaner full strength and a stiff brush. Let stand 2 minutes and scrub thoroughly. Wipe with a clean, soft rag.
Nylon or synthetic fabrics	For normal stains, use the same procedures you would for washing cloth upholstery. If the fabric is extremely dirty, use a multi-purpose cleaner full strength with a stiff scrub brush. Scrub thoroughly in all directions and wipe with a cotton towel or soft rag.

TORQUE SPECIFICATIONS

Component	U.S.	Metric
Door hinge-to-chassis bolts		
1985–88	16–22 ft. lbs.	22–29 Nm
1989–92	22–27 ft. lbs.	29–37 Nm
Door hinge-to-door bolts	22–27 ft. lbs.	29–37 Nm
Door striker-to-chassis bolts	9–12 ft. lbs.	13–16 Nm
Front bumper reinforcement-to-chassis		
Bolts:		
1985–88	12–15 ft. lbs.	16–21 Nm
1989–92	80–101 ft. lbs.	108–137 Nm
Nut:		
1985–88	6.7–8.7 ft. lbs.	9.1–11.8 Nm
Front seat-to-chassis bolts:		
1985–88	18–23 ft. lbs.	25–31 Nm
1989–92	32–41 ft. lbs.	43–55 Nm
Gas stay-to-hood bolt(s)		
1985–88	3.9–5.3 ft. lbs.	5.3–7.2 Nm
1989–92	6.2–8.0 ft. lbs.	8.4–10.8 Nm
Hood-to-hinge bolts		
1985–88	6.7–8.7 ft. lbs.	9.1–11.8 Nm
1989–92	12–15 ft. lbs.	16–21 Nm
Inside door handle-to-door screws	1.7–2.2 ft. lbs.	2.3–3.0 Nm
Outside door handle-to-door nuts	2.7–3.7 ft. lbs.	3.7–5.0 Nm
Power lock-to-door bolts:		
1985–88	2.7–3.7 ft. lbs.	3.7–5.0 Nm
1989–92	3.8–4.8 ft. lbs.	5.1–6.5 Nm
Power mirror-to-chassis bolts	2.7–3.4 ft. lbs.	3.6–4.6 Nm
Power window motor-to-door bolts	2.7–3.7 ft. lbs.	3.7–5.0 Nm
Rear bumper reinforcement-to-chassis		
Bolts:		
1985–88		
Station Wagon	20–27 ft. lbs.	26–36 Nm
1989–92	80–101 ft. lbs.	108–137 Nm
Nuts		
1985–88		
Sedan	6.7–8.7 ft. lbs.	9.1–11.8 Nm
Station Wagon	5.8–8.0 ft. lbs.	8–11 Nm
1989–92	9–12 ft. lbs.	13–16 Nm
Rear seat		
Sedan		
Lower seat-to-chassis bolts:		
1985–88	3.8–4.8 ft. lbs.	5.1–6.5 Nm
1989–92	15–20 ft. lbs.	21–26 Nm
Upper seat-to-chassis bolts:		
1985–88	3.8–4.8 ft. lbs.	5.1–6.5 Nm
1989–92	15–20 ft. lbs.	21–26 Nm
Station Wagon		
Lower rear seat-to-chassis bolts	3.8–4.8 ft. lbs.	5.1–6.5 Nm
Upper center seat-to-chassis bolts	32–41 ft. lbs.	43–55 Nm
Upper end seat-to-chassis bolts	3.8–4.8 ft. lbs.	5.1–6.5 Nm
Upper seat backs-to-hinge bolts	9–12 ft. lbs.	13–16 Nm
Tailgate lid-to-hinge bolts	12–15 ft. lbs.	16–21 Nm
Trunk lid-to-hinge bolts	3.3–4.0 ft. lbs.	4.4–5.4 Nm
Trunk lid striker bolts		
1985–88	3.3–4.0 ft. lbs.	4.4–5.4 Nm
1989–92	3.8–4.8 ft. lbs.	5.1–6.5 Nm

GLOSSARY

AIR/FUEL RATIO: The ratio of air to gasoline by weight in the fuel mixture drawn into the engine.

AIR INJECTION: One method of reducing harmful exhaust emissions by injecting air into each of the exhaust ports of an engine. The fresh air entering the hot exhaust manifold causes any remaining fuel to be burned before it can exit the tailpipe.

ALTERNATOR: A device used for converting mechanical energy into electrical energy.

AMMETER: An instrument, calibrated in amperes, used to measure the flow of an electrical current in a circuit. Ammeters are always connected in series with the circuit being tested.

AMPERE: The rate of flow of electrical current present when one volt of electrical pressure is applied against one ohm of electrical resistance.

ANALOG COMPUTER: Any microprocessor that uses similar (analogous) electrical signals to make its calculations.

ARMATURE: A laminated, soft iron core wrapped by a wire that converts electrical energy to mechanical energy as in a motor or relay. When rotated in a magnetic field, it changes mechanical energy into electrical energy as in a generator.

ATMOSPHERIC PRESSURE: The pressure on the Earth's surface caused by the weight of the air in the atmosphere. At sea level, this pressure is 14.7 psi at 32°F (101 kPa at 0°C).

ATOMIZATION: The breaking down of a liquid into a fine mist that can be suspended in air.

AXIAL PLAY: Movement parallel to a shaft or bearing bore.

BACKFIRE: The sudden combustion of gases in the intake or exhaust system that results in a loud explosion.

BACKLASH: The clearance or play between two parts, such as meshed gears.

BACKPRESSURE: Restrictions in the exhaust system that slow the exit of exhaust gases from the combustion chamber.

BAKELITE: A heat resistant, plastic insulator material commonly used in printed circuit boards and transistorized components.

BALL BEARING: A bearing made up of hardened inner and outer races between which hardened steel balls roll.

BALLAST RESISTOR: A resistor in the primary ignition circuit that lowers voltage after the engine is started to reduce wear on ignition components.

BEARING: A friction reducing, supportive device usually located between a stationary part and a moving part.

BIMETAL TEMPERATURE SENSOR: Any sensor or switch made of two dissimilar types of metal that bend when heated or cooled due to the different expansion rates of the alloys. These types of sensors usually function as an on/off switch.

BLOWBY: Combustion gases, composed of water vapor and unburned fuel, that leak past the piston rings into the crankcase during normal engine operation. These gases are removed by the PCV system to prevent the buildup of harmful acids in the crankcase.

BRAKE PAD: A brake shoe and lining assembly used with disc brakes.

BRAKE SHOE: The backing for the brake lining. The term is, however, usually applied to the assembly of the brake backing and lining.

BUSHING: A liner, usually removable, for a bearing; an anti-friction liner used in place of a bearing.

BYPASS: System used to bypass ballast resistor during engine cranking to increase voltage supplied to the coil.

CALIPER: A hydraulically activated device in a disc brake system, which is mounted straddling the brake rotor (disc). The caliper contains at least one piston and two brake pads. Hydraulic pressure on the piston(s) forces the pads against the rotor.

CAMSHAFT: A shaft in the engine on which are the lobes (cams) which operate the valves. The camshaft is driven by the crankshaft, via a belt, chain or gears, at one half the crankshaft speed.

CAPACITOR: A device which stores an electrical charge.

CARBON MONOXIDE (CO): A colorless, odorless gas given off as a normal byproduct of combustion. It is poisonous and extremely dangerous in confined areas, building up slowly to toxic levels without warning if adequate ventilation is not available.

CARBURETOR: A device, usually mounted on the intake manifold of an engine, which mixes the air and fuel in the proper proportion to allow even combustion.

CATALYTIC CONVERTER: A device installed in the exhaust system, like a muffler, that converts harmful byproducts of combustion into carbon dioxide and water vapor by means of a heat-producing chemical reaction.

CENTRIFUGAL ADVANCE: A mechanical method of advancing the spark timing by using fly weights in the distributor that react to centrifugal force generated by the distributor shaft rotation.

CHECK VALVE: Any one-way valve installed to permit the flow of air, fuel or vacuum in one direction only.

CHOKE: A device, usually a movable valve, placed in the intake path of a carburetor to restrict the flow of air.

CIRCUIT: Any unbroken path through which an electrical current can flow. Also used to describe fuel flow in some instances.

CIRCUIT BREAKER: A switch which protects an electrical circuit from overload by opening the circuit when the current flow exceeds a predetermined level. Some circuit breakers must be reset manually, while most reset automatically

COIL (IGNITION): A transformer in the ignition circuit which steps up the voltage provided to the spark plugs.

COMBINATION MANIFOLD: An assembly which includes both the intake and exhaust manifolds in one casting.

COMBINATION VALVE: A device used in some fuel systems that routes fuel vapors to a charcoal storage canister instead of venting them into the atmosphere. The valve relieves fuel tank pressure and allows fresh air into the tank as the fuel level drops to prevent a vapor lock situation.

COMPRESSION RATIO: The comparison of the total volume of the cylinder and combustion chamber with the piston at BDC and the piston at TDC.

CONDENSER: 1. An electrical device which acts to store an electrical charge, preventing voltage surges.
  2. A radiator-like device in the air conditioning system in which refrigerant gas condenses into a liquid, giving off heat.

CONDUCTOR: Any material through which an electrical current can be transmitted easily.

CONTINUITY: Continuous or complete circuit. Can be checked with an ohmmeter.

COUNTERSHAFT: An intermediate shaft which is rotated by a mainshaft and transmits, in turn, that rotation to a working part.

CRANKCASE: The lower part of an engine in which the crankshaft and related parts operate.

CRANKSHAFT: The main driving shaft of an engine which receives reciprocating motion from the pistons and converts it to rotary motion.

CYLINDER: In an engine, the round hole in the engine block in which the piston(s) ride.

CYLINDER BLOCK: The main structural member of an engine in which is found the cylinders, crankshaft and other principal parts.

CYLINDER HEAD: The detachable portion of the engine, fastened, usually, to the top of the cylinder block, containing all or most of the combustion chambers. On overhead valve engines, it contains the valves and their operating parts. On overhead cam engines, it contains the camshaft as well.

DEAD CENTER: The extreme top or bottom of the piston stroke.

DETONATION: An unwanted explosion of the air/fuel mixture in the combustion chamber caused by excess heat and compression, advanced timing, or an overly lean mixture. Also referred to as "ping".

DIAPHRAGM: A thin, flexible wall separating two cavities, such as in a vacuum advance unit.

DIESELING: A condition in which hot spots in the combustion chamber cause the engine to run on after the key is turned off.

DIFFERENTIAL: A geared assembly which allows the transmission of motion between drive axles, giving one axle the ability to turn faster than the other.

DIODE: An electrical device that will allow current to flow in one direction only.

DISC BRAKE: A hydraulic braking assembly consisting of a brake disc, or rotor, mounted on an axle, and a caliper assembly containing, usually two brake pads which are activated by hydraulic pressure. The pads are forced against the sides of the disc, creating friction which slows the vehicle.

DISTRIBUTOR: A mechanically driven device on an engine which is responsible for electrically firing the spark plug at a predetermined point of the piston stroke.

DOWEL PIN: A pin, inserted in mating holes in two different parts allowing those parts to maintain a fixed relationship.

DRUM BRAKE: A braking system which consists of two brake shoes and one or two wheel cylinders, mounted on a fixed backing plate, and a brake drum, mounted on an axle, which revolves around the assembly. Hydraulic action applied to the wheel cylinders forces the shoes outward against the drum, creating friction, slowing the vehicle.

DWELL: The rate, measured in degrees of shaft rotation, at which an electrical circuit cycles on and off.

ELECTRONIC CONTROL UNIT (ECU): Ignition module, amplifier or igniter. See Module for definition.

ELECTRONIC IGNITION: A system in which the timing and firing of the spark plugs is controlled by an electronic control unit, usually called a module. These systems have no points or condenser.

ENDPLAY: The measured amount of axial movement in a shaft.

ENGINE: A device that converts heat into mechanical energy.

EXHAUST MANIFOLD: A set of cast passages or pipes which conduct exhaust gases from the engine.

FEELER GAUGE: A blade, usually metal, of precisely predetermined thickness, used to measure the clearance between two parts. These blades usually are available in sets of assorted thicknesses.

F-HEAD: An engine configuration in which the intake valves are in the cylinder head, while the camshaft and exhaust valves are located in the cylinder block. The camshaft operates the intake valves via lifters and pushrods, while it operates the exhaust valves directly.

FIRING ORDER: The order in which combustion occurs in the cylinders of an engine. Also the order in which spark is distributed to the plugs by the distributor.

FLATHEAD: An engine configuration in which the camshaft and all the valves are located in the cylinder block.

FLOODING: The presence of too much fuel in the intake manifold and combustion chamber which prevents the air/fuel mixture from firing, thereby causing a no-start situation.

FLYWHEEL: A disc shaped part bolted to the rear end of the crankshaft. Around the outer perimeter is affixed the ring gear. The starter drive engages the ring gear, turning the flywheel, which rotates the crankshaft, imparting the initial starting motion to the engine.

FOOT POUND (ft.lb. or sometimes, ft. lbs.): The amount of energy or work needed to raise an item weighing one pound, a distance of one foot.

FUSE: A protective device in a circuit which prevents circuit overload by breaking the circuit when a specific amperage is present. The device is constructed around a strip or wire of a lower amperage rating than the circuit it is designed to protect. When an amperage higher than that stamped on the fuse is present in the circuit, the strip or wire melts, opening the circuit.

GEAR RATIO: The ratio between the number of teeth on meshing gears.

GENERATOR: A device which converts mechanical energy into electrical energy.

HEAT RANGE: The measure of a spark plug's ability to dissipate heat from its firing end. The higher the heat range, the hotter the plug fires.

HUB: The center part of a wheel or gear.

HYDROCARBON (HC): Any chemical compound made up of hydrogen and carbon. A major pollutant formed by the engine as a byproduct of combustion.

HYDROMETER: An instrument used to measure the specific gravity of a solution.

INCH POUND (in.lb. or sometimes, in. lbs.): One twelfth of a foot pound.

INDUCTION: A means of transferring electrical energy in the form of a magnetic field. Principle used in the ignition coil to increase voltage.

INJECTION PUMP: A device, usually mechanically operated, which meters and delivers fuel under pressure to the fuel injector.

INJECTOR: A device which receives metered fuel under relatively low pressure and is activated to inject the fuel into the engine under relatively high pressure at a predetermined time.

INPUT SHAFT: The shaft to which torque is applied, usually carrying the driving gear or gears.

INTAKE MANIFOLD: A casting of passages or pipes used to conduct air or a fuel/air mixture to the cylinders.

JOURNAL: The bearing surface within which a shaft operates.

KEY: A small block usually fitted in a notch between a shaft and a hub to prevent slippage of the two parts.

MANIFOLD: A casting of passages or set of pipes which connect the cylinders to an inlet or outlet source.

MANIFOLD VACUUM: Low pressure in an engine intake manifold formed just below the throttle plates. Manifold vacuum is highest at idle and drops under acceleration.

MASTER CYLINDER: The primary fluid pressurizing device in a hydraulic system. In automotive use, it is found in brake and hydraulic clutch systems and is pedal activated, either directly or, in a power brake system, through the power booster.

MODULE: Electronic control unit, amplifier or igniter of solid state or integrated design which controls the current flow in the ignition primary circuit based on input from the pick-up coil. When the module opens the primary circuit, the high secondary voltage is induced in the coil.

NEEDLE BEARING: A bearing which consists of a number (usually a large number) of long, thin rollers.

OHM:(Ω) The unit used to measure the resistance of conductor to electrical flow. One ohm is the amount of resistance that limits current flow to one ampere in a circuit with one volt of pressure.

OHMMETER: An instrument used for measuring the resistance, in ohms, in an electrical circuit.

OUTPUT SHAFT: The shaft which transmits torque from a device, such as a transmission.

OVERDRIVE: A gear assembly which produces more shaft revolutions than that transmitted to it.

OVERHEAD CAMSHAFT (OHC): An engine configuration in which the camshaft is mounted on top of the cylinder head and operates the valves either directly or by means of rocker arms.

OVERHEAD VALVE (OHV): An engine configuration in which all of the valves are located in the cylinder head and the camshaft is located in the cylinder block. The camshaft operates the valves via lifters and pushrods.

OXIDES OF NITROGEN (NOx): Chemical compounds of nitrogen produced as a byproduct of combustion. They combine with hydrocarbons to produce smog.

OXYGEN SENSOR: Used with the feedback system to sense the presence of oxygen in the exhaust gas and signal the computer which can reference the voltage signal to an air/fuel ratio.

PINION: The smaller of two meshing gears.

PISTON RING: An open ended ring which fits into a groove on the outer diameter of the piston. Its chief function is to form a seal between the piston and cylinder wall. Most automotive pistons have three rings: two for compression sealing; one for oil sealing.

PRELOAD: A predetermined load placed on a bearing during assembly or by adjustment.

PRIMARY CIRCUIT: Is the low voltage side of the ignition system which consists of the ignition switch, ballast resistor or resistance wire, bypass, coil, electronic control unit and pick-up coil as well as the connecting wires and harnesses.

PRESS FIT: The mating of two parts under pressure, due to the inner diameter of one being smaller than the outer diameter of the other, or vice versa; an interference fit.

RACE: The surface on the inner or outer ring of a bearing on which the balls, needles or rollers move.

REGULATOR: A device which maintains the amperage and/or voltage levels of a circuit at predetermined values.

RELAY: A switch which automatically opens and/or closes a circuit.

RESISTANCE: The opposition to the flow of current through a circuit or electrical device, and is measured in ohms. Resistance is equal to the voltage divided by the amperage.

RESISTOR: A device, usually made of wire, which offers a preset amount of resistance in an electrical circuit.

RING GEAR: The name given to a ring-shaped gear attached to a differential case, or affixed to a flywheel or as part a planetary gear set.

ROLLER BEARING: A bearing made up of hardened inner and outer races between which hardened steel rollers move.

ROTOR: 1. The disc-shaped part of a disc brake assembly, upon which the brake pads bear; also called, brake disc.
2. The device mounted atop the distributor shaft, which passes current to the distributor cap tower contacts.

SECONDARY CIRCUIT: The high voltage side of the ignition system, usually above 20,000 volts. The secondary includes the ignition coil, coil wire, distributor cap and rotor, spark plug wires and spark plugs.

SENDING UNIT: A mechanical, electrical, hydraulic or electromagnetic device which transmits information to a gauge.

SENSOR: Any device designed to measure engine operating conditions or ambient pressures and temperatures. Usually electronic in nature and designed to send a voltage signal to an on-board computer, some sensors may operate as a simple on/off switch or they may provide a variable voltage signal (like a potentiometer) as conditions or measured parameters change.

SHIM: Spacers of precise, predetermined thickness used between parts to establish a proper working relationship.

SLAVE CYLINDER: In automotive use, a device in the hydraulic clutch system which is activated by hydraulic force, disengaging the clutch.

SOLENOID: A coil used to produce a magnetic field, the effect of which is to produce work.

SPARK PLUG: A device screwed into the combustion chamber of a spark ignition engine. The basic construction is a conductive core inside of a ceramic insulator, mounted in an outer conductive base. An electrical charge from the spark plug wire travels along the conductive core and jumps a preset air gap to a grounding point or points at the end of the conductive base. The resultant spark ignites the fuel/air mixture in the combustion chamber.

SPLINES: Ridges machined or cast onto the outer diameter of a shaft or inner diameter of a bore to enable parts to mate without rotation.

TACHOMETER: A device used to measure the rotary speed of an engine, shaft, gear, etc., usually in rotations per minute.

THERMOSTAT: A valve, located in the cooling system of an engine, which is closed when cold and opens gradually in response to engine heating, controlling the temperature of the coolant and rate of coolant flow.

TOP DEAD CENTER (TDC): The point at which the piston reaches the top of its travel on the compression stroke.

TORQUE: The twisting force applied to an object.

TORQUE CONVERTER: A turbine used to transmit power from a driving member to a driven member via hydraulic action, providing changes in drive ratio and torque. In automotive use, it links the driveplate at the rear of the engine to the automatic transmission.

TRANSDUCER: A device used to change a force into an electrical signal.

TRANSISTOR: A semi-conductor component which can be actuated by a small voltage to perform an electrical switching function.

TUNE-UP: A regular maintenance function, usually associated with the replacement and adjustment of parts and components in the electrical and fuel systems of a vehicle for the purpose of attaining optimum performance.

TURBOCHARGER: An exhaust driven pump which compresses intake air and forces it into the combustion chambers at higher than atmospheric pressures. The increased air pressure allows more fuel to be burned and results in increased horsepower being produced.

VACUUM ADVANCE: A device which advances the ignition timing in response to increased engine vacuum.

VACUUM GAUGE: An instrument used to measure the presence of vacuum in a chamber.

VALVE: A device which control the pressure, direction of flow or rate of flow of a liquid or gas.

VALVE CLEARANCE: The measured gap between the end of the valve stem and the rocker arm, cam lobe or follower that activates the valve.

VISCOSITY: The rating of a liquid's internal resistance to flow.

VOLTMETER: An instrument used for measuring electrical force in units called volts. Voltmeters are always connected parallel with the circuit being tested.

WHEEL CYLINDER: Found in the automotive drum brake assembly, it is a device, actuated by hydraulic pressure, which, through internal pistons, pushes the brake shoes outward against the drums.

MASTER

INDEX